Frommer's®

Hawaii
from $80 a Day

35th Edition

by Jeanette Foster

Here's what the critics say about Frommer's:

"Amazingly easy to use. Very portable, very complete."

—*Booklist*

"Detailed, accurate, and easy-to-read information for all price ranges."
—*Glamour Magazine*

"Hotel information is close to encyclopedic."

—*Des Moines Sunday Register*

"Frommer's Guides have a way of giving you a real feel for a place."
—*Knight Ridder Newspapers*

WILEY

Wiley Publishing, Inc.

About the Author

A resident of the Big Island, **Jeanette Foster** has skied the slopes of Mauna Kea—during a Fourth of July ski meet, no less—and gone scuba diving with manta rays off the Kona Coast. A prolific writer widely published in travel, sports, and adventure magazines, she's also a contributing editor to *Hawaii* magazine and the editor of *Zagat's Survey to Hawaii's Top Restaurants*. In addition to this guide, Jeanette is the author of *Frommer's Maui*, *Frommer's Hawaii*, *Frommer's Honolulu, Waikiki & Oahu*, *Frommer's Kauai*, and *Frommer's Hawaii with Kids*.

Published by:

Wiley Publishing, Inc.

111 River St.
Hoboken, NJ 07030-5774

ISBN-13: 978-0-7645-9589-9
ISBN-10: 0-7645-9589-X

Editor: Christina Summers
Production Editor: Melissa S. Bennett
Cartographer: Andrew Murphy
Photo Editor: Richard Fox
Production by Wiley Indianapolis Composition Services

For information on our other products and services or to obtain technical support, please contact our Customer Care Department within the U.S. at 800-762-2974, outside the U.S. at 317-572-3993 or fax 317-572-4002.

Wiley also publishes its books in a variety of electronic formats. Some content that appears in print may not be available in electronic formats.

Manufactured in the United States of America

5 4 3 2 1

Contents

10 Kauai: The Garden Isle   511

Appendix: Hawaii in Depth   594

Index   612

List of Maps

An Invitation to the Reader

In researching this book, we discovered many wonderful places—hotels, restaurants, shops, and more. We're sure you'll find others. Please tell us about them, so we can share the information with your fellow travelers in upcoming editions. If you were disappointed with a recommendation, we'd love to know that, too. Please write to:

Frommer's Hawaii from $80 a Day, 35th Edition
Wiley Publishing, Inc. • 111 River St. • Hoboken, NJ 07030-5774

An Additional Note

Please be advised that travel information is subject to change at any time—and this is especially true of prices. We therefore suggest that you write or call ahead for confirmation when making your travel plans. The authors, editors, and publisher cannot be held responsible for the experiences of readers while traveling. Your safety is important to us, however, so we encourage you to stay alert and be aware of your surroundings. Keep a close eye on cameras, purses, and wallets, all favorite targets of thieves and pickpockets.

Other Great Guides for Your Trip:

Frommer's Hawaii

Frommer's Maui

Frommer's Honolulu, Waikiki & Oahu

Frommer's Kauai

Frommer's Hawaii with Kids

Hawaii For Dummies

Frommer's Star Ratings, Icons & Abbreviations

Every hotel, restaurant, and attraction listing in this guide has been ranked for quality, value, service, amenities, and special features using a **star-rating system.** In country, state, and regional guides, we also rate towns and regions to help you narrow down your choices and budget your time accordingly. Hotels and restaurants are rated on a scale of zero (recommended) to three stars (exceptional). Attractions, shopping, nightlife, towns, and regions are rated according to the following scale: zero stars (recommended), one star (highly recommended), two stars (very highly recommended), and three stars (must-see).

In addition to the star-rating system, we also use **seven feature icons** that point you to the great deals, in-the-know advice, and unique experiences that separate travelers from tourists. Throughout the book, look for:

Finds	Special finds—those places only insiders know about
Fun Fact	Fun facts—details that make travelers more informed and their trips more fun
Kids	Best bets for kids and advice for the whole family
Moments	Special moments—those experiences that memories are made of
Overrated	Places or experiences not worth your time or money
Tips	Insider tips—great ways to save time and money
Value	Great values—where to get the best deals

The following **abbreviations** are used for credit cards:

AE	American Express	DISC	Discover	V	Visa
DC	Diners Club	MC	MasterCard		

Frommers.com

Now that you have the guidebook to a great trip, visit our website at **www.frommers.com** for travel information on more than 3,000 destinations. With features updated regularly, we give you instant access to the most current trip-planning information available. At Frommers.com, you'll also find the best prices on airfares, accommodations, and car rentals—and you can even book travel online through our travel booking partners. At Frommers.com, you'll also find the following:

- Online updates to our most popular guidebooks
- Vacation sweepstakes and contest giveaways
- Newsletter highlighting the hottest travel trends
- Online travel message boards with featured travel discussions

What's New in Hawaii

Hawaii is suddenly the "in" spot to vacation. The Hawaii Visitors and Convention Bureau reports double-digit percentage increases in the number of tourists. One of the main reasons Hawaii continues to attract around seven million visitors a year is the islands' ability to improve, renovate, and reinvent everything from cultural experiences to restaurants to activities. Even Waikiki is a different place today than it was last year, and by the end of 2006 it will reveal its new face-lift.

OAHU The City and County of Honolulu performed a "makeover" of **Waikiki Beach** by creating a parklike atmosphere, complete with water features, grassy areas, and streams along the waterfront and then upgrading the sidewalks of the world's most famous beachside city. If that wasn't enough, the City added some 400 new trees to give Waikiki a verdant boulevard look.

And the renovations keep coming. One of the biggest projects in decades is the total renovation of an 8-acre area called the **Waikiki Beach Walk.** The project, which started in 2005 and hopefully will be completed by 2006, is estimated to cost some $420 million and affects 11 different hotels. When finished, the now very congested area with its narrow streets (and lots of delivery trucks double parked) and old, outdated buildings will be replaced with wider sidewalks, tropical foliage, water features, open space, and newly renovated hotels.

When the project is completed, the near-oceanfront area will go from budget hotels, neighborhood eateries, and small shops to luxury (higher-priced) properties with swank shops and restaurants to match. Plus there will be 30 different retail shops and six restaurants. The entire revised area will be linked through pedestrian bridges and connecting walkways.

Where to Dine D. K. Kodama, who wowed Maui's restaurant community with his **Sansei Seafood Restaurant and Sushi Bar,** has moved on to Oahu. First, he decided to move his Oahu Sansei Restaurant from its prime location in Restaurant Row to an even better location in the Waikiki Beach Marriott Resort. He also moved **Vino Italian Tapas & Wine Bar,** a copy of his Italian tapas restaurant on Maui, into the former space that Sansei occupied in Restaurant Row.

Kodama then leased the other half of his old Sansei location to L'Uraku Chef Hiroshi Fukui, who then opened **Hiroshi Eurasian Tapas.** The result is fabulous, especially for foodies who want to sample several items off the menu of this unique fusion of European and Asian cuisine.

Shopping Big changes are in progress in the two major shopping centers in Waikiki: The Royal Hawaiian and the International Market Place.

The Royal Hawaiian Shopping Center is undergoing a massive renovation—to the tune of $84 million—and is expected to be completed in late 2006.

The new design and renovations are adding more gardens and more open space to the formerly, mostly enclosed mall. Added will be a 30,000-square-foot landscaped gathering area with gardens around a central performance center. The biggest change will be the open-air bridge between the mall and the Royal Hawaiian Hotel.

In the past few decades, the **International Market Place** had become a sea of schlock. The 4.5-acre open market, bordered by Kuhio and Kalakaua avenues, was squeezed in amongst the high-rises of Waikiki contributing to its claustrophobic atmosphere. Those days are gone. At the end of 2005, after 48 years, the International Market Place and all the venders were shut down and a $150-million total restoration began and is expected to be completed by early 2008. The Queen Emma Foundation is bringing back the stream that used to run through the area (albeit as a water feature), and building an amphitheatre and a hula mound. Surrounding the area will be 230,000 square feet of 8 to 10 clustered buildings, ranging from one to three stories tall and featuring shops and restaurants.

After Dark   The last Friday of every month (except Nov and Dec), the place to be after the sun goes down is the **Honolulu Academy of Arts' ARTafterDark**, a *pau-hana* (after work) mixer in the art museum that brings residents and visitors together by combining art with food, music, and dancing. In addition to the exhibits in the gallery, ARTafterDark also features visual and live performances. Last year the "themes" included "'80s Night," "Turkish Delights," "Cool Nights, Hot Jazz and Blues," and "Havana Heat." The entry fee is $7, and the party gets going about 6pm and lasts to 9pm. The crowd ranges in age from 20s to 50s; the dress is everything from jeans and T-shirts to designer cocktail-party attire.

BIG ISLAND   In Big Island accommodation news, the **Palms Cliff House,** located oceanside of Akaka Falls in Honomu, has added lots of extra activities from hula to cooking classes to yoga to keep their guests entertained and happy. For a cultural experience of a different sort, every Saturday afternoon, they have a High English Tea served on their wraparound lanai, complete with pastries and savories.

Where to Dine   There's a lot of cooking going on in Kailua-Kona, where several restaurants have opened recently. **Jackie Rey's Ohana Grill** sits off the beaten tourist path and offers something for everyone (think sports bar meets dance club meets neighborhood cafe). This is a great place to eat at wallet-pleasing prices.

Pa Leo opened in the former Gallery Restaurant location, right on Alii Drive facing the ocean. Pa Leo is dishing up some very good fresh fish, fresh salads, and yummy desserts.

Rooster's The Restaurant is hidden in the back of a hodge-podge shopping enclave, also on Alii Drive in Kailua-Kona. Not only is it a culinary treat but they also feature live jazz Thursday through Saturday.

A couple of very inexpensive eateries also have opened. Pint-sized **Aki's Café** has three things going for it: terrific food, cheap prices, and an oceanfront location. In Keauhou, **Habanero's** has great, fast, Mexican food at budget prices.

Seeing the Sights   Pua Mau Place, one of Hawaii's most unusual botanical gardens, offers guests a 45-acre oasis with breathtaking views of both the ocean and the majestic mountains. This is a great place for families (children are welcome and invited to feed the large number of birds in the aviary). Visitors can take the self-guided tour along mulched pathways meandering through the gardens, where every plant is clearly marked.

MAUI   Recently opened is the fabulous budget **Pineapple Inn Maui,** in Kihei. Located in the residential Maui Meadows area, this charming inn (only four rooms, plus a darling two-bedroom cottage) is not only an exquisite find, but the prices are terrific and include panoramic ocean views, a saltwater pool, and a Jacuzzi.

Other great budget deals in Kihei are the newly renovated **Sunseeker Resort** and **Wailana Inn,** both recently purchased by the same owners and massively renovationed.

In that same area, **Bello Realty,** one of our favorite vacation rental management companies, has added the **Wailani Kai** condominium to its collection of very inexpensive units. Just a 1-minute walk to the beach, this is a frugal traveler's dream accommodation.

Where to Dine   A couple of new restaurants opened recently. The **Main Street Bistro,** located on Main Street in Wailuku, is now owned by Chef Tom Selman (formerly of David Paul's Lahaina Grill) and serves what he calls "refined comfort food." **Cilantro: Fresh Mexican Grill,** located in Lahaina, dishes up fabulous Mexican food at frugal prices.

When Vino Restaurant opened in August 2003, it featured terrific Italian food and a view to die for, overlooking the rolling hills of the Kapalua Golf Course. Always wanting to be on the cutting edge, Chef D. K. Kodama rebranded the restaurant in December 2004 to **Vino Italian Tapas & Wine Bar** because he wanted his loyal following to be able to sample even more items on the menu with small plates.

After Dark   The Ritz-Carlton Kapalua has added a couple of "not to be missed" cultural activities to their list of things to do after dark: **The Legends of Kaulula'au** every Tuesday night at the indoor amphitheater and the **Masters of Hawaiian Slack Key Guitar Series.**

KAUAI   In the rolling hills behind Kapaa, the **Kauai Country Inn** offers visitors on a budget a terrific deal. Each of the four suites is uniquely decorated in Hawaiian art deco, complete with hardwood floors, private baths, kitchen or kitchenette, your own computer with high-speed connection, and lots of little amenities that will make you break out into laughter at the host's sense of humor.

Seeing the Sights   The best way to see the sights on Kauai is via helicopter. Just recently, **Blue Hawaiian Helicopter,** our favorite helicopter company on both Maui and the Big Island, opened up a branch on Kauai. We recommend booking with Blue Hawaiian for a flight that will remain with you long after your tan has faded.

Believe it or not, a sacred Hindu temple is being carved out of rocks from India and constructed on the banks of the Wailua River. The **San Marga Iraivan Temple** is being built to last "a thousand years or more" on the 458-acre site of the Saiva Siddhanta Church monastery, just outside Kapaa. Not expected to be completed until 2010, the Chola-style temple is the result of a vision by the late Satguru Sivaya Subramuniyaswami, known to his followers as Gurudeva. He specifically selected this site in 1970, recognizing that the Hawaiians also felt the spiritual power of this place, which the Hawaiians call *pihanakalani* (where heaven touches the earth). The public is welcome to the monastery temple dedicated to the Hindu god Shiva. There is also a weekly-guided tour of the grounds.

1

The Best of Hawaii from $80 a Day

There's no place on earth quite like this handful of sun-drenched mid-Pacific islands. Here you'll find palm-fringed blue lagoons, lush rainforests, hidden gardens, cascading waterfalls, wild rivers running through rugged canyons, and volcanoes soaring 2 miles into the sky. And oh, those beaches—gold, red, black, and even green sands caressed by endless surf.

Unfortunately, even paradise has its share of stifling crowds and tourist schlock. If you're not careful, your trip to Hawaii could turn into a nightmare of tourist traps selling shells from the Philippines, the hokey faux culture of cellophane-skirted hula dancers, overpriced exotic drinks, and a 4-hour timeshare lecture before you get on that "free" sailing trip. That's where this guide comes in. As Hawaii residents, we can tell the extraordinary from the merely ordinary. We're here to steer you away from the crowded, the overrated, and the overpriced—and toward the best Hawaii has to offer. This guide will make sure that your every dollar is well spent.

THE HAWAII FROM $80 A DAY PREMISE

This premise might seem like a pipe dream, but it's not. The idea is this: With good planning and a watchful eye, you can keep your basic daily living costs—accommodations and three meals a day—down to as little as $80 per person. This budget model works best for two adults traveling together who have at least $160 a day to work with and can share a double room (single rooms are much less cost-efficient). This way, if you aim for accommodations costing around $100 for a double, you'll be left with about $30 per person per day for food (less drinks and tips).

If you want to keep things even cheaper, we'll show you how to do that, too. But, in defining this basic premise, we at Frommer's have assumed that you want to travel comfortably, probably with your own room rather than a hostel bunk (even if it does mean a shared bathroom), and dining on good food rather than fast food at every meal. This book will also serve you well even if you don't need to keep your two-person budget to an absolutely strict $160 a day, but you want to keep the tabs down and get the most for your money at every turn. It will, on the other side of the coin, also meet your needs if you want to travel on the ultra-cheap—for less than $80 a day—by camping out in clean hostels and eating as cheaply as possible.

Of course, the cost of sightseeing, transportation, and entertainment are all extras. But don't worry—although many of Hawaii's outings and eco-adventures are quite pricey, we've got plenty of suggestions on how to keep those bills down, too. Only you know how much money you have to spend; but with our advice, you'll be able to make informed decisions on what to see and do. If you stick to our recommendations, it'll be money well spent.

The Hawaiian Islands

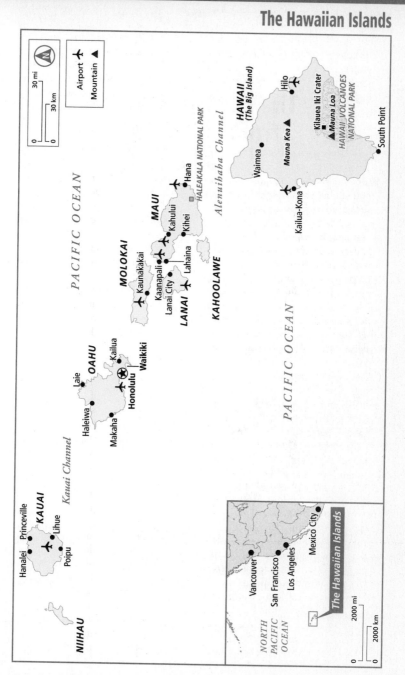

N

Airport ✈
Mountain ▲

30 mi
30 km

KAUAI
Hanalei
Princeville
Lihue
Poipu

NIIHAU

PACIFIC OCEAN

Kauai Channel

OAHU
Laie
Kailua
Haleiwa
Honolulu
Waikiki
Makaha

MOLOKAI
Kaunakakai

MAUI
Kahului
Kihei
Kaanapali
Lahaina
Hana
HALEAKALA NATIONAL PARK

LANAI
Lanai City

KAHOOLAWE

Alenuihaha Channel

PACIFIC OCEAN

HAWAII
(The Big Island)
Hilo
Waimea
Mauna Kea ▲
Kilauea Iki Crater
Mauna Loa ▲
HAWAII VOLCANOES
NATIONAL PARK
Kailua-Kona
South Point

NORTH
PACIFIC
OCEAN

Vancouver
San Francisco
Los Angeles
Mexico City

The Hawaiian Islands

2000 mi
2000 km

1 The Best Beaches

- **Lanikai Beach** (Oahu): Too gorgeous to be real, this stretch along the Windward Coast is one of Hawaii's postcard-perfect beaches—a mile of golden sand as soft as powdered sugar bordering translucent turquoise waters. The year-round swimming pool–calm waters are excellent for swimming, snorkeling, and kayaking. To complete the picture, there are two tiny offshore islands that function not only as scenic backdrops but also as bird sanctuaries. See "Beaches" in chapter 5.

- **Hapuna Beach** (Big Island): This half-mile–long crescent regularly wins kudos in the world's top travel magazines as the most beautiful beach in Hawaii—some consider it one of the most beautiful beaches in the whole world. One look and you'll see why: Perfect cream-colored sand slopes down to crystal-clear waters that, in the summer, are great for swimming, snorkeling, and bodysurfing; come winter, waves thunder in like stampeding wild horses. The facilities for picnicking and camping are top-notch, and there's plenty of parking. See p. 283.

- **Kapalua Beach** (Maui): On an island of many great beaches, Kapalua takes the prize. This golden crescent with swaying palms is protected from strong winds and currents by two outstretched lava-rock promontories. Its calm waters are perfect for snorkeling, swimming, and kayaking. The beach borders the Kapalua Bay Hotel, but it's long enough for everyone to enjoy. Facilities include showers, restrooms, and lifeguards. See "Beaches" in chapter 7.

- **Papohaku Beach** (Molokai): One of Hawaii's longest beaches, these gold sands stretch on for some 3 miles, and are about as wide as a football field. Offshore, the ocean churns mightily in winter, but the waves die down in summer, making the calm waters inviting for swimming. Papohaku is also great for picnics, beach walks, and sunset watching. See "Beaches" in chapter 8.

- **Hulopoe Beach** (Lanai): This golden, palm-fringed beach off the south coast of Lanai gently slopes down to the azure waters of a Marine Life Conservation District, where clouds of tropical fish flourish and spinner dolphins come to play. A tide pool in the lava rocks defines one side of the bay, while the other is lorded over by the Manele Bay Hotel, which sits prominently on the hill above. Offshore, you'll find good swimming, snorkeling, and diving. Onshore, there's a full complement of beach facilities, from restrooms to camping areas. See "Beaches" in chapter 9.

- **Haena Beach** (Kauai): Backed by verdant cliffs, this curvaceous North Shore beach has starred as Paradise in many a movie. It's easy to see why Hollywood loves Haena Beach, with its grainy golden sand and translucent turquoise waters. Summer months bring calm waters for swimming and snorkeling, while winter brings mighty waves for surfers. There are plenty of facilities on hand, including picnic tables, restrooms, and showers. See "Beaches" in chapter 10.

2 The Best Destinations for Low-Cost Vacations

- **The Hamakua Coast** (the Big Island): For an affordable vacation with plenty of hiking and ocean swimming among some of Hawaii's greatest natural beauty, come to the Hamakua Coast. Steeped in myth, the majestic Waipio Valley once supported a community of 40,000 Hawaiians in a garden of Eden etched by streams and waterfalls. Today, only about 50 Hawaiians live in this sacred place, which stretches from a black-sand beach to the cathedral-like cliffs that mark the valley wall some 6 miles away. Affordable B&Bs abound in nearby Kukuihaele and the historic village of Honokaa, which also has a good number of reasonably priced restaurants. See chapter 6.

- **Hilo** (the Big Island): This quaint, misty, flower-filled city by the bay offers bargains galore for the traveler on a tight budget. Comfy rooms start at just $55 for two, filling Hawaiian-style plate lunches go for only $7, and there are plenty of bargains to be found in the unique boutique shops downtown. Explore nearby waterfalls and tropical gardens, take in the historic sites, and lazily drift in the warm ocean waters offshore. Spectacular Hawaii Volcanoes National Park—with its still-spewing volcano, miles of trails through desolate lava deserts and verdant rainforests, and the bargain-basement admission fee of just $10 per car (good for an entire week!)—is less than an hour's drive away. See chapter 6.

- **Huelo** (Maui): This place is so special and such a deal, we almost hate to spill the secret. On the road to Hana, on steep ocean cliffs out past the congestion of Kahului and the funky, bustling windsurfing capital of Paia, lies the quiet community of Huelo. This is the place to get away from it all. Those staying at Huelo's one-of-a-kind B&Bs wake early to catch the sunrise over the Pacific; they venture out to waterfalls and swimming holes after a leisurely breakfast; in winter, they scan for whales from vantage points along the cliffs. At sunset, they dine on simple meals they've prepared themselves as they watch the sky fade from blue to magenta. Huelo is ideal for a quiet, simple vacation rich in nature, serenity, and affordability. See chapter 7.

- **Molokai:** Often called "the real Hawaii," Molokai is the kind of place where time moves more slowly. Reasonably priced condos and B&Bs dot the island; you can even stay on the ocean for just $80 a night. Restaurants cater to the locals, for whom eating out is a treat, not a necessity, so prices are low. Entertainment is homemade: early-morning swims, day hikes through the forest, sunset picnics on the beach. Best of all, a stay on Molokai is a sojourn back to an era where people smile and wave to strangers, and nothing is more important than stopping to appreciate natural beauty. See chapter 8.

- **Kauai's Coconut Coast:** This once-royal land on the road to the North Shore abounds with sparkling waterfalls and lush rainforest as well as bargain-priced accommodations and restaurants. With lots of activities to offer—from water-skiing on the Wailua River to offshore kayaking—this is heaven for active travelers. At the center of the action is Kapaa, a restored plantation town that hasn't lost its funky charm. And the central location makes this a great base for exploring the entire island—nothing is much more than an hour away. See chapter 10.

3 The Best Free or Cheap Experiences

- **Hitting the Beach:** A beach is a beach is a beach, right? Not in Hawaii. With 132 islets, shoals, and reefs in the tropical Pacific and a general coastline of 750 miles, Hawaii has beaches of all different sizes, shapes, and colors, from white to black; the variety on the six major islands is astonishing. You can go to a different beach every day for years and still not see them all. And, whether you're looking for a scene or want to get away from it all, there's one for everyone. See the "Beaches" sections in the individual island chapters.

- **Taking the Plunge:** Don mask, fin, and snorkel and explore the magical world beneath the waves—exotic corals and kaleidoscopic clouds of tropical fish; a sea turtle may even come over to check you out. Can't swim? Rent a life jacket that will keep you afloat while you peer below the surface. Whatever you do, don't miss the opportunity to go under—if you come to Hawaii and don't see the underwater world, you're missing half the fun.

- **Reliving the Tragedy of Pearl Harbor** (Oahu): After December 7, 1941, the day that Japanese warplanes bombed Pearl Harbor, the United States could turn its back on World War II no longer. Standing on the deck of the USS *Arizona* Memorial, which stands as an eternal tomb for the 1,177 sailors and Marines trapped below when the battleship sank in 9 minutes, is a moving experience you'll never forget. Admission is absolutely free. See p. 184.

- **Meeting Local Folks:** Get out of the resort areas to learn about Hawaii and its people. Just smile and say "Owzit?" ("How is it?"). "It's good," is the usual response—and you'll usually make a new friend. Hawaii is remarkably cosmopolitan—every ethnic group in the world seems to be represented here—and it's fascinating to discover the varieties of food, culture, language, and customs.

- **Touring an Entire Island for Just a Couple of Bucks** (Oahu): A buck-fifty gets you around the island of Oahu on TheBus's Circle Island line. From Ala Moana Center, no. 52 goes clockwise around the island, and no. 55 goes counterclockwise. It takes 3 to 4½ hours to circumnavigate the island, in which time you'll see the majority of its scenic beauty. It's the best sightseeing deal in the islands, hands down. See chapter 5.

- **Watching the Hula Being Performed:** On Kauai, the **Coconut Market Place** hosts free hula shows every day at 5pm. Get there early to get a good seat for the hour-long performances of both *kahiko* (ancient) and *auwana* (modern) hula. The real show-stoppers are the *keiki* (children) who perform. Don't forget your camera! See chapter 10.

- **Ogling the Day's Catch** (the Big Island): Daily weigh-ins of big game fish catch usually get underway at the Honokohau Harbor Fuel Dock between 4 and 5pm. It doesn't cost a thing to sit in the bleachers at the weigh-in area and watch as 1,000-pound Pacific blue marlin, fat yellowfin tunas in the 100- to 200-pound range, and a host of other eye-popping catches are strung up to the scale and weighed. See p. 293.

- **Visiting the National Parks:** Hawaii's national parks are the nation's most unusual. Maui's Haleakala National Park features one of the biggest volcanic craters on earth; it's an otherworldly place that holds the secrets of past millennia. Sunrise here is a mystical experience. The Big Island's Hawaii Volcanoes National Park, on the other hand, holds the key to the future: At its heart is still-erupting Kilauea volcano, where you can watch nature in action, sculpting the island before your eyes. You can actually walk up to the flow and watch it ooze along for an up-close-and-personal encounter, or you can stand at the shoreline and watch with awe as 2,000°F (1,093°C) molten fire pours into the ocean, adding to the island's density. If you have to choose just one park in Hawaii, choose Hawaii Volcanoes; it's simply spectacular. See "Seeing the Sights" in chapters 6 and 7.

- **Hiking into Kalaupapa (Molokai):** Even if you can't afford to fly or ride a mule in, don't pass up the opportunity to see this hauntingly beautiful peninsula. It takes nothing more than a pair of hiking boots, a permit (available at the trail head), and some grit. Hike down the 2.5-mile trail (with 26 switchbacks, it can be a bit tricky) to Molokai's legendary leper colony. The views are breathtaking: You'll see the world's highest sea cliffs and waterfalls plunging thousands of feet into the ocean. See p. 479.

4 The Best Adventures for Special Splurges

Branch out while you're in Hawaii; do something you wouldn't normally do—after all, you're on vacation. Following is a list of adventures we highly recommend. They may be pricey, but these splurges are worth every penny.

- **Year-Round Whale-Watching with Captain Dan** (the Big Island; *C* **808/ 322-0028**): During humpback season—roughly December to April—when Hawaii's most impressive visitors return to the waters off the Kona Coast, Capt. Dan McSweeney will take you right to them. In the other months of the year, he'll take you out to see Hawaii's year-round whales: pilot, sperm, false killer, melon-headed, pygmy killer, and beaked whales. A whale researcher for more than 20 years, Captain Dan has no problem finding whales—in fact, he guarantees a sighting, or he'll take you out again for free. He frequently drops an underwater microphone or video camera into the depths so you can listen to whale songs or actually see what's going on. See p. 289.

- **Night Diving with Manta Rays** (the Big Island): These harmless creatures of the deep, with wingspans of 10 to 14 feet, frequent the waters of Kona looking for a meal of microscopic plankton, which are attracted to the shore lights. Watching these graceful fish spin, barrel roll, and pirouette in the lights is an experience you'll never forget. See p. 292.

- **Big-Game Fishing off the Kona Coast** (the Big Island): Don't pass up the opportunity to try your luck in the big-game fishing capital of the world. This is one of the few places where 1,000-pound marlin are taken from the seas just about every month of the year. Not looking to set a world record? Kona's charter boat captains specialize in conservation, and will be glad to "tag and release" any fish you angle, letting the fish go so someone else can have the fun of fighting a big game fish. See "Watersports" in chapter 6.

- **Riding a Mule to Kalaupapa** (Molokai): Even if you have only a single day to spend on Molokai, spend it on a mule. The trek from "topside" Molokai to the Kalaupapa National Historic Park, Father Damien's world-famous leper colony, with **Molokai Mule Ride** (C 800/ 567-7550 or 808/567-6088) is a once-in-a-lifetime adventure. The cliffs are taller than 300-story sky-scrapers—but Buzzy Sproat's mules go up and down the narrow 2.9-mile trail daily, rain or shine, without ever losing a rider or mount on any of the 26 switchbacks. From 1,600 feet on the nearly perpendicular ridge, the sure-footed mules step down the muddy trail, pausing often to calculate their next move. Each switchback is numbered; by the time you get to number 4, you'll catch your breath, put the mule on cruise control, and begin to enjoy Hawaii's most awesome trail ride. See p. 484.

- **Day Tripping to Lanai:** If you'd like to visit Lanai, but you only have a day to spare, the best way to go is on **Trilogy Excursions'** (C 800/874-2666 or 808/661-4743) daylong sailing, snorkeling, swimming, and whale-watching adventure from Maui. For more than 2 decades, the members of the Coon family have taken visitors on personalized tours of their favorite island. They make the 6:30am departure as painless as possible with their home-baked hot cinnamon rolls (mom's own secret recipe) and just-brewed Kona coffee. After several hours of snorkeling, swimming, and just laying around in the sun, the crew whips up a Hawaiian-style barbecue, after which they take you on a guided van tour of the island. The afternoon sail back can be relaxing or wet 'n' wild, depending on the wind gods. See p. 410.

- **A Helicopter Ride over the Na Pali Coast** (Kauai): Streaking low over razor-thin cliffs, fluttering past sparkling waterfalls and down into the canyons and valleys of the fabled Na Pali Coast—there's almost too much beauty to absorb as you fly over this spectacular, surreal landscape. It's the best way to see the dazzling beauty of Kauai. See "Seeing the Sights," in chapter 10 for recommended outfitters.

5 The Best of Natural Hawaii

- **Volcanoes:** The entire island chain is made of volcanoes; don't miss the opportunity to see one. On Oahu, the entire family can hike to the top of the ancient volcano, world-famous **Diamond Head.** At the other end of the spectrum is fire-breathing Kilauea at **Hawaii Volcanoes National Park,** on the Big Island, where you can get an up-close-and-personal experience with the red-hot lava ooze. On Maui, **Haleakala National Park** provides a bird's-eye view into a long-dormant volcanic crater. See chapters 5, 6, and 7.

- **Waterfalls:** Rushing waterfalls thundering downward into sparkling freshwater pools are some of Hawaii's most beautiful natural wonders. If you're on the Big Island, stop by **Rainbow Falls,** in Hilo, or the spectacular 442-foot **Akaka Falls,** just outside the city. On Maui, the Road to Hana offers numerous viewing opportunities; at the end of the drive, you'll find **Oheo Gulch** (also known as the Seven Sacred Pools), with some of the most dramatic and accessible waterfalls on the islands. Kauai is loaded with waterfalls, especially along the North Shore and in the Wailua area, where you'll find 40-foot **Opaekaa Falls,** probably the best-looking drive-up waterfall on Kauai. With scenic mountain peaks in the background and a restored Hawaiian village on the nearby river banks, the Opaekaa Falls are what the tourist-bureau folks call an eye-popping photo op. See "Seeing the Sights," in chapters 6, 7, and 10.

- **Gardens:** The islands are redolent with the sweet scent of flowers. On Oahu, amid the high-rises of down-town Honolulu, the leafy oasis of **Foster Botanical Garden** showcases 24 native Hawaiian trees and the last stand of several rare trees, including an East African whose white flowers bloom only at night. On the Big Island, **Liliuokalani Gardens**—the largest formal Japanese garden this side of Tokyo—resembles a postcard from Asia, with bonsai, carp ponds, pagodas, and even a moon gate bridge. At Maui's **Kula Botanical Garden,** you can take a leisurely self-guided stroll through more than 700 native and exotic plants, including orchids, proteas, and bromeliads. On lush Kauai, do not miss the incredible magical **Na Aina Kai Botanical Gardens,** on some 240 acres, sprinkled with some 70 life-size (some larger than life) whimsical bronze statues, hidden off the beaten path of the North Shore. See "Seeing the Sights," in chapters 5, 6, 7, and 10.

- **Marine Life Conservation Areas:** Nine underwater parks are spread across Hawaii, most notably **Waikiki Beach** and **Hanauma Bay,** on Oahu; the Big Island's **Kealakekua Bay; Molokini,** just off the coast of Maui;

and Lanai's **Manele and Hulopoe bays.** Be sure to bring snorkel gear to at least one of these wonderful places during your vacation here. See "Water-sports," in chapters 5, 6, 7, and 9.

- **Garden of the Gods** (Lanai): Out on Lanai's North Shore lies the ultimate rock garden: a rugged, barren, beautiful place full of rocks strewn by volcanic forces and shaped by the elements into a variety of shapes and colors—brilliant reds, oranges, ochers, and yellows. Scientists use phrases such as "ongoing post-erosional event" or "plain and simple badlands" to describe the desolate, windswept place. The ancient Hawaiians, however, considered the Garden of the Gods to be an entirely supernatural phenomenon. Natural badlands or mystical garden? Take a four-wheel-drive trip out here and decide for yourself. See "Seeing the Sights," in chapter 9.

- **The Grand Canyon of the Pacific—Waimea Canyon** (Kauai): This valley, known for its reddish lava beds, reminds everyone who sees it of Arizona's Grand Canyon. Kauai's version is bursting with ever-changing color, just like its namesake, but it's smaller—only a mile wide, 3,567 feet deep, and 12 miles long. All this grandeur was caused by a massive earthquake that sent all the streams flowing into a single river, which then carved this picturesque canyon. You can stop by the road and look at it, hike down into it, or swoop through it by helicopter. See p. 578.

6 The Best Golf Courses with Reasonable Greens Fees

Believe it or not, there are golfing bargains to be had in Hawaii—not at the world-famous resort or PGA courses, but at little-known local ones offering breathtaking views, challenging play, and affordable greens fees.

- **Kahuku Golf Course** (Oahu; ✆ **808/293-5842**): We admit that this nine-hole budget course is a bit funky: There are no facilities (except a few pull carts that disappear with the first handful of golfers), no club rentals, and no clubhouse. But golfing here is a great way to experience the tranquillity and natural beauty of Oahu's North Shore. The views are fantastic, especially from holes 3, 4, 7, and 8, which are right on the ocean. Duffers will love the ease of this recreational course. The cost for this experience? Just $8 on weekdays and $10 on weekends for 9 holes. See p. 173.

- **Hamakua Country Club** (the Big Island; ℂ **808/775-7244**): This par-33, 2,520-yard course was built in the 1920s on a very steep hill overlooking the ocean. With really only enough room for about 4½ holes, architect Frank Anderson somehow managed to squeeze in 9 by criss-crossing holes across the fairway. The cost to play this course—open weekdays to nonmembers—is just $15. See p. 299.

- **Pukalani Country Club** (Maui; ℂ **808/572-1314**): This cool par-72, 6,962-yard course at 1,100 feet elevation is a fun one to play. High-handicap golfers will love it, and more experienced players can make it more challenging by playing from the back tee. Greens fees, including carts, are only $55 for 18 holes, even cheaper after 11am. See p. 424.

- **Ironwood Hills Golf Course** (Molokai; ℂ **808/567-6000**): One of the oldest golf courses in the state, Ironwood Hills is a real find. Built in 1929 by the Del Monte Plantation for its executives, this unusual course delights with its rich foliage, open fairways, and spectacular views of the rest of the island. Greens fees range from $15 to $20, depending on how many holes you play. See p. 480.

- **Cavendish Golf Course** (Lanai): To play this 9-hole course next to the Lodge at Koele in Lanai City, just show up and put a donation ($5–$10 would be nice) into the little wooden box next to the first tee. The par-30, 3,071-yard course was built by the Dole plantation in 1947 for its employees. The greens are a bit bumpy—nothing will roll straight here—but the views of Lanai are great. See p. 504.

- **Kukuiolono Golf Course** (Kauai; ℂ **808/332-9151**): This fun 9-hole course has spectacular views of Kauai's entire south coast. You can't beat the price: $7 for the day, no matter how many holes you play—you can even play the course twice, if you like. This course is well maintained and relatively straightforward, with few fairway hazards, but there are plenty of trees in this wooded area to keep you on your game. When you get to the second tee box, check out the coconut tree dotted with yellow, pink, orange, and white golf balls that have been driven into the bark. Don't laugh—your next shot might add to the decor! See p. 571.

7 The Best Cultural Experiences

Hawaii isn't just any other beach destination. It has a wonderfully rich, ancient history and culture that's worth getting to know while you're in the islands.

- **Watching the Ancient Hawaiian Sport of Canoe Paddling** (Oahu): From February to September, on weekday evenings and weekend days, hundreds of canoe paddlers gather at Ala Wai Canal and practice the Hawaiian sport of canoe paddling. Find a comfortable spot at Ala Wai Park, next to the canal, and watch this ancient sport come to life. See p. 174.

- **Attending a Hawaiian-Language Church Service** (Oahu): Kawaiahao Church (ℂ **808/522-1333**) is the Westminster Abbey of Hawaii; the vestibule is lined with portraits of the Hawaiian monarchy, many of whom were crowned in this very building. The coral church is a perfect setting to experience an all-Hawaiian service, held every Sunday at 10:30am, complete with Hawaiian song. Admission is free; let your conscience be your guide as to a donation. See p. 174.

- **Buying a Lei in Chinatown** (Oahu): There's actually a host of cultural sights and experiences to be had in Honolulu's Chinatown. Wander through this several-square-block area with its jumble of exotic shops offering herbs, Chinese groceries, and acupuncture services. Before you leave, be sure to check out the lei sellers on Maunakea Street (near N. Hotel St.), where Hawaii's finest leis go for as little as $3.50. See chapter 5.

- **Visiting Ancient Hawaii's Most Sacred Temple** (the Big Island): On the Kohala Coast, where King Kamehameha the Great was born, stands Hawaii's oldest, largest, and most sacred religious site—the 1,500-year-old Mookini Heiau, used by kings to pray and offer human sacrifices. The massive three-story stone temple, dedicated to Ku, the Hawaiian god of war, was erected in A.D. 480. Each stone is said to have been passed hand-to-hand from Pololu Valley, 14 miles away, by 18,000 men who worked from sunset to sunrise. Go in late afternoon when the setting sun strikes the lava rock walls and creates a primal mood. See p. 310.

- **Hunting for Petroglyphs** (the Big Island): Archaeologists are still unsure who made these ancient rock carvings—the majority of which are found in the 233-acre Puako Petroglyph Archaeological District, near Mauna Lani Resort, on the Kohala Coast—or why. The best time to hunt for intricate depictions of

ancient life is either early in the morning or late afternoon, when the angle of the sun lets you see the forms clearly. See "Seeing the Sights" in chapter 6.

- **Exploring Puuhonua O Honaunau National Historic Park** (the Big Island): This sacred site on the South Kona Coast was once a place of refuge and a revered place of rejuvenation. Today, you can walk the same consecrated grounds where priests once conducted holy ceremonies and glimpse the ancient way of life in pre-contact Hawaii in the re-created 180-acre village. See p. 305.

- **Visiting the Most Hawaiian Isle:** A time capsule of 19th-century Hawaii, Molokai allows visitors to experience real Hawaiian life in its most unsullied form. The island's people have woven the cultural values of ancient times into modern life. In addition to this rich community, you'll find the magnificent natural wonders it so cherishes: Hawaii's highest waterfall and greatest collection of fish ponds; the world's tallest sea cliffs; plus sand dunes, coral reefs, rainforests, and empty, gloriously empty, beaches—pretty much the same Molokai of generations ago. See chapter 8.

- **Watching Salt Being Made** (Kauai): At Salt Pond Beach Park, Hawaiian families have practiced the ancient art of salt making for generations. During the summer, families—from the littlest *keiki* to eldest *kupuna*—work together in the ponds, evaporate the salt water, rake up the salt, and bag the Hawaiian salt, which is used in cooking and medicine. See p. 553.

- **Discovering the Legendary Little People** (Kauai): According to ancient Hawaiian legend, among Kauai's earliest settlers were the Menehune, a race of small people who worked at night to accomplish magnificent feats. The Menehune Fish Pond—which at one time extended 25 miles—is said to have been built in just one night, with two rows of thousands of Menehune passing stones hand to hand. The Menehune were promised that no one would watch them work, but one person did; when they discovered the spy, they stopped working immediately, leaving two gaps in the wall. Kayakers can paddle up Huleia Stream to see it up close. See p. 577.

8 The Best Affordable Accommodations

- **Royal Grove Hotel** (Oahu; ℂ 808/923-7691; www.royalgrovehotel.com): This small, family-owned hotel, with plenty of old-fashioned aloha, has *the* bargain of Waikiki. For $45 (about the same price a couple would pay to stay in a private room at the hostel in Waikiki), you get a clean room in the older Mauka Wing, with a double bed or two twins, plus a kitchenette with refrigerator and stove. And it's only a 3-minute walk to the beach. See p. 119.

- **Backpackers Vacation Inn** (Oahu; ℂ 808/638-7838; www.backpackers-hawaii.com): If your dream of Hawaii is staying on the North Shore of Oahu where monstrous waves roll in during the winter, this multi-accommodation property is for you. It's not just for backpackers (although they do have dorm beds starting at $20 and private rooms for $66). This North Shore property has oceanfront studios, which sleep four, starting at $96, and other oceanview homes at budget prices. See p. 129.

- **Kona Islander Inn** (Big Island; ℂ 800/622-5348; www.konahawaii.com): This is the most affordable condo in Kailua-Kona with studio apartments beginning at $80 a night. These plantation-style, three-story buildings are surrounded by lush, palm-tree–lined gardens with torchlit pathways that make it hard to believe you're smack-dab in the middle of downtown. The central location—across the street from the historic Kona Inn Shops—is convenient but can be noisy; but at these rates, you can afford earplugs. See p. 243.

- **Kona Tiki Hotel** (the Big Island; ℂ 808/329-1425): Right on the ocean, away from the hustle and bustle of downtown Kailua-Kona, is one of the hottest budget deals in Hawaii. Although it's called a hotel, this small, family-run operation is more like a large bed-and-breakfast, with a continental breakfast buffet served by the pool every morning. The price? Just $61 to $75 for a double, or $84 for a room with kitchenette. See p. 244.

- **Makai Inn** (Maui; ℂ 808/662-3200; www.makaiinn.net) This small apartment complex located right on the water (okay, no white-sand beach out front, but what do you want at these eye-popping prices that start at $75 a room). The closest white-sand beach is just a 10-minute stroll, and the center of Lahaina town is a 20-minute walk away. The units are small (400 sq. ft.) but clean and filled with everything you could possible need for your vacation: full kitchens, views of the ocean (in most units), separate bedrooms, and a quiet neighborhood. See p. 359.

- **Pineapple Inn Maui** (Maui; ℂ 877-212-MAUI, ext. 6284; www.pineappleinnmaui.com): This charming inn (only four rooms, plus a darling two-bedroom cottage) is not only an exquisite find, but the prices, at just $99, are terrific. Located in the residential area, with panoramic ocean views, this two-story inn is expertly landscaped in tropical flowers and plants with a lily pond in the front and a giant saltwater pool and Jacuzzi overlooking the ocean. Each of the soundproof rooms is professionally decorated with a small kitchenette (fridge, coffeemaker, toaster, and microwave), comfy bed, free wireless Internet access, TV/VCR, and an incredible view off your own private lanai. See p. 367.

- **Kamalo Plantation Bed-and-Breakfast** (Molokai; © **808/558-8236;** www.molokai.com/kamalo): This lush 5-acre spread includes an ancient *heiau* ruin in the front yard, plus leafy tropical gardens and a working fruit orchard. The plantation-style cottage is tucked under flowering trees and surrounded by swaying palms and tropical foliage. It has its own lanai, a big living room with a queen sofa bed, and a separate bedroom with a king bed, so it can sleep four comfortably. The kitchen is fully equipped (it even has spices), and there's a barbecue outside. A breakfast of fruit and freshly baked bread is served every morning, all for just $85 for a double. See p. 468.

- **Kauai Country Inn** (Kauai; © **808/ 821-0207;** www.kauaicountryinn. com): Run to the phone right now and book this place! Hard to believe that nestled in the rolling hills behind Kapaa, this old-fashioned country inn exists. Starting at $95, each of the four suites is uniquely decorated in Hawaiian art deco with a touch of humor—complete with hardwood floors, private baths, kitchen or kitchenette, your own computer with high-speed connection, and lots of little amenities. Everything is top drawer, from the furniture to the Sub-Zero refrigerator. See p. 530.

- **Victoria Place** (Kauai; © **808/ 332-9300;** www.hshawaii.com/kvp/ victoria): Hostess Edee Seymour lavishes her guests with attention and aloha in her spacious, skylit, U-shaped house that wraps around the swimming pool and garden of bougainvillea, hibiscus, gardenia, and ginger. There's also a secluded studio apartment ("Victoria's Other Secret") down a private path. Edee's breakfasts are truly a big deal: at least five different tropical fruits, followed by something from the oven, such as homemade bread, scones, or muffins—all for just $90. See p. 522.

9 The Best Affordable Family Accommodations

- **Aloha Punawai** (Oahu; © **808/923-5211;** www.alternative-hawaii.com/ alohapunawai): Here's one of Waikiki's best-kept secrets: a low-profile, family-operated (since 1959) apartment hotel just 2 blocks from the beach and within walking distance of most Waikiki attractions. The Aloha Punawai offers some of the lowest prices in Waikiki ($95 for studios and $105 for a one-bedroom); if you stay a week, prices drop even more. And the location is great, just across the street from Fort DeRussy Park and 2 blocks to Grey's Beach—the same great beach facing the luxury Halekulani and Sheraton Waikiki hotels. See p. 109.

- **Schrader's Windward Marine Resort** (Oahu; © **800/735-5071** or 808/239-5711; www.hawaiiscene. com/schrader): Nestled in a tranquil, tropical setting on Kaneohe Bay, only a 30-minute drive from Waikiki, this complex is made up of older cottage-style motels and a collection of older homes with budget prices starting at $72 for a one-bedroom, $127 for a two-bedroom, $226 for a three-bedroom, and $446 for a four-bedroom. See p. 127.

- **Volcano Guest House** (Big Island; ℂ 808/967-7775; www.volcanoguesthouse.com): If you're planning to visit Hawaii Volcanoes National Park, here's the place to bring the family. A mother herself, Bonnie Gooddell has completely child-proofed her house and installed a basketball hoop in the driveway; her truckload of toys will keep the kids happy for hours. You can make yourself right at home in Bonnie's free-standing two-story guest cottage, which comes outfitted with everything, even down to extra wool socks for cold nights. And at $85 for two plus $15 for each of the kids, it's easy on the family budget. See p. 260.

- **The Spinnaker** (Maui; ℂ 808/662-3200; www.makaiinn.net): This residential complex on a side street in Lahaina offers extremely affordable one- and two-bedroom budget apartments offered only by the week, but at prices that families can afford ($500 a week for the one-bedroom or $600 a week for the two-bedroom). All units have full kitchens, phones, television, and all the comforts of home. There is a pool in the complex and a whirlpool and barbecue area. There's no maid service, but at these prices you can clean up on your own. See p. 359.

- **Wailana Kai** (Maui; ℂ 800/541-3060; www.bellomaui.com): Bello Realty, which has searched out the best deals in Kihei, has added this renovated, two-story, 10-unit one- and two-bedroom apartments to its collection. With one-bedroom units starting at $85, this is a deal that will not last long. It's located at the end of a cul-de-sac street and just a 1-minute walk to the beach. All units have full kitchens, concrete walls (soundproof!), and the second floor has ocean views. Also on property are a small pool, coin-operated laundry, and a barbecue area. See p. 369.

- **Moanui Beach House** (Molokai; ℂ 808/558-8236; www.molokai.com/kamalo): If you're looking for a quiet, remote beach house, this is it: a two-bedroom beach house, right across the street from a secluded white-sand cove beach. The A-frame has a shaded lanai facing the ocean, a screened-in lanai on the side of the house, a full kitchen, and an ocean view that's worth the price alone, which is just $140. See p. 468.

- **Nihi Kai Villas, Poipu Crater Resort,** and **Waikomo Stream Villas** (Kauai; ℂ 800/325-5701; www.grantham-resorts.com). Here's a deal for you: These three wonderful Poipu properties with large, perfectly wonderful one- and two-bedroom condos a stone's throw from the beach—from just $89 a night! What you're not getting is new carpet, new furniture, new drapes, and a prime location on the sands. What you are getting is a clean, well-located, well-cared for unit at a bargain price. The sofa bed in the living room allows even the one-bedroom condos to sleep four comfortably. Such on-site amenities as swimming pools, tennis and paddle courts, and barbecue and picnic areas make these value properties an even better bargain. See p. 523 and p. 524.

10 The Best Hawaii Websites

- **Big Island Home Page (www.big island.com):** Though not the most beautifully designed site, it does include lots of listings for dining, lodging, and activities, most with links to more information and images.

- **Hawaii Visitors & Convention Bureau (www.gohawaii.com):** This site provides an excellent, all-around guide to activities, tours, lodging, and events, plus a huge section on weddings and honeymoons. But keep in mind that only members of the HVCB are listed.

- **Internet Hawaii Radio (www.hot spots.hawaii.com):** A great way to get into the mood, this eclectic site features great Hawaiian music, with opportunities to order a CD or cassette. You can also purchase a respectable assortment of Hawaiian historical and cultural books.

- **Kauai: Island of Discovery (www. kauai-hawaii.com):** Extensive listings cover activities, events, recreation, attractions, beaches, and much more. The Vacation Directory includes information on golf, fishing, and island tours; some listings include e-mail addresses and links to websites. You'll also find a clickable map of the island with listings organized by region.

- **Maui Island Currents (www.island currents.com):** Specializing in arts and culture, Island Currents gives the most detailed lowdown on current exhibitions and performance art. Gallery listings are organized by town, while in-depth articles highlight local artists. Consult restaurant reviews from the *Maui News* "Best of Maui" poll for suggestions and prices.

- **Maui Net (www.maui.net):** The clients of this Internet service provider are featured in this extensive directory of links to accommodations, activities, and shopping. The Activity Desk has links to outfitters' sites, where you can learn more and set up excursions before you arrive.

- **Molokai: The Most Hawaiian Island (www.molokai-hawaii.com):** This is a complete site for activities, events, nightlife, accommodations, and family vacations. Enjoy the landscape by viewing a virtual photo tour, get driving times between various points, and learn about local history.

- **Visit Lanai (www.visitlanai.net):** Everything you wanted to know about the island of Lanai from activities and accommodations to maps, a calendar of events, even romance.

- **Visit Oahu (www.visit-oahu.com):** This site provides an extensive guide to activities, dining, lodging, parks, shopping, and more from the Oahu chapter of the Hawaii Visitors and Convention Bureau.

2

Planning an Affordable Trip to Hawaii

Hawaii has so many places to explore, things to do, and sights to see that it can be bewildering to plan your trip with so much vying for your attention. Where to start? That's where we come in. In the pages that follow, we've compiled everything you need to know to plan your ideal trip to Hawaii.

The first thing to do: Decide where you want to go. You may stare at a map of Hawaii, looking at the six major islands—Oahu, the Big Island of Hawaii, Maui, Molokai, Lanai, and Kauai—and wonder how to choose. Each island is distinct from the others and has its own personality. Read through section 2 of this chapter, "The Islands in Brief," to see which islands appeal to you.

We strongly recommend that you **limit your island-hopping to one island per week.** If you decide to go to more than one in a week, be warned: You could spend much of your precious vacation time in airports, waiting to board flights and for your luggage to arrive, and checking in and out of hotels. Not much fun!

Our second tip is to **fly directly to the island of your choice;** doing so can save you a 2-hour layover in Honolulu and another plane ride. There are no direct flights from the mainland to Molokai or Lanai. You will have to fly into Honolulu and then take a commuter plane to these islands.

You may still be wondering: How can I see and do everything without going flat broke? You can, using our insider advice and money-saving tips. If you stick to our recommendations for great places to stay and eat, you can keep your basic living costs—a comfortable room and three meals a day—down to as little as $80 a day. (We assume that two adults are traveling together and that you have at least $160 per day between the two of you.) The costs of sightseeing, outdoor activities, transportation, and entertainment are all extras, but don't worry; we'll provide tips on saving money in those areas as well.

So let's get started.

1 55 Money-Saving Tips

WHEN TO GO

1. The best bargain rates on hotels and airfares are available in the spring (from mid-Apr to mid-June) and fall (from Sept to mid-Dec)—a paradox, since these months bring Hawaii's best weather. There's one exception to this rule, and that's from the last week in April to the first week in May, which is Japan's "Golden Week." A flood of holiday visitors from Japan causes crowds and prices to rise briefly. See "When to Go" on p. 30 for more information on Hawaii's seasons and weather.

PACKAGE DEALS

2. Booking a package deal that includes some combination of airfare, accommodations, rental car, meals, airport and baggage transfers, sightseeing, and more is usually the most cost-effective way to travel to Hawaii. **Liberty Travel** (© 888/271-1584; www.libertytravel. com), for instance, is one of the biggest packagers in the Northeast. **American Express Travel** (© 800/AXP-6898; www.americanexpress.com/travel) can also book you a well-priced Hawaiian vacation. **Pleasant Hawaiian Holidays** (© 800/2-HAWAII or 800/242-9244; www.pleasantholidays.com) is by far the biggest and most comprehensive packager to Hawaii. Other reliable packagers include the airlines themselves, which often package their flights together with accommodations. **United Vacations** (© 800/328-6877; www.unitedvacations.com) is the most comprehensive airline packager to Hawaii, offering great air-inclusive and land-only deals on a surprisingly wide selection of accommodations throughout the islands. Other airlines offering good-value packages to the islands are **American Airlines Vacations** (© 800/321-2121; www.aa.com), **Continental Airlines Vacations** (© 800/634-5555 or 800/301-3800; www.cool vacations.com), and **Delta Dream Vacations** (© 800/872-7786; www.deltavacations.com). If you're traveling to the islands from Canada, ask your travel agent about package deals through **Air Canada Vacations** (© 800/776-3000; www.aircanada.ca).

3. Hawaii's major **hotel chains** have a host of packages that will save you big bucks on accommodations. **Ohana Hotels** (© 800/462-6262; www.ohanahotels.com), **Outrigger** properties (© 800/OUTRIGGER; www.outrigger.com), the **Aston** chain (© 800/92-ASTON; www.aston-hotels.com), **Marc Resorts Hawaii** (© 800/535-0085; www.marcresorts.com), and **Castle Resorts and Hotels** (© 800/367-5004; www.castleresorts.com) offer an array of deals: multi-night stays, fly-drive packages, family plans, senior rates, golf packages, and much more. See p. 113 for more details.

4. You may be able to save substantially on inter-island airfares and car rentals (and sometimes even accommodations) by getting a **fly/drive package.** Ask your travel agent, or call **Hawaiian Airlines** (© 800/367-5320; www.hawaiianair.com) or **Aloha Airlines** (© 800/367-5250; www.alohaairlines.com) directly.

5. Confused by all your options? No problem—**visit a travel agent.** Travel agents can find you the cheapest airfares, room rates, package deals, and other travel bargains that you could never find—all at no charge to you (most travel agents work on commissions paid by the airlines, hotels, car rental companies, and tour operators).

AIR TRAVEL

6. Buy your ticket well in advance. Most airlines offer deep discounts on airfares purchased 7, 14, or 21 days before the departure date. And cheap seats always sell out first.

7. Or, buy your ticket at the last minute. Sometimes, when a flight is only half sold 72 hours before take-off, the airlines kick into high gear to fill those empty seats—and you can get deep, deep discounts. Be warned, however: There's no guarantee that the last-minute approach will work. You run the risk of being stuck with a really expensive ticket—or no ticket at all. This is a better strategy in the off season, when flights are more likely to have empty seats. Some websites to

check for last-minute deals are: **LastMinuteTravel.com** (www.last minutetravel.com), **Go4Less** (www.go4less.com), **Moment's Notice** (www.moments-notice.com), **Web-Flyer** (www.webflyer.com), and **Price-line.com** (www.priceline.com).

8. Go directly to the airlines' websites. Sometimes purchasing via the Internet will save you 10% to 30%, even more if the airline has a deal going. Not Internet savvy? Then call the airlines directly. Be sure to ask for the cheapest fare, not just the coach fare. Be flexible in your schedule if you can—flying on Tuesday, Wednesday, or Thursday can save you money with some airlines; the prime Friday through Monday flights are often priced higher. And ask about night flights; the red eye may leave you bleary, but if it's substantially cheaper, it might be worth it—you can make up the sleep later.

9. If you're a **senior**, speak up—you'll be surprised how much you can save with many airlines. Also ask about children's fares, student fares, family fares, military discounts, and any other special airfare rates you might qualify for.

10. Check for discounted fares with **consolidators.** Also known as bucket shops, consolidators are a good place to find low fares, often below even the airlines' discounted rates. Basically, these companies are just big travel agents that get discounts for buying in bulk and pass some of the savings on to you. Be aware that consolidator tickets are usually nonrefundable or come with stiff cancellation penalties. Among the safest bets are **Cheap Tickets** (✆ 800/377-1000; www.cheaptickets.com), **Lowestfare.com** (✆ 888/278-8830; www.lowestfare.com), **1-800-AIR-FARE** (www.1800airfare.com), **Cheap Seats** (✆ 800/451-7200; www.cheap seatstravel.com), and **1-800-FLY-CHEAP** (www.flycheap.com).

11. Search the **Internet** for cheap advance-purchase fares. Online booking services can be especially useful because they show you all the options, and some even make lower-priced suggestions on alternatives to your requested itinerary. A few of the better-respected virtual travel agents are **Travelocity** (www.travelocity.com), **Expedia** (www.expedia.com), **Yahoo! Travel** (http://travel.yahoo.com), and **Orbitz** (www.orbitz.com). **Smarter Living** (www.smarterliving.com) is a great source for discount Internet deals. And, of course, **Frommer's** website (www.frommers.com) keeps a running list of current deals on its website; plus you can book a trip online.

12. Sign up for **E-Savers** so airlines will e-mail you their best bargain airfares on a weekly basis. Once a week, subscribers receive a list of discounted flights to and from various destinations, both international and domestic. These fares are usually available only for specific travel dates. Some of the participating airlines include **American** (www.americanair.com), **Continental** (www.continental.com), **United** (www.ual.com), and **Northwest** (www.nwa.com). **Concierge Travel** (www.concierge.com) allows you to sign up for all these airline e-mail lists at once.

13. Taxis are the most expensive way to travel to and from an airport. Oahu has **shuttle vans** to most major hotels, as well as a good public transportation network (see chapter 5 for details), and the Big Island and Maui have SpeediShuttle vans that will take you where you want to go (see chapters 6 and 7 for details). Some hotels will even pick you up at the airport

for free, so be sure to ask when you book your room.

CAR RENTALS

14. Call all the major rental firms and **compare rates** before you book. Even after you've made your reservations, call again and check rates a few days or weeks later—you may stumble upon a cheaper rate. When getting quotes, keep in mind that Hawaii has a per-day state highway fund surcharge. The car rental companies don't include this surcharge, or Hawaii state taxes, when they quote rates. See p. 60 for further details on car rentals.

15. Book via the car company's website; sometimes you can save 10% to 30% by booking direct. If you don't speak Internet, then call the toll-free number for each car company and ask for the **cheapest rate on the smallest car.** If there are only two of you traveling, get a subcompact or compact (sometimes called an economy car). The $5 or more per day you save can add up—and you'll save money on gas and have an easier time parking. If the agent tells you that all the economy cars are booked, this may be a ploy to get you to upgrade; thank them and book with another company.

16. Book at **weekly rates** when possible—you can save a bundle. If you're going to more than one island, ask the car rental firm if they offer multi-island bookings. Setting up your rental contract this way allows you to book at cheaper weekly rates even if you're moving from island to island every few days.

17. There are **car-rental booking agencies** that work to find you the best deal available from the major car-rental companies. By combining the promotional specials that the major chains offer to travel agents with the discounts you may be entitled to as a member of a national organization (such as AARP, Costco, USAA, AAA, and so on), they get you the best deal possible—as much as 10% to 30% off what you'd pay by booking directly. The following companies book cars on every island, except Molokai and Lanai: **AA Aloha Cars-R-Us** (© 800/655-7989 or 808/879-7989; www.maui.net/~dante) and **Hookipa Haven Vacation Services** (© 800/398-6284 or 808/579-8202; www.hookipa.com).

18. If you arrive at the rental desk with a valid car reservation with a confirmation number, the agents are obligated to honor the rate you were quoted—even if they have to give you an upgrade. A ploy some rental companies use when they're all out of the grade of car you booked (economy cars often get booked up first) is to tell you that for just a few more dollars a day, they'll put you in a "better car." Make them stick to their original quote.

19. Hawaii's "no fault" insurance laws have sent the price of insurance sky-high, thereby forcing most independent car rental companies (the "Rent-A-Wreck" types) out of business. But Oahu still has one family-run company offering discount rates—**Tradewinds** (© 888/388-7368; www.tradewindsudrive.com), which has a fleet of some 300 cars. On Maui, the most accessible used-car-rental firm is **Word of Mouth Rent-a-Used-Car** ⭐, in Kahului (© 800/533-5929 or 808/877-2436; www.mauirentacar.com).

20. Always **return your rental car full of gas.** The prices the rental companies charge you to fill your tank when you don't are often double or triple the already high price per gallon charged at local filling stations. On Kauai, the cheapest gas station near the airport is **Hanamaulu Shell Station,** 3–4280

Kuhio Hwy., just outside Lihue (© **808/245-7220**). On the Big Island, where gas in Kona is 15¢ more per gallon than it is on the other side of the island in Hilo, head to **Costco**, 73-5600 Maiau Kona St. (© **808/334-0770,** in the new industrial area) before dropping your car off at the airport. It's the cheapest gas on the Big Island, but you must be a Costco member and pay with an American Express or Costco credit card. On Maui, try **BHP Gas Express,** 243 Puunene Ave., Kahului (© **808/877-0604**). And remember: Don't bother putting expensive gas in the tank. After all, it is a rental.

ACCOMMODATIONS
HOTELS

21. To get the cheapest room, **book early.** The more advance notice you can give, the more likely you are to get the budget rooms—and many of Hawaii's best bargains are small places that fill up quickly with returning guests.

22. **Don't just accept the rack rate**— there's almost always a lower rate available. When booking, ask about discounts for seniors, families, or any national organizations that you might belong to (especially AAA and AARP). Ask about package deals— sometimes you can get a car rental for just a few bucks more—discounts on longer stays, and special promotions.

23. Many hotels have **Internet-only deals** that can save you from 20% to 50% off rack rates. Use the toll-free numbers; at some chains, only the operators at the 800 number know about package deals that can save you money. Try all the approaches and see which one yields the best deal.

24. If you don't have a reservation, **bargain at the front desk.** This won't work during the high season, when most hotels are nearly full. But in the off season, you might be able to strike a very favorable deal. Empty rooms generate no income at all, so some hoteliers are happy to discount a room just to get some return on it, especially if you arrive in the late afternoon/early evening. If the front-desk clerk is unhelpful, ask to speak to the hotel manager, who is often the only employee who can make decisions on discounts.

25. Some hotel chains, like **Aston** (© **800/92-ASTON**), have **package deals** that give you a discount if you stay at their hotels for 7 nights, even if you move from island to island. Loyalty to one chain can save you up to 30%.

26. Check the daily rate for **parking,** especially at Waikiki hotels. The extra $8 to $15 a day you might be required to pay may blow your budget. Ways to get around this are to ask if there's local street parking (tough to find in Waikiki) or a cheaper parking lot (make sure you can pay by the day, not hourly) nearby.

27. In a fiercely competitive market, more and more hotels are offering **free continental breakfast** with coffee as an enticement. Find out from your hotel or travel agent if this is available at your hotel; the savings can really add up.

28. Consider **getting a room with kitchen facilities.** The cost of a kitchenette is usually well worth the extra few dollars—and it makes life a lot easier, especially if you're traveling with your family.

29. Rooms with an ocean view, especially on the upper floors, are the most expensive. Mountain or garden views are usually much cheaper, and in some cases you can save enough money to stay a day longer.

30. Consider **staying away from the ocean** altogether. It's wonderful to be steps away from the surf, but hotels away from the beach—especially in Waikiki—are much, much cheaper. If you don't mind a long walk or a short drive to the beach, you'll save a bundle.

31. If you're traveling with children, check to see if they can stay in your room for free. Or better yet, consider getting a one-bedroom suite with a pull-out sofa in the living room; one suite is usually cheaper than two hotel rooms, and you'll still have privacy.

32. **Don't make local calls from your hotel room** if you can avoid it. Hotels generally charge from 75¢ to $1.50 per local phone call, so you may want to pull out your cellphone or take your quarters and dimes (local phone calls are 50¢) and head to the lobby instead, where there's always a pay phone. Some hotels even tack a fee onto credit card calls, so check with the hotel before you start dialing.

CONDOMINIUM UNITS

33. If you're staying on one island for a week or more, consider a condominium unit, especially if you're traveling with children. Condos can be cost-effective, as they usually have a sleeper sofa as extra bedding, a kitchen that lets you prepare some of your own meals, and a pool.

34. The longer you stay at a condo, the lower the day rate goes. The rates at even high-end properties can become very attractive.

35. Ask about **condo/car deals** and, in some cases, inter-island airfare package deals. The prices are often so low that you practically fly and drive for free.

BED-AND-BREAKFASTS

36. You can generally save money at a B&B if you're willing to **share a bathroom.** Europeans seem to have no problem with the idea of sharing a bathroom, but Americans tend to balk at the idea. Decide for yourself if it's worth the savings to share.

37. Although they may call themselves bed-and-breakfasts, not all B&Bs in Hawaii serve breakfast. This can make a big difference in your daily budget. In the accommodations listings in the following chapters, we note if breakfast is served, and whether it's continental or full.

38. If you don't have the time to do extensive research on your own, using **a booking agency** may end up being the dollar-wise way to go, since agents will likely be able to lead you directly to the best deals. Some agencies charge you a flat fee to research and make all the arrangements for your trip; others get their commissions from the B&B, so their services cost you nothing. Be sure you discuss commissions and fees with the agency up front so there are no misunderstandings later. The top reservations service in the state is **Hawaii's Best Bed-and-Breakfasts** (© **800/ 262-9912** or 808/962-0100; www. bestbnb.com). When booking through an agency, be sure to discuss what happens if you arrive at the B&B and find that the accommodations don't meet your expectations.

VACATION HOMES

39. If you want the conveniences of a condominium, but with more privacy, you might consider renting a vacation home. The bigger your party, the better the deal. Two- and three-bedroom homes can be gotten for as low as $25 to $50 per person per night. For vacation rentals, contact **Hawaii Beachfront Vacation Homes** (© **808/247-3637** or 808/235-2644; www.hibeach. com). **Hawaii Condo Exchange**

(© **800/442-0404;** http://hawaii condoexchange.com) acts as a consolidator for condo and vacation-rental properties.

DINING

40. The **Hawaii Entertainment Book,** the budget bible, has become even more valuable. Putting its money where its mouth is, it reduced its price by $8 a few years ago. You can stretch your dollars by ordering this book for $35 (up to 50% off if you buy on the Internet) and using the hundreds of coupons. Contact **Entertainment Publications, Inc.,** 4211 Waialae Ave., Honolulu, HI 96816 (© **808/737-3252;** www. entertainment.com), for a list of participants or to order a book.

41. Plan daytime and romantic sunset **picnics.** Take to the heights or a nearby beach park with an inexpensive plate lunch, a tasty bento, sushi, Vietnamese shrimp rolls, or any of the many take-out treats available from corner stores and markets. Some stores slash their prices on bentos and prepared foods around mid- or late-afternoon, when the morning rush is over. Perfectly delicious prepared foods are available at greatly reduced prices in supermarkets throughout the islands.

42. **Early-bird specials** can mean substantial savings on meals. Call ahead to see if the restaurant of your choice has such a special and, if so, what the hours are. The really chic spots won't usually offer an early-bird, but when a neighborhood oasis does (such as Sushi King in the Moiliili section of Honolulu), it's worth knowing about. And **happy hour** specials don't always apply just to drinks. At some places, happy-hour appetizers are also a steal. Check out places like Ocean Club in Honolulu and Coconuts on Kauai.

43. Inquire about **children's discounts.** *Keiki* (child) menus are widely available throughout Hawaii, enabling your kids to eat at a fraction of the regular adult prices.

44. Look for **prix-fixe menus** at the pricier restaurants, or splurge on a special meal at lunch rather than dinner. You'd be surprised at the difference between lunch and dinner prices at some of the finer restaurants.

45. Take advantage of Hawaii's many **ethnic restaurants** and their affordable, tasty offerings. Vietnamese, Chinese, Laotian, and other Asian culinary traditions line the streets of Chinatown with their exotic tastes and smells.

46. **Buffets** are no longer the culinary pariah they used to be. In response to a demand for greater value, many Chinese restaurants in Honolulu—including some dim sum restaurants—have added buffet-style dining. Seafood buffets also are increasingly popular, even among the high-end eateries, the Waikiki Parc's Parc Cafe has one of Honolulu's best affordable buffets; on the Big Island, the Friday-night seafood buffet at the Hilo Hawaiian Hotel is a magnet for those who like unlimited portions of Dungeness crab.

SIGHTSEEING & ACTIVITIES

47. Before you leave the airport, wander over to the visitor's publications rack and **grab a few of the visitor magazines**—they're packed with coupons that will save you money on activities. Especially popular is *This Week* magazine, available on the major islands: Maps, dining reviews, recipes, feature articles, dining and shopping directories, and discount coupons give these pocket-size giveaways a good wallop. On Oahu, Maui, and the Big Island also look for the *"Guides"* magazines; each issue is filled with money-saving coupons.

On Maui, *Maui Gold* magazine offers discount coupons for a host of activities. On Kauai and the Big Island, pick up the *Beach and Activity Guide.* Also use the coupon books dispensed at some car-rental agencies.

48. Book activities through **discount activity centers.** Many activity booking agencies will "split" their commission with you, giving themselves a smaller commission to get your business—and you get up to a 10% discount on activities. On Maui, call **Tom Barefoot's Cashback Tours,** 834 Front St., Lahaina (© **888/ 222-3601** or 808/661-8889; www. tombarefoot.com). Although they are located on Maui, Tom's offers a 10% discount on all tours, activities, and adventures when you pay in cash or with traveler's checks on Maui, Oahu, Kauai, and the Big Island. If you pay with a credit card or personal check, he'll give you a 7% discount. We found Tom's to be very reliable and honest. On the Big Island, check out the **Activity Connection,** Bougainvillea Plaza, Ste. 102, 75-5656 Kuakini Hwy., Kailua-Kona (© **800/459-7156** or 808/329-1038; fax 808/327-9411; www.beachactivityguide.com). They offer up to 15% off on various island activities. If you don't go with these reliable choices, at least be wary of those activity centers offering discounts as fronts for timeshare sales presentations.

49. You can save 10% to 25% on nearly 100 different activities statewide by buying an **Activities and Attractions Association of Hawaii Gold Card,** 355 Hukilike St., no. 202, Kahului, HI 96732 (© **800/398-9698** or 808/871-7947; fax 808/877-3104; www.hawaiifun.org), for just $30. The Gold Card gives your entire family (up to four people) discounts on car rentals, helicopter tours, sailing tours, dinner cruises, horseback riding, kayaking, luaus, submarine tours, and more. Note that you must buy the card before you arrive in Hawaii.

50. If you're a senior, student, or active member of the military, be sure to **bring identification** with you. Several activities and attractions around the islands offer discounts, but you'll have to have a valid ID to qualify for the bargain rate.

51. Check the ***Honolulu Advertiser*** on the first of every month for a list of free events that month.

SHOPPING

52. **Hilo Hattie** is a budgeter's bonanza on all the major islands, offering free shuttle service to and from its stores. A shuttle from Waikiki departs every 20 minutes and takes you not only to its store on Nimitz Highway, but also to Ala Moana Shopping Center, Dole Cannery, and Aloha Tower Marketplace. They even throw in a free 10-minute tour of downtown Honolulu. Hilo Hattie guarantees the lowest price in the state on 4.5-ounce cans of Mauna Loa macadamia nuts. They've also greatly expanded their two-for-one specials at several local attractions.

53. The **Waikele Center** on Oahu is Hawaii's discount-outlet center, with reduced prices on everything from china to fashions, cosmetics to hardware. Shoppers descend there in droves to take advantage of new, marked-down goods. Closer to town, **Ross** and **Nordstrom's Rack** brim with department-store bargains, and **Sports Authority** is the sports lover's bargain central.

NIGHTLIFE

54. Some clubs have ladies' nights and selected theme nights, with lowered cover charges and reduced prices on drinks. Ask your concierge, or call the clubs directly.

55. On Oahu, head for the heart of Waikiki, **Kuhio Beach,** for free hula performances daily at 6:30pm (unless it rains). On Monday through Thursday, a couple of dancers perform, but on Friday, Saturday, and Sunday, a full hula troupe appears, and it can be quite dramatic against the Waikiki sunset.

2 The Islands in Brief

Each of the six main islands is separate and distinct, larger than life, and infinitely complex. There's far too much to see and do on any 2-week vacation, which is why so many people return to the Aloha State year after year.

OAHU

Oahu is home to **Honolulu,** Hawaii's largest city, and about 80% of the state's residents. Some 900,000 people live here, and 9 out of every 10 visitors to Hawaii make at least a pit stop here—so leave Oahu, the most urban island, off your itinerary if you're looking to get away from it all. And while there's much about Honolulu and the rest of Oahu that's naturally beautiful and genuinely Hawaiian, this is also the land of Don Ho. Those of you with a low tolerance for kitsch should beware.

On the other hand, Oahu isn't popular for nothing. This is where you'll find Hawaii's biggest sights (like **Pearl Harbor**) and best restaurants, shopping, and nightlife. And **Waikiki Beach** really *is* fabulous. There's a reason why travelers from the world over regularly converge on this sunny little spot.

There are also parts of Oahu that aren't crowded at all. Less than an hour's drive from Honolulu—but a world away in terms of crowds—are Oahu's North Shore, Windward Coast, and Leeward Coast. Small B&Bs, empty beaches, and residential neighborhoods await your visit in these less-touristy areas. The Banzai Pipeline and several other of Hawaii's best surfing beaches (with waves topping 30 ft. in winter) are here, too.

Still, Honolulu can feel like Los Angeles (well, on a really good day in L.A., anyway), and if you visit only Oahu, you'll get the wrong idea about Hawaii—that it's more crowded, overbuilt, and theme-park-y than real tropical paradise. Don't be ashamed to stay in Waikiki, but be sure to pair your stay with a visit to at least one of the neighbor islands for a more balanced experience.

HAWAII: THE BIG ISLAND

The real name of this island is Hawaii, but everybody calls it the Big Island to differentiate it from the entire chain. The Big Island is twice as big as all the other islands combined, and its size is reflected in its diversity of attractions. You can ski down a 14,000-foot mountain and snorkel in a placid bay on the same day. You can hike through a tropical rainforest, or gape at slow-moving lava as it spews from an active volcano and wanders down the hillside to the sea. Or you can plop yourself on one of the fabulous beaches on the Kona coast and do absolutely nothing.

Hawaii Volcanoes National Park is the premier inland attraction on the Big Island. It's been spewing lava for the last 17 years and shows no sign of stopping anytime soon. The hikes through rainforest and dried lava fields are incredible at any time, but seeing red-hot lava is more of a crapshoot. (Sometimes, it's just not going in the right places, and you won't be able to see it up close. At other times, you may get lucky and witness unbelievably dramatic volcanic activity.) The area surrounding the national park and, in fact, this entire half of the island, is full of beautiful, lush rainforest.

The **Kona-Kohala Coast** is home to some of the most luxurious resorts in the world. The beaches, carved out of lava fields, are stunning, and the sun shines almost every day. In particular, we love the turquoise waters, multicolored coral gardens, and kaleidoscopic array of tropical fish at **Kealakekua Bay,** which we consider the best snorkeling spot in all of Hawaii. (However, salt-and-pepper beaches and stark lava fields may not be everyone's idea of tropical paradise; some travelers prefer the lush scenery of Maui or Kauai.)

Keep in mind the sheer size of the Big Island. You can't experience it all in a few days. You'll need a week just to see the coast and the volcano. And that doesn't even leave much time for Hilo, the green sand beach, helicopter tours, and hikes to waterfalls. . . .

MAUI

When many people think Hawaiian paradise, they think Maui. There's something about Maui that wins people over, sends them home with a gleam in their eye and plans to hop the next plane back ASAP. *Condé Nast Traveler* has named Maui the world's best island for 9 years running.

The Valley Isle is home to many of Hawaii's **best beaches.** It's also home to **Haleakala National Park,** a dormant volcanic crater so big and deep that it could swallow the island of Manhattan whole. One of the best driving tours in the world, the 50-mile heavenly **Road to Hana,** is also here. There are **outdoor adventures** galore, ranging from bicycle rides down the side of a mountain to snorkeling and scuba diving cruises to the nearby island of Molokini. And **Lahaina** may just be the quintessential beach town. In recent years, chefs who transformed the face of Hawaiian cuisine on Oahu have opened branches of their restaurants on Maui, too, making the dining scene here as good, if not better, than that found in Honolulu.

It's not all paradise, of course. The highways and mini-malls and L.A.-style traffic jams will look familiar. Indeed, Maui is more like the mainland than any other place in Hawaii, even more so than Honolulu. And prices for hotels, restaurants, and activities are as high as you'd expect in such a popular place. Don't let this deter you, though. We'll tell you where the best deals are to be had.

MOLOKAI

Molokai is known as the most Hawaiian island because it has the fewest mainland influences. That's great for people who want to get back to nature or escape from it all. But it's not so great for people who can't live without creature comforts like air-conditioning (there isn't any A/C anywhere on the island), upscale restaurants, nightlife, or resorts. There's only one resort on the island, and it's not really up to the prices it charges.

Molokai is the birthplace of the hula, and has a larger native Hawaiian population than any other island in the chain. What it lacks in tourist facilities, it more than makes up for it in **stunning natural beauty.** Here you'll find Hawaii's highest waterfall, the world's tallest sea cliffs, challenging hikes, and, of course, countless miles of gloriously empty beaches.

Molokai admittedly isn't for everyone. But if you like to do your sightseeing from a sea kayak, from a hiking trail, or on horseback, rather than from a rental car, it may be just your speed.

LANAI

Before 1990, Lanai was so sleepy it made Molokai look busy. The smallest of the six major islands, Lanai has only 30 miles of paved roads, and very little lining them— no strip malls, no taxis, no fast-food restaurants, and only one ATM for the entire island.

But the super-luxe Lodge at Koele opened its doors in 1990, followed a year later by the even more posh Manele Bay

Hotel, transforming Lanai into a getaway for the rich and famous. Gulfstream jets now ply the runway at tiny Lanai airport, where propellers once held sway. Shuttle buses link the luxury hotels, the airport, the best golf courses, and top snorkeling beaches, but only guests at the big hotels are allowed on board.

The good news is that the best of what Lanai has to offer is absolutely free. There's snorkeling and swimming in the sapphire waters of **Hulopoe Bay,** more than 100 miles of underused hiking trails, whale-watching along deserted beaches, and overwhelming natural beauty everywhere you look. There's even a public golf course where you pay your greens fees (you decide on an appropriate amount) in an honor box. Lanai's waters are the clearest in Hawaii, primarily because they haven't been polluted by development.

Lanai's appeal to the glitterati *has* benefited budget travelers when it comes to nightlife. The **Lanai Visiting Artists Program,** sponsored by the Lodge at Koele, brings top name musicians, writers, actors, chefs, and other creative types to the island to talk and/or perform in an intimate setting. The program is free and is open to anyone, not just hotel guests. It's about the only nightlife there is on Lanai.

KAUAI

Kauai is nicknamed "the Garden Isle," and after one look at the incredibly lush **North Shore,** you'll know why. Hollywood loves filming here, especially when it needs a landscape that looks like an uncharted South Pacific island. The impenetrable (to cars, anyway) **Na Pali coast** and other thickly forested areas around Kauai have played that role in dozens of movies ranging from *Raiders of the Lost Ark* to *Jurassic Park.*

Kauai is the ideal place to get away from it all, but with enough luxuries (including some fine restaurants) to make it feel like vacation. Don't come expecting Cancún-style nightlife or St. Thomas–worthy shopping. Instead, what you'll get is an ancient island whose wind-carved cliffs, beautiful vistas, and powder fine beaches are picture-perfect Hawaii. Really! You can try a different **gorgeously uncrowded beach** every day of your Kauai vacation. Or check out **Waimea Canyon,** the so-called "Grand Canyon of the Pacific."

The price to be paid for all this paradise is unpredictable weather, especially in winter. It can rain anywhere on the island December through April, and often does so steadily on the North Shore. Seas that are glassy calm in summer turn too rough for swimming or snorkeling in these months.

Kauai is a budget traveler's dream, with lots of affordable condos, cabins, and B&Bs scattered among its shores (you won't find any towering hotels here; by law, no building can be taller than a palm tree). Tours of the inaccessible Na Pali coast, either by boat or helicopter, are expensive. But for the natural beauty they allow you to access (the only other way to see it is via a grueling 11-mile hike), we think you'll find them worth a splurge.

3 Visitor Information

For information about traveling in Hawaii, contact the **Hawaii Visitors and Convention Bureau (HVCB),** Waikiki Business Plaza, 2270 Kalakaua Ave., Suite 801, Honolulu, HI 96815 (© **800/GO-HAWAII** or 808/923-1811; www.go hawaii.com). The bureau publishes the helpful *Accommodations and Car Rental Guide* and supplies free brochures, maps, and the *Islands of Aloha* magazine, the official HVCB publication. If you want information about working and living in Hawaii, contact the **Chamber of Commerce of Hawaii,** 1132 Bishop St., Suite 402, Honolulu, HI 96813 (© **808/ 545-4300**).

INFORMATION ON HAWAII'S PARKS

The following offices can supply you with hiking and camping information:

- On the **Big Island: Hawaii Volcanoes National Park,** P.O. Box 52, Hawaii National Park, HI 96718 (© 808/985-6000;   www.nps.gov/havo); **Puuhonua O Honaunau National Historical Park,** P.O. Box 129, Honaunau, HI 96726 (© 808/328-2326; www.nps.gov/puho); **Puukohola Heiau National Historic Site,** P.O. Box 44340, Kawaihae, HI 96743 (© 808/882-7218; www.nps.gov/puhe); and **Kaloko-Honokohau National Historical Park,** 72–4786 Kanalani St., Kailua-Kona, HI 96740 (© 808/329-6881; www.nps.gov/kaho).
- On **Maui: Haleakala National Park,** P.O. Box 369, Makawao, HI 96768 (© 808/572-9306; www.nps.gov/hale).
- On **Molokai: Kalaupapa National Historical Park,** P.O. Box 2222, Kalaupapa, HI 96742 (© 808/567-6802; www.nps.gov/kala).
- On **Oahu:** USS *Arizona* **Memorial at Pearl Harbor** (© 808/422-0561; www.nps.gov/usar).

To find out more about Hawaii's state parks, contact the **Hawaii State Department of Land and Natural Resources,** 1151 Punchbowl St., no. 130, Honolulu, HI 96813 (© **808/587-0300;** www. hawaii.gov). The office can provide you with information on hiking and camping at the parks and will send you free topographic trail maps.

HAWAII ON THE WEB

Listed below are some of the most useful sites.

- **Hawaii Visitors & Convention Bureau:** www.gohawaii.com
- **Hawaii State Vacation Planner:** www.hshawaii.com
- **Ulukau, a Hawaiian Language Electronic Library:** http://ulukau. org/english.php
- **Planet Hawaii:** www.planet-hawaii. com
- **Oahu Visitors Bureau:** www.visit-oahu.com
- Big Island's **Kona-Kohala Resort Association:** www.kkra.org
- **Big Island Visitors Bureau:** www. bigisland.org
- **Maui Visitors Bureau:** www.visit maui.com
- **Maui information:** www.maui.net
- **Maui's Kaanapali Beach Resort Association:** www.maui.net/~kbra
- **Molokai information:** www.molokai-hawaii.com
- **Kauai Visitors Bureau:** www.kauai visitorsbureau.org
- Kauai's **Poipu Beach Resort Association:** www.poipu-beach.org
- **Lanai Visitors Bureau:** www.visit lanai.net
- **Weather information:** http://weather. hawaii.edu or www.weather.com or www.cnn.com/weather

4 Money

Hawaii pioneered the use of ATMs more than two decades ago, and now they're everywhere. You'll find them at most banks, in supermarkets, at Longs Drugs, at Honolulu International Airport, and in some resorts and shopping centers. It's actually cheaper and faster to get cash from an ATM than to fuss with traveler's checks. Credit cards are accepted just about everywhere.

The U.S. dollar is the coin of the realm in Hawaii, but you can easily exchange most major foreign currencies (see "Money" in chapter 3).

Be prepared for a bit of sticker shock—many items in Hawaii have high prices,

> **Tips Dear Visa: I'm Off to Kapalua, Kapaa, and Kaneohe!**
>
> Some credit card companies recommend that you notify them of any impending trip across the seas so that they don't become suspicious when the card is used numerous times in an exotic destination and have your charges blocked. Even if you don't call your credit card company in advance, you can call the card's toll-free emergency number if a charge is refused—another good reason to carry the phone number with you. But perhaps the most important lesson is to bring more than one credit card on your trip. If one card doesn't work for any number of reasons, you'll have a backup card just in case.

since so many things have to be shipped in. Expect to pay more for groceries and gasoline than you would back home on the mainland.

5 When to Go

Most visitors don't come to Hawaii when the weather's best in the islands; rather, they come when it's at its worst everywhere else. Thus, the **high season**—when prices are up and resorts are often booked to capacity—is generally from mid-December to March or mid-April. The last 2 weeks of December in particular are the prime time for travel to Hawaii. If you're planning a holiday trip, make your reservations as early as possible, expect crowds, and prepare to pay top dollar for accommodations, car rentals, and airfare.

The **off season,** when the best bargain rates are available and the islands are less crowded, is spring (from mid-Apr to mid-June) and fall (from Sept to mid-Dec)—a paradox, since these are the best seasons to be in Hawaii, in terms of reliably great weather. If you're looking to save money, or if you just want to avoid the crowds, this is the time to visit. Hotel rates and airfares tend to be significantly lower, and good packages and special deals are often available.

Note: If you plan to come to Hawaii during the last week in April and the first week in May, be sure you book your accommodations, inter-island air reservations, and car rentals in advance. In Japan, the last week of April is called **Golden Week,** because three Japanese holidays take place one after the other. Waikiki is especially busy with Japanese tourists during this time, but the neighbor islands also see dramatic increases.

CLIMATE

Since Hawaii lies at the edge of the tropical zone, it technically has only two seasons, both of them warm. There's a dry season that corresponds to **summer,** and a rainy season in **winter** from November to March. It rains every day somewhere in the islands any time of the year, but the rainy season sometimes brings gray weather that can spoil your tanning opportunities. Fortunately, it seldom rains in one spot for more than 3 days straight.

The **year-round temperature** usually varies no more than 15°F (9°C). At the beach, the average daytime high in summer is 85°F (29°C), while the average daytime high in winter is 78°F (26°C); nighttime lows are usually about 10°F (-12°C) cooler. But how warm it is on any given day really depends on *where* you are on the island.

Each island has a leeward side (the side sheltered from the wind) and a windward side (the side that gets the wind's full force). The **leeward** sides (the west and south) are usually hot and dry, while the **windward** sides (east and north) are generally cooler and moist. When you want arid, sun-baked, desertlike weather, go leeward. When you want lush, sometimes wet, junglelike weather, go windward.

Hawaii is also full of **microclimates,** thanks to its interior valleys, coastal plains, and mountain peaks. Kauai's Mount Waialeale is the wettest spot on earth, yet Waimea Canyon, just a few miles away, is almost a desert. On the Big Island, Hilo is the wettest city in the nation, with 180 inches of rainfall a year, while at Puako, only 60 miles away, it rains less than 6 inches a year. If you travel into the mountains, the climate can change from summer to winter in a matter of hours since it's cooler the higher you go. So, if the weather doesn't suit you, just go to the other side of the island—or head into the hills.

On rare occasions, the weather can be disastrous, as when Hurricane Iniki crushed Kauai in September 1992 with 225mph winds. Tsunamis, huge tidal waves caused by far-off earthquakes, have swept Hilo and the south shore of Oahu. But those are extreme exceptions. Mostly, one day follows another here in glorious, sunny procession, each quite like the other.

HOLIDAYS

When Hawaii observes holidays, especially those over a long weekend, travel between the islands increases, inter-island airline seats are fully booked, rental cars are at a premium, and hotels and restaurants are busier.

Federal, state, and county government offices are closed on all federal holidays: January 1 (New Year's Day), the third Monday in January (Martin Luther King Jr. Day), the third Monday in February (Presidents' Day),, the last Monday in May (Memorial Day), July 4th (Independence Day), the first Monday in September (Labor Day), the second Monday in October (Columbus Day), November 11 (Veterans' Day), the fourth Thursday in November (Thanksgiving Day), and December 25 (Christmas).

State and county offices are also closed on local holidays, including Prince Kuhio Day (Mar 26), honoring the birthday of Hawaii's first delegate to the U.S. Congress; King Kamehameha Day (June 11), a statewide holiday commemorating Kamehameha the Great, who united the islands and ruled from 1795 to 1819; and Admissions Day (the third Fri in Aug), which honors the admittance of Hawaii as the 50th state on August 21, 1959.

Other special days celebrated in Hawaii by many people but which involve no closing of federal, state, and county offices are the Chinese New Year (which can fall in Jan or Feb), Girls' Day (Mar 3), Buddha's Birthday (Apr 8), Father Damien's Day (Apr 15), Boys' Day (May 5), Samoan Flag Day (in Aug), Aloha Festivals (in Sept and Oct), and Pearl Harbor Day (Dec 7).

Tips   Travel Tip

Your best bets for total year-round sun are **Waikiki Beach** and the **Ko Olina** (southwest) coast of Oahu, the Big Island's **Kona-Kohala Coast,** the south **(Kihei-Wailea)** and west **(Lahaina-Kapalua)** Maui coasts, and **Poipu Beach** and the southwest coast of Kauai.

HAWAII CALENDAR OF EVENTS

Please note that, as with any schedule of upcoming events, the following information is subject to change. Always confirm the details before you plan your trip around an event. For a complete and up-to-date list of events throughout the islands, check out **www.calendar.go hawaii.com**.

January

Morey World Bodyboarding Championship, Banzai Pipeline, North Shore, Oahu. Competition is determined by the best wave selection and maneuvers on the wave. Call ℡ **808/ 396-2326.** Early January.

PGA Kapalua Mercedes Championship, Kapalua Resort, Maui. Top PGA golfers compete for $1 million. Call ℡ **808/669-2440; www.kapalua maui.com**. Early January.

Sony Open, Waialae Country Club, Oahu. A $1.2-million PGA golf event featuring the top men in golf. Call ℡ **808/734-2151.** Early to mid-January.

MasterCard Championship, Jack Nicklaus Signature Course, Four Seasons Resort Hualalai, Kona, Big Island. Formerly known as the Tournament of Champions, this is the season-opening competition for golfers who have won a Senior PGA Tour event. Call ℡ **800/ 417-2770** or 808/325-8000; www. pgatour.com. Late January.

Ka Molokai Makahiki, Kaunakakai Town Baseball Park, Mitchell Pauole Center, Kaunakakai, Molokai. Makahiki, a traditional time of peace in ancient Hawaii, is re-created with music, dance, games, sports, crafts, and food. It's a wonderful chance to experience the Hawaii of yesteryear. Call ℡ **800/ 800-6367** or 808/553-3876; www. molokai-hawaii.com. Late January.

Ala Wai Challenge, Ala Wai Park, Waikiki, Oahu. This all-day event features ancient Hawaiian games, like *ulu maika* (bowling a round stone through pegs), *oo ihe* (spear throwing at an upright target), *huki kaula* (tug of war), and a ¼-mile outrigger canoe race. It's also a great place to hear Hawaiian music. Call ℡ **808/923-1802.** Last weekend in January.

Senior Skins Tournament, Gold Course, Wailea Golf Courses, Maui. Longtime golfing greats participate in this four-man tournament for $600,000 in prize money. Call ℡ **800/ 332-1614;** www.seniorskinswailea. com. Played during Super Bowl weekend.

Hula Bowl Football All-Star Classic, War Memorial Stadium, Maui. An annual all-star football classic featuring America's top college players. Call ℡ **808/874-9500; www.hulabowl maui.com**. Ticket orders are processed beginning April 1 for the next year's game.

Chinese New Year, Maui. Lahaina town rolls out the red carpet for this important event with a traditional lion dance at the historic Wo Hing Temple on Front Street, accompanied by fireworks, food booths, and a host of activities. Call ℡ **888/310-1117** or 808/667-9175. Also on Market Street in Wailuku; call ℡ **808/270-7414.** On Oahu, a big celebration takes place in Chinatown; call ℡ **808/533-3181** for details. Jan 29, 2006, starts the year of the dog.

Narcissus Festival, Honolulu, Oahu. Taking place around the Chinese New Year, this cultural festival includes a queen pageant, cooking demonstrations, and a cultural fair. Call ℡ **808/ 533-3181** for details.

Whalefest Week, Maui. This event celebrates Maui's best-known winter visitors, the humpback whales. Activities include seminars, art exhibits, sailing, snorkeling and diving tours, and numerous events for children. Call © 808/667-9175 or 808/879-8860; www.calendarmaui.com. Late January or early February.

February

NFL Pro Bowl, Aloha Stadium, Honolulu, Oahu. The National Football League's best pro players square-off in this annual gridiron all-star game. Call © 808/486-9300; www.nfl.com. Early February.

Waimea Town Celebration, Waimea, Kauai. This annual party on Kauai's west side celebrates the Hawaiian and multiethnic history of the town where Captain Cook first landed. This is the island's biggest 2-day event, drawing some 10,000 people. Top Hawaiian entertainers, sporting events, rodeo, and lots of food are on tap during the weekend celebration. Call © 808/245-3971. Second or third week of February.

Sand Castle Building Contest, Kailua Beach Park, Oahu. Students from the University of Hawaii School of Architecture compete against professional architects to see who can build the best, most unusual, and most outrageous sand sculpture. Call © 808/956-7225.

The Great Aloha Run, Oahu. Thousands run 8¼ miles from Aloha Tower to Aloha Stadium. Call © 808/528-7388. Presidents' Day (third Mon in Feb).

Buffalo's Big Board Classic, Makaha Beach, Oahu. This contest involves traditional Hawaiian surfing, long boarding, and canoe-surfing. Call © 808/951-7877. Depending on the surf, it can be held in February or March.

March

Run to the Sun, Paia to Haleakala, Maui. The world's top ultra-marathoners make the journey from sea level to the top of 10,000-foot Haleakala in 37 miles. Call © 808/573-7584 or 808/741-2726; www.virr.com. Generally, late March.

Hawaii Challenge International Sportkite Championship, Kapiolani Park, Oahu. The longest-running sportkite competition in the world attracts top kite pilots from around the globe. Call © 808/735-9059. First weekend in March.

Annual St. Patrick's Day Parade, Waikiki (Fort DeRussy to Kapiolani Park), Oahu. Bagpipers, bands, clowns, and marching groups parade through the heart of Waikiki, with lots of Irish celebrations all day. Call © 808/524-0722. March 17.

Kona Brewer's Festival, King Kamehameha's Kona Beach Hotel Luau Grounds, Kailua-Kona, Big Island. This annual event features microbreweries from around the world, with beer tasting, food, and entertainment. Call © 808/334-1133. Second Saturday in March.

Prince Kuhio Day Celebrations, all islands. State holiday. Various festivals throughout the state celebrate the birth of Jonah Kuhio Kalanianaole, who was born on March 26, 1871, and elected to Congress in 1902. Kauai, his birthplace, stages a huge celebration in Lihue; call © 808/826-9272 for details. Molokai also hosts a daylong celebration; call © 808/553-5215 to learn more.

April

East Maui Taro Festival, Hana, Maui. Taro, a Hawaiian staple food, is celebrated through music, hula, arts, crafts, and, of course, food. Call ⓒ 808/248-8972; www.tarofestival. org. Early April or late March.

Buddha Day, Lahaina Jodo Mission, Lahaina, Maui. Each year this historic mission holds a flower festival pageant honoring the birth of Buddha. Call ⓒ 808/661-4303. First Saturday in April.

Annual Ritz-Carlton Kapalua Celebration of the Arts, Ritz-Carlton Kapalua, Maui. Contemporary and traditional artists give free hands-on lessons. Call ⓒ 808/669-6200. The 4-day festival begins the Thursday before Easter.

Annual Easter Sunrise Service, National Cemetery of the Pacific, Punchbowl Crater, Honolulu, Oahu. For a century, people have gathered at this famous cemetery for Easter sunrise services. Call ⓒ 808/566-1430.

Merrie Monarch Hula Festival, Hilo, Big Island. Hawaii's biggest hula festival features three nights of modern *(auana)* and ancient *(kahiko)* dance competition in honor of King David Kalakaua, the "Merrie Monarch," who revived the dance. Tickets sell out by January 30, so reserve early. Call ⓒ 808/935-9168. The week after Easter.

David Malo Day, Lahainaluna High School, Lahaina, Maui. This daylong event with hula and other Hawaiian cultural celebrations commemorates Hawaii's famous scholar and ends with a luau. Mid-April. Call ⓒ 808/662-4000.

Honolulu International Bed Race Festival, Honolulu, Oahu. This popular fund-raiser event allows visitors a small taste of Honolulu, with food booths sponsored by local restaurants, live entertainment, a *keiki* (children's) carnival with games and rides, and a race through the streets of Honolulu with runners pushing beds to raise money for local charities. Call ⓒ 808/696-2424. Mid-April.

Ulupalakua Thing! Maui County Agricultural Trade Show and Sampling, Ulupalakua Ranch and Tedeschi Winery, Ulupalakua, Maui. The name may be long and cumbersome, but this event is hot, hot, hot. It features local-product exhibits, food booths, and live entertainment. Call ⓒ 808/875-0457. Last Saturday in April.

May

Outrigger Canoe Season, all islands. From May to September nearly every weekend, canoe paddlers across the state participate in outrigger canoe races. Call ⓒ 808/261-6615, or go to www.y2kanu.com for this year's schedule of events.

Annual Lei Day Celebrations, various locations on all islands. May Day is Lei Day in Hawaii, celebrated with lei-making contests, pageantry, Arts and Crafts, and the real highlight, a Brothers Cazimero concert at the Waikiki Shell. Call ⓒ 808/924-8934 or 808/524-0722 for Oahu events (ⓒ 808/597-1888 for the Brothers Cazimero show); ⓒ 808/886-1655 for Big Island events; ⓒ 808/879-1922 for Maui events; or ⓒ 808/245-6931 for Kauai events. May 1.

World Fire-Knife Dance Championships and Samoan Festival, Polynesian Cultural Center, Laie, Oahu. Junior and adult fire-knife dancers from around the world converge on the center for one of the most amazing performances you'll ever see. Authentic Samoan food and cultural festivities round out the fun. Call ⓒ 808/293-3333; www. polynesianculturalcenter.com. Mid-May.

International Festival of Canoes, West Maui. Celebration of the Pacific islands' seafaring heritage. Events include canoe paddling and sailing regattas, a luau feast, cultural arts demonstrations, canoe-building exhibits, and music. Call © **888/310-1117; www.calendarmaui.com.** Mid- to late May.

Molokai Ka Hula Piko, Papohaku Beach Park, Kaluakoi, Molokai. This daylong celebration of the hula takes place on the island where it was born, featuring performances by dancers from hula schools, musicians, and singers from across Hawaii, as well as local food and Hawaiian crafts, including quilting, woodworking, feather work, and deer-horn scrimshaw. Call © **800/800-6367** or 808/553-3876; www.molokai-hawaii.com. Third Saturday in May.

Memorial Day, National Memorial Cemetery of the Pacific, Punchbowl, Honolulu, Oahu. The armed forces hold a ceremony recognizing those who died for their country, beginning at 9am. Call © **808/532-3720.**

June

Hawaiian Slack-Key Guitar Festival, Maui Arts and Cultural Center, Kahului, Maui. Great music performed by the best musicians in Hawaii. It's 5 hours long and absolutely free. Call © **808/239-4336** or e-mail kahoku productions@yahoo.com.

King Kamehameha Celebration, all islands. It's a state holiday with a massive floral parade, *hoolaulea* (party), and much more. Call © **808/586-0333** for Oahu events; © **808/329-1603** for Big Island events; © **808/667-9175** for Maui events; © **808/553-3876** for Molokai events; and © **808/245-3971** for Kauai events, or visit www.state.hi.us/dags/kkcc. June 10.

Maui Film Festival, Wailea Resort, Maui. Five days and nights of screenings of premieres and special films, along with traditional Hawaiian storytelling, chants, hula, and contemporary music. Call © **808/579-9996; www.mauifilmfestival.com.** June.

King Kamehameha Hula Competition, Neal Blaisdell Center, Honolulu, Oahu. This is one of the top hula competitions in the world, with dancers from as far away as Japan. Call © **808/586-0333;** www.state.hi.us/dags/kkcc. Third weekend in June.

Taste of Honolulu, Civic Center Grounds, Honolulu, Oahu. Hawaii's premier outdoor food festival features tasting from 30 restaurants, as well as entertainment, beer and wine tasting, cooking demos, a gourmet marketplace, and children's activities. Call © **808/536-1015;** www.easterseals.org. Mid- to late June.

Makana Aloha, Molokai. The Makana Aloha is a celebration of all things Hawaiian, from the ancient Kahiko and Oli to the sweet sounds of Falsetto. The Competition is free and there will be plenty of good food prepared by Molokai's finest cooks, wonderful arts and crafts, event memorabilia and games for the kids, too! Call © **808-552-2800** or www.molokaievents.com. Last Saturday in June.

July

Parker Ranch Rodeo, Waimea, Big Island. This is a hot rodeo competition in the heart of cowboy country. Call © **808/885-7311** or go to www.rodeo hawaii.com. July 4.

Annual Lanai Pineapple Festival, Lanai City, Lanai. A celebration of Lanai's past of pineapple plantation and ranching and includes a pineapple eating contest, pineapple cooking contest, entertainment, arts and crafts, food and fireworks. © **808/565-7600** or www.visitlanai.net. First Saturday in July.

Turtle Independence Day, Mauna Lani Resort and Bungalows, Kohala

Coast, Big Island. Scores of endangered green sea turtles, which have been raised in captivity, race down to the sea each year when they're released from the historic fish ponds at Mauna Lani. Call © **808/885-6677;** www. maunalani.com. July 4.

Great Waikoloa Food, Wine & Music Festival, Hilton Waikoloa Village, Big Island. One of the Big Island's best food and wine festivals features Hawaii's top chefs (and a few mainland chefs) showing off their culinary talents, wines from around the world, and an excellent jazz concert with fireworks. Not to be missed. Call © **808/886-1234;** www. hiltonwaikoloavillage.com. Weekend closest to July 4th.

Hawaii International Jazz Festival, Sheraton Waikiki, Honolulu, Oahu. This festival includes evening concerts and daily jam sessions, the University of Southern California jazz band, many popular jazz and blues artists, plus scholarship giveaways. Call © **808/ 941-9974.** Mid-July.

Crater Rim Run and Marathon, Hawaii Volcanoes National Park, Big Island. Some 1,000 runners from around the globe line up to compete in 5-, 10- and 26-mile races over uneven lava terrain, up the walls of volcanic craters, and through lush rainforests. Call © **808/967-8222.** Late July.

Quicksilver Molokai to Oahu Paddleboard Race, starting on Molokai and finishing on Oahu. Some 70 participants from an international field of paddleboard racing journey to Molokai to compete in this 32-mile race, considered to be the world championship of long distance paddleboard racing. Race begins at Kaluakoi Beach on Molokai at 7:00am and finishes at Maunaloa Bay, Oahu around 12:30pm. Call © **808/ 638-8208.** Mid- to late July.

August

Queen Liliuokalani Keiki Hula Competition, Neal Blaisdell Center, Honolulu, Oahu. More than 500 *keiki* (children) representing 22 *halau* (hula schools) from the islands compete in this dance fest. The event is broadcast a week later on KITV-TV. Call © **808/ 521-6905.** Early August or last weekend in July.

Hawaii State Farm Fair, Aloha Stadium, Honolulu, Oahu. The annual state fair is a great one. It features displays of Hawaiian agricultural products (including orchids), educational and cultural exhibits, entertainment, and local-style food. Call © **808/ 531-3531.** Early August.

Annual Hawaiian International Billfish Tournament, Kailua-Kona, Big Island. One of the world's most prestigious billfish tournaments, the HIBT attracts teams from around the globe. Call © **808/329-6155;** www.kona billfish.com.

Puukohola Heiau National Historic Site Anniversary Celebration, Kawaihae, Big Island. This is a weekend of Hawaiian crafts, workshops, and games. Call © **808/882-7218.** Mid-August.

September

Aloha Festivals, various locations statewide. Parades and other events celebrate Hawaiian culture and friendliness throughout the state. Call © **800/ 852-7690,** 808/545-1771, or 808/ 885-8086, or visit www.alohafestivals. com for a schedule of events.

Na Wahine O Ke Kai, Molokai to Oahu. Women's 32-mile canoe race. Watch the sunrise and the start of the race beginning at 7am on Sunday morning. The Finish line is fronting the shores of the Hilton Hawaiian Village. **Contact** © **808/259-7112** or http:// holoholo.org/wahine. Mid-Sept.

Aloha Festivals Poke Recipe Contest, Hapuna Beach Prince Hotel and Mauna Kea Beach Resort, Kohala Coast, Big Island. Top chefs from across Hawaii and the U.S. mainland, as well as local amateurs, compete in making this Hawaiian delicacy, *poke* (pronounced po-*kay*): chopped raw fish mixed with seaweed and spices. Here's your chance to sample *poke* at its best. Call © **808/885-8086.** Early to mid-September.

Long Distance Outrigger Canoe Races, Kailua Pier to Honaunau and back, Big Island. Some 2,500 paddlers from all over Hawaii, the U.S. mainland, Canada, and the Pacific Islands vie in the world's longest canoe event. Call © **808/329-7787.** Labor Day weekend.

A Taste of Lahaina, Lahaina Civic Center, Maui. Some 30,000 people show up to sample 40 signature entrees of Maui's premier chefs during this weekend festival, which includes cooking demonstrations, wine tasting, and live entertainment. The event begins Friday night with Maui Chefs Present, a dinner/cocktail party featuring about a dozen of Maui's best chefs. Call © **888/310-1117** or www.visitmaui. com. Second weekend in September.

Maui Marathon, Kahului to Kaanapali, Maui. Runners line up at the Maui Mall before daybreak and head off for Kaanapali. Call © **808/871-6441;** www.mauimarathon.com. Sunday in mid-September.

LifeFest Maui, Kapalua, Maui. An all-new health-and-wellness 3-day event featuring lectures and panel presentations by leaders in the health-and-wellness field (Dr. Deepak Chopra, Bob Greene, Dr. Julian Whitaker, and others), plus ocean sporting events, fitness activities, a health-and-wellness expo, and sumptuous culinary gala dinners.

Call © **800/KAPALUA;** www.lifefest kapalua.com.

October

Emalani Festival, Kokee State Park, Kauai. This festival honors Her Majesty Queen Emma, an inveterate gardener and Hawaii's first environmental queen, who made a forest trek to Kokee with 100 friends in 1871. Call © **808/245-3971.**

Aloha Classic World Wavesailing Championship, Hookipa Beach, Maui. The top windsurfers in the world gather for this final event in the Pro Boardsailing World Tour. If you're on Maui, don't miss it—it's spectacular to watch. Call © **808/575-9151.**

Hamakua Music Festival, Hamakua, Big Island. This event features a surprisingly eclectic mix of well-known musicians, ranging from blues and jazz to rock 'n' roll, Hawaiian, and even classical. Call © **808/775-3378.** Early October.

Maui County Fair, War Memorial Complex, Wailuku, Maui. The oldest county fair in Hawaii features a parade, amusement rides, live entertainment, and exhibits. Call © **800/525-MAUI** or 808/244-3530. First weekend in October.

Molokai Hoe, Molokai to Oahu. The course of this men's 40-mile outrigger contest runs across the channel from Molokai to finish at Fort DeRussy Beach in Waikiki. Call © **808/261-6615;** www.molokai-hawaii.com. Mid-October.

Ironman Triathlon World Championship, Kailua-Kona, Big Island. Some 1,500-plus world-class athletes swim 2½ miles, bike 112 miles, and run a full marathon on the Kona-Kohala coast of the Big Island. Spectators can watch the action along the route for free. Call © **808/329-0063;**

www.ironmanlive.com. Saturday closest to the full moon in October.

Halloween in Lahaina, Maui. There's Carnaval in Rio, Mardi Gras in New Orleans, and Halloween in Lahaina. Come to this giant costume party (some 20,000 people show up) on the streets of Lahaina. Front Street is closed off for the festivities. Call ℂ **808/667-9175.** October 31.

November

Annual Kona Coffee Cultural Festival, Kailua-Kona, Big Island. Celebrate the coffee harvest with a bean-picking contest, lei contests, song and dance, and the Miss Kona Coffee pageant. Call ℂ **808/326-7820** or go to www.konacoffee.com for this year's schedule.

Hawaii International Film Festival, various locations throughout the state. This cinema festival with a cross-cultural spin features filmmakers from Asia, the Pacific Islands, and the United States. Call ℂ **808/528-FILM,** or visit www.hiff.org. First 2 weeks in November.

MasterCard PGA Grand Slam, Poipu Bay Resort Golf Course, Kauai. Top golfers compete for $1 million in prize money. Call ℂ **800/PGA-TCKT** or 888/744-0888; www.pga.com. Last weekend in November.

Triple Crown of Surfing, North Shore, Oahu. The world's top professional surfers compete in events for more than $1 million in prize money. Call ℂ **808/638-7266** or visit www.triplecrownofsurfing.com. Triple Crown of Surfing is held during the best days of surfing from mid-November to late-December.

December

Festival of Trees, Honolulu, Oahu. This downtown display of one-of-a-kind decorated trees, wreaths, and decorations benefits Queen's Medical Center. The lighting takes place the first or second week of the month. Call ℂ **808/547-4371.**

Old-Fashioned Holiday Celebration, Lahaina, Maui. This day of Christmas carolers, Santa Claus, live music and entertainment, a crafts fair, Christmas baked goods, and activities for children takes place in the Banyan Tree Park on Front Street. Call ℂ **888/310-1117** or www.visitlahaina.com. Second Saturday in December.

Festival of Lights, all islands. On Oahu, the mayor throws the switch to light up the 40-foot-tall Norfolk pine and other trees in front of Honolulu Hale, while on Maui, marching bands, floats, and Santa roll down Lahaina's Front Street in an annual parade. Molokai celebrates with a host of activities in Kaunakakai. On Kauai, the lighting ceremony takes place in front of the former county building on Rice Street, Lihue. Call ℂ **808/547-4397** on Oahu; ℂ **808/667-9175** on Maui; ℂ **808/567-6361** on Molokai; and ℂ **808/828-0014** on Kauai. Early December.

Honolulu Marathon, Honolulu, Oahu. This is one of the largest marathons in the world, with more than 30,000 competitors. Call ℂ **808/734-7200** or go to www.honolulumarathon.org. Second Sunday in December.

Aloha Bowl, Aloha Stadium, Honolulu, Oahu. A Pac-10 team plays a Big 12 team in this nationally televised collegiate football classic. Call ℂ **808/545-7171.** Christmas Day.

Rainbow Classic, University of Hawaii, Manoa Valley, Oahu. Eight of the best NCAA basketball teams compete at the Special Events Arena. Call ℂ **808/956-6501.** The week after Christmas.

First Night, Maui Arts and Cultural Center, Maui, and Kailua-Kona, Big Island. Hawaii's largest festival of arts and entertainment takes place on two different islands. For 12 hours, musicians, dancers, actors, jugglers, magicians, and mimes perform. Afterwards, fireworks bring in the New Year. Alcohol-free. Call © **808/326-7820** on the Big Island, or © **808/242-7469** on Maui. December 31.

6 What to Pack

Hawaii is very informal. Shorts, T-shirts, and tennis shoes will get you by at most restaurants and attractions; a casual dress or a polo shirt and khakis are fine even in the fanciest places. Aloha wear is acceptable everywhere, so you may want to plan on buying an aloha shirt or a *muumuu* (a Hawaiian-style dress) while you're in the islands.

So bring T-shirts, shorts, long pants, a couple of bathing suits, a long-sleeve cover-up (to throw on at the beach when you've had enough sun for the day), tennis shoes, rubber water shoes or flip-flops, and hiking boots and good socks, if you plan on hiking.

The tropical sun poses the greatest threat to anyone who ventures into the great outdoors, so be sure to bring **sun protection:** a good pair of sunglasses, strong sunscreen, a light hat (like a baseball cap or a sun visor), and a canteen or water bottle if you'll be hiking—you'll easily dehydrate in the tropical heat, so figure on carrying 2 liters of water per day on any hike. Campers should bring water-purification tablets or devices.

You won't have to stuff your suitcase with 2 weeks' worth of shorts and T-shirts. Almost all of Hawaii's hotels and resorts—even the high-end ones—have **laundry facilities.** If your accommodation doesn't have a washer and dryer or laundry service, there will likely be a Laundromat nearby. The only exception to this is Hana on Maui; this tiny town has no launderette, so check with the place where you're staying beforehand.

One last thing: **It really can get cold in Hawaii.** If you plan to see the sunrise from the top of Maui's Haleakala Crater, venture into the Big Island's Hawaii Volcanoes National Park, or spend time in Kokee State Park on Kauai, bring a warm jacket; 40°F (4°C) upcountry temperatures, even in summer when it's 80°F (27°C) at the beach, are not uncommon. It's always a good idea to bring at least a windbreaker, a sweater, or a light jacket. And be sure to toss some **rain gear** into your suitcase if you'll be in Hawaii between November and March.

7 The Active Vacation Planner

If all you want is a fabulous beach and a perfectly mixed mai tai, then Hawaii has what you're looking for. But the islands' wealth of natural wonders is equally hard to resist; the year-round tropical climate and spectacular scenery tend to inspire almost everyone to get outside and explore.

If you have your own snorkel gear or other watersports equipment, bring it if you can. However, if you don't have it, don't fret: Everything you'll need is available for rent in the islands. We discuss all kinds of places to rent or buy gear in the individual island chapters that follow. From binoculars to golf clubs to kayaks, the best all-around place to rent any number of toys is the **Activity Warehouse** (www.travelhawaii.com) on Maui (© **800/923-4004**); on Kauai (© **800/688-0580**);

on the Big Island (© **877/862-4355**); and on Oahu (© **800/923-4004**). See also the note on **Snorkel Bob's,** later in this chapter.

SETTING OUT ON YOUR OWN VERSUS USING AN OUTFITTER

There are two ways to go: Plan all the details before you leave and either rent gear or schlepp your stuff 2,500 miles across the Pacific, or go with an outfitter or a guide and let someone else worry about the details.

Experienced outdoors enthusiasts may head to coastal campgrounds or even trek to the 13,796-foot-high summit of Mauna Loa on their own. But in Hawaii, it's often preferable to go with a local guide who is familiar with the conditions at both sea level and summit peaks, knows the land and its flora and fauna in detail, and has all the gear you'll need. It's also good to go with a guide if time is an issue, or if you have specialized interests. Should you really want to see native birds, for instance, an experienced guide will take you directly to the best areas for sightings. And many forests and valleys in the interior of the islands are either on private property or in wilderness preserves accessible only on guided tours.

The downside? If you go with a guide, plan on spending at least $100 a day per person. We've recommended the best local outfitters and tour-guide operators on each island in the chapters that follow.

But if you have the time, already own the gear, and love doing the research and planning, try exploring on your own. Each island chapter discusses the best spots to set out on your own, from the top offshore snorkel and dive spots to great daylong hikes, as well as the federal, state, and county agencies that can help you with hikes on public property. We also list references for spotting birds, plants, and sea life. We recommend that you always use the resources available to inquire about weather, trail, or surf conditions, water availability, and other conditions before you take off on your adventure.

For hikers, a great alternative to hiring a private guide is taking a guided hike offered by the **Nature Conservancy of Hawaii,** 1116 Smith St., no. 210, Honolulu, HI 96817 (© **808/537-4508** on Oahu; © **808/572-7849** on Maui; © **808/553-5236** on Molokai; www.tnc.org/hawaii), or the **Hawaii Chapter of the Sierra Club,** P.O. Box 2577, Honolulu, HI 96803 (© **808/538-6616** on Oahu; www.hi.sierraclub.org). Both organizations offer guided hikes in preserves and special areas during the year, as well as day- to weeklong work trips to restore habitats and trails and to root out invasive plants. It might not sound like a dream vacation to everyone, but it's a chance to see the "real" Hawaii—including wilderness areas that are ordinarily off-limits.

All Nature Conservancy hikes and work trips are free (donations are appreciated). However, you must reserve a spot for yourself, and a deposit is required for guided hikes to ensure that you'll show up; your deposit is refunded once you do. The hikes are generally offered once a month on Maui, Molokai, and Lanai, and twice a month on Oahu. For all islands, call the Oahu office for reservations. Write for a schedule of guided hikes and other programs.

The Sierra Club offers weekly hikes on Oahu and Maui. Hikes are led by certified Sierra Club volunteers and are classified as easy, moderate, or strenuous. These half-day or full-day affairs cost $1 for Sierra Club members and $3 for nonmembers (bring exact change). For a copy of the club newsletter, which lists all outings and trail-repair work, send $2 to the address above.

Local ecotourism opportunities are also discussed in each island chapter. For more information, contact the **Hawaii Ecotourism Association** (© **877/300/7058**; www.hawaiiecotourism.org).

OUTDOOR ACTIVITIES A TO Z

Here's a brief rundown of the many outdoor activities available in Hawaii. For our recommendations on the best places to go, the best shops for renting equipment, and the best outfitters to use, see the individual island chapters later in this book.

BIRDING   Many of Hawaii's tropical birds are found nowhere else on earth. There are curved-bill honeycreepers, black-winged red birds, and the rare o'o, whose yellow feathers Hawaiians once plucked to make royal capes. When you go birding, take along *A Field Guide to the Birds of Hawaii and the Tropical Pacific,* by H. Douglas Pratt, Phillip L. Bruner, and Delwyn G. Berett (Princeton University Press, 1987). If you go bird-watching with a local guide, you'll usually be provided with a good pair of binoculars; you can also rent them from gear-rental locations throughout the islands.

Kauai and **Molokai,** in particular, are great places to go birding. On Kauai, large colonies of seabirds nest at Kilauea National Wildlife Refuge and along the Na Pali Coast. The lush rainforest of Molokai's Kamakou Preserve is home to the Molokai thrush and Molokai creeper, which live only on this 30-mile-long island.

BOATING   Almost every type of nautical experience is available in the islands. You can go to sea on old-fashioned Polynesian outrigger canoes, high-tech kayaks, fast-moving catamarans, inflatable rubber Zodiac boats, smooth-moving SWATH vessels that promise not to make you seasick, gaff-rigged schooners, America's Cup racing sloops, submarines, and even an inter-island cruise ship. You'll find details on all these seafaring experiences in the individual island chapters.

No matter which vessel and type you choose, be sure to see the Hawaiian islands from offshore if you can afford it. It's easy to combine multiple activities into one cruise: Lots of snorkel boats double as sightseeing cruises and, in winter, whale-watching cruises. The main harbors for visitor activities are Kewalo Basin, Oahu; Honokohau, Kailua-Kona, and Kawaihae on the Big Island; Lahaina and Maalaea, Maui; Nawiliwili and Port Allen, Kauai; and Kaunakakai, Molokai.

BODYBOARDING   (BOOGIE BOARDING) & BODYSURFING Bodysurfing—riding the waves without a board, becoming one with the rolling water—is a way of life in Hawaii. Some bodysurfers just rely on their outstretched hands (or hands at their sides) to ride the waves; others use hand boards (flat, paddlelike gloves). For additional maneuverability, try a boogie board or bodyboard (also known as belly boards or *paipo* boards). These 3-foot-long vehicles, which support the upper part of your body, are easy to carry and very maneuverable in the water. Both bodysurfing and bodyboarding require a pair of open-heeled swim fins to help propel you through the water. Both kinds of wave riding are very popular in the islands, as the equipment is inexpensive and easy to carry, and both sports can be practiced in the small, gentle waves. See the individual island chapters for details on where to rent boards and where to go.

CAMPING   Hawaii's year-round balmy climate makes camping a breeze. However, tropical campers should always be ready for rain, especially in Hawaii's wet winter season, but even in the dry summer season as well. And remember that mosquitoes are abundant when the air is still; bring a good mosquito repellent. If you're heading to the top of Hawaii's volcanoes, you'll need your down mummy bag. If you plan to camp on the beach, bring your mosquito net and rain poncho. Always be prepared to deal with contaminated water (purify it by boiling, filtration, or using iodine tablets) and the tropical sun (protect yourself with sunscreen, a hat, and a long-sleeved shirt).

> **Tips Travel Tip**
>
> When planning sunset activities, be aware that Hawaii, like other places close to the equator, has a very short (5–10 min.) twilight period after the sun sets. After that, it's dark. If you hike out to watch the sunset, be sure you can make it back quickly, or take a flashlight.

Also be sure to check out "Staying Healthy," later in this chapter, for hiking and camping tips.

But, in general, camping is ideal in the islands. There are many established campgrounds at beach parks, including Kauai's Anini Beach, Oahu's Malaekahana Beach, Maui's Waianapanapa Beach, and the Big Island's Hapuna Beach. Campgrounds are also located in the interior at Maui's Haleakala National Park and the Big Island's Hawaii Volcanoes National Park, as well as at Kalalau Beach on Kauai's Na Pali Coast and in the cool uplands of Kokee State Park. See "Beaches" and "Hiking & Camping" in the individual island chapters for the best places to camp. For details on who to contact for regulations and information on camping in any of Hawaii's national or state parks, see section 3 of this chapter, "Visitor Information."

Hawaiian Trail and Mountain Club, P.O. Box 2238, Honolulu, HI 96804, offers an information packet on hiking and camping throughout the islands. Send $2 and a legal-size, self-addressed, stamped envelope for information. Another good source is the *Hiking/Camping Information Packet,* available for $7 from **Hawaii Geographic Maps and Books,** 49 S. Hotel St., Honolulu, HI 96813 (© **800/538-3950** or 808/538-3952). The **University of Hawaii Press,** 2840 Kolowalo St., Honolulu, HI 96822 (© **888/847-7737;** www.uhpress.hawaii.edu), has an excellent selection of hiking, backpacking, and bird-watching guides.

GOLF   Nowhere else on earth can you tee off to whale spouts, putt under rainbows, and play around a live volcano.

Hawaii has some of the world's top-rated golf courses. But be forewarned: Each course features hellish natural hazards, like razor-sharp lava, gusty trade winds, an occasional wild pig, and the tropical heat. And greens fees tend to be very expensive. Still, golfers flock here from around the world and love every minute of it. See the individual island chapters for coverage of the best resort courses worth splurging on (with details, where applicable, on money-saving twilight rates), as well as the best budget and municipal courses.

Tip: There's generally wind—10 to 30mph is not unusual between 10am and 2pm—so you may have to play two to three clubs up or down to compensate. Bring extra balls. The rough is thick, water hazards are everywhere, and the wind wreaks havoc with your game. On the greens, your putt will *always* break toward the ocean. Hit deeper and more aggressively in the sand, because the type of sand used on most Hawaii courses is firmer and more compact than usual (lighter sand would blow away in the constant wind). And bring a camera—you'll kick yourself if you don't capture those spectacular views.

See our coverage in each island chapter, and see also "The Best Golf Courses with Reasonable Greens Fees," in chapter 1.

HIKING   Hiking in Hawaii is a breathtaking experience. The islands have hundreds of miles of trails, many of which reward you with a hidden beach, a private waterfall, an Eden-like valley, or simply an unforgettable view. However, rock climbers are, sadly, out of luck: Most of

Hawaii's volcanic cliffs are too steep and too brittle to scale.

Hawaiian Trail and Mountain Club, P.O. Box 2238, Honolulu, HI 96804, offers an information packet on hiking and camping in Hawaii; to receive a copy, send $2 and a legal-size, self-addressed, stamped envelope. **Hawaii Geographic Maps and Books,** 49 S. Hotel St., Honolulu, HI 96813 (℃ **800/538-3950** or 808/538-3952), offers a *Hiking/Camping Information Packet* for $7. Also note that the **Hawaii State Department of Land and Natural Resources,** 1151 Punchbowl St., no. 131, Honolulu, HI 96809 (℃ **808/587-0300;** www.hawaii.gov), will send you free topographical trail maps.

The **Nature Conservancy of Hawaii** (℃ **808/537-4508** on Oahu; ℃ **808/572-7849** on Maui; ℃ **808/553-5236** on Molokai; www.tnc.org/hawaii) and the **Hawaii Chapter of the Sierra Club,** P.O. Box 2577, Honolulu, HI 96803 (℃ **808/538-6616**), both offer guided hikes in preserves and special areas during the year. Also see the individual island chapters for complete details on the best hikes for all ability levels.

Before you set out on the trail, see p. 41 for tips on hiking safety.

HORSEBACK RIDING One of the best ways to see Hawaii is on horseback; almost all the islands offer riding opportunities for just about every age and level of experience. You can ride into Maui's Haleakala Crater, along Kauai's Mahaulepu Beach, or through Oahu's remote windward valleys on Kualoa Ranch, or you can gallop across the wide-open spaces of the

---

Value **Fun for Less: Don't Leave Home Without a Gold Card**

Almost any activity you can think of, from submarine rides to Polynesian luaus, can be purchased at a discount by using the **Activities and Attractions Association of Hawaii Gold Card,** 355 Hukilike St., no. 202, Kahului, HI 96732 (℃ **800/398-9698** or 808/871-7947; fax 808/877-3104; www.hawaii fun.org). The Gold Card, accepted by members on Oahu, the Big Island, Maui, Molokai, Lanai, and Kauai, offers a discount of 10% to 25% off activities and meals for up to four people; it's good for a year from the purchase date and costs $30.

You can save big bucks with the Gold Card. For example, if you have your heart set on taking a helicopter ride that goes for $149, you'll pay only $119.20 with your Gold Card, saving you nearly $30 per person—almost $120 in savings for a family of four. With just one activity alone, you've gotten the cost of the card back in savings. And there are hundreds of activities to choose from: air tours, attractions, bicycling tours, dinner cruises, fishing, guided tours, helicopter tours, horseback riding, kayaking, luaus, snorkeling, rafting, sailing, scuba diving, submarine rides, and more. It even gets you discounts on rental cars, restaurants, and golf!

Here's how it works: You contact Activities and Attractions Association via mail, e-mail, fax, phone, or Internet (see above). They issue you the card, good for discounts for 1 year after the date you purchased it. You contact the activity (restaurant, rental car, and so on) directly, give them your Gold Card number, and get discounts ranging from 10% to 25%.

Big Island's Parker Ranch, one of the largest privately owned ranches in the United States. See the individual island chapters for details. Be sure to bring a pair of jeans and closed-toed shoes to wear on your ride.

KAYAKING Hawaii is one of the world's most popular destinations for ocean kayaking. Beginners can paddle across a tropical lagoon to two uninhabited islets off Lanikai Beach on Oahu, while more experienced kayakers can take on Kauai's awesome Na Pali Coast. In summer, experts take advantage of the usually flat conditions on the North Shore of Molokai, where the sea cliffs are the steepest on earth and the remote valleys can be reached only by sea. See "Watersports" in chapters 5 through 9 for local outfitters and tour guides.

SCUBA DIVING Some people come to the islands solely to take the plunge into the tropical Pacific and explore the underwater world. Hawaii is one of the world's top 10 dive destinations, according to *Rodale's Scuba Diving Magazine.* Here you can see the great variety of tropical marine life (more than 100 endemic species found nowhere else on the planet), explore sea caves, and swim with sea turtles and monk seals in clear, tropical water. If you're not certified, try to **take classes before you come to Hawaii** so you don't waste time learning and can dive right in.

If you dive, **go early in the morning.** Trade winds often rough up the seas in the afternoon, especially on Maui, so most operators schedule early morning dives that end at noon. To organize a dive on your own, order the *Dive Hawaii Guide,* which describes sites on the various Hawaiian Islands, by sending $2 to **UH/SGES,** Attention: Dive Guide, 2525 Correa Rd., HIG 237, Honolulu, HI 96822.

Tip: It's usually worth the extra bucks to go with a good dive operator. Check "Scuba Diving" in the island chapters; we've listed the operators that'll give you the most for your money.

SNORKELING Snorkeling is one of Hawaii's main attractions—and almost anyone can do it. All you need is a mask, a snorkel, fins, and some basic swimming skills. In many places, all you have to do is wade into the water and look down at the magical underwater world.

If you've never snorkeled before, most resorts and excursion boats offer snorkeling

---

Tips Snorkel Bob's

If you're planning on visiting several islands and would like to rent snorkel gear on one island and keep it with you for your whole trip, try **Snorkel Bob's** (© 800/262-7725; www.snorkelbob.com), which lets you rent snorkels, masks, fins, boogie boards, life jackets, and wet suits on any one island and return them on another. The basic set of snorkel gear is $3.50 a day, or $9 a week—a very good deal. The best gear is $6.50 a day, or $29 a week; if you're nearsighted and need a prescription mask, it's $9 a day, or $39 a week.

You can find Snorkel Bob's on **Oahu** at 702 Kapahulu Ave. (at Date Street), Honolulu (© 808/735-7944); on **Maui** at 1217 Front St., in Lahaina (© 808/661-4421), at Napili Village, 5425-C Lower Honapiilani Hwy., Napili (© 808/669-9603), and in South Maui at Kamole Beach Center, 2411 S. Kihei Rd., Kihei (© 808/879-7449); on the **Big Island** at 75–5831 Kahakai St. (off Alii Drive, next to Huggo's and the Royal Kona Resort), and Kailua-Kona (© 808/329-0770); and on **Kauai** at 4–734 Kuhio Hwy. (just north of Coconut Plantation Marketplace), in Kapaa (© 808/823-9433), and in Koloa at 3236 Poipu Rd., near Poipu Beach (© 808/742-2206).

equipment and lessons. You don't really need lessons, however; it's plenty easy to figure out for yourself, especially once you're at the beach, where everybody around you will be doing it. If you don't have your own gear, you can rent it from dozens of dive shops and activity booths, discussed in the individual island chapters that follow.

While everyone heads for Oahu's Hanauma Bay—the perfect spot for first-timers—other favorite snorkel spots include Kee Beach on Kauai, Kahaluu Beach on the Big Island, Hulopoe Bay on Lanai, and Kapalua Bay on Maui. Although snorkeling is excellent on all the islands, the Big Island, with its recent lava formations and abrupt drop-offs, offers some particularly spectacular opportunities. Some of the best snorkel spots in the islands—notably, the Big Island's Kealakekua Bay and Molokini Crater just off Maui—are accessible only by boat. For tips on the islands' top snorkel boats, see "Watersports" in the individual island chapters.

Tips: Always snorkel with a buddy. Look up every once in a while to see where you are and if there's any boat traffic. Don't touch anything; not only can you damage coral, but camouflaged fish and shells with poisonous spines may surprise you. Always check with a dive shop, lifeguards, or others on the beach about the area in which you plan to snorkel: Are there any dangerous conditions you should know about?

SPORTFISHING   Big-game fishing at its best is found **off the Big Island of Hawaii at Kailua-Kona,** where the deep blue waters offshore yield trophy marlin year-round. You can also try for spearfish, swordfish, various tuna, mahimahi (dorado), rainbow runners, wahoo, barracuda, trevallies, bonefish, and various bottom fish like snappers and groupers. Each island offers deep-sea boat charters for good-eating fish like tuna, wahoo,

and mahimahi. Visiting anglers currently need no license.

Charter fishing boats range widely both in size—from small 24-foot open skiffs to luxurious 50-foot-plus yachts—and in price—from about $100 per person to "share" a boat with other anglers for a half-day to more than $1,000 a day to book an entire luxury sportfishing yacht on an exclusive basis. Shop around. Prices vary according to the boat, the crowd, and the captain. See the individual island chapters for details. Also, many boat captains tag and release marlin, or keep the fish for themselves (sorry, that's Hawaii style). If you want to eat your mahimahi for dinner or have your marlin mounted, tell the captain before you go.

Money-saving tip: Try contacting the charter boat captain directly and bargaining. Many charter captains pay a 20% to 30% commission to charter-booking agencies and may be willing to give you a discount if you book directly.

SURFING   The ancient Hawaiian practice of *hee nalu* ("wave sliding") is probably the sport most people picture when they think of Hawaii. Believe it or not, you too can do some wave sliding—just sign up at any one of the numerous surfing schools located throughout the islands; see "Surfing" in chapters 5, 6, 7, and 10. On world-famous Waikiki Beach, just head over to one of the surf stands that line the sand; these guys say they can get anybody up and standing on a board. If you're already a big kahuna in surfing, check the same chapters for the best deals on rental equipment and the best places to hang ten.

TENNIS   Tennis is a popular sport in the islands. Each island chapter lists details on free municipal courts as well as the best deals on private courts. The etiquette at the free county courts is to play only 45 minutes if someone is waiting.

WHALE-WATCHING   Every winter, pods of Pacific humpback whales make the 3,000-mile swim from the chilly

Not So Close! They Hardly Know You

In the excitement of seeing a whale or a school of dolphins, don't forget that they're protected under the Marine Mammals Protection Act. You must stay at least 100 yards (the length of a football field) away from all whales, dolphins, and other marine mammals. This applies to swimmers, kayakers, and windsurfers. And yes, visitors have been prosecuted for swimming with dolphins! If you have any questions, call the **National Marine Fisheries Service** (© 808/541-2727) or the **Hawaiian Islands Humpback Whale National Marine Sanctuary** (© 800/831-4888).

waters of Alaska to bask in Hawaii's summery shallows, fluking, spy hopping, spouting, breaching, and having an all-around swell time. About 1,500 to 3,000 humpback whales appear in Hawaiian waters each year.

Humpbacks are one of the world's oldest, most impressive inhabitants. Adults grow to be about 45 feet long and weigh a hefty 40 tons. Humpbacks are officially an endangered species; in 1992, the waters around Maui, Molokai, and Lanai were designated a Humpback Whale National Marine Sanctuary. Despite the world's newfound ecological awareness, humpbacks and their habitats and food resources are still under threat from whalers and pollution.

The season's first whale is usually spotted in November, but the best time to see humpback whales in Hawaii is between **January and April,** from any island. Just look out to sea. Each island also offers a variety of whale-watching cruises, which will bring you up close and personal with the mammoth mammals; see the individual island chapters for details.

Money-saving tip: Book a snorkeling cruise during the winter whale-watching months. The captain of the boat will often take you through the best local whale-watching areas on the way, and you'll get two activities for the price of one. It's well worth the money.

WINDSURFING Maui is Hawaii's top windsurfing destination. World-class windsurfers head for Hookipa Beach, where the wind roars through Maui's isthmus and creates some of the best windsurfing conditions in the world. Funky Paia, a derelict sugar town saved from extinction by surfers, is now the world capital of big-wave board sailing. And along Maui's Hana Highway, there are lookouts where you can watch the pros flip off the lip of 10-foot waves and gain hang time in the air.

Others, especially beginners, set their sails for Oahu's Kailua Bay or Kauai's Anini Beach, where gentle onshore breezes make learning this sport a snap. See the individual island chapters for outfitters and local instructors.

8 Staying Healthy

ON LAND

Like any tropical climate, Hawaii is home to lots of bugs. Most of them won't harm you. However, three insects—mosquitoes, centipedes, and scorpions—do sting, and may cause anything from mild annoyance to severe swelling and pain.

MOSQUITOES These pesky insects are not native to Hawaii, but arrived as larvae stowed away in water barrels on the ship *Wellington* in 1826, when it anchored in Lahaina. There's not a whole lot you can do about them, except to apply commercial repellent, burn mosquito punk or citronella candles, and use ointments (which you can pick up at any drugstore) after you've been stung to ease the itching and swelling.

CENTIPEDES These segmented insects with a jillion legs come in two varieties: 6- to 8-inch-long brown ones and 2- to 3-inch-long blue guys. Both can really pack a wallop with their sting. Centipedes are generally found in damp, wet places, such as under wood piles or compost heaps; wearing closed-toe shoes can help prevent stings if you happen to accidentally unearth one. If you're stung, the reaction can range from something similar to a mild bee sting to severe pain; apply ice at once to prevent swelling. See a doctor if you experience extreme pain, swelling, nausea, or any other severe reaction.

SCORPIONS Rarely seen, scorpions are found in arid, warm regions; their stings can be serious. Campers in dry areas should always check their boots before putting them on, and shake out sleeping bags and bed rolls. Symptoms of a scorpion sting include shortness of breath, hives, swelling, and nausea. In the unlikely event that you're stung, apply diluted household ammonia and cold compresses to the area of the sting and seek medical help immediately.

HIKING SAFETY

In addition to taking the appropriate precautions regarding Hawaii's bug population, hikers should always let someone know where they're heading, when they're going, and when they plan to return. Too many hikers get lost in Hawaii because they don't let others know their basic plans.

Always check weather conditions with the **National Weather Service** (© 808/ 973-4381 on Oahu; see individual island chapters for local weather information) before you go. Hike with a pal, never alone. Wear hiking boots, a sun hat, clothes to protect you from the sun and from getting scratches, and high-SPF sunscreen on all exposed areas of skin. Take water. Stay on the trail. Watch your step. It's easy to slip off precipitous trails and into steep canyons. Incapacitated hikers are often plucked to safety by fire and rescue squads, who must use helicopters to gain access to remote sites. Many experienced hikers and boaters today pack a cellphone in case of emergency; just dial © **911.**

VOG (VOLCANIC SMOG)

The volcanic haze dubbed *vog* is caused by gases released when molten lava— from the continuous eruption of Kilauea volcano on the Big Island—pours into the ocean. This hazy air, which looks like urban smog, limits viewing from scenic vistas and wreaks havoc with photographers trying to get clear panoramic shots. Some people claim that long-term exposure has even caused bronchial ailments, but it's highly unlikely to cause you any harm in the course of your visit.

There actually is a vog season in Hawaii: the fall and winter months, when the trade winds that blow the fumes out

Tips   A Few Words of Warning about Crime

Although Hawaii is generally a safe tourist destination, visitors have been crime victims, so stay alert. The most common crime against tourists is rental-car break-ins. Never leave any valuables in your car, not even in your trunk: Be especially leery of high-risk areas, such as beaches, resorts, scenic lookouts, and other visitor attractions. Also, never carry large amounts of cash. Stay in well-lighted areas after dark.

Tips Don't Get Burned: Smart Tanning Tips

Hawaii's Caucasian population has the highest incidence of malignant melanoma (deadly skin cancer) in the world. And nobody is completely safe from the sun's harmful rays: All skin types and races can burn. To ensure that your vacation won't be ruined by painful sunburn, here are some helpful tips.

- **Wear a strong sunscreen at all times.** Use a sunscreen with a sun-protection factor (SPF) of 15 or higher; people with a light complexion should use 30. Apply it liberally, and reapply every 2 hours.

- **Prevent wrinkles.** Wrinkles, sagging skin, and other signs of premature aging can be caused by Ultraviolet A (UVA) rays. For years, sunscreens concentrated on blocking out just Ultraviolet B (UVB) rays. The best protection from UVA rays is zinc oxide (the white goo that lifeguards wear on their noses), but other ingredients also provide protection. Read the label, and get another brand if your sunscreen doesn't contain one of the following: zinc oxide, benzophenone, oxybenzone, sulisobenzone, titanium dioxide, or avobenzone (also known as Parsol 1789).

- **Wear a hat and sunglasses.** The hat should have a brim (all the way around, to cover not only your face but also the sensitive back of your neck). Make sure your sunglasses have UV filters.

- **Protect children from the sun.** Infants under 6 months should not be in the sun at all. Older babies need zinc oxide to protect their fragile skin, and all children should be slathered with sunscreen frequently.

- **If you start to turn red, get out of the sun.** Contrary to popular belief, you don't have to turn red to tan; if your skin is red, it's burned, and that's serious. The best remedy for sunburn is to get out of the sun immediately and stay out of the sun until all the redness is gone. Aloe vera (straight from the plant or from a commercial preparation), cool compresses, cold baths, and anesthetic benzocaine also help with the pain of sunburn.

to sea die down. The vog is felt not only on the Big Island but also as far away as Maui and Oahu.

One more word of caution: If you're pregnant or have heart or breathing problems, you might want to think twice about visiting the Big Island's Hawaii Volcanoes National Park. You're cautioned to avoid exposure to the sulfuric fumes that are ever-present in and around the park's calderas.

OCEAN SAFETY
Because most people coming to Hawaii are unfamiliar with the ocean environment, they're often unaware of the natural

hazards it holds. With just a few precautions, your ocean experience can be a safe and happy one. An excellent book is *All Stings Considered: First Aid and Medical Treatment of Hawaii's Marine Injuries* (University of Hawaii Press, 1997), by Craig Thomas and Susan Scott.

Note that sharks are not a big problem in Hawaii; in fact, they appear so infrequently that locals look forward to seeing them. Since records have been kept, starting in 1779, there have been only about 100 shark attacks in Hawaii, of which 40% have been fatal. Most attacks occurred after someone fell into the ocean from the shore or from a boat; in these cases, the sharks probably attacked after the person was dead. But general rules for avoiding sharks are: Don't swim at sunrise, sunset, or where the water is murky due to stream runoff—sharks may mistake you for one of their usual meals. And don't swim where there are bloody fish in the water, as sharks become aggressive around blood.

SEASICKNESS   The waters in Hawaii can range from calm as glass (off the Kona Coast on the Big Island) to downright frightening (in storm conditions), and they usually fall somewhere in between. In general, expect rougher conditions in winter than in summer.

Some 90% of the population tends toward seasickness. If you've never been out on a boat, or if you've been seasick in the past, you might want to avoid alcohol, caffeine, citrus and other acidic juices, and greasy, spicy, or hard-to-digest foods the day before you go out. Take or use whatever seasickness prevention works best for you—medication, an acupressure wristband, gingerroot tea or capsules, or any combination. But do it *before* you board; once you set sail, it's generally too late. While you're on the boat, stay as low and as near the center of the boat as possible. Avoid the fumes (especially if it's a diesel boat); stay out in the fresh air and watch the horizon. Do not read. If you start to feel queasy, drink clear fluids like water, and eat something bland, such as a soda cracker.

STINGS   The most common stings in Hawaii come from jellyfish, particularly Portuguese man-of-war and box jellyfish. Since the poisons they inject are very different, you need to treat each sting differently.

A bluish-purple floating bubble with a long tail, the **Portuguese man-of-war** causes some 6,500 stings a year on Oahu alone. These stings, although painful and a nuisance, are rarely harmful; fewer than 1 in 1,000 requires medical treatment. The best prevention is to watch for these floating bubbles as you snorkel (look for the hanging tentacles below the surface). Get out of the water if anyone near you spots these jellyfish.

Reactions to stings range from mild burning and reddening to severe welts and blisters. *All Stings Considered* recommends the following treatment: First, pick off any visible tentacles with a gloved hand, a stick, or anything handy; then rinse the sting with salt- or freshwater, and apply ice to prevent swelling and to help control pain. Hawaii folklore advises using vinegar, meat tenderizer, baking soda, papain, or alcohol, or even urinating on the wound. Studies have shown that these remedies may actually cause further damage. Most Portuguese man-of-war stings will disappear by themselves within 15 to 20 minutes if you do nothing at all to treat them. Still, be sure to see a doctor if pain persists or a rash or other symptoms develop.

Transparent, square-shaped **box jellyfish** are nearly impossible to see in the water. Fortunately, they seem to follow a monthly cycle: 8 to 10 days after the full moon, they appear in the waters on the leeward side of each island and hang around for about 3 days. Also, they seem to sting more in the morning hours, when they're on or near the surface. The best prevention is to get out of the water.

The stings can cause anything from no visible marks to red, hivelike welts, blisters, and pain (a burning sensation) lasting from 10 minutes to 8 hours. *All Stings Considered* recommends the following treatment: First, pour regular household vinegar on the sting; this may not relieve the pain, but it will stop additional burning. Do not rub the area. Pick off any vinegar-soaked tentacles with a stick. For pain, apply an ice pack. Seek additional medical treatment if you experience shortness of breath, weakness, palpitations, muscle cramps, or any other severe symptoms. Again, ignore any folk remedies. Most box jellyfish stings disappear by themselves without any treatment.

PUNCTURES   Most sea-related punctures come from stepping on or brushing against the needlelike spines of sea urchins (known locally as *wana*). Be careful when you're in the water; don't put your foot down (even if you have booties or fins on) if you can't clearly see the bottom. Waves can push you into *wana* in a surge zone in shallow water. The spines can even puncture a wet suit.

A sea-urchin puncture can result in burning, aching, swelling, and discoloration (black or purple) around the area where the spines entered your skin. The best thing to do is to pull any protruding spines out. The body will absorb the spines within 24 hours to 3 weeks, or the remainder of the spines will work themselves out. Again, contrary to popular wisdom, do not urinate or pour vinegar on the embedded spines—this will not help.

CUTS   All cuts obtained in the marine environment must be taken seriously, because the high level of bacteria present in the water can quickly cause the cut to become infected. The most common cuts are from coral. Contrary to popular belief, coral cannot grow inside your body. Bacteria, however, can. The best way to prevent cuts is to wear a wet suit, gloves, and reef shoes. Never, under any circumstances, should you touch a coral head; not only can you get cut, but you can also damage a living organism that took decades to grow.

The symptoms of a coral cut can range from a slight scratch to severe welts and blisters. *All Stings Considered* recommends gently pulling the edges of the skin open and removing any embedded coral or grains of sand with tweezers. Next, scrub the cut well with fresh water. Never use ocean water to clean a cut. If you're bleeding, press a clean cloth against the wound until it stops. If the bleeding continues, or the edges of the injury are jagged or gaping, seek medical treatment.

9 Getting Married in the Islands (Without Going Broke)

Hawaii is a great place for a wedding. The islands exude romance and natural beauty, and after the ceremony, you're already on your honeymoon. And the members of your wedding party will most likely be delighted, since you've given them the perfect excuse for their own island vacation.

More than 20,000 marriages are performed annually on the islands, mostly on Oahu; nearly half are for couples from somewhere else. The booming wedding business has spawned more than 70 companies that can help you organize a long-distance event and stage an unforgettable wedding, Hawaiian style or your style. However, you can also plan your own island wedding, even from afar, and not spend a fortune doing it.

THE PAPERWORK

The state of Hawaii has some very minimal procedures for obtaining a marriage license. The first thing you should do is contact the **Honolulu Marriage License Office,** State Department of Health Building, 1250 Punchbowl St., Honolulu, HI 96813 (© **808/586-4545;** www.state.hi.us/doh/records/vr_marri.html), which is open Monday through Friday from 8am to 4pm. The office will mail you the brochure *Getting Married* and direct you to the marriage-licensing agent closest to where you'll be staying in Hawaii.

Once in Hawaii, the prospective bride and groom must go together to the marriage-licensing agent to get the license, which costs $60 and is good for 30 days.

Both parties must be 15 years of age or older (couples 15–17 years old must have proof of age, written consent of both parents, and written approval of the judge of the family court) and not more closely related than first cousins. That's it.

Gay couples cannot marry in Hawaii. After a protracted legal battle, and much discussion in the state legislature, in late 1999 the Hawaii Supreme Court ruled that the state will not issue marriage licenses to same-sex couples.

PLANNING THE WEDDING

DOING IT YOURSELF   The marriage-licensing agents, who range from employees of the governor's satellite office in Kona to private individuals, are usually friendly, helpful people who can steer you to a nondenominational minister or marriage performer who's licensed by the state of Hawaii. These marriage performers are great sources of information for budget weddings. They usually know wonderful places to have the ceremony for free or for a nominal fee.

If you don't want to use a wedding planner (see below), but you do want to make arrangements before you arrive in Hawaii, our best advice is to get a copy of the daily newspaper on the island where you want to have the wedding. People willing and qualified to conduct weddings advertise in the classifieds. They're great sources of information, as they know the best places to have the ceremony and can recommend caterers, florists, and everything else you'll need. If you want to have your wedding on the Kona/Waimea side of the Big Island, get *West Hawaii Today,* P.O. Box 789, Kailua-Kona, HI 96745 (© 808/329-9311; www.westhawaiitoday.com); for the Hilo/Puna side, try the *Hawaii Tribune Herald,* P.O. Box 767, Hilo, HI 96720

(© 808/935-6621; www.hilohawaii tribune.com). On Maui, get the *Maui News,* P.O. Box 550, Wailuku, HI 96793 (© 808/244-3981). On Kauai, try the *Garden Island,* 3137 Kuhio Hwy., Lihue, HI 96766 (© 808/245-3681; www.kauai world.com). And on Oahu, check out the *Honolulu Advertiser,* P.O. Box 3110, Honolulu, HI 96802 (© 808/525-8000; www.honoluluadvertiser.com); the *Honolulu Star Bulletin,* 7 Waterfront Plaza, Suite 500, Honolulu, HI 96813 (© 808/529-4700; www.honolulustarbulletin. com); and *MidWeek,* 45–525 Luluku Rd., Kaneohe, HI 96744 (© 808/235-5881; www.midweek.com).

USING A WEDDING PLANNER
Wedding planners—many of whom are marriage-licensing agents as well—can arrange everything for you, from a small, private, outdoor affair to a full-blown formal ceremony in a tropical setting. They charge anywhere from $225 to a small fortune—it all depends on what you want. On the Big Island, contact **Paradise Weddings Hawaii** (© **800/428-5844** or 808/883-9067; www.paradiseweddingshawaii. com); on Maui, contact **First Class Weddings** (© **800/262-8433** or 808/877-1411; www.firstclassweddings.com); on Kauai try **Coconut Coast Weddings & Honeymoons** (© **800/585-5595** or 808/826-5557; www.kauaiwedding.com); on Oahu contact Rev. Toni Baran and Rev. Jerry Le Lesch at **Love Hawaii** (© **808/235-6966;** www.lovehawaii.com), which offers wedding services starting at $95. The Hawaii Visitors and Convention Bureau (see section 1 of this chapter) can provide contact information for other wedding coordinators, and many of the big resorts have their own coordinators on staff.

10 Specialized Travel Resources

FOR TRAVELERS WITH DISABILITIES

Travelers with disabilities are made to feel very welcome in Hawaii. There are more than 2,000 ramped curbs in Oahu alone, hotels are usually equipped with wheelchair-accessible rooms, and tour companies provide many special services. The **Hawaii Center for Independent Living,** 414 Kauwili St., Suite 102, Honolulu, HI 96817 (© **808/522-5400;** fax 808/586-8129 www.diverseabilities.org), can provide information.

The only travel agency in Hawaii specializing in needs for travelers with disabilities is **Access Aloha Travel** (© **800/480-1143;** www.accessalohatravel.com), which can book anything, including rental vans (available on Maui and Oahu only), accommodations, tours, cruises, airfare, and anything else you can think of. For more details on wheelchair transportation and tours around the islands, see "Getting Around" in the island chapters.

For travelers with disabilities who wish to do their own driving, hand-controlled cars can be rented from **Avis** (© **800/331-1212;** www.avis.com) and **Hertz** (© **800/654-3131;** www.hertz.com). The number of hand-controlled cars in Hawaii is limited, so be sure to book well in advance. Vision-impaired travelers who use a Seeing Eye dog can now come to Hawaii without the hassle of quarantine. A recent court decision ruled that visitors with Seeing Eye dogs only need to present documentation that the dog is a trained Seeing Eye dog and has had rabies shots. For more information, contact the **Animal Quarantine Facility** (© **808/483-7171;** www.hawaii.gov).

Many travel agencies offer customized tours and itineraries for travelers with disabilities. **Flying Wheels Travel** (© **507/451-5005;** www.flyingwheelstravel.com) offers escorted tours and cruises that emphasize sports and private tours in minivans with lifts. **Access-Able Travel Source** (© **303/232-2979;** www.access-able.com) offers extensive access information and advice for traveling around the world with disabilities. **Accessible Journeys** (© **800/846-4537** or 610/521-0339; www.disabilitytravel.com) caters specifically to slow walkers and wheelchair travelers and their families and friends.

Organizations that offer assistance to travelers with disabilities include **MossRehab** (www.mossresourcenet.org), which provides a library of accessible-travel resources online; **SATH (Society for Accessible Travel & Hospitality)** (© **212/447-7284;** www.sath.org; annual membership fees: $45 adults, $30 seniors and students), which offers a wealth of travel resources for all types of disabilities and informed recommendations on destinations, access guides, travel agents, tour operators, vehicle rentals, and companion services; and the **American Foundation for the Blind (AFB)** (© **800/232-5463;** www.afb.org), a referral resource for the blind or visually impaired that includes information on traveling with Seeing Eye dogs.

FOR GAY & LESBIAN TRAVELERS

Hawaii is known for its acceptance of all groups. The number of gay- or lesbian-specific accommodations on the islands is limited, but most properties welcome gays and lesbians like any other travelers.

The Center, mailing address: P.O. Box 22718, Honolulu, HI 96823 or 2424 S. Beretania St. (between Isenberg and University), Honolulu, HI 96823 (© **808/951-7000;** fax 808/951-7001; www.thecenterhawaii.org), open Monday through Friday from 10am to 6pm and on Saturday from noon to 4pm, is a referral center for nearly every kind of gay-related service you can think of, including the latest happenings on Oahu. Check out their community newspaper, *Outlook,* published quarterly focusing on local issues in the gay community on the islands.

For information on Kauai's gay community and related events, contact the **Gay/Lesbian/Bisexual/Transgender Audio Bulletin Board** (© 808/823-6248).

On the Big Island check out the website for **Out in Hawaii,** www.outin hawaii.com, for information on vacation ideas on the Big Island.

The International Gay & Lesbian Travel Association (IGLTA) (© 800/448-8550 or 954/776-2626; www.iglta. org) is the trade association for the gay and lesbian travel industry, and offers an online directory of gay- and lesbian-friendly travel businesses; go to their website and click on "Members."

Many agencies offer tours and travel itineraries specifically for gay and lesbian travelers. **Pacific Ocean Holidays** (© 800/735-6600 or 808/923-2400; www.gayhawaii.com), offers vacation packages that feature gay-owned and gay-friendly lodgings. Also on their website is *A Guide for Gay Visitors & Kamaaina.*

FOR SENIORS

Discounts for seniors are available at almost all of Hawaii's major attractions, and occasionally at hotels and restaurants. The Outrigger hotel chain, for instance, offers travelers ages 50 and older a 20% discount off regular published rates—and an additional 5% off for members of AARP. Always ask when making hotel reservations or buying tickets. And always carry identification with proof of your age—it can really pay off.

Don't forget to mention your age when you book your airline tickets; most U.S. airlines offer substantial senior discounts.

Members of the AARP (© 800/424-3410 or 202/434-2277; www.aarp.org)

are usually eligible for many discounts; AARP also puts together organized tour packages at moderate rates through the AARP Travel Service.

There are some great, low-cost trips to Hawaii available for those ages 55 and older through **Elderhostel** (© 617/426-7788; www.elderhostel.org), a nonprofit group that offers travel and study programs around the world. Trips usually include moderately priced accommodations and meals in one low-cost package.

If you're 62 or older and plan to visit Hawaii's national parks, you can save sightseeing dollars by picking up a **Golden Age Passport** from any national park, recreation area, or monument. This lifetime pass has a one-time fee of $10 and provides free admission to all the parks in the system, plus a 50% savings on camping and recreation fees. You can pick one up at any park entrance; be sure to have proof of your age with you.

FOR FAMILIES

Hawaii is paradise for children: beaches to run on, water to splash in, and unusual sights to see. Be sure to check out the boxes in each island chapter for kid-friendly places to stay and family activities.

The larger hotels and resorts offer supervised programs for children and can refer you to qualified babysitters. By state law, hotels can accept only children ages 5 to 12 in supervised activities programs, but they often accommodate younger children by simply hiring babysitters to watch over them. You can also contact **People Attentive to Children (PATCH),** which can refer you to babysitters who have taken a training course on child care. On Oahu, call © 808/839-1988; on the Big Island, call © 808/325-3864 in Kona and © 808/961-3169 in Hilo; on Maui, call © 808/242-9232; on Kauai, call © 808/246-0622; on Molokai and Lanai, call © 800/498-4145; or visit www.patchhawaii.org.

Baby's Away (www.babysaway.com) rents cribs, strollers, high chairs, playpens, infant seats, and the like on Maui (© **800/ 942-9030** or 808/875-9030), the Big Island (© **800/996-9030** or 808/987-9236), and Oahu (© **800/496-6386** or 808/222-6041). The staff will deliver whatever you need to wherever you're staying and pick it up when you're done.

Recommended family-travel Internet sites include **Family Travel Forum** (www. familytravelforum.com), a comprehensive site that offers customized trip planning; **Family Travel Network** (www.familytravel network.com), an award-winning site that offers travel features, deals, and tips; and **Family Travel Files** (www.thefamily travelfiles.com), which offers an online magazine and a directory of off-the-beaten-path tours and tour operators for families. Also look for the just-released, first edition of *Frommer's Hawaii with Kids.*

11 Money-Saving Package Deals

SURFING FOR AIRFARES

The "big three" online travel agencies, **Expedia.com, Travelocity.com,** and **Orbitz.com** sell most of the air tickets bought on the Internet. (Canadian travelers should try Expedia.ca and Travelocity. ca; U.K. residents can go for Expedia. co.uk and Opodo.co.uk.) Each has different business deals with the airlines and may offer different fares on the same flights so it's wise to shop around. Expedia and Travelocity will also send you **e-mail notification** when a cheap fare becomes available to your favorite destination.

Also remember to check **airline websites.** You can often shave a few bucks from a fare by booking directly through the airline and avoiding a travel agency's transaction fee. But you'll get these discounts only by **booking online:** Most airlines now offer online-only fares that even their phone agents know nothing about. For the websites of airlines that fly to and from your destination, go to "Getting There & Getting Around" below.

If you're willing to give up some control over your flight details, use what is called an **"opaque" fare service** like **Priceline** (www.priceline.com; www.priceline.co.uk for Europeans) or its smaller competitor **Hotwire** (www.hotwire.com). Both offer rock-bottom prices in exchange for travel on a "mystery airline" at a mysterious time of day, often with a mysterious change of planes en route. The mystery airlines are all major, well-known carriers—and the possibility of being sent from Philadelphia to Chicago via Tampa is remote; the airlines' routing computers have gotten a lot better than they used to be. But your chances of getting a 6am or 11pm flight are pretty high. Hotwire tells you flight prices before you buy; Priceline usually has better deals than Hotwire, but you have to play their "name our price" game. If you're new at this, the helpful folks at **BiddingForTravel** (www.biddingfortravel. com) do a good job of demystifying Priceline's prices and strategies. Priceline and Hotwire are great for flights within North America and between the U.S. and Europe. But for flights to other parts of the world, consolidators will almost always beat their fares. *Note:* In 2004, Priceline added non-opaque service to its roster. You now have

---

No Smoking: Hawaii's Restaurants Are Smoke Free

All restaurants in Hawaii are smoke free. Only Kauai allows smoking in a bar. About one out of every five Hawaii residents smokes; according to the State Department of Health, that's slightly less than the national average.

Frommers.com: The Complete Travel Resource

For an excellent travel-planning resource, we highly recommend **Frommers. com** (www.frommers.com), voted Best Travel Site by *PC Magazine*. We're a little biased, of course, but we guarantee that you'll find the travel tips, reviews, monthly vacation giveaways, bookstore, and online-booking capabilities thoroughly indispensable. Among the special features are our popular **Destinations** section, where you'll get expert travel tips, hotel and dining recommendations, and advice on the sights to see for more than 3,500 destinations around the globe; the **Frommers.com Newsletter,** with the latest deals, travel trends, and money-saving secrets; our **Community** area featuring **Message Boards,** where Frommer's readers post queries and share advice (sometimes even our authors show up to answer questions); and our **Photo Center,** where you can post queries and share money-saving tips. When your research is done, the **Online Reservations System** (www. frommers.com/book_a_trip) takes you to Frommer's preferred online partners for booking your vacation at affordable prices.

the option to pick exact flights, times, and airlines from a list of offers—or opt to bid on opaque fares as before.

For much more about airfares and savvy air-travel tips and advice, pick up a copy of *Frommer's Fly Safe, Fly Smart* (Wiley Publishing, Inc.).

SURFING FOR HOTELS

Shopping online for hotels is generally done one of two ways: by booking through the hotel's own website or through an independent booking agency (or a fare-service agency like Priceline; see below). These Internet hotel agencies have multiplied in mind-boggling numbers of late, competing for the business of millions of consumers surfing for accommodations around the world. This competitiveness can be a boon to consumers who have the patience and time to shop and compare the online sites for good deals—but shop they must, for prices can vary considerably from site to site. And keep in mind that hotels at the top of a site's listing may be there for no other reason than that they paid money to get the placement.

Of the "big three" sites, **Expedia** offers a long list of special deals and "virtual tours" or photos of available rooms so you can see what you're paying for (a feature that helps counter the claims that the best rooms are often held back from bargain-booking websites). **Travelocity** posts unvarnished customer reviews and ranks its properties according to the AAA rating system. Also reliable are **Hotels.com** and **Quikbook.com.** An excellent free program, **TravelAxe** (www.travelaxe.net), can help you search multiple hotel sites at once, even ones you may never have heard of—and conveniently lists the total price of the room, including the taxes and service charges. Another booking site, **Travelweb** (www.travelweb.com), is partly owned by the hotels it represents (including the Hilton, Hyatt, and Starwood chains) and is therefore plugged directly into the hotels' reservations systems—unlike independent online agencies, which have to fax or e-mail reservation requests to the hotel, some of which get misplaced in the shuffle. To be fair, many of the major sites are undergoing improvements in service and ease of

> **Tips   A Package-Buying Tip**
>
> For one-stop shopping on the Web, **Pleasant Hawaiian Holidays** (© **800/2-HAWAII** or 800/242-9244; www.pleasantholidays.com) is by far the biggest and most comprehensive packager to Hawaii. It offers an extensive, high-quality collection of 50 condos and hotels in every price range. Or, go to **www.vacationpackager.com**, a search engine that can link you up with many different package-tour operations; be sure to look under both "Hawaii" and "Hawaiian Islands."

use, and Expedia will soon be able to plug directly into the reservations systems of many hotel chains. In the meantime, it's a good idea to **get a confirmation number** and **make a printout** of any online booking transaction.

In the opaque website category, **Priceline** and **Hotwire** are even better for hotels than for airfares; with both, you're allowed to pick the neighborhood and quality level of your hotel before offering up your money. Priceline's hotel product even covers Europe and Asia, though it's much better at getting five-star lodging for three-star prices than at finding anything at the bottom of the scale. On the downside, many hotels stick Priceline guests in their least desirable rooms. Be sure to go to the BiddingForTravel website (see above) before bidding on a hotel room on Priceline; it features a fairly up-to-date list of hotels that Priceline uses in major cities. For both Priceline and Hotwire, you pay upfront, and the fee is nonrefundable. *Note:* Some hotels do not provide loyalty program credits or points or other frequent-stay amenities when you book a room through opaque online services.

SURFING FOR RENTAL CARS

For booking rental cars online, the best deals are usually found at rental-car company websites, although all the major online travel agencies also offer rental-car reservations services. Priceline and Hotwire work well for rental cars, too; the only "mystery" is which major rental company you get, and for most travelers the difference between Hertz, Avis, and Budget is negligible.

12 The 21st-Century Traveler

INTERNET ACCESS AWAY FROM HOME

Travelers have any number of ways to check their e-mail and access the Internet on the road. Of course, using your own laptop—or even a PDA or electronic organizer with a modem—gives you the most flexibility. But even if you don't have a computer, you can still access your e-mail and even your office computer from cybercafes.

WITHOUT YOUR OWN COMPUTER

It's hard nowadays to find a city that *doesn't* have a few cybercafes. Although there's no definitive directory for cybercafes—these are independent businesses, after all—three places to start looking are at **www.cybercaptive.com**, **www.netcafeguide.com**, and **www.cybercafe.com**.

Aside from formal cybercafes, most **public libraries** across the world offer Internet access free or for a small charge. **Hotel business centers** generally provide access, but most charge exorbitant rates.

To retrieve your e-mail, ask your **Internet Service Provider (ISP)** if it has a Web-based interface tied to your existing e-mail account. If your ISP doesn't have such an interface, you can use the free

mail2web service (www.mail2web.com) to view (but not reply to) your home e-mail. For more flexibility, you may want to open a free, Web-based e-mail account with **Yahoo! Mail** (mail.yahoo.com). (Microsoft's Hotmail is another popular option, but Hotmail has severe spam problems.) Your home ISP may be able to forward your e-mail to the Web-based account automatically.

WITH YOUR OWN COMPUTER

Wi-Fi (Wireless Fidelity) is the buzzword in computer access, and more and more hotels, cafes, and retailers are signing on. You can get a Wi-Fi connection one of several ways. Many laptops sold in the last year have built-in Wi-Fi capability (an 802.11b wireless Ethernet connection). Mac owners have their own networking technology, Apple AirPort. For those with older computers, an 802.11b/ **Wi-Fi card** (around $50) can be plugged into your laptop. You sign up for wireless access service much as you do cellphone service, through a plan offered by one of several commercial companies that have made wireless service available in airports, hotel lobbies, and coffee shops, primarily in the U.S. (followed by the U.K. and Japan). **T-Mobile Hotspot** (www.t-mobile.com/hotspot) serves up wireless connections at more than 1,000 Starbucks coffee shops nationwide. **Boingo** (www.boingo.com) and **Wayport** (www.wayport.com) have set up networks in airports and high-class hotel lobbies. IPass providers (see below) also give you access to a few hundred wireless hotel lobby setups. Best of all, you don't need to be staying at the Four Seasons to use the hotel's network; just set yourself up on a nice couch in the lobby.

There are also places that provide **free wireless networks** in cities around the world. To locate these free hotspots, go to **www.personaltelco.net/index.cgi/ WirelessCommunities**.

If Wi-Fi is not available at your destination, most business-class hotels throughout the world offer dataports for laptop modems, and a few thousand hotels in the U.S. and Europe now offer free high-speed Internet access using an Ethernet network cable. You can bring your own cables, but most hotels rent them for around $10. **Call your hotel in advance** to see what your options are.

In addition, major Internet Service Providers (ISPs) have **local access numbers** around the world, allowing you to go online by simply placing a local call. Check your ISP's website or call its toll-free number and ask how you can use your current account away from home and how much it will cost.

If you're traveling outside the reach of your ISP, the **iPass** network has dial-up numbers in most of the world's countries. You'll have to sign up with an iPass provider who will then tell you how to set up your computer for your destination(s). For a list of iPass providers, go to www.ipass.com and click on "Individuals Buy Now." One solid provider is **i2roam** (© **866/811-6209** or 920/235-0475; www.i2roam.com).

USING A CELLPHONE

Just because your cellphone works at home doesn't mean it'll work in Hawaii (thanks to our fragmented cellphone system). Take a look at your wireless company's coverage map on its website before heading out.

13 Getting There & Getting Around

For additional advice on travel within each island, see "Getting Around" in the individual island chapters that follow.

Don't forget to **refer back to section 1 of this chapter, "55 Money-Saving Tips."** Tips 6 through 13 offer some great advice about finding the best airfare, including a list of consolidators.

ARRIVING IN THE ISLANDS

Most major U.S. and many international carriers fly to Honolulu International Airport. Some also offer direct flights to Kailua-Kona, on the Big Island; Kahului, Maui; and Lihue, Kauai.

United Airlines (© 800/225-5825; www.ual.com) offers the most frequent service from the U.S. mainland, flying not only to Honolulu, but also offering nonstop flights from Los Angeles and San Francisco to the Big Island, Maui, and Kauai. Aloha Airlines (© 800/367-5250 or 808/484-1111; www.alohaairlines.com) has direct flights from Oakland and Orange County to Maui, Kona, and Honolulu, and from Orange County, California, to Honolulu and Maui. American Airlines (© 800/433-7300; www.aa.com) offers flights from Dallas, Chicago, San Francisco, San Jose, and Los Angeles to Honolulu, plus several direct flights to Maui and Kona. Continental Airlines (© 800/231-0856; www.continental. com) offers the only daily nonstop from the New York area (Newark) to Honolulu. Delta Air Lines (© 800/221-1212; www. delta.com) flies nonstop from the West Coast to both Honolulu and Maui. Hawaiian Airlines (© 800/367-5320; www.hawaiianair.com) offers nonstop flights to Honolulu from several West Coast cities (including new service from San Diego), plus nonstop flights from Los Angeles to Maui. Northwest Airlines (© 800/225-2525; www.nwa.com) has a daily nonstop from Detroit to Honolulu.

For information on airlines serving Hawaii from places other than the U.S. mainland, see chapter 3. For details on navigating Hawaii's airports, see each island chapter.

LONG-HAUL FLIGHTS: HOW TO STAY COMFORTABLE

Long flights can be trying; stuffy air and cramped seats can make you feel as if you're being sent parcel post in a small box. But with a little advance planning, you can make an otherwise unpleasant experience almost bearable.

- Your choice of airline and airplane will definitely affect your leg room. Among U.S. airlines, American Airlines has the best average seat pitch (the distance between a seat and the row in front of it). Find more details at www.seatguru.com, which has extensive details about almost every seat on six major U.S. airlines.

- Emergency exit seats and bulkhead seats typically have the most legroom. Emergency exit seats are usually held back to be assigned the day of a flight (to ensure that the seat is filled by someone able-bodied); it's worth getting to the ticket counter early to snag one of these spots for a long flight. Keep in mind that bulkheads are where airlines often put baby bassinets, so you may be sitting next to an infant.

- To have two seats for yourself, try for an aisle seat in a center section toward the back of coach. If you're traveling with a companion, book an aisle and a window seat. Middle seats are usually booked last, so chances are good you'll end up with three seats to yourselves. And, in the event that a third passenger is assigned the middle seat, he or she will probably be more than happy to trade for a window or an aisle.

- To sleep, avoid the last row of any section or a row in front of an emergency exit, as these seats are the least likely to recline. Avoid seats near highly trafficked toilet areas. You also may want to reserve a window seat so that you can rest your head and avoid being bumped in the aisle.

- Get up, walk around, and stretch every 60 to 90 minutes to keep your blood flowing. This helps avoid deep vein thrombosis, or "economy-class syndrome," a rare and deadly condition that can be caused by sitting in cramped conditions for too long.

- Drink water before, during, and after your flight to combat the lack of humidity in airplane cabins—which can be drier than the Sahara. Bring a bottle of water on board. Avoid alcohol, which will dehydrate you.

- If you're flying with kids, don't forget to carry on toys, books, pacifiers, and chewing gum (to help them relieve ear pressure buildup during ascent and descent). Let each child pack his or her own backpack with favorite toys.

AGRICULTURAL SCREENING AT THE AIRPORTS   At Honolulu International and the neighbor-island airports, baggage and passengers bound for the mainland must be screened by agricultural officials before boarding. The process is usually quick and easy. Officials will confiscate fresh avocados, bananas, mangoes, and many other kinds of local produce in the name of fruit-fly control. Pineapples, coconuts, and papayas inspected and certified for export, boxed flowers, leis without seeds, and processed foods (macadamia nuts, coffee, jams, dried fruit, and the like) will pass. Call federal or state agricultural officials before leaving for the airport if you're not sure about your trophy.

INTER-ISLAND FLIGHTS

Don't expect to jump a ferry between any of the Hawaiian islands. Today, everyone island-hops by plane. In the past year, due to the September 11, 2001, terrorist attacks and the not-so-bright-economic-picture for the airline industry in Hawaii, the two inter-island carriers have cut way, way, way back on the number of inter-island flights. Gone are the days when you could catch a flight every 30 to 40

Tips   Coping with Jet Lag

Jetlag is a pitfall of traveling across time zones. If you're flying north-south and you feel sluggish when you touch down, your symptoms will be caused by dehydration and the general stress of air travel. When you travel east to west, like going to Hawaii, however, your body becomes thoroughly confused about what time it is, and everything from your digestion to your brain gets knocked for a loop. Traveling east, say, from Maui to Los Angeles, is more difficult on your internal clock than traveling west, say from Atlanta to Hawaii, as most peoples' bodies find it more acceptable to stay up late than to fall asleep early. Here are some tips for combating jet lag:

- **Reset your watch** to your destination time before you board the plane.
- **Drink lots of water** before, during, and after your flight. Avoid alcohol.
- **Exercise and sleep well** for a few days before your trip.
- If you have trouble sleeping on planes, **fly eastward on morning flights.**
- **Daylight** is the key to resetting your body clock. At the website for **Outside In** (www.bodyclock.com), you can get a customized plan of when to seek and avoid light.
- If you need help getting to sleep earlier than you usually would, doctors recommend taking either the hormone melatonin or the sleeping pill Ambien—but not together. Take 2 to 5 milligrams of melatonin about 2 hours before your planned bedtime.

Tips **Flying with Film & Video**

Never pack film—developed or undeveloped—in checked bags, as the new, more powerful scanners in U.S. airports can fog film. The film you carry with you can be damaged by scanners as well. X-ray damage is cumulative; the slower the film, and the more times you put it through a scanner, the more likely the damage. Film under 800 ASA is usually safe for up to five scans. If you're taking your film through additional scans, U.S. regulations permit you to demand hand inspections.

Most photo supply stores sell protective pouches designed to block damaging X-rays. The pouches fit both film and loaded cameras. They should protect your film in checked baggage, but they also may raise alarms and result in a hand inspection.

An organization called **Film Safety for Traveling on Planes, FSTOP** (© **888/ 301-2665**; www.f-stop.org), can provide additional tips for traveling with film and equipment.

Carry-on scanners will not damage **videotape** in video cameras, but the magnetic fields emitted by the walk-through security gateways and handheld inspection wands will. Always place your loaded camcorder on the screening conveyor belt or have it hand-inspected. Be sure your batteries are charged; you will probably be required to turn the device on to ensure that it's what it appears to be.

---

minutes. The number of flights is fewer and you have to book in advance. The airlines warn you to show up at least 90 minutes before your flight and, believe me, with all the recent inspections (bag inspections, security inspections, and so on) you will need all 90 minutes to catch your flight. If you miss it, you are out of luck. For details on making inter-island connections at Honolulu International Airport, see section 1 of chapter 5.

Aloha Airlines (© **800/367-5250** or 808/484-1111; www.alohaairlines.com) is the state's largest provider of inter-island air transport service. It offers an all-jet fleet of Boeing 737 aircraft. Aloha's sibling company, **Island Air** (© **800/323-3345** or 808/484-2222), serves Hawaii's small inter-island airports on Maui, Molokai, and Lanai.

Hawaiian Airlines (© **800/367-5320** or 808/835-3700; www.hawaiianair.com), Hawaii's first inter-island airline has carried more than 100 million passengers to and around the state.

CAR RENTALS

Hawaii has some of the lowest car-rental rates in the country. (An exception is the island of Lanai, where they're very expensive.) The average non-discounted, unlimited-mileage rate for a 1-day rental for an intermediate-size car in Honolulu was $41 (plus $3 a day in state fees) in 2003; that's the lowest rate in the country, compared with the national average of $54 a day. To rent a car in Hawaii, you must be at least 25 years of age and have a valid driver's license and credit card.

Refer back to section 1 of this chapter, "55 Money-Saving Tips." Tips 14 through 20 offer great advice on getting the best car rental deal.

At Honolulu International Airport and most neighbor-island airports, you'll find most major rental-car agencies, including

Alamo (℃ 800/327-9633; www.goalamo. com), **Avis** (℃ 800/321-3712; www.avis. com), **Budget** (℃ 800/935-6878; www. budgetrentacar.com), **Dollar** (℃ 800/800-4000; www.dollarcar.com), **Enterprise** (℃ 800/325-8007; www.enterprise.com), **Hertz** (℃ 800/654-3011; www.hertz. com), **National** (℃ 800/227-7368; www. nationalcar.com), and **Thrifty** (℃ 800/367-2277; www.thrifty.com). It's almost always cheaper to rent a car at the airport than in Waikiki or through your hotel (unless there's one already included in your package deal).

Rental cars are usually at a premium on Kauai, Molokai, and Lanai and may be sold out on the neighbor islands on holiday weekends, so be sure to book well ahead.

INSURANCE Hawaii is a no-fault state, which means that if you don't have collision-damage insurance, you are required to pay for all damages before you

---

Tips **Traveling Inter-Island**

Jumping on an inter-island flight is not as quick and easy as it was before the September 11, 2001, terrorist attacks. Due to increased security, be sure to check in at least 90 minutes before an inter-island flight and 2 hours before a flight to the mainland.

Be prepared to stand in line. The first line you will stand in for inter-island travel is the ticket line. Once you make your way to the counter, be prepared to show a photo ID (driver's license is best), keep your ID out, as you will have to show it at several other check points.

After you have your ticket, you will then get in another line to have your luggage screened. *Do not lock your luggage.* Baggage screeners may have to open your luggage if they see anything out of the norm. We suggest that you go to a hardware store and get plastic tie locks (like mini-handcuffs). If the baggage screeners need to open your luggage, they will just cut the plastic and replace it with their own "certified" inspected plastic tie locks. This way when you pick up your bag it should either have your plastic ties or the "certified" ties from security. If your lock is missing and there is no "certified" lock replacing it—someone has gotten into your bag. Report it to the airline at once.

Once you and your luggage are checked in (only one carry-on is allowed past this point, this is *strictly* enforced), proceed to the security area to get you into the airport gates.

Here again you have to show your photo ID and your ticket. If you have a laptop, remove it from its carrying case to go through the x-ray scanning device.

You may be asked to remove your shoes and/or to have your carry-on luggage hand inspected.

At the gate area, you will once again go through another inspection (have photo ID and tickets ready) before you board the airplane. Random checks will pull some passengers out of the boarding line and you and your carry-on will be searched again.

These various lines and check points quickly take up the full 90 minutes.

A Cruise Through the Islands

If you're looking for a taste of several islands in a single week, consider taking a cruise with **Norwegian Cruise Line** (✆ **800/327-7030;** www.ncl.com) the only cruise line that operates year-round in the Hawaiian Islands.

Norwegian Cruise Line's 91,000-ton, 2,240-passenger ship, *Norwegian Star,* leaves every Sunday from Honolulu and makes stops on The Big Island, Maui, Kauai, and Fanning Island in the Republic of Kiribati, before returning to Honolulu the following Sunday. Prices start at $1,099 per person, based on double occupancy in a budget cabin, and go way up for the nicer staterooms and suites. Better deals are often available through travel agents

The disadvantage of a cruise is that you won't be able to see any of the islands in depth or at leisure; the advantage is that you can spend your days exploring the island where the ship is docked and your nights aboard ship sailing to the next port of call.

leave the state, whether or not the accident was your fault. Your personal car insurance may provide rental-car coverage; read your policy or call your insurer before you leave home. Bring your insurance identification card if you decline the optional insurance, which usually costs from $12 to $20 a day. Obtain the name of your company's local claim representative before you go. Some credit card companies also provide collision-damage insurance (but not liability coverage) for their customers; check with yours before you rely on this coverage.

DRIVING RULES   Hawaiian state law mandates that all car passengers must wear a **seat belt,** and all infants must be strapped into car seats. The fine is enforced with vigilance, so buckle up—you'll pay a $50 fine if you don't. **Pedestrians** always have the right of way, even if they're not in the crosswalk. You can turn **right on red** from the right lane after a full and complete stop, unless there's a sign forbidding you to do so.

ROAD MAPS   The best and most detailed maps for activities are published by **Franko's Maps** (www.frankosmaps.com); they feature a host of island maps, plus a terrific "Hawaiian Reef Creatures Guide" for snorkelers curious about those fish they spot under water. The island maps come either foldable ($6) or laminated ($10). Free road maps are published by *This Week Magazine,* a free visitor publication available on Oahu, the Big Island, Maui, and Kauai. For island maps, check out the University of Hawaii Press maps. Updated periodically, they include a detailed network of island roads, large-scale insets of towns, historical and contemporary points of interest, parks, beaches, and hiking trails. They cost about $3 each, or about $15 for a complete set. If you can't find them in a bookstore near you, contact **University of Hawaii Press,** 2840 Kolowalu St., Honolulu, HI 96822 (✆ **888/847-7737;** www.uhpress.hawaii.edu). For topographic and other maps of the islands, go to the **Hawaii Geographic Society,** 49 S. Hotel St., Honolulu, or contact P.O. Box 1698, Honolulu, HI 96806 (✆ **800/538-3950** or 808/538-3952).

14 Tips on Accommodations

Hawaii offers all kinds of accommodations, from simple rooms in restored plantation homes and quaint cottages on the beach to luxurious oceanview condo units and opulent suites in beachfront resorts. Each type has its pluses and minuses—so before you book, make sure you know what you're getting into.

TYPES OF ACCOMMODATIONS

HOTELS   In Hawaii, "hotel" can indicate a wide range of options, from few or no on-site amenities to enough extras to qualify as a miniresort. Generally, a hotel offers daily maid service and has a restaurant, on-site laundry facilities, a pool, and a sundries/convenience–type shop (rather than the shopping arcades that most resorts have these days). Top hotels also have activities desks, concierge and valet service, room service (though it may be limited), business centers, airport shuttles, bars and/or lounges, and perhaps a few more shops.

The advantages of staying in a hotel are privacy and convenience; the disadvantage is generally noise (either thin walls between rooms or loud music from a lobby lounge late into the night). Hotels are often a short walk from the beach rather than right on the beachfront (although there are exceptions).

RESORTS   In Hawaii, a resort offers everything a hotel does—and more. You can expect such extras as direct beach access, with beach cabanas and lounge chairs; pools (often more than one) and a Jacuzzi; a spa and fitness center; restaurants, bars, and lounges; a 24-hour front desk; concierge, valet, and bellhop services; room service (often around the clock); an activities desk; tennis and golf (some of the world's best courses are at Hawaii's resorts); ocean activities; a business center; children's programs; and more.

The advantages of a resort are that you have everything you could possibly want in the way of services and things to do; the disadvantage is that the price generally reflects this. Hawaii has dozens of incredibly expensive resorts that are way out of our price range. But we have found some places that offer resort amenities at a reasonable price; we've reviewed many in the chapters that follow.

And don't be misled by a name—just because a place is called "ABC Resort" doesn't mean it actually *is* a resort. Make sure you're getting what you pay for.

CONDOS   The roominess and convenience of a condo—which is usually a fully

---

Tips   **What If Your Dream Hotel Becomes a Nightmare?**

To avoid any unpleasant surprises, find out when you make your reservation exactly what the accommodation is offering you: cost, minimum stay, included amenities. Ask if there's any penalty for leaving early. Discuss with the property or booking agency what the cancellation policy is if the accommodation fails to meet your expectations—and get this policy in writing.

When you arrive, if you're not satisfied with your room, notify the front desk or booking agency immediately. Approach the management in a calm, reasonable manner, and suggest a solution (like moving to another unit). Be willing to compromise. Do not leave; if you do, you may not get your deposit back.

If all else fails, when you get home, write to any association the accommodation may be a member of (the Hawaii Visitors and Convention Bureau, a resort association, or an island association). Describe your complaint and why the issue was not resolved to your satisfaction. And be sure to let us know if you have a problem with a place we recommend in this book!

equipped, multiple-bedroom apartment—makes this a great choice for families. Condominium properties in Hawaii generally consist of several apartments set in either a single high-rise or a cluster of low-rise units. Condos usually have amenities such as some maid service (ranging from daily to weekly; it may or may not be included in your rate, so be sure to ask), a pool, laundry facilities (either in your unit or in a central location), and an on-site front desk or a live-in property manager. Condos vary in price according to size, location, and amenities. Many of them are on or near the beach, and they tend to be clustered in resort areas. While there are some very high-end condos, most are quite affordable, especially if you're traveling in a group that's large enough to require more than one bedroom.

The advantages of a condo are privacy, space, and conveniences—which usually include a full kitchen, a washer and dryer, a private phone, and more. The downsides are the standard lack of an on-site restaurant and the density of the units (versus the privacy of a single-unit vacation rental).

BED & BREAKFASTS   Hawaii has a wide range of places that call themselves B&Bs: everything from a traditional B&B—several bedrooms (which may or may not share a bathroom) in a home,

with breakfast served in the morning—to what is essentially a vacation rental on an owner's property that comes with fixings for you to make your own breakfast. Make sure that the B&B you're booking matches your own mental picture. Would you prefer conversation around a big dining-room table as you eat a hearty breakfast, or just a muffin and juice to enjoy in your own private place? Note that laundry facilities and private phones are not always available. We've reviewed lots of wonderful B&Bs in the island chapters that follow. If you have to share a bathroom, we've spelled it out in the listings; otherwise, you can assume that you will have your own.

The advantages of a traditional B&B are its individual style and congenial atmosphere. Bed-and-breakfasts are great places to meet other visitors to Hawaii, and the host is generally happy to act as your own private concierge, giving you tips on where to go and what to do. In addition, they're usually an affordable way to go (though fancier ones can run $150 or more). The disadvantages are lack of privacy, usually a set time for breakfast, few amenities, generally no maid service, and the fact that you'll have to share the quarters beyond your bedroom with others. Also, B&B owners usually require a minimum stay of 2 or 3 nights, and it's often a drive to the beach.

Tips   B&B Etiquette

In Hawaii, it's customary to remove your shoes before entering anyone's home. The same is true for most bed-and-breakfasts. Most hosts post signs or will politely ask you to remove your shoes before entering the B&B. Not only does this keep the B&B clean, but you'll be amazed how relaxed you feel walking around barefoot. If this custom is unpleasant to you, a B&B may not be for you. Consider a condo or hotel, where no one will be particular about your shoes.

Hotels, resorts, condos, and vacation rentals generally allow smoking in guest rooms (most also have nonsmoking rooms available), but most B&Bs forbid smoking in the rooms. If this matters to you, be sure to check the policy of your accommodation before you book.

VACATION RENTALS This is another great choice for families and for long-term stays. "Vacation rental" usually means that there will be no one on the property where you're staying. The actual accommodation can range from an apartment in a condominium building to a two-room cottage on the beach to an entire fully equipped house. Generally, vacation rentals allow you to settle in and make yourself at home for a while. They have kitchen facilities (which can be either a complete kitchen or just a kitchenette with microwave, refrigerator, burners, and coffeemaker), on-site laundry facilities, and phone; some also come outfitted with such extras as a TV, VCR, and stereo.

The advantages of a vacation rental are complete privacy, your own kitchen (which can save you money on meals), and lots of conveniences. The disadvantages are a lack of an on-site property manager and generally no maid service; often, a minimum stay is required (sometimes as much as a week). If you book a vacation rental, be sure that you have a 24-hour contact to call if the toilet won't flush or you can't figure out how to turn on the air-conditioning.

BARGAINING ON PRICES

Rates can sometimes be bargained down, but it depends on the place. In general, each type of accommodation allows a different amount of latitude in bargaining on their rack (published) rates.

The best bargaining can be had at **hotels** and **resorts.** Both regularly pay travel agents a commission of as much as 30%; if business is slow, some places may give you the benefit of at least part of this commission if you book directly instead of going through an agent. Most hotels and resorts also have *kamaaina* (local) rates for islanders, which they may extend to visitors during slow periods. It never hurts to ask about discounted or local rates; a host of special rates are available for the military, seniors, members of the travel industry, families, corporate travelers, and long-term stays. Also ask about **package deals,** which might include a car rental or free breakfast for the same price as a room by itself. Hotels and resorts offer packages for everyone: golfers, tennis players, families, honeymooners, and more (see "Money-Saving Package Deals" on p. 54). We've found that it's worth the extra few cents to make a local call to the hotel. Sometimes the local reservations person knows about package deals that the toll-free operators are unaware of, and vice-versa, so it's best to try both numbers and compare what you're quoted. If all else fails, try to get the hotel or resort to upgrade you to a better room for the same price as a budget room, or waive the parking fee or extra fees for children. Persistence and polite inquiries can pay off.

It's harder to bargain at **bed-and-breakfasts.** You may be able to negotiate down the minimum stay, or get a discount if you're staying a week or longer. But generally, a B&B owner has only a few rooms and has already priced the property at a competitive rate; expect to pay what's asked.

You have somewhat more leeway to negotiate at **vacation rentals** and **condos.** In addition to asking for a discount on a multinight stay, also ask if they can throw in a rental car to sweeten the deal; believe it or not, they often will.

USING A BOOKING AGENCY VERSUS DOING IT YOURSELF

If you don't have the time to call several places yourself to bargain for prices and to make sure they offer the amenities you'd like, you might consider a booking agency. The time an agency spends on your behalf may be well worth any fees you'll have to pay.

The top reservations service in the state is **Hawaii's Best Bed & Breakfasts** ★ (© **800/262-9912** or 808/985-7488; fax 808/967-8610; www.bestbnb.com). This service charges $15 to book the first two locations and $5 for each additional location. Barbara and Susan Campbell personally select the traditional homestays, cottages, and inns, based on each one's hospitality, distinctive charm, and attention to detail. They also book vacation rentals, hotels, and resorts.

Another great statewide booking agent is **Bed-and-Breakfast Hawaii** (© 800/733-1632 or 808/822-7771; fax 808/822-

2723; www.bandb-hawaii.com), offering a range of accommodations from vacation homes to B&Bs, starting at $75 a night.

For vacation rentals, contact **Hawaii Beachfront Vacation Homes** (© 808/247-3637 or 808/235-2644). **Hawaii Condo Exchange** (© 800/442-0404; http://hawaiicondoexchange.com) acts as a consolidator for condo and vacation-rental properties.

15 Recommended Reading

In addition to the books discussed below, those planning an extended trip to other islands in Hawaii should check out *Frommer's Hawaii 2006, Frommer's Maui 2006,* and *Frommer's Honolulu, Waikiki and Oahu.*

FICTION

The first book people think about is James A. Michener's *Hawaii* (Fawcett Crest, 1974). This epic novel is a fictionalization of Hawaii's history. It manages to put the island's history into chronological order, but remember, it is still fiction, and very sanitized fiction too. For a more contemporary look at life in Hawaii today, one of the best novels is *Shark Dialogue* by Kiana Davenport (Plume, 1995). The novel tells the story of Pono, the larger-than-life matriarch, and her four daughters of mixed races. Davenport skillfully weaves legends and myths of Hawaii into the "real life" reality that Pono and her family face in the complex Hawaii of today. Lois-Ann Yamanaka, a recent emerging writer from Hawaii, uses a very "local" voice and stark depictions of life in the islands in her fabulous novels *Wild Meat and the Bully Burgers* (Farrar, Straus, Giroux, 1996), *Blu's Hanging* (Avon, 1997), and *Heads by Harry* (Avon, 1999).

NONFICTION

Mark Twain's writing on Hawaii in the 1860s offers a wonderful introduction to Hawaii's history. One of his best books is

Mark Twain in Hawaii: Roughing It in the Sandwich Islands (Mutual Publishing, 1990). Another great depiction of the Hawaii of 1889 is *Travels in Hawaii* (University of Hawaii Press, 1973) by Robert Louis Stevenson. For contemporary voices on Hawaii's unique culture, one of the best books to get is *Voices of Wisdom: Hawaiian Elders Speak* by M. J. Harden (Aka Press, 1999). Some 24 different *kahuna* (experts) in their fields were interviewed about their talent, skill, or artistic practice. These living treasures talk about how Hawaiians of yesteryear viewed nature, spirituality and healing, preservation and history, dance and music, Arts and Crafts, canoes, and the next generation.

Recently re-released *Native Planters in Old Hawaii: Their Life, Lore and Environment* (Bishop Museum Press, 2004), was originally published in 1972, but still is one of the most important ethnographic works on traditional Hawaiian culture, portraying the lives of the common folk and their relationship with the land before the arrival of Westerners. This revised edition, with one of the best indices which allows you to find anything, is an excellent resource for any one interested in Hawaii.

FLORA & FAUNA

Because Hawaii is so lush with nature and blessed with plants, animals, and reef fish seen nowhere else on the planet, a few reference books can help you identify what you're looking at and make your trip more interesting. In the botanical world, Angela Kay Kepler's *Hawaiian Heritage Plants* (University of Hawaii Press, 1998) is the standard for plant reference. In a series of essays, Kepler weaves culture, history, geography, botany, and even spirituality into her vivid descriptions of plants. You'll never look at plants the same way. There are great color photos and drawings to help you sort thorough the myriad species. Another great plant book is *Tropicals* (Timber Press, 1988) by Gordon Courtright, which is filled with color photos identifying everything from hibiscus and heliconia to trees and palms. As Courtright puts it, "This book is intended to be a visual plant dictionary."

The other necessary reference guide to have in Hawaii is a book identifying the colorful reef fish you will see while snorkeling. The best reference book is John E. Randall's *Shore Fishes of Hawaii* (University of Hawaii Press, 1998). Randall is the expert on everything that swims underwater, and his book is one of the best. Two other books on reef fish identification, with easy-to-use spiral bindings, are *Hawaiian Reef Fish—The Identification Book* (Blue Kirio Publishing, 1993) by Casey Mahaney and *Hawaiian Reef Fish* (Island Heritage, 1998) by Astrid Witte and Casey Mahaney.

For birders, or those who just wonder about Hawaii's unique birds, H. Douglas Pratt's *A Pocket Guide to Hawaii's Birds* (Mutual Publishing, 1996) gives you everything you need to identify Hawaii's birds.

For fans of the Hawaiian lei, *Na Lei Makamae: The Treasured Lei*, (University of Hawaii Press, 2003) by Marie McDonald and Paul Weissich is a comprehensive work on this incredible art form. McDonald is one of Hawaii's top lei makers and Weissich is the direct emeritus of Honolulu Botanical Gardens, and together, they cover some 88 flowers and plants used for leis.

HISTORY

There are many great books on Hawaii's history, but one of the best places to start is with the formation of the Hawaiian islands, vividly described in David E. Eyre's *By Wind, By Wave: An Introduction to Hawaii's Natural History* (Bess Press, 2000). In addition to chronicling the natural history of Hawaii, Eyre also describes the complex and necessary interrelationships among the plants, animals, ocean, and people. Eyre points out that Hawaii has become the "extinction capital of the world," but rather than dwelling on that fact, he urges readers to do something about it and carefully spells out how.

For history of "pre-contact" Hawaii (before Westerners arrived), David Malo's *Hawaiian Antiquities* (Bishop Museum Press, 1976) is the preeminent source. Malo was born around 1793, and wrote about the Hawaiian lifestyle at that time, as well as the beliefs and religion of his people. It's an excellent reference book, but not a fast read. For more readable books on old Hawaii, try *Stories of Old Hawaii* (Bess Press, 1997) by Roy Kakulu Alameide on myths and legends; *Hawaiian Folk Tales* (Mutual Publishing, 1998) by Thomas G. Thrum; and *The Legends and Myths of Hawaii* (Charles E. Tuttle Company, 1992) by His Hawaiian Majesty King David Kalakaua.

The best book on the overthrow of the Hawaiian monarchy in 1898 is told by the woman who experienced it, Queen Liliuokalani, in her book *Hawaii's Story by Hawaii's Queen Liliuokalani* (Mutual Publishing, 1990). When it was written at the turn of the 20th century it was an international plea for justice for her people, but it is a poignant read even today. It's also a "must-read" for people interested in current events and the recent rally in the 50th state for sovereignty. Two contemporary books on the question of Hawaii's sovereignty are Tom Coffman's *Nation Within—The Story of America's Annexation of the Nation of Hawaii* (Epicenter, 1998) and *Hawaiian Sovereignty: Do the Facts Matter?* (Goodale, 2000) by Thurston Twigg-Smith, which explores the opposite view. Twigg-Smith, former publisher of the statewide newspaper *The Honolulu Advertiser*, is the grandson of Lorrin A. Thurston, one of the architects of the 1893 overthrow of the monarchy. His so-called "politically incorrect" views present a different look on this hotly debated topic.

For more recent history, Lawrence H. Fuchs' *Hawaii Pono* (Bess Press, 1991) is a carefully researched tome on the contributions made by each of Hawaii's main immigrant communities (Chinese, Japanese, and Filipino) between 1893 and 1959.

FAST FACTS: The Hawaiian Islands

AAA Hawaii's only American Automobile Association (AAA) office is at 1130 N Nimitz, Suite A-170, in Honolulu (℡ 808/593-2221). Some car-rental agencies now provide auto club–type services, so you should inquire about their availability when you rent your car.

American Express For 24-hour traveler's-check refunds and purchase information, call ℡ 800/221-7282. For local offices, see the "Fast Facts" sections in the individual island chapters.

Area Code All the Hawaiian Islands are in the **808** area code. Note that if you're calling one island from another, you'll have to dial 1-808 first.

Business Hours Most offices are open Monday through Friday from 8am to 5pm. Bank hours are Monday through Thursday from 8:30am to 3pm and Friday from 8:30am to 6pm; some banks are open on Saturday as well. Shopping centers are open Monday through Friday from 10am to 9pm, Saturday 10am to 5:30pm, and Sunday from noon to 5 or 6pm.

Emergencies Dial ℡ **911** for police, fire, or ambulance.

Liquor Laws The legal drinking age in Hawaii is 21. Bars are allowed to stay open daily until 2am; places with cabaret licenses are able to keep the booze flowing until 4am. Grocery and convenience stores are allowed to sell beer, wine, and liquor 7 days a week.

Smoking It's against the law to smoke in public buildings, including airports, grocery stores, retail shops, movie theaters, banks, and all government buildings and facilities. There is no smoking in restaurants and, depending on the island, smoking may or may not be permitted in stand-alone bars. Most bed-and-breakfasts prohibit smoking indoors.

Taxes Hawaii's sales tax is 4%. The hotel-occupancy tax is 7.25%, and hoteliers are allowed by the state to tack on an additional 0.1666% excise tax. Thus, expect taxes of about 11.42% to be added to your hotel bill.

Time Zone There's no daylight savings time here. During Standard Time on the mainland, Hawaii is 2 hours behind Pacific Standard Time and 5 hours behind Eastern Standard Time. In other words, in winter when it's noon in Hawaii, it's 2pm in California and 5pm in New York. However, when daylight savings time goes in effect on the mainland, Hawaii is 3 hours behind the West Coast and 6 hours behind the East Coast. In summer, when it's noon in Hawaii, it's 3pm in California and 6pm in New York.

Hawaii is east of the international date line, putting it on the same day as the U.S. mainland and Canada, and a day behind Australia, New Zealand, and Asia.

3

For International Visitors

The pervasiveness of American culture around the world may make the United States feel like familiar territory to foreign visitors, but leaving your own country for the States—especially the unique island state of Hawaii—still requires some additional planning.

1 Preparing for Your Trip

ENTRY REQUIREMENTS

Check at any U.S. embassy or consulate for current information and requirements. You can also obtain a visa application and other information online at the **U.S. State Department**'s website, at **www. travel.state.gov**. Click on "Visas for Foreign Citizens" for the latest entry requirements, while "Foreign Consular Offices" and "Links to Foreign Embassies" will provide you with contact information for U.S. embassies and consulates worldwide.

VISAS The U.S. State Department has a **Visa Waiver Program** allowing citizens of certain countries to enter the United States without a visa for stays of up to 90 days. At press time, these included Andorra, Australia, Austria, Belgium, Brunei, Denmark, Finland, France, Germany, Iceland, Ireland, Italy, Japan, Liechtenstein, Luxembourg, Monaco, the Netherlands, New Zealand, Norway, Portugal, San Marino, Singapore, Slovenia, Spain, Sweden, Switzerland, and the United Kingdom. Citizens of these countries need only a valid passport and a round-trip air or cruise ticket in their possession upon arrival. If they first enter the United States, they may also visit Mexico, Canada, Bermuda, and/or the Caribbean islands and return to the United States without a visa. Further

information is available from any U.S. embassy or consulate. Canadian citizens may enter the United States without visas; they need only proof of residence.

Citizens of all other countries must have (1) a valid passport that expires at least 6 months later than the scheduled end of their visit to the United States, and (2) a tourist visa, which may be obtained without charge from any U.S. consulate.

To obtain a visa, the traveler must submit a completed application form (either in person or by mail) with a 1½-inch-square photo, and must demonstrate binding ties to a residence abroad. Usually you can obtain a visa at once or within 24 hours, but it may take longer during the summer rush from June through August. If you cannot go in person, contact the nearest U.S. embassy or consulate for directions on applying by mail. Your travel agent or airline office may also be able to provide you with visa applications and instructions. The U.S. consulate or embassy that issues your visa will determine whether you will be issued a multiple- or single-entry visa and any restrictions regarding the length of your stay.

British subjects can obtain up-to-date visa information by calling the **U.S. Embassy Visa Information Line** (© **0891/200-290**) or by visiting the

"Consular Services" section of the American Embassy London's website at www.usembassy.org.uk.

Irish citizens can find visa information through the **Embassy of the USA Dublin,** 42 Elgin Rd., Dublin 4, Ireland (© **353/1-668-8777**), or by checking the "Consular Services" section of the website at http://dublin.usembassy.gov.

Information **for Australian** citizens is available by contacting the **U.S. Embassy Canberra,** Moonah Place, Yarralumla, ACT 2600 (© **02/6214-5600**), or by checking the U.S. Diplomatic Mission's website at http://usembassy-australia.state.gov/consular.

Citizens of **New Zealand** can contact the **U.S. Embassy New Zealand,** 29 Fitzherbert Terrace, Thorndon, Wellington (© **644/472-2068**), or get the information directly from the "For New Zealanders" section of the website at http://usembassy.org.nz.

MEDICAL REQUIREMENTS   Unless you're arriving from an area known to be suffering from an epidemic (particularly cholera or yellow fever), inoculations or vaccinations are not required for entry into the United States. If you have a medical condition that requires **syringe-administered medications,** carry a valid signed prescription from your physician—the Federal Aviation Administration (FAA) no longer allows airline passengers to pack syringes in their carry-on baggage without documented proof of medical need. If you have a disease that requires treatment with **narcotics,** you should also carry documented proof with you—smuggling narcotics aboard a plane is a serious offense that carries severe penalties in the U.S.

For **HIV-positive visitors,** requirements for entering the United States are somewhat vague and change frequently. According to the latest publication of *HIV and Immigrants: A Manual for AIDS Service Providers,* the Immigration and Naturalization Service (INS) doesn't require a medical exam for entry into the United States, but INS officials may stop individuals because they look sick or because they are carrying AIDS/HIV medicine.

DRIVER'S LICENSES   Most foreign driver's licenses are recognized in the U.S., although you may want to get an international driver's license if your home license is not written in English.

PASSPORT INFORMATION

Safeguard your passport in an inconspicuous, secure place like a money belt. Copy critical pages, including the passport number, and store it in a safe place, separate from the passport itself. If you lose your passport, visit the nearest consulate of your native country as soon as possible for a replacement.

Note: The International Civil Aviation Organization has recommended a policy requiring that *every* individual who travels by air have a passport. In response, many countries are now requiring that children be issued their own passports to travel internationally; previously, those under 16 may have been allowed to travel on a parent or guardian's passport.

CUSTOMS
WHAT YOU CAN BRING IN

Every visitor over 21 years of age may bring in, free of duty, the following: (1) 1 liter of wine or hard liquor; (2) 200 cigarettes, 100 cigars (but not from Cuba), or 3 pounds of smoking tobacco; and (3) $100 worth of gifts. These exemptions are offered to travelers who spend at least 72 hours in the United States and who have not claimed them within the preceding 6 months. It is altogether forbidden to bring into the country foodstuffs (particularly fruit, cooked meats, and canned goods) and plants (vegetables, seeds, tropical plants, and the like). Foreign tourists may bring in or take out up to $10,000 in U.S. or foreign currency with no formalities; larger sums must be declared to U.S. Customs on entering or leaving, which includes filing form CM 4790. For more specific information regarding U.S. Customs, contact your nearest U.S. embassy or consulate, or the **U.S. Customs** office (© **202/927-1770** or www.customs.ustreas.gov).

WHAT YOU CAN TAKE HOME

Rules governing what you can bring back duty-free vary from country to country and are subject to change. Generally, checking postings on the web can give you the most up-to-date information. **U.K. citizens returning from a non-EU country** should contact HM Customs & Excise at © **0845/010-9000** (from outside the U.K., 020/8929-0152), or consult their website at www.hmce.gov.uk. For a clear summary of **Canadian** rules, request the booklet *I Declare,* issued by the **Canada Customs and Revenue Agency** (© **800/461-9999** in Canada, or 204/983-3500; www.ccra-adrc.gc.ca). A helpful brochure available from **Australian** consulates or Customs offices is *Know Before You Go.* For more information, call the **Australian Customs Service** at © **1300/363-263,** or log on to www.customs.gov.au. For those returning to **New Zealand,** most questions are answered in a free pamphlet available at New Zealand consulates and Customs offices: *New Zealand Customs Guide for Travellers, Notice No. 4.* For more information, contact **New Zealand Customs,** The Customhouse, 17–21 Whitmore St., Box 2218, Wellington (© **0800/428-786** or 04/473-6099; www.customs.govt.nz).

HEALTH INSURANCE

Although it's not required of travelers, health insurance is highly recommended. Unlike many European countries, the United States does not usually offer free or low-cost medical care to its citizens or visitors. Doctors and hospitals are expensive, and in most cases will require advance payment or proof of coverage before they render their services. See "Insurance" in chapter 2 for more information.

Packages such as **Europ Assistance's "Worldwide Healthcare Plan"** are sold by European automobile clubs and travel agencies at attractive rates. **Worldwide Assistance Services Inc.** (© **800/821-2828;** www.worldwideassistance.com) is the agent for Europ Assistance in the United States.

Though lack of health insurance may prevent you from being admitted to a hospital in nonemergencies, don't worry about being left on a street corner to die: The American way is to fix you now and bill the living daylights out of you later.

MONEY

CURRENCY   The U.S. monetary system is very simple. The most common **bills** are the $1 (colloquially, a "buck"), $5, $10, and $20 denominations. There are also $2 bills (seldom encountered), $50 bills, and $100 bills (the last two are usually not welcome as payment for small purchases). All the paper money was recently redesigned, making the famous faces adorning them disproportionately large. The old-style bills are still legal tender.

There are seven denominations of **coins**: 1¢ (1 cent, or a penny); 5¢ (5 cents, or a nickel); 10¢ (10 cents, or a dime); 25¢ (25 cents, or a quarter); 50¢ (50 cents, or a half dollar); the new gold "Sacagawea" coin worth $1; and, prized by collectors, the rare, older silver-dollar coin.

The "foreign-exchange bureaus" so common in Europe are rare even at airports in the United States, and nonexistent outside major cities. It's best not to change foreign money (or traveler's checks denominated in a currency other than U.S. dollars) at a small-town bank, or even a branch in a big city; in fact, leave any currency other than U.S. dollars at home—it may prove a greater nuisance to you than it's worth.

EXCHANGING CURRENCY Exchanging foreign currency for U.S. dollars is usually best done in Oahu. Generally, the best rates of exchange are available through major banks, most of which exchange foreign currency. In Waikiki go to **Pacific Money Exchange,** 339 Royal Hawaiian Ave. (© **808/924-9318**). There also are currency services at **Honolulu International Airport.** Most of the major hotels offer currency-exchange services, but generally the rate of exchange is not as good as what you'll get at a bank.

On the other islands, it's not so easy. None of the other airports have currency-exchange facilities. You'll need to either go to a bank (call first to see if currency exchange is available) or use your hotel.

TRAVELER'S CHECKS Though traveler's checks are widely accepted at most hotels, restaurants, and large stores, *make sure that they're denominated in U.S. dollars,* as foreign-currency checks are often difficult to exchange. The three traveler's checks that are most widely recognized—and least likely to be denied—are **Visa, American Express,** and **Thomas Cook/MasterCard.** Be sure to record the numbers of the checks, and keep that information separate from the checks in case they get lost or stolen. Most businesses are pretty good about taking traveler's checks, but you're better off cashing them in at a bank (in small amounts, of course) and paying in cash. *Remember:* You'll need identification, such as a driver's license or passport, to change a traveler's check. It's generally easier to use ATMs than to bother with traveler's checks.

CREDIT CARDS & ATMS Credit cards are widely used in Hawaii. You can save yourself trouble by using plastic rather than cash or traveler's checks.

It is strongly recommended that you bring at least one major credit card, the most popular being MasterCard and Visa. You will also see American Express, Diners Card, and Discover. You must have a credit or charge card to rent a car. Hotels and airlines usually require a credit-card imprint as a deposit against expenses, and in an emergency, a credit card can be priceless.

You'll find **automated teller machines (ATMs)** on just about every block—at least in almost every town. Some ATMs will allow you to draw U.S. currency against your bank and credit cards. Check with your bank before leaving home, and remember that you will need your personal identification number (PIN) to do so. Expect to be charged up to $3 per transaction, however, if you're not using your own bank's ATM.

SAFETY

GENERAL SAFETY Although tourist areas are generally safe, visitors should always stay alert, even in laid-back Hawaii (and especially in Waikiki). If you're in doubt about which neighborhoods are safe, it's wise to ask the island tourist office.

DRIVING SAFETY Safety while driving is particularly important. Ask your rental agency about personal safety, or request a brochure of traveler safety tips when you pick up your car. Get written directions or a map with the route marked in red showing you how to get to your destination.

For more information on driving rules and getting around by car in Hawaii, see "Getting There & Getting Around," in chapter 2.

2 Getting to & Around the United States

Airlines serving Hawaii from places other than the U.S. mainland include **Air Canada** (© 800/776-3000; www.air canada.ca); **Air New Zealand** (© 0800/737-000 in Auckland, 643/379-5200 in Christchurch, 800/926-7255 in the U.S.; www.airnewzealand.com), which runs 40 flights per week between Auckland and Hawaii; **Qantas** (© 008/177-767 in Australia, 800/227-4500 in the U.S.; www.qantas.com.au), which flies between Sydney and Honolulu daily (plus additional flights 4 days a week); **Japan Air Lines** (© 03/5489-1111 in Tokyo, 800/525-3663 in the U.S.; www.japanair.com); **All Nippon Airways (ANA)** (© 03/5489-1212 in Tokyo, 800/235-9262 in the U.S.; www.fly-ana.com); **China Airlines** (© 02/715-1212 in Taipei, 800/227-5118 in the U.S.; www.china-airlines.com); **Air Pacific,** serving Fiji, Australia, New Zealand, and the South Pacific (© 800/227-4446; www.airpacific.com); **Korean Air** (© 02/656-2000 in Seoul, 800/223-1155 on the East Coast, 800/421-8200 on the West Coast, 800/438-5000 from Hawaii; www.koreanair.com); and **Philippine Airlines** (© 631/816-6691 in Manila, 800/435-9725 in the U.S.; www.philippineair.com).

If you're traveling in the United States beyond Hawaii, some large U.S. airlines—such as **American, Delta, Northwest, TWA,** and **United**—offer travelers on transatlantic or transpacific flights special discount tickets under the name **Visit USA,** allowing travel between any U.S. destinations at reduced rates. These tickets must be purchased before you leave your foreign point of departure. This system is the best, easiest, and fastest way to see the United States at low cost; but be sure to obtain information well in advance as conditions attached to discount tickets can change without notice.

Visitors arriving by air should stock up on patience. Getting through immigration may take as long as 2 hours, especially summer weekends. Allow generous allowance for this delay when planning connections between international and domestic flights—2 to 3 hours at least.

For further information about travel to Hawaii, see "Getting There & Getting Around" in chapter 2.

FAST FACTS: For International Travelers

Automobile Organizations Auto clubs supply maps, suggested routes, guide-books, accident/bail-bond insurance, and emergency road service. The major auto club in the United States is the **American Automobile Association (AAA; often called "Triple A").** Foreign auto club members have reciprocal arrangements with AAA and enjoy its services at no charge. Check with your auto club before you leave. AAA can also provide you with an **International Driving Permit** validating your foreign license. To inquire about joining AAA, call © **800/736-2886** or visit www.aaa.com.

Oahu's local AAA office is in the Nimitz Center, 1130 Nimitz Hwy., Honolulu (© **808/593-2221**). Some car-rental agencies provide automobile club–type services, so ask when you rent your car.

Automobile Rentals To rent a car in the United States, you need a valid driver's license, a passport, and a major credit card. The minimum age is usually 25, but some companies will rent to younger people and add a surcharge. It's a good idea to buy maximum insurance coverage unless you're positive your own auto or credit card insurance is sufficient. Rates vary, so it pays to call around.

Business Hours See "Fast Facts: The Hawaiian Islands" in chapter 2.

Climate See "When to Go" in chapter 2.

Drinking Laws See "Fast Facts: Liquor Laws" in chapter 2.

Electricity Hawaii, like the U.S. mainland and Canada, uses 110–120 volts (60 cycles), compared to the 220–240 volts (50 cycles) used in most of Europe and in other areas of the world, including Australia and New Zealand. Small appliances of non-American manufacture, such as hair dryers or shavers, will require a plug adapter with two flat, parallel pins; larger ones will require a 100-volt transformer.

Embassies & Consulates All embassies are in Washington, D.C. Some countries have consulates generally in major U.S. cities, and most have a mission to the United Nations in New York City. If your country isn't listed below, call directory information in Washington, D.C. (© **202/555-1212**), or log onto **www. embassy.org/embassies**.

The embassy of **Australia** is at 1601 Massachusetts Ave. NW, Washington, DC 20008 (© **202/797-3000**; www.austemb.org). There is also an Australian consulate in Hawaii at 1000 Bishop St., Penthouse Suite, Honolulu, HI 96813 (© 808/524-5050).

The embassy of **Canada** is at 501 Pennsylvania Ave. NW, Washington, DC 20001 (© **202/682-1740**; www.canadianembassy.org). Canadian consulates are also at 1251 Ave. of the Americas, New York, NY 10020 (© 212/596-1628), and at 550 S. Hope St., 9th Floor, Los Angeles, CA 90071 (© 213/346-2700).

The embassy of **Japan** is at 2520 Massachusetts Ave. NW, Washington, DC 20008 (© **202/238-6700**; www.embjapan.org). The consulate general of Japan is located at 1742 Nuuanu Ave., Honolulu, HI 96817 (© 808/543-3111).

The embassy of **New Zealand** is at 37 Observatory Circle NW, Washington, DC 20008 (© **202/328-4800**; www.nzemb.org). The only New Zealand consulate in the United States is at 780 Third Ave., New York, NY 10017 (© 202/328-4800).

The embassy of the **Republic of Ireland** is at 2234 Massachusetts Ave. NW, Washington, DC 20008 (© **202/462-3939**; www.irelandemb.org). There's a consulate office in San Francisco at 44 Montgomery St., Suite 3830, San Francisco, CA 94104 (© 415/392-4214).

The embassy of the **United Kingdom** is at 3100 Massachusetts Ave. NW, Washington, DC 20008 (© **202/588-6640**; www.fco.gov.uk/directory). British consulates are at 845 Third Ave., New York, NY 10022 (© 212/745-0200), and 11766 Wilshire Blvd., Suite 400, Los Angeles, CA 90025 (© 310/477-3322).

Emergencies Call © **911** to report a fire, contact the police, or get an ambulance.

Gasoline (Petrol) One U.S. gallon equals 3.8 liters, while 1.2 U.S. gallons equal 1 Imperial gallon. You'll notice there are several grades (and price levels) of gasoline available at most gas stations (the names of which change from one company to the next). The gasoline grades with the highest octane are the most expensive, but most rental cars take the least expensive "regular" gas, with an octane rating of 87.

Holidays See "When to Go" in chapter 2.

Legal Aid The ordinary tourist will probably never become involved with the American legal system. If you're pulled over for a minor traffic infraction (for example, driving faster than the speed limit), never attempt to pay the fine directly to a police officer; you may wind up arrested on the much more serious charge of attempted bribery. Pay fines by mail or directly into the hands of the clerk of the court. If accused of a more serious offense, it's wise to say and do nothing before consulting a lawyer (under the U.S. Constitution, you have the rights both to remain silent and to consult an attorney). Under U.S. law, an arrested person is allowed one telephone call to a party of his or her choice; call your embassy or consulate.

Mail Mailboxes, which are generally found at intersections, are blue with a blue-and-white eagle logo and carry the inscription U.S. POSTAL SERVICE. If your mail is addressed to a U.S. destination, don't forget to add the five-figure postal code, or zip code, after the two-letter abbreviation of the state to which the mail is addressed. The abbreviation for Hawaii is HI.

At press time, domestic postage rates were 23¢ for a postcard and 37¢ for a letter. For international mail, a first-class letter of up to 1 ounce costs 80¢ (60¢ to Canada and Mexico); a first-class postcard costs 70¢ (50¢ to Canada and Mexico); and a preprinted postal aerogramme costs 70¢. Point your Web browser to **www.usps.com** for complete U.S. postal information, or call ℂ **800/275-8777** for information on the nearest post office.

Taxes The United States has no VAT (value-added tax) or other indirect taxes at a national level. Every state, and every city in it, has the right to levy its own local tax on all purchases, including hotel and restaurant checks, airline tickets, and so on. In Hawaii, sales tax is 4%; there's also a 7.25% hotel-room tax and a small excise tax, so the total tax on your hotel bill will be 11.42%.

Telephone & Fax The telephone system in the United States is run by private corporations, so rates, particularly for long-distance service and operator-assisted calls, can vary widely. Local calls—that is, calls to other locations on the island you're on—made from public phones in Hawaii cost 50¢.

Generally, hotel surcharges on long-distance and local calls are astronomical. You are usually better off using a **public pay telephone.**

Most **long-distance** and **international calls** can be dialed directly from any phone. **For calls within the United States and to Canada,** dial 1 followed by the area code and the seven-digit number. **For other international calls,** dial 011 followed by the country code, city code, and the telephone number of the person you are calling.

If you're calling the **United States from another country,** the country code is 01.

In Hawaii, inter-island phone calls are considered long-distance and are often as costly as calling the U.S. mainland. The international country code for Hawaii is 1, just as it is for the rest of the United States and Canada.

For **reversed-charge** or **collect calls,** and for **person-to-person calls,** dial 0 (zero, not the letter "O"), followed by the area code and number you want; an operator will then come on the line, and you should specify that you are calling collect, person-to-person, or both. If your operator-assisted call is international, ask for the overseas operator.

Note that all phone numbers with the area code 800, 888, 866, and 877 are toll-free. However, calls to numbers in area codes 700 and 900 (chat lines, "dating" services, and so on) can be very expensive—usually a charge of 95¢ to $3 or more per minute.

For **local directory assistance** ("information"), dial ✆ 411. For **long-distance information,** dial 1, then the appropriate area code and 555-1212; for **directory assistance for another island,** dial 1, then 808, then 555-1212.

Fax facilities are widely available and can be found in most hotels and many other establishments. Try **The UPS Store, FedEx Kinko's** (check the local Yellow Pages), or any photocopying shop.

Telephone Directories There are two kinds of telephone directories in the United States. The general directory, the so-called White Pages, lists private and business subscribers in alphabetical order. The second directory, printed on yellow paper (hence its name, Yellow Pages), lists all local services, businesses, and industries by type of activity, with an index at the front.

Time Zone See "Fast Facts: Time Zone" in chapter 2.

Tipping It's part of the American way of life to tip. Many service employees receive little direct salary and must depend on tips for their income. The following are some general rules:

In **hotels,** tip bellhops at least $1 per piece of luggage ($2–$3 if you have a lot of luggage), and tip the housekeeping staff $1 per person, per day. Tip the doorman or concierge only if he or she has provided you with some specific service (for example, calling a cab for you or obtaining difficult-to-get theater tickets). Tip the valet-parking attendant $1 to $2 every time you get your car.

In **restaurants, bars,** and **nightclubs,** tip service staff 15% to 20% of the check, tip bartenders 10% to 15%, and tip valet-parking attendants $1 to $2 per vehicle. Tip the doorman only if he or she has provided you with some specific service (such as calling a cab for you). Tipping is not expected in cafeterias and fast-food restaurants.

Tip **cab drivers** 15% of the fare.

As for **other service personnel,** tip skycaps at airports at least $1 per piece ($2–$3 if you have a lot of luggage), and tip hairdressers and barbers 15% to 20%. Tipping ushers at theaters is not expected.

Toilets Foreign visitors often complain that public toilets are hard to find. True, there are none on the streets, but visitors can usually find one in a bar, fast-food outlet, restaurant, hotel, museum, or department store—and it will probably be clean. (The cleanliness of toilets at service stations, parks, and beaches is more open to question.)

4

Suggested Hawaii Itineraries

Yes, Virginia: It *is* possible to have a fabulous vacation in Hawaii and not have to take out a second mortgage. The most common question I get from reader is "What should I do in Hawaii?" The purpose of this chapter is to give you my expert advice on the best things to see and do on each island, and how to do them on a budget.

First, here's the best advice I can give you: Do not plan to see more than one island per week. With the exception of the ferry between Maui and Lanai, getting from one island to another is an all-day affair once you figure in packing, checking out of and into hotels, driving to and from the airport, and dealing with rental cars, not to mention time actually spent at the airport and on the flight. Don't waste a day of your vacation seeing our inter-island air terminals.

Second, don't max out your days. This is Hawaii—allow some time to do nothing but relax. Remember that you will most likely arrive jet-lagged. Ease into your vacation. In fact, exposure to sunlight can help reset your internal clock, so I include time at the beach on day one of these itineraries.

Finally, keep in mind that the following itineraries are designed to appeal to a wide range of people. If you're a golf enthusiast or a scuba diver, check out chapter 1, "The Best of Hawaii from $80 a Day," to plan your trip around your passion.

One last thing: You will need a car to get around the islands. Oahu has an adequate public transportation service, but it is set up for Hawaii residents, not tourists carrying coolers and beach toys (all carryons must fit under the bus seat). So plan to rent a car. But also plan to get out of the car as much as possible. Hawaii is not a place to "view" from your car window. You have to get out to smell the sweet perfume of plumerias, to hear the sound of the wind through a bamboo forest, and to plunge into the gentle waters of the Pacific.

1 A Week on Oahu

The island of Oahu is so stunning that the *alii* (the kings of Hawaii) made it the capital of the island nation. I've presumed that you are staying in Waikiki; if you are in another location, be sure to factor in the time for traveling.

Day ❶: Arrival & Waikiki Beach ★★★
After you get off the plane, lather up in sunscreen, grab your sunglasses and a hat, and plop down on the most famous beach in the world—Waikiki Beach (p. 153). If you have kids in tow, or an hour in

Hawaii's intense sun is all you can handle, you might consider checking out Hawaii's water world by dropping by the **Waikiki Aquarium** (p. 189), or learning about Hawaii's unique culture at the **Bishop Museum Kalia** (p. 183), or taking

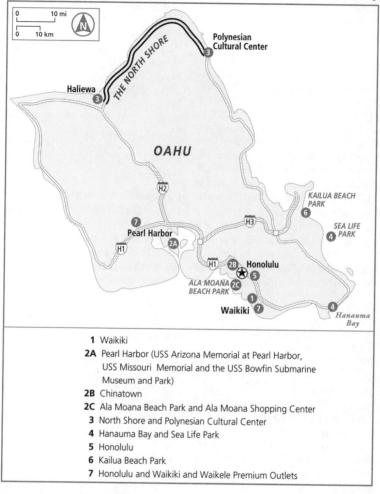

1 Waikiki
2A Pearl Harbor (USS Arizona Memorial at Pearl Harbor,
   USS Missouri Memorial and the USS Bowfin Submarine
   Museum and Park)
2B Chinatown
2C Ala Moana Beach Park and Ala Moana Shopping Center
3 North Shore and Polynesian Cultural Center
4 Hanauma Bay and Sea Life Park
5 Honolulu
6 Kailua Beach Park
7 Honolulu and Waikiki and Waikele Premium Outlets

the family to the **Honolulu Zoo** (p. 187).
For insight into Waikiki's past, take the
Waikiki Historic Trail (p. 179), a 2-mile
trail marked with bronzed surfboards. Be
sure to catch the sunset (anywhere on
Waikiki Beach will do) and get an early
dinner.

Day ❷: Pearl Harbor ⭐⭐⭐ **&**
Honolulu's Chinatown ⭐⭐⭐
Head to the **USS *Arizona* Memorial at
Pearl Harbor** (p. 184). Get there as early

as possible—by the afternoon the lines
are 2 hours long. While you are there,
stop by the **USS *Missouri* Memorial**
(p. 185) and the **USS *Bowfin* Submarine
Museum and Park** (p. 185). On your
way back, stop in **Chinatown** for lunch
and take a self-guided tour (p. 191). In
the afternoon, consider taking a nap,
heading for the beach at **Ala Moana
Beach Park** (p. 153), or shopping across
the street at the **Ala Moana Shopping**

Center (p. 216). Plan a dinner in Honolulu or surrounding area.

Day ❸: North Shore ★★★ & the Polynesian Cultural Center ★

Start your day with a drive to the **North Shore** (p. 101). If you are up early enough, stop for breakfast in the quaint town of **Haleiwa.** If not, at least stop and get a picnic lunch before beach hopping your way down the coast of the North Shore, home to some of the world's most beautiful beaches: **Waimea Bay, Sunset Beach, Bonzai,** and **Pipeline** (p. 160). Any time after 12:30pm, head for the **Polynesian Cultural Center** in Laie (p. 201). Allow at least 2 hours to tour this mini-glimpse of the Pacific. Continue driving down the coast road to the small town of **Kailua;** in fact, stay here for dinner to avoid the traffic over the Pali back to Waikiki.

Day ❹: Snorkeling in Hanauma Bay ★★ & Watching Marine Life at Sea Life Park ★

If it's not Tuesday (when the park is closed), head out in the morning for the spectacular snorkeling at **Hanauma Bay** (p. 156). After a couple of hours, wander down the coast to **Sea Life Park** (p. 189). If you have kids, this is a must-stop. Otherwise, you can continue beach-hopping down the coastline with stops at **Sandy Beach, Makapuu Point and Makapuu Beach Park,** and **Waimanalo Beach,** before turning back to take the Pali Highway (be sure to stop at the **Pali Lookout;** p. 190) back to Waikiki.

Day ❺: Rainforest Hike ★★, Historic Honolulu & Hawaiian Culture

For a beach-free day, try a short hike into the rainforest, just a 15-minute drive from downtown Honolulu. Good hiking or trail shoes are a must for the **Manoa Falls Trail** hike (p. 168) as is mosquito repellant. Next, head for downtown and take in the sites of historic Honolulu, including the **Iolani Palace** (p. 183), **Kawaiahao Church** (p. 184), **Mission Houses Museum** (p. 184), and the **Hawaii Maritime Center** (p. 183). For a view of where you've been, go to the top of the **Aloha Tower,** at the Aloha Tower Marketplace, for a bird's eye view of Honolulu. Stop for lunch either at the Marketplace or one of the nearby restaurants. Spend the afternoon at the **Bishop Museum** (p. 179) to immerse yourself in Hawaiian culture.

Day ❻: Kailua Beach ★★★

On your last full day on Oahu, travel over the Pali Highway to the Windward side of the island and spend a day at **Kailua Beach.** Pick up a picnic lunch at **Good to Go** (p. 150). This is the perfect beach to just relax or snorkel, or try something different like kayaking or windsurfing. You can spend the entire day here, or you can take an afternoon hike at the **Hoomaluhia Gardens** (p. 170).

Day ❼: Final Day: Adventure, Art, or Shopping

Depending on your available time and energy, you could spend your last day in Hawaii a number of ways, including just hanging out in Waikiki and perhaps taking a surfing lesson, riding a surfing canoe, or venturing underwater in Atlantis Submarine (p. 165). For the energetic, get up early and climb Diamond Head (p. 167). Art lovers should check out the Honolulu Academy of Art (p. 188), the Contemporary Museum (p. 188), and the Hawaii State Art Museum (p. 188). On your way back to the airport, be sure to stop on Maunakea Street in Chinatown and buy a lei from one of the numerous lei makers along the street (p. 174) to take back as a sweet smelling memory of your trip.

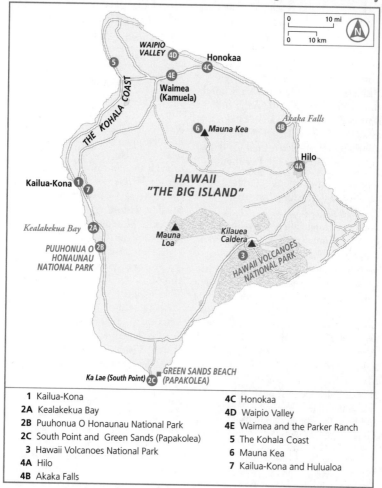

2 A Week on the Big Island of Hawaii

A week is barely enough time to see the entire Big Island of Hawaii; 2 weeks would be better. But if your schedule doesn't allow more time, this itinerary will steer you to the highlights of this huge island (twice the size of all the other islands combined). This schedule is set up for people staying either in Kailua-Kona or on the Kohala Coast. I suggest you spend at least 2 nights in Volcano Village to really enjoy one of the stars of the Big Island, the Hawaii Volcanoes National Park.

Day ❶: Arrival & Beach Time

After you settle into your hotel, head for the beach. Snorkelers should go to **Kahaluu Beach Park** (p. 282), surfers to **White Sands Beach** (p. 282), privacy buffs to **Kekaha Kai (Kona Coast) State**

Park (p. 282), and beach aficionados can choose from **Anaehoomalu Bay, Hapuna Beach,** or **Kaunaoa Beach (Mauna Kea Beach)** (p. 283). When the sun starts to wane, head for old **Kailua-Kona** town and wander through the **Hulihee Palace, Mokuaikaua Church,** and **Kamehameha's Compound at Kamakahonu Bay** (p. 304). Find a spot to watch the sunset (either on the pier or along the seawall), then head for dinner in either **Kailua-Kona** or **Keauhou.**

Day ❷: Water Time & a Drive to Hawaii Volcanoes National Park ⭑⭑⭑

Book a morning sailing/snorkeling sail on the **Fair Winds** (p. 290) to **Kealakekua Bay,** now a marine life preserve but once the site of the death of Captain James Cook. Spend the afternoon floating in a rainbowed sea of fish and sailing on the catamaran. In the afternoon, drive south. Great stops include **Puuhonua O Honaunau National Park** (p. 305), **South Point** (p. 308), and **Green Sands (Papakolea) Beach** (p. 288). Then head up **Mauna Kea Mountain** (p. 312) to the **Hawaii Volcanoes National Park** (p. 321) and stay at one of the many quaint bed-and-breakfasts in the tiny village of **Volcano** (p. 339).

Day ❸: Exploring an Active Volcano ⭑⭑⭑

The highlight of your trip most likely will be the time you spend in the incredible **Hawaii Volcanoes National Park** (p. 321). I recommend spending the morning exploring the park and taking hikes. Your first stop should be the Kilauea Visitors Center. Then explore **Halemaumau Crater, Thurston Lava Tube, Devastation Trail,** among other sites in the crater. Find out from the rangers how to get to the current lava flow and walk out as far as the rangers will allow. Eat a nice dinner in Volcano and then return to the flow after dark, armed with flashlight,

water bottle, and jacket. This is a full and tiring day, so I recommend spending another night in Volcano.

Day ❹: Touring Old Hawaii: Hilo Town ⭑⭑⭑, Akaka Falls ⭑⭑⭑, Valley of the Kings ⭑⭑⭑ & Cowboy Country

It's just a 45-minute drive from Volcano to **Hilo** (p. 236), so plan to arrive early in the morning, grab a cup of coffee at **Bears' Coffee** (p. 269), and wander through the old town, being sure to see **Banyan Drive** (p. 318), **Liliuokalani Gardens** (p. 318), **Lyman Museum & Mission House** (p. 318), **the Pacific Tsunami Museum** (p. 320), and **Nani Mau Gardens** (p. 320). Head up the Hamakua Coast, stopping at **Akaka Falls** (p. 316) and planning a lunch stop in **Honokaa.** After lunch, be sure to see **Waipio Valley** (p. 317), the birthplace of Hawaii's kings, before heading for **Waimea** (p. 333). Spend some time in this cowboy town and at the **Parker Ranch Visitor Center and Museum** (p. 312). Stay the night along the Kona Coast.

Day ❺: The Kohala Coast: Stepping Back in Time ⭑⭑⭑

Time travelers should plan to get an early start. First stop is just south of Kawaihae, at the **Puukohola Heiau National Historic Site** (p. 308), the temple Kamehameha built to the war god to insure his success in battle. Allow at least an hour to view the temple and wander through the visitor center. Keep driving up Highway 270 to the **Lapakahi State Historical Park** (p. 309) for a view of a typical 14th-century Hawaiian village. Plan a lunch stop in Hawi or Kapaau at either **Bamboo** (see p. 272) or **Kohala Rainbow Café** (p. 272) and stop by the **Original King Kamehameha Statue** (p. 310) in Kapaau. The final stop on your journey is at the end of the road and the **Pololu Valley Lookout** (p. 311). On your way back, in the late afternoon (the best time for viewing), be sure to stop at the **Puako Petroglyph Archaeological District** (p. 309). If it is Friday, make reservations at the **Kona Village Luau** (p. 341) for one of the best luaus in the state.

Day ❻: Mauna Kea: Where the gods Live ★★★

Sleep in, have a lazy morning at the beach, and in the afternoon, plan to explore Hawaii's tallest mountain (and dormant volcano), **Mauna Kea** (p. 312). You will need a four-wheel-drive vehicle

to climb to the top of the 13,796-foot Mauna Kea, so I recommend that you book with the experts, **Mauna Kea Summit Adventures** (p. 314), for a 7-to-8-hour sojourn up this mountain.

Day ❼: Beach or Shopping Day

Depending on how much time you have on your final day, you can choose from relaxing on the beach, or shopping for souvenirs and bargains. Shoppers can wander through the shops from Kailua-Kona to the tiny village of Hulualoa (p. 327).

3 A Week on Maui

I've outlined the highlights of Maui for those who just have 7 days and want to see everything. Two things I suggest: plan to spend 2 nights in Hana, a decision you will not regret, and take the Trilogy boat trip to Lanai for the day—expensive, but well worth the splurge. I've designed this itinerary on staying in West Maui for 5 days. If you are staying elsewhere (like Wailea or Kihei), allow extra driving time.

Day ❶: Arrival & Kapalua Beach ★★

Settle into your hotel, then head for **Kapalua Beach** (p. 402). Don't overdue the sun on your first day. After an hour or two at the beach, drive to **Lahaina** (p. 348) and spend a couple of hours walking the historic old town. To really feel like you are in Hawaii, go to the **Old Lahaina Luau** (p. 387) at sunset to immerse yourself into the Hawaiian culture.

Day ❷: Up a 10,000-Foot Dormant Volcano & Down Again ★★★

You'll likely wake up early on your first day in Hawaii, so take advantage of it and head up to the 10,000-foot (dormant) volcano, **Haleakala.** Plan either to **hike in the crater** (p. 420), **speed down the mountain on a bicycle** (p. 425), or just wander about the **Haleakala National Park.** You don't have to be at the top for sunrise, but I have to tell you—it is an experience you'll never forget. On your way back down, stop and tour **Upcountry Maui** (p. 350). In fact,

plan to have an early sunset dinner in **Paia** or **Kuau.**

Day ❸: Hana Highway: World's Most Scenic Tropical Road ★★★

Pack a lunch and spend the entire day driving the **Hana Highway** (p. 351). Pull over often, get out to take photos, smell the flowers, jump in the mountain stream pools. Wave to everyone, move off the road for those speeding by, breath in Hawaii. Plan to spend at least 2 nights in Hana.

Day ❹: A Day in Heavenly Hana ★★★

An entire day in paradise, so many things to do. Take an early morning hike along the black sands of **Waianapanapa State Park** (p. 408), then explore the tiny town of **Hana** (p. 437), making sure to see the **Hana Museum Cultural Center, Hasagawa General Store,** and **Hotel Hana-Maui Gallery.** Grab a picnic lunch and drive out to the Kipihulu end of the

Maui Itinerary

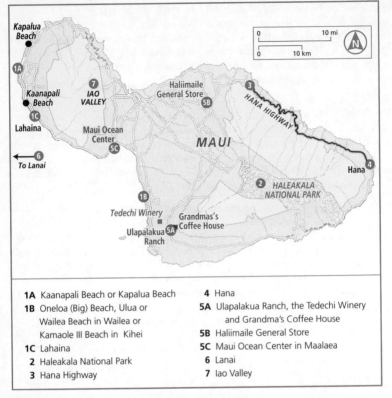

1A Kaanapali Beach or Kapalua Beach	**4** Hana
1B Oneloa (Big) Beach, Ulua or Wailea Beach in Wailea or Kamaole III Beach in Kihei	**5A** Ulapalakua Ranch, the Tedechi Winery and Grandma's Coffee House
1C Lahaina	**5B** Haliimaile General Store
2 Haleakala National Park	**5C** Maui Ocean Center in Maalaea
3 Hana Highway	**6** Lanai
	7 Iao Valley

Haleakala National Park at **Oheo Gulch** (p. 442). Hike to the waterfalls, swim in the pools, take lots of photos. Splurge on dinner and eat at the dining room at the **Hotel Hana Maui.** Spend another night in Hana.

Day ⑤: Wine, Food & (Hawaiian) Song

Continue driving around the island, past **Kaupo,** and up to the **Ulupalakua Ranch** (p. 443) and the **Tedeschi Winery** (p. 436). Stop at **Grandma's Coffee House** (p. 398) for a cup of java and head down the mountain, with a stop for lunch at **Haliimaile General Store** (p. 397). Spend the afternoon at the **Maui Ocean Center** (p. 432) checking out the marine life, especially the sharks.

Day ⑥: Sailing to Lanai ★★★

Trilogy (p. 410) is the best sailing/snorkeling trip in Hawaii, so don't miss it. You'll spend the day (breakfast and lunch included) sailing to the island of Lanai, snorkeling, touring the island, and sailing back to Lahaina. Plus you still have the afternoon to go shopping for souvenirs or take a nap.

Day ⑦: Relaxing & Shopping

Depending on how much time you have on your final day, you can choose from relaxing on the beach or shopping for souvenirs and bargains. Shopping aficionados should check out my favorites (p. 443). If you have a late flight, you might want to check out Iao Valley (p. 429).

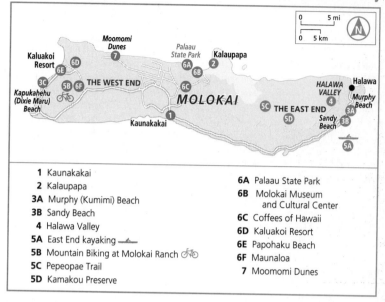

1 Kaunakakai
2 Kalaupapa
3A Murphy (Kumimi) Beach
3B Sandy Beach
4 Halawa Valley
5A East End kayaking
5B Mountain Biking at Molokai Ranch
5C Pepeopae Trail
5D Kamakou Preserve

6A Palaau State Park
6B Molokai Museum
   and Cultural Center
6C Coffees of Hawaii
6D Kaluakoi Resort
6E Papohaku Beach
6F Maunaloa
7 Moomomi Dunes

4 A Week on Molokai

The island of Molokai is for people trying to get away from everything or those looking for adventure. There are no direct flights from the mainland to Molokai, so you will have to fly into Honolulu and then take a commuter plane to Molokai.

Day ❶: Arrival & Kaunakakai

If you are staying in a condo or a vacation rental, head into **Kaunakakai** and stock up on groceries and supplies. While you're there, wander around the old two-street town and check out all the stores. Be sure to stop at the **Kapuaiwa Coconut Grove in Kiowea Park** (p. 481) and watch the sunset.

Day ❷: Riding a Mule to Kalaupapa ★★★

Your internal clock will still be set to mainland time, so you will have no problem getting up early and getting out to the **Molokai Mule Ride** (p. 484). If you're in terrific shape, consider hiking down the 26 switchbacks and the 1,600-foot cliff,

and then joining up with the tour of the **Kalaupapa Peninsula,** where sufferers of leprosy have lived for decades. Don't forget, you'll have to hike back up the 1,600-foot cliffs too.

Day ❸: Heading for the Beach

Molokai not only has terrific beaches, but on weekdays they generally are empty! Depending on the time of year and the weather, great beaches for snorkeling are **Murphy (Kumimi) Beach** and **Sandy Beach** (p. 473) on the East End and **Kapukahehu (Dixie Maru) Beach** (p. 477) on the West End. Pack a picnic lunch or stop by the **Outpost Natural Foods** or the **Sundown Deli** in Kaunakakai (p. 471). Stay all day. Relax.

Day ❹: Hiking in a Tropical Valley & Venture into Paradise ⚝

After a day at the beach, you'll be ready for a hike into the tropical jungle of **Halawa Valley.** Book with the **Lodge at Molokai Ranch** (p. 479) before you head out, as you cannot venture into the valley without trespassing. Bring a picnic lunch for after the hike, and then either spend the day on the beach at Halawa or beach hop your way along the East End coastline. Stop to see the **fish ponds** (p. 487) before you leave the East End.

Day ❺: Outdoor Adventure

Spend a day kayaking, bicycling, or hiking on this Hawaiian oasis. **Molokai Outdoors Activities** (p. 476) can set you up with whatever equipment you need. I recommend kayaking along the shallow water of the East End. Mountain bikers should know the best off-road bicycle trails in the state are on **Molokai Ranch property** (p. 460), and hikers should check out **Pepeopae Trail** (p. 478) or the **Kamakou Preserve** (p. 486).

Day ❻: Touring the West End ⚝⚝

Since you've already seen the East End, spend a day touring the rest of the island. Start out with a tour of the central part of the island by driving out to **Palaau State Park** (p. 483), overlooking the Kalaupapa Peninsula. Then stop off at the **Molokai Museum and Cultural Center** (p. 482) and stop by for a coffee break at **Coffees of Hawaii** (p. 482). Next, head for the 3-mile-long, white-sand **Papohaku Beach.** After an hour or so at the beach, drive up to the cool air in **Maunaloa** town to see the best store on the island: the **Big Wind Kite Factory & the Plantation Gallery** (p. 491).

Day ❼: Moomomi Dunes: Archaeology Heaven

Before you catch your plane back, stop by the Moomomi Dunes. This wild, sand-covered coast is a treasure trove for archaeologists. Buried in the mounds are ancient Hawaiian burial sites, fossils, Hawaiian artifacts, and even the bones of prehistoric birds. If you have enough time, take the 20-mile easy walk west to Kawaaloa Bay, the perfect place to say aloha to Molokai.

5 A Week on Lanai

The smallest of all the Hawaiian island, Lanai was once a big pineapple plantation and now is home to two exclusive resorts, hundreds of years of history, and just one small town with some of the friendliest people you will ever meet. Like the island of Molokai, there are no direct flights from the mainland to Lanai. You will have to fly into Honolulu and then take a commuter plane to Lanai.

Day ❶: Arrival & Hulopoe Bay ⚝⚝

After you settle into your hotel, head for the beach. The best beach on the island is the marine preserve at **Hulopoe Bay.** It is generally safe for swimming, and because it's a marine preserve, no one can take the fish, which means snorkeling is terrific and the fish so friendly that you have to shoo them away. On the way back, stop at the **Luahiwa Petroglyph Fields** (p. 506).

Day ❷: Touring the Island in a Four-Wheel-Drive Vehicle

Lanai is a fantastic place to go four-wheeling. Generally you will not need a car if you are staying at the Hotel Lanai (they provide shuttle bus service). So splurge and rent a four-wheel-drive vehicle. Get a picnic lunch from **Pele's Other Garden** (p. 499) and head out of Lanai City to the **Kanepuu Preserve** (p. 507), a 590-acre dry-land forest. Next stop is

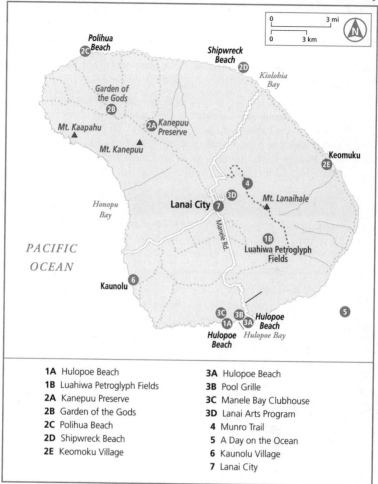

1A Hulopoe Beach
1B Luahiwa Petroglyph Fields
2A Kanepuu Preserve
2B Garden of the Gods
2C Polihua Beach
2D Shipwreck Beach
2E Keomoku Village

3A Hulopoe Beach
3B Pool Grille
3C Manele Bay Clubhouse
3D Lanai Arts Program
4 Munro Trail
5 A Day on the Ocean
6 Kaunolu Village
7 Lanai City

Garden of the Gods (p. 505) and a picnic lunch at **Polihua Beach** (p. 502), Lanai's largest white-sand beach. The beach generally is not safe for swimming and it can be windy here, but it most likely will be deserted and you'll have a great view of Molokai in the distance. After lunch, reverse directions and head for another beach, **Shipwreck Beach** (p. 501), and then on to **Keomoku Village** (p. 507).

Day ❸: A Day at the Beach

Plan a lazy day at Hulopoe Beach. Get a good book or watch the kids play in the surf, or take a long slow walk around the crescent-shaped bay. Take a picnic lunch, plan a nap for the afternoon, or try your hand at art at the **Lanai Arts Program** (p. 509).

Day ❹: Hiking (or Driving) the Munro Trail

If it has not been raining and the ground is dry, do a little exploring. The adventurous will spend the day (all day, plan on at least 7 hours) climbing to the top of Lanai at Lanaihale on the **Munro Trail** (p. 504). The not-so-adventurous will take a four-wheel-drive vehicle. Consider a soak in the hot tub upon your return.

Day ❺: A Trip to Maui ★★
Catch an early ferry (**Expeditions Lahaina/ Lanai Ferry;** p. 494) to Lahaina on Maui. Spend the day exploring the old whaling town, have a leisurely lunch, and then, at sunset, take the ferry back to Lanai.

Day ❻: A Day Back in Time
Pack a lunch, grab the sunscreen, and spend the day at a slower pace by taking a four-wheel-drive vehicle tour to the historic ruins of the old **Kaunolu Village** (p. 507).

Day ❼: Lanai's Great Shopping
Lanai City has some terrific, unique boutique shops. Don't miss visiting Dis 'N Dat, Gifts of Aloha, Local Gentry, and Mike Carroll Gallery (p. 508).

6 A Week on Kauai

Hawaii's oldest island, ringed with white-sand beaches, is small and easy to circumnavigate in a week. But there are so many wonderful things to do and see that you may find yourself wishing you had more time.

Day ❶: Arrival & Beach Time
Settle into your hotel and head for the beach. If you are staying on the south side, **Poipu Beach** (p. 553) is your best bet; on the east, in the Coconut Coast area, go to **Lydgate State Beach** (p. 554); and if you are on the North Shore try **Anini, Hanalei, Haena,** or **Ke'e Beaches** (p. 555, p. 556 and p. 558).

Day ❷: Touring the North Shore ★★
It rains often on the Garden Isle of Kauai, so the first sunny day, head out for the **North Shore** (p. 515). Drive all the way to the end of the road to Ke'e Beach. Plan to hike on the famous **Na Pali Coast trail** (p. 565). A half-hour on the trail will give you an idea of the spectacular coastline. The hearty may want to hike to the **Hanakapiai Beach,** a 2-hour trip one-way. Be sure to take a look at Ke'e Beach's **Ka Ulu O Laka Heiau** (p. 584). Head into **Hanalei** (p. 516) for lunch; then drive down to **Hanalei Bay** (p. 516) for a quiet afternoon on the beach, or book at tour with **Na Aina Kai Botanical Gardens** (p. 585) to see one of Kauai's most beautiful (and whimsical) gardens. Plan

to have dinner along **Kauai's North Shore** (p. 550).

Day ❸: Touring Kauai by Helicopter ★★★
Book a **helicopter tour** (p. 575), but not until 10 or 11am at the earliest to avoid the bumper to bumper commuter traffic. After your tour, head to the **Coconut Coast** for lunch (p. 546). In the afternoon, travel back in Hawaiian history at the **Wailua River State Park** (p. 580); hike up **Sleeping Giant Mountain** (p. 582); tour the **Hindu Temple** (p. 581); or take a boat ride up to the **Fern Grotto** (p. 580).

Day ❹: Hiking Kokee & Waimea Canyon ★★★
Get an early start and drive up to the 4,640-acre **Kokee State Park** (p. 566), where you will find a range of hiking trails to fit any ability. Birders, hikers, and sightseers will love wandering around this park. You can get lunch at the **Kokee Lodge Restaurant** (p. 567). Be sure to stop by the **Kokee Natural History Museum** (p. 579), which is full of great information as well as trail maps. In the

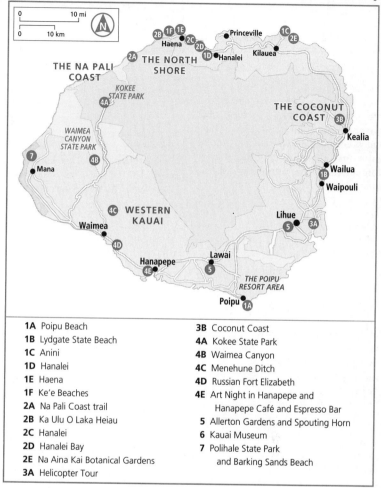

1A	Poipu Beach	**3B**	Coconut Coast
1B	Lydgate State Beach	**4A**	Kokee State Park
1C	Anini	**4B**	Waimea Canyon
1D	Hanalei	**4C**	Menehune Ditch
1E	Haena	**4D**	Russian Fort Elizabeth
1F	Ke'e Beaches	**4E**	Art Night in Hanapepe and
2A	Na Pali Coast trail		Hanapepe Café and Espresso Bar
2B	Ka Ulu O Laka Heiau	**5**	Allerton Gardens and Spouting Horn
2C	Hanalei	**6**	Kauai Museum
2D	Hanalei Bay	**7**	Polihale State Park
2E	Na Aina Kai Botanical Gardens		and Barking Sands Beach
3A	Helicopter Tour		

afternoon, stop at the "Grand Canyon of the Pacific," **Waimea Canyon** (p. 578), with more great hiking. On your way out of Waimea town, ditch the hiking boots and check out the **Menehune Ditch** (p. 578) and the **Russian Fort Elizabeth** (p. 578). *Tip:* A great time to plan this trip to Kokee and Waimea is on a Friday. Since you are already on the west side, you can attend Friday nights' **Art Night in Hanapepe** (p. 593), and the terrific

Hanapepe Café and Espresso Bar (p. 593) will be open for dinner.

Day ⑤: Beach Day

Kauai has the best beaches in Hawaii, so you should devote at least 1 day to beaching it. Check out our **beach recommendations**, starting on p. 552. If sunning on the sand isn't your style, book a kayak or snorkel tour (especially a tour of the **Na Pali Coast;** p. 516). If you've had enough sun, take a tour at the **Allerton Gardens**

(p. 578). On your way back from the Gardens, stop and marvel at the very unusual geological **Spouting Horn** (p. 577).

Day ⑥: Rainy Day

It's best to plan for at least one rainy day on Kauai. You may luck out and not get any rain, but our rainy day suggestions are just as much fun to do when it's not rainy. Great rainy day activities include exploring the treasure-filled **Kauai Museum** (p. 576) or **shopping** at Kauai's unique markets (p. 586).

Day ⑦: Embarking to Barking Sands Beach

Before heading back home, go as far west as you can to **Polihale State Park** (p. 554). This mini-Sahara on the west end of the island is Hawaii's biggest beach—7 miles long and as wide as three football fields. This is a wonderful place to get away from it all, but don't forget your flip-flops because the midday sand is hotter than a lava flow. The state park includes ancient Hawaiian *heiau* (temple) and burial sites, a view of the "forbidden" island of Niihau, and the famed **Barking Sands Beach.**

Oahu: The Gathering Place

A wise Hawaiian *kahuna* once said that the islands are like children—each is special yet different, and each is to be loved for its individual qualities. One thing's for sure: You'll never find another island like Oahu, the commercial and population center of Hawaii.

Honolulu offers a fast-paced urban setting, with Hawaii's hottest nightlife, its best shopping, and a huge array of restaurants. Yet at the same time, the North Shore and the Windward side of the island present a different face: miles of white-sand beaches and a slower, country way of life. If just the thought of rush-hour traffic, freeways, high-rise towers, and having to pay for parking makes your back molars hurt, then either head for the North Shore or take the next plane out to a quieter neighbor island.

It's astounding to spend hours flying across the barren blue of the Pacific and then suddenly see below the whites and pastels of Honolulu, the most remote big city on earth, a 26-mile-long metropolis of some 903,000 souls living in the middle of nowhere. Once on its streets, you'll find bright city lights, excellent restaurants, nightclubs, world-class shopping, a vibrant arts scene, and grand old hotels.

Nine out of ten visitors to Hawaii—some five million a year—stop on Oahu, and most of them end up along the canyon-like streets of Waikiki, Honolulu's well-known hotel district and its most densely populated neighborhood. Some days, it seems like the entire world is sunning itself on Waikiki's famous beach. Beyond Waikiki, Honolulu is clean and easy to enjoy. The city is coming of age for the 21st century: The old port town has built a brand-new convention center and is reshaping its waterfront, altering its skyline, opening new world-class hotels, and all the while trying to preserve its historic roots and revive its Polynesian heritage.

Out in the country, Oahu can be as down-home as a slack-key guitar. This is where you'll find a big blue sky, perfect waves, empty beaches, rainbows and waterfalls, sweet tropical flowers, and fiery Pacific sunsets. In fact, nowhere else within 60 minutes of a major American city can you snorkel in a crystal-clear lagoon, climb an old volcano, surf monster waves, kayak to a desert isle, picnic on a sandbar, soar in a glider over tide pools, skin dive over a sunken airplane, bicycle through a rainforest, golf a championship course, or sail into the setting sun.

And weather-wise, no other Hawaiian island has it as fine as Oahu. The Big Island is hotter, Kauai is wetter, Maui has more wind, Molokai and Lanai are drier. But Oahu enjoys a kind of perpetual late spring, with light trade winds and 82°F (28°C) days almost year-round. In fact, the climate is supposed to be the best on the planet. Once you have that, the rest is easy.

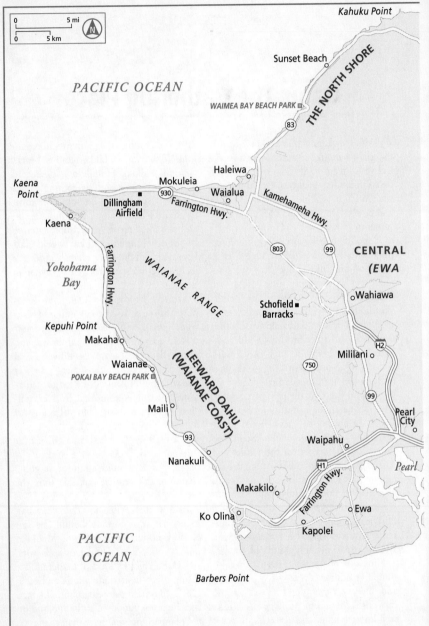

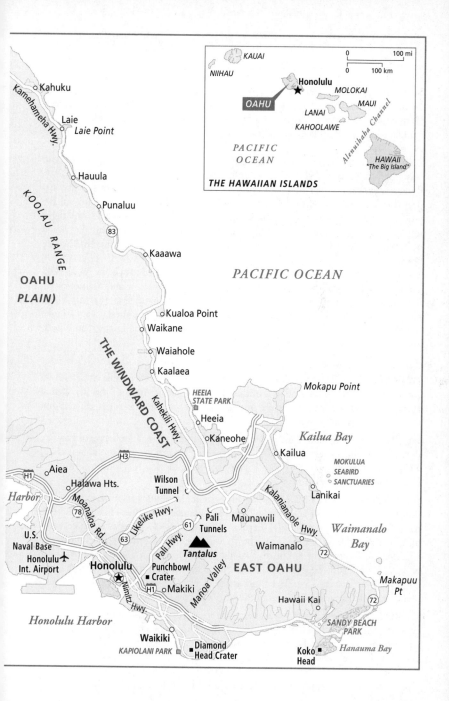

KAUAI

NIIHAU

Honolulu

OAHU

MOLOKAI

MAUI

LANAI

KAHOOLAWE

Alenuihaha Channel

PACIFIC
OCEAN

HAWAII
"The Big Island"

THE HAWAIIAN ISLANDS

0   100 mi
0   100 km

Kahuku

Kamehameha Hwy.

Laie
Laie Point

Hauula

KOOLAU RANGE

Punaluu

83

Kaaawa

OAHU
PLAIN)

PACIFIC OCEAN

Kualoa Point

Waikane

Waiahole

Kaalaea

THE WINDWARD COAST

Kahekili Hwy.

HEEIA
STATE PARK

Heeia

Mokapu Point

Kaneohe

Kailua Bay

Kailua

MOKULUA
SEABIRD
SANCTUARIES

H3

Aiea

H1

Halawa Hts.

Moanalua Rd.

78

Harbor

Wilson
Tunnel

Likelike Hwy.

63

Lanikai

Pali
Tunnels

61

Maunawili

Kalanianaole Hwy.

Waimanalo
Bay

U.S.
Naval Base

Honolulu
Int. Airport

Pali Hwy.

Tantalus

Waimanalo

72

Honolulu

Punchbowl
Crater

Makiki

H1

Nimitz Hwy.

Manoa Valley

EAST OAHU

Makapuu
Pt

Hawaii Kai

72

Honolulu Harbor

SANDY BEACH
PARK

Waikiki

KAPIOLANI PARK

Diamond
Head Crater

Koko
Head

Hanauma Bay

1 Orientation

ARRIVING

Honolulu is your gateway to the Hawaiian Islands; chances are, no matter which islands you're visiting, you'll come to Oahu first. Honolulu International Airport sits on the south shore of Oahu, west of downtown Honolulu and Waikiki, near Pearl Harbor. All major U.S. and many international carriers fly to Honolulu from the mainland; see "Getting There & Getting Around" in chapter 2 for a list of carriers and their toll-free numbers.

While the airport is large and constantly expanding, the layout is quite simple and easy to grasp. It ought to be, with the number of people arriving every day from far-flung places around the globe. You can walk or take the **Wiki-Wiki Bus,** a free airport shuttle, from your arrival gate to the main terminal and baggage claim, on the ground level. After collecting your bags—unless you're getting on an inter-island flight immediately—exit to the palm-lined street, where uniformed attendants flag down taxis, Waikiki shuttles, and rental car vans; they can also direct you to TheBus (see below).

Passengers connecting to neighboring island flights will need to take the Wiki-Wiki shuttle, or walk along the connecting corridor to the large inter-island terminal serving Aloha and Hawaiian Airlines. For the more distant commuter terminal, which serves the smaller airlines like Pacific Wings and Island Air, you might want to take the Wiki-Wiki shuttle, as it's a much longer walk. (For details on inter-island flights, see "Getting There & Getting Around" in chapter 2.)

GETTING TO & FROM THE AIRPORT

BY RENTAL CAR   All major rental companies have cars available at Honolulu International Airport (see section 2 of this chapter, "Getting Around," below). Rental agency vans will pick you up at the middle curbside area outside baggage claim and take you to their off-site lot.

BY TAXI   Taxis are abundant at the airport; an attendant will be happy to flag one down for you. Taxi fare from Honolulu International to downtown Honolulu is about $18, to Waikiki about $25 to $30. If you need to call a taxi, see "Getting Around," below, for a list of cab companies.

BY AIRPORT SHUTTLE   Shuttle vans operate 24 hours a day every day of the year between the airport and all 350 hotels and condos in Waikiki. The shuttle service to Waikiki is **Airport Waikiki Express** (© **808/566-7333;** www.hawaii.gov/dot/airports/oahu/hnl/hnl_ground_trans.htm), with 24-hour service in air-conditioned vans for just $8 from the airport to Waikiki ($14 round-trip). You'll find the shuttle at street level outside baggage claim. You can board with two pieces of luggage and a carry-on at no extra charge. Backpacks are okay. Tips are welcome. For advance purchase of group or family tickets, call the number above.

BY BUS   **TheBus** is by far the cheapest way to get to Waikiki—but you've got to be traveling light to use it. TheBus nos. 19 and 20 (Waikiki Beach and Hotels) run from the airport to downtown Honolulu and Waikiki. The first bus from Waikiki to the airport is at 4:50am on weekdays and 5:25am on weekends; the last bus departs the airport for Waikiki at 11:45pm on weekdays, 11:25pm on weekends. There are two bus stops on the main terminal's upper level; a third is on the second level of the Inter-Island terminal.

> ### *Tips* Tips to Make Life Easier
>
> When departing the islands or making inter-island connections, allow yourself plenty of time—at least 90 minutes for inter-island flights, more than 2 hours' lead for mainland international flights. Like most major airports, Honolulu sprawls over a huge area—larger than you want to sprint around in the tropical heat. Allow time to fit the island-style schedule.

You can board TheBus with a carry-on or small suitcase as long as it fits under the seat and doesn't disrupt other passengers; otherwise, you'll have to take a shuttle or taxi. The approximate travel time to Waikiki is an hour. The one-way fare is $2adults and $1 for students ages 6 to 19, exact change only. For information on routes and schedules, call **TheBus** at ✆ **808/848-5555,** daily from 5:30am to 10pm; for recorded information available 24 hours a day, call ✆ **808/296-1818,** then press 8287; or check out **www.TheBus.org**, which provides timetables and maps for all routes, plus directions to the many local attractions (sometimes, taking TheBus is easier than trying to park).

VISITOR INFORMATION

The **Hawaii Visitors and Convention Bureau** is located at 2270 Kalakaua Ave., 7th floor, Suite 801, Honolulu, HI 96815 (✆ **800/GO-HAWAII** or 808/923-1811; www.gohawaii.com). The bureau supplies free brochures, maps, accommodation guides, and *Islands of Aloha,* the official magazine. The **Oahu Visitors Bureau,** 735 Bishop St., Suite 1872, Honolulu, HI 96813 (✆ **877/525-OAHU** or 808/524-0722; www.visitoahu.com), distributes a free travel planner and map.

A number of free publications, including *This Week* and *Guide to Oahu,* are packed with money-saving coupons offering discounts on dining, shops, and activities around the island; look for them on the visitor's publication racks at the airport and around town.

THE ISLAND IN BRIEF
HONOLULU

Honolulu looks like any other big metropolitan center with tall buildings. In fact, some cynics refer to it as "Los Angeles West." But within Honolulu's boundaries, you'll find rainforests, deep canyons, valleys and waterfalls, a nearly mile-high mountain range, coral reefs, and gold-sand beaches. The city proper—where most of Honolulu's 850,000 residents live—is approximately 12 miles wide and 26 miles long, running east-west, roughly between Diamond Head and Pearl Harbor. Within the city are seven hills laced by seven streams that run to Mamala Bay.

Surrounding the central area is a plethora of neighborhoods, ranging from the quiet suburbs of **Hawaii Kai** to *kamaaina* (old-timer) neighborhoods like **Manoa.** These areas are generally quieter and more residential than Waikiki, but they're still within minutes of beaches, shopping, and all the activities Oahu has to offer.

WAIKIKI   Some say that Waikiki is past its prime—that everybody goes to Maui now. If it has fallen out of favor, you couldn't prove it by us. Waikiki is the very incarnation of Yogi Berra's comment about Toots Shor's famous New York restaurant: "Nobody goes there anymore. It's too crowded."

Honolulu's Neighborhoods in Brief

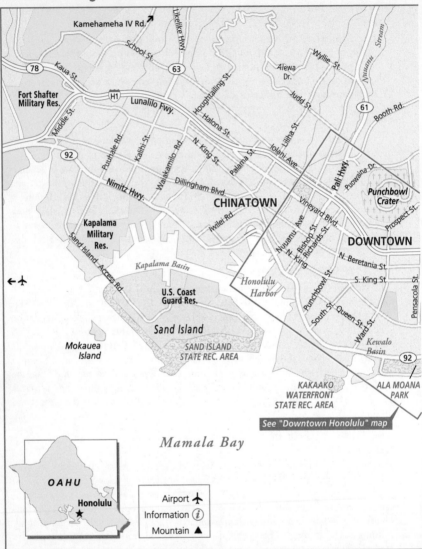

When King Kalakaua played in Waikiki, it was "a hamlet of plain cottages . . . its excitements caused by the activity of insect tribes and the occasional fall of a coconut." The Merrie Monarch, who gave his name to Waikiki's main street, would love the scene today. Some five million tourists visit Oahu every year, and nine out of ten of them stay in Waikiki. This urban beach is where all the action is; it's backed by 175 high-rise hotels with more than 33,000 guest rooms and hundreds of bars and restaurants, all in a 1½-square-mile beach zone. Waikiki means honeymooners and sun seekers,

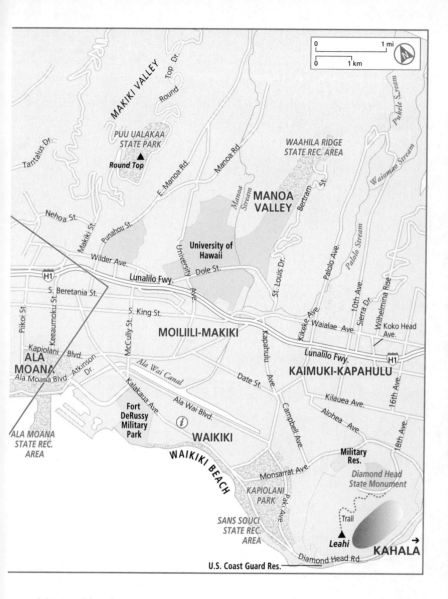

bikinis and bare buns, a round-the-clock beach party every day of the year—and it's all because of a thin crescent of sand that was shipped over from Molokai. Staying in Waikiki puts you in the heart of it all, but also be aware that this is an on-the-go place with traffic noise 24 hours a day and its share of crime—and it's almost always crowded.

ALA MOANA   A great beach as well as a famous shopping mall, Ala Moana is the retail and transportation heart of Honolulu, a place where you can both shop and sun-tan in one afternoon. All bus routes lead to the open-air **Ala Moana Center,** across

Downtown Honolulu

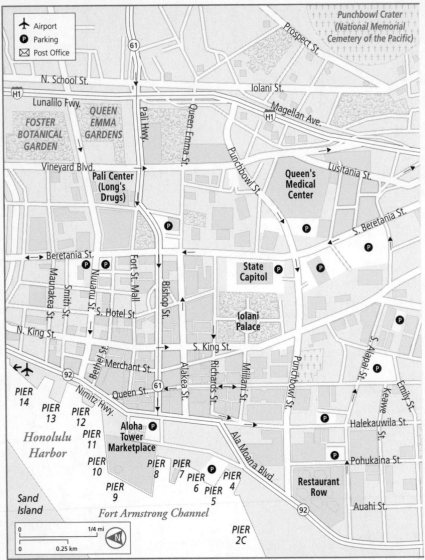

the street from **Ala Moana Beach Park.** This 50-acre, 200-shop behemoth attracts 56 million customers a year (people fly up from Tahiti just to buy their Christmas gifts here). Every European designer from Armani to Vuitton is represented in Honolulu's answer to Beverly Hills's Rodeo Drive. For our purposes, the neighborhood called "Ala Moana" extends along Ala Moana Boulevard from Waikiki in the direction of Diamond Head to downtown Honolulu in the Ewa direction (west), and includes the **Ward Centre** and **Ward Warehouse** complexes as well as **Restaurant Row.**

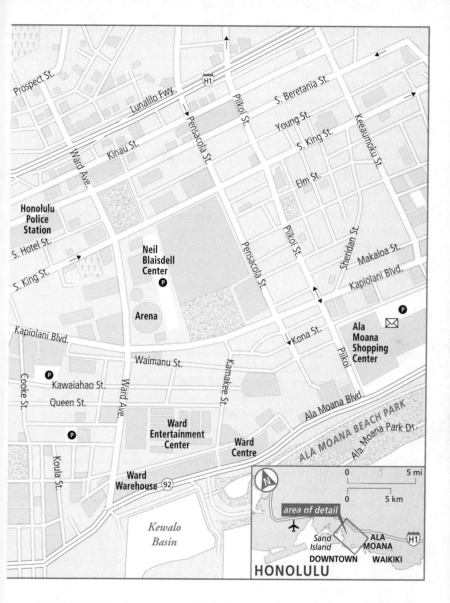

DOWNTOWN A tiny cluster of high-rises west of Waikiki, downtown Honolulu is the financial, business, and government center of Hawaii. On the waterfront stands the iconic 1926 Aloha Tower, now the centerpiece of a harborfront shopping and restaurant complex known as the **Aloha Tower Marketplace.** The whole history of Honolulu can be seen in just a few short blocks: Street vendors sell papayas from trucks on skyscraper-lined concrete canyons; joggers and BMWs rush by a lacy palace where U.S. Marines overthrew Hawaii's last queen and stole her kingdom; burly bus drivers sport fragrant white ginger flowers on their dashboards; Methodist churches look like Asian temples; and businessmen wear aloha shirts to billion-dollar meetings.

On the edge of downtown is the **Chinatown Historic District,** the oldest Chinatown in America and still one of Honolulu's liveliest neighborhoods, a nonstop pageant of people, sights, sounds, smells, and tastes—not all Chinese, now that Southeast Asians, including many Vietnamese, share the old storefronts. Go on Saturday morning, when everyone shops here for fresh goods such as gingerroot, fern fronds, and hogs' heads.

Among the historic buildings and pan-Pacific corporate headquarters are a few hotels, mainly geared toward business travelers. Most visitors prefer the sun and excitement of Waikiki or choose a quieter neighborhood outside the city.

MANOA VALLEY First inhabited by white settlers, the Manoa Valley above Waikiki still has vintage *kamaaina* (old-timer) homes, one of Hawaii's premier botanical gardens in the Lyon Arboretum, the ever-gushing Manoa Falls, and the 320-acre campus of the University of Hawaii, where 50,000 students hit the books when they're not on the beach.

TO THE EAST: KAHALA Except for the estates of world-class millionaires and the luxurious Kahala Mandarin Oriental Hotel (home of Hoku's, an outstanding beachfront restaurant), there's not much out this way that's of interest to visitors.

EAST OAHU

Beyond Kahala lies East Honolulu and suburban bedroom communities like Aina Haina, Niu Valley, and Hawaii Kai, among others, all linked by the Kalanianaole Highway and loaded with homes, condos, fast-food joints, and shopping malls. It looks like Southern California on a good day. There are only a few reasons to come here: to have dinner at **Roy's,** the original and still-outstanding Hawaii Regional Cuisine restaurant, in Hawaii Kai; to snorkel at **Hanauma Bay** or watch daredevil surfers at **Sandy Beach;** or just to enjoy the natural splendor of the lovely coastline, which might include a hike to **Makapuu Lighthouse.**

THE WINDWARD COAST

The Windward side is the opposite side of the island from Waikiki. On this coast, trade winds blow cooling breezes over gorgeous beaches; rain squalls inspire lush, tropical vegetation; and miles of subdivisions dot the landscape. Bed-and-breakfasts, ranging from oceanfront estates to tiny cottages on quiet residential streets, are everywhere. Vacations here are spent enjoying ocean activities and exploring the surrounding areas. Waikiki is just a quick 15-minute drive away.

KAILUA The biggest little beach town in Hawaii, Kailua sits at the foot of the sheer green Koolau Mountains, on a great bay with two of Hawaii's best beaches. The town itself is a funky low-rise cluster of timeworn shops, homes, and fun restaurants. Kailua has become the B&B capital of Hawaii; it's an affordable alternative to Waikiki, with rooms and vacation rentals from $50 a day and up. With the prevailing trade winds whipping up a cooling breeze, Kailua attracts windsurfers from around the world.

KANEOHE Helter-skelter suburbia sprawls around the edges of Kaneohe, one of the most scenic bays in the Pacific. A handful of B&Bs dots its edge. After you clear the trafficky maze of town, Oahu returns to its more natural state. This great bay beckons you to get out on the water; you can depart from Heeia Boat Harbor on snorkel or fishing charters and visit Ahu a Laka a, the sandbar that appears and disappears in the middle of the bay. From here, you'll have a panoramic view of the Koolau Range.

KUALOA/LAIE   The upper northeast shore is one of Oahu's most sacred places, an early Hawaiian landing spot where kings dipped their sails, cliffs hold ancient burial sites, and ghosts still march in the night. Sheer cliffs stab the reef-fringed seacoast, while old fish ponds are tucked along the two-lane coast road that winds past empty gold-sand beaches around beautiful Kahana Bay. Thousands "explore" the South Pacific at the **Polynesian Cultural Center,** in Laie, a Mormon settlement with its own Tabernacle Choir of sweet Samoan harmony.

THE NORTH SHORE

Here's the Hawaii of Hollywood—giant waves, surfers galore, tropical jungles, water-falls, and mysterious Hawaiian temples. If you're looking for a quieter vacation, closer to nature, and filled with swimming, snorkeling, diving, surfing, or just plain hanging out on some of the world's most beautiful beaches, the North Shore is your place. The artsy little beach town of **Haleiwa** and the surrounding shoreline seem a world away from Waikiki. The North Shore boasts good restaurants, shopping, and cultural activities—but here they come with the quiet of country living. Bed-and-breakfasts are the most common accommodations, but there's one first-class hotel and some vacation rentals as well. Be forewarned: It's a long trip—nearly an hour's drive—to Honolulu and Waikiki, and it's about twice as rainy on the North Shore as in Honolulu.

CENTRAL OAHU: THE EWA PLAIN

Flanked by the Koolau and Waianae mountain ranges, the hot, sun-baked Ewa Plain runs up and down the center of Oahu. Once covered with sandalwood forests (hacked down for the China trade) and later the sugarcane and pineapple backbone of Hawaii, Ewa today sports a new crop: suburban houses stretching to the sea. But let your eye wander west to the Waianae Range and Mount Kaala, at 4,020 feet the highest summit on Oahu; up there in the misty rainforest, native birds thrive in the hummocky bog. In 1914, the U.S. Army pitched a tent camp on the plain; author James Jones would later call **Schofield Barracks** "the most beautiful army post in the world." The movie version of Jones's *From Here to Eternity* was filmed here.

LEEWARD OAHU: THE WAIANAE COAST

The west coast of Oahu is a hot and dry place of dramatic beauty: white-sand beaches bordering the deep blue ocean, steep verdant green cliffs, and miles of Mother

---

Tips **Finding Your Way Around, Oahu Style**

Mainlanders sometimes find the directions given by locals a bit confusing. Seldom will you hear the terms east, west, north, and south; instead, islanders refer to directions as either *makai* (ma-*kae*), meaning toward the sea, or *mauka* (*mow*-kah), toward the mountains. In Honolulu, people use **Diamond Head** as a direction meaning to the east (in the direction of the world-famous crater called Diamond Head), and **Ewa** as a direction meaning to the west (toward the town called Ewa, on the other side of Pearl Harbor).

So, if you ask a local for directions, this is what you're likely to hear: "Drive 2 blocks *makai* (toward the sea), then turn Diamond Head (east) at the stoplight. Go 1 block, and turn *mauka* (toward the mountains). It's on the Ewa (western) side of the street."

Nature's wildness. Except for the luxurious J. W. Marriott Ihilani Resort and Spa in the Ko Olina Resort and the Makaha Golf Course, you'll find virtually no tourist services out here. The funky west-coast villages of Nanakuli, Waianae, and Makaha are the last stands of native Hawaiians. This side of Oahu is seldom visited, except by surfers bound for **Yokohama Bay** and those coming to see needle-nose **Kaena Point** (the island's westernmost outpost), which has a coastal wilderness park.

2 Getting Around

BY CAR   Oahu residents own 600,000 registered vehicles, but they have only 1,500 miles of mostly two-lane roads. That's 400 cars for every mile, a fact that becomes abundantly clear during morning and evening rush hours. You can avoid the gridlock by driving between 9am and 3pm or after 6pm.

All the major car-rental firms have agencies on Oahu, at the airport and in Waikiki. For a complete list, as well as tips on insurance, driving rules, and getting the best rate, see "Car Rentals" under "Getting There & Getting Around," on p. 60 of chapter 2. It's almost always cheaper to rent a car at the airport than in Waikiki or through your hotel (unless there's one already included in your package deal). A local competitor to the big national chains is **Tradewinds,** 2875-A Koapaka St., Honolulu (© **888/388-7368** or 808/834-1465; www.tradewindsudrive.com), a small, family-run company with a fleet of some 300 cars. Daily rentals start at $20; weekly (starting at $120) and monthly (starting at $476) rentals offer super savings. Book in advance. Look for their courtesy phone at the airport.

BY BUS   One of the best deals anywhere, **TheBus** (© **808/848-5555,** or 808/296-1818 for recorded information; www.TheBus.org) will take you around the whole island for $2. You can buy a **Visitors Pass** for $20 at any ABC store in Waikiki (ABC stores are literally everywhere in Waikiki). It's good for unlimited rides anywhere on Oahu for 4 consecutive days. In fact, more than 260,000 people use the system's 68 lines and 4,000 bus stops daily.

TheBus goes almost everywhere almost all the time. The most popular route is **no. 8,** which shuttles people between Waikiki and Ala Moana Center every 10 minutes or so (the ride is 15–20 min.); the **no. 19** (Airport/Hickam), **no. 20** (Airport/Halawa Gate), **no. 47** (Waipahu), and **no. 58** (Waikiki/Ala Moana) also cover the same stretch. Waikiki service begins daily at 5am and runs until midnight; buses run about every 15 minutes during the day and every 30 minutes in the evening.

The Circle Island–North Shore route is **no. 52** (Wahiawa/Circle Island); it leaves from Ala Moana Center every 30 minutes, and takes about 4½ hours to circle the island. The Circle Island–South Shore route is **no. 55** (Kaneohe/Circle Island) and also leaves Ala Moana every half-hour and takes about 3 to 4½ hours to circle the island. *Warning:* Some visitors waiting for a bus along the North Shore have been attacked and robbed in broad daylight recently. You might want to consider splurging on a rental car to visit the North Shore.

BY TROLLEY   It's fun to ride the 34-seat, open-air, motorized **Waikiki Trolley** (© **800/824-8804** or 808/596-2822; www.enoa.com), which looks like a San Francisco cable car (see "Organized Tours," p. 177, in section 10 of this chapter). The trolley loops around Waikiki and downtown Honolulu, stopping every 40 minutes at 12 key places: Hilton Hawaiian Village, Iolani Palace, Wo Fat's in Chinatown, the State Capitol, King Kamehameha's Statue, the Mission House Museum, the Aloha Tower, the Honolulu Academy of Arts, the Hawaii Maritime Museum, Ward Centre, Fisherman's Wharf, and Restaurant Row. The driver provides commentary along the way. A 1-day trolley pass—which costs $25 for adults, $18 for seniors over 62, and $12 for kids ages 4 to 11—allows you to jump on and off all day long (8:30am–11:35pm). Four-day passes cost $45 for adults, $27 for seniors, and $18 for kids 4 to 11.

BY TAXI   Oahu's major cab companies offer islandwide, 24-hour, radio-dispatched service, with multilingual drivers and air-conditioned cars, limos, vans, and vehicles equipped with wheelchair lifts (there's a $5 charge for wheelchairs). Fares are standard for all taxi firms; from the airport, expect to pay about $25 to $30 (plus tip) to Waikiki, about $18 to downtown, about $40 to $45 to Kailua, about $40 to $45 to Hawaii Kai, and about $85 to $95 to the North Shore. For a flat fee of $22, **Star Taxi** ★ (*©* **800/ 671-2999** or 808/942-STAR; www.hawaiistartaxi.net) will take up to five passengers from the airport to Waikiki (with no extra charge for baggage); however, you must book in advance. After you have arrived and before you pick up your luggage, re-call Star to make sure that they will be outside waiting for you when your luggage arrives.

For a metered cab, try **Charley's Taxi & Tours** (*©* 808/531-1333), **Elite Limousine Service** (*©* 808/735-2431), and **V.I.P. Transportation** (*©* 808/836-0317). **Robert's Taxi and Shuttle** (*©* 808/261-8555) serves windward Oahu, and **Hawaii Kai Hui/Koko Head Taxi** (*©* 808/396-6633) serves east Honolulu/southeast Oahu.

WHEELCHAIR TRANSPORTATION   Handicabs of the Pacific (*©* **808/524- 3866**) offers taxi services as well as a range of complete tours for wheelchair-bound travelers. Serving Oahu since 1973, Handicabs has air-conditioned vehicles that are specially equipped with ramps and wheelchair lockdowns. Airport pickup to Waikiki hotels is $41 one-way; transportation within Waikiki is $20.

FAST FACTS: Oahu

American Express The Honolulu office is at 1440 Kapiolani Blvd., Suite 104 (*©* **808/946-7741**), and is open Monday through Friday from 8am to 5pm. There's also an office at **Hilton Hawaiian Village,** 2005 Kalia Rd. (*©* **808/947- 2607** or 808/951-0644), and one at the **Hyatt Regency Waikiki,** 2424 Kalakaua Ave. (*©* **808/926-5441**); both offer financial services daily from 8am to 8pm.

Dentists If you need dental attention on Oahu, contact the **Hawaii Dental Association** (*©* **808/593-2135**).

Doctors **Straub Doctors on Call,** 2222 Kalakaua Ave., at Lewers Street, Honolulu (*©* **808/971-6000**), can dispatch a van if you need help getting to the main clinic or to any of their additional clinics at the Royal Hawaiian Hotel, Hyatt Regency Waikiki, Hilton Hawaiian Village, Kahala Mandarin Oriental, and J. W. Marriott Ihilani Resort & Spa.

Emergencies Call *©* **911** for police, fire, and ambulance. The **Poison Control Center** is at 1319 Punahou St. (*©* **808/941-4411**).

Hospitals Hospitals offering 24-hour emergency care include **Queens Medical Center,** 1301 Punchbowl St. (*©* 808/538-9011); **Kuakini Medical Center,** 347 Kuakini St. (*©* 808/536-2236); **Straub Clinic and Hospital,** 888 S. King St. (*©* 808/ 522-4000); **Moanalua Medical Center,** 3288 Moanalua Rd. (*©* 808/834-5333);

TheBus

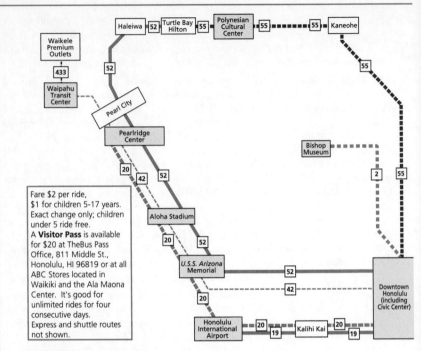

Fare $2 per ride, $1 for children 5-17 years. Exact change only; children under 5 ride free. A **Visitor Pass** is available for $20 at TheBus Pass Office, 811 Middle St., Honolulu, HI 96819 or at all ABC Stores located in Waikiki and the Ala Maona Center. It's good for unlimited rides for four consecutive days. Express and shuttle routes not shown.

Common Bus Routes:

Ala Moana Shopping Center: Take bus #19 & #20 AIRPORT. Return via #19 WAIKIKI, or cross Ala Moana Blvd. for #20.

Bishop Museum: Take #2 SCHOOL STREET. Get off at Kapalama St., cross School St., walk down Bernice St. Return to School St. and take #2 WAIKIKI.

Byodo-In Temple: Take bus #2 to Hotel-Alakea St. (TRF) to #55 KANEOHE-KAHALUU. Get off at Valley of the Temple cemetery. Also #19 and #20 AIRPORT to King-Alakea St., (TRF) on Alakea St. to #55 KANEOHE-KAHALUU.

Circle Island: Take a bus to ALA MOANA CENTER (TRF) to #52 WAHIAWA CIRCLE ISLAND or #55 KANEOHE CIRCLE ISLAND. This is a 4-hour bus ride.

Chinatown or Downtown: Take any #2 bus going out of Waikiki to Hotel St. Return, take #2 WAIKIKI on Hotel St., or #19 or #20 on King St.

The Contemporary Museum & Punchbowl (National Cemetery of the Pacific): Take #2 bus (TRF) at Alapai St. to #15 MAKIKI-PACIFIC HGTS. Return, take #15 and get off at King St., area (TRF) #2 WAIKIKI.

Diamond Head Crater: Take #22 HAWAII KAI-SEA LIFE PARK to the crater. Take a flashlight. Return to the same area and take #22 WAIKIKI.

Dole Plantation: Take bus to ALA MOANA CENTER (TRF) to #52 WAHIAWA CIRCLE ISLAND.

Foster Botanic Gardens: Take #2 bus to Hotel-Riviera St. Walk to Vineyard Blvd. Return to Hotel St. Take #2 WAIKIKI, or take #4 NUUANU and get off at Nuuanu-Vineyard. Cross Nuuanu Ave. and walk one block to the gardens.

Aloha Tower Marketplace & Hawaii Maritime Center: Take #19-#20 AIRPORT and get off at Alakea–Ala Moana. Cross the street to the Aloha Tower.

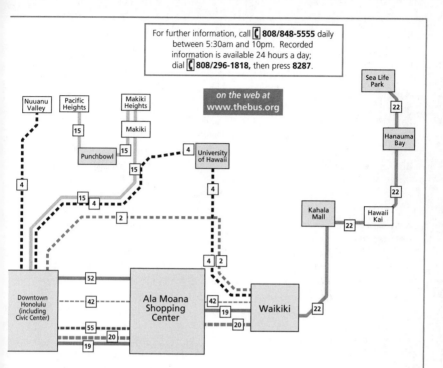

For further information, call ☎ **808/848-5555** daily between 5:30am and 10pm. Recorded information is available 24 hours a day; dial ☎ **808/296-1818,** then press **8287.**

on the web at **www.thebus.org**

Nuuanu Valley

Pacific Heights

Makiki Heights

Makiki

15

Punchbowl

15

15

4

University of Hawaii

4

Sea Life Park

22

Hanauma Bay

22

4

15

4

2

Kahala Mall

22

Hawaii Kai

4 **2**

52

Downtown Honolulu (including Civic Center)

42

Ala Moana Shopping Center

42

19

Waikiki

22

55

20

20

19

Honolulu Zoo: Take any bus on Kuhio Ave. going DIAMOND HEAD direction to Kapahulu Ave.

Iolani Palace (also **State Capitol, Honolulu Hale, Kawaihao Church, Mission Houses, Queen's Hospital, King Kamehameha Statue, State Judiciary Bldg.**) Take any #2 bus and get off at Punchbowl and Beretania St. Walk to King St. Return #2 WAIKIKI on King St.

Kahala Mall: Take #22 HAWAII KAI–SEA LIFE PARK to Kilauea Ave. Return, #22 WAIKIKI.

Pearl Harbor (*Arizona* **Memorial):** Take #20 AIRPORT. Get off across from Memorial, or take a bus to ALA MOANA CENTER (TRF) to #52.

Polynesian Cultural Center: Take a bus to ALA MOANA CENTER (TRF) to #55 KANEOHE CIRCLE ISLAND. Bus ride takes 2 hours one-way.

Queen Emma's Summer Home: Take #4 NUUANU, or board a bus to ALA MOANA CENTER (TRF) to #55 KANEOHE.

Sea Life Park: Take #22 HAWAII KAI-SEA LIFE PARK. #22 will stop at Hanauma Bay en route to the park.

University of Hawaii: Take #4 NUUANU. The bus will go to the University en route to Nuuanu.

Waimea Valley & Adventure Park: Take a bus to ALA MOANA CENTER (TRF) to #52 WAHIAWA CIRCLE ISLAND or #55 KANEOHE CIRCLE ISLAND.

Waikele Premium Outlets: Take bus #42 from Waikiki to Wapahu Transit Center, then bus #433 to Waikele.

Kapiolani Medical Center for Women and Children, 1319 Punahou St. (© 808/973-8511); and **Kapiolani Medical Center** at Pali Momi, 98–1079 Moanalua Rd. (© 808/486-6000). Central Oahu has **Wahiawa General Hospital,** 128 Lehua St. (© 808/621-8411). On the windward side is **Castle Medical Center,** 640 Ulukahiki St., Kailua (© 808/263-5500).

Internet Access If your hotel doesn't have Web access, head to **Web Site Story Café,** 2555 Cartwright Rd. (in the Hotel Waikiki), Waikiki (© **808/922-1677**). It's open daily from 7am to 11pm, and serves drinks.

Newspapers The *Honolulu Advertiser* and *Honolulu Star-Bulletin* are Oahu's daily papers. *Pacific Business News* and *Honolulu Weekly* are weekly papers. *Honolulu Weekly,* available free at restaurants, clubs, shops, and newspaper racks around Oahu, is the best source for what's going on around town.

Post Office To find the location nearest you, call © 800/275-8777. The downtown location is in the old U.S. Post Office, Customs, and Court House Building (referred to as the "old Federal Building") at 335 Merchant St., across from Iolani Palace and next to the Kamehameha Statue (TheBus: 2). Other branch offices include the Waikiki Post Office, 330 Saratoga Ave. (Diamond Head side of Fort DeRussy; TheBus: 19 or 20), and in the Ala Moana Center (TheBus: 8, 19, or 20).

Safety Recently, there has been a series of purse-snatching incidents in Oahu. Thieves in slow-moving cars or on foot have snatched handbags from female pedestrians (in some instances, dragging women who refuse to let go of their pocketbooks down the street). The Honolulu police department advises women to carry their purses on the shoulder away from the street or, better yet, to wear the strap across the chest instead of on one shoulder. Women with clutch bags should hold them close to their chest.

Weather For National Weather Service recorded forecasts for Honolulu, call © **808/973-4380**; for elsewhere on the island, call © **808/973-4381**. For marine reports, call © **808/973-4382**. For surf reports, call © **808/973-4383**.

See "Fast Facts: The Hawaiian Islands," in chapter 2 for more details.

3 Accommodations You Can Afford

Contrary to popular belief, you don't have to go into serious debt to vacation on Oahu. This island is Hawaii's king of accommodations; some 33,000 units, ranging from hostel bunks to plush penthouse apartments, are available here—and among them are some fabulous deals. Believe it or not, it's possible to stay in clean, comfortable, well-located accommodations—some within minutes of the beach—for as low as $45 a day for two (rack rate at the Royal Grove Hotel). A family of four can even stay in a one-bedroom luxury condominium in the heart of Waikiki for as little as $35 each (rack rate at the Royal Kuhio).

The challenge, of course, is finding the bargains. That's where we come in: We've done all the legwork for you. We've scoured the island, inspecting thousands of possibilities to fit all kinds of budgets and tastes. Below, you'll find the results of that work: a complete guide to the best affordable accommodations Oahu has to offer. If a hotel, condominium, or bed-and-breakfast wasn't clean and comfortable enough that we'd be willing to stay there ourselves, or if the accommodations were priced way out of proportion for what you get, you won't find it in this book. If a lodging was in an area whose safety was questionable after dark, it, too, was scratched. Those places where we found the aloha spirit lacking were also excised from our recommendations.

Check for Internet rates first. We have noted when the Internet rates (you have to book direct online to get the deals) will save you big bucks.

A few general words on **Ohana Hotels** (© **800/462-6262;** www.ohanahotels.com), the largest hotel chain in Waikiki: Ohana (formerly called Outrigger) Hotels offers excellent budget accommodations, with dependable, clean, well-appointed rooms at all of its locations, many of which are reviewed below. The chain's price structure is based entirely on location, room size, and amenities. Also consider the alternatives to the big hotels: hostels, the Y, and bed-and-breakfasts. We've also included vacation rentals in our list of recommendable accommodations; these are individual units that you'll have all to yourself, outfitted with everything you need to enjoy your stay in Hawaii—a particularly good choice if you're planning on an extended stay.

Remember, you don't have to stay in Waikiki to enjoy it. Oahu is a small island, and Waikiki is within a half-hour of most of the rest of the island, which has a wonderful selection of places to stay. The only exception is the North Shore, which is a little too far afield to allow a quick jaunt to Waikiki—but it has its own fantastic beaches.

Before choosing a place to stay, you might want to review "55 Money-Saving Tips" in chapter 2 for tips on using reservation booking agencies, advice on how to negotiate better deals, and tips on when you can expect to get the best deals on Oahu—and during what months you should resign yourself to paying top dollar.

A few caveats: Be sure to add the 11.42% accommodation tax to the prices listed below. Street parking in Waikiki and some parts of Honolulu is unheard of, so you most likely will have to cough up the parking costs; they're included in the information provided below.

WAIKIKI
EWA WAIKIKI
All the hotels listed below are located from the ocean to Ala Wai Boulevard., and between Ala Wai Terrace in the Ewa direction (or western side of Waikiki) and Olohana Street through Fort DeRussy Park in the Diamond Head direction (or eastern side of Waikiki).

Ambassador Hotel *Value*   Back when entertainers like the Smothers Brothers and Liberace were A-list performers, the Ambassador was *the* happening Waikiki hotel. That's no longer true, but $59 for two in a studio or $85 for four in a one bedroom (if you book on the Internet), in a centrally located hotel, is still a great deal. Most Waikiki attractions are within walking distance, and the on-site Keo's Restaurant offers some of Hawaii's best Thai cuisine.

Those are the pluses—now for the minuses. The Ambassador is not on the beach, nor is it close to the beach. It's located at a crowded intersection, where the wait to cross the street can be almost as long as the 15-minute walk through Fort DeRussy Park to the beach. Then there's the building itself: The Ambassador feels like a high-rise motel, as all of the hallways are on the outside (expect traffic noise). There have been what the hotel terms "major renovations," but this still isn't an upscale hotel. The rooms, although clean, show some wear. They're on the small side, with small lanais, and either a kitchenette (with a full-size refrigerator) or a full kitchen.

2040 Kuhio Ave. (entry on Namahana St., 1 block from corner of Kuhio and Kalakaua aves.), Honolulu, HI 96815. ✆ **800/923-2620** or 808/941-7777. Fax 808/941-4717. www.ambassadorwaikiki.com. 221 units (with shower only). High season $135–$165 studio double, $185–$195 1-bedroom (up to 4); low season $125–$155 studio double, $175–$185 1-bedroom (up to 4). Always check Internet rates, which can start from $59 studio double, $85 1-bedroom double. Extra person $25. AE, MC, V. Parking $7. TheBus: 19 or 20. **Amenities:** Excellent restaurant (Thai); small outdoor pool; coin-op washer/dryers. *In room:* A/C, TV, kitchenette, fridge, coffeemaker, hair dryer, iron (on request), safe.

Hawaii Polo Inn and Tower

Until recently, the Hawaii Polo Inn was just another aging hotel going to seed. Then along came the brand-new Hawaii Convention Center, which opened in 1998 just a few blocks away, and the management saw new potential in their property. This place has been totally transformed; what was once a crone is now a beauty. It still isn't the Ritz, but this boutique hotel, located within walking distance of Ala Moana Center, offers nicely decorated rooms with modern conveniences at budget prices; be sure to book on the Internet where prices started at $74 when we went to press. The tired rooms have been redone with new tile, new furniture, all-new amenities, and a fresh tropical motif. The suites have microwaves and hot plates. In 2002, they added additional studio units (with kitchenettes, two-burner stove, dishwasher, microwave, and so on) next door at the Polo Tower (which also houses the Aqua Marina Hotel) for even more options. Ala Moana Boulevard is noisy, but the minute you step inside the rattan-furnished lobby, you'll feel like you're in another world. Staff members are fluent in several languages, and all seem knowledgeable about local adventures and activities.

1696 Ala Moana Blvd. (between Hobron Lane and Ala Wai Canal), Honolulu, HI 96815. ✆ **800/949-0061** or 808/949-0061. Fax 808/949-4906. www.hawaiipolo.com. 68 units (with shower only). $98–$119 double; $129 mini-suite with kitchenette for 2; $125–$145 studios with kitchenettes in Polo Tower next door. Internet and convention rates start as low as $74. Extra person $10. Children 18 and under stay free in parent's room. AE, DC, DISC, MC, V. TheBus: 19 or 20. **Amenities:** Tiny outdoor wading pool; activity desk; car-rental desk; coin-op washer/dryers. *In room:* A/C, TV, fridge, coffeemaker; hair dryers, irons, and safes available at the front desk.

Holiday Inn—Waikiki

Just 2 blocks from the beach, 2 blocks from Ala Moana Center, and a 7-minute walk from the Convention Center, this Holiday Inn has a great location and offers this chain's usual amenities for prices that are quite reasonable (for Waikiki, anyway). All rooms, which have a modern Japanese look, come with either a king or two double beds. The property sits back from the street, so noise is at a minimum. The staff is unbelievably friendly.

1830 Ala Moana Blvd. (between Hobron Lane and Kalia Rd.), Honolulu, HI 96815. ✆ **888/992-4545** or 808/955-1111. Fax 808/947-1799. www.waikikihi.holiday-inn.com. 199 units. $120–$130 double. Extra person $15. Children 19 and under stay free in parent's room using existing bedding. AE, DC, DISC, MC, V. Parking $6. TheBus: 19 or 20. **Amenities:** Restaurant; outdoor pool; small fitness room; activities desk; limited room service; coin-op washer/dryers; laundry service; dry cleaning. *In room:* A/C, TV, dataport, high-speed Internet ($9.95/day), fridge, coffeemaker, hair dryer, iron, safe.

Ohana Maile Sky Court 🌴 *Kids*

As soon as you enter this family-friendly branch of the Ohana chain, you'll know you've arrived in Hawaii. Where else would you find a spectacular waterfall in the open-air lobby of your hotel? When booking, first ask for the Simple Saver rate of $69 per room, then ask for a room on one of the upper floors of this 44-story skyscraper; the views of Fort DeRussy Park (a great place for the kids to run off energy) and Waikiki Beach are terrific. As with most Ohanas, the rooms are small, but tastefully done (all were renovated in 2001). The kitchenettes come with a hot plate, refrigerator, toaster, and coffeemaker. There's a pool and Jacuzzi on the property, as well as an outpost of the T.G.I. Friday's restaurant chain. This is a great location for people who love to shop. An extra plus for those relying on public transportation to explore Oahu: TheBus stops right out front. The only downside is that rooms lack lanais.

2058 Kuhio Ave. (at Olohana St.), Honolulu, HI 96815. © 800/462-6262 or 808/947-2828. Fax 800/622-4852 or 808/943-0504. www.ohanahotels.com. 596 units. $139–$159 double; $149–$199 double with kitchenette; $239 suite with kitchenette for up to 4. Ask about Simple Saver rates, which were only $69 at press time. Extra person $15. AE, DC, DISC, MC, V. Parking $8. TheBus: 19 or 20. **Amenities:** Restaurant (family-style); 1 pool bar; outdoor pool with big wraparound deck; huge Jacuzzi; children's program; activity desk; sundries shop; salon; coin-op washer/dryers. *In room:* A/C, TV, kitchenettes (some units), fridge, coffeemaker, hair dryer, iron (on request), safe.

Royal Garden at Waikiki ★ *(Finds* For people looking for a quieter stay, this elegant boutique hotel, tucked away on a tree-lined side street, offers a lobby filled with European marble and chandeliers in addition to the plush guest rooms, which feature a pantry kitchenette, marble bathroom, lanai, lots of closet space, and views. The beach is a few blocks away, but if you can get the Internet special price of $105, it's worth the hike.

440 Olohana St. (between Kuhio Ave. and Ala Wai Blvd.), Honolulu, HI 96815. © 800/367-5666 or 808/943-0202. Fax 808/946-8777. www.royalgardens.com. 210 units. $150–$250 double; from $350 suite. Internet rates start at $105. Packages galore. Extra person $25. Children under 12 stay free in parent's room. AE, DC, DISC, MC, V. Parking $9. TheBus: 19 or 20. **Amenities:** Restaurant (Japanese cuisine); lounge (with DJ); 2 freshwater outdoor pools (1 with cascading waterfall); small fitness room; 2 Jacuzzis; 2 saunas; small business center; coin-op washer/dryers; laundry service; dry cleaning. *In room:* A/C, TV, dataport, kitchenette, fridge, coffeemaker, hair dryer, iron, safe.

For Members of the Military Only

Hale Koa Hotel ★★ *(Value* We wish we could stay here—but we're not allowed. This is a very exclusive hotel, for active-duty and retired military and their families only. The Hale Koa is a first-class hotel, right on Waikiki Beach, with the grassy lawns of Fort DeRussy on the other side and vendors offering watersports equipment rentals nearby. The price structure, which depends on military rank (lower ranks get cheaper rates), is 50% to 75% less than what comparable Waikiki hotels charge. The facilities here are terrific, including three swimming pools, 66 landscaped acres with picnic tables and barbecues, jogging trails, four restaurants, and lots of sports facilities. The only drawback is that the hotel is always booked; some guests reserve up to a year in advance.

2055 Kalia Rd. (across from Fort DeRussy, between Dewey Way and Saratoga Rd.), Honolulu, HI 96815. © 800/367-6027 or 808/955-0555. Fax 800/HALE-FAX. www.halekoa.com. 814 units. $74–$190 double, depending on room views and military rank. Rates include continental breakfast and orientation the morning after check-in. Extra person $15; singles deduct $2 from double rate. AE, DC, DISC, MC, V. Parking $3. TheBus: 19 or 20. **Amenities:** 4 restaurants and bars (occasional dinner shows); 3 outdoor pools; 4 lit tennis courts; fitness room; Jacuzzi; sauna; racquetball and volleyball courts; concierge desk; activity desk; car-rental desk; business center; shopping arcade; salon; room service; babysitting; coin-op washer/dryers; laundry service; dry cleaning. *In room:* A/C, TV/VCR, dataport, fridge, coffeemaker, hair dryer, iron, safe.

MID-WAIKIKI, MAKAI

All of the hotels listed below are between Kalakaua Avenue and the ocean, and between Saratoga Road in the Ewa direction and Royal Hawaiian Avenue in the Diamond Head direction.

Aloha Punawai *(Value* Here's one of Waikiki's best-kept secrets: a low-profile, family-operated (since 1959) apartment hotel just 2 blocks from the beach and within walking distance of most Waikiki attractions. The Aloha Punawai offers some of the lowest prices in Waikiki; if you stay a week, prices drop even more. And the location is great, just across the street from Fort DeRussy Park and 2 blocks to Grey's Beach—the

Waikiki Accommodations & Dining

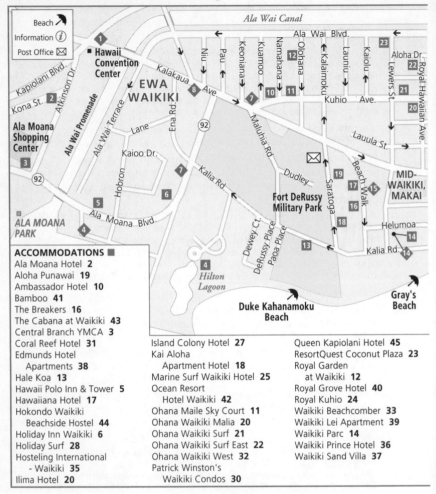

Beach

Information (i)

Post Office ✉

ACCOMMODATIONS ■

Ala Moana Hotel **2**
Aloha Punawai **19**
Ambassador Hotel **10**
Bamboo **41**
The Breakers **16**
The Cabana at Waikiki **43**
Central Branch YMCA **3**
Coral Reef Hotel **31**
Edmunds Hotel
    Apartments **38**
Hale Koa **13**
Hawaii Polo Inn & Tower **5**
Hawaiiana Hotel **17**
Hokondo Waikiki
    Beachside Hostel **44**
Holiday Inn Waikiki **6**
Holiday Surf **28**
Hosteling International
    - Waikiki **35**
Ilima Hotel **20**

Island Colony Hotel **27**
Kai Aloha
    Apartment Hotel **18**
Marine Surf Waikiki Hotel **25**
Ocean Resort
    Hotel Waikiki **42**
Ohana Maile Sky Court **11**
Ohana Waikiki Malia **20**
Ohana Waikiki Surf **21**
Ohana Waikiki Surf East **22**
Ohana Waikiki West **32**
Patrick Winston's
    Waikiki Condos **30**

Queen Kapiolani Hotel **45**
ResortQuest Coconut Plaza **23**
Royal Garden
    at Waikiki **12**
Royal Grove Hotel **40**
Royal Kuhio **24**
Waikiki Beachcomber **33**
Waikiki Lei Apartment **39**
Waikiki Parc **14**
Waikiki Prince Hotel **36**
Waikiki Sand Villa **37**

same great beach facing the luxury Halekulani and Sheraton Waikiki hotels. The apartments contain a mishmash of furniture and come with full kitchens and lanais. Don't expect the Ritz (or any interior decoration, for that matter)—just sparkling clean accommodations in a great location. Towels and linens are provided. The phone wiring has been installed and is ready for service; you have to pay for hookup.

305 Saratoga Rd. (across from Fort DeRussy and the Waikiki Post Office, between Kalia Rd. and Kalakaua Ave.), Honolulu, HI 96815. ✆ 808/923-5211. Fax 808/622-4688. www.alternative-hawaii.com/alohapunawai. 19 units (studios have shower only). $95–$105 studio double; $105–$135 1-bedroom double (sleeps up to 5). Children 16 and under stay free with parents and existing bedding. Extra person $10. Discounts for weeklong (or longer) stays. MC, V. Parking $9. TheBus: 19 or 20. **Amenities:** Coin-op washer/dryers. *In room:* A/C, TV, kitchen, fridge, coffeemaker.

The Breakers 🌺 *(Value* The Breakers is full of old-fashioned Hawaiian aloha—and it's only steps from the sands of Waikiki. This two-story hotel has a friendly staff and

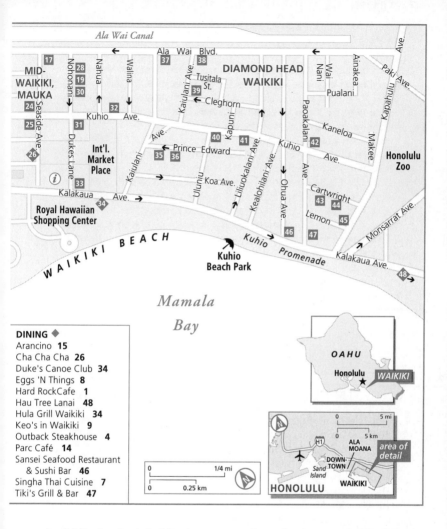

Ala Wai Canal

Ala Wai Blvd.

MID-WAIKIKI, MAUKA

DIAMOND HEAD WAIKIKI

Nohonani
Nahua
Walina
Kaiulani Ave.
Tusitala St.
Cleghorn
Wai Nani
Ainakea
Paki Ave.
Kapahulu Ave.

Seaside Ave.
Dukes Lane

Kuhio Ave.
Kapuni
Paoakalani
Pualani
Kaneloa
Makee

Int'l. Market Place
Kaiulani
Prince Edward
Uluniu
Koa Ave.
Kuhio Ave.
Liliuokalani Ave.
Kealohilani Ave.
Ohua Ave.

Honolulu Zoo

Kalakaua Ave.

Royal Hawaiian Shopping Center

Cartwright
Lemon
Monsarrat Ave.

Kalakaua Ave.

WAIKIKI BEACH

Kuhio Promenade

Kuhio Beach Park

Mamala Bay

DINING ◆
Arancino **15**
Cha Cha Cha **26**
Duke's Canoe Club **34**
Eggs 'N Things **8**
Hard RockCafe **1**
Hau Tree Lanai **48**
Hula Grill Waikiki **34**
Keo's in Waikiki **9**
Outback Steakhouse **4**
Parc Café **14**
Sansei Seafood Restaurant
  & Sushi Bar **46**
Singha Thai Cuisine **7**
Tiki's Grill & Bar **47**

OAHU

Honolulu ★ *WAIKIKI*

0   5 mi
0   5 km

ALA MOANA
DOWN-TOWN
Sand Island
area of detail

HONOLULU   **WAIKIKI**

0   1/4 mi
0   0.25 km

a loyal following. Its six buildings are set around a pool and a tropical garden blooming with brilliant red and yellow hibiscus; wooden jalousies and shoji doors further the tropical ambience. Each of the tastefully decorated, slightly oversize rooms comes with a lanai and a kitchenette. Every Wednesday and Friday, you're invited to a formal Japanese tea ceremony from 10am to noon. One of the best things about the Breakers is the location, just a 2-minute walk to numerous restaurants, shopping, and Waikiki Beach.

250 Beach Walk (between Kalakaua Ave. and Kalia Rd.), Honolulu, HI 96815. © **800/426-0494** or 808/923-3181. Fax 808/923-7174. www.breakers-hawaii.com. 64 units (shower only). $99–$105 double; $145 garden studio double. Extra person $10. AE, DC, MC, V. Limited parking, $9 across the street. TheBus: 19 or 20. **Amenities:** Limited Restaurant (poolside bar open Mon–Fri, and grill for lunch on Fri only); free coffee in lobby all day; outdoor pool; coin-op washer/dryers; dry cleaning. *In room:* A/C, TV, kitchenette, fridge, hair dryer (on request), iron (on request), safe.

Big Changes for Waikiki

One of the biggest projects to take place in Waikiki in decades is the total renovation of an 8-acre area (bounded by Saratoga Rd., Kalakaua Ave., Lewers St., and Kalia Rd.) called the **Waikiki Beach Walk**. The project, which is being done by Outrigger Enterprises, is estimated to cost some $420 million and will directly affect 11 different hotels.

Phase One, which got underway in the spring of 2005, is expected to be completed by the end of 2006. When finished, the now very-congested-area, with narrow streets (and lots of delivery trucks double parked), and old, outdated buildings will be replaced with a new look with wider sidewalks, tropical foliage, water features, open space, and new, totally renovated hotels ready for the 21st century. Some 11 hotels will be either razed, combined, upgraded, or changed to suites or condos so that only five hotels and timeshare condominiums will remain. Not only will all the small restaurants and shops be gone, but when the project is completed, the near-oceanfront area will go from budget hotels, neighborhood eateries, and small shops to luxury (higher-priced) properties with swank shops and restaurants to match. Plus there will be a two-level, 90,000-square-foot complex of retail shops and restaurants. The entire revised area will be linked through pedestrian bridges and connecting walkways.

Here are the changes to the hotels:

- The former 480-room Ohana Reef Towers will be replaced by 193 timeshare condominium units, operated by Outrigger, and renamed Fairfield Hawaii at Waikiki Beach Walk.
- The Ohana Edgewater and Ohana Coral Seas will be razed and replaced by a two-story, 90,000-square-foot retail/entertainment complex to include 40 retail shops, four major restaurants, three or four smaller food and beverage places, and an open pedestrian plaza.
- The former Ohana Waikiki Village and the Ohana Waikiki Tower hotels, which had a total of 881 rooms, will be redeveloped into a 421-suite Embassy Suites-Waikiki Beach Walk.
- The Outrigger Reef on the Beach will be totally refurbished throughout 2006, and all 858 rooms will redone, along with renovations to the Serenity Spa, two restaurants, retail shops, and all public areas.
- The Ohana Islander Waikiki, on the corner of Kalakaua Avenue and Lewers Street, will also undergo renovations to the 280 units.

During the construction, this will not be a fun area to visit. The neighbors, Halakulani, Waikiki Parc, and other non-Outrigger hotels are not exactly thrilled with the scheduled disruptions to traffic and the serenity of their guests. But plans are afoot to minimize the impacts to everyone.

Hawaiiana Hotel ✮ *Finds*   The hotel's slogan—"The spirit of old Hawaii"—says it all. The lush tropical flowers and carved tiki at the entrance on tiny Beach Walk set the tone for this intimate low-rise hotel. From the moment you arrive, you'll be embraced by the aloha spirit: At check-in, you're given a pineapple, and every morning, complimentary Kona coffee and tropical juice are served poolside. All the concrete, hollow-tiled guest rooms feature kitchenettes, two beds (a double and a single or a queen plus a sofa bed), and a view of the gardens and two swimming pools. Hawaiian entertainment is featured every week. The hotel is about a block from the beach and within walking distance of Waikiki shopping and nightlife.

260 Beach Walk (near Kalakaua Ave.), Honolulu, HI 96815. © **800/367-5122** or 808/923-3811. Fax 808/926-5728. www.hawaiianahotelatwaikiki.com. 95 units (some with shower only). $95–$105 double; $165–$195 deluxe studio with kitchenette; $175 1-bedroom with kitchenette (sleeps up to 4). Extra person $10. AE, DC, DISC, MC, V. Parking $10. TheBus: 19 or 20. **Amenities:** Cafe (serving sandwiches, hot dogs, shave ice, and coffee); 2 good-size outdoor pools; coin-op washer/dryers. *In room:* A/C, TV, kitchenette, fridge, coffeemaker, iron, safe.

Kai Aloha Apartment Hotel 🄥Value If you want to experience what Waikiki was like 40 years ago, stay here. This small apartment hotel just a block from the beach is reminiscent of the low-key hotels that used to line the blocks of Waikiki in the good old days. It offers one-bedroom apartments and studios, all furnished in modest rattan and colorful island prints. Each of the one-bedroom units has a bedroom with either a queen bed or two twins, a living room with a couch and two additional twins (Hawaiian houses of 40 years ago all had extra beds in the living room, called *punee,* for guests to sleep on), a full kitchen, plus a dining table, and even voice mail. These rooms are even large enough to accommodate a roll-away bed for a fifth person. Glass jalousies take advantage of the cooling trade winds, but there's also air-conditioning for very hot days. The studios have two twin beds, a kitchenette, a balcony, a Plexiglas roof in the bathroom (the forerunner of the skylight), and a screen door for ventilation. The units aren't exactly designer showrooms, but they do have a homey, comfortable feel and provide daily maid service. You're sure to forgive the lack of aesthetics when you're presented with the bill. A large deck on the second floor is a great place to sip early morning coffee or watch the sun sink into the Pacific.

235 Saratoga Rd. (across from Fort DeRussy and Waikiki Post Office, between Kalakaua Ave. and Kalia Rd.), Honolulu, HI 96815. © **808/923-6723.** Fax 808/922-7592. www.magickhawaii.com/kaialoha. 18 units. $65–$70 studio double; $73–$76 1-bedroom double; $85–$90 1-bedroom for 3; $95–$105 1-bedroom for 4. Extra person $15. 3-night minimum. AE, MC, V. Parking at separate pay lot across the street. TheBus: 19 or 20. **Amenities:** Coin-op washer/dryers. *In room:* A/C, TV, kitchenette, fridge, coffeemaker.

Hot Package Deals

Waikiki Parc 🄫 Terrifically located just 100 yards from the beach, this hotel is for people who want a taste of the Halekulani's elegance, grace, and style but at a more reasonable price. It's tucked just behind the Halekulani and is owned and operated by the same company. The compact, beautifully appointed rooms all have lanais with ocean, mountain, or city views; ceramic-tile floors with plush carpeting; and conversation areas with a writing desk and rattan couch and chair. Nice extras include adjustable floor-to-ceiling shutters for those who want to sleep in.

The Parc features the same level of service that has made the Halekulani famous and offers two excellent restaurants. On a recent visit, I asked room service for a few items that were not on the menu—not only did they happily comply, but the manager also checked back later to make sure I got what I wanted.

Though the rack rates are way over our price range, it's often possible to land a package deal here that's a great bargain. At press time, room/car packages started at $235, including a double room (usually $229 a night), a compact car, breakfast for two, and free parking. The Parc Sunrise package featured a double room, the daily buffet breakfast for two (usually $15 each), and free parking (usually $15). For families, the hotel was featuring the Parc Bonus Plan, which takes 54% off your second room—a minimum savings of $112—when you book your first at the normal rack rate.

2233 Helumoa Rd. (at Lewers St.), Honolulu, HI 96815. ℂ **800/422-0450** or 808/921-7272. Fax 808/923-1336. www.waikikiparchotel.com. 297 units. $229–$339 double. Extra person $50. Children 17 and under stay free in parent's room. Ask about room/car, bed-and-breakfast, and family packages. AE, DC, MC, V. Self- or valet parking $15. TheBus: 19 or 20. **Amenities:** 2 restaurants (fine buffet restaurant, Kyoto-style Japanese restaurant); concierge; activities desk; business center; limited room service; babysitting; coin-op washer/dryers; same-day laundry and dry cleaning. *In room:* A/C, TV, dataport, high-speed Internet access (fee), fridge, hair dryer, safe.

MID-WAIKIKI, MAUKA

These mid-Waikiki hotels, on the mountain side of Kalakaua Avenue, are a little farther away from the beach than those listed above. They're all between Kalakaua and Ala Wai Boulevard, and between Kalaimoku Street in the Ewa direction and Kaiulani Street in the Diamond Head direction.

ResortQuest Hawaii *Value* This small hotel is showing signs of wear and in need of renovation—hallways need painting, rooms look worn, etc. but it does offers perks that are rare in Waikiki, such as free continental breakfast and the kind of personalized service that only a small hotel can provide. Also, if you can get the Internet price of $79, you'll have a fantastic deal. The property has a tropical-plantation feel, with big, airy, island-style rooms, terra-cotta tile, and lots of greenery. The bedrooms, done in rattan and earth tones, all have private lanais, ceramic-tile bathrooms, and daily maid service. The units with kitchenettes are especially good deals. Most rooms have views of the Ala Wai Canal and the mountains (if you prefer quiet, ask for a city-view room). Ala Wai Golf Course is just across the canal, and the beach is 4 blocks away.

450 Lewers St. (at Ala Wai Blvd.), Honolulu, HI 96815. ℂ **877/997-6667** or 808/923-8828. Fax 808/922-8785. www.resortquesthawaii.com. 80 units. $105 double; $125 suite with kitchenette; $140 1-bedroom; $190 for junior suite. Rates include continental breakfast. Extra person $12. (check Internet, where rates start at $79). AE, DC, MC, V. Parking $9. TheBus: 19 or 20. **Amenities:** Tiny outdoor pool with sun deck; activities desk; coin-op washer/dryers. *In room:* A/C, TV, kitchenette, fridge, coffeemaker, hair dryer, iron, safe.

Coral Reef Hotel If you're looking for a roomy, mid-priced hotel and don't mind a short walk to the beach, this 15-story Aston-operated hotel may be the one for you. It was built in 1969, but totally renovated in 1998. The last room renovations took place just before 2000. Price differences are based on views: The higher up you go, the better the view—and the higher the price. Located 1 block from the International Market Place and Kuhio Mall and 3 blocks from the beach, the Coral Reef has a good central location; the only problem is that Kuhio Avenue is very busy and noisy, both day and night.

2299 Kuhio Ave. (at Duke's Lane), Honolulu, HI 96815. ℂ **800/92-ASTON** (Aston Hotels) or 808/922-1262. Fax 808/ 922-5048 or 808/922-8785. www.aston-hotels.com. 247 units. High season $145–$155 for up to 4, $165–$175 junior suite for up to 4, $185–$195 1-bedroom suite for up to 4; low season $115–$125 for up to 4, $135–$145 junior suite for up to 4, $155–$165 1-bedroom suite for up to 4. Discounts and packages available; at press time, Internet "ePricebreaker" rates were from $83 double. Extra person $15. AE, DC, DISC, MC, V. Limited parking $10. TheBus: 19 or 20. **Amenities:** 2 restaurants; bar; outdoor pool; travel desk; sundries shop. *In room:* A/C, TV, dataport, some kitchenettes with coffeemakers, fridge, hair dryer, iron, safe.

Holiday Surf *Value* Three blocks and about a 10- to 15-minute walk from Waikiki Beach lies this 1960s apartment hotel, run since 1964 by the Chun family. Overlooking the Ala Wai Canal, this six-story building can be noisy, but the location is within walking distance of Waikiki attractions, dining, and shopping. The 315-square-foot studios are composed of an immaculately clean bedroom/living room/kitchen combo, with a bed on one side and a full kitchen across the room. Air-conditioning drowns out the street noise. The one-bedroom units are larger and have separate bedrooms (great for families). Some of the rooms have been upgraded, thus the range in prices. *Hot tip:* If you are on a budget, ask for the "Manager's Special Rates" at $79 for a studio or $89 for one bedroom (note, that these are not the deluxe upgraded units, but still clean and very functional, this is a great deal). They also added a spa with massage and a floating salon.

2303 Ala Wai Blvd. (corner of Nohonani St.), Honolulu, HI 96815. © **808/923-8488.** Fax 808/923-1475. 34 units. $125–$175 studio double; $225 1-bedroom double. Ask about special discounts, such as the Manager Special Rates offered at press time (from $79 studio double, from $89 1-bedroom double). Extra person $20. AE, MC, V. Parking $6.25 TheBus: 19 or 20. **Amenities:** Spa; coin-op washer/dryers. *In room:* A/C, TV/VCR/DVD, Internet access ($9/day), kitchen, fridge, coffeemaker.

Ilima Hotel 🌸 *Kids*   The Teruya brothers, former owners of Hawaii's Times Supermarket, wanted to offer comfortable accommodations that Hawaii residents could afford, and they've succeeded. One of Hawaii's small, well-located condo-style hotels, the 17-story, pale pink Ilima (named for the native orange flower used in royal leis) offers value for your money. Rooms are huge, the location (near the International Market Place and the Royal Hawaiian Shopping Center; 2 blocks to Waikiki Beach) is great, and prices are low. A tasteful koa-wood lobby lined with works by Hawaiian artists greets you upon arrival. Perks include free local phone calls (a nice plus), and a full kitchen in every unit; in addition, all the couches fold out into beds, making this a particularly good deal for families. The one-bedroom units now have a Jacuzzi tub to soak in. There are three sun decks, a dry sauna, and truly nice people staffing the front desk to help you enjoy your vacation. The only caveat: no ocean views.

445 Nohonani St. (near Ala Wai Blvd.), Honolulu, HI 96815. © **800/801-9366** or 808/923-1877. Fax 808/924-2617. www.ilima.com. 99 units. $135–$145 double; $189–$219 1-bedroom (rate for 4); $265–$285 2-bedroom (rate for 4, sleeps up to 6); $395 3-bedroom (rate for 6, sleeps up to 8). Extra person $10. Discounts available for seniors and business travelers. AE, DC, DISC, MC, V. Limited free parking, $10 across the street. TheBus: 19 or 20. **Amenities:** Outdoor pool with sauna; exercise room; Jacuzzi in 1-bedroom units; tour desk; coin-op washer/dryers. *In room:* A/C, TV, free high-speed Internet for deluxe rooms floors 10–16, kitchen, fridge, coffeemaker, hair dryer, iron, safe, free local phone calls.

Island Colony Hotel 🌸   This elegant hotel combines the spaciousness of a condominium property with the amenities of a hotel, such as daily maid service. All units have private lanais. The studio units (which can sleep up to four) have kitchenettes, and the one-bedrooms (which can sleep up to five) have full kitchens. And the views are spectacular: the jagged mountains and lush valleys, well-known Diamond Head, or the sparkling Pacific Ocean. The only caveat is the minuscule bathrooms: Ours was so small that the door didn't clear the toilet (it doesn't sound like a big deal, but it was annoying). The tub/shower combo was also *very* cramped. Access via car (always tricky on Waikiki's one-way streets) is very convenient from Ala Wai Boulevard. *Hot tip:* Book on the Internet for rates as low as $69 (almost $100 off rack rates).

445 Seaside Ave. (at Ala Wai Blvd.), Honolulu, HI 96815. © **800/367-5004** or 808/923-2345. Fax 808/921-7105. www.castleresorts.com. 347 units. $160–165 double; $180–$185 studio with kitchenette; $230–$275 1-bedroom with kitchen for 4. Check for Internet specials, which were $69 double at press time. Extra person $25. AE, DC, DISC, MC, V. Parking $8. TheBus: 19 or 20. **Amenities:** Restaurant (Chinese); outdoor pool; Jacuzzi; sauna; activity desk; car-rental desk; coin-op washer/dryers. *In room:* A/C, TV, dataport, full kitchen or kitchenette (some units), fridge, coffeemaker, hair dryer.

Marine Surf Waikiki Hotel   Located in the heart of Waikiki, this high-rise is part privately owned condo units and part spacious studio apartments—only the studios are available for rent. Each one has a complete kitchen, two extra-long double beds, and a small lanai. Prices vary with the views (the best views are from floors 17–22). Located just a half-block from Kuhio Mall and the International Market Place, the hotel is about 1½ blocks from the beach.

364 Seaside Ave. (at Kuhio Ave.), Honolulu, HI 96815. 🕿 **888/456-SURF** or 808/923-0277. Fax 808/926-5915. 110 units. www.marinesurf.com. $107–$140 double; $180–$205 1-bedroom penthouse suite double. Internet specials from $83. Extra person $10. DC, DISC, MC, V. Parking $5. TheBus: 19 or 20. **Amenities:** Restaurant (Italian); bar; outdoor pool; activity desk; coin-op washer/dryers. *In room:* A/C, TV, kitchen, fridge, coffeemaker, hair dryer, iron, safe.

Ohana Waikiki Malia *(Kids*   This large hotel, part of the cluster of Ohana Hotels on Kuhio and surrounding blocks, offers very large rooms with either a king bed or twins, and lanais. Recently added are the one-bedroom suites with kitchenettes, great for families. Like those at most Ohana Hotels, the windows have black-out curtains, which not only keep the blaring morning sun out, but also help with the noise from busy Kuhio Avenue. There's no pool, but guests are welcome to use the pool at the Ohana Waikiki Surf West across the street. But why bother? One of the most famous beaches in the world is just 3 blocks away. Wheelchair-accessible rooms outfitted with wide doorways and special grips in the bathroom are available.

2211 Kuhio Ave. (between Royal Hawaiian Ave. and Lewers St.), Honolulu, HI 96815. 🕿 **800/462-6262** or 808/923-7621. Fax 800/622-4852 or 808/921-4804. www.ohanahotels.com. 327 units. $159–$169 double; $219 1-bedroom suite with kitchenette for up to 4. Ask about promotions and packages, including Simple Saver rates, which were only $69 at press time. Extra person $15. AE, DC, DISC, MC, V. Parking $8. TheBus: 19 or 20. **Amenities:** Restaurant (24-hr. coffee shop); bar; roof-top tennis courts; children's program; activity desk; room service (5am–10pm); laundry service. *In room:* A/C, TV, kitchenette (some units), fridge, coffeemaker, hair dryer, iron (on request), safe.

Ohana Waikiki Surf *(Value*   This budget Outrigger offers all the necessities in a comfortable setting at very good rates. The recently renovated rooms are a bit small, with miniature lanais. Only 16 rooms have tub/shower combinations, but most rooms have kitchenettes. A brand-new pool is on-site; there are no restaurants, but a 24-hour coffee shop is available across the street at the Ohana Malia. Waikiki activities are all within walking distance—it's just 3 blocks to the beach—and TheBus stops right outside.

2200 Kuhio Ave. (at Lewers St.), Honolulu, HI 96815. 🕿 **800/462-6262** or 808/923-7671. Fax 808/921-4959 or 800/622-4852. www.ohana.com. 302 units (most with shower only). $139 double; $159 double with kitchenette; $209 1-bedroom with kitchenette for up to 4. Ask about promotions and packages, including Simple Saver rates, which were only $69 at press time. Extra person $15. AE, DC, DISC, MC, V. Parking $8. TheBus: 19 or 20. **Amenities:** Outdoor pool; children's program; activity desk; laundry service. *In room:* A/C, TV, kitchenette (most rooms), fridge, coffeemaker, hair dryer, iron (on request), safe.

Ohana Waikiki Surf East   Deep in the heart of Ohanaville—the 3- or 4-block area where it seems every hotel is an Ohana—is this 12-story moderately priced hotel offering the chain's clean, comfortable rooms and dependable service. The rooms here open to outdoor hallways, making it feel a bit like a high-rise motel; they're carefully color-coordinated, and all have kitchenettes (completely renovated in 1998). There's a small pool (half of it is under the hotel, half in the sun), and dozens of restaurants are just a few footsteps away on Kuhio Avenue. This section of Waikiki is quieter than most, but you'll have to walk about 5 blocks to the beach.

422 Royal Hawaiian Ave. (between Manukai and Aloha Dr., 1 block from Kuhio Ave.), Honolulu, HI 96815. 🕿 **800/462-6262** or 808/923-7671. Fax 800/622-4852 or 808/921-4141. www.ohana.com. 102 units (with kitchenette, shower only). $139 double with kitchenette for up to 4; $189 1-bedroom with kitchenette for up to 4. Ask about

promotions and packages, including Simple Saver rates, which were only $69 at press time. AE, DC, DISC, MC, V. Parking $8. TheBus: 19 or 20. **Amenities:** Tiny indoor/outdoor pool; children's program; coin-op washer/dryers. *In room:* A/C, TV, kitchenette, fridge, coffeemaker, hair dryer, iron (on request), safe.

Ohana Waikiki West   On the upside, this Ohana hotel has lots of guest services and facilities. The downside is that it's located on a very busy, noisy part of Kuhio Avenue. The rooms were redone in 1995; those with kitchenettes also have two-burner stoves and ovens. Waikiki Beach is 2 blocks away, and restaurants, shopping, and nightlife are all no more than a 10-minute walk. International Market Place is across the street.

2330 Kuhio Ave. (between Nahua and Walina sts.), Honolulu, HI 96815. ℂ **800/462-6262** or 808/922-5022. Fax 800/622-4852 or 808/924-6414. www.ohana.com. 663 units (with shower only). $159 double; $169–$179 double with kitchenette. Ask about promotions and packages, including Simple Saver rates, which were only $69 at press time. Extra person $15. AE, DC, DISC, MC, V. Parking $8. TheBus: 19 or 20. **Amenities:** 2 restaurants (a Chili's franchise, a bakery/deli); 2 bars (1 poolside, 1 country and western); outdoor pool; children's program; activity desk; shopping arcade (with a pharmacy); limited room service; coin-op washer/dryers. *In room:* A/C, TV, kitchenette (some units), fridge, coffeemaker, hair dryer, iron, safe.

Patrick Winston's Waikiki Condos ★ *Finds*   Looking for a condo priced to fit a tight budget, with a hefty dose of old-fashioned aloha thrown in? Try Patrick Winston's rentals, located on a quiet side street. When this five-story condominium hotel was built in 1981, Winston bought one unit; he has since acquired 24 more, spent hundreds of thousands of dollars on refurbishment, and put his spacious suites on the market at frugal prices. Staying here is like having a personal concierge; Winston has lots of terrific tips on where to eat, where to shop, and how to get the most for your money, and he can book any activity you want.

Four types of units are available: standard/budget rooms, one-bedroom suites, ground-floor junior business suites, and one two-bedroom unit. All have sofa beds, separate bedrooms, lanais with breakfast table and chairs, ceiling fans, and full kitchens; most have a washer and dryer. All are individually decorated. Eight units are "standard budget," which means the carpet has not been replaced or the walls need repainting but are otherwise a terrific deal for those looking for a condominium unit at a penny-pincher price. Waikiki Beach is just a 10- to 15-minute walk away, shopping is a half block away, and restaurants are within a 5- to 10-minute walk. This area of Waikiki is a little scary at night, not totally safe for a single woman to be wandering about by herself.

Hawaiian King Building, 417 Nohonani St., Suite 409 (between Kuhio Ave. and Ala Wai Blvd.), Honolulu, HI 96815. ℂ **800/545-1948** or 808/924-3332. Fax 808/922-3894. www.winstonswaikikicondos.com. 24 units (shower only). $89–$109 double budget units; $99–$119 double family suite; $115–$135 1-bedroom; $125–$145 business suite; $135–$155 2-bedroom unit. Extra person $10. 7-night minimum. Ask for the Frommer's reader's discount. AE, DC, DISC, MC, V. Parking $7. TheBus: 19 or 20. **Amenities:** Bar; small outdoor pool surrounded by a tropical courtyard; babysitting; coin-op washer/dryers. *In room:* A/C, TV, dataport, kitchen, fridge, coffeemaker, hair dryer, iron, washer/dryer (in most units).

Royal Kuhio ★ *Kids*   Families, take note: This is one of the best deals in Waikiki. All the units in this high-rise condo are privately owned, and some are owner-occupied. Several companies handle apartments here, but Paradise Management offers some of the best deals. Each of its units has a full kitchen, separate bedrooms, and a living area with a lanai. Because the units are individually owned, they're all decorated and furnished uniquely. It's 2 blocks from Waikiki Beach and within walking distance of everything else of interest. And this is one of the few places in Waikiki where parking is free.

Tips: Ask for a corner unit (they're the nicest); if you plan to go in February, be sure to book a year in advance (it's the condo's busiest month).

2240 Kuhio Ave. (between Royal Hawaiian Ave. and Seaside Ave.), c/o Paradise Mgmt., 50 S. Beretania St., Suite C207, Honolulu, HI 96813. ℂ **808/538-7145.** Fax 808/538-7149. pmchi@verizon.net. 389 units. $140–$145 apt for 4. Extra person $15. AE, DISC, MC, V. Free parking. TheBus: 19 or 20. **Amenities:** Small fitness room; sauna; game room; coin-op washer/dryers; volleyball; billiards; basketball court; shuffleboard; putting green. *In room:* A/C, TV, dataport, kitchen, fridge, coffeemaker, iron.

Hot Package Deals

Waikiki Beachcomber   A room/car package makes this stylish Waikiki hotel a real deal. Room and car for two is just $145 a night (or you can choose their room and breakfast for two for $145). Internet specials start at $110 a night, and Seniors can get up to 50% off the regular rack rate. In addition to the package deals, one of the main pluses of this hotel is the great location—a block from Waikiki Beach, across the street from the upscale Royal Hawaiian Shopping Center, and next door to bargain shopping at the International Market Place. The rooms feature Berber carpets, TV armoires, contemporary furniture, handheld showers, convenient hot pots for making coffee or tea, and voice mail. Yet another reason to stay at this conveniently located hotel is that it hosts *The Magic of Polynesia,* a show with illusionist John Hirokana and the king of Hawaiian entertainment, Don Ho, a Hawaii legend for more than 40 years.

2300 Kalakaua Ave. (at Duke's Lane), Honolulu, HI 96815. ℂ **800/622-4646** or 808/922-4646. Fax 808/926-9973. www.waikikibeachcomber.com. 495 units (shower only). $245–$295 double; from $415 suite. Extra person $30. Internet rates from $110. Room/car packages from $149. AE, DC, MC, V. Parking $10. TheBus: 19 or 20. **Amenities:** Restaurant (poolside coffee shop); Hawaiian entertainment show; outdoor pool; children's program July–Aug; activities desk; car-rental desk; small shopping arcade; limited room service (6am–11am); coin-op washer/dryers; laundry service; dry cleaning. *In room:* A/C, TV, fridge, coffeemaker, hair dryer, iron (on request), safe.

WAIKIKI: DIAMOND HEAD END

You'll find all of these hotels between Ala Wai Boulevard and the ocean, and between Kaiulani Street (1 block Diamond Head from the International Market Place) in the Ewa direction and world-famous Diamond Head itself.

Bamboo *★ Value*   This boutique hotel was so successful they made it into individually owned condos, now managed by Aqua Resorts. Formerly a very neglected budget hotel, just a block from Waikiki Beach, Bamboo has been transformed into a contemporary "condotel" (a condominium/hotel), decorated with an Asian flair. The rooms are stylish and functional with modern furniture, marble bathrooms and with kitchenettes or kitchens. It's in a good location (behind the Hyatt Regency), within walking distance to numerous restaurants and shopping, the Honolulu Zoo, and just 3 minutes to the beach. Since it is small, the staff gives guests personalized attention. When booking, be sure to "reserve" a parking space, as the parking lot has a limited number of spaces.

2425 Kuhio Ave. (Kaiulani Ave.), Honolulu, HI 96815. ℂ **800/367-5004** or 808/922-7777. Fax 808/922-9473. www.aquaresorts.com. 90 units. $99–$175 double; $142–$175 studio double; $158–$235 1-bedroom for 4. Extra person $17. Check out Internet rates which begin at $145 for room and car package. Parking $5. TheBus: 19 or 20. **Amenities:** outdoor pool; Jacuzzi; sauna; concierge; laundry service; dry cleaning. *In room:* A/C, TV, dataport, kitchenette or kitchen, fridge, coffeemaker, hair dryer, iron, safe.

Ocean Resort Hotel Waikiki   Book on the Internet for nearly 50% off the rack rates at this large twin-tower hotel, located on a relatively quiet (for Waikiki) street. The property has been totally renovated and has a brighter, cleaner look. The Diamond

Tower houses the budget rooms; at 325 square feet, they boast new carpet, bedspreads, drapes, and other interior redesigns. These budget rooms have showers only; tub/shower combos are available in the more expensive Pali Tower rooms. All rooms in both towers have refrigerators, and the rooms with kitchenettes have a two-burner hot plate and cooking utensils; those from the ninth floor up also have small lanais. Only a few rooms have coffeemakers, so if you want one, ask for it when you reserve. You'll be a short walk from the Honolulu Zoo, Kapiolani Park, and the Waikiki Aquarium, and just 2 minutes from the beach.

175 Paoakalani Ave. (near Kuhio Ave.), Honolulu, HI 96815. © **800/367-2317** or 808/922-3861. Fax 808/924-1982. www.oceanresort.com. 450 units (some with shower only). $137–$173 double; $183–$230 studio with kitchenette. Internet specials start at $75. Extra person $25. AE, DC, DISC, MC, V. Parking $8. TheBus: 19 or 20. **Amenities:** Restaurant (steak/seafood with live Hawaiian music during dinner); bar; 2 outdoor pools; activity desk; shopping arcade; salon; babysitting; laundry service; currency exchange desk. *In room:* A/C, TV, kitchenette (some units), fridge, coffeemaker (on request), hair dryer, iron, safe.

Queen Kapiolani Hotel   Named for Queen Kapiolani (1834–99), the wife of Hawaii's last king, David Kalakaua (1836–91), this hotel harks back to the days of the Hawaiian monarchs. The 19th-century flavor of the place reflects those grand days, with 10-foot chandeliers in the main dining room and a full-size portrait of the queen in the lobby. The plush decor, however, doesn't extend to the budget rooms, which are quite small. For just a few bucks more, get the superior room. Not only is it double in size but the shoreline views are vastly—well, superior. The property's location is great: just across the street from Kapiolani Park, a half-block to the beach, and within walking distance of the Honolulu Zoo, the Waikiki Aquarium, and the activities of Waikiki. For even more savings, book on the Internet where rates are nearly 50% off rack rates.

150 Kapahulu Ave. (at Lemon Rd., across from Kapiolani Park), Honolulu, HI 96815. © Castle Resorts and Hotels, **800/367-5004** or 808/922-1941. Fax 808/596-0518 or 808/922-2694. www.queenkapiolani.com. 315 units. $130–$220 double; $225–$250 studio double with kitchenette; $325–$425 1-bedroom suite with kitchenette (sleeps up to 4). Check for Internet specials which start at $72. Extra person $17. Children 18 and under stay free in parent's room using existing bedding. AE, DC, DISC, MC, V. Parking $7. TheBus: 19 or 20. **Amenities:** 2 restaurants (one with a tasty, budget-priced buffet); bar; large outdoor pool; municipal tennis courts nearby; concierge; activity desk; salon; babysitting; coin-op washer/dryers; laundry service; dry cleaning. *In room:* A/C, TV, some kitchenettes, fridge, coffeemaker, hair dryer (available on request), iron (on request), safe.

Royal Grove Hotel ⭐ *Value*   This is a great bargain for frugal travelers. You can't miss the Royal Grove—it's bright pink. Among Waikiki's canyons of corporate-owned high-rises, it's also a rarity in another way: The Royal Grove is a small, family-owned hotel. What you get here is old-fashioned aloha in cozy accommodations along the lines of Motel 6—basic and clean. For years *Frommer's* readers have written about the aloha spirit of the Fong family; they love the potluck dinners and get-togethers the Fongs have organized so their guests can get to know one another. And you can't do better for the price—this has to be *the* bargain of Waikiki. For $45 (about the same price a couple would pay to stay in a private room at the hostel in Waikiki), you get a clean room in the older Mauka Wing, with a double bed or two twins, plus a kitchenette with refrigerator and stove. I suggest that you spend a few dollars more and go for an air-conditioned room ($62) to help drown out the street noise. Even the most expensive unit, a one-bedroom suite with three beds and kitchenette for $75 to $77, is half the price of similar accommodations elsewhere. At these rates, you won't mind that maid service is only twice a week.

The hotel is built around a courtyard pool, and the beach is just a 3-minute walk away. All of Waikiki's attractions are within walking distance. *Tip:* If you book 7 nights or more from April to November, you'll get a discount on the already low rates.

151 Uluniu Ave. (between Prince Edward and Kuhio aves.), Honolulu, HI 96815. © **808/923-7691.** Fax 808/922-7508. www.royalgrovehotel.com. 85 units. $45 double (no A/C); $62 standard double; $75–$77 standard 1-bedroom. Extra person $10. AE, DC, DISC, MC, V. Parking nearby $6. TheBus: 19 or 20. **Amenities:** Pool; activities desk; coin-op washer/dryers. *In room:* A/C (most rooms), TV, kitchen, fridge.

Waikiki Sand Villa   Budget travelers, take note: This very affordable hotel is located on the quieter side of Waikiki, across the street from the Ala Wai Canal. The 10-story tower has medium-size rooms, most with a double bed plus a single bed (convenient for families) and a lanai with great views of the green mountains. The adjacent three-story building features studio apartments with kitchenettes (refrigerator, stove, and microwave). Another plus for families is the Nintendo system in every room (available for $7.95 an hour). For guests arriving early or catching a late flight, there's a hospitality room (complete with shower) for late checkout and a luggage-storage area.

2375 Ala Wai Blvd. (entrance on Kanekapolei Ave.), Honolulu, HI 96815. © **800/247-1903** or 808/922-4744. Fax 808/923-2541. www.waikiki-hotel.com. 214 units. $125–$168 double; $220–$347 studio with kitchenette. Internet specials start as low as $81. Rates include continental breakfast served poolside every morning. Extra person $20. Children under 12 stay free in parent's room using existing bedding. AE, DC, DISC, MC, V. Parking $9. TheBus: 19 or 20. **Amenities:** 70-ft. outdoor pool, which has its own island in the middle and an adjoining whirlpool spa; activities desk; coin-op washer/dryers; laundry service; dry cleaning. *In room:* A/C, TV w/Nintendo, dataport (with free Internet access), kitchenette (in some rooms), fridge (in some rooms), coffeemaker (in some rooms), safe.

An Especially Gay-Friendly Hotel
The Cabana at Waikiki   Located on a quiet street in Waikiki, this boutique hotel caters to a clientele of gay men and features exquisitely decorated rooms. Each has a queen bed and pullout sofa bed, entertainment center with VCR and CD player, lanai, and well-equipped kitchenette. A free continental breakfast is served every morning. Free Internet access is available in the lobby. A giant, eight-person spa also is on the property. The Cabana is within walking distance of gay nightclubs and the gay scene at Queen's Surf Beach.

2551 Cartwright Rd. (between Paoakalani and Kapahulu aves.), Honolulu, HI 96815. © **877/902-2121** or 808/926-5555. Fax 808/926-5566. www.cabana-waikiki.com. 15 units. $129–$175 double. Rates include continental breakfast. Internet rates start at $99. Extra person $15. AE, DC, DISC, MC, V. Parking $8. TheBus: 19 or 20. **Amenities:** Complimentary access to nearby (about a 15-min. walk) fitness complex; Jacuzzi; concierge; coin-op washer/dryers. *In room:* A/C, TV, dataport, kitchenette, fridge, coffeemaker, hair dryer, iron, safe.

For Month-Long Stays
Waikiki Lei Apartments ✓*Value*   If you plan to be on Oahu for a month, these fully furnished studio apartments work out to be quite a deal—just about $25 a day. Built in 1967, the four-story walk-up (no elevator) building has been well maintained through the years and offers clean, comfortable budget apartments on a long-term basis. It's located in a residential neighborhood of apartment and condo buildings, 5 blocks from the beach and 1 block from the bus stop. Don't expect *Architectural Digest* interiors—or even matching furnishings—but each apartment has a full kitchen, two twin beds, a dresser, a dining room table and chairs, towels, and bed linens. The manager's name is Charlie; tell him Frommer's sent you.

241 Kaiulani Ave. (between Cleghorn and Tusitala sts., 1 block from Kuhio Ave.), Honolulu, HI 96815. © **808/923-6656.** Fax 808/922-9105. www.waikikileiapartments.com. 20 studios. $750–$850 per month double (students $650 a month). 30-night minimum. No credit cards. Limited parking available. TheBus: 19 or 20. **Amenities:** Coin-op washer/dryers. *In room:* TV, kitchen, fridge, coffeemaker, no phone.

Super-Cheap Sleeps

Edmunds Hotel Apartments (*Value*)   This small, modest place isn't for everyone, but students and travelers on extra-tight budgets will be delighted to find these clean and neat studios. Don't expect color-coordinated interiors—don't even expect a phone. These are basic studios with beds, bathrooms, TVs, and small kitchenettes with stove, refrigerator, toaster, and pots and pans. There's no air-conditioning, and leaving the windows wide open means even more noise from the constantly bustling Ala Wai Boulevard. But with rates this low, you can invest in some earplugs.

2411 Ala Wai Blvd. (at Kaiulani St.), Honolulu, HI 96815. © 808/923-8381. 8 studios (with shower only). $75 double in high season; $45 double in low season. Extra person $10. 2-night minimum. No credit cards. No parking. The-Bus: 19 or 20. *In room:* TV, kitchenette, fridge, coffeemaker.

Hokondo Waikiki Beachside Hostel   Once an apartment building, now an unique configuration for a hostel. Each former apartment unit is now a four- to eight-person dorm (bed linens are provided), complete with a full kitchen (equipped with pots, pans, and dishware), cable television, private bathroom, safebox, lanai, daily housekeeping, air conditioner, and phone. Dorm rooms are either co-ed or female only. For those who are not fans of dorm rooms and want a little more privacy, there are semi-private bedrooms with your own lanai and a lockable door. The semi-private rooms are located in the bedroom of the former apartment units. You'll share kitchen and bathroom with one to four other travelers who are in single, dorm-type beds in the living room. Also on property is a high-speed Internet cafe with 10 computers you may use for only $1 for 10 minutes. The hostel has lots of free amenities like ocean toys (rafts and beach mats), electronic safes, local calls, and daily continental break-fast. Even the rooms offer more than most hostels: storage facilities for extra luggage; air conditioning; full kitchens used by no more than eight people; telephones; cable television, daily housekeeping; and parking ($5 a day). All this and just a half block to the beach and 1 block to Kapiolani Park with the Honolulu Zoo and Waikiki Shell.

2556 Lemon (Kapahulu Blvd), Honolulu, Hi 96815. © 866/478-3888 or 808/923-9566. Fax 808/923-7525. www. hokondo.com. 155 dorm beds and 14 semi-private rooms. $18 per person for 8-person dorm; $24–$27 per person for 4-person dorm; $50–$59 double semi-private. Parking $5. AE, DISC, MC, V. TheBus: 19 or 20. **Amenities:** Complimentary beach mats, rafts, safes, local phone calls, continental breakfast; high-speed Internet cafe; beach equipment rental; coin-op laundry; barbecue area; message and mail service. *In-room:* A/C, TV, full kitchen, daily maid service.

Hostelling International–Waikiki   A couple of blocks from the beach is a safe, clean alternative for travelers on a shoestring budget. Housed in a converted apartment building, this hostel features the option of dorm rooms (four beds to a room with a shared bathroom) or private studios that sleep two people, with their own private bathroom. The common areas include an immaculately clean full kitchen and a lounge area with TV and VCR; the covered patio area is great for lounging, and there's a complimentary locked storage area adjacent. The staff is friendly, the guests tend to be a young international crowd, and the price is easy on the wallet. Note that there is a maximum stay of 7 nights.

2417 Prince Edward St. (between Kaiulani and Uluniu sts.), Honolulu, HI 96815. © 808/926-8313. Fax 808/922-3798. www.hostelsaloha.com. 50 dorm beds; 4 studios with private bathrooms (showers only). $20 bed for Hostelling International members; $23 bed for nonmembers; $48 studio double for Hostelling International members; $54 studio double for nonmembers. AE, MC, V. Parking $5. TheBus: 19 or 20. **Amenities:** Coin-op washer/dryers; Internet access on their computer 10¢ a min.

Waikiki Prince Hotel   Located next door to the Hostelling International, this is a step up from a hostel, in that you actually get a room, ranging from a teeny, tiny, unbelievably small room (for $45) to a room with a kitchenette (for $65–$75). Single women should be aware that this is not the greatest neighborhood to be walking around by yourself after dark, and, in fact, you will notice lots of deadbolts and other security measures here. The 30 rooms in this six story ultra-budget property face outside and all have private bathrooms, air conditioning, a lanai, TV, microwave, and small refrigerator. For a few bucks more you can upgrade to a room with a kitchenette (stove, rice cooker, toaster). The only thing they do not have is phones in the rooms. All rooms are nonsmoking. Maid service is weekly, but you can pick up clean towels every day from the front desk. There is very limited parking (make sure to reserve when you book) and there are coin-operated laundry facilities on property.

2431 Prince Edward St. (between Kaiulani and Uluniu sts.), Honolulu, HI 96815. (✆ 808/922-1544. Fax 808/924-3712. www.waikikiprince.com. 30 units. $45–$55 double (extremely small room); $50–$55 small room; $60–65 small room with kitchenette; $65–$75 standard room with kitchenette. Additional person $6 day. AE, MC, V. Parking $5. TheBus: 19 or 20. **Amenities:** Coin-op washer/dryers. *In room:* AC, TV, kitchenette (some rooms), fridge, microwave, weekly maid service. No Phones.

JUST BEYOND WAIKIKI: ALA MOANA
SUPER-CHEAP SLEEPS
Central Branch YMCA *Value*   If you can't afford Waikiki's prices, the Central Y is a good alternative; it's ultra-cheap, and just a short 5-minute walk from Waikiki. Women are welcome here, but in the rooms with private bathrooms only. The rooms are small and furnished in monkish style: bed, desk, phone, and shower—no air-conditioning, no TV. There's a common room with a TV. Guests also have use of all the Y's facilities—sauna, outdoor pool, gym, handball courts, and other athletic facilities—at no additional charge. Meals are available at the low-cost restaurant in the building. Absolutely no smoking.

401 Atkinson Dr. (at Ala Moana Blvd., across from Ala Moana Center), Honolulu, HI 96814. (✆ 808/941-3344. 114 units. $35 single with shared bathroom (men only); $41 double with shared bathroom (men only); $43 single with private bathroom; $53 double with private bathroom. AE, DC, MC, V. Free parking 6pm–6am. TheBus: 6, 8, or 20. **Amenities:** Small Japanese-style deli; outdoor pool; full fitness facilities; coin-op washer/dryers.

WORTH A SPLURGE
Ala Moana Hotel   This hotel's 1,152 rooms on 36 floors make it feel like a metropolis. Its proximity to Waikiki, the downtown financial and business district, the new convention center, and Hawaii's largest mall, the Ala Moana Center, makes it a popular spot for out-of-state visitors and locals alike. Lots of Asian tourists choose the Ala Moana Hotel, probably because the management does an excellent job of providing a multilingual staff and translators. Most guests are people attending a convention at the convention center, a short 2-minute walk away, or shoppers, mostly from neighboring islands (especially in Dec). The rooms vary in size according to price: The cheaper rooms are small, but all come with two double beds and all the amenities you'll need to make your stay comfortable. The views of Waikiki and Honolulu from the upper floors are spectacular.

410 Atkinson Dr. (at Kona St., next to Ala Moana Center), Honolulu, HI 96814. (✆ 800/367-6025 or 808/955-4811. Fax 808/944-6839. www.alamoanahotel.com. 1,152 units. $135–$235 double; from $285 suite. Internet specials as low as $109. Extra person $30. Children under 18 stay free in parent's room. AE, DC, DISC, MC, V. Valet parking $14, self-parking $10. TheBus: 19 or 20. **Amenities:** 5 restaurants (from coffee shop to exquisite Japanese food); 2 bars (plus a Polynesian show); large outdoor pool; small fitness room; game room; concierge; activities desk; business center; shopping arcade; salon; limited room service (6:30am–10:30pm); coin-op washer/dryers; laundry service; dry cleaning. *In room:* A/C, TV, dataport, fridge, coffeemaker, hair dryer, iron, safe.

HONOLULU BEYOND WAIKIKI

Once you move beyond the confines of Waikiki—and away from that world-famous beach—to other areas of the city, your options widen to include some wonderful B&Bs and inns in lovely, leafy residential neighborhoods; inexpensive family-owned hotels usually catering to neighbor islanders, but with lots of aloha spirit for new-comers as well; and some great bargain bunks for travelers on a shoestring budget. (If you're looking for a place to stay near the airport, see "Near Honolulu International Airport," below.)

Aloha B&B   Perched on a hillside in the residential community of Hawaii Kai is this very affordable B&B, complete with swimming pool, panoramic ocean views, and a continental breakfast served on the outdoor lanai. The three bedrooms (one with a king bed, one queen and one with twins) share a bath and a half (no waiting for the toilet!). It's a 10-minute drive to snorkeling in Hanauma Bay and about a 15-minute drive to Waikiki and downtown Honolulu. Hostess Phyllis Young has lots of beach toys (including coolers, mats, boogie boards, and beach chairs) that she'll loan you for the day. Self laundry for $4. No smoking inside or outside.

909 Kahauloa Place, Honolulu, HI 96825. ✆ **808/395-6694.** Fax 808/396-2020. http://home.hawaii.rr.com/aloha phyllis. 3 units with shared bathrooms. $60–$75 double. Rates include continental breakfast. 2-night minimum. No credit cards. Free parking. TheBus: 22 (stops at the bottom of a steep, up-hill climb. **Amenities:** Pool; laundry facilities. *In room:* TV.

Diamond Head Bed & Breakfast ✦ *Finds*   Hostess Joanne and her longtime housekeeper, Sumiko, offer a quiet, relaxing place to stay on the far side of Kapiolani Park, away from the hustle and bustle of Waikiki. Staying here is like venturing back 50 years to a time when kamaaina (native-born) families built huge houses with airy rooms opening onto big lanais and tropical gardens. The house is filled with family heirlooms and Joanne's artwork. One of the two rooms features the beyond-king-size carved koa bed that once belonged to Princess Ruth, a member of Hawaii's royal family. You'll feel like royalty sleeping in it.

Noela Dr. (at Paki Ave., off Diamond Head Rd.), Honolulu. Reservations: Hawaii's Best Bed & Breakfasts, P.O. Box 758, Volcano, HI 96785. ✆ **800/262-9912** or 808/985-7488. Fax 808/967-8610. www.bestbnb.com. 2 units. $115 double. Rates include full breakfast. Extra person $30. 2-night minimum. No credit cards. Free parking. TheBus: 2. *In room:* TV, fridge, hair dryer.

J&B's Haven   Brits Joan and Barbara Webb have had a successful bed-and-breakfast on Oahu since 1982. Both Joan, who moved to Hawaii in 1981, and her daughter Barbara, who has lived here since 1970, are knowledgeable about Oahu's attractions and love introducing guests to Hawaii. They recently moved to this beautiful house in Hawaii Kai, just 15 minutes east of Waikiki (on the other side of Diamond Head) and close to Hanauma Bay, Sandy Beach, and Sea Life Park, as well as within easy reach of three shopping centers with excellent restaurants. There are two rooms in the house: the large master bedroom, with private bathroom, king bed, mini-refrigerator, and microwave; and a smaller room with a small refrigerator. *Note:* This is a smoke-free house. They have two very friendly dogs that live inside, so if you are allergic to canine roommates, you might look elsewhere.

Kahena St. (at Ainapo St., off Hawaii Kai Dr.), Hawaii Kai. Reservations: P.O. Box 25907, Honolulu, HI 96825. ✆ **808/396-9462.** http://home.hawaii.rr.com/jnbshaven. 2 units. $75–$85 double. Rates include continental breakfast. Extra person $10. 2-night minimum. No credit cards. Free parking. TheBus: 1. *In room:* TV, fridge, microwave.

Manoa Valley Inn ⋆ (Finds)   It's completely off the tourist trail and far from the beach, but that doesn't stop travelers from heading to this historic 1915 Carpenter Gothic home, on a quiet residential street near the University of Hawaii. This eight-room Manoa landmark—it's on the National Register of Historic Places—offers a glimpse into the lifestyles of the rich and famous of early Honolulu.

Those who find resorts impersonal will find the eclectically furnished inn refreshing. Each room has its own unique decor, and each has been named for a prominent figure in Hawaii's history. The John Guild Suite, for instance, has a parlor with antiques and old-fashioned rose wallpaper; the adjoining bedroom contains a king-size koa bed, while the bathroom features an old-style tub as well as a separate modern shower. The three top-floor rooms share a full bathroom; the others have private bathrooms. A genteel ambience pervades the entire place. Guests regularly gather in the parlor to listen to the Victrola or play the nickelodeon. There's also a billiards room with an antique billiards table, a piano in the living room, and croquet set up in the backyard.

2001 Vancouver Dr. (at University Ave.), Honolulu, HI 96822. ℂ 808/947-6019. Fax 808/946-6168. www.manoavalley inn.com. 10 units (3 with shared bathroom). $99–$125 double with shared bathroom; $140–$170 double with private bathroom (shower only); $150 cottage double. Rates include continental breakfast. MC, V. Free parking. TheBus: 4 or 6. Children 8 and older preferred. **Amenities:** In-room massage; laundry service. *In room:* A/C (some rooms), TV (some rooms), dataport, safe.

Pagoda Hotel   This is where local residents from neighbor islands stay when they come to Honolulu. Close to shopping and downtown, the Pagoda has been serving Hawaii's island community for decades. This modest hotel has very plain (motel-ish) rooms: clean and utilitarian with no extra frills. For a quieter room, ask for the mountain view, where you'll be away from the street noise. Kitchenettes are available. There's easy access to Waikiki via TheBus—the nearest stop is just a half block away. Ask about the car packages: For the price of most rooms, you can get a free car. Studios and one- and two-bedroom units have kitchenettes. *Tip:* Rates Sunday through Thursday are cheaper than weekend rates.

1525 Rycroft St. (between Keeaumoku and Kaheka sts.), Honolulu, HI 96814. ℂ 800/367-6060 or 808/923-4511. Fax 808/922-8061. www.pagodahotel.com. 361 units. $113–$133 studio double; $138–$158 1-bedroom double (sleeps up to 4); $163–$193 1-bedroom deluxe double (sleeps up to 6); $173–$203 2-bedroom double (sleeps up to 5). Extra person $15. Free cribs available. Ask about free breakfast packages (from $95) and excellent car/room deals (from $100). AE, DC, DISC, MC, V. Parking $5. TheBus: 5 or 6. **Amenities:** Restaurant; bar; 2 outdoor pools; activities desk; salon; babysitting; coin-op washer/dryers; laundry service; dry cleaning. *In room:* A/C, TV, dataport, kitchenette (some units), fridge, coffeemaker, hair dryer, iron, safe.

SUPER-CHEAP SLEEPS

Fernhurst YWCA (Finds)   This Y, located in a quiet residential area, offers accommodations for women only. Each room in the 1950s-style dorms has two beds, two dressers, a phone, and shares a bathroom with the adjacent room. For a quieter unit, ask for a room facing Poki Street and away from Wilder Avenue. The Y recently renovated all the rooms, bringing in a bright, airy, modern look. Extremely safe (only guests are allowed in the dorm area) and budget priced (breakfast and dinner Mon–Fri are included in the cost), this is a good alternative for women traveling solo. Guests have use of all the facilities: swimming pool, laundry room, lounge area, piano, TV, and sewing machine. Nearby bus routes will get you anywhere you want to go on Oahu.

1566 Wilder Ave. (at Punahou Ave.), Honolulu, HI 96822. ℂ 808/941-2231. Fax 808/949-0266. www.ywcaoahu.org. 100 units (all with shared bathroom). $48 per person. Rates include breakfast and dinner Mon–Fri. After 3 nights, you must join the YWCA ($30 per year; $15 a year for women over 65). MC, V. Parking $3. TheBus: 4 or 5. Men not accepted.

Hostelling International—Honolulu   A block from the University of Hawaii is this cheap alternative place to stay. Tucked into the crowded residential community of Manoa, this spotless oasis is surrounded by plants, picnic tables, and the sound of dozens of languages being spoken. Mrs. Akau makes sure that guests are happy and that the house rules are met. The rooms are dormitory style, with three to four beds in each room with a shared bathroom. For an additional $10, your hostess will happily arrange the beds so a party of two to four can share the same room. Guests also have use of a full kitchen and a recently renovated common room with TV, VCR, stereo, and games. A blackboard lists all the activities available, ranging from low-cost tours to hiking trips. Off-street parking is extremely limited and street parking is unheard of in this neighborhood, so think twice about staying here if you rent a car. A nearby bus stop gives you access to Waikiki and the rest of Oahu.

2323-A Seaview Ave. (at University Ave.), Honolulu, HI 96822. © 808/946-0591. Fax 808/946-5904. www.hostels aloha.com. 43 beds (with shared bathroom, shower only), 2 private units (with shared bathroom). $16 dorm beds for members of Hostelling International; $19 dorm beds for nonmembers; $42 double private room for members, $48 for nonmembers. AE, MC, V. Free limited parking. TheBus: 4 or 6.

Nuuanu YMCA *Value*   This modern facility offers accommodations for single men only. Budget travelers will welcome the $30-a-night rate—they'll also love the fact that buses stop right in front of the building. The rooms feature a single bed, desk, and dresser. Only two units have private bathrooms, so book early. Guests have use of all facilities: fitness center, pool, weight room, cardiovascular workout room, martial arts center, and aerobic classes. Other perks include a jogging path, video games, and a microwave. *Hot tip:* Request a room that doesn't face the noisy Pali Highway.

1441 Pali Hwy. (at Vineyard St.), Honolulu, HI 96813. © 808/536-3556. Fax 808/521-1182. 70 units (some with shared bathroom; showers only). $30 single with shared bathroom; $37 single with private bathroom. AE, MC, V. Free parking. TheBus: 1, 2, 4, 6. Women and children not accepted. **Amenities:** Cafeteria (open 6:30am–6:30pm); pool; 2 tennis courts (lit for night play); full fitness facilities; sauna; coin-op washer/dryers.

NEAR HONOLULU INTERNATIONAL AIRPORT

Best Western—The Plaza Hotel   If you've got a flight that arrives late or leaves early, this is an okay place to spend the night. But the prices are high and the rooms only so-so, so don't stay here for more than just a layover. There's free shuttle service to the airport (less than 5 min. away).

3253 N. Nimitz Hwy. (at Paiea St.), Honolulu, HI 96819. © 800/800-4683 or 808/836-3636. Fax 808/834-7406. www.bestwesternhonolulu.com. 274 units. $159–$169 double. Internet specials from $115. Extra person $20. AE, DC, DISC, MC, V. Free parking. Free shuttle van to and from airport. TheBus: 19 or 20. **Amenities:** Restaurant; bar; outdoor pool; limited room service; coin-op washer/dryers; laundry/dry cleaning service; airport shuttle service. *In room:* A/C, TV, fridge, coffeemaker, hair dryer.

Honolulu Airport Hotel   Just minutes from the airport via a free shuttle, this convenient airport hotel is the best of the lot, but still recommended only for a quick layover. Two four-story buildings wrap around an outdoor swimming pool and garden. There are noise problems here, though; the walls seem thin. If you don't have a lot of luggage, ask for a room well away from the elevator (late at night, lively guests tend to get louder). Nonsmoking and wheelchair-accessible rooms are available.

3401 N. Nimitz Hwy. (Rodgers St.), Honolulu, HI 96819. © 800/800-3477 or 808/833-0661. Fax 808/833-1738. www.honoluluairporthotel.com. 308 units. $125–$146 double. Internet special at press time was $95, or a car/room package for $115. Extra person $20. AE, DISC, MC, V. Free parking. TheBus: 19 or 20. **Amenities:** Restaurant and bar with entertainment; outdoor pool; coin-op washer/dryers; airport shuttle service. *In room:* A/C, TV, fridge, coffeemaker, hair dryer.

EN ROUTE TO PEARL HARBOR: PEARL CITY

Rainbow Inn ℛ *Finds*   Here's one of Oahu's best bed-and-breakfast deals. This private tropical garden studio, downstairs from the home of retired military officer Gene Smith and his wife, Betty, has panoramic views of Pearl Harbor, the entire south coast of Oahu, and the Waianae and Koolau mountains. A large stone deck and full-size pool are just outside the apartment's door; inside, the apartment features a double bed, washer/dryer, and kitchen. The Smiths are happy to lend their guests any beach and picnic equipment they might need—ice chests of all sizes and shapes, beach mats and chairs, even wine glasses. Located close to Pearl Ridge Shopping Center, Rainbow Inn is close to all of Oahu's attractions, yet far enough way to provide you with lots of peace and quiet. Reserve early.

98–1049 Mahola Place (off Kaonohi St., 2 miles from Kamehameha Hwy.), Pearl Ridge, Aiea, HI 96701. ✆ **808/ 488-7525.** Fax 808/487-1879. http://hometown.aol.com/gsmith3777/myhomepage/business.html. 1 apt. $95 double. Rates include refrigerator very well-stocked with breakfast items. Extra person $10. 3-night minimum. No credit cards. Free parking. TheBus: 20, 50, 51, or 52. **Amenities:** Outdoor pool. *In room:* A/C, TV/VCR, kitchen, fridge, coffeemaker, washer/dryer.

THE WINDWARD COAST

All of these accommodations are located on the other side of the Koolau Range on the lush Windward Coast, in or near the quiet residential communities of Kailua and Kaneohe. These communities are about a 30-minute drive from Waikiki and Honolulu.

Alii Bluffs Windward Bed-and-Breakfast   Located on a quiet residential street just 15 minutes from the beach, this traditional B&B is filled with antiques and collectibles as well as the owners' original art. The guest wing has two rooms, one with a double bed and adjacent bathroom, the other with two extra-long twins and a bathroom across the hall. The yard blooms with tropical plants, and the view of Kaneohe Bay from the pool area is breathtaking. Lots of extras make this B&B stand out from the crowd: daily maid service, a large breakfast served on the poolside lanai, afternoon tea, and sewing kits in the bathroom—they'll even lend you anything you need for the beach.

46–251 Ikiiki St. (off Kamehameha Hwy.), Kaneohe, HI 96744. ✆ **800/235-1151** or 808/235-1124. Fax 808/236- 4877. www.hawaiiscene.com/aliibluffs. 2 units. $65–$75 double. Rates include continental breakfast. 3-night minimum. MC, V. Free parking. TheBus: 55 or 65. Children must be 16 or older. **Amenities:** Outdoor pool. *In room:* Hair dryer, no phone.

Fairway View Bed-and-Breakfast *Value*   Hostess Louise "Weezie" Wooden calls her bed-and-breakfast a "homestay," because after staying with her and her husband, Neal (a retired naval aviator and communicator), you'll feel completely at home. Located on the second fairway of the Mid-Pacific Golf Course and just a half-mile from Kailua Beach, Fairway View offers comfortable accommodations at a budget price. The two guest rooms share a large bathroom with tub and shower: one features a queen bed, koa furniture, a small TV, and a minifridge; the other has white wicker twin beds, koa-framed Hawaiian art, and a minifridge. Most of the action, including breakfast, takes place in the family room, which has a spectacular view of the golf course and the Koolau Mountains in the background. Smokers can light up out on the adjacent covered lanai.

515 Paumakua Place, Kailua, HI 96734. ✆ **888/263-6439,** 808/263-6439, or 808/262-0485. www.fairwayview bnb.com. 2 units (with shared bathroom). $45–$60 single; $50–$65 double. Rates include continental breakfast. 3- night minimum. No credit cards. Free parking. TheBus: 56, 57, or 70. *In room:* TV, minifridge.

Kailua Tradewinds *(Finds)*   This is really more of a vacation rental, since no breakfast is served. Hosts Jona and Ken Williams offer two guest rooms with private entrances, both renovated in 2002. Each of the studios has a queen bed and a well-equipped kitchenette, and they open onto a swimming pool and a large garden. The location, in a safe, quiet neighborhood, is excellent, and it's just a few minutes' drive to Kailua's restaurants and shopping. Jona has all kinds of beach accessories—towels, mats, chairs, and coolers—that you're welcome to take with you to Kailua Beach, which is only a short walk away.

391 Auwinala Rd. (at Wanaao Rd., next to Enchanted Lakes, a neighborhood within Kailua), Kailua, HI 96734. (✆ **808/262-1008.** Fax 808/261-0316. www.kailuaoahuhawaii.com/kt.htm. 2 units. $80. Extra person $10. 3-night minimum. No credit cards. Free parking. TheBus: 57. **Amenities:** Outdoor swimming pool. *In room:* A/C, TV, kitchenette, fridge, coffeemaker.

Manu Mele Bed-and-Breakfast *(Finds)*   Just a few minutes' walk from Kailua Bay is Manu Mele ("bird song"), a vacation rental with two separate units around the garden and swimming pool. The largest unit, the Hibiscus Room, features a king bed and large bathroom with double vanity. The smaller Pikake Room has a queen bed and full bathroom. Both rooms have tile floors, a nice mix of antiques and modern furniture, Laura Ashley linens, and a kitchenette. Hostess Carol Isaacs, originally from England, has been running Manu Mele for more than a decade; she loves helping travelers plan their visit to Oahu. She stocks the refrigerators with 3 days' worth of muffins, fruit, and coffee to get her visitors started.

153 Kailuana Place (at Kalaheo Ave.), Kailua, HI 96734. (✆ **808/262-0016.** www.pixi.com/~manumele. 2 units (with shower only). $80–$90 double. Rates include continental breakfast items in refrigerator at beginning of stay. 2-night minimum. No credit cards. Free parking. TheBus: 52, 55, or 56. **Amenities:** Outdoor pool. *In room:* A/C, TV, kitchenette, fridge, coffeemaker.

Papaya Paradise *(Finds)*   The two units here have private entrances and are furnished in tropical rattan and wicker. Each has two beds and a ceiling fan, and they both open onto a pool and Jacuzzi surrounded by tropical plants and flowers. A refrigerator and microwave are also available. Bob and his wife Jeanette, who have been doing this for 17 years, love sitting on the poolside lanai at breakfast, sharing stories with their guests (Bob has many, many stories). Visitors include a large number of German tourists and people with a sense of humor.

395 Auwinala Rd. (at Wanaao Rd., next to the Enchanted Lake area), Kailua, HI 96734. (✆ and fax **808/261-0316.** www.kailuaoahuhawaii.com. 2 units (with shower only). $95–$100 double. Rate includes continental breakfast. Extra person $15. 3-night minimum. No credit cards. Free parking. TheBus: 56 or 57. **Amenities:** Outdoor pool. *In room:* A/C, TV, kitchenette, fridge, coffeemaker.

Schrader's Windward Marine Resort   Despite the name, the ambience here is more motel than resort, but Schrader's offers a good alternative for families. The property is nestled in a tranquil, tropical setting on Kaneohe Bay, only a 30-minute drive from Waikiki. The complex is made up of cottage-style motels and a collection of older homes. Cottages contain either a kitchenette with refrigerator and microwave or a full kitchen. There's also a picnic area with barbecue grills. Prices are based on the views; depending on how much you're willing to pay, you can look out over a Kahuluu fish pond, the Koolau Mountains, or Kaneohe Bay. Lots of watersports are available at an additional cost; don't miss the complimentary boat cruise on Wednesday and Saturday. *Hot tip:* When booking, ask for a unit with a lanai; that way, you'll end up with at least a partial view of the bay.

47–039 Lihikai Dr. (off Kamehameha Hwy.), Kaneohe, HI 96744. ☎ **800/735-5071** or 808/239-5711. Fax 808/239-6658. www.hawaiiscene.com/schrader. 20 units. $72–$143 1-bedroom double; $127–$215 2-bedroom for 4; $226–$358 3-bedroom for 6; $446–$501 4-bedroom for 8. Rates include continental breakfast. Additional person $7.50. 2-night minimum. AE, DC, DISC, MC, V. Free parking. TheBus: 52, 55, or 56. **Amenities:** Outdoor pool; watersports/equipment rentals. *In room:* TV, kitchenette, fridge, coffeemaker.

Sharon's Serenity ☆ *(Finds)*   What a setting! In the backyard, beyond the pool and the deck and the grassy lawn, run the slow-moving waters of a canal, framed by the greens of the Mid-Pacific Golf Course and the lush Koolau Range in the distance. Serenity is indeed the word. Hostess Sharon Price has a warm, welcoming attitude that makes you feel at home. And what a home it is—a huge living area with three large couches, a giant kitchen, and two guest rooms to choose from: one with pool view and a king bed as well as a twin, the other with a queen bed in a more romantic ambience. Kailua Beach is just a couple of blocks away, but the atmosphere is so relaxing here that sometimes guests may not want to leave. Sharon has an adorably chubby Bichon Frise who loves everyone, plus another dog and a couple of indoor-outdoor cats.

127 Kakahiaka St. (Mahelani St.), Kailua, HI 96734. ☎ **800/914-2271**, 808/263-3634, or 808/262-5621. www.sharonsserenity.com. 2 units. $70–$85 double. Rates include continental breakfast. Extra person $10. 3-night minimum. No credit cards. Free parking. TheBus: 56 or 57. **Amenities:** Outdoor pool. *In room:* TV, fridge, iron.

Sheffield House *(Kids)*   Unlike many other B&Bs, Sheffield House welcomes children. The owners, Paul Sheffield and his wife, Rachel, have three kids, so things like a portable baby bed are no problem. There are two units here, a one-bedroom and a studio (which is fully wheelchair-accessible), each with a private entry (through elaborately landscaped tropical gardens), with full kitchen. The two units can be combined and rented as two-bedroom/two-bathroom accommodations.

131 Kuulei Rd. (at Kalaheo Dr.), Kailua, HI 96734. ☎ and fax **808/262-0721**. Rachel@hawaiisheffieldhouse.com. 2 units. $75 double studio (shower only); $95 double apt. (some lower rates depending on the season). Rates include 1st day's continental breakfast. Extra person $10. 3-night minimum. MC, V. Free parking. TheBus: 56 or 57. *In room:* TV, kitchen, fridge, coffeemaker.

THE NORTH SHORE

Laie Inn   This two-story, plantation-style hotel, within walking distance of the Polynesian Cultural Center, Brigham Young University Hawaii, and the Mormon Temple, is scheduled to be torn down and replaced with four separate three-story buildings on the eight-acre site. As we went to press, there was no firm date on construction, so the Laie Inn, which is badly in need of renovation (bedding and towels are old and worn, paint is peeling, some air conditioners sound like they are on their last leg), will remain open. The staff, however, is as friendly as you will find anywhere in Hawaii. They know that the old place is not up to par, and they make up for it in cheerfulness and helpfulness. The rates do include a small continental breakfast (if you are still hungry, there's a McDonald's across the street).

55–109 Laniloa St. (off Kamehameha Hwy., near the Polynesian Cultural Center), Laie, HI 96762. ☎ **800/526-4562** or 808/293-9282. Fax 808/293-8115. www.laieinn.com. 49 units. $89–$99 double. Extra person $10. Children under 18 stay free in parent's room. AE, DISC, MC, V. Free parking. TheBus: 52 or 55. **Amenities:** Outdoor pool; activities desk; coin-op washer/dryers. *In room:* A/C, TV, fridge.

Ke Iki Beach Bungalows   This collection of rustic studio, one-, and two-bedroom duplex cottages, located on a beautiful white-sand beach, was under total renovation, to the tune of $1 million, as we went to press. All units are being remodeled and the studios were being razed. Everything should be complete in 2006; the end product will have no resemblance to the old ramshackle budget bungalows which have stood here for decades. Prices have gone up, but considering the units are snuggled on a large lot with its own 200-foot stretch of white-sand beach between two legendary surf spots, Waimea Bay and Banzai Pipeline, the units are still affordable. The winter waves are rough stuff; we regular folks can only venture in to swim in the flat summer seas. But there's a large lava reef nearby with tide pools to explore and, on the other side, Shark's Cove, a relatively protected snorkeling area. Nearby are tennis courts and a jogging path. All units have full kitchens and their own barbecue area. *Tip:* Stay on the beach side, where the views are well worth the extra bucks.

59–579 Ke Iki Rd. (off Kamehameha Hwy.), Haleiwa, HI 96712. © 866/638-8229 or 808/638-8829. Fax 808/637-6100. www.keikibeach.com. 11 units. $110–$130 double 1-bedroom gardenview; $150–$170 double 1-bedroom beachfront; $140–$180 double for 2-bedroom gardenview; $190–$220 double for 2-bedroom beachfront. AE, MC, V. Free parking. TheBus: 52. **Amenities:** Complimentary watersports equipment and bicycles; barbecue facilities, in-room massage; coin-op washer/dryers. *In room:* TV, kitchen, fridge, coffeemaker, CD player.

Ulu Wehi Bed-and-Breakfast *Finds*

Set above the North Shore's famous beaches is Ulu Wehu, a B&B that doubles as a working nursery and flower and fruit farm. The plantation-style bunkhouse is a tiny separate building with a double bed in an antique metal frame, a kitchenette with a small refrigerator and microwave, and a VCR; outside is a bathhouse with an outdoor shower (open at the top to the sun and the stars, but with a privacy fence around the pertinent parts). In the orchids, you'll find an old-fashioned bathtub. Also on the property—in addition to the gorgeous plants—is a 75-foot lap pool, a large video library, a fire-pit for bonfires, a horseshoe pit, and sports equipment (boogie boards, beach stuff) you can use for free. There's also an outdoor shower to wash off the sand when you return from the beach. It's a 10-minute drive to the shops and restaurants of Haleiwa, and just minutes to the North Shore's beaches and hiking and biking trails. The only caveat is the long hike uphill—to 900 feet—from the closest bus stop.

59–416 Alapio Rd. (off Pupukea Rd.), Haleiwa, HI 96712. © and fax 808/638-8161. 1 studio bunkhouse (with separate bathhouse). $85 double. Rates include continental breakfast. Extra person $15. No credit cards. Free parking. TheBus: 52. **Amenities:** Huge 75-ft. lap pool, complimentary watersports equipment. *In room:* VCR (no TV reception), kitchenette, fridge, coffeemaker, hair dryer, iron (on request).

SUPER-CHEAP SLEEPS

Backpackers Vacation Inn *Kids* Located just across from Three Tables at Pupukea Beach, Backpackers has something for just about every kind of budget traveler. The backpacking set might choose the inexpensive, basic accommodations in hostel-type facilities consisting of four bunks to a room with a shared bathroom. There's a common living room with TV and kitchen. For a bit more money, private rooms are available. For families, we recommend the recently renovated oceanfront studios and oceanview cabins. The one-room studios are the best deal: They're right on the beach, and feature a big, airy room with terra-cotta tile floors, two double beds, kitchen, and TV. *Hot tip:* If you're booking an oceanfront studio, ask for one on the second floor for a better view. The swimming, snorkeling, and diving here are excellent in summer; in the winter, this is a great place to sit on the beach and watch the pros ride the wild waves. The management offers free airport pickup, a real plus.

59–788 Kamehameha Hwy., Haleiwa, HI 96712. © 808/638-7838. Fax 808/638-7515. www.backpackers-hawaii.com. 20 units, 8 studios, 4 cabins. $20–$23 dorm bed with shared bathroom; $66 private double with shared bathroom and kitchen; $96–$114 ocean-front studio (sleeps 4); $132–$200 2, 3, or 4 bedroom oceanview cabin for up to 8. MC, V. Free parking. TheBus: 52.

4 Great Deals on Dining

For budget travelers, ethnic eateries are the saving grace of Oahu's restaurant scene. With a Vietnamese *pho* house around every corner and affordable take-out sushi houses dotting the neighborhoods, it's possible to dine well without breaking the bank. Although the abundance of ethnic restaurants and plate-lunch palaces makes it easy to eat cheaply on Oahu, the challenge is finding your way around the maze of Honolulu's illogically arranged streets to get to those local finds.

As for the glamour chefs, they're moving into their own spheres beyond hotel properties and walk-in traffic, creating their own destinations and loyal clienteles who are willing to find them in unexpected neighborhoods. Chefs such as Alan Wong, George Mavrothalassitis, Sam Choy, and Roy Yamaguchi are worth seeking out when you're in the mood for that special splurge.

The recommendations below are organized by location, beginning with Waikiki, then neighborhoods west of Waikiki, neighborhoods east of Waikiki, and finally the Windward Coast and the North Shore.

If you have a room or apartment with kitchen facilities, you may want to prepare some of your own meals to save money. The "Edibles" sections under "Shopping" (later in this chapter) feature a wide variety of markets and shops—including produce stands, bakeries, health-food stores, gourmet shops, and fish markets—in Honolulu and around the island where you can pick up Oahu's best foodstuffs to prepare meals for yourself. Many of them also feature very affordable prepared meals (just heat and serve) and takeout.

A new website, **Anytime Grinds** (www.anytimegrinds.com), might help you decide where to eat on Oahu. This interactive online restaurant guide lets you view basic restaurant information (name, address, phone, if they are open for breakfast/lunch/dinner, and type of cuisine). The site is sorted by name, type of cuisine, location, and price range. There are no restaurant reviews, but it can give you an idea of various restaurants in a general area. The site also has daily information on live entertainment.

WAIKIKI

To locate the restaurants reviewed in this section, see the "Waikiki Accommodations & Dining" map on p. 110.

Arancino ITALIAN   When jaded Honolulu residents venture into Waikiki for dinner, it had better be good. Arancino is worth the hunt. You'll find a cheerful cafe of Monet-yellow walls and tile floors, serving respectable pastas, wonderful pizzas, fabulous red-pepper salsa and rock-salt focaccia, we-try-harder service, and reasonable prices. The risotto changes daily. Don't miss the Gorgonzola-asparagus pizza if it's on the menu. Arancino is frequently filled, with a line outside on the sidewalk.

255 Beach Walk. (©) 808/923-5557. Main courses $10–$20. AE, DC, MC, V. Daily 11:30am–2:30pm and 5–10:30pm.

Cha Cha Cha MEXICAN/CARIBBEAN   Its heroic margaritas, cheap happy-hour beer, pupu, excellent homemade chips, and all-around lovable menu make this a Waikiki treasure. From the beans to the salsa to the grilled Jamaican chicken, there's nothing wimpy about the flavors here. The lime, coconut, and Caribbean spices make Cha Cha Cha more than plain ol' Mex, adding zing to the blackened mahimahi and fresh fish burritos, the jerk chicken breast, and the grilled veggies in a spinach tortilla. Tacos, tamales, quesadillas, soups, enchiladas, chimichangas, and a host of spicy pork, chicken, and fish ensembles are real pleasers. Ask about the specials, because they're likely to be wonderful. Blackened swordfish, curried fresh grilled vegetables, and homemade desserts (including a creamy toasted coconut custard you won't want to miss) are some of the highlights. Its location, across from two of Waikiki's three movie theaters, makes it a choice spot for pre- and after-theater dining.

342 Seaside Ave. ✆ 808/923-7797. Complete dinners $7–$13. MC, V. Daily 11:30am–11pm; happy hour 4–6pm and 9–11pm.

Duke's Canoe Club Restaurant & Barefoot Bar ✿ STEAK/SEAFOOD   Hip, busy, and oceanfront, Duke's is what dining in Waikiki should be. There's hardly a time when the open-air dining room isn't filled with good Hawaiian music. It's crowded at sunset, though. Although Duke's is popular among singles, don't dismiss it as just another pick-up bar—its ambience is stellar. Named after fabled surfer Duke Kahanamoku, this casual, upbeat hot spot buzzes with diners and Hawaiian-music lovers throughout the day. Lunch and the Barefoot Bar menu include pizza, sand-wiches, burgers, salads, and appetizers such as mac-nut and crab wontons and the ever-popular grilled chicken quesadillas. Dinner fare is steak and seafood, with decent marks for the fresh catch, prepared in your choice of the five styles. There's live enter-tainment nightly from 4pm to midnight, with no cover.

In the Outrigger Waikiki on the Beach, 2335 Kalakaua Ave. ✆ 808/922-2268. www.hulapie.com. Reservations rec-ommended for dinner. Main courses $10–$20; breakfast buffet $12. AE, DC, MC, V. Daily 7am–midnight.

Eggs 'n Things ✿✿ Finds BREAKFAST   Like the mythical Phoenix, this breakfast-only eatery was resurrected within a year of the Christmas 2001 fire. This popular place is famous not only for its great food but also for its all-night hours (drop in at 3am and check out the clientele scarfing down the humongous breakfasts). Go when you are hungry, you'll find the fluffiest omelets (which come with pancakes, potatoes, and toast), melt-in-your-mouth waffles (piled high with fruit and whipped cream), and a constant stream of hot coffee being poured into your cup. Prices are surprisingly reasonable, worth standing in line for.

1911-B Kalakaua Ave. (at Ala Moana Blvd.). ✆ 808/949-0820. Breakfast entrees in the $7–$12 range. No credit cards. Daily 11pm–2pm.

Hula Grill Waikiki ✿✿ Value HAWAIIAN REGIONAL   Even if you are not staying at the Outrigger Waikiki, this is the best place for breakfast in Waikiki: Not only does it have a terrific view of all of Waikiki (clear to Diamond Head), but the food is fab-ulous and fantastically priced (especially for Waikiki). Breakfast is a great selection of pancakes (banana, mac nut, pineapple, even coconut) and eggs (from crab cake eggs Benedict to a mushroom-spinach-cheese omelet). Dinner is romantic. The second floor restaurant is decorated in a 1930's Hawaii waterfront home theme with touches like the ohia log bar, a hula doll collection, slate flooring and lauhala line soffited ceil-ings. Signature dinner dishes at this beachside bistro include Hawaiian ceviche, fire grilled ono, screamin' sesame opah, and a nightly collection of specials.

In the Outrigger Waikiki on the Beach, 2335 Kalakaua Ave. ✆ 808/923-HULA. www.hulagrillwaikiki.com. Reserva-tions recommended for dinner. Breakfast $5–13. Main courses $16–$29. AE, DC, MC, V. Daily 6:30–10:30am and 5–10pm.

Keo's in Waikiki ✿ THAI   With its freshly spiced and spirited dishes and familiar menu of Thai delights, Keo's arrived in Waikiki with a splashy tropical ambience and a menu that islanders and visitors love. Owner Keo Sananikone grows his own herbs, fruits, and vegetables—without pesticides—on his North Shore farm. Sate shrimp, basil-infused eggplant with tofu, evil jungle prince (shrimp, chicken, or vegetables in a basil-coconut-chile sauce), Thai garlic shrimp with mushrooms, pad Thai noodles, and the ever-delectable panang, green, and yellow curries are among his abiding delights. The menu includes a heat rating for spiciness, a plus for the delicate palate.

2028 Kuhio Ave. (C) **808/951-9355**. www.keosthaicuisine.com. Reservations recommended. Main courses $10–$14; prix fixe $30 per person. AE, DC, DISC, MC, V. Daily 7am–2pm; Sun–Thurs 5–10:30pm; Fri–Sat 5–11pm.

Parc Cafe ☆ GOURMET BUFFET As the saying goes, Wow! Laulau! The Halekulani's sister hotel has redefined the buffet and made it—surprise!—a culinary attraction. Breakfast, sushi lunch, noodles, Hawaiian, and seafood or prime rib are among the buffet themes featured throughout the week. The Hawaiian buffet is great for visitors—it gives them a taste of real, down-home Hawaiian food with an elegance that is nonthreatening. It's multicultural, too, so you have roast duck and Portuguese bean soup among the Hawaiian staples of laulau, beef stew, chicken long rice, kalua pig, squid luau, and the pièce de résistance, Kauai (or sometimes, Molokai) taro au gratin, a brilliant treatment of the Hawaiian corn that is too often misunderstood. Chafing dishes notwithstanding, this is gourmet fare, using fresh, fine ingredients. A carving station serves up rotisserie duck and prime rib, and the seafood soup is reliably good.

In the Waikiki Parc Hotel, 2233 Helumoa Rd. (C) **808/931-6643**. www.waikikiparchotel.com. Reservations recommended. Breakfast buffet $15, lunch buffet $13–$18, and dinner buffet $29. AE, DC, DISC, MC, V. Daily 6–10am; Wed–Sat 11:30am–2pm; Mon–Thurs 5:30–9pm; Fri–Sun 5:30–9:30pm.

Singha Thai Cuisine THAI The Royal Thai dancers arch their graceful fingers nightly in classical Thai dance on the small center stage, but you may be too busy tucking into your Thai chili, fresh fish, or blackened ahi summer rolls to notice. Imaginative combination dinners and the use of local organic ingredients are among the special touches of this Thai-Hawaiian fusion restaurant. Complete dinners for two to five cover many tastes, and they are an ideal way for the uninitiated to sample this cuisine, as well as the elements of Hawaii Regional Cuisine that have had considerable influence on the chef. Some highlights of a diverse menu: local fresh catch with Thai chili and light blackbean sauce; red, green, yellow, and vegetarian curries; ginseng chicken soup; and many seafood dishes. Such extensive use of fresh fish (mahimahi, ono, ahi, opakapaka, onaga, and uku) in traditional Thai preparations is unusual for a Thai restaurant. The entertainment and indoor-outdoor dining add to this first-class experience.

1910 Ala Moana Blvd. (at the Ala Moana end of Waikiki). (C) **808/941-2898**. Reservations recommended. Main courses $15–$36. AE, DC, DISC, MC, V. Daily 4–11pm.

Tiki's Grill & Bar AMERICAN/PACIFIC RIM When the newly renovated Aston Waikiki Beach Hotel opened in 2002, the surprise was not the renovations but the great food coming from the kitchen of Chef Fred DeAngelo (formerly of Palomino fame). Located on the second floor of the hotel and overlooking Waikiki Beach (get an outside table on the lanai at sunset), this casual eatery is decorated in palm wood flooring with fish nets hanging from the ceiling and lava-rock walls. A 30-foot volcano is the showpiece in the bar (where you can snack on pupus). DeAngelo's cuisine is good ol' American, with his particular touch of Pacific Rim, apparent in all his fish dishes. His signature dish is king salmon ($18), glazed with lemon-grass beurre blanc. Also high on the list is the mahimahi ($15) grilled with a spicy seafood salsa. Save room for pastry chef Ron Villoria's coconut banana bread pudding and outstanding *lilikoi* (yellow passion fruit) cheesecake with basil syrup. Check out the live Hawaiian music in the bar every night.

Aston Waikiki Beach Hotel, 2570 Kalakaua Ave. (at Paoakalani St.). © 808/923-TIKI. Lunch entrees $8–$17; dinner main courses $11–$37. AE, DC, DISC, MC, V. Daily 10:30am–midnight.

WORTH A SPLURGE

Hau Tree Lanai ⋆ PACIFIC RIM Informal and delightful, this Honolulu institution scores higher on ambience than on food. The outdoor setting and earnest menu make it a popular informal dining spot; an ancient hau tree provides shade and charm for diners. A diverse parade of beachgoers at Sans Souci Beach (called "Dig Me Beach" for its eye-candy sunbathers) is part of the scenery. Breakfast here is a must: Choices include salmon Florentine, served with a fresh-baked scone; poi pancakes; Belgian waffles; eggs Benedict; and the Hawaiian platter of miniature poi pancakes, eggs, and a medley of island sausages. Lunchtime offerings include house-cured Atlantic salmon and an assortment of burgers, sandwiches, salads, and fresh-fish and pasta specialties. Dinner selections are more ambitious and less reliable: fresh moonfish, red snapper, opakapaka, ahi, and chef's specials, in preparations ranging from plain grilled to stuffed and over-the-top rich.

In the New Otani Kaimana Beach Hotel, 2863 Kalakaua Ave. © 808/921-7066. Reservations recommended. Main courses $18–$39. AE, DC, DISC, MC, V. Mon–Sat 7–11am, 11:30am–2pm, and 5:30–9pm; Sun 7–11am, noon–2pm, and 5:30–9pm. Late lunch in the open-air bar daily 2–4pm. On the 2nd and 4th Sun of every month, breakfast with limited menu 7am–8:30am, and buffet only 10am–2pm.

Sansei Seafood Restaurant and Sushi Bar ⋆⋆ SUSHI/ASIAN-PACIFIC RIM Perpetual award-winner D. K. Kodama, who built Kapalua's Sansei into one of Maui's most popular eateries, has become something of a local legend with his exuberant brand of sushi and fusion cooking. Although some of the flavors (sweet Thai chile sauce with cilantro, for example) may be too fussy for sushi purists, there are ample choices. On the extensive menu appear Sansei's trademark, award-winning Asian rock shrimp cake and Sansei special sushi (crab, cilantro, cucumber, and avocado with a

Sunday Brunch at the Waikiki Block Party

Waikiki, the state's main visitor destination, continues to reinvent itself. The latest attraction is Sunday brunch. The current mayor of Honolulu has cut back on the Sunday Brunch Block Party from once a month to once a quarter. But, on these days, the city closes down all traffic on Kalakaua Avenue, from Kaiulani to Liliuokalani avenues, from 9:30am to 1:30pm and has a giant block party.

Astroturf is rolled out into the street and tables, chairs, and bright tropical umbrellas are set up. The hotels and restaurants of Waikiki send their chefs out on the sidewalks where you can purchase everything from just-made pastries to finger-licking ribs. Entertainment ranges from a 60-member chorus to a hula troop of children. For information on dates, call © 808/523-2489.

If you are staying in Waikiki, you can just wander out to the party, but if you are coming from another part of the island, parking can be a problem. I suggest either parking on the streets around the Honolulu Zoo and Kapiolani Park, where a shuttle will run you down to the brunch, or for $1 you can park at the Royal Hawaiian Shopping Center or the Waikiki Trade Center.

sweet chile sauce), as well as Spam musubi (help!) and miso scallops. More traditional selections range from very fresh yellowtail sushi to Japanese miso eggplant. There's entertainment on Fridays when, after 10pm, the restaurant (along with d.k. Steakhouse next door) transforms into a "hot" nightclub, Club 25 (yes, you have to be 25 to get in; see review p. 226).

Waikiki Beach Marriott Resort, 2552 Kalakaua Ave., Third Floor. ℂ **808/931-6286.** www.sanseihawaii.com. Reservations recommended. Sushi $3–$17, entrees $17–$40. AE, DISC, MC, V. Mon–Thurs and Sun 5:30–10pm; Fri–Sat 5:30pm–1am.

HONOLULU BEYOND WAIKIKI
ALA MOANA & KAKAAKO

One of the city's largest food courts, great for grabbing a quick, affordable meal on the run, is the Makai Court in the **Ala Moana Center,** at Ala Moana Boulevard between Atkinson Drive and Piikoi Street (ℂ **808/946-2811**). The newly expanded center features nearly two dozen different vendors in this busy, noisy complex on the ground floor of the rambling mall. Favorites: Tsuruya Noodles (the Tenzaru is excellent), Panini Grill Too, Orleans Express, and the Thirst Aid Station, with its smoothies and fresh fruit juices. Korean, Italian, Thai, Chinese, and other ethnic foods, as well as health foods, are also available. Open Monday to Saturday from 9:30am to 9pm and Sunday from 10am to 5pm.

Akasaka 𝒜𝒜 JAPANESE/SUSHI BAR   Cozy, busy, casual, and occasionally smoky, with a tiny tatami room for small groups, Akasaka wins high marks for sushi, sizzling tofu and scallops, miso-clam soup, and the overall quality of its cuisine. Highlights include the zesty, spicy tuna hand-roll *(temaki)*; scallop roll with flying-fish roe; and hamachi. During soft-shell crab season, you can order these spiny delicacies in sushi— a novel, tasty treat. Lunch and dinner specials help ease the bite of the bill, and ordering noodles or other less expensive a la carte items can also reduce the cost considerably.

1646B Kona St. ℂ **808/942-4466.** Reservations recommended. Main courses $10–$25. AE, DC, DISC, MC, V. Mon–Sat 11am–2:30pm and 5pm–2am; Sun 5pm–midnight.

Assaggio 𝒜 ITALIAN   The wildly popular chain, until recently the toast of suburban Oahu, moved into Ala Moana Center to a roar of approval and immediate success. Townies can now enjoy Assaggio's extensive, high-quality Italian offerings—at good prices. The lighter lunch menu features pasta dishes and house specialties (shrimp scampi, rigatoni alla ricotta) at prices around $10 and less. At dinner, a panoply of pastas and specialties streams out of the kitchen: at least nine chicken entrees, pasta dishes ranging from mushroom and clam to linguine primavera, and eight veal choices. One of Assaggio's best features is its prodigious seafood selection: shrimp, scallops, mussels, calamari, and fresh fish in so many preparations, ranging from plain garlic and olive oil to spicy tomato and wine sauces. Assaggio's excellent service and the fact that entrees are priced under $20 deserve our applause.

In the Ala Moana Center, 1450 Ala Moana Blvd. ℂ **808/942-3446.** Reservations recommended. Main courses $9–$15 lunch, $11–$21 dinner. AE, DC, DISC, MC, V. Daily 11am–3pm; Sun–Thurs 4:30–9:30pm; Fri–Sat 4:30–10pm.

Angelo Pietro PIZZA/SPAGHETTI   Two motifs go over well here: the create-your-own pasta and the quirky take on Italian food that could come only from Japan. At this Italian-Japanese pasta house, you can order raw potato salad with any of four dressings—shoyu, ginger, ume (plum), and sesame-miso—and chase it with one of more than four dozen spaghetti choices, with sauces and toppings ranging from several types each of mushroom, shrimp, chicken, spinach, and sausage to squid ink and egg-plant. Pescatore, carbonara with asparagus, pickled mustard cabbage with sausage, codfish eggs—everything is grist for the spaghetti mill at the hands of Angelo Pietro. Garlic lovers adore the crisp garlic chips that are heaped atop some of the selections.

1585 Kapiolani Blvd. ✆ **808/941-0555**. Reservations accepted for groups of 5 or more. Main courses $7–$14. AE, DC, DISC, MC, V. Sun–Thurs 11am–10pm; Fri–Sat 11am–11pm.

Brew Moon PACIFIC RIM/AMERICAN   Award-winning beers and an eclectic menu of sandwiches, pizza, seafood, and ethnic specialties (the ahi sampler of poke, blackened ahi, and sashimi is popular) are featured at this industrial-tropical micro-brewery in the Ward Centre. Diners, many of them under 30, can sit indoors or on the terrace to sample the wide-ranging menu. Poke, chicken curry, barbecued ribs, and items from East and West draw the lunchtime and late-night crowd. Brew Moon's physical space was an attempt at an architectural statement, featuring curved banquettes, high ceilings, surprising niches, and views of mountain and sea. Live entertainment begins at 9pm on Friday nights, when R&B, jazz, funk, or contemporary Hawaiian music takes center stage. Sunday brunch is offered from 11am to 2pm and lunch from 2 to 4pm, after which, dinner service begins.

Budget tip: Zero Gravity hours, when drink prices are slashed ($3 for beer, $4 for house wines, and discounted pupu menu) are daily from 3 to 6pm.

In the Ward Centre, 1200 Ala Moana Blvd. ✆ **808/593-0088**. Reservations recommended. Main courses $8–$28. AE, DC, MC, V. Daily 11am–10pm, bar until 2am.

Compadres Mexican Bar & Grill (Kids) MEXICAN   Memorable margaritas, tequila festivals, Cinco de Mayo, fundraisers, live Hawaiian music on Fridays—Compadres looks for any excuse to throw a party. The atmosphere here is festive, with one wall of glass windows looking out toward Ala Moana Park. The food—from chimichangas to enchilada platters to the simple pleasures of guacamole and salsa—includes some nifty choices for children, who get their own special *keiki* menu. Those with heftier appetites can choose huevos rancheros; eight different types of enchiladas; steak, chicken, and fish combination plates; fajitas; and nachos. For the reckless, there's the back-bar margarita, made with Gold tequila, Grand Marnier, fresh lime, sweet-and-sour, and orange juice.

In the Ward Centre, 1200 Ala Moana Blvd. ✆ **808/591-8307**. Reservations recommended. Main courses $8–$19. AE, DC, DISC, MC, V. Mon–Thurs ↑ am–11pm; Fri–Sat 11am–midnight; Sun 11am–10pm; bar daily 11am–2am, depending on business.

Dixie Grill AMERICAN   Popcorn, video games, a TV bar, and a lusty, noisy atmosphere—that's Dixie Grill, the busiest (and perhaps noisiest) spot on Ward Avenue. You can't miss it—just look for the fire-engine–red walls and turquoise painted fence. You can sit outside at wooden tables (with a view of Sports Authority), or indoors in a high-decibel, quirky atmosphere much loved by families with kids. The all-American menu features barbecued ribs, burgers, shrimp, salads, sandwiches, and a "mess o' crabs." Watch for the "Screamin' Mai Tai" specials.

404 Ward Ave. ✆ **808/596-8359**. Reservations accepted for groups of 8 or more. Sandwiches and entrees $7–$20. AE, DC, DISC, MC, V. Sun–Thurs 11am–10pm; Fri–Sat 11am–11pm.

I ♥ Country Cafe INTERNATIONAL   Give yourself time to peruse the lengthy list of specials posted on the menu board, as well as the prodigious printed menu. Stand in line at the counter, place your order and pay, and find a Formica-topped

Dining Beyond Waikiki

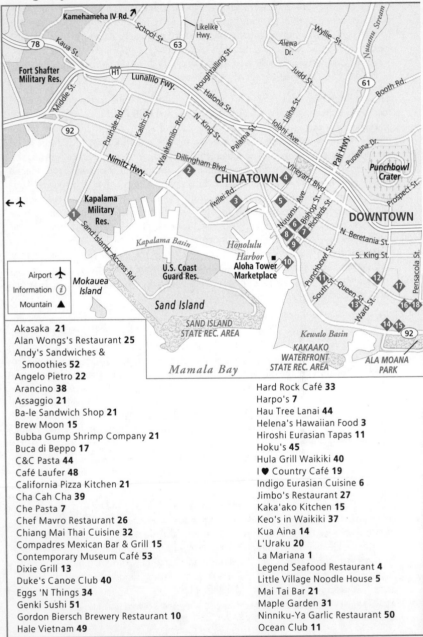

Akasaka **21**
Alan Wongs's Restaurant **25**
Andy's Sandwiches & Smoothies **52**
Angelo Pietro **22**
Arancino **38**
Assaggio **21**
Ba-le Sandwich Shop **21**
Brew Moon **15**
Bubba Gump Shrimp Company **21**
Buca di Beppo **17**
C&C Pasta **44**
Café Laufer **48**
California Pizza Kitchen **21**
Cha Cah Cha **39**
Che Pasta **7**
Chef Mavro Restaurant **26**
Chiang Mai Thai Cuisine **32**
Compadres Mexican Bar & Grill **15**
Contemporary Museum Café **53**
Dixie Grill **13**
Duke's Canoe Club **40**
Eggs 'N Things **34**
Genki Sushi **51**
Gordon Biersch Brewery Restaurant **10**
Hale Vietnam **49**

Hard Rock Café **33**
Harpo's **7**
Hau Tree Lanai **44**
Helena's Hawaiian Food **3**
Hiroshi Eurasian Tapas **11**
Hoku's **45**
Hula Grill Waikiki **40**
I ♥ Country Café **19**
Indigo Eurasian Cuisine **6**
Jimbo's Restaurant **27**
Kaka'ako Kitchen **15**
Keo's in Waikiki **37**
Kua Aina **14**
L'Uraku **20**
La Mariana **1**
Legend Seafood Restaurant **4**
Little Village Noodle House **5**
Mai Tai Bar **21**
Maple Garden **31**
Ninniku-Ya Garlic Restaurant **50**
Ocean Club **11**

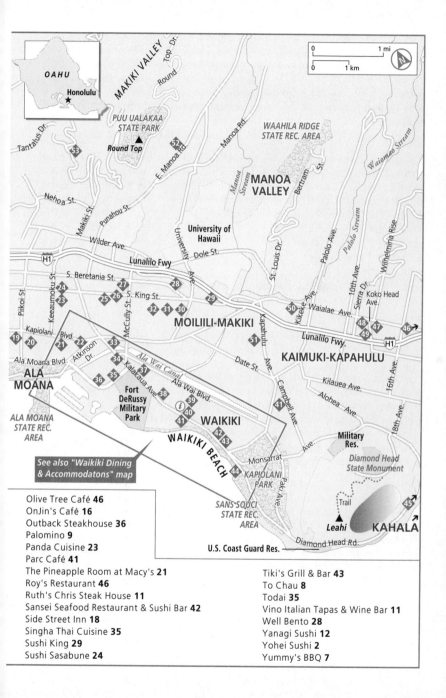

OAHU

Honolulu

MAKIKI VALLEY

PUU UALAKAA STATE PARK

Round Top

WAAHILA RIDGE STATE REC. AREA

MANOA VALLEY

University of Hawaii

MOILIILI-MAKIKI

KAIMUKI-KAPAHULU

ALA MOANA

Fort DeRussy Military Park

WAIKIKI

ALA MOANA STATE REC. AREA

WAIKIKI BEACH

KAPIOLANI PARK

SANS-SOUCI STATE REC. AREA

Diamond Head State Monument

Military Res.

Leahi

KAHALA

U.S. Coast Guard Res.

See also "Waikiki Dining & Accommodatons" map

Olive Tree Café **46**
OnJin's Café **16**
Outback Steakhouse **36**
Palomino **9**
Panda Cuisine **23**
Parc Café **41**
The Pineapple Room at Macy's **21**
Roy's Restaurant **46**
Ruth's Chris Steak House **11**
Sansei Seafood Restaurant & Sushi Bar **42**
Side Street Inn **18**
Singha Thai Cuisine **35**
Sushi King **29**
Sushi Sasabune **24**

Tiki's Grill & Bar **43**
To Chau **8**
Todai **35**
Vino Italian Tapas & Wine Bar **11**
Well Bento **28**
Yanagi Sushi **12**
Yohei Sushi **2**
Yummy's BBQ **7**

table; or wait about 10 minutes for your takeout order to appear on a Styrofoam plate heaped with salad and other accompaniments. The mind-boggling selection includes nine types of cheese steaks (including vegetarian tofu), Cajun meatloaf, Thai curries, various stir-fries, shoyu chicken, vegetarian or eggplant lasagna, chicken Dijon, Cajun-style ahi, and other choices spanning many cultures and tastes. Take a good look at the diners, and you'll see that the menu appeals equally to bodybuilders and hedonists.

In Ala Moana Plaza, 451 Piikoi St. ✆ 808/596-8108. Main courses $5–$8.75. AE, DC, DISC, MC, V. Daily 8am–9pm.

Kaka'ako Kitchen 🌟🌟 *Finds* GOURMET PLATE LUNCHES This popular industrial-style plate-lunch haven is busier than ever since it moved to the trendy Ward Centre in March 2000, with an expanded concept that includes dinner and breakfast service. You'll get excellent home-style cooking (it's owned by Chef Russell Siu, of 3660 on the Rise) served on Styrofoam plates, in a warehouse ambience, at budget prices. The menu, which changes every 3 to 4 months, includes a seared ahi sandwich with *tobiko* (flying-fish roe) aioli, the signature charbroiled ahi steak, sandwiches, beef stew, five-spice shoyu chicken, the very popular meatloaf, and other multiethnic entrees.

In Ward Centre, 1200 Ala Moana Blvd. ✆ 808/596-7488. Breakfast $5–$8; lunch and dinner main courses $7–$13. AE, DC, MC, V. Mon–Thurs 7am–9pm; Fri–Sat 7am–10pm; Sun 7am–5pm.

Kua Aina *Value* AMERICAN The ultimate sandwich shop, for years a North Shore fixture, expanded to the Ward Centre area (near Borders and Starbucks), and the result is dizzying. Phone in your order if you can. During lunch and dinner hours, people wait patiently in long lines for the famous burgers and sandwiches: the beef burgers with heroic toppings; mahimahi with ortega and cheese; grilled eggplant and peppers; roast turkey; tuna andavocado; roast beef and avocado; and about a dozen other selections on Kaiser rolls, multigrain wheat, or rye breads. The sandwiches are excellent, the fries legendary, and the outdoor section with tables, thank God, has grown—but there still may be a wait during lunch hour. The takeout business is brisk.

In Ward Village, 1116 Auahi St. ✆ 808/591-9133. Sandwiches and burgers $4.20–$6.75. No credit cards. Daily 10:30am–9pm.

OnJin's Café 🌟🌟 *Finds* FRENCH/ASIAN OnJin's offers a fabulous bargain for lunch, with gourmet fare at plate-lunch prices. Although dinner is more expensive, it still offers good value (most restaurants serving a menu like this would charge twice as much). OnJin Kim is a brilliant chef who serves excellent fare at excellent prices. Expect long lines at lunch, a more relaxed mood at dinner, pleasant service, and an indoor-outdoor setting in a rapidly developing part of Kakaako. (A movie-theater multiplex is coming up nearby.) At lunch, you order and pay at the counter, but your superbly prepared snapper with lemon caper beurre blanc or salmon misoyaki arrives on a real plate—for less than $7. Specials (beef bourguignonne, seafood jambalaya) change daily. For dinner, there's charred ahi with seven Japanese spices and a selection of entrees (soft-shell crab lightly fried in almond flour or the top-of-the-line bouilla-baisse) remarkable not only for their friendly prices, but also for the sophisticated execution that is OnJin's signature.

401 Kamakee St. ✆ 808/589-1666. Reservations for lunch for 6 or more. Dinner reservations suggested. Lunch main courses $6.50–$9; dinner main courses $8–$22. AE, MC, V. Daily 11am–9pm.

Panda Cuisine DIM SUM/SEAFOOD/HONG-KONG STYLE CHINESE   This is dim sum heaven, not only for the selection, but for the rare late-night dim sum service (usually reserved for morning and lunchtime in Hong Kong). Panda's dim sum selection—spinach-scallop, chive, taro, shrimp dumplings, pork hash, and some 50-plus others—is a real pleaser. (*Tip:* The spinach-scallop and taro puff varieties are a cut above.) The reckless can spring for the live Maine lobster and Dungeness crab in season or the king clam and steamed fresh fish, but the steaming bamboo carts yielding toothsome surprises are hard to resist. Noodles and sizzling platters are good accompaniments to the dim sum, and the sautéed shrimp with honey-roasted walnuts is a favorite.

641 Keeaumoku St. © **808/947-1688.** Main courses $8–$29. AE, MC, V. Mon–Sat 10:30am–2:30pm and 5pm–2am; Sun 5–10pm.

Side Street Inn ★ *(Finds* LOCAL   After their own fancy kitchens have closed, some of Honolulu's top chefs head to this off-the-beaten-track neighborhood bar with TV sets on the walls, a back room with a dart board, and Miller Lite and Budweiser neon lights. Very camp. The terrific food is a surprise; this small side street near Ala Moana Center is noted more for its seedy bars than for pesto-crusted ahi and gourmet Nalo greens. But hey—the grinds (that's local slang for eats) are fabulous, with no pretensions and a spirited local feeling. The barbecued baby back ribs in lilikoi sauce are tender, flavorful, and a steal at $13, and you can find 10- to 16-ounce steaks, charbroiled or on sizzling platters, for $17 to $19. Plus they offer half orders ($5.25–$8.75) on most popular dishes. My faves are the blackened ahi, pesto-crusted ahi, fresh steamed manila clams (tender, in a wine-garlic broth), shrimp scampi, and escargots. By the end of the meal, your clothes may smell like smoke—but chances are, you'll return.

1225 Hopaka St. © **808/591-0253.** Reservations accepted, usually for parties of 4 or more. Plate lunches $4.50–$7.50; dinner main courses $7–$20. AE, DC, DISC, MC, V. Mon–Fri 10:30am–1:30pm; daily 4pm–12:30am.

Worth a Splurge

L'Uraku ★★ *(Value* ASIAN FUSION   L'Uraku's pleasant, light-filled dining room and expanded fusion menu make it a great spot for lunch or dinner. It's not overly fussy but still has the right touch of elegance for dining in style without breaking the bank. Chef Hiroshi Fukui, who has been at the helm of this eatery since it opened in 1996, left recently to open his own restaurant, Hiroshi Eurasian Tapas (p. 141), but the new culinary team of sous Chef Edison Ching, corporate Chef Shuji Abe, and kitchen manager Kawika Cahill has continued the same great culinary experience of Japanese *kaiseki* combined with fresh island ingredients and European cooking styles. I doubt if any diners have noticed the difference. Dishes such as seared scallops, garlic steak, and superb misoyaki butterfish are among the many stellar offerings. The $16 "Weekender lunch" is an unbelievable value: crab cake or shrimp, salad, and a choice of entree such as fresh salmon, almond-crusted fresh snapper, or the succulent misoyaki butterfish. Vegetarians should find comfort and pleasure in the Vegetarian's Dream, a medley of grilled tomatoes, eggplant, portobello mushrooms, and seasonal vegetables with a lively tofu sauce. L'Uraku is a find that has only gotten better with the years.

1341 Kapiolani Blvd. © **808/955-0552.** www.luraku.com. Reservations recommended. Main courses $9.50–$21 lunch, $17–$32 dinner; $38 prix fixe; $52 prix fixe with wine. AE, DC, MC, V. Daily 11am–2pm and 5:30–10pm

The Pineapple Room at Macy's ★★ HAWAII REGIONAL   Yes it's in a department store, but the chef is Alan Wong, a culinary icon. The food is terrific, particularly anything with fresh island fish (such as the ahi "meat" loaf) or kalua pig (such as

Local Chains & Familiar Names

Todai, 1910 Ala Moana Blvd. (© 808/947-1000), a string of Japanese seafood buffet restaurants with locations ranging from Dallas to Portland to Beverly Center, is packing 'em in at the gateway to Waikiki with bountiful tables of sushi (40 kinds), hot seafood entrees (tempura, calamari, fresh fish, gyoza, king crab legs, teppanyaki), and delectable desserts. There's not much ambience, but no one cares; the food is terrific, the selection impressive, and the operation as smooth as the green tea cheesecake.

Ala Moana Center's third floor is a mecca for dining and schmoozing. The open-air **Mai Tai Bar** is a popular watering hole. Next door are the boisterous **Bubba Gump Shrimp Company** (© 808/949-4867) and the **California Pizza Kitchen** (© 808/941-7715), which also maintains branches in Kahala Mall, 4211 Waialae Ave. (© 808/737-9446), and Pearlridge, 98–1005 Moanalua Rd. (© 808/487-7741).

L&L Drive-Inn remains a plate-lunch bonanza islandwide, with 45 locations in Hawaii (36 on Oahu alone). **Zippy's Restaurants** ℝ—at last count 21 of them on Oahu—is the maestro of quick meals, with a surprisingly good selection of fresh seafood, saimin, chili, and local fare, plus the wholesome new low-fat, vegetarian "Shintani Cuisine," sold in selected branches and deli counters. Every restaurant offers a daily Shintani special, and at several locations (Kahala, Vineyard, Pearlridge, Kapolei, Waipio) you can order cold Shintani items in 2-pound portions to take home and heat up.

It's hard to spend more than $7 for the French and Vietnamese specials at the **Ba-le Sandwich Shops:** pho, croissants as good as the espresso, and wonderful taro/tapioca desserts. Among Ba-le's 20 locations are those at Ala Moana Center (© 808/944-4752) and 333 Ward Ave. (© 808/591-0935). A Ba-le location at Manoa Marketplace, 2855 E. Manoa Rd. (© 808/988-1407), serves a terrific selection of Thai dishes in an enlarged dining area, making it as much a restaurant as a place for takeout food. For smoothies, head to **Jamba Juice,** with seven locations at last count, from Kahala Mall to Ward Village, Ewa Beach, Kapahulu, Pearlridge, Kailua, and the new DFS Galleria on Kalakaua Avenue (© 808/926-4944). The ubiquitous **Boston's North End Pizza Bakery** chain claims an enthusiastic following with its reasonable prices and generous toppings. Boston's can be found in Kaimuki, Kailua, Kaneohe, Pearlridge, and Makakilo.

For Italian food, the American chain **Buca di Beppo** (© 808/591-0880) is in the Ward Entertainment Center, 1030 Auahi St. Heaping plates of Italian food, enough to feed a very hungry family, make this place quite popular, along with the reasonable prices. Reservations are a must.

In Waikiki, the local **Hard Rock Cafe** is at 1837 Kapiolani Blvd. (© 808/955-7383), while at the Ala Moana end of Waikiki, **Outback Steakhouse,** 1765 Ala Moana Blvd. (© 808/951-6274), serves great steaks and is always full. In downtown's Restaurant Row, beef eaters can also chow down at **Ruth's Chris Steak House,** 500 Ala Moana Blvd. (© 808/599-3860).

the kalua pig BLT). Wong conjures culinary masterpieces that will probably leave you wanting to come back and try breakfast, lunch, and dinner, just to see what he will present. The room features an open kitchen with a lava-rock wall and abundant natural light, but these are details in a room where food is king. The menu changes regularly, but keep an eye out for the crispy Asian slaw (with cilantro and mac nuts), the miso glazed salmon, the black pepper ahi (with risotto) and pineapple barbecued baby back ribs (with garlic mashed potatoes and sautéed corn).

Macy's, 1450 Ala Moana Blvd. (🕿) 808/945-8881. www.alanwongs.com. Reservations recommended for lunch and dinner. Main courses $10–$17 lunch, $17–$24 prix fixe lunch; $20–$34 dinner, $60 sampling dinner. AE, DC, MC, V. Mon–Fri 11am–8:30pm; Sat 8am–8:30pm; Sun 9am–3pm.

Sushi Sasabune 🟊 SUSHI   The only time Sasabune would fit into a budget-saver's day is at lunch, when four combination specials offer the opportunity to sample the fresh-from-the-sea sushi. The four new lunch specials are divine: choose the crab, salmon belly, and tuna rolls for $7.50; or the sushi combo (seven-pieces and one-roll) for $13. The $11 *chirashi* special is brilliant, a perfect ensemble of warm rice topped with top-quality nori and several kinds of fresh fish and teriyaki octopus, daintily presented in a rectangular "box" as if you were in Japan. Specials come with seaweed salad, miso soup, and azuki bean ice cream. You can always choose to dine at the sushi bar, where strict rules apply: Obey the chef, eat what's served, and God help you if you drop a grain of rice or dip in wasabi without permission. This will cost you dearly, but serious sushi lovers might find it a worthy splurge.

1419 S. King St. (🕿) 808/947-3800. Reservations recommended. Sushi $4–$7; sashimi $3–$15. AE, DC, DISC, MC, V. Tues–Fri noon–2pm; Mon–Sat 5:30–10pm.

DOWNTOWN

Downtowners love the informal walk-in cafes lining one side of attractive **Bishop Square,** at 1001 Bishop St. (at King Street), in the middle of the business district, where free entertainment is offered every Friday during lunch hour. The popular **Che Pasta** is a stalwart of the square, chic enough for business meetings and not too formal (or expensive) for a spontaneous rendezvous over pasta and minestrone soup. With its sandwiches, salads, and pasta, and sprinkling of tables outdoors, nearby **Yummy's BBQ** serves Korean plate lunches, while **Harpo's** caters to the pizza set. Some operations open for breakfast and lunch, others open only for lunch, but most of them close when the business offices empty.

Helena's Hawaiian Foods HAWAIIAN   This small neighborhood restaurant received the prestigious James Beard Foundation "Regional Classic" award for the yummy Hawaiian food that has been coming out of the kitchen for nearly 60 years. This is the real McCoy of Hawaiian food, the best poke (raw fish), the tastiest luau squid (squid with coconut milk), and the ono-licious pipikaula shortribs. Everything comes with poi on the side and haupia, a coconut pudding-type dessert. Forget going to a commercial luau; the food here is much better.

1240 N. School St. (🕿) 808/845-8044. Most items under $10. No credit cards. Tues–Fri 10am–7:30pm.

Hiroshi Eurasian Tapas 🟊🟊 EURO-ASIAN FUSION   Part of the new trend in cuisine, tapas, or small plates (named after the appetizers served in Spanish bars) is the star here, produce by star Chef Hiroshi Fukui. For 8 years, he was at the helm of L'U-raku (p. 139), but in 2004, he opened this restaurant (along with Hawaii's only master sommelier, Chuck Furuya, and manager, Cheryle Gomez) of fusion of European and Asian cuisine. The result is fabulous, especially for foodies who want to sample several items off the menu. These small plates—the staff recommends three dishes per person—offer a range of tastes: from the simple and straight forward spinach salad, spice tuna in a cucumber boat, or shrimp chawanmushi soup to the more complex both in taste and in texture, such as soft shell crab ooze (kabocha puree, wilted spinach and ginger with lemon jelee), seared scallops (with bacon takana ragout), or sizzlin' moi carpaccio (with ginger, tomato, tofu and ponzu vinaigrette topped with micro greens) to the most complicated crab stuffed Kona lobster tail (with sautéed beets and micro herbs), seared foie gras (with sweet miso, grilled eggplant, and creamy yuzu vinaigrette) or red wine braised veal cheek (with cilantro pesto crust, succotash and scallop potato). Go with as many people as possible so you can sample more items. Try to hold out for dessert: a delicious green tea crème brulee, a wicked chocolate cake with chocolate ooze, or a great panna cotta.

Restaurant Row, 500 Ala Moana Blvd. ✆ **808/533-HIRO.** Reservations recommended. Tapas $6.75–$22. AE, DISC, MC, V. Daily 6–10pm.

Legend Seafood Restaurant 🏖 DIM SUM/SEAFOOD   It's like dining in Hong Kong here, with a Chinese-speaking clientele poring over Chinese newspapers and the clatter of chopsticks punctuating conversations. Excellent dim sum comes in bamboo steamers that beckon seductively from carts. Although dining here is a form of assertiveness training (you must wave madly to catch the server's eye and then point to what you want), the system doesn't deter fans from returning. Among our favorites: deep-fried taro puffs and prawn dumplings; shrimp dim sum; vegetable dumplings; and the open-faced seafood with shiitake, scallops, and a tofu product called *aburage*. Dim sum is served only at lunch, but dinnertime seafood dishes comfort sufficiently. Not a very elegant restaurant, but the food is serious and great.

In the Chinese Cultural Plaza, 100 N. Beretania St. ✆ **808/532-1868.** Reservations recommended for dinner. Most items under $15. AE, DC, MC, V. Mon–Fri 10:30am–2pm and 5:30–10pm; Sat–Sun 8am–2pm and 5:30–10pm.

Little Village Noodle House *Finds* CHINESE   Ignore the decor (no, not the usual lack of decor that Chinese restaurants affect): The interior design here reminds me of a French bistro with overhanging roof, similar to eating on the back porch of a small place in Provence. No matter, the food here is "simple and healthy" (their motto) and authentic Chinese (Northern, Canton, and Hong Kong–style). Our picks are the Shanghai noodles with stir-friend veggies, the walnut shrimp and the butterfish in black bean sauce. The menu is eclectic and offers some interesting selections you don't often see. The service is not only friendly (a rarity in Chinatown) but the wait staff are quite knowledgeable about the dishes. Yes, there is take out, but even more unique (for Chinatown) they have parking in the back!

1113 Smith St. ✆ **808/545-3008.** Most items under $10. AE, DISC, MC, V. Sun–Thurs 10:30am–10:30pm; Fri–Sat 10am–midnight.

Ocean Club ★ SEAFOOD   Part restaurant, part nightclub, this sleek, chic magnet has redefined happy hour with its extended hours of slashed prices, excellent appetizer-only seafood menu, and ultra-cool ambience for the 30 and under set. Galvanized steel counters, mahogany bars lined with shoyu bottles, linoleum tile floors, and oddly attractive pillars resembling *pahu* (Hawaiian drums) make for a wonderfully eclectic mix. Add DJs in hip garb spinning hip-hop, and you get the picture. The menu of appetizers lives up to its "ultimate cocktail hour" claim, especially from 4:30

to 8pm nightly, when great seafood is slashed to half-price and the upbeat mood starts spiraling. A happy-hour sampling includes toothsome dips of spinach—artichoke or crab—served with tortilla chips, salsa, and sour cream; ahi tacos and sashimi for a pittance; and standards such as buffalo wings and fried calamari.

On Restaurant Row, 500 Ala Moana Blvd. ✆ 808/526-9888. www.oceanclubonline.com. No T-shirts, athletic wear, or beachwear (including rubber slippers) allowed. Minimum age 23. Appetizer sized items $1–$5 before 8pm and $2–$9 after 8pm. AE, DISC, MC, V. Tues–Fri 4:30pm–2am; Sat 7pm–3am.

To Chau ⭐ *(Value* VIETNAMESE/PHO   The stars are strictly for the *pho,* which many think is the best in a city studded with *pho* houses. Ambience is nil, you'll have to stand in a line that normally numbers 13 to 15 hopefuls, and service can be brusque. But that's all part of the charm of this no-nonsense Formica-style *pho* house, located in a stone building along a river and marked, without fail, by a queue of Asian customers. The anticipation is heightened by the view of diners relishing their steaming, long-awaited orders, visible through the windows as you await your turn on the sidewalk—a Dickensian touch that vanishes as soon as your own order appears. There are shrimp and spring rolls and chicken and pork chop plates, but we've never seen anyone order anything but *pho,* the classic Vietnamese noodle soup. And what a soup it is! The broth is clear, hearty and marvelously flavored with hints of cinnamon and spice. You can order it with several choices of steak, and it comes with a heaping platter of fresh bean sprouts, basil, hot green peppers, and an Asian green called *boke* (*bokay*). It's worth the wait, and so inexpensive.

1007 River St., Chinatown. ✆ 808/533-4549. Reservations not accepted. Pho $4–$5.50. No credit cards. Daily 8:30am–2:30pm (or until they run out of food).

Vino Italian Tapas & Wine Bar ⭐ *(Finds* ITALIAN   Two Japanese guys, famous Japanese guys that is—d.k. Kodama, chef and owner of Sansei Seafood Restaurant and Sushi Bars and D.K. Steakhouse (see above), and Hawaii's only master sommelier, Chuck Furuya, teamed up to create a culinary adventure for foodies. The cozy room, with murals of a vineyard hillside and a kitchen with barrels of wine on the walls and a sky of white puffy clouds on the ceiling, makes you ready for the mouth watering Italian creations by Chef Tom Selman. The menu, similar to Vino on Maui, features *tapas,* or small plates. I'd recommend any ravioli on the menu, but if they have the butternut squash and goat cheese mushroom ravioli, don't miss it. Other great eats are the seared froi gras, Dungeness crab and pasta in a truffle broth, the warm buffalo mozzarella and heirloom tomatoes with a tangy balsamic vinaigrette, and Tuscan skirt steak with baby arugula and petite osso buco. Plus, Furuyu has put together an amazing array of wines by the glass, dispensed from a custom crafted 20-spigot wine cruvinet. The idea here is to enjoy great wines and be able to taste great Italian food.

Restaurant Row, 500 Ala Moana Blvd. ✆ 808/524-8466. Reservations recommended. Tapas $5–$17. AE, DISC, MC, V. Wed–Thurs 5:30–9:30pm and Fri–Sat 5:30–10:30pm.

Yanagi Sushi ⭐ JAPANESE   We love the late-night hours, the sushi bar, and the extensive choices of combination lunches and dinners. But we also love the a la carte Japanese menu, which covers everything from *chazuke* (a comfort food of rice with tea, salmon, seaweed, and other condiments) to *shabu-shabu* and other steaming earthenware-pot dishes. Complete dinners come with choices of sashimi, shrimp tempura, broiled salmon, New York steak, and many other possibilities. You can dine here affordably ($6 noodles) or extravagantly ($30 lobster nabe). Consistently crisp tempura and fine spicy ahi hand-rolled sushi also make Yanagi worth remembering.

762 Kapiolani Blvd. ℂ **808/597-1525.** Reservations recommended. Main courses $8–$33; complete dinners $16–$19. AE, DC, DISC, MC, V. Daily 11am–2pm; Mon–Sat 5:30pm–2am; Sun 5:30–10pm.

Worth a Splurge

Indigo Eurasian Cuisine ✸✸ EURASIAN Hardwood floors, red brick, wicker, high ceilings, and an overall feeling of Indochina luxury give Indigo a stylish edge. You can dine indoors or in a garden setting on menu offerings such as pot stickers, Buddhist bao buns, savory brochettes, tandoori chicken breast, vegetable tarts, Asian-style noodles and dumplings, lilikoi-glazed baby back ribs, and cleverly named offerings from East and West. Chef Glenn Chu is popular, but many claim that Indigo is more style than flavor. We disagree—this is a great restaurant. The adjoining Green Room is packed and smoky.

1121 Nuuanu Ave. ℂ **808/521-2900.** Reservations recommended. Lunch $16–$22; dinner main dishes $19–$30. DC, DISC, MC, V. Tues–Fri 11:30am–2pm; Tues–Sat 6–9:30pm; martini time in the Green Room Tues–Fri 4–7pm.

Palomino ✸✸ AMERICAN REGIONAL Palomino offers splendid harbor views, interesting architecture, conscientious service, and respectable food. Combined, they make up for the dubious (and ubiquitous) artworks. It is more Chicago than Hawaii, lacking in a sense of place but proffering dishes that will likely bring you back. We return for the wild mushroom salad and cedar-plank roasted salmon, and because it's walking distance from Hawaii Theatre. The pizzas (one with caramelized onion and spinach), roasted garlic, shrimp in grape leaves, and kiawe-grilled fish get high marks, as does the devastating dessert called Caffe Affogato (white-chocolate ice cream, espresso, and whipped cream).

66 Queen St., in the Harbor Court Building, mezzanine. ℂ **808/528-2400.** Reservations recommended. Main dishes $7–$27. AE, DC, DISC, MC, V. Mon–Fri 11am–2:30pm; Sun–Thurs 5–10pm; Fri–Sat 5–11pm; late-night bar menu Mon–Fri till 11pm; Fri–Sat till 1am.

ALOHA TOWER MARKETPLACE

Gordon Biersch Brewery Restaurant NEW AMERICAN/PACIFIC RIM German-style lagers brewed on the premises would be enough of a draw, but the food is also a lure at Gordon Biersch, one of Honolulu's liveliest after-work hangouts. Fresh Pacific and Island seafood highlights the eclectic menu. The lanai bar and the brewery bar—open until 1am—are the brightest spots in the marketplace, teeming with downtown types who nosh on pot stickers, grilled steaks, baby back ribs, chicken pizza, garlic fries, and any number of American classics with deft cross-cultural touches. Extensive renovations in 1999 created a stage area for live music, a popular weekend feature.

Aloha Tower Marketplace, 1 Aloha Tower Dr. ℂ **808/599-4877.** Reservations recommended. Main courses $8–$20. AE, DC, DISC, MC, V. Sun–Thurs 10am–10pm; Fri–Sat 10am–11pm; daily late-night menu till midnight.

KALIHI/SAND ISLAND

La Mariana (Finds) AMERICAN Just try to find a spot more evocative or nostalgic than this South Seas oasis at lagoon's edge in the bowels of industrial Honolulu, with carved tikis, glass balls suspended in fishing nets, shell chandeliers, and old tables made from koa trees. In the rear section, the entire ceiling is made of tree limbs. This unique 46-year-old restaurant is popular for lunch, sunset appetizers, and impromptu Friday- and Saturday-night sing-alongs at the piano bar, where a colorful crowd (including some Don Ho look-alikes) gathers to sing Hawaiian classics like a 1950s high school glee club. It is delightful. The seared Cajun-style ahi is your best bet as an appetizer or entree; La Mariana is more about spirit, ambience, and uniqueness than gourmet grinds.

50 Sand Island Rd. ℂ **808/848-2800.** Reservations recommended, especially on weekends. Main courses $6–$12 lunch, $10–$22 dinner. AE, MC, V. Daily 11am–3pm, pupu 3–5pm; dinner 5–9pm. Turn makai (toward the ocean) on Sand Island Rd. from Nimitz Hwy.; immediately after the first stoplight on Sand Island, take a right and drive toward the ocean; it's not far from the airport.

Yohei Sushi ✿ JAPANESE/SUSHI BAR   Yohei is difficult to find; it's tucked away in a small, nondescript complex just before Dillingham crosses the bridge into Kalihi, Honolulu's industrial area. But it's well worth the hunt, especially for lovers of authentic Tokyo-style sushi. Try the sweet shrimp *(amaebi)*, surf clam *(akagai)*, yellowtail tuna *(hamachi)*, butterfly tuna *(negi toro temaki)*, bluefish *(kohada gari chiso temaki)*, and a wonderful assortment of seafood, fresh as can be. An evening at Yohei is like a trip to a Tokyo sushi bar, where regulars know the chef, and even familiar gastronomic territory can be a grand adventure.

1111 Dillingham Blvd., across from Honolulu Community College. ℂ **808/841-3773.** Reservations recommended. Lunch entrees $6–$15; complete dinners $15–$26. DC, MC, V. Mon–Sat 11am–1:45pm and 5–9:30pm.

MANOA VALLEY/MOILIILI/MAKIKI

Chiang Mai Thai Cuisine THAI   Chiang Mai made sticky rice famous in Honolulu, serving it in bamboo steamers with fish and exotic curries that have retained a following. Menu items include toothsome red, green, and yellow curries; the signature Cornish game hen in lemon grass and spices; and a garlic-infused green papaya salad marinated in tamarind sauce. Spicy shrimp soup, eggplant with basil and tofu, and the vegetarian green curry are favorites.

2239 S. King St. ℂ **808/941-1151.** Reservations recommended for dinner. Main courses $7.50–$14. AE, DC, DISC, MC, V. Mon–Fri 11am–2pm; daily 5:30–10pm.

Contemporary Museum Cafe ✿✿ HEALTHY GOURMET   The surroundings are an integral part of the dining experience at this tiny lunchtime cafe, part of an art museum nestled on the slopes of Tantalus amid carefully cultivated Asian gardens, with a breathtaking view of Diamond Head and priceless contemporary artwork displayed indoors and out. The menu is limited to sandwiches, soups, salads, and appetizers, but you won't leave disappointed: They're the perfect lunchtime fare, especially in this environment. Before crowning the meal with flourless chocolate cake, consider the grilled vegetable bruschetta, Gorgonzola-walnut spread, garden burger, black-bean pita wrap, or fresh-fish specials. If Noreen Lam's fresh-baked chocolate chip cookies are hiding in the kitchen, snatch 'em.

2411 Makiki Heights Dr., in the Contemporary Museum.ℂ **808/523-3362.** www.tcmhi.org. Reservations recommended. Main courses $8–$12. AE, MC, V. Tues–Sat 11:30am–2:30pm; Sun noon–2:30pm.

Jimbo's Restaurant ✿✿ *Value* JAPANESE   Jimbo's is the quintessential neighborhood restaurant—small, with a line of regulars outside, everything good and affordable. A must for any noodle lover, Jimbo's serves homemade udon in a flawless broth with a subtly smoky flavor, then tops the works with shrimp tempura, chicken, eggs, vegetables, seaweed, roasted mochi, and a variety of accompaniments of your choice. Cold noodles (the *Tanuki* salad is wonderful!), stir-fried noodles, *donburi* rice dishes with assorted toppings, and combination dinners are other delights. The earthenware pot of noodles, with shiitake mushrooms, vegetables, and udon, plus a platter of tempura on the side, is the top-of-the-line combo. But our fave is the *namesake* (an earthenware pot of udon with tempura on top). Owner Jimbo Motojima, a perfectionist, uses only the finest ingredients from Japan.

1936 S. King St. ✆ **808/947-2211.** Reservations not accepted. Main courses $5–$11. MC, V. Daily 11am–2:50pm; Sun–Thurs 5–9:50pm; Fri–Sat 5–10:30pm.

Maple Garden 🍴 SZECHUAN   It hums like a top and rarely disappoints. Maple Garden is known for its garlic eggplant, Peking duck, and Chinaman's Hat, a version of mu shu pork, available in a vegetarian version as well. The crisp green beans are out of this world. Other hits: braised scallops with Chinese mushrooms, sautéed spinach, and prawns in chili sauce. There are ample vegetarian selections and dozens of seafood entrees—everything from sea cucumbers and braised salmon to lobster with black-bean sauce. An ever-expanding visual feast adorns the dining-room walls, covered with noted artist John Young's original drawings, sketches, and murals.

909 Isenberg St. ✆ **808/941-6641.** Main courses $5–$23 (most $8–$9). DC, DISC, MC, V. Daily 11am–2pm and 5:30–10pm.

Sushi King 🍴 *Value* JAPANESE   This is a top value for lovers of Japanese food. Brusque service can't deter the throngs that arrive for the excellent lunch specials. At arrestingly low prices, the jumbo platters come with soup, pickles, California roll sushi, and your choice of chicken teriyaki, beef teriyaki, shrimp and vegetable tempura, or calamari and vegetable tempura. Other combination lunches offer generous choices that include sashimi, tempura, butterfish, fried oysters, and noodles hot and cold. Early-bird specials are offered daily from 5:30 to 6:30pm.

2700 S. King St. ✆ **808/947-2836.** Reservations recommended, especially for 5 or more on weekends. Lunch $7–$10; dinner main courses $12–$25. AE, DC, DISC, MC, V. Daily 11:30am–2pm; Wed–Mon 5:30pm–2am; Tues 5:30–10pm.

Well Bento *Value* GOURMET HEALTH/ORGANIC PLATE LUNCHES   Can such healthy organic food, without the use of eggs, refined sugar, or dairy products, be satisfying? Countless plate lunches later, we can report that Well Bento will make a guiltless gourmet out of even the fussiest palate. Each plate is aesthetically pleasing, wholesome, and tasty. Louisiana *tempeh,* salmon grilled over lava rocks or poached with shiitake mushrooms, Cajun-style chicken, and creative vegetarian selections ("plant-based plates") make this a place worth trying. Bean salad, cabbage and seaweed salads, and organic brown rice accompany each plate and are as decorative as they are delicious. This is a good picnic choice, as it's mostly takeout, and only a few seats are provided.

2570 S. Beretania St., 2nd Floor. ✆ **808/941-5261.** Plate lunches $5.95–$8.50. No credit cards. Mon–Fri 10:30am–8pm; Sun 10:30am–7pm.

Super-Cheap Eats

Andy's Sandwiches & Smoothies *Value* GOURMET HEALTH FOOD   It started as a health-food restaurant, expanded into a juice bar, and today is a neighborhood fixture for fresh baked bread, healthy breakfasts and lunches (its mango muffins are famous), and vegetarian fare. Andy's roadside stops always carry fresh papayas, sandwiches, and healthy snacks for folks on the run. The ahi deluxe sandwich is tops, but the fresh roasted turkey sandwich is the acclaimed favorite.

2904 E. Manoa Rd., opposite Manoa Marketplace. ✆ **808/988-6161.** Most items less than $5. MC, V. Mon–Thurs 7am–5:30pm; Fri 7am–4pm; Sun 7am–2:30pm.

Worth a Splurge

Alan Wong's Restaurant ★★★ HAWAII REGIONAL CUISINE   Alan Wong is one of Hawaii's most popular chefs, but the service at his bustling eatery has often suffered because of his popularity. Long waits in front of the elevator have angered many. But the worshipful foodies come from all over the state, drawn by the food—which is brilliant—and a menu that is irresistible. The 90-seat room has a glassed-in terrace and open kitchen. Sensitive lighting and curly-koa wall panels accent an unobtrusively pleasing environment—casual but not too. The menu's cutting-edge offerings sizzle with the Asian flavors of lemon grass, sweet-and-sour, garlic, and wasabi, deftly melded with the fresh seafood and produce of the islands. The California roll is a triumph, made with salmon roe, wasabi, and Kona lobster instead of rice, and served warm. We love the opihi shooters, nori-wrapped ahi, chilled vine-ripened tomato soup, and "luau lumpia," a dish of kalua pig, butterfish, and taro greens in a crisp lumpia wrapper. But don't get attached to any one item, as the menu changes daily.

1857 S. King St., 3rd floor. ✆ 808/949-2526. www.alanwongs.com. Reservations recommended. Main courses $26–$48; 5-course sampling menu $65 ($90 with wine); Chef's tasting menu $85 ($120 with wine). AE, DC, MC, V. Daily 5–10pm.

Chef Mavro Restaurant ★★★ PROVENÇAL/HAWAII REGIONAL   Chef/owner George Mavrothalassitis, a native of Provence, has fans all over the world who have admired his creativity since his days at Halekulani's La Mer and Seasons at the Four Seasons Resort Wailea. Winner of the 2003 prestigious James Beard award for Best Chef for Hawaii and the Pacific Northwest, this is a must-do for all serious foodies. His restaurant is the only independently operated AAA Four-Diamond restaurant in Hawaii, located in a conveniently accessible, nontouristy neighborhood in McCully where you can order prix fixe or a la carte, with or without wine pairings. And they are dazzling pairings. To his list of signature items (filet of moi with crisp scales, sautéed mushrooms, and saffron coulis; award-winning *onaga* baked in Hawaiian-salt crust), he's added new favorites: Keahole lobster in an Asian broth; a Hawaiian/Marseilles bouillabaisse; and you-can-cut-it-with-a-fork filet of beef tenderloin crusted with red-wine confit onion. Hints of Tahitian vanilla, lemon grass, ogo, rosemary, and Madras curry add exotic flavors to the French-inspired cooking and fresh island ingredients. The desserts are extraordinary, especially the all-American apple tart with Hawaiian vanilla yogurt ice cream. The split-level room is quietly cordial, and the menu changes monthly to highlight seasonal ingredients.

1969 S. King St. ✆ 808/944-4714. www.chefmavro.com. Reservations recommended. Main courses $32–$42; prix fixe $56–$93 ($81–$136 with wine pairings). AE, DC, DISC, MC, V. Tues–Sun 6–9:30pm.

KAIMUKI/KAPAHULU

C & C Pasta ★★ (Finds) ITALIAN   First primarily a takeout, and now Honolulu's best Italian eatery (still with great sauces and homemade pasta to go), this tiny neighborhood gem really sizzles. Be sure to make a reservation, because there's always a line for dinner. Oenophiles gather regularly to uncork their best bottles of red while an eclectic crowd of pasta lovers tucks into toe-tingling feasts: a sublime mushroom risotto with truffle butter, excellent bruschetta and raviolis, and my perpetual favorites, linguine with clams and spaghetti puttanesca. Other excellent choices include the lasagna (meat and vegetarian), penne with roasted eggplant, and many of the specials on the menu blackboard, such as a linguine I had recently that was generously flavored with spinach and roasted garlic. Owner Carla Magziar recently added pizza to the menu (with garlic, Gorgonzola, and other such tasty toppings) and a heroic salad of mixed greens, Gorgonzola, hazelnuts, roasted onions, and peppers, with fig balsamic dressing. The quality is tops at C & C, the atmosphere is casual, and even the pickiest palates should find something to rave about. *Tip:* If the bread pudding and tiramisu are on the menu, they're a must. And if you're in a rush, there's always a pot of puttanesca sauce simmering, and it's great to go. Although service can lag when it's busy, the food is hard to beat.

3605 Waialae Ave. (C) **808/732-5999.** Reservations required for dinner. Main courses $14–$20. MC, V. Tues–Sat 11am–3pm; Tues–Thurs and Sun 5–9pm; Fri–Sat 5pm–10pm.

Cafe Laufer ⭑ BAKERY/SANDWICH SHOP   This small, cheerful cafe features frilly decor and sublime pastries—from apple scones and linzer tortes to fruit flan, decadent chocolate mousse, and carrot cake—to accompany the latte and espresso. Fans drop in for simple soups and deli sandwiches on fresh-baked breads; biscotti during a coffee break; or a hearty loaf of seven-grain, rye, pumpernickel, or French. The place is a solid hit for lunch; the small but satisfying menu includes soup/salad/sandwich specials for a song, a fabulous spinach salad with dried cranberries and Gorgonzola, and gourmet greens with mango-infused honey-mustard dressing. The orange-seared shrimp salad and the Chinese chicken salad are great for light eaters, and the smoked Atlantic salmon with fresh pumpernickel bread and cream cheese, Maui onions, and capers, is excellent. The special Saturday-night desserts draw a brisk post-movie business.

3565 Waialae Ave. (C) **808/735-7717.** Most items less than $9. AE, DC, DISC, MC, V. Sun–Mon and Wed–Thurs 10am–9pm; Fri–Sat 10am–10pm

Genki Sushi ⭑ (Kids) SUSHI   Fun! Crowded! Entertaining! Take your place in line for a seat at one of the U-shaped counters and watch the conveyor belts parade by with freshly made sushi, usually two pieces per color-coded plate, priced inexpensively. The possibilities are dizzying: spicy tuna topped with scallions, ahi, scallops with mayonnaise, Canadian roll (like California roll, except with salmon), sea urchin, flavored octopus, sweet shrimp, surf clam, corn, tuna salad, and so on. Genki starts with a Japanese culinary tradition and takes liberties with it, so purists miss out on some fun. By the end of the meal, the piled-high plates are tallied up by color and presto, your bill appears, much smaller than the pleasure. Brilliant combination platters are available for takeout.

900 Kapahulu Ave. (C) **808/735-7700.** A la carte sushi from $1.20 for 2 pieces; combination platters $8–$39. AE, DC, DISC, MC, V. Sun–Thurs 11am–9pm; Fri–Sat 11am–10pm; takeout available daily 11am–9pm.

Hale Vietnam VIETNAMESE   Duck into this house of *pho* and brave the no-frills service for the steaming noodle soups, the house specialty. The stock is simmered and skimmed for many hours and is accompanied by noodles, beef, chicken, and a platter of bean sprouts and fresh herbs. Approach the green chiles with caution. We love the chicken soup and shrimp vermicelli, as well as the seafood *pho* and spicy chicken with eggplant. Sautéed green beans, a seasonal offering, are not to be missed if available, nor is the *bun,* cold noodles heaped with sliced veggies and herbs, a fabulous sauce, and spring rolls. Be advised that this restaurant, like most other Vietnamese eateries, uses MSG, and that the *pho,* although respectable, does not equal that of **To Chau** (p. 143) in Chinatown.

1140 12th Ave. (C) **808/735-7581.** Reservations recommended for groups. Main courses $4.50–$16. AE, DISC, MC, V. Daily 10am–10pm.

Worth a Splurge
Ninniku-Ya Garlic Restaurant ⭐ EURO-ASIAN   This is a great garlic restaurant, a paean to the stinking rose. Ninniku-Ya is located in a cozy old home, with tables in a split-level dining room and under venerable old trees outdoors. The menu titillates with many garlic surprises and specials. Seasonal offerings (winter pumpkin in garlic potatoes, opah in winter, beet-colored sauces for Valentine's Day) are fine but not necessary, as the staples are quite wonderful. The three-mushroom pasta is sublime, the hot-stone filet mignon tender and tasty, and the garlic rice a meal in itself. Every garlic lover should experience the garlic toast and the roasted garlic with blue cheese. Everything contains garlic, even the house-made garlic gelato (really quite good), but it doesn't overpower. Look for the festive fairy lights lining the building.

3196 Waialae Ave. ⓒ **808/735-0784**. Reservations recommended. Main dishes $15–$32. AE, DC, DISC, MC, V. Tues–Sun 5:30–9:30pm (last seating).

EAST OF HONOLULU & WAIKIKI
Olive Tree Cafe ⭐⭐ *Finds* GREEK/EASTERN MEDITERRANEAN   Delectables at bargain prices stream out of the tiny open kitchen here. Recently voted "best restaurant in Hawaii under $20" in a local survey, the Olive Tree is every neighborhood's dream—a totally hip restaurant with divine Greek fare and friendly prices. There are umbrella tables outside and a few seats indoors, and you order and pay at the counter. Larger parties now have an awning over the sturdy wooden tables on the Koko Head side. The mussel ceviche is broke-the-mouth fabulous, with lemon, lime, capers, herbs, and olive oil—a perfect blend of flavors. The creamy, tender chicken saffron, a frequent special, always elicits groans of pleasure, as does the robust and generous Greek salad, another Olive Tree attraction. We also love the souvlakia, ranging from fresh fish to chicken and lamb, spruced up with the chef's signature yogurt-dill sauce, made with house-made yogurt. A large group can dine here like sultans without breaking the bank, and take in a movie next door, too. BYOB.

4614 Kilauea Ave., next to Kahala Mall. ⓒ **808/737-0303**. Main courses $5–$10. No credit cards; checks accepted. Mon–Thurs 5–10pm; Fri–Sun 11am–10pm.

WORTH A SPLURGE
Hoku's ⭐⭐⭐ HAWAIIAN REGIONAL   Elegant without being stuffy and creative without being overwrought, the fine-dining room of the Kahala Mandarin offers elegant lunches and dinners combining European finesse with an island touch. This is fusion that really works. The ocean view, open kitchen, and astonishing bamboo floor are stellar features. Reflecting the restaurant's cross-cultural influences, the kitchen is equipped with a kiawe grill; an Indian tandoori oven for its chicken and naan bread; and Szechuan woks for the prawn, lobster, tofu, and other stir-fried specialties. The steamed Hong Kong–style whole fresh fish is worthy of a special occasion, and at lunch, the warm Caesar salad, with kiawe-grilled tiger prawns, is smashing. (It's hard to order anything else once you've tried it.) The chef's daily selection of appetizers could include sashimi, dim sum, and other dainty tastings and is a good choice for the curious. Rack of lamb, pan-seared ahi steak, and the full range of East-West specialties appeal to many tastes. Sunday brunch is not to be missed.

5000 Kahala Ave., in the Kahala Mandarin Oriental Hotel. ⓒ **808/739-8780**. Reservations recommended. Main courses $24–$36. AE, DC, DISC, MC, V. Daily 11:30am–2:30pm and 5:30–10pm.

HAWAII KAI
WORTH A SPLURGE

Roy's Restaurant ★★★ EUROPEAN/ASIAN   This was the first of Roy Yamaguchi's six signature restaurants in Hawaii (out of the two dozen throughout Hawaii, the mainland, Japan, and Guam). It is still the flagship and many people's favorite, true to its Euro-Asian roots and Yamaguchi's winning formula: open kitchen, fresh ingredients, ethnic touches, and a good dose of nostalgia mingled with European techniques. The menu changes nightly, but you can generally count on individual pizzas, a varied appetizer menu (crab cakes, ahi poke, potstickers, and spring rolls), a small pasta selection, and entrees such as lemon grass–roasted chicken, garlic-mustard short ribs, hibachi-style salmon in *ponzu* sauce, and several types of fresh catch. One of Hawaii's most popular restaurants, Roy's is lit up at night with tiki torches outside; the view from within is of scenic Maunalua Bay. Roy's is also renowned for its high-decibel style of dining—it's always full and noisy. Look for live music Friday and Saturday evenings from 7:30 to 10:30pm and Sundays from 6:30 to 9:30pm.

6600 Kalanianaole Hwy. ℂ **808/396-7697.** www.roysrestaurant.com. Reservations recommended. Main courses $16–$30. AE, DC, DISC, MC, V. Mon–Thur 5:30–9pm; Fri 5:30–9:30pm; Sat 5–9:30pm; Sun 5–9pm.

THE WINDWARD COAST

Boots and Kimo's Homestyle Kitchen LOCAL FOOD   It's worth the ride from Waikiki over the Pali to Kailua to eat the melt-in-your-mouth banana pancakes with macadamia nut sauce. This is a great breakfast spot, with a menu ranging from giant omelets to those great pancakes. Lunch has some mouth watering items like the hamburger steak with grilled onions and mushrooms and a local favorite, pulehu ribs, which is shortribs, covered with the grilled onions and mushrooms, but the secret is the Hawaiian salt seasoning. Don't expect much in the way of atmosphere in this tiny diner. Believe me, it's worth the wait.

131 Hekili St., Kailua. ℂ **808/263-7929.** Most items under $10. No credit cards. Tues–Fri 7am–2pm; Sat–Sun 6am–2pm.

Buzz's Original Steak House STEAK/SEAFOOD   A Lanikai fixture for 40 years, Buzz's is a few feet from Kailua Beach (windsurfing central), just past the bridge that leads into Lanikai. (Though it's on the beach, shirt and shoes are required.) A small deck, varnished koa bar, rattan furniture, and wood walls covered with snapshots and surf pictures will put you immediately at ease. Buzz's has the perfect Gauguinesque tropical ambience to go with its offerings: great burgers at lunch (including a terrific mushroom garden burger), fresh catch, superb artichoke appetizer, and steak-and-lobster combos, all much loved by fans. Dinner offerings are pricier, but include Alaskan king crab legs (market price), prime rib, fresh fish, and wonderful items at the soup and salad bar.

413 Kawailoa Rd., Lanikai. ℂ **808/261-4661.** Reservations required. Lunch main courses $6.95–$13; dinner main courses $11–$29. No credit cards. Daily 11am–3pm and 5–10pm; appetizers from 11am–10pm.

Good to Go ★★ *(finds)* DELI   Hidden on the back streets of Kailua is this amazing sandwich/soup/entree deli with healthy food to eat in or take home. Daily specials range from fresh ahi and papaya salsa to teriyaki salmon. Huge salads, just-made sandwiches on homemade bread and blue plate specials (starting at just $4.50) make this a must-stop for a picnic at the beach, or something to take back to the hotel or condo to eat for dinner.

307 Uluniu St., Kailua. ℂ **808/266-4646.** Sandwiches $5.50–$6.75. No credit cards. Mon–Fri 10am–7pm.

Junie's Coffee Shop COFFEE SHOP   *Attention garlic lovers:* This tiny neighborhood coffee shop is for you. It's small (a mini counter and a handful of tables) and old (even the Formica counter has seen better days), but the garlic dishes coming out of the kitchen are wonderful. Regulars rave about the (garlic) corned beef hash and the (garlic) fried pork chops covered in gravy and onions. Not for those counting calories or for non-garlic eaters.

46-022 Kamehameha Hwy., Kaneohe. (£) 808/247-1607. Most items under $10. No credit cards. Daily 6:30am–1pm.

Lucy's Grill 'n Bar ★★ HAWAII REGIONAL CUISINE   This is one of Kailua's most popular restaurants, not just because of the open-air bar and the outdoor lanai seating, but because the food is terrific. The menu is eclectic Hawaii Regional Cuisine with lots of choices and giant-size portions. The dress is casual, and the clientele is from the neighborhood. Be sure to order the spicy ahi tower with sushi rice, avocado, wasabi cream, and roasted nori to get you started. Any of the fresh fish or seafood is wonderful, especially the Szechuan spiced jumbo tiger prawns with black-bean cream and penne pasta or the lemon grass–crusted scallops with yellow Thai curry. Save room for desserts: crème brûlée with Tahitian vanilla bean, dark chocolate soufflé cake, or their "damn fine" apple pie—a la mode, of course. *Budget tip:* Early Bird Special, 5 to 6:30pm nightly, has a terrific dinner for just $12.

33 Aulike St., Kailua. (£) 808/230-8188. Reservations recommended. Main courses $14–$28. MC, V. Daily 5–10pm.

The Shrimp Trucks ★★

Maybe it's a Hawaii-thing, but the best, sweetest, most juicy shrimp you are ever going to eat will be from a shrimp truck on Oahu's North Shore. There are several trucks that line up around Kahuku on the Kamehameha Hwy, but our two favorites are: **Giovanni's Original White Shrimp Truck** and **Kahuku Famous Shrimp.**

Giovanni's (which usually parks in the middle of Kahuku; (£) 808/293-1839) claims to be the first shrimp truck to serve the delicious aquaculture shrimp farmed in the surrounding area. The menu is simple: spicy, garlic, or lemon and butter shrimp. Skip the lemon and butter shrimp (boring) and go to the garlic (my fave) or the spicy (they are not kidding when they say spicy, it's very, very, very spicy). The battered white truck has picnic tables under the awning outside, so you can munch away right there.

The other truck, Kahuku Famous Shrimp (usually parked in front of the old sugar mill in Kahuku, (£) 808/455-1803) has a bit more extensive menu with shrimp (garlic, spicy, or coconut lemon), squid, shrimp and steak, and shrimp and vegetable stir fry.

The trucks are usually in place before noon and stay until about sunset. Depending on how much shrimp you can down, expect to spend no more than $12 per person.

THE NORTH SHORE

Cafe Haleiwa BREAKFAST/LUNCH/MEXICAN   Haleiwa's legendary breakfast joint is a big hit with surfers, urban gentry with weekend country homes, reclusive artists, and anyone who loves mahimahi plate lunches and heroic sandwiches. It's a wake-up-and-hit-the-beach kind of place, serving generous omelets with names like Off the Wall, Off the Lip, and Breakfast in a Barrel. Surf pictures line the walls, and the ambience is Formica-style casual. And what could be better than an espresso bar to start the day?

66–460 Kamehameha Hwy., Haleiwa. ℂ **808/637-5516.** Reservations not accepted. Main courses $6–$11. AE, MC, V. Daily 7am–2pm.

Cholos Homestyle Mexican II *(Value)* MEXICAN   There's usually a wait at this popular North Shore eatery, where some of the tables have leather stools without backs, and the excellent spinach quesadillas and roasted veggie combination plate are presented with so-so service. Still, this is the unhurried North Shore, and the biggest rush for most folks is getting to and from the beach. I recommend the above-mentioned spinach quesadilla, a generous serving filled with black beans, cheese, and fresh vegetables; the chicken fajita plate, a winner; and the fish taco plate, a steal at $7.50 (just $4.50 a la carte). There are tables and stools outdoors; indoors, it's dark and cave-like, with loud music, Mexican handicrafts all over the place, and great home-style Mexican food, down to the last drop of fresh salsa.

North Shore Marketplace, 66–250 Kamehameha Hwy. ℂ **808/637-3059.** Combination plates $6.50–$10. AE, DISC, MC, V. Mon–Thurs 10am–9pm; Fri 10am–9:30pm; Sat 9am–9:30pm; Sun 9am–9pm.

Haleiwa Joe's ✪ AMERICAN/SEAFOOD   Next to the Haleiwa bridge, with a great harbor and sunset view, Haleiwa Joe's serves up fresh local seafood such as whole Hawaiian moi, opakapaka, ahi, and whatever comes in fresh that day. This is a steak-and-seafood harborside restaurant with indoor-outdoor seating and a surf-and-turf menu that could include Parker Ranch New York steak, coconut shrimp, black-and-blue sashimi, and smoked Hawaiian ono. With sandwiches and salads, it's a great lunch stop, too. There are only two Haleiwa restaurants close to the ocean, and this is one of them.

66–0011 Kamehameha Hwy., Haleiwa. ℂ **808/637-8005.** Reservations not accepted. Main courses $14–$27. V. Mon–Thurs 11:30am–9:30pm (limited menu 4:15–5:30pm); Fri–Sat 11:30am–10:30pm (limited menu 4:15–5:30pm, bar until midnight); Sun 11:30am–9:30pm (limited menu 3:45–5pm).

Jameson's by the Sea SEAFOOD   Duck into this roadside watering hole across the street from the ocean for cocktails, sashimi, or the celebrated salmon pâté, or for other hot and cold appetizers, salads, and sandwiches. The grilled crab-and-shrimp sandwich (pardon the mayonnaise) on sourdough bread is a perennial favorite, and it's hard to go wrong with the fresh-fish sandwich of the day, grilled plain and simple. Upstairs, the much pricier dining room opens its doors 5 nights a week for the usual surf-and-turf choices: fresh opakapaka, *ulua* (Hawaiian jack fish), and mahimahi; scallops in lemon butter and capers; lobster tail; New York steak; and filet mignon.

62–540 Kamehameha Hwy., Haleiwa. ℂ **808/637-4336.** Reservations recommended. Main courses $13–$39 in upstairs dining room; downstairs lunch menu $7–$19. AE, DC, DISC, MC, V. Mon–Fri 10:30am–9pm; Sat–Sun 9am–9pm.

Kua Aina ✪ *(Value)* AMERICAN   "What's the name of that sandwich shop on the North Shore?" I hear that often. Recently, after 29 years at the same spot, they moved some 450 feet down the street and opened a new 75-seat eatery. It's as busy as ever, and many diners get their burgers to go and head for the beach. Kua Aina's thin and spindly french fries are renowned islandwide and are the perfect accompaniment to its legendary burgers. Fat, moist, and homemade, the burgers can be ordered with avocado, bacon, and many other accompaniments, including Ortega chiles and cheese. The tuna/avocado, roast turkey, and mahimahi sandwiches are excellent alternatives to the burgers. Kua Aina is unparalleled on the island and is a North Shore must, eclipsing its fancier competitors at lunch.

66–160 Kamehameha Hwy., Haleiwa. © 808/637-6067. Sandwiches and Burgers $4.20–$6.75. No credit cards. Daily 11am–8pm.

Paradise Found Cafe (Value VEGETARIAN A tiny cafe behind Celestial Natural Foods, Paradise Found is a bit of a hunt, but stick with it. For more than a few townies, the North Shore sojourn begins at Paradise, the only pure vegetarian restaurant in these parts. Their smoothies (especially the Waimea Shorebreak!) are legendary, and their organic soups, fresh pressed vegetable juices, sandwiches, and healthy plate lunches are a great launch to a Haleiwa day. Vegan substitutes are willingly made in place of dairy products or to accommodate dietary needs.

66–443 Kamehameha Hwy., Haleiwa. © 808/637-4540. All items less than $7. No credit cards. Mon–Sat 9am–5pm; Sun 9am–4pm.

THE LEEWARD COAST

Aloha Aina Café ★ (Finds HEALTHY It's hard to believe that one of the best healthy food cafes on Oahu is in Waianae, an area filled with fast food and takeout chains. But the Waianae Community Redevelopment Corporation formed a co-op consisting of a farm and this cafe. The food here is so fresh, it may have been picked just hours ago up the street. Located in a tiny wood house on the main highway through Waianae, this friendly cafe gets humming at breakfast with great French toast make from either taro bread or Hawaiian sweet bread, or for the really hungry eaters, a chili and rice omelet. For lunch, try the taro burger, Hawaii's version of the hamburger.

85–773 Farrington Hwy., Waianae. © 808/697-8808. All items under $10. No credit cards. Mon–Sat. 6am–4pm.

5 Beaches

THE WAIKIKI COAST

ALA MOANA BEACH PARK ★★

Quite possibly America's best urban beach, gold-sand Ala Moana ("by the sea"), on sunny Mamala Bay, stretches for more than a mile along Honolulu's coast between downtown and Waikiki. This 76-acre midtown beach park, with spreading lawns shaded by banyans and palms, is one of the island's most popular playgrounds. It has a man-made beach, created in the 1930s by filling a coral reef with Waianae Coast sand, as well as its own lagoon, yacht harbor, tennis courts, music pavilion, bathhouses, picnic tables, and enough wide-open green spaces to accommodate four million visitors a year. The water is calm almost year-round, protected by black lava rocks set offshore. There's a large parking lot as well as metered street parking.

WAIKIKI BEACH ★★★

No beach anywhere is so widely known or so universally sought after as this narrow, 1½-mile-long crescent of imported sand (from Molokai) at the foot of a string of high-rise hotels. Home to the world's longest-running beach party, Waikiki attracts nearly

Beaches & Outdoor Pursuits on Oahu

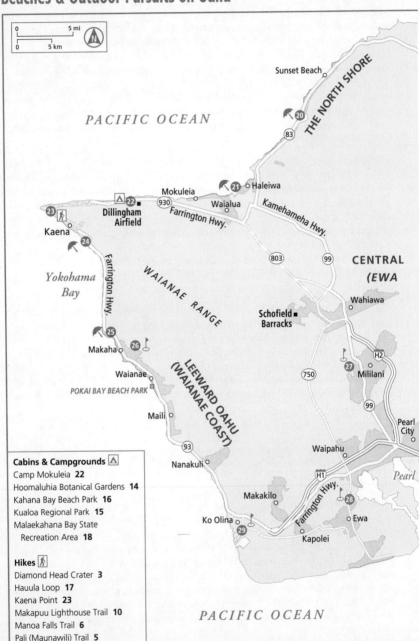

Cabins & Campgrounds ⛺
Camp Mokuleia **22**
Hoomaluhia Botanical Gardens **14**
Kahana Bay Beach Park **16**
Kualoa Regional Park **15**
Malaekahana Bay State
   Recreation Area **18**

Hikes 🚶
Diamond Head Crater **3**
Hauula Loop **17**
Kaena Point **23**
Makapuu Lighthouse Trail **10**
Manoa Falls Trail **6**
Pali (Maunawili) Trail **5**

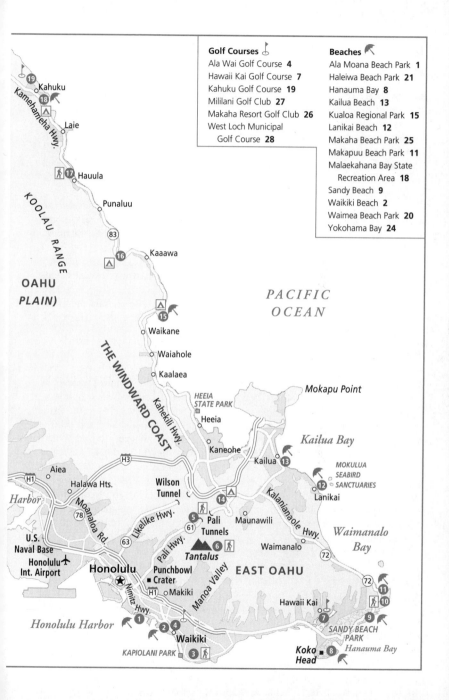

Golf Courses ⛳
Ala Wai Golf Course **4**
Hawaii Kai Golf Course **7**
Kahuku Golf Course **19**
Mililani Golf Club **27**
Makaha Resort Golf Club **26**
West Loch Municipal
  Golf Course **28**

Beaches ☂
Ala Moana Beach Park **1**
Haleiwa Beach Park **21**
Hanauma Bay **8**
Kailua Beach **13**
Kualoa Regional Park **15**
Lanikai Beach **12**
Makaha Beach Park **25**
Makapuu Beach Park **11**
Malaekahana Bay State
  Recreation Area **18**
Sandy Beach **9**
Waikiki Beach **2**
Waimea Beach Park **20**
Yokohama Bay **24**

Kahuku
Kamehameha Hwy.
Laie
Hauula
Punaluu
83
Kaaawa
KOOLAU RANGE
OAHU PLAIN)
PACIFIC OCEAN
Waikane
Waiahole
Kaalaea
THE WINDWARD COAST
Kahekili Hwy.
HEEIA STATE PARK
Mokapu Point
Heeia
Kaneohe
Kailua
Kailua Bay
MOKULUA SEABIRD SANCTUARIES
Lanikai
H3
Aiea
Halawa Hts.
Wilson Tunnel
Kalanianaole Hwy.
Waimanalo Bay
H1
Harbor
Moanalua Rd.
78
Likelike Hwy.
Pali Tunnels
61
Maunawili
Waimanalo
72
U.S. Naval Base
63
Pali Hwy.
Tantalus
Waimanalo
Honolulu Int. Airport
EAST OAHU
72
Honolulu
Punchbowl Crater
Nimitz Hwy.
H1
Makiki
Manoa Valley
Hawaii Kai
Honolulu Harbor
Waikiki
KAPIOLANI PARK
SANDY BEACH PARK
Koko Head
Hanauma Bay

155

five million visitors a year from every corner of the planet. First-timers are always amazed to discover how small Waikiki Beach actually is, but there's always a place for them under the tropical sun here.

Waikiki is actually a string of beaches that extends between **Sans Souci State Recreational Area,** near Diamond Head to the east, and **Duke Kahanamoku Beach,** in front of the Hilton Hawaiian Village, to the west. Great stretches along Waikiki include **Kuhio Beach,** next to the Sheraton Moana Surfrider, which provides the quickest access to the Waikiki shoreline; the stretch in front of the Royal Hawaiian Hotel known as **Grey's Beach,** which is canted so it catches the rays perfectly; and **Sans Souci,** the small, popular beach in front of the New Otani Kaimana Beach Hotel that's locally known as "Dig Me" Beach because of all the gorgeous bods who strut their stuff here.

The City and County of Honolulu just completed the first phase of a makeover to Waikiki at Kuhio Beach Park, a $12.75 million improvement project that has changed the beachfront from tacky to tasteful, adding stone-like walkways, rock waterfalls, more coconut trees, plush grass, and hula mounds.

Waikiki is fabulous for swimming, board- and bodysurfing, outrigger canoeing, diving, sailing, snorkeling, and pole fishing. Every imaginable type of marine equipment is available for rent here. There are posted lifeguards, and the facilities include showers, restrooms, grills, picnic tables, and pavilions at the **Queen's Surf** end of the beach (at Kapiolani Park, between the zoo and the aquarium). The best place to park is at Kapiolani Park, near Sans Souci.

EAST OAHU
HANAUMA BAY ★★
Oahu's most popular snorkeling spot is this volcanic crater with a broken sea wall; its small, curved, 2,000-foot gold-sand beach is packed elbow-to-elbow with people year-round. The bay's shallow shoreline water and abundant marine life are the main attractions, but this good-looking beach is also popular for sunbathing and people-watching. Serious divers shoot "the slot" (a passage through the reef) to gain Witch's Brew, a turbulent cove, and then brave strong currents in 70-foot depths at the bay mouth to see coral gardens, turtles, and—that's right—sharks. (***Divers:*** Beware the Molokai Express, a strong current.) Snorkelers hug the safe, shallow (10 ft.) inner bay that, depending on when you go, can be similar to swimming in a fish-feeding frenzy or bathing with 300,000 honeymooners. Since Hanauma Bay is a conservation district, you may look at but not touch or take any marine life here. Feeding the fish is also prohibited.

A new $13-million Marine Education Center just opened with exhibits and a 7-minute video orienting visitors on this Marine Life Sanctuary. The 10,000-square-foot center includes a training room, gift shop, public restrooms, snack bar and staging area for the motorized tram, which for a fee will take you down the steep road to the beach. There are lifeguards here, and facilities include parking, restrooms, a pavilion, a grass volleyball court, barbecues, picnic tables, and food concessions. Alcohol is prohibited in the park; there is no smoking past the visitor center. Expect to pay $1 per vehicle to park and a $3 per person entrance fee (children 12 and under are free). If you're driving, take Kalanianaole Highway to Koko Head Regional Park. Avoid the crowds by going early, about 8am, on a weekday morning; once the parking lot's full, you're out of luck. Or, take TheBus to escape the parking problem: The Hanauma Bay Shuttle runs from Waikiki to Hanauma Bay every half hour from 8:45am to 1pm; you can catch it at the Ala Moana Hotel, the Ilikai Hotel, or any city bus stop. It returns every hour from noon to 4:30pm. Hanauma Bay is closed on Tuesdays so the fish can have a day off.

SANDY BEACH ☞

Sandy Beach is one of the best bodysurfing beaches on Oahu; it's also one of the most dangerous. It's better to just stand and watch the daredevils literally risk their necks at this 1,200-foot-long gold-sand beach that's pounded by wild waves and haunted by a dangerous shore break and strong backwash. Weak swimmers and children should definitely stay out of the water here; Sandy Beach's heroic lifeguards make more rescues in a year than those at any other beach. Visitors, easily fooled by experienced bodysurfers who make wave-riding look easy, often fall victim to the bone-crunching waves. Lifeguards post flags to alert beachgoers to the day's surf: Green means safe, yellow caution, and red indicates very dangerous water conditions; always check the flags before you dive in.

Facilities include restrooms and parking. Go weekdays to avoid the crowds, weekends to catch the bodysurfers in action. From Waikiki, drive east on the H-1, which becomes Kalanianaole Highway, proceed past Hawaii Kai, up the hill to Hanauma Bay, past the Halona Blow Hole, and along the coast. The next big, gold, sandy beach you see ahead on the right is Sandy Beach. TheBus no. 22 will also get you here.

MAKAPUU BEACH PARK ☞

Makapuu Beach, the most famous bodysurfing beach in Hawaii, is a beautiful, 1,000-foot-long, gold-sand beach cupped in the stark black Koolau cliffs on Oahu's easternmost point. Even if you never venture into the water, it's worth a visit just to enjoy the great natural beauty of this classic Hawaiian beach. You've probably already seen it in countless TV shows, from *Hawaii Five-O* to *Magnum, P.I.*

In summer, the ocean here is as gentle as a Jacuzzi and swimming and diving are perfect; come winter, however, Makapuu is hit with big, pounding waves that are ideal for expert bodysurfers, but too dangerous for regular swimmers. Small boards—3 feet or less with no skeg (bottom fin)—are permitted; regular board surfing is banned by state law.

Facilities include restrooms, lifeguards, barbecue grills, picnic tables, and parking. To get here, follow Kalanianaole Highway toward Waimanalo, or take TheBus no. 57 or 58.

THE WINDWARD COAST
LANIKAI BEACH ☞☞

One of Hawaii's best spots for swimming, gold-sand Lanikai's crystal-clear lagoon is like a giant saltwater swimming pool that you're lucky enough to be able to share with the resident tropical fish and sea turtles. Too gorgeous to be real, this is one of Hawaii's postcard-perfect beaches: It's a mile long and thin in places, but the sand's as soft as talcum powder. Prevailing onshore trade winds make this an excellent place for sailing and windsurfing. Kayakers often paddle out to the two tiny offshore Mokulua islands, which are seabird sanctuaries. Because Lanikai is in a residential neighborhood, it's less crowded than other Oahu beaches; it's the perfect place to enjoy a quiet day. Sun worshipers should arrive in the morning, though, as the Koolau Range blocks the afternoon rays.

There are no facilities here, just off-street parking. From Waikiki, take the H-1 to the Pali Highway (Hwy. 61) through the Nuuanu Pali Tunnel to Kailua, where the Pali Highway becomes Kailua Road as it proceeds through town. At Kalaheo Avenue,

Cheap Thrills: What to See & Do for Free (or Almost) on Oahu, Part I

- **Get a Tan on Waikiki Beach.** The best place for catching the rays on the world-famous beach is in front of the Royal Hawaiian Hotel (the big pink one)—the beach here is sloped at the perfect angle for sunning. It's also a great spot for people-watching. Get there early; by midday, it's packed towel-to-towel.

- **Explore Oahu's Rainforests.** Colorful birds flit among giant ferns and hanging vines, and towering tropical trees form a thick emerald canopy that shelters all below in cool shadows. Try Manoa Falls Trail, a walk of about a mile that ends at a freshwater pool and waterfall.

- **Take a Dip in the Warm Waters of the Pacific.** The perfect place for this is San Souci Beach, the small stretch of Waikiki in front of the New Otani Kaimana Beach Hotel. The water is calm, the temperature perfect, and the gorgeous bodies that strut around have given this beach its nickname, "Dig Me" Beach. Go in the morning when the ocean is calmer.

- **Snorkel the Glistening Waters of Hanauma Bay.** This underwater park, once a volcanic crater, is teeming with a rainbow of tropical fish. Bordered by a 2,000-foot golden-sand beach, the bay's shallow water (10 ft. in places) is the perfect set-up for neophyte snorkelers to enjoy the underwater world. Get there early, before it gets crowded—and don't forget that the bay is closed on Tuesday. There's a $3 fee per person. The closest place to rent snorkeling gear is the **Aloha Dive Shop,** Koko Marina Shopping Center (© **808/395-5922**).

- **Marvel at the Daredevil Bodysurfers at Sandy Beach.** One of the best free shows on the island is when the surf is up at Sandy's. The 1,200-foot-long sand beach is pounded by wild waves, yet troupes of dedicated bodysurfers plunge into this dangerous shore break to ride the charging surf. It may look easy, but don't be tempted to try it yourself—just lie back and enjoy the show.

turn right and follow the coast about 2 miles to Kailua Beach Park; just past it, turn left at the T intersection and drive uphill on Aalapapa Drive, a one-way street that loops back as Mokulua Drive. Park on Mokulua Drive and walk down any of the eight public-access lanes to the shore. Or, take TheBus no. 56 or 57 (Kailua), then transfer to the shuttle bus.

KAILUA BEACH ✦✦✦

Windward Oahu's premier beach is a 2-mile-long, wide golden strand with dunes, palm trees, panoramic views, and offshore islets that are home to seabirds. The swimming is excellent, and the azure waters are usually decorated with bright sails; this is Oahu's premier windsurfing beach as well. It's also a favorite spot to sail catamarans, bodysurf the gentle waves, or paddle a kayak. Water conditions are quite

- **When the Surf's Up, Head to Waimea Bay.** From November to March, monstrous waves—some 30 feet tall—roll into Waimea. When the waves break on the shore, the ground actually shakes, an explosive sound fills the air, and everyone on the beach is covered with salt spray mist. The best surfers in the world paddle out to challenge these freight trains. When the surfers catch a ride, it's amazing to see how small they appear on the lip of the giant waves. It's an experience you'll never forget—and it won't cost you a dime.

- **Hike to the Top of Diamond Head Crater.** Nearly everyone can make this hike to the top of Hawaii's most famous landmark. The 1.4-mile round-trip goes up to the top of the 750-foot volcanic cone, where you have a 360-degree view of Oahu. Allow an hour for the trip up and back, and don't forget your camera.

- **Watch the Sun Set from a 1,048-foot Hill Named after a Sweet Potato.** Actually, it's more romantic than it sounds. Puu Ualakaa State Park, at the end of Round Hill Drive, translates into "rolling sweet potato hill" (which was how the early Hawaiians harvested the crop). The majestic view of the sunset from here is not to be missed.

- **Greet the Sunrise from the Beach at Lanikai.** Watch the sky slowly move from pitch black to wisps of gray to burnt orange as the sun begins to rise over the two tiny offshore islands called Mokulua. This is a multi-sensory experience: Birds sing the sun up; gentle breezes kiss your face; the taste of salt and the smell of the ocean, the sand, and the flowers' fragrances fill the air; and the sky becomes a kaleidoscope of colors as another day dawns.

- **Hike Out to Where the Souls Depart.** At Kaena Point, on the western tip of Oahu, lies Pohaku O Kauai, the point where Hawaiians believed the souls of Oahu's dearly departed left this world for the next. If you go early in the morning, you may not see souls jumping off into the here-after, but you will likely see schools of dolphins swimming offshore.

safe, especially at the mouth of Kaelepulu Stream, where toddlers play in the fresh-water shallows at the middle of the beach park. The water's usually about 78°F (26°C), the views are spectacular, and the setting, at the foot of the sheer, green Koolaus, is idyllic. Best of all, the crowds haven't found it yet.

The 35-acre beach park is intersected by a freshwater stream and watched over by lifeguards. Facilities include picnic tables, barbecues, restrooms, a volleyball court, a public boat ramp, free parking, and an open-air cafe. Kailua's new bike path weaves through the park, and windsurf boards and kayak rentals are available as well. To get here, take Pali Highway (Hwy. 61) to Kailua, drive through town, turn right on Kala-heo Avenue, and go a mile until you see the beach on your left. Or, take TheBus no. 56 or 57 into Kailua, then the no. 70 shuttle.

KUALOA REGIONAL PARK 🐾🐾

This 150-acre coco palm–fringed peninsula is the biggest beach park on the windward side and one of Hawaii's most scenic. It's located on Kaneohe Bay's north shore, at the foot of the spiky Koolau Ridge. The park has a broad, grassy lawn and a long, narrow, white-sand beach ideal for swimming, walking, beachcombing, kite-flying, or just enjoying the natural beauty of this once-sacred Hawaiian shore, listed on the National Register of Historic Places. The waters are shallow and safe for swimming year-round. Offshore is Mokolii, the picturesque islet otherwise known as Chinaman's Hat. At low tide, you can swim or wade out to the island, which has a small, sandy beach and is a bird preserve—so don't spook the red-footed boobies. Lifeguards are on duty.

The park is located on Kamehameha Highway (Hwy. 83) in Kualoa; you can get here via TheBus no. 55.

THE NORTH SHORE

MALAEKAHANA BAY STATE RECREATION AREA 🐾🐾

This almost mile-long white-sand crescent lives up to just about everyone's image of the perfect Hawaii beach. It's excellent for swimming. On a weekday, you may be the only one here; but should some net fisherman—or kindred soul—intrude upon your delicious privacy, you can swim out to Goat Island (or wade across at low tide) and play Robinson Crusoe. (The islet is a sanctuary for seabirds and turtles, so no chase 'em, brah.) Facilities include restrooms, barbecue grills, picnic tables, outdoor showers, and parking.

To get here, take Kamehameha Highway (Hwy. 83) 2 miles north of the Polynesian Cultural Center; as you enter the main gate, you'll come upon the wooded beach park. Or, you can take TheBus no. 52.

WAIMEA BEACH PARK 🐾🐾

This deep, sandy bowl has gentle summer waves that are excellent for swimming, snorkeling, and bodysurfing. To one side of the bay is a huge rock that local kids like to climb up and dive from. In this placid scene, the only clues of what's to come in winter are those evacuation whistles on poles beside the road. But what a difference a season makes: Winter waves pound the narrow bay, sometimes rising to 50 feet high. When the surf's really up, very strong currents and shore breaks sweep the bay—and it seems like everyone on Oahu drives out to Waimea to get a look at the monster waves and those who ride them. Weekends are great for watching the surfers; to avoid the crowds, go on weekdays. *A safety tip:* Don't get too distracted by the waves and forget to pay attention when parking or crossing the road.

Lifeguards are posted and facilities include restrooms, showers, parking, and nearby restaurants and shops in Haleiwa town. The beach is located on Kamehameha Highway (Hwy. 83); from Waikiki, you can take TheBus no. 52.

LEEWARD OAHU/THE WAIANAE COAST

MAKAHA BEACH PARK 🐾🐾

When surf's up here, it's spectacular: Monstrous waves pound the beach. This is the original home of Hawaii's big-wave surfing championship; surfers today know it as the home of Buffalo's Big Board Surf Classic, where surfers ride the waves on 10-foot-long wooden boards in the old Hawaiian style of surfing. Nearly a mile long, this half-moon, gold-sand beach is tucked between 231-foot Lahilahi Point, which locals call Black Rock, and Kepuhi Point, a toe of the Waianae mountain range. Summer is the best time to hit this beach—the waves are small, the sand abundant, and the water safe for swimming. Children hug the shore on the north side of the beach, near the life-guard stand, while surfers dodge the rocks and divers seek an offshore channel full of big fish. *A caveat:* This is a "local" beach; you are welcome, of course, but you can expect "stink eye" (mild approbation) if you are not respectful of the beach and the local residents who use the facility all the time.

Facilities include restrooms and parking. Lifeguards are on duty. To get here, take the H-1 freeway to the end of the line, where it becomes Farrington Highway (Hwy. 93), and follow it to the beach; or you can take TheBus no. 51.

YOKOHAMA BAY 𝒜

Where Farrington Highway (Hwy. 93) ends, the wilderness of Kaena Point State Park begins. It's a remote 853-acre coastline park of empty beaches, sand dunes, cliffs, and deep-blue water. This is the last sandy stretch of shore on the northwest coast of Oahu. Sometimes, it's known as Keawalua Beach or Puau Beach, but everybody here calls it Yokohama, after the Japanese immigrants who came from that port city to work the cane fields and fished along this shoreline. When the surf's calm—mainly in sum-mer—this is a good area for snorkeling, diving, swimming, shore fishing, and pic-nicking. When surf's up, board and bodysurfers are out in droves; don't go in the water then unless you're an expert. There are no lifeguards or facilities, except at the park entrance, where there's a restroom and a lifeguard stand. No bus service.

6 Watersports

For general advice on the activities listed below, see "The Active Vacation Planner," in chapter 2.

If you want to rent beach toys (like a mask, snorkel, and fins; boogie boards; surf-boards; kayaks; and more), check out the following rental shops: **Snorkel Bob's,** on the way to Hanauma Bay at 700 Kapahulu Ave. (at Date St.), Honolulu (© **808/735-7944;** www.snorkelbob.com); and **Aloha Beach Service,** in the Sheraton Moana Surfrider Hotel, 2365 Kalakaua Ave. (© **808/922-3111,** ext. 2341), in Waikiki. On Oahu's windward side, try **Kailua Sailboards & Kayaks,** 130 Kailua Rd., a block from the Kailua Beach Park (© **808/262-2555;** www.kailuasailboards.com). On the North Shore, get equipment from **Surf-N-Sea,** 62–595 Kamehameha Hwy., Haleiwa (© **808/637-9887;** www.surfnsea.com).

BOATING

A funny thing happens to people when they come to Hawaii: Maybe it's the salt air, the warm tropical nights, or the blue Hawaiian moonlight, but otherwise-rational people who have never set foot on a boat in their life suddenly want to go out to sea. You can opt for a "booze cruise" with a thousand loud, rum-soaked strangers, or you can sail on one of these special yachts, all of which will take you out **whale-watching** in season (roughly Dec–Apr). For fishing charters, see "Sportfishing," below.

Captain Bob's Adventure Cruises 𝒜   See the majestic Windward Coast the way it should be seen—from a boat. Captain Bob will take you on a 4-hour, lazy-day sail of Kaneohe Bay aboard his 42-foot catamaran, which skims across the almost-always calm water above the shallow coral reef, lands at the disappearing sandbar Ahu o Laka, and takes you past two small islands to snorkel spots full of tropical fish and, some-times, turtles. The color of the water alone is worth the price. This is an all-day affair, but hey, getting out on the water is the reason you came to Hawaii, right? A shuttle will pick you up at your Waikiki hotel between 9 and 9:30am and bring you back at about 4pm—it's a lot quicker than taking TheBus (no. 55 or 56).

Kaneohe Bay. ⓒ **808/942-5077.** $72 adults, $61 children 13–17, $51 children 12 and under. Rates include all-you-can-eat barbecue lunch and transportation from Waikiki hotels. No cruises Sun and holidays. TheBus: 55 or 56.

Dream Cruises 🐬 If you aren't lucky enough to be in Hawaii during humpback-whale season (roughly Dec–Apr), you can go **dolphin watching** 🐬 instead. Dream Cruises offers year-round dolphin-watching cruises that check out friendly pods of bottle-nosed and spinner dolphins near Yokohama Bay on the northern end of Oahu. This might be your only chance to get "up-close and personal" with these protected marine mammals. During whale season, the company guarantees that if you don't see whales, you can sail again for free. Departing from the Kewalo Basin are a range of cruises, including a snorkel/splash tour that anchors off Waikiki for snorkeling, swimming, and lunch; a 3-hour Pearl Harbor coastal cruise; and a 2-hour sunset dinner-and-dancing cruise with views of the Waikiki skyline.

Kewalo Basin and Waianae Small Boat Harbor. ⓒ **800/400-7300** or 808/592-5200. www.dream-cruises.com. $28–$66 adults, $19–$40 children 4–12. Rates include hotel pickup and drop-off, plus some meals.

Navatek I 🐬🐬 You've never been on a boat, you don't want to be on a boat, but here you are being dragged aboard one. Why are you boarding this weird-looking vessel? It guarantees that you'll be "seasick-free," that's why. The 140-foot-long *Navatek I* isn't even called a boat; it's actually a SWATH (Small Waterplane Area Twin Hull) vessel. That means the ship's superstructure—the part you ride on—rests on twin torpedo-like hulls that cut through the water so you don't bob like a cork and spill your mai tai. It's the smoothest ride on Mamala Bay. In fact, *Navatek I* is the only dinner cruise ship to receive U.S. Coast Guard certification to travel beyond Diamond Head.

Sunset dinner cruises leave Pier 6 (across from the Hawaii Maritime Museum) nightly. If you have your heart set on seeing the city lights, take the royal Sunset Dinner Cruise, which runs from 5:15 to 7:15pm. The best deal is the **lunch cruise,** with full buffet lunch and a great view of Oahu offshore. During the **whale season** (roughly Dec–Apr), you get whales to boot. The lunch cruise lasts from 11:30am to 2pm. Both cruises include live Hawaiian music.

Aloha Tower Marketplace, Pier 6. ⓒ **808/973-1311.** www.go-atlantis.com. Dinner cruises $63–$100 adults, $42–$63 children 2–12; lunch cruises $53 adults, $34 children 2–11. Validated parking before 4:30pm $3, after 4:30pm flat parking fee of $2. TheBus: 8, 19, 20, 55, 56, or 57; or the Waikiki Trolley to stop no. 7.

BODYBOARDING (BOOGIE BOARDING) & BODYSURFING

Good places to learn to bodyboard are in the small waves of **Waikiki Beach** and **Kailua Beach,** and **Bellows Field Beach Park,** off Kalanianaole Highway (Hwy. 72) in Waimanalo, which is open to the public on weekends (from noon Friday to midnight on Sun and holidays). To get here, turn toward the ocean on Hughs Road, then right on Tinker Road, which takes you right to the park.

See above for a list of rental shops where you can get a boogie board.

OCEAN KAYAKING

For a wonderful adventure, rent a kayak, arrive at Lanikai Beach just as the sun is appearing, and paddle across the emerald lagoon to the pyramid-shaped islands off the beach called Mokulua—it's an experience you won't forget. Kayak equipment rental starts at $10 an hour for a single kayak and $16 an hour for a double kayak. In Waikiki try **Prime Time Sports,** Fort DeRussy Beach (ⓒ **808/949-8952**); on the windward side, check out **Kailua Sailboards & Kayaks,** 130 Kailua Rd., a block from Kailua Beach Park (© **808/262-2555;** www.kailuasailboards.com), where single kayaks rent for $39 for a half-day and a double kayak for $49 for a half-day. On the North Shore, **Surf-N-Sea,** 62–595 Kamehameha Hwy., Haleiwa (© **808/637-9887;** fax 808/637-3008; www.surfnsea.com), not only rents kayaks ($10 an hour for single and $15 an hour for double), but it also has clear kayaks (see the fish swim underneath you) for $20 an hour.

First-timers should go to **Kailua Sailboards & Kayaks** (see above), where the company offers a guided tour with the novice in mind in a safe, protected environment. Included in the tour are lunch, all equipment, and transportation from Waikiki hotels for $89; kayak lessons at $35 an hour; and self-guided trips for $59.

SCUBA DIVING

Oahu is a wonderful place to scuba dive, especially for those interested in wreck diving. One of the more famous wrecks in Hawaii is the *Mahi,* a 185-foot former minesweeper easily accessible just south of Waianae. Abundant marine life makes this a great place to shoot photos—schools of lemon butterfly fish and taape are so comfortable with divers and photographers that they practically pose. Eagle rays, green sea turtles, manta rays, and white-tipped sharks occasionally cruise by as well, and eels peer out from the wreck.

For non-wreck diving, one of the best dive spots in summer is **Kahuna Canyon.** In Hawaiian, *kahuna* means priest, wise man, or sorcerer; this massive amphitheater, located near Mokuleia, is a perfect example of something a sorcerer might conjure up. Walls rising from the ocean floor create the illusion of an underwater Grand Canyon. Inside the amphitheater, crabs, octopi, slippers, and spiny lobsters abound (be aware that taking them in summer is illegal), and giant trevally, parrot fish, and unicorn fish congregate as well. Outside the amphitheater, you're likely to see an occasional shark in the distance.

Because Oahu's best dives are offshore, your best bet is to book a two-tank dive from a dive boat. Hawaii's oldest and largest outfitter is **Aaron's Dive Shop,** 307 Hahani St., Kailua (© **808/262-2333;** www.hawaii-scuba.com), which offers boat and beach dive excursions off the coast. The boat dives cost from $125 per person, including two tanks and transportation from the Kailua shop. The beach dive off the North Shore in summer or the Waianae Coast in winter is the same price as a boat dive, including all gear and transportation, so Aaron's recommends the boat dive.

In Waikiki, **South Sea Aquatics,** 2155 Kalakaua, Suite 112 (next to Planet Hollywood; © **808/922-0852;** www.ssahawaii.com), features two-tank boat dives, with transportation to and from Waikiki hotels, for $85 to $95 without gear and $16 extra for equipment. On the North Shore, **Surf-N-Sea,** 62–595 Kamehameha Hwy., Haleiwa (© **808/637-9887;** fax 808/637-3008; www.surfnsea.com), has dive tours from the shore (starting at $65 for one tank), from a boat ($110 for two tanks), and at night ($100 for one tank). Surf-N-Sea also rents equipment and can point you to the best dive sites in the area.

Another great resource for diving on your own is the University of Hawaii Sea Grant's *Dive Hawaii Guide,* which describes 44 dive sites on the various Hawaiian islands, including Oahu. Send $2 to UH/SGES, Attn: Dive Guide, 2525 Correa Rd., HIG 237, Honolulu, HI 96822.

SNORKELING

Some of the best snorkeling in Oahu is at the underwater park at **Hanauma Bay** ★★. It's crowded—sometimes it seems there are more people than fish, but Hanauma has clear, warm, protected waters and an abundance of friendly reef fish—including Moorish idols, scores of butterfly fish, damsel fish, and wrasses. Hanauma Bay has two reefs, an inner and an outer—the first for novices, the other for experts. The inner reef is calm and shallow (less than 10 ft.); in some places, you can just wade and put your face in the water. Go early: It's packed by 10am and closed on Tuesdays. For details, see "Beaches," on p. 153.

Braver snorkelers may want to head to **Shark's Cove,** on the North Shore just off Kamehameha Highway, between Haleiwa and Pupukea. Sounds risky, we know, but we've never seen or heard of any sharks in this cove, and in summer, this big, lava-edged pool is one of Oahu's best snorkel spots. Waves splash over the natural lava grotto and cascade like waterfalls into the pool full of tropical fish. To the right of the cove are deep-sea caves to explore.

The uninitiated might feel better after a lesson and a snorkel tour. **Surf-N-Sea,** 62–595 Kamehameha Hwy., Haleiwa (✆ **808/637-9887;** www.surfnsea.com), has 2-hour tours, with equipment, starting at $45.

SPORTFISHING

Kewalo Basin, located between the Honolulu International Airport and Waikiki, is the main location for charter fishing boats on Oahu. From Waikiki, take Kalakaua

---

Moments **Experiencing Jaws: Up Close and Personal**

You're four miles out from land, which is just a speck on the horizon, with hundreds of feet of open ocean. Suddenly, from out of the blue depths, a shape emerges: the sleek, pale shadow of a 6-foot-long, gray reef shark, followed quickly by a couple of 10-foot-long galapagos sharks. Within a couple of heart beats, you are surrounded by sharks on all sides. Do you panic? No, you paid $120 to be in the midst of these jaws of the deep. Of course, there is a 6-foot by 6-foot by 10-foot aluminum shark cage separating you from all those teeth. It happens everyday on the **North Shore Shark Adventure** (✆ **808/256-2769;** www.hawaiisharkadventures.com), the dream of Capt. Joe Pavsek, who decided after some 30 years of surfing and diving to share the experience of seeing a shark with visitors. To make sure that the predators of the deep will show up for the viewing, Captain Pavsek heaves "chum," a not very appetizing concoction of fish trimmings and entrails, over the side of his 26-foot boat, *Kailolo.* Similar to ringing the dinner bell, after a few minutes, the sharks (generally gray reef, galapagos, and sandbars, ranging from 5–15 ft.) show up—sometimes just a few, sometimes a couple dozen. Depending on the sea conditions and the weather, snorkelers can stay in the cage as long as they wish, with the sharks just inches away. The shark cage, connected to the boat with wire line, floats several feet back holding two snorkelers comfortably and four snuggly. You can stay on the boat and view the sharks from a more respectable distance for just $60. The brave and adventuresome will be down in that cage, just thin aluminum separating them from jaws. It definitely will be a memory you won't forget.

Ewa (west) beyond Ala Moana Center; Kewalo Basin is on the left, across from Ward Centre. Look for charter boats all in a row in their slips; on lucky days, the captains display the catch of the day in the afternoon. You can also take TheBus no. 19 or 20 (Airport).

The best way to book a sportfishing charter is through the experts; the best booking desk in the state is **Sportfish Hawaii** ★ (© **877/388-1376** or 808/396-2607; www.sportfishhawaii.com), which not only books boats on Oahu, but on all islands. These fishing vessels have been inspected and must meet rigorous criteria to guarantee that you will have a great time. Prices range from $721 to $914 for a full-day exclusive charter (you, plus five friends, get the entire boat to yourself), $550 to $625 for a half-day exclusive, or from $170 for a full-day share charter (you share the boat with five other people).

SUBMARINE DIVES

Here's your chance to play Jules Verne and experience the underwater world from the comfort of a submarine, which will take you on an adventure below the surface in high-tech comfort. The entire trip is narrated as you watch tropical fish and sunken ships just outside the sub; if swimming's not your thing, this is a great way to see Hawaii's spectacular sea life. Shuttle boats to the sub leave from Hilton Hawaiian Village Pier. The cost is $80 for adults (book on the Internet for just $68), $42 ($36 booked on-line) for kids 12 and under (children must be at least 36 in. tall). Call **Atlantis Submarines** ★ (© **800/548-6262** or 808/973-9811; www.go-atlantis.com) to reserve. *A word of warning:* The ride is safe for everyone, but, if you suffer from claustrophobia, skip it.

SURFING

In summer, when the water's warm and there's a soft breeze in the air, the south swell comes up. It's surf season in Waikiki, the best place to learn how to surf on Oahu. For lessons, go early to **Aloha Beach Service,** next to the Sheraton Moana Surfrider, 2365 Kalakaua Ave., Waikiki (© **808/922-3111**). The beach boys offer surfing lessons for $30 an hour; board rentals are $10 for the first hour and $5 for every hour after that. You must know how to swim.

On the North Shore, there's no excuse not to learn to surf in Hawaii: Hans Hedemann, a champion surfer with 34 years of competition under his hang-ten toes, has opened the **Hans Hedemann Surf School** at the Turtle Bay Resort (© **808/924-7778;** www.hhsurf.com). His classes range from one-on-one private sessions to group lessons (four students to one teacher) and begin at $50 an hour. If you aren't staying at the Turtle Bay, he will provide complimentary hotel transportation from Waikiki hotels to one of his three locations: North Shore, Waikiki, and the Kohala Mandarin.

Surfboards are also available for rent on the North Shore at **Surf-N-Sea,** 62–595 Kamehameha Hwy., Haleiwa (© **808/637-9887;** www.surfnsea.com), for $5 to $7 an hour. They also offer lessons for $65 for 2 hours. For the best surf shops, where you can soak in the culture as well as pick up gear, also see "Shopping A to Z" later in this chapter.

On the windward side, call **Kimo's Surf Hut,** 151 Hekili St., across from Daiei, in Kailua (© **808/262-1644**). Kimo and his wife, Ruth, couldn't be more friendly and helpful. In addition to surfboards ($30 a day) and body boards for rent, Kimo has his own personal collection of vintage surfboards, lovingly displayed on the walls of his shop. If you have the time, Kimo will gladly tell you the pedigree and history of each board. Although Kimo doesn't offer formal surfing lessons, he'd be happy to give you pointers.

More experienced surfers should drop in on any surf shop around Oahu, or call the **Surf News Network Surfline** (℗ **808/596-SURF**) to get the latest surf conditions. **The Cliffs,** at the base of Diamond Head, is a good spot for advanced surfers; 4- to 6-foot waves churn here, allowing high-performance surfing.

If you're in Hawaii in winter and want to see the serious surfers catch the really big waves, bring your binoculars and grab a front-row seat on the beach near **Kalalua Point.** To get there from Waikiki, take the H-1 toward the North Shore, veering off at H-2, which becomes Kamehameha Highway (Hwy. 83). Keep going to the funky surf town of Haleiwa and Waimea Bay; the big waves will be on your left, just past Pupukea Beach Park.

WATERSKIING

To learn to water ski, or to just go out and have a good time, call the oldest water ski company in Hawaii, **Hawaii Water Sports,** Koko Marina Shopping Center (℗ **808/ 395-3773;** www.hisports.com; TheBus: 58). Lessons and boat rental are $59 for 20 minutes and $79 for a half-hour, including the boat and all equipment rentals (maximum of five people).

WINDSURFING

Windward Oahu's **Kailua Beach** is the home of champion and pioneer windsurfer Robbie Naish; it's also the best place to learn to windsurf. The oldest and most established windsurfing business in Hawaii is **Naish Hawaii/Naish Windsurfing Hawaii,** 155-A Hamakua Dr., Kailua (℗ **800/767-6068** or 808/262-6068; www.naish.com). The company offers everything: sales, rentals, instruction, repair, and free advice on where to go when the wind and waves are happening. Private lessons start at $75 for one, $100 for two for a 60- to 90-minute lesson (depending on your skill level); beginner equipment rental is $25 for 2 hours and $35 for a full day. Kite surfing lessons are also available ($100 for 1½ hr.). Kite board rentals are $25 a day. **Kailua Sailboards & Kayaks,** 130 Kailua Rd., a block from the Kailua Beach Park (℗ **808/262-2555;** www.kailuasailboards.com), offers 3-hour small-group lessons ($79 per person, including all gear, plus lunch) and rentals of windsurfing equipment, surfboards, snorkel gear, and ocean kayaks.

Windsurfer wannabes on the North Shore can contact **Surf-N-Sea,** 62–595 Kamehameha Hwy., Haleiwa (℗ **808/637-9887;** www.surfnsea.com), which offers equipment rental ($12 an hour or $45 for the day), as well as private lessons (beginning at $65 for 2–3 hr.).

7 Nature Hikes

People think Oahu is just one big urban island, so they're always surprised to discover that the great outdoors is less than an hour away from downtown Honolulu. Highlights of the island's 33 major hiking trails include razor-thin ridge backs and deep waterfall valleys.

Check out Stuart Ball's *The Hikers Guide to Oahu* (University of Hawaii Press, 1993) before you go. Another good source of hiking information on Oahu is the state's **Na Ala Hele Program** (Trails to Go On) (℗ **808/973-9782** or 808/587-0058).

For a free Oahu recreation map listing all 33 trails, write to the **Department of Land and Natural Resources,** 1151 Punchbowl St., Room 131, Honolulu, HI 96813

(© **808/587-0300**). The department will also send free topographic trail maps on request and issue camping permits.

Another good source of information is the *Hiking/Camping Information Packet,* which costs $7 (postage included); to order, contact **Hawaii Geographic Maps and Books,** 49 S. Hotel St., Honolulu, HI 96813 (© **800/538-3950** or 808/538-3952). This store also carries a full line of United States Geographic Survey topographic maps, very handy for hikers.

Also be sure to get a copy of *Hiking on Oahu: The Official Guide,* a hiking safety brochure that includes instructions on hiking preparation, safety procedures, emergency phone numbers, and necessary equipment; for a copy, contact Erin Lau, Trails and Access Manager, **City and County of Honolulu** (© **808/973-9782**); the **Hawaii Nature Center,** 2131 Makiki Heights Dr. (© **808/955-0100**); or **The Bike Shop,** 1149 S. King St. (© **808/596-0588**).

The **Hawaiian Trail and Mountain Club,** P.O. Box 2238, Honolulu, HI 96804, offers regular hikes on Oahu. You bring your own lunch and drinking water and meet up with the club at the Iolani Palace to join them on a hike. The club also has an information packet on hiking and camping in Hawaii, as well as a schedule of all upcoming hikes; send $2 plus a legal-size, self-addressed, stamped envelope to the address above.

Other organizations that offer regularly scheduled hikes are the **Sierra Club,** P.O. Box 2577, Honolulu, HI 96803 (www.hi.sierraclub.org); the **Nature Conservancy,** 1116 Smith St., Suite 201, Honolulu, HI 96817 (© **808/537-4508,** ext. 220); and the **Hawaii Nature Center,** 2131 Makiki Heights Dr. (© **808/955-0100**).

Casual hikers and walkers will enjoy the maps put out by the Hawaii Department of Health on great places to walk. The two brochures are *The Honolulu Walking Map,* with 16 routes in Honolulu ranging from 1.5 miles to 3.6 miles, and *The Fun Fitness Map,* with 12 walking adventures all over Oahu. To get a free copy of each, send a self-addressed, stamped envelope (with four 37¢ stamps) to Angela Wagner, Health, Promotions and Education Branch, Room 217, 1250 Punchbowl St., Honolulu, HI 96813. For more information, call © **808/586-4661.**

HONOLULU AREA HIKES
DIAMOND HEAD CRATER ✸✸✸
This is a moderate, but steep, walk to the summit of Hawaii's most famous landmark. Kids love to look out from the top of the 760-foot volcanic cone, where they have 360-degree views of Oahu up the Leeward Coast from Waikiki. The 1.4-mile round-trip takes about 1½ hours; entry fee is $1.

Diamond Head was created by a volcanic explosion about half a million years ago. The Hawaiians called the crater *Leahi* (meaning the brow of the ahi, or tuna, referring to the shape of the crater). Diamond Head was considered a sacred spot; King Kamehameha offered human sacrifices at a *heiau* (temple) on the western slope. It wasn't until the 19th century that Mount Leahi got its current name: A group of sailors found what they thought were diamonds in the crater; it turned out they were just worthless calcite crystals, but the Diamond Head moniker stuck.

Before you begin your journey to the top of the crater, put on some decent shoes (rubber-soled tennies are fine) and gather a flashlight (you'll walk through several dark tunnels), binoculars (for better viewing at the top), water (very important), a hat to protect you from the sun, and a camera. You might want to put all your gear in a pack to leave your hands free for the climb. If you don't have a flashlight, or if your hotel can't lend you one, you can buy a small one for a few dollars as part of a Diamond Head climbers' "kit" at the gift shop at the **New Otani Kaimana Beach Hotel,** on the Diamond Head end of Kalakaua Avenue, just past the Waikiki Aquarium and across from Kapiolani Park.

Go early, preferably just after the 6:30am opening, before the midday sun starts beating down. The hike to the summit of Diamond Head starts at Monsarrat and 18th avenues on the crater's inland (or *mauka*) side. To get here, take TheBus no. 58 from the Ala Moana Center or drive to the intersection of Diamond Head Road and 18th Avenue. Follow the road through the tunnel (which is closed from 6pm–6am) and park in the lot. The trail head starts in the parking lot and proceeds along a paved walkway (with handrails) as it climbs up the slope. You'll pass old World War I and II pillboxes, gun emplacements, and tunnels built as part of the Pacific defense network. Several steps take you up to the top observation post on Point Leahi. The views are indescribable.

If you want to go with a guide, the Clean Air Team leads a free guided hike to the top of Diamond Head every Saturday. The group gathers at 9am, near the front entrance to the Honolulu Zoo (look for the rainbow windsock). Hikers should bring a flashlight. Each person will be given a bag and asked to help keep the trail clean by picking up litter. For more information, call © **808/948-3299.**

MANOA FALLS TRAIL ✿✿

This easy, ¾-mile (one-way) hike is terrific for families; it takes less than an hour to reach idyllic Manoa Falls. The trail head, marked by a footbridge, is at the end of Manoa Road, past Lyon Arboretum. The staff at the arboretum prefers that hikers do not park in their lot, so the best place to park is in the residential area below Paradise Park; you can also get to the arboretum via TheBus no. 5. The often-muddy trail follows Waihi Stream and meanders through the forest reserve past guavas, mountain apples, and wild ginger. The forest is moist and humid and is inhabited by giant bloodthirsty mosquitoes, so bring repellent. If it has rained recently, stay on the trail and step carefully, as it can be very slippery (and it's a long way down if you slide off the side). As we went to press, the state of Hawaii was still assessing the safety of the trail after a series of landslides. Before you venture out, call © **808/587-0300** to check if the trail is open.

EAST OAHU HIKES
MAKAPUU LIGHTHOUSE TRAIL ✿

You've seen this famous old lighthouse on episodes of *Magnum, P.I.* and *Hawaii Five-O.* No longer manned by the Coast Guard (it's fully automated now), the lighthouse is the goal of hikers who challenge a precipitous cliff trail to gain an airy perch over the Windward Coast, Manana (Rabbit) Island, and the azure Pacific. It's about a 45-minute, mile-long hike from Kalanianaole Highway (Hwy. 72), along a paved road that begins across from Hawaii Kai Executive Golf Course and winds around the 646-foot-high sea bluff to the lighthouse lookout.

To get to the trail head from Waikiki, take Kalanianaole Highway (Hwy. 72) past Hanauma Bay and Sandy Beach to Makapuu Head, the southeastern tip of the island; you can also take TheBus no. 57 or 58. Look for a sign that says NO VEHICLES ALLOWED on a gate to the right, a few hundred yards past the entrance to the golf course. The trail isn't marked, but it's fairly obvious: Just follow the abandoned road that leads gradually uphill to a trail that wraps around Makapuu Point. It's a little precarious, but anyone in reasonably good shape can handle it.

Blowhole alert: When the south swell is running, usually in summer, there are a couple of blowholes on the south side of Makapuu Head that put the famous Halona blowhole to shame.

WINDWARD OAHU HIKES
HAUULA LOOP 🎯

For one of the best views of the coast and the ocean, follow the Hauula Loop Trail on the windward side of the island. It's an easy, 2.5-mile loop on a well-maintained path that passes through a whispering ironwood forest and a grove of tall Norfolk pines. The trip takes about 3 hours and gains some 600 feet in elevation.

To get to the trail, take TheBus no. 55 or follow Highway 83 to Hauula Beach Park. Turn toward the mountains on Hauula Homestead Road; when it forks to the left at Maakua Road, park on the side of the road. Walk along Maakua Road to the wide, grassy trail that begins the hike into the mountains. The climb is fairly steep for about 300 yards, but continues to easier-on-the-calves switchbacks as you go up the ridge. Look down as you climb: You'll spot wildflowers and mushrooms among the matted needles. The trail continues up, crossing Waipilopilo Gulch, where you'll see several forms of native plant life. Eventually, you reach the top of the ridge, where the views are spectacular.

Camping is permitted along the trail, but it's difficult to find a place to pitch a tent on the steep slopes and in the dense forest growth. There are a few places along the ridge, however, that are wide enough for a tent. Contact the **Division of Forestry and Wildlife,** 1151 Punchbowl St., Honolulu, HI 96813 (© **808/587-0166**), for information on camping permits.

PALI (MAUNAWILI) TRAIL 🎯

For a million-dollar view of the Windward Coast, take this easy 11-mile (one-way) foothill trail. The trail head is about 6 miles from downtown Honolulu, on the windward side of the Nuuanu Pali Tunnel, at the scenic lookout just beyond the hairpin turn of the Pali Highway (Hwy. 61). Just as you begin the turn, look for the scenic overlook sign, slow down, and pull off the highway into the parking lot (sorry, no bus service available).

The mostly flat, well-marked, easy-to-moderate trail goes through the forest on the lower slopes of the 3,000-foot Koolau Mountain range and ends up in the backyard of the coastal Hawaiian village of Waimanalo. Go halfway to get the view and return to your car, or have someone meet you in 'Nalo.

TO LAND'S END: A LEEWARD OAHU HIKE
KAENA POINT 🎯

At the very western tip of Oahu lie the dry, barren lands of Kaena Point State Park; 853 acres consisting of a remote, wild coastline of jagged sea cliffs, deep gulches, sand dunes, endangered plant life, and a wind- and surf-battered coastline. *Kaena* means "red-hot" or "glowing" in Hawaiian; the name refers to the brilliant sunsets visible from the point.

Kaena is steeped in numerous legends. A popular one concerns the demigod Maui: Maui had a famous hook that he used to raise islands from the sea. He decided that he wanted to bring the islands of Oahu and Kauai closer together, so one day he threw his hook across the Kauai Channel and snagged Kauai (which is actually visible from Kaena Point on clear days). Using all his might, Maui was able to pull loose a huge boulder, which fell into the waters very close to the present lighthouse at Kaena. The rock is still called Pohaku o Kauai (the rock from Kauai). Like Black Rock in Kaanapali on Maui, Kaena is thought of as the point on Oahu from which souls depart.

To hike out to the departing place, take the clearly marked trail from the parking lot of Kaena Point State Park. The moderate, 5-mile round-trip to the point will take a couple of hours. The trail along the cliff passes tide pools abundant in marine life and rugged protrusions of lava reaching out to the turbulent sea; seabirds circle overhead. There are no sandy beaches, and the water is nearly always turbulent. In winter, when a big north swell is running, the waves at Kaena are the biggest in the state, averaging heights of 30 to 40 feet. Even when the water appears calm, offshore currents are powerful, so don't plan to swim. Go early in the morning to see the schools of porpoises that frequent the area just offshore.

To get to the trail head from Honolulu or Waikiki, take the H-1 west to its end; continue on Highway 93 past Makaha and follow Highway 930 to the end of the road. There's no bus service.

8 Camping & Wilderness Cabins

If you plan to camp, you must bring your own gear or buy it here—no one on Oahu rents gear. You can buy gear at **Tents and Events,** 94–158 Leole St. (from H-2 take the second Waipahu exit, then at the first light, make a right on to Leole St.), Waipahu (✆ **808/677-8785**). Also check out "Surf & Sports" under "Shopping A to Z" later in this chapter. If you are bringing your own equipment, remember that you can not transport fuel (even in a canister) on the plane. Also, if your fuel is butane, don't bother bringing it, as butane is very difficult to find in Hawaii.

The best places to camp on Oahu are listed below. TheBus's Circle Island route can get you to or near all these sites, but remember: On TheBus, you're allowed only one bag, which has to fit under the seat. If you have more gear, you're going to have to drive or take a cab.

WINDWARD OAHU
HOOMALUHIA BOTANICAL GARDENS ✦
This windward campground outside Kaneohe is an almost secret place and a real treasure. It's hard to believe that you're just a half hour from downtown Honolulu.

Hoomaluhia, or "peace and tranquillity," accurately describes this 400-acre botanical garden at the foot of the jagged Koolaus. In this lush, tropical setting, gardens are devoted to plants that are native to Hawaii and to others that are specific to tropical America, Polynesia, India, Sri Lanka, and Africa. A 32-acre lake sits in the middle of the scenic park (no swimming or boating are allowed, though), and there are numerous hiking trails. The visitor center offers free guided walks Saturday at 10am and Sunday at 1pm.

Facilities for this tent-camp area include restrooms, cold showers, dishwashing stations, picnic tables, and water. A public phone is available at the visitor center. Shopping and gas are available in Kaneohe, 2 miles away. Permits are free, but stays are limited to 3 nights (Fri, Sat, and Sun only); the office is closed on Sunday. The gate is locked at 4pm and doesn't open again until 9am, so you're locked in for the night.

Hoomaluhia Botanical Gardens are at 45–680 Luluku Rd. (at Kamehameha Hwy.), Kaneohe (✆ **808/233-7323**). From Waikiki, take H-1 to the Pali Highway (Hwy. 61); turn left on Kamehameha Highway (Hwy. 83); at the fourth light, turn left on Luluku Road. TheBus nos. 55 and 56 stop nearby on Kamehameha Highway; from here, you have to walk 2 miles to the visitor center.

KUALOA REGIONAL PARK 🏕🏕

This park has a spectacular setting on a peninsula on Kaneohe Bay. The gold-sand beach is excellent for snorkeling, and fishing can be rewarding as well (see section 5, "Beaches," earlier in this chapter). There are two campgrounds: Campground A—located in a wooded area with a sandy beach and palm, ironwood, kamani, and monkeypod trees—is mainly used for groups. It does have a few sites for families, except during the summer (June–Aug), when the Department of Parks and Recreation conducts a children's camping program here. Campground B is on the main beach; it has fewer shade trees but a great view of Mokolii Island. Facilities at both sites include restrooms, showers, picnic tables, drinking fountains, and a public phone. Campground A also has sinks for dishwashing, a volleyball court, and a kitchen building. Gas and groceries are available in Kaaawa, 2½ miles away. The gate hours at Kualoa Regional Park are 7am to 8pm; if you're not back to the park by 8pm, you're locked out for the night.

Permits are free but limited to 5 days (no camping on Wed and Thurs). Contact the **Honolulu Department of Parks and Recreation,** 650 S. King St., Honolulu, HI 96713 (© **808/523-4525**), for information and permits. Kualoa Regional Park is located in the 49–600 area of Kamehameha Highway, across from Mokolii Island. Take the Likelike Highway (Hwy. 63); after the Wilson Tunnel, get in the right lane and turn off on Kahakili Highway (Hwy. 83). Or, take TheBus no. 55.

KAHANA BAY BEACH PARK 🏕🏕🏕

Lying under Tahiti-like cliffs, with a beautiful, gold-sand crescent beach framed by pine-needle casuarina trees, Kahana Bay Beach Park is a place of serene beauty. You can swim, bodysurf, fish, hike, and picnic, or just sit and listen to the trade winds whistle through the beach pines. Only tent and vehicle camping are allowed at this oceanside oasis. Facilities include restrooms, picnic tables, drinking water, public phones, and a boat-launching ramp. Note that the restrooms are located at the north end of the beach, far away from the camping area, and that there are no showers.

There's a $5 fee for camping, and you must get a permit. Permits are limited to 5 nights; contact the **Department of Land and Natural Resources,** State Parks Division, P.O. Box 621, Honolulu, HI 96809 (© **808/587-0300**; www.state.hi.us/dlnr). Kahana Bay Beach Park is located in the 52–222 block of Kamehameha Highway (Hwy. 83) in Kahana. From Waikiki, take the H-1 west to the Likelike Highway (Hwy. 63). Continue north on the Likelike, through the Wilson Tunnel, turning left on Highway 83; Kahana Bay is 13 miles down the road on the right. You can also get here via TheBus no. 55.

THE NORTH SHORE

MALAEKAHANA BAY STATE RECREATION AREA 🏕🏕🏕

This is one of the most beautiful beach-camping areas in the state, with a mile-long gold-sand beach on Oahu's Windward Coast (see section 5, "Beaches," earlier in this chapter, for details). There are two areas for tent camping. Facilities include picnic tables, restrooms, showers, sinks, drinking water, and a phone. For your safety, the park gate is closed between 6:45pm and 7am; vehicles cannot enter or exit during those hours. Groceries and gas are available in Laie and Kahuku, less than a mile away.

Permits are $5 and limited to 5 nights; they may be obtained at any state park office, including the **Department of Land and Natural Resources,** State Parks Division, P.O. Box 621, Honolulu, HI 96809 (© **808/587-0300**; www.state.hi.us/dlnr).

The recreation area is located on Kamehameha Highway (Hwy. 83) between Laie and Kahuku. Take the H-2 to Highway 99 to Highway 83 (both roads are called Kamehameha Hwy.); continue on Highway 83 just past Kahuku. You can also get here via TheBus no. 55.

CAMP MOKULEIA 🐾

The centerpiece of this 9-acre campground is a quiet, isolated beach on Oahu's North Shore, 4 miles from Kaena Point. Camping is available on the beach or in a grassy, wooded area. Activities include swimming, surfing, shore fishing, and beachcombing. This place makes a great getaway. Facilities include tent camping, cabins, and lodge accommodations. The tent-camping site has portable chemical toilets, a water spigot, and outdoor showers; there are no picnic tables or barbecue grills, so come prepared. The cabins sleep up to 22 people in bunk beds. The cabins are $160 per night for the 14-bed cabin and $240 per night for the 22-bed cabin. Rooms at the lodge (must have a group of 15) are $65 for a shared bathroom and $75 for a private bathroom. Tent camping is $7 per person, per night. Many groups use the camp, but there's a real sense of privacy. Parking is $3 per day. Reservations are required; contact **Camp Mokuleia,** 68–729 Farrington Hwy., Waialua, HI 96791 (✆ **808/637-6241;** www.campmokuleia.org/default.htm).

Camp Mokuleia is located on Farrington Highway, west of Haleiwa. From Waikiki, take the H-1 to the H-2 exit; stay on H-2 until the end. Where the road forks, bear left to Waialua on Highway 803, which turns into Highway 930 to Kaena Point. Look for the green fence on the right, where a small sign at the driveway reads CAMP MOKULEIA, EPISCOPAL CHURCH OF HAWAII.

9 Golf & Other Affordable Outdoor Activities

GOLF

Oahu has nearly three dozen golf courses, ranging from bare-bones municipal courses to exclusive country-club courses with membership fees running to six figures a year. Below are the best of a great bunch.

Windward courses play much differently than the leeward courses. On the windward side, the prevailing winds blow from the ocean to shore, and the grain direction of the greens tends to run the same way—from the ocean to the mountains. Leeward golf courses have the opposite tendency: The winds usually blow from the mountains to the ocean, with the grain direction of the greens corresponding.

Tips on beating the crowds and saving money: Oahu's golf courses tend to be crowded, so we suggest that you golf midweek if you can. Also, most island courses have twilight rates that offer substantial discounts if you're willing to tee off in the afternoon, usually between 1 and 3pm; these are included in the listings below, where applicable.

Transportation note: TheBus does not allow golf-club bags on board, so if you want to use TheBus to get to a course, you're going to have to rent clubs there.

WAIKIKI

Ala Wai Municipal Golf Course   The Guinness Book of World Records lists this as the busiest golf course in the world; some 500 rounds a day are played on this 18-hole municipal course within walking distance of Waikiki's hotels. For years, we've held off recommending this par 70, 6,020-yard course because it was so busy (tee times taken

Value **Insider Tip**

For last-minute and discount tee times, call **Stand-by Golf** (© **888/645-BOOK;** www.stand-bygolf.com) which offers discounted tee times for same-day or next-day golfing. Call between 7am and 11pm for a guaranteed tee time at up to 50% discount.

by local retirees), but a recent scandal, involving telephone company employees tapping into the tee time reservation system to get tee times for themselves and their friends, has shaken up the old system, and visitors now have a better chance of playing here. It still is a challenge to get a tee time, and the computerized tee reservations system for all of Oahu's municipal courses will only allow you to book 3 days in advance, but keep trying. Ala Wai basically is a flat layout, bordered by the Ala Wai Canal one side and the Manoa-Palolo Stream on the other. It's less windy than most Oahu courses, but pay attention to the 372-yard, par-4, first hole which demands a straight and long shot to the very tiny green. If you miss, you can make it up on the 478-yard, par-5 10th hole—the green is reachable in two, so with a two-putt, a birdie is within reach.

404 Kapahulu Ave., Waikiki. © **808/733-7387** (golf course) or 808/296-2000 tee time reservations. www.co.honolulu.hi.us/des/golf/alawai.htm. Greens fee: $42, twilight half-price. From Waikiki turn left on Kapahulu Ave.; the course is on the mauka side of Ala Wai Canal. TheBus: 19, 20, or 22.

EAST OAHU
Hawaii Kai Golf Course   This is actually two golf courses in one. The par-72, 6,222-yard **Hawaii Kai Championship Golf Course** is moderately challenging, with scenic vistas. The course is forgiving to high-handicap golfers, although it does have a few surprises. The par-3 **Hawaii Kai Executive Golf Course** is fun for beginners and those just getting back in the game after a few years. The course has lots of hills and valleys, with no water hazards and only a few sand traps. Lockers are available.

8902 Kalanianaole Hwy., Honolulu. © **808/395-2358**. www.hawaiikaigolf.com. Greens fees: Champion Course $90 Mon–Fri, $100 Sat–Sun, with twilight rates $60; Executive Course $37 Mon–Fri, $42 Sat–Sun. Take H-1 east past Hawaii Kai; it's immediately past Sandy Beach on the left. TheBus: 58.

THE NORTH SHORE
Kahuku Golf Course *Finds*   Okay, so this 9-hole budget golf course is a bit funky. There are no facilities, except a few pull carts that disappear with the first handful of golfers—no club rentals, no clubhouse. But playing here, at this scenic oceanside course, amidst the tranquillity of the North Shore, is quite an experience nonetheless. Duffers will love the ease of this recreational course, and weight watchers will be happy to walk the gently sloping greens. Don't forget to bring your camera for the views (especially at holes 3, 4, 7, and 8, which are right on the ocean). No reservations are taken; tee times are doled out on a first-come, first-served basis—and with plenty of retirees happy to sit and wait, the competition is fierce for early tee times. Bring your own clubs and call ahead to check the weather. The cost for this experience? Eight bucks!

56-501 Kamehameha Hwy., Kajuku. © **808/293-5842**. Greens fees: $8 weekdays, $10 weekends for 9 holes. Take H-1 west to H-2; follow H-2 through Wahiawa to Kamehameha Hwy. (Hwy. 99, then Hwy. 83); follow it to Kahuku.

CENTRAL OAHU
Mililani Golf Club   This par-72, 6,455-yard public course is home to the Sports Shinko Rainbow Open, where Hawaii's top professionals compete. Located between

More Cheap Thrills: What to See & Do for Free (or Almost) on Oahu, Part II

- **Tour the Entire Island for Just a Couple of Bucks.** For $2, the "Circle the Island" city buses will take you all the way around the island of Oahu. From Ala Moana Center, TheBus no. 52 goes clockwise around the island, and no. 55 goes counterclockwise. It takes up to 5 hours to see the entire scope of Oahu's scenic beauty.

- **Watch the Ancient Hawaiian Sport of Canoe Paddling.** On weekday evenings and weekend days from February to September, hundreds of canoe paddlers gather at Ala Wai Canal and practice paddling traditional Hawaiian canoes out to sea. Find a comfortable spot at Ala Wai Park, next to the canal, and watch the canoe paddlers re-create this centuries-old sport.

- **Get a Bargain at the Aloha Flea Market.** Just 50¢ will get you into this all-day show at the Aloha Stadium parking lot, where more than 1,000 vendors sell everything from junk to jewels. Go early for the best deals. Open Wednesday, Saturday, and Sunday from 6am to 3pm.

- **Attend a Hawaiian-Language Church Service.** Built in 1842, Kawaiahao Church, 957 Punchbowl St., near King Street, is the Westminster Abbey of Hawaii; the vestibule is lined with portraits of the Hawaiian monarchy, many of whom were coronated in this very building. The coral church is a perfect setting to experience an all-Hawaiian service, complete with Hawaiian song. Hawaiian-language services are held every Sunday at 10:30am and admission is free—let your conscience be your guide as to a donation.

- **Visit the Lei Sellers in Chinatown.** Wander Honolulu's Chinatown, taking in its jumble of exotic shops offering herbs, Chinese groceries, and acupuncture services. On Maunakea Street (near North Hotel St.), Hawaii's finest leis go for as little as $3.50.

- **Experience a Turning Point in America's History: The Bombing of Pearl Harbor.** Standing on the deck of the USS *Arizona* Memorial at Pearl Harbor, with the ship underneath, is an experience you'll never forget. On that fateful day—December 7, 1941—the 608-foot *Arizona* sank in just 9 minutes after being bombed during the Japanese air raid. The 1,177 men on board plunged to a fiery death—and the U.S. went to war. Admission

the Koolau and Waianae mountain ranges on the Leilehua Plateau, this is one of Oahu's most scenic courses, with views of mountains from every hole. Unfortunately, there are also lots of views of trees, especially eucalyptus, Norfolk pine, and coconut palm; it's a lesson in patience to stay on the fairways and away from the trees. The two signature holes, the par-4 number 4 (a classic middle hole with water, flowers, and bunkers) and the par-3 number 12 (a comfortable tee shot over a ravine filled with is free, and a $1 bus ride will get you there. Go early; you'll wait 2 to 3 hours if you wait until midday.

- **Wander the "Hill of Sacrifice" at the National Cemetery of the Pacific at Punchbowl.** The old volcanic crater that the ancient Hawaiians called Puowaina ("hill of sacrifice") is a burial ground for 35,000 victims of three American wars: World War II, Korea, and Vietnam. The air is still, the atmosphere reflective, and the experience intensely personal.

- **See a *Heiau* Where Ancient Hawaiians Were Sacrificed.** Puu O Mahuka Heiau, once the largest sacrificial temple on Oahu, is now a state historic site. Encompassing some 5 acres, the *heiau* is composed of a huge rectangle of stones twice as big as a football field; the upper section has a raised mound surrounded by stones, creating what appears to be an altar. People still come here to pray; you may see offerings such as ti-leaves, flowers, and fruit left behind. Don't disturb the offerings or walk on the stones (this is very disrespectful). The view from this 300-foot bluff—from Waimea Bay all the way to Kaena Point—is awe-inspiring.

- **Order a Shave Ice in a Tropical Flavor.** When you're in Haleiwa, stop at Matsumoto Shave Ice, 66–087 Kamehameha Hwy., for a snow cone with an exotic flavor poured over the top, such as the local favorite *li hing mui,* or sweet Japanese azuki beans hidden inside. This taste of tropical paradise goes for just $1.

- **Watch the Sun Set from Kuhio Beach.** There are few more pleasing spots in Waikiki than the benches at the water's edge at Kuhio Beach, where lovers of all ages stop to peruse the sinking sun. A short walk across the intersection of Kalakaua and Kapahulu avenues takes you to the Duke Kahanamoku statue on Kuhio Beach where, on weekends, there's a thoroughly delightful torch-lighting ceremony with hula dancing. It's completely free of charge, and a wonderful way to end the day.

- **Listen to the Soothing Sounds of Hawaiian Music.** You can sit under the huge canopy of the banyan tree at the Sheraton Moana Surfrider's Banyan Veranda in Waikiki and sway to the live Hawaiian music any night of the week. You'll just have to order a drink to maintain your seat (a Coke is $3). *Budget tip:* Get yours from the ground-level beach bar, where drinks are much cheaper, if less elegantly served (in plastic cups), than they are on the veranda.

tropical flowers that jumps to the undulating green with bunkers on each side) are so scenic, you'll forgive the challenges they pose.

95–176 Kuahelani Ave., Mililani. ⓒ **808/623-2222.** www.mililanigolf.com. Greens fees: $85 Mon–Fri, $85 Sat–Sun and holidays. From Waikiki, take H-1 west (toward Ewa), past Aloha Stadium; at the split in the freeway, turn off onto H-2. Exit at Mililani (exit 5B) onto Meheula Pkwy.; go to the third stoplight (about 2 miles from the exit), and turn right onto Kuahelani Ave. TheBus: 52.

LEEWARD OAHU

Makaha Resort Golf Club ★★ This challenging course—recently named "The Best Golf Course on Oahu" by *Honolulu* magazine—sits some 45 miles west of Honolulu, in Makaha Valley. Designed by William Bell, the par-72, 7,091-yard course meanders toward the ocean before turning and heading into the valley. Sheer volcanic walls tower 1,500 feet above the course, which is surrounded by swaying palm trees and neon-bright bougainvillea; an occasional peacock will even strut across the fairways. The beauty here could make it difficult to keep your mind on the game if it weren't for the course's many challenges: eight water hazards, 107 bunkers, and frequent brisk winds. This course is packed on weekends, so it's best to try weekdays. Facilities include a pro shop, bag storage, and snack shop.

84–627 Makaha Valley Rd., Waianae. © **808/695-7111** or 808/695-5239. www.makahavalleycc.com. Greens fees: $100. Take H-1 west until it turns into Hwy. 93, which winds through the coastal towns of Nanakuli, Waianae, and Makaha. Turn right on Makaha Valley Rd. and follow it to the fork; the course is on the left. TheBus: 51. Shuttle: 75.

West Loch Municipal Golf Course *Value* This par-72, 6,615-yard course located just 30 minutes from Waikiki, in Ewa Beach, offers golfers a challenge at bargain rates. The difficulties on this municipal course are water (lots of hazards), wind (constant trade winds), and narrow fairways. To help you out, the course features a "water" driving range (with a lake) to practice your drives. After a few practice swings on the driving range, you'll be ready to take on this unusual course, designed by Robin Nelson and Rodney Wright. The first hole starts in front of the clubhouse; the course crosses a freeway for the next 10 holes and then goes back across for holes 12 to 18. West Loch has practice greens, a pro shop, and a restaurant. *Note:* Booking a week in advance is recommended.

91–1126 Okupe St., Ewa Beach. © **808/675-6076.** www.gvhawaii.com/westloch/westloch.htm. Greens fees: $42, $21 twilight. Booking a week in advance is recommended. Take H-1 west to the Hwy. 76 exit; stay in the left lane and turn left at West Loch Estates, just opposite St. Francis Medical Center. To park, take 2 immediate right turns. TheBus: 50.

BIKING

Biking is a great way to see Oahu. Most streets here have bike lanes. For information on trails, races, and tours, check out **www.bikehawaii.com**. For information on bikeways and maps, contact the **Honolulu City and County Bike Coordinator** (© **808/527-5044**).

If you're in Waikiki, you can rent a bike for as little as $10 for a half-day and $16 for 24 hours at **Wiki Wiki Wheels,** 1827 Ala Moana, Suite 201 (© **808/951-5787;** www.bigkahunarentals.com). On the North Shore, for a full-suspension mountain bike, try **Raging Isle,** 66–250 Kamehameha Hwy., Haleiwa (© **808/637-7707;** www.ragingisle.com), which rents full-suspension mountain bikes for $40 for 24 hours.

For a bike and hike adventure, call **Bike Hawaii** (© **877-MTV-RIDE** or 808/734-4214; www.bikehawaii.com); they have a variety of group tours, like their Downhill Coasting Ride, which gives you a bird's-eye view of Oahu from 1,800 feet above Waikiki. The tour includes coasting down 5 miles on a paved mountain road with scenic views above Waikiki, Honolulu, and Manoa Valley. Listen to the songs of birds, the wind through the trees, and learn about the culture, plants, and geology of the Hawaiian Islands. After that, you leave your bike for a 2-mile round-trip hike to a 200-foot waterfall. The 9am to 2pm trip, which includes van transportation from your hotel, continental-style breakfast, bike, helmet, snacks, water bottle, and guide, costs $75 for adults and $65 for children 14 and under.

If you'd like to join in on some club rides, contact the **Hawaii Bicycle League** (☎ **808/735-5756**), which offers rides every weekend, as well as several annual events. The league can also provide a schedule of upcoming rides, races, and outings.

HORSEBACK RIDING

You can gallop on the beach at the **Turtle Bay Resort,** 57–091 Kamehameha Hwy., Kahuku (☎ **808/293-8811;** www.turtlebayresort.com; TheBus: 52 or 55), where 45-minute rides along sandy beaches with spectacular ocean views and through a forest of ironwood trees cost $45 for adults and $30 for children 7 to 12 (they must be at least 4 ft. 4 in. tall). Romantic evening rides take place on Friday, Saturday, and Sunday from 5 to 6:30pm ($65 per person). Advanced riders can sign up for a 60-minute trot-and-canter ride along Kawela Bay ($100).

TENNIS

Oahu has 181 free public tennis courts. To get a complete list of all facilities or information on upcoming tournaments, send a self-addressed, stamped envelope to **Department of Parks and Recreation,** Tennis Unit, 650 S. King St., Honolulu, HI 96813.

In Waikiki, try the Diamond Head courts at 3908 Paki Ave., across from the Kapiolani Park; call ☎ **808/971-7150.** The courts are available on a first-come, first-served basis; playing time is limited to 45 minutes if others are waiting. If those courts are full, try the **Ilikai Tennis Center** at the Ilikai Hotel, 1777 Ala Moana Blvd., at Hobron Lane (☎ **800/367-8434** or 808/949-3811; TheBus: 19 or 20), which has six courts, equipment rental, lessons, and repair service. Courts cost $8 per person per hour; private lessons are $50 per hour.

On the North Shore, the **Turtle Bay Resort,** 57–091 Kamehameha Hwy., Kahuku (☎ **808/293-8811,** ext. 24; TheBus: 52 or 55), has 10 courts, 4 of which are lit for night play. You must reserve the night courts in advance, as they're very popular. Court time is $10 for 1½ hours, equipment rental and lessons are also available.

10 Organized Tours

If your time is limited, you might want to consider a guided tour. These tours are informative and entertaining—you'll probably be surprised at how much you enjoy yourself.

Waikiki Trolley Tours ✿, 1141 Waimanu St., Suite 105, Honolulu (☎ **800/824-8804** or 808/596-2199; www.waikikitrolley.com), offers three fun tours of sightseeing, entertainment, dining, and shopping. These tours are a great way to get the lay of the land. You can get on and off the trolley as needed (trolleys come along every 2–20 min.). An all-day pass (8:30am–11:35pm) is $25 for adults, $18 for seniors, and $12 for children (4–11); a 4-day pass is $45 for adults, $27 for seniors, and $18 for children (4–11). For the same price, you can experience the new 2-hour narrated Ocean Coastline tour of the southeast side of Oahu, an easy way to see the stunning views.

If you'd rather go touring on your own, **TourTalk-Oahu** (☎ **877/585-7499;** www.tourtalkhawaii.com) offers a complete package of 2½-hour narrated compact disks (or cassettes), driving instructions and a 72-page booklet containing color maps, photos, site information, and Hawaii facts for $25. The self-guided driving tour not only guides you around the island to see the most popular sites, it has cultural and historical information as well.

WAIKIKI & HONOLULU WALKING TOURS

DOWNTOWN HONOLULU   The **Mission Houses Museum,** 553 S. King St., at Kawaiahao Street (© **808/531-0481;** TheBus: 2), offers a guided walking tour of historic downtown Honolulu, on Thursday and Saturday, 9:30am to 12:45pm. The fee is $15 for adults, $12 for seniors, $10 children 6 and up, age 5 and under free; rates includes the regular Mission Houses tour (see "Attractions In & Around Honolulu & Waikiki," below). The tour includes the capitol district, making stops at sites such as Iolani Place, the Kamehameha Statue, the Royal Tomb, and James Kekela's grave. Reserve a day ahead in person or by phone.

CHINATOWN HISTORIC DISTRICT   Two 3-hour guided tours of Chinatown are offered Tuesdays at 9:30am by the **Chinese Chamber of Commerce** ★, 42 N. King St., at Smith Street (© **808/533-3181;** TheBus: 2). The cost is $5 per person; call to reserve.

The **Hawaii Heritage Center** (© **808/521-2749**) also conducts 2-hour walking tours that focus on the history, culture, and multicultural aspects of Chinatown. Tours begin Fridays at 9:30am at the Ramsay Gallery, 1128 Smith St., at N. King Street (TheBus: 2 or 13; get off on Hotel and Smith sts.); the cost is $5 per person.

Moments   A Bird's-Eye View

To understand why Oahu was the island of kings, you need to see it from the air. **Island Seaplane Service** ★★ (© **808/836-6273;** www.islandseaplane.com) operates flights departing from a floating dock in the protected waters of Keehi Lagoon in either a six-passenger DeHavilland Beaver or a four-passenger Cessna 206. There's nothing quite like feeling the slap of the waves as the plane skims across the water and then effortlessly lifts into the air.

Your tour will give you aerial views of Waikiki Beach, Diamond Head Crater, Kahala's luxury estates, and the sparkling waters of Hanauma and Kaneohe bays. The half-hour tour ($99) ends here, while the 1-hour tour ($179) continues on to Chinaman's Hat, the Polynesian Cultural Center, and the rolling surf of the North Shore. The flight returns across the island, flying over Hawaii's historic wartime sites: Schofield Barracks and the USS *Arizona* and *Missouri* memorials in Pearl Harbor.

Capt. Pat Magie, company president and chief pilot, has logged more than 32,000 hours of flight time without an accident (26,000 hr. in seaplanes in Alaska, Canada, the Arctic, and the Caribbean). Any day now, he'll break the world record for seaplane hours.

The **Hawaii Geographic Society** (© **808/538-3952**) presents numerous interesting and unusual tours, such as "A Temple Tour," which includes Chinese, Japanese, Christian, and Jewish houses of worship; an archaeology tour in and around downtown Honolulu; and others. Each is guided by an expert from the Hawaii Geographic Society and must have a minimum of three people; the cost is $10 per person. The society's brochure, *Historic Downtown Honolulu Walking Tour,* is a fascinating self-guided tour of the 200-year-old city center. If you'd like a copy, send $3 to **Hawaii Geographic Maps and Books,** 49 S. Hotel St. (P.O. Box 1698), Honolulu, HI 96808.

For a self-guided tour of the neighborhood, see "A Stroll Through Historic Chinatown," which begins on p. 191.

GUIDED ECOTOURS

Oahu isn't just high-rises in Waikiki or urban sprawl in Honolulu, but extinct craters, hidden waterfalls, lush rainforests, forgotten coastlines, and rainbow-filled valleys. To experience the other side of Oahu, contact **Oahu Nature Tours** (𝕮 **808/924-2473; www.oahunaturetours.org**). They have seven different ecotours, starting at $20 a person. They provide everything: experts in geology, history, Hawaiian mythology and archaeology, round-trip transportation, entrance fees, bottled water, snacks, use of day packs, binoculars, flash lights, and rain gear.

If you want to explore a hidden, ancient Hawaii that even most lifelong residents have never seen, book a tour with **Mauka Makai Excursions** 🦀, 350 Ward Ave., Honolulu (𝕮 **808/593-3525**), a Hawaiian-owned and -operated ecotour company specializing in field trips to off-the-beaten-path (and sometimes hidden in the jungle) ancient temples, sea caves, sacred stones, petroglyphs, and other cultural treasures. Tours range from a half-day ($43 adults, $32 children 6–17) to a full day ($75 adults, $63 children). They provide bottled water, insect repellent, rain gear, beach gear, fishing tackle, and hotel pickup; you bring your imagination.

11 Attractions In & Around Honolulu & Waikiki

HISTORIC HONOLULU

The Waikiki you see today bears no resemblance to the Waikiki of yesteryear, a place of vast taro fields extending from the ocean to deep into Manoa Valley, dotted with numerous fish ponds and gardens tended by thousands of people. This picture of old Waikiki can be recaptured by following the emerging **Waikiki Historic Trail** 🦀, a meandering 2-mile walk with 20 bronze surfboard markers (standing 6 ft., 5 in. tall, you can't miss 'em), complete with descriptions and archive photos of the historic sites. The markers note everything from Waikiki's ancient fish ponds to the history of the Ala Wai Canal. The trail begins at Kuhio Beach and ends at the King Kalakaua statue, at the intersection of Kuhio and Kalakaua avenues. Free, guided walking tours, sponsored by the Native Hawaiian Hospitality Association are given every Tuesday, Thursday, and Saturday. Meet at the Royal Hawaiian Shopping Center stage, near the fountain, at 9am. For more information, call 𝕮 **808/737-6442** or www.waikikihistorictrail.com.

A hula performance is a popular way for visitors to get a taste of traditional Hawaiian culture. Unfortunately the **Kodak Hula Show** at the Waikiki Band Shell at Kapiolani Park closed in 2002. For a more genuine Hawaiian hula experience, catch the hula *halau* performed Monday through Friday at 1pm at the **Bishop Museum** (see below).

Bishop Museum 🦀🦀 (Kids) This forbidding, four-story, Romanesque, lava-rock structure (it looks like something out of a Charles Addams cartoon) holds safe the world's greatest collection of natural and cultural artifacts from Hawaii and the Pacific. It's a great rainy-day diversion; plan to spend about half a day here. The museum was founded by a Hawaiian princess, Bernice Pauahi, who collected priceless artifacts and in her will instructed her husband, Charles Reed Bishop, to establish a Hawaiian museum "to enrich and delight" the people of Hawaii. The institution is now home to Dr. Yoshihiko Sinoto, the last in a proud line of adventuring archaeologists who explored more of the Pacific than Captain Cook and traced Hawaii's history and culture through its fish hooks.

Honolulu Attractions

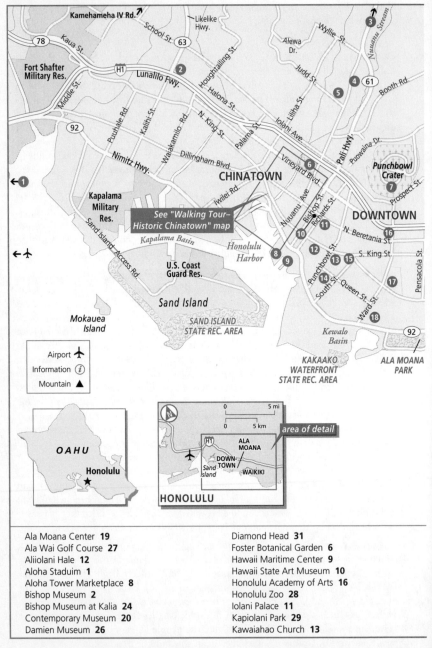

Ala Moana Center **19**
Ala Wai Golf Course **27**
Aliiolani Hale **12**
Aloha Stadium **1**
Aloha Tower Marketplace **8**
Bishop Museum **2**
Bishop Museum at Kalia **24**
Contemporary Museum **20**
Damien Museum **26**

Diamond Head **31**
Foster Botanical Garden **6**
Hawaii Maritime Center **9**
Hawaii State Art Museum **10**
Honolulu Academy of Arts **16**
Honolulu Zoo **28**
Iolani Palace **11**
Kapiolani Park **29**
Kawaiahao Church **13**

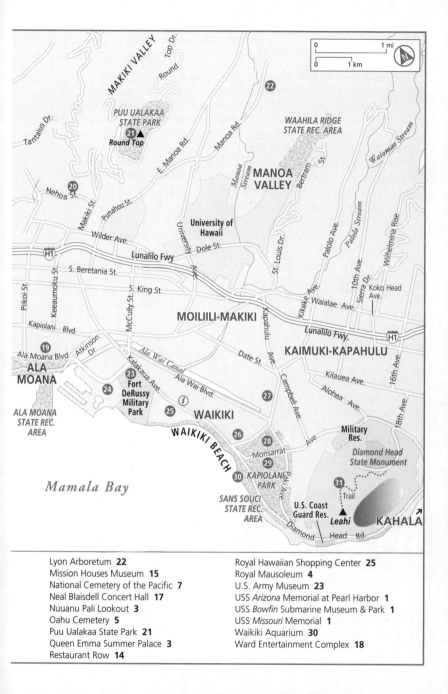

Kids Especially for Kids

Visiting the Honolulu Zoo (p. 187)   Visit Africa in Hawaii at Waikiki's Kapiolani Park. The lions, giraffes, zebras, and elephants delight youngsters and parents alike. But the great new thrill is the Zoo by Moonlight tour—so kids can see and hear what really goes bump in the night.

Shopping the Aloha Flea Market   Most kids hate to shop. But the Aloha Flea Market, a giant outdoor bazaar at Aloha Stadium every Wednesday, Saturday, and Sunday, is more than shopping. It's an experience akin to a carnival, full of strange food, odd goods, and bold barkers. Nobody ever leaves this place empty-handed—or without having had lots of fun.

Seeing the World's Only Wholphin (p. 189)   It's a freak of nature, a cross between a whale and a dolphin—and you can see it at Sea Life Park. Kids love this marine amusement park, where trained dolphins, whales, and seals do their thing.

Flying a Kite at Kapiolani Park   Great open expanses of green and constant trade winds make this urban park one of Hawaii's prime locations for kite-flying. You can watch the pros fly dragon kites and stage kite-fighting contests; or join in the fun after checking out the convenient kite shop across the street in New Otani's arcade.

Eating Shave Ice at Haleiwa (p. 204)   No visit to Hawaii is complete without an authentic shave ice. You can find shave ice in all kinds of tropical flavors throughout the islands, but for some reason, it tastes better in this funky North Shore surf town.

Beating Bamboo Drums in a Fijian Village (p. 201)   The Polynesian Cultural Center introduces kids to the games played by Polynesian and Melanesian children. The activities, which range from face painting to Hawaiian bowling, go on every day from 12:30 to 5:30pm.

The Bishop is jam-packed with acquisitions—from insect specimens and ceremonial spears to calabashes and old photos of topless hula dancers. A visit here will give you a good basis for understanding Hawaiian life and culture. You'll see the great feathered capes of kings, the last grass shack in Hawaii, pre-industrial Polynesian art, even the skeleton of a 50-foot sperm whale. There are also seashells, koa-wood bowls, nose flutes, and Dr. Sinoto's major collection of fish hooks.

Hula performances take place daily at 11am and 2pm, and various Hawaiian crafts like lei-making, featherworking, and quilting are demonstrated. This daily cultural event is worth making time for. For a look at spectacular artifacts, such as the ancient feather cloak of King Kamehameha and other items not shown to the general public, take the "Behind the Scenes Tour," offered weekdays at 1:30pm for an additional fee of $15.

1525 Bernice St., just off Kalihi St. (also known as Likelike Hwy.). © 808/847-3511. www.bishopmuseum.org. Admission $15 adults, $12 children 4–12 and seniors. Daily 9am–5pm. TheBus: 2.

Bishop Museum at Kalia ★★★ *(Kids)*   Now in Waikiki, this "mini" version of the Bishop Museum is just right for visitors who want to get an insider's view of Hawaiian culture but are pressed for time. Located in the Kalia Tower of the Hilton Hawaiian Village Beach Resort and Spa, the Bishop Musuem at Kalia features cultural interpreters to walk you through the story of life in Waikiki from ancient times to today. Allow at least an hour (1½ hours would be better). You can participate in a variety of interactive, hands-on-activities, such as lei making, weaving cordage from coconut fibers, pounding kapa into cloth, learning the basic motions of the hula, or trying your hand at playing a Hawaiian instrument, such as the pahu (shark skin drum), ohe hano ihu (nose flute), or uli uli (feathered gourd rattle). As you move from ancient times into the arrival of the missionaries, the royal monarchy, and into Waikiki of the 20th century (with great old surfing movies), you will be amazed at how time flies. Not to be missed!

2005 Kalia Rd. © **808/946-9478**. www.bishopmuseum.org. Admission $7 adults, children 12 and under free. Daily 9am–5pm. TheBus: 19 or 20.

Hawaii Maritime Center ★ *(Finds)*   You can easily spend a couple of hours here, wandering around and learning the story of Hawaii's rich maritime past, from the ancient journey of Polynesian voyagers to the nostalgic days of the *Lurline,* which once brought tourists from San Francisco on 4-day cruises. Inside the Hawaii Maritime Center's Kalakaua Boat House, patterned after His Majesty King David Kalakaua's own canoe house, are more than 30 exhibits, including Matson cruise ships (which brought the first tourists to Waikiki), flying boats that delivered the mail, and the skeleton of a Pacific humpback whale that beached on Kahoolawe. Outside, the *Hokulea,* a double-hulled sailing canoe that, in 1976, reenacted the Polynesian voyage of discovery, is moored next to the *Falls of Clyde,* a four-masted schooner that once ran tea from China to the West Coast.

Pier 7 (next to Aloha Tower), Honolulu Harbor. © **808/536-6373**. www.bishopmuseum.org. Admission $7.50 adults, $4.50 children 6–17. Daily 8:30am–5pm. TheBus: 19 or 20.

Iolani Palace ★   If you want to really "understand" Hawaii, this 45-minute tour is well worth the time. The Iolani Palace was built by King David Kalakaua, who spared no expense. The 4-year project, completed in 1882, cost $360,000—and nearly bankrupted the Hawaiian kingdom. This four-story Italian Renaissance palace was the first electrified building in Honolulu (it had electricity before the White House and Buckingham Palace). Royals lived here for 11 years, until Queen Liliuokalani was deposed in a palace coup led by U.S. Marines on January 17, 1893, at the demand of sugar planters and missionary descendants, and the Hawaiian monarchy fell forever.

Cherished by latter-day royalists, the 10-room palace stands as an architectural statement of the monarchy period. Iolani attracts 100,000 visitors a year in groups of 20; everyone must don denim booties to scoot across the royal floors. Tours are either a comprehensive **Grand Tour** ★, which is 90 minutes long and covers the Palace history, the Palace grounds, and the Palace itself; or the **Galleries Tour,** a self-guided tour of the Palace Galleries (complete with crown jewels, the ancient feathered cloaks, the Royal china, etc.).

At S. King and Richards sts. © **800/532-1051** or 808/522-0832. www.iolanipalace.org. Grand Tour $20 adults, $5 children 5–17; Galleries Tour $6 adults, $3 children 5–17. Tues–Sat 8:30am–2pm; call ahead to reserve the Grand Tour. Children under 5 not permitted. Extremely limited parking on palace grounds, try metered parking on the street. TheBus: 2.

Kawaiahao Church In 1842, Kawaiahao Church stood complete at last, the crowning achievement of missionaries and Hawaiians working together for the first time on a common project. Designed by Rev. Hiram Bingham and supervised by Kamehameha III, who ordered his people to help build it, the project took 5 years. Workers quarried 14,000 1,000-pound coral blocks from the offshore reefs and cut timber in the forests for the beams.

This proud stone church, complete with bell tower and colonial colonnade, was the first permanent Western house of worship in the islands. It became the church of the Hawaiian royalty and remains in use today by Hawaiians who conduct services in the Hawaiian language (which probably sets old Rev. Bingham spinning in his grave). Some fine portraits of Hawaiian royalty hang inside. The best time to come is for the **Hawaiian-language services** ⟨★★⟩, conducted on Sundays at 10:30am.

957 Punchbowl St. (at King St.). ⟨✆⟩ **808/522-1333**. Free admission (small donations appreciated). Mon–Fri 9am–3pm; Sun services 10:30am. TheBus: 2.

Mission Houses Museum This museum tells the dramatic story of cultural change in 19th-century Hawaii. American Protestant missionaries established their headquarters here in 1820. Included in the complex are a visitor center and three historic mission buildings, which have been restored and refurnished to reflect the daily life and work of the missionaries.

Insider's tip: The best way to see the museum is as part of a walking tour of historic downtown buildings, offered on Thursday and Friday mornings (museum admission is included in the tour price); for details, see "Organized Tours," above.

553 S. King St. (at Kawaiahao St.). ⟨✆⟩ **808/531-0481**. www.missionhouses.org. Admission $10 adults, $8 military personnel and seniors, $6 students and youths 6–18, children under 5 free. Tues–Sat 9am–4pm. TheBus: 2.

Queen Emma Summer Palace Hanaiakamalama, the name of the country estate of Kamehameha IV and Queen Emma, was once in the secluded uplands of Nuuanu Valley. These days, it's adjacent to a six-lane highway full of speeding cars that sound remarkably like surf as they zip by. This simple, seven-room New England–style house, built in 1848 and restored by the Daughters of Hawaii, is worth about an hour of your time to see the interesting blend of Victorian furniture and hallmarks of Hawaiian royalty, including feather cloaks and *kahili,* the feathered standards that mark the presence of *alii* (royalty). Other royal treasures include a canoe-shaped cradle for Queen Emma's baby, Prince Albert, who died at the age of 4. (Kauai's ultra-ritzy Princeville Resort is named for the little prince.)

2913 Pali Hwy. (at Old Pali Rd.). ⟨✆⟩ **808/595-3167**. Admission $5 adults, $4 seniors, $1 children 11 and under. Daily 9am–4pm. TheBus: 4, 55, 56, 57, or 65.

WARTIME HONOLULU

USS Arizona Memorial at Pearl Harbor ⟨★★★⟩ On December 7, 1941, the USS *Arizona,* while moored here in Pearl Harbor, was bombed in a Japanese air raid. The 608-foot battleship sank in 9 minutes without firing a shot, taking 1,177 sailors and Marines to their deaths—and catapulting the United States into World War II.

Nobody who visits the memorial will ever forget it. The deck of the ship lies 6 feet below the surface of the sea. Oil still oozes slowly up from the *Arizona's* engine room to stain the harbor's calm, blue water; some say the ship still weeps for its lost crew. The memorial is a stark white 184-foot rectangle that spans the sunken hull of the ship; it was designed by Alfred Pries, a German architect interned on Sand Island during the war. It contains the ship's bell, recovered from the wreckage, and a shrine room with the names of the dead carved in stone.

Today, free U.S. Navy launches take visitors to the *Arizona*. Try to arrive early at the visitor center (no later than 1:30pm), operated jointly by the National Park Service and the U.S. Navy, to avoid the huge crowds; waits of 1 to 3 hours are common, and they don't take reservations. While you're waiting for the shuttle to take you out to the ship—you'll be issued a number and time of departure, which you must pick up yourself—you can explore the interesting museum's personal mementos, photographs, and historic documents. A moving 20-minute film, more solemn and accurate than the recent Disney blockbuster version of events—precedes your trip to the ship. Allow a total of at least 4 hours for your visit.

Due to increased security measures, visitors cannot carry purses, handbags, fanny packs, backpacks, camera bags, diaper bags, or other items that offer concealment on the boat. However, there is a container to store carry-on-size items (no bigger than 30'×30'×18') for a fee of $2 per item.

Parents: Note that baby strollers, baby carriages, and baby backpacks are not allowed in the theater, on the boat, or on the USS *Arizona* Memorial. All babies must be carried. *One last note:* Most unfortunately, the USS *Arizona* Memorial is a high-theft area—leave your valuables at the hotel.

Pearl Harbor. © **808/422-0561** (recorded info) or 808/422-2771. www.nps.gov/usar. Free admission. Daily 7:30am–5pm (programs run 8am–3pm). Children under 12 should be accompanied by an adult. Shirts and shoes required; no swimsuits or flip-flops allowed (shorts are okay). Wheelchairs gladly accommodated. Drive west on H-1 past the airport; take the USS *Arizona* Memorial exit and follow the green-and-white signs; there's ample free parking. TheBus: 20 and 47; or Arizona Memorial Shuttle Bus (© **808/839-0911**), which picks up at Waikiki hotels 6:50am–1pm ($6 round-trip).

USS Bowfin Submarine Museum & Park ⭐

The USS *Bowfin* is one of only 15 World War II submarines still in existence today. You can go below deck of this famous submarine—nicknamed the "Pearl Harbor Avenger" for its successful attacks on the Japanese—and see how the 80-man crew lived during wartime. The *Bowfin* Museum has an impressive collection of submarine-related artifacts. The Waterfront Memorial honors submariners lost during World War II.

11 Arizona Memorial Dr. (next to the USS *Arizona* Memorial Visitor Center). © **808/423-1341**. Admission $8 adults, $6 active-duty military personnel, $3 children 4–12. Daily 8am–5pm. See USS *Arizona* Memorial, above, for driving, bus, and shuttle directions.

USS Missouri Memorial ⭐

On the deck of this 58,000-ton battleship (the last one the Navy built), World War II came to an end with the signing of the Japanese surrender on September 2, 1945. The *Missouri* was part of the force that carried out bombing raids over Tokyo and provided firepower in the battles of Iwo Jima and Okinawa. In 1955, the Navy decommissioned the ship and placed it in mothballs at the Puget Sound Naval Shipyard, in Washington State. But the *Missouri* was modernized and called back into action in 1986, eventually being deployed in the Persian Gulf War, before retiring once again in 1992. Here it sat until another battle ensued, this time over who would get the right to keep this living legend. Hawaii won that battle and brought the ship to Pearl Harbor in 1998. The next year, the 887-foot ship, like a phoenix, rose again into the public spotlight; it's now open to visitors as a museum memorial.

If you have the time, take the tour, which begins at the visitor center. Guests are shuttled to Ford Island on military-style buses while listening to a 1940s-style radio program (complete with news clips, wartime commercials, and music). Once on the ship, guests watch an informational film and are then free to explore on their own or take a guided tour. Highlights of this massive (more than 200-ft. tall) battleship include the forecastle (or *foc's'le,* in Navy talk), where the 30,000-pound anchors are "dropped" on 1,080 feet of anchor chain; the 16-inch guns (each 65 ft. long and weighing 116 tons), which can accurately fire a 2,700-pound shell some 23 miles in 50 seconds; and the spot where the Instrument of Surrender was signed as Douglas MacArthur, Chester Nimitz, and William "Bull" Halsey looked on.

Battleship Row, Pearl Harbor. ☎ 808/423-2263. www.ussmissouri.com. Admission $16 adults, $8 children 4–12 (hour-long guided tours, available 9:30am–4:30pm, cost $22 adults and $14 children—admission included). Daily 9am–5pm. Check in at the visitor center of the USS *Bowfin* Memorial, next to the USS *Arizona* Memorial. Drive west on H-1 past the airport, take the USS *Arizona* Memorial exit, and follow the green-and-white signs; there's ample free parking. TheBus: 20 or 47.

National Cemetery of the Pacific   The National Cemetery of the Pacific (also known as "the Punchbowl") is an ash-and-lava tuff cone that exploded about 150,000 years ago—like Diamond Head, only smaller. Early Hawaiians called it Puowaina, or "hill of sacrifice." The old crater is a burial ground for 35,000 victims of three American wars in Asia and the Pacific: World War II, Korea, and Vietnam. Among the graves, you'll find many unmarked ones with the date December 7, 1941 carved in stone. Some will be unknown forever; others are famous, like that of war correspondent Ernie Pyle, killed by a Japanese sniper in April 1945 on Okinawa; still others buried here are remembered only by family and surviving buddies. The white stone tablets, known as the Courts of the Missing, bear the names of 28,788 Americans missing in action in World War II.

Survivors come here often to reflect on the meaning of war and to remember those, like themselves, who stood in harm's way to win peace a half-century ago. Some fight back tears, remembering lost buddies, lost missions, and the sacrifices of those who died.

Punchbowl Crater, 2177 Puowaina Dr. (at the end of the road). ☎ 808/541-1434. Free admission. Daily 8am–5:30pm (Mar–Sept to 6:30pm). TheBus: 15.

JUST BEYOND PEARL HARBOR

Hawaiian Railway *(Kids)*   All aboard! This is a train ride back into history. Between 1890 and 1947, the chief mode of transportation for Oahu's sugar mills was the Oahu Railway and Land Co.'s narrow-gauge trains. The line carried not only equipment, raw sugar, and supplies, but also passengers from one side of the island to the other. You can relive those days every Sunday with a 1½-hour narrated ride through Ko Olina Resort and out to Makaha.

As an added attraction, on the second Sunday of the month, you can ride on the nearly-100-year-old, custom-built parlor-observation car belonging to Benjamin F. Dillingham, founder of the Oahu Railway and Land Co.; the fare is $15 (no kids under 13), and you must reserve in advance.

Ewa Station, Ewa Beach. ☎ 808/681-5461. www.hawaiianrailway.com. Admission $10 adults, $5 seniors and children 2–12. Departures Sun 1 and 3pm and weekdays by appointment. Take H-1 west to exit 5A; take Hwy. 76 south for 2½ miles to Tesoro Gas; turn right on Renton Rd. and drive 1½ miles to end of paved section. The station is on the left. TheBus: C-Express to Kapalei, then transfer to no. 41, which goes through Ewa and drops you off outside the gate.

Hawaiian Waters Adventure Park *(Kids)*   If you have kids, you have to take them here! This 29-acre water-themed amusement park opened in spring 1999 with some $14 million in attractions. Plan to spend the day. Highlights are a football field–size wave pool for bodysurfing, two 65-foot-high free-fall slides, two water-toboggan bullet slides, inner-tube slides, body flume slides, a continuous river for floating inner tubes, and separate pools for adults, teens, and children. In addition, there are restaurants, food carts, Hawaiian performances, and shops.

400 Farrington Hwy., Kapolei. © 808/674-9283. www.hawaiianwaters.com. Admission $35 adults, $24 children 4–11, free for children under 3. Hours vary, but generally the park is open daily 10:30am–4 or 5pm in peak season (summer); during off-peak season 10:30am–3:30 or 4pm; closed some weekdays. Take H-1 west to exit 1 (Campbell Industrial Park). Make an immediate left turn to Farrington Hwy.; the park is on your left.

Hawaii's Plantation Village   The hour-long tour of this restored 50-acre village offers a glimpse back in time to when sugar planters from America shaped the land, economy, and culture of territorial Hawaii. From 1852, when the first contract laborers arrived here from China, to 1947, when the plantation era ended, more than 400,000 men, women, and children from China, Japan, Portugal, Puerto Rico, Korea, and the Philippines came to work the sugarcane fields. The "talk story" tour brings the old village alive with 30 faithfully restored camp houses, Chinese and Japanese temples, the Plantation Store, and even a sumo-wrestling ring.

Waipahu Cultural Garden Park, 94–695 Waipahu St. (at Waipahu Depot Rd.), Waipahu. © 808/677-0110. www.hawaii plantationvillage.org. Admission (including escorted tour) $10 adults, $7 military personnel and seniors, $4 children 5–17. Mon–Fri 9am–3pm; Sat 10am–3pm. Take H-1 west to Waikele-Waipahu exit (exit 7); get in the left lane on exit and turn left on Paiwa St.; at the 5th light, turn right onto Waipahu St.; after the 2nd light, turn left. TheBus: 47.

FISH, FLORA & FAUNA

Foster Botanical Garden ★★ (Finds)   You could spend days in this unique and historic garden, a leafy oasis amid the high-rises of downtown Honolulu, but your schedule will probably only allow a couple of hours. Combine a tour of the Garden with a trip to Chinatown (just across the street) to maximize your time. The giant trees that tower over the main terrace were planted in the 1850s by William Hillebrand, a German physician and botanist, on royal land leased from Queen Emma. Today, this 14-acre public garden, on the north side of Chinatown, is a living museum of plants, some rare and endangered, collected from the tropical regions of the world. Of special interest are 26 "Exceptional Trees" protected by state law, a large palm collection, a primitive cycad garden, and a hybrid orchid collection.

50 N. Vineyard Blvd. (at Nuuanu Ave.). © 808/522-7066. Admission $5 adults, $1 children 6–12. Daily 9am–4pm; guided tours Mon–Fri at 1pm (reservations recommended). TheBus: 2, 4, or 13.

Honolulu Zoo ★ (Kids)   Nobody comes to Hawaii to see an Indian elephant, or African lions and zebras. Right? Wrong. This 43-acre municipal zoo in Waikiki attracts visitors in droves. If you've got kids, allot at least half a day or more. The highlight is the new African Savannah, a 10-acre wild preserve exhibit with more than 40 uncapped African critters roaming around in the open. The zoo also has a rare Hawaiian nene goose, a Hawaiian pig, and mouflon sheep. (Only the goose, an evolved version of the Canadian honker, is considered to be truly Hawaiian; the others are imported from Polynesia, India, and elsewhere.)

For a real treat, take the **Zoo by Moonlight** tour, which offers a rare behind-the-scenes look into the lives of the zoo's nocturnal residents. Tours are offered 2 days before, during, and 2 days after the full moon, from 7 to 9pm; the cost is $7 for adults and $5 for children.

151 Kapahulu Ave. (between Paki and Kalakaua aves.), at entrance to Kapiolani Park. © 808/971-7171. www. honoluluzoo.org. Admission $6 adults, $1 children 6–12. Daily 9am–4:30pm. TheBus: 2, 8, 19, 20, or 47.

Oahu's Vibrant Art Scene

MUSEUMS   Passionate art lovers should head straight to Hawaii's three top cultural resources: the Contemporary Museum, the Honolulu Academy of Arts and the State Art Museum, which opened in 2002.

The acclaimed **Honolulu Academy of Arts** ★★, 900 S. Beretania St. (© **808/532-8700,** or 808/532-8701 for recording), is considered Hawaii's premier example of *kamaaina*-style architecture, the Academy is the state's only general fine-arts museum and has expanded steadily over the last decade. It boasts one of the top Asian art collections in the country. Open Tuesday through Saturday from 10am to 4:30pm, Sunday from 1 to 5pm; tours are Tuesday through Saturday at 11am and on Sunday at 1:15pm. Admission is $7 for adults and $4 for students, seniors, and military personnel; children under 12 enter free.

Set up on the slopes of Tantalus, one of Honolulu's upscale residential communities, the **Contemporary Museum,** 2411 Makiki Heights Dr. (© **808/ 526-0232;** www.tcmhi.org), is renowned for its 3 acres of Asian gardens (with reflecting pools, sun-drenched terraces, views of Diamond Head, and stone benches for quiet contemplation). Open Tuesday through Saturday from 10am to 4pm, Sunday from noon to 4pm. A 1-day membership is $5 for adults, $3 for seniors and students, and free for children 12 and under. The third Thursday of each month is free. Ask about the daily docent-led tours, and look for the excellent cafe and shop.

Just opened in 2002 is the **Hawaii State Art Museum,** housed in the original Royal Hawaiian Hotel built in 1872, during the reign of King Kamehameha V, at 250 S. Hotel St. (at Richards St.) (© **808/586-0900**). All of the 360 pieces currently displayed were all purchased by the state thanks to a 1967 law which said that 1 % of the cost of state buildings will be used to acquire works of art. Nearly 4 decades later, that state has amassed some

Lyon Arboretum ★   The Lyon Arboretum dates back to 1918, when the Hawaiian Sugar Planters Association wanted to demonstration the value of watershed for reforestation. In 1953, it became part of the University of Hawaii, where they continued to expand the extensive collection of tropical plants. Six-story-tall breadfruit trees, yellow orchids no bigger than a bus token, ferns with fuzzy buds as big as a human head . . . These are just a few of the botanical wonders you'll find at 194-acre Lyon Arboretum. A whole different world opens up to you along the self-guided 20-minute hike through the arboretum to Inspiration Point. You'll pass more than 5,000 exotic tropical plants full of singing birds in this cultivated rainforest (a University of Hawaii research facility) at the head of Manoa Valley. As we went to press, a University of Hawaii task force was deciding whether to keep the Arboretum for research and educational programs or relinquish the botanical garden to a conservancy group.

3860 Manoa Rd. (near the top of the road). © **808/988-0456.** www.hawaii.edu/lyonarboretum. $7 adults, $4 seniors and students, $3 children 12 and under. Mon–Fri 9am–4pm. TheBus: 5.

5,000 pieces. Open Tuesday through Saturday, 11am to 2pm, admission is free. Take the no. 2 bus from Waikiki. If you are driving, look for street (metered) parking.

GALLERIES   Galleries come and go in Chinatown, where efforts to revitalize the area have moved in fits and spurts. Two exceptions are the **Ramsay Galleries,** Tan Sing Building, 1128 Smith St. (© **808/537-2787**), and the **Pegge Hopper Gallery,** 1164 Nuuanu Ave. (© **808/524-1160**). Both are housed in historic Chinatown buildings that have been renovated and transformed into stunning showplaces.

The **Gallery at Ward Centre** in the Ward Centre, 1200 Ala Moana Blvd. (© **808/597-8034**), a cooperative gallery of Oahu artists, features fine works in all media, including paper, clay, scratchboard, oils, watercolors, collages, woodblocks, lithographs, glass, jewelry, and more.

Hawaii's most unusual gallery, listed on the Hawaii Register of Historic Places, is perched on the slopes of Punchbowl. The **Tennent Art Foundation Gallery,** 203 Prospect St. (© **808/531-1987**), is devoted to the oeuvre of artist Madge Tennent, whose paintings hang in the National Museum of Women alongside the works of Georgia O'Keeffe. Open limited hours and by appointment, so call before you go.

Art lovers now have a wonderful new resource: a 34-page brochure offering an overview of the music, theater, history, music, and visual arts of Oahu. The free brochure, which includes a map, phone numbers, websites, and more information, is put out by Arts with Aloha, representing 11 major Honolulu cultural organizations. Send a legal-size, self-addressed, stamped (55¢) envelope to **Arts with Aloha,** c/o Honolulu Academy of Arts, 900 S. Beretania St., Honolulu, HI 96814, or call the 24-hour hot line at © **808/532-8713.**

Sea Life Park ⭐ *Kids*   This 62-acre ocean theme park, located in East Oahu, is one of the island's most popular attractions. It features whales from Puget Sound, Atlantic bottle-nosed dolphins, California sea lions, and penguins going through their hoops to the delight of kids of all ages. If you have kids, allow all day to take in the sights. There's also a Hawaiian reef tank full of tropical fish; a "touch" pool, where you can touch a real sea cucumber (commonly found in tide pools); and a bird sanctuary, where you can see birds like the red-footed booby and the frigate bird. The chief curiosity, though, is the world's only "wholphin"—a cross between a false killer whale and an Atlantic bottle-nosed dolphin. On-site, marine biologists operate a recovery center for endangered marine life; during your visit, you'll be able to see rehabilitated Hawaiian monk seals and seabirds.

41–202 Kalanianaole Hwy. (at Makapuu Point), Honolulu. © **808/259-7933.** Admission $25 adults, $13 children 4–12. Daily 9:30am–5pm. Parking $3. Shuttle buses from Waikiki $5. TheBus: 22 or 58.

Waikiki Aquarium ⭐⭐⭐ *Kids*   Do not miss this! Half of Hawaii is its underwater world; plan to spend at least 2 hours discovering it. Behold the chambered nautilus, nature's submarine and inspiration for Jules Verne's *20,000 Leagues Under the Sea*. You may see this tropical spiral-shelled cephalopod mollusk—the only living one born in captivity—any day of the week here. Its natural habitat is the deep waters of Micronesia, but aquarium director Bruce Carlson not only succeeded in trapping the pearly shell in 1,500 feet of water (by dangling chunks of raw tuna), but also managed to breed this ancient relative of the octopus. There are also plenty of other fish in this small but first-class aquarium located on a live coral reef. The Hawaiian reef habitat features sharks, eels, a touch tank, and habitats for the endangered Hawaiian monk seal and green sea turtle. They have recently added a rotating biodiversity exhibit and interactive displays focusing on corals and coral reefs.

2777 Kalakaua Ave. (across from Kapiolani Park). ℂ 808/923-9741. www.waquarium.org. Admission $9 adults, $6 active military, seniors, and college students, $4 children 13–17, children under 12 free. Daily 9am–5pm. TheBus: 2

OTHER NATURAL WONDERS & SPECTACULAR VIEWS

In addition to the attractions listed below, check out "Diamond Head Crater" under "Nature Hikes," on p. 167; almost everybody can handle this hike, and the 360-degree views from the top are fabulous.

Nuuanu Pali Lookout ★ *Moments*   Gale-force winds sometimes howl through the mountain pass at this 1,186-foot-high perch guarded by 3,000-foot peaks, so hold on to your hat—and small children. But if you walk up from the parking lot to the precipice, you'll be rewarded with a view that'll blow you away. At the edge, the dizzying panorama of Oahu's windward side is breathtaking: Clouds low enough to pinch scoot by on trade winds; pinnacles of the *pali* (cliffs), green with ferns, often disappear in the mist. From on high, the tropical palette of green and blue runs down to the sea. Combine this 10-minute stop with a trip over the Pali to the windward side.

Near the summit of Pali Hwy. (Hwy. 61); take the Nuuanu Pali Lookout turnoff.

Nuuanu Valley Rain Forest *Finds*   It's not the same as a peaceful nature walk, but if time is short and hiking isn't your thing, Honolulu has a rainforest you can drive through. It's only a few minutes from downtown Honolulu in verdant Nuuanu Valley, where it rains nearly 300 inches a year. And it's easy to reach: As the Pali Highway leaves residential Nuuanu and begins its climb though the forest, the last stoplight is the Nuuanu Pali Road turnoff; turn right for a jungly detour of about 2 miles under a thick canopy strung with liana vines, past giant bamboo that creaks in the wind, Norfolk pines, and wild shell ginger. The road rises and the vegetation clears, blinking in the bright light of day, as you drive past a small mountain reservoir.

Soon the road rejoins the Pali Highway. Kailua is to the right and Honolulu to the left—but it can be a hair-raising turn. Instead, turn right, go half a mile to the Nuuanu Pali Lookout (see above), stop for a panoramic view of Oahu's windward side, and return to the town-bound highway on the other side.

Take the Old Nuuanu Pali Rd. exit off Pali Hwy. (Hwy. 61).

Puu Ualakaa State Park ★ *Moments*   The best **sunset view** of Honolulu is from a 1,048-foot-high hill named for sweet potatoes. Actually, the poetic Hawaiian name means "rolling sweet potato hill," which is how early planters used to use gravity to harvest their crop. The panorama is sweeping and majestic. On a clear day—which is almost always—you can see from Diamond Head to the Waianae Range; almost the length of Oahu. At night, several scenic overlooks provide romantic spots for young lovers who like to smooch under the stars with the city lights at their feet. It's a top-of-the-world experience—the view, that is.

At the end of Round Hill Dr. Daily 7am–6:45pm (to 7:45pm in summer). From Waikiki, take Ala Wai Blvd. to McCully St., turn right, and drive *mauka* (inland) beyond the H-1 on-ramps to Wilder St.; turn left and go to Makiki St.; turn right, and continue onward and upward about 3 miles.

MORE MUSEUMS

For details on Honolulu's three wonderful art museums, the **Contemporary Museum,** the **Honolulu Academy of Arts,** and the **Hawaii State Art Museum,** see the box titled "Oahu's Vibrant Art Scene" on p. 188.

Aliiolani Hale   Don't be surprised if this place looks familiar; you probably saw it on *Magnum, P.I.* This gingerbread Italianate building, designed by Australian Thomas Rowe in Renaissance revival style, was built in 1874 and was originally intended to be a palace. Instead, Aliiolani Hale ("chief unto heavens") became the Supreme Court and Parliament government office building. Inside, there's a **Judiciary History Center** ★, which features a multimedia presentation, a restored historic courtroom, and exhibits tracing Hawaii's transition from pre-contact Hawaiian law to Western law.

417 S. King St. (between Mililani and Punchbowl sts.). ✆ **808/539-4999.** Fax 808/539-4996. www.jhchawaii.org. Free admission. Mon–Fri 9am–4pm; reservations for group tours only. TheBus: 1, 2, 3, 4, 8, 11, or 12. Limited parking meter parking on street.

Damien Museum   This is a tiny museum about a large subject in Hawaii's history: Father Damien's work with leprosy victims on the island of Molokai. The museum contains prayer books used by Father Damien in his ministry as well as his personal items. Don't miss the award-winning video on Damien's story.

130 Ohua St. (between Kuhio and Kalakaua aves., behind St. Augustine's Catholic Church). ✆ **808/923-2690.** Donations accepted. Mon–Fri 9am–3pm. TheBus: 8, 19, or 20.

U.S. Army Museum   This museum, built in 1909 and used in defense of Honolulu and Pearl Harbor, houses military memorabilia ranging from ancient Hawaiian warfare items to modern-day high-tech munitions. On the upper deck, the Corps of Engineers Pacific Regional Visitors Center shows how the corps works with the civilian community to manage water resources in an island environment.

Fort DeRussy Park, Waikiki. ✆ **808/438-2822.** Free admission. Tues–Sun 10am–4:30pm. TheBus: 8.

WALKING TOUR   A STROLL THROUGH HISTORIC CHINATOWN

Getting There	From Waikiki, take TheBus no. 2 or 20 toward downtown; get off on North Hotel Street (after Maunakea Street). If you're driving, take Ala Moana Boulevard and turn right on Smith Street; make a left on Beretania Street and a left again at Maunakea Street. The city parking garage (50¢ per hr.) is on the Ewa (west) side of Maunakea Street, between North Hotel and North King streets.
Start and Finish	North Hotel and Maunakea streets.
Time	1 to 2 hours, depending on how much time you spend browsing.
Best Times	Daylight hours.

Chinese laborers from the Guangdong Province first came to work on Hawaii's sugar and pineapple plantations in the 1850s. They quickly figured out that they would never get rich working in the fields; once their contracts were up, a few of the ambitious started up small shops and restaurants in the area around River Street.

Chinatown was twice devastated by fire, once in 1886 and again in 1900. The second fire still intrigues historians. In December 1899, bubonic plague broke out in the area, and the Board of Health immediately quarantined its 7,000 Chinese and Japanese residents. But the plague continued to spread. On January 20, 1900, the Board decided to burn down plague-infected homes, starting at the corner of Beretania Street and Nuuanu Avenue. But the fire department wasn't quite ready; a sudden wind quickly spread the flames from one wooden building to another in the densely built area, and soon Chinatown's entire 40 acres were leveled. Many historians believe that the "out-of-control" fire may have been purposely set to drive the Chinese merchants—who were becoming economically powerful and controlled prime real estate—out of Honolulu. If this was indeed the case, it didn't work: The determined merchants built a new Chinatown in the same spot.

Chinatown reached its peak in the 1930s. In the days before air travel, visitors arrived here by cruise ship. Just a block up the street was the pier where they disembarked—and they often headed straight for the shops and restaurants of Chinatown, which mainlanders considered an exotic treat. In the '40s, military personnel on leave flocked here looking for different kinds of exotic treats—in the form of pool halls, tattoo joints, and houses of ill repute.

Today, Chinatown is again rising from the ashes. After deteriorating over the years into a tawdry district of seedy bars, drug dealing, and homeless squatters, the neighborhood recently underwent extensive urban renewal. There's still just enough sleaze on the fringes (a few peep shows and a couple of topless bars) to keep it from being some theme park–style tourist attraction, but Chinatown is poised to relive its glory days.

It's not exactly a microcosm of China, however. What you'll find is a mix of Asian cultures, all packed into a small area where tangy spices rule the cuisine, open-air markets have kept out the minimalls, and the way to good health is through acupuncture and herbalists. The jumble of streets comes alive every day with bustling residents and visitors from all over the world; a cacophony of sounds, from the high-pitched bleating of vendors in the market to the lyrical dialects of the retired men "talking story" over a game of mahjong; and brilliant reds, blues, and greens trimming buildings and goods everywhere you look. No trip to Honolulu is complete without a visit to this exotic, historic district.

Start your walk on the Ewa (west) side of Maunakea Street at:

❶ Hotel Street

During World War II, Hotel Street was synonymous with good times. Pool halls and beer parlors lined the blocks, and prostitutes were plentiful. Nowadays, the more nefarious establishments have been replaced with small shops, from art galleries to specialty boutiques, and urban professionals and recent immigrants look for bargains where the sailors once roamed.

Once you're done wandering through the shops, head to the intersection with Smith Street. On the Diamond Head (east) side of Smith, you'll notice stones in the sidewalk; they were taken from the sandalwood ships, which came to Hawaii empty of cargo except for these stones, which were used as ballast on the trip over. The stones were removed and the ships' hulls were filled with sandalwood for the return to the mainland.

From Hotel Street, turn toward the ocean on Maunakea and proceed to the corner of King Street to the:

Walking Tour—Historic Chinatown

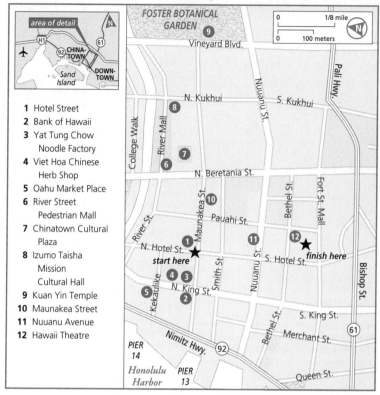

1 Hotel Street
2 Bank of Hawaii
3 Yat Tung Chow
   Noodle Factory
4 Viet Hoa Chinese
   Herb Shop
5 Oahu Market Place
6 River Street
   Pedestrian Mall
7 Chinatown Cultural
   Plaza
8 Izumo Taisha
   Mission
   Cultural Hall
9 Kuan Yin Temple
10 Maunakea Street
11 Nuuanu Avenue
12 Hawaii Theatre

Map labels: FOSTER BOTANICAL GARDEN · area of detail · CHINA-TOWN · DOWN-TOWN · Sand Island · Vineyard Blvd. · N. Kukhui · S. Kukhui · Nuuanu St. · Pali Hwy. · N. Beretania St. · College Walk · River Mall · River St. · Maunakea St. · Pauahi St. · Bethel St. · Fort St. Mall · N. Hotel St. · start here · S. Hotel St. · finish here · Smith St. · Nuuanu St. · Kekaulike · N. King St. · S. King St. · Bishop St. · Bethel St. · Nimitz Hwy. · Merchant St. · PIER 14 · Honolulu Harbor · PIER 13 · Queen St.

❷ Bank of Hawaii

This unusual-looking bank is not the conservative edifice you'd expect—it's guarded by two fire-breathing dragon statues.

At 162 N. King St. is another interesting stop:

❸ Yat Tung Chow Noodle Factory

The delicious, delicate noodles that star in numerous Asian dishes are made here, ranging from thread-like noodles (literally no thicker than embroidery thread) to fat udon noodles. There aren't any tours of the factory, but you can look through the window, past the white cloud of flour that hangs in the air, and watch as dough is fed into rollers at one end of the noodle machines; perfectly cut noodles emerge at the other end.

Turn right onto King Street, where you'll pass the shops of various Chinese herbalists, including the one at 150 N. King St.:

❹ Viet Hoa Chinese Herb Shop

Here, Chinese herbalists act as both doctors and dispensers of herbs. Patients come in and tell the herbalist what ails them; the herbalist then decides which of the myriad herbs to mix together. Usually, there's a wall of tiny drawers all labeled in Chinese characters; the herbalist quickly pulls from the drawers various objects that range from dried flowers and ground-up roots to such exotics as mashed antelope antler. The patient then takes the concoction home to brew into a strong tea.

Cross to the south side of King Street, where, just west of Kekaulike Street, you'll come to the most visited part of Chinatown, the open-air market known as:

❺ Oahu Market Place

Those interested in Asian cooking will find all the necessary ingredients here, including pigs' heads, poultry (some still squawking), fresh octopi, salted jellyfish, pungent fish sauce, fresh herbs, and thousand-year-old eggs. The friendly vendors are happy to explain their wares and give instructions on how to prepare these exotic treats. The market, which has been at this spot since 1904, is divided into meats, poultry, fish, vegetables, and fruits. Past the open market are several grocery stores with fresh produce on display on the sidewalk. You're bound to spot some varieties here that you're not used to seeing at your local supermarket.

Follow King down to River Street and turn right toward the mountains. A range of inexpensive restaurants lines River Street from King to Beretania. You can get the best Vietnamese and Filipino food in town in these blocks, but go early—lines for lunch start at 11:15am. Beyond Beretania Street is the:

❻ River Street Pedestrian Mall

Here, River Street ends and the pedestrian mall begins with the **statue of Chinese revolutionary leader Sun Yat-Sen.** The wide mall, which borders the Nuuanu Stream, is lined with shade trees, park benches, and tables where seniors gather to pay mahjong and checkers. There are plenty of take-out restaurants nearby if you'd like to eat lunch outdoors. If you're up early (5:30am in summer and 6am in winter), you'll see senior citizens practicing tai chi.

Along the River Street Mall, extending nearly a block over to Maunakea Street, is the:

❼ Chinatown Cultural Plaza

This modern complex is filled with shops featuring everything from tailors to calligraphers (most somewhat more expensive than their streetside counterparts), as well as numerous restaurants—a great idea,

but in reality, people seem to prefer wandering Chinatown's crowded streets to venturing into a modern mall. A couple of interesting shops here specialize in Asian magazines; there's also a small post office tucked away in a corner of the plaza, for those who want to mail cards home with the "Chinatown" postmark. The best feature of the plaza is the **Moongate Stage** in the center, the site of many cultural presentations, especially around the Chinese New Year.

Continue up the River Street Mall and cross the Nuuanu Stream via the bridge at Kukui Street, which will bring you to the:

❽ Izumo Taisha Mission Cultural Hall

This small, wooden Shinto shrine, built in 1923, houses a male deity (look for the X-shaped crosses on the top). Members of the faith ring the bell out front as an act of purification when they come to pray. Inside the temple is a 100-pound sack of rice, symbolizing good health. During World War II, the shrine was confiscated by the city of Honolulu and wasn't returned to the congregation until 1962.

If temples interest you, walk a block toward the mountains to Vineyard Boulevard; cross back over Nuuanu Stream, past the entrance of Foster Botanical Gardens, to:

❾ Kuan Yin Temple

This Buddhist temple, painted in a brilliant red with a green ceramic-tiled roof, is dedicated to Kuan Yin Bodhisattva, the goddess of mercy, whose statue towers in the prayer hall. The aroma of burning incense is your clue that the temple is still a house of worship, not an exhibit, so enter with respect and leave your shoes outside. You may see people burning paper "money" for prosperity and good luck, or leaving flowers and fruits at the altar (gifts to the goddess). A common offering is the pomelo, a grapefruit-like fruit that's a fertility symbol as well as a gift, indicating a request for the blessing of children.

Continue down Vineyard and then turn right (toward the ocean) on:

⑩ Maunakea Street

Between Beretania and King streets are numerous **lei shops** (with lei-makers working away right on the premises). The air is heavy with the aroma of flowers being woven into beautiful treasures. Not only is this the best place in all of Hawaii to get a deal on leis, but the size, color, and design of the leis made here are exceptional. Wander through the shops before you decide which lei you want.

TAKE A BREAK If you have a sweet tooth, stop in at **Shung Chong Yuein,** 1027 Maunakea St. (near Hotel St.), for delicious Asian pastries like moon cakes and almond cookies, all at very reasonable prices. The shop also has a wide selection of dried and sugared candies (like ginger, pineapple, and lotus root) that you can eat as you stroll or give as an exotic gift to friends back home.

Turn left on Hotel Street, and walk in the Diamond Head (east) direction to:

⑪ Nuuanu Avenue

You may notice that the sidewalks on Nuuanu are made of granite blocks; they came from the ballasts of ships that brought tea from China to Hawaii in the 1800s. On the corner of Nuuanu Avenue and Hotel Street is **Lai Fong Department Store,** a classic Chinatown store owned by the same family for more than three-quarters of a century. Walking into Lai Fong is like stepping back in time. The old store sells everything from precious antiques to god-awful knick-knacks to rare turn-of-the-century Hawaiian postcards—but it has built its reputation on its fabulous selection of Chinese silks, brocades, and custom dresses.

Between Hotel and Pauahi streets is the **Pegge Hopper Gallery,** 1164 Nuuanu Ave., where you can admire Pegge's well-known paintings of beautiful Hawaiian women (see "Oahu's Vibrant Art Scene," on p. 188).

Bargaining: A Way of Life in Chinatown

In Chinatown, nearly every purchase—from haggling over the price of chicken's feet to buying an 18-carat gold necklace—is made by bargaining. It's the way of life for most Asian countries—and part of the fun and charm of shopping in Chinatown.

The main rule of thumb when negotiating a price is **respect.** The customer must have respect for the merchant and understand that he's in business to make money. This respect is coupled with the understanding that the customer does not want to be taken advantage of and would like the best deal possible.

Keep in mind two rules when bargaining: **cash** and **volume.** Don't even begin haggling if you're not planning to pay cash. The second you pull out a credit card (if the merchant or vendor will even accept it), all deals are off. And remember, the more you buy, the better the deal the merchant will extend to you.

Significant savings can be realized for high-ticket items like jewelry. The price of gold in Chinatown is based on the posted price of the *tael* (a unit of weight, slightly more than an ounce), which is listed for 14-, 18-, and 24-carat gold, plus the value of the labor. There's no negotiating on the tael price, but the cost of the labor is where the bargaining begins.

At Pauahi Street, turn right (toward Diamond Head) and walk up to Bethel Street and the:

⑫ **Hawaii Theatre**

This restored 1920 Art Deco theater is a work of art in itself. It hosts a variety of programs, from the Hawaii International Film Festival to beauty pageants (see section 14, "Oahu After Dark," at the end of this chapter, for how to find out what's on).

Turn right onto Bethel and walk toward the ocean. Turn right again onto Hotel Street, which will lead you back to where you started.

12 Beyond Honolulu: Exploring the Island by Car

The moment always arrives—usually after a couple of days at the beach, snorkeling in the warm, blue-green waters of Hanauma Bay, enjoying sundown mai tais—when a certain curiosity kicks in about the rest of Oahu, largely unknown to most visitors. It's time to find the rental car in the hotel garage and set out around the island. You can also explore Oahu using **TheBus** (see section 2 of this chapter, "Getting Around").

For great places to stop for a bite to eat while you're exploring, see section 4, "Great Deals on Dining," earlier in this chapter. You also might want to check out "Shopping," in section 13 of this chapter. Beaches, nature hikes, camping, and other outdoor activities outside of Honolulu have all been covered earlier in this chapter.

OAHU'S SOUTHEAST COAST

From the high-rises of Waikiki, venture down Kalakaua Avenue through tree-lined Kapiolani Park to take a look at a different side of Oahu, the arid South Shore. The landscape here is more moonscape, with prickly cacti onshore and, in winter, spouting whales cavorting in the water. Some call it the South Shore, others Sandy's (after the mile-long beach here), but Hawaiians call it **Ka Iwi,** which means "the bone"— no doubt because of all the bone-cracking shore breaks along this popular bodyboarding coastline. The beaches here are long, wide, and popular with local daredevils.

This open, scenic coast is the best place on Oahu to watch sea, shore, and even land birds. It's also a good whale-watching spot in season, and the night sky is ideal for amateur astronomers on the lookout for meteors, comets, and stars.

To get to this coast, follow Kalakaua Avenue past the multi-tiered Dillingham Fountain and around the bend in the road, which now becomes Poni Moi Road. Make a right on Diamond Head Road and begin the climb up the side of the old crater. At the top are several lookout points, so if the official Diamond Head Lookout is jammed with cars, try one of the other lookouts just down the road. The view of the rolling waves is spectacular; take the time to pull over.

Diamond Head Road rolls downhill now into the ritzy community of **Kahala.** At the V in the road at the triangular Fort Ruger Park, veer to your right and continue on the palm-tree–lined Kahala Avenue. Make a left on Hunakai Street, then a right on Kilauea Avenue, and look for the sign: H-1 WEST—WAIMANALO. Turn right at the sign, although you won't get on the H-1 freeway; get on the Kalanianaole Highway, a four-lane highway interrupted every few blocks by a stoplight. This is the suburban bedroom community to Honolulu, marked by malls on the left and beach parks on the right.

About half an hour outside of Waikiki, you'll see the turnoff to **Hanauma Bay** ✦✦ (p. 156) on the right. This marine preserve is a great place to stop for a swim; you'll find the friendliest fish on the island here. *A reminder:* The beach park is closed on Tuesdays.

Eastern Oahu & the Windward Coast

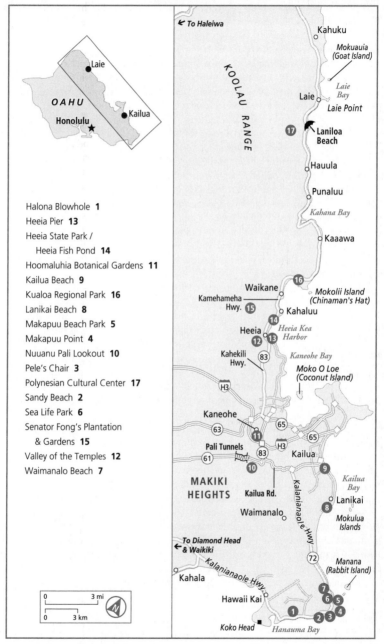

Halona Blowhole **1**

Heeia Pier **13**

Heeia State Park /
   Heeia Fish Pond **14**

Hoomaluhia Botanical Gardens **11**

Kailua Beach **9**

Kualoa Regional Park **16**

Lanikai Beach **8**

Makapuu Beach Park **5**

Makapuu Point **4**

Nuuanu Pali Lookout **10**

Pele's Chair **3**

Polynesian Cultural Center **17**

Sandy Beach **2**

Sea Life Park **6**

Senator Fong's Plantation
   & Gardens **15**

Valley of the Temples **12**

Waimanalo Beach **7**

0   3 mi

0   3 km

Around mile marker 11, the jagged lava coast itself spouts sea foam at the **Halona Blowhole.** Look out to sea from Halona over Sandy Beach and across the 26-mile gulf to neighboring Molokai and the faint triangular shadow of Lanai on the far horizon. **Sandy Beach** (p. 157) is Oahu's most dangerous beach; it's the only one with an ambulance always standing by to whisk injured wave catchers to the hospital. Body-boarders just love it.

The coast looks raw and empty along this stretch, but the road weaves past old Hawaiian fish ponds and the famous formation known as **Pele's Chair,** just off Kala-nianaole Highway (Hwy. 72) above Queen's Beach. From a distance, the lava-rock outcropping looks like a mighty throne; it's believed to be the fire goddess's last rest-ing place on Oahu before she flew off to continue her work on other islands.

Ahead lies 647-foot-high **Makapuu Point,** with a lighthouse that once signaled safe passage for steamship passengers arriving from San Francisco. The automated light now brightens Oahu's south coast for passing tankers, fishing boats, and sailors. You can take a short hike up here for a spectacular vista (p. 168).

If you're with the kids, you may want to spend the day at **Sea Life Park** ♠, a marine amusement park described earlier in this chapter (p. 189).

Turn the corner at Makapuu, and you're on Oahu's windward side, where cooling trade winds propel windsurfers across turquoise bays; the waves at **Makapuu Beach Park** are perfect for bodysurfing (p. 157).

Ahead, the coastal vista is a profusion of fluted green mountains and strange peaks, edged by golden beaches and the blue, blue Pacific. The 3,000-foot-high sheer green Koolau Mountains plunge almost straight down, presenting an irresistible jumping-off spot for hang-glider pilots, who catch the thermals on hours-long rides.

Winding up the coast, Kalanianaole Highway (Hwy. 72) leads through rural **Waimanalo,** a country beach town of nurseries and stables, fresh-fruit stands, and some of the island's best conch and triton shell specimens at roadside stands. Nearly 4 miles long, **Waimanalo Beach** is Oahu's longest beach and the most popular for bodysurfing. Take a swim here or head on to **Kailua Beach** ♠♠, one of Hawaii's best (p. 158).

If it's still early in the day, you can head up the lush, green Windward Coast by turning right at the Castle Junction, Highway 72, and Highway 61 (which is also Kailua Road on the *makai* [seaward] side of the junction, and Kalanianaole Highway on the *mauka* [inland] side of the junction), and continuing down Kailua Road (Hwy. 61). After Kailua Road crosses the Kaelepulu Stream, the name of the road changes to Kuulei Road. When Kuulei Road ends, turn left onto Kalaheo Avenue, which becomes Kaneohe Bay Drive after it crosses the Kawainui Channel. Follow this scenic drive around the peninsula until it crosses Kamehameha Highway (Hwy. 83); turn right and continue on Kamehameha Highway for a scenic drive along the ocean.

If you're in a hurry to get back to Waikiki, turn left at Castle Junction and head over the Pali Highway (Hwy. 61), which becomes Bishop Street in Honolulu and ends at Ala Moana. Turn left for Waikiki; it's the second beach on the right.

THE WINDWARD COAST

From the **Nuuanu Pali Lookout** ♠, near the summit of the Pali Highway (Hwy. 61), you get the first hint of the other side of Oahu, a region so green and lovely that it could be an island sibling of Tahiti. With its many beaches and bays, the scenic 30-mile Windward Coast parallels the corduroy-ridged, nearly perpendicular cliffs of the Koolau Range, which separates the windward side of the island from Honolulu and the rest of Oahu. As you descend on the serpentine Pali Highway beneath often gushing waterfalls, you'll see the nearly 1,000-foot spike of **Olomana,** the bold pinnacle that always reminds us of that mountain in *Close Encounters,* and beyond, the Hawaiian village of **Waimanalo.**

From the Pali Highway, to the right is **Kailua,** Hawaii's biggest beach town, with more than 50,000 residents and two special **beaches,** Kailua and Lanikai, begging for visitors (p. 157). Funky little Kailua is lined with million-dollar houses next to tarpaper shacks, antiques shops, and bed-and-breakfasts. Although the Pali Highway (Hwy. 61) proceeds directly to the coast, it undergoes two name changes, becoming first Kalanianaole Highway—from the intersection of Kamehameha Highway (Hwy. 83)—and then Kailua Road as it heads into Kailua town; but the road remains Highway 61 the whole way. Kailua Road ends at the T intersection at Kalaheo Drive, which follows the coast in a northerly and southerly direction. Turn right on South Kalaheo Drive to get to Kailua Beach Park and Lanikai Beach. No signs point the way, but you can't miss them.

If you spend a day at the beach here, stick around for sunset, when the sun sinks behind the Koolau Range and tints the clouds pink and orange. After a hard day at the beach, you'll work up an appetite, and Kailua has several great, inexpensive restaurants (see section 4, "Great Deals on Dining," earlier in this chapter).

If you want to skip the beaches this time, turn left on North Kalaheo Drive, which becomes Kaneohe Bay Drive as it skirts Kaneohe Bay and leads back to Kamehameha Highway (Hwy. 83), which then passes through Kaneohe. The suburban maze of Kaneohe is one giant strip mall of retail excess that mars one of the Pacific's most picturesque bays. After clearing this obstacle, the place begins to look like Hawaii again.

Incredibly scenic Kaneohe Bay is spiked with islets and lined with gold-sand beach parks like **Kualoa,** a favorite picnic spot (p. 160). The bay has a barrier reef and four tiny islets, one of which is known as Moku o loe, or Coconut Island. Don't be surprised if it looks familiar—it appeared in *Gilligan's Island.*

At Heeia State Park is **Heeia Fish Pond,** which ancient Hawaiians built by enclosing natural bays with rocks to trap fish on the incoming tide. The 88-acre fish pond, which is made of lava rock with four watchtowers (to observe fish movement) and several sluice gates along the 5,000-foot-long wall, is now in the process of being restored.

Stop by the **Heeia Pier,** which juts onto Kaneohe Bay. You can take a snorkel cruise here, or sail out to a sandbar in the middle of the bay for an incredible view of Oahu that most people, even those who live here, never see. If it's Tuesday through Sunday between 7am and 6pm, stop in and see Ernie Choy at the **Deli on Heeia Kea Pier** (© **808/235-2192**). He has served fishermen, sailors, and kayakers the beach town's best omelets and plate lunches at reasonable prices since 1979.

Everyone calls it **Chinaman's Hat,** but the tiny island off the eastern shore of Kualoa Regional Park is really named **Mokolii.** It's a sacred *puu honua,* or place of refuge, like the restored Puu Honua Honaunau on the Big Island of Hawaii. Excavations have unearthed evidence that this area was the home of ancient *alii* (royalty). Early Hawaiians believed that Mokolii ("fin of the lizard") is all that remains of a *mo'o,* or lizard, slain by Pele's sister, Hiiaka, and hurled into the sea. At low tide, you can swim out to the island, but keep watch on the changing tide, which can sweep you out to sea. The islet has a small, sandy beach and is a bird preserve, so don't spook the red-footed boobies.

Little poly-voweled beach towns like **Kaaawa, Hauula, Punaluu,** and **Kahaluu** pop up along the coast, offering passersby shell shops and art galleries to explore.

Famed hula photographer **Kim Taylor Reece** lives on this coast; his gallery at 53–866 Kamehameha Hwy., near Sacred Falls (✆ **808/293-2000**), is open daily from noon to 6pm. You'll also see working cattle ranches, fishermen's wharves, and roadside fruit and flower stands vending ice-cold coconuts (to drink) and tree-ripened mangoes, papayas, and apple bananas.

Sugar, once the sole industry of this region, is gone. But **Kahuku,** the former sugar-plantation town, has found new life as a small aquaculture community with prawn farms that supply island restaurants.

From here, continue along Kamehameha Highway (Hwy. 83) to the North Shore.

ATTRACTIONS ALONG THE WINDWARD COAST

The attractions below are arranged geographically as you drive up the coast from south to north.

Hoomaluhia Botanical Gardens ★

This 400-acre botanical garden at the foot of the steepled Koolau Mountains is the perfect place for a picnic. Its name means "a peaceful refuge" and that's exactly what the Army Corps of Engineers created when they installed a flood-control project here, which resulted in a 32-acre freshwater lake and garden. Just unfold a beach mat, lie back, and watch the clouds race across the rippled cliffs of the majestic Koolau Range. This is one of the few public places on Oahu that provides a close-up view of the steepled cliffs. The park has hiking trails and—best of all—the island's only free inland campground (p. 170). If you like hiking and nature, plan to spend at least a half a day here.

45–680 Luluku Rd., Kaneohe. ✆ 808/233-7323. www.co.honolulu.hi.us/parks/hbg/hmbg.htm. Free admission. Daily 9am–4pm. Guided nature hikes Sat 10am and Sun 1pm. Take H-1 to the Pali Hwy. (Hwy. 61); turn left on Kamehameha Hwy. (Hwy. 83); at the 4th light, turn left onto Luluku Rd. TheBus: 55 or 56 will stop on Kamehameha Hwy.; it's a 2-mile walk to the visitor center.

Valley of the Temples

This famous cemetery in a cleft of the pali is stalked by wild peacocks and about 700 curious people a day, who pay to see the 9-foot medita-tion Buddha, 2 acres of ponds full of more than 10,000 Japanese koi carp, and a replica of Japan's 900-year-old Byodo-in Temple of Equality. The original, made of wood, stands in Uji, on the outskirts of Kyoto; the Hawaiian version, made of con-crete, was erected in 1968 to commemorate the 100th anniversary of the arrival of the first Japanese immigrants to Hawaii. It's not the same as seeing the original, but it's worth a detour. A 3-ton brass temple bell brings good luck to those who can ring it—although the gongs do jar the Zen-like serenity of this little bit of Japan. If you are in a rush, you can sail through here in an hour, but you'll want to stay longer.

47–200 Kahekili Hwy. (across the street from Temple Valley Shopping Center), Kaneohe. ✆ 808/239-8811. Admis-sion $2 adults, $1 children under 12 and seniors 65 and over. Daily 8:30am–4:30pm. Take the H-1 to the Likelike Hwy. (Hwy. 63); after the Wilson Tunnel, get in the right lane and take the Kahekili Hwy. (Hwy. 63); at the 6th traffic light is the entrance to the cemetery (on the left). TheBus: 65.

Senator Fong's Plantation & Gardens

Senator Hiram Fong, the first Chinese American elected to the U.S. Senate, served 17 years before retiring to tropical gar-dening years ago. Now you can ride an open-air tram through five gardens named for the American presidents he served. His 725-acre private estate includes 75 edible nuts and fruits. It's definitely worth an hour—if you haven't already seen enough botanics to last a lifetime.

47–285 Pulama Rd., Kaneohe. ✆ 808/239-6775. www.fonggarden.net. Admission $15 adults, $13 seniors, $9 children 5–12. Daily 10am–4pm; 45-min. narrated tram tours daily from 10:30am, last tour 3pm. Take the H-1 to the Likelike Hwy.

(Hwy. 63); turn left at Kahekili Hwy. (Hwy. 83); continue to Kaneohe and turn left on Pulama Rd. TheBus: 55; it's a mile walk uphill from the stop.

Polynesian Cultural Center ⭐ *Kids*   Even if you never leave Hawaii, you can still experience the natural beauty and culture of the vast Pacific in a single day at the Polynesian Cultural Center, a kind of living museum of Polynesia. Here, you can see first-hand the lifestyles, songs, dance, costumes, and architecture of seven Pacific islands—Fiji, New Zealand, Marquesas, Samoa, Tahiti, Tonga, and Hawaii—in the re-created villages scattered throughout the 42-acre lagoon park. A new $1.1 million renovation project has improved the front entrance and added an exhibit on the story of the Polynesian immigration.

You "travel" through this museum by foot or in a canoe on a man-made freshwater lagoon. Each village is "inhabited" by native students from Polynesia who attend Hawaii's Brigham Young University. The park, which is operated by the Mormon Church, also features a variety of stage shows celebrating the music, dance, history, and culture of Polynesia. There's a luau every evening. Since a visit can take up to 8 hours, it's a good idea to arrive before 2pm.

Just beyond the center is the **Hawaii Temple** of the Church of Jesus Christ of Latter-Day Saints, which is built of volcanic rock and concrete in the form of a Greek cross and includes reflecting pools, formal gardens, and royal palms. Completed in 1919, it was the first Mormon temple built outside the continental U.S. An optional tour of the Temple Visitors Center, as well as neighboring Brigham Young University–Hawaii, is included in the package admission prices.

55–370 Kamehameha Hwy., Laie. ⓒ **800/367-7060**, 808/293-3333, or 808/923-2911. www.polynesia.com. Admission $50 adults, $34 children 3–11. Admission, IMAX, luau, and nightly show $80 adults, $56 children. Ambassador VIP (deluxe) tour $110–$195 adults, $76–$135 children. Mon–Sat 12:30–9:30pm. Take H-1 to Pali Hwy. (Hwy. 61) and turn left on Kamehameha Hwy. (Hwy. 83). TheBus: 55. Polynesian Cultural Center coaches $15 round-trip; call numbers above to book.

CENTRAL OAHU & THE NORTH SHORE

If you can afford the splurge, rent a bright, shiny convertible—the perfect car for Oahu, since you can tan as you go—and head for the North Shore and Hawaii's surf city: **Haleiwa** ⭐, a quaint turn-of-the-20th-century sugar-plantation town designated a historic site. A collection of faded clapboard stores with a picturesque harbor, Haleiwa has evolved into a surfer outpost and major roadside attraction with art galleries, restaurants, and shops that sell hand-decorated clothing, jewelry, and sports gear (see section 13, "Shopping," later in this chapter).

Getting here is half the fun. You have two choices: The first is to meander north along the lush Windward Coast, through country hamlets with roadside stands selling mangoes, bright tropical pareus, fresh corn, and pond-raised prawns. Attractions along that route are discussed in the previous section.

The second choice is to cruise up the H-2 through Oahu's broad and fertile central valley, past Pearl Harbor and the Schofield Barracks of *From Here to Eternity* fame and on through the red-earthed heart of the island, where pineapple and sugarcane fields stretch from the Koolau to the Waianae mountains, until the sea reappears on the horizon. If you take this route, the tough part is getting on and off the H-1 freeway from Waikiki, which is done by way of convoluted routing on neighborhood streets. Try McCully Street off Ala Wai Boulevard, which is always crowded but usually the most direct route.

Central & Leeward Oahu

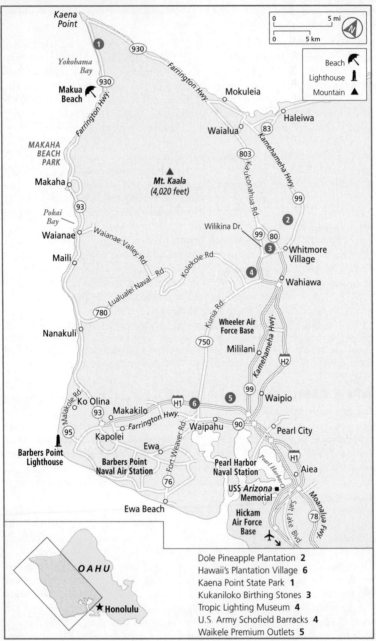

Kaena Point

Yokohama Bay

Makua Beach

Mokuleia

930

Farrington Hwy.

Haleiwa

Waialua

83

Kamehameha Hwy.

MAKAHA BEACH PARK

803

Mt. Kaala (4,020 feet)

Kaukonahua Rd.

99

Makaha

2

Pokai Bay

93

Wilikina Dr.

Whitmore Village

Waianae

Waianae Valley Rd.

99 80

3

Maili

Kolekole Rd.

4

Wahiawa

780

Lualualei Naval Rd.

Kunia Rd.

Wheeler Air Force Base

Nanakuli

750

Mililani

Kamehameha Hwy.

H2

Ko Olina

H1 6

5

99

Waipio

93

Makakilo

Malakole Rd.

95

Farrington Hwy.

Waipahu

90

Pearl City

Kapolei

Ewa

Fort Weaver Rd.

H1

Aiea

Barbers Point Lighthouse

Barbers Point Naval Air Station

76

Pearl Harbor Naval Station

Pearl Harbor

Moanalua Hwy.

USS Arizona Memorial

Salt Lake Blvd.

78

Ewa Beach

Hickam Air Force Base

Legend:
- Beach
- Lighthouse
- Mountain

0   5 mi
0   5 km

OAHU

★ Honolulu

Dole Pineapple Plantation **2**
Hawaii's Plantation Village **6**
Kaena Point State Park **1**
Kukaniloko Birthing Stones **3**
Tropic Lighting Museum **4**
U.S. Army Schofield Barracks **4**
Waikele Premium Outlets **5**

Once you're on H-1, stay to the right side; the freeway tends to divide abruptly. Keep following the signs for the H-1 (it separates off to Hwy. 78 at the airport and reunites later on; either way will get you there), then the H-1/H-2. Leave the H-1 where the two "interstates" divide; take the H-2 up the middle of the island, heading north toward the town of Wahiawa. That's what the sign will say—not North Shore or Haleiwa, but Wahiawa.

The H-2 runs out and becomes a two-lane country road about 18 miles outside downtown Honolulu, near Schofield Barracks (see below). The highway becomes Kamehameha Highway (Hwy. 99 and later Hwy. 83) at Wahiawa. Just past Wahiawa, about a half-hour out of Honolulu, the **Dole Pineapple Plantation,** 64–1550 Kamehameha Hwy. (© **808/621-8408;** fax 808/621-1926; www.dole-plantation.com; TheBus: 52), offers a rest stop with pineapples, pineapple history, pineapple trinkets, and pineapple juice, open daily from 9am to 6pm. This agricultural exhibit/retail area also features a maze that kids will love to wander through, open daily from 9am to 5pm; admission is $5 for adults and $3 for children 4 to 12 (3 and under are free). The latest attraction is the Pineapple Express, a single-engine diesel locomotive with four cars that takes a 22-minute tour around 2¼ miles of the plantation's grounds, with an educational spiel on the legacy of the pineapple and agriculture in Hawaii. The first tour departs at 9:30am, and the last tour gets back to the station at 5:20pm. Cost is $7.50 for adults, $5.50 for children 4 to 12 (3 and under are free). The latest attraction is the Plantation Garden tour, a self-guided tour through the various crops that have been grown on Oahu's North Shore. The tour costs $3.75 for adults and $3 for children. "Kam" Highway, as everyone calls it, will be your road for most of the rest of the trip to Haleiwa.

CENTRAL OAHU ATTRACTIONS

On the central plains of Oahu, tract homes and malls with factory-outlet stores are now spreading across abandoned sugarcane fields, where sandalwood forests used to stand at the foot of Mount Kaala, the mighty summit of Oahu. Hawaiian chiefs once sent commoners into thick sandalwood forests to cut down trees, which were then sold to China traders for small fortunes. The scantily clad natives caught cold in the cool uplands, and many died.

On these plains in 1908, the U.S. Army pitched a tent that later become a fort. And on December 7, 1941, Japanese pilots came screaming through Kolekole Pass to shoot up the Art Deco barracks at Schofield, sending soldiers running for cover, and then flew on to sink ships at Pearl Harbor.

U.S. Army Schofield Barracks   James Jones, author of *From Here to Eternity,* called Schofield Barracks "the most beautiful army post the U.S. has or ever had." The *Honolulu Star Bulletin* called it a country club. More than a million soldiers have called Schofield Barracks home. With its broad, palm-lined boulevards and Art Deco buildings, this old Army cavalry post is still the largest operated by the U.S. Army outside the continental United States. And it's still one of the best places to be a soldier.

The history of Schofield Barracks and the 25th Infantry Division is told in the small **Tropic Lightning Museum,** Schofield Barracks, Bldg. 361, Waianae Avenue (© **808/655-0438;** troplight1@juno.com). Displays range from a 1917 bunker exhibit to a replica of Vietnam's infamous Cu Chi tunnels.

Free admission. Open Tues–Sat from 10am–4pm. TheBus: 52 to Wahiawa; transfer at California Ave. to no. 72, Schofield Barracks Shuttle.

Kukaniloko Birthing Stones   This is the most sacred site in central Oahu. Two rows of 18 lava rocks once flanked a central birthing stone, where women of ancient Hawaii gave birth to potential *alii* (royalty). The rocks, according to Hawaiian belief, held the power to ease the labor pains of childbirth. Birth rituals involved 48 chiefs who pounded drums to announce the arrival of newborns likely to become chiefs. Children born here were taken to the now-destroyed Holonopahu Heiau in the pineapple field, where chiefs ceremoniously cut the umbilical cord.

Used by Oahu's *alii* for generations of births, the *pohaku* (rocks), many in bowl-like shapes, now lie strewn in a grove of trees that stands in a pineapple field here. Some think the site also may have served ancient astronomers—like a Hawaiian Stonehenge. Petroglyphs of human forms and circles appear on some of the stones. The Wahiawa Hawaiian Civic Club recently erected two interpretive signs, one explaining why this was chosen as a birth site and the other telling how the stones were used to aid in the birth process.

Off Kamehameha Hwy. between Wahiawa and Haleiwa, on Plantation Rd. opposite the road to Whitmore Village.

SURF CITY: HALEIWA

Only 28 miles from Waikiki is Haleiwa, the funky ex–sugar-plantation town that's the world capital of big-wave surfing. This beach town really comes alive in winter, when waves rise up, light rain falls, and temperatures dip into the 70s; then, it seems, every surfer in the world is here to see and be seen.

Officially designated a historic cultural and scenic district, Haleiwa thrives in a time warp recalling the turn of the 20th century, when it was founded by sugar baron Benjamin Dillingham, who built a 30-mile railroad to link his Honolulu and North Shore plantations in 1899. He opened a Victorian hotel overlooking Kaiaka Bay and named it Haleiwa, or "house of the Iwa," the tropical seabird often seen here. The hotel and railroad are gone, but Haleiwa, which was rediscovered in the late 1960s by hippies, resonates with rare rustic charm. Tofu, not taro, is a staple in the local diet. Arts and crafts, boutiques, and burger stands line both sides of the town. There's also a busy fishing harbor full of charter boats and captains who hunt the Kauai Channel daily for tuna, mahimahi, and marlin. The bartenders at **Jameson's** ✪, 62–540 Kamehameha Hwy. (© **808/637-6272**), make the best mai tais on the North Shore; they use the original recipe by Trader Vic Bergeron.

Once in Haleiwa, the hot and thirsty traveler should report directly to the nearest shave-ice stand, usually **Matsumoto Shave Ice** ✪✪, 66–087 Kamehameha Hwy. (© **808/637-4827**). For 40 years, this small, humble shop operated by the Matsumoto family has served a popular rendition of the Hawaii-style snow cone flavored with tropical tastes. The cooling treat is also available at neighboring stores, some of which still shave the ice with a hand-crank device.

Just down the road are some of the fabled shrines of surfing—**Waimea Beach, Banzai Pipeline, Sunset Beach**—where some of the world's largest waves, reaching 20 feet and more, rise up between November and January. They draw professional surfers as well as reckless daredevils and hordes of onlookers, who jump in their cars and head north when word goes out that "surf's up." Don't forget your binoculars. (For more details on North Shore beaches, see p. 160.)

North Shore Surf and Cultural Museum   Even if you've never set foot on a surfboard, you'll want to visit Oahu's only surf museum to learn the history of this Hawaiian sport of kings. This collection of memorabilia traces the evolution of surfboards from

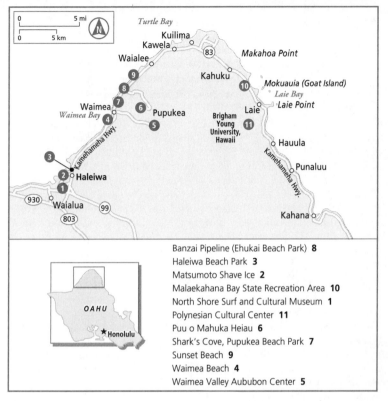

Banzai Pipeline (Ehukai Beach Park) **8**
Haleiwa Beach Park **3**
Matsumoto Shave Ice **2**
Malaekahana Bay State Recreation Area **10**
North Shore Surf and Cultural Museum **1**
Polynesian Cultural Center **11**
Puu o Mahuka Heiau **6**
Shark's Cove, Pupukea Beach Park **7**
Sunset Beach **9**
Waimea Beach **4**
Waimea Valley Aububon Center **5**

an enormous, weathered redwood board made in the 1930s for Turkey Love, one of Waikiki's legendary beach boys, to the modern-day equivalent—a light, sleek, racy, foam-and-fiberglass board made for big-wave surfer Mark Foo, who drowned while surfing in California in 1994. Other items include classic 1950s surf-meet posters, 1960s surf-music album covers, old beach movie posters with Frankie Avalon and Sandra Dee, the early black-and-white photos by legendary surf photographer LeRoy Grannis, and trophies won by surfing's greatest. Curator Steve Gould is working on a new exhibit of surfing in the ancient Hawaiian culture, complete with Hawaiian artifacts.

North Shore Marketplace, 66–250 Kamehameha Hwy. (behind KFC), Haleiwa. © **808/637-8888**. www.captain rick.com/surf_museum.htm. Free admission. Tues–Sun noon–5pm.

MORE NORTH SHORE ATTRACTIONS

Puu o Mahuka Heiau ⭐ *Moments*   Go around sundown to feel the *mana* (sacred spirit) of this Hawaiian place. The largest sacrificial temple on Oahu, it's associated with the great Kaopulupulu, who sought peace between Oahu and Kauai. This prescient *kahuna* predicted that the island would be overrun by strangers from a distant land. In 1794, three of Captain George Vancouver's men of the *Daedalus* were sacrificed here. In 1819, the year before New England missionaries landed in Hawaii, King Kamehameha II ordered all idols here to be destroyed.

A national historic landmark, this 18th-century *heiau*, known as the "hill of escape," sits on a 5-acre, 300-foot bluff overlooking Waimea Bay and 25 miles of Oahu's wave-lashed North Coast—all the way to Kaena Point, where the Waianae Range ends in a spirit leap to the other world. The *heiau* appears as a huge rectangle of rocks twice as big as a football field (170 ft. by 575 ft.), with an altar often covered by the flower and fruit offerings left by native Hawaiians.

1 mile past Waimea Bay. Take Pupukea Rd. *mauka* (inland) off Kamehameha Hwy. at Foodland, and drive 0.7 miles up a switchback road. TheBus: 52, then walk up Pupukea Rd.

Waimea Valley Audubon Center ⋆ *Kids*   For nearly 3 decades, Waimea Falls Park has hosted visitors to the 1,875-acre park (home to some 6,000 species of plants and trees) and activity center (from cliff diving and hula performances to kayaking and ATV tours). In 2003, the City and County of Honolulu awarded the lease to the valley to the National Audubon Society. The Audubon Society has renamed the park Waimea Valley Audubon Center and is focusing on protecting and interpreting the valley's cultural, botanical, and ecological resources. Activities (kayaking, ATV tours, and others) have been eliminated, along with the cliff diving and hula; instead, the emphasis is on education and preservation. The public is invited to hike the trails, wander through, and spend a day in this quiet oasis. Admission prices have been lowered and parking now is free.

59–864 Kamehameha Hwy. ⓒ 808/638-9199. www.audubon.org. Admission $8 adults, $5 children 4–12 and seniors. Daily 10am–5:30pm. TheBus: 52.

13 Shopping

Shopping competes with surfing, sightseeing, and golf as a bona fide Honolulu activity. And why not? The proliferation of top-notch made-in-Hawaii products, the vitality of the local crafts scene, and the unquenchable thirst for mementos of the islands make this a terrific place to shop. And Oahu is a haven for mall mavens. More than a thousand stores occupy the 11 major shopping centers on this island.

From T-shirts to Versace, posh European to down-home local, avant-garde to unspeakably tacky, Oahu's offerings are wide-ranging indeed. Here's the rub: You must sometimes wade through oceans of schlock to arrive at the mother lode.

The section that follows is not about finding cheap souvenirs or tony items from designer fashion chains. Instead, we'll guide you to those special treasures that lie somewhere in between.

IN & AROUND HONOLULU & WAIKIKI
ALOHA WEAR

One of Hawaii's lasting afflictions is the penchant visitors have for wearing loud, matching aloha shirts and muumuus. We applaud such visitors' good intentions (to act local), but no local resident would be caught dead in such a get-up. Muumuus and aloha shirts are wonderful, but the real thing is what island folks wear on Aloha Friday (every Fri), to the Brothers Cazimero Lei Day Concert (every May 1), or to work (where allowed). It's what they wear at home and to special parties where the invitation reads "Aloha Attire."

Aside from the vintage Hawaiian wear (from the 1930s through 1950s) found only in collectibles shops and swap meets, our favorite contemporary aloha-wear designer is Hawaii's **Tori Richards. Tommy Bahama,** which never calls its shirts "aloha shirts" but claims, instead, a Caribbean influence, is another Hawaii shirt icon, and so is the

International Market Place

"What it once was, it can be again," said Mark Hastert, president of the Queen Emma Foundation, owner of the International Market Place, on the renovations and resurrection of this once proud and famous shopping area.

In the past few decades, this 4.5-acre open market, squeezed in among the high-rises of Waikiki and bordered by Kuhio and Kalakaua avenues, had become a sea of schlock with an army of small carts selling trinkets (most cheaply made overseas), shoddy T-shirts, and lots of junk.

Those days are gone. At the end of 2005, after 48 years, the International Market Place and all the vendors were shut down, and a $150-million total restoration began that is expected to be completed by early 2008. The Queen Emma Foundation is bringing back the stream that used to run through the area (albeit as a water feature), and building an amphitheatre and a hula mound. Surrounding the area will be 230,000 square feet of retail in clusters of 8 to 10 buildings, from one to three stories tall, featuring shops and restaurants.

"We want it to once again be an exciting place, a central gathering place for Waikiki," said Hastert. "The aim is to re-create this once historic spot where visitors and residents can come for ceremonies and performances, to shop and eat, and enjoy Waikiki."

up-and-coming **Tiki** brand, quirky and distinctive, with fabulous fabric prints and retro elements that hark back to 1950s bowling shirts and James Dean charisma.

Unless you score at a garage sale or swap meet, the best aloha shirts are pricey these days, going for $80 to $125 and some, especially in places such as Kapaa, Kauai for $110! For the vintage look, **Avanti** has a corner on the market with its stunning line of silk shirts and dresses in authentic 1930s to 1950s patterns. The $60 shirts boast all the qualities of a vintage silky but without the high price or the web-thin fragility of an authentic antique. Women's dresses, tea timers from the 1940s, pants sets, and many other styles are the epitome of island chic, comfort, and nostalgic good looks. The line is distributed in better boutiques and department stores throughout Hawaii. In Waikiki, the major retail outlet is **Avanti Fashion,** at 2229 Kuhio Ave. (© **808/ 924-1668**); Waikiki Shopping Plaza, 2250 Kalakaua Ave. (© **808/922-2828**); 307 Lewers St. (© **808-926-6886**); and 2160 Kalakaua Ave. (© **808/924-3232**), or www.avantishirts.com.

The surf lines have hopped on the aloha-shirt bandwagon, with some viable styles put out by **Quiksilver's Silver Edition** line. Also popular is **Kahala Sportswear,** a well-known local company established in 1936. Kahala has faithfully reproduced, with astounding success, the linoleum-block prints of noted Maui artist Avi Kiriaty and the designs of other contemporary artists, including noted Islander Yvonne Cheng and surfer John Severson. Kahala is sold in department stores (from Macy's to Nordstrom), surf shops, and stylish boutiques throughout Hawaii and the mainland.

For the most culturally correct aloha wear, check out the shirts, dresses, and pareus of **Sig Zane Designs,** available at his Hilo (Big Island) and Wailuku (Maui) stores.

Zane, an accomplished hula dancer married to one of Hawaii's most revered hula masters, has an unmistakable visual style and a profound knowledge of Hawaiian culture that brings depth and meaning to his boldly styled renditions. Each Sig Zane aloha shirt, in pure cotton, tells a story. No wonder it's the garb of the cultural connoisseurs, who also buy fabrics by the yard for cushions, curtains, and interior accents.

Reyn Spooner is another source of attractive aloha shirts and muumuus in traditional and contemporary styles, with stores in Ala Moana Center, Kahala Mall, and the Sheraton Waikiki. Reyn, years ago, popularized the reverse-print aloha shirt—the uniform of downtown boardrooms—and has also jumped aboard the vintage-look bandwagon with old-Hawaii cotton and rayon prints, some of them in attractive two-color pareu patterns.

Well-known muumuu labels in Hawaii include **Mamo Howell,** with a boutique in Ward Warehouse, and **Princess Kaiulani** and **Bete** for the dressier mumus, sold along with many other lines at Macy's and other department stores. **Hilo Hattie's** new Ala Moana store (© 808/973-3266) is a gold mine of affordable aloha wear. Hilo Hattie's also offers free daily shuttle service from Waikiki to its retail outlet on Nimitz Highway (© 808/537-2926), and to Aloha Tower Marketplace, Ala Moana Center, and Waikiki. You'll also find macadamia nuts, Hawaii coffees, and other souvenirs at these Hilo Hattie's stores, as well as live Hawaiian entertainment. Quality and selection have improved noticeably in recent years.

Bailey's Antiques & Aloha Shirts   A large selection (thousands) of vintage, secondhand, and nearly new aloha shirts and other collectibles fills this eclectic emporium. It looks as though the owners regularly scour Hollywood movie costume departments for odd ball gowns, feather boas, fur stoles, leather jackets, 1930s dresses, and scads of other garments from periods past. Bailey's has one of the largest vintage aloha-shirt collections in Honolulu, with prices ranging from inexpensive to sky-high. Old Levi's jeans, mandarin jackets, vintage vases, household items, shawls, purses, and an eye-popping assortment of bark-cloth fabrics (the real thing, not repros) are among the mementos in this monumental collection. 517 Kapahulu Ave. © 808/734-7628.

Hilo Hattie *Value*   Hilo Hattie, the largest manufacturer of Hawaiian fashions, attracts more than a million visitors to its ever-expanding empire throughout the state. Its Ala Moana store is a leap in image, quality, range of merchandise, and overall shopping options. You can find great gifts here, from coconut utensils to food products and aloha shirts in all price ranges and motifs. There are some inexpensive silk aloha shirts as well as brand-name aloha shirts like Tommy Bahama and the store's own label. Hilo Hattie's also offers free daily shuttle service from Waikiki to its various locations. Quality and selection have improved noticeably in recent years. 1450 Ala Moana Blvd., Ala Moana Center. © 808/973-3266. Also at 700 N. Nimitz Hwy. © 808/544-3500.

Kamehameha Garment Co.   This Ward Centre shop carries dresses and aloha shirts by the time-honored Kamehameha label. Aloha shirts and dresses, many of them with a vintage look, fill the cordial room with a sense of nostalgia. Wide variety, good styling, and striking fabric patterns make this a must for those in search of the perfect aloha shirt. In the Ward Centre, 1200 Ala Moana Blvd. © 808/597-1503.

Macy's   If it's aloha wear, Macy's (formerly Liberty House) has it. The extensive aloha shirt and muumuu departments feature every label you can conjure, with a selection that changes with the times, and in all price ranges. 1450 Ala Moana Blvd., Ala Moana Center. © 808/941-2345.

Reyn's   Reyn's used to be a prosaic line but has stepped up its selection of women's and men's aloha wear with contemporary fabric prints and stylings, appealing to a hipper clientele. 1450 Ala Moana Blvd., Ala Moana Center. © 808/949-5929. Also at 4211 Waialae Ave., Kahala Mall. © 808/737-8313.

ANTIQUES & COLLECTIBLES

See also the listing for **Bailey's Antiques & Aloha Shirts,** above, in the section on "Aloha Wear."

Aloha Antiques and Collectables   This is arguably the largest antiques mall in Hawaii, with shops strung together in a mind-boggling labyrinth of treasures. This is not for the weak-kneed: the chockablock, multilevel stores can put you in sensory overload. But if the shopping gods are good to you, you may find rare Japanese plates or a priceless Lalique among the tchotchkes that fill every square inch of this dizzying miniemporium, where the items literally spill out onto the sidewalk. You'll have to look hard, but it's worth it—the prices are good and the rewards substantial. Jewelry, vintage aloha shirts, vases, silver, Asian lacquer, Hawaiian collectibles, and countless eclectic items make up this collection of junk, treasures, and nostalgia. 930 Maunakea St. (at the harbor end of the street). © 808/536-6187.

Anchor House Antiques   This highly eclectic collection of Hawaiian, Asian, and European pieces sprawls over thousands of square feet. You'll find wooden calabashes, camphor chests, paintings, Hawaiian artifacts, and trinkets, priced from $10 to $2,000. 471 Kapahulu Ave. © 808/732-3884.

Antique Alley   This narrow shop is chockablock with the passionate collections of several vendors under one roof. With its expanded collection of old Hawaiian artifacts and surfing and hula nostalgia, it's a sure winner for eclectic tastes. The showcases include estate jewelry, antique silver, Hawaiian bottles, collectible toys, pottery, cameras, Depression glass, linens, plantation photos and ephemera, and a wide selection of nostalgic items from Hawaii and across America. At the rear is a small, attractive selection of Soiree clothing, made by Julie Lauster, of antique kimonos and obis. 1347 Kapiolani Blvd. © 808/941-8551.

Antique House   Small but tasteful, the low-profile Antique House is hidden below the lobby level of the illustrious Royal Hawaiian Hotel. Come here for small items, such as Asian antiques, Chinese and Japanese porcelains, and a stunning selection of snuff bottles, bronzes, vases, and china. In the Royal Hawaiian Hotel, 2259 Kalakaua Ave. © 808/923-5101.

T. Fujii Japanese Antiques   This is a long-standing icon in Hawaii's antiques world and an impeccable source for ukiyo-e prints, scrolls, obis, Imari porcelain, tansus, tea-ceremony bowls, and screens, as well as contemporary ceramics from Mashiko and Kasama, with prices from $25 to $18,000. 1016 Kapahulu Ave., © 808/732-7860.

Garakuta-Do   This huge warehouse/store at the gateway to Waikiki has a sublime collection of Japanese antiques. In its expanded space on the Ala Wai Canal, across from the Convention Center, it offers ample free parking. It's worth finding for its late-Edo period (1800s–early 1900s) antiques, collected and sold by cheerful owner Wataru Harada. The selection of gorgeous tansus, mingei folk art, Japanese screens, scrolls, Imari plates, bronze sculptures, kimonos, obis, modern woodblock prints, and stone objects makes shopping here a treasure hunt. Noritake lovers, listen up: The shop now carries a sizable collection of old Noritake china from 1891 to the 1940s. Yum. 1833 Kalakaua Ave., Ste. 100. © 808/955-2099.

Robyn Buntin   Robyn Buntin's 5,000-square-foot gallery and picture-framing department, called Robyn Buntin's Picture Framing and Oceania Gallery, and his gallery for Hawaiian art, at 820 S. Beretania St., are among the features of this burgeoning art resource, located three doors from the Honolulu Academy of Art. This is Honolulu's stellar source of museum-quality Asian art and contemporary and traditional Hawaiian art. The gracious and authoritative Robyn Buntin is an expert in netsuke and a highly esteemed resource in Asian art. As much a gallery as an antiques store, Robyn Buntin radiates a tasteful serenity. The offerings include jade; scholar's table items; Buddhist sculpture; Japanese prints; contemporary Chinese, Japanese, and Korean pictorial (graphic) art; and a large and magnificent collection of Hawaiiana. Some pieces are 5,000 years old, while many others are hot off the presses from Tokyo, Seoul, and Beijing. The brilliant selection of netsuke and Japanese carvings is complemented with Hawaiian works by Isami Doi, Avi Kiriaty, Guy Buffet, Mark Kadota, and others. Few people know that John Kelly's legacy includes Asian works; they're here, along with rare etchings and prints that move swiftly to waiting collectors. 848 S. Beretania St. ✆ **808/523-5913.**

BOOKSTORES

Barnes & Noble   With more than 150,000 titles, a respectable music department, and strong Hawaiiana, fiction, and new-release departments, as well as a popular coffee bar, Barnes & Noble has become the second home of Honolulu's casual readers and bibliophiles. Kahala Mall, 4211 Waialae Ave. ✆ **808/737-3323.**

Bestsellers Books & Music   Hawaii's largest independent bookstore, located in downtown Honolulu, has a complete selection of nonfiction and fiction titles with an emphasis on Hawaiian books and music. There's another Bestsellers in the Hilton Hawaiian Village (2005 Kalia Rd.). 1001 Bishop St. ✆ **808/528-2378.**

Borders   Borders is a beehive of literary activity, with weekly signings, prominent local and mainland musicians at least monthly, and special events almost daily that make this store a major Honolulu attraction. Ward Centre, 1200 Ala Moana Blvd. ✆ **808/591-8995.** Waikele Center, 94–821 Lumiaina St. (✆ **808/676-6699**).

Pacific Book House   Denis Perron, connoisseur of rare books, continues to build and expand his rare and out-of-print book inventory. He has also expanded into paintings, antiques, and estate jewelry, even offering appraisals of rare books and paintings and handling restorations others are afraid to touch. When you tire of book browsing, look into the selection of antique silver and china. Literati still come here for finds in Hawaiiana, rare prints, collectible books, and other out-of-print treasures. 1249 S. Beretania St. ✆ **808/591-1599.**

Rainbow Books and Records   A little weird but totally lovable, especially among students and eccentrics (and insatiable readers), Rainbow Books is notable for its selection of popular fiction, records, and Hawaii-themed books, secondhand and reduced. Because it's located in the university area, it's always bulging with textbooks, Hawaiiana, and popular music. It's about the size of a large closet, but you'll be surprised by what you'll find. 1010 University Ave. ✆ **808/955-7994.**

CONSIGNMENT SHOPS

comme ci comme ca   Great finds abound here, especially if your timing is good. Brand-new Prada bags, old Hermès jackets and dresses in pristine condition, an occasional Ferragamo purse, Armani suits, and vintage fur-collared sweaters straight out of 1940s Hollywood are some of the pleasures awaiting. Timing is paramount here;

finds—such as a made-in-Italy, brand-new, mostly cashmere Donna Karan for Men jacket—disappear to the early birds, but you can always count on great finds in designer clothes, bags, shoes, jewelry, and stylish vintage treasures. 3464 Waialae Ave., Kaimuki. © 808/734-8869.

The Ultimate You   In this resale boutique, the clothes are current (the fashions of the last 2 years) and not always cheap, but always 50% to 90% off retail. This means designer suits and dresses, often new or barely worn, from such names as Escada, Chanel, Prada, Gianfranco Ferre, Donna Karan, Yves St. Laurent, Armani, Ralph Lauren, Laura Ashley, and Ann Taylor. You'll also find aisles of separates, cashmere sweaters, dresses, shoes, scarves, and purses. When a red star appears on the tag, it means another big chunk off the bill. In its new Ward Centre location, it's spiffier than ever. In the Ward Centre, 1200 Ala Moana Blvd. © 808/591-8388.

EDIBLES

In addition to the stores listed below, I also recommend **Executive Chef** (© 808/596-2433), in the Ward Warehouse, and **Islands' Best** (© 808/949-5345), in the Ala Moana Center. Both shops contain wide-ranging selections that include Hawaii's specialty food items.

If you're looking for a bakery, **Saint-Germain,** in Shirokiya at Ala Moana Center (© 808/955-1711), and near Times Supermarket, 1296 S. Beretania St. (© 808/593-8711), sells baguettes, country loaves, and oddball delicacies such as mini mushroom-and-spinach pizzas. The reigning queen of bakers, though, is **Cafe Laufer,** 3565 Waialae Ave. (© 808/735-7717; p. 148). Nearby, old-timers still line up at **Sconees,** 1117 12th Ave. (© 808/734-4024), formerly Bea's Pies. Sconees has fantastic scones, pumpkin-custard pies, and danishes. And don't forget **Mary Catherine's** (see below), a great place for quality cakes and European pastries.

Asian Grocery   Asian Grocery supplies many of Honolulu's Thai, Vietnamese, Chinese, Indonesian, and Filipino restaurants with authentic spices, rice, noodles, produce, sauces, herbs, and adventurous ingredients. Browse among the kafir lime leaves, tamarind and fish pastes, red and green chiles, curries, chutneys, lotus leaves, gingko nuts, jasmine and basmati rice, and shelf upon shelf of medium to hot chile sauces. 1319 S. Beretania St. © 808/593-8440. www.asianfoodtrading.com.

Daiei   Stands offering takeout sushi, Korean *kal bi,* pizza, Chinese food, flowers, Mrs. Fields cookies, and other items for self and home surround this huge emporium. Inside, you'll find household products, a pharmacy, and inexpensive clothing, but it's the prepared foods and produce that excel. The fresh-seafood section is one of Honolulu's best, not far from where regulars line up for the bento lunches and individually wrapped sushi. When Kau navel oranges, macadamia nuts, Kona coffee, Chinese taro, and other Hawaii products are on sale, savvy locals arrive in droves to take advantage of the high quality and good value. 801 Kaheka St.; © 808/973-4800. 345 Hahani St, Kailua; © 808/266-4400. 850 Kamehameha Hwy., Pearl City; © 808/453-5509. 94–144 Farrington Hwy., Waipahu; © 808/678-6800.

Fujioka's Wine Merchants   Oenophiles flock here for a mouthwatering selection of wines, single-malt Scotches, excellent Italian wines, and affordable, farm-raised caviar—food and libations for all occasions. Everyday wines, special-occasion wines, and esoteric wines are priced lower here than at most places. The wine-tasting bar at the rear of the store is a new attraction. Market City Shopping Center, 2919 Kapiolani Blvd., lower level. © 808/739-9463.

Honolulu Chocolate Co.   Life's greatest pleasures are dispensed here with abandon: expensive gourmet chocolates made in Honolulu, Italian and Hawaiian biscotti, boulder-size turtles (caramel and pecans covered with chocolate), truffles, chocolate-covered coffee beans, and jumbo apricots in white and dark chocolate, to name a few. There are also tinned biscuits, European candies, and sweets in a million disguises. You pay dearly for them, but the dark-chocolate-dipped macadamia-nut clusters are beyond compare. Ward Centre, 1200 Ala Moana Blvd. ℂ 808/591-2997.

It's Chili in Hawaii   This is *the* oasis for chile-heads, a house of heat with endorphins aplenty and good food to accompany the hot sauces from around the world, including a fabulous selection of made-in-Hawaii products. Scoville units (measurements of heat in food) are the topic of the day in this shop, lined with thousands of bottles of hot sauces, salsas, and other chile-based food products. Not everything is scorching, however; some products, like Dave's Soyabi and the limu-habañero sauce called Makai, are everyday flavor enhancers that can be used on rice, salads, meats, and pasta. If you're eating in, the fresh-frozen tamales, in several varieties (including meatless), are now in regular supply. Every Saturday, free samples of green-chile stew are dished up to go with the generous hot-sauce tastings. Located by McCully Street, across the street from McDonald's. 2080 S. King St., Suite 105. ℂ 808/945-7070.

Mary Catherine's Bakery   This top-notch European bakery sells everything from lavishly tiered wedding cakes to killer carrot cakes and a chocolate decadence cake that is moist, rich, and extravagant. Cookies, cakes, scones, pastries, tortes, and all manner of baked sweets line the counters. Long a favorite of locals. 2820 S. King St., across from the Hawaiian Humane Society. ℂ 808/946-4333.

Fish Markets

Tamashiro Market, 802 N. King St., Kalihi (ℂ 808/841-8047), is the grandfather of fish markets and the ace in the hole for home chefs with bouillabaisse or paella in mind. A separate counter sells seaweed salad, prepared poke, Filipino and Puerto Rican ti-wrapped steamed rice, and dozens of other ethnic foods.

For more mainstream shoppers, **Safeway** on Beretania Street (ℂ 808/591-8315) has a seafood counter with fresh choices and a staff that takes pride in its deftness with prepared foods (like fresh ahi poke, seaweed salad, shrimp cocktail, and marinated crab—don't be shy about asking for a taste).

Neighbor islanders have been known to drive directly from the airport to **Yama's Fish Market,** 2203 Young St., Moiliili (ℂ 808/941-9994), for one of the best plate lunches in town. But Yama's is also known for its inexpensive fresh fish, tasty poke, and lomi salmon. Chilled beer, boiled peanuts, and fresh ahi sliced into sashimi are popular for local-style gatherings, sunset beach parties, and festive *pau hana* (end of work) celebrations. New standouts include a fabulous assortment of chocolate biscotti and chocolate chip cookies, sweet-potato and custard mochi and a haupia (coconut pudding) pie layered with bright-purple Okinawa sweet potato.

Mauna Kea Marketplace Food Court   Hungry patrons line up in front of these no-nonsense food booths that sell everything from pizza and plate lunches to quick, authentic, and inexpensive Vietnamese, Thai, Italian, Chinese, Japanese, and Filipino dishes. The best seafood fried rice comes from the woks of **Malee Thai/Vietnamese Cuisine,** at the *mauka* (inland) end of the marketplace—perfectly flavored with morsels of fish, squid, and shrimp. Right next to it is Tandoori Chicken Cafe, a fount of Indian culinary pleasures, from curries and jasmine-chicken rice balls to spiced rounds of curried potatoes and a wonderful lentil dal. On the other side of Malee, **Masa's** serves bento and Japanese dishes, such as miso eggplant, that are famous. A few stalls *makai,* you'll find the best dessert around at **Pho Lau,** which serves haupia (coconut pudding), tapioca, and taro in individual baskets made of pandanus. Walk the few steps down to the produce stalls (pungent odors, fish heads, and chicken feet on counters—not for the squeamish) and join in the spirit of discovery. Vendors sell everything from fresh ahi and whole snapper to yams and taro, seaweed, and fresh fruits and vegetables of every shape and size. 1120 Maunakea St., Chinatown. © 808/524-3409.

Paradise Produce Co.   Neat rows of mangoes, top-quality papayas, and reasonably priced and very fresh produce make this a paradise for food lovers. When mangoes are in season, you'll find Yee's Orchard Haydens set apart from the less desirable Mexican mangoes and, if you're lucky, a stash of ambrosial Pirie mangoes (they sell out quickly). Chinese taro, litchi and asparagus in season, local eggplant, and dozens of fruits and vegetables are offered up fresh, neat, and colorful. 83 N. King St., Chinatown. © 808/533-2125.

People's Open Markets   Truck farmers from all over the island bring their produce to Oahu's neighborhoods in regularly scheduled, city-sponsored open markets, held Monday through Saturday at various locations. Among the tables of ong choy, choi sum, Okinawan spinach, opal basil, papayas, mangoes, seaweed, and fresh fish, you'll find homemade banana bread, Chinese pomelo (like large grapefruit), fresh fiddleheads (fern shoots) when available, and colorful, bountiful harvests from land and sea. Various sites around town. Call to find the open market nearest you. © 808/527-5167.

R. Field Wine Co.   Foodland has won countless new converts since Richard Field—oenophile, gourmet, and cigar aficionado—moved his wine shop from Ward Centre to this new location within lower Makiki's Foodland. The thriving gourmet store offers gemlike vine-ripened tomatoes and juicy Clementines, sparkling bags of Nalo gourmet greens, designer cheeses, caviar, Langenstein Farms macadamia nuts, vegetarian and salmon mousses, vinegars, and all manner of epicurean delights, including wines and single-malt Scotches. *A huge hit:* the warm, just-baked breads (rosemary/olive oil, whole-wheat, organic wheat, and others) baked on the premises with dough flown in from Los Angeles's famous La Brea Bakery. Foodland Super Market, 1460 S. Beretania St. © 808/596-9463.

Sushi Company   It's not easy to find premium-grade *hamachi* (yellowtail tuna), ahi, *ikura* (salmon roe), *ika* (cuttlefish), and other top-grade fresh ingredients in anything but a bona-fide sit-down sushi bar. But here it is; a small, sparkling gem of a sushi maker that sells fast-food sushi of non-fast-food quality, at great prices. Order ahead or wait while they make it. The combinations range from minisets (27 pieces) to large-variety sets (43–51 pieces), ideal for picnics and potlucks. Individual hand rolls range from 99¢ to $1.55, and the nigiri comes in orders of two and more. An expanded menu now offers excellent miso soup, salmon skin sushi to go, scallop, sea urchin, and spicy tuna. A newcomer to the neighborhood and already a mainstay, Sushi Company has one small two-person table; most of the business is takeout. 1111 McCully St. (at Young St.) ℂ **808/947-5411.**

FLOWERS & LEIS

At most lei shops, simple leis sell for $3 and up, deluxe leis for $10 and up. For a special-occasion designer bouquet or lei, you can't do better than Michael Miyashiro of **Rainforest Plantes et Fleurs** (ℂ **808/942-1550** or 808/591-5999). He's an ecologically aware, highly gifted lei-maker—his leis are pricey, but worth it. He is the consummate lei designer who custom-creates the lei for the person, occasion, and even destination. (Many of his original designs have been adopted by the Chinatown lei makers.) Order by phone or stop by the Ward Warehouse, where his tiny shop is an oasis of green and beauty. Upon request, Miyashiro's leis will come in ti-leaf bundles, called *pu`olo;* custom gift baskets (in woven green coconut baskets), and special arrangements. You can even request the card sentiments in Hawaiian, with English translations.

The other primary sources for flowers and leis are the shops lining the streets of Moiliili and Chinatown. Moiliili favorites include **Rudy's Flowers,** 2722 S. King St. (ℂ **808/944-8844**), a local institution with the best prices on roses, Micronesian ginger lei, and a variety of cut blooms. Across the street, **Flowers for a Friend,** 2739 S. King St. (ℂ **808/955-4227**), has good prices on leis, floral arrangements, and cut flowers. Nearby, **Flowers by Jr. and Lou,** 2652 S. King St. (ℂ **808/941-2022**), offers calla lilies, Gerbera daisies, a riot of potted orchids, and the full range of cut flowers along with its lei selection.

In Chinatown, lei vendors line Beretania and Maunakea streets, and the fragrances of their wares mix with the earthy scents of incense and ethnic foods. Our top picks are **Lita's Leis,** 59 N. Beretania St. (ℂ **808/521-9065**), which has fresh puakenikeni, gardenias that last, and a supply of fresh and reasonable leis; **Sweetheart's Leis,** 69 N. Beretania St. (ℂ **808/537-3011**), with a worthy selection of the classics at fair prices; **Lin's Lei Shop,** 1017–A Maunakea St. (ℂ **808/537-4112**), with creatively fashioned, unusual leis; and **Cindy's Lei Shoppe,** 1034 Maunakea St. (ℂ **808/536-6538**), with terrific sources for unusual leis such as feather dendrobiums, firecracker combinations, and everyday favorites like ginger, tuberose, orchid, and pikake. Ask Cindy's about its unique "curb service," available with phone orders. Just give them your car's color and model, and you can pick up your lei curbside—a great convenience on this busy street.

HAWAIIANA & GIFT ITEMS

Our top recommendations are the fabulous, newly expanded **Academy Shop,** at the Honolulu Academy of Arts, 900 S. Beretania St. (ℂ **808/523-8703**), and the **Contemporary Museum Gift Shop,** 2411 Makiki Heights Rd. (ℂ **808/523-3447**), two of the finest shopping stops on Oahu and worth a special trip whether or not you want to see the museums themselves. (And you will want to see the museums, especially the recently expanded Honolulu Academy of Arts.) The Academy Shop offers a brilliant selection of art books, jewelry, basketry, ethnic fabrics and native crafts from all over the world, posters and books, and fiber vessels and accessories. The Contemporary Museum shop focuses on arts and crafts such as avant-garde jewelry, cards and stationery, books, home accessories, and gift items made by artists from Hawaii and across the country. We love the glam selection of jewelry and novelties, such as the twisted-wire wall hangings.

Hula Supply Center   Hawaiiana meets kitsch in this shop's marvelous selection of Day-Glo cellophane skirts, bamboo nose flutes, T-shirts, hula drums, shell leis, feathered

Health-Food Stores

In the university district, **Down to Earth,** 2525 S. King St., Moiliili (📞 **808/ 947-7678**), is a respectable source of organic vegetables and vegetarian bulk foods, with good prices, a strong selection of supplements and herbs, and a vegetarian juice-and-sandwich bar. But my favorite is nearby **Kokua Market,** 2643 S. King St. (📞 **808/941-1922**), a health-food cooperative and Honolulu's best source for organic vegetables. It also has an excellent variety of cheeses, pastas and bulk grains, sandwiches, salads, and prepared foods, organic wines, and an expanded vitamin section.

Tiny but powerful, with a loyal clientele, **House of Health,** 1541 S. Beretania St. (at Kalakaua Ave) (📞 **808/955-6168**), has competitive prices and a wide selection of health-food supplements. There's no produce, but there are frozen vegetarian foods, bulk grains, and healthful snacks. In Nuuanu Valley, *mauka* (inland) of downtown Honolulu, **Huckleberry Farms,** 1613 Nuuanu Ave. (at School St.) (📞 **808/524-7960**), has a wide range of produce, vitamins, cosmetics, books, and prepared vegetarian foods. A few doors down, the beauty and vitamin retail outlet is stocked with cosmetics, nutritional supplements, and nonperishable, nongrocery health products.

rattle gourds, lauhala accessories, fiber mats, and a wide assortment of pareu fabrics. Although hula dancers shop here for their dance accoutrements, it's not all serious shopping. This is fertile ground for souvenirs and memorabilia of Hawaii, rooted somewhere between irreverent humor and cultural integrity. A great stop for Hawaiian and Polynesian gift items. Hawaiian Traders, its new adjoining store, is a showcase for made-in-Hawaii products. 2346 S. King St., Moiliili. 📞 808/941-5379.

**Macy's Ku`u Home Island Gifts**    The fourth-floor island lifestyle department, called Ku`u Home ("my home") Island Gifts, is the best thing this department store has done in recent memory. Cultural/retail wizards Donna Burns and Maile Meyer of the enormously successful Native Books & Beautiful Things (see below) contacted 65 Hawaii artists and created a department of more than 600 unique, made-in-Hawaii products, skillfully displayed in a warm, real-life setting. Furniture, lamps, books, cushions, baskets, Hawaiian implements, quilts, lauhala and coconut home accessories, glassware, fabrics, gifts, personal adornments—the selection is eclectic and wonderful, capturing a distinctive Hawaii flavor that has its own strong identity within the store. The "Hawaii Artist of the Month" series brings the artists into the store to talk about their works. More than a shopping must, Ku`u Home is a cultural and aesthetic eye-opener. In the Ala Moana Center, 1450 Ala Moana Blvd. 📞 808/945-5636.

Native Books & Beautiful Things *Finds*   Come to either of the two locations of this *hui* (association) of artists and craftspeople and you'll be enveloped in a love of things Hawaiian, from musical instruments to calabashes, jewelry, leis, books, and items of woven fibers—beautiful things of Hawaii. You'll find contemporary Hawaiian clothing, handmade koa journals, Hawaii-themed home accessories, lauhala handbags and accessories, jams and jellies and food products, etched glass, hand-painted fabrics and clothing, stone poi pounders, and other high-quality gift items. Some of

Hawaii's finest artists in all craft media have their works available here on a regular basis, and the Hawaiian-book selection is tops. The 5,000-square-foot emporium at Ward Warehouse is a browser's paradise and features new artists every month. Ward Warehouse, 1050 Ala Moana Blvd. (📞 808/596-8885).

Nohea Gallery   A fine showcase for contemporary Hawaii art, Nohea celebrates the islands with thoughtful, attractive selections in all media, from pit-fired raku and finely turned wood vessels to jewelry, hand-blown glass, paintings, prints, fabrics (including Hawaiian-quilt cushions), and furniture. Nohea's selection is always evolving and growing, with 90% of the works by Hawaii artists and a thoughtful selection of works representing Hawaii's best in all media. This is a terrific source of art and unique gift items from Hawaii. In the Ward Warehouse, 1050 Ala Moana Blvd. 📞 808/596-0074; Kahala Mandarin Oriental Hawaii, 5000 Kahala Ave. (📞 808/737-8688); Ohana Reef Towers Hotel, 227 Lewers St. (📞 808/926-2224); Sheraton Moana Surfrider Hotel, 2365 Kalakaua Ave. (📞 808/923-6644).

Nui Mono   We love this tiny shop's kimonos, clothing, and accessories and the contemporary clothes made from ethnic fabrics. Other items include handbags made of patchwork vintage fabrics and priceless kimono silks, drapey Asian shapes and ikat fabrics, and richly textured vests and skirts. Warm, rich colors are the Nui Mono signature—and everything's moderately priced. 2745 S. King St., Moiliili. 📞 808/946-7407.

Shop Pacifica   Local crafts, lauhala and Cook Island woven coconut, Hawaiian music tapes and CDs, pareus, and a vast selection of Hawaii-themed books anchor this gift shop. Hawaiian-quilt cushion kits, jewelry, glassware, seed and Niihau shell leis, cookbooks, and many other gift possibilities will keep you occupied between stargazing in the planetarium and pondering the shells and antiquities of the esteemed historical museum. In the Bishop Museum, 1525 Bernice St. 📞 808/848-4158.

SHOPPING CENTERS

Ala Moana Center   The new third level is abuzz with eateries and shops, while the ponds on the mall level are thriving with taro and Hawaiian plants, even hapu`u ferns and koa trees. At press time, the finishing touches are being applied to the parking areas, but most of the shops are in, and many of them are the familiar names of mainland chains, such as **DKNY, Old Navy,** and **Eddie Bauer.** The three-story, super-luxe Neiman Marcus, which opened in September 1998, was a bold move in Hawaii's troubled economy and has retained its position as the shrine of the fashionistas. But there are practical touches in the center, too, such as banks and a foreign-exchange service (**Thomas Cook**), a U.S. Post Office, several optical companies (including 1-hour service by **LensCrafters**), **Foodland Supermarket, Longs Drugs,** and a handful of photo-processing services. The smaller, locally-owned stores (alas, fewer by the year) are scattered among the behemoths, mostly on the ground floor. Approximately 250 shops and services sprawl over several blocks (and 1.8 million sq. ft. of store space) on this 50-acre site, catering to every imaginable need; from over-the-top upscale to mainland chains such as the **Gap, Banana Republic, Body Shop, Sharper Image, Ann Taylor,** and **Polo/Ralph Lauren.** Department stores such as **Macy's** sell fashion, food, cosmetics, shoes, and household needs. Shoes? They're a kick at **Nordstrom,** and newcomer **Walking Co.** has first-rate comfort styles by Mephisto, Ecco, and Naot. **Sephora,** the cosmetics emporium to top all, neighbors **Williams-Sonoma,** which will appeal to anyone who loves food, or even the smell of it.

A good stop for gifts is **Islands' Best,** which spills over with Hawaiian-made foodstuffs, ceramics, fragrances, and more. **Splash! Hawaii** is a good source for women's swimwear; for aloha shirts and men's swimwear, try **Macy's, Town & Country Surf, Reyn's,** or the terminally hip **Hawaiian Island Creations.** Lovers of Polynesian wear and pareus shouldn't miss **Tahiti Imports.** The **food court** is abuzz with dozens of stalls purveying Cajun food, ramen, pizza, plate lunches, vegetarian fare, green tea and fruit freezes (like frozen yogurt), panini, and countless other treats. Monday through Saturday 9:30am-9:00pm, and Sunday 10am to 7pm. 1450 Ala Moana Blvd. ℰ 808/955-9517. The Bus: 8, 19, or 20. Ala Moana Shuttle Bus runs daily every 15 min. from 7 stops in Waikiki; Waikiki Trolley also stops at Ala Moana.

Aloha Tower Marketplace   There is a perpetual parking shortage here, and when you find a parking spot, the parking rates are ridiculously sky high. Take the trolley if you can. Or skip the hassle all together and go somewhere else. Once you get to the new harbor-front complex, however, a sense of nostalgia, of what it must have been like in the "Boat Days" of the 1920s to 1940s, will inevitably take over. Sleek ocean liners (as well as malodorous fishing boats) still tie up across the harbor, and the refurbished Aloha Tower stands high over the complex, as it did in the days when it was the tallest structure in Honolulu.

   Hawaiian House is a hit with its island-style interiors and home accents. Dining and shopping prospects abound: **Martin & MacArthur** gift shop, **Hawaiian Ukulele Company, Sunglass Hut, Don Ho's Island Grill, Chai's Island Bistro,** and **Gordon Biersch Brewery.** Retail shops are open Monday through Saturday 9am to 9pm and Sunday 9am to 6pm. Dining and entertainment is daily 8am to midnight. 1 Aloha Tower Dr., on the waterfront between piers 8 and 11, Honolulu Harbor. ℰ 808/528-5700, or ℰ 808/566-2333 for the Aloha Tower Entertainment Hotline. Various Honolulu trolleys stop here; if you want a direct ride from Waikiki, take the free Hilo Hattie's trolley or the Waikiki Red Line trolley, which continues on to Hilo Hattie's in Iwilei.

DFS Galleria   "Boat days" is the theme at this newly renovated (to the tune of $65 million) Waikiki emporium, a three-floor extravaganza of shops ranging from the very tony to the very touristy. This is a tacky addition to Waikiki, but there are some great Hawaiian food products, ranging from the incomparable Big Island Candies short-bread cookies to a spate of coffees and preserves. Servers bearing warm, fresh-from-the-oven cookies are a nice touch. The Tube, a walk-through aquarium complete with spotted rays and sting rays, is a big attraction, visible from indoors and on the sidewalk at the corner of Kalakaua and Royal Hawaiian avenues. There are multitudes of aloha shirts and T-shirts, a virtual golf course, surf and skate equipment, a terrific Hawaiian music department, and a labyrinth of boutiques once you get past the Waikiki Walk. Fragrances and cosmetics make a big splash at DFS—they're a big part of the upper floors. **Starbucks** and **Jamba Juice** are always buzzing with coffee and smoothies, and **Kalia Grill** offers rotisserie and deli items for casual dining. *One caveat:* Some sections are restricted to international travelers only. Free live Hawaiian entertainment, featuring hula styles from the 1920s to 1940s, takes place nightly at 7pm. Corner of Kalakaua and Royal Hawaiian aves., 330 Royal Hawaiian Ave. ℰ 808/931-2655.

Kahala Mall   Chic, manageable, and unfrenzied, Kahala Mall is home to some of Honolulu's best shops. Located east of Waikiki in the posh neighborhood of Kahala, the mall has everything from a small **Macy's** to chain stores such as **Banana Republic** and the **Gap**—nearly 100 specialty shops (including dozens of eateries and eight movie theaters) in an enclosed, air-conditioned area. **Starbucks** is a java magnet, a stone's throw from the **Gourmet Express** with its fast, healthy salads, tortilla wraps, and fresh juices and smoothies. **Jamba Juice** is the hot spot of the mall, with lines of smoothie lovers waiting for their Citrus Squeeze or Kiwi-Berry Burner. For gift, fashion, and specialty stores, our picks of the mall's best and brightest are: **Riches,** a tiny kiosk with a big, bold selection of jewelry; the **Compleat Kitchen;** the **Paperie,** with an impressive selection of everything you'll need in stationery, cards, napkins and paper goods; and the sprawling **Hawaiian House.** Anchoring the mall are stalwarts **Longs Drugs, Macy's, Star Market,** and **Barnes & Noble** with its books, coffee bar, and inviting nooks. Look also for the **Macy's West Men's Store** at the *mauka* (inland) corner of the mall, under a separate roof from the main store. 4211 Waialae Ave., Kahala. ℂ 808/732-7736.

Royal Hawaiian Shopping Center   Unfortunately for budget travelers, "upscale" is the operative word here. Although there are drugstores, lei stands, restaurants, and food kiosks, the most conspicuous stores are the European designer boutiques (**Chanel, Cartier, Hermès,** and more) that cater largely to visitors from Japan. But one of our favorite stops is the **Little Hawaiian Craft Shop,** which features a distinctive collection of Niihau shell leis, museum replicas of Hawaiian artifacts, and works by Hawaii artists, as well as South Pacific crafts. **Beretania Florist,** located in the hut under the large banyan tree, will ship cut tropical flowers anywhere in the United States. 2201 Kalakaua Ave. ℂ 808/922-0588.

Waikele Premium Outlets *Value*   Just say the word "Waikele" and our eyes glaze over. So many shops, so little time! And so much money to be saved while spending for what you don't need. There are two sections to this sprawling discount shopping mecca: the **Waikele Premium Outlets,** some 51 retailers offering designer and name-brand merchandise; and the **Waikele Value Center** across the street, with another 25 stores more practical than fashion-oriented (Eagle Hardware, Sports Authority, Borders). The 64-acre complex has made discount shopping a major activity and a travel pursuit in itself, with shopping tours for visitor groups and carloads of neighbor islanders and Oahu residents making pilgrimages from all corners of the state. They

Royal Hawaiian Shopping Center: Under Construction

The Royal Hawaiian Shopping Center is undergoing a massive renovation, to the tune of $84 million and is expected to be completed in late 2006.

The mall is redefining itself by expanding into more gardens, more open space and less dense atmosphere. The central performance area will be remodeled into a 30,000-square-foot landscaped, gathering area with gardens. The entire mall will have more windows, more open space and a nine-restaurant food court on the second level.

The biggest change will be the exterior finish, which will have a Polynesian kapa look, and elimination of the three thick-concrete bridges that connect to the wings of the mall. They will be combined into one open-air bridge, creating a panoramic view of the Royal Hawaiian Hotel.

During construction, the shops will remain open, and the renovations will be conducted behind barricades. Occasionally, one lane on Kalakaua Avenue may be blocked for construction.

come to hunt down bargains on everything from perfumes, luggage, and hardware to sporting goods, fashions, vitamins, and china. Examples: **Geoffrey Beene, Donna Karan, Saks Fifth Avenue, Anne Klein, Max Studio, Levi's, Converse, Vitamin World, Mikasa, Kenneth Cole, Banana Republic,** and dozens of other name brands at a fraction of retail. The ultra-chic **Barneys** has added new cachet to this shopping haven. 94–790 Lumiaina St., Waikele (about 20 miles from Waikiki). ℂ **808/676-5656.** Take H-1 west toward Waianae and turn off at exit 7. TheBus: no. 42 from Waikiki to Waipahu Transit Center, then 433 from Transit Center to Waikele. To find out which companies offer shopping tours with Waikiki pickups, call the Information Center at ℂ 808/678-0786.

Ward Centre   Although it has a high turnover and a changeable profile, Ward Centre is a standout for its concentration of restaurants and shops. **Ryan's** and **Kakaako Kitchen** are as popular as ever, the former looking out over Ala Moana Park and the latter with lanai views of the sprawling **Pier 1 Imports** across the street. Across from Pier 1, **Nordstrom Rack** and **Office Depot** have sprouted in a new development area that also includes a 16-theater movie megaplex now being built. All these establishments are part of developer Victoria Ward's Kakaako projects, which take up several blocks in this area: Ward Centre, Ward Farmers' Market, Ward Village Shops, Ward Gateway Center, and Ward Warehouse.

Ward Centre's gift shops and galleries include **Kamehameha Garment Company** for aloha shirts, **Vagabond House, Paper Roses** for wonderful paper products, **Honolulu Chocolate Co.** (see "Edibles," above), and the very attractive **Gallery at Ward Centre. Handblock** proffers wonderful table linens, clothing, and household accents, while **Borders** is action central, bustling with browsers. 1200 Ala Moana Blvd. ℂ 808/591-8411.

Ward Warehouse   Older than its sister property, Ward Centre, and endowed with an endearing patina, Ward Warehouse remains a popular stop for dining and shopping. **Native Books & Beautiful Things** and the **Nohea Gallery** (see "Hawaiiana & Gift Items," above for both) are excellent sources for quality Hawaii-made arts and crafts.

Other recommended stops in the low-rise wooden structure include the ever-colorful **C. June Shoes,** with flamboyant designer women's shoes and handbags (tony, expensive, and oh-so-entertaining!); **Executive Chef,** for gourmet Hawaii food items and household accessories; **Out of Africa,** for pottery, beads, and interior accents; **Mamo Howell,** for distinctive aloha wear; and **Private World,** for delicate sachets, linens, and fragrances. Another great stop is **Bambini,** brimming with tasteful gifts for kids and babies. For T-shirts and swimwear, check out the **Town & Country Surf Shop,** and for an excellent selection of sunglasses, knapsacks, and footwear to take you from the beach to the ridgetops, don't miss **Thongs 'N Things.** 1050 Ala Moana Blvd. ℂ 808/591-8411.

Ward Entertainment Center   This large, multiblock complex includes Ward Centre and Ward Warehouse, mentioned above, at the corner of Auahi and Kamakee streets. The complex has undergone enormous expansion, beginning with a new 16-movie megaplex, and a new retail and restaurant complex, with eateries like **Dave & Buster's** (with virtual golf, games, interactive entertainment, bars, and a restaurant), **Buca di Beppo, Wolfgang Puck Express,** and **Cold Stone Creamery.** Open Monday through Saturday 10am to 10pm, Sunday 10am to 9pm. Auahi and Kamakee Streets. ℂ 808/591-8411. www.victoriaward.com.

SURF & SPORTS

The surf-and-sports shops scattered throughout Honolulu are a highly competitive lot, with each trying to capture your interest (and dollars). The top sources for sports gear and accessories in town are **McCully Bicycle & Sporting Goods,** 2124 S. King St. (© **808/955-6329**), with everything from bicycles and fishing gear to athletic shoes and accessories, along with a stunning selection of sunglasses; and **The Bike Shop,** 1149 S. King St., near Piikoi St. (© **808/596-0588**), excellent for cycling and backpacking equipment for all levels, with major camping lines such as North Face, MSR, and Kelty. Avid cyclists coming to Oahu should make this a definite stop, as it's the hub of cycling news on the island, offering night tours of downtown Honolulu by bicycle and other cycling activities islandwide. The **Sports Authority,** at 333 Ward Ave. (© **808/596-0166**) and at Waikele Center (© **808/677-9933**), is a discount megaoutlet offering clothing, cycles, and equipment.

Surf shops, centers of fashion as well as definers of daring, include **Local Motion,** in Waikiki and Windward Mall (© **808/979-7873**); **Town and Country** in Ala Moana Center and Ward Warehouse; and **Hawaiian Island Creations,** at Ala Moana Center (© **808/941-4491**). Local Motion is the icon of surfers and skateboarders, both professionals and wannabes; the shop offers surfboards, T-shirts, aloha and casual wear, boogie boards, and countless accessories for life in the sun. Hawaiian Island Creations is another supercool surf shop offering sunglasses, sun lotions, surfwear, and accessories galore.

SHOPPING IN WINDWARD OAHU

KAILUA

All of the listings below can be found in the town of **Kailua,** whose shopping nexus is formed by **Long's Drugs** and **Macy's** department store, located side by side on Kailua Road.

Agnes Portuguese Bake Shop *Finds*   This Kailua treasure is the long-time favorite of Hawaii's *malassada* mavens. *Malassadas*—sugary Portuguese dumplings that look and taste like doughnuts without holes—fly out of the bakery, infusing the entire neighborhood with an irresistible aroma. The Bake Shop also offers a variety of pastries, cookies, scones, Portuguese bean and other soups, and local- and European-style breads. 46 Hoolai St. © **808/262-5367.**

Alii Antiques of Kailua II   Abandon all restraint, particularly if you have a weakness for vintage Hawaiiana. Koa lamps and rattan furniture from the 1930s and 1940s, hula nodders, rare 1940s koa tables, Roseville vases, Don Blanding dinnerware, and a breathtaking array of vintage etched-glass vases and trays are some of the items in this unforgettable shop. Across the street, the owner's wife runs **Alii Antiques of Kailua,** which is chockablock with all the things that won't fit here: jewelry, clothing, Bauer and Fiestaware, linens, Bakelite bracelets, and floor-to-ceiling collectibles. 9–A Maluniu Ave., Kailua. © **808/261-1705.**

BookEnds   BookEnds is the quintessential neighborhood bookstore, run by a pro who buys good books and knows how to find the ones she doesn't have. There are more than 60,000 titles here, new and used, from *Celtic Mandalas* to C. S. Lewis's *Chronicles of Narnia* and the full roster of current bestsellers. Volumes on child care, cooking, and self-improvement; a hefty periodicals section; and mainstream and offbeat titles are among the treasures to be found. 600 Kailua Rd., Kailua. © **808/261-1996.**

KANEOHE

Windward Oahu's largest shopping complex is **Windward Mall,** 46–056 Kamehameha Hwy., in Kaneohe (© **808/235-1143**), open Monday through Saturday from 10am to 9pm and Sunday from 10am to 5pm. The 100 stores and services at this standard suburban mall include **Macy's West** and **Sears,** health stores, airline counters, surf shops, and **LensCrafters.** A small food court serves pizza, Chinese fare, tacos, and other morsels, and the new theaters are a big draw for windwardites. If you like movies, the 10-screen theater complex has recently-released films.

SHOPPING IN HALEIWA: JEWEL OF THE NORTH SHORE

Like Hilo on the Big Island and Maui's upcountry Makawao, Haleiwa means serious shopping for those who know that the unhurried pace of rural life can conceal vast material treasures. Ask the legions of townies who drive an hour each way just to stock up on wine and clothes at Haleiwa stores.

ART, GIFTS & CRAFTS

Haleiwa's shops and galleries display a combination of marine art, watercolors, sculptures, and a plethora of crafts trying to masquerade as fine art. This is the town for gifts, fashions, and surf stuff—mostly casual, despite some very high price tags. **Haleiwa Gallery** in North Shore Marketplace displays a lot of local art of the nonmarine variety, and some of it is appealing.

Global Creations Interiors You'll find casual clothing as well as international imports for the home, including Balinese bamboo furniture and colorful hammocks for the carefree life. There are gifts and crafts by 115 local potters, painters, and artists of other media. 66–079 Kamehameha Hwy. © **808/637-1505**.

EDIBLES

Haleiwa is best known for its roadside shave-ice stands: the famous **Matsumoto Shave Ice** ⋆, with the perennial queue snaking along Kamehameha Highway, and nearby **Aoki's.** Shave ice is the popular island version of a snow cone, topped with your choice of syrups, such as strawberry, rainbow, root beer, vanilla, or passion fruit. Aficionados order it with a scoop of ice cream and sweetened black adzuki beans nestled in the middle.

For food-and-wine shopping, our mightiest accolades go to **Fujioka Super Market,** 66–190 Kamehameha Hwy. (© **808/637-4520**). Oenophiles and tony wine clubs from town shop here for the best prices on California reds, coveted Italian reds, and a growing selection of cabernets, merlots, and French vintages. Fresh produce and no-cholesterol, vegetarian health foods, in addition to the standards, fill the aisles of this third-generation store.

Tiny, funky **Celestial Natural Foods,** 66–443 Kamehameha Hwy. (© **808/637-6729**), is the health foodies' Grand Central for everything from wooden spine-massagers to health supplements, produce, cosmetics, and bulk foods.

FASHION

Although Haleiwa used to be an incense-infused surfer outpost where zoris and tank tops were the regional uniform and the Beach Boys and Ravi Shankar the music of the day, today it's one of the top shopping destinations for those with unconventional tastes. Specialty shops abound.

Top-drawer **Silver Moon Emporium,** North Shore Marketplace, 66–250 Kamehameha Hwy. (© **808/637-7710**), is an islandwide phenomenon, featuring the terrific finds of owner Lucie Talbot-Holu. Exquisite clothing and handbags, reasonably-priced footwear, hats straight out of *Vogue,* jewelry, scarves, and a full gamut of other treasures pepper the attractive boutique. Tastes run from the conventional to the outrageous; you'll find shoes, handbags, suits, dresses, jewelry, bags, and accessories for all occasions, from weddings to work, parties, and everything in between.

In addition to Silver Moon, other highlights of the prominent North Shore Marketplace include **Patagonia** (© 808/637-1245) for high-quality surf, swim, hiking, kayaking, and all-around adventure wear; **North Shore Swimwear** (© 808/637-6859) for excellent mix-and-match bikinis and one-piece suits, custom ordered or off the rack; **Kama`ainas Haleiwa** (© 808/637-1907), the new gallery-gift store for quality island crafts, Hawaiian quilts, soaps, hats, accessories, clothing, and food specialties; and **Jungle Gems** (© 808/637-6609), the mother lode of gemstones, crystals, silver, and beadwork.

Nearby **Oceania,** 66–208 Kamehameha Hwy. (© 808/637-4581), also has some treasures among its racks of casual and leisure wear. Foldable straw hats, diaphanous dresses, dressy T-shirts, friendly service, and good prices are what we've found here. **Oogenesis Boutique,** 66–249 Kamehameha Hwy. (© 808/637-4580), in the southern part of Haleiwa, features a storefront lined with vintage-looking dresses that flutter prettily in the North Shore breeze.

Amid all these hip Haleiwa newcomers, the perennial favorite remains the old-fashioned, longtime neighborhood staple, **H. Miura Store and Tailor Shop,** 66–057 Kamehameha Hwy. (© 808/637-4845). You can custom-order swim trunks, an aloha shirt, or a muumuu from bolts of Polynesian-printed fabrics, from tapa designs to two-color pareu prints. It's the most versatile tailor shop we've ever seen, with coconut-shell bikini tops, fake hula skirts, and heaps of cheap and glorious tchotchkes lining the aisles.

SURF SHOPS

Haleiwa's ubiquitous surf shops are the best on earth, surfers say. At the top of the heap is **Northshore Boardriders Club,** North Shore Marketplace, 66–250 Kamehameha Hwy. (© 808/637-5026), the mecca of the board-riding elite, with sleek, fast, elegant, and top-of-the-line boards designed by North Shore legends such as longboard shaper Barry Kanaiaupuni, John Carper, Jeff Bushman, and Pat Rawson. This is a Quiksilver "concept store," which means that it's the testing ground for the newest and hottest trends in surfwear put out by the retail giant. Kanaiaupuni's other store, **B K Ocean Sports,** in the old Haleiwa Post Office, 66–215 Kamehameha Hwy. (© 808/637-4966), is a more casual version, appealing to surfers and watersports enthusiasts of all levels. Across the street, **Hawaii Surf & Sail,** 66–214 Kamehameha Hwy. (© 808/637-5373), offers new and used surfboards and accessories for surfers, bodyboarders, and sailboarders.

Strong Current Surf Design, North Shore Marketplace (© 808/637-3406), is the North Shore's nexus for memorabilia and surf nostalgia because of the passion of its owners, Bonnie and John Moore, who expanded the commercial surf-shop space to encompass the Haleiwa Surf Museum. From head level on down, Strong Current displays shorts, ocean sportswear, hats, jewelry, towels, and popular new items of Hawaiiana; from head level up, the walls and ceilings are lined with vintage boards, posters, and pictures from the 1950s and 1960s. Also in the North Shore Marketplace, **Barnfield's Raging Isle Sports** (© 808/637-7707) is the surf-and-cycle center of the area, with everything from wet suits and surfboards to surf gear and clothing for men, women, and children. The adjoining surfboard factory puts out custom-built boards of high renown. There's also a large inventory of mountain bikes for rent and sale.

A longtime favorite among old-timers is the newly expanded **Surf & Sea Surf Sail & Dive Shop,** 62–595 Kamehameha Hwy. (© **808/637-9887**), a flamboyant road-side structure just over the bridge, with old wood floors, blowing fans, and a tangle of surf and swimwear, T-shirts, surfboards, boogie boards, fins, watches, sunglasses, and countless other miscellany; you can also rent surf and snorkel equipment here.

Tropical Rush, 62–620-A Kamehameha Hwy. (© **808/637-8886**), has a huge inventory of surf and swim gear: surfboards, longboards, bodyboards, Sector 9 skate-boards, and all the accessories to go with an ocean-minded life, like slippers and swimwear for men and women. T-shirts, hats, sunglasses, and visors are among the scads of cool gear, and you can rent equipment and arrange surf lessons, too. An added feature is the shop's surf report line for the up-to-the-minute lowdown on wave action (© **808/638-7874**); it covers the day's surf and weather details for all of Oahu.

14 Oahu After Dark

Nightlife in Hawaii begins at sunset, when all eyes turn westward to see how the day will end. Like seeing the same pod of whales or school of spinner dolphins, sunset view-ers seem to bond in the mutual enjoyment of a natural spectacle. People in Hawaii are fortunate to have a benign environment that encourages this cultural ritual.

On Fridays and Saturdays at 6:30pm, as the sun casts its golden glow on the beach and surfers and beach boys paddle in for the day, **Kuhio Beach,** where Kalakaua Avenue intersects with Kaiulani, eases into evening with hula dancing and a torch-lighting ceremony. This is a thoroughly delightful, free weekend offering. Start off ear-lier with a picnic basket and your favorite libations and walk along the oceanside path fronting Queen's Surf, near the Waikiki Aquarium. (You can park along Kapiolani Park or near the Honolulu Zoo.) There are few more pleasing spots in Waikiki than the benches at the water's edge at the Diamond Head end of Kalakaua Avenue, where lovers and families of all ages stop to peruse the sinking sun. A short walk across the intersection of Kalakaua and Kapahulu avenues takes you to the Duke Kahanamoku statue on Kuhio Beach and the nearby Wizard Stones. Here, you can view the torch-lighting and hula and gear up for the strolling musicians who amble down Kalakaua Avenue every Friday from 8 to 10pm. The musicians begin at Beachwalk Avenue at the Ewa (western) end of Waikiki and end up at the statue.

BARS

ON THE BEACH   Waikiki's beachfront bars also offer many possibilities, from the Royal Hawaiian Hotel's **Mai Tai Bar** (© **808/923-7311**), a few feet from the sand, to the unfailingly enchanting **House Without a Key at the Halekulani** (© **808/923-2311**), where the breathtaking **Kanoelehua Miller** dances hula to the riffs of Hawai-ian steel-pedal guitar under a century-old kiawe tree. With the sunset and ocean glow-ing behind her and Diamond Head visible in the distance, the scene is straight out of Somerset Maugham—romantic, evocative, nostalgic. It doesn't hurt, either, that the Halekulani happens to make the best mai tais in the world. Halekulani has the after-dinner hours covered, too, with nightly light jazz by local artists from 10:15pm to midnight.

See also p. 131 for a review of **Duke's Canoe Club,** a classic spot for casual ocean-front drinks on Waikiki.

Moments **Mai Tais at Sunset**

One of my favorite times in life is sunset at Ke Iki Beach. When the sun is low, it's time to assemble the ingredients: fresh lime juice, fresh lemon juice, fresh orange juice, passion-orange-guava juice, and fresh grapefruit juice. Pour this mix on ice in tall, frosty glasses, and then add Meyer's rum, in which Tahitian vanilla beans have been soaking for days. (You can also add cinnamon if you like, or soak a cinnamon stick with the rum and vanilla beans.) A dash of Angostura bitters, a few drops of Southern Comfort as a float, a sprig of mint, a garnish of fresh lime, and voilà! The homemade Ke Iki mai tai: a cross between planter's punch and the classic Trader Vic's mai tai. As the sun sets, lift your glasses and savor the moment, the setting, and the first sip—not a bad way to end the day.

In Hawaii, the mai tai is more than a libation. It's a festive, happy ritual that signals holiday, vacation, or a time of play, not work. Mai tais and computers don't mix. Mai tais and hammocks do. And mai tais and sunsets go hand in hand.

ALOHA TOWER MARKETPLACE   The landmark Aloha Tower at Honolulu Harbor, once Oahu's tallest building, has always occupied Honolulu's prime downtown location—on the water, at a naturally sheltered bay, near the business and civic center of Honolulu. Since the Aloha Tower Marketplace, 1 Aloha Tower Dr., on the waterfront between piers 8 and 11, Honolulu Harbor (© 808/528-5700), was constructed, it's gained popularity as an entertainment and nightlife spot, with more than 100 shops and restaurants, including several venues for Honolulu's leading musical groups.

Unlike Waikiki, there are no swaying palm trees at your fingertips here, but you will see tugboats and cruise ships from the popular open-air **Pier Bar** (© 808/536-2166) and various other venues in the marketplace offering live music throughout the week. There's live music nightly at the Pier Bar: contemporary Hawaiian, swing, alternative rock, and jazz. The Pier Bar's main stage, the **Gordon Biersch Brewery Restaurant,** and the **Atrium Center Court** feature ongoing programs of foot-stomping good times. At the recently expanded Gordon Biersch, where a new stage area was added, diners swing to jazz, blues, and island riffs. Most notable, however, are **Don Ho's Island Grill** and **Chai's Island Bistro,** Honolulu's hottest nightspots (see "Hawaiian Music," below, for more on Chai's).

Across the street from Aloha Tower Marketplace, the bar and lounge of **Palomino** (© 808/528-2400) is a magnet for revelers, often two deep at the bar. You'll find great appetizers, pizzas, service, and drinks.

DOWNTOWN   The downtown scene is awakening from a long slumber, thanks to the **Hawaii Theatre** and some tenacious entrepreneurs who want everyone to love Nuuanu Avenue as much as they do. The occasional block parties along Nuuanu Avenue, called "Nuuanu Nights," are now a regular monthly event.

Hank's Cafe, between Hotel and King streets on Nuuanu (© 808/526-1410), is noteworthy and always jumping, a tiny, kitschy, friendly pub that spells FUN with its live music, open-mike nights, and special events that attract great talent and a supportive crowd—and it's open for lunch, too. (Their cilantro-laden chili is famous.) On some nights the music spills out into the street and it's so packed you have to press your nose against the window to see what's happening.

At the *makai* (ocean) end of Nuuanu, **Murphy's Bar & Grill** (© 808/531-0422) and **O'Toole's Pub** (© 808/536-6360) are the downtown ale houses and media haunts that have kept Irish eyes smiling for years.

CLUB SCENE

The nightclub scene in Waikiki and Honolulu is just as hot as the sun kissed beaches during the day. It's not New York (or Chicago or LA) but a laid back version where the dress is casual (no slippers, tank tops, or athletic wear) and there's no point in even showing up until midnight. The **Wave Waikiki,** 1877 Kalakaua Ave (between Ala Wai Blvd. and Ena Rd.; © 808/941-0424; www.wavewaikiki.com), is one of Hawaii's top dance clubs with two levels (and two bars, no waiting) featuring a huge variety of live music and every type of DJ you can think of. Open nightly, from 9pm to 4am, the weekday cover is $5 and weekends $7 (except for special events, then expect to pay more). Dress code is so laid back, all they care about is that you have something on your back and on your feet.

Twice the size of the Wave and filled with dancing, darts, pool, and sports bar with huge TV screens is the **Pipeline,** 805 Pohukaina St. (in Kakaako; © 808/589-1999; www.pipelinecafe.net). Patrons here tend to be younger than the Wave (you can get in at 18 years old) and they are dressed to go clubbing. Cover charge generally is $1 to $3; concerts are around $15.

The 20-something crowd, visitors, and military tend to head to **Moose McGilly-cuddy's,** 310 Lewers, Waikiki (© 808/923-0751; www.maui.net/~mooses/mooses_waikiki). Downstairs is a cafe serving breakfast, lunch, and dinner; upstairs is a happening live entertainment and dancing nightclub ("get loose at the moose"). Open nightly with bikini contests on Sunday, Ladies Night on Wednesday, and Tuesday is $1 drink night.

At the edge of Chinatown is something from a 1940s film noir, **Indigo's,** 1121 Nuuanu Ave. (© 808/521-2900; www.indigo-hawaii.com), which serves sizzling food during the day, then turns to cool jazz in the early evening, and progresses to late night DJs spinning Top 40, disco, rock, funk, and other assorted music. Two venues to choose from include the Green Room and the Opium Den and Champagne Bar.

The college-age crowd flocks to **Blue Tropix,** 1700 Kapiolani Blvd. (© 808/944-0001), which is known for its monkey in a cage (which recently was relocated to the Panaewa Rainforest Zoo, outside of Hilo), features a small, 100-square-foot dance floor, and lively DJ jams of Top 40, hip-hop, and R&B dance music. There's a $5 cover charge. Open daily from 10pm to 2am.

Downstairs in the lobby of the Ala Moana Hotel, **Rumours Nightclub** (© 808/955-4811) is the disco of choice for those who remember Paul McCartney as something other than Stella's father. The theme changes by the month, but generally, it's the "Big Chill" '60s, '70s, and '80s music on Friday; the "Little Chill" on Saturday; ballroom dancing from 5 to 9pm on Sunday; Top 40 on Tuesday; karaoke on Wednesday; and an "after-work office party" to midnight on Thursday. A spacious dance floor, good sound system, and Top 40 music draw a mix of generations.

At Restaurant Row, **Ocean Club** (500 Ala Moana Blvd.; © 808/526-9888; ocean clubonline.com), is the Row's hottest and hippest spot. Good seafood appetizers, attractive happy-hour prices, a fabulous quirky interior, and passionate DJs in alternative garb make up a dizzyingly successful formula. The minimum age is 23 (except on Thursdays), and the dress code calls for "smart-casual"—no T-shirts, slippers, hats, athletic wear, ripped jeans, or beachwear (see also the dining review on p. 142).

The latest hot spot in Waikiki for dancing is **Club 25,** in the Sansei Seafood Restaurant and adjoining d.k. Steak House, on the third floor of the Waikiki Beach Marriott Resort, 2552 Kalakaua Ave. (© **808/931-6286**). First of all, you have to be 25 to be let in. Second, you better be "dressed to go clubbing" (no jeans, T-shirts, athletic gear, and so on) or you won't make it in. Every Friday, from 10pm to 2am, the duo restaurants turn into one of Waikiki's "in" spots for dancing (DJ) and great eats (half-price sushi). Cover is $10 and worth it.

HAWAIIAN MUSIC

Oahu has several key spots for Hawaiian music. A delightful (and powerful) addition to the Waikiki music scene is Hawaii's queen of falsetto, **Genoa Keawe,** who fills the Lobby Bar of the Hawaiian Regent Hotel (© **808/922-6611**) with her larger-than-life voice. You'll find her here from 5:30 to 8:30pm every Thursday; the rest of the week, except Monday, other contemporary Hawaiian musicians fill in.

Brothers Cazimero remain one of Hawaii's most gifted duos (Robert on bass, Roland on 12-string guitar), appearing every Wednesday at 7pm at **Chai's Island Bistro** (© **808/585-0011;** www.chaisislandbistro.com) in the Aloha Tower Marketplace. Also at Chai's: Robert Cazimero solos on the piano on Tuesday at 7pm and **Jerry Santos** and **Olomana** perform on Monday at 7pm. In the past couple of years, Chai's has emerged as the leading venue for Hawaiian entertainment. But if you're here on May 1, Lei Day, try to make it to the special concert the Brothers Caz give every year at the Waikiki Shell—it's one of the loveliest events in Hawaii. Locals dress up in their leis and best aloha shirts, the air smells like pikake and pakalana, and if you're lucky, you'll see the moon rise over Diamond Head.

Impromptu hula and spirited music from the family and friends of the performers are an island tradition at places such as the Hilton Hawaiian Village's **Paradise Lounge** (© **808/949-4321**), which serves as a large living room for the full-bodied music of **Olomana.** The group plays Friday and Saturday from 8pm to midnight (no cover, one-drink minimum).

Nearby, the Sheraton Moana Surfrider offers a regular nightly program of live Hawaiian music and piano in its **Banyan Veranda** (© **808/922-3111**), which surrounds an islet-size canopy of banyan tree and roots where Robert Louis Stevenson loved to linger. The Veranda serves afternoon tea, a sunset buffet, and cocktails. Still sizzling in the Polynesian revue world is Sheraton Princess Kaiulani's new *Creation— A Polynesian Odyssey* (© **808/931-4660**), in the hotel's second-floor Ainahau Showroom. Produced by Tihati, the state's largest entertainment company, the show is a theatrical journey of fire dancing, special effects, illusions, and Polynesian dances from Hawaii and the South Pacific. The dinner show is at 5:15pm, deluxe dinner, lei greeting and preferred seating is $106, dinner and admission is $63, and the cocktail show, priced at $33, is at 6pm. No shows on Monday and Wednesday.

My best advice for lovers of Hawaiian music is to scan the local dailies or the *Honolulu Weekly* to see if and where the following Hawaiian entertainers are appearing: **Kekuhi Kanahele,** accomplished chanter and *kahiko* (ancient hula) dancer whose award-winning recordings have redefined Hawaiian music; **Ho'okena,** a symphonically rich quintet featuring **Manu Boyd,** one of the most prolific songwriters and chanters in Hawaii; **Keali'i Reichel,** premier chanter, dancer, and award-winning recording artist; **Robbie Kahakalau,** another award-winning musician; **Kapena,** for contemporary Hawaiian music; **Na Leo Pilimehana,** a trio of angelic Hawaiian singers; the **Makaha Sons of Niihau,** pioneers in the Hawaiian cultural renaissance; **Fiji;** and slack-key guitar master **Raymond Kane.**

Consider the gods beneficent if you happen to be here when the hula halau of **Frank Kawaikapuokalani Hewett** is holding its annual fund-raiser in windward Oahu. It's a rousing, inspired, family effort for a good cause, and it always features the best in ancient and contemporary Hawaiian music. For the best in ancient and modern hula, check the dailies for halau fund-raisers, which are always authentic, enriching, and local to the core.

Showroom acts that have maintained a following are led by the tireless, disarming **Don Ho,** who still sings "Tiny Bubbles" and remains a fixture at the supper club **Waikiki Beachcomber** (© 808/923-3981). He's very generous in sharing his stage with other Hawaii performers, so guests are often in for surprise appearances by leading Hawaii performers. The **Outrigger Waikiki on the Beach** (© 808/923-0711) features the **Society of Seven's** nightclub act (a blend of skits, Broadway hits, popular music, and costumed musical acts) in its 30th year—no small feat for performers.

THE BLUES

The blues are alive and well in Hawaii, with quality acts, both local and from the mainland, drawing enthusiastic crowds. **Junior Wells, Willie & Lobo, War,** and surprise appearances by the likes of **Bonnie Raitt** are among the past successes of this genre of big-time licks. The best-loved Oahu venue is **Anna Bannanas,** 2440 S. Beretania St., between University Avenue and Isenberg Street (© 808/946-5190), still rocking after 30 years in the business, with reggae, blues, and rock—plus video games and darts.

Get Down with ARTafterDark ★★★

The last Friday of every month (except Nov and Dec), the place to be after the sun goes down is the **Honolulu Academy of Arts' ARTafterDark,** a *pau-hana* (after work) mixer in the art museum that brings residents and visitors together around a theme combining art with food, music, and dancing. In addition to the exhibits in the gallery, ARTafterDark also features visual and live performances. Last year the themes ranged from "Plant Rice," with rice and sake-tastings, rice dishes, and Asian beers with live Asian fusion music, and a tour of the "Art of Rice" exhibit, to "'80s Night," "Turkish Delights," "Cool Nights, Hot Jazz and Blues," and "Havana Heat."

The entry fee is $7. The party gets going about 6pm and lasts to 9pm, and the crowd ranges from 20s to 50s. The dress is everything from jeans and T-shirts to designer cocktail party attire. For more information, call © 808/532-6091.

Top 40 from the Top

Aaron's Atop the Ala Moana, Ala Moana Hotel, 410 Atkinson Dr. (© **808/955-4466**), has the best view: Take the express elevator to the 36th floor of the hotel (p. 122), then watch the Honolulu city lights wrap around the room and cha-cha-cha to the vertigo! There's live music and dancing nightly, a great dinner menu, and an appetizer menu nightly from 5pm.

JAZZ

Jazz lovers should watch for the Great Hawaiian Jazz Blowout every March (2006 will be its 9th year), at Mid-Pacific Institute's Bakken Hall (at the south end of Honolulu, near Diamond Head). To find out what's happening in the jazz scene while you're in town, check out www.honolulujazzscene.net. **Diamond Head Grill** (© **808/922-3734**) features live music nightly, and **Duc's Bistro** (© **808/531-6325**), downtown, presents live jazz nightly except Thursday, when vocalist Mihana Souza brings her style of Hawaiian music to the cozy venue. **Nick's Fishmarket,** Waikiki Gateway Hotel, 2070 Kalakaua Ave. (© **808/955-6333**), still offers live entertainment nightly in its lounge—mild jazz or Top 40 contemporary hits.

Tops in taste and ambience is the perennially alluring **Lewers Lounge,** in the Halekulani, 2199 Kalia Rd. (© **808/923-2311;** www.halekulani.com). Recently renovated (higher ceiling, contemporary color scheme and comfy intimate seating round the pillars), not only is this a great spot for contemporary jazz nightly from 8:30pm to midnight, but with expert mixologist Dale DeGroff (the "king of cocktails"), now the hotel's director of beverage, the drinks are better than ever. Be sure to try the Hpnotiq Liqueur, a blend of premium vodka, cognac and fruit juices from France, served over ice or in various concoctions, which Dale has created.

Outside of Waikiki, the **Veranda,** at the Kohala Mandarin Oriental Hawaii, 5000 Kahala Ave. (© **808/739-8888;** www.mandarinoriental.com), is a popular spot for the over 40 crowd with nightly jazz music and a dance floor.

Around town, watch for **Sandy Tsukiyama,** a gifted singer (Brazilian, Latin, jazz) and one of Honolulu's great assets, and jazz singers **Rachel Gonzales** and **Loretta Ables.** Other groups in jazz, blues, and R&B include **Blue Budda, Bongo Tribe, Secondhand Smoke, Bluzilla, Piranha Brothers,** and the **Greg Pai Trio.**

THE PERFORMING ARTS

"Aloha shirt to Armani" is how I describe the night scene in Honolulu—mostly casual but with ample opportunity to dress up if you dare to part with your flip-flops.

Audiences have stomped to the big off-Broadway percussion hit *Stomp* and have enjoyed the talent of *Tap Dogs,* Momix, Forever Tango, Cool Heat, Urban Beat, the Jim Nabors Christmas show, the Hawaii International Jazz Festival, the American Repertory Dance Company, barbershop quartets, and John Ka'imikaua's halau—all at the **Hawaii Theatre,** 1130 Bethel St., downtown (© **808/528-0506**), still basking in its renaissance following a 4-year, $22-million renovation. The neoclassical Beaux Arts landmark features a 1922 dome, 1,400 plush seats, a hydraulically elevated organ, a mezzanine lobby with two full bars, Corinthian columns, and gilt galore. Breathtaking murals, including a restored proscenium centerpiece lauded as Lionel Walden's "greatest creation," create an atmosphere that's making the theater a leading multi-purpose center for the performing arts.

The **Honolulu Symphony Orchestra** has booked some of its performances at the new theater, but it still performs at the Waikiki Shell and the **Neal Blaisdell Concert Hall** (© 808/591-2211). Meanwhile, the highly successful **Hawaii Opera Theatre,** in its 41st season (past hits have included *La Bohème, Carmen, Turandot, Romeo and Juliet, Rigoletto,* and *Aïda*), still draws fans to the Neal Blaisdell Concert Hall, as do many of the performances of Hawaii's four ballet companies: **Hawaii Ballet Theatre, Ballet Hawaii, Hawaii State Ballet,** and **Honolulu Dance Theatre.** Contemporary performances by **Dances We Dance** and the **Iona Pear Dance Company,** a strikingly creative Butoh group, are worth tracking down if you love the avant-garde.

LUAU!

Regrettably, there's no commercial luau on Oahu that comes close to Maui's Old Lahaina Luau, or Hawaii Island's legendary Kona Village luau. The two major choices on Oahu are **Germaine's** (© 808/941-3338; www.germainesluau.com) and **Paradise Cove Luau** (© 808/842-5911; www.paradisecovehawaii.com), both located about a 40-minute drive away from Waikiki on the Leeward Coast. TheBus pickups and drop-offs in Waikiki are part of the deal.

Germaine's tries awfully hard and is a much more intimate affair than those legendary shows, but the experience is not as complete. Cost for Germaine's is $58 per adult, $48 for 14- to 20-year-olds, and $36 for 6- to 13-year-olds, 5 years and younger are free; the prices include tax and transportation. The shows are held nightly from 5:30 to 9:30pm.

Paradise Cove, too, is a mixed bag, with 600 to 800 guests a night. The small thatched village makes it more of a Hawaiian theme park, with Hawaiian games, *huk-ilau* net throwing and gathering, craft demonstrations, and a beautiful shoreline looking out over what is usually a storybook sunset. Tahitian dance and ancient and modern hula make this a fun-filled evening for those spirited enough to join in. The food is safe, though not breathtaking: Hawaiian kalua pig, lomi salmon, poi, and coconut pudding and cake, as well as more traditional fare. Paradise Cove is extremely popular because of its idyllic setting and good entertainment quality. Tickets, including transportation and taxes, are $65 for adults, $55 for ages 13 to 18, $45 for ages 4 to 12, and free for those 3 and under. Shows are held nightly from 5 to 8:30pm.

6

Hawaii: The Big Island

The Big Island of Hawaii—the island that lends its name to the entire 1,500-mile-long Hawaiian archipelago—is where Mother Nature pulled out all the stops. Simply put, it's spectacular.

The Big Island has it all: fiery volcanoes and sparkling waterfalls, black-lava deserts and snowcapped mountain peaks, tropical rainforests and alpine meadows, a glacial lake and miles of golden-, black-, and green-sand beaches. The Big Island has an unmatched diversity of terrain and climate. A 50-mile drive will take you from snowy winter to sultry summer, passing through spring or fall along the way. The island looks like the inside of a barbecue pit on one side, and a lush jungle on the other.

The Big Island is the largest island in the Hawaiian chain (4,038 sq. miles—about the size of Connecticut), the youngest (800,000 years), and the least populated (with 30 people per sq. mile). It has the nation's wettest city, the southernmost point in the United States, the world's biggest telescope, the ocean's biggest trophy marlin, and America's greatest collection of tropical luxury resorts. It also has the highest peaks in the Pacific, the most volcanoes of any Hawaiian island, and the newest land on earth.

Five volcanoes—one still erupting—have created this continental island, which is growing bigger daily. At its heart is snowcapped Mauna Kea, the world's tallest sea mountain (measured from the ocean floor), complete with its own glacial lake. Mauna Kea's nearest neighbor is

Mauna Loa (or "Long Mountain"), creator of one-sixth of the island; it's the largest volcano on earth, rising 30,000 feet out of the ocean floor (of course, you can see only the 13,796 ft. that are above sea level). Erupting Kilauea makes the Big Island bigger every day—and, if you're lucky, and your timing is good, you can stand just a few feet away and watch it do its work. (In just a week, Kilauea volcano can produce enough lava to fill the Astrodome.)

Steeped in tradition and shrouded in the primal mist of creation, the Big Island called to the Polynesians across 2,000 miles of open ocean. In fact, ancient Hawaiian chants talk about a great burning in the night skies that guided the sojourners to the land of volcanoes. The Big Island radiates what the Hawaiians call *mana,* a sense of spirituality that's still apparent through the acres of petroglyphs etched in the black lava, the numerous *heiau* (ancient temples), burial caves scattered in the cliffs, sacred shrines both on land and in the sea, and even in the sound the wind makes as it blows across the desolate lava fields.

The Big Island is not for everyone, however. It refuses to fit the stereotype of a tropical island. Some tourists are taken aback at the sight of stark fields of lava or black-sand beaches. You must remember that it's *big* (expect to do lots of driving). And you may have to go out of your way if you're looking for traditional tropical beauty, such as a quintessential white-sand beach.

On the other hand, if you're into watersports, this is paradise. The two tall volcanoes mean 350 days of calm water on the leeward side. The underwater landscape of caves, cliffs, and tunnels attracts a stunning array of colorful marine life just waiting to be visited by divers and snorkelers. The island's west coast is one of the best destinations in the world for big-game fishing. And its miles of remote coastline are a kayaker's dream of caves, secluded coves, and crescent-shaped beaches reachable only by sea.

On land, hikers, bikers, and horseback riders can head up and down a volcano, across black-sand beaches, into remote valleys, and through rainforests without seeing another soul. Bird-watchers are rewarded with sightings of the rare, rapidly dwindling native birds of Hawaii. Golfers can find nirvana on top championship courses, less-crowded municipal courses, and even some unusual, off-the-beaten-track choices.

This is the least-explored island in the Hawaiian chain, but if you're looking to get away from it all and back to nature in its most primal state, that might be the best thing of all about it. Where else can you witness fiery creation and swim with dolphins, ponder the stars from the world's tallest mountain, catch a blue marlin, downhill ski, and surf the waves in a single day? You can do all this, and more, on only one island in the world: the Big Island of Hawaii.

1 Orientation

If you think you can "do" the Big Island in a day, forget it. You need about 3 days just to do Hawaii Volcanoes National Park justice. If you hope to catch more than a glimpse of the island through the window of a speeding rental car, plan on spending a week on the Big Island.

ARRIVING

Most people arrive on the Big Island at **Kona International Airport,** on the island's west coast. From there, you can go around the island clockwise or counterclockwise. From Kona, head south, or counterclockwise to get to Kilauea volcano; north, or clockwise, takes you to the ritzy Kohala Coast.

You can also land in **Hilo,** on the eastern side of the island, which is much closer to the volcano, but not nearly as close to the Kohala Coast. If you want to see both the volcano and the fabulous beaches but don't want to make a full 360-degree tour of the island, consider flying into one airport and out of the other. Doing so generally isn't any more expensive, but check with your airline. (Your car rental company may charge you a $50 drop-off fee, but it might be worth it to save 2 or 3 hr. of driving.)

The Kona Airport receives direct overseas flights from Japan (Japan Airlines), as well as direct mainland flights from Los Angeles and San Francisco on **United Airlines** (© **800/241-6522;** www.ual.com), from Los Angeles on **American Airlines** (© **800/433-7300;** www.aa.com), and from Oakland and Orange County on **Aloha Airlines** (© **800/367-5250;** www.alohaairlines.com). Otherwise, you'll have to pick up an inter-island flight in Honolulu. Both **Aloha Airlines** (see above) and **Hawaiian Airlines** (© **800/367-5320;** www.hawaiianair.com) offer jet service to both Big Island airports. All major rental companies have cars available at both airports. See "Getting There & Getting Around" in chapter 2 for more details on inter-island travel and car rentals.

If you're not renting a car, the cheapest way to get from the airport to your accommodations is via **SpeediShuttle** (© **808/329-5433;** www.speedishuttle.com), which

The Big Island

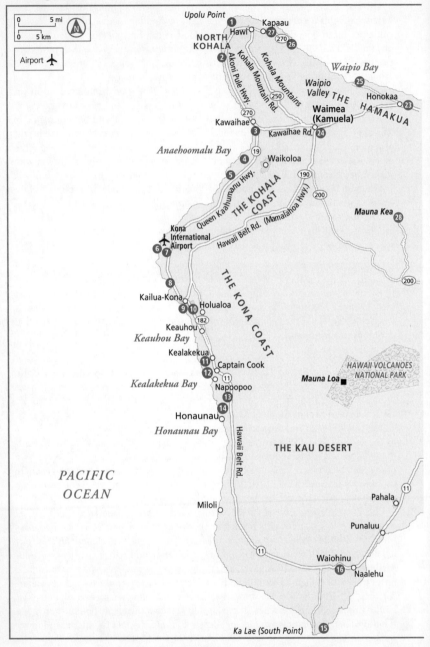

Scale: 0 — 5 mi / 0 — 5 km

Airport ✈

PACIFIC OCEAN

Upolu Point
Kapaau
Hawi ○ ❶ ㉗ 270
NORTH KOHALA ❷ ㉖
Akoni Pule Hwy. *Waipio Bay*
Kohala Mountain Rd. 250 ㉕
Kohala Mountains
Waipio Valley **THE HAMAKUA**
270 Honokaa ○ ㉓
Kawaihae ○ ❸
Kawaihae Rd. ㉔
Waimea (Kamuela)
Anaehoomalu Bay
19 ❹ Waikoloa ○
❺ Queen Kaahumanu Hwy. **THE KOHALA COAST**
190 200
Mauna Kea ㉘
Hawaii Belt Rd. (Mamalahoa Hwy.)
Kona International Airport ✈ ❻ ❼
❽
Kailua-Kona ○ ❾ ❿ Holualoa ○
182
Keauhou ○ **THE KONA COAST**
Keauhou Bay
Kealakekua ○ ⓫
⓬ Captain Cook ○
11 200
Kealakekua Bay Napoopoo ○ ⓭
⓮
Honaunau ○
Honaunau Bay Hawaii Belt Rd.
Mauna Loa ■
HAWAII VOLCANOES NATIONAL PARK
THE KAU DESERT
Pahala ○ 11
Miloli ○ Punaluu ○
11 Waiohinu ○ ⓰ Naalehu ○
Ka Lae (South Point) ⓯

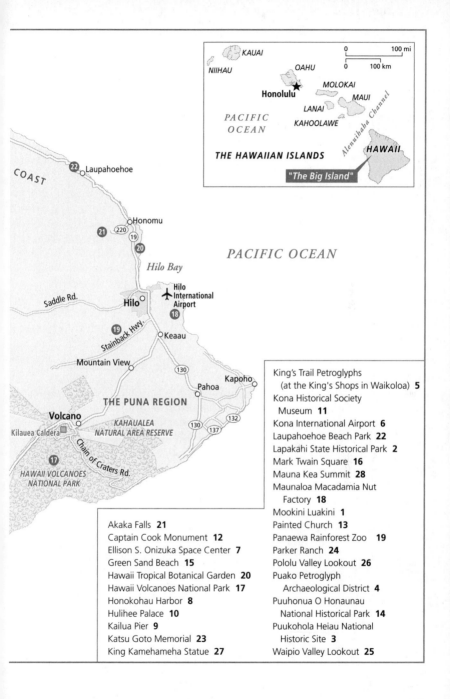

King's Trail Petroglyphs
(at the King's Shops in Waikoloa) **5**
Kona Historical Society
Museum **11**
Kona International Airport **6**
Laupahoehoe Beach Park **22**
Lapakahi State Historical Park **2**
Mark Twain Square **16**
Mauna Kea Summit **28**
Maunaloa Macadamia Nut
Factory **18**
Mookini Luakini **1**
Painted Church **13**
Panaewa Rainforest Zoo **19**
Parker Ranch **24**
Pololu Valley Lookout **26**
Puako Petroglyph
Archaeological District **4**
Puuhonua O Honaunau
National Historical Park **14**
Puukohola Heiau National
Historic Site **3**
Waipio Valley Lookout **25**

Akaka Falls **21**
Captain Cook Monument **12**
Ellison S. Onizuka Space Center **7**
Green Sand Beach **15**
Hawaii Tropical Botanical Garden **20**
Hawaii Volcanoes National Park **17**
Honokohau Harbor **8**
Hulihee Palace **10**
Kailua Pier **9**
Katsu Goto Memorial **23**
King Kamehameha Statue **27**

233

offers inexpensive transportation in its 7- and 10-passenger air-conditioned vans. Book in advance; from the airport to Kailua-Kona the rate is $18 for one passenger and $20 for two. Be sure and carry exact change, as the driver does not always have change and you may end up giving a bigger tip than you anticipated.

VISITOR INFORMATION

The **Big Island Visitors Bureau** has two offices on the Big Island: one at 250 Keawe St., Hilo, HI 96720 (© **808/961-5797;** fax 808/961-2126); and on the other side of the island at 250 Waikoloa Beach Dr., Waikoloa, HI 96738 (© **808/886-1652**). Its website is www.bigisland.org. Ask for *Hawaii's Big Island Driving Tour,* a step-by-step guide that takes you on the Big Island's Circle Island tour, pointing out all the wonders along the way, with legends, facts, and bits of trivia thrown in for fun.

On the west side of the island, there are two additional sources to contact for information: the **Kona-Kohala Resort Association,** 69–275 Waikoloa Beach Dr., Kamuela, HI 96743 (© **800/318-3637** or 808/886-4915; fax 808/886-1044; www.kkra.org); and **Destination Kona,** P.O. Box 2850, Kailua-Kona, HI 96745 (© **808/322-6809;** fax 808/322-8899). On the east side, you can contact **Destination Hilo,** P.O. Box 1391, Hilo, HI 96721 (© **808/935-5294;** fax 808/969-1984). And in the middle, contact the **Waimea Visitor Center,** P.O. Box 6570, Kamuela, HI 96743 (© **808/885-6707;** fax 808/885-0885).

The Big Island's best free tourist publications are *This Week,* the *Beach and Activity Guide,* and *101 Things to Do on Hawaii the Big Island.* All three offer lots of useful information, as well as discount coupons on a variety of island adventures. Copies are easy to find all around the island.

The *Beach and Activity Guide* is affiliated with the **Activity Connection,** Bougainvillea Plaza, Suite 102, 75-5656 Kuakini Hwy., Kailua-Kona (© **800/459-7156** or 808/329-1038; fax 808/327-9411; www.beachactivityguide.com), a discount activity desk offering real savings (no fees, no timeshares) of up to 15% on activities including island tours, snorkel and dive trips, submarine and horseback rides, luaus, and more. The office is open daily from 7:30am to 5:30pm.

THE ISLAND IN BRIEF
THE KONA COAST

One Hawaiian word everyone seems to know is Kona, probably because it's synonymous with great coffee and big fish—both of which are found in abundance along this 70-mile-long stretch of black lava–covered coast.

A collection of tiny communities devoted to farming and fishing along the sun-baked leeward side of the island, the Kona Coast has an amazingly diverse geography and climate for such a compact area. The oceanfront town of **Kailua-Kona,** a quaint fishing village that now caters more to tourists than boat captains, is its commercial center. The lands of Kona range from stark, black, dry coastal desert to cool, cloudy upcountry so fertile that it seems anything could grow here. And it does—glossy green coffee, macadamia nuts, tropical fruit, and a riotous profusion of flowers cover the jagged steep slopes. Among the coffee fields, you'll find the funky, artsy village of **Holualoa.** Higher yet in elevation are native forests of giant trees filled with tiny, colorful birds, some perilously close to extinction. About 7 miles south of Kailua-Kona, bordering the ocean, is the resort area of **Keauhou,** a suburban-like series of upscale condominiums, a shopping center, and homes in the seven-figure range.

Kona means "leeward side" in Hawaiian—and that means full-on summer sun every day of the year. This is an affordable vacation spot; an ample selection of mid-priced condo units, peppered with a few older hotels and B&Bs, lines the shore, which is mostly rocky lava reef, interrupted by an occasional pocket beach. Here, too, stand two world-class resorts: Kona Village, the site of one of the best luaus in the islands, and Hawaii's newest luxury retreat, the Four Seasons at Hualalai.

Away from the bright lights of the town of Kailua lies the rural **South Kona Coast,** home to coffee farmers, macadamia-nut growers, and people escaping to the country. The serrated South Kona Coast is indented with numerous bays, starting with **Kealakekua,** a marine-life preserve that's the island's best diving spot and the place where Captain James Cook met his demise; down to **Honaunau,** where a national historic park recalls the days of old Hawaii. Accommodations in this area are mainly inexpensive B&Bs; everything from the very frugal Japanese Manago Hotel to the very classy Horizon Guest House. This coast is a great place to stay if you want to get away from crowds and experience peaceful country living. You'll be within driving distance of beaches and the sites of Kailua.

THE KOHALA COAST

Fringes of palms and flowers, brilliant blankets of emerald green, and an occasional flash of white buildings are your only clues from the road that this black-lava coast north of Kona is more than bleak and barren. But, oh, is it! Down by the sea, pleasure domes rise like palaces no Hawaiian king ever imagined. This is where the Lear jet set escapes to play in world-class beachfront hotels set like jewels in the golden sand. But you don't have to be a billionaire to visit the Waikoloa, Mauna Lani, and Mauna Kea resorts: The fabulous beaches and abundant historic sites are open to the public, with parking and other facilities provided by the resorts, including restaurants, golf courses, and shopping.

NORTH KOHALA

Seven sugar mills once shipped enough sugar to sweeten all the coffee in San Francisco from three harbors on this knob of land at the northernmost reaches of the island. **Hawi,** the region's hub and home to the Kohala Sugar Co., was a flourishing town. Today, Hawi's quaint, 3-block-long strip of sun-faded, false-fronted buildings and 1920s vintage shops lives on as a minor tourist stop in one of Hawaii's most scenic rural regions, most famous as the birthplace of King Kamehameha the Great; a statue commemorates the royal site. It's also home to the islands' most sacred site, the 1,500-year-old **Mookini Heiau** (p. 310).

WAIMEA (KAMUELA)

This old upcountry cow town on the northern road between the coasts is set in lovely country: rolling green pastures, wide-open spaces dotted by *puu* (hills), and real Marlboro-smoking cowpokes who ride mammoth **Parker Ranch,** Hawaii's largest working ranch. The town is also headquarters for the **Keck Telescope,** the largest and most powerful in the world, bringing world-class, starry-eyed astronomers to town. The nightlife here is far out, in the galactic sense; bring your own telescope if you have one. Waimea is home to several affordable B&Bs, and Merriman's Restaurant is a popular foodie outpost at Opelo Plaza.

THE HAMAKUA COAST

This emerald coast, a 52-mile stretch from Honokaa to Hilo on the island's windward northeast side, was once planted with sugarcane; it now blooms with flowers, macadamia nuts, papayas, and marijuana, also known as *pakalolo* (still Hawaii's number-one cash crop). Resort-free and virtually without beaches, the Hamakua Coast still has a few major destinations, such as spectacular **Waipio Valley,** a picture-perfect valley with impossibly steep sides, taro patches, a green riot of wild plants, and a winding stream leading to a broad, black-sand beach; and the historic plantation town of **Honokaa,** making a comeback as the B&B capital on the coastal trail. Akaka Falls and Laupahoehoe Beach Park (p. 316) are also worth seeking out.

HILO

When the sun shines in Hilo, it's one of the most beautiful tropical cities in the Pacific. Being here is an entirely different kind of island experience: Hawaii's largest metropolis after Honolulu is a quaint, misty, flower-filled city of Victorian houses overlooking a half-moon bay, with a restored historic downtown and a clear view of Mauna Loa's often snowcapped peak. Hilo catches everyone's eye until it rains—it rains a lot in Hilo—and when it rains, it pours.

Hilo is America's wettest town, with 128 inches of rain annually. It's ideal for growing ferns, orchids, and anthuriums, but not for catching a few rays. Yet there's a lot to see and do in Hilo, so grab your umbrella. The rain is warm (the temperature seldom dips below 70°F (21°C), and there's usually a rainbow afterward.

Hilo's oversized airport and hotels are remnants of a dream: The city wanted to be Hawaii's major port of entry. That didn't happen, but the facilities here are excellent. Hilo is also Hawaii's best bargain for budget travelers. It has plenty of hotel rooms—most of the year, that is. Hilo's magic moment comes in spring, the week after Easter, when hula *halau* (schools) arrive for the annual **Merrie Monarch Festival** hula competition (see "Hawaii Calendar of Events," in chapter 2, for details). This is a full-on Hawaiian spectacle and a wonderful cultural event. Plan ahead if you want to go: Tickets are sold out the first week in January for the post-Easter event, and the hotels within 30 miles are usually booked solid.

Hilo is also the gateway to Hawaii Volcanoes National Park; it's just an hour's drive up-slope.

HAWAII VOLCANOES NATIONAL PARK

This is the location of America's most exciting national park, where a live volcano called Kilauea erupts daily. (If you're lucky, it will be a spectacular sight. At other times, you may not be able to see the molten lava at all, but there's still a lot to see and learn.) Ideally, you should plan to spend 3 days at the park, exploring the trails, watching the volcano, visiting the rainforest, and just enjoying this most unusual, spectacular place. But even if you have only a day, get here, it's worth the trip. Bring your sweats or jacket (honest!); it's cool up here, especially at night.

If you plan to dally in the park—and you should—the sleepy hamlet of Volcano Village (located in a rainforest just outside the National Park entrance) has some great places to stay. Several terrifically cozy B&Bs, some with fireplaces, hide under tree ferns in this cool mountain hideaway. The tiny highland (elev. 4,000 ft.) community, first settled by Japanese immigrants, is now inhabited by artists, soul-searchers, and others who like the crisp air of Hawaii's high country. It has just enough civilization to sustain a good life: a few stores, a handful of eateries, a gas station, and a golf course.

KA LAE: SOUTH POINT

This is the Plymouth Rock of Hawaii, where the first Polynesians arrived in seagoing canoes, probably from the Marquesas Islands or Tahiti, around A.D. 500. You'll feel like you're at the end of the world on this lonely, windswept place, the southernmost point of the United States (a geographic claim that belonged to Key West, Florida, until 1959, when Hawaii became the 50th state). Hawaii ends in a sharp black-lava point. Bold 500-foot cliffs stand against the blue sea to the west and shelter the old fishing village of Waiahukini, which was born in A.D. 750 and lasted until the 1860s. Ancient canoe moorings, shelter caves, and *heiau* (temples) poke through windblown pili grass. The East Coast curves inland to reveal a lonely, green-sand beach, a world-famous anomaly that's accessible only by foot or four-wheel-drive. For most, the only reason to venture down to the southern tip is to say you did, or to experience the empty vista of land's end.

Everything in the two wide spots in the road, called **Naalehu** and **Waiohinu,** that pass for towns at South Point, claims to be the southernmost this or that. Except for a monkeypod tree planted by Mark Twain in 1866, there's not much else to crow about. There is, thankfully, a gas station, along with a couple of places to eat, a fruit stand, and a few B&Bs. These end-of-the-world towns are just about as far removed from the real world as you can get.

2 Getting Around

You'll need a rental car on the Big Island; not having one will really limit what you'll be able to see and do.

BY CAR   Rental cars are available at both major airports and at the Kohala Coast resorts from **Alamo** (☎ 800/327-9633); **Avis** (☎ 800/321-3712); **Budget** (☎ 800/527-0700); **Dollar** (☎ 800/800-4000); **Hertz** (☎ 800/654-3011); and **National** (☎ 800/227-7368). See "55 Money-Saving Tips" in chapter 2; tips 14 through 20 will help you get the best deal on a car rental. Also see "Car Rentals" under "Getting There & Getting Around" in chapter 2 for details on insurance and driving rules. Unfortunately, the Big Island has no discount "Rent-a-Wreck"–type car rental agencies.

There are more than 480 miles of paved road on the Big Island, but only two main highways. The one main highway that circles the island is called the Hawaii Belt Road. On the Kona side of the island you have two choices: the scenic "upper" road, Mamalahoa Highway (Hwy. 190), or the speedier "lower" road, Queen Kaahumanu Highway (Hwy. 19). The road that links east to west is called the Saddle Road (Hwy. 200), because it crosses the "saddle" between Mauna Kea and Mauna Loa. Saddle Road is the one rental car agencies ask you to avoid, because it's rough and narrow and the weather conditions can be a handful for motorists.

BY TAXI   Taxis are readily available at both Keahole and Hilo airports. In Hilo, call **Ace-1** (☎ **808/935-8303**). In Kailua-Kona, call **Kona Airport Taxi** (☎ **808/329-7779**). Taxis will take you wherever you want to go on the Big Island, but it's prohibitively expensive to use them for long distances.

BY BUS & SHUTTLE   For transportation from the Kona Airport, call **Speed-iShuttle** (☎ **808/329-5433**; www.speedishuttle.com).

There is an islandwide bus system, but all it does is take passengers from Kona to Hilo and back (and does not stop at the airports). It's the **Hele-On Bus** (☎ **808/961-8744**), and it leaves Kailua-Kona from the Lanihau Shopping Center, at Palani Road and Queen Kaahumanu Highway, every morning at 6:45am, getting into Hilo at 9:30am. The afternoon return trip leaves the bus terminal on Kamehameha Avenue at Mamo Street, in Hilo, at 1:30pm, arriving back in Kailua-Kona at 4:30pm. The fare is $5.25 each way.

For transportation around Kailua-Kona all the way to Keauhou, take the **Alii Shuttle** (© 808/938-1112), which travels up and down Alii Drive (the coastal road) and Palani Road (the main entrance to Kailua-Kona) from the Lanihau Shopping Center to Ohana Keauhou Bay Resort, stopping just about anywhere you want on Palai Road or Alii Drive (just flag the bus down). The buses run about every hour and a half. The cost is $2 one-way; the current hours of operation (subject to change, so call to check) are from 8:30am (leaving Keauhou Bay heading north to Kailua Village) to 7pm. No buses on Sunday.

FAST FACTS: The Big Island

American Express There's an office on the Kohala Coast at the **Hilton Waikoloa Village** (© 808/886-7958) and the **Fairmont Orchid** in Mauna Lani Resort (© 808/885-2000). To report lost or stolen traveler's checks, call © 800/221-7282.

Dentists In an emergency, contact **Dr. Craig C. Kimura** at Kamuela Office Center (© 808/885-5947); in Kona, call **Dr. Frank Sayre,** Frame 10 Center, behind Lanihau Shopping Center on Palani Rd. (© 808/329-8067); in Hilo, call **Hawaii Smile Center,** Hilo Lagoon Center, 101 Aupuni St. (© 808/961-9181).

Doctors **Hilo Medical Center** is at 1190 Waianuenue Ave., Hilo (© 808/974-4700); on the Kona side, call **Hualalai Urgent Care,** Hualalai Medical Center, 75–1028 Henry St. (across the street from Safeway) (© 808/327-HELP).

Emergencies For ambulance, fire, and rescue, dial © **911.** The Poison Control Center hot line is © 800/362-3585.

Hospitals Hospitals offering 24-hour urgent-care facilities include **Hilo Medical Center,** 1190 Waianuenue Ave., Hilo (© 808/974-4700); **North Hawaii Community Hospital,** Kamuela (Waimea) (© 808/885-4444); and **Kona Community Hospital,** on the Kona coast in Kealakekua (© 808/322-9311).

Police Dial © **911,** or call the Hawaii Police Department at © 808/326-4646 in Kona or © 808/961-2213 in Hilo.

Post Office There are local branches in Hilo, at 1299 Kekuanaoa Ave.; in Kailua-Kona, at 74–5577 Palani Rd.; and in Waimea, on Lindsey Road. Call © 800/275-8777 to reach any of these post offices.

Weather For conditions in and around Hilo, call © 808/935-8555; for the rest of the Big Island, call © 808/961-5582. For marine forecasts, call © 808/935-9883.

See "Fast Facts: The Hawaiian Islands" in chapter 2 for more information.

---

3 Accommodations You Can Afford

We've scoured the entire Big Island for affordable places to stay and included the best of the bunch below. There's something for everyone, from romantic B&Bs just a stone's throw from the volcano to inexpensive beachfront condos for the entire family.

Before you reach for the phone to book your vacation dream house, refer back to chapter 2 to read up on the types of accommodations available to make sure you book the kind of place you want. Also remember that the Big Island is really big; see "The Island in Brief," on p. 234, to make sure you choose the best area to base yourself.

In the listings below, all rooms have full private bathrooms (with tubs and showers) and free parking unless otherwise noted. Remember to add Hawaii's 11.42% accommodation tax to your final bill.

A bed-and-breakfast booking agency can save you time and money by matching you up with the right accommodations for your needs and budget. We recommend **Hawaii's Best Bed-and-Breakfasts** (© **800/262-9912** or 808/962-0100; fax 808/962-6360; www.bestbnb.com), which represents only the *crème de la crème* of B&Bs across the state.

Knutson & Associates (© **800/800-6202** or 808/329-6311; www.konahawaiirentals.com) is one of Kona's best vacation-rental brokers, offering dozens of oceanfront properties (from condos to houses) to fit every budget. Marilyn Knutson has high standards for the properties she chooses to represent.

Sun Quest Vacations (© **800/367-5168** or 808/329-6488; www.sunquest-hawaii.com) handles a variety of condos south of Kailua-Kona in Keauhou, with prices starting at $80 a night.

THE KONA COAST: IN & AROUND KAILUA-KONA

Boynton's B&B ★ *Kids*   Just 3 miles from Kailua-Kona, but up in the cooler, rolling hills, is this quaint two-bedroom B&B, perfect for a family vacation. The house is perched at 1,000 feet in a quiet country neighborhood; guests can enjoy views of the coastline from the lanai. A private entrance leads you into the complete kitchen, which is stocked with breakfast fixings (including eggs, cereals, muffins, and juice). One bedroom looks out on tropical greenery, the other has an ocean view. Hosts Peter and Tracy Boynton have lovingly created a little bit of heaven here, complete with a hot tub on the deck outside. The beach is just a 5-minute drive away.

74-4920-A Palani Rd., Kailua-Kona, HI 96740 © 808/329-4178. Fax 808/326-1510. www.konabandb.com. 1 2-bedroom unit. $120 double. Extra person $15. 3-night minimum. No credit cards. **Amenities:** Hot tub. *In room:* TV, kitchen, fridge, coffeemaker, hair dryer, iron.

Casa de Emdeko *Kids*   These older condo units are individually owned, so they vary in style and decor, but they're all comfortable. They offer ocean views from their private lanais (even the garden rooms have partial ocean views), and are kept in great shape (the management won't keep units in the rental pool unless the owners renovate regularly). The shoreline here is rocky, and the waters aren't safe for swimming or snorkeling (it's 1½ miles to the nearest swimming beach). But there's a big recreation area and barbecue facilities, plus a small shopping complex with a general store and other small shops so you don't have to schlep into town. The management office is located on the property, so if you have any problems, they're right on the spot. Maid service is available for an extra fee. All in all, this is a good-value choice for families.

Alii Dr. (2½ miles south of Kailua-Kona), Reservations c/o Knutson and Assoc., 75–6082 Alii Dr., Apt. 8, Kailua-Kona, HI 96740. © 800/800-6202 or 808/329-6311. Fax 808/326-2178. www.konahawaiirentals.com. 100 units. High season $105 garden 1-bedroom, $130 oceanview 1-bedroom, $155–$165 2-bedroom; low season $90 garden 1-bedroom, $110 oceanview 1-bedroom, $140–$150 2-bedroom. 3-night minimum. 25% discount for stays of a month or longer. No credit cards. **Amenities:** 2 outdoor pools (1 saltwater, 1 freshwater); shopping arcade; coin-op washer/dryers. *In room:* A/C, TV, kitchen, fridge, coffeemaker; no phone.

Kona Billfisher ★ *Value* *Kids*   This is our favorite of all the affordable condos on this coast. It's within walking distance of downtown Kailua-Kona, and the big, blue Pacific is just across the street. (Unfortunately, the ocean here is not good for swimming or snorkeling, but there's a pool on-site, and the Kailua Pier, just a mile away, has a good swimming area.) The property is very well maintained (the interiors were renovated in 1998). Each unit comes with a full kitchen and a balcony, and features new furnishings and king-size beds. The one-bedroom units have sliding-glass doors that allow you to close off the living room and make it into another private bedroom, so for the price of a one-bedroom unit, you can have a two-bedroom—a real deal. Other on-site facilities include a barbecue area. Book well in advance.

Alii Dr. (across from the Royal Kona Resort), c/o Hawaii Resort Management, P.O. Box 39, Kailua-Kona, HI 96745. ℭ **800/622-5348** or 808/329-3333. Fax 808/326-4137. www.konahawaii.com. 60 units. High season $105 1-bedroom, $135 2-bedroom; low season $90 1-bedroom, $115 2-bedroom. AE, DC, DISC, MC, V. **Amenities:** Outdoor pool; nearby coin-op washer/dryer. *In room:* A/C, TV, kitchen, fridge, coffeemaker, iron.

Kona Isle *Kids* This beautifully landscaped three-story oceanfront complex—built about 3 decades ago but renovated constantly—has individually owned, comfortably decorated condo units with full kitchens, washer and dryer, sofa beds in the open living/dining room area, and ocean views from the lanai. Most units have air-conditioning, but some don't, so, if it matters to you, ask when you reserve. A large grassy area slopes down to a man-made beach, but the water here isn't safe for swimming and snorkeling; you can laze around the pool, or venture about 1½ miles down Alii Drive to a beach that's great for swimming and snorkeling. Like its sister Knutson properties (Casa de Emdeko and Kona Riviera Villas), this place is very well managed and kept in excellent shape. It's 2½ miles to town, but the distance can be a blessing if you like peace and quiet. Book early in the winter, as return guests reserve far in advance.

Alii Dr. (2½ miles south of Kailua-Kona, next to Casa de Emdeko), c/o Knutson and Assoc., 75–6082 Alii Dr., Apt. 8, Kailua-Kona, HI 96740. ℭ **800/800-6202** or 808/329-6311. Fax 808/326-2178. www.konahawaiirentals.com. 90 units. High season $700–$770 per week 1-bedroom condo; low season $395–$645 perweek 1-bedroom condo. 1-week minimum. No credit cards. **Amenities:** Outdoor pool. *In room:* TV, kitchen, fridge, coffeemaker, washer/dryer.

Kona Magic Sands *★ Value* If you want to stay right on the ocean without spending a fortune, this is the place to do it—it's one of the best oceanfront deals you'll find on a Kona condo, and the only one with a beach right next door for swimming and snorkeling. Every unit in this older complex has a lanai that steps out over the ocean and sunset views that you'll dream about long after you return home. These studio units aren't luxurious; they're small (two people max) and cozy, great for people who want to be lulled to sleep by the sound of the waves crashing on the shore. Each consists of one long, narrow room with a small kitchen at one end and the lanai at the other, with a living room/dining room/bedroom combo in between.

77–6452 Alii Dr. (next to Magic Sands Beach Park), c/o Hawaii Resort Management, P.O. Box 39, Kailua-Kona, HI 96745. ℭ **800/622-5348** or 808/329-3333. Fax 808/326-4137. www.konahawaii.com. 37 units (shower only). High season $125 double; low season $95 double. DISC, MC, V. **Amenities:** Excellent seafood restaurant (Jameson's by the Sea); bar; oceanfront outdoor pool. *In room:* TV, kitchen, fridge, coffeemaker.

Kona Riviera Villas *Kids* For those who love the idea of being on the ocean but can't get to sleep with all the racket it makes, this place may be your answer. An older condominium set back from the ocean—still keeping the view but lessening the sound of the waves—Kona Riviera Villas also has a waterfront freshwater swimming pool surrounded by a patio with barbecue facilities. Ocean swimming is too rough here, but it's fun to watch the surfers when the waves roll in. All of the individually owned units are one-bedrooms that comfortably sleep up to four; some have sofa beds, most

Kona Coast Accommodations

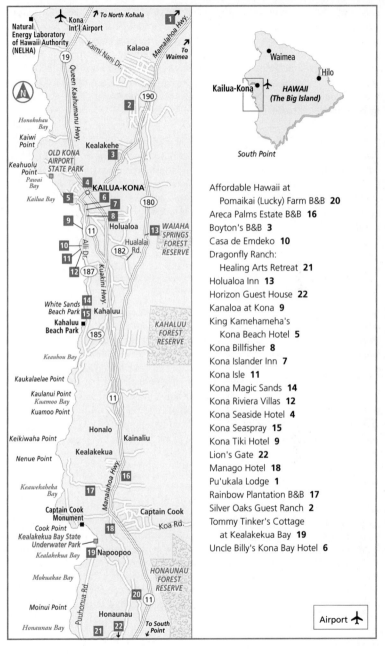

Affordable Hawaii at
   Pomaikai (Lucky) Farm B&B **20**
Areca Palms Estate B&B **16**
Boyton's B&B **3**
Casa de Emdeko **10**
Dragonfly Ranch:
   Healing Arts Retreat **21**
Holualoa Inn **13**
Horizon Guest House **22**
Kanaloa at Kona **9**
King Kamehameha's
   Kona Beach Hotel **5**
Kona Billfisher **8**
Kona Islander Inn **7**
Kona Isle **11**
Kona Magic Sands **14**
Kona Riviera Villas **12**
Kona Seaside Hotel **4**
Kona Seaspray **15**
Kona Tiki Hotel **9**
Lion's Gate **22**
Manago Hotel **18**
Pu'ukala Lodge **1**
Rainbow Plantation B&B **17**
Silver Oaks Guest Ranch **2**
Tommy Tinker's Cottage
   at Kealakekua Bay **19**
Uncle Billy's Kona Bay Hotel **6**

Airport ✈

have ocean views from the lanai. All have ceiling fans (but no A/C) and fully equipped kitchens. Decor varies, from tropical rattan to modern Scandinavian. Like its sister Knutson properties (Casa de Emdeko and Kona Isle), this complex is well managed and well maintained (management requires that units be constantly renovated and updated to remain in the rental pool). Book early, as the word is out on this place.

Alii Dr. (2½ miles south of Kailua-Kona, next to Kona Isle), c/o Knudson & Associates, 75–6082 Alii Dr., Kailua-Kona, HI 96740. ☎ **800/800-6202** or 808/329-6311. Fax 808/326-2178. www.konahawaiirentals.com. 12 units. High season $95–$115 double; low season $80–$115 double. 3-night minimum. No credit cards. **Amenities:** Outdoor pool; coin-op washer/dryers. *In room:* TV, kitchen, fridge, coffeemaker.

Kona Seaside Hotel   The package deal here is great: For just a few dollars more than the regular room rate, you can have a rental car thrown in, too. This budget hotel, located in the heart of Kailua-Kona, is just steps away from Kailua Bay and Kailua-Kona's shopping, restaurants, and historic sites. The rooms are large and comfy (even if they don't have fancy soaps and extra amenities), but they can be noisy (ask for one away from the road). You may want to splurge on one of the 14 rooms with kitchenettes.

75–5646 Palani Rd. (at Kuakini Hwy.), Kailua-Kona, HI 96740. ☎ 800/560-5558 or 808/329-2455. Fax 808/329-6157. www.sand-seaside.com. 225 units. $118–$150 double; $150 double with kitchenette. Extra person $20. Children under 12 stay free in parent's room. Room/car packages available from $118 ($29 extra for car). Parking $5. AE, DC, MC, V. **Amenities:** Restaurant; bar; 2 small outdoor pools; laundry/dry cleaning service; coin-op washer/dryers. *In room:* A/C, TV, dataports (some units), kitchenette (some units), fridge.

Kona Seaspray ☆ *Value*   The Kona Seaspray has a couple of great things going for it: location and price. It's just across from the Kahaluu Beach Park, possibly the best snorkeling area in Kona. The rates are a great deal when you consider that the one-bedroom apartments easily sleep four and the two-bedroom (one-bathroom) unit can sleep six. Recently under new ownership, all the units are undergoing renovation with upgraded furniture, new carpets, and a whole new look. Each apartment has a full kitchen, complete with all the amenities of home, plus a lanai and a fabulous ocean view. Golf and tennis are nearby. This is the place to book if you're going to spend a lot of time lounging around or if you need the extra space.

78–6671 Alii Dr., c/o Johnson Resort Properties, 78–6665 Alii Dr., Kailua-Kona, HI 96740. ☎ **808/322-2403**. Fax 808/ 322-0105. www.konaseaspray.com. 12 units. $105–$130 1-bedroom double; $135–$150 1-bedroom/2 bathroom double; $140 2-bedroom/1 bathroom for 4; $130–$175 2-bedroom/2 bathroom for 4. 3 nights minimum. Extra person $20. AE, DISC, MC, V. **Amenities:** Gorgeous outdoor pool with waterfall; whirlpool hot tub; barbecue area; washer/dryers. *In room:* TV/VCR, kitchen, fridge, coffeemaker, hair dryer, iron.

Silver Oaks Guest Ranch ☆☆ *Finds*   Book this place! Not a bed-and-breakfast or a condo, this is a true "guest ranch," consisting of two cottages spread over a 10-acre working ranch (with friendly horses—no horseback riding, just petting—the cutest Nigerian dwarf goats, chickens, even wild turkeys that come to get fed once a day). Located at 1,300 feet, where the temperatures are in the 70s (low to mid-20s Celsius) year-round, the ranch has units ranging from one-bedroom to family-size units. The views are spectacular, some 40 miles of coastline from the ocean to Mauna Loa, yet it's just 5 miles from the airport and 5 miles from downtown Kailua-Kona. Hosts Amy and Rick Decker have impeccable taste, and every unit is uniquely decorated. All the units have a private bathroom and a complete kitchen, and are stocked with breakfast items (cereals, milk, yogurt, coffee, fruit basket, and bread) for your first day. They have a closet full of free beach gear for guests, not to mention all the books, videos, binoculars, and even a couple of backpacks.

Reservations: 75–1027 Henry St., Suite 310, Kailua-Kona, HI 96740. ℰ **877/325-2300** or 808/325-2000. Fax 808/325-2200. www.silveroaksranch.com. 2 units. $195 Rates includes breakfast items. Extra person $15. 3-night minimum. MC, V. **Amenities:** Outdoor pool; Jacuzzi; washer/dryers. *In room:* TV/VCR, high dataport, kitchen, fridge, coffeemaker.

Uncle Billy's Kona Bay Hotel   An institution in Kona, Uncle Billy's is where visitors from the other islands stay when they come to this coast. A thatched roof hangs over the lobby area, and a Polynesian longhouse restaurant is next door. The rooms are standard fare: They're old, but comfortable, and come with large lanais. Most also have minifridges (request one at booking if you want one), and 16 are condo-style units with kitchens. This budget hotel is a good place to sleep, but don't expect new furniture or carpets or fancy soap in the bathroom. It can be noisy at night when big groups check in; avoid Labor Day weekend, when all the canoe paddlers in the state want to stay here and rehash the race into the wee morning hours.

75–5739 Alii Dr., Kailua-Kona, HI 96740. ℰ **800/367-5102** or 808/961-5818. Fax 808/935-7903. www.unclebilly. com. 139 units. $94–$99 double; $99 double with kitchenettes. Check Internet for specials starting at $84 and car/room deals for just $30 more a night. Extra person $14. Children 18 and under stay free in parent's room. AE, DC, DISC, MC, V. **Amenities:** Restaurant (buffet); bar (with Hawaiian entertainment); 2 outdoor pools (1 just for children); watersports equipment/rentals; activities desk; coin-op washer/dryers. *In room:* A/C, TV, dataport, kitchenette (in some rooms), fridge, hair dryers (in some rooms).

GREAT PACKAGE DEALS

The **Kona Seaside Hotel** and **Uncle Billy's Kona Bay Hotel,** mentioned above, also have great package deals.

King Kamehameha's Kona Beach Hotel 🄥alue   The location is terrific, downtown Kailua Kona, right on the ocean. The problem here is that this is an old (30-plus years) hotel, and very little remodeling, renovation and general maintenance has been done in the past few years. It looks tired. Rooms are showing their age, but they are clean and can have views of an ancient banyan tree, the Kona Pier, or sparkling Kailua Bay. The hotel's own small, gold-sand beach is right out the front door. The hotel's restaurant is forgettable, but you're within walking distance of dozens of other options. The best deal at this convenient downtown Kailua-Kona hotel is the Paradise on Wheels, which comes with a double room, a compact car, and breakfast for two, starting at just $170—a price that makes the "King Kam" (as locals call it) attractive to travelers on a budget.

75–5660 Palani Rd., Kailua-Kona, HI 96740. ℰ **800/367-6060** or 808/329-2911. Fax 808/922-8061. www.kona beachhotel.com. 460 units. $160–$250 double. Paradise on Wheels (including room, car, and breakfast) from $170 (subject to availability). Extra person $30. AE, DC, DISC, MC, V. Parking $7. **Amenities:** 1 restaurant; outdoor bar with Hawaiian entertainment; outdoor pool; 4 tennis courts; Jacuzzi; watersports equipment/rentals; activities desk; shopping arcade; salon; limited room service; laundry/dry cleaning service; coin-op washer/dryers. *In room:* A/C, TV, dataport, fridge, coffeemaker, hair dryer, iron, safe.

SUPER-CHEAP SLEEPS

If you're traveling in the low season, also consider **Casa de Emdeko,** the **Kona Billfisher,** and the **Kona Isle,** above, where off-season rates are quite low.

Kona Islander Inn 🄥alue   This is the most affordable place to stay in Kailua-Kona. These plantation-style, three-story buildings are surrounded by lush, palm tree–lined gardens with torch-lit pathways that make it hard to believe you're smack-dab in the middle of downtown. The central location—across the street from the historic Kona Inn Shops—is convenient, but can be noisy. Built in 1962, the complex is showing some signs of age, but the units were recently outfitted with new appliances, new bedspreads and curtains, and a fresh coat of paint. The studios are small, but extras like lanais and kitchenettes outfitted with microwaves, minifridges, and coffeemakers make up for the lack of space.

75–5776 Kuakini Hwy. (south of Hualalai Rd.), Kailua-Kona. c/o Hawaii Resort Management, P.O. Box 39, Kailua-Kona, HI 96745. © **800/622-5348** or 808/329-3333. Fax 808/326-4137. www.konahawaii.com. 80 studios. $80–$90 double. DC, DISC, MC, V. **Amenities:** Outdoor pool; hot tub; activities desk; coin-op washer/dryers. *In room:* A/C, TV, kitchenette, fridge, coffeemaker.

Kona Tiki Hotel ⭐⭐ *Finds* It's hard to believe that places like this still exist. The Kona Tiki, located right on the ocean, away from the hustle and bustle of downtown Kailua-Kona, is one of the best budget deals in Hawaii. All of the rooms are tastefully decorated and feature queen beds, ceiling fans, minifridges, and private lanais overlooking the ocean. Although it's called a hotel, this small, family-run operation is more like a large B&B, with lots of aloha and plenty of friendly conversation at the morning breakfast buffet around the pool. The staff is helpful in planning activities. There are no TVs or phones in the rooms, but there's a pay phone in the lobby. If a double with a kitchenette is available, grab it—the extra few dollars will save you a bundle in food costs. Book way, way, way in advance.

75–5968 Alii Dr. (about a mile from downtown Kailua-Kona), Kailua-Kona, HI 96740. © **808/329-1425.** Fax 808/327-9402. www.konatiki.com. 15 units. $61–$75 double; $84 double with kitchenette. Rates include continental breakfast. Extra person $9; children 2–12 $6. 3-night minimum. No credit cards. **Amenities:** Outdoor pool. *In room:* Kitchenettes (in some rooms), fridge, no phone.

Pu'ukala Lodge *Value* This four-unit lodge, located above the Kona Airport, away from the heat and humidity of Kailua-Kona at a cool 1,500 feet, is one of the bargains of Kona. This gorgeous, high-ceilinged wooden home with wraparound lanais has fabulous coastline views and sunsets that will remain in your memory long after the tan has faded. The location is terrific: just 7 miles from Kona and 1 mile from a public golf course. Big, delicious, gourmet breakfasts (fresh fruit from the garden, waffles, sausage, etc.) are served every morning and innkeeper Tom serenades the guests with his guitar as the sun sinks into the Pacific. The rooms range from a small room (with TV and queen bed) to spacious suites to a two-room apartment with full kitchen.

P.O. Box 2967, Kailua-Kona, HI 96745. © **888/325-1729** or 808/325-1729. www.puukala-lodge.com. 4 units. $90–$100 double; $85–$110 suite double; $150–$165 2-bedroom suite (with kitchen) for 4 (sleeps up to 6). Rates include full breakfast. For a rental car, call for rates. Extra person $25. 2-night minimum. MC, V. *In room:* TV, kitchenette (some units), fridge, coffeemaker, hair dryer, iron.

WORTH A SPLURGE

Holualoa Inn ⭐⭐ *Finds* The quiet, secluded setting of this B&B—40 pastoral acres just off the main drag of the artsy village of Holualoa, on the slopes at 1,350 feet above Kailua-Kona—provides stunning panoramic views of the entire coast. Owned by a *kamaaina* (old-line) family, this contemporary 7,000-square-foot Hawaiian home, built of golden woods, has six private suites and window-walls that roll back to embrace the gardens and views. Cows graze on the bucolic pastures below the garden Jacuzzi and pool, and the coffee plantation on the property is the source of the morning brew. The inn offers several nice features, such as a gas grill for a romantic dinner beside the pool, a telescope for stargazing, and a billiard table. It's a 15-minute drive down the hill to busy Kailua-Kona and about 20 minutes to the beach, but the pool has a stunning view of Kailua-Kona and the sparkling Pacific below.

76–5932 Mamalahoa Hwy. (P.O. Box 222), Holualoa, HI 96725. © **800/392-1812** or 808/324-1121. Fax 808/322-2472. www.holualoainn.com. 6 units (1 with shower only). $175–$225 double. Rates include full breakfast and sunset pupu platter. Extra person $30. 15% discount for 7 nights or more. AE, DC, DISC, MC, V. On Mamalahoa Hwy., just after the Holualoa Post Office, look for Paul's Place General Store; the next driveway is the inn. Children must be 13 or older. **Amenities:** Huge outdoor pool; Jacuzzi. *In room:* Hair dryer, no phone.

THE SOUTH KONA COAST

Areca Palms Estate Bed-and-Breakfast (formerly Merryman's Bed-and-Breakfast) 🌟 *finds*   Everything about this upcountry B&B is impeccable: the landscaping, the furnishings, the fresh flowers in every room—even breakfast is served with attention to every detail. This charming cedar home, surrounded by immaculate park-like landscaping, sits above the Captain Cook–Kealakekua area, close to beaches, shopping, and restaurants. Guests enjoy watching the sun sink into the ocean from the large lanai or gazing at the starry sky as they soak in the hot tub. Hosts Janice and Steve Glass took over from Don and Penny Merryman, but continue the tradition of memorable breakfasts (orange-oatmeal quiche, tropical stuffed French toast, tree-ripened banana cakes), offer daily maid service, provide guests with beach equipment, and gladly help with reservations for activities and dinner.

P.O. Box 489, Captain Cook, HI 96704. © **800/545-4390** or 808/323-2276. Fax 808/323-3749. www.konabedandbreakfast.com. 4 units. $90–$125 double. Rates include full breakfast. Extra person $25. 2-night minimum. MC, V. From Hwy. 11, make a left at the Pacific Island Tire dealer (after mile marker 111) and follow the signs. **Amenities:** Outdoor Jacuzzi. *In room:* TV, hair dryer, no phone.

Dragonfly Ranch: Healing Arts Retreat *finds*   Some may find the Dragonfly Ranch too rustic. But if you want to enjoy Hawaii's tropical outdoors, and you're thrilled by the island's most unique architecture—structures that bring the outdoors inside—this may be the place for you. The location is ideal, with Puuhonua o Honaunau National Historic Park just down the road and five bays offering great swimming and diving just minutes away. The place itself, with freestanding cabins tucked away on 2 acres of fruit trees and exotic flowers, truly is a tropical fantasy.

P.O. Box 675 (19 miles south of Kailua-Kona on Hwy. 160), Honaunau, HI 96726. © **800/487-2159** or 808/328-2159. Fax 808/328-9570. www.dragonflyranch.com. 5 units (4 with private bathroom; 1 with shower only). $100–$150 double; $175–$250 suite. Rates include continental breakfast. Extra person $20. 3-night minimum. MC, V. From Hwy. 11, turn onto Hwy. 160 (the road to Puuhonua O Honaunau National Historic Park), between mile markers 103 and 104; after 1½ miles, look for the Dragonfly Ranch mailbox. **Amenities:** Yoga studio and fitness room; watersports equipment/rentals; activities desk; car-rental desk; massage; babysitting; laundry service. *In room:* TV, wireless high-speed Internet access, kitchenette (in some rooms), fridge, coffeemaker, hair dryer, iron.

Kanaloa at Kona 🌟🌟 *Kids*   These big, comfortable, well-managed, and spacious vacation condos border the rocky coast beside Keauhou Bay, 6 miles south of Kailua-Kona. They're exceptional units, ideal for families, with comforts such as huge bathrooms with whirlpool bathtubs, dressing rooms, and bidets. In addition, the spacious lanais, tropical decor, and many appliances make for free and easy living. It's easy to stock up on supplies at the supermarket at the new mall just up the hill, but the ocean-front restaurant offers an alternative to your own cooking. Guests receive discounted rates at the two 18-hole golf courses at a nearby country club.

78–261 Manukai St., Kailua-Kona, HI 96740. © **800/688-7444** or 808/322-9625. Fax 800/622-4852. www.outrigger.com. 76 units. $205–$290 1-bedroom apt (sleeps up to 4); $220–$330 2-bedroom apt (sleeps up to 6); $305–$360 2-bedroom apt with loft (sleeps up to 8). AE, DC, DISC, MC, V. **Amenities:** Restaurant; ocean-side bar; 3 outdoor pools (1 for adults only); 2 tennis courts (lighted); 3 Jacuzzis; concierge; activities desk; babysitting; coin-op washer/dryers. *In room:* TV, kitchen, fridge, coffeemaker, hair dryer, iron, safe.

Lion's Gate *finds*   Located on a beautifully landscaped, working macadamia nut and coffee farm, this two-story house features four units with private entrances. Rooms are either doubles or two-room suites. The decor is nothing to brag about, but the house is comfortably furnished. The units share a large lanai with a hot tub, a barbecue, and a common area with a TV and VCR, refrigerator, microwave, and coffeemaker. Hosts Bill and Diane Shriner opened their B&B in 1993 as a complement to their 10-acre farm, where they grow their own Lion's Gate Coffee. It's well off the main highway, but still convenient to beaches and about a 30-minute drive to Kailua-Kona.

P.O. Box 761, Honaunau (26 miles south of Kailua-Kona), HI 96726. **©** **800/955-2332** or 808/328-2335. Fax 808/328-2335. www.coffeeofkona.com. 4 units. $110 double; $175–$180 2-room suite for 4. Rates include continental breakfast. Extra person $15. MC, V. From Hwy. 11, turn right after 105 mile marker; follow driveway for ¼ mile to house. **Amenities:** Outdoor Jacuzzi. *In room:* No phone.

Rainbow Plantation Bed-and-Breakfast *(Finds)*

The key word here is "rustic." Everything at this upcountry place at elevation 1,200 feet is clean, but this is a very rural environment—with chickens running around and all the paraphernalia of a working coffee farm—so don't expect lush landscaping. The large rooms are equally rustic, but comfortable, with private entrances and queen beds. You can even stay in a converted 34-foot fishing boat. Guests have use of a "jungle kitchenette" with a barbecue grill, a counter top, and a sink for preparing meals (all the rooms have private minifridges for storing food). Hostess Marianna Schrepter speaks German, French, and some Spanish, and she's fluent in the language of aloha.

P.O. Box 122 (7 miles south of Kailua-Kona), Captain Cook, HI 96704. **©** **800/494-2829** or 808/323-2393. Fax 808/323-9445. www.aloha.net/~konabnb. 3 units, 1 converted boat. $79–$99 double; $89 converted 34-foot boat. Rates include full breakfast. Extra person $15. 2-night minimum. AE, MC, V. From Hwy. 11, turn right between mile markers 110 and 111, just north of Napoopoo Rd. (which leads to the Kealakekua Bay Marine Life Sanctuary). *In room:* TV, fridge, coffeemaker, no phone.

FOR LONG-TERM FAMILY STAYS

Tommy Tinker's Cottage at Kealakekua Bay *(Kids)*

For a half-hour beyond Kailua-Kona, the road meanders through coffee country and wild avocados, finally arriving at Kealakekua Bay (of "Little Grass Shack" fame), whose underwater sights draw snorkelers on day cruises and dolphin lovers hoping for a swim with a friendly spinner. Perched right on the edge of all this natural wonder is this box-like ocean-front cottage, perfectly located, roomy, and priced right for families. The cottage rents by the week, which is a good deal for four people ($60 per person per day). The interior is open and airy. They've improved the furnishings in the past few years, but the location and amenities (full kitchen, two bedrooms, a sofa bed in the living room, and two bathrooms) are the stars here. Good swimming beaches line the coast here, and 4 miles to the south, Puuhonua O Honaunau National Historic Park is a fascinating spot to learn about local history and culture.

P.O. Box 599, Kapaau, HI 96755. **©** **808/889-5584.** Fax 808-889-0573. www.kokua.com/ocean. 1 cottage. $1,670 for 2–6 people per week. MC, V. *In room:* TV, kitchen, fridge, coffeemaker, iron, washer/dryer, no phone.

SUPER-CHEAP SLEEPS

Affordable Hawaii at Pomaikai (Lucky) Farm Bed-and-Breakfast *(Value)*

True to its name, Affordable Hawaii offers an inexpensive perch from which to explore the South Kona Coast. Come share ex-Californian Nita Isherwood's century-old 4-acre farm, which is overflowing with macadamia-nut trees, coffee, tropical fruits, avocados as big as footballs, and even *jaboticaba,* an exotic fruit that makes a zingy jam and local wine. The least expensive room is inside the old farmhouse (hey, at $60 a night, including a private bathroom, this is a deal!). The recent addition, the Greenhouse wing, has two rooms with wooden floors, big windows with screens, full private bathrooms, and private entrances. The most unique accommodation is the old coffee barn, updated into a rustic room for two with a raised queen bed, a fabulous view of the coastline, a private bathroom (with toilet and sink only), and an outdoor shower. Guests can use a common kitchen with a refrigerator, microwave, hot plate, and barbecue grill.

83–5465 Mamalahoa Hwy. (south of Kailua-Kona, after mile marker 107), Captain Cook, HI 96704. ℂ 800/325-6427 or 808/328-2112. Fax 808/328-2112. www.luckyfarm.com. 4 units. $60–$75 double. Rates include full farm breakfast. Extra person $10; kids under 6 are $5. 2-night minimum. AE, DISC, M/C, V. *In room:* No phone.

Manago Hotel 🌟 *(Value)*   If you want to experience the history and culture of the 50th state, the Manago Hotel may be the place for you. This living relic is still operated by the third generation of the same Japanese family that opened it in 1917. It offers clean accommodations, tasty home cooking (see the review of the **Manago Hotel Restaurant** on p. 268), and generous helpings of aloha, all at budget prices. The older rooms (with community bathrooms) are ultra-spartan—strictly for desperate budget travelers. The rooms with private bathrooms in the new wing are still pretty spare (freshly painted walls with no decoration and no TV), but they're spotlessly clean and surrounded by Japanese gardens with a koi pond. The room prices increase as you go up; the third-floor units have the most spectacular views of the Kona coastline. Adventuresome travelers might want to try the Japanese rooms with tatami mats to sleep on and *furo* (deep hot tubs) in each room to soak in. By the end of your stay, you may leave with new friends (the Manago family is very friendly).

P.O. Box 145, Captain Cook, HI 96704. ℂ **808/323-2642.** Fax 808/323-3451. www.managohotel.com. 63 units (some with shared bathroom). $31 double with shared bathroom; $51–$56 double with private bathroom; $70 double Japanese room with small *furo* tub and private bathroom. Extra person $3. DISC, MC, V. **Amenities:** Restaurant; bar. *In room:* No phone.

WORTH A SPLURGE

Horizon Guest House 🌟🌟 *(Finds)*   Host Clem Classen spent 2 years researching the elements of a perfect bed-and-breakfast. The Horizon Guest House is the result. Its 40 acres of pastureland are located at 1,100 feet. You can see 25 miles of coastline from Kealakekua to just about South Point, yet you cannot see another structure or hear any sounds of civilization. The carefully thought-out individual units (all under one roof, but positioned at an angle to each other so you don't see any other units) are filled with Hawaiian furniture, including hand-quilted Hawaiian bedspreads, writing desks, luxurious robes, and private lanais with coastline views. The property features a spectacular ocean view, top-drawer barbecue facilities, gardens everywhere, an outdoor shower, and all the ocean and beach toys you can think of. Clem whips up a gourmet breakfast in the octagonal kitchen in the main house, which also features a media room with library, video collection, TV (which you can take to your room, if you promise to use the headphones so you won't disturb other guests), DVD, VCR, and cordless phone. At first glance, the rate may seem high, but once ensconced on the unique property, we think you'll agree it's worth every penny.

P.O. Box 268, Honaunau, HI 96726. ℂ **888/328-8301** or 808/328-2540. Fax 808/328-8707. www.horizonguesthouse.com. 4 units. $250 double. Rates include full gourmet breakfast. 2-night minimum. MC, V. 21 miles south of Kailua-Kona on Hwy. 11, just before mile marker 100. Children must be 14 or older. **Amenities:** Large outdoor pool that's worthy of a big resort; Jacuzzi perfectly placed to watch the sunset behind Kealakekua Bay; washer/dryers; dataport; wireless Internet access. *In room:* Fridge, coffeemaker, hair dryer, no phone.

WAIMEA (KAMUELA)

Aaah the Views Bed-and-Breakfast ✦ *Value*   At this quiet B&B, just 15 minutes from the fabulous beaches of the Kohala Coast and 5 minutes from the cowboy town of Waimea, you have the choice of a two-bedroom apartment (with private entrance), a separate new garden cottage, or a room in the main house. New owners Erika and Derek Stuart recently took over this B&B and have added a new deck to the stream-side property. True to its name, every one of the four units has huge picture windows to watch the moon rise or to hear the babble of the stream outside and the sounds of birds in the surrounding trees in the morning. One unit is a studio apartment, complete with kitchen. Two rooms share one bath and the fourth unit has its own private bathroom down the hall.

P.O. Box 6593, Kamuela, HI 96743. © 808/885-3455. Fax 808/885-4031. www.aaahtheviews.com. 4 units. $75–$145 double. Rates include continental breakfast. Extra person $15. 2-night minimum. MC, V. *In room:* TV/VCR, dataport, kitchenette, fridge, coffeemaker, hair dryer, iron.

Aloha Vacation Cottages ✦ *Finds*   Hostess Heidi Staab cannot do enough for her guests. She makes sure she has every kind of beach toy you can think of, and if you have children, she'll loan you a playpen, high chair, or whatever else you need. Staying with her is like having your own private concierge to make sure that your vacation is everything you want it to be. Heidi has two units available. The small, intimate guesthouse has a full kitchen, a separate bedroom, washer and dryer, high-speed Internet, and all the comforts of home, including a selection of pillows and a mattress with an adjustable "comfort level" on each side. The larger, stand-alone cottage has all the same amenities, plus more space. Guests are greeted with a fruit basket. Heidi provides daily maid service (she's also a massage therapist—don't miss one of her massages). The cottages are on the "dry" or "sunny" side of Waimea, just about a 10- to 15-minute drive to the beach and just a few minutes to the restaurants of Waimea.

P.O. Box 1395 Kamuela, HI 96743. © 877/875-1722 or 808/885-6535. www.alohacottages.net. 2 units. $95–$135. Extra person $15. 3-night minimum. MC, V. *In room:* TV/VCR, washer/dryer, dataport, hair dryer, iron, robes and slippers, beach gear, BBQ.

Belle Vue ✦ *Finds*   This two-story vacation rental has a truly beautiful view. Sitting in the hills overlooking Waimea and surrounded by manicured gardens, the charming home is just 15 minutes from the Kohala Coast beaches. The penthouse unit is a large, cathedral-ceilinged studio apartment with a small kitchen, huge bedroom, luxurious bathroom, and view of Mauna Loa and Mauna Kea mountains down to the Pacific Ocean. The one-bedroom apartment has a full kitchen, fireplace, and sofa bed. Each unit has a separate entrance. The rates include breakfast fixings (toast, juice, fruit, cereal, coffee) inside the kitchenettes.

1351 Konokohau Rd., off Opelo Rd. (P.O. Box 1295), Kamuela, HI 96743. © 800/772-5044, or 808/885-7732 local phone and fax. www.hawaii-bellevue.com. 3 units. $95–$185 double. Extra person $25. AE, MC, V. *In room:* TV, dataport, kitchenette, fridge, coffeemaker, hair dryer, iron.

Kamuela Inn   The best deals at this rambling inn set high in the hills are the kitchenette suites, which are roomier than the standard rooms and come equipped with everything you need to fix basic meals. The regular doubles are small and seem crowded, with a double bed taking up most of the space. For a bit more breathing room, spend the extra money on a suite, which also comes with a lanai. The clientele generally consists of parents of students at nearby Hawaii Preparatory Academy, a private boarding school.

Kawaihae Rd. (P.O. Box 1994), Kamuela, HI 96743. © 808/885-4243. Fax 808/885-8857. www.hawaii-bnb. com/kamuela.html. 31 units. $59–$85 double; $89–$185 suite. Rates include continental breakfast. Extra person $10. AE, DC, DISC, MC, V. *In room:* TV, kitchenettes (in some), fridges (in some), coffeemakers (in some), no phone.

Kamuela's Mauna Kea View Suite and Cottage *Finds*   Location, location, location—this B&B has it. Retired Parker Ranch manager Richard Mitchell must've used his ranch connections to get this fabulous property, which borders Parker Ranch's 225,000 acres and looks straight up at 14,000-foot Mauna Kea. The 1,000-square-foot suite features two bedrooms (the master bedroom has bay and ranch views), full kitchen, dining area, living room with fireplace (handy on chilly winter nights), covered deck, and Jacuzzi. The 440-square-foot cottage is a chalet-style studio with a separate second sleeping area, kitchenette, and deck. The same attention to detail that Richard contributed to Parker Ranch's success he now applies to making sure that his guests are happy. Since opening in 1988, he has had visitors from 34 countries and 49 states (would someone from North Dakota please stay here and make Richard's life complete?).

P.O. Box 6375, Kamuela, HI 96743. © 808/885-8425. Fax 808/885-6514. 1 suite, 1 cottage (with shower only). $77 cottage double; $89 suite. Rates include continental breakfast. Extra person $18. 2-night minimum. AE, MC, V. From junction of Hwy. 19 and Hwy. 190, continue east on Hwy. 19 for 3 miles. *In room:* TV, kitchenette, fridge, coffeemaker.

Puu Kapu *Value*   This charming French country–style home sits just off the main highway in Waimea. Inside, it's got lacy curtains, old-fashioned flowered wallpaper, and quilts on the bed, and outside are a pond, fountain, gazebo, and hot tub. The accommodations range from small, but quaint, rooms to a spacious one-bedroom suite. The smallest room shares the bathroom with the owner, but each room has a private entrance. The one-bedroom suite has a full kitchen, lanai, and barbecue area. The views are fabulous, but the location has pluses (close to Waimea and just 15 minutes to beaches) and minuses (some noise from the road).

P.O. Box 2864, Kamuela, HI 96740. © 808/885-6821. www.kamuela.com/puukapu. 3 units (1 with shared bathroom). $65–$85 double. Rates include continental breakfast. Extra person $10. MC, V. **Amenities:** Hot tub. *In room:* TV, kitchenettes (in some), fridge, coffeemaker, microwave, no phone.

WORTH A SPLURGE
Waimea Garden Cottages ★★ *Finds*   Imagine rolling hills on pastoral ranchland. Then add a babbling stream. Now set two cozy Hawaiian cottages in the scene, and complete the picture with mountain views—and you have Waimea Garden Cottages. One unit has the feel of an old English country cottage, with oak floors, a fireplace, and French doors opening onto a spacious brick patio. The other is a remodeled century-old Hawaiian wash house, filled with antiques, eucalyptus-wood floors, and a full kitchen. Extra touches keep guests returning again and again: plush English robes, sandalwood soaps in the bath, mints next to the bed, and fresh flower arrangements throughout. Hosts Barbara and Charlie Campbell live on the 1½-acre property.

Off Mamalahoa Hwy., 2 miles west of Waimea town center. Reservations: c/o Hawaii's Best Bed & Breakfasts, P.O. Box 758, Volcano, HI 96785. © 800/262-9912 or 808/985-7488. Fax 808/962-6360. 2 cottages. $140–$160 double. Rates include continental breakfast. Extra person $20. 3-night minimum. No credit cards. *In room:* TV/VCR, kitchen, fridge, coffeemaker, hair dryer, iron, whirlpool bathtub (in 1 unit), fireplace (in 1 unit).

THE HAMAKUA COAST
The Cliff House ★★ *Finds*   Perched on the cliffs above the ocean is this romantic two-bedroom getaway, surrounded by horse pastures and million-dollar views. A large deck takes in that ocean vista, where whales frolic offshore in winter. Impeccably decorated

(the owner also owns Waipio Valley Artworks), the unit features a full kitchen (stocked with everything you could possibly want—even a salad spinner), two large bedrooms, and a full bathroom. Lots of little touches make this property stand out from the others: an answering machine for the phone, a pair of binoculars, a chess set, and even an umbrella for the rain squalls. Four people could comfortably share this unit.

P.O. Box 5070, Kukuihaele, HI 96727. © 800/492-4746 or 808/775-0005. Fax 808/775-0058. www.cliffhouse hawaii.com. 1 unit. $195 double. Extra person $25. 2-night minimum. MC, V. *In room:* TV, dataport, kitchen, fridge, coffeemaker, hair dryer, iron.

Hale Kukui *Finds*   The draw of this remote cottage is its tropical bird's-eye view into the mouth of Waipio Valley, with haunting sea cliffs and waves crashing along miles of coastline—simply mesmerizing. Architect-hosts William and Sarah McCowatt created an otherworldly environment in this clever structure (which expands or contracts to suit the size of each party) near their home, surrounding it with lush gardens and tropical flowers. Each unit has a kitchenette and a lanai with a fabulous view, which can include rare glimpses of native birds and whales calving in winter.

P.O. Box 5044 (7 miles outside of Honokaa), Kukuihaele, HI 96727. © 800/444-7130 or 808/775-7130. Fax 808/775-7472. www.halekukui.com. 1 studio and 1 two-bedroom apt in 1 cottage (can be combined into 1 3-bedroom unit). $145 studio; $180 apt; $195 for entire cottage. Extra person $15. No credit cards. Turn off Hwy. 240 into the village of Kukuihaele; after a mile, look for the Hale Kukui sign on ocean side of road. **Amenities:** Jet tub. *In room:* TV, kitchenette, fridge, coffeemaker, no phone.

Luana Ola B&B Cottages ★ *Finds*   These off-the-beaten-path, plantation-style, open-room cottages hark back to the romantic 1940s. Furnished in rattan and wicker, each features a kitchenette and sleeps up to four. One unit has a spectacular ocean view, the other an ocean view that's not as panoramic, but hostess Marsha Tokareff has made up for it with a satellite TV. She leaves all the fixings for breakfast in your kitchen so you can get up at your leisure. The cottages are within walking distance to Honokaa town, yet far enough away to feel the peace and quiet of this bucolic area. Laundry facilities are available.

P.O. Box 1967, Honokaa, HI 96727. © 800/357-7727 or 808/775-1150. luanacottages@yahoo.com. 2 units. $100. Extra person $15. 2-night minimum. MC, V. **Amenities:** Laundry facilities. *In room:* TV (in 1 unit); DVD (in 1 unit), kitchenette, fridge, coffee maker, hair dryer, iron, CD player.

Mountain Meadow Ranch Bed-and-Breakfast ★ *Kids*   Located on the slopes of Mauna Kea at 2,000 feet, this B&B is for people who want everything: a serene retreat in a remote woodland with world-class beaches just a half-hour away. The setting is magical; on moonlit nights, the surrounding eucalyptus trees come alive as they dance in the gentle breeze. Each of the two guest rooms has its own private entrance, which opens into a cozy living/dining room with two skylights. The bedrooms have great views, and share the full bathroom, separate dry sauna, and small kitchenette. (*Tip:* Book both bedrooms and have the entire place to yourself.) The cottage is tucked away on a hill behind a large macadamia nut tree and banana grove. It has two good-size bedrooms (it can sleep up to six people), a full kitchen, and a big lanai overlooking rolling hills dotted with horses. Hosts Bill and Gay George make this place special. Bill is a retired Aloha Airlines pilot, now a video producer. Gay, who is half-Hawaiian, is the Hawaiian expert. Sitting in this bit of paradise, listening to Gay weave Hawaiian legends and culture into stories, you can almost see history spring to life.

46–3895 Kapuna Rd. (P.O. Box 1697), Ahualoa, Honokaa, HI 96727. © 808/775-9376. Fax 808/775-8033. www. mountainmeadowranch.com. 2 units (with shared bathroom), 1 cottage. $95 double; $135 cottage. Rates include continental breakfast. Extra person $40. 3-night minimum for cottage. AE, MC, V. **Amenities:** Washer/dryers. *In room:* TV/VCR, kitchen (in cottage only), fridge, coffeemaker, no phone.

Waipio Ridge Vacation Rental *(Value)*   On the top ridge of Waipio Valley, this budget cottage and 24-foot Airstream trailer, next door, have an eye-popping, jaw-dropping view of the entire valley, including the turquoise waves rolling onto the black-sand beach. Owner Roger Lasko, a former high school woodshop teacher, built the private cottage in 1990 to share the view and meet folks from around the globe. With a queen bed, private bathroom, and kitchenette, the small cottage isn't the lap of luxury, but it's very functional. The trailer has a bedroom, kitchen, bathroom and outdoor shower and a 10×24-foot deck outside. It's the view that guests come for, and Roger knows it: Out on the lawn, he has set up a gas grill, a picnic table, and lounge chairs that let you kick back and soak in the awe-inspiring view of Waipio's straight-edged cliffs and the verdant valley below—spectacular.

P.O. Box 5039, Kukuihaele, HI 96727. © **808/775-0603.** www.cyberrentals.com/HI/LaskoBIGI.html. 1 cottage (with shower only), 2 studios. Cottage $85 double; studios $75–$85 double. Extra person $15. No credit cards. Follow Hwy. 240 to Waipio Valley Lookout; proceed down the 4WD road for just a few feet, and take the first road on the left; the driveway is on the right. *In room:* TV/VCR, kitchenette, fridge, coffeemaker, no phone.

Waipio Wayside B&B Inn 🌺🌺 *(Finds)*   Jackie Horne's restored Hamakua Sugar supervisor's home, built in 1938, sits nestled among fruit trees and surrounded by sweet-smelling ginger, fragile orchids, and blooming birds-of-paradise. The comfort-able house, done in old Hawaii style, abounds with thoughtful touches, such as the help-yourself tea-and-cookies bar with 26 different kinds of tea. A sunny lanai with hammocks overlooks a yard lush with five kinds of banana trees plus lemon, lime, tan-gerine, and avocado trees; the cliffside gazebo has views of the ocean 600 feet below. There are five vintage rooms to choose from: Our favorite is the master bedroom suite (dubbed the "bird's-eye" room) with double doors that open onto the deck; we also love the Library Room, which has an ocean view, hundreds of books, and a skylight in the shower. Jackie's friendly hospitality and excellent breakfasts (such as pesto scrambled eggs with blueberry muffins) round out the experience. A shared TV with DVD and VCR is in the communal living room.

P.O. Box 840, Honokaa, HI 96727. © **800/833-8849** or 808/775-0275. www.waipiowayside.com. 5 units. $95–$175 double. Rates include full, organic, tropical continental breakfast with coffee, fruit (sunrise papayas, mangoes, and fresh tangerines), granola, yogurts, and muffins. Extra person $25. MC, V. On Hwy. 240, 2 miles from the Honokaa Post Office; look on the right for a long, white picket fence and sign on the ocean side of the road; the 2nd driveway is the parking lot. **Amenities:** Concierge.

SUPER-CHEAP SLEEPS

Akiko's Buddhist Bed-and-Breakfast *(Value)*   You don't have to be a Buddhist to stay here. Tucked away in the mountains, the once-thriving sugar village of Wailea is now home to just 12 families, and this spartan, Zen-like B&B, converted from the town's old garage, tailor shop, and tofu factory. It is the handiwork of Akiko Masuda: Buddhist, artist, children's book author, farmer, and one-woman renovation/reclamation team. Accommodations are simple (bedrooms have a futon on the floor and one low table) and immaculately clean, with one shared toilet and an outside stone bathhouse with a shower. Several rooms in the house are set aside for meditation (daily at 5:30am). The plantation-style kitchen is where Akiko makes daily breakfasts of organic fruits and smoothies, fresh bread, locally grown banana pancakes, and a wicked French toast. The real reason to stay here is the incredible feeling of peace in this tranquil community. Great walks on old country roads past waterfalls, mountain streams, and tropic forests. No smoking.

P.O. Box 272 (located in the tiny village of Wailea), Hakalau, HI 96710. (C) and fax **808/963-6422.** www.alternative-hawaii.com/akiko. 4 units (all with shared bathroom). $40 single; $55 double. Cooking facilities available. Rates include breakfast. No credit cards. Look for mile marker 15 on Hamakua Hwy. and WAILEA sign. Turn towards mountain, road will turn and parallel highway. Drive for ½ mile to 1-block town of Wailea. No children under age 11. *In room:* No phone.

Hotel Honokaa Club *(Value)* This funky and humble old place has been sheltering guests—mostly sugarland workers—for nearly 100 years. The sugar mills have closed down, but the Honokaa Club refuses to die, attracting bicyclists, adventure travelers, and anyone traveling on a tight budget. Some private rooms have ocean views (ask for no. 10 to see the sunrise and no. 16 to see the sunset), but don't expect much beyond a clean room and a bed. You can keep to yourself here, but once you venture into the lobby or restaurant, the overflowing aloha will lure you into the extended *ohana* (family). The 1950s-style cafe serves three meals a day—nothing fancy, but tasty and cheap fare. One terrific plus is the entire hotel is a no-smoking facility. The employees are used to meeting travelers from around the globe and aren't shy about starting up a conversation with you and introducing you to the other guests and regular town folks who drop by to "talk story."

P.O. Box 247 (at the Hilo end of Honokaa town, across from the Recreation Park), Honokaa, HI 96727. (C) **800/808-0678** or 808/775-0678. Fax 808/775-0678. www.hotelhonokaa.com. 14 units, 6 hostel dorm beds (shared room or private). $18 dorm single; $38 dorm double; $28 private dorm single; $50–$75 hotel room double with private bathroom. Rates include free continental breakfast for hotel room only. Extra person $15 (children $10). AE, MC, V. **Amenities:** High-speed Internet access. *In room:* No phone.

HILO

The accommodations described in this section are shown on the map of Hilo on p. 319.

The Bay House *(Finds)* Overlooking Hilo Bay, this brand-new B&B offers immaculate rooms (each with oak-wood floors, king-size bed, sofa, private bathroom, and oceanview lanai) at reasonable prices. A full breakfast (fruit, yogurt, eggs, granola, muffins, and so on) is set out in a common area every morning (which also has a refrigerator, coffeemaker, toaster, and microwave for common use); you can take all you want to eat back to your lanai and watch the sun rise over Hilo Bay. The only minus is the lack of laundry facilities, but there are plenty in nearby Hilo.

42 Pukihae St., Hilo, HI 96720. (C) **888/235-8195,** or 808/961-6311 local phone and fax. www.bayhousehawaii.com. 3 units. $105–$120 double. Rates include continental breakfast. Extra person $15. AE, MC, V. Amenities: hot tub. *In room:* TV, hair dryer.

Dolphin Bay Hotel *(Value)* This two-story motel-like building, 4 blocks from downtown, is a clean, family-run property that offers good value in a quiet garden setting. Ripe star fruit hang from the trees, flowers abound, and there's a jungle-like trail by a stream. The tidy concrete-block apartments are small and often breezeless, but they're equipped with ceiling fans and jalousie windows. Rooms are brightly painted and outfitted with rattan furniture and Hawaiian prints. There are no phones in the rooms, but there's one in the lobby. You're welcome to all the papayas and bananas you can eat.

333 Iliahi St., Hilo, HI 96720. (C) **808/935-1466.** Fax 808/935-1523. www.dolphinbayhilo.com. 18 units. $79–$89 studio double; $109 1-bedroom apt double; $129 2-bedroom apt double. Extra person $10. From Hwy. 19, turn mauka

(toward the mountains) on Hwy. 200 (Waianuenue St.), then right on Puueo St.; go over the bridge and turn left on Iliahi St. **Amenities:** Concierge; car-rental desk; coin-op washer/dryer. *In room:* TV, dataport, kitchenette, fridge, coffeemaker, hair dryer (on request), iron.

Hale Kai Hawaii ⋆ *Value*   An eye-popping view of the ocean runs the entire length of this house; you can sit on the wide deck and watch the surfers slide down the waves. All rooms have that fabulous ocean view through sliding-glass doors. There's one suite, with a living room, kitchenette, and separate bedroom. Guests have access to a pool, hot tub, and small guest area with fridge, telephone, and library. Breakfast is a treat: homemade macadamia-nut waffles, a double cheese soufflé, or banana pancakes. Landscape designer Maria Macias and photographer Ricardo Zepeda recently bought this B&B and have breathed new life into it: The rooms are now all painted in vibrant tropical colors, Maria has improved the landscaping, they've installed privacy barriers between each room, and in the future they plan to move the hot tub to a more private location and expand the pool deck.

111 Honolii Pali, Hilo, HI 96720. © **808/935-6330.** Fax 808/935-8439. www.halekaihawaii.com. 4 units. $110–$125 double; $135 suite. Rates include gourmet breakfast. Extra person $20. 2-night minimum. MC, V. **Amenities:** Oceanfront outdoor pool; Jacuzzi. *In room:* TV, no phone.

Hawaii Naniloa Resort   Hilo's biggest hotel offers nice rooms with lanais and enjoys a quiet, leafy Banyan Drive setting on the ocean. The hotel is a little old and tired (but so are all the other hotels on Banyan Drive—in terms of comfort and amenities, this is one of the best that Hilo has to offer). Although it needs work (new carpet, a paint job, and overall remodeling), the rooms are clean and the oceanfront views are spectacular. Not only can you see the ocean, but, on a cloudless day, to the top of Mauna Kea. The rack rates are on the high side, but it's usually pretty easy to snag one of the cheapest rooms (which have only partial ocean views and no balconies).

93 Banyan Dr. (off Hwy. 19), Hilo, HI 96720. © **800/367-5360** or 808/969-3333. Fax 808/969-6622. www.naniloa. com. 325 units. $100–$160 double; from $190 suite. Internet rates from $70. AE, DC, DISC, MC, V. **Amenities:** 2 restaurants; bar; 2 outdoor pools; 18-hole golf course nearby with special rates for guests; $5 fee for fitness center with Jacuzzi and sauna; salon; very limited room service; coin-op washer/dryers; laundry/dry cleaning service. *In room:* A/C, TV, fridge (some rooms), coffeemaker (some rooms), hair dryer (some rooms), iron (on request), safe.

The Inn at Kulaniapia ⋆ *Finds*   The view from this off-the-beaten-track inn is worth the price alone: the 120-foot Kulaniapia Waterfall in one direction and the entire town of Hilo sprawled out 850 feet below in another direction. This is *the* place for a romantic getaway. Not only are you nestled in luxury accommodations, but you are given a royal breakfast with egg dishes, fresh fruit grown on the 22-acre property, and just-baked breads. Wander along the 2-mile pathways that follow the Waiau River (check out the exotic bamboo garden) or swim at the base of the waterfall in the 300-foot pond. The rooms are well appointed with private bathrooms (marble) and balconies (to enjoy those views). It's just 15 minutes from Hilo, but feels a zillion miles away from everything in the peaceful surroundings of a 2,000-acre macadamia-nut grove.

P.O. Box 11338, Hilo, HI 96720. © **866/935-6789** or 808/935-6789. Fax 808/935-6789. www.waterfall.net. 4 units. $109. Rates include breakfast. Extra person $20. AE, MC, V. **Amenities:** Hot tub; high-speed Internet access; Ohana Room with TV, phone. *In room:* No phone.

The Old Hawaiian B&B *Value*   Bargain hunters take note: This old plantation house from the 1930s has been renovated and upgraded and offers great room rates that include breakfast. Located on the Wailuku River, the house features a large lanai, where guests have use of a phone, refrigerator, and microwave. The rooms range from tiny to large with its own sitting area and sunken bathtub and separate shower. All have their own private entrances and private bathrooms. Hosts Stewart and Lory Hunter prepare a beautiful breakfast of fruit cup, fruit smoothie, juice, coffee and tea, and two types of homemade bread (you'll want seconds of Lory's mac-nut scones). The Hunters happily help guests with sightseeing plans.

1492 Wailuku Dr., Hilo, HI 96720. © **877/961-2816** or 808/961-2816. www.thebigislandvacation.com. 3 units. $75–$95. Extra person $10. MC, V. *In room:* Wireless Internet access, hair dryer, iron (on request).

GREAT PACKAGE DEALS

Uncle Billy's Hilo Bay Hotel   Uncle Billy's is the least expensive place to stay along Hilo's hotel row, Banyan Drive. This oceanfront budget hotel boasts a dynamite location, and the car/room package offers an extra incentive to stay here. You enter via a tiny lobby, gussied up Polynesian style; it's slightly overdone, with sagging fishnets and tapa-covered walls. The guest rooms are simple: bed, TV, phone, closet, and soap and clean towels in the bathroom—that's about it. The walls seem paper thin, and it can get very noisy at night (you may want to bring ear plugs), but at rates like these, you're still getting your money's worth. As we went to press you could get three nights (four days) of room, car and free breakfast for $375. If you want to stay at Uncle Billy's in Hilo and in Kona, as of press time you could get a car-room-breakfast for $693 for seven nights.

87 Banyan Dr. (off Hwy. 19), Hilo, HI 96720. © **800/367-5102** or 808/961-5818. Fax 808/935-7903. www.unclebilly. com. 144 units. $84–$89 double; $94 studio with kitchenette. Car/room packages and special senior rates available. Extra person $14. Children 18 and under stay free in parent's room. AE, DC, DISC, MC, V. **Amenities:** Restaurant; bar with hula show nightly; oceanfront outdoor pool; activities desk; coin-op washer/dryers. *In room:* A/C, TV, kitchenette (some rooms), fridge, coffeemaker (some rooms), hair dryers (some rooms), iron (some rooms).

SUPER-CHEAP SLEEPS

Arnott's Lodge ⭐ (Kids) (Value)   If you aren't too picky about decor but want a clean, safe place to stay within walking distance of beaches, Arnott's is the place for you. This is *the* budget buy in Hilo. A step up from a hostel, this former apartment building was converted to dorms and suites in 1990. In 1998, Arnott, a native Australian, did a major renovation on the public areas, adding to the collection of more than 200 videos, and upgrading wheelchair-accessible facilities. The spartan apartments are basic: hollow-tile walls, tiny kitchens, and bathrooms. Guests include European backpackers and families on a budget. Arnott sees no reason why his guests have to rent a car; he provides shuttle service to the airport and charges $2 for a shuttle to Hilo. He also provides a long list of activities, from twice-weekly barbecues to hiking to the lava flows at night. He also has inexpensive access to the Internet, brand-new laundry facilities, and a separate camping area for tents.

98 Apapane Rd. (off Hwy.19, just after Keaukaha Beach Park), Hilo, HI 96720. © **808/969-7097.** Fax 808/961-9638. www.arnottslodge.com. 36 bunk beds in 3 apts and 6 additional apts, set up as singles, doubles, and suites (all with shared bathrooms and kitchens) and 4 2-bedroom houses. $17 bunk; $37 single; $47 double; $57 double with private bathroom; $120 2-bedroom house double. Extra person $15 in suite and house. AE, DC, DISC, MC, V. Free airport shuttle. **Amenities:** Activity desk; car-rental desk; coin-op washer/dryers. *In room:* TV, kitchen, fridge, coffeemaker, no phone.

Butterfly Inn ⭐ (Value)   All women, gay and straight, but women only, are welcome at this secluded two-story home on a lush acre blooming with fruit trees, exotic flowers, and tropical plants. The upper floor of the house is for guests' use, including the full kitchen, the living room with entertainment center, and an enclosed deck. Also on the property is an outdoor steam house and hot tub. A massage therapist is on call to help relax those who arrive stressed-out.

P.O. Box 667 (2 miles off Hwy.11, off Huina Rd.), Kurtistown, HI 96760. ✆ **800/54MAGIC** or 808/966-7936. www.the butterflyinn.com. 2 units (with shared bathroom and kitchen). $55 single; $65 double. Rates include continental breakfast. Extra person $25. MC, V. **Amenities:** Jacuzzi. *In room:* TV, fridge, coffeemaker, no phone.

Lihi Kai ⚡ (*Value*)   Amy Gamble Lannan began renting out her two extra bedrooms in 1981, and she's been full ever since. When Amy turned 80, her regular guests gave her a present: A vacation at one of Hawaii's luxury hotels. "Oh, those places are nice," Amy said in her usual direct manner, "but expensive. Really, we have the same thing here—ocean view, nice rooms, and lots of service." She's absolutely right. Her beautifully designed house—with mahogany floors, huge sliding glass doors, and large lanai—is perched on the edge of a cliff that has a beautiful wide-angle view of Hilo Bay. The sound of the surf wafts into the two garden-view bedrooms, which share a bathroom and a half. The smell of coffee fills the early morning air as Amy sets a continental breakfast next to the pool on the covered lanai (passing squalls are frequent in Hilo). Considering the location, the price is unbelievable. The house really isn't appropriate for children (there's that cliff), but babes in arms are welcome.

30 Kahoa Rd. (at Alae Point), Hilo, HI 96720. ✆ **808/935-7865.** 2 units (with shared bathroom). $65 double. 3-night minimum. No credit cards. **Amenities:** Outdoor swimming pool. *In room:* No phone.

Maureen's Bed and Breakfast (*Finds*)   The old Saiki mansion, built in 1932 and totally restored by Maureen Goto, is again the grande dame it was always meant to be. Staying here is like taking a trip back in time: The house, constructed of redwood and cedar, features arched windows and doorways and a formal Japanese tearoom; large lanais overlook koi ponds and the carefully maintained botanical gardens. The two smallest rooms are perfect for singles; the others are comfy for two, but would be crowded with three. Breakfast, served in the formal dining room, starts with fresh fruit and moves on to quiche or waffles. Maureen's is comfortable and conveniently located, across the street from good swimming and snorkeling, and just 10 minutes from downtown Hilo. Maureen has dogs, so if you have allergies, be warned.

1896 Kalanianaole Ave. (2.7 miles from Ken's House of Pancakes), Hilo, HI 96720. ✆ **800/935-9018** or 808/935-9018. www.maureenbnb.com. 6 units (5 with shared bathroom). $50 single; $75 double; $100 double with private bath. Rates include full breakfast. 10% discount for 7 nights or more. No credit cards. No children under 7. *In room:* No phone.

WORTH A SPLURGE

The Palms Cliff House ⚡⚡ (*Finds*)   The newest accommodation in the Hilo area actually is a 15-minute drive north of Hilo town, at Honomu (where Akaka Falls is located). Perched on the side of a cliff, this grand old Victorian-style inn is surrounded by manicured lawns, a grove of macadamia nut trees, plus lemon, banana, lime, orange, avocado, papaya, star fruit, breadfruit, grapefruit, and mango trees. Eight oversize suites, filled with antiques, DVD players, fireplaces, and private lanais, all overlook the ocean. Four rooms have private Jacuzzis; other extras include custom-made Italian lace sheets, cooking classes, yoga classes, and private massage. A gourmet hot breakfast (fresh fruit, home-baked bread, and entrees ranging from banana–mac nut pancakes to asparagus–sweet potato quiche) are served on the wraparound lanai overlooking the rolling surf. This magnificent getaway is not to be missed.

P.O. Box 189, Honomu, 96728 ✆ **808/963-6076.** Fax 808/963-6316. www.palmscliffhouse.com. 8 units. $175–$375. Rates include full gourmet breakfast, Sat afternoon high tea. AE, DC, DISC, MC, V. **Amenities:** Hot tub. *In room:* A/C (only upper units), TV/DVD, dataport, fridge, hair dryer, iron, Jacuzzi (in some rooms).

Shipman House Bed-and-Breakfast ★/★ *Finds* Built in 1900, the Shipman House is on both the national and state registers of historic places. This Victorian mansion has been totally restored by Barbara Andersen, the great-granddaughter of the original owner, and her husband, Gary. Despite the home's historic appearance, Barbara has made sure that its conveniences are strictly 21st century, including full bathrooms with all the amenities. All five guest bedrooms are large, with 10- to 12-foot ceilings, with extras such as cotton kimonos, heirloom furnishings, hand-woven lauhala mats, ceiling fans, and fresh flowers. Wake up to a large continental breakfast buffet. *Tip:* For a real Hawaiian experience, stay on a Wednesday, when guests can join in with the hula class practicing on the lanai.

131 Kaiulani St., Hilo, HI 96720. © 800/627-8447 or 808/934-8002. Fax 808/934-8002. www.hilo-hawaii.com. 5 units. $199–$219 double. Rates include continental breakfast. Extra person $25. AE, MC, V. From Hwy. 19, take Waianuenue Ave.; turn right on Kaiulani St. and go 1 block over the wooden bridge; look for the large house on the left. *In room:* No phone.

HAWAII VOLCANOES NATIONAL PARK & VOLCANO VILLAGE

Carson's Volcano Cottage ★ *Finds* Recently Jeanne and Bill Winslow took over this well-known B&B from Tom and Brenda Carson, who owned the property for a decade and a half. The property has two suites inside the main house, two units in another building and one free-standing cottage, all with private entrances and private bathrooms, done in Asian, 1940s, and 1950s Hawaiiana themes. They also rent another two cottages and a larger house in the neighborhood. Several of the deluxe cottages even have their own hot tubs and free-standing fireplaces. The property also has a hot tub tucked under the ferns for guests' use. The Winslows are continuing the tradition of serving a hearty breakfast in the dining room. Some of the units were showing their age, and the Winslows are repainting, renovating, and replacing things as quickly as they can to bring the property back up to its usual tip-top shape. Note that the three cottages do not have private phones or TV, so if that's important to you, speak up when you are booking.

P.O. Box 503 (in Mauna Loa Estates, 501 Sixth St., at Jade Ave.), Volcano, HI 96785. © 800/845-5282 or 808/967-7683. Fax 808/967-8094. www.carsonsvolcanocottage.com. 9 units. Guest rooms (shower only) $110 double; suites $125 double; 3 cottages $125–$165 double; houses $125–$135. Rates include full buffet breakfast. Extra person $15–$20. AE, DISC, MC, V. **Amenities:** Hot tub. *In room:* Kitchen (in some rooms), fridge, coffeemaker.

Country Goose *Finds* An avid hiker, Joan Early volunteered to house some of the runners in the first Volcanoes Marathon in 1987. Almost two decades later, her B&B and booking service are well known throughout the islands. Joan's quaint country home is decorated with—you guessed it—all manner of country geese: wooden geese, ceramic geese, stuffed cloth geese (most of them sent to her from around the globe by her guests). We think the secret to Joan's success is her hearty breakfasts: sour cream pancakes with fresh strawberries, bacon and scrambled eggs, waffles with whipped cream and berries, or maybe baked eggs and ham. Joan only has two guest rooms in her house—one king room and one queen room, both with private entrances and bathrooms—so book in advance.

P.O. Box 597 (at Eighth St. and Ruby Ave.), Volcano, HI 96785. © 800/238-7101 or 808/967-7759. Fax 808/965-8673. www.countrygoose.com. 2 units. $90 double. Rates include full breakfast. Extra person $10. 2-night minimum. DISC, MC, V. *In room:* TV, no phone.

Hale Ohia Cottages ★ *Finds* Take a step back in time to the 1930s. Here you'll have a choice of suites, each with private entrance, located in the main residence or a

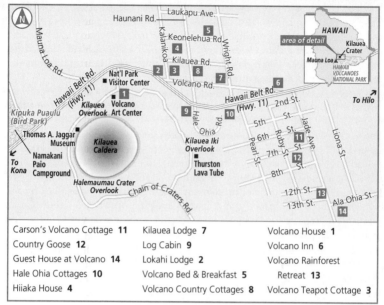

Carson's Volcano Cottage **11**	Kilauea Lodge **7**	Volcano House **1**
Country Goose **12**	Log Cabin **9**	Volcano Inn **6**
Guest House at Volcano **14**	Lokahi Lodge **2**	Volcano Rainforest
Hale Ohia Cottages **10**	Volcano Bed & Breakfast **5**	Retreat **13**
Hiiaka House **4**	Volcano Country Cottages **8**	Volcano Teapot Cottage **3**

cottage. There are also four guest cottages, ranging from one bedroom to three. The surrounding botanical gardens contribute to the overall tranquil ambience of the estate. They were groomed in the 1930s by a resident Japanese gardener, who worked with the natural volcanic terrain but gently tamed the flora into soothing shapes and designs. The lush grounds are just a mile from Hawaii Volcanoes National Park. New this year: a cozy cottage with a fireplace, a hot tub, and a bedroom made from a round, redwood water tank (very, very romantic!).

P.O. Box 758 (Hale Ohia Rd., off Hwy. 11), Volcano, HI 96785. © 800/455-3803 or 808/967-7986. Fax 808/967-8610. www.haleohia.com. 4 units, 4 cottages. $95–$165 double. Rates include continental breakfast. Extra person $20. MC, V. *In room:* Fridge, coffeemaker, hair dryer, no phone.

Hi'iaka House 🎏 *(Kids)*   This is a quite a deal: An entire 1930s vacation home, outfitted with everything you need to enjoy a vacation in the rainforest, is available for less than $30 per person per night, if you're traveling in a party of eight. A big porch welcomes you as you first approach the house; you'll then step into a large living/dining room with a wood-burning stove. This house is a throwback to a time when days were slower and people had time to sit in the overstuffed rattan chairs and read, play croquet on the rolling lawn, or produce multi-course meals out of the full kitchen. It's equipped with everything from a washer and dryer to a TV, VCR, and deluxe stereo system (complete with a selection of music). Three large bedrooms (with space heaters for chilly winter nights), a comfortable sofa bed in the living room, landscaped grounds, and the sounds of birds in the rainforest make this a great choice for families.

P.O. Box 159 (19–4079 Haunani Rd., between Kilauea and Keonelehua rds.), Volcano, HI 96785. © 877/967-7990 or 808/967-7990. www.volcanoplaces.com. 3-bedroom, 1½-bath house for up to 8. $135 double. Rate includes ingredients for making your own breakfast. Extra person $15. 2-night minimum. DISC, MC, V. *In room:* TV/VCR, kitchen, fridge, coffeemaker, iron, washer/dryer, no phone.

Kilauea Lodge 🏕 This crowded and popular roadside lodge, built in 1938 as a YMCA camp, sits on 10 wooded and landscaped acres. Its rooms offer heating systems and hot-towel warmers, beautiful art on the walls, fresh flowers, and, in some, fireplaces. There's also a 1929 two-bedroom cottage with a fireplace and a full kitchen, just a couple of blocks down the street. A full gourmet breakfast is served to guests at the restaurant, which is open to the public for dinner (see the review on p. 281).

P.O. Box 116 (1 block off Hwy. 11 on Old Volcano Rd.), Volcano, HI 96785. 📞 808/967-7366. Fax 808/967-7367. www.kilauealodge.com. 14 units, 3 cottages. $140–$160 double room; $160–$190 cottages. Rates include full breakfast. Extra person $15. AE, MC, V. **Amenities:** Restaurant; hot tub. *In room:* Coffeemaker, no phone.

Log Cabin 🧒 Here's an old log cabin for the young at heart. Nearly a century old, it's built with notched ohia logs (no nails) and set in a forest of native tree ferns, wild ginger, and virgin cedars. One of the first homes built in Volcano (it served as a cowboy hangout and a speakeasy before becoming a one-of-a-kind historic hideaway), it's fully equipped with all the modern conveniences, including a wood-burning fireplace (vital in Hawaii's high country), full kitchen and bathroom, and VCR. Rustic and romantic, it sleeps up to four on the second floor (two in a master bedroom and two in an antechamber), up a double spiral staircase with ohia handrails.

At Hale Ohia and Volcano rds. Reservations: c/o Cynthia R. Rubinstein, 1123 11th Ave., Suite 404, Honolulu, HI 96816. 📞 808/262-7249. Fax 808/261-3440. www.crubinstein.com. 1 cabin. $125 for 2; $150 for 4; $175 for 6. No credit cards. *In room:* TV/VCR, kitchen, fridge, coffeemaker.

Lokahi Lodge Offering restful accommodations since 1992, Lokahi Lodge is located on a quiet side street in Volcano village. Part of the "Chalet Kilauea Collection," this small inn promises a quiet, restful vacation with all the amenities. Four of the guest rooms at this large lodge have private entrances and two double beds; decor ranges from feminine, with flower bedspreads and matching curtains, to masculine, with darker furniture and bolder colors. The 1,000-square-foot fifth room has a king bed, private wet bar, and sitting and dining area. The common living room features a fireplace, piano, and shelves filled with books you're welcome to read.

P.O. Box 998 (on Kalanikoa Rd., between Old Volcano and Kilauea rds.), Volcano, HI 96785. 📞 800/937-7786 or 808/967-7786. Fax 808/967-8660. www.volcano-hawaii.com. 5 units. $99–$149 double. Rates include continental breakfast. Extra person $15. MC, V. *In room:* TV.

Volcano Country Cottages 🏕 *Value* These cottages are tucked away in the midst of magnificent towering pines, yet centrally located, within walking distance of Volcano's two grocery stores and Kilauea Lodge for dinner. The Artist's House is a two-bedroom, one-bathroom house with a fully-equipped kitchen and woodstove, built in 1944. For years an artist's residence, it's adorned with works by an impressive list of Big Island artists. Owner Kathleen Ing Porter, who lives with her family on the property, still keeps art supplies and an easel in the living room for the guests' use ("You'd be surprised how many people who have never painted before use the art supplies, and their work is wonderful!"). Next door, located behind the main family house, is the Ohelo Berry Cottage, a sweet little studio with a minikitchen and queen bed—very private, a perfect place for honeymooners to stay.

P.O. Box 545 (on Old Volcano Rd., near Haunani Rd.), Volcano, HI 96785. 📞 888/446-3910 or 808/967-7960. Fax 808/967-7960 www.volcanocottages.com. 1 studio, 1 2-bedroom house. $95 double studio; $120 double house. 2-night minimum. Extra person $15. MC, V. *In room:* TV, kitchen, fridge, coffeemaker, no phone.

Volcano House Volcano House has a great location—inside the boundaries of the National Park. This mountain lodge, which evolved out of a grass lean-to in 1865, is

Hawaii's oldest visitor accommodation. It stands on the edge of Halemaumau's bubbling crater, and its edgy view of the crater is still an awesome sight. The rooms are very plain, and quite pricey for what you get. This historic hotel deserves better. A novel treat: Rooms are heated with volcanic steam. A major drawback: The lodge is a major tour-bus lunch stop; you might want to stop for ohelo berry pie and coffee (or something stronger) at Uncle George's Lounge and bring it back to enjoy in front of the eerie crater.

P.O. Box 53 (Hawaii Volcanoes National Park), HI 96718. ℂ 808/967-7321. Fax 808/967-8429. www.volcano househotel.com. 42 units. $95–$225 double. AE, DC, DISC, MC, V. **Amenities:** Restaurant with great view; bar.

Volcano Inn *(Finds)*   Located in the rainforest, this AAA-rated property is a combination of a four-room inn in the heart of Volcano village and four fully equipped cedar cabins (with complete kitchens) a few blocks away. Guests in all units (both the inn rooms and the cottages) enjoy a family-style breakfast with eggs, granola, breads, pastries, and coffee, tea, and juice. The rooms at the inn are quite luxurious for the price; each comes with a fireplace, daily maid service, and comfy robes for the cool mornings. The cottages are best for families.

19–3820 Old Volcano Rd., Volcano, HI 96785. ℂ 800/997-2292 or 808/967-7293. Fax 808/985-7349. www.volcano inn.com. 8 units. $95–$136 double. AE, DC, DISC, MC, V. **Amenities:** Bike rentals; car-rental desk. *In room:* TV/VCR, dataport, kitchen (cottages only), fridge, coffeemaker, hair dryer, iron.

Volcano Rainforest Retreat *(Finds)*   This charming property is on an acre of fern-filled land. The "guest" cottage has a full kitchen, a sleeping loft, and a bathroom that looks right into the jungle. The eight-sided "Forest Hale" studio is a new addition with a private forest entrance, queen bed, gas fireplace, kitchenette, skylight dome, and private bathroom. The six-sided "sanctuary" cottage started out as a meditation house, but once guests saw it, they begged the Goldens to rent it out. The only drawback is the half-bath, but next door, open to the forest, is a handcrafted Japanese *furo* (hot tub) with an outdoor shower. The newest "bamboo guest house" has an open beam living room with gas fireplace and entertainment center, with a 6-foot skylight. Shoji screen doors open to the bedroom, and two futons are available for additional guests.

P.O. Box 957, Volcano, HI 96785. ℂ 800/550-8696, or 808/985-8696 local phone and fax. www.volcanoretreat.com. 4 units (1 with half-bathroom). $110–$185 cottage double; $245 new bamboo guest house. Rates include continental breakfast. 2-night minimum. Extra person $15. MC, V. **Amenities:** Hot tub. *In room:* Kitchenette, fridge, coffeemaker, phones in cottages only.

Volcano Teapot Cottage *(R) (Finds)*   As one B&B owner told us, "The Volcano Teapot Cottage is the standard that we all try to live up to." This quaint cottage, built in 1914 (but lovingly renovated in 1996), was a guest cottage to the Dillingham estate. Everything in the house has been carefully collected over the past 15 years by owner Antoinette Dullough, including the hats in the hat rack, the antique rugs, the wood-burning stove, the four-poster bed, and the lace curtains and old-fashioned bedspreads; there's even the original claw-foot tub in the bathroom. The atmosphere is very F. Scott Fitzgerald. The master bedroom has a queen bed; the second bedroom, outfitted with twin beds, is perfect for children. Despite its old-fashioned ambience, Antoinette has made sure that the full kitchen is completely outfitted and up-to-date; there's also a TV/VCR in the living room and a washer and dryer on the back porch. Located in the older section of Volcano Village, the cottage sits on 2½ acres of fruit and pine trees, camellias, hapu ferns, and native ohia and koa trees.

P.O. Box 511 (19–4041 Kilauea Rd., off Haunani Rd.), Volcano, HI 96785. Ⓒ **800/670-8345** or 808/967-7112. Fax 808/967-7112. www.volcanoteapot.com. 1 cottage. $165 double. Rate includes kitchen stocked with breakfast foods. Extra person $15. 2-night minimum. No credit cards. **Amenities:** Washer/dryer. *In room:* TV/VCR, kitchen, fridge, coffeemaker, no phone.

SUPER-CHEAP SLEEPS

Volcano Bed-and-Breakfast *(Value)*   Frugal travelers looking for comfortable, clean, and quiet lodgings, this is quite a bargain. A charming restored 1912 historic home sits on beautifully landscaped grounds. The rooms are small, but clean and inviting; all share bathrooms. The common rooms include a living room with TV, VCR, and piano; a reading room; and a sunroom.

P.O. Box 998 (on Keonelehua St., off Hwy. 11 on Wright Rd.), Volcano, HI 96785. Ⓒ **800/937-7786** or 808/967-7779. Fax 808/967-8660. www.volcano-hawaii.com. 6 units (none with private bathroom). $49–$69 double. Rates include continental breakfast. Extra person $15. AE, DC, DISC, MC, V. From Hwy. 11, turn north onto Wright Rd.; go 1 mile to Chalet Kilauea on the right, where you'll check in. *In room:* No phone.

Volcano Guest House *(Kids)*   Here's the ideal place to stay with the kids. A mother herself, Bonnie Gooddell has completely child-proofed her cottages ("There's nothing they can ruin") and filled the large porches with children's toys; there's even a basketball hoop in the driveway and a swing set in the yard. All of the guesthouses are freestanding, and three are completely wheelchair accessible. One unit is a two-story cottage that can sleep a large family: The upstairs bedroom has two twin beds and one queen bed, and the couch in the living room pulls out into a double bed. Each has a full kitchen, bathroom, telephone, TV, and everything else you might need, down to extra wool socks for cold nights. There's even a forest trail in the backyard, which goes all the way through 2 miles of tropical rainforest to the Thurston Lava Tube in Hawaii Volcanoes National Park.

11–3733 Ala Ohia (off Jade Ave.; P.O. Box 6), Volcano, HI 96785. Ⓒ **808/967-7775.** Fax 808/985-7505. www.volcano guesthouse.com. 4 units. $85–$105 double. Extra person $15. 2-night minimum. No credit cards. **Amenities:** Laundry room. *In room:* TV, kitchen, fridge, coffeemaker.

SOUTH POINT

Macadamia Meadows Bed-and-Breakfast ★ *(Value)*   Near the southernmost point in the United States, and just 45 minutes from Volcanoes National Park, lays one of the Big Island's most welcoming B&Bs. It's located on an 8-acre working macadamia-nut farm, in a great place for stargazing. The warmth and hospitality of host Charlene Cowan is unsurpassed: Each guest is treated like a favorite relative. Accommodations include a two-bedroom suite, a private room, and a honeymoon suite, which has an antique claw-foot tub on a private lanai. All rooms have private entrances and are immaculately clean.

94–6263 Kamaoa Rd., Waiohinu. Reservations: P.O. Box 756, Naalehu, HI 96772. Ⓒ **888/929-8118** or 808/929-8097. Fax 808/929-8097. www.macadamiameadows.com. 4 units. $75–$135 double; $120 for 4 in suite. Rates include continental breakfast. Extra person $10–$15; children under 5 stay free. AE, DISC, MC, V. **Amenities:** Resort-size outdoor pool; tennis courts; activities desk. *In room:* TV, fridge, microwave, no phone.

South Point Banyan Tree House ★ *(Finds)*   Couples looking for an exotic place to nest should try this treehouse, nestled inside a huge Chinese banyan tree. The cottage comes complete with see-through roof that lets the outside in, plus a comfy, just-for-two hot tub on the wraparound deck. Inside, there's a queen bed and a kitchen with microwave, and two-burner stove. The sweet scent of ginger brings you sweet dreams at night, while the twitter of birds greets you in the morning.

At Hwy. 11 and Pinao St., Waiohinu. Reservations: c/o Janette LeGault, 11172 W. Edwards Rd., Saxon, WI 54559. ☎ 949/492-1258 or 949/842-0051. www.southpointbth.com. 1 cottage. $150 double. 2-night minimum. No credit cards. **Amenities:** Hot tub; washer/dryer, outside grill. *In room:* TV/VCR, kitchen, fridge, coffeemaker.

SUPER-CHEAP SLEEPS

Bougainvillea Bed-and-Breakfast ⋆ *Finds*   Don and Martie Jean Nitsche bought this 3-acre property in the Hawaiian Rancho subdivision of Ocean View and had a *Field of Dreams* experience: They decided that if they built a bed-and-breakfast, people would come. Where some people just saw lava, the Nitsches saw the ancient Hawaiian path that went from the mountain to the sea. So they built. And out of the lava came gardens—first colorful bougainvillea, then flowers and a pineapple patch, then a fish pond to add to the pool and hot tub, and finally a barbecue area and satellite for TV reception. Word got out. Martie's breakfast—her secret-recipe banana-nut pancakes, plus sausage, fruit, and coffee—drew people from all over. Things got so good, they had to add more rooms (all with their own private entrances) and expand the living room (complete with TV, VCR, and video library) and dining room. Guests usually take their breakfast plates out to the lanai, which boasts ocean views.

P.O. Box 6045, Ocean View, HI 96737. ☎ **800/688-1763** or 808/929-7089. Fax 808/929-7089. http://hawaii-inn.com/bouga or www.bougainvilleabedandbreakfast.com. 4 units. $80 double. Rates include full breakfast. Extra person $15. AE, DC, DISC, MC, V. **Amenities:** Big outdoor pool; hot tub; concierge; car-rental desk; massage; Satellite TV; minikitchen in pavilion; game area; barbecue area; microwave. *In room:* VCR, hair dryer, no phone.

4 Great Deals on Dining

So many restaurants, so little time. What's a traveler to do? Even with a so-so budget, you keep yourself very, very busy grazing your way across the vast culinary landscape of Hawaii. It is a volcano of flavors, an island of daunting size and sizable offerings for palates of every stripe.

The island's volcanic soil produces fine tomatoes, lettuces, beets, beans, fruit, and basic herbs and vegetables that were once difficult to find locally. Southeast Asian fruit, such as mangosteen and rambutan, are beginning to appear in markets, along with the low-acid white pineapple that is, by now a well-established Big Island crop. Along with the lamb and beef from Big Island ranches and seafood from local fishermen, the freshness of the produce forms the backbone of ethnic cookery and Hawaii Regional Cuisine. The island has produced its share of celebrity chefs, but it's also known for its home-style flair and its abundance of small neighborhood ethnic restaurants, especially in Hilo. You'll find an extraordinary diversity of dining choices, from el-cheapo to splurge.

Kailua-Kona is teeming with restaurants for all pocketbooks. Although most of them are touristy and many overpriced, there are some commendable restaurants in town. Budget breakfast at Aki's Café on Alii Drive, terrific dinner at Jackie Rey's Ohana Grill, at the Pottery Terrace on Kuakini Highway and Izakaya Kai for Japanese cuisine at wallet-pleasing prices. For a splurge choice, head to the Keauhou Shopping Center and have a dinner you will long remember at Kenichi Pacific.

Because this is a budget guide, we haven't reviewed most of the purveyors of haute cuisine that dominate the **Kohala Coast.** If you feel like a splurge, however, know that North Kona's Four Seasons Resort Hualalai and the Kohala Coast's Mauna Kea Beach Hotel, Hapuna Beach Prince Hotel, Fairmont Mauna Lani (formerly the Orchid at Mauna Lani), and Mauna Lani Bay Hotel and Bungalows offer endless sumptuous opportunities to put a volcano-size dent in your pocketbook.

Waimea is a thriving upcountry community, a haven for yuppies, techies, and retirees who know a good place when they see one. Merriman's is a notable force in the island's culinary offerings. Also in Waimea Tako Taco Taqueria offers innovative and healthy Mexican cuisine at budget prices.

In **Hawi,** North Kohala, expect bakeries, neighborhood diners, and one tropical-chic restaurant, Bamboo, that's worth a special trip.

In **Hilo,** you'll find pockets of trendiness (don't miss the Hilo Bay Café) among the precious old Japanese and ethnic restaurants that provide honest, tasty, and affordable meals in unpretentious surroundings. For a splurge night on the town, Restaurant Kaikodo is the best choice.

In the listings below, reservations are not required unless otherwise noted.

In section 10 of this chapter, "Shops & Galleries," you'll find a wide variety of markets and shops around the island where you can pick up the island's best foodstuffs to prepare meals for yourself. Many of them also feature very affordable prepared meals and takeout.

THE KONA COAST: IN & AROUND KAILUA-KONA

For an inexpensive meal, also consider the more casual room at the Kona Inn Restaurant, the **Cafe Grill** (see "Worth a Splurge," below).

Aki's Café ★ *Value* AMERICAN/JAPANESE   This tiny, neighborhood eatery has three things going for it: terrific food, cheap prices, and it is oceanfront on Alii Drive. The most popular meal is breakfast, where regulars can be seen standing around waiting for the 8am opening. But lunch and dinner (same menu, same great prices) bring in a crowd looking for authentic Japanese food or delicious American hamburgers. Lunch and dinner features everything from chicken katsu ($13) to noodle dishes (ramen, yakisuba, even spaghetti) to sandwiches (from fresh fish to buffalo).

75-5699 Alii Dr., Kailua-Kona, HI. ℂ 808/329-0090. Breakfast $4–$8.50; Lunch and dinner $3.50–$11. AE, MC, V. Daily 8am–8:30pm.

Basil's Pizzeria *Value* PIZZA/ITALIAN   Two dining rooms seat 100 in a garlic-infused atmosphere where pizza is king, sauces sizzle, and pasta is cheap. The ocean-view restaurant, in a prime location in Kailua-Kona, is redolent with cheeses, garlic, and fresh organic herbs (a big plus). Shrimp pesto and the original barbecue-chicken pizzas are long-standing favorites, as is the artichokes/olives/capers version, a Greek-Italian hybrid.

75-5707 Alii Dr., Kailua-Kona. ℂ 808/326-7836. Main courses $8–$15; ndividual pizzas $9.95–$11. MC, V. Daily 11am–10pm.

Big Island Grill ★ *Finds* AMERICAN   One of the best kept secrets among local residents is the Big Island Grill, where you get huge servings of home cooking at 1970's prices. The place is always packed from the first cup of coffee at breakfast to the last bite of dessert at night. Chef Bruce Goold has been cooking in Kona for decades and has a loyal following for his "localized" American cuisine. This is a place to take the family for dinner (excellent fresh salmon, generous-sized salads and world's tastiest mash potatoes) without having to go into debt. Warning: be prepared to wait (no reservations) and then have a sense of humor about the sometimes slow service once you finally land a table.

75-5702 Kuakini Hwy., Kailua-Kona. ℂ 808/326-1153. Main courses $6.25–$16. MC, V. Mon–Sat 6–10am, 11am–2pm and 5–9pm.

Jackie Rey's Ohana Grill ★★ *Finds* ECLECTIC   Off the beaten tourist path lies this hard-to-categorize eatery: part sports bar, part family restaurant, part music and dancing (salsa, country western), and part neighborhood cafe. Jackie Rey's is all of that and more: great food at wallet-pleasing prices. Lunches are filled with a local crowd squeezing in a midday meal on burgers, roasted turkey sandwiches, seared ahi poki, and crispy chicken finger sandwiches (with spicy hoisin sauce). After the lunch crowd disappears, during weekdays, a happy-hour crowd arrives and downs a few brews and pupu (appetizers). Starting at 5pm, families with kids in tow show up for the best curry crusted ahi (over organic greens), grilled fresh catch over soba noodles and stir fried veggies, pan-seared pork chops, filet mignon and shrimp (with crumbled blue cheese), and beef short ribs (with a ko-chu-jang glazed sauce). There are music and dancing on weekends from 8:30pm on.

75-5995 Kuakini Hwy., Kailua-Koha. ☎ **808/327-0209.** Reservations recommended for dinner. Lunch entrees $7–$12; dinner entrees $11–$24; pupu menu $5–$12. Mon–Fri 11am–9pm; Sat 5–9pm.

Habanero's *Value* MEXICAN   Great, fast, Mexican food at budget prices. This small eatery is for people on the run, no leisurely dining here. You order at one counter and pick up at another. Stools and counters are scattered around the room, but people tend to eat and go. Habanero's starts off with breakfast (huevos rancheros to a range of egg dishes from Mexican style to a chorizo-egg burrito) from 9 to 11:30am. The remainder of the day features burritos (the fish with black bean is our favorite), soft and hard tacos (the veggie is surprisingly tasting and filling), nachos, tostadas, quesadillas, enchiladas and daily specials (Friday night is shrimp Vallarta). Bring cash, they don't take cards.

Keauhou Shopping Center, Keauhou. ☎ **808/324-HOTT.** All items under $7.50. No credit cards. Mon–Sat 9am–9pm.

Izakaya Kai ★★ *Value* JAPANESE/SUSHI BAR   Tucked away on a side street, off the hustle and bustle of Alii Drive, is a "hidden" restaurant, Izakaya Kai, serving Japanese cuisine in a relaxing atmosphere with surprisingly inexpensive prices. Izakaya, which means "pub" in Japanese, and "Kai," which translates as "oar," is already well known to local residents, but off the beaten path for visitors. Owners Fusako and Kunihiko Imai already have one of the top Japanese restaurants in the U.S. (selected by the readers of *Zagat Survey*), Syun Izakaya in Hillsboro, Oregon. They brought their talents, their knowledge of food, and their willingness to create a fabulous restaurant to Hawaii. The "pub" is stocked with a wide selection of more than 20 different kinds of sake, the dishes feature top-grade fish, and the prices are unbelievably low. Don't leave without trying their specialty, the Volcano don (fresh tuna artistically arranged over sushi rice).

75-5719 Alii Dr. (restaurant actually is around the corner on Sarona St.), Kailua-Kona. ☎ **808/329-2002.** Sushi under $5; most items $7 and under. AE, DC, DISC, MC, V. Daily 5–11pm.

Lu Lu's AMERICAN   As it often is with joints that are popular, Lu Lu's has fallen prey to the deadly sin of self-importance. Service is brisk and can be downright rude. It is casual, noisy, and corny (black velvet paintings at the entrance!), but it's undeniably popular, with open-air dining, ocean views, and a sports-bar atmosphere. Other elements include capiz-shell lamps, clam-shell sconces, and hula girl replicas. The offerings: appetizers, sandwiches, salads, burgers, fresh fish tacos, and fresh fish and meats in the evening. Okay for certain folks, but not for romantics in search of a quiet, intimate evening.

75–5819 Alii Dr. (in the Coconut Grove Market Place), Kailua-Kona. (C) **808/331-2633.** www.luluskona.com. Reservations not accepted. Main courses $9–$15. DC, DISC, MC, V. Daily 11am–10pm; bar until 2am Fri–Sun, till 1:30am Mon–Thurs.

Ocean View Inn AMERICAN/CHINESE/HAWAIIAN   The Hawaiian food, rare in this town, and the local color are reasons enough to come here. This is a no-non-sense, unpretentious restaurant that's been a Kailua landmark for as long as anyone can remember. Don't expect epicurean fare; concentrate instead on the ocean view, because the Ocean View Inn is as much a Kona fixture as the sunsets that curl around Kailua Pier across the street. Stew and rice, roast pork, kalua pork and cabbage, a vegetarian selection, and local staples, such as shoyu chicken and broiled ahi, appear on a menu with dozens of Chinese dishes. A refreshing change, definitely, from the more touristy waterfront eateries, and especially appealing on Sundays, when old-timers from along the coast appear in their haku leis and muumuu.

75–5683 Alii Dr., Kailua-Kona. (C) **808/329-9998.** Main courses $8–$11. No credit cards. Tues–Sun 6:30am–2:45pm and 5:15–9pm.

Quinn's Almost by the Sea ★★ STEAK/SEAFOOD   Always, dependably good food, especially late at night when every other restaurant on the coast is closed. Quinn's, located at the northern gateway to town, has a nautical/sports bar atmosphere. There's casual alfresco dining on a garden lanai, with an air-conditioned, no-smoking area also available. The menu is surf-and-turf basic: burgers, sandwiches, and a limited dinner menu of fresh fish, filet mignon, and a few shrimp dishes. There are six burger selections, and, when available, fresh ahi or ono sandwiches.

75–5655-A Palani Rd., Kailua-Kona. (C) **808/329-3822.** Main courses $7–$19. MC, V. Daily 11am–11pm.

Rooster's The Restaurant ★ *Finds* CONTINENTAL   Hidden in the back of this hodge-podge shopping enclave is a culinary treat that features live jazz Thursday through Saturday. Barely more than a hole in the wall (a very cute, romantically decorated hole, that is), Rooster's features service inside or out in the courtyard. You won't believe the amount of food they dish up for these wonderfully low prices (plus, for just $4 more, they will add an organic salad to your meal). Whatever fresh fish is being served the night you go, grab it. Other musts are the crab cakes (with sweet blue crab), chicken cordon bleu, baby back ribs (with homemade guava barbecue sauce) and rib-eye steak. Open for lunch with terrific sandwiches (from a cheeseburger for just $7 to a yummy Italian club with ham, turkey, Swiss, pepperoni, salami and provolone). If you are a jazz fan, make reservations for Thursday, Friday or Saturday nights when some of the Big Island's best jazz musicians play from 6 to 9pm.

75-566 Alii Dr., Kailua-Kona. (C) **808/327-9453.** Reservations a must on Jazz nights, Thurs–Sat. Lunch entrees $7–$11; dinner entrees $15–$25. AE, MC, V. Mon–Fri 11am–3pm; daily 5:30–9pm.

Sibu Cafe ★ *Value* INDONESIAN/SOUTHEAST ASIAN   An affordable favorite for many years, Sibu offers curries, homemade condiments, and a very popular, spicy grilled Balinese chicken with peanut sauce. Fresh catch is available daily, and weekday lunch specials are a good value, especially the Kona Combo: spring roll, chicken or beef satay, vegetable stir-fry, and cucumber salad with rice. The vegetarian combo or a small *gado gado* (a large, peanut-sauced Indonesian salad) is recommended. The Indonesian decor, courtyard dining, and excellent *satays* (traditional grilled skewers of vegetables, seafood, and meats) are the Sibu signature. The larger combination plates pamper all palates, while the vegetable curries and stir-fries appeal to vegetarians. Top off your order with the homemade three-jalapeño, red-chile, or spicy coconut condiment (or all three). Wine and beer are available; white sugar and MSG are not.

75–5695 Alii Dr. (in Banyan Court), Kailua-Kona. ⓒ 808/329-1112. Reservations recommended for lunch and dinner. Most items less than $14. MC, V. Lunch Tues–Fri 11:30am–2:30pm, Sat–Sun 12–3pm; dinner Sun–Thurs 4–9pm, Fri–Sat 4:30-9:30pm.

WORTH A SPLURGE

Beach Tree Bar and Grill ★★ CASUAL GOURMET   Here's an example of outstanding cuisine in a perfect setting, without being fancy or fussy. The bar on the sand is a sunset paradise. Diners on a budget might concentrate on the sandwiches, seafood, and grilled items at the casual outdoor restaurant (a few feet from the bar). They're in a class of their own—simple, excellent, prepared with no short cuts and imagination that overflows. The regular menu, the same for lunch and dinner, features vegetable summer rolls (a good bet), grilled fresh fish with melted Gruyère on a toasted Maui onion roll, and a selection of salads, sandwiches, and entrees. The gazpacho soup with cumin yogurt is excellent; entrees include grilled fresh fish, linguine with shrimp and spinach-tomato pesto, and an excellent fresh-tuna sandwich. An added attraction: entertainment from 5 to 8pm nightly.

In the Four Seasons Resort Hualalai, Queen Kaahumanu Hwy., Kaupulehu-Kona. ⓒ 808/325-8000. Reservations recommended for Saturday night buffet. Lunch main courses $10–$19; dinner main courses $23–$37. AE, DC, DISC, MC, V. Daily 11:30am–8:30pm.

Hualalai Club Grille ★★ CONTEMPORARY PACIFIC   This open-air oasis of koa, marble, and island artwork just got better. Chef Alan Wong, who put the Canoe House Restaurant on the map and was one of the founders of Hawaii Regional Cuisine, has taken the helm at this popular golf club restaurant. Wong's distinctive cooking (see "Alan Wong's Restaurant" and "The Pineapple Room at Macy's" in the Oahu chapter) is the star in this already star-studded location (overlooking the golf course and the Pacific) and decor. Lunch features soups (including Wong's famous chilled red-and-yellow tomato soup poured in a yin-yang design), sandwiches (his burger consists of grass-fed Kamuela beef with bacon, cheese, avocado, and salsa), and daily specials (seared peppered ahi over crispy Asian slaw). Dinner entrees include gingercrusted onaga, steamed moi (raised on property at Hualalai Resort), mac-nut–crusted lamb chops, and a host of other mouthwatering offerings. Save room for dessert: chocolate crunch bars, caramel sea salt cheesecake and other tempting delights. The only thing missing is service. I have had two kinds of service here: service with an "attitude" (hard to believe that these members of the waitstaff were working for tips) or very bad service.

In the Hualalai Resort, Queen Kaahumanu Hwy., Kaupulehu-Kona. ⓒ 808/325-8525. www.hualalairesort.com. Reservations recommended. Main courses $10–$20 lunch, $28–$55 dinner. AE, DC, MC, V. Daily 11:30am–2:30pm; dinner 5–9pm.

Huggo's ★ PACIFIC RIM/SEAFOOD   The main Huggo's dining room still hums with diners murmuring dreamily about the view, but it's the thatched-bar fantasy that's *really* on the rocks. **Huggo's on the Rocks** ★, a mound of thatch, rock, and grassy-sandy ground right next to Huggo's, is a sunset lover's nirvana. At sundown it's choked with people either on chaises or at the 50-seat thatched bar, sipping mai tais and noshing on salads, poke, sandwiches, plate lunches, sashimi, and fish and chips. From 6:30 to 11am, this same location turns into the **Java on the Rocks** ★★ espresso bar, which is *not* to be missed—sip Kona coffee, enjoy your eggs, and watch the waves roll onto the shore. Island-style pupus are offered here from 11:30am to 10pm, and from 5:30pm to 1am there's dancing at the water's edge.

At the senior Huggo's, fresh seafood remains the signature, as does the coral-strewn beach with tide pools just beyond the wooden deck. The tables are so close to the water you can see the entire curve of Kailua Bay. Feast on sautéed mahimahi or steamed clams, or seared ahi or imu-style chicken cooked in ti leaves. At lunch, specialties include kalua chicken quesadillas, brick-oven pizzas, and sandwiches ranging from hot turkey to prime rib and fresh fish.

75–5828 Kahakai Rd., Kailua-Kona. © 808/329-1493. www.huggos.com. Reservations requested. Main courses $9–$23 lunch, $18–$46 dinner. AE, DC, DISC, MC, V. Daily 11:30am–2pm and 5:30–10pm.

Kenichi Pacific ✶✶✶ *(Finds)* PACIFIC RIM FUSION/SUSHI BAR Hidden in the Keauhou Shopping Center is this gem of a restaurant, decorated in muted tones and understated furnishings, featuring both Pacific Rim fusion cuisine and a sushi bar. The food is fantastic, the service efficient, and the experience leaves you smiling. The appetizer menu is so tempting, you might just want to graze from one dish to the next of ginger-marinated squid, blackened tuna, Dungeness crab cakes, and fresh lobster summer rolls. Entrees include pan-seared mahimahi with eggplant mousse; hearts of palm and asparagus in a miso beurre blanc sauce; macadamia-crusted lamb accompanied by taro risotto; ono tataki; lemongrass ahi; and bamboo salmon. If you love duck, don't miss Kenichi's Duck Confit which has Chinese five-spice cured duck leg with celeriac puree, ali'i mushrooms, pea tendrils, red pepper coulis and balsamic reduction. Whatever you order, leave room for the warm, flourless molten cake, covered with espresso crème anglaise and served with Kona coffee-chip ice cream.

Keauhou Shopping Center, Keauhou. © 808/322-6400. Reservations recommended for dinner. Entrees $17–$32. AE, DISC, MC, V. Tues–Fri 11:30am–1:30pm; daily 5–9:30pm.

Kona Inn Restaurant ✶ AMERICAN/SEAFOOD Sure, it's touristy, but dining here can be a very pleasant experience if the sun is setting or you've just arrived from the airport and don't want your hotel's offerings. The wide-ranging menu and fresh seafood in the open-air oceanfront setting tell you why you have come to Kailua-Kona. The large, open room and panoramic view of the Kailua shoreline are the most attractive features, especially for sunset cocktails and appetizers. It's a huge menu, so the choices are vast, with some affordable choices that include everything from nachos and chicken Caesar salad to sandwiches, pasta, and stir-fried dishes. The highlight is the fresh fish, served Cajun-style or broiled and basted in lemon butter. Watch for the daily specials on the less-expensive Cafe Grill menu.

75–5744 Alii Dr. (in Kona Inn Shopping Village), Kailua-Kona. © 808/329-4455. Reservations recommended at dinner. Main courses $16–$36; Cafe Grill $7–$13. AE, MC, V. Dinner menu daily 5:30–9pm; Cafe Grill daily 11:30am–9:30pm.

La Bourgogne ✶✶ *(Finds)* CLASSIC FRENCH An intimate spot with 10 tables, La Bourgogne serves classic French fare with simple, skillful elegance. Baked Brie in puff pastry is a taste treat, and the fresh Maine lobster salad, served on a bed of greens with mango slices and a passion-fruit vinaigrette, is a masterstroke. Other offerings: classic onion soup, fresh catch of the day (market price), and *osso buco,* a former special added back on to the menu by popular demand. Also in demand are the New Zealand mussels steamed in apple cider, thyme, shallots, and cognac. The roast duck breast with raspberries and pine nuts is exactly the kind of dish that characterizes La Bourgogne— done to perfection, presented attractively, and with an unbeatable match of flavors and textures. Classically trained chef Ron Gallaher expresses his allegiance to *la cuisine Française* down to the last morsel of flourless chocolate cake and lemon tartlets.

Hwy. 11, 3 miles south of Kailua-Kona. ☎ **808/329-6711.** Reservations recommended. Main courses $25–$32. AE, DC, DISC, MC, V. Tues–Sat 6–10pm.

Pa Leo PACIFIC RIM   Just as we went to press, this new restaurant opened in the location of the former Gallery Restaurant, right on Alii Drive facing the ocean. The location is so good, that they could serve dog food and it still would get business. Fortunately, Pa Leo is dishing up some very good fresh fish (crusted with taro and drizzled with lehua honey-lime tartar sauce), chicken (in a pineapple ginger-apple sauce), and meats (rack of lamb served with ginger cream). According to the menu it "overlooks the pier and Ahuena Heiau (King Kamehameha's temple)," which is true, but it also overlooks the alley where there is a constant stream of what looks like drug deals taking place. The new owners have redone the old second story restaurant into bold colors (one wall red, one wall blue, and so on) and filled it with orchids. Although our service was very slow (after we had to wait 15 min. for our 7:30pm reservation), we attributed this to working out the opening bugs and hope they will hire additional waitstaff. One very pressing problem is that there is virtually no parking. Your options are to park in the pay lot at the King Kamehameha Hotel across the street, to wander the street for the very little parking, or to take your chances and park in the alley where what looked like nefarious activities were taking place.

Alii Dr., Kailua-Kona. ☎ **808/329-5550.** Reservations a must. Entrees $12–$28. AE, MC, V. Daily 5:30–9pm.

O's Bistro 🐟 NOODLES/PASTA   Chef Amy Ferguson-Ota's wildly popular gourmet noodle house Oodles of Noodles has been replaced by O's Bistro, but offers nearly the same menu with a staggering assortment of noodles from far-flung cultures and countries. Diners can tuck into udon, cake noodles, saimin, ramen, spaghetti, orzo, somen, spring rolls, chow fun, linguine, and other noodle wonders. If you're looking for the fresh local-style steamed fish, fish prepared Provençal style, Peking duck in fresh plum sauce, or rib-eye steak (with old fashion mash potatoes), this is your place. The late breakfast specials include hearty egg and fish dishes, a healthy breakfast taco, and French toast with pecans and maple syrup.

75–1027 Henry St. (in Crossroads Shopping Center), Kailua-Kona.☎ **808/329-9222.** Main course $23–$26. AE, DC, DISC, MC, V. Daily 10am–9pm.

THE SOUTH KONA COAST

Aloha Angel Cafe ISLAND CUISINE   The former Aloha Cafe is under new management, but they kept the trademark large servings, heroic burgers and sandwiches, and a home-style menu for vegetarians and carnivores alike. Breakfast and lunch are served on the veranda that wraps around the old Aloha Theatre with sweeping views down from the coffee fields to the shoreline. Dinner is in the tiny dining room (which unfortunately has no view); space is limited so phone ahead to assure that you get a table. The cheaper daytime staples include omelets, burritos, tostadas, quesadillas, and home-baked goods (breakfast is served all day). Most of the produce is organic, and fresh-squeezed orange juice and fresh-fruit smoothies are served daily. Sandwiches, from turkey to tofu-avocado and a wonderful fresh ahi, are heaped with vegetables on tasty whole-wheat buns, still generous after all these years. The dinner entrees cover the basics, from fresh catch to grilled New York steak and Cajun chicken with tropical salsa.

Hwy. 11, Kainaliu. ℂ 808/322-3383. Reservations recommended (dinner only). Breakfast $5.50–$9; dinner main courses $14–$21. AE, MC, V. Mon–Tues 8am–2:30pm; Wed–Sun 8am–2:30pm and 5–9pm.

The Coffee Shack ★★ *Kids* COFFEEHOUSE/DELI   Great food, crisp air, and a sweeping ocean view make The Coffee Shack one of South Kona's great finds. It's an informal place with counter service, pool chairs, and white trellises on the deck framed by ferns, palms, and banana trees. Especially charming is the wooden deck near a towering old tree that droops with the weight of avocados. The fare is equally inviting: French toast made with homemade poi bread; lemon bars and carrot cake; eggs Benedict with a delectable hollandaise. At lunch: a cheerful assortment of imported beers, excellent sandwiches on home-baked breads, and fresh, hearty salads made with organic lettuces. Let the kids order peanut-butter-and-jelly or grilled-cheese sandwiches, while you head for the smoked Alaskan salmon sandwich or the hot, authentic Reuben.

Hwy. 11, 1 mile south of Capt. Cook. ℂ 808/328-9555. Most items less than $7.95; pizzas $9–$13. DISC, MC, V. Daily 7am–4pm.

Keei Cafe *Overrated* MEDITERRANEAN/LATINO/ISLAND   When this bistro cafe opened in a former fish market in Keei, it was fabulous in every respect: delicious food at frugal prices, friendly service and quirky, but cute, decor. The restaurant became so popular that they moved a few years ago to a new location with hardwood floors, first-class artwork, and a view of the coast. They got really big, really fast, and didn't seem to keep up with the rapid growth. The first thing that went was seating people on time. Reservations meant nothing. The last time, we waited more than an hour for a 7:30 reservation. The staff was unapologetic, a shrug and a quick "we're very busy" was mumbled, with the added caveat: "If you don't like it, you can go somewhere else." The next thing that went was the food, once the draw, the food was no longer dependably good. We can no longer recommend this once terrific cafe, not only because of the not-up-to par food and the slow service, but more because of the cavalier attitude: They are making money (right now) and don't really care how they treat their clientele.

By the 113 mile marker on Hwy. 11, in Kalakekua. ℂ 808/322-9992. Main courses $12–$20. No credit cards. Tues–Sat 5:15–9pm.

Manago Hotel Restaurant *Value* AMERICAN   The dining room of the decades-old Manago Hotel is a local legend; greatly loved for its unpretentious, tasty food at family prices. At breakfast, $4.50 buys you eggs, bacon, papaya, rice, and coffee. At lunch or dinner, you can dine handsomely on local favorites: a 12-ounce T-bone, fried ahi, opelu, or, the house specialty, pork chops. Manago T-shirts announce "the best pork chops in town": The restaurant serves nearly 1,500 pounds monthly. When the akule or opelu are running, count on a rush by the regular customers. This place is nothing fancy, and there's a lot of frying going on in the big kitchen, but the local folks would riot if anything were to change after so many years.

In the Manago Hotel, Hwy. 11, Captain Cook. ℂ 808/323-2642. Reservations recommended for dinner. Main courses $8–$14. DISC, MC, V. Tues–Sun 7–9am, 11am–2pm, and 5–7:30pm.

Nasturtium Café ★★ *Finds* HEALTHY GOURMET   This tiny cafe is a true find for those who love healthy gourmet food, with an international flair, at budget prices. Chef Diane Tomac-Campogan is in the kitchen cooking up interesting dishes like Moroccan chicken wrap (range-fed and hormone- and antibiotic-free chicken that is), to-die-for fresh fish burger, a mean Mexican corn soup, and a Korean spinach salad

Kona Coffee Craze!

Coffeehouses are booming on the Big Island. Why not? This is, after all, the home of Kona coffee, and it's a wide-open field for the dozens of vendors competing for your loyalty and dollars.

Most of the farms are concentrated in the North and South Kona districts, where coffee remains a viable industry. Notable among them is the **Kona Blue Sky Coffee Company,** in Holualoa (© 877/322-1700 or 808/322-1700), which handles its own beans exclusively. The Christian Twigg-Smith family and staff grow, hand-pick, sun-dry, roast, grind, and sell their coffee, whole or ground, on a 400-acre estate, at elevations from 1,400 to 3,400 feet. There are only a few retail locations for Kona Blue Sky coffee, and one of them is the farm itself, where visitors are welcome to see the operation from field to final product. You can also find Blue Sky at the cheerful outdoor market, Alii Marketplace Gardens in Kailua-Kona, open Wednesday through Sunday.

Also in Holualoa, 10 minutes above Kailua-Kona, **Holualoa Kona Coffee Company** (© 800/334-0348 or 808/322-9937) purveys organic Kona from its own farm and other growers: unsprayed, hand-picked, sun-dried, and carefully roasted. Not only can you buy premium Kona coffee here, but you can also witness the hulling, sorting, roasting, and packaging of beans on a farm tour, Monday through Friday from 8am to 4pm. Also in this village, the **Holuakoa Cafe,** Highway 180 (© 808/322-2233), is famous for its high-octane espresso, ground from fresh-roasted pure Kona Blue Sky beans.

Some other coffees to watch for: **Bong Brothers** (© 808/328-9289) thrives with its coffees, roadside fruit stand, B&B, and natural-foods deli. Aficionados know that **Langenstein Farms** (© 808/328-8356), a name associated with quality and integrity, distributes excellent Kona coffee and distinctively tasty macadamia nuts in the town of Honaunau. **Rooster Farms,** in Honaunau (© 808/328-9173), enjoys an excellent reputation for the quality of its organic coffee beans. The **Bad Ass Coffee Company** has franchises in Kainaliu, Kawaihae, Honokaa, Keauhou, and Kailua-Kona, all selling its 100% Kona coffee as well as coffees from Molokai, Kauai, and other tropical regions.

In Waimea, the **Waimea Coffee Company,** Parker Square, Highway 19 (© 808/885-4472), a deli/coffeehouse/retail operation, is a whirl of activity. The owners are friendly and their coffee is top-of-the-line: organic pure Kona from Sakamoto Estate, organic Hamakua Coast coffee from Carter's Coffee Farm, pure water-processed decaf—an impressive selection of the island's best estate-grown coffees, plus signature blends and coffee from Molokai Plantation. The homemade quiches, sandwiches, and pastas draw a lively lunchtime crowd. Island-made gourmet foods make great gift baskets, and local artists display their work on the walls.

A good bet in Hilo is **Bears' Coffee,** 106 Keawe St. (© 808/935-0708), the quintessential sidewalk coffeehouse and a Hilo stalwart. Regulars love to start their day here, with coffee and specialties such as souffléed eggs, cooked light and fluffy in the espresso machine and served in a croissant. It's a great lunchtime spot as well.

that will keep you smiling all afternoon. Do not leave this culinary heaven without dessert: ginger macadamia-nut tart (wheat and dairy free), fresh ginger spice cake, homemade fruit crisp ala mode, and the very yummy chocolate mousse (which Chef Diane claims is cholesterol free). They also have takeout, so you can take your mouth-watering treats and go to the beach for a picnic. They recently opened for dinner with a very creative menu. Our only lament is that they are closed on weekends.

79–7491-B Mamalahoa Hwy. (Hwy. 11), Kainaliu ⓒ **808/322-5083.** Reservations recommended. Most lunch items under $12; dinner entrees under $25. MC, V. Mon–Fri 10:30am–7:30pm.

Teshima's JAPANESE/AMERICAN   This is local style all the way. Shizuko Teshima has a strong following among those who have made her miso soup and sukiyaki an integral part of their lives. The early morning crowd starts gathering while it's still dark for omelets or Japanese breakfasts (soup, rice, and fish). As the day progresses, the orders pour in for shrimp tempura and sukiyaki. By dinner, Number 3 teishoku trays—miso soup, sashimi, sukiyaki, shrimp, pickles, and other delights—are streaming out of the kitchen. Other combinations include steak and shrimp tempura; beef teriyaki and shrimp tempura; and the deep-sea trio of shrimp tempura, fried fish, and sashimi.

Hwy. 11, Honalo. ⓒ **808/322-9140.** Reservations recommended for large parties. Complete dinners $16 and under. No credit cards. Daily 6:30am–1:45pm and 5–9pm.

THE KOHALA COAST

Cafe Pesto ⭐⭐ MEDITERRANEAN/ITALIAN   Fans drive long miles for these gourmet pizzas, calzones, and fresh organic greens grown from Kealakekua to Kamuela. The herb-infused Italian pies are adorned with lobster from the aquaculture farms on Keahole Point (south on the coastline), shiitake mushrooms from a few miles *mauka* (inland), and fresh fish, shrimp, and crab. Honey-miso crab cakes, Santa Fe chicken pasta, sweet roasted peppers, and herb-garlic Gorgonzola dressing are other favorites.

In Kawaihae Shopping Center, at Kawaihae Harbor, Pule Hwy. and Kawaihae Rd. ⓒ **808/882-1071.** Main courses $10–$26. AE, DC, DISC, MC, V. Sun–Thurs 11am–9pm; Fri–Sat 11am–10pm.

Merriman's Market Café ⭐ MEDITERRANEAN/DELI   Peter Merriman, who has long reigned as king of Hawaii Regional Cuisine with Merriman's Restaurant in Waimea (p. 273), has opened this tiny "market cafe" featuring cuisines of the Mediterranean, made with fresh local produce, house-made sausages, artisan-style breads, and great cheese and wines. This is a fun place for lunch or a light dinner. The 3,000-square-foot restaurant and deli features full-service indoor and outdoor dining in a casual atmosphere and a gourmet deli with daily specials. Lunch ranges from salads to sandwiches. Dinner has small-plate dishes, small pizzas, and entrees from grilled fish to large salads.

Kings' Shops at Waikoloa Beach Resort, 250 Waikoloa Beach Dr., Waikoloa. ⓒ **808/886-1700.** www.merrimans hawaii.com. Main courses $6.95–$16 lunch, $14–$29 dinner. AE, MC, V. Daily 11am–9:30pm.

WORTH A SPLURGE

Brown's Beach House ⭐⭐ HAWAII REGIONAL   The nearby lagoon takes on the pink-orange glow of sunset, while torches flicker between the coconut trees. With white tablecloths, candles, and seating near the lagoon, this is a spectacular setting, complemented by a menu that keeps getting better by the year. They've redone the kitchen so it is now an open, exhibition kitchen, and there have been many menu changes from *chef de cuisine* Stephen Rouelle, whose Pacific Rim includes unusual dishes like sautéed grilled moi and soft-shell crab, green garlic and herb roasted free-range chicken, Big Island swordfish poached in seasoned olive oil, sizzling ahi tataki with local exotic mushrooms and crab-crusted sautéed opakapaka. Next door is the just-opened **Brown's Deli,** with freshly made breads, pastries and espresso coffees for breakfast, and pizza, salad, paninis, and sandwiches for lunch and dinner. There are even grill tables along the oceanfront where you can grill your own food.

At the Fairmont Orchid, Hawaii, 1 N. Kaniku Dr. (*C*) **808/885-2000.** Reservations recommended for dinner. Main courses $12–$18 lunch; $24–$36 dinner. AE, DC, DISC, MC, V. Daily 6–10pm.

CanoeHouse ★★ HAWAII REGIONAL

The setting is as gorgeous as ever, but it is not the same restaurant as it was when Alan Wong was the chef and the food coming out of the kitchen was nothing short of extraordinary. However, Wong didn't take the ambience with him, and the legendary sunset views remain, along with a koa canoe hanging from the ceiling in the open-air dining room. *Tip:* Ask for a table outside and go at sunset to get the real flavor of this incredible setting. The menu, which changes seasonally, includes great fish items (Shanghai lobster, sautéed moi, steamed opakapaka), meats (honey-roasted rack of lamb, grilled beef tenderloin, and braised short rib of beef), and even vegetarian items (spiced-lacquered tofu). Save room for dessert, especially the dark and sticky chocolate cake or warm coconut-pudding cake with lilikoi sauce or the chocolate fondue.

At Mauna Lani Bay Hotel and Bungalows, 68–1400 Mauna Lani Dr. (*C*) **808/885-6622.** Reservations recommended. Main courses $27–$42. AE, DC, DISC, MC, V. Daily summer 5:30–9pm; winter 6–9:30pm.

Coast Grille ★★ STEAK/SEAFOOD/HAWAII REGIONAL

It's a 3-minute walk from the main lobby to the open-air Grille, but the view along the way is nothing to complain about and will help you work up an appetite. The split-level dining room has banquettes and wicker furniture, open-air seating, and an oyster bar that is famous. The extensive seafood selection includes poke, clams, and fresh oysters from all over the world, as well as fresh seafood from island waters, served in multicultural preparations. Kona lobster-tempura sushi and an excellent clam chowder are among the finer pleasures.

In the Hapuna Beach Prince Hotel, 62–100 Kaunaoa Dr. (*C*) **808/880-1111.** www.hapunabeachprincehotel.com. Reservations recommended. Main courses $28–$34. AE, DISC, MC, V. Daily 6–9:30pm.

Roy's Waikoloa Bar & Grill ★ PACIFIC RIM/EURO-ASIAN

Don't let the strip mall location fool you. Roy's Waikoloa has several distinctive and inviting features: a golf-course view, large windows overlooking part of a 10-acre lake, and the East-West cuisine and upbeat service that are Roy Yamaguchi signatures. This is a clone of his Oahu restaurant, offering dishes we've come to love, like Szechuan baby back ribs, blackened island ahi, and six other types of fresh fish prepared charred, steamed, or seared, and topped with exotic sauces, such as shiitake miso and gingered lime-chile butter. Always in demand are the hibachi-style salmon and, at lunch, the "lumpia basket" of fresh fish and stir-fried vegetables. Yamaguchi's tireless exploration of local ingredients and world traditions produces food that keeps him at Hawaii's culinary cutting edge.

In the Waikoloa Beach Resort, Kings' Shops, 250 Waikoloa Beach Dr. (*C*) **808/886-4321.** Main courses $7.95–$13.75 lunch; $17–$27 dinner. AE, DC, DISC, MC, V. Daily 11:30am–2pm and 5:30–9:30pm.

NORTH KOHALA

Bamboo ★★ *Finds* PACIFIC RIM   Serving fresh fish and Asian specialties in a turn-of-the-20th-century building, Hawaii's self-professed "tropical saloon" is a major attraction on the island's northern coastline. The exotic interior is a nod to nostalgia, with high wicker chairs from Waikiki's historic Moana Hotel, works by local artists, and old Matson liner menus accenting the bamboo-lined walls. The fare, island favorites in sophisticated presentations, is a match for all this style: imu-smoked pork quesadillas, fish prepared several ways, sesame nori-crusted or tequila-lime shrimp, and selections of pork, beef, and chicken. There are even some local faves, such as teriyaki chicken and fried noodles served vegetarian, with chicken, or with shrimp. Produce from nearby gardens and fish fresh off the chef's own hook are among the highlights. At Sunday brunch, diners gather for eggs Bamboo (eggs Benedict with a lilikoi-hollandaise sauce) and the famous passion-fruit margaritas. Hawaiian music wafts through the Bamboo from 7pm to closing on weekends. Next door, on the second floor, is a gallery of furniture and arts and crafts, some very good, and most locally made.

Hwy. 270, Hawi. ② **808/889-5555.** Reservations recommended. Main courses $13–$33 (full- and half-size portions available). MC, V. Tues–Sat 11:30am–2:30pm and 6–9pm; Sun 11:30am–2:30pm (brunch).

Kohala Rainbow Cafe *Value* GOURMET DELI   This place is known for its healthful fare and made-with-care wraps. They serve fresh soups and giant salads and homemade sandwiches and burgers, but most in demand are the wraps—herb-garlic flatbread filled with local organic baby greens and vine-ripened organic tomatoes, cheese, and various fillings. The Kamehameha Wrap features kalua pork, two different cheeses, and a Maui onion dressing. My favorite: the Mexican Veggie Wrap of greens, tomatoes, avocado, roasted peppers, cheese, and refried beans. There are about 30 seats indoors and a few outdoors next to an art gallery with a striking mural.

Hwy. 270, Kapaau, in front of the King Kamehameha Statue. ② **808/889-0099.** Main courses under $10. MC, V. Daily 10am–6pm.

WAIMEA

Aioli's ★ AMERICAN ECLECTIC   Most of the breads for the sandwiches are homemade, the turkey is roasted in Aioli's own kitchen, the prices are reasonable, and on Saturday mornings, the scent of fresh-baked cinnamon rolls wafts through the neighborhood. Specialty salads, homemade cookies and desserts, and daily hot sandwich specials (fresh catch on fresh bread can hardly be beat!) have kept the diners coming. Lunch is informal: order, pay at the counter, and find a table. The evening bistro menu changes every 3 weeks. Recent offerings include herb-crusted Black Angus prime rib with baked potato and vegetables; seared sea scallops with a coconut curry sauce; rack of lamb with cranberry orange sauce; and vegetarian items.

Opelo Plaza, Hwy. 19., Waimea ② **808/885-6325.** Main courses $3.95–$8.95 lunch, $12–$23 dinner. DISC, MC, V. Tues–Thurs 11am–8pm; Fri–Sat 11am–9pm.

Tako Taco Taqueria ★ *Value* HEALTHY MEXICAN   This literally is a tiny "hole-in-the-wall" type of eatery with the most delicious (and healthy) Mexican food you'll eat on the Big Island. There are about eight chairs at the counter inside, or you can opt to sit on the patio outside, but most people do "take-away" and zip off to the beach. The most expensive items are $8.50 (and that includes a full meal of entree, rice, and black or pinto beans), but most items fall in the $6 to $7 range, making this a terrific bargain. Along with daily specials, the fresh-fish burrito (with beans, rice, cheese, guacamole, sour cream, slaw, and salsa) is a hot deal at $8.50. There are plenty of vegetarian selections. If the Mexican chocolate-chip wedding cookies are available, grab one (they're huge, and only $1 each).

65-1271 Kawaihae Rd., Waimea. ✆ **808/887-1717**. All items $8.50 and under. MC, V. Sun–Fri 11am–8pm.

SUPER-CHEAP EATS

The Little Juice Shack JUICE BAR/DELI   When you want a sudden jolt of energy that isn't caffeine, Juice Shack comes to the rescue. There's nothing like fresh-squeezed carrot-apple juice to put a spring in your step, and this is the place to get it. The smoothies and sandwiches here are wholesome and the produce fresh, green, and varied. All juices are made fresh to order: orange, pear, apple, pineapple, carrot, tomato, and many combinations, including vegetable drinks and spirulina powder. Smoothies (Bananarama, Nutty Monkey, Hawaii 5-0) are witty, creamy, and healthful, made with low-fat yogurt mix. Bagels and luscious toppings (pesto, smoked salmon, tapenade); vegetarian chili; and hearty soups, salads, and sandwiches (Thai curry vegetable soup, Greek salad, ahi-tuna sandwich) are guiltless and guileless.

In Parker Ranch Shopping Center, Hwy. 19., Wailea. ✆ **808/885-1686**. Most items less than $6. No credit cards. Mon–Fri 7am–4pm; Sat 9am–4pm.

WORTH A SPLURGE

Daniel Thiebaut Restaurant ✿ FRENCH-ASIAN   It took 2 years to renovate the 100-year-old Chock Inn Store, and, when it finally opened as Daniel Thiebaut's, it did not disappoint the chef's eager and loyal fans. Daniel Thiebaut and his partner, Chuck Clarke, left no stone unturned in their lengthy restoration. Hilo designer Sig Zane has an unmistakable aesthetic presence in everything from upholstery to concept in the seven dining rooms, and the menu and its execution are stellar. The restaurant, with a gaily lit plantation-style veranda, is full of intimate enclaves allowing anything from an intimate tête-à-tête to a celebration for groups of 40 and more. The menu highlights Big Island products (Kamuela Pride beef, Kahua Ranch lettuces, Hirabara Farms field greens, herbs and greens from Adaptations in South Kona) interpreted by the French-trained Thiebaut. Highlights include a greaseless, perfect kalua-duck lumpia; vegetarian spring rolls; wok-fried scallops; and fresh mahimahi in kaffir lime reduction. Waimea strawberries are prominent on the dessert menu, in cheesecake, *crème brulée*, gratin, with ice cream, and fresh—sold outside the restaurant during the day, as in bygone times. However, we lowered the rating on this eatery due to a pattern of disappointments we experienced on our last few visits: the service, once sterling, has become snippy and sometimes rude, and the amount of the food served on your plate has decreased, while the prices have increased.

65–1259 Kawaihae Rd. (the Historic Yellow Building). ✆ **808/887-2200**. www.danielthiebaut.com. Reservations recommended. Main course $7.50–$15 lunch; $22–$35 dinner; $4.50–$8 desserts. AE, DISC, MC, V. Lunch Mon–Sat 11:30am–2pm; dinner daily 5:30–9pm; Sun brunch 10am–1:30pm.

Merriman's ✿✿✿ HAWAII REGIONAL   Merriman's is peerless. Although founder/owner/chef Peter Merriman now commutes between the Big Island and Maui, where he runs the Hula Grill and his new Merriman's Bamboo Bistro, he manages to maintain the sizzle that has made Merriman's a premier Hawaii attraction. Order anything from saimin to poisson cru for lunch; at dinner, choose from the signature wok-charred ahi, kung pao shrimp, lamb from nearby Kahua Ranch, and a noteworthy vegetarian selection. Peter's Caesar with sashimi, Pahoa corn and shrimp fritters, and sautéed, sesame-crusted fresh catch with spicy lilikoi sauce are among our many favorites. An organic spinach salad (like most things on the menu, grown nearby), Lokelani tomatoes, kalua pig quesadillas, and his famous platters of seafood and meats are among the many reasons this is still the best, and busiest, dining spot in Waimea.

In Opelu Plaza, Hwy. 19, Waimea. ✆ **808/885-6822.** Reservations recommended. Main courses $9–$14 lunch, $30–$36 dinner (market price for ranch lamb or ahi). AE, MC, V. Mon–Fri 11:30am–1:30pm; daily 5:30–9pm.

THE HAMAKUA COAST

Cafe Il Mondo ⭐ PIZZA/ESPRESSO BAR   A tiny cafe with a big spirit has taken over the Andrade Building in the heart of Honokaa. Tropical watercolors and local art, the irresistible aromas of garlic sauces and pizzas, and a 1924 koa bar meld gracefully in Sergio and Dena Ramirez's tribute to the Old World. A classical and flamenco guitarist, Sergio occasionally plays solo guitar in his restaurant while contented drinkers tuck into the stone oven–baked pizzas. The Waipio vegetable pizza is a bestseller, but the Sergio—pesto with marinated artichokes and mushrooms—is the one folks remember. Sandwiches come cradled in fresh French, onion, or rosemary buns, all made by local bakeries. There's fresh soup daily, roasted chicken and other specials, and fresh pasta; all greens are fresh, local, and organic.

Mamane St., Honokaa. ✆ **808/775-7711.** Pizzas $10–$19; sandwiches $5.75–$6; pasta $9.95. No credit cards. Tues–Sat 11am–8pm.

Jolene's Kau Kau Korner AMERICAN/LOCAL   It's homey and friendly, with eight tables and windows that look out into a scene much like an old western town, but for the cars. The Hawaiian food has been dropped from the menu, leaving us with saimin, stir-fried tempeh with vegetables, sandwiches (including a good vegetarian tempeh burger), and plate lunches—mahimahi, fried chicken, shrimp, beef stew, and familiar selections of local food. Nothing fancy, although Jolene's has upped the choices (and prices) for dinner, with New York steak, chicken katsu, combination "kau kau plates," and the usual American fare with a local twist.

At Mamane St. and Lehua, Honokaa. ✆ **808/775-9498.** Plate lunches $5.95–$7.95; dinner main courses $7.95–$19. No credit cards. Mon, Wed, Fri 10am–8pm; Tues and Thurs 10am–3pm.

Tex Drive In & Restaurant AMERICAN/LOCAL ETHNIC   When Ada Lamme bought the old Tex Drive In, she made significant changes, such as improving upon an ages-old recipe for Portuguese *malassadas,* a cakelike doughnut without a hole. Tex sells tens of thousands of these sugar-rolled morsels a month, including *malassadas* filled with pineapple-papaya preserves, pepper jelly, or Bavarian cream. The menu has a local flavor and features ethnic specialties: Korean chicken, teriyaki meat, kalua pork with cabbage, and Filipino specials. Hamburgers, on buns baked by Mamane Street Bakery, are a big seller. New on the menu are Tex wraps, served with homemade sweet-potato chips. With its gift shop and visitor center, Tex is a roadside attraction and a local hangout; residents have been gathering there for decades over early morning coffee and breakfast.

Hwy. 19, Honokaa. ✆ **808/775-0598.** Main courses $6.95–$9.95. DC, DISC, MC, V. Daily 6:30am–8:30pm.

SUPER-CHEAP EATS

Mamane Street Bakery BAKERY/CAFE   Honokaa's gourmet bake shop serves espresso, cappuccino, sandwiches, and snacks, including a legendary focaccia. Most sandwich lovers on the island have tasted these breads, as the Mamane Street Bakery also wholesales breads and pastries, including its well-known burger buns, to the Big

Island's most prominent eateries. Portuguese sweet bread and honey-nut muffins are the big sellers in this easygoing, informal coffeehouse with lower-than-coffeehouse prices: Breads sell for $2.25 to $3.25, and most pastries are less than $1.50. The Danishes are to die for. Edible gift products made on the island, such as Lilikoi Gold jams and local coffees, are a recent addition.

Mamane St., Honokaa. © 808/775-9478. Most items less than $3. MC, V. Mon–Fri 6am–noon.

Simply Natural ★ *(Value* HEALTH FOOD/SANDWICH SHOP   Simply Natural is a superb find on Honokaa's main street. We love this charming deli with its friendly staff, wholesome food, and vintage interior. It offers a counter and a few small tables with bright tablecloths and fresh anthuriums. Don't be fooled by the unpretentiousness of the place; we had the best smoked chicken sandwich we've ever tasted here. The owner's mother proudly displayed the gloriously plump whole chicken, smoked by her neighbor in Honokaa, before slicing and serving it on freshly baked onion bread from the Big Island Bakery. The menu is wholesome, with no sacrifice in flavor: sautéed mushroom-onion sandwiches, tempeh burgers, and breakfast delights that include taro-banana pancakes. Even a simple vegetable-mushroom sandwich is special, made to order with grilled mushrooms and onions, luscious fresh tomato, and your choice of squaw, onion, or rosemary bread. Top it off with premium ice cream by Hilo Homemade (another favorite) or a smoothie. The mango-pineapple-banana-strawberry version is sublime.

Mamane St., Honokaa. © 808/775-0119. Deli items $3.50–$7.95. No credit cards. Mon–Sat 8am–3:30pm.

What's Shakin' ★ *(Finds* HEALTH FOOD   Look for the cheerful plantation-style wooden house in yellow and white, with a green roof, 2 miles north of the Hawaii Tropical Botanical Garden. This is where many of the bananas and papayas from Patsy and Tim Withers's 20-acre farm end up: in fresh-fruit smoothies, with names like Papaya Paradise, an ambrosial blend of pineapples, coconuts, papayas, and bananas or one of the other eight different types of smoothies offered. If you're in the mood for something more substantial, try the Blue Hawaii blue-corn tamale with homemade salsa, or the teriyaki-ginger tempeh burger. There are several lunch specials daily, and every plate arrives with fresh fruit and a green salad topped with Patsy's Oriental sesame dressing. You can sit outdoors in the garden, where bunches of bananas hang for the taking, and the ocean view is staggering.

27–999 Old Mamalahoa Hwy. (on the 4-mile scenic drive), Pepeekeo. © 808/964-3080. Most items less than $7.50; smoothies $3.85–$4.45. MC, V. Daily 10am–5pm.

HILO

Cafe Pesto Hilo Bay ★★ PIZZA/PACIFIC RIM   The Italian brick oven burns many bushels of ohia and kiawe wood to turn out its toothsome pizzas, topped with fresh organic herbs and island-grown produce. The high-ceilinged 1912 room, with windows looking out over Hilo's bay front, is filled with seductive aromas. It's difficult to resist the wild mushroom and artichoke pizza or the chipotle and tomato–drenched Southwestern. But go with the Four Seasons—dripping with prosciutto, bell peppers, and mushrooms—it won't disappoint. Other personal favorites are the Milolii, a crab-shrimp-mushroom sandwich with basil pesto; the chile-grilled shrimp pizza; and the flash-seared poke salad on a bed of spinach. There are many raves on this tried-and-true menu.

In the S. Hata Building, 308 Kamehameha Ave., Hilo © 808/969-6640. Pizzas $8–$18. AE, DC, DISC, MC, V. Mon–Thurs 11am–9pm; Fri–Sat 11am–10pm.

Hilo Bay Café ★★ *(Finds)* PACIFIC RIM   Foodie alert: In the midst of a suburban shopping mall is this upscale, elegant eatery, like something out of SoHo. It was created by the people from the Island Naturals Market and Deli, located on the other side of the shopping center. When you enter, the cascade of orchids sitting on the marble bar is the first thing you see. Mellow jazz wafts from speakers and plush chairs at low tables fill out the room. The creative menu ranges from house-made ravioli (stuffed with artichoke hearts, roasted garlic and cream cheese) to potato-crusted fresh catch to grilled pork loin with bordelaise sauce. Lunch features salads (such as seared ahi Caesar), sandwiches (grilled free-range chicken breast), and entrees (flaky-crust vegetarian pot pie, slow-cooked pork BBQ ribs, or crispy spanakopita). There's also a terrific wine list and great martinis. Don't miss eating here.

Waiakea Center, 315 Makaala St., Hilo. ⓒ **808/935-4939.** Reservations recommended for dinner. Lunch $6–$15. Dinner entrees $8–$24. AE, DC, DISC, MC, V. Mon–Sat 11am–9:30pm; Sun 5-9pm.

Miyo's ★ JAPANESE   Often cited by local publications as the island's "best Japanese restaurant," Miyo's offers home-cooked, healthy food, served in an open-air room on Wailoa Pond, where an idyll of curving footpaths and greenery fills the horizon. Sliding shoji doors bordering the dining area are left open so you can take in the view and gaze at Mauna Kea on a clear day. Although sesame chicken (deep-fried and boneless with a spine-tingling sesame sauce) is a bestseller, the entire menu is appealing. For vegetarians, there are constantly changing specials such as vegetable tempura, vegetarian *shabu-shabu* (cooked in a chafing dish at your table, then dipped in a special sauce), and noodle and seaweed dishes. Other choices include mouthwatering sashimi, beef teriyaki, fried oysters, tempura, ahi *donburi* (seasoned and steamed in a bowl of rice), sukiyaki, and generous combination dinners. All orders are served with rice, soup, and pickled vegetables. The miso soup is a wonder, and the ahi tempura plate is one of Hilo's stellar buys. Special diets (low-sodium, sugarless) are cheerfully accommodated, and no MSG is used.

In Waiakea Villas, 400 Hualani St., Hilo. ⓒ **808/935-2273.** Main courses $6–$10 lunch, $9–$11 lunch combinations; $6–$11 dinner, $10–$14 dinner combinations. MC, V. Mon–Sat 11am–2pm and 5:30–8:30pm.

Naung Mai ★ *(Value)* THAI   This quintessential hole-in-the-wall has gained an extra room, but even with 26 seats, it fills up quickly. In a short time, Naung Mai has gained the respect of Hilo residents for its curries and pad Thai noodles and its use of fresh local ingredients. The flavors are assertive, the produce comes straight from the Hilo Farmers' Market, and the prices are good. The four curries—green, red, yellow, and Mussaman (Thai Muslim)—go with the jasmine, brown, white, and sticky rice. The pad Thai rice noodles, served with tofu and fresh vegetables, come with a choice of chicken, pork, or shrimp, and are sprinkled with fresh peanuts. You can order your curry Thai-spicy (incendiary) or American-spicy (moderately hot), but even mild, the flavors are outstanding. Known for her magic with spices, owner-chef Alisa Rung Khongnok makes outstanding spring rolls and a Tom Yum spicy soup that is legendary. Lunch specials are a steal. Naung Mai is obscured behind the Garden Exchange, so it may take some looking. BYOB.

86 Kilauea Ave., Hilo. ⓒ **808/934-7540.** Reservations recommended. Main dishes $10–$14. MC, V. Mon–Fri 11am–2pm; Mon–Thurs 5–8:30pm; Fri–Sat 5–9pm.

Nihon Restaurant & Cultural Center ★ JAPANESE   The room offers a beautiful view of Hilo Bay on one side and the soothing green sprawl of Liliuokalani Gardens on the other. This is a magnificent part of Hilo that's often overlooked because of its location away from the central business district. The reasonably-priced menu features steak-and-seafood combination dinners and selections from the sushi bar, including the innovative poke and lomi salmon hand rolls. The "Businessman's Lunch," a terrific deal, comes with sushi, potato salad, soup, vegetables, and two choices from the following: butterfish, shrimp tempura, sashimi, chicken, and other morsels. This isn't inexpensive dining, but the value is sky-high, with a presentation that matches the serenity of the room and its stunning view of the bay.

Overlooking Liliuokalani Gardens and Hilo Bay, 123 Lihiwai St., Hilo. 🕐 808/969-1133. Reservations recommended. Main courses $9–$20; combination dinner $19. AE, DC, DISC, MC, V. Mon–Sat 11am–1:30pm and 5–8pm.

Ocean Sushi Deli 🌸 SUSHI   Now that sister restaurant Tsunami (see below) has opened across the street, the lines aren't so long at Ocean Sushi Deli, Hilo's nexus of affordable sushi. This tiny take-out sushi shop, Hilo's spot for poetic-license sushi at friendly prices, is very popular. Local-style specials stretch purist boundaries but are so much fun: lomi salmon, oyster nigiri, opihi nigiri, unagi avocado hand roll, ahi poke roll, and special new rolls that use thin sheets of tofu skins and cooked egg. For traditionalists, there are ample shrimp, salmon, hamachi, clam, and other sushi delights—a long menu of them, including handy ready-to-cook sukiyaki and *shabu-shabu* sets.

239 Keawe St., Hilo. 🕐 **808/961-6625.** Sushi boxes $4–$23; sushi family platters $20–$50. MC, V. Mon–Sat 10am–2pm and 4:30–9pm.

Queen's Court Restaurant AMERICAN/BUFFET   Many of those with a "not me!" attitude toward buffets have been disarmed by the Hilo Hawaiian's generous and well-rounded offerings at budget-friendly prices. A la carte menu items are offered Monday through Thursday, but the Hawaiian, seafood, and Dungeness crab and prime rib buffets throughout the week (particularly the seafood buffet) cover the bases and draw throngs of local families. Hawaiian food lovers also come for the Wednesday and Friday Hawaiian lunch buffet.

In the Hilo Hawaiian Hotel, 71 Banyan Dr., Hilo. 🕐 **808/935-9361.** Reservations recommended. Mon–Thurs prime rib/crab buffet $25; Fri Hawaiian lunch buffet $14; Fri–Sun seafood buffet $28. AE, DC, DISC, MC, V. Mon–Sat 6:30am–9:15am and 11:15am–1:15pm; Sun 6:30am–9:15am and 10:30am–1:30pm (brunch); daily 5:30–9pm.

Restaurant Miwa 🌸 JAPANESE   Duck around a corner of the shopping center and discover sensational seafood in this quintessential neighborhood sushi bar. This self-contained slice of Japan is a pleasant surprise in an otherwise unremarkable mall. *Shabu shabu* (you cook your own ingredients in a heavy pot), tempura, fresh catch, and a full sushi selection are among the offerings. The top-of-the-line dinner, the steak-and-lobster combination, is a splurge you can enjoy without dressing up. Some items, such as the fresh catch, may be ordered American style. The *haupia* (coconut pudding) cream-cheese pie is a Miwa signature, but is not offered daily; blueberry cream-cheese pie is the alternative.

In the Hilo Shopping Center, 1261 Kilauea Ave., Hilo. 🕐 **808/961-4454.** Reservations recommended. Main courses $9–$37 (most $10–$15). AE, DC, DISC, MC, V. Mon–Sat 11am–2pm and 5–10pm; Sun 5–9pm.

Royal Siam Thai Restaurant 🌸 THAI   A popular neighborhood restaurant, the Royal Siam serves consistently good Thai curries in a simple room just off the sidewalk. Fresh herbs and vegetables from the owner's gardens add an extra zip to the platters of noodles, soups, curries, and specialties that pour out of the kitchen in clouds of spicy fragrance. The Buddha Rama, a wonderful concoction of spinach, chicken, and peanut sauce, is a scene-stealer and a personal favorite. The Thai garlic chicken, in sweet basil with garlic and coconut milk, is equally superb.

70 Mamo St., Hilo. © **808/961-6100.** Main courses $9–$13. AE, DC, DISC, MC, V. Mon–Sat 11am–2pm; daily 5–9pm.

Seaside Restaurant ★★ STEAK/SEAFOOD   This is a casual local favorite; not fancy, but quite an experience—a Hilo signature with a character all its own. How fresh are the trout, catfish, mullet, golden perch, and *aholehole,* the silvery mountain bass, devoured passionately by island fish lovers? Fished out of the pond shortly before you arrive, that's how fresh. The restaurant has large windows overlooking the glassy ponds that spawned your dinner, so you can't be sentimental. Colin Nakagawa and his family raise the fish and cook them in two unadorned styles: fried, or steamed in ti leaves with lemon juice and onions. Daily specials include steamed opakapaka, onaga, or parrot fish; steak and lobster; *paniolo*-style prime rib; salmon encrusted with a nori-wasabi sprinkle; New York steak; and shrimp. *You must call ahead* so your order can be fished from the ponds and whisked from kitchen to table. The outdoor tables are fabulous at dusk, when the light reflects on the ponds with an otherworldly glow.

1790 Kalanianaole Ave., Hilo. © **808/935-8825.** Reservations recommended. Main courses $11–$28. AE, DC, MC, V. Tues–Thurs and Sun 5–8:30pm; Fri–Sat 5–9pm.

Tsunami Grill & Tempura ★ *Value* JAPANESE/AMERICAN   Like its sister restaurant across the street, Ocean Sushi Deli, Tsunami proves that you can dine well in Hilo without breaking the bank. You'll discover here what local residents love to eat: cheap, tasty appetizers, such as gyoza and steamed clams, for under $5; complete dinners of ahi tempura, chicken yakitori, mahimahi, or beef teriyaki, accompanied by rice, miso soup, and salad—for an astonishing $6.50; *bentos* (lavish assortments of sushi, tempura, salmon, noodles, tofu, and other treats) for $8.45; *donburi* (meats and fish steamed atop rice in a bowl) for under $7; and Japanese curries and tempura for just $4.95 and up. What a find! If you want to get fancier, there are stuffed seafood dinners and New York steak. The lunch and dinner buffets are a top value, and the Sunday seafood buffet includes sushi from Ocean Sushi Deli.

250 Keawe St., Hilo. © **808/961-6789.** Main courses $7–$13. AE, DC, DISC, MC, V. Mon–Sat 10am–2pm and 5–9pm; Sun 5–8pm.

SUPER-CHEAP EATS
Ken's House of Pancakes AMERICAN/LOCAL   The only 24-hour coffee shop in Hilo, Ken's fulfills basic dining needs simply and efficiently, with a good dose of local color. Lighter servings and more health-conscious meals and salads have been added to the menu, a clever antidote to the more than dozen pies available. Omelets, pancakes, French toast made with Portuguese sweet bread, saimin, sandwiches, soup—what they call a "poi dog menu"—stream out of the busy kitchen. Other affordable selections include fried chicken, steak, prime rib, and grilled fish. Wednesday is prime rib night, and Sunday is the "All-You-Can-Eat Spaghetti Night." Very local, very Hilo.

1730 Kamehameha Ave., Hilo. © **808/935-8711.** Most items less than $8. AE, DC, DISC, MC, V. Daily 24 hr.

Kuhio Grille AMERICAN/HAWAIIAN   The "home of the 1-pound laulau" is quite the local hangout, a coffee/saimin shop with a few tables outdoors and a bustling business indoors. Taro and taro leaves from Waipio Valley are featured in the popular Hawaiian plate, but there are other local specialties: saimin, miso-saimin, taro-corned-beef hash, chicken yakitori, burgers, fried rice (famous!), and eclectic selections such as nacho salad and spaghetti. The famous "Kanak Atak" is a 1-pound lau, kalua pig, lomi salmon, pickled onions, haupia, rice, and poi, for $12. Regulars make a beeline for the counter, where desserts (such as the superb chocolate cake with custard filling) are ordered apace before they run out.

In Prince Kuhio Plaza., Hilo. © **808/959-2336**. Main courses $7–$20. AE, DISC, MC, V. Sun–Thurs 6am–10pm; Fri–Sat 6am–midnight.

Nori's Saimin & Snacks ✿ *Finds* SAIMIN/NOODLE SHOP   Nori's requires some looking, but it's worth it. Unmarked and not visible from the street, it's located across from the Hilo Lanes bowling alley, down a short driveway into an obscure parking lot. You'll wonder what you're doing here, but stroll into the tiny noodle house with the neon sign of chopsticks and a bowl, grab a plywood booth or Formica table, and prepare to enjoy the best saimin on the island. Saimin comes fried or in a savory homemade broth—the key to its success—with various embellishments, from seaweed to wonton dumplings. Ramen, soba, udon, and *mundoo* (a Korean noodle soup) are among the 16 varieties of noodle soups. Barbecued chicken or beef sticks are part of the saimin ritual, smoky and marvelous. Cold noodles, plate lunches (teriyaki beef, ahi, Korean short ribs), and sandwiches give diners ample choices from morning to late night, but noodles are the star. The "big plate" dinners feature ahi, barbecue beef, fried noodles, kal bi ribs, and salad—not for junior appetites. The desserts at Nori's are also legendary, with its signature pies—haupia, sweet potato—flying out the door almost as fast as the famous chocolate mochi cookies and cakes.

688 Kinoole St., Hilo. © **808/935-9133**. Most items less than $7.95; "big plate" dinner for 2 $18. MC, V. Mon 10:30am–3pm; Tues–Thurs 10:30am–3pm and 4pm–midnight; Fri–Sat 4pm–1am; Sun 10:30am–9:30pm.

WORTH A SPLURGE

Harrington's ✿ SEAFOOD/STEAK   This is arguably the prettiest location in Hilo, on a clear rocky pool teeming with koi (carp) at Reeds Bay, close to the waterfront but not on it. The house specialty, thinly sliced Slavic steak swimming in butter and garlic, is part of the old-fashioned steak-and-seafood formula that makes the Harrington's experience a predictable one. But the Caesar salad is zesty and noteworthy, and for those oblivious to calories, the escargots—baked en casserole on a bed of spinach and topped with lightly browned cheeses—are a rewarding choice. The meunière-style fresh catch, sautéed in white wine and topped with a lightly browned lemon-butter sauce, is also popular. The strongest feature of Harrington's is the tranquil beauty of Reeds Pond (also known as Ice Pond), one of Hilo's visual wonders. With the open-air restaurant perched on the pond's shores, the ambience is sublime.

135 Kalanianaole Ave., Hilo. © **808/961-4966**. Reservations recommended. Main courses $8–$15 lunch; $16–market price dinner. MC, V. Daily 11am–3pm; Mon–Sat 5:30–9:30pm; Sun 5:30–9pm.

Pescatore ✿ SOUTHERN ITALIAN   In a town of ethnic eateries and casual mom-and-pop diners, this is a special-occasion restaurant, dressier and pricier than most of the Hilo choices. It's ornate, especially for Hilo, with gilded frames on antique paintings, chairs of vintage velvet, koa walls, and a tile floor. The fresh catch is offered in several preparations, including reduced-cream and Parmesan or capers and wine. The paper-thin ahi carpaccio is garnished with capers, red onion, garlic, lemon, olive oil, and shaved Parmesan—and it's superb. Chicken, veal, and fish Marsala, a rich and garlicky scampi Alfredo, and the *Fra Diavolo* (a spicy seafood marinara) are among the dinner offerings, which come with soup and salad. Lighter fare, such as simple pasta marinara and chicken Parmesan, prevails at lunch.

235 Keawe St., Hilo. ✆ 808/969-9090. Reservations recommended for dinner. Main courses $5–$12 lunch, $16–$29 dinner. AE, DC, DISC, MC, V. Daily 7:30am–2pm and 5–9pm.

Restaurant Kaikodo ✪✪✪ PACIFIC RIM/SUSHI BAR   This is Hilo's best restaurant, period. Owners Howard and Mary Ann Rogers, who are art historians and collectors, bought this 100-year-old Toyama Building (a former Masonic temple and then a bank, which is listed on the National Register of Historic Buildings) and transformed it into a light-filled, elegant restaurant with a 19-foot mahogany bar from England, 100-year-old cut-glass doors from China, a bedchamber from China, and a wine cellar in the former bank's vault. Their East-meets-West cuisine includes coconut- and lentil-crusted baked ono with Hawaiian pumpkin puree; tapioca-crusted mahimahi with Thai eggplant and sweet chili sauce; five-fragrance pork and baby back ribs; or Mahana red ale–braised lamb shank. Lunch is equally as appetizing: house-made pumpkin ravioli, sherry-and-oyster-sauce grilled steak sandwich, even a teriyaki-basted bacon cheeseburger. Who would believe that Hilo could have one of Hawaii's most sophisticated and elegant restaurants?

60 Keawe St., Hilo. ✆ 808/961-2558. www.restaurantkaikodo.com. Reservations a must. Main courses: $8–$12 lunch, $17–$28 dinner. AE, MC, V. Mon–Thurs 11am–2:30pm and 5–9pm; Fri–Sat 11am–2:30pm and 5–9:30pm; Sun 10:30am–2pm and 5–9pm.

VOLCANO VILLAGE & HAWAII VOLCANOES NATIONAL PARK

Lava Rock Café ✪ AMERICAN/LOCAL   Surprise! Volcano Village's newest favorite spot isn't a rocky lava cave, but a cheerful, airy oasis in knotty pine, with tables and booths indoors and semi-outdoors, under a clear corrugated-plastic ceiling. The cross-cultural menu includes everything from chow fun to fajitas. The choices include three-egg omelets and pancakes with wonderful house-made lilikoi butter, teriyaki beef and chicken, serious desserts (lilikoi, mango, or ohelo cheesecake!), fresh catch, T-bone steak, and steak-and-shrimp combos. The lunchtime winners are the "seismic sandwiches" (which the cafe will pack for hikers), chili, quarter-pound burgers, and a host of salads, plate lunches, and "volcanic" heavies, such as Southern-fried chicken and grilled meats.

Hwy. 11 (Volcano Village exit, next to Kilauea Kreations), Volcano. ✆ 808/967-8526. Main courses $4.50–$7 lunch; $7–$18 dinner. MC, V. Sun 7:30am–4pm; Mon 7:30am–5pm; Tues–Sat 7:30am–9pm.

Thai Thai Restaurant THAI   Volcano's first Thai restaurant adds warming curries to the chill of upcountry life. It's a welcome touch: spicy curries and rich satays, intense garlic flavors and coconut-rich soups, noodles and rice, and sweet-and-sour stir-fries of fish, vegetables, beef, cashew chicken, and garlic shrimp. A big hit is the green papaya salad, made with tomatoes, crunchy green beans, green onions, and a heap of raw and roasted peanuts—heat and texture and a full symphony of color, aroma, and flavor. There are five types of curries, each with its own array of choices and each quite rich with coconut milk and spices.

19-4084 Old Volcano Rd., Volcano. ✆ 808/967-7969. Main courses $9–$15. AE, DISC, MC, V. Daily 5–9pm.

Volcano Golf & Country Club AMERICAN/LOCAL   One of the first two eateries in the area, this golf-course clubhouse has kept its niche as a low-key purveyor of local favorites. The food ranges from okay to good, while the room—looking out over a fairway—is cordial. It's not as clichéd as it sounds, especially when the mists are rolling in and the greens and grays assume an eye-popping intensity; we've even seen nene geese from our table. In the typically cool Volcano air, local favorites, such as chili, saimin, and Hawaiian stew with rice, become especially comforting. Also featured are prime rib, on special occasions, teriyaki beef or chicken, stir-fry, and corned beef and cabbage (also on occasion).

Hwy. 11 (at mile marker 30), Volcano. ℭ **808/967-8228.** Reservations recommended for large groups. Breakfast items under $6.50; lunch items under $9.75. AE, DC, DISC, MC, V. Mon–Fri 8am–4pm; Sat–Sun 7am–5pm.

WORTH A SPLURGE

Kiawe Kitchen PIZZA/MEDITERANEAN   Although it has a somewhat limited menu, this small eatery offers a great place to stop for hot soup or fresh salad after viewing the volcano. The pizza is excellent (all fresh ingredients) but pricey; I'd recommend the insalada caprese and a bowl of soup for lunch. Dinners include lamb (both rack and shank), pasta dishes, a vegetarian item, and usually beef. The menu changes daily (whatever they can get fresh that day). There's an interesting beer list (all from Hawaii) and yummy espresso drinks (including Kona coffees). You can eat on the lanai or inside the restaurant.

19–4005 Haunani Rd., Volcano. ℭ **808/967-7711.** Main courses $8.50–$13 lunch, $16–$20 dinner. MC. V. Daily noon–2:30pm and 5:30–9:30pm.

Kilauea Lodge & Restaurant ✦ CONTINENTAL   Diners travel long distances to drive through the lava-rock pillars lined with hydrangeas and escape from the crisp upland air into the warmth of the high-ceilinged lodge. The decor is a cross between chalet-cozy and volcano-rugged; the sofa in front of the 1938 fireplace is especially inviting when a fire is roaring. The European cooking is a fine culinary act on the big volcano. Favorites: the fresh catch, hasenpfeffer, potato-leek soup (all flavor and no cream), and Alsatian soup. All dinners come with soup, a loaf of freshly baked bread, and salad.

Hwy. 11 (Volcano Village exit), Volcano. ℭ **808/967-7366.** Reservations recommended. Main courses $19–$38. MC, V. Daily 5:30–9pm.

NAALEHU/SOUTH POINT

Shaka Restaurant AMERICAN/LOCAL   You can't miss the Shaka sign from the highway. This welcome addition to the very slim Naalehu restaurant scene has white tile floors, long tables, an espresso machine, and a friendly, casual atmosphere (including a new "garden room" for smokers). The serviceable menu of plate lunches and American fare will seem like foie gras on the long drive through the Ka'u desert. The servings are humongous, especially the Mauna Loa–sized burrito, brimming with cheese, beans, olives, onions, and zucchini—highly recommended if you have a hefty appetite. Locals come here for the plate lunches, sandwiches (the shaka burger is very popular), and honey-dipped fried chicken; and at dinner, for the fresh catch—grilled, deep-fried, or prepared in a special potato crust with a ginger-mango sauce.

Hwy. 11. Naalehu. ℭ **808/929-7404.** Reservations recommended for dinner. Main courses $6.50–$8.95 lunch; $10–$17 dinner. MC, V. Daily 10am–9pm.

SUPER-CHEAP EATS

Naalehu Fruit Stand AMERICAN/PIZZA   This little roadside attraction is a bright spot on the long southern route; the liveliest nook in pleasingly sleepy Naalehu. You can buy sandwiches, pizza, fresh salads, and baked goods—the best-loved items here—and then nosh away at one of the few tables on the front porch while panting canines stare longingly from truck beds. Big Island macadamia nuts, hefty quiches, fresh local papayas, and Ka'u navel oranges are usually good here, and the pastries are famous, especially the macadamia-nut pie made with whole nuts and the new mac-nut bars and passion fruit-cream cheese bars.

Hwy. 11, Naalehu. ⊘ **808/929-9009.** Most items less than $10. MC, V. Mon–Thurs 9am–6pm; Fri–Sat 9am–7pm; Sun 9am–5pm.

5 Beaches

Too young geologically to have many great beaches, the Big Island instead has an odd collection of unusual ones: brand-new black-sand beaches, green-sand beaches, salt-and-pepper beaches, and even a rare white-sand beach.

THE KONA COAST
KAHALUU BEACH PARK 𝒜𝒜
This is the most popular beach on the Kona Coast; these reef-protected lagoons attract a thousand people a day almost year-round. Kahaluu is the best all-around beach on Alii Drive, with coconut trees lining a narrow salt-and-pepper–sand shore that gently slopes to turquoise pools. The schools of brilliantly colored tropical fish that weave in and out of the well-established reef make this a great place to snorkel. It's also an ideal spot for children and beginning snorkelers to get their fins wet; the water is so shallow that you can literally stand up if you feel uncomfortable. Be careful in winter, though: The placid waters become turbulent, and there's a rip current when high surf rolls in; look for the lifeguard warnings.

Kahaluu isn't the biggest beach on the island, but it's one of the best equipped, with off-road parking, beach-gear rentals, a covered pavilion, and a food concession. It gets crowded, so come early to stake out a beach blanket–sized spot.

KEKAHA KAI STATE PARK (KONA COAST STATE PARK) 𝒜
You'll glimpse this beach as your plane makes its final approach to Kona Airport. It's about 2 miles north of the airport on Queen Kaahumanu Highway; turn left at a sign pointing improbably down a bumpy road. You won't need a four-wheel-drive vehicle to make it down here—just drive slowly and watch out for potholes. What you'll find at the end is 5 miles of shoreline with a half-dozen long, curving beaches and a big cove on Mahaiula Bay, as well as archaeological and historical sites. The series of well-protected coves is excellent for swimming, and there's great snorkeling and diving offshore; the big winter waves attract surfers.

Facilities include restrooms, picnic tables, and barbecue pits; you'll have to bring your own drinking water. Since it's a state park, the beach is open daily from 8am to 8pm (the closing is strictly enforced, and there's no overnight camping).

WHITE SANDS BEACH 𝒜
As you cruise Alii Drive, blink and you'll miss White Sands Beach. This small, white-sand, pocket beach about 4½ miles south of Kailua-Kona—very unusual on this lava-rock coast—is sometimes called Disappearing Beach because it does just that, especially at high tide or during storms. It vanished completely when Hurricane Iniki hit in 1991, but it's now back in place. (At least it was the last time we looked.) On calm days, the water is perfect for swimming and snorkeling. Locals use the elementary waves to teach their children how to surf and boogie board. In winter, the waves

swell to expert levels, attracting both surfers and spectators. Facilities include rest-rooms, showers, and a small parking lot; lifeguards are on duty.

THE KOHALA COAST
HAPUNA BEACH ★★★

Just off Queen Kaahumanu Highway, south of the Hapuna Beach Prince Hotel, lies this crescent of gold sand—big, wide, and a half-mile long. In summer, when the beach is widest, the ocean calmest, and the crowds biggest, this is the island's best beach for swimming, snorkeling, and bodysurfing. But beware Hapuna in winter, when its thundering waves, strong rip currents, and lack of lifeguards can be danger-ous. Facilities include A-frame cabins for camping, pavilions, restrooms, showers, and plenty of parking.

KAUNAOA BEACH (MAUNA KEA BEACH) ★★★

Since 1965, this gold-sand beach at the foot of Mauna Kea Beach Hotel has been the top vacation spot among America's corporate chiefs. Everyone calls it Mauna Kea Beach, but its real name is Hawaiian for "native dodder," a lacy, yellow-orange vine that once thrived on the shore. A coconut grove sweeps around this golden crescent, where the water is calm and protected by two black-lava points. The sandy bottom slopes gently into the bay, which often fills with not only schools of tropical fish but also green sea turtles and manta rays, especially at night, when the hotel lights flood the shore. Swimming is excellent year-round, except in rare winter storms. Snorkelers prefer the rocky points, where fish thrive in the surge. Facilities include restrooms, showers, and ample parking, but there's no lifeguard.

ANAEHOOMALU BAY (A-BAY) ★★

The Big Island makes up for its dearth of beaches with a few spectacular ones, like Anaehoomalu, or A-Bay, as the locals call it. This popular, peppered, gold-sand beach, fringed by a grove of palms and backed by royal fish ponds still full of mul-let, is one of Hawaii's most beautiful. It fronts the Outrigger Waikoloa Beach Resort and is enjoyed by guests and locals alike (it's a little busier in summer, but doesn't ever get truly crowded). The beach slopes gently from shallow to deep water; swimming, snorkeling, diving, kayaking, and windsurfing are all excellent here. Equipment rental and snorkeling, scuba, and windsurfing instruction are available at the north end of the beach. At the far edge of the bay is a rare turtle cleaning station, where snorkelers and divers can watch endangered green sea turtles line up, waiting their turn to be cleaned by small fish. Facilities include restrooms, showers, picnic tables, and plenty of parking.

HILO
LELEIWI BEACH PARK ★

Hilo's beaches may be few, but Leleiwi is one of Hawaii's most beautiful. This unusual cove of palm-fringed black-lava tide pools fed by freshwater springs and rippled by gentle waves is a photographer's delight—and the perfect place to take a plunge. In winter, big waves can splash these ponds, but the shallow pools are generally free of currents and ideal for families with children, especially in the protected inlets at the center of the park. Leleiwi often attracts endangered sea turtles, making this one of Hawaii's most popular snorkeling spots. The beach is 4 miles out of town on Kalani-anaole Avenue. Facilities include restrooms, showers, lifeguards, picnic pavilions, and paved walkways. There's also a marine-life facility here.

Beaches & Outdoor Pursuits on the Big Island

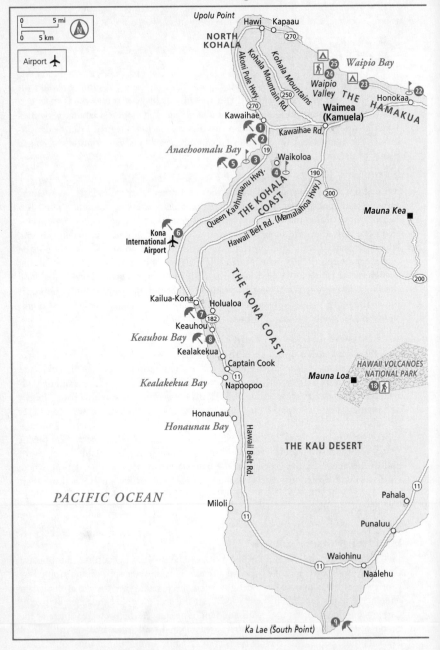

0   5 mi
0   5 km

Airport ✈

Upolu Point
Hawi   Kapaau
270
NORTH
KOHALA
Kohala Mountain Rd.
Akoni Pule Hwy.
Kohala Mountains
250
Waipio Bay
25
24
Waipio
Valley
THE
HAMAKUA
23
Honokaa
22
270
Waimea
(Kamuela)
Kawaihae
1
Kawaihae Rd.
2
Anaehoomalu Bay
19
3
Waikoloa
5
4
190
THE KOHALA COAST
Queen Kaahumanu Hwy.
200
Hawaii Belt Rd. (Mamalahoa Hwy.)
Mauna Kea
Kona
International
Airport
6
200
Kailua-Kona
Holualoa
THE KONA COAST
7
182
Keauhou
Keauhou Bay
8
Kealakekua
Captain Cook
Kealakekua Bay
11
Napoopoo
HAWAII VOLCANOES
NATIONAL PARK
Mauna Loa
18
Honaunau
Honaunau Bay
Hawaii Belt Rd.
THE KAU DESERT
PACIFIC OCEAN
Pahala
11
Miloli
Punaluu
11
Waiohinu
11
Naalehu
Ka Lae (South Point)
9

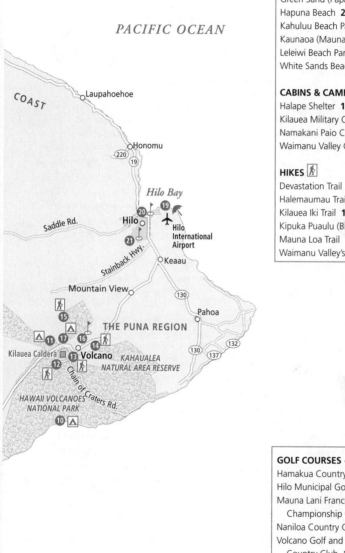

PACIFIC OCEAN

COAST

Laupahoehoe

Honomu
220
19

Hilo Bay

Saddle Rd.
20
19
Hilo
21
Hilo
International
Airport

Stainback Hwy.
Keaau

Mountain View
130

15
Pahoa
THE PUNA REGION
11 17 16
14
Kilauea Caldera 13 Volcano
130 132
KAHAUALEA
12
NATURAL AREA RESERVE
137
Chain of Craters Rd.
HAWAII VOLCANOES
NATIONAL PARK
10

BEACHES

Anaehoomalu Bay (A-Bay) **5**
Green Sand (Papakolea) Beach **9**
Hapuna Beach **2**
Kahuluu Beach Park **8**
Kaunaoa (Mauna Kea) Beach **1**
Leleiwi Beach Park **19**
White Sands Beach **7**

CABINS & CAMPGROUNDS

Halape Shelter **10**
Kilauea Military Camp **17**
Namakani Paio Campground **16**
Waimanu Valley Campground **27**

HIKES

Devastation Trail **18**
Halemaumau Trail **17**
Kilauea Iki Trail **19**
Kipuka Puaulu (Bird Park) Trail **16**
Mauna Loa Trail **15**
Waimanu Valley's Muliwai Trail **26**

GOLF COURSES

Hamakua Country Club **22**
Hilo Municipal Golf Course **21**
Mauna Lani Frances I'i Brown
    Championship Courses **5**
Naniloa Country Club **20**
Volcano Golf and
    Country Club **16**
Waikoloa Beach Course **4**
Waikoloa Kings' Course **4**

Cheap Thrills: What to See & Do for Free (or Almost) on the Big Island

- **Creep Up to the Ooze.** Hawaii Volcanoes National Park is a work in progress thanks to Kilauea Volcano, which has been pouring red-hot lava into the sea and adding land to the already big Big Island every day since it erupted in 1983. If the lava is oozing and bubbling to the surface in the right places, you can walk right up to it for an up-close-and-personal encounter.

- **Go Underwater at Kealakekua Bay.** The islands have lots of extraordinary snorkel and dive sites, but none are so easily accessible or have as much to offer as mile-wide Kealakekua Bay, an uncrowded marine preserve on the south Kona Coast. You can swim with sea turtles, octopuses, and every species of tropical fish that calls Hawaii's waters home. For as little as $4.50, you can rent a mask, fins, and snorkel for an entire day of exploration.

- **Cross the Lava Fields to Kona Coast State Park.** The road across the lava fields of Kona seems too surreal for words: It looks like a thousand bulldozers pulverized the tarmac of 10,000 airport runways. Everyone should drive this bumpy 1.7-mile road to an oasis-like beach at least once, if only to marvel at the incredible power of a single volcano.

- **Gawk at the Day's Catch in Honokohau Harbor.** Every afternoon between 4 and 5pm local fishermen pull into the fuel dock to weigh-in their big game fish. And when we say big, we mean it. We're talking 1,000-pound blue marlins and 200-pound yellowfin tunas, and other Pacific billfish. It doesn't cost a dime to sit on the bleachers here and check out these magnificent creatures.

- **Discover Old Hawaii in Puuhonua O Honaunau National Historic Park.** Protected by a huge rock wall, this sacred Honaunau site was once a refuge for ancient Hawaiian warriors. Today, for just $2, you can walk the consecrated grounds and glimpse a former way of life in a partially restored 16th-century village, complete with thatched huts, canoes, forbidding idols, and a temple that holds the bones of 23 Hawaiian chiefs.

- **Hang Out in Waipio Valley.** Pack a picnic and head for this gorgeously lush valley that time forgot. Delve deep into the jungle on foot, comb the black-sand beach, or just laze the day away by a babbling stream, the tail-end of a 1,000-foot waterfall.

- **Stargaze from Mauna Kea.** A jacket, beach mat, and binoculars are all you need to see the Milky Way from here. Every star and planet shines brightly in this ultra-clean atmosphere, where the visibility is so keen that 11 nations have set up telescopes to probe deep space.

- **Witness the "Green Flash" at Sunset.** The Kona sunset is renowned for the "green flash," which occurs on a clear night just after the sun sinks into the Pacific. It illuminates the entire horizon, but don't blink, because the flash lasts for less than a second. Good places to watch from are along the seawall on Alii Drive in downtown Kailua-Kona, on the sands at Kona Coast State Park, on the side of Mamalahoa Highway in upcountry Holu-aloa, and under the coconut trees at Puuhonua O Honaunau National Historical Park.

- **Watch Whales.** Humpback whales pass through waters off the Kona Coast every winter from December to April—and you don't have to shell out big bucks for a boat ride to see them. Just head to the Keahole National Energy Lab, just south of the Kona airport, and keep your eyes peeled as you walk the shoreline. Since humpbacks are so big—up to 45 feet—you can see them for miles when they come out of the water.

- **Savor a Cup of Kona Coffee.** It's just one of those things you have to do while you're on the Big Island. Most of the coffee craze centers on the north and south Kona districts, but for a truly authentic cup of java, we suggest that you head up-country to **Holuakoa Cafe** (Hwy. 180; © **808/ 322-2233**), in Hulualoa, where they buy green beans from local farmers, roast them, grind them, and then pour you the freshest cup of coffee you've ever had.

- **Hunt for Petroglyphs.** Archaeologists still aren't sure who's responsible for these ancient rock carvings, but the majority of Hawaii's are found in the 233-acre **Puako Petroglyph Archaeological District,** near Mauna Lani Resort. The best time to go looking for canoes, paddlers, turtles, sails, marchers, dancers, and family groups is either early morning or late after-noon, when it's cool. There are more than 3,000 petroglyphs in this area alone—see how many you can spot!

- **Chase Rainbows at Akaka Falls.** When the light is right, a perfect prism is formed and a rainbow leaps out of this spectacular 442-foot waterfall, located about 11 miles north of Hilo. There's no charge to revel in the soothing sounds and mellowing mist of this natural wonder.

- **Taste the Ice Cream at Tropical Dreams.** After a long day of sunbathing and sightseeing, treat your tastebuds to a scoop of the locally produced Tropical Dreams Ice Cream. Go for a refreshing poha or pikake sorbet, or try white chocolate mango or lilikoi ice cream. A variety of places sell this Hawaiian specialty. You'll find it in the Kress Building in Hilo, Sugar & Spice in Waimea, and along Highway 270 in Kapaau.

- **Shop at the Hilo Farmers' Market.** For less than $10, you can buy a pound of *rambutan* (a sweet Indonesian fruit), a bouquet of tropical orchids, and a couple of tasty foot-long Hawaiian laulaus (pork, chicken, or fish steamed in ti leaves). Be sure to arrive early—the mar-ket opens at sunrise, and many of the 60 or so vendors quickly sell out of their island specialties.

SOUTH POINT

GREEN SAND BEACH (PAPAKOLEA BEACH) ⊛

Hawaii's famous green-sand beach is located at the base of Puu o Mahana, an old cinder cone spilling into the sea. The place has its problems: It's difficult to reach; the open bay is often rough; there are no facilities, fresh water, or shade from the relentless sun; and howling winds scour the point. Nevertheless, each year the unusual emerald-green sands attract thousands of oglers, who follow a well-worn four-wheel-drive–only road for 2½ miles to the top of a cliff, which you have to climb down to reach the beach (the south end offers the safest path). The "sand" is actually crushed olivine, a green semiprecious mineral found in eruptive rocks and meteorites. If the surf's up, just check out the beach from the cliff's edge; if the water's calm, it's generally safe to swim and dive.

To get to Green Sand Beach from the boat ramp at South Point, follow the four-wheel-drive trail; even if you have a four-wheel-drive vehicle, you may want to walk, as the trail is very, very bad in parts. Make sure you have appropriate closed-toed footwear: tennis shoes or hiking boots. The trail is relatively flat, but you're usually walking into the wind as you head toward the beach. The beginning of the trail is lava. After the first 10 to 15 minutes of walking, the lava disappears and the trail begins to cross pastureland. After about 30 to 40 minutes more, you'll see an eroded cinder cone by the water; continue to the edge, and there lie the green sands below.

The best way to reach the beach is to go over the edge from the cinder cone. (It looks like walking around the south side of the cone would be easier, but it's not.) From the cinder cone, go over the overhang of the rock, and you'll see a trail.

Going down to the beach is very difficult and treacherous, as you'll be able to see from the top. You'll have to make it over and around big lava boulders, dropping down 4 feet to 5 feet from boulder to boulder in certain spots. And don't forget that you'll have to climb back up. Look before you start; if you have any hesitation, don't go down (you get a pretty good view from the top, anyway).

Warning: When you get to the beach, watch the waves for about 15 minutes and make sure they don't break over the entire beach. If you walk on the beach, always keep one eye on the ocean and stick close to the rock wall. There can be strong rip currents here, and it's imperative to avoid them. Allow a minimum of 2 to 3 hours for this entire excursion.

6 Watersports

The Big Island is big on watersports. Its waters are warm, clear, and usually calm year-round, especially on the leeward Kona-Kohala Coast. Underwater coral formations and dramatic drop-offs attract a kaleidoscope of marine life, making for great snorkeling, diving, and fishing, especially on the Kona side, where the seas are small, the wind is light, and it's summery year-round. Local afternoon breezes make sailing and windsurfing exciting. In winter, you can see humpback whales from shore or boat, and winter waves keep body- and boardsurfers happy. Some of the activities listed below are expensive (boat trips start at about $50 per person), but there are plenty that won't break the bank.

For general advice on watersports and other activities, see "The Active Vacation Planner" in chapter 2.

If you want to rent beach toys, like snorkel gear or boogie boards, the beach concessions at all the big resorts, plus tour desks and dive shops, all offer equipment rentals and sometimes lessons for beginners. Perhaps the cheapest place to get great rental equipment is **Snorkel Bob's,** in the parking lot of Huggo's Restaurant at 75–5831 Kahakai Rd., at Alii Drive, Kailua-Kona (© **808/329-0770;** www.snorkelbob.com), or **Kona Coast Divers,** Honokohau Harbor (© **808/329-8802;** www.konacoast divers.com).

BOATING

For fishing charters, see "Sportfishing: The Hunt for Granders," later in this section.

Body Glove Cruises ⭐ The *Body Glove,* a 55-foot trimaran that carries up to 100 passengers, runs an adventurous sail/snorkel/dive cruise at a reasonable price. You'll be greeted with fresh Kona coffee, fruit, and breakfast pastries; you'll then sail north of Kailua to Pawai Bay, a marine preserve where you can snorkel, scuba dive, swim, or just hang out on the deck for a couple of hours. After a buffet deli lunch spread, you might want to take the plunge off the boat's water slide or diving board before heading back to Kailua Pier. The boat departs daily from the pier at 9am and returns at 1:30pm. The only thing you need to bring is a towel, as snorkeling equipment (and scuba equipment, if you choose to dive) is provided. *Money-saving tip:* The afternoon trip is $35 cheaper for adults.

Kailua Pier. © **800/551-8911** or 808/326-7122. www.bodyglovehawaii.com. Morning cruise $94 adults, $54 children 6–12, free for children 5 and under; afternoon cruise $59 adults, $39 children 6–12, free for children 5 and under; additional $43 for certified scuba divers with own equipment ($53 without own equipment) and $63 additional for introductory scuba; whale-watching with Greenpeace Hawaii (Dec–Apr) $59 adults, $37 children 6–12, free for children 5 and under.

Captain Beans' Cruises Captain Beans runs Kona's most popular dinner sails on a 150-foot catamaran, which can accommodate about 290 passengers. The 2-hour cruise includes dinner, cocktails, dancing, and Hawaiian entertainment.

Kailua Pier. © **800/831-5541** or 808/329-2955. www.robertshawaii.com. $61 per adult and $34 children ages 4–11.

Captain Dan McSweeney's Year-Round Whale-Watching Adventures ⭐⭐⭐ Hawaii's most impressive visitors—45-foot humpback whales—return to the waters off Kona every winter. Captain Dan McSweeney, a whale researcher for more than 25 years, is always here to greet them, as well as other whales that spend the warmer months in Hawaiian waters. Since Captain Dan works daily with the whales, he has no problem finding them. Frequently, he drops an underwater microphone into the water so you can listen to their songs. If the whales aren't singing, he may use his underwater video camera to show you what's going on. In humpback season—roughly December to April—Dan makes two 3½-hour trips a day. From July 1 to December 20, he schedules one morning trip on Tuesday, Thursday, and Saturday to look for pilot, sperm, false killer, melon-headed, pygmy killer, and beaked whales. Captain Dan guarantees a sighting, or he'll take you out again for free. There are no cruises in May and June; that's when he goes whale-watching in Alaska.

Honokohau Harbor. © **888/WHALE6** or 808/322-0028. www.ilovewhales.com. $60 adults, $40 children under 11.

Captain Zodiac If you'd prefer to take a snorkel cruise to Kealakekua Bay in a small boat, go in Captain Zodiac's 16-passenger, 24-foot inflatable rubber life raft. The boat takes you on a wild ride 14 miles down the Kona Coast to Kealakekua, where you'll spend about an hour snorkeling in the bay, and then enjoy snacks and beverages at the picnic snorkel site. Trips are twice daily, from 8am to 12:15pm and from 12:45 to 5pm. *Warning:* Pregnant women and those with bad backs should avoid this often-bumpy ride.

Gentry's Marina, Honokohau Harbor. © **808/329-3199.** www.captainzodiac.com. $82 adults, $67 children 3–12.

Fair Wind Snorkeling and Diving Adventures ★★★ (Kids)   One of the best ways to snorkel Kealakekua Bay, the marine-life preserve that's one of the best snorkel spots in Hawaii, is on Fair Wind's half-day **sail-and-snorkel cruise to Kealakekua.** The company's 60-foot catamaran holds up to 100 passengers. The morning cruise, which leaves from Keauhou Bay at 9am and returns at 1:30pm, includes breakfast, lunch, snorkel gear, and lessons; it goes for $99 for adults and $59 for children ages 4 to 12 ($29 for those 3 and under). The afternoon cruise is a little shorter and a little cheaper: It runs from 2 to 5:30pm and includes snacks, sailing, and snorkeling, at a cost of $65 for adults, $39 for kids 4 to 12 (no charge for toddlers ages 3 and under).

The deluxe afternoon cruise, from 2 to 6pm, with hot lunch of cheeseburgers, garden burgers, hot dogs, pasta salad, fruit, and cookies; the same great snorkeling/sailing trip is $93 adults, $55 children ages 4 to 12 years, and no charge for toddlers ages 3 and under.

78-7130 Kaleiopapa Street, Kailua-Kona. ✆ **800/677-9461** or 808/322-2788. www.fair-wind.com. $65–$99 adults, $39–$59 children (prices vary depending on cruise).

Kamanu Charters ★★ (Value)   This sleek catamaran, 36 feet long and 22 feet wide, provides a laid-back sail/snorkel cruise from Honokohau Harbor to Pawai Bay. The 3½-hour trip includes a tropical lunch (deli sandwiches, chips, fresh island fruit, and beverages), snorkeling gear, and personalized instruction for first-time snorkelers. The *Kamanu* sails Monday through Saturday (weather permitting) at 9am and 1:30pm; it can hold up to 24 people.

Honokohau Harbor. ✆ **800/348-3091** or 808/329-2021. www.kamanu.com. $75 adults, $45 children under 12.

BODYBOARDING (BOOGIE BOARDING) & BODYSURFING

On the Kona side of the island, the best beaches for bodyboarding and bodysurfing are **Hapuna Beach, White Sands Beach,** and **Kekaha Kai State Park.** On the east side, try **Leleiwi Beach.**

No one offers formal boogie-boarding lessons, but the staff at Snorkel Bob's (see above) can give you pointers and tell you where waves appropriate for beginners are rolling in.

KAYAKING

OCEAN KAYAKING   Imagine sitting at sea level, eye-to-eye with a turtle, a dolphin, even a whale—it's possible in an oceangoing kayak. Anyone can kayak: Just get in, find your balance, and paddle. After a few minutes of instruction and a little practice in a calm area (like the lagoon in front of the **King Kamehameha's Kona Beach Hotel**), you'll be ready to explore. Beginners can practice their skills in **Kailua** and **Kealakekua bays;** intermediates might try paddling from **Honokohau Harbor** to **Kekaha Kai Beach Park;** the **Hamakua Coast** is a challenge for experienced kayakers.

You can rent one- and two-person kayaks (and other ocean toys) from **Aloha Kayak** ★★★ (✆ **877/322-1441** or 808/322-2868; www.alohakayak.com) for $20 for a half-day single and $30 double ($25 for a full-day single and $40 for a full-day double). They also have a unique tour from Keauhou Bay and the Captain Cook Monument, with Hawaiian guides showing you their "secret" spots (including sea caves) and snorkeling areas, abundant with fish and turtles. The tours are either 4 hours ($65 adults, $33 for children ages 12 and under) or 2½ hours ($50 adults, $25 children 12 and under) and include all equipment, beverages, snorkeling gear, and snacks.

FRESHWATER FLUMING   Years ago, the best thing to do on a hot summer day was to grab an old inner tube and go "fluming" down the Kohala Sugar Plantation irrigation system. There were only two problems: You had to trespass to get to the elaborate ditch system, and the water was cold. But the opportunity to float past a pristine rainforest, over ravines, and under waterfalls was worth the risk of getting caught (and worth a numb rear end). You no longer have to worry about either problem. **Fluming da Ditch** (② **808/889-6922;** www.kohalakayaks.com) offers perfectly legal access to this North Kohala area, and guided tours in high-tech, double-hulled inflatable kayaks, with knowledgeable guides "talking story" about the history, culture, and legends of the area, followed by snacks. When the operation first started years ago it was fabulous, but on our last trip we were somewhat disappointed. To insure a good trip, tell them you want to be in the kayak with the guide (otherwise, you will miss out on all the history, culture, and so on). Wear a swimsuit or bring a change of clothing, as the kayaks pass under waterfalls and through water pouring in from the intake systems—getting wet is part of the fun, and the whole experience is one you won't forget. The 2½-hour cruises are $99 for adults, $68 for kids 5 to 18. No experience is necessary, but children must be at least 5.

PARASAILING

Get a bird's-eye view of Hawaii's pristine waters with **UFO Parasail** (② **800/FLY-4UFO** or 808/325-5836; www.ufoparasail.net). UFO offers parasail rides daily from 8am to 2pm from Kailua Pier. The cost is $52 for the standard flight of 7 minutes of air time at 400 feet and $62 for a deluxe 10-minute ride at 800 feet. You can go up alone or with a friend; no experience is necessary. *Tip:* Take the early-bird special (when the light is fantastic and the price is right) at 8am for just $47 (for 400 ft.) and $57 (for 800 ft.).

SCUBA DIVING

The Big Island's Leeward Coast offers some of the best diving in the world, as the water is calm (protected by the two 13,000-ft. volcanoes), warm (75–81°F/24–27°C), and clear (visibility is 100-plus-ft. year-round). Want to swim with fast-moving game fish? Try **Ulua Cave** at the north end of the Kohala Coast. There are nearly two dozen dive operators on the west side of the Big Island, plus a couple in Hilo. They offer everything from scuba certification courses to guided boat dives.

"This is not your mother or father's dive shop," said Jeff Kirschner, of the newly opened **BottomTime,** 74–5590 Luhia St. (② **866-GO-DIVEN** or 808/331-1858; www.bottomtimehawaii.com). "This is a dive shop for today's diver," Kirschner said. What sets BottomTime apart is their willingness to take their 34-foot catamaran (complete with hot-water showers, TV, and restrooms) to unusual dive sites, and "not those sites just 2 minutes from the mouth of the harbor." BottomTime also offers free introductory dives in enriched air (Nitrox) for $130 and two-tank dives for $110.

One of Kona's oldest dive shops, **Jack's Diving Locker,** 75–5819 Alii Dr. (② **800/345-4807** or 808/329-7585; www.jacksdivinglocker.com), has recently expanded their former 600-square-foot retail store into an 8,000-square-foot dive center with swimming pool (with underwater viewing windows), retail store, classrooms, full-service rentals, and a full-service sports diving and technical diving facility. They offer two-tank morning or sunset dives off either a 23-foot boat or a 38-foot boat, starting at $95 per person for morning or $115 for sunset dive with your own gear. Jack's also offers shore dives for those who tend to get seasick on a boat; the cost is $55 per person for one tank, including gear. Plus they have an array of programs for kids, the largest in the state, ranges from swimming lessons (from infants 6 months old and up) to bubble-maker parties to kids' sea camps during school vacations.

HOT-LAVA DIVES   Hilo's **Nautilus Dive Center,** 382 Kamehameha Ave., between Open Market and the Shell Gas Station (© **808/935-6939;** www.nautilusdivehilo.com), offers a very unusual opportunity for advanced divers: diving where the lava flows into the ocean. For $150 to $200 each, four divers can take two-tank dives where the molten lava pours into the ocean. "Sometimes you can feel the pressure from the sound waves as the lava explodes," owner Bill De Rooy says. "Sometimes you have perfect visibility to the color show of your life." As we went to press, these hot-lava dives were currently on hold (an unstable collapse of a recent lava field sent 20 acres of lava into the ocean; fortunately no one was injured). Call to see if the dives have resumed.

NIGHT DIVING WITH MANTA RAYS 🤿🤿   A little less risky—but still something you'll never forget—is swimming with manta rays on a night dive. These giant, totally harmless creatures, with wingspans that reach up to 14 feet, glide gracefully through the water to feed on plankton. **Kona Coast Divers,** Honokahau Harbor (© **800/KOA-DIVE** or 808/329-8802; www.konacoastdivers.com), offers a "Manta Ray Madness" dive among their menu of custom boat dives, which takes place about 5 minutes north of Honokohau Harbor (just a 20-min. boat ride) at a depth of 30 to 50 feet. Everyone from beginners through experts will love this dive. They do not guarantee that these wild creatures will show up every night, but they do boast more than 90% sightings record. Cost for this one-tank dive is $99. If they are booked, try **Sandwich Isle Divers,** 75–5729 Alii Dr., in the back of the Kona Market Place (© **888/743-3483** or 808/329-9188; www.sandwichisledivers.com). They also offer one-tank nighttime manta dives for $75, including equipment ($65 if you have your own gear).

WEEKLONG DIVES   If you're looking for an all-diving vacation, you might think about spending a week on the 80-foot *Kona Aggressor II* 🤿 (© **800/344-5662** or 808/329-8182; www.pac-aggressor.com), a live-aboard dive boat that promises to provide you with unlimited underwater exploration, including day and night dives, along 85 miles of the Big Island's coastline. You may spot harmless 70-foot whale sharks, plus not-so-harmless tiger and hammerhead sharks, as well as dolphins, whales, monk seals, and sea turtles. You'll navigate through caves and lava tubes, glide along huge reefs, and take on the open ocean, too. Ten divers are accommodated in five staterooms. Guided dives are available, but as long as you're certified, just log in with the dive master and you're free to follow the limits of your dive computer. It's $2,195 for 7 days (without gear), which isn't so bad when you consider the excellent accommodations and the all-inclusive meals. Rental gear, from cameras (starting at $100 a week) to dive gear ($120) to computers ($100), is available.

SNORKELING

If you come to Hawaii and don't snorkel, you'll miss half the fun. The year-round calm waters along the Kona and Kohala coasts are home to spectacular marine life. Some of the best snorkeling areas on the Kona-Kohala Coast include **Hapuna Beach Cove,** at the foot of the Hapuna Beach Prince Hotel, a secret little cove where you can snorkel not only with schools of yellow tangs, needlefish, and green sea turtles, but also, once in a while, with somebody rich and famous. But if you've never snorkeled in your life,

Kahaluu Beach Park is the best place to start. Just wade in and look down at the schools of fish in the bay's black-lava tide pools. Another "hidden" snorkeling spot is off the rocks north of the boat launch ramp at **Honaunau Bay.** Other great snorkel sites include **White Sands Beach,** as well as **Kekaha Kai State Park, Hookena, Honaunau, Puako,** and **Spencer** beach parks.

SNORKELING CRUISES TO KEALAKEKUA BAY ★★★   Probably the best snorkeling for all levels can be found in **Kealakekua Bay.** The calm waters of this underwater preserve teem with a wealth of marine life. Coral heads, lava tubes, and underwater caves all provide an excellent habitat for Hawaii's vast array of tropical fish, making mile-wide Kealakekua the Big Island's best accessible spot for snorkeling and diving. Without looking very hard, you can see octopi, free-swimming moray eels, parrot fish, and goat fish; once in a while, a pod of spinner dolphins streaks across the bay.

Kealakekua is reachable only by boat; in addition to **Fair Wind** and **Captain Zodiac** (see "Boating," earlier in this section), check out **Sea Quest Snorkeling and Rafting Adventures** (© **808/329-RAFT;** www.seaquesthawaii.com), which offers unique coastal adventures through sea caves and lava tubes on the Kona Coast, as well as snorkeling plunges into the ocean at the Historic Place of Refuge in Honaunau and at the Captain Cook Monument at Kealakekua. The small size of the rigid-hull, inflatable rafts allows the six-passenger vessels to go where larger boats can't. The 4-hour morning tour is $85 for adults, and $54 for children. During whale season they have a 3-hour whale-watching cruise for $53 for adults and children. They do not allow children under 6 years old, pregnant women, or people with bad backs.

SNUBA

If you're not quite ready to make the commitment to scuba but you want more time underwater than snorkeling allows, **Big Island Snuba** (© **808/326-7446;** www. snubabigisland.com) may be the answer. Just like in scuba, the diver wears a regulator and mask; however, the tank floats on the surface on a raft, and is connected to the diver's regulator by a hose that allows the diver to go 20 to 25 feet down. Snuba can actually be easier than snorkeling, as the water is calmer beneath the surface. With just 15 minutes of instruction, neophytes can be down under. It costs $69 for a 1½-hour dive from the beach, $110 for 1 day aboard a boat, and $135 for two dives; children must be at least 8 years old.

SPORTFISHING: THE HUNT FOR GRANDERS ★★

If you want to catch fish, it doesn't get any better than the Kona Coast, known internationally as the marlin capital of the world. Big-game fish, including gigantic blue marlin and other Pacific billfish, tuna, mahimahi, sailfish, swordfish, ono (also known as wahoo), and giant trevellies (ulua) roam the waters here. When anglers here catch marlin that weigh 1,000 pounds or more, they call them *granders;* there's even a "wall of fame" on Kailua-Kona's Waterfront Row, honoring 40 anglers who've nailed more than 20 tons of fighting fish.

Nearly 100 charter boats, with professional captains and crew, offer fishing charters out of **Keauhou, Kawaihae, Honokohau,** and **Kailua Bay** harbors. If you're not an expert angler, the best way to arrange a charter is through a booking agency like the **Charter Desk at Honokohau Marina** (© **888/KONA-4-US** or 808/329-5735; www.charterdesk.com) or **Charter Services Hawaii** (© **800/567-2650** or 808/334-1881; www.konazone.com). Either one will sort through the more than 40 different types of vessels, fishing specialties, and personalities to match you with the right boat. Prices range from $375 to $850 or so for a full-day exclusive charter (you and up to five of your friends have the entire boat to yourself) and about $225 to $550 for a half-day charter on a six-passenger boat.

Serious sportfishers should call the boats directly. They include **Anxious** (© 808/ 326-1229; www.alohazone.com), **Marlin Magic** (© 808/325-7138), **Ihu Nui** (© 808/325-1513), and the **Sundowner** (© 808/329-7253), which is run by TV personality Captain Norm Isaacs. If you aren't into hooking a 1,000-pound marlin or 200-pound tuna and just want to go out to catch some smaller fish and have fun, we recommend **Reel Action Light Tackle Sportfishing** ☆☆ (© 808/325-6811). Light-tackle anglers and saltwater fly fishermen should contact **Sea Genie II** ☆☆ (© 808/325-5355), which has helped several anglers set world records. All of the above outfitters operate out of Honokohau Harbor.

Most big-game charter boats carry six passengers max, and the boats supply all equipment, bait, tackle, and lures. No license is required. Many captains now tag and release marlins and keep other fish to sell—that's island style. If you want to eat your catch or have your trophy marlin mounted, tell the captain before you go.

SUBMARINE DIVES

This is the stuff movies are made of: venturing 100 feet below the sea in a high-tech, 65-foot submarine. On a 1-hour trip, you'll be able to explore a 25-acre coral reef that's teeming with schools of colorful tropical fish. Look closely, and you may catch glimpses of moray eels—or even a shark—in and around the reef. On selected trips, you'll watch as divers swim among these aquatic creatures, luring them to the view-ports for face-to-face observation. Call **Atlantis Submarines** ☆, 75–5669 Alii Dr. (across the street from Kailua Pier, underneath Flashback's Restaurant), Kailua-Kona (© 800/548-6262; www.goatlantis.com). Trips leave daily between 10am and 3pm. The cost is $78 for adults and $38 for children under 12. *Note:* The ride is safe for everyone, but skip it if you suffer from claustrophobia.

SURFING

Most surfing off the Big Island is for the experienced only. As a general rule, the beaches on the north and west shores of the island get northern swells in winter, while those on the south and east shores get southern swells in summer. Experienced surfers should check out the waves at **Pine Trees** (north of Kailua-Kona), **Lyman's** (off Alii Drive in Kailua-Kona), and **Banyan's** (also off Alii Drive); reliable spots on the east side of the island include **Honolii Point** (outside Hilo), **Hilo Bay Front Park,** and **Keaukaha Beach Park.** But there are a few sites where beginners can catch a wave, too: You might want to try **Kahuluu Beach,** where the waves are manage-able most of the year, other surfers are around to give you pointers, and there's a life-guard on shore.

Ocean Eco Tours (© 808/324-SURF; www.oceanecotours.com), owned and oper-ated by two veteran surfers, is one of the few companies on the Big Island that teaches surfing. Private lessons cost $150 per person (including all equipment) and usually last a minimum of 2 hours; 2- to 3-hour group lessons go for $95 (also including all equip-ment), with a maximum of four students. Both guys love this ancient Hawaiian sport, and their enthusiasm is contagious. The minimum age is 8, and you must be a fairly good swimmer. As we went to press, Hawaii County was in the process of regulating commercial use of the ocean for private operators teaching surfing. Ocean Eco Tours assured us that they have fully cooperated with the county on all levels, and, if permits are given, they should be the first in line to obtain one.

Your only Big Island choice for surfboard rentals is **Pacific Vibrations,** 75–5702 Likana Lane (just off Alii Dr., across from the pier), Kailua-Kona (© **808/329-4140**), where they're $10 for 24 hours.

WINDSURFING

Anaehoomalu Bay (A-Bay), on the Kohala Coast, is one of the best beaches for windsurfing, as there are constant 5- to 25-knot winds blowing toward the beach. If you get into trouble, the wind brings you back to shore, instead of taking you out to sea. **Ocean Sports,** at the Outrigger Waikoloa Beach Hotel (© **808/885-5555**), starts beginners on a land simulator to teach them how to handle the sail and "come about" (turn around and come back). Instruction is $60 an hour; after a half-hour or so of instruction on land, you're ready to hit the water. If you already know how to windsurf, equipment rental is $30 an hour. Advanced windsurfers should head to **Puako** and **Hilo Bay.**

7 Hiking & Camping

Hikers get to see a face of the Big Island that most visitors don't. Both day-hikers and backpackers can step into the heart of a still-active volcano, experience the solitude of the tropical rainforest, and discover remote, hidden beaches.

For information on camping and hiking, contact **Hawaii Volcanoes National Park,** P.O. Box 52, Hawaii National Park, HI 96718 (© 808/985-6000; www.nps.gov/havo); **Puuhonua O Honaunau National Historic Park,** Honaunau, HI 96726 (© 808/ 328-2288; www.nps.gov/puho); the **State Division of Forestry and Wildlife,** P.O. Box 4849, Hilo, HI 96720 (© 808/947-4221; www.hawaii.gov); the **State Division of Parks,** P.O. Box 936, Hilo, HI 96721 (© 808/974-6200; www.hawaii.gov); the **County Department of Parks and Recreation,** 25 Aupuni St., Hilo, HI 96720 (© 808/961-8311; www.hawaii-county.com); or the **Hawaii Sierra Club** (© 808/ 959-0452; www.hi.sierraclub.org). For other sources and general tips on hiking and camping in Hawaii, see "The Active Vacation Planner" in chapter 2.

Camping equipment is *not* available for rent on the Big Island. Plan to bring your own or buy it at **Hilo Surplus Store** (© **808/935-6398**).

GUIDED NIGHT HIKES For an off-the-beaten-track experience, **Arnott's Lodge,** 98 Apapane Rd., Hilo (© **808/969-7097;** www.arnottslodge.com), offers a day-long tour of Hawaii Volcanoes National Park, followed by a night lava hike right up to the fiery flow. The 9½-hour tour leaves the lodge at noon and spends most of the afternoon in the park. The lava hike (a 4-hr. round-trip, somewhat strenuous experience) takes place as the sun is setting, so you can see the glow of the flow both during and after sunset. The cost is $80.

HAWAII VOLCANOES NATIONAL PARK ★★★

This national park is a wilderness wonderland. Miles of trails not only lace the lava, but also cross deserts, rainforests, beaches, and, in winter, snow at 13,650 feet. Trail maps are sold at park headquarters and are highly recommended. Check conditions before you head out. Come prepared for hot sun, cold rain, and hard wind any time of year. Always wear sunscreen and bring plenty of drinking water.

Warning: If you have heart or respiratory problems, or if you're pregnant, don't attempt any hike in the park; the fumes will get to you.

TRAILS IN THE PARK

KILAUEA IKI TRAIL You'll experience the work of the volcano goddess, Pele, firsthand on this hike. The 4-mile trail begins at the visitor center, descends through a forest of ferns into still-fuming Kilauea Iki Crater, and then crosses the crater floor past the vent where a 1959 lava blast shot a fountain of fire 1,900 feet into the air for 36 days. Allow 2 hours for this fair-to-moderate hike.

HALEMAUMAU TRAIL This moderate 3½-mile hike starts at the visitor center, goes down 500 feet to the floor of Kilauea crater, crosses the crater, and ends at Halemaumau Overlook.

DEVASTATION TRAIL Up on the rim of Kilauea Iki Crater, you can see what an erupting volcano did to a once-flourishing ohia forest. The scorched earth, with its ghostly tree skeletons, stands in sharp contrast to the rest of the nearby lush forest that escaped the rain of hot molten lava, cinder, and debris. Everyone can—and should—take this half-mile hike on a paved path across the eerie bed of black cinders. The trail head is on Crater Rim Road at Puu Puai Overlook.

KIPUKA PUAULU (BIRD PARK) TRAIL This easy 1½-mile, hour-long hike lets you see native Hawaiian flora and fauna in a little oasis of living nature in a field of lava. For some reason (gravity or rate of flow, or perhaps the protection of the volcano goddess, Pele), the once red-hot lava skirted this miniforest and let it survive. At the trail head on Mauna Loa Road is a display of plants and birds you'll see on the walk. Go early in the morning or in the evening (or even better, just after a rain) to see native birds, such as the *apapane* (a small, bright-red bird with black wings and tail that sips the nectar of the red-blossom ohia lehua trees) and the *iiwi* (larger and orange-vermilion colored, with a curved orange bill). Native trees along the trail include giant ohia, koa, soapberry, kolea, and mamani.

MAUNA LOA TRAIL Probably the most challenging hike in Hawaii, this 7½-mile trail goes from the lookout to a cabin at the Red Hill at 10,035 feet, then 11.6 more miles up to the primitive Mauna Loa summit cabin at 13,250 feet, where the climate is called sub-arctic, whiteouts are common, and overnight temperatures are below freezing year-round; there's often snow in July. This 4-day round-trip requires advance planning, great physical condition, and registration at the visitor center. Call ✆ **808/985-6000** for maps and details. The trail head begins where Mauna Loa Road ends, 13½ miles north of Highway 11.

CAMPGROUNDS & WILDERNESS CABINS IN THE PARK

The only park campground accessible by car is **Namakani Paio,** which has a pavilion with picnic tables and a fireplace (no wood is provided). Tent camping is free; no reservations are required. Stays are limited to 7 days per year. Backpack camping at hiker shelters and cabins is available on a first-come, shared basis, but you must register at the visitor center.

Kilauea Military Camp, a mile from the visitor center, is a rest-and-recreation camp for active and retired military personnel. Facilities include 75 one- to four-bedroom cabins with fireplaces (rates are based on rank, ranging from $52 to $133 a night), cafeteria, bowling alley, bar, general store, weight room, and tennis and basketball courts. Call ✆ **808/967-8333** on the Big Island, or ✆ **808/438-6707** on Oahu (www.kmc-volcano.com).

The following cabins and campgrounds are the best of what the park and surrounding area have to offer.

HALAPE SHELTER   This backcountry site, about 7 miles from the nearest road, is the place for those who want to get away from it all and enjoy their own private white-sand beach. The small, three-sided stone shelter, with a roof but no floor, can accommodate two people comfortably, but four's a crowd. You could pitch a tent inside, but if the weather is nice, you're better off setting up outside. There's a catchment water tank, but check with rangers on the water situation before hiking in (sometimes they don't have accurate information on the water level; bring extra water just in case). The only other facility is a pit toilet. Go on weekdays if you're really looking for an escape. It's free to stay here, but you're limited to 3 nights. Permits are available at the visitor center on a first-come, first-served basis; you can't get a permit any earlier than noon on the day before your trip. For more information, call ✆ **808/985-6000.**

NAMAKANI PAIO CAMPGROUNDS & CABINS   Just 5 miles west of the park entrance is a tall eucalyptus forest where you can pitch a tent in an open grassy field. The trail to Kilauea Crater is just a half-mile away. No permit is needed, but stays are limited to 7 days. Facilities include pavilions with barbecues and a fireplace, picnic tables, outdoor dishwashing areas, restrooms, and drinking water. There are also 10 cabins that accommodate up to four people each. Each cabin has a covered picnic table at the entrance and a fireplace with a grill. Toilets, sinks, and hot showers are available in a separate building. You can get groceries and gas in the town of Volcano, 4 miles away. Make cabin reservations through **Volcano House,** P.O. Box 53, Hawaii National Park, HI 96718 (✆ **808/967-7321**); the cost is $40 per night for two adults (and two children), $48 for three adults, and $56 for four adults.

WAIMANU VALLEY'S MULIWAI TRAIL

This difficult 2- to 3-day backpacking adventure—only for the hardy—takes you to a hidden valley some call Eden. It probably looks just as it did when Captain James Cook first saw it, with virgin waterfalls and pools and spectacular views. The trail, which goes from sea level to 1,350 feet and down to the sea again, takes more than 9 hours to hike in and more than 10 hours to hike out. Be prepared for clouds of blood-thirsty mosquitoes, and look out for wild pigs. If it's raining, forget it: You'll have 13 streams to cross before you reach the rim of Waimanu Valley, and rain means flash floods.

You must get permission to camp in Waimanu Valley from the **Division of Forestry and Wildlife,** P.O. Box 4849, Hilo, HI 96720-0849 (✆ **808/974-4221**). Permits to the nine designated campsites are assigned by number. They're free, but you're limited to a 7-day stay. Facilities are limited to two composting pit toilets. The best water in the valley is from the stream on the western wall, a 15-minute walk up a trail from the beach. All water must be treated before drinking. The water from the Waimanu Stream drains from a swamp, so skip it. Be sure to pack out what you take in.

To get to the trail head, take Highway 19 to the turnoff for Honokaa; drive 9½ miles to the Waipio Valley Lookout. Unless you have four-wheel drive, this is where your hike begins. Walk down the road and wade the Wailoa Stream; then cross the beach and go to the northwest wall. The trail starts here and goes up the valley floor, past a swamp, and into a forest before beginning a series of switchbacks that parallel the coastline. These switchbacks go up and down about 14 gulches. At the ninth gulch, about two-thirds of the way along the trail, is a shelter. After the shelter, the trail descends into Waimanu Valley, which looks like a smaller version of Waipio Valley, but without a sign of human intrusion.

8 Golf & Other Affordable Outdoor Activities

The not-for-profit group **Friends for Fitness,** P.O. Box 1671, Kailua-Kona, HI 96745 (© **808/322-0033**), offers a free brochure on physical activities (from aerobic classes to dancing to yoga) in West Hawaii; they will gladly mail it to you upon request.

GOLF

The Big Island's resort courses are known around the world for their beauty as well as their bestiality, courses where the pros play throughout the year. You'll encounter tracts where barren, black fields of lava have been turned into spectacular fairways and manicured greens, with malevolent bunkers and mind-boggling water hazards. The only problem is that these courses are also known for their pricey greens fees—some resorts charge non-guests as much as $200-plus for 18 holes.

But don't put your clubs away yet. It is possible to play an affordable round of golf on the Big Island. At the more expensive clubs and resorts, reserve a tee time in the late afternoon when cheaper **"twilight" rates** are in effect (sometimes greens fees are cut in half). For last-minute and discount tee times, call **Stand-by Golf** (© **888/645-BOOK** or 808/322-BOOK) between 7am and 11pm. Stand-by offers discounted (10%–40%), guaranteed tee times for same-day or next-day golfing.

If your game's a little rusty, head for the **Swing Zone,** 74–5562 Makala Blvd. (corner of Kuikuni Hwy., by the Old Airport Park), in Kailua-Kona (© **808/329-6909**). They have everything to polish up your game: 35 stall golf driving ranges, 25 mats, and 10 grass tee spaces. A bucket of 60 balls is $6, and the practice putting green and chipping area is free with a bucket of balls. The Pro Shop has limited golf supplies for sale, but rental clubs are available. For $6, you can play a round on the 18-hole, all-grass putting course built in the shape of the Big Island (they'll even supply the putter and a ball for free).

THE KOHALA COAST

Mauna Lani Frances I'i Brown Championship Courses 𝒜𝒜𝒜   The **Mauna Lani South Course,** a 7,029-yard, par-72, has an unforgettable ocean hole: the downhill, 221-yard, par-3 7th, which is bordered by the sea, a salt-and-pepper sand dune, and lush kiawe trees. Depending on the wind, you may need anything from a wood to a wedge to hit the green. The **North Course** may not have the drama of the oceanfront holes, but because it was built on older lava flows, the more extensive indigenous vegetation gives the course a Scottish feel. The hole that's cursed the most is the 140-yard, par-3 17th: It's absolutely beautiful but plays right into the surrounding lava field. Facilities include two driving ranges, a golf shop (with teaching pros), a restaurant, and putting greens.

Mauna Lani Dr., off Hwy. 19 (20 miles north of Kona Airport), Waikoloa. © 808/885-6655. www.maunalani.com. Greens fees: $195 ($130 for resort guests); twilight fees are $75 for everyone all year.

Waikoloa Beach Course 𝒜   This pristine 18-hole, par-70 course certainly reflects designer Robert Trent Jones, Jr.'s motto: "Hard par, easy bogey." Most golfers remember the par-5, 505-yard 12th hole, a sharp dogleg left with bunkers in the corner and an elevated tee surrounded by lava. Facilities include a golf shop, restaurant, and driving range.

1020 Keana Pl. (adjacent to the Marriott Waikoloa and Hilton Waikoloa Village), Waikoloa. © 877/WAIKOLOA or 808/886-6060. www.waikoloagolf.com. Greens fees: $175 ($125 for resort guests); twilight fees: $75.

Waikoloa Kings' Course ⛳ This sister course to the Waikoloa Beach Course is about 500 yards longer. Designed by Tom Weiskopf and Jay Morrish, the 18-hole links-style tract features a double green at the 3rd and 6th holes and several carefully placed bunkers that often come into play due to the ever-present trade winds. Facilities include a pro shop and showers.

600 Waikoloa Beach Dr. (adjacent to the Marriott Waikoloa and Hilton Waikoloa Village), Waikoloa. ⓒ 877/WAIKOLOA or 808/886-7888. www.waikoloagolf.com. Greens fees: $175 ($125 for resort guests); twilight fees: $75.

Waikoloa Village Golf Club *Value* This semiprivate 18-hole course, with a par-72 for each of the three sets of tees, is hidden in the town of Waikoloa and usually overshadowed by the glamour resort courses along the Kohala Coast. Not only is it a beautiful course with great views, but it also offers some great golfing. The wind can play havoc with your game here (like most Hawaii golf courses), so choose your clubs with caution. Robert Trent Jones, Jr., designed this challenging course, inserting his trademark sand traps, slick greens, and great fairways. We're particularly fond of the 18th hole: This par-5, 490-yard thriller doglegs to the left, and the last 75 yards up to the green are water, water, water—always a great way to end the day. Take time to check out the fabulous views of Mauna Kea and Mauna Loa, and, on a very clear day, Maui's Haleakala in the distance.

Waikoloa Rd., Waikoloa Village, off Hwy. 19 (18 miles north of Kona Airport), Waikoloa. ⓒ **808/883-9621.** www.waikoloa.org. Greens fees: $100 before 1pm, $65 after 1pm. Turn left at the Waikoloa sign; it's about 6 miles up, on your left.

THE HAMAKUA COAST

Hamakua Country Club ⛳ *Value* As you approach the sugar town of Honokaa, you can't miss this funky 9-hole course, built in the 1920s on a very steep hill overlooking the ocean. It's a par-33, 2,520-yard course that really has room for only about 4½ holes; but somehow, architect Frank Anderson managed to squeeze in 9 by crisscrossing holes across fairways—you may never see a layout like this again. The best part about Hamakua, though, is the price; just $15. The course is open to nonmembers on weekdays only; you don't need a tee time—just show up. If no one's around, simply drop your $15 in the box and head right to the first tee. Carts aren't allowed because of the steep hills.

On the ocean side of Hwy. 19 (41 miles from Hilo), Honokaa. ⓒ **808/775-7244.** Greens fees: $15.

HILO

Hilo Municipal Golf Course This is a great course for the casual golfer: It's flat, scenic, and often fun. *Warning:* Don't go after a heavy rain (especially in winter), as the fairways can get really soggy and play can slow way down. The rain does keep the course green and beautiful, though. Wonderful trees (monkeypods, coconuts, eucalyptus, banyans) dot the grounds, and the views—of Mauna Kea on one side and Hilo Bay on the other—are breathtaking. This is a course where you can challenge yourself. There are four sets of tees, with a par-71 from all; if you carry a medium handicap, go ahead and play from the back (black) tees (6,325 yd. of play). Getting a tee time can be a challenge as well, since lots of Hilo golfers love this course; weekdays are your best bet.

340 Haihai St. (between Kinoole and Iwalani sts.), Hilo. ⓒ **808/959-7711.** www.gvhawaii.com. Greens fees: $29 weekdays, $34 Sat–Sun and holidays; cart fee is $16. From Hilo, take Hwy. 11 toward Volcano; turn right at Puainako St. (at Prince Kuhio Shopping Center), left on Kinoole, and then right on Haihai St.

Naniloa Country Club   At first glance, this semiprivate, 9-hole course looks pretty flat and short, but once you get beyond the 1st hole—a wide, straightforward 330-yard, par-4—the challenges come. The tree-lined fairways require straight drives, and the huge lake on the 2nd and 5th holes is sure to haunt you. This course is very popular with locals and visitors alike. Rental clubs are available.

120 Banyan Dr. (at the intersection of Hwy. 11 and Hwy. 19), Hilo. ⓒ 808/935-3000. www.gvhawaii.com. Green fees: $25 ($15 Naniloa Hotel guests) Mon–Fri; $30 ($20 Naniloa Hotel guests) Sat–Sun (if you can get a tee time); twilight rates (after 3pm) are $10 less; cart fee is $14.

VOLCANO VILLAGE

Volcano Golf and Country Club   Located at 4,200 feet, this public course got its start in 1922, when the Blackshear family put in a green, using old tomato cans for the holes. It now has three sets of tees to choose from, all with a par of 72. The course is unusually landscaped, making use of a few ancient lava flows among the pine and ohia trees. It's considered challenging by locals. *Some tips from the regulars:* Since the course is up at 4,200 feet, the ball travels farther than you're probably used to, so club down. If you hit the ball off the fairway, take the stroke—you don't want to look for your ball in the lava. Also, play a pitch-and-run game, as the greens are slick and your ball just won't stick.

Hwy. 11, on the right side, just after the entrance to Hawaii Volcanoes National Park, Volcano. ⓒ 808/967-7331. www.gvhawaii.com. Greens fees: $63; includes a shared cart.

BICYCLING & MOUNTAIN BIKING

When was the last time you bicycled around a tropical island? Jump on a 21-speed mountain bike and do it here. A novice can complete the 225-mile Circle Island tour in 6 days or less; serious bikers do it in 2.

Some tips if you're going to make your way around the island: Plan your trip. Make advance reservations. Get a bike that fits. Go early in the day—just after sunrise is best. Wear lightweight bike togs and a helmet. Take two water bottles and sunscreen. Bring rain gear. Stay on the road, as razor-sharp lava and kiawe thorns cause blowouts. Bring a patch kit, cables, and a lock. But most important, have fun!

For mountain- and cross-training bike rentals in Kona, see **Dave's Bike and Triathlon Shop,** 75–5669 Alii Dr., across from the Kailua Pier, behind Atlantis Submarine (ⓒ 808/329-4522). Dave rents brand-name mountain bikes (with full-suspension) for $15 a day or $60 a week (including helmet and water bottle). Feel free to ask Dave for riding advice (such as which routes are the most scenic) and local weather reports. To carry your rented bike around, be sure to get a bike rack for your car ($10 a week).

Hawaiian Pedals ⚡, Kona Inn Shopping Village, Alii Drive, Kailua-Kona (ⓒ 808/329-2294), and **Hawaiian Pedals Bike Works,** Hale Hana Centre, 74-5583 Luhia St., Kailua-Kona, (ⓒ 808-326-2453; www.hawaiianpedals.com), have a huge selection of bikes, from mountain bikes and hybrids ($35 a day) to racing bikes and front-suspension mountain bikes ($45 a day). Bike racks go for $5 a day, and you pay only for the days you actually use it (the honor system): If you have the rack for a week but only use it for 2 days, you'll be charged just $10. The folks at the shops are friendly and knowledgeable about cycling routes all over the Big Island.

GUIDED TOURS   **Mauna Kea Mountain Bikes, Inc.** (ⓒ 888/MTB-TOUR or 808/883-0130, or cell 808/936-TOUR; www.bikehawaii.com) offers everything from

3-hour downhill cruises in the historic Kohala Mountains to advanced rides down monstrous Mauna Kea. Prices range from $75 to $115.

Contact the **Big Island Mountain Bike Association,** P.O. Box 6819, Hilo, HI 96720 (✆ **808/961-4452;** www.interpac.net/~mtbike), for its free brochure, *Big Island Mountain Biking,* which has useful safety tips on biking as well as great off-road trails for both beginner and advanced riders. Check out www.bikehawaii.com for information on trails and access. Another good contact for biking information and maps is **PATH** (✆ **808/326-9495**).

BIRDING

Native Hawaiian birds are few—and dwindling. Though Hawaii may be the endangered bird capital of the world, it still offers extraordinary birding for anyone nimble enough to traverse tough, mucky landscape. And the best birding is on the Big Island; birders the world over come here hoping to see three Hawaiian birds in particular: *akiapolaau,* a woodpecker wannabe with a war club–like head; *nukupuu,* an elusive little yellow bird with a curved beak, one of the crown jewels of Hawaiian birding; and *alala,* the critically endangered Hawaiian crow that's now almost impossible to see in the wild.

The following places are good spots to see native Hawaiian and other birds.

HAWAII VOLCANOES NATIONAL PARK   The best places for accomplished birders to go on their own are the ohia forests of this national park, usually at sunrise or sunset, when the little forest birds seem to be most active. The Hawaiian nene goose can be spotted at the park's Kipuka Nene Campground, a favorite nesting habitat. Geese and pheasants sometimes appear on the Volcano Golf Course in the afternoon. The white-tailed tropic bird often rides the thermals caused by steam inside Halemaumau Crater.

HAKALAU FOREST NATIONAL WILDLIFE REFUGE   The first national wildlife refuge established solely for forest-bird management is on the eastern slope of Mauna Kea above the Hamakua Coast. It's open for birding by permit only on the last weekend of each month and can be reached only by four-wheel-drive vehicle. Contact Refuge Manager Richard Wass, Hakalau Forest, 154 Waianuenue Ave., Room 219, Hilo, HI 96720 (✆ **808/933-6915;** Richard_Wass@mail.fws.gov).

HILO PONDS   Ducks, coots, herons (night and great blue), cattle egrets, even Canada and snow geese fly into these popular coastal wetlands in Hilo, near the airport. Take Kalanianaole Highway about 3 miles east, past the industrial port facilities to Loko Waka Pond and Waiakea Pond.

HORSEBACK RIDING

Kohala Na'alapa ✯, on Kohala Mountain Road (Hwy. 250) at mile marker 11 (ask for directions to the stables at the security-guard station; ✆ **808/889-0022**), offers unforgettable journeys into the rolling hills of Kahua and Kohala ranches, past ancient Hawaiian ruins, through lush pastures with grazing sheep and cows, and along mountaintops with panoramic coastal views. The horses and various riding areas are suited to everyone from first-timers to experienced equestrians. There are two trips a day: a 2½-hour tour at 9am for $89 and a 1½-hour tour at 1:30pm for $68. No riders over 230 pounds, no pregnant riders, and no children under 8 permitted.

Experienced riders should call **King's Trail Rides, Tack, and Gift Shop** ✯✯, Highway 11 at mile marker 111, Kealakekua (✆ **808/323-2388;** www.konacowboy.com).

These 4-hour trips, with 2 hours of riding, are limited to four people. The trip heads down the mountain along Monument Trail to the Captain Cook Monument in Kealakekua Bay, where you'll stop for lunch and an hour of snorkeling. The $135 weekday ($150 weekends) price tag isn't so bad when you consider that it includes both lunch and gear.

To see Waipio Valley on horseback, call **Waipio Na'alapa Trail Rides** ⚡ (© 808/ 775-0419). The 2-hour tours of this gorgeous tropical valley depart Monday through Saturday at 9:30am and 1pm (don't forget your camera). The guides are well versed in Hawaiian history and provide running commentary as you move through this historic place. The cost is $89 for adults. No kids under 8, no pregnant riders, and no riders over 230 pounds.

RIDING PARKER RANCH   Visitors now have a rare opportunity to explore **Parker Ranch** (© 808/885-7655; www.parkerranch.com/horseback.html) and its vast 175,000-acre, working cattle ranch. Visitors learn first-hand about Parker Ranch, its history, variety of plant life, and may even catch glimpses of pheasant, francolins, or wild pigs. Rides are available three times daily at 8:15am, 12:15pm, and a special sunset ride at 4:00pm. Morning and noon rides are 2 hours, and the sunset ride is 1½ hours; each of the three rides costs $79 per person. Minimum age requirement is 7 years and older, making this an ideal family activity, whether family members are beginners, intermediate, or advanced riders. Riders will feel like Hawaiian *paniolo* (cowboys) as they ride through stone corrals where up to 5,000 Hereford cattle were rounded up after being brought down from the slopes of Mauna Kea. A visit to the racetrack, where Parker Ranch thoroughbreds were trained and still hold the record for speed, is included in the excursion. The rides all begin at the Blacksmith Shop on Pukalani Road.

TENNIS

You can play for free at any Hawaii County tennis court; for a detailed list of all courts on the island, contact **Hawaii County Department of Parks and Recreation,** 25 Aupuni St., Hilo, HI 96720 (© 808/961-8720). The best courts in Hilo are at the Hoolulu Tennis Stadium, located next to the Civic Auditorium on Manono Street; in Kona the best courts are at Old Airport Park.

Most of the resorts in the Kona-Kohala area do not allow nonguests to use their tennis facilities.

9 Seeing the Sights

The Big Island is big, really big, with an area of some 4,028 square miles—that's more than twice the size of all the other Hawaiian Islands combined. Circling the island's roadways, which cover more than 200 miles, takes time, so plan on taking 5 days to circumnavigate the Big Island. Anything less is a big mistake—everything will just fly by in a blur.

THE KONA COAST
IN & AROUND KAILUA-KONA

Ellison S. Onizuka Space Center *Kids*   This small museum has a real moon rock and memorabilia in honor of Big Island–born astronaut Ellison Onizuka, who died in the 1986 *Challenger* space shuttle disaster. Fun displays in the museum include a gravity well, which illustrates orbital motion, and an interactive rocket-propulsion exhibit, where you can launch your own miniature space shuttle.

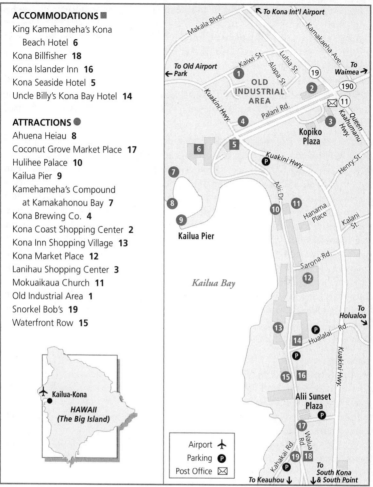

ACCOMMODATIONS ■

King Kamehameha's Kona
  Beach Hotel **6**
Kona Billfisher **18**
Kona Islander Inn **16**
Kona Seaside Hotel **5**
Uncle Billy's Kona Bay Hotel **14**

ATTRACTIONS ●

Ahuena Heiau **8**
Coconut Grove Market Place **17**
Hulihee Palace **10**
Kailua Pier **9**
Kamehameha's Compound
  at Kamakahonou Bay **7**
Kona Brewing Co. **4**
Kona Coast Shopping Center **2**
Kona Inn Shopping Village **13**
Kona Market Place **12**
Lanihau Shopping Center **3**
Mokuaikaua Church **11**
Old Industrial Area **1**
Snorkel Bob's **19**
Waterfront Row **15**

HAWAII
(The Big Island)
Kailua-Kona

Airport ✈
Parking ℗
Post Office ✉

At Kona International Airport, Kailua-Kona. © **808/329-3441.** Admission $3 adults, $1 children 12 and under. Daily 8:30am–4:30pm. Parking in airport lot, $2 per hour.

Hulihee Palace 👁👁   This two-story New England–style mansion of lava rock and coral mortar, erected in 1838 by the governor of the island of Hawaii, John Adams Kuakini, overlooks the harbor at Kailua-Kona. The largest, most elegant residence on the island when it was erected, Hulihee (the name means "turn and flee") was the gracious summer home of Hawaii's royalty, making it the other royal palace in the United States (the most famous being Oahu's Iolani Palace). Now run by Daughters of Hawaii, it features many 19th-century mementos and gorgeous koa furniture. You'll get lots of background and royal lore on the guided tour. No photography is allowed.

The Palace hosts 12 **Hawaiian music and hula concerts** a year, each dedicated to a Hawaiian monarch, at 4pm on the last Sunday of the month (except June and Dec, when the performances are held in conjunction with King Kamehameha Day and Christmas).

Across the street is **Mokuaikaua Church** (© **808/329-1589**), the oldest Christian church in Hawaii. It's constructed of lava stones, but its architecture is New England–style all the way. The 112-foot steeple is still the tallest man-made structure in Kailua-Kona.

75–5718 Alii Dr., Kailua-Kona. © 808/329-1877. www.daughtersofhawaii.org/hulihee. Admission $5 adults, $4 seniors, $1 students, 50¢ children under 12. Daily 9am–4pm. Daily tours held throughout the day (arrive at least an hour before closing).

Kamehameha's Compound at Kamakahonu Bay ★★
On the ocean side of the Kona Beach Hotel is a restored area of deep spiritual meaning to Hawaiians. This was the spot that King Kamehameha the Great chose to retreat to in 1812 after conquering the Hawaiian Islands. He stayed until his death in 1819. The king built a temple, Ahuena Heiau, and used it as a gathering place for his *kahunas* (priests) to counsel him on governing his people in times of peace. In 1820, it was on this sacred ground that Kamehameha's son, Liholiho, as king, sat down to eat with his mother, Keopuolani, and Kamehameha's principal queen, Kaahumanu, thus breaking the ancient *kapu* (taboo) against eating with women; this act established a new order in the Hawaiian kingdom. Although the temple grounds are now just a third of their original size, they're still impressive. You're free to come and wander the grounds, envisioning the days when King Kamehameha appealed to the gods to help him rule with the spirit of humanity's highest nature.

On the grounds of King Kamehameha's Kona Beach Hotel, 75–5660 Palani Rd., Kailua-Kona. © 808/329-2911. Free admission. Daily 9am–4pm; guided tours Mon–Fri at 1:30pm.

Kona Brewing Co. and Brew Pub
This microbrewery is the first of its kind on the Big Island. Spoon and Pops, a father-and-son duo from Oregon, brought their brewing talents here and now produce about 25 barrels (about 124,000 gallons) per year. Drop by any time during their business hours and take a quick, informal tour of the brewery, after which you get to taste the product. A brewpub on the property serves gourmet pizza, salads, and fresh brewed Hawaiian ales.

75–5629 Kuakini Hwy. (at Palani Rd.), Kailua-Kona. © 808/334-BREW. www.konabrewingco.com. Free tours and tastings. Tours Mon–Fri 10:30am and 3:30pm. Turn into Firestone's parking lot on Palani Rd. at Kuakini Hwy.; the brewery is at the back of the shopping center (behind Zac's Photo)—look for the orange gecko on the door.

Kona Pier
This is action central for water adventures. Fishing charters, snorkel cruises, and party boats all come and go here. Stop by around 4pm, when the captains weigh in with the catch of the day, usually huge marlin—the record-setters often come in here. It's also a great place to watch the sunset.

On the waterfront outside Honokohau Harbor, Kailua-Kona. © 808/329-7494.

Natural Energy Laboratory of Hawaii Authority
Technology buffs should consider a visit to NELHA, the only site in the world where the hot tropical sun, in combination with a complex pumping system that brings 42°F (6°C) ocean water from 2,000 feet deep up to land, is used to develop innovations in agriculture, aquaculture, and ocean conservation. The interesting 1½-hour tour takes in all areas of the high-tech ocean science and technology park, including the seawater delivery system, the energy-conversion process, and some of the park's more interesting tenants, from Maine lobsters to giant clams.

73–4460 Queen Kaahumanu Hwy. (at mile marker 94), Kailua-Kona. ✆ 808/329-7341. www.nelha.org. Public presentation tours $5 adults, children 8 and under free. Wed–Thurs 10am; reservations required.

UPCOUNTRY KONA: HOLUALOA

On the slope of Hualalai volcano above Kailua-Kona sits the small village of Holualoa, which attracts travelers weary of super-resorts. Here you'll find a little art and culture—and shade.

This funky upcountry town, centered on two-lane Mamalaloa Highway, is nestled amid a lush, tropical landscape where avocados grow as big as footballs. Little more than a wide spot in the road, Holualoa is a cluster of brightly painted, tin-roofed plantation shacks enjoying a revival as B&Bs, art galleries, and quaint shops (see "Shops & Galleries," p. 327, for details). In 2 blocks, it manages to pack in two first-rate galleries, a frame shop, a potter, a glassworks, a goldsmith, an old-fashioned general store, a vintage 1930s gas station, a tiny post office, a Catholic church, and the **Kona Hotel,** a hot-pink clapboard structure that looks like a Western movie set—you're welcome to peek in, and you should.

The cool upslope village is the best place in Hawaii for a coffee break. That's because Holualoa is in the heart of the coffee belt; a 20-mile-long strip at an elevation of between 1,000 and 1,400 feet, where all the Kona coffee in the world is grown in the rich volcanic soil of the cool uplands. Everyone's backyard seems to teem with glossy green leaves and ruby-red cherries (that's why they call it coffee on the vine, because it's a fruit), and the air smells like a San Francisco espresso bar. The **Holuakoa Cafe,** on Mamalahoa Highway (Hwy. 180) in Holualoa (✆ **808/322-2233**), is a great place to get a freshly brewed cup.

To reach Holualoa, follow narrow, winding Hualalai Road up the hill from Highway 19; it's about a 15-minute drive.

SOUTH KONA

The Painted Church 🖈 *Finds*   Oh, those Belgian priests—what a talented lot. At the turn of the century, Father John Berchman Velghe borrowed a page from Michelangelo and painted biblical scenes inside St. Benedict's Catholic Church, so the illiterate Hawaiians could visualize the white man's version of creation.

Hwy. 19, Honaunau. ✆ 808/328-2227.

Puuhonua O Honaunau National Historical Park 🖈🖈🖈   With its fierce, haunting idols, this sacred site on the black-lava Kona Coast certainly looks forbidding. To ancient Hawaiians, however, it must have been a welcome sight, for Puuhonua O Honaunau served as a 16th-century place of refuge, providing sanctuary for defeated warriors and *kapu* (taboo) violators. A great rock wall—1,000 feet long, 10 feet high, and 17 feet thick—defines the refuge where Hawaiians found safety. On the wall's north end is Hale O Keawe Heiau, which holds the bones of 23 Hawaiian chiefs. Other archaeological finds include burial sites, old trails, and a portion of an ancient village. On a self-guided tour of the 180-acre site—which has been restored to its pre-contact state—you can see and learn about reconstructed thatched huts, canoes, and idols and feel the *mana* (power) of old Hawaii.

A cultural festival, usually held in June, allows you to join in games, learn crafts, sample Hawaiian food, see traditional hula, and experience life in the islands before outsiders arrived in the late 1700s. Every Labor Day weekend, one of Hawaii's major outrigger canoe races starts here and ends in Kailua-Kona. Call for details on both events.

Kids Especially for Kids

Walking through Thurston Lava Tube at Hawaii Volcanoes National Park (p. 236)   It's scary, it's spooky, and it's perfect for any kid. You hike downhill through a rainforest full of little chittering native birds to enter this huge, silent black hole full of drips, cobwebs, and tree roots that stretches underground for almost a half-mile. At the end, there's a fork in the tunnel, which leads either up a stairway to our world or—here's the best part—down an unexplored hole that probably goes all the way to China.

Snorkeling Kahaluu Beach Park (p. 293)   The shallow, calm waters off Kahaluu Beach are the perfect place to take kids snorkeling. The waters are protected by a barrier reef, and the abundance of fish will keep the kids' attention. You might want to pick up a fish identification card at any dive shop and make a game out of seeing how many fish the kids can find.

Riding a Submarine into the Underwater World (p. 294)   The huge viewing windows will have the kids enthralled as the high-tech sub leaves the surface and plunges 120 feet down through the mysterious Neptunian waters. The hour-long trip is just enough time to hold the young ones' attention as the sub passes through clouds of reef fish and past prehistoric-looking corals.

Launching Your Own Space Shuttle (p. 302)   Okay, it's a model of a space shuttle, but it's close enough to the real thing to be a real blast. The Ellison S. Onizuka Space Center has dozens of interactive displays to thrill budding young astronauts, such as a hands-on experience with gyroscopic stabilization. Great video clips of astronauts working and living in space may inspire your kids as well.

Hunting for Petroglyphs (p. 309)   There's plenty of space to run around and discover ancient stone carvings at either the Puako Petroglyph Archaeological District, at Mauna Lani Resort, or at the King's Trail, by the Outrigger Waikoloan. And finding the petroglyphs is only part of the game—once you find them, you have to guess what the designs mean.

Watching the Volcano (p. 236)   Any kid who doesn't get a kick out of watching a live volcano set the night on fire has been watching too much television. Take hot dogs, bottled water, flashlights, and sturdy shoes and follow the ranger's instructions on where to view the lava safely. You might want to make the trip during daylight first so the kids can see the Technicolor difference in experiencing a lava flow in the dark.

Hwy. 160 (off Hwy. 11 at mile marker 104), Honaunau. ℂ **808/328-2288.** www.nps.gov/puho. Admission $5 per vehicle or $3 per person; children 16 and under free. Visitor center daily 8am–4:30pm; park Mon–Thurs 6am–8pm, Fri–Sun 6am–11pm. From Hwy. 11, it's 3½ miles to the park entrance.

Kona Historical Society Museum 🐵🐵   Built in 1875 by Henry Nicholas Greenwell out of native stone and lime mortar made from burnt coral, this well-organized pocket museum is housed in the historic Greenwell Store. Antiques, artifacts, and photos tell the story of this fabled coast. The museum is filled with items that were common to everyday life here in the last century, when coffee-growing and cattle-raising were the main industries. Serious history buffs should sign up for one of the museum's walking tours; see "Guided Walking Tours," below.

Hwy. 11 (between mile markers 111 and 112), Kealakekua. © 808/323-3222 or 808/323-2006. www.konahistorical. org. Admission free (donations accepted). Mon–Fri 9am–3pm. Parking on grassy area next to Kona Specialty Meats parking lot.

Kula Kai Caverns and Lava Tubes ★★ (Finds

Before you trudge up to Pele's volcanic eruption, take a look at her underground handiwork. Ric Elhard and Rose Herrera have explored and mapped out the labyrinth of lava tubes and caves, carved out over the last 1,000 years or so, that crisscross their property on the southwest rift zone on the slopes of Mauna Loa near South Point. As soon as you enter their thatched-yurt field office (which resembles something out of an Indiana Jones movie), you know you're in for an amazing tour. Choices range from an easy half-hour tour on a well-lit underground route ($12 for adults, $6 for children ages 5–12) to a more adventuresome 2-hour caving trip ($45 for adults). Helmets, lights, gloves, and knee pads are all included. Sturdy shoes are recommended for caving.

Off Hwy. 11, (between mile markers 79 and 78), Ocean View. © 808/929-7539. www.kulakaicaverns.com. Tours by appointment.

ORGANIZED TOURS ON THE KONA COAST

GUIDED WALKING TOURS   The **Kona Historical Society** (© 808/323-2005; www.konahistorical.org) hosts two historic walking tours in the Kona region. All walks must be booked in advance; call for reservations and departure locations. The 75-minute **Historic Kailua Village Walking Tour** ★ is the most comprehensive tour of the Kona Coast. It takes you all around Kailua-Kona, from King Kamehameha's last seat of government to the summer palace of the Hawaiian royal family and beyond, with lots of Hawaiian history and colorful lore along the way. Tours depart from the King Kamehameha Hotel lobby Monday through Friday, 9 and 11am. Tickets are $20 for adults, $10 for children ages 5 to 12. Call © 808/323-3222 for reservations (www.konahistorical.org/tours/walking.shtml).

The 1-hour **Living History Tour** takes you through the everyday life of a Japanese family on the historic Uchida Coffee Farm from the 1920s through the 1940s. Interact with costumed interpreters as they go about life on a coffee farm. The tour is offered Monday through Friday on the hour from 9am to 2pm, at a cost of $15 for adults and $7.50 for kids ages 5 to 12. Meet at the Kona Historical Society office, 81–6551 Mamalahoa Hwy. (next to Kona Specialty Meats), across from mile marker 110, Kealakekua. To call ahead for reservations, dial © 808/323-2006.

A SELF-GUIDED DRIVING TOUR   There's a self-guided audio tour on CD, **Big Island Audio Tour** (© 808/896-4275; www.bigislandaudiotour.com), which features 36 tracks of information on seeing the Big Island. Not only does it give directions to the well-known sites, but it also has tracks on various beaches, short hikes, and side trips, as well as information on pronouncing Hawaiian words, and Hawaiian history and culture. The cost is $20 plus $2 for shipping.

If you're interested in seeing how your morning cup of joe goes from beans to brew, get a copy of the **Coffee Country Driving Tour.** This self-guided drive will take you farm by farm through Kona's famous coffee country; it also features a fascinating history of the area, the lowdown on coffee-making lingo, some insider tips on how to make a great cup, and even a recipe for Kona coffee macadamia-nut chocolate-chunk pie (goes great with a cup of java). The free brochure is available at the **Big Island Visitors Bureau,** 250 Waikoloa Beach Dr., Waikoloa, HI 96738 (© **808/886-1652;** www.gohawaii.com/bigisland).

SOUTH POINT: LAND'S END

The history of Hawaii is condensed here, at the end of 11 miles of bad road that peters out at Kaulana Bay, in the lee of a jagged, black-lava point—the tail end of the United States. No historic marker marks the spot or gives any clue as to the geographical significance of the place. If you walk out to the very tip, beware of the big waves that lash the shore.

The nearest continental landfall is Antarctica, 7,500 miles away.

It's a 2½-mile four-wheel-drive trip and a hike down a cliff from South Point to the anomaly known as **Green Sand Beach** 𝕽 (see "Beaches," p. 288).

Back on the Mamalahoa Highway (Hwy. 11), about 20 miles east, is the small town of Pahoa; turn off the highway and travel about 5 miles through this once-thriving sugar plantation and beyond to the **Wood Valley Temple and Retreat Center** 𝕽 (© **808/928-8539**), also known as *Nechung Drayang Ling* ("Island of Melodious Sound"). It's an oasis of tranquillity tucked into the rainforest. Built by Japanese sugarcane workers, the temple, retreat center, and surrounding gardens were rededicated by the Dalai Lama in 1980 to serve as a spiritual center for Tibetan Buddhism. You can walk the beautiful grounds, attend morning or evening services, and breathe in the quiet mindfulness of this serene area.

THE KOHALA COAST

Puukohola Heiau National Historic Site 𝕽𝕽𝕽   This seacoast temple, called "the hill of the whale," is the single most imposing and dramatic structure created by the ancient Hawaiians. It was built by Kamehameha I from 1790 to 1791. The temple stands 224 feet long by 100 feet wide, with three narrow terraces on the seaside and an amphitheater to view canoes. Kamehameha built this temple of sacrifice with mortarless stone after a prophet told him he would conquer and unite the islands if he did so; 4 years later, he fulfilled his kingly goal. The site also includes the house of John Young, trusted advisor to Kamehameha, and, offshore, the submerged ruins of Hale O Ka Puni, a shrine dedicated to the shark gods.

Hwy. 270, near Kawaihae Harbor. © 808/882-7218. www.nps.gov/puhe. Free admission. Daily 7:30am–4pm. The visitor center is on Hwy. 270; the *heiau* is a short walk away. The trail is closed when it's too windy, so call ahead if you're in doubt.

ANCIENT HAWAIIAN FISH PONDS

Like their Polynesian forefathers, Hawaiians were among the first aquaculturists on the planet. Scientists still marvel at the ways they used the brackish ponds along the shoreline to stock and harvest fish. There are actually two different types of ancient fish ponds *(loko i'a)*. Closed ponds, inshore and closed off from the ocean, were used to raise mullet and milkfish, while open ponds were open to the sea, with rock walls as a barrier to the ocean and sluice gates that connected the ponds to the ocean. The gates were woven vines, with just enough room for juvenile fish to swim in at high tide while keeping the bigger, fatter fish from swimming out. Generally, the Hawaiians raised mullet, milkfish, and shrimp in these open ponds; juvenile manini, papio, eels, and barracuda found their way in during high tides.

The **Kalahuipuaa Fish Ponds,** at Mauna Lani Resort (✆ **808/885-6622**), are great examples of both types of ponds in a lush tropical setting. South of the Mauna Lani Resort are **Kuualii** and **Kahapapa Fish Ponds,** at the Outrigger Waikoloa Beach Resort (✆ **808/885-6789**). Both resorts have taken great pains to restore the ponds to their original state and to preserve them for future generations; call ahead to arrange a free guided tour.

KOHALA COAST PETROGLYPHS

The Hawaiian petroglyph is a great enigma of the Pacific. No one knows who made them or why, only that they're here. Petroglyphs appear at 135 different sites on six inhabited islands, but most of them are found on the Big Island.

At first glance, the huge slate of pahoehoe looks like any other smooth black slate of lava on the seacoast of the Big Island—until gradually, in slanting rays of the sun, a wonderful cast of characters leaps to life before your eyes. You might see dancers and paddlers, fishermen and chiefs, hundreds of marchers all in a row. Pictures of the tools of daily life are everywhere: fish hooks, spears, poi pounders, canoes. The most common representations are family groups: father, mother, and child. There are also post–European contact petroglyphs of ships, anchors, goats, horses, and guns.

The largest concentration of these stone symbols in the Pacific lies within the 233-acre **Puako Petroglyph Archaeological District** ✿, near Mauna Lani Resort. Once hard to find, the enigmatic graffiti is now easily reachable. The 1.4-mile **Malama Trail** starts north of Mauna Lani Resort; take Highway 19 to the resort turnoff and drive toward the coast on North Kaniku Drive, which ends at a parking lot; the trail head is marked by a sign and interpretive kiosk. Go in the early morning or late afternoon, when it's cool. A total of 3,000 designs have been identified, including paddlers, sails, marchers, dancers, and family groups, as well as dog, chicken, turtle, and deity symbols.

The **Kings' Shops** (✆ **808/886-8811**), at the Waikoloa Beach Resort, offers a free tour of the surrounding petroglyphs Tuesday through Friday at 10:30am and Saturday at 8:30am; it meets in front of the Food Pavilion.

Disabled visitors, as well as others, can explore petroglyphs at **Kaupulehu Petroglyphs** ✿ in the **Kona Village Resort,** Queen Kaahumanu Highway (✆ **808/325-5555**). Free guided tours are offered three times a week, but reservations are required (or you won't get past the gatehouse). Here you can see some of the finest images in the Hawaiian Islands. There are many petroglyphs of sails, canoes, fish, and chiefs in headdresses, plus a burial scene with three stick figures. Kite motifs—rare in rock art—similar to those found in New Zealand are also here. This is Hawaii's only ADA accessible petroglyph trail.

Warning: The petroglyphs are thousands of years old and easily destroyed. Do not walk on them or attempt to take a "rubbing" (there's a special area in the Puako Preserve for doing so). The best way to capture a petroglyph is with a photo in the late afternoon, when the shadows are long.

NORTH KOHALA

Lapakahi State Historical Park ✿ *(Kids)*   This 14th-century fishing village, on a hot, dry, dusty stretch of coast, offers a glimpse into the lifestyle of the ancients. Lapakahi is the best-preserved fishing village in Hawaii. Take the self-guided, mile-long loop trail past stone platforms, fish shrines, rock shelters, salt pans, and restored *hale* (houses) to a coral-sand beach and the deep blue sea (good snorkeling). Wear good hiking shoes or tennies; it's a hearty 45-minute walk. Go early or later in the afternoon, as the sun is hot and shade is at a premium.

Hwy. 270, Mahukona. © 808/889-5566. Free admission. Daily 8am–4pm. Guided tours by appointment.

Mookini Heiau ★★ (Moments)   On the coast where King Kamehameha the Great was born stands Hawaii's oldest, largest, and most sacred religious site, now a national historic landmark—the 1,500-year-old Mookini Heiau ★, used by kings to pray and offer human sacrifices. You need four-wheel drive to get here, as the road is rough, but it's worth the trip. The massive three-story stone temple, dedicated to Ku, the Hawaiian god of war, was erected in A.D. 480; each stone is said to have been passed hand to hand from Pololu Valley, 14 miles away, by 18,000 men who worked from sunset to sunrise. Kamehameha, born nearby under Halley's Comet, sought spiritual guidance here before embarking on his campaign to unite Hawaii. The temple is not open to the public, but you can see it on the third Saturday of every month, when a group of volunteers meets at the site to pull weeds and clean up property surrounding the temple. If you are interested, call the Mo'okini Preservation Foundation, on Oahu (© **808/373-8000**), and be prepared to do some work.

On the North Shore, near Upolu Point Airport.

The Original King Kamehameha Statue ★★   Here stands King Kamehameha the Great, right arm outstretched, left arm holding a spear, as if guarding the seniors who have turned a century-old New England–style courthouse into an airy center for their golden years. The center is worth a stop just to meet the town elders, who are quick to point out the local sights, hand you a free *Guide to Historic North Kohala,* and give you a brief tour of the courthouse, where a faded photo of FDR looms over the judge's dais, and the walls are covered with the faces of innocent-looking local boys killed in World War II, Korea, and Vietnam.

But the statue is the main attraction here. There's one just like it in Honolulu, across the street from Iolani Palace, but this is the original: an 8-foot, 6-inch bronze by Thomas R. Gould, a Boston sculptor. It was cast in Europe in 1880 but was lost at sea on its way to Hawaii. A sea captain eventually recovered and returned the statue, which was finally placed here, near Kamehameha's Kohala birthplace, in 1912.

Kamehameha was born in 1750, became ruler of Hawaii in 1810, and died in Kailua-Kona in 1819. His burial site remains a mystery.

Hwy. 270, Kapaau.

Pua Mau Place   Perched on the sun-kissed western slopes of the Kohala Mountains, and dotted with deep, craggy ravines, lies one of Hawaii's most unusual botanical gardens, Pua Mau Place, a 45-acre oasis with breath-taking, views of both the ocean and the majestic mountains, dedicated to plants that are "ever blooming," an expansive collection of continuously flowering tropical flowers, trees, and shrubs. That would be worth the price of admission alone, but the gardens also have an aviary of exotic birds, and a unique hibiscus maze, planted with some 200 varieties of hibiscus. This is a great place for families (children are welcome and invited to feed the large number of birds in the aviary); visitors can take the self guided tour (along with a booklet filled with the names and descriptions of all the plants) along mulched pathways meandering through the gardens, where every plant is clearly marked.

10 Ala Kahua, Kawaihae. © 808/882-0888. www.puamau.com. Admission $10 adults, $8 for seniors and students, free for kids 12 and under. Daily 10am–4pm. Located off Hwy. 270 on Ala Kahua Dr. (in Kohala Estates) just north of Kawaihae. Turn at the 6 mile marker, ½ mile up the hill to the gate at a lava-rock wall.

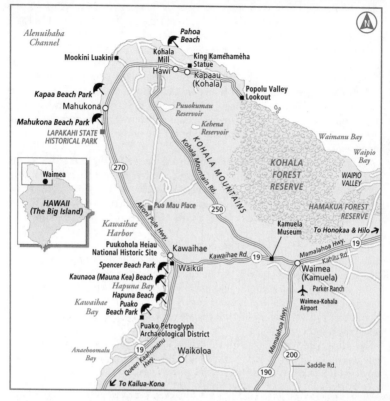

Pololu Valley Lookout ★★★ At this end-of-the-road scenic lookout, you can gaze at the vertical jade-green cliffs of the Hamakua Coast and two islets offshore. The view may look familiar once you get here—it often appears on travel posters. Most people race up, jump out, take a snapshot, and turn around and drive off; but it's a beautiful scene, so linger if you can. For the more adventurous, a switchback trail leads to a secluded black-sand beach at the mouth of a wild valley once planted in taro; bring water and bug spray.

At the end of Hwy. 270, Makapala.

WAIMEA (KAMUELA)

Kamuela Museum It takes only about an hour to explore tiny Kamuela Museum. Its eclectic collection includes an early Hawaiian dogtoothed death cup, which sits next to a piece of rope used on the *Apollo* mission, which, in turn, sits near ancient artifacts from the royal family.

At the junction of Hwy. 19 and Hwy. 250, Waimea. © 808/885-4724. www.hawaiimuseums.org/mc/ishawaii_kamuela.htm. Admission $5 adults, $2 children under 12. Daily 8am–5pm.

Parker Ranch ★ The *paniolo* (cowboy) tradition began here in 1809, when John Parker, a 19-year-old New England sailor, jumped ship and rounded up wild cows for King Kamehameha. There's some evidence that Hawaiian cowboys were the first to be taught by the great Spanish horsemen, the *vaqueros;* they were wrangling 40 years before their counterparts in California, Texas, and the Pacific Northwest. The Parker Ranch, after six generations of cowboys, is smaller today than in its glory, but it still is a working ranch of some 12 cowboys, 250 horses, and 30,000 to 35,000 head of cattle on 200,000 acres.

The **Visitor Center,** located at the Parker Ranch Shopping Center on Highway 190 (© 808/885-7655), is open daily from 9am to 5pm and houses the **Parker Ranch Museum,** which displays items that have been used throughout the ranch's history, dating from 1847, and illustrates six generations of Parker family history. An interesting video takes you inside the ranch and captures the essence of day-to-day life when it was a working ranch.

You can also tour two historic homes on the ranch. In 1989, the late Richard Smart—the sixth-generation heir who sought a career on Broadway—opened his 8,000-square-foot yellow Victorian home, **Puuopelu,** to art lovers. The French Regency gallery here includes original works by Renoir, Degas, Dufy, Corot, Utrillo, and Pissarro. Next door is **Mana Hale,** a little New England saltbox built from koa wood 140 years ago.

If you want to get out and see the ranch itself, a 45-minute narrated **Kohala Carriage Tour** (Tues–Sat) takes place in an old-fashioned covered wagon—pulled by two large Belgian draft horses—with seating for 20, roll-down protection from the elements, and warm blankets for the upcountry temperatures. The tour rolls past ancient Hawaiian artifacts, 19th-century stone corrals (still in use), and miles of vast rolling hills; it stops at a working cowboy station, where visitors can get out, take photos, and stretch their legs.

See "Horseback Riding" (p. 301) for details on riding tours of Parker Ranch.

Parker Ranch Center, Waimea. © 808/885-7655 for visitor center. www.parkerranch.com. Admission $6.50 to museum only, $4.50 for children 12 and under; $8.50 tour of ranch homes, $6 for children 12 and under; $15 adults for the Wagon Tour, $12 for children 12 and under. Visitor center and museum open Mon–Sat 9am–5pm. If you're seeing the museum only, you can arrive as late as 4pm; the last museum/ranch homes tickets are sold at 4pm; the final museum/Wagon Tour tickets are sold at 2pm. Allow about 1½ hr. to see everything.

MAUNA KEA

Some people just have to be on top of things. If you're one of them, head for the summit of Mauna Kea, which is the world's tallest mountain if you measure it from its base on the ocean floor.

Mauna Kea's summit is the best place on earth for astronomical observations, because its mid-Pacific site is near the equator and because it enjoys clear, pollution-free skies and pitch-black nights with no urban light to interfere. That's why Mauna Kea is home to the world's largest telescope. Needless to say, the stargazing from here is fantastic, even with the naked eye.

SETTING OUT You'll need a four-wheel-drive vehicle to climb to the peak, **Observatory Hill.** A standard car will get you as far as the visitor center, but check your rental agreement before you go; some agencies prohibit you from taking your car on the Saddle Road, which is narrow and rutted and has a soft shoulder.

SAFETY TIPS Always check the weather and Mauna Kea road conditions before you head out (© 808/969-3218). Dress warmly, as the temperatures drop into the 30s (-1°C to 4°C) after dark. Drink as much liquid as possible, avoiding alcohol and coffee, in the 36 hours surrounding your trip to avoid dehydration. Don't go within 24 hours of scuba diving—you could get the bends. The day before you go, avoid gas-pro-ducing foods, such as beans, cabbage, onions, soft drinks, or starches. If you smoke, take a break for 48 hours before to allow the carbon monoxide in your bloodstream to dissipate—you need all the oxygen you can get. Wear dark sunglasses to avoid snow blindness, and use lots of sunscreen and lip balm. Pregnant women and anyone under 16 or with a heart condition or lung ailment are advised to stay below. Once you're at the top, don't overexert yourself; it's bad for your heart. Take it easy up here.

ACCESS POINTS & VISITOR CENTERS   Before you climb the mountain, you've got to find it. It's about an hour from Hilo or Waimea to the visitor center and another 30 to 45 minutes from here to the summit. Take the Saddle Road (Hwy. 200) from Highway 190; it's about 19 miles to Mauna Kea State Recreation Area, a good place to stop and stretch your legs. Go another 9 miles to the unmarked Summit Road turnoff, at mile marker 28 (about 9,300 ft.), across from the Hunter's Check-in Station. The higher you go, the more lightheaded you get, sometimes even dizzy; it usu-ally sets in after the 9,600-foot marker (about 6.2 miles up the Summit Road), the site of the last comfort zone and the **Onizuka Visitor Center** (✆ **808/961-2180**). Named in memory of Hawaii's fallen astronaut, a native of the Big Island and a vic-tim of the *Challenger* explosion, the center is open daily from 9am to 10pm.

TOURS & PROGRAMS   If you'd rather not go it alone to the top, you can car-avan up as part of a **free summit tour,** offered Saturday and Sunday at 1pm from the visitor center (returns at 5pm). You must be 16 or older and in good health (no cardiopulmonary problems), not pregnant, and have a four-wheel-drive vehicle. The tours explain the development of the facilities on Mauna Kea and include a walking tour of an observatory at 13,796 feet. Call ✆ **808/961-2180** if you'd like to participate.

Every night from 6 to 10pm, you can do some serious **stargazing** from the **Onizuka Visitor Center.** There's a free lecture at 6pm, followed by a video, a ques-tion-and-answer session, and your chance to peer through 11-inch, 14-inch, and 16-inch telescopes. Bring a snack and, if you've got them, your own telescope or binoculars, along with a flashlight (with a red filter). Dress for 30°F to 40°F (-1°C–4°C) temperatures, but call for the weather report first (✆ **808/961-5582**). Families are welcome.

Another telescope tour is offered, free, during the day, by the **Subaru Telescope** (✆ **808/934-5056** or www.subarutelescope.org), Monday through Friday, at 10:30, 11:30am, and 1:30pm on a first-to-sign-up basis. The Subaru Telescope is one of 13 world-class telescopes (representing 11 countries) on the summit of Mauna Kea. You will need a four-wheel-drive to make the trip up. They recommend that you stop for at least 30 minutes at the Onizuka Visitor Center at 9,000 feet to acclimatize. Because of the risk of altitude sickness, the 30-minute tour is closed to pregnant women, chil-dren under 16 and anyone with health concerns that could be aggravated by low-oxygen and high altitude. Scuba divers are advised to schedule dives on a day separate from the tour.

You can see a model of the world's largest telescope, which sits atop Mauna Kea, at the **Keck Control Center,** 65–1120 Mamalahoa Hwy. (Hwy. 19), across from the North Hawaii Community Hospital, Waimea (✆ **808/885-7887**); open Monday through Friday from 8am to 4:30pm. A 10-minute video explains the Keck's search for objects in deep space.

Moments **Experiencing Where the Gods Live**

"The ancient Hawaiians thought of the top of Mauna Kea as heaven, or at least where the Gods and Goddess lived," said Monte "Pat" Wright, owner and chief guide of **Mauna Kea Summit Adventures.**

Wright, the first guide to take people up to the top of the Mauna Kea, the world's tallest mountain when measured from the base, and an astonishing 13,796 feet when measured from the sea, said he fell in love with this often-snow capped peak the first time he saw it.

Mauna Kea Summit Adventures offer a luxurious trip to the top of the world. The 7- to 8-hour adventure actually begins mid-afternoon with pick up along the Kona-Kohala coast in one of their brand new, $65,000, custom Ford, four-wheel-drive, turbo-diesel vans.

As the passengers make the drive up the mountain, the extensively trained guides discuss the geography, geology, natural history, and Hawaiian culture along the way.

The first stop is at the Onizuka Visitor's Center, at the 9,000-foot level.

"We let people out to stretch, get acclimatized to the altitude, and to eat dinner," Wright said.

As guests gear up with Mauna Kea Summit's heavy, arctic-style hooded parkas and gloves (30°F/-1°C is the average temperature on the mountain), the guide describes why the world's largest telescopes are located on Mauna Kea and also tells stories about the lifestyle of astronomers who live for a clear, night sky.

After a dinner of gourmet sandwiches (turkey, Black Forest ham, or lacto-veggie on a fresh baguette roll), vegetarian onion soup, and hot chocolate, coffee, or tea, everyone climbs back into the van for the half-hour ride to the summit.

Arriving in time to catch the sun sinking into the Pacific nearly 14,000 feet below, the guide points out the various world-renown telescopes as the

---

MAKING THE CLIMB   If you're heading up on your own, stop at the visitor center for about a half-hour to get acquainted with the altitude, walk around, eat a banana, drink some water, and take deep breaths of the crystal-clear air before you press on and upward, in low gear, engine whining. It takes about 30 to 45 minutes to get to the top from here. The trip is a mere 6 miles, but you climb from 9,000 to nearly 14,000 feet.

AT THE SUMMIT   Up here, 11 nations, including Japan, France, and Canada, have set up peerless infrared telescopes to look into deep space. Among them sits the **Keck Telescope,** the world's largest. Developed by the University of California and the California Institute of Technology, it's eight stories high, weighs 150 tons, and has a 33-foot–diameter mirror made of 36 perfectly attuned hexagon mirrors, like a fly's eye, rather than one conventional lens.

Also at the summit, up a narrow footpath, is a **cairn of rocks;** from it, you can see across the Pacific Ocean in a 360-degree view that's beyond words and pictures. When observatories open and the high-tech, multi-mirrored telescopes rotate into position for the night viewing.

After the last trace of sunset colors has disappeared from the sky, the tour again descends down to mid-mountain, where the climate is more agreeable for stargazing. Each tour has Celestron Celestar 8 deluxe telescopes, capable of 30-175x magnification and gather up to 500x more light than the unaided eye.

Wright does caution people to book the adventure early in their vacation.

"Although we do cancel about 25 trips a year due to weather, we want to be able to accommodate everyone," he said. An extensive series of live Web cameras, live weather stats, and a full-time meteorologist constantly feed weather information on the mountain. If guests book at the beginning of their holiday and the trip is canceled due to weather, then Mauna Kea Summit will attempt to reschedule another day.

Wright also points out that, due to the summit's low oxygen level (40% less oxygen than sea level) and the diminished air pressure (also 40% less air pressure than sea level), the lack of oxygen can be a serious problem for people with heart or lung problems or for scuba divers who have been diving in the previous 24 hours.

Pregnant women, children under 13 years old, or obese people should not travel to the summit due to the decreased oxygen. Since the roads to the summit are bumpy, anyone with a back injury might want to reconsider the trip.

The cost for this celestial adventure is $166 (discounted if you book on the Internet, www.maunakea.com, 2 weeks in advance). For more information, contact ✆ **888-322-2366** (toll-free) or ✆ 808/322-2366.

it's socked in (and that can happen while you're standing here), you get a surreal look at the summits of Mauna Loa and Maui's Haleakala poking through the puffy white cumulus clouds beneath your feet.

Inside a cinder cone just below the summit is **Lake Waiau,** the only glacial lake in the mid-Pacific and the third-highest lake in the United States (13,020 ft. above sea level). The lake never dries up, even though it gets only 15 inches of rain a year and sits in porous lava where there are no springs. Nobody quite knows what to make of this, although scientists suspect the lake is replenished by snow melt and permafrost from submerged lava tubes. You can't see the lake from Summit Road; you must take a brief, high-altitude hike. But it's easy: On the final approach to the summit area, upon regaining the blacktop road, go about 200 yards to the major switchback and make a hard right turn. Park on the shoulder of the road (which, if you brought your altimeter, is at 13,200 ft.). No sign points the way, but there's an obvious half-mile trail that goes down to the lake about 200 feet across the lava. Follow the base of the big cinder cone on your left; you should have the summit of Mauna Loa in view directly ahead as you walk.

THE HAMAKUA COAST

The rich history of 117 years of the sugar industry, along the scenic 45-mile coastline from Hilo to Hamakua, comes alive in the interpretive *Hilo-Hamakua Heritage Coast* drive guide, produced by the **Hawaii Island Economic Development Board,** 200 Kanoelehua Ave., Suite 103, Hilo, HI 96720 (② **808/966-5416**).

The free guide not only points out the historic sites and museums, scenic photo opportunities, restaurants and stores, and even restrooms along the Hawaii Belt Road (Hwy. 19), but also has corresponding brown-and-white points-of-interest signs on the highway. Visitor information centers anchored at either end in Hilo and in Hamakua offer additional information on the area.

NATURAL WONDERS ALONG THE COAST

Akaka Falls ✦✦✦   See one of Hawaii's most scenic waterfalls via an easy, 1-mile paved loop through a rainforest, past bamboo and ginger and down to an observation point. You'll have a perfect view of 442-foot Akaka and nearby Kahuna Falls, which is a mere 100-footer. Keep your eyes peeled for rainbows.

On Hwy. 19, Honomu (8 miles north of Hilo). Turn left at Honomu and head 3.6 miles inland on Akaka Falls Rd. (Hwy. 220).

Hawaii Tropical Botanical Garden ✦✦   More than 1,800 species of tropical plants thrive in this little-known Eden by the sea. The 40-acre garden, nestled between the crashing surf and a thundering waterfall, has the world's largest selection of tropical plants growing in a natural environment, including a torch ginger forest, a banyan canyon, an orchid garden, a banana grove, a bromeliad hill, and a golden bamboo grove, which rattles like a jungle drum in the trade winds. The torch gingers tower on 12-foot stalks. Each spectacular specimen is named by genus and species, and caretakers point out new or rare buds in bloom. Some endangered Hawaiian specimens, such as the rare *Gardenia remyi,* are flourishing in this habitat. The gardens are seldom crowded; you can wander around by yourself all day.

Off Hwy. 19 on the 4-mile Scenic Route, Onomea Bay (8 miles north of Hilo). ② **808/964-5233.** www.htbg.com. Admission $15 adults, $5 children 6–16. Daily 8:30am–4pm.

Laupahoehoe Beach Park ✦   This idyllic place holds a grim reminder of nature's fury. In 1946, a tidal wave swept across the village that once stood on this lava-leaf (that's what *laupahoehoe* means) peninsula and claimed the lives of 20 students and four teachers. A memorial in this pretty little park recalls the tragedy. The land here ends in black sea stacks that resemble tombstones. It's not a place for swimming, but the views are spectacular.

Laupahoehoe Point exit off Hwy. 19.

World Botanical Garden ✦✦   Just north of Hilo is Hawaii's largest botanical garden in the state, with some 5,000 species, and, still growing. When the fruits are in season, they hand out free chilled juices. One of the most spectacular sites is the quarter-mile rainforest walk, which is also wheelchair accessible, along a stream, on a path lined with flowers, to the viewing area of the three-tiered, 300 foot Umauma Falls. Parents will appreciate the children's maze, nearly the size of a football field, where the "prize" is a playing field near the exit. The mock orange hedge, which defines the various paths in the maze, is only 5 feet tall, so most parents can peer over the edge to keep an eye on their *keiki*. Under construction, when we went to press, are an educational visitor's center, scheduled to be open by the end of the year, a Hawaii wellness garden with medicinal Hawaiian plants, an etho-botanical garden, an arboretum, and a phylogenetic garden with various plants and trees arranged in roughly the same sequence they first appeared on Earth.

Off Hwy. 19 near the 16-mile marker in Umauma. P.O. Box 324, Honomu, HI 96728. (©) **808/963-5427.** www.world botanicalgardens.com. Admission $8.50 adults, $4.25 teens ages 13–19, $2 children 5–12 years, free for children under 5. Guided tours: $40 adults, $30 teens ages 13–19, $20 children 5–12 years, free for children under 5. Mon–Sat 9am–5:30pm.

HONOKAA

Honokaa is worth a visit to see the remnants of plantation life when sugar was king. This is a real place that hasn't yet been boutiqued into a shopping mall; it looks as if someone has kept it in a bell jar since 1920. There's a real barber shop, a real Filipino store, some good shopping (see section 10 of this chapter, "Shops & Galleries"), and a hotel with creaky floorboards that dishes up hearty food. The town also serves as the gateway to spectacular Waipio Valley (see below).

Honokaa has no attractions per se, but you might want to check out the **Katsu Goto Memorial,** next to the library at the Hilo end of town. Katsu Goto, one of the first indentured Japanese immigrants, arrived in Honokaa in the late 1800s to work on the sugar plantations. He learned English, quit the plantation, and aided his fellow immigrants in labor disputes with American planters. On October 23, 1889, he was hanged from a lamppost in Honokaa, a victim of local-style justice. Today, a memorial recalls Goto's heroic human-rights struggle.

THE END OF THE ROAD: WAIPIO VALLEY

Long ago, this lush, tropical place was the valley of kings, who called it the valley of "curving water" (which is what *Waipio* means). From the black-sand bay at its mouth, Waipio sweeps back 6 miles between sheer, cathedral-like walls that reach almost a mile high. Here, 40,000 Hawaiians lived amid taro, red bananas, and wild guavas in an area etched by streams and waterfalls. Only about 50 Hawaiians live in the valley today, tending taro, fishing, and soaking up the ambience of this old Hawaiian place.

Many of the ancient royals are buried in Waipio's hidden crevices; some believe they rise up to become Marchers of the Night, whose chants reverberate through the valley. It's here that the caskets of Hawaiian chiefs Liloa and Lono Ika Makahiki, recently stolen from Bishop Museum, are believed to have been returned by Hawaiians. The sacred valley is steeped in myth and legend, some of which you may hear, usually after dark in the company of Hawaiian elders.

To get to Waipio Valley, take Highway 19 from Hilo to Honokaa, then Highway 240 to **Waipio Valley Lookout** ★★★, a grassy park on the edge of Waipio Valley's sheer cliffs with splendid views of the wild oasis below. This is a great place for a picnic; you can sit at old redwood picnic tables and watch the white combers race upon the black-sand beach at the mouth of Waipio Valley.

From the lookout, you can hike down into the valley. Do not, repeat *do not,* attempt to drive your rental car down into the valley (even if you see someone else doing it). The problem is not so much going down as coming back up. Every day, rental cars have to be "rescued" and towed back up to the top, at great expense to the driver. Instead, take the **Waipio Valley Shuttle** (© **808/775-7121**) on a 90-minute guided tour. The shuttle runs Monday through Saturday from 9am to 4pm; tickets are

$45 for adults, $20 for kids 11 and under. Get your tickets at **Waipio Valley Art Works,** on Highway 240, 2 miles from the lookout (© **808/775-0958**).

You can also explore the valley on a narrated, 90-minute **Waipio Valley Wagon Tour** (© **808/775-9518**), a historical ride by mule-drawn surrey. Tours are offered every 2 hours on Monday through Saturday starting at 9:30am until 3:30pm. It costs $45 for adults, $23 for children 4 to 12; call for reservations.

If you want to spend more than a day in the valley, plan ahead. A few simple B&Bs are situated on the ridge overlooking the valley and require advance reservations (see "Accommodations You Can Afford," p. 238). While it's possible to camp, it does put a strain on the natural environment here.

HILO

Contact or stop by the **Downtown Hilo Improvement Association,** 252 Kamehameha Ave., Hilo, HI 96720 (© **808/935-8850;** www.downtownhilo.com) for a copy of its very informative self-guided walking tour of 18 historic sites in Hilo, focusing on various sites from the 1870s to the present.

ON THE WATERFRONT

Old banyan trees shade **Banyan Drive** 🎔🎔, the lane that curves along the waterfront to the Hilo Bay hotels. Most of the trees were planted in the mid-1930s by memorable visitors like Cecil B. DeMille (who was here in 1933 filming *Four Frightened People*), Babe Ruth (his tree is in front of Hilo Hawaiian Hotel), King George V, and Amelia Earhart, but many were planted by celebrities whose fleeting fame didn't last as long as the trees themselves.

It's worth a stop along Banyan Drive—especially if the coast is clear and the summit of Mauna Kea is free of clouds—to make the short walk across the concrete-arch bridge in front of the Naniloa Hotel to **Coconut Island** 🎔, if only to gain a panoramic sense of the place.

Also along Banyan Drive is **Liliuokalani Gardens** 🎔🎔, the largest formal Japanese garden this side of Tokyo. This 30-acre park, named for Hawaii's last monarch, Queen Liliuokalani, is as pretty as a postcard from the East, with bonsai, carp ponds, pagodas, and a moon-gate bridge. Admission is free; open 24 hours.

OTHER HILO SIGHTS

Lyman Museum & Mission House 🎔 *Kids*   The oldest wood-frame house on the island was built in 1839 by David and Sarah Lyman, a missionary couple who arrived from New England in 1832. This hybrid combined New England– and Hawaiian-style architecture with a pitched thatch roof. Built of hand-hewn koa planks and timbers, it's crowned by Hawaii's first corrugated zinc roof, imported from England in 1856. Here, the Lymans served as the spiritual center of Hilo, receiving such guests as Mark Twain, Robert Louis Stevenson, and Hawaii's own monarchs. The well-preserved house is the best example of missionary life and times in Hawaii. You'll find lots of artifacts from the last century, including furniture and clothing from the Lymans and one of the first mirrors in Hawaii. The 21st century has also entered the museum, which now offers online computers and interactive, high-tech exhibits.

The **Earth Heritage Gallery** next door continues the story of the islands with geology and astronomy exhibits, a mineral rock collection that's rated one of the top 10 in the country, and a section on local flora and fauna. Upstairs is the **Island Heritage Gallery,** which features displays on native Hawaiian culture, including a replica of a grass hut, as well as other cultures transplanted to Hawaii's shores.

Hilo

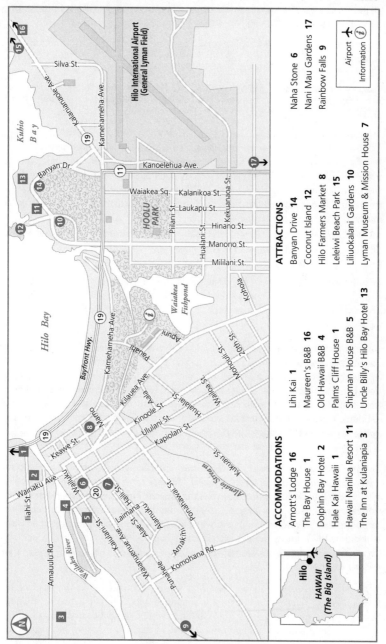

Hilo International Airport
(General Lyman Field)

Silva St.

Kalaniaole Ave.

Kamehameha Ave.

*Kuhio
Bay*

Banyan Dr.

Kanoelehua Ave.

Waiakea Sq.   Kalanikoa St.

Piliani St.

HOOLU
PARK

Laukapu St.

Kekuanaoa St.

Hinano St.

Manono St.

Mililani St.

Hualani St.

Hilo Bay

*Waiakea
Fishpond*

Kiholo

Bayfront Hwy.

Kamehameha Ave.

Apuni

Pauahi

Manu

Kilauea Ave.

Aala St.

Kinoole St.

Ululani St.

Kapiolani St.

Keawe St.

Wailuku

Wainaku Ave.

Iliahi St.

Mamo

Hualalai St.

Waianuenue Ave.

Aae St.

Haili St.

Laimana

Abanuku

Ponahawai St.

Kukuau St.

20th St.

Mohouli St.

Waiola St.

Almaio Stream

Kilauea

Amauulu Rd.

Wailuku River

Kaulani St.

Punahele

Amakihi

Komohana Rd.

ACCOMMODATIONS

Arnott's Lodge **16**
The Bay House **1**
Dolphin Bay Hotel **2**
Hale Kai Hawaii **1**
Hawaii Naniloa Resort **11**
The Inn at Kulaniapia **3**

Lihi Kai **1**
Maureen's B&B **16**
Old Hawaii B&B **4**
Palms Cliff House **1**
Shipman House B&B **5**
Uncle Billy's Hilo Bay Hotel **13**

ATTRACTIONS

Banyan Drive **14**
Coconut Island **12**
Hilo Farmers Market **8**
Leleiwi Beach Park **15**
Liliuokalani Gardens **10**
Lyman Museum & Mission House **7**

Naha Stone **6**
Nani Mau Gardens **17**
Rainbow Falls **9**

Airport ✈
Information ⓘ

Hilo

HAWAII
(The Big Island)

276 Haili St. (at Kapiolani St.), Hilo. © **808/935-5021.** www.lymanmuseum.org. Admission $10 adults, $8 seniors over 60, $3 children 6–17, $21 per family. Mon–Sat 9am–4:30pm.

Mauna Loa Macadamia Nut Factory
Explore this unique factory and learn how Hawaii's favorite nut is grown and processed. And, of course, you'll want to sample the tasty mac nuts, too.

Macadamia Nut Rd. (8 miles from Hilo, off Hwy. 11), Hilo. © **888/MAUNA LOA** or 808/966-8618. www.mauna loa.com. Free admission, self-guided factory tours. Daily 8:30am–5pm. From Hwy. 11, turn on Macadamia Nut Rd.; go 3 miles down the road to the factory.

Mokupapapa: Discovery Center for Hawaii's Remote Coral Reef
This 4,000-square-foot center is perfect for kids to explore Hawaii's Northwest Hawaiian Islands coral-reef ecosystem. Through interactive displays, engaging three-dimensional models, and an immersion theater, the kids can learn natural science, culture, and history while having a great time. A 2,500-gallon salt-water aquarium provides a habitat for a collection of fish from the Northwest Hawaiian Islands reefs. Way too much fun at a terrific price: free.

308 Kamehameha Ave, Suite 109, Hilo. © **808/933-8198**; www.hawaiireef.noaa.gov. Free admission. Mon–Sat. 9am–4pm.

Naha Stone
This 2½-ton stone was used as a test of royal strength: Ancient legend said that whoever could move the stone would conquer and unite the islands. As a 14-year-old boy, King Kamehameha the Great moved the stone—and later fulfilled his destiny. The Pinao stone, next to it, once guarded an ancient temple.

300 Waianuenue Ave., in front of Hilo Public Library, Hilo.

Nani Mau Gardens ✦
Just outside Hilo is Nani Mau ("forever beautiful"), where Makato Nitahara, who turned a 20-acre papaya patch into a tropical garden, claims to have every flowering plant in Hawaii. His collection includes more than 2,000 varieties, from fragile hibiscus, whose blooms last only a day, to durable red anthuriums imported from South America. There are also Japanese gardens, an orchid walkway, a botanical museum, a house full of butterflies, and a restaurant that's open for lunch and dinner.

421 Makalika St., Hilo. © **808/959-3500.** www.nanimau.com. Admission $10 adults, $5 children 4–10. Tram tours $7 extra. Daily 8:30am–5pm. Go 3 miles south of Hilo Airport on Hwy. 11, turn on Makalika St., and continue ¾ miles.

Pacific Tsunami Museum ✦
The most interesting artifacts here are not the exhibits, but the volunteers who survived Hawaii's most deadly "walls of water" in 1946 and 1960, both of which reshaped the town of Hilo. Visitors can listen to their stories of terror and view a range of exhibits, from interactive computers to a children's section to a display on what happens when a local earthquake triggers a seismic wave, as it did in 1975 during the Big Island's last tsunami.

130 Kamehameha Ave., Hilo. © **808/935-0926.** www.tsunami.org. Admission $7adults, $6 seniors, $2 students and children. Mon–Sat 9am–4pm.

Panaewa Rainforest Zoo ✦ *(Kids)*
This 12-acre zoo, nestled in the heart of the Panaewa Forest Reserve south of Hilo, is the only outdoor rainforest zoo in the United States. Some 50 species of animals from rainforests around the globe call Panaewa home—including several endangered Hawaiian birds. All of them are exhibited in a natural setting. This is one of the few zoos where you can observe Sumatran tigers, Brazilian tapirs, and the rare pygmy hippopotamus, an endangered "minihippo" found in Western Africa.

Stainback Highway (off Hwy. 11), Hilo. © **808/959-7224.** Free admission. Daily 9am–4pm.

Rainbow Falls ★ *Moments*   Go in the morning, around 9 or 10am, just as the sun comes over the mango trees, to see Rainbow Falls at its best. The 80-foot falls spill into a big round natural pool surrounded by wild ginger. If you like legends, try this: Hina, the mother of Maui, lives in the cave behind the falls. In the old days, before liability suits and lawyers, people swam in the pool, but that's now prohibited.

West on Waianuenue Ave., past Kaumana Dr., Hilo.

HAWAII VOLCANOES NATIONAL PARK ★★★

Yellowstone, Yosemite, and other national parks are spectacular, no doubt about it. But in our opinion, they're all ho-hum compared to this one: Here, nothing less than the miracle of creation is the daily attraction.

In the 19th century, before tourism became Hawaii's middle name, the islands' singular attraction for world travelers wasn't the beach, but the volcano. From the world over, curious spectators gathered on the rim of Kilauea's Halemaumau crater to see one of the greatest wonders of the globe. Nearly a century after it was named a National Park (in 1916), Hawaii Volcanoes remains the state's premier natural attraction.

Visiting the park is a yin/yang experience. It's the only rainforest in the U.S. National Park system—and the only park that's home to an active volcano. Most people drive through the park (it has 50 miles of good roads, some of them often covered by lava flows) and call it a day. But it takes at least 3 days to explore the whole park, including such oddities as **Halemaumau Crater,** a still-fuming pit of steam and sulfur; the intestinal-looking **Thurston Lava Tube; Devastation Trail,** a short hike through a desolated area destroyed by lava, right next to a rainforest; and finally, the end of **Chain of Craters Road,** where lava regularly spills across the man-made two-lane blacktop to create its own red-hot freeway to the sea. In addition to some of the world's weirdest landscapes, the park also has hiking trails, rainforests, campgrounds, a historic old hotel on the crater's rim, and that spectacular, still-erupting volcano.

NOTES ON THE ERUPTING VOLCANO   In Hawaii, volcanoes aren't violent killers like Mount Pinatubo in the Philippines or even Mount St. Helens in Washington State. Vulcanologists refer to Hawaii's volcanic eruptions as "quiet" eruptions, since gases escape slowly instead of building up and exploding violently all at once. Hawaii's eruptions produce slow-moving, oozing lava that provides excellent, safe viewing most of the time. In Hawaii, people run to volcanoes instead of fleeing from them.

Since the current eruption of Kilauea began on January 3, 1983, lava has covered some 16,000 acres of lowland and rainforest, threatening rare hawks, honeycreeper birds, spiders, and bats, while destroying power and telephone lines and eliminating water service possibly forever. Some areas have been mantled repeatedly and are now buried underneath 80 feet of lava.

Even though people haven't had to run from this flow, it has still caused its share of destruction. At last count, in early 2000, the lava flow had destroyed nearly 200 homes and businesses, wiped out Kaimu Black Sand Beach (once Hawaii's most photographed beach) and Queen's Bath, obliterated entire towns and subdivisions (Kalapana, Royal Gardens, Kalapana Gardens, and Kapaahu Homesteads), and buried natural and historic landmarks (a 12th-century *heiau,* the century-old Kalapana Mauna Kea Church, Wahaulu Visitor Center, and thousands of archaeological artifacts and sites). The cost of the destruction—so far—is estimated at $100 million. But how do you price the destruction of a 700-year-old temple or a 100-year-old church?

However, Kilauea has not only destroyed; it has also added—more than 560 acres of new land to the island by the beginning of 2000. The volume of erupted lava over the last 2 decades measures nearly two billion cubic yards—enough new rock to pave a two-lane highway 1.2 million miles long, circling the Earth some 50 times. Or, as a spokesperson for the park puts it: "Every 5 days, there is enough lava coming out of Kilauea volcano's eruption to place a thin veneer over Washington, D.C.—all 63 square miles."

The most prominent vent of the eruption has been Puu Oo, a 760-foot-high cinder-and-spatter cone. The most recent flow—the one you'll be able to see, if you're lucky—follows a 7-mile-long tube from the Puu Oo vent area to the sea. This lava flow has extended the Big Island's shoreline seaward and added hundreds of acres of new land along the steep southern slopes. Periodically, the new land proves unstable, falls under its own weight, and slides into the ocean. (These areas of ground gained and lost are not included in the tally of new acreage—only the land that sticks counts.)

Scientists are also keeping an eye on Mauna Loa, which has been swelling since its last eruption in 1983. If there's a new eruption, there could be a fast-moving flow down the southwest side of the island, possibly into South Kona or Kau.

WHAT YOU'RE LIKELY TO SEE   Hopefully, the volcano will still be streaming rivers of red lava when you visit the park, but a continuous eruption of this length (more than 2 decades) is setting new ground, so to speak. Kilauea continues to perplex vulcanologists, since most major eruptions in the past have ended abruptly after only several months.

But neither Mother Nature nor Madame Pele (the volcano goddess) runs on a schedule. The volcano could be shooting fountains of lava hundreds of feet into the air on the day you arrive, or it could be completely quiet—there are no guarantees with nature. On many days, the lava flows right by accessible roads, and you can get as close as the heat will allow; sometimes, however, the flow is miles away from the nearest access point, visible only in the distance or in underground tubes where you can't see it. Always ask the park rangers before you set out on any lava-viewing expedition.

VOLCANO VOCABULARY   The volcano has its own unique, poetic vocabulary that describes in Hawaiian what cannot be said so well in English. The lava that looks like swirls of chocolate cake frosting is called **pahoehoe (pa-*hoy*-hoy)**; it results from a fast-moving flow that curls artistically as it flows. The big, blocky, jumbled lava that looks like a chopped-up parking lot is called **aa** (ah-AH); it's caused by lava that moves slowly, pulling apart as it overruns itself.

Newer words include **vog**, which is volcanic smog made of volcanic gases and smoke from forests set on fire by aa and pahoehoe. **Laze** results when sulfuric acid hits

---

Tips **A Volcano-Visiting Tip**

Thanks to its higher elevation and windward (rainier) location, this neck of the woods is always colder than it is at the beach. If you're coming from the Kona side of the island in summer, expect it to be at least 10° to 20° cooler at the volcano; bring a sweater or light jacket. In the winter months, expect temperatures to be in the 40s or 50s, (4°C–15°C) and dress accordingly. Always have rain gear on hand, especially in winter.

Hawaii Volcanoes National Park

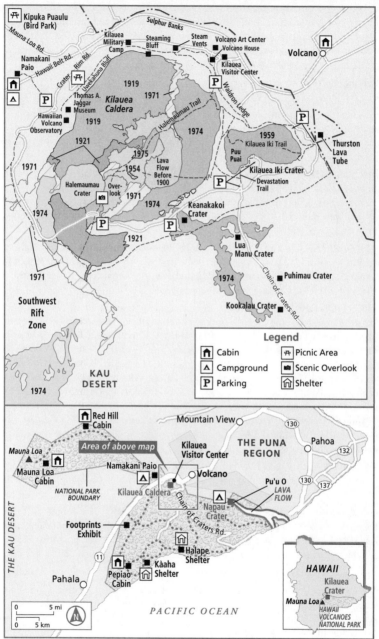

Kipuka Puaulu (Bird Park)

Mauna Loa Rd.

Hawaii Belt Rd.

Crater Rim Rd.

Sulphur Banks

Namakani Paio

Kilauea Military Camp

Steaming Bluff

Steam Vents

Volcano Art Center
Volcano House

Volcano

Kilauea Visitor Center

Uwekahuna Bluff

1919

1971

Kilauea Caldera

Waldron Ledge

Thomas A. Jaggar Museum

1919

Halemaumau Trail

1974

1971

Kilauea Iki Trail

1959

Hawaiian Volcano Observatory

1921

1975

1954

Lava Flow Before 1900

Puu Puai

Kilauea Iki Crater

Thurston Lava Tube

1971

Halemaumau Crater

Overlook

1971

1974

1974

Keanakakoi Crater

Devastation Trail

1921

Lua Manu Crater

1971

1974

Chain of Craters Rd.

Puhimau Crater

Kookalau Crater

Southwest Rift Zone

KAU DESERT

1974

Legend

🏠	Cabin	🪧	Picnic Area
⛺	Campground	📷	Scenic Overlook
🅿	Parking	🏚	Shelter

Red Hill Cabin

Mountain View

130

Pahoa

132

Mauna Loa

Area of above map

Kilauea Visitor Center

THE PUNA REGION

Mauna Loa Cabin

Namakani Paio

Volcano

NATIONAL PARK BOUNDARY

Kilauea Caldera

Chain of Craters Rd.

Pu'u O

LAVA FLOW

130

137

Napau Crater

THE KAU DESERT

Footprints Exhibit

11

Halape Shelter

Pahala

Pepiao Cabin

Kàaha Shelter

0   5 mi

0   5 km

PACIFIC OCEAN

HAWAII

Kilauea Crater

Mauna Loa

HAWAII VOLCANOES NATIONAL PARK

the water and vaporizes and mixes with chlorine to become, as any chemistry student knows, hydrochloric acid. Both vog and laze sting your eyes and can cause respiratory illness; don't expose yourself to either for too long. Pregnant women and anyone with heart or breathing trouble should avoid both vog and laze.

JUST THE FACTS

WHEN TO GO   The best time to go is when Kilauea is really pumping. If you're lucky, you'll be in the park when the volcano is active and fountaining; mostly, the lava runs like a red river downslope into the sea. If you're on another island and hear a TV news bulletin that the volcano is acting up, catch the next flight to Hilo to see the spectacle. You won't be sorry—and your favorite beach will still be there when you get back.

ACCESS POINTS   Hawaii Volcanoes National Park is 29 miles from Hilo, on Hawaii Belt Road (Hwy. 11). If you're staying in Kailua-Kona, it's 100 miles, or about a 2½-hour drive, to the park. Admission is $10 per vehicle; you can come and go as often as you want for 7 days. Hikers and bicyclists pay $5; bikes are allowed only on roads and paved trails.

VISITOR CENTERS & INFORMATION   Contact **Hawaii Volcanoes National Park,** P.O. Box 52, Hawaii Volcanoes National Park, HI 96718 (© **808/985-6000;** www.nps.gov/havo). **Kilauea Visitor Center** is at the entrance to the park, just off Highway 11; it's open daily from 7:45am to 5pm.

ERUPTION UPDATES   Everything you wanted to know about Hawaii's volcanoes, from what's going on with the current eruptions to where the next eruption is likely to be, is now available on the Hawaiian Volcano Observatory's new website, **http://hvo.wr.usgs.gov/kilauea/update/main.html**. The site is divided into areas on Kilauea (the currently erupting volcano), Mauna Loa (which last erupted in 1984), and Hawaii's other volcanoes (including Lo'ihi, the submerged volcano off the coast of the Big Island). Each section provides photos, maps, eruption summaries, and historical information.

You can also get the latest on volcanic activity in the park by calling the park's **24-hour hot line** (© **808/985-6000**). Updates on volcanic activity are also posted daily on the bulletin board at the visitor center.

HIKING & CAMPING IN THE PARK   Hawaii Volcanoes National Park offers a wealth of hiking and camping possibilities. See "Hiking & Camping" (p. 295) for details.

ACCOMMODATIONS IN & AROUND THE PARK   If camping isn't your thing, don't worry. There's a hotel, **Volcano House,** within the park boundary, on the rim of Halemaumau Crater; Volcano Village, just outside the park, has plenty of comfortable and convenient hotels and restaurants. See p. 256 through 280 for reviews.

SEEING THE HIGHLIGHTS

Your first stop should be the newly renovated **Kilauea Visitor Center** ★★, a rustic structure in a shady grove of trees just inside the entrance to the park. Here, you can get up-to-the-minute reports on the volcano's activity, learn how volcanoes work, see a film showing blasts from the past, get information on hiking and camping, and pick up the obligatory postcards.

Filled with a new understanding of vulcanology and the volcano goddess, Pele, you should then walk across the street to **Volcano House;** go through the lobby and out

Drive Up to an Erupting Volcano

When the hot tropical sun quits for the day, do not miss seeing the eruption—after dark. At night, it's the greatest show on earth: Red rivers of fire flow just below the surface, visible through the fissures between your feet, and Jell-O–like globs of molten lava inch their way down the mountain and pour into the steaming Pacific, creating the newest land on earth. The ongoing eruption has been pouring out lava for more than 20 years, with no sign of it stopping. Visitors wanting to see the lava flow have had difficulties in the past, as Madame Pele would roll her lava across the very roads leading to the eruption. Be sure to call ahead and check where the current eruption is and how to get there (© **808/985-6000**).

Every time you go, the eruption will be different. The best plan is to go about 1 to 2 hours before sunset. Before you jump in your car, be sure to bring a flashlight, plenty of water, sturdy closed-toed shoes and a jacket for after the sun has set. Some even pack sandwiches and juice, and a banana and an apple (for later, to rid your mouth of the lingering sulfur taste), plus an extra jug of water because it's hot out there on the lava, even after dark.

By the time you can see the telltale plume of smog that rises 1,000 feet in the sky, like a giant exclamation point, you will be near the end of the road. Park rangers will direct you where to park your car. From there you usually can see ruby rivers of lava running to the sea. Close to the parking area is a pile of steaming black pillowy-looking stuff with a silvery sheen— it's actually rock-hard pahoehoe lava, like swirls of chocolate frosting.

The first step onto the hardened lava is scary. It crunches like crushed glass under your heels (you'll be happy you have closed-toed shoes or hiking boots). In the distance you can see a red road map of molten lava glowing in the cracks and flowing in fiery rivulets about a foot below the surface. Depending on where the eruption is, you will have to walk a quarter-mile to a mile, in pitch-black darkness (except for your flashlight), to the intersection of lava and sea—but it's a walk that is well worth the trouble.

Silhouetted against the fire, visitors stand at the edge of the earth like primal natives witnessing the double act of creation and destruction. The lava hisses and spits and crackles as it moves, snakelike, in its perpetual flow to the sea, dripping like candle wax into the wavy surf—fire and water, the very stuff of the islands. The lava still burns underwater until the vast Pacific Ocean finally douses the fire and transforms the flow into yet more black-sand beach.

It's a sight you will never forget.

the other side, where you can get a good look at **Kilauea Caldera** ✫✫✫, a 2½-mile-wide, 500-foot-deep pit. The caldera used to be a bubbling pit of fountaining lava; today, you can still see wisps of steam that might, while you're standing there, turn into something more.

Now get out on the road and drive by the **Sulphur Banks** ✫, which smell like rotten eggs, and the **Steam Vents** ✫✫✫, where trails of smoke, once molten lava, rise from within the inner reaches of the earth. This is one of the few places where you feel that the volcano is really alive. Stop at the **Thomas A. Jaggar Museum** ✯✯✯ (open daily from 8:30am–5pm; free admission) for a good look at Halemaumau Crater, which is a half-mile across and 1,000 feet deep. On a clear day, you might also see Mauna Loa, 20 miles to the west. The museum shows video from days when the volcano is really spewing, explains the Pele legend in murals, and monitors earthquakes (a precursor of eruptions) on a seismograph, recording every twitch in the earth.

Once you've seen the museum, drive around the caldera to the south side, park, and take the short walk to Halemaumau Crater's edge, past stinky sulfur banks and steam vents, to stand at the overlook and stare in awe at this once-fuming old firepit, which still generates ferocious heat out of vestigial vents.

If you feel the need to cool off now, go to the **Thurston Lava Tube** ✯✯✯, the coolest place in the park. You'll hike down into a natural bowl in the earth, a forest preserve the lava didn't touch—full of native bird songs and giant tree ferns. Then you'll see a black hole in the earth; step in. It's all drippy and cool here, with bare roots hanging down. You can either resurface into the bright daylight or, if you have a flashlight, poke on deeper into the tube, which goes for another quarter-mile or so.

If you're still game for a good hike, try **Kilauea Iki Crater** ✯, a 4-mile, 2-hour hike across the floor of the crater, which became a bubbling pool of lava in 1959 and sent fountains of lava 1,900 feet in the air, completely devastating a nearby ohia forest and leaving another popular hike ominously known as **Devastation Trail** ✯✯✯. This half-mile walk is a startling look at the powers of a volcanic eruption on the environment. (See "Hiking & Camping," p. 295, for details on these and other park hikes.)

For a glimpse of ancient Hawaiian art, check out the **Puu Loa Petroglyphs** ✯, around the 15-mile marker down Chain of Craters Road. Look for the stack of rocks on the road. A brief, half-mile walk will bring you to a circular boardwalk where you can see thousands of mysterious Hawaiian petroglyphs carved in stone. This area, Puu Loa, was a sacred place for generations; fathers came here to bury their newborn's umbilical cord in the numerous small holes in the lava, thus ensuring a long life for the child. *Warning:* It's very easy to destroy these ancient works of art. Do not leave the boardwalk, and do not walk on or around the petroglyphs. Rubbings of petroglyphs will destroy them; the best way to capture them is by taking a photo.

THE VOLCANO AFTER DARK   If the volcano is erupting, be sure to see it after dark as brilliant red lava snakes down the side of the mountain and pours into the sea. It's a vivid display you'll never forget. About an hour and a half before sunset, find out from the park rangers the best way to get to the lava flow. From here (depending on the flow), it's about a mile walk over sharp-crusted lava; park rangers will tell you how to get to the best viewing locations. Be forewarned that the flow changes constantly, and on some days may be too far from the road to hike, in which case you'll have to be content with seeing it from a distance. Be sure to heed the rangers: In the past, a handful of hikers who ignored these directions died en route; new lava can be unstable and break off without warning. Take water, a flashlight, and your camera, and wear sturdy shoes.

A BIRD'S-EYE VIEW   The best way to see Kilauea's bubbling caldera is from on high, in a helicopter. It's a big splurge, of course, but this bird's-eye view puts the enormity of it all into perspective. We recommend **Blue Hawaiian Helicopter** ✯✯✯ (© **800/745-BLUE** or 808/886-1768; www.bluehawaiian.com), a professionally run, locally based company with an excellent safety record; comfortable, top-of-the-line 'copters; and pilots who are extremely knowledgeable about everything from vulcanology to Hawaii lore. The company flies out of both Hilo and Waikoloa (Hilo is cheaper because it's closer). From Hilo, the 45-minute **Circle of Fire** tour takes you over the boiling volcano and then on to a bird's-eye view of the destruction the lava has caused and remote beaches ($165 per person). From Waikoloa, the 2-hour **Big Island Spectacular** stars the volcano, tropical valleys, Hamakua Coast waterfalls, and the Kohala Mountains ($340, and worth every penny).

10 Shops & Galleries

While chefs and farmers tout this island as fertile ground for crops and food, artists point to its primal, volcanic energy as a boost to their creative endeavors, too. Art communities and galleries are sprinkled across the Big Island, in villages like Holualoa and Volcano, where fine works in pottery, wood-turning, handmade glass, and other two- and three-dimensional media are sold in serene settings.

Although the visual arts are flourishing on this island, the line between shop and gallery can often be too fine to define. Too many self-proclaimed "galleries" purvey schlock or a mixture of arts, crafts, and tacky souvenirs. Alas, T-shirts and Kona coffee mugs are a souvenir staple in many so-called galleries.

The galleries and shops below offer a broad mix in many media. Items for the home, jewelry and accessories, vintage Hawaiiana, and accoutrements at various prices and for various tastes can make great gifts to go, as can locally-made food products such as preserves, cookies, flowers, Kona coffee, and macadamia nuts. You'll find that bowls made of rare native woods, such as koa, are especially abundant on the Big Island. This is an area in which politics and art intersect: Although reforestation efforts are underway to plant new koa trees, the decline of old-growth forests is causing many artists to turn to equally beautiful, and more environmentally correct, alternative woods.

THE KONA COAST: IN & AROUND KAILUA-KONA

Kailua-Kona's shopping prospects pour out into the streets in a festival atmosphere of T-shirts, trinkets, and dime-a-dozen souvenirs, with Alii Drive at the center of this activity. But the **Coconut Grove Market Place**, on Alii Drive, across the street from the seawall, has changed that image and added some great new shops around a sand volleyball court. Next door, in the **Alii Sunset Plaza,** next to Hard Rock Cafe, beaders can make a beeline for **Kona Beads** (© **808/331-2161**) and peruse a dizzying—and handsome—collection of beads from all over the world.

Shopping stalwarts in Kona, in more familiar shopping territory, are the **Kona Square,** across from **King Kamehameha's Kona Beach Hotel;** the hotel's shopping mall, with close to two dozen shops; and the **Kona Inn Shopping Village,** on Alii Drive. All include the usual assortment of T-shirt shops. One highlight is **Alii Gardens Marketplace** at the southern end of Kailua-Kona, a pleasant, tented outdoor marketplace with fresh fruit, flowers, imports, local crafts, and a wonderful selection of orchid plants. There's cheesy stuff there, too, but somehow it's less noticeable outdoors.

EDIBLES & EVERYDAY THINGS

The Big Island's **greenmarkets** are notable for the quality of produce and the abundance of island specialties at better-than-usual prices. Look for the cheerful green kiosks of the **Alii Gardens Marketplace,** 75–6129 Alii Dr. (at the south end), where local farmers and artists set up their wares daily from 8am to 5pm. This is not your garden-variety marketplace; some vendors are permanent, some drive over from Hilo, and the owners have planted shade trees and foliage to make the 5-acre plot a Kona landmark. There are 40 to 50 vendors on any given day, selling jewelry, woodcrafts, produce, macadamia nuts, orchids, and—our favorite—the fresh juices of Kay Reeves, owner of Wau, who gets up before dawn to make her sensational fresh lilikoi and lime juices with healthy ingredients. Kona Blue Sky Coffee is also here, as is Lynn Cappell, a fine painter of island landscapes, and Laura de Rosa's A la Dreams lotions and oils—sensational.

For produce and flowers straight from the farm, go to the **Kona Farmers' Market** in Kaiwi Square, in Kona's old industrial area (follow the sign on the Queen Kaahumanu Hwy.). Open on Saturday and Wednesday from 8:30am to 2:30pm, it teems with dedicated vendors and eager shoppers. You'll find live catfish, taro, organic vine-ripened tomatoes, Kamuela string beans, lettuces, potatoes, and just-picked blooms, such as anthuriums and feathery, sturdy protea.

Java junkies jump-start their day at **Island Lava Java** (© **808/327-2161**), the hot new magnet for coffee lovers at the Coconut Grove Market Place, on Alii Drive. At the other end of Kailua-Kona, the hand-made, hand-dipped candies of **Kailua Candy Company** (© **808/329-2522;** or 800/622-2462 for orders) also beckon, especially the macadamia-nut clusters with ground ginger or the legendary macadamia-nut *honu* (turtle). Other products include truffles, pure Kona coffee, shortbread cookies, toffee, macadamia nuts, T-shirts, mugs, mustards, and other gift items.

Good news for wine lovers: **Kona Wine Market,** in the King Kamehameha Mall (© **808/329-9400**), has a noteworthy selection, including some esoteric vintages, at prices you'll love. This is a wine lover's store, with selections from California, Europe, and points beyond, as well as gift baskets, cheeses, cigars, oils and vinegars, specialty pastas and condiments, Riedel glassware, and friendly, knowledgeable service.

For everyday grocery needs, **KTA Stores** (in the Kona Coast Shopping Center, at Palani Rd. and the Queen Kaahumanu Hwy., and in the Keauhou Shopping Village, on Alii Dr.) are always our first choice. Through its Mountain Apple brand, KTA sells hundreds of top-notch local products—from Kona smoked marlin and Hilo-grown rainbow trout to cookies, breads, jams and jellies, taro chips, and *kulolo,* the decadently dense taro-coconut steamed pudding—by dozens of local vendors. The fresh-fish department is always an adventure; if anything esoteric is running, such as the flashy red aweoweo, it's sure to be on KTA's counters, along with a large spread of prepared foods for sunset picnics and barbecues.

Our other favorite is **Kona Natural Foods,** in the Crossroads Center (© **808/329-2296**). It's been upgraded from a health-food store to a full-on healthy supermarket. And it's the only full-service health-food store for miles, selling bulk grains and cereals, vitamins, snacks, fresh-fruit smoothies, and sandwiches and salads from its take-out deli. Organic greens, grown in the South Kona area, are a small but strong feature of the produce section.

GIFTS & FASHION
Alapaki's Hawaiian Gifts   Lovers of Polynesian crafts will appreciate this selection of gift items, made by more than 100 craftspeople from five of the Hawaiian Islands, with a small percentage of the inventory from Fiji, Samoa, Tonga, Tahiti, and other Polynesian islands. Alapaki's includes jewelry, original paintings, feather hat bands, ceramics, and handblown glass. Photography by noted Big Island photographer G. Brad Lewis,

Art Appreciation

The finest art on the Kona Coast hangs in, of all places, a bank. Award-winning **First Hawaiian Bank,** 74–5593 Palani Rd. (© **808/329-2461**), has art lovers making special trips to view Hiroki Morinoue's mural, John Buck's prints, Chiu Leong's ceramic sculpture, Franco Salmoiraghi's photographs, Setsuko Morinoue's abstract fiber wallpiece, and other works that were incorporated as part of the bank's design, rather than added on as an afterthought. Artists Yvonne Cheng and Sharon Carter Smith, whose works are included, assembled this exhibition, a sterling example of corporate sponsorship of the arts.

who specializes in volcanoes, is among the items for sale. In Keauhou Shopping Center, Alii Dr. © **808/322-2007.**

Hawaiian Country   Noe Kimi Buchanan and her husband, Alika Buchanan, make a fine team on the main drag of Kailua-Kona. He does all the weaving of the fans and hats, while she makes the trims. Their colorful display, in the open air across from the Kailua Bay seawall, is a celebration of things Hawaiian: good weather, generosity of spirit, love of fibers and textures, and old-fashioned ingenuity. The hats are visible from up and down the street—and they're wonderfully affordable (you can find a great one for $12 and a fabulous one for more). Lauhala, raffia, straw, you name it—it's here, just waiting to soothe the sunburned brow. And every woman who buys one gets a free lauhala hat pin, made by the Buchanans. 75–5693 Alii Dr., outdoors below Stan's Restaurant. No phone.

Honolua Surf Company   This shop targets the surf-and-sun enthusiast with good things for good times: towels, flip-flops, body boards, sunglasses, swimsuits, and everything else you need for ocean and shore action. Quiksilver, Tommy Bahama, Roxy, Billabong, and Kahala are among the top menswear labels here, but we also like the quirky, colorful Toes on the Nose. Also popular is the full line of products with the Honolua Surf Co. label, including T-shirts, hats, bags, dresses, sweatshirts, aloha shirts, and swimwear. At Kona Inn Shopping Village, Alii Dr. © **808/329-1001.**

Kailua Village Artists Gallery   A co-op of four dozen Hawaii island artists, plus a few guest artists, display their works in various media: watercolors, paintings, prints, handblown and blasted glass, and photography. Books, pottery, and an attractive assortment of greeting cards are among the lower-priced items. In King Kamehameha's Kona Beach Hotel, 75–5660 Palani Rd. © **808/329-6653.**

Noelani Farms   Noelani Whittington's grandfather planted the coffee trees on this farm when he was 85 years old. The trees are still yielding tasty coffee beans that Noelani and her husband, Rick, sell wholesale and retail. The 100% Kona coffee is available by phone order. The beans are hand-roasted—only 15 pounds at a time—and packed with lots of TLC. You can also order the seasonally available pincushion and miniature king protea, and the dazzling Telopa protea, which resemble torch gingers in all red and all white. Protea are sturdy, showy flowers with a long afterlife—they dry beautifully. The selection varies, depending on the time of year, so there are always surprises. Whittington also sells gift baskets and wreaths, and ships just about anywhere. Phone orders © **877/322-3579** or 808/322-3579.

UPCOUNTRY KONA: HOLUALOA

Charming Holualoa, 1,400 feet and 10 minutes above Kailua-Kona at the top of Hualalai Road, is a place for strong espresso, leisurely gallery hopping, and nostalgic explorations across several cultural and time zones. One narrow road takes you across generations and cultures.

Paul's Place is Holualoa's only all-purpose general store, a time warp tucked between frame shops, galleries, and studios.

Prominent Holualoa artists include the jewelry maker/sculptor Sam Rosen, who, years ago, set the pace for found-object art, and today, makes beautiful pieces at the rear of Chestnut Gallery; the furniture maker and wood sculptor Gerald Ben; the printmaker Nora Yamanoha; the glass artist Wilfred Yamazawa; the sculptor Cal Hashimoto; and Hiroki and Setsuko Morinoue of Studio 7 gallery. All galleries listed are on the main street, Mamalahoa Highway, and all are within walking distance of each other.

Cinderella Unlimited *(Finds)*   Most of the treasures here are tucked away, so don't be shy about asking the owner, Cindi Nespor, where she keeps her prized antique engravings or her out-of-print naturalists' books of hand-painted engravings. There are engravings of old Hawaii, rare prints and vases, kimonos, lamps, and home accessories. The rare books will quicken a book lover's heart, while the estate jewelry, vintage linens, rattan furniture, and hats make this a brilliant browse. Gorgeous antique shawls, long-extinct Chanel perfumes, and 1940s Garbo-style hats are among the treasures found here. Call ahead, though; the owner keeps flexible, island-style hours. Mamalahoa Hwy. ℂ **808/322-2474.**

Dovetail Gallery and Design   Located behind the old historic post office, Dovetail features contemporary and abstract art and the works of high-end, fine craftsmen and furniture makers. But the gallery's custom woodworking shop separates it from all the other galleries lining the Mamalahoa Highway. It features top craftsmen and the design work of Gerald Ben, who not only is a skilled ceramicist, but also has been a custom woodworker for 22 years. His expertise is designing furniture and wood accessories for his clients, which include collectors, home owners, interior designers, and architects. 76–5942 Mamalahoa Hwy. ℂ **808/322-4046.**

Holualoa Gallery   Owners Matthew and Mary Lovein show their own work as well as the work of selected Hawaii artists in this roadside gallery in Holualoa. Sculptures, paintings, koa furniture, fused-glass bowls, raku ceramics, and creations in paper, bronze, metal, and glass are among the gallery's offerings. 76–5921 Mamalahoa Hwy. ℂ **808/322-8484.**

Kimura Lauhala Shop   Everyone loves Kimura's and the masterpieces of weaving that spill out of the tiny shop. It's lined with lauhala, from rolled-up mats and wide-brimmed hats to tote bags, coasters, and coin purses. The fragrant, resilient fiber, woven from the spiny leaves of the *hala* (pandanus) tree, is smooth to the touch and becomes softer with use. Lauhala also varies in color, according to region and growing conditions. Although Kimura employs a covey of local weavers who use the renowned hala leaves of Kona, some South Pacific imports bolster the supply. At Mamalahoa Hwy. and Hualalai Rd. ℂ **808/324-0053.**

Studio 7 *(Finds)*   Some of Hawaii's most respected artists, among them gallery owners Setsuko and Hiroki Morinoue, exhibit their works in this serenely beautiful studio. Smooth pebbles, stark woods, and a garden setting provide the backdrop for Hiroki's paintings and prints and Setsuko's pottery, paper collages, and wall pieces. The Main

Gallery houses multimedia art, the Print Gallery has sculptural pieces and two-dimensional works, and the Ceramic Gallery holds the works of Clayton Amemiya, Chiu Leong, and Gerald Ben, whose mixed-media sculptures, made of ceramic raku and wood, continue to be a pleasing attraction. This is the hub of the Holualoa art community; activities include workshops, classes, and special events by visiting artists. Mamalahoa Hwy. ℭ 808/324-1335.

SOUTH KONA
EDIBLES

In Kealakekua, the **Kamigaki Market,** on Highway 11, also called Mamalahoa Highway, is a reliable source of food items, especially for regional specialties such as macadamia nuts and Kona coffee.

In Honaunau, farther south, keep an eye out for the **Bong Brothers' Store,** on Highway 11, and its eye-catching selections of fresh local fruit—from cherimoya (in season) to star fruit and white **Sugarloaf pineapples.** The Bongs are known for their deli items, produce, and Kona coffee fresh from their own roasting room, but we think their black, very hip Bong Brothers and Bong Sistah T-shirts are the find of the region and season. The juice bar offers homemade soups and smoothies made with fresh local fruit.

In Captain Cook, look for the big "Banana Bread" sign (you can't miss it) across the street from the fire station on Highway 11, and you'll come across the **Captain Cook Baking Company,** which bakes excellent banana bread with macadamia nuts, under the "Auntie Helen's" label. This bakery/sandwich shop also sells Lilikoi Gold passion butter, cheesecake brownies, and submarine sandwiches on its own house-made breads. The banana breads are made with Big Island bananas and macadamia nut honey, and are baked right there in the kitchen.

GIFTS & FASHION

Antiques and Orchids   Beverly Napolitan and her husband took over the oldest building in Captain Cook (built in 1906) and filled it with an eclectic array of antiques, collectibles, and fresh orchids. There are a few vintage Hawaiian items, lots of tea cups, raspberry-colored walls, linens, old kimonos, celadon, etched glass and crystal lamps, a Queen Liliuokalani lanai sofa from the 1800s, and a red wooden veranda where tea is served at the Saturday high tea (11am–4pm); complete with homemade scones, Devonshire cream, and English tea cups. You can't miss the green building with white trim, on the *mauka* (mountain) side of the highway in Captain Cook. Hwy. 11, Captain Cook. ℭ 808/323-9851.

The Grass Shack   The Grass Shack has been here for more than 3 decades with its large selection of local woodcrafts, Niihau shell and wiliwili-seed leis, packaged coffee, pahu drums, nose flutes, and lauhala (woven pandanus leaves) in every form. Bowls, boxes, and accessories of Norfolk pine, the rare kou, and other local woods also take up a sizable portion of the shop. Lauhala baskets, made of fiber from the region and the Hamakua Coast, are among the Shack's finest offerings, as are the custom ukuleles and feather gourds for hula dancing. Hwy. 11, Kealakekua. ℭ 808/323-2877.

Island Framing Company and Gifts   The owners of this tiny frame shop have great taste, and they've filled their shop with their favorite things: excellent soaps and candles (including Votivo, very chichi), line lights in fabulous designs (such as Japanese lanterns), framed prints, koa frames, Indonesian imports, umbrellas, and household accessories and accents that would liven up any home. Look closely and you might spot a treasure, such as the beautiful lacquer chest I saw for $1,285. The shop is in a charming green plantation house with a small veranda, on the ocean side of the street at the border of Kainaliu and Kealakekua. Hwy. 11, Kealakekua. ✆ 808/322-4397.

Kimura Store *(Finds)*   This old-fashioned general store is one of those places you'll be glad you found—a store with spirit and character, plus everything you need and don't need. You'll see Hawaii's finest selection of yardage, enough cookware for a multi-course dinner, aspirin, Shiseido cosmetics, and an eye-popping assortment of buttons, zippers, and quilting materials. Irene Kimura, the family matriarch, who presided over the store for more than 60 years until she passed away recently, said she quit counting the fabric bolts at 8,000 but knew there were more than 10,000. Kimura's is the spot for pareu and Hawaiian fabrics, brocades, silks, and offbeat gift items, such as Japanese china and *tabi*, the comfortable cloth footwear. Hwy. 11, Kainaliu. ✆ 808/322-3771.

THE KOHALA COAST

Shops on the Kohala Coast, with Gold-Coast prices, are concentrated in and around the resorts, listed below.

HILTON WAIKOLOA VILLAGE   Among the hotel's shops, **Sandal Tree** carries footwear with style and kick: Italian sandals at non-Italian prices, designer pumps, and other footwear to carry you from sailing deck to dance floor.

KING'S SHOPS   These stores are located near the Hilton. A recent find here—and a lifesaving one!—is **Walking in Paradise.** The footwear—much of it made in France (Mephisto, Arche)—can be expensive, but it's worthwhile for anyone seeking comfort while exploring the harsh lava terrain of this island or the pedestrian culture of Kailua's Alii Drive. Toward the *mauka* (mountain side) end is **Noa Noa,** filled with exotic arti-facts from Java and Borneo and tropical clothing for easygoing life on the Pacific Rim. At **Under the Koa Tree,** some of the island's finest artists display their prints, wood-crafts, and paintings. For snacks, ice, sunscreen, wine, postcards, newspapers, and everyday essentials, there's the **Whalers General Store,** and for dining on the run, a small food court with pizza, plate lunches, and the **Wild Boar Juice & Java** bar for fresh-pressed carrot/ginger juice or a steaming cup of brew.

HUALALAI RESORT   **Ka'upulehu Store,** in the Four Seasons Resort Hualalai, is a perfect blend of high quality and cultural integrity. Located within the award-win-ning Ka'upulehu Cultural Center, the store carries items made in Hawaii: handmade paper, hand-painted silks, seed lei, greeting cards, koa bowls, wreaths, John Kelly prints, and a selection of Hawaii-themed books. **Hualalai Sports Club and Spa,** in the same resort, has a winning retail section of beauty, aromatherapy, and treatment products, including Hana Nai'a Aromatherapy products. The products include mango and jasmine perfumes, Bulgarian rose water, and herbal lotions and potions.

MAUNA LANI RESORT   In the Fairmont Orchid, at **Spa Without Walls,** the finest European beauty treatments, a well-trained staff, and products using seaweeds, salts, herbs, and essential oils make it hard to resist the spa's refined allure.

NORTH KOHALA

Ackerman Gallery   Crafts and fine arts are housed in two separate galleries a few blocks apart. Artist Gary Ackerman and his wife, Yesan, display gifts, crafts, and the works of award-winning Big Island artists, including Ackerman's own Impressionis-tic paintings. There are Kelly Dunn's hand-turned Norfolk pine bowls, Jer Houston's heirloom-quality koa-and-ebony desks, and Wilfred Yamazawa's handblown-glass perfume bottles and sculptures. Primitive artifacts, Asian antiques, jewelry, and Cal Hashimoto's bamboo sculptures are also among the discoveries here. The crafts-and-gifts gallery, across from the King Kamehameha statue, has recently doubled in size; it features gift ideas in all media and price ranges. Hwy. 270 (across from the Kamehameha statue; also 3 blocks away, on the opposite side of the street), Kapaau. *C* 808/889-5971.

As Hawi Turns   You never know what you'll find in this whimsical, delightful shop of women's clothing and accessories. The windows may be filled with painted paper lanterns in the shapes of stars, or retro painted switch plates, or kicky straw hats paired with bias-cut silk dresses and quirky jewelry. This is the perfect place to pamper yourself with such fripperies as tatami zoris and flamboyant accessories for a colorful tropical life. Hwy. 270 (Akoni Pule Hwy.), Hawi. *C* 808/889-5023.

Elements   John Flynn designs jewelry and his wife, Prakash, assembles fountains and other treasures, and together they've filled their quiet gallery with an assortment of arts and crafts from the Big Island, including local artist Margaret Ann Hoy's wonderful watercolors of island scenes. The lauhala accessories, jewelry, and fountains—simple bowls filled with smooth gemstones such as amethyst and rose quartz, with a water pump for the movement—make great gifts and accessories. Hwy. 270 (Akoni Pule Hwy.), Kapaau. *C* 808/889-0760.

Harbor Gallery   Formerly Kohala Kollection, this two-story gallery seems to have made a seamless transition, remaining a big draw next to the Cafe Pesto in this industrial harbor area of Kawaihae. Harry Wishard paintings, Miles Fry's museum-quality model canoes and ships, Kathy Long pencil drawings, and Frances Dennis's painted island scenes on canvas are among the works by more than 150 artists, primarily from the Big Island. The range is vast—from jewelry to basketry to ceramics, carved native woods and heirloom-quality koa furniture. In Kawaihae Shopping Center, Hwy. 270, just north of Hwy. 19. *C* 808/882-1510.

Kohala Book Shop   Jan and Frank Morgan's new-and-used bookstore—the largest such store in Hawaii—is a huge success and a major attraction in the town's historic Hotel Nanbu building. The yellow building with red-and-green trim is beautifully and faithfully restored; all the better to house a priceless collection that includes out-of-print first editions, the $22,500 set of *Captain Cook's Journals, The Morals of Confucius* (dated 1691 and priced at $350), and thousands of other treasures. You'll see popular fiction and everyday books, too, along with titles on Hawaii and Oceania; at last count, the inventory was 20,000 and climbing. Thoughtful signs, good prices, and an attractive and welcoming environment are only some of the winning features. Hwy. 270 (Akoni Pule Hwy.), a block from the Kamehameha statue, Kapaau. *C* 808/889-6732.

WAIMEA

Shops here range from the small roadside storefronts lining Highway 19 and Highway 190, which intersect in the middle of town, to complexes such as **Waimea Center,** where you'll find the trusty old **KTA Super Store,** the one-stop shop for all your basic necessities, plus a glorious profusion of interesting local foods. (Unfortunately, the nightmarish parking lot breeds road rage.) Across the street at **Parker Ranch Shopping Center,** you'll find **Big Island Coffee Co., The Little Juice Shack,** and a smattering of shops and casual eateries, including the ever-popular **Reyn's,** but generally this complex is uninspired. With its upscale galleries and shops, **Parker Square** will likely be your most rewarding stop.

Small and sublime, the **Waimea Farmers' Market,** Highway 19, at mile marker 55 on the Hamakua side of Waimea town (on the lawn in front of the Department of Hawaiian Home Lands, West Hawaii office), draws a loyal crowd on Saturdays from 7am to noon. Waimea is lei country as well as the island's breadbasket, so look for protea, vegetables, vine-ripened tomatoes, and tuberose stalks here at reasonable prices. Mainstays include **Honopua Farm** and **Hufford's Farm,** side by side, selling flowers and organic vegetables. And the flowers: freesias, irises, heather, stars-of-Bethlehem, Australian teas, and cleomes, all freshly clipped. You'll find **Marie McDonald,** one of Hawaii's premier lei-makers, at the booth. (If you want one of her designer Waimea leis, you have to order ahead; call © **808/885-4148.**) Also here is **Bernice Berdon,** considered the best maker of akulikuli leis, a Waimea signature that comes in yellows, oranges, and fuchsias. Ask about her bat-face kika, the cigar-flower lei with bat-faced blossoms. If you're here around Christmas, the protea wreaths are phenomenal.

At the other end of Waimea, the **Parker School Farmers' Market,** held Saturdays from 7:30am to noon, is smaller and more subdued, but with choice items as well. The Kalopa macadamia nuts are the sweetest and tastiest we've ever had.

Hilo's wonderful **Dan De Luz Woods** (p. 337) has a branch at 64–1013 Mamalahoa Hwy., in front of the True Value hardware store.

Bentley's Home & Garden Collection

To its lavish list of glassware, linens, chenille throws, home fragrances, stuffed animals, and Wild West gift wraps, Bentley's has added casual country clothing in linens and cottons. Dresses, sweaters, raffia hats, top-drawer Western shirts, handbags, woven shoes, and all things Martha Stewart adorn this fragrant, gardenesque shop. This is for people who like to raise flowers and herbs, cook with them, breathe potpourried air, and make everything from scratch. In Parker Square, Hwy. 19. © 808/885-5565.

Gallery of Great Things

Here's an eye-popping assemblage of local art and Pacific Rim artifacts. Browse under the watchful gaze of an antique Tongan war club (not for sale) and authentic rhinoceros- and deer-horn blowguns from Borneo among the plethora of treasures from Polynesia, Micronesia, and Indonesia. You'll find jewelry, glassware, photographs, greeting cards, fiber baskets, and hand-turned bowls of beautifully grained woods. Photos by Victoria McCormick, Kathy Long sketches, feather masks by Bety McCormick, and the paintings of Yvonne Cheng are among the treasures by local artists. There are a few pieces of etched glass and vintage clothing, too, along with a small, gorgeous collection of antique kimonos. In Parker Square, Hwy. 19. © 808/885-7706.

Mauna Kea Galleries (Finds)

This is the new and expanded version of the gallery we've come to know and love in Hilo, which is now open by appointment only. Mark Blackburn, who wrote *Hawaiiana: The Best of Hawaiian Design,* has made this his showcase for the treasures he loves to collect. He and his wife, Carolyn, amass vintage Hawaiiana in mint condition from estate sales and collectors all over the country, then respectfully display it. Their collection includes monarchy and Ming jewelry; mint-condition Santa Anita and Don Blanding dinnerware, including very rare pieces; adz-hewn, not lathed, koa- and kou-wood bowls; and vintage photography and menus, all individually stored in plastic sleeves ($10–$300). Rare books and prints, including hand-colored 1870s lithographs; old koa furniture; original Hawaiian fish prints from the early 1900s; and limited-edition, museum-quality reproductions of hula-girl photos from the 1890s are also among the finds. 65–1298 Kawaihae Rd., Waimea. © 808/969-1184.

Silk Road Gallery   Now doubled in size from its original location, Silk Road offers a rare experience of beauty in a large corner of Parker Square. It's worth a special stop if you love Asian antiques: porcelain tea cups, jade cups, kimonos, lacquerware, Buddhas, tansus, bronze bells and chimes, Indonesian woven baskets, Japanese screens, and all manner of delights for elevated living. Fine textiles and baskets, antique dolls, rare woodblock prints, and books, cards, and prints are some of its offerings. You can part with $15 for a bronze bell, thousands for an antique tansu, or something in between. The gallery overflows with Asian treasures, so leave time for an unhurried look. In Parker Square, Hwy. 19. (℃ **808/885-7474.**

Sweet Wind   Because the owner loves beauty and harmonious things, you'll find chimes, carved dolphins, crystals, geodes, incense (an excellent selection), beads, jewelry, gems, essential oils, and thoughtfully selected books worth more than a casual glance. The books cover self-help, health, metaphysics, Hawaiian spirituality, yoga, meditation, and other topics for wholesome living. In Parker Square, Hwy. 19. (℃ **808/885-0562.**

Upcountry Connection   This warm, gleaming gallery and gift shop offers an even mix of fine art, antiques, and crafts, all of impeccable taste, plus a recently expanded collection of home accessories, gifts, and decorative pieces. You may not be looking for a koa chest, but it's here, along with antique koa mirrors, fine crocheted linens, jewelry boxes, hand-turned Norfolk pine bowls, and all kinds of collectibles and contemporary art. Other great discoveries: the original oils, limited prints, cards, and books of Herb Kawainui Kane, a living treasure of Hawaii; and the vibrant paintings of Harry Wishard. The gallery has expanded its line of sterling and hand-beaded jewelry, accessories, and clothing. In Mauna Kea Center, Hwy. 19 and Hwy. 190. (℃ **808/885-0623.**

Waimea General Store   This charming, unpretentious country store has always offered a superb assortment of Hawaii-themed books, soaps and toiletries, cookbooks and kitchen accessories, candles, linens, greeting cards, dolls, Japanese hapi coats, island teas, rare kiawe honey, preserves, and countless gift items from the practical to the whimsical. This is a great stop for Crabtree and Evelyn soaps, fragrances, and cookies—and 1,000 other delights. In Parker Square, Hwy. 19. (℃ **808/885-4479.**

THE HAMAKUA COAST

Waipio Valley Artworks   Housed in an old wooden building at the end of the road before the Waipio Valley, this gallery/boutique offers treasures for the home. The focus here is strictly local, with a strong emphasis on woodwork—one of the largest selections, if not the largest, in the state. A recent expansion has brought more chests and tables and gift items by Big Island artists. All the luminaries of wood-turning have works here: Jack Straka, Robert Butts, Scott Hare, Kevin Parks. Their bowls, rocking chairs, and jewelry boxes exhibit flawless craftsmanship and richly burnished grains. More affordable are the pens and hair accessories. Deli sandwiches and Tropical Dreams ice cream are served in the expanded cafe. In Kukuihaele. (℃ **808/775-0958.**

HONOKAA

Mamane Street Bakery (p. 274), on the main drag, will fill all your coffee-shop needs. Fresh-baked breads, pies, and pastries (including melt-in-your-mouth danishes) are served with good coffee in a tiny cafe lined with old photographs.

Honokaa Market Place   We've noticed a proliferation of Balinese imports (not a good sign) mingling with the old and new Hawaiiana. The eclectic selection of Hawaiian, Asian, and Indonesian handicrafts includes wood crafts, Hawaiian prints, and Hawaiian quilts, from wall hangings and pillows to the full-sized quilts, plus a few pieces of jewelry. 45–3321 Mamane St. ✆ **808/775-8255.**

Honokaa Trading Company   "Rustic, tacky, rare—there's something for everyone," says owner Grace Walker. Every inch of this labyrinthine, 2,200-square-foot bazaar is occupied by antiques and collectibles, new and used goods, and countless treasures of plantation memorabilia and Hawaiiana. Bark-cloth fabrics from the 1940s, rhinestone jewelry and rattan furniture from the 1930s, vintage ukuleles, Depression glass, dinnerware from Honolulu's landmark Willows restaurant, koa lamps, Francis Oda airbrush paintings, vintage kimonos and linens. This is a Honokaa landmark, a plantation museum, and a major attraction for treasure hunters. It's an unbelievable conglomeration, with surprises in every corner. Vigilant collectors make regular forays here to scoop up the 1950s ivory jewelry and John Kelly prints. Mamane St. ✆ **808/775-0808.**

Kamaaina Woods   The showroom is adjacent to the workshop, so visitors can watch the craftspeople at work on the other side of the glass panel. Local woods are the specialty here, with a strong emphasis on koa and milo bowls. Boxes, carvings, albums, and smaller accessories are also included in the mix, but bowl-turning is clearly the focus. Prices begin at about $10. Lehua St. (down the hill from the post office). ✆ **808/775-7722.**

Maya's Clothing and Gifts   The Hawaiian-print table runners and locally made soaps and ceramics are only part of the growing selection at this Honokaa newcomer. Napkins, place mats, hula girl lamps, koa accessories, quilted Hawaiian pot holders, aloha shirts, jams and jellies, T-shirts, sportswear, jewelry boxes—it's an eclectic selection for all tastes. Mamane St. ✆ **808/775-1016.**

Seconds to Go   Elaine Carlsmith spends a lot of time collecting vintage pottery, glassware, kimonos, fabrics, and other treasures, only to release them to eager seekers of nostalgia. Many beautiful things have passed through her doors, including antique koa furniture, old maps, music sheets, rare and out-of-print books, and reams of ephemera. The vintage ivory jewelry and Don Blanding dinnerware are grabbed up quickly. The main store is a few doors away from the warehouse, where furniture and larger pieces are displayed. Mamane St. ✆ **808/775-9212.**

Starseed   Shop here for offbeat holographic bumper stickers, jewelry, beads, incense, and New Age amulets. The selection of beads and crystals is impressive. The owner has a special camera that purportedly photographs people's auras, or electromagnetic fields. Find out what your colors are, or look for them in the hundreds of boxes of beads, some of them rare European and Asian imports. Mamane St. ✆ **808/775-9344.**

Taro Patch Gifts   Taro Patch carries an eclectic assortment of Hawaiian music tapes and CDs, switch plates printed with Hawaiian labels, Ka'u coffee, local jams and jellies, soaps, pareus, books, ceramics, sushi candles, essential oils, and sportswear, such as Hawaiian-print cowboy shirts. The Hawaiian seed lei selection is the best in town: kamani, blue marble, wiliwili, double sheep eye, betel nut, and several other attractive native species. Mamane St. ✆ **808/776-1602.**

HILO

Shopping in Hilo is centered on the **Kaiko'o Hilo Mall,** 777 Kilauea Ave., near the state and county buildings; the **Prince Kuhio Shopping Plaza,** 111 E. Puainako, just off Highway 11 on the road north to Volcano, where you'll find a supermarket, drugstore,

Macy's West (formerly Liberty House), and other standards; the **Bayfront area** downtown, where the hippest new businesses have taken up residence in the historic buildings lining Kamehameha Avenue; and the new **Waiakea Plaza,** where the big-box retailers (Ross, Office Max, Borders, Wal-Mart) have moved in. For practical needs, there's a **KTA Super Store** at 323 Keawe St. and another at 50 E. Puainako St. Also see "Edibles," below.

Basically Books   Our favorite Hilo bookstore, affectionately called "the map shop," is a sanctuary for lovers of books, maps, and the environment. They have expanded their selection of Hawaii-themed gift items while they maintain the engaging selection of printed materials covering geology, history, topography, botany, mythology, and more. Get your bearings by browsing among the nautical charts, U.S. Geological Survey maps, street maps, raised relief maps, atlases, and compasses, and books on travel, natural history, music, spirituality, and countless other topics. Specializing in Hawaii and the Pacific, this is a bountiful source of information that will enhance any visit. Even the most knowledgeable residents stop by here to keep current and conscious. 160 Kamehameha Ave. ⓒ 808/961-0144.

Dan De Luz Woods   The unstoppable Dan De Luz has been turning bowls for more than 30 years. His studio, on the highway on the way to Volcano, is a larger, more stunning showcase than his previous location in Hilo. He turns koa, milo, mango, kamani, kou, sandalwood, hau, and other island woods, some very rare, into bowls, trays, and accessories of all shapes and sizes. You can find bookmarks, rice and stir-fry paddles, letter openers, and calabashes, priced from $3 to $1,000. Hwy. 11, Kurtistown. ⓒ 808/935-5587.

Dragon Mama *(Finds*   For a dreamy stop in Hilo, head for this haven of all-natural comforters, cushions, futons, meditation pillows, hemp yarns and shirts, antique kimonos and obis, tatami mats sold by the panel, and all manner of comforts in the elegantly spare Japanese esthetic. The bolts of lavish silks and pure, crisp cottons, sold by the yard, can be used in clothing or interior decorating. Dragon Mama also offers custom sewing, and you know she's good: She sewed the futon and bedding for the Dalai Lama when he visited the island a few years ago. 266 Kamehameha Ave. ⓒ 808/934-9081.

Ets'ko   Shop and be entertained by the dizzying selection of loungewear, porcelains, teapots, home accessories, purses, and miscellaneous good things the owner collects from the design centers of the world. Futuristic wine racks, minimalist jewelry, neckties, photo frames, handblown-glass pens, Japanese furniture and accessories, and ultraluxe candles are included in the glittering assortment. 35 Waianuenue Ave. ⓒ 808/961-3778.

Hana Hou *(Finds*   Michele Zane-Faridi has done a superlative job of assembling, designing, and collecting objects of beauty that evoke old and new Hawaii. Vintage shirts, china, books, furniture, lamps, jewelry, handbags, accessories, and fabrics are displayed in surprising corners. The bark-cloth lampshades and collector's dreams— such as vintage silver-and-ivory jewelry by Ming—disappear quickly. Mundorff prints, 1940s sheet music, and the nicest dressing room on the island (with a mango-wood bench made from the same tree as the desk) are more reasons for a standing ovation. 164 Kamehameha Ave. ⓒ 808/935-4555.

Hawaiian Force   Artist Craig Neff and his wife, Luana, hang their shingle at the original location of Sig Zane Designs (good karma), where they sell bold, wonderful T-shirt dresses, mamaki tea they gather themselves, lauhala fans and trivets, surf wear, aloha shirts, and jewelry made of opihi and Niihau shells. Everything here is Hawaiian, most of it made or designed by the Neffs. Their handsome, two-toned T-shirt dresses are a Hawaiian Force signature, ideal for Island living, and very popular. 140 Kilauea Ave. (℃ 808/934-7171.

Sig Zane Designs *Finds* Our favorite stop in Hilo, Sig Zane Designs evokes such loyalty that people make special trips from the outer islands for this inspired line of authentic Hawaiian wear. The spirit of this place complements the high esthetic standards; everyone involved is completely immersed in Hawaiian culture and dance. The partnership of Zane and his wife, the revered hula master Nalani Kanaka'ole, is stunningly creative. The shop is awash in gleaming woods, lauhala mats, and clothing and accessories—handmade house slippers, aloha shirts, pareus, muumuus, T-shirts, duffel bags, and high-quality, made-in-Hawaii crafts. They all center on the Sig Zane fabric designs. New designs appear constantly, yet the classics remain fresh and compelling: ti, koa, kukui, taro, the lehua blossoms of the ohia tree. The Sig Zane bedcovers, cushions, fabrics, and custom-ordered upholstery bring the rainforest into your room. To add to the delight, Sig and his staff take time to "talk story" and explain the significance of the images, or simply chat about Hilo, hula, and Hawaiian culture. 122 Kamehameha Ave. (℃ 808/935-7077.

EDIBLES
Abundant Life Natural Foods Stock up here on healthful snacks, fresh organic produce, vitamins and supplements, bulk grains, baked goods, and the latest in health foods. There's a sound selection of natural remedies and herbal body, face, and hair products. The take-out deli makes fresh-fruit smoothies and sprout- and nutrient-rich sandwiches and salads. Seniors get a 10% discount. 292 Kamehameha Ave. (℃ 808/935-7411.

Big Island Candies Abandon all restraint. The smell of butter mixing with chocolate is as thick as honey, and the chocolate-dipped shortbread and macadamia nuts will make it very hard to be sensible. Owner Alan Ikawa has turned cookie-making into an art and a spectator sport. Large viewing windows allow you to watch the hand-dipping from huge vats of chocolate while the aroma of butter fills the room. Ikawa uses eggs straight from a nearby farm, pure butter, Hawaiian cane sugar, no preservatives, and premium chocolate. Gift boxes are available, and they're carted inter-island—or shipped all over the country—in staggering volumes. The Hawaiian Da Kine line is irrepressibly local: mochi crunch, fortune cookies, animal crackers, and other morsels—all dipped in chocolate. By far, the best are the shortbread cookies, dipped in chocolate, peanut butter, and white chocolate. 585 Hinano St. (℃ 808/935-8890; or (℃ 800/935-5510 for mail orders.

Hilo Farmers' Market *Finds* This has grown into the state's best farmers' market, embodying what we love most in Hawaii: local color, good soil and weather, the mixing of cultures, and new adventures in taste. More than 120 vendors from around the island bring their flowers, produce, and baked goods to this teeming corner of Hilo every Wednesday and Saturday from sunrise to 4pm. Because many of the vendors sell out early, go as early as you can. Expect to find a stunning assortment: fresh, homegrown oyster mushrooms from Kona—three or four different colors and sizes—for about $5 a pound; the creamy, sweet, queenly Indonesian fruit called mangosteen; warm breads, from focaccia to walnut; an array of flowers; fresh aquacultured seaweed; corn from Pahoa; Waimea strawberries; taro and taro products; foot-long, miso-flavored, and traditional Hawaiian laulau; made-from-scratch tamales; and fabulous ethnic vegetables with unpronounceable names. The selection changes by the week, but it's always reasonable, fresh, and appealing, with a good cross section of the island's specialties. Although it's open daily, Wednesday and Saturday are the days when all the vendors are there. Kamehameha Ave. at Mamo St. © **808/933-1000.**

O'Keefe & Sons   You can enjoy O'Keefe's breads throughout the island, served in the best delis, coffee shops, and restaurants. But come to the source, this friendly Hilo bakery, for the full selection of artisan breads and pastries hot from the oven: Hilo nori bread, black-pepper/cilantro bread, focaccia in many flavors, cracked rye, challah, three types of sourdough, carrot-herb bread, and the classic French country loaf. Located opposite the Hawaii Tribune Herald building, O'Keefe's serves sandwiches, soups, and quiche for lunch. 374 Kinoole St. © **808/934-9334.**

THE VOLCANO AREA

In volcano you have the option of exploring a unique array of shops and galleries (the rainforest seems to create an atmosphere of creativity) or visiting a local artist's studio. If you make an appointment, most artists are happy to give you a tour of their studios and will sell their work directly to you (avoiding the middle man and giving you 50%–60% off the price in a gallery).

STUDIO VISITS

The airy Volcano studio/showroom of **Phan Barker** (© **808/985-8636**), an international artist, is a mountain idyll and splendid backdrop for her art, which ranges from batik paintings on silk, acrylic painting on wood, oil on paper, dye on paper, and mixed media sculptures. Her work has been exhibited in galleries and museums ranging from the Smithsonian to Saigon. In addition to studio visits (by appointment only), she also offers classes in painting on silk and drawing for beginners.

Adding to the vitality of the Volcano arts environment are the studio visits offered by the **Volcano Village Art Studios.** Several respected artists in various media open their studios to the public by appointment. Artists in the hui include **Ira Ono** (© **808/967-7261**), who makes masks, water containers, fountains, paste-paper journals, garden vessels, and goddesses out of clay and found objects; **Pam Barton** (© **808/967-7247**), who transforms vines, leaves, roots, bark, and tree sheddings into stunning fiber sculptures and vessels, from baskets to handmade paper and books; raku and jewelry artist **Zeke Israel** (© **808/965-8820**); and sculptor **Randy Takaki** (© **808/985-8756**), who works in wood, metal, and ceramics.

SHOPS & GALLERIES

Kilauea Kreations   This is the quilting center of Volcano, a co-op made up of local Volcano artists and crafters who make quilts, jewelry, feather leis, ceramics, baskets, and fiber arts. Gift items made by Volcano artists are also sold here, but it's the quilts and quilting materials that distinguish the shop. Starter kits are available to initiate the needleworthy into this Hawaiian and American craft. We also like the Hawaiian seed leis and items made of lauhala, as well as the locally made soaps and bath products and the greeting cards, picture frames, and candles. Old Volcano Rd. © **808/967-8090.**

Volcano Art Center   The Volcano Island's frontier spirit and raw, primal energy have spawned a close-knit community of artists. Although their works appear in galleries and gift shops throughout the island, the Volcano Art Center (VAC) is the hub of the island's arts activity. Housed in the original 1877 Volcano House, VAC is a not-for-profit art-education center that offers exhibits and shows that change monthly, as well as workshops and retail space. Marian Berger's watercolors of endangered birds, Dietrich Varez oils and block prints, Avi Kiriaty oils, Kelly Dunn and Jack Straka woods, Brad Lewis photography, Harry Wishard paintings, Ira Ono goddess masks, and Mike Riley furnishings are among the works you'll see. Of the 300 artists represented, 90% come from the Big Island. The fine crafts include baskets, jewelry, mixed-media pieces, stone and wood carvings, and the journals and wood diaries of Jesus Sanchez, a third-generation Vatican bookbinder who has turned his skills to the island woods. In Hawaii Volcanoes National Park. ℂ **808/967-8222.**

Volcano Store   Walk up the wooden steps into a wonderland of flowers and local specialties. Tangy lilikoi butter (transportable, and worth a special trip) and flamboyant sprays of cymbidiums, tuberoses, dendrobiums, anthuriums, hanging plants, mixed bouquets, and calla lilies (splendid when grown in Volcano) make a breathtaking assemblage in the enclosed front porch. Volcano residents are lucky to have these blooms at such prices. The flowers can also be shipped (orders are taken by phone); Marie and Ronald Onouye and their staff pack them meticulously. If mainland weather is too humid or frosty for reliable shipping, they'll let you know. Produce, stone cookies (as in hard-as-stone) from Mountain View, Hilo taro chips, cookies, bottled water (a necessity in Volcano), local *poha* (gooseberry) jam, and bowls of chile rice (a local favorite) round out the selection. Even if you're just visiting the park for the day, it's worth turning off to stop for gas here; kindly clerks give directions. At Huanani and Old Volcano Hwy. ℂ **808/967-7210.**

Volcano Winery   Lift a glass of Volcano Blush or Macadamia Nut Honey and toast Pele at this boutique winery, where the local wines are made from tropical honey (no grapes) and tropical fruit blends (half-grape and half-fruit). It's open daily from 10am to 5:30pm; tastings are free. Pii Mauna Dr., off Hwy. 11 at mile marker 30, all the way to the end. ℂ **808/967-7479.**

11 The Big Island After Dark

Jokes abound about neighbor-island nightlife being an oxymoron, but there are a few pockets of entertainment here, largely in the Kailua-Kona and Kohala Coast resorts. Your best bet is to check the local newspapers—*Honolulu Advertiser* and *West Hawaii Today*—for special shows, such as fund-raisers, that are held at local venues. Other than that, regular entertainment in the local clubs usually consists of mellow Hawaiian music at sunset, small hula groups, or jazz trios.

Some of the island's best events are held at **Kahilu Theatre,** in Waimea (ℂ **808/ 885-6017;** www.kahilutheatre.org), so be on the lookout for any mention of it during your stay. Hula, the top Hawaiian music groups from all over Hawaii, drama, and all aspects of the performing arts use Kahilu as a venue.

LIVE MUSIC/DANCING

A host of bars and restaurant featuring dancing and live music when the sun goes down, all of them on Alii Drive in Kailua-Kona. Starting from the south end of Alii Drive, **Huggo's on the Rocks** (ℂ **808/329-1493**) has dancing and live music on weekends, and next door at **Huggo's Restaurant,** there are jazz and blues and a piano bar. Across the street from Huggo's, **Durty Jake's Café & Bar** (ℂ **808/329-7366**) in the Coconut Marketplace has live rock 'n' roll on Saturday and karaoke during weeknights. Upstairs, **Lulu's** (ℂ **808/321-2633**) draws a 20-something crowd with music to match on Friday and Saturday, with dancing till 1:00 in the am.

Just down the street, the **Hard Rock Cafe** (© **808329-8866),** in the **Alii Sunset Plaza,** has music most nights, sometimes live, sometimes DJ, but always a happening kind of place.

If you are in the mood for a few laughs, the **Big Island Comedy Club** usually has a live performance once a week of stand-up comedians on tour; performances are at the Royal Kona Resort. To check the current line up, call © **808/329-4368.**

THE BEST LUAU ON THE BIG ISLAND

Kona Village Luau *Moments*   The longest continuously running luau on the island is still the best—a combination of an authentic Polynesian venue with a menu that works, impressive entertainment, and the spirit of old Hawaii. The feast begins with a ceremony in a sandy kiawe grove, where the pig is unearthed after a full day of cooking in a rock-heated underground oven. In the open-air dining room, next to prehistoric lagoons and tropical gardens, you'll sample a Polynesian buffet: poisson cru, poi, laulau (butterfish, seasoned pork, and taro leaves cooked in ti leaves), lomi salmon, squid luau (cooked taro leaves with steamed octopus and coconut milk), ahi poke, *opihi* (fresh limpets), coconut pudding, taro chips, sweet potatoes, chicken long rice, steamed breadfruit, and the shredded kalua pig. The generosity is striking. The Polynesian revue, a fast-moving, mesmerizing tour of South Pacific cultures, manages— miraculously—to avoid being clichéd or corny. Friday at 5:30pm. In Kona Village Resort. © 808/325-5555. Reservations required. Part of the full American plan for Kona Village guests; for non-guests, $76 adults, $46 children 6–12, $22 children 2–5.

THE KOHALA COAST RESORTS

Evening entertainment here usually takes the form of a luau or indistinctive lounge music at scenic terrace bars with scintillating sunset views. But Marriott Waikoloa's **Hawaii Calls** restaurant and adjoining **Clipper Lounge** are a bright new venue for local musicians, with live music nightly from 8:30 to 11:30pm (see also "Great Deals on Dining," p. 261).

The Friday luau at the **Kona Village Resort** (see above) is the best choice on the island. Otherwise, the resort roundup includes the Hilton Waikoloa Village's **Legends of the Pacific** Friday dinner show, $72 adults, $36 children ages 5 to 12 (© **808/885-1234)** and the Tuesday luau at the **Mauna Kea Beach Hotel** (© **808/882-7222),** $76 adults, $38 children ages 5 to 12.

A popular night spot on the Kohala Coast is the **Honu Bar** (© **808/885-6622)** at the Mauna Lani Bay Hotel, a sleek, chic place for light supper, live light jazz with dancing, gourmet desserts, fine wines, and after-dinner drinks. When most other restaurants are closing, you can still order toothsome pastas and light suppers with fine wines by the glass.

If you get a chance to see the **Lim Family,** don't miss them. Immensely talented in hula and song, members of the family perform in the intimate setting of the Mauna Lani Bay Hotel's **Atrium Bar** (© **808/885-6622)** and at the Hapuna Beach Prince Hotel's open-air **Reef Lounge** (© **808/880-1111).** Also at the Hapuna Beach Prince Hotel is a new night club, **Splash At Hapuna** (© **808/880-1111),** featuring live music and dancing Monday through Saturday, with Hawaii's best musicians playing top 40's, jazz, or Hawaiian.

The **Hilton Waikoloa Beach's** newly opened Malolo Lounge (© **808/886-1234;** www.hiltonwaikoloavillage.com) has nightly live entertainment of Hawaiian music (5–8pm) and jazz (9pm–midnight).

Just beyond the resorts, lies a great music spot, the **Blue Dolphin Restaurant,** 61–3616 Kawaihae Rd., Kawaihae (© **808/882-7771**), where an eclectic mix of music happens Wednesday through Saturday, featuring jazz, rock, swing, Hawaiian, and even big band music.

HILO

Hilo's most notable events are special or annual occasions such as the **Merrie Monarch Hula Festival,** the state's largest, which continues for a week after Easter Sunday. The festivities include hula competitions with competitors from all over the world, demonstrations, and crafts fairs. A staggering spirit of pageantry takes over the entire town. Tickets are always hard to come by; call © **808/935-9168** well ahead of time, and see the "Hawaii Calendar of Events" (p. 32), for more information.

A special new venue is the old **Palace Theater,** 38 Haili St. (© **808/934-7010**), restored and in action thanks to the diligent efforts of the Friends of the Palace Theater. The neoclassical wonder first opened in 1925, was last restored in 1940, and has reopened for first-run movies while restoration continues. Film festivals, art movies, hula, community events, concerts (including the Slack Key Guitar Festival), and all manner of special entertainment take place at this historical marvel.

Special concerts are also held at the **Hawaii Naniloa Hotel's Crown Room** (© **808/969-3333**), the Hilo venue for big-name performers from Oahu and the outer islands. You can always count on a great act here, whether it's the Brothers Cazimero or Willie K.

Maui: The Valley Isle

Maui meets all the criteria for a tropical paradise: swaying palm trees bordering perfect white-sand coves; free-falling waterfalls etching the faces of mountains; voluptuous jungles bursting with bright color and birdsong; moonlight sparkling on calm, turquoise seas.

And everybody, it seems, knows it. Next to Waikiki, Maui is Hawaii's most popular destination, welcoming 2½ million people each year to its sunny shores. As soon as you arrive at Kahului Airport, a huge banner will tell you that readers of *Condé Nast Traveler* voted Maui the best island *in the world*—and they've done so 11 years running. *Travel and Leisure*'s readers also ranked Maui as their favorite island and top travel destination.

Maui has become *the* hip travel destination. Indeed, sometimes it feels a little too well-known—especially when you're stuck in bumper-to-bumper traffic or the wall-to-wall boat jam at Maui's popular snorkeling-diving atoll, Molokini Crater. However, the congestion here pales in comparison to big-city Honolulu's; Maui is really just a casual collection of small towns. Once you move beyond the resort areas, you'll find a slower, more peaceful way of life, where car horns are used only to greet friends, posted store hours mean nothing if the surf's up, and taking time to watch the sunset is part of the daily routine.

Visitors from other small towns in America and elsewhere find Maui just right: warm and friendly and not too foreign, with an easygoing lifestyle that's perfect for relaxing. But Maui also has an underlying energy that can nudge devout sunbathers right off the beach. People get inspired to do things they might not do otherwise, like rise before dawn to catch the sunrise over Haleakala Crater, then mount a bicycle to coast 37 switchbacked miles down to sea level; head out to sea on a kayak to look for wintering humpback whales; swim in the clear pool of a waterfall; or discover a whole new world of exotic flowers and tropical fish.

On a map, Maui doesn't look like much, but it's bigger than you might think. The 727-square-mile island has three peaks more than a mile high, thousands of waterfalls, 120 miles of shoreline, and more than 80 golden-sand beaches (including two that are more than a mile long). The island is the result of a marriage of two shield volcanoes, 10,023-foot-high Haleakala and 5,788-foot-high Puu Kukui, that spilled enough lava between them to create a valley—and inspire the island's nickname. Thanks to this unusual makeup, Maui packs a lot of nature in and around its landscape, and its microclimates offer distinct variations on the tropical-island theme: The island's as lush as an equatorial rainforest in Hana, as dry as the Arizona desert in Makena, as hot as Mexico in Lahaina, and as cool and misty as Oregon up in Kula. The shores of Hookipa are ideal for windsurfers, while channel breezes challenge golfers in Kapalua.

It is possible to have a fabulous vacation on Maui without having to take out a second mortgage. This chapter will give you all the info you need.

Maui

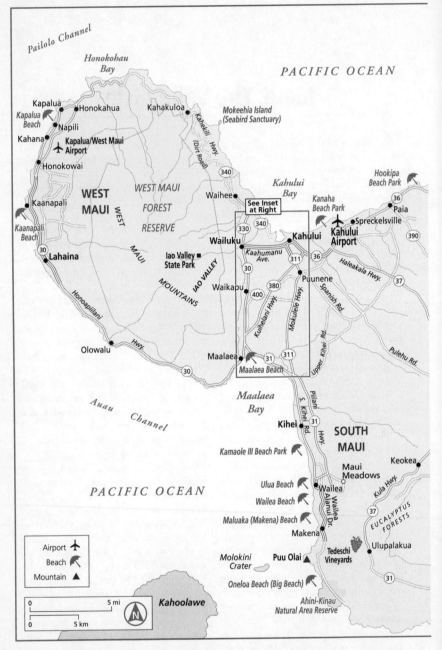

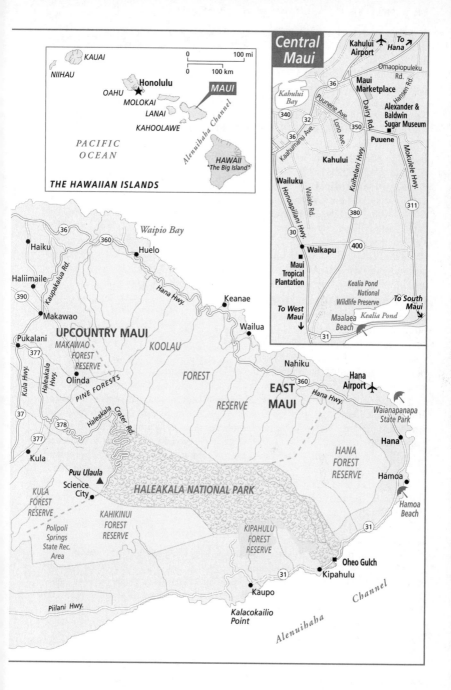

THE HAWAIIAN ISLANDS

KAUAI

NIIHAU

OAHU
Honolulu

MOLOKAI
LANAI
MAUI
KAHOOLAWE

PACIFIC
OCEAN

Alenuihaha Channel

HAWAII
"The Big Island"

0   100 mi
0   100 km

Central Maui

Kahului
Airport

To Hana

Omaopiopuleku Rd.

Maui
Marketplace

Kahului
Bay

Hansen Rd.

Alexander &
Baldwin
Sugar Museum

Puuene

Puunene Ave.

Lono Ave.

Dairy Rd.

Kahului

Kaahumanu Ave.

Kuihelani Hwy.

Mokulele Hwy.

Wailuku

Waiale Rd.

Honoapiilani Hwy.

Waikapu

Maui
Tropical
Plantation

Kealia Pond
National
Wildlife Preserve

To West
Maui

Maalaea
Beach

Kealia Pond

To South
Maui

Waipio Bay

Haiku

Huelo

Haliimaile

Kaupakalua Rd.

Makawao

Hana Hwy.

Keanae

Wailua

UPCOUNTRY MAUI

MAKAWAO
FOREST
RESERVE

KOOLAU

Pukalani

Olinda

Kula Hwy.

Haleakala Hwy.

PINE FORESTS

FOREST

Nahiku

Hana
Airport

EAST
MAUI

Hana Hwy.

Waianapanapa
State Park

RESERVE

Hana

Haleakala

Crater Rd.

Kula

Puu Ulaula
Science
City

HALEAKALA NATIONAL PARK

HANA
FOREST
RESERVE

Hamoa

Hamoa
Beach

KULA
FOREST
RESERVE

Polipoli
Springs
State Rec.
Area

KAHIKINUI
FOREST
RESERVE

KIPAHULU
FOREST
RESERVE

Oheo Gulch

Kipahulu

Kaupo

Kalacokailio
Point

Piilani Hwy.

Alenuihaha   Channel

1 Orientation

ARRIVING

If you think of the island of Maui as the shape of a person's head and shoulders, you'll probably arrive on its neck, at **Kahului Airport.**

As of press time, six airlines fly directly from the mainland to Maui. **United Airlines** (© **800/241-6522;** www.ual.com) has nonstop service from Los Angeles and San Francisco; **Hawaiian Airlines** (© **800/367-5320;** www.hawaiianair.com) offers direct flights from Los Angeles, San Francisco, Portland, and Seattle; **American Airlines** (© **800/433-7300;** www.aa.com) has direct service from Los Angeles; **Delta Airlines** (© **800/221-1212;** www.delta.com) flies direct from San Francisco and Los Angeles; **Aloha Airlines** (© **800/367-5250** or 808/484-1111; www.alohaair.com) has direct flights from Oakland and Orange County, California; and **American Trans Air** (© **808/435-9282;** www.ata.com) offers direct flights from San Francisco, Los Angeles, and Phoenix several times a week.

The other major carriers fly to Honolulu, where you'll have to pick up an inter-island flight to Maui. **Aloha Airlines** (© **800/367-5250** or 808/484-1111; www.aloha air.com) and **Hawaiian Airlines** (© **800/367-5320** or 808/838-1555; www.hawaiian air.com) both offer jet service from Honolulu and the other neighbor islands.

LANDING AT KAHULUI   Kahului airport is so small that a single plane can cause a long wait at the baggage carousel, rental car van pickup area, and rental car checkout desk—the three obstacles you must clear to get out onto the highway.

The Kahului Airport bottleneck is further compounded by poor urban planning. Maui expanded its small, friendly inter-island airport into a major international airport, and then built a busy retail complex just a mile from the end of the runway where three traffic-choked roads converge, usually the minute you arrive.

If there's a long wait at baggage claim, step over to the state-operated **Visitor Information Center** and pick up brochures and the latest issue of *This Week Maui,* which features great regional maps of the islands. After collecting your bags from the pokey carousels, step out, take a deep breath, and proceed to your right to the rental car pickup area (located behind the car rental desks), and wait for the appropriate shuttle van to take you a half-mile away to the rental car check-out desk, where there's usually another long line. This process can take as long as 20 to 30 minutes, sometimes more. Be patient. Look for rainbows. Notice how clouds form over Iao Valley. Try whistling "Tiny Bubbles." (All the major rental companies have branches at Kahului; see p. 57, "Getting There & Getting Around," in chapter 2, for details on renting in Hawaii.)

If you're not renting a car, the cheapest way to get to your hotel is **SpeediShuttle** (© **808/875-8070;** www.speedishuttle.com), which can take you between Kahului Airport and all the major resorts between 6am and 11pm daily. Rates vary, but figure on $30 for one to Wailea (one-way), $41 one-way to Kaanapali and $57 one-way to Kapalua. Be sure to call ahead of time to arrange pickup.

You'll see taxis outside the airport terminal, but note that they are quite expensive—expect to spend around $60 to $75 for a ride from Kahului to Kaanapali and $50 from the airport to Wailea.

If possible, avoid landing on Maui between 3 and 6pm, when the working stiffs on the island are "pau work" (finished with work) and a major traffic jam occurs at the first intersection.

AVOIDING KAHULUI   If you're planning to stay at any of the hotels in Kapalua or at the Kaanapali resorts, you might consider flying **Island Air** (© **800/323-3345**) from Honolulu to **Kapalua–West Maui Airport.** From this airport, it's only a 10- to 15-minute drive to most hotels in West Maui, as opposed to an hour from Kahului. **Pacific Wings** (© **888/873-0877** or 808/575-4546; www.pacificwings.com) flies eight-passenger, twin-engine Cessna 402C aircraft into tiny **Hana Airport,** but you have to make a connection at Kahului to get there.

VISITOR INFORMATION

The **Maui Visitors Bureau** is at 1727 Wili Pa Loop, Wailuku, Maui, HI 96793 (© **800/525-MAUI** or 808/244-3530; fax 808/244-1337; www.visitmaui.com). To get here from the airport, go right on Highway 36 (Hana Hwy.) to Kaahumanu Avenue (Hwy. 32); follow it past Maui Community College and Wailuku War Memorial Park onto East Main Street in Wailuku. At North Market Street, turn right, and then right again on Mill Street; go left on Imi Kala Street and left again onto Wili Pa Loop.

For those staying in the Lahaina-Kaanapali Area, the **Kaanapali Beach Resort Association,** at 2530 Kekaa Dr., Suite 1–B, Kaanapali-Lahaina, HI 96761 (© **800/ 245-9229** or 808/661-3271; www.maui.net/~kbra), can be helpful for information.

THE ISLAND IN BRIEF
CENTRAL MAUI

Maui's main airport lies in this flat, often windy corridor between Maui's two volcanoes, and this is where most of the island's population lives. You'll find good shopping and dining bargains here, as well as the heart of the business community and the local government.

KAHULUI   This is "Dream City," home to thousands of former sugarcane workers whose dream in life was to own their own home away from the sugar plantation. There's wonderful shopping here (especially at discount stores), but this is not a place to spend your vacation.

WAILUKU   Wailuku is like a time capsule, with its faded wooden storefronts, old plantation homes, shops straight out of the 1950s, and relaxed way of life. While most people race through on their way to see the natural beauty of **Iao Valley,** this quaint little town is worth a brief visit, if only to see a real place where real people actually appear to be working at something other than a suntan. This is the county seat, so you'll see men in neckties and women in dressy suits on important missions in the tropical heat. The town has a spectacular view of Haleakala Crater, great budget restaurants, some interesting bungalow architecture, a Frank Lloyd Wright building on the outskirts, a wonderful historic B&B, and the always-endearing Bailey House Museum.

WEST MAUI

This is the fabled Maui you see on postcards, with the jagged peaks of the West Maui mountains and green velvet valleys. The beaches here are some of the islands' best. And it's no secret: This stretch of coastline along Maui's "forehead," from Kapalua to the historic port of Lahaina, is the island's most bustling resort area (with South Maui close behind). Expect a few mainland-style traffic jams.

If you want to book into a resort or condo on this coast, first consider what community you'd like to base yourself in. Starting at the southern end of West Maui and moving northward, the coastal communities look like this:

LAHAINA   This old seaport is a tame version of its former self, when whalers swaggered ashore in search of women and grog. Today, the village teems with restaurants, T-shirt shops, and galleries, and parts of it are downright tacky, but there's still lots of real history to be found amid the gimcrackery. Lahaina is a great place to stay; accommodation choices include a few old hotels (such as the newly restored 1901 Pioneer Inn on the harbor), quaint bed-and-breakfasts, and a handful of oceanfront condos.

KAANAPALI   Farther north along the West Maui Coast is Hawaii's first master-planned family resort. Pricey midrise hotels line nearly 3 miles of gold-sand beach; they're linked by a landscaped parkway and a walking path along the sand. Golf greens wrap around the slope between beachfront and hillside properties. **Whalers Village**— a seaside mall with 48 shops and restaurants, including such fancy names as Tiffany and Louis Vuitton, plus the best little whale museum in Hawaii—and other restaurants are easy to reach on foot along the oceanfront walkway or by resort shuttle, which also serves the small West Maui airport just to the north. Shuttles also go to Lahaina (see above), 3 miles to the south, for shopping, dining, entertainment, and boat tours. Kaanapali is popular with meeting groups and families—especially those with teenagers, who like all the action.

HONOKOWAI, KAHANA & NAPILI   In the building binge of the 1970s, condominiums sprouted along this gorgeous coastline like mushrooms after a rain. Today, these older oceanside units offer excellent bargains. The great location—along sandy beaches, within minutes of both the Kapalua and Kaanapali resort areas, and close enough to the goings-on in Lahaina town—makes this area an accommodations heaven for the budget-minded.

In **Honokowai** and **Mahinahina,** you'll find mostly older units that tend to be cheaper. There's not much shopping here (mostly convenience stores), but you'll have easy access to the shops and restaurants of Kaanapali.

Kahana is a little more upscale than Honokowai and Mahinahina. Most of its condos are big high-rise types, newer than those immediately to the south. You'll find a nice selection of shops and restaurants in the area, and Kapalua–West Maui Airport is nearby.

Napili is a much-sought-after area for condo seekers: It's quiet; has great beaches, restaurants, and shops; and is close to Kapalua. Units are generally more expensive here (although we've found a few hidden gems at affordable prices).

KAPALUA   North beyond Kaanapali and the shopping centers of Napili and Kahana, the road starts to climb and the vista opens up to fields of silver-green pineapple and manicured golf fairways. Turn down the country lane of Pacific pines toward the sea, and you could only be in Kapalua. It's the very exclusive domain of two gracious—and expensive—hotels set on one of Hawaii's best gold-sand beaches, next to two bays that are marine-life preserves (with fabulous surfing in winter).

Even if you don't stay here, you're welcome to come and enjoy Kapalua. Both of the fancy hotels here provide public parking and beach access. The resort champions innovative environmental programs; it also has an art school where you can learn local crafts, as well as three favorite golf courses, historic features, a collection of swanky condos and homes (many available for vacation rental at astronomical prices), and wide-open spaces that include a rainforest preserve—all open to the general public.

SOUTH MAUI

This is the hottest, sunniest, driest, most popular coastline on Maui for sun lovers— Arizona by the sea. Rain rarely falls here, and temperatures stick around 85°F (29°C) year-round. On this former scrubland from Maalaea to Makena, where cacti once grew wild and cows grazed, there are now four distinctive areas—Maalaea, Kihei, Wailea, and Makena—and a surprising amount of traffic.

MAALAEA If West Maui is the island's head, Maalaea is just under the chin. This windy, oceanfront village centers on the small boat harbor (with a general store and a couple of restaurants) and the **Maui Ocean Center,** an aquarium/ocean complex. Visitors staying here should be aware that it's often—like, 350 days a year—very windy. All the wind from the Pacific is funneled between the West Maui Mountains and Haleakala and comes out in Maalaea.

KIHEI Kihei is less a proper town than a nearly continuous series of condos and mini-malls lining South Kihei Road. This is Maui's best vacation bargain. Budget travelers swarm like sun-seeking geckos over the eight sandy beaches along this scalloped, condo-packed, 7-mile stretch of coast. Kihei is neither charming nor quaint; what it lacks in aesthetics, though, it more than makes up for in sunshine, affordability, and convenience. If you want a latte in the morning, the beach in the afternoon, and Hawaii Regional Cuisine in the evening—all at budget prices—head to Kihei.

WAILEA Only 25 years ago, this was wall-to-wall scrub kiawe trees, but now Wailea is a manicured oasis of multimillion-dollar resort hotels along 2 miles of palm-fringed gold coast—sort of Beverly Hills by the sea, except California never had it so good. You'll find warm, clear water full of tropical fish; year-round golden sunshine and clear blue skies; and hedonistic pleasure palaces on 1,500 acres of black-lava shore indented by five beautiful beaches. Amazing what a billion dollars can do.

This is the playground of the stretch-limo set. The planned resort development—practically a well-heeled town—has a shopping village, three prized golf courses of its own and three more in close range, and a tennis complex. A growing number of large homes sprawl over the upper hillside, some offering excellent bed-and-breakfast units at reasonable prices. The resorts along this fantasy coast are spectacular, to say the least. Next door to the Four Seasons, the most elegant, is the Grand Wailea Resort and Spa, a public display of ego by Tokyo mogul Takeshi Sekiguchi, who dropped $600 million in 1991 to create his own mini-city. There's nothing like it in Hawaii. Stop in and take a look—it's so gauche you've gotta see it.

Appealing natural features include the coastal trail, a 3-mile round-trip path along the oceanfront with pleasing views everywhere you look—out to sea and to the neighboring islands, or inland to the broad lawns and gardens of the hotels. The trail's south end borders an extensive native coastal plant garden, as well as ancient lava-rock house ruins juxtaposed with elegant oceanfront condos. But the chief attractions, of course, are those five outstanding beaches (the best is Wailea).

MAKENA Suddenly, the road enters raw wilderness. After Wailea's overdone density, the thorny landscape is a welcome relief. Although beautiful, this is an end-of-the-road kind of place: It's a long drive from Makena to anywhere on Maui. If you're looking for an activity-filled vacation, you might want to try somewhere else, or you'll spend most of your vacation in the car. But if you want a quiet, relaxing respite, where the biggest trip of the day is from your bed to the beach, Makena is the place.

Beyond Makena, you'll discover Haleakala's last lava flow, which ran to the sea in 1790; the bay named for French explorer La Pérouse; and a chunky lava trail known as the King's Highway, which leads around Maui's empty south shore past ruins and fish camps. Puu Olai stands like Maui's Diamond Head on the shore, where a sunken crater shelters tropical fish and empty golden-sand beaches stand at the end of dirt roads.

UPCOUNTRY MAUI

After a few days at the beach, you'll probably take notice of the 10,000-foot mountain in the middle of Maui. The slopes of Haleakala ("House of the Sun") are home to cowboys, growers, and other country people who wave back as you drive by. They're all up here enjoying the crisp air, emerald pastures, eucalyptus, and flower farms of this tropical Olympus—there's even a misty California redwood grove. You can see a thousand tropical sunsets reflected in the windows of houses old and new, strung along a road that runs like a loose hound from Makawao to Kula, where the road leads up to the crater and **Haleakala National Park.** The rumpled, two-lane blacktop of Highway 37 narrows on the other side of Tedeschi Winery, where wine grapes and wild elk flourish on the Ulupalakua Ranch, the biggest on Maui. A stay upcountry is usually affordable and a nice contrast to the sizzling beaches and busy resorts below.

MAKAWAO   Until recently, this small, two-street upcountry town was little more than a post office, a gas station, a feed store, a bakery, and a restaurant/bar serving the cowboys and farmers living in the surrounding community; the hitching posts outside storefronts were really used to tie up horses. As the population of Maui started expanding in the 1970s, a health-food store sprang up, followed by boutiques, a chiropractic clinic, and a host of health-conscious restaurants. The result is an eclectic amalgam of old *paniolo* Hawaii and the baby-boomer trends of transplanted mainlanders. **Hui No'Eau Visual Arts Center,** Hawaii's premier arts collective, is definitely worth a peek. The only accommodations here are reasonably priced bed-and-breakfasts, perfect for those who enjoy great views and don't mind slightly chilly nights.

KULA   A feeling of pastoral remoteness prevails in this upcountry community of old flower farms, humble cottages, and new suburban ranch houses with million-dollar views that take in the ocean, the isthmus, the West Maui Mountains, and, at night, the string of pearls that lights the gold coast from Maalaea to Puu Olai. Everything flourishes at a cool 3,000 feet (bring a jacket), just below the cloud line, along a winding road on the way up to Haleakala National Park. Everyone here grows something—Maui onions, carnations, orchids, and proteas, that strange-looking blossom that looks like a *Star Trek* prop—and B&Bs cater to guests seeking cool tropic nights, panoramic views, and a rural upland escape. Here you'll find the true peace and quiet that only rural farming country can offer—yet you're still just 30 to 40 minutes away from the beach and an hour's drive from Lahaina.

EAST MAUI

ON THE ROAD TO HANA   When old sugar towns die, they usually fade away in rust and red dirt. Not **Paia.** The tangled spaghetti of electrical, phone, and cable wires hanging overhead symbolizes the town's ability to adapt to the times—it may look messy, but it works. Here, trendy restaurants, eclectic boutiques, and high-tech windsurf shops stand next door to a ma-and-pa grocery, a fish market, and stores that have been serving customers since plantation days. Hippies took over in the 1970s; although their macrobiotic restaurants and old-style artists' co-op have made way for Hawaii regional cuisine and galleries featuring the works of renowned international artists, Paia still manages to maintain a pleasantly granola vibe. The town's main attraction, though, is **Hookipa Beach Park,** where the wind that roars through the isthmus of Maui brings windsurfers from around the world. A few B&Bs are located just outside Paia in the tiny community of **Kuau.**

Ten minutes down the road from Paia and up the hill from the Hana Highway—the connector road to the entire east side of Maui—is **Haiku.** Once a pineapple-plantation village, complete with working cannery (today a shopping complex), Haiku offers vacation rentals and B&Bs in a quiet, pastoral setting: the perfect base for those who want to get off the beaten path and experience the quieter side of Maui, but don't want to feel too removed (the beach is only 10 min. away).

About 15 to 20 minutes past Haiku is the largely unknown community of **Huelo.** Every day, thousands of cars whiz by on the road to Hana; most barely glance at the double row of mailboxes overseen by a fading Hawaii Visitors Bureau sign. But down the gun-metal road lies a hidden Hawaii: a Hawaii of an earlier time, where Mother Nature is still sensual and wild, where ocean waves pummel soaring lava cliffs, and where an indescribable sense of serenity prevails. Huelo is not for everyone—but those who hunger for the magic of a place still largely untouched by "progress" should check into a B&B or vacation rental here.

HANA   Set between an emerald rainforest and the blue Pacific is a village probably best defined by what it lacks: golf courses, shopping malls, McDonald's. Except for a gas station and a bank with an ATM, you'll find little of what passes for progress here. Instead, you'll discover the simple joys of fragrant tropical flowers, the sweet taste of backyard bananas and papayas, and the easy calm and unabashed small-town aloha spirit of old Hawaii. What saved "Heavenly" Hana from the inevitable march of progress? The 52-mile **Hana Highway,** which winds around 600 curves and crosses more than 50 one-lane bridges on its way from Kahului. You can go to Hana for the day—it's a 3-hour drive from Kihei and Lahaina (and a half-century away)—but 3 days are better.

2 Getting Around

BY CAR   The only way to really see Maui is by rental car; there's no islandwide public transit. All of the major car-rental firms have agencies on Maui, usually at both Kahului and West Maui airports (for a complete list, as well as tips on insurance and driving rules, see chapter 2). Cars are usually plentiful, except on holiday weekends, which in Hawaii also means Prince Kuhio Day (Mar 26), King Kamehameha Day (June 11), and Admission Day (third Fri in Aug).

There are also a few frugal car-rental agencies offering used cars at discount prices. **Word of Mouth Rent-a-Used-Car** ✿, in **Kahului** (© **800/533-5929** or 808/877-2436; www.mauirentacar.com), offers a four-door compact without air-conditioning for $120 a week, plus tax; with air-conditioning, it's $145 a week, plus tax.

Maui has only a handful of major roads, and you can expect to encounter a traffic jam or two in the major resort areas. Two of them follow the coastline around the two volcanoes that form the island, Haleakala and Puu Kukui (the West Maui Mountain); one road goes up to Haleakala's summit; one road goes to Hana; one goes to Wailea; and one goes to Lahaina. It sounds simple, right? Well, it isn't, because the names of the few roads change en route. Study an island map before you set out.

Traffic advisory: The road from Central Maui to Kihei and Wailea, Mokulele Highway (Hwy. 311), is a dangerous strip that's often the scene of head-on crashes involving intoxicated and speeding drivers; be careful. Also, be alert on the Honoapiilani Highway (Hwy. 30) en route to Lahaina, since drivers who spot whales in the channel between Maui and Lanai often slam on the brakes and cause major tie-ups and accidents. Since this is the only main road connecting the west side to the rest of the island, if there is an accident, flooding, rock slide, or any other road hazard, traffic can back up for 1 to 8 hours (no joking)—plan accordingly.

BY MOPED   Mopeds are available for rent from **Wheels USA** at either of its two locations: 578 Front St., Lahaina (© **808/667-7751**), and in the Rainbow Mall, 2439 S. Kihei Rd., Kihei (© **808/875-1221**). Mopeds, which start at $10 for 2 hours or $22 per 24 hours, are little more than motorized bicycles that get up to around 35 mph (with a good wind at your back), so I suggest using them only locally (to get to the beach or to go shopping). Don't take them out on the highway; they can't keep up with traffic.

BY TAXI & SHUTTLE   Alii Taxi (© 808/661-3688) offers 24-hour service island-wide. You can also call **Kihei Taxi** (© **808/879-3000**), **Islandwide Taxi & Tours** (© **808/874-TAXI**), or **Sunshine Cabs of Maui** (© **808/879-2220**) if you need a ride.

Holo Ka'a Public Transit is a public/private partnership that has convenient, economical, and air-conditioned shuttle buses in Central, West, and South Maui. The costs range from free shuttle vans within the resort areas of Kaanapali, Kapalua, and Wailea to $1 for routes in Kaanapali-Lahaina, $2 for routes in Kapalua-Kaanapali to $5 for stops from Wailea to Maalaea. For more information, call © **808/879-2828** or go to www.akinatours.com.

FAST FACTS: Maui

American Express Offices are located in South Maui at the **Grand Wailea Resort** (© **808/875-4526**), and in West Maui at the **Westin Maui** at Kaanapali Beach (© **808/661-7155**).

Dentists Emergency dental care is available at **Kihei Dental Center,** 1847 S. Kihei Rd., Kihei (© **808/874-8401**), or in Lahaina at the **Aloha Lahaina Dentists,** 134 Luakini St. (in the Maui Medical Group Building), Lahaina (© **808/661-4005**).

Doctors **West Maui Healthcare Center,** Whalers Village, 2435 Kaanapali Pkwy., Suite H–7 (near Leilani's Restaurant), Kaanapali (© **808/667-9721**), is open 365 days a year until 10pm nightly; no appointment is necessary. In Kihei, call **Urgent Care Maui,** 1325 S. Kihei Rd, Suite 103 (at Lipoa St., across from Star Market), Kihei (© **808/879-7781**), which is open daily from 6am to midnight.

Emergencies Call © **911** for police, fire, and ambulance service. District stations are located in Lahaina (© **808/661-4441**) and in Hana (© **808/248-8311**).

Hospitals In Central Maui, **Maui Memorial Hospital** is at 221 Mahalani, Wailuku (© **808/244-9056**). East Maui's **Hana Medical Center** is on Hana Highway (© **808/248-8924**). In upcountry Maui, **Kula Hospital** is at 204 Kula Hwy., Kula (© **808/878-1221**).

Post Office To find the nearest post office, call © **800/ASK-USPS.** In Lahaina, there are branches at the Lahaina Civic Center, 1760 Honoapiilani Hwy., and at the Lahaina Shopping Center, 132 Papalaua St. In Kahului, there's a branch at 138 S. Puunene Ave.; and in Kihei, there's one at 1254 S. Kihei Rd.

Weather For the current weather, call © **808/871-5054;** for Haleakala National Park weather, call © **808/572-9306;** for marine weather and surf and wave conditions, call © **808/877-3477.**

3 Accommodations You Can Afford

Before you book, be sure to read "The Island in Brief," earlier in this chapter; it'll help you settle on a location. Also check out chapter 2, section 1, "55 Money-Saving Tips"; tips 21 to 39 have valuable advice on booking your accommodations. Also in chapter 2, section 14, "Tips on Accommodations" (starting on p. 62) defines the various options and points you to the state's best booking agencies.

Remember to add Hawaii's 11.42% accommodations tax to your final bill. Parking is free unless otherwise noted.

CENTRAL MAUI

If you're arriving late at night, or you have an early morning flight out, the best choice near Kahului Airport is the **Maui Beach Hotel,** 170 Kaahumanu Ave. (© **888/649-3222**). The nondescript, motel-like rooms start at $120 ($105 if you book online) and include free airport shuttle service. It's okay for a night, but not a place to spend your vacation.

WAILUKU

Old Wailuku Inn at Ulupono ★★ *Finds* This 1924 former plantation manager's home, lovingly restored by innkeepers Janice and Thomas Fairbanks, offers a genuine old-Hawaii experience. The theme is Hawaii of the 1920s and 1930s, with decor, design, and landscaping to match. The spacious rooms are gorgeously outfitted with exotic ohia-wood floors, high ceilings, and traditional Hawaiian quilts. The mammoth bathrooms (some with claw-foot tubs, others with Jacuzzis) have plush towels and earth-friendly toiletries on hand. Recently, the Fairbanks added an additional building, the "Vagabond House," a modern three-room complex in the inn's lavishly landscaped backyard. The rooms are decorated in island-designer Sig Zane's floral prints with rare framed prints of indigenous Hawaiian flowers, plus all the modern amenities you can imagine (TV/VCR, coffeemaker, A/C, and an ultra luxurious multihead shower). Whether you stay in the main house or the Vagabond House, a full gourmet breakfast is served on the enclosed back lanai. You'll feel right at home lounging on the generously sized living-room sofa or watching the world go by from an old wicker chair on the lanai. The inn is located in the old historic area of Wailuku, just a few minutes' walk from the Maui County Seat Government Building, the courthouse, and a wonderful stretch of antiques shops.

2199 Kahookele St. (at High St., across from the Wailuku School), Wailuku, HI 96732. © **800/305-4899** or 808/244-5897. Fax 808/242-9600. www.mauiinn.com. 10 units. $125–$180 double. Rates include full breakfast. Extra person $20. 2-night minimum. MC, V. **Amenities:** Jacuzzi; laundry service; dry cleaning. *In room:* A/C, TV/VCR, dataport, coffeemaker, DSL.

Super-Cheap Sleeps

Banana Bungalow Maui ★ *Value* For years this place was . . . well, a dump. Today, not only is this budget hostel a safe, clean place to stay, it is a virtual cornucopia of affordable activities. It's still a hostel with dorm rooms, shared bathrooms, creaking stairs, and thin walls, but it's been totally renovated inside and out, and now has added amenities and a range of free island tours and outings. For those who would rather cook for themselves, a clean kitchen area has refrigerators, freezers, a stove, an oven, and a barbecue area. Management encourages guests to pick the papayas, mangoes, and bananas on the property. Other pluses include free Internet access, free morning beach shuttle and airport shuttle, cable TV with movie channels in the common area, and discounts on car rentals.

310 North Market St. (at Kapoai St., just past Iao Stream in Happy Valley), Wailuku, HI 96793. ✆ **800/846-7835** or 808/244-5090. Fax 808/244-3678. www.mauihostel.com. 30 units (all with shared bathroom with shower only). $20 single in shared dorm room; $40 single in private room; $50 double in private room. Children stay free in parent's room. MC, V.

Happy Valley Hale Maui *(Value)*   The Kong family, owners of Nona Lani Cottages in Kihei (p. 369), have taken the same loving care of this old plantation home and created a tiny oasis in the midst of this economically challenged area. Keep in mind these are frugal, budget accommodations—really an alternative to a youth hostel. However, it's immaculately clean, and the Kongs have done extensive renovations to this plantation home. There are four bedrooms, each with twin beds, small refrigerator, dresser and closet, and two shared baths. It's like staying in a family home, with a shared kitchen (no stove, but microwave, griddle, coffeemaker, and so on) and shared common room with television and comfy sofas. There are coin-operated laundry facilities on site. The front yard sports a barbecue and picnic area. The only drawback is that Happy Valley is not exactly a resort area—public housing is just across the street. But for those on extremely tight budgets, this could mean a few extra days on Maui.

332 Alahe'e Dr. Wailuku, HI 96793. ✆ **800/733-2688** or 808/357-3737. www.nonalanicottages.com. 4 rooms, $25–$30 per bed shared room; $45–$50 per bed private room. Extra person $10–$15. 3-night minimum. No credit cards. **Amenities:** Shared kitchen; coin-op laundry. *In room:* Small fridges, no phone.

Northshore Hostel   Down an alley in old Wailuku town, where a big banyan tree has taken over the landscape, is the entry to this hostel, which has had several names over the years, such as the Northwind Inn, Aloha Windsurfers, and Northshore Inn. Once upon a time it was the old Wailuku Grand Hotel (grand in its day, but that was a long time ago); the landmark has been renovated and upgraded into a hostel-type operation. The small rooms—each of which has a minifridge and fan—are mainly outfitted as dorms, with four to six bunk beds in each room, but there are some one- and two-bedroom units. All guests share the six bathrooms (with showers only) and a nook of a lobby/common area with a TV and VCR; off to the side is a full kitchen (with free coffee all day) and a room for surfboards, windsurfing equipment, and anything else you might need to store. The friendly staff makes up for the mish-mash of furniture and the rather funky surroundings. *A note of warning:* Though it's a perfectly fine neighborhood during the day, this is not a safe area for women walking alone at night.

2080 Vineyard St. (between Market and Central sts.), Wailuku, HI 96793. ✆ **800/9HOSTEL** or 808/242-1448. www.northshorehostel.com. 20 dorm-style units (shared bathrooms with shower only). $23 shared dorm room; $45 private single room; $55 private double room. AE, MC, V.

WEST MAUI
IN & AROUND LAHAINA
Best Western Pioneer Inn   This once-rowdy home-away-from-home for sailors now seems almost respectable—even charming. The hotel is a two-story plantation-style

structure with big verandas that overlook the streets of Lahaina and the harbor, which is just 50 feet away. All rooms have been remodeled, with vintage bathrooms and new curtains and carpets. The quietest rooms face either the garden courtyard—devoted to refined outdoor dining accompanied by live (but quiet) music—or the square-block-sized banyan tree next door. We recommend room no. 31, over the banyan court, with a view of the ocean and the harbor. If you want a front-row seat for all the Front Street action, book no. 49 or 36.

658 Wharf St. (in front of Lahaina Pier), Lahaina, HI 96761. © 800/457-5457 or 808/661-3636. Fax 808/667-5708. www.pioneerinnmaui.com. 34 units. $115–$155 double; suites from $165. Extra person $15 (12 or older). AE, DC, DISC, MC, V. Parking included in room rate. **Amenities:** Restaurant (good for breakfast); bar with live music; outdoor pool; big shopping arcade; laundry service. In room: A/C, TV, fridge, coffeemaker, hair dryer, iron

Garden Gate Bed-and-Breakfast (Finds)   This oasis of a B&B, located on a quiet residential street just outside Lahaina town, is only a 5-minute drive to the beach. The six units all have private entrances and private bathrooms, plus garden or ocean views. The deluxe suites have private Jacuzzi tubs, refrigerators, microwaves, decks, and a separate pull-out sofa for kids. Hosts Jamie and Bill Mosley can answer any questions about things to do or places to eat. Bicycles, boogie boards, beach chairs, and mats are available for guests' use at no charge. You can also use the barbecue area and the large refrigerator.

67 Kaniau Rd., Lahaina, HI 96761. © 800/939-3217 or 808/661-8800. Fax 808/661-0209. www.gardengatebb.com. 6 units. $89–$159 double. 3-night minimum. Extra person $15. Rates include continental breakfast. AE, DC, DISC, MC, V. **Amenities:** Washer/dryer. In room: A/C, TV (VCR available on request), fridge, coffeemaker, microwave, hair dryer, iron.

Guest House ★★ (Finds)   This is one of Lahaina's great bed-and-breakfast deals: a charming house with more amenities than the expensive Kaanapali hotels just down the road. The roomy home features parquet floors and floor-to-ceiling windows; its swimming pool—surrounded by a deck and comfortable lounge chairs—is larger than some at high-priced condos. Every guest room has a quiet lanai and a romantic hot tub. The large kitchen (with every gadget imaginable) is available for guests' use. The Guest House also operates Trinity Tours and offers discounts on car rentals and just about every island activity. Tennis courts are nearby, and the nearest beach is about a block away.

1620 Ainakea Rd. (off Fleming Rd., north of Lahaina town), Lahaina, HI 96761. © 800/621-8942 or 808/661-8085. Fax 808/661-1896. www.mauiguesthouse.com. 4 units. $129 double, $115 single. Rates include full breakfast. AE, DC, DISC, MC, V. Take Fleming Rd. off Hwy. 30; turn left on Ainakea; it's 2 blocks down. **Amenities:** Huge outdoor pool; watersports equipment/rentals; concierge; activity desk; car-rental desk; self-service washer/dryers. In room: A/C, TV/VCR/DVD, fridge, free high-speed wireless Internet access, Jacuzzi.

House of Fountains Bed-and-Breakfast   This 7,000-square-foot contemporary home, in a quiet residential subdivision at the north end of town, is popular with visitors from around the world. This place is immaculate (hostess Daniela Atay provides daily maid service). The oversized rooms are fresh and quiet, with white ceramic-tile floors, handmade koa furniture, Hawaiian quilt bedspreads, and a Hawaiiana theme; the four downstairs rooms all open onto flower-filled private patios. In fact, in 2002, Daniela won the prestigious "Most Hawaiian Accommodation" award from the Hawaii Visitors and Convention Bureau. Guests share the fully equipped guest kitchen and barbecue area, and are welcome to curl up on the living-room sofa facing the fireplace (not really needed in Lahaina) with a book from the library. The nearest beach is about a 5 minute drive away, and tennis courts are nearby. Around the pool

Lahaina

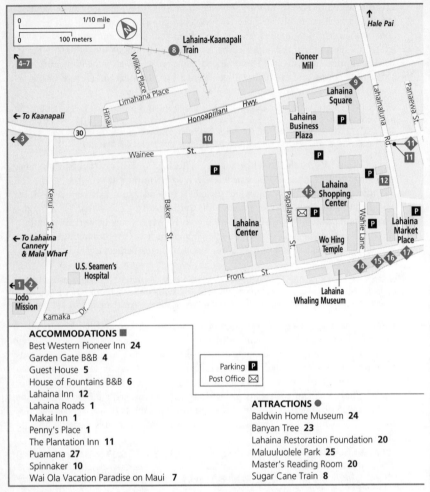

ACCOMMODATIONS ■
Best Western Pioneer Inn **24**
Garden Gate B&B **4**
Guest House **5**
House of Fountains B&B **6**
Lahaina Inn **12**
Lahaina Roads **1**
Makai Inn **1**
Penny's Place **1**
The Plantation Inn **11**
Puamana **27**
Spinnaker **10**
Wai Ola Vacation Paradise on Maui **7**

Parking **P**
Post Office ✉

ATTRACTIONS ●
Baldwin Home Museum **24**
Banyan Tree **23**
Lahaina Restoration Foundation **20**
Maluuluolele Park **25**
Master's Reading Room **20**
Sugar Cane Train **8**

is a thatch hut for weekly hula performances, an imu pit for luaus, and an area that's perfect for Hawaiian weddings.

1579 Lokia St. (off Fleming Rd., north of Lahaina town), Lahaina, HI 96761. ℂ **800/789-6865** or 808/667-2121. Fax 808/667-2120. www.alohahouse.com. 6 units (shower only). $105–$160 double (2 people per room). Rates include full breakfast. MC, AE, V (additional 5% charge if using credit card). From Hwy. 30, take the Fleming Rd. exit; turn left on Ainakea; after 2 blocks, turn right on Malanai St.; go 3 blocks, and turn left onto Lokia St. **Amenities:** Outdoor pool; Jacuzzi; washer/dryers. *In room:* A/C, TV/VCR, fridge, hair dryer, phone.

Lahaina Inn ✦   If you like old hotels that have genuine historic touches, you'll love this place. As in many old hotels, some of these Victorian antique–stuffed rooms are small; if that's a problem for you, ask for a larger unit. All come with private bathrooms and lanais. The best room in the house is no. 7 ($109), which overlooks the beach, the town, and the island of Lanai; you can watch the action below or close the

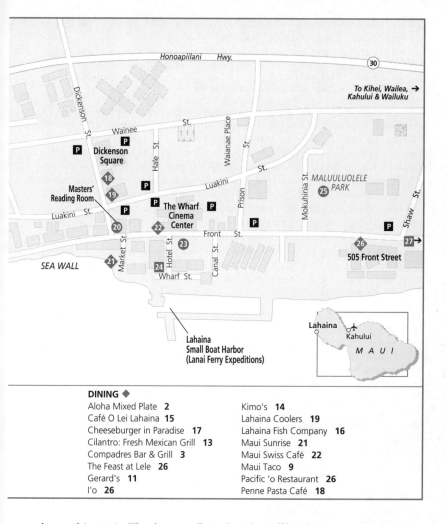

door and ignore it. There's an excellent, though unaffiliated, restaurant in the same building (David Paul's Lahaina Grill), with a bar downstairs.

127 Lahainaluna Rd. (near Front St.), Lahaina, HI 96761. ✆ **800/669-3444** or 808/661-0577. Fax 808/667-9480. www.lahainainn.com. 12 units (most bathrooms have shower only). $125–$175 double. AE, MC, V. $7 parking next door. **Amenities:** Bar; concierge; activity desk. *In room:* A/C, hair dryer, iron.

Lahaina Roads *Value*   If you dream of an oceanfront condo but your budget is on the slim side, here's your place. This condominium complex offers small, reasonably priced units in an older building located in the quiet part of Lahaina, away from the noisy, crowded downtown area, overlooking the boats in the Mala Wharf roadstead (a protected place to anchor near the shore). The compact units come with full kitchens. The bedrooms face the road, while the living rooms and lanais overlook the ocean and the island of Lanai. The soundproofed walls are a real plus. The building is about 35 years old but well maintained. Two drawbacks are no air conditioning (it can it boiling hot in Lahaina) and no laundry facilities.

1403 Front St. (1 block north of Lahaina Cannery Shopping Center). Reservations: c/o Klahani Travel, Lahaina Cannery Mall, 1221 Honoapiilani Hwy., Lahaina, HI 96761. ℂ **800/669-MAUI** or 808/667-2712. Fax 808/661-5875. www.klahani.com. 17 units. $125 1-bedroom (sleeps up to 4). 3-night minimum. AE, DC, DISC, MC, V. **Amenities:** Ocean-side outdoor pool. *In room:* TV, kitchen, fridge, coffeemaker, hair dryer, iron.

Penny's Place in Paradise *(Finds)*

No attention to detail has been spared in this Victorian-style bed-and-breakfast, just 50 feet from the water, with a fabulous view of Molokai and Lanai from the front porch. Each of the four rooms is uniquely decorated, with themes ranging from contemporary Hawaii (with a canopy bed and a traditional island quilt) to formal Victorian (with a four-poster cherry bed and an antique gentleman's night chest). Guests are welcome to use the balcony kitchenette (fridge, microwave, toaster, coffeemaker, and ice machine). Only the location is a problem—Penny's is located in a small island bounded by Honoapiilani Highway on one side and busy Front Street on the other. The house is soundproof, and air-conditioning in each room drowns out the noise. Recently Penny enclosed the outside lanai area so you can enjoy your breakfast without the highway noise.

1440 Front St., Lahaina, HI 96761. ℂ **877/431-1235** or 808/661-1068. Fax 808/667-7102. www.pennysplace.net. 4 units. $88–$124 double. Rates include continental breakfast Mon-Sat. 3-night minimum. AE, DISC, MC, V. *In room:* A/C, TV, free wireless Internet access, iron.

Puamana

These 28 acres of town houses set right on the water are ideal for those who want to be able to retreat from the crowds and cacophony of downtown Lahaina into the serene quiet of an elegant neighborhood. Private and peaceful are apt descriptions for this complex: Each unit is a privately-owned individual home, with no neighbors above or below. Most are exquisitely decorated, and all come with full kitchen, lanai, barbecue, and at least two bathrooms. Puamana was once a private estate in the 1920s, part of the sugar plantations that dominated Lahaina; the plantation manager's house has been converted into a clubhouse with an oceanfront lanai, library, card room, sauna, table-tennis tables, and an office. We've found the best rates by booking through Klahani Travel (contact information below), but their office is not on site, which has caused some problems with guests getting assistance. If you'd rather book with the Puamana Association office, contact Puamana Community Association, 34 Puailima Place, Lahina, HI 96761 (ℂ **808/661-3423;** fax 808/667/0398; office@ puamana.us).

Front St. (at the extreme southern end of Lahaina, ½ mile from downtown). Reservations: c/o Klahani Travel, Lahaina Cannery Mall, 1221 Honoapiilani Hwy., Lahaina, HI 96761. ℂ **800/669-6284** or 808/667-2712. Fax 808/661-5875. www.klahani-travel.com. 40 units. $125–$200 1-bedroom unit; $150–$275 2-bedroom; $300–$500 3-bedroom. 3-night minimum. AE, DC, DISC, MC, V. **Amenities:** 3 pools (1 for adults only); tennis court; Jacuzzi; game room; activity desk; on-site laundry. *In room:* TV, kitchen, fridge, coffeemaker, hair dryer, iron, washer/dryer (in some units).

Wai Ola Vacation Paradise on Maui *(Finds)*

Just 2 blocks from the beach, in a quiet, residential development behind a tall concrete wall, lies this lovely retreat, with shade trees, sitting areas, gardens, a pool, an ocean mural, and a range of accommodations (from a small studio to a couple of suites inside the home, to a separate honeymoon cottage, a 1-bedroom apartment, or the entire 5,000-sq.-ft. house). Kim and Jim Wicker recently took over this vacation paradise and are more than willing to provide any information you need to make your vacation fabulous. Every unit has a welcome fruit basket when you arrive, plus coffee beans for the coffee maker. Kim loves to bake, and she surprises her guests with "a little something" from her kitchen like cheesecake or heavenly brownies. You'll also find a deck, huge pool, Jacuzzi, barbecue facilities, free wireless Internet access, and an outdoor wet bar on the property; there's a great beach just a 3-minute drive away and tennis courts are nearby.

1565 Kuuipo St. (P.O. Box 12580), Lahaina, HI 96761. ℂ **800/492-4652** or 808/661-7901. Fax 808/661-1119. www. waiola.com. 5 units. $95 double; $135 suite; $150 1-bedroom apt; $175 honeymoon cottage; entire house $725–$900. Extra person $15. AE, DISC, MC, V. **Amenities:** Outdoor pool; Jacuzzi; complimentary use of watersports equipment; free self-service washer/dryers. *In room:* A/C, TV/DVD/VCR, dataport, kitchenette, fridge, coffeemaker, hair dryer, iron.

Super-Cheap Sleeps

Makai Inn *Value*   Budget travelers take note: here's a small apartment complex located right on the water (okay, no white-sand beach out front but what do you want at these eye-popping prices). The closest white-sand beach is just a 10-minute stroll and the center of Lahaina town is a 20-minute walk away. The units are small (400 sq. ft.) but clean and filled with everything you could possibly need for your vacation: full kitchens, views of the ocean (in most units), separate bedrooms, and a quiet neighborhood. There are no phones or TVs, but you're on vacation; you don't need television. And if you don't have a cell phone, there's a public phone by the office, along with coin-operated laundry service. In the middle of the complex is a tropical garden. I recommend the Ginger Hideway unit with windows on two sides overlooking the ocean for just $130. Families will like the Pineapple Suite, the only two-bedroom unit (800 sq. ft. of space) for just $130.

1415 Front St., Lahaina, HI 96761. ℂ **808/662-3200.** Fax 808/661-9027. www.makaiinn.net. 18 units. $75–$130 double. Extra person $10. MC, V. **Amenities:** Coin-op laundry facilities. *In room:* Kitchen, no phone.

The Spinnaker *Value*   Run by the same people who have the Makai Inn (see above), they offer seven units in this residential complex on a side street in Lahaina town. Extremely affordable one- and two-bedroom budget apartments are offered only by the week, but at prices that families can afford. All units have full kitchens, phones, television, and all the comforts of home. There is a pool in the complex and a whirlpool and barbecue area. No maid service, but at these prices, you can clean up on your own.

760 Wainae St., Lahaina, HI 96761. ℂ **808/662-3200.** Fax 808/661-9027. www.makaiinn.net. 7 units. $500/week 1-bedroom; $600/week 2-bedroom. 7-night minimum. MC, V. **Amenities:** Swimming pool; whirlpool; barbecue area; coin-op laundry facilities. *In room:* A/C, TV, kitchen, iron.

Worth a Splurge

The Plantation Inn ★★ *Finds*   Attention, romance-seeking couples: Look no further. This charming Victorian-style inn, located a couple of blocks from the water, looks like it's been here 100 years or more, but it's actually of 1990s vintage—an artful deception. The rooms are romantic to the max, tastefully done with period furniture, hardwood floors, stained glass, and ceiling fans. There are four-poster canopy beds and armoires in some rooms, brass beds and wicker in others. All units are soundproofed (a plus in Lahaina) and come with a private lanai; the suites have kitchenettes. The rooms wrap around the large pool and deck. Also on the property are a pavilion lounge and Gerard's, an outstanding French restaurant (it can be pricey, but hotel guests get a discount on dinner; see p. 387). Breakfast is served around the pool and in the elegant pavilion lounge.

174 Lahainaluna Rd. (between Wainee and Luakini sts., 1 block from Hwy. 30), Lahaina, HI 96761. ℂ **800/433-6815** or 808/667-9225. Fax 808/667-9293. www.theplantationinn.com. 19 units (some bathrooms with shower only).

$160–$265 double. Check the Internet for great package deals. Rates include full breakfast. Extra person $25. AE, DC, DISC, MC, V. **Amenities:** Acclaimed restaurant and bar; large outdoor pool; Jacuzzi; concierge; activity desk; coin-op washer/dryers. *In room:* A/C, TV/VCR, kitchenettes (in suites), fridge, hair dryer, iron, safe.

HONOKOWAI, KAHANA & NAPILI

Blue Horizons *(Finds)* The only bed-and-breakfast on the west side of the island outside of Lahaina, Blue Horizons is located in Honokowai, 1 block from the Honoapiilani Highway; it's about a 10-minute drive from Lahaina and about a 5-minute walk to sandy beaches. The four units, in a custom-built home in a subdivision, range from compact to spacious suites with separate bedrooms and a living-room area with sofa bed. Three units have kitchenettes and all four are air-conditioned, which helps not only with the heat of Mahinahina but also with the noise of the subdivision. A lavish breakfast is served in the screened dining area, where the ocean view may distract you from the banana pancakes. Amenities on site include a tile lap pool, washer/dryer, gas barbecue, and video library.

3894 Mahinahina Dr. (just south of the West Maui airport), Lahaina, HI 96761. © **800/669-1948** or 808/669-1965. Fax 808/665-1615. www.bluehorizonsmaui.com. 4 units. $99–$139 double. 2-night minimum. Rates include breakfast Mon–Sat. Extra person $15. AE, MC, V. **Amenities:** Small outdoor lap pool; complimentary laundry facilities. *In room:* A/C, TV/VCR, kitchenette (some rooms), fridge, coffeemaker (some rooms).

Hale Kai *(Kids)* This small, two-story condo complex is ideally located, right on the beach and next door to a county park. Shops, restaurants, and ocean activities are all within a 6-mile radius. The units are older but in excellent shape, and come with well-equipped kitchens (each with a dishwasher, disposal, microwave, and even a blender), and louvered windows that open to the trade winds. Lots of guests clamor for the oceanfront pool units, but we find the park-view units cooler, and they still have ocean views (upstairs units also have cathedral ceilings). Book early, as this place fills up fast; repeat guests make up most of the clientele.

3691 Lower Honoapiilani Rd. (in Honokowai), Lahaina, HI 96761. © **800/446-7307** or 808/669-6333. Fax 808/669-7474. www.halekai.com. 25 units. High season $130 1-bedroom double, $165–$170 2-bedroom (rates for up to 4), $225 3-bedroom (up to 6); low season $115 1-bedroom, $150–$155 2-bedroom, $225 3-bedroom. Extra person $15. 5-night minimum. MC, V. **Amenities:** Outdoor pool; concierge; car-rental desk; coin-op washer/dryers. *In room:* TV/VCR, kitchen, fridge, coffeemaker, hair dryer, iron.

Hale Maui Apartment Hotel *(Finds)* For decades, Hans and Eva Zimmerman have made this tiny apartment hotel a piece of paradise. Their spirit is 100% aloha: They personally greet each guest, make sure their new friends are happy and comfortable in their accommodations, and willingly offer suggestions on everything from where to eat to where to find the best beaches (Hans's favorite is right out in front of the complex). One guest told us he keeps coming back to Hale Maui because Hans and Eva are like family. The one-bedroom suites can sleep up to five guests, and all come with private lanais and complete kitchens. There's no pool, but a private path leads to the great swimming beach.

3711 Lower Honoapiilani Hwy. (P.O. Box 516), Honokowai, Lahaina, HI 96767. © **888/621-1736** or 808/669-6312. Fax 808/669-1302. www.maui.net/~halemaui. 12 apts. $85–$105 double. Extra person $10. MC, V. *In room:* TV, kitchen, fridge, coffeemaker, iron.

Hoyochi Nikko *(Finds)* Only 17 units share 180 feet of oceanfront at this tropical hideaway. The one-bedroom units are older, but well maintained and outfitted with everything you could need. All face the ocean and have fabulous views of Molokai and

Accommodations & Dining in Honokowai, Kahana, Napili & Kapalua

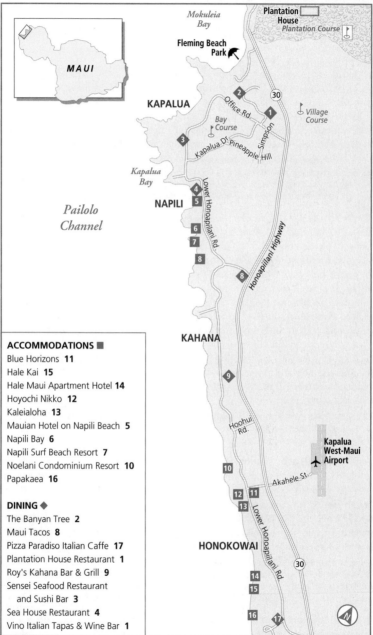

Mokuleia Bay

Plantation House
Plantation Course

Fleming Beach Park

MAUI

KAPALUA

Office Rd.

Village Course

Bay Course

Simpson

Kapalua Dr. Pineapple Hill

Kapalua Bay

Lower Honoapiilani Rd.

NAPILI

Pailolo Channel

Honoapiilani Highway

KAHANA

Hoohui Rd.

Kapalua West-Maui Airport

Akahele St.

Lower Honoapiilani Rd.

HONOKOWAI

ACCOMMODATIONS ■
Blue Horizons **11**
Hale Kai **15**
Hale Maui Apartment Hotel **14**
Hoyochi Nikko **12**
Kaleialoha **13**
Mauian Hotel on Napili Beach **5**
Napili Bay **6**
Napili Surf Beach Resort **7**
Noelani Condominium Resort **10**
Papakaea **16**

DINING ◆
The Banyan Tree **2**
Maui Tacos **8**
Pizza Paradiso Italian Caffe **17**
Plantation House Restaurant **1**
Roy's Kahana Bar & Grill **9**
Sensei Seafood Restaurant
    and Sushi Bar **3**
Sea House Restaurant **4**
Vino Italian Tapas & Wine Bar **1**

Lanai across the channel. The property may be small, but it has a pool, a sandy beach, and a great offshore snorkeling area.

3901 Lower Honoapiilani Rd. (in Honokowai), Lahaina, HI 96761. © 800/487-6002 or 808/669-8343. www.maui lodging.com. 17 units. $115–$170 double. Extra person $10. 1-week minimum. No credit cards. **Amenities:** Outdoor pool. *In room:* A/C, TV/VCR, kitchen, fridge, coffeemaker, hair dryer, iron, washer/dryer.

Kaleialoha This condo complex for the budget-minded has recently been upgraded, with new paint, bedspreads, and drapes in each apartment. Each one-bedroom unit has a sofa bed in the living room, which allows you to comfortably sleep four. All of the island-style units feature fully-equipped kitchens, with everything from dishwashers to washer/dryers (the only thing not supplied is beach towels; bring your own). There's great ocean swimming just off the rock wall (no sandy beach); a protective reef mows waves down and allows even timid swimmers to relax.

3785 Lower Honoapiilani Rd. (in Honokowai), Lahaina, HI 96761. © 800/222-8688 or 808/669-8197. Fax 808/ 669-2502. www.mauicondosoceanfront.com. 21 units. $125–$135 1-bedroom double. Extra person $10. Children 3 and under stay free. 3-night minimum. $70 cleaning fee for less than 7-night stay. MC, V. **Amenities:** Outdoor pool; concierge; activity desk; coin-op washer/dryers. *In room:* TV, kitchen, fridge, coffeemaker, washer/dryer.

Napili Bay ☆ *(Finds)* One of Maui's best secret bargains is this small, two-story complex right on Napili's beautiful half-mile white-sand beach. It's perfect for a romantic getaway: The atmosphere is comfortable and relaxing, the ocean lulls you to sleep at night, and birdsong wakes you in the morning. The beach here is one of the best on the coast, with great swimming and snorkeling—in fact, it's so beautiful that people staying at much more expensive resorts down the road frequently haul all their beach paraphernalia here for the day. The studio apartments are definitely small, but they pack in everything you need to feel at home, from a full kitchen to a comfortable queen bed, and a roomy lanai that's great for watching the sun set over the Pacific. There's no air-conditioning, but louvered windows and ceiling fans keep the units fairly cool during the day. There are lots of restaurants and a convenience store within walking distance, and you're about 10 to 15 minutes away from Lahaina and some great golf courses. All this for as little as $95 a night—unbelievable! Book early, and tell 'em Frommer's sent you.

33 Hui Dr. (off Lower Honoapiilani Hwy., in Napili). Reservations: c/o Aloha Condos Hawaii, P.O. Box 396681, Keauhou, Hi 96740. © 877/782-5642. www.alohacondos.com. 33 units. $95–$225 studio for 2. 5-night minimum. MC, V. **Amenities:** Coin-op washer/dryers. *In room:* TV, kitchen, fridge, coffeemaker.

Napili Surf Beach Resort ☆ *(Finds)* This well-maintained, superbly landscaped condo complex has a great location on Napili Beach. The well-furnished units (all with full kitchen) were renovated in 1997; free daily maid service—a rarity in condo properties—keeps the units clean. Management encourages socializing: In addition to weekly mai tai parties and coffee socials, the resort hosts annual shuffleboard and golf tournaments, as well as holiday get-togethers. Many guests arrange their travel plans around these events at the Napili Surf. Three gas barbecue grills encourage cookouts.

50 Napili Place (off Lower Honoapiilani Rd., in Napili), Lahaina, HI 96761. © 800/541-0638 or 808/669-8002. Fax 808/669-8004. www.napilisurf.com. 53 units (some w/shower only). $140–$200 studio (sleeps up to 3); $215–$290 1-bedroom (sleeps up to 4). Extra person $15. No credit cards. **Amenities:** 2 freshwater swimming pools; shuffle-board; barbecue grills; coin-op washer/dryers. *In room:* TV/VCR, kitchen, fridge, coffeemaker, iron, safe.

Noelani Condominium Resort ☆☆ *(Kids)* *(Finds)* This oceanfront condo is a great value, whether you stay in a studio or a three-bedroom unit (ideal for large families). Everything is first-class, from the furnishings to the oceanfront location. Though it's on the water, there's no sandy beach here—but next door is a sandy cove at the new county park, just opened in 2001. All units feature complete kitchens, entertainment centers, and spectacular views (the one-, two-, and three-bedroom units also have their own washer/dryers and dishwashers). Our favorites are in the Anthurium Building, where the condos have oceanfront lanais just 20 feet from the water. Frugal travelers will love the deluxe studios in the Orchid Building, with great ocean views and all the amenities for just $107 in the low season and $122 in high season. Guests are invited to mai tai parties at night; there are also oceanfront barbecue grills for guest use.

4095 Lower Honoapiilani Rd. (in Kahana), Lahaina, HI 96761. ℂ 800/367-6030 or 808/669-8374. Fax 808/669-7904. www.noelani-condo-resort.com. 50 units. $107–$150 studio double; $157–$180 1-bedroom (sleeps up to 4); $237–$257 2-bedroom (sleeps up to 6); $299–$317 3-bedroom (sleeps up to 8). Rates include continental breakfast on first morning. Extra person $10. Children under 18 stay free in parent's room. Packages for honeymooners, seniors, and AAA members available. 3-night minimum. AE, MC, V. **Amenities:** 2 freshwater swimming pools (1 heated for night swimming); access to nearby health club; oceanfront Jacuzzi; concierge; activity desk; car-rental desk; coin-op washer/dryers. *In room:* TV/VCR, kitchen, fridge, coffeemaker, hair dryer, iron, safe, washer/dryer (in larger units).

Papakea   Just a mile down the beach from Kaanapali lie these low-rise buildings, surrounded by manicured, landscaped grounds and ocean views galore. Palm trees and tropical plants dot the property, a putting green wraps around two kidney-shaped pools, and a foot bridge arches over a lily pond brimming with carp. Each pool has its own private cabana with sauna, Jacuzzi, and barbecue grills; a poolside shop rents snorkel gear for exploring the offshore reefs. The studios have Murphy beds that fold into the wall to save space during the day. Definitely a good value.

3600 Lower Honoapiilani Rd. (in Honokowai). Reservations: Maui Resort Management, Lahaina, HI 96761. ℂ 800/367-5037 or 808/669-1902. Fax 808/669-8790. www.mauigetaway.com. 364 units. $115–$135 studio double; $150–$210 1-bedroom (sleeps up to 4); $190–$220 2-bedroom (sleeps up to 6). 7-night minimum. MC, V. **Amenities:** 2 outdoor pools; 3 tennis courts; 2 Jacuzzis; watersports equipment/rentals. *In room:* A/C, TV/VCR, kitchen, fridge, coffeemaker, washer/dryer.

Worth a Splurge

Mauian Hotel on Napili Beach ⭐   The Mauian is perched above a beautiful ½-mile long white-sand beach with great swimming and snorkeling; there's a pool with chaise lounges, umbrellas, and tables on the sun deck; and the verdant grounds are bursting with tropical color. The rooms feature hardwood floors, Indonesian-style furniture, and big lanais with great views. Thoughtful little touches include fresh flowers in rooms upon arrival, plus chilled champagne for guests celebrating a special occasion. There are no phones and no TVs in the rooms (this place really is about getting away from it all), but the large ohana (family) room does have a TV with a VCR and an extensive library for those who can't bear the solitude. There's complimentary coffee; phones and fax service are available in the business center. Great restaurants are just a 5-minute walk away, and Kapalua Resort is up the street. The nightly sunsets off the beach are spectacular.

5441 Lower Honoapiilani Rd. (in Napili), Lahaina, HI 96761. ℂ 800/367-5034 or 808/669-6205. Fax 808/669-0129. www.mauian.com. 44 units. High season $165–$195 double; low season $150–$185 double (sleeps up to 4). Rates include continental breakfast. Extra person $10. Children under 5 stay free in parent's room. AE, DISC, MC, V. **Amenities:** Outdoor pool; shuffleboard court; barbeques; golf course nearby; tennis courts nearby; activity desk; coin-op washer/dryer. *In room:* Kitchen, fridge, coffeemaker, no phone.

SOUTH MAUI

Aloha Journeys *(Finds)*   Tucked into the residential neighborhood of Maui Meadows (and a 5-min. drive from the nearest good beach) is an oasis of fruit trees, a flower garden, and a sun deck with picnic table, chairs, and a hot tub overlooking the ocean. Both rental cottages have their own TVs, VCRs, CD players, and washer/dryers. The two-bedroom Ginger Cottage is best for families, with full kitchen, two separate bedrooms and an enclosed lanai. The one-bedroom Palm Cottage makes a cozy honeymoon cottage (it also has a sofa bed). Guests are welcome to gather fresh fruits for their breakfast. Other great amenities for guests: numerous beach toysand snorkel gear. Occasionally, owner/hostess Karen will waive the 5-night minimum for last-minute bookings. They also rent a three-bedroom, million-dollar vacation home for just $265 double; and a another 3-bedroom (only one bath) house for $140 double.

490 Mikioi Place (Maui Meadows), Kihei, HI 96753. © 800/871-5032 or 808/875-4840. Fax 808/879-3998. www.aloha journeys.com. 2 units. Apr 16–Dec 14 $95 double (plus $50 cleaning fee), extra person $15; Dec 15–Apr 15 $115 double (plus $50 cleaning fee), extra person $20. 5-night minimum. MC, V. **Amenities:** Jacuzzi; laundry facilities. *In room:* A/C, TV/VCR/DVD, kitchen, fridge, coffeemaker, hair dryer, stereo, answering machine.

Hale Kamaole *(Value* These low-rise apartments are situated on sprawling grounds just across the street from Kamaole Beach Park III, which is great for swimming and sunset watching. The location makes this quiet complex a good choice (shops and restaurants are also just a walk away). All units are tastefully decorated and come with complete kitchens; the large rooms have lanais that overlook either the swimming pool or the tropical gardens. The two-bedroom units have only one bathroom.

2737 S. Kihei Rd. (on the mountain side of Kihei Rd. between Keonekai Rd. and Kilohana St., at Wailea end of Kihei), Kihei, HI 96753. © 800/367-2970 or 808/879-1221. Fax 808/879-5576. www.maui.net/~coop/HKChome.html. 105 units. High season $122 1-bedroom double, $167–$177 2-bedroom for 4; low season $95–$105 1-bedroom double, $123–$150 2-bedroom for 4. Extra person $10. 3-night minimum. AE, MC, V. **Amenities:** 2 outdoor pools; tennis court; babysitting; coin-op washer/dryers. *In room:* A/C, TV/VCR, dataport, kitchen, fridge, coffeemaker, iron.

Hale Kumulani *(Finds* At the top of Maui Meadows subdivision, right on the Wailea border, about a 5-minute drive to the beach, lies this half-acre (chemical-free) property, surrounded by a 40,000-acre wilderness area with two quaint units. A darling, one-room cottage with full kitchen, wood flooring, high beam ceilings, living room area (with TV/VCR, stereo, and full-size guest sofa/futon), large deck, and outdoor shower. Underneath the main house, but with private entrance and complete privacy, is the waterfall suite with a kitchenette, a giant outdoor patio with an overhang that provides shade and is landscaped with a waterfall and banana and papaya trees. Both units have access to the organic vegetable garden, numerous fruit trees, and beach equipment. Hosts Ron and Merry couldn't be more gracious in helping you navigate the island. They also accommodate children with both a full-size crib and junior beds available (as well as a stroller).

874 Kumulani Dr., Maui Meadows, Kihei, HI 96753. © 808/891-0425. Fax 808/891-0269. www.cottagemaui.com. 2 units. $125 double suite; $145 cottage double. 4-night minimum. MC, V. **Amenities:** 6 championship golf courses within 5 miles; aquatic center with 3 pools nearby (a 7-min. drive). *In room:* TV/VCR, kitchen (in cottage), kitchenette (in suite), fridge, coffeemaker, hair dryer, iron, washer/dryer.

Kealia Resort *(Value* This oceanfront property, at the northern end of Kihei, is well maintained and nicely furnished—and the price is excellent. But as tempting as the $80 studio units may sound, don't give in: They face noisy Kihei Road and are near a major junction, so big trucks downshifting can be especially noisy at night. Instead, spend a little more and go for one of the oceanview units, which all have full kitchens and private lanais. The grounds face a 5-mile stretch of white-sand beach. The management goes out of its way to provide opportunities for guests to meet; social gatherings include free coffee-and-doughnut get-togethers every Friday morning and pupu parties on Wednesdays.

South Maui Accommodations & Dining

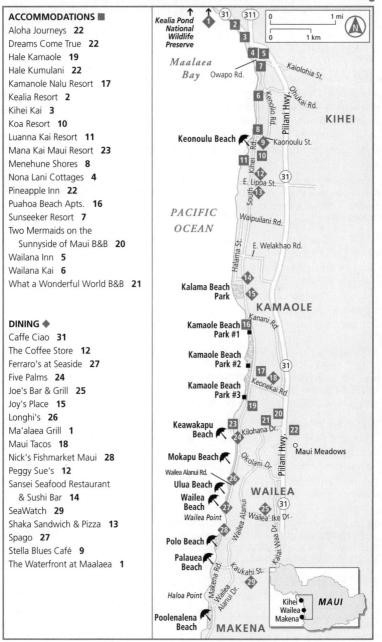

191 N. Kihei Rd. (north of Hwy. 31, at the Maalaea end of Kihei), Kihei, HI 96753. ℂ 800/265-0686 or 808/879-0952. Fax 808/875-1540. www.kealiaresort.com. 51 units. $80–$100 studio; $120–$170 1-bedroom double; $185–$220 2-bedroom (sleeps up to 4). Extra person $10. Children 12 and under stay free in parent's room. 4-night minimum. MC, V. **Amenities:** Recently retiled outdoor pool. *In room:* TV, kitchen, fridge, coffeemaker, hair dryer, iron, washer/dryer.

Kihei Kai *(Kids (Value)* Set back from noisy Kihei Road, this oceanfront complex fronts a long sandy beach, with restaurants and bars nearby. Affordable prices, roomy floor plans, and a great location make Kihei Kai ideal for families. The protected cove out front is ideal for safe swimming, even for kids. The units, all one-bedroom apartments, easily sleep four. The rooms were recently renovated and outfitted with new bedspreads, curtains, and carpets. Fully equipped kitchens, big living rooms, and private lanais (most with ocean views) add extra value to the budget rates. All in all, this is a very good deal.

61 N. Kihei Rd. (north of Hwy. 31 at the Maalaea end of Kihei), Kihei, HI 96753. ℂ 888/778-7717 or 808/891-0780. Fax 808/874-4960. www.kiheirentals.com. 22 units. $100–$140 double. Extra person $10. 4-night minimum. MC, V. **Amenities:** Outdoor pool; coin-op washer/dryers. *In room:* A/C, TV/VCR, dataport, kitchen, fridge, coffeemaker, iron.

Koa Resort *(⭐ (Kids)* Located just across the street from the ocean, Koa Resort consists of five two-story wooden buildings on more than 5½ acres of landscaped grounds. The spacious, privately owned one-, two-, and three-bedroom units are decorated with care and come fully equipped, right down to the dishwasher and disposal in the kitchens. The larger condos have both showers and tubs; the smaller units have showers only. All feature large lanais, ceiling fans, and washer/dryers. For maximum peace and quiet, ask for a unit far from Kihei Road. Bars, restaurants, and a golf course are nearby.

811 S. Kihei Rd. (between Kulanihakoi St. and Namauu Place). Reservations: c/o Bello Realty, P.O. Box 1776, Kihei, HI 96753. ℂ 800/541-3060 or 808/879-3328. Fax 808/875-1483. www.bellomaui.com. 54 units (some with shower only). High season $110 1-bedroom; $120–$130 2-bedroom; $180 3-bedroom; low season $85 1-bedroom; $100–$110 2-bedroom; $160 3-bedroom. V, MC. **Amenities:** Outdoor pool; putting green; 2 tennis courts; Jacuzzi. *In room:* TV, kitchen, fridge, coffeemaker, iron, safe, washer/dryer.

Luana Kai Resort *(Kids)* This older three-story condo complex lies on 8 acres of landscaped grounds, with extras like a sauna, a putting green, and barbecue area, not to mention the big blue Pacific just steps from each unit. The condos have recently been renovated and look like new. Families will love the prices and the grassy lawn in the center of the complex, which is a great place for the kids to let off steam. Ask for a unit away from Kihei Road for more peace and quiet; for a better view, don't get a ground unit.

940 S. Kihei Rd. (between Kulanihakoi St and Namauu Place), Kihei, HI 96753. ℂ 800/669-1127 or 808/879-1268. Fax 808/879-1455. www.luanakai.com. 113 units. $99–$179 1-bedroom; $119–$199 2-bedroom.; $219–$269 3-bedroom. 4-night minimum. AE, DC, DISC, MC, V. **Amenities:** Outdoor pool; tennis courts; Jacuzzi. *In room:* TV/VCR, dataport, kitchen, fridge, coffeemaker, iron, washer/dryer.

Mana Kai Maui Resort *(⭐ (Kids)* This eight-story complex, situated on a beautiful white-sand cove, is an unusual combination of hotel and condominium. The hotel rooms, which account for half of the total number of units, are small but nicely furnished. The condo units feature full kitchens and open living rooms with sliding-glass doors that lead to small lanais overlooking the sandy beach and ocean. Some units are beginning to show their age (the building is more than 20 years old), but they're all clean and comfortable. One of the best snorkeling beaches on the coast is just steps away; a golf course and tennis courts are nearby.

2960 S. Kihei Rd. (between Kilohana and Keonekai rds., at the Wailea end of Kihei), Kihei, HI 96753. ℰ **800/ 367-5242** or 808/879-2778. Fax 808/879-7825. www.crhmaui.com. 105 units. $130 hotel-room double; $180–$255 1-bedroom (sleeps up to 4); $230–$310 2-bedroom (up to 6). AE, MC, V. **Amenities:** Restaurant (Five Palms, p. 394); bar; outdoor pool; concierge; coin-op washer/dryers. *In room:* A/C (in hotel rooms only), TV, kitchen (in condo units), fridge, coffeemaker, safe.

Pineapple Inn Maui *Finds* ⋆⋆   Just opened at the end of 2004, this charming inn (only four rooms, plus a darling two-bedroom cottage) is not only an exquisite find, but the prices are terrific. Located in the residential Maui Meadows area, with panoramic ocean views, this two story inn (one side of the building is the owner's home) is expertly landscaped in tropical flowers and plants with a lily pond in the front and a giant saltwater pool and Jacuzzi overlooking the ocean. Each of the sound-proof rooms is expertly decorated with a small kitchenette (fridge, coffeemaker, toaster, and microwave), which is stocked with juice, pastries, and drinks on your arrival, comfy bed, free wireless Internet access, TV/VCR, and an incredible view off your own private lanai. If you need more room, they also offer a darling two-bedroom, one-bath cottage (wood floors, beautiful artwork) with everything you could possibly need: full kitchen (even a dishwasher), private lanai, and landscaped for maximum privacy.

3170 Akala Dr., Klihei, HI 96753. ℰ **877-212-MAUI** (6284) or 808/298-4403. www.pineappleinnmaui.com. 4 rooms; 1 2-bedroom cottage. $99–$119 room double; $165 cottage for 4. 3-night minimum for rooms. 6-night minimum for cottage. No credit cards. **Amenities:** Large saltwater pool; Jacuzzi; barbecue area; complimentary laundry facilities. *In room:* A/C, TV/VCR, complimentary wireless Internet access, kitchenette (in rooms), full kitchen (in cottage), fridge, coffeemaker, hair dryer, phone/answering machine (in cottage), no phone (in rooms).

Punahoa Beach Apts ⋆ *Value*   Book this place! We can't put it any more simply than that. The location—off noisy, traffic-ridden Kihei Road, on a quiet side street with ocean frontage—is fabulous. A grassy lawn rolls about 50 feet down to the beach, where there's great snorkeling just offshore and a popular surfing spot next door; shopping and restaurants are all within walking distance. All of the beautifully decorated units in this small, four-story building have fully equipped kitchens and lanais with great ocean views. Rooms go quickly in winter, so reserve early.

2142 Iliili Rd. (off S. Kihei Rd., 300 ft. from Kamaole Beach I), Kihei, HI 96753. ℰ **800/564-43**?? or 808/879-2720. Fax 808/875-9147. www.punahoabeach.com. 13 units. High season $130 studio double; $185–$198 1-bedroom double; $220 2-bedroom double. Low season $94 studio; $130–$145 1-bedroom; $160 2-bedroom. Extra person $15. 5-night minimum. AE, MC, V. **Amenities:** Coin-op washer/dryer. *In room:* TV, kitchen, fridge, coffeemaker, iron.

Sunseeker Resort *Finds*   This former budget property, located just across the street from a terrific white-sand beach, has been recently sold, and the new management team has spiffed up the studio and one-bedroom units with custom furniture, and has added air conditioning and several amenities not usually seen at small properties, such as high-speed Internet access and concierge services. The re-done units have been tastefully decorated. Studios offer terrific, wallet-pleasing prices. The one bedrooms, which have a pullout sofa in the living room and new appliances in the kitchen, offer a deal at $160, but definitely not a deal during the high season at $200. All units have private lanais with ocean views with the beach just a few steps away.

551 S. Kihei Rd. (P.O. Box 276), Kihei, HI 96753 (ℰ **800/532-MAUI** or 808/879-1261. Fax 808/874-3877. www.maui sunseeker.com. 4 units. $85–$125 studio, $160–$200 1-bedroom. 3-night minimum. Extra person $15. AE, DISC, MC, V. **Amenities:** Hot tub; concierge; coin-op washer and dryer; same-day laundry service; complimentary local phone calls; gas-barbecue grill area. *In room:* A/C, TV/VCR, high-speed Internet access, full kitchen (1 bedroom), kitchenette (studio), coffeemaker, hair dryer, answering machine.

Two Mermaids on the Sunnyside of Maui B&B ⭐ *Finds* The two mermaids, Juddee and Miranda, both avid scuba divers, have a friendly accommodation, professionally decorated in brilliant, tropical colors, complete with hand-painted art of the island (above and below the water) in a quiet neighborhood just a short 10-minute walk from the beach. Our favorite is the "ocean ohana" a large one-bedroom (with option of a second connecting bedroom) apartment, complete with kitchenette (full-sized refrigerator, microwave, coffeemaker), huge private deck, private entryway and your own giant hot tub. Equally cute is the "poolside suite," with private entry next to the outdoor pool. This studio (with the option of a connecting separate bedroom) is a living room during the day, and, at night, it converts to a bedroom with a pull down hide-a-bed. Continental breakfast, with some of the best homemade bread on the island, is placed on your doorstep every morning (so you can sleep in). There are many amenities, such as guitars in every unit (in case you get the urge to strum a few songs), a range of complimentary beach equipment, microwave popcorn, barbecue area, and swimming pool. Juddee is also a licensed minister and performs weddings and vow renewal.

2840 Umalu Place, Kihei, 96753. ℂ **800/598-9550** or 808/874-8687. Fax 808/875-1833. www.twomermaids.com. 2 units. $120 studio double; $165 studio plus connecting bedroom double; $145 1-bedroom apartment; $185 with connecting 2nd bedroom. Rates include continental breakfast. No credit cards. 3-night minimum stay. **Amenities:** Outdoor pool; golf nearby; tennis courts nearby; massage; babysitting; barbecue area. *In room:* TV, VCR/DVD on request, kitchen, fridge, coffeemaker, hair dryer, iron, free local phone calls.

Wailana Inn *Finds* As we went to press, the new owners of Sunseeker Resort (see above) just purchased this tiny, one-bedroom apartment complex. They revamped everything and put in slate in the bathroom, new tile on the floor, new furniture, and repainted. The units are small (but hey, just how much time are you going to be hanging out in the apartment?), but the lanais are large and the price is right. The result is a terrific moderately-priced property, with the beach just across the street. An unusual amenity they offer is a secluded "clothing-optional" rooftop where you can get an overall tan or sit in the hot tub with great ocean views.

Wailana Pl., Kihei, HI 96753. ℂ **800/399-3885** or 808/874-3131. 12 units. $80–$120 standard room double; $100–$140 studio double; $140–$180 junior suite. Extra person $15. AE, DISC, MC, V. **Amenities:** Hot tub; concierge; same-day laundry service; coin-op washer/dryer; complimentary local phone calls; gas barbecue area. *In room:* A/C, TV/VCR, high-speed Internet access, kitchen, coffeemaker, hair dryer, answering machine.

SUPER CHEAP SLEEPS

Dreams Come True on Maui *Value* This bed-and-breakfast (where "you are never just renting a room") was the dream come true for hosts Tom Croly and Denise Mc-Kinnon, who, after several years of vacationing to Maui, opened this three-unit property in 2002. Centrally located in the Maui Meadows subdivision (just a few minutes' drive to golf courses, tennis courts, white-sand beaches, shopping, and restaurants in Kihei and Wailea), they offer a one-bedroom, oceanview cottage (great for long stays) with its own (high-speed) Internet-connected computer, a gourmet kitchen, two TV sets, washer/dryer, and wraparound decks (6-night minimum). They also offer two rooms in the house (one with king bed, one with queen bed) with TV, private entrance, kitchenettes (plus outdoor cooking area with barbecue grill, sink, and microwave), use of washer/dryer, and lots of other amenities not usually found in B&Bs (3- to 4-night minimum). Every guest is greeted and given personal concierge treatment, from the low-down on good snorkeling to a tour of the property. Guests are invited to use the centrally located oceanview deck and the living room in the house with its computer (with high-speed Internet connection). In the evenings Tom shows movies on the 8-foot-wide movie screen and frequently helps guests transfer their digital images to a CD, so they can go out and shoot more photos of Maui. They recently acquired a two-bedroom/two-bath condo, across the street from the beach, which they rent for $109 for two and $149 for three or more (6 night minimum).

3259 Akala Dr., Kihei, HI 96753. ☎ **877/782-9628** or 808/879-7099. Fax 808/879-7099. www.dreamscometrueon maui.com. 3 units. $75–$99 rooms in house (3- to 4-night minimum); $105–$125 cottage (6-night minimum). MC, V. **Amenities:** Concierge service; washer/dryer. *In room:* A/C, TV/VCR, kitchen or kitchenette, fridge, coffeemaker, hair dryer, CD player.

Nona Lani Cottages ★ *Finds*   Picture this: a grassy expanse dotted with eight cottages tucked among palm, fruit, and sweet-smelling flower trees, right across the street from a white-sand beach. This is one of the great hidden deals in Kihei. The cottages are tiny, but contain everything you'll need: a small but complete kitchen, twin beds that double as couches in the living room, a separate bedroom with a queen bed, and a lanai with table and chairs. The cottages were renovated recently with new ceramic flooring. The real attraction, however, is the garden setting next to the beach. There are no phones in the cabins (a blessing if you're trying to escape civilization), but there's a public one by the registration/check-in area.

If the cabins are booked, or if you want a bit more luxury, you might opt for one of the private guest rooms, with private entrance and private bath. These beautiful units feature plush carpet, koa bed frames, air-conditioning, and lanais. The industrious Kong family, hosts here, also run Happy Valley Hale Maui, hostel accommodations on the other side of the island in Happy Valley, next to Wailuku.

455 S. Kihei Rd. (just south of Hwy. 31; P.O. Box 655), Kihei, HI 96753. ☎ **800/733-2688** or 808/879-2497. www.nonalanicottages.com. 11 units. $75–$95 double; $90–$105 cottage. Extra person $12–$15. 3-night minimum for rooms; 4-night minimum for cottages. No credit cards. **Amenities:** Coin-op washer/dryers. *In room:* A/C, TV, kitchen (in cottages), fridge, coffeemaker, no phone.

Wailana Kai *Value* ★   Bello Realty, which has searched out the best deals in Kihei, has added this renovated, two-story, 10-unit, one- and two-bedroom apartments to its collection. With one-bedroom units starting at $85, this is a deal that will not last long. Once they get a reputation, the prices most likely will go up. Located at the end of a cul-de-sac street, and just a 1-minute walk to the beach, the property was totally renovated in 2004 with two types of units: standard (perfectly acceptable, clean, with new paint, furniture, and so on) and deluxe (the ones we recommend, for only a few dollars more). All units have full kitchens and concrete walls (sound proof!), and the second floor has ocean views. Also on property are a small pool, coin-operated laundry facilities, and a barbecue area.

34 Wailana Place. Reservations: c/o Bello Realty, P.O. Box 1776, Kihei, HI 96753. ☎ **800/541-3060** or 808/879-3328. Fax 808/875-1483. www.bellomaui.com. 10 units. $85–$100 1-bedroom; $110–$125 2-bedroom. V, MC. **Amenities:** Outdoor pool; barbecue area; coin-op laundry facilities. *In room:* TV/VCR, kitchen, fridge, coffeemaker, iron.

What a Wonderful World B&B ★ *Value*   We couldn't believe what we'd discovered here: an impeccably done B&B with a great location, excellent rates, and thought and care put into every room. Then we met hostess Eva Tantillo, who not only has a full-service travel agency, but also a master's degree in hotel management. The result? One of Maui's finest bed-and-breakfasts, centrally located in Kihei (a half-mile to Kamaole II Beach Park, 5 min. from Wailea golf courses, and convenient to shopping and restaurants). Choose from one of four units: the master suite (with small fridge, coffeemaker, and barbecue grill on the lanai), studio apartment (with fully-equipped kitchen), or two one-bedroom apartments (also with full kitchens). Each has a private entrance. You're also welcome to use the communal barbecue. Eva serves a family-style breakfast on her lanai, which boasts views of white-sand beaches, the West Maui Mountains, and Haleakala.

2828 Umalu Place (off Keonakai St., near Hwy. 31), Kihei, HI 96753. © **800/943-5804** or 808/879-9103. Fax 808/874-9352. www.amauibedandbreakfast.com. 4 units. $75 double; $89 studio double; $99 1-bedroom apt. (5% discount for cash). Rates include full breakfast. Children 11 and under stay free in parents' room. AE, MC, V. **Amenities:** Hot tub; laundry facilities. *In room:* TV, kitchenette, fridge, coffeemaker, hair dryer, iron.

GREAT PACKAGE DEALS

Menehune Shores *Value* If you plan to stay on Maui for a week, you might want to look into the car/condo packages here; they're a real deal, especially for families on a budget. The six-story Menehune Shores is about 30 years old and is showing its age in some places, but all units are well maintained and have ocean views. The design is straight out of the 1970s, but the views from the private lanais are timeless. The kitchens are fully equipped, and the oceanfront location guarantees a steady breeze that keeps the rooms cool (there's no air-conditioning). The building sits in front of the ancient Hawaiian fish ponds of Kalepolepo; some Hawaiians still fish them using traditional throw nets, but, generally, the pond serves as protection from the ocean waves, making it safe for children to swim in the relatively calm waters. There are also shuffleboard courts and a whale-watching platform on the roof garden.

760 S. Kihei Rd. (between Kaonoulu and Hoonani sts., P.O. Box 1327), Kihei, HI 96753. © **800/558-9117** or 808/879-3428. Fax 808/879-5218. www.menehunereservations.com. 70 units. $115–$145 1-bedroom double ($939/week w/car); $140–$190 2-bedroom double ($1099–$1289/week w/car); $185–$240 3-bedroom for up to 6 ($1,589/week w/car). 3-night minimum. Extra person $7.50. No credit cards. **Amenities:** Restaurant (Hawaiian/Pacific Rim); bar; outdoor pool. *In room:* TV/VCR, kitchen, fridge, coffeemaker, washer/dryers.

OFF-SEASON VALUES

Kamaole Nalu Resort This six-story condominium complex is located between two beach parks, Kamaole I and Kamaole II, and right across the street from a shopping complex. Units have fabulous ocean views, large living rooms, and private lanais; the kitchens are a bit small but come fully equipped. We recommend no. 306 for its wonderful bird's-eye view. The property also has an oceanside pool and great barbecue facilities. Restaurants, bars, a golf course, and tennis courts are nearby; shopping is across the street. *Be warned:* Since the building is right on Kihei Road, it can be noisy.

2450 S. Kihei Rd. (between Kanani and Keonekai rds., next to Kamaole Beach Park II), Kihei, HI 96753. © **800/767-1497** or 808/879-1006. Fax 808/879-8693. www.kamaolenalu.com. 36 units. High season $155–$215 double; low season $135–$195 double. Extra person $15. 5-night minimum. MC, V. **Amenities:** Outdoor pool; activity desk; car-rental desk. *In room:* TV, kitchen, fridge, coffeemaker, hair dryer, iron, safe, washer/dryer.

UPCOUNTRY MAUI

You'll find it cool and peaceful up here; be sure to bring a sweater.

MAKAWAO & OLINDA

Here you'll be (relatively) close to Haleakala National Park; Makawao and Olinda are approximately 90 minutes from the entrance to the park at the 7,000-foot level (you still have 3,000 ft. and another 30–45 min. to get to the top). Accommodations in

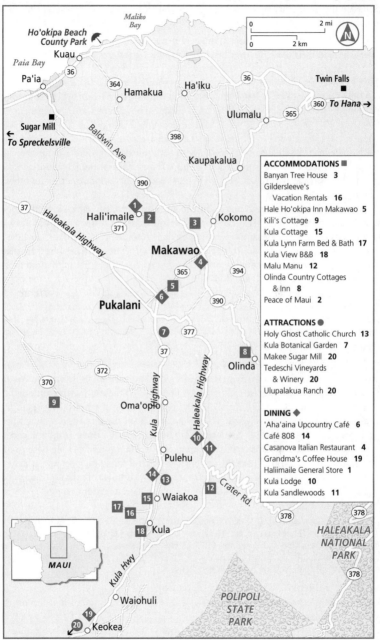

ACCOMMODATIONS ■
Banyan Tree House **3**
Gildersleeve's
  Vacation Rentals **16**
Hale Ho'okipa Inn Makawao **5**
Kili's Cottage **9**
Kula Cottage **15**
Kula Lynn Farm Bed & Bath **17**
Kula View B&B **18**
Malu Manu **12**
Olinda Country Cottages
  & Inn **8**
Peace of Maui **2**

ATTRACTIONS ●
Holy Ghost Catholic Church **13**
Kula Botanical Garden **7**
Makee Sugar Mill **20**
Tedeschi Vineyards
  & Winery **20**
Ulupalakua Ranch **20**

DINING ◆
'Aha'aina Upcountry Café **6**
Café 808 **14**
Casanova Italian Restaurant **4**
Grandma's Coffee House **19**
Haliimaile General Store **1**
Kula Lodge **10**
Kula Sandlewoods **11**

Kula are the only other options that will get you closer to the park so you can make the sunrise.

Banyan Tree House 🌀   Huge monkeypod trees (complete with swing and hammock) extend their branches over this property like a giant green canopy. The restored 1920s plantation manager's house is decorated with Hawaiian furniture from the 1930s. It can accommodate a big family or a group of friends, since it has three spacious bedrooms with big, comfortable beds and three private, marble-tiled bathrooms. A fireplace stands at one end of the huge living room, a large lanai runs the entire length of the house, and the hardwood floors shine throughout. The four smaller guest cottages have been totally renovated and also feature hardwood floors and marble bathrooms. The small cottage has a queen bed, private bathroom, microwave, coffee pot, and access to the fridge in the laundry room. Each of the larger cottages has two beds, a private bathroom, and a TV. One cottage has a kitchenette, the other a full kitchen.

New additions to this grand property include a full-size, saltwater swimming pool and Jacuzzi with a fabulous ocean view. The quiet neighborhood and old Hawaii ambience give this place a comfortable, easygoing atmosphere. Restaurants and shops are just minutes away in Makawao, and the beach is a 15-minute drive—but this place is so relaxing that you may find yourself wanting to do nothing more than lie in the hammock and watch the clouds float by.

3265 Baldwin Ave. (next to Veteran's Cemetery, less than a mile below Makawao), Makawao, HI 96768. ✆ 808/ 572-9021. Fax 808/573-5072. www.hawaii-mauirentals.com. 1 house, 4 cottages. $85–$115 cottage for 2; $350 3-bedroom house (sleeps up to 9). Extra person $20. Children age 12 and under stay free in parent's room. 3-night minimum for house. No credit cards. **Amenities:** Outdoor pool; Jacuzzi; babysitting; small charge for self-serve washer/dryer. *In room:* Kitchen or kitchenette, fridge, coffeemaker.

Hale Ho'okipa Inn Makawao 🌀 *(Finds)*   Step back in time at this 1924 plantation-style home, rescued by owner Cherie Attix in 1996 and restored to its original charm. Cherie lovingly refurbished the old wooden floors, filled the rooms with antique furniture from the 1920s, and hung works by local artists on the walls. The result is a charming, serene place to stay, just a 5-minute walk from the shops and restaurants of Makawao town, 15 minutes from beaches, and a 1½-hour drive from the top of Haleakala. The guest rooms have separate outside entrances and private bathrooms. The house's front and back porches are both wonderful for sipping tea and watching the sunset. The Kona Wing is a two-bedroom suite with private bathroom and use of the kitchen. Recently, Cherie has added a separate cottage next door with one bed and bath, plus a sleeping loft with half bath upstairs for $145 double.

32 Pakani Place, Makawao, HI 96768. ✆ 877/572-6698 or 808/572-6698. Fax 808/573-2580. www.maui-bed-and-breakfast.com. 4 units (2 w/shower only). $95–$125 double; $145–$165 suite with full kitchen; $145 double cottage. Rates include continental breakfast. Extra person $10. MC, V. From Haleakala Hwy., turn left on Makawao Ave., then turn right on the 5th street on the right off Makawao Ave. (Pakani Place); 2nd to the last house on the right (green house w/white picket fence and water tower). *In room:* TV, hair dryer.

Worth a Splurge

Olinda Country Cottages & Inn 🌀🌀 *(Finds)*   This charming B&B is set on the slopes of Haleakala in the crisp, clean air of Olinda, on an 8½-acre farm dotted with the surreal protea plants and surrounded by 35,000 acres of ranchlands (with miles of great hiking trails). The 5,000-square-foot country home, outfitted with a professional eye to detail, has large windows with incredible panoramic views of all of Maui. Upstairs are two guest rooms with country furnishings, private full bathrooms, and separate entryways. Connected to the main house but with its own private entrance, the Pineapple Sweet has a full kitchen, an antiques-filled living room, and a marble-tiled full bathroom. A separate 1,000-square-foot cottage is the epitome of cozy country luxury, with a fireplace, a queen bedroom, cushioned window seats (with great sunset views), and cathedral ceilings. The 950-square-foot Hidden Cottage (located in a truly secluded spot surrounded by protea flowers) features three decks, 8-foot French glass doors, a full kitchen, a washer/dryer, and a private tub for two on the deck.

Restaurants are a 15-minute drive away in Makawao, and beaches are another 15 minutes beyond that. Once ensconced, however, you may never want to leave this enchanting inn.

2660 Olinda Rd. (near the top of Olinda Rd., a 15-min. drive from Makawao), Makawao, HI 96768. ☎ **800/932-3435** or 808/572-1453. Fax 808/573-5326. www.mauibnbcottages.com. 5 units. $140 room and suite double; $195–$245 cottage for 2 (sleeps up to 5). Extra person $25. 2-night minimum for rooms and suite; 3-night minimum for cottages. No credit cards. *In room:* TV, kitchen (in cottages), washer/dryer (in cottages) fridge, coffeemaker.

Super-Cheap Sleeps
Peace of Maui ⭑ *Kids* *Value*   If you're looking for a clean, safe, quiet, well-located, and inexpensive place to stay, you can't beat this quiet lodge, just 10 minutes from the Kahului Airport and the north shore beaches, in the small plantation town of Haliimaile. Owners John and Tammi Cadman both worked for years in the hotel industry; when they started a family, they decided to convert the downstairs of their house into a seven-bedroom lodge so they could stay at home with their children. Each room has a double or queen bed, a TV, and a minifridge; they share a full kitchen, living room, shower room, and toilet room. Outside is a covered patio with a view of the rolling pineapple fields and the north shore beaches. The lodge is quiet (loud parties are not allowed) and kept immaculately clean by Tammi, who provides daily maid service. Also on the property is a separate private cottage with wood floors, full kitchen, two bedrooms, and a deck; the entire place can sleep up to six comfortably. The Cadmans welcome children (they have plenty of toys and acres of property for kids to roam). Ask about their excellent rates on car rentals.

1290 Haliimaile Rd. (just outside of Haliimaile town), Haliimaile, HI 96768. ☎ **888/475-5045** or 808/572-5045. www.peaceofmaui.com. 7 units (some with shared bathroom, shower only), 1 cottage. $50 single (w/shared bathroom; $55 double (w/shared bathroom); $100 double cottage. Extra person $10. AE, MC, V. **Amenities:** Jacuzzi; coin-op washer/dryer, free wireless Internet access, barbecue area. *In room:* TV/VCR, fridge.

IN KULA
Lodgings in Kula are the closest options to the entrance of Haleakala National Park (about 60 min. away).

Gildersleeve's Vacation Rentals *Value*   Located on a quiet side street, on the slopes of Haleakala, at 2,000 feet—just 25 minutes from Kahului Airport and the north shore beaches—is Elaine and Murray Gildersleeve's two-story pole house (on elevated telephone pole–sized stilts), set on their 2½-acre tropical-fruit farm. Guests have the downstairs: a large living room with a fireplace; a lanai that runs the length of the house, offering panoramic views of Maui from the ocean to Haleakala; a fully-equipped kitchen; and three oversized guest bedrooms, each with a private entrance. At this rural oasis, the nights are filled with quiet calm, and the hospitality of the hosts is always warm and welcoming.

2112 Naalae Rd. (1½ miles from Kula Hwy.), Kula, HI 96790. ☎ **808/878-6623**. Fax 808/878-2619. papag@ hawaii.rr.com. 2 units. $70 double. 3-night minimum. No credit cards.

Kili's Cottage ☆ *Value*   If you're looking for a quiet getaway in the cool elevation of Kula, this sweet cottage, situated on 2 acres, is the place. The amenities are numerous: large lanai, full kitchen, gas barbecue, washer/dryer, views, and even toys for the kids. The hostess, Kili Namau'u, who is the director of a Hawaiian-language immersion school, greets each guest with royal aloha—from the flowers (picked from the garden) that fill the house to the welcome basket filled with tropical produce grown on the property.

Kula. Reservations: c/o Hawaii's Best Bed & Breakfast, P.O. Box 758, Volcano, HI 96785. ℂ 800/262-9912 or 808/985-7488. Fax 808/967-8610. www.bestbnb.com. 1 3-bedroom/2-bathroom house. $115 double. Extra person $15. 2-night minimum. No credit cards. *In room:* TV, kitchen, fridge, coffeemaker, washer/dryer.

Kula Cottage ☆ *Finds*   We can't imagine having a less-than-fantastic vacation here. Tucked away on a quiet street amid a half-acre of blooming papaya and banana trees, Cecilia and Larry Gilbert's romantic honeymoon cottage is very private—it even has its own driveway and carport. The 700-square-foot cottage has a full kitchen (complete with dishwasher), and three huge closets that offer enough storage space for you to move in permanently. An outside lanai has a big gas barbecue and an umbrella table and chairs. Cecilia delivers a continental breakfast daily. Groceries and a small take-out lunch counter are within walking distance; it's a 30-minute drive to the beach.

40 Puakea Place (off Lower Kula Rd.), Kula, HI 96790. ℂ **808/878-2043** or 808/871-6230. Fax 808/871-9187. www.kulacottage.com. 1 cottage. $95 double. Rate includes continental breakfast. 2-night minimum. No credit cards. *In room:* TV, kitchen, fridge, coffeemaker, washer/dryer.

Kula Lynn Farm Bed & Bath ☆ *Kids*   The Coons, the same great family that runs Maui's best sailing adventure on the *Trilogy,* offer this spectacular 1,600-square-foot unit on the ground floor of their custom-built pole house. From its location on the slopes of Haleakala, the panoramic view (across Maui's central valley, with the islands of Lanai and Kahoolawe in the distance) is worth the price alone. Wall-to-wall windows and high ceilings add to the feeling of spaciousness throughout. The two bedrooms, two bathrooms, and two queen sofa beds in the living room make this the perfect place for a family. No expense has been spared in the European-style kitchen, with top appliances and Italian marble floors. This place should appeal to those who enjoy a quiet location and such activities as barbecuing on the lanai and watching the sunset.

P.O. Box 847, Kula, HI 96790. ℂ **800/874-2666**, ext. 211, or 808/878-6176. Fax 808/878-6320. captcoon@ verizon.net. 1 unit. $119 double. 5-night minimum. Rate includes breakfast fixings. Extra person $20. No credit cards. *In room:* TV/VCR, kitchen, fridge, coffeemaker, iron.

Kula View *Finds*   Susan Kauai's quaint studio suite is located on the upper level of her home, which sits at 2,000 feet on the slopes of Haleakala. A private entrance takes you up the stairs to a wide deck with views, views, views (in one direction, Haleakala rises majestically; in another, all of Maui is spread out before you). Surrounding the B&B are 2 lush acres blooming with fruits, flowers, and banana and coffee trees. The unit is tastefully decorated and outfitted with a queen-size bed, a reading area, a wicker breakfast nook with small kitchenette, and a private shower. Susan's family has been in the islands since the 1800s; she's an expert on everything Maui has to offer and is happy to help you plan your stay, loan warm clothes for your trip up Haleakala, or take you for a tour of her garden.

P.O. Box 322, Kula, HI 96790. ℂ **808/878-6736.** www.kulaview.com. 1 suite. $95 double. Rate includes continental breakfast. 2-night minimum. *In room:* Fridge, coffeemaker.

Worth a Splurge

Malu Manu ★★ *(Finds)*   This is one of the most romantic places to stay on Maui, with a panoramic view of the entire island from the front door. Tucked into the side of Haleakala Volcano, at 4,000 feet, this is an old Hawaiian estate with a single-room log cabin (built as a writer's retreat in the early 1900s) and a separate 30-year-old family home. The writer's cabin has a full kitchen, a fireplace, and antiques galore. The two-bedroom, two-and-a-half-bathroom home also has antiques, koa walls, and beautiful eucalyptus floors. It's an ideal retreat for a romantic couple, a family, or two couples traveling together. The 7-acre property is filled with native forest, organic gardens—help yourself to lemons, avocados, and whatever else is ripe—a paddle-tennis court, and a Japanese-style outdoor soaking tub. If you're a dog person, the resident golden retriever, Alohi, may come over and make your acquaintance. This is one of the closest accommodations to Haleakala; restaurants are about a 15-minute drive away.

446 Cooke Rd. (P.O. Box 175), Kula, HI 96790. (*C*) 888/878-6161 or 808/878-6111. www.mauisunrise.com. 2 units. $150 double in log cabin; $185 double in 2-bedroom house. Extra person $10. 3-night minimum. MC, V. **Amenities:** Hot tub; paddle-tennis court; massage; laundry facilities. *In room:* Kitchen, fridge, coffeemaker, iron.

EAST MAUI

See "The Road to Hana" map on p. 438 and the "Hana" map on p. 442.

ON THE ROAD TO HANA

Halfway to Hana House *(Finds)*   This cozy private guest studio has its own entrance, a covered patio, and 180-degree wraparound ocean views. Decorated in Polynesian style in rattan and wicker, it has a double bed, original island art, owner Gail Pickholz's dazzling flower arrangements (freshly picked from her 2 acres), and just about all the comforts of home, including a CD player. Also provided is everything you need for a trip to the beach. Freshwater pools and waterfalls are just a few minutes' walk from the studio.

Off Hana Hwy., nearly a half-mile past Twin Falls Bridge. P.O. Box 675, Haiku, HI 96708. (*C*) 808/572-1176. Fax 808/572-3609. www.halfwaytohana.com. 1 studio. $85–$105 double. Breakfast available for $8 per person ($15 for 2). 3-night minimum. No credit cards. **Amenities:** Laundry facilities available ($5 a load). *In room:* TV, kitchenette, fridge, coffeemaker, hair dryer, iron.

Maui Dream Cottages *(Kids) (Value)*   Essentially a vacation rental, this 2-acre country estate is located atop a hill overlooking the ocean. The grounds are dotted with fruit trees (bananas, papayas, and avocados, all free for the picking), and the front lawn is comfortably equipped with a double hammock, chaise longues, and table and chairs. One cottage has two bedrooms, a full kitchen, a washer/dryer, and an entertainment center. The other is basically the same, but with only one bedroom (plus a sofa bed in the living room). They're both very well maintained and comfortably outfitted with furniture that's attractive but casual. The Haiku location is quiet and restful and offers the opportunity to see how real islanders live. However, you'll have to drive a good 20 to 25 minutes to restaurants in Makawao or Paia. Hookipa Beach is about a 20-minute drive, and Baldwin Beach (good swimming) is 25 minutes away.

265 W. Kuiaha Rd. (1 block from Pauwela Cafe), Haiku, HI 96708. (*C*) 808/575-9079. Fax 808/575-9477. 2 cottages (shower only). $80 for 4. 7-night minimum. MC, V. *In room:* TV, kitchen, fridge, coffeemaker, washer/dryer.

Over Yonder Maui   If you don't mind sharing a house with the host, this hidden bed-and-breakfast offers a quiet, relaxing vacation in a home on 2 acres in Haiku.

Host Nina Cahoj has the perfect eye for decorating and has created an absolutely gorgeous, comfy home. You have your own entrance into the sunroom with floor-to-ceiling windows that overlook the lush, tropical jungle of koa, with guava and kukui-nut trees. Two rooms are available: the antiques-filled ginger room, and the plumeria suite that features a bathroom with an old Chinese sideboard converted into a sink enclosure. The entire house is decorated with wonderful antiques and one-of-a-kind art and furniture. Guests have use of the kitchen, living room, sunroom, and television room. A breakfast of coffee and tea, cereal, banana bread or toast, and fruit is served every morning. Nina's two dogs, Liza, a Belgian Shepard, and Dodger, a yellow lab, are happy to provide canine company if your are missing your pooch at home.

2555 Lemi Pl., Haiku, HI 96708. (C) 888/222-2466 or 808/573-5320. www.overyondermaui.com. 2 rooms. $90–$100. No credit cards. **Amenities:** TV/VCR; use of kitchen; washer/dryer.

Pilialoha B&B Cottage ⭐   The minute you arrive at this split-level country cottage, located on 2 acres of half-century-old eucalyptus trees, you'll see owner Machiko Heyde's artistry at work. Just in front of the quaint cottage (which is great for couples but can sleep up to five) is a garden blooming with some 200 varieties of roses. You'll find more of Machiko's handiwork inside. There's a queen bed in the master bedroom, a twin bed in a small adjoining room, and a queen sofa bed in the living room. A large lanai extends from the master bedroom. There's a great movie collection for rainy days or cool country nights, and a garage. Machiko delivers breakfast daily; if you plan on an early-morning ride to the top of Haleakala, she'll make sure you go with a thermos of coffee and her homemade bread.

2512 Kaupakalua Rd. (½ mile from Kokomo intersection), Haiku, HI 96708. (C) **808/572-1440.** Fax 808/572-4612. www.pilialoha.com. 1 cottage. $130 double. Rates include continental breakfast. Extra person $20. 3-night minimum. No credit cards. **Amenities:** Complimentary use of beach paraphernalia (including snorkel equipment); complimentary use of washer/dryer. *In room:* TV, kitchenette, fridge, coffeemaker.

Tea House Cottage *Finds*   Here's your chance to *really* get away—so far away that you park your car on the dirt road and follow a fern-lined path to this secluded hideaway in the jungle. Alternative energy (no electric poles!) powers the place, allowing you to use all the modern conveniences, including phone, TV, CD player—you can even plug in your laptop. The house has a screened porch, compact living room and kitchen, separate bedroom, and antique bathhouse next door.

P.O. Box 335, Haiku, HI 96708. (C) **808/572-5610.** www.mauiteahouse.com. 1 cottage. $105 single; $125 double. Rates include breakfast fixings. 3-night minimum. No credit cards. About ½-mile past the mile marker 2 on the Hana Hwy., turn onto a gravel road and wind your way around to Hoolawa Rd., another ½-mile down this dirt road. *In room:* TV, kitchen, fridge, coffeemaker.

Wild Ginger ⭐⭐ *Finds*   This cozy, romantic, intimate cottage, hidden in Miliko Gulch, overlooking a stream with a waterfall, bamboo, sweet-smelling ginger, and banana trees, is perfect for honeymooners, lovers, and fans of Hawaiiana art. The moment you step into this 400-square-foot, artistically-decorated Hawaiian cottage (with additional 156-sq.-ft. screened deck), you will be delighted at the carefully placed memorabilia (ukulele tile, canoe paddle, and the like) found throughout. The cottage has a full kitchen with everything you could possibly need for cooking. The Hawaiian theme carries into the living room with VCR behind a tropical painted cabinet and stereo. The comfy queen bed opens to the living area. The screened porch has table, chairs, and couch, perfect for curling up with a good book. Outside there's a barbecue, plus all the beach toys you could want to borrow. Your hosts are Bob, a ceramic artist (with his creations throughout the cottage), and his wife, Sunny, who manages Dolphin Galleries (where she has selected the best-of-the-best artwork for the cottage).

355 Kaluanui Rd., Makawao, HI 96768. ℂ and fax **808/573-1173**. www.wildgingerfalls.com. 1 unit. $125 double, 3-night minimum. No credit cards. *In room:* VCR, kitchen, fridge, coffeemaker, iron, hair dryer, washer/dryer.

Super-Cheap Sleeps

Aloha Maui B&B *Value*   On 2 acres of jungle, tucked away in the Twin Falls area, is this budget-traveler accommodation. Three separate bungalows offer a back-to-nature experience. The rustic, but clean and well outfitted, cabins are all landscaped to offer privacy and offer good value for the price. The cabins range from the Mango cottage with hardwood floors, full kitchen, and big bedroom with ocean view to the Banana Room, a small room with kitchenette (two burners, full fridge, microwave, toaster, coffeemaker), and a CD player. All rooms are stocked with coffee or tea and locally-grown fruit (some comes from right outside your front door) in season. Host Ken knows all the hiking and biking trails (he will loan you his mountain bikes to go exploring) and secret waterfalls. This is the perfect place if you are on a tight budget and looking for a vacation in Maui's rainforest.

P.O. Box 790210, Paia, HI 96779. ℂ **808/572-0298**. www.alohamauicottages.com. 5 units (2 with shared bathroom). $70–$135 double. Extra person $5. 3-night minimum. DISC, MC, V. **Amenities:** Gas barbecue. *In room:* Kitchen or kitchenette, CD player.

Hale Akua Shangri-la Retreat Center *Value*   This place isn't for everyone. The hang-loose atmosphere might or might not be your style. Way off the beaten path, Hale Akua is a collection of eclectic buildings on 2 tropical acres where, at certain times of the year, guests can choose to go "clothing optional." The main house on the property has breathtaking ocean views and private lanais off most rooms; guests share the living room, bathroom, and kitchen. The Cabana building, next to the 60-foot pool, is a two-story house with five separate rooms, two kitchens, and a dining area. Also on the property is a cottage with two rooms, one pyramid-shaped. Other on-site features include a hot tub, fountain, lily pond, hammock, trampoline, and maze formed by panex trees. Yoga classes are available.

Star Rte. 1, Box 161 (off Hana Hwy., between mile markers 3 and 4), Haiku, HI 96708. ℂ **888/368-5305** or 808/572-9300. Fax 808/572-6666. www.haleakua.com. 18 units (some w/shared bathroom). $60–$160 double. Rates include breakfast. Extra person $25 (except for the Villa). AE, DISC, MC, V. **Amenities:** Giant pool; hot tub; Internet access; massage; coin-operated laundry; yoga classes; use of kitchen.

Worth a Splurge

Huelo Point Flower Farm ★ *Finds*   Here's a little Eden by the sea on a spectacular, remote, 300-foot sea cliff near a waterfall stream. This 2-acre estate overlooking Waipio Bay has two guest cottages, a guest house, and a main house available for rent. The studio-sized Gazebo Cottage has a glass-walled ocean front, a koa-wood captain's bed, a TV, a stereo, a kitchenette, a private oceanside patio, a private hot tub, and a half-bathroom with outdoor shower. The new, 900-square-foot Carriage House apartment sleeps four and has glass walls facing the mountain and sea, plus a kitchen, a den, decks, and a loft bedroom. The two-bedroom main house contains an exercise room, a fireplace, a sunken Roman bath, cathedral ceilings, and other extras. On site is a natural pool with a waterfall and an oceanfront hot tub. You're welcome to pick fruit, vegetables, and flowers from the extensive garden. Homemade scones, tree-ripened papayas, and fresh-roasted coffee start your day. Despite its seclusion, off the crooked road to Hana, it's just a half-hour to Kahului, or about 20 minutes to Paia's shops and restaurants.

Off Hana Hwy., between mile markers 3 and 4. P.O. Box 791808, Paia, HI 96779. (C) **808/572-1850.** www.maui flowerfarm.com. 4 units. $160 cottage double; $190 carriage-house double; $350 guest-house double; $450 main-house double (sleeps 8). Extra person $20–$35. 2-night minimum for smaller houses, 5-night minimum for main house. No credit cards. **Amenities:** Outdoor pool; 3 Jacuzzis; self-serve washer/dryer. *In room:* TV, kitchenette (in cottage), kitchen (in houses), fridge, coffeemaker, hair dryer.

Mama's Beachfront Cottages ☆
The fabulous location (nestled in a coconut grove on secluded Kuau Beach), beautifully decorated interior (with island-style rattan furniture and works by Hawaiian artists), full kitchen, and extras (Weber gas barbecue, huge 27-in. TVs, and all the beach toys you can think of) make this place a gem for those seeking a centrally-located vacation rental. It has everything; even Mama's Fish House next door, where guests get a discount off lunch and dinner. The one-bedrooms are nestled in tropical jungle (red ginger surrounds the garden patio), while the two-bedrooms face the beach. Both have terra-cotta floors, complete kitchens (even dishwashers), sofa beds, and laundry facilities.

799 Poho Place (off the Hana Hwy. in Kuau), Paia, HI 96779. (C) **800/860-HULA** or 808/579-9764. Fax 808/579-8594. www.mamasfishhouse.com. 9 units. $175 1-bedroom (sleeps up to 4); $475 2-bedroom (up to 6). 3-night minimum stay. AE, DISC, DC, MC, V. *In room:* A/C, TV/VCR, kitchen, fridge, coffeemaker, iron, hair dryer.

AT THE END OF THE ROAD IN HANA
Hana Kai Maui Resort
Hana's only vacation condo complex, Hana Kai offers studio and one-bedroom units overlooking Hana Bay. All units have large kitchens and private lanais. Each one-bedroom unit has a sliding door that separates the bedroom from the living room, plus a sofa bed that sleeps two additional guests. There are no TVs or phones in the units (a pay phone is located on the property), so you can really get away from it all. Ask for a corner unit with wraparound ocean views.

1533 Uakea Rd. (P.O. Box 38), Hana, HI 96713. (C) **800/346-2772** or 808/248-8426. Fax 808/248-7482. www.hana kai.com. 17 units. $125–$135 studio double; $145–$195 1-bedroom (sleeps up to 4). Children under 8 stay free in parent's room. AE, MC, V. *In room:* Kitchen, fridge, coffeemaker, no phone.

Hana's Tradewinds Cottage ☆ (Value)
Nestled among the ginger and heliconias on a 5-acre flower farm are two separate cottages, each with full kitchen, carport, barbecue, private hot tub, TV, ceiling fans, and sofa bed. The studio cottage sleeps up to four; a bamboo shoji blind separates the sleeping area (with queen bed) from the sofa bed in the living room. The Tradewinds cottage has two bedrooms (with a queen bed in one room and two twins in the other), one bathroom (shower only), and a huge front porch. The atmosphere is quiet and relaxing, and hostess Rebecca Buckley, who has been in business for a decade, welcomes families (she has two children, a cat, and a very sweet golden retriever). You can use the laundry facilities at no extra charge.

135 Alalele Place (the airport road), P.O. Box 385, Hana, HI 96713. (C) **800/327-8097** or 808/248-8980. Fax 808/248-7735. www.hanamaui.net. 2 cottages. $120 studio double; $145 2-bedroom double. Extra person $10. 2-night minimum. AE, DISC, MC, V. *In room:* TV, kitchen, fridge, coffeemaker, no phone.

Super-Cheap Sleeps
Aloha Cottages (Value)
Mrs. Nakamura has been renting vacation houses in Hana since the 1970s. She started with one unit and now has five. All located in residential areas close to Hana Bay, her budget rentals are simple but adequately furnished cottages, which vary in size from a roomy studio with a kitchenette to three-bedroom/

two-bathroom homes. They're fully equipped, clean, and fairly well kept. Not all units have TVs, and none have phones, but Mrs. N. is more than happy to take messages.

83 Keawa Place (off Hana Hwy.). P.O. Box 205, Hana, HI 96713. © **808/248-8420.** 5 cottages. $65–$95 double. Extra person $10–$15. No credit cards. *In room:* TV (some units), kitchen (some units), fridge (some units), coffeemaker (some units), no phone.

Joe's Place *Value*   This is as close to a hostel as you can get in Hana. Joe's is a rambling large house, located just spitting distance from Hana Bay. Seven spartan, but clean, bedrooms share showers and bathroom; one has private facilities. All the guests are welcome to the large living room with TV and adjoining communal kitchen (free coffee available all day). Other facilities include a rec room, barbecue, and owner Ed Hill himself. He'll tell you the long story about the name if you ask, and can also talk all day about what to do and see in Hana if you let him.

4870 Ua'kea Rd. Reservations: P.O. Box 746, Hana, HI 96713. © **808/248-7033.** www.joesrentals.com. 8 units (7 with shared bathroom). $45 double (shared bathroom); $55 double (private bathroom). Extra person $10. No credit cards.

Kulani's Hideway in Hana, Maui ⭑ *Value*   On the road to Waianapanapa State Park is Hana's best deal: two one-bedroom units (with pull-out sofa bed in the living room) with cable TV (a plus in Hana), within walking distance of a fabulous black-sand beach. Outside is a large lanai, for watching the clouds go by, with a barbecue area and a picnic table in the yard. Book early.

Reservations: P.O. Box 483, Hana, HI 96713. © and fax **808/248-8234** or 808/248-4815. kulanis@maui.net. 2 units. $80 double. Extra person $15. *In room:* TV, kitchen, fridge, coffeemaker, washer/dryer, no phone.

Waianapanapa State Park Cabins *Value* *Kids*   These 12 rustic cabins are a steal. Everyone knows it, too—so make your reservations early (up to 6 months in advance). The cabins are warm and dry and come complete with kitchen, living room, bedroom, and bathroom with hot shower; furnishings include bedding, linens, towels, dishes, and very basic cooking and eating utensils. Don't expect luxury—this is a step above camping, albeit in a beautiful tropical jungle setting. The key attraction at this 120-acre state beach park is the unusual horseshoe-shaped black-sand beach on Pailoa Bay, popular for shore fishing, snorkeling, and swimming. There's a caretaker on-site, along with restrooms, showers, picnic tables, shoreline hiking trails, and historic sites. But bring mosquito protection—this *is* the jungle, after all.

Off Hana Hwy. Reservations: c/o State Parks Division, 54 S. High St., Room 101, Wailuku, HI 96793. © **808/984-8109.** 12 cabins. $45 for 4 (sleeps up to 6). Extra person $5. 5-night maximum. No credit cards. *In room:* Kitchen, fridge, coffeemaker, no phone.

Worth a Splurge

Ekena ⭑   Just one glance at the 360-degree view, and you can see why hosts Robin and Gaylord gave up their careers on the mainland and moved here. This 8½-acre piece of paradise in rural Hana boasts ocean and rainforest views; the floor-to-ceiling glass doors in the spacious Hawaiian-style pole house bring the outside in. The elegant two-story home is exquisitely furnished, from the comfortable U-shaped couch that invites you to relax and take in the view to the top-of-the-line mattress on the king bed. The kitchen is fully equipped with every high-tech convenience you can imagine (guests have made complete holiday meals here). Only one floor (and one two-bedroom unit) is rented at any one time to ensure privacy. The grounds are impeccably groomed and dotted with tropical plants and fruit trees. Hiking trails into the rainforest start right on the property, and beaches and waterfalls are just minutes away. Robin places fresh flowers in every room and makes sure you're comfortable; after that, she's available to answer questions, but she also respects your privacy.

P.O. Box 728 (off Hana Hwy., above Hana Airport), Hana, HI 96713. ℂ **808/248-7047.** Fax 808/248-7047. www. ekenamaui.com. 2 units. $185 for 2; $250–$350 for 4. Extra person $25. 3-night minimum. No credit cards. **Amenities:** Complimentary use of washer/dryers. *In room:* TV, kitchen, fridge, coffeemaker, iron.

Hamoa Bay Bungalow 🎬 *(Finds)*

Down a country lane guarded by two Balinese statues stands a little bit of Indonesia in Hawaii: a carefully crafted bungalow and an Asian-inspired two-bedroom house overlooking Hamoa Bay. This enchanting retreat is just 2 miles beyond Hasegawa's general store on the way to Kipahulu. It sits on 4 verdant acres within walking distance of Hamoa Beach. The 600-square-foot Balinese-style cottage is distinctly tropical—with giant bamboo furniture from Indonesia, batik prints, a king bed, a full kitchen, and a screened porch with hot tub and shower. Hidden from the cottage is a 1,300-square-foot home with a soaking tub and private outdoor stone shower. It offers a bamboo king bed in one room, a queen bed in another, a screened-in sleeping porch, a full kitchen, and wonderful ocean views.

P.O. Box 773, Hana, HI 96713. ℂ **808/248-7884.** Fax 808/248-7047. www.hamoabay.com. 2 units. $195 cottage (sleeps only 2); $250 house for 2; $350 house for 4. 3-night minimum. No credit cards. **Amenities:** Hot tub; complimentary use of washer/dryers. *In room:* TV, kitchen, fridge, coffeemaker, iron.

Hotel Hana-Maui 🎬🎬🎬 *(Kids)*

Picture Shangri-La, Hawaiian-style: 66 acres rolling down to the sea in a remote Hawaiian village, with a wellness center, two pools, and access to one of the best beaches in Hana. This is the atmosphere, the landscape, and the culture of old Hawaii set in 21st-century accommodations. Every unit is excellent, but my favorites are the Sea Ranch Cottages (especially units 215–218 for the best views of turtles frolicking in the ocean), where individual duplex bungalows look out over the craggy shoreline to the rolling surf. You step out of the oversize, open, airy units (with floor-to-ceiling sliding doors) onto a huge lanai with views that will stay with you long after your tan has faded. These comfy units have been totally redecorated with every amenity you can think of, and you won't be nickle-and-dimed for things like coffee and water—everything they give you, from the homemade banana bread to the bottled water, is complimentary. Cathedral ceilings, a plush feather bed, a giant-size soaking tub, Hawaiian art work, bamboo hardwood floors—this is luxury. The white-sand beach (just a 5 min. shuttle away), top notch wellness center with some of the best massage therapists in Hawaii, and numerous activities (horseback riding, mountain biking, tennis, pitch-and-putt golf) all add up to make this one of the top resorts in the state. There's no TV in the rooms, but the Club Room has a giant-screen TV, plus VCR and Internet access. I highly recommend this little slice of paradise.

Hana, Maui 96713. ℂ **800/321-HANA** or 808/248-8211; fax 808/248-7202; www.hotelhanamaui.com. 66 units. $395–$455 Bay Cottages double; $525–$895 Sea Ranch Cottages double; $1,295 2-bedroom suite for 4; 2-bedroom Plantation Guest House from $2,500. AE, DC, DISC, MC, V. **Amenities:** Restaurant (with Hawaiian entertainment twice a week); bar (entertainment 4 times a week); 2 outdoor pools; complimentary use of the 3-hole practice golf courses (clubs are complimentary); complimentary tennis courts; fitness center; full-service spa; game room; concierge; activity desk; car-rental desk; business center; small shopping arcade; salon; limited room service; babysitting; laundry service. *In room:* Dataport, kitchenette, fridge, coffeemaker, hair dryer, iron, safe.

4 Dining

The Valley Isle is fertile ground for Hawaii's enterprising chefs. The great news in affordable dining on Maui is the proliferation of informal, budget-friendly restaurants. While the palaces of Hawaii Regional Cuisine have burgeoned as well, towns such as Wailuku, Paia, and even touristy Lahaina have sprouted some welcome new dining options offering good, simple food for the value-conscious.

Inexpensive noodle houses and Mexican restaurants are on the rise. When Hawaii Regional Cuisine chef Mark Ellman opened **Maui Tacos** in Napili, and then expanded the take-out chain to Kahului, Kihei, and Lahaina, he started a trend that is now a fever on Maui: home-style, south-of-the-border cooking. Now you'll find easygoing Mexican restaurants all over the island, and top-notch made-on-Maui tortillas and salsas for sale in supermarkets and health-food stores. Noodle houses, such as **Sam Sato's** in Wailuku, and casual gourmet diners, such as Café O'Lei (Maalaea and Lahaina), are a thriving part of dining on Maui. And the classic old-timer's mom-and-pop diner is not yet an anachronism for those who venture off the resort circuit.

In the listings below, reservations are not necessary unless otherwise noted.

CENTRAL MAUI

The **Queen Kaahumanu Center,** the structure that looks like a white *Star Wars* umbrella in the center of Kahului, at 275 Kaahumanu Ave. (5 min. from Kahului Airport on Hwy. 32), has a very popular food court. Busy shoppers seem more than willing to dispense with fine china and other formalities to enjoy a no-nonsense meal on foam plates. **Edo Japan** teppanyaki is a real find; its flat Benihana-like grill dispensing marvelous, flavorful mounds of grilled fresh vegetables and chicken teriyaki for $5.70. **Maui Mixed Plate** dishes out "local style" cuisine of meat with rice and macaroni salad in the $4.45 to $7 range. **Yummy Korean B-B-Q** offers the assertive flavors of Korea ranging from $4.75 to $7.50; **Panda Express** serves tasty Chinese food; and **Sushi Go** is a great place for fast sushi. Outside of the food court, but still in the shopping center, is the **Coffee Store** (p. 393), which sells sandwiches, salads, pasta, and nearly two dozen different coffee drinks; **Ruby's,** dishing out hamburgers, fries and shakes; and **Starbucks** for the java fans. When you leave Kaahumanu Center, take a moment to gaze at the West Maui Mountains to your left from the parking lot. They are one of Maui's wonders.

There's a branch of **Maui Tacos** (p. 390) in Kaahumanu Center, Kahului (✆ **808/871-7726**).

Class Act ✿ GLOBAL   Part of a program run by the distinguished Food Service Department of Maui Community College (now housed in a new state-of-the-art, $15-million culinary facility), this restaurant has a following. Student chefs show their stuff with a flourish in their "classroom," where they pull out all the stops. Linen, china, servers in ties and white shirts, and a four-course lunch make this a unique value. The appetizer, soup, salad, and dessert are set, but you can choose between the regular entrees and a heart-healthy main course prepared in the culinary tradition of the week. The menu roams the globe with highlights of Italy, Mexico, Maui, Napa valley, France, New Orleans, and other locales. The day we dined, the menu was pastrami-cured salmon gravlax with Yukon gold potato blini and lemon relish (appetizer), farm greens with warm goat cheese and choice of entree: pan seared fish with citrus brown butter and parsnip puree, crispy duck-leg confit with orange gastrique and haricot vert, or green lentil crepe with oven-dried tomato relish and dessert coffee or tea.

Maui Community College, 310 Kaahumanu Ave., Wailuku. ✆ 808/984-3480. www.hawaii.edu/maui/mca. Reservations recommended. 4-course lunch $25. MC. V. Wed and Fri 11am–12:30pm; closed May–Aug for summer vacation. Menu and cuisine type change weekly.

Ichiban *Finds* JAPANESE/SUSHI   What a find: an informal neighborhood restaurant that serves inexpensive, home-cooked Japanese food *and* good sushi at realistic prices. Local residents consider Ichiban a staple for breakfast, lunch, or dinner and a haven of comforts: egg-white omelets; great saimin; combination plates of teriyaki chicken, teriyaki meat, *tonkatsu* (pork cutlet), rice, and pickled cabbage; chicken yakitori; and sushi—everything from unagi and scallop to California roll. The sushi items may not be cheap, but like the specials, such as steamed opakapaka, they're a good value. We love the tempura, miso soup, and spicy ahi hand roll.

Kahului Shopping Center, 47 Kaahumanu Ave., Kahului. © **808/871-6977**. Main courses $4.25–$5.25 breakfast; from $4.25 lunch (combination plates $8.50); $4.95–$27 dinner (combination dinner $12, dinner specials from $8.95). DC, MC, V. Mon–Fri 6:30am–2pm and 5–9pm; Sat 10:30am–2pm and 5–9pm.

Main Street Bistro *Value* AMERICAN   Formerly the Who's the Boss? restaurant, before that Iao Café (and before that the Café O Lei), this popular eatery, located on the main street of Wailuku, is now owned by Chef Tom Selman, well know in culinary circles on Maui. He was formerly the Chef du Cuisine at David Paul's Lahaina Grill and also was Corporate Chef for the Sansei/Vino restaurants. As we went to press, the restaurant was only open for lunch, but Selman was talking about possibly creating a "pau hana pupu" menu (after-work appetizers) and a wine list to come. Chef Selman calls his food "refined comfort food," with signature menu items that range from onion rings with house-made smoky ketchup, to roasted Chinese chicken salad (with won tons), blackened chicken and shrimp pastas salad (with a creamy avocado ranch dressing), slow-cooked baby back ribs (with poha honey mustard glaze) and "mother's roast beef sandwich" (served open faced on a French roll). The chef will happily customize any menu item for people who prefer low calorie, low-fat or low-carbohydrates options. Daily specials range from grilled steak to roasted eggplant terrine.

2051 Main St., Wailuku. © **808/244-6816**. Entrees $9–$11, daily lunch specials $6.95–$15. No credit cards. Mon–Fri 10:30am–2:30pm.

Mañana Garage ✶✶✶ *Finds* LATIN AMERICAN   Chef Tom Lelli, formerly of Haliimaile General Store, is serving up some incomparable fare at this central Maui hot spot. The industrial motif features table bases like hubcaps, a vertical garage door as a divider for private parties, blown-glass chandeliers, and gleaming chrome and cobalt walls with orange accents. The menu is brilliantly conceived and executed. Fried green tomatoes are done just right and served with slivered red onions. Three different kinds of ceviche, each one perfectly balances flavors and textures: lime, cilantro, chile, coconut, and fresh fish. They even have barbecued ribs! Mañana Garage has raised the bar and introduced exciting new flavors to Maui's dining options. If you are on this side of the island, don't miss this incredible experience.

33 Lono Ave., Kahului. © **808/873-0220**. Reservations recommended. Main courses $7–$13 lunch; $16–$29 dinner. AE, DISC, MC, V. Mon 11am–9pm; Wed–Sat 11am–10:30pm; Sun 5–9pm.

Marco's Grill & Deli ITALIAN   Located in the thick of central Maui, where the roads to upcountry, west, and south Maui converge, Marco's is popular among area residents for its homemade Italian fare and friendly informality. Everything—from the meatballs, sausages, and burgers to the sauces, salad dressings, and raviolis—is made in-house. The 35 different choices of hot and cold sandwiches and entrees are served all day, and they include vodka rigatoni with imported prosciutto, *pasta e' fagiolo* (a house specialty: smoked ham hock, simmered for hours in tomato sauce, with red and white beans), and simple pasta with marinara sauce. This is one of those comfortable neighborhood fixtures favored by all generations. Locals stop here for breakfast, lunch, and dinner; before and after movies; and on the way to and from baseball games and concerts. The antipasto salad, vegetarian lasagna, and roasted peppers are taste treats, but the meatballs and Italian sausage are famous in central Maui.

Dairy Center, 395 Dairy Rd., Kahului. ℂ 808/877-4446. Main courses $11–$27. AE, DC, DISC, MC, V. Daily 7:30am–10pm.

A Saigon Cafe ★★ (Finds) VIETNAMESE   Jennifer Nguyen has stuck to her guns and steadfastly refused to erect a sign, and diners will come anyway. That's how good the food is. Fans drive from all over the island for her crisped, spiced Dungeness crab, her steamed opakapaka with ginger and garlic, and her wok-cooked Vietnamese specials tangy with spices, herbs, and lemon grass. There are a dozen different soups, cold and hot noodles (including the popular beef noodle soup called *pho*), and chicken and shrimp cooked in a clay pot. You can create your own Vietnamese "burritos" from a platter of tofu, noodles, and vegetables that you wrap in rice paper and dip in garlic sauce. Among our favorites are the shrimp lemongrass, savory and refreshing, and the tofu curry, swimming in herbs and vegetables straight from the garden. The *Nhung Dam,* the Vietnamese version of fondue—a hearty spread of basil, cucumbers, mint, romaine, bean sprouts, pickled carrots, turnips, and vermicelli, wrapped in rice paper and dipped in a legendary sauce—is cooked at your table.

1792 Main St., Wailuku. ℂ 808/243-9560. Main courses $6.50–$17. MC, V. Mon–Sat 10am–9:30pm; Sun 10am–8:30pm. Heading into Wailuku from Kahului, go over the bridge and take the 1st right onto Central Ave, then the 1st right on Nani St. At the next stop sign, look for the building with the neon sign that says OPEN.

SUPER-CHEAP EATS

Maui Bake Shop BAKERY/DELI   Sleepy Vineyard Street has seen many a mom-and-pop business come and go, but Maui Bake Shop is here to stay. Maui native Claire Fujii-Krall and her husband, baker José Krall (who was trained in the south of France), are turning out buttery brioches, healthful nine-grain and two-tone rye breads, focaccia, strudels, sumptuous fresh-fruit gâteaux, puff pastries, and dozens of other baked goods and confections. The breads are baked in one of Maui's oldest brick ovens, installed in 1935; a high-tech European diesel oven handles the rest. The front window displays more than 100 bakery and deli items, among them salads, a popular eggplant marinara focaccia, homemade quiches, and an inexpensive calzone filled with chicken, pesto, mushroom, and cheese. Homemade soups (clam chowder, minestrone, cream of asparagus) team up nicely with sandwiches on freshly baked bread. The food here is light enough (well, almost) to justify the Ultimate Dessert: white-chocolate macadamia-nut cheesecake.

2092 Vineyard St., Wailuku. ℂ 808/242-0064. Most items under $5. AE, DISC, MC, V. Mon–Fri 6am–3pm; Sat 7am–1pm.

Sam Sato's NOODLES/PLATE LUNCHES   Sam Sato's is a Maui institution, not only for its noodles (saimin, dry noodles, chow fun), but also its flaky baked *manju,* filled with sweetened lima beans or adzuki beans. Sam opened his family eatery in 1933, and his daughter, Lynne Toma, still makes the broth the old-fashioned way: from scratch. The saimin and the dry noodles, with broth that comes in a separate bowl, are big sellers. One regular comes to the counter, with its wooden stools and homemade salt and pepper shakers, for his "usual:" two barbecued meat sticks, two scoops of rice, and three macaroni salads. The peach, apple, coconut, and pineapple turnovers fly out the door, too, as do take-out noodles by the tray. *Tip:* If you want them to hold the MSG, be sure to make your request early.

Millyard Plaza, 1750 Wili Pa Loop, Wailuku. ⓒ **808/244-7124**. Plate lunches $5.75–$6.75. No credit cards. Mon–Sat 7am–2pm.

Wei Wei BBQ and Noodle House CHINESE/NOODLES
Noodles are rapidly gaining on Big Macs as the fast-food choice of Hawaii, and Wei Wei is the darling of Maui's on-the-go, noodle-loving crowd. You order at the counter, fast-food style, from a menu that includes Chinese classics: saimin with roast duck, shrimp-vegetable chow mein, dim sum, and the extremely popular house-fried noodles. American favorites— hamburgers, a teriyaki chicken burger, a turkey sandwich, and the popular chicken katsu burger—win fans, too.

Millyard Plaza, 210 Imi Kala St., Wailuku. ⓒ **808/242-7928**. Combination plates $4.95–$6.95; main courses $5.95–$8.50. No credit cards. Daily 9:30am–9pm.

WEST MAUI
LAHAINA
There's a **Maui Tacos** (p. 390) in Lahaina Square (ⓒ **808/661-8883**). Maui's branch of the **Hard Rock Cafe** is in Lahaina at 900 Front St. (ⓒ **808/667-7400**).

To locate the restaurants in this section, see the "Lahaina" map on p. 356.

Aloha Mixed Plate ★ *Value* PLATE LUNCHES/BEACHSIDE GRILL
Look for the festive turquoise-and-yellow, plantation-style front with the red corrugated-iron roof and adorable bar, tiny and busy, directly across from the Lahaina Cannery Mall. Grab a picnic table at ocean's edge, in the shade of large kiawe and milo trees, where you can watch the bobbing sailboats and two islands on the near horizon. (On the upper level, there are umbrellas and plumeria trees—just as charming.) Then tuck into inexpensive mahimahi, kalua pig and cabbage, shoyu chicken, teriyaki beef, and other local plate-lunch specials, all at budget-friendly prices, served with macaroni salad and rice. The shoyu chicken is the best we've had, fork tender and tasty, and the spicy chicken drumettes come from a fabled family recipe. (The bestsellers are the coconut prawns and Aloha Mixed Plate of shoyu chicken, teriyaki beef, and mahimahi.) We don't know of anywhere else where you can order a mai tai with a plate lunch and enjoy table service with an ocean view.

1285 Front St., Lahaina. ⓒ **808/661-3322**. Main courses $4.95–$9.95. MC, V. Daily 10:30am–10pm.

Café O'Lei Lahaina AMERICAN ★★ *Value*
About a dozen years ago, restaurateurs Dana and Michael Pastula (Dana has managed such premier restaurants as Hulo'poe Court and Ihilani in Manele Bay Resort on Lanai and Pacific Grill at Four Seasons Maui, and Michael has been a chef for more than 25 years, including stints at the Swan Court in the Hyatt Regency Maui and Wailea Maui Marriott) opened their first Café O'Lei in Makawao. A tiny, hidden eatery, it was packed from day one. The duo has brought their unique blend of island fresh ingredients and zippy preparations to Lahaina (and Maalaea). The location could not be better: al fresco dining on upper and lower decks, both with an unobstructed 180 degree view of the ocean and the island of Lanai in the distance. Despite the fact that this is Front Street, Lahaina, the Pastulas still have great food and reasonable prices; the plate lunch special is only $6.95. Because the view is so romantic, I recommend that you go here for dinner before the sun sets to take in that ocean panorama as you dine on seared ahi, sautéed mahi, macadamia-nut roast duckling, thai coconut lobster, jumbo shrimp, or calamari. Best prices in town!

839 Front St., Lahaina. © **808/661-9491.** Reservations recommended. Main courses $6.50–$11 lunch, $14–$23 dinner. AE, DISC, MC, V. Daily 10:30am–9:30pm.

Cheeseburger in Paradise AMERICAN   Wildly successful, always crowded, highly visible, and very noisy with its live music in the evenings, Cheeseburger is a shrine to the American classic. The home of three-napkin cheeseburgers with attitude, this is burger country, tropical style, with everything from tofu and garden burgers to the biggest, juiciest beef and chicken burgers, served on whole-wheat and sesame buns baked fresh daily. There are good reasons the two-story green-and-white building next to the seawall is always packed: good value, good grinds, and a great ocean view. The Cheeseburger in Paradise—a hefty hunk with Jack and cheddar cheeses, sautéed onions, lettuce, fresh tomatoes, and Thousand Island dressing—is a paean to the basics. You can build your own burger by adding sautéed mushrooms, bacon, grilled ortega chiles, and other condiments for an extra charge. Onion rings, chili-cheese fries, and cold beer complete the carefree fantasy.

811 Front St., Lahaina. © **808/661-4855.** www.cheeseburgerland.com. Burgers $7–$10. AE, DISC, MC, V. Daily 8am–10pm.

Cilantro: Fresh Mexican Grill ★ (Finds   For fabulous Mexican food at frugal prices, this is Maui's best by far. And, believe it or not, it's a healthy, fast-food Mexican eatery that serves fresh food! Chef and owner Pris Nabavi, creator of Maui's Pizza Paradiso Italian Kitchen, wanted the "challenge of something different." So he took off to Mexico to find out how the Mexican chefs cooked in "the old days." He's back on Maui with this unbelievably delicious eatery where everything is made from scratch or, as Nabavi puts it, "slow cooked food that's served fast." Even the corn tortillas are hand-made daily. Signature dishes include the citrus-and-herb marinated chipotle rotisserie chicken, the veggie Mariposa salad, and the popular "mother clucker" flautas. Plus lip-smacking "al pastor" style adobo pork. All this and budget-pleasing prices. Great place to take the kids, where the Los Niños menu items are under $3.75.

170 Papalaua Ave., Lahaina © **808/667-5444.** www.cilantrogrill.com. Entrees $3.25–$8.95. MC, V. Mon–Thurs 11am–9:30pm; Fri–Sat 11am–10pm and Sun 11am–8pm.

Compadres Bar & Grill MEXICAN   Despite its concrete floor and high industrial ceilings, Compadres exudes good cheer. And that cheer has burgeoned lately with a new open-air seating area and a take-out taqueria window for diners on the run. The food is classic Tex-Mex, good any time of the day, beginning with huevos rancheros, egg burritos, hotcakes, and omelets (the Acapulco is heroic), and progressing to enchiladas and appetizers for the Margarita-happy crowd. Stay spare (vegetable enchilada in fresh spinach tortilla) or get hefty (Texas T-bone and enchiladas). This is a carefree place with a large capacity for merrymaking.

Lahaina Cannery Mall, 1221 Honoapiilani Hwy., Lahaina. © **808/661-7189.** Main courses $10–$23. AE, DC, DISC, MC, V. Daily 8am–10pm.

Kimo's STEAK/SEAFOOD   Kimo's has a loyal following that keeps it from falling into the faceless morass of waterfront restaurants serving surf-and-turf with great sunset views. It's a formula restaurant (sibling to Leilani's and Hula Grill) that works not only because of its oceanfront patio and upstairs dining room, but also because, for the price, there are some satisfying choices. It's always crowded, buzzing with people on a deck offering views of Molokai, Lanai, and Kahoolawe. Burgers and sandwiches are affordable and consistent, and the fresh catch in garlic-lemon and a sweet-basil glaze is a top seller. The waistline-defying hula pie—macadamia-nut ice cream in a chocolate-wafer crust with fudge and whipped cream—originated here.

845 Front St., Lahaina. ℂ 808/661-4811. www.kimosmaui.com. Reservations recommended for dinner. Main courses $8–$12 lunch, $17–$26 dinner. AE, DC, DISC, MC, V. Daily 11am–3:30pm and 5–10:30pm; bar open 11am–1:30am.

Lahaina Coolers AMERICAN/INTERNATIONAL   A huge marlin hangs above the bar, epic wave shots and wall sconces made of surfboard fins line the walls, and open windows on three sides of this ultracasual indoor/outdoor restaurant take advantage of the shade trees to create a cheerful ambience. This is a great breakfast joint, with feta-cheese Mediterranean omelets, huevos rancheros, and fried rice made with jasmine rice, Kula vegetables, and Portuguese sausage. There are three types of eggs Benedict—the classic, a vegetarian version (with Kula vegetables, excellent), and the local, with Portuguese sausage and sweetbread. At lunch, burgers rule; and the sandwiches, from grilled portobellos to the classic tuna melt, are ideal for casual Lahaina. Made fresh daily, the pasta is prepared Asian style (chicken breast in a spicy Thai peanut sauce), with pesto, and vegetarian, in a spicy Creole sauce. Pizzas, pastas, fresh catch, steak, and enchiladas round out the entrees, and everything can be prepared vegetarian upon request.

180 Dickensen St., Lahaina. ℂ **808/661-7082.** www.lahainacoolers.com. Main courses $7.50–$11 lunch; $14–$25 dinner. AE, DC, DISC, MC, V. Daily 8am–2am (full menu until midnight).

Lahaina Fish Company SEAFOOD   The open-air dining room is literally over the water, with flickering torches after sunset and an affordable menu that covers the seafood-pasta basics. Head to an ocean-side table and order a cheeseburger, chicken burger, fish burger, generous basket of peel-and-eat shrimp, or sashimi—lingering is highly recommended. The light-lunch/grill menu offers appetizers (sashimi, seared ahi, spring rolls, and potstickers), salads, and soups. The restaurant has spiffed up its dinner selections to include hand-carved steaks, several pasta choices, and local fare such as stir-fry dishes, teriyaki chicken, and luau-style ribs. The specialty, though, remains the fresh seafood: four types of fresh fish are offered nightly, in three preparations, and Pacific Rim specials include fresh ahi, seared spicy or cooked in a sweet ginger-soy sauce.

831 Front St., Lahaina. ℂ **808/661-3472.** Main courses $10–$36. AE, MC, V. Daily 11am–11pm.

Maui Sunrise Café *Value* GOURMET DELI/CAFE   If you want to know where the best breakfasts or the most filling lunch on a budget are, follow the surfers to this teeny, tiny cafe located on Front Street, next door to the library. Eat in the patio garden out back or take your lunch to the beach. You'll find huge breakfasts, delicious gourmet sandwiches, and filling lunch plates all at bargain prices. It's tough to find a parking spot nearby (and you can't park at the library), but you'll probably want a brisk walk after eating here anyway.

693A Front St., Lahaina. ℂ **808/661-8558.** Breakfast under $10, lunch $6–$10. No cards. Daily 6am–6pm.

Maui Swiss Cafe SANDWICHES/PIZZA   Having gone from a sandwich-and-pizza shop to a European-style sidewalk Internet cafe, Maui Swiss Cafe still serves inexpensive lunch specials and low-price ice cream and remains a welcome stop in hot Lahaina. Top-quality breads baked fresh daily, Dijon mustard, good Swiss cheese, and keen attention to sandwich fillings and pizza toppings make this a very special sandwich shop. The Swiss owner, Dominique Martin, has imbued this corner of Lahaina with a European flavor, down to the menus printed in English and German and the Swiss breakfast of sliced ham, Emmentaler cheese, hard-boiled egg, and freshly baked croissant. *Tip:* The "signature melt" sandwiches, with imported Emmentaler cheese baked on an Italian Parmesan crust, are something to watch for, and there are excellent vegetarian and turkey sandwiches. The only problem is lack of free parking.

640 Front St., Lahaina. © **808/661-6776.** www.swisscafe.net. Sandwiches and 8-inch pizzas $6.50–$8.95. No credit cards. Daily 9am–8pm.

Super-Cheap Eats

Penne Pasta Café ★ *Finds* ITALIAN/MEDITERRANEAN   Bargain hunters don't pass up this neighborhood cafe, under the helm of Chef Mark Ellman (of Maui Taco fame), which features delicious Italian and Mediterranean cuisine. You'll get a sit-down meal at takeout prices, and mama mia—those are big plates of pasta, pizzas, salads, and sandwiches. So, what's the catch? No wait help. You order at the counter and the manager delivers your *molto bene* linguine pesto, baked penne, olive/caper/basil/roasted-pepper pizza, or whatever you ordered. Wine (less than $5.50 a glass) and beer are available, too.

180 Dickenson St., Lahaina. © **808/661-6633.** Basic menu items under $10, specials up to $14. AE, DC, DISC, MC, V. Mon–Fri 11am–9:30pm; Sat–Sun 5pm–9:30pm.

Worth a Splurge

The Feast at Lele ★★ POLYNESIAN   The owners of the Old Lahaina Luau, I'o, and Pacific'o have outdone themselves with their lavish cultural concoction, the Feast at Lele. Chef James McDonald's culinary prowess, the outdoor oceanfront setting, and the exquisite dancers of the Old Lahaina Luau add up to an intoxicating experience, definitely worth considering if you can afford the big splurge. As if the sunset weren't heady enough, dances from Hawaii, New Zealand, Tahiti, and Samoa are presented, up close and personal, in full costumed splendor. Chanting, singing, drumming, dancing, the swish of ti-leaf skirts, the scent of plumeria—it's a full culinary-cultural adventure. Guests sit at white-clothed, candlelit tables set on the sand (unlike the luau, where seating is en masse) and dine on kalua pig, tasty steamed moi, and savory pohole ferns and hearts of palm. From New Zealand comes sea-bean duck salad with poha berry dressing, Kuku patties (which are fish cakes with salmon, mussels, and scallops), Harore Kumara (consisting of roasted mushrooms, orange sweet potatoes, onions and garlic in a brown sauce); from Tahiti, steamed chicken and taro leaf in coconut milk; and, from Samoa, grilled fish in banana leaf. Particularly mesmerizing is the evening's opening: A softly lit canoe carries three people ashore to the sound of conch shells.

505 Front St., Lahaina. © **886/244-5353** or 808/667-5353. www.feastatlele.com. Reservations a must. Set 5-course menu $99 for adults, $69 for children 2–12; gratuity not included. AE, MC, V. Apr 1–Sept 30 daily 6–9pm; Oct 1–Mar 31 daily 5:30–8:30pm.

Gerard's ★★★ *Finds* FRENCH   The charm of Gerard's—soft lighting, Edith Piaf on the sound system, excellent service—is matched by a menu of uncompromising standards. Gerard Reversade never runs out of creative offerings, yet stays true to his French roots. A frequent winner of the *Wine Spectator* Award of Excellence, Gerard's offers roasted opakapaka with star anise, fennel fondue, and hints of orange and ginger, a stellar entree on a menu of winners. If you're feeling extravagant, the Kona lobster ragout with pasta and morels promises ecstasy, and the spinach salad with scallops is among the finest we've tasted. Gerard's has an excellent appetizer menu, with shiitake and oyster mushrooms in puff pastry, fresh ahi and smoked salmon carpaccio, and a very rich, highly touted escargot ragout with burgundy butter and garlic cream.

In the Plantation Inn, 174 Lahainaluna Rd., Lahaina. *C* **808/661-8939.** Reservations recommended. Main courses $30–$39. AE, DC, DISC, MC, V. Daily 6–9pm.

I'o ✦ PACIFIC RIM   I'o is a fantasy of sleek curves and etched glass, co-owned by chef James McDonald. He offers an impressive selection of appetizers (his strong suit) and some lavish Asian-Polynesian interpretations of seafood, such as stir-fried lobster with mango-Thai curry sauce, fresh ahi in a nori panko crust, and lemongrass coconut fish. Unless you're sold on entrees, our advice is to go heavy on the superb appetizers, especially the silken purse, a brilliant concoction of tricolored potstickers stuffed with roasted peppers, mushrooms, spinach, macadamia nuts, and silken tofu. Oyster lovers, take heed: The memorable Pan-Asian Rockefellers are baked on a bed of spinach and served with a hint of star anise coconut cream.

505 Front St., Lahaina. *C* **808/661-8422.** Reservations recommended. Main courses $23–$59. AE, DC, MC, V. Daily 5:30–10pm.

Pacific'o Restaurant ✦ PACIFIC RIM/CONTEMPORARY PACIFIC   You can't get any closer to the ocean than the tables here, which are literally on the beach. With good food complementing this sensational setting, foodies and aesthetes have much to enjoy. The split-level dining starts at the top, near the entrance, with a long bar (where you can also order lunch or dinner) and a few tables along the railing. Steps lead to the outdoor tables, where the award-winning seafood dishes come to you with the backdrop of Lanai across the channel. The prawn and basil wontons, fresh fish over wilted arugula and bean sprouts, and ahi and ono tempura with miso and lime-basil sauce are among Pacific'o's memorable offerings. The vegetarian special, a marinated, roasted tofu steak crowned with quinoa, Maui onions, red lentils, and a heavenly dose of shiitake mushrooms, is a long-time favorite. If you like seafood, sunsets, and touches of India and Indonesia in your fresh-from-the-sea dining choices, you should be happy here.

505 Front St., Lahaina. *C* **808/667-4341.** Reservations recommended. Main courses $11–$14 lunch; $26–$32 dinner. AE, DC, MC, V. Daily 11am–4pm and 5:30–10pm.

KAANAPALI

Beachside Grill and Leilani's on the Beach *Kids* STEAK/SEAFOOD   The Beachside Grill is the informal, less-expensive room downstairs on the beach, where folks wander in off the sand for a frothy beer and a beachside burger. Leilani's is the dinner-only room, with more expensive but still not outrageously-priced steak and seafood offerings. At Leilani's, you can order everything from affordable spinach, cheese, and mushroom ravioli to lobster and steak. Children can get a quarter-pound hamburger for under $5 or a broiled chicken breast for a couple of dollars more—a value, for sure. Pasta, rack of lamb, filet mignon, and Alaskan king crab at market price are among the choices in the upstairs room. Although the steak-and-lobster combinations can be pricey, the good thing about Leilani's is the strong middle range of entree prices, especially the fresh fish for around $20 to $25. All of this, of course, comes with an ocean view. There's live Hawaiian music every afternoon except Fridays, when the Rock 'n' Roll Aloha Friday set gets those decibels climbing. Free concerts are usually offered on a stage outside the restaurant on the last Sunday of the month.

In Whalers Village, 2435 Kaanapali Pkwy., Kaanapali. © **808/661-4495**. www.leilanis.com. Reservations suggested for dinner at both restaurants. Lunch and dinner (Beachside Grill) $6.95–$13; dinner (Leilani's) from $18–$25. AE, DC, DISC, MC, V. Beachside Grill daily 11am–11pm (bar daily until 12:30am); Leilani's daily 5–10pm.

Hula Grill ☆ *Kids* HAWAII REGIONAL/SEAFOOD   Who wouldn't want to be tucking into crab-and-corn cakes, banana-glazed opah, mac-nut–roasted opakapaka, or crab wontons under a thatched umbrella, with a sand floor and palm trees at arm's length and a view of Lanai across the channel? Peter Merriman, one of the originators of Hawaii Regional Cuisine, segued seamlessly from his smallish, Big Island upcountry enclave to this large, high-volume, open-air dining room on the beach. Hula Grill offers a wide range of prices and choices; it can be expensive but doesn't have to be. The menu includes Merriman's signature wok-charred ahi, firecracker mahimahi, seafood potstickers, and several different fresh-fish preparations, including his famous ahi poke rolls, lightly sautéed rare ahi wrapped in rice paper with Maui onions. At lunch, the menu is more limited, with a choice of sandwiches, three entrees, pizza, appetizers, and salads. There's happy-hour entertainment and Hawaiian music daily. For those wanting a more casual atmosphere, the Barefoot Bar, located on the beach, offers burgers, fish, pizza, and salads.

In Whalers Village, 2435 Kaanapali Pkwy., Kaanapali. © **808/667-6636**. www.hulagrill.com. Reservations recommended for dinner. Lunch and Barefoot Bar menus $8–$16; dinner main courses from $16–$32. AE, DC, DISC, MC, V. Daily 11am–10:30pm.

Super-Cheap Eats

Whalers Village has a food court where you can buy pizza, very good Japanese food (including tempura soba and other noodle dishes), Korean plates, and fast-food burgers at serve-yourself counters and courtyard tables. It's an inexpensive alternative and a quick, handy stop for shoppers and Kaanapali beachgoers.

CJ's Deli and Diner ☆ *Value* AMERICAN/DELI   Eat here! If you are staying in Kaanapali, it is walking distance from your resort (up to the highway); if you're not staying in Kaanapali, it's worth the drive to sample the "comfort food" (as they call it) at this hip, happening eatery with prices so low you can't believe you are on Maui (nothing over $13 on the entire menu). A huge billboard menu hangs from the yellow and gold textured wall, with the staff standing in the open-air kitchen waiting to cook something up for you. Highly-polished wooden floors give the roadside eatery a homey feeling. You can eat in or take out (hey, they even have "chefs-to-go" to come to your accommodations and cook for you), the atmosphere is friendly and there's even a computer with high-speed Internet connection to keep the techies humming. Huge, delicious breakfasts start at 6:30am (for those up that early, check out the $4.95 early-bird special of two eggs, bacon or sausage, rice and coffee) and for those who sleep in late, no worries—breakfast is served until 11am. They have a wide selection of egg dishes (from omelets to eggs Benedict), plus pancakes and waffles, and don't forget the tempting delights from the bakery. Lunch ranges from deli sandwiches, burgers, and hot sandwiches to pot roast, ribs and fish dishes. If you are on your way to Hana or to the top of Haleakala, stop by and get a box lunch. They even have a menu for the kids.

Kaanapali Fairway Shops, 2580 Keka'a Drive (just off the Honoapiilani Hwy.), Kaanapali Resort. © **808/667-0968**. Breakfast items $1.75–$9.50, lunch $6.50–$9.95. AE, MC, V. Daily 6:30am–7:30pm.

Nikki's Pizza PIZZA   Formerly Pizza Paradiso, Nikki's has a full menu of pastas, pizzas, and desserts, including smoothies, coffee, and ice cream. This is a welcome addition to the Kaanapali scene, where casual is king and good food doesn't have to be fancy. The pizza reflects a simple and effective formula that has won acclaim through the years: good crust, true-blue sauces, and toppings loyal to tradition but with just enough edge for those who want it. Create your own pizza with roasted eggplant, mushrooms, anchovies, artichoke hearts, spicy sausages, cheeses, and a slew of other toppings. Pizza Paradiso offers some heroic choices, from the Veg Wedge to the Maui Wowie (ham and Maui pineapple) and the Godfather (roasted chicken, artichoke hearts, sun-dried tomatoes).

In Whalers Village, 2435 Kaanapali Pkwy., Kaanapali. ℂ **808/667-0333**. Gourmet pizza $3.85–$4.65 (by the slice); whole pizzas $12–$27. MC, V. Daily 11am–10pm.

KAHANA, HONOKOWAI & NAPILI

To locate the restaurants reviewed below, see the "Accommodations & Dining in Honokowai, Kahana, Napili & Kapalua" map on p. 361.

Pizza Paradiso Italian Caffe PIZZA/ITALIAN   Owner Paris Nabavi had such success with his Pizza Paradiso in Whalers Village (see above) that he opened up in the marketplace—and can hardly keep up with demand. Order at the counter (pastas, gourmet pizza whole or by the slice, salads, and desserts) and find a seat at one of the few tables. The pasta sauces—marinara, pescatore, Alfredo, Florentine, and pesto, with options and add-ons—are as popular as the pizzas and panini sandwiches. The Massimo, a pesto sauce with artichoke hearts, sun-dried tomatoes, and capers, comes with a choice of chicken, shrimp, or clams, and is so good it was a Taste of Lahaina winner in 1999. Take out or dine in, this is a hot spot in the neighborhood, with free delivery.

Honokowai Marketplace, 3350 Lower Honoapiilani Rd., Honokowai. ℂ **808/667-2929**. www.pizzaparadiso.com. Pastas $7.95–$9.25; pizzas $13–$27. MC, V. Daily 11am–10pm.

Super-Cheap Eats

Maui Tacos *Kids* MEXICAN   Mark Ellman's Maui Tacos chain has grown faster than you can say "Haleakala." Ellman put gourmet Mexican on paper plates and on the island's culinary map long before the island became known as Hawaii's center of salsa and chimichangas. Barely more than a take-out counter with a few tables, this and the six other Maui Tacos in Hawaii (four on Maui alone) are the rage of hungry surfers, discerning diners, burrito buffs, and Hollywood glitterati like Sharon Stone, whose picture adorns a wall or two. Choices include excellent fresh-fish tacos (garlicky and flavorful), chimichangas, and mouth-breaking compositions such as the Hookipa, a "surf burrito" of fresh fish, black beans, and salsa and a personal favorite. The greenspinach burrito contains four kinds of beans, rice, and potatoes—it's a knockout, requiring a siesta afterward.

In Napili Plaza, 5095 Napili Hau St., Napili ℂ **808/665-0222**. Also in Kaahumanu Center, Kahului (ℂ 808/871-7726); Lahaina Square, Lahaina (ℂ 808/661-8883); and Kamaole Beach Center, Kihei (ℂ 808/879-5005). Most items less than $7.50. AE, DC, DISC, MC, V. Daily 9am–9pm.

Worth a Splurge

Roy's Kahana Bar & Grill *⋆⋆* EURO-ASIAN   Despite the lack of dramatic view and an upstairs location in a shopping mall, Roy's remains crowded and extremely popular for one reason—fabulous food! In fact, it bustle with young, hip servers impeccably trained to deliver blackened ahi or perfectly seared lemongrass *shutome* (broadbill swordfish) hot to your table, in rooms that sizzle with cross-cultural tastings. Known for Roy's famous rack of lamb and fresh seafood (usually eight or nine choices), and for the chain's large, open kitchens that turn out everything from pizza to sake-grilled New York steak. If polenta is on the menu, don't resist; on my last visit, the polenta was rich and fabulous, with garlic, cream, spinach, and wild mushrooms. Large picture windows open up Roy's Kahana but don't quell the noise, another tireless trait long ago established by Roy's Restaurant in Honolulu, the flagship of Yamaguchi's burgeoning empire.

In the Kahana Gateway Shopping Center, 4405 Honoapiilani Hwy., Kahana. ⓒ 808/669-6999.www.roysrestaurant. com. Reservations strongly recommended. Main courses $14–$31. AE, DC, DISC, MC, V. Daily 5:30–10pm.

Sea House Restaurant ASIAN/PACIFIC   The Sea House is not glamorous, famous, or hip, but it's worth mentioning for its gorgeous view of Napili Bay. It is spectacular. The Napili Kai Beach Club, where Sea House is located, is a charming throwback to the days when hotels blended in with their surroundings, had lush tropical foliage, and were sprawling rather than vertical. Dinner entrees come complete with soup or salad, vegetables, and rice or potato. The lighter appetizer menu is a delight—more than a dozen choices ranging from sautéed or blackened crab cake to crisp Pacific Rim sushi of ahi capped in nori and cooked tempura-style. They share top billing with the million-dollar view.

In Napili Kai Beach Resort, 5900 Honoapiilani Hwy., Napili. ⓒ 808/669-1500. Reservations required for dinner. Main courses $18–$49; pupu menu $5–$14. AE, DISC, MC, V. Sun–Fri 8–10:30am, noon–2pm, and 5:30–9pm; pupu menu Sat–Thurs 2–9pm, Fri 2–9pm, and Sat 5:30–9pm.

KAPALUA

Sansei Seafood Restaurant and Sushi Bar ✦✦✦ PACIFIC RIM   Perpetual award-winner Sansei proffers an extensive menu of Japanese and East-West delicacies. Furiously fusion, part Hawaii Regional Cuisine, and all parts sushi, Sansei is tirelessly creative, with a menu that scores higher with adventurous palates than with purists (although there are endless traditional choices as well). Maki is the mantra here. If you don't like cilantro, watch out for those complex spicy crab rolls. Other choices include panko-crusted ahi sashimi, sashimi trio, ahi carpaccio, noodle dishes, lobster, Asian rock-shrimp cakes, traditional Japanese tempura, and sauces that surprise, in creative combinations such as ginger-lime chile butter and cilantro pesto. But there's simpler fare as well, such as shrimp tempura, noodles, and wok-tossed upcountry vegetables. Desserts are not to be missed. If it's autumn, don't pass up persimmon crème brûlée, made with Kula persimmons. In other seasons, opt for tempura-fried ice cream with chocolate sauce. Recently, they added a new branch of this mouth-watering restaurant in Kihei.

At the Kapalua Shops, 115 Bay Dr., Kapalua ⓒ 808/669-6286. Also in Kihei at the Kihei Town Center, ⓒ 808/879-0004. www.sanseihawaii.com. Reservations recommended. Main courses $19–$29. AE, DISC, MC, V. Daily 5:30–10pm. Thurs–Fri pupu and bar menu with karaoke until 1am.

Vino Italian Tapas & Wine Bar ✦✦✦ Finds ITALIAN   When two Japanese guys— famous Japanese guys, that is—D. K. Kodama, chef and owner of Sansei Seafood Restaurants and Sushi Bar (see above) and master sommelier Chuck Furuya teamed up to create a culinary adventure for foodies, Vino opened in August 2003 to big, big accolades. Probably the best Italian food on Maui is served at this exquisite restaurant, overlooking the rolling hills of the Kapalua Golf Course. Always wanting to be on the cutting edge, the duo rebranded the restaurant in December 2004 to Vino Italian Tapas & Wine Bar because they wanted their clients to be able to sample even more items on the menu with small plates. The new menu features more than two dozen tapas (small plate) items, ranging from the signature asparagus Milanese (just $5.95) to slow butter-poached Kona lobster ($18). Plus, they have retained the "favorite" large-plate dishes like fresh mahimahi with artichokes and grape tomatoes on capellini, Mudicca-crusted pan-fried veal stuffed with prosciutto, and osso bucco with spinach risotto. Go to Vino's early during your stay on Maui; most likely, you will want to return.

Kapalua Village Course Golf Club House, Kapalua Resort. ✆ **808/661-VINO**. Reservations recommended. $5.95–$18 tapas; large plates $19–$25. AE, DISC, MC, V. Daily 11am–2pm lunch and 6–9:30pm dinner.

Worth a Splurge
The Banyan Tree Restaurant 𝒦𝒦𝒦 CONTEMPORARY AUSTRALIAN   Fasten your seat belts food fans; this is one of the hottest, most creative chefs to come to Hawaii in decades. Australian Chef Antony Scholtmeyer said his philosophy is "dining shouldn't be safe, but a sexy blend of flavors and textures to create an exciting and sensual experience." His combinations may sound like a walk on the wild side, but once you've tasted his "sexy" cuisine, you're hooked for life. It takes a creative mind to come up with a signature *amuse bouche* of foie gras ice cream (don't laugh until you've tried it) with the taste of duck a'la orange (thanks to the confit orange zest and fresh orange segments) and the creamy taste of foie gras. Other zingers are crispy skin moi (the Hawaiian fish of royalty) with lentil dhal, raita and micro cilantro, or honey-roasted duck breast with celery root and chive risotto and pineapple jus. Save room for his warm, bitter-chocolate "meltaway" with sour cream sorbet, lilikoi sauce, and local berries. *Food and Wine Magazine* named him the "Chef to Watch." Word is out; book a reservation at the Ritz-Carlton's signature restaurant before you leave home, or you'll never get in.

Ritz-Carlton Kapalua Resort, Kapalua. ✆ **808/669-6200**. Reservations recommended for dinner. $32–$48 dinner entrees; $80 4-course meal. AE, DISC, MC, V. Daily lunch 11am–2pm, dinner 5:30–9pm.

SOUTH MAUI
KIHEI & MAALAEA
In addition to their Kapalua location, **Sansei Seafood Restaurant and Sushi Bar** opened a new restaurant in Kihei (see review above; ✆ **808/879-0004**).

Ma'alaea Grill 𝒦 *Finds* PACIFIC RIM   This charming eatery is another great restaurant from the people behind Café O'Lei Lahaina (reviewed earlier in this chapter) and is superbly located, overlooking the Maalaea Small Boat Harbor. There is outside seating, but the harbor is almost always windy; so if you don't want your lettuce blown across the shopping center, eat inside. Lunches include creative salads (curry chicken salad), hefty sandwiches (crab club), and reasonably-priced entrees (blackened mahimahi for just $9). Dinner features appetizers so interesting you could make a meal out of them (fried ahi-stuffed calamari, tempura potato cakes, grilled seafood tower), mouthwatering main courses (macadamia-nut roast duckling, kiawe-grilled New York steak and calamari, and stir-fried vegetable pad Thai), and yummy desserts.

Maalaea Harbor Village, 300 Maalaea Rd., Maalaea (the triangle between Honoapiilani Hwy. and Maalaea Rd.). ✆ **808/243-2206**. Reservations recommended. $7–$11 lunch; $16–$21 dinner. AE, MC, V. Open Tues–Sun 10:30am–5pm and 5:30–9pm.

Peggy Sue's *Kids* AMERICAN   Just for a moment, forget that diet and take a leap. It's Peggy Sue's to the rescue! This 1950s-style diner has oodles of charm and is a swell place to spring for the best chocolate malt on the island. You'll also find sodas, shakes, floats, egg creams, milk shakes, and scoops of made-on-Maui Roselani brand gourmet ice cream—14 flavors. Old-fashioned soda-shop stools, an Elvis Presley Boulevard sign, and jukeboxes on every Formica table serve as a backdrop for the famous burgers (and garden burgers), brushed with teriyaki sauce and served with all the goodies. The fries are great too.

In Azeka Place II, 1279 S. Kihei Rd., Kihei ℂ **808/875-8944.** Burgers $7–$11; plate lunches $5.99–$12. AE, DISC, MC, V. Sun–Thurs 11am–9pm; Fri–Sat 11am–10pm.

Shaka Sandwich & Pizza PIZZA   At this south-shore old-timer, award-winning pizzas share the limelight with New York–style heroes and Philly cheese steaks, calzones, salads, homemade garlic bread, and homemade meatball sandwiches. Shaka uses fresh Maui produce, long-simmering sauces, and homemade Italian bread. Choose thin or Sicilian thick crust with gourmet toppings: Maui onions, spinach, anchovies, jalapeños, and a spate of other vegetables. Don't be misled by the whiteness of the white pizza; with the perfectly balanced flavors of olive oil, garlic, and cheese, you won't even miss the tomato sauce. Clam-and-garlic pizza, spinach pizza (with olive oil, spinach, garlic, and mozzarella), and the Shaka Supreme (with at least 10 toppings!) will satisfy even the insatiable.

1295 S. Kihei Rd., Kihei. ℂ **808/874-0331.** Sandwiches $4.35–$11; pizzas $13–$26. No credit cards. Daily 10:30am–9pm.

Stella Blues Cafe AMERICAN   Stella Blues gets going at breakfast and continues through to dinner with something for everyone—vegetarians, kids, pasta and sandwich lovers, hefty steak eaters, and sensible diners who go for the inexpensive fresh Kula green salad. Grateful Dead posters line the walls, and a covey of gleaming motorcycles is invariably parked outside. It's loud and lively, irreverent, and unpretentious. Sandwiches are the highlight, ranging from Tofu Extraordinaire to Mom's Egg Salad on a croissant to garden burgers and grilled chicken. Tofu wraps and mountain-size Cobb salads are popular, and for the reckless, large coffee shakes with mounds of whipped cream. Daily specials include fresh seafood and other surprises—all homestyle cooking, made from scratch, down to the pesto mayonnaise and herb bread. At dinner, selections are geared toward good-value family dining, from affordable full dinners to pastas and burgers.

Azeka II Shopping Center, 1279 S. Kihei Rd., Kihei. ℂ **808/874-3779.** Main courses $7–$23. AE, DC, DISC, MC, V. Daily 7:30am–10pm.

Super-Cheap Eats

There's a **Maui Tacos** at Kamaole Beach Center in Kihei (ℂ **808/879-5005**).

The Coffee Store COFFEEHOUSE   This simple, classic coffeehouse for caffeine connoisseurs serves two dozen different types of coffee and coffee drinks, from mochas and lattes to cappuccinos, espressos, and toddies. Breakfast items include smoothies, lox and bagels, quiches, granola, and assorted pastries. Pizza, salads, vegetarian lasagna, veggie-and-shrimp quesadillas, and sandwiches (garden burger, tuna, turkey, ham, grilled veggie panini) also move briskly from the take-out counter. If that's too tame, the turkey-and-veggie wraps are a local legend. There are only a few small tables, and they fill up fast, often with musicians and artists who've spent the previous evening entertaining at the Wailea and Kihei resorts.

In Azeka Place II, 1279 Kihei Rd., Kihei. ℂ **808/875-4244.** All items less than $8.50. AE, DC, DISC, MC, V. Mon–Sat 6:30am–8pm, Sun 6:30am–7pm.

Joy's Place *(Value)* HEALTHY DELI/SANDWICHES   If you are in Kihei and are looking for a healthy, delicious lunch at rock-bottom prices, it's worth hunting around for Joy's Place. Mostly organic, this tiny hole-in-the-wall has humongous sandwiches, wheat-free wraps, fresh salads, hot items (falafel burger, turkey or tuna pizza melt and spinach quinoa burger), soups and desserts. There are a few places to sit in the deli, but the beach is just a couple minutes' walk away.

Island Surf Building, 1993 South Kihei Rd. (entrance to the restaurant is on Auhana St.), Kihei. (*C*) **808/879-9258.** All items under $10. No credit cards. Mon–Sat 10am– 5pm.

Worth a Splurge

Five Palms ⭐ PACIFIC RIM   This is the best lunch and breakfast spot in Kihei—open-air, with tables a few feet from the beach and up-close-and-personal views of Kahoolawe and Molokini. You'll have to walk through a nondescript parking area and the modest entrance of the Mana Kai Resort to reach this unpretentious place. Both lunch and breakfast is served until 2pm. So, if you are jet-lagged and still on mainland time, you can get a snow-crab and avocado omelet at 2pm or a huge, juicy Angus beef hamburger at 8am. Other great choices include: Kula greens; burgers; sandwiches on homemade focaccia; capellini with shiitake mushrooms, sun-dried tomatoes, and white-wine sauce; and other appealing choices, including a perfectly grilled vegetable platter. At dinner, with the torches lit on the beach and the main dining room open, the ambience shifts to evening romantic, but still casual.

In the Mana Kai Resort, 2960 S. Kihei Rd., Kihei. (*C*) **808/879-2607.** Reservations recommended for dinner. Breakfast and lunch $10–$15; dinner main courses $19–$40. AE, DC, MC, V. Daily breakfast and lunch, 8am–2:30pm, pupus from 2:30–6pm and dinner from 5–9pm.

The Waterfront at Maalaea ⭐⭐ SEAFOOD   The family-owned Waterfront has won many prestigious awards for wine excellence, service, and seafood, but its biggest boost is word of mouth. Loyal diners rave about the friendly staff and seafood, fresh off the boat in nearby Maalaea Harbor, prepared with care. The bay and harbor view is one you'll never forget, especially at sunset. You have nine choices of preparations for the several varieties of fresh Hawaiian fish, ranging from *en papillote* (baked in buttered parchment) to Southwestern (smoked chile and cilantro butter) to Cajun spiced and Island style (sautéed, broiled, poached, or baked and paired with tiger prawns). Other choices: Kula onion soup, an excellent Caesar salad, the signature lobster chowder, and grilled eggplant layered with Maui onions, tomatoes, and spinach, served with red-pepper coulis and Big Island goat cheese. Like the seafood, it's superb.

Maalaea Harbor, 50 Hauoli St., Maalaea. (*C*) **808/244-9028.** Reservations recommended. Main courses $19–$35. AE, DC, DISC, MC, V. Opens daily at 5pm; last seating at 8:30pm.

WAILEA

Caffé Ciao ⭐ ITALIAN   There are two parts to this charming trattoria: the deli and take-out section, and the tables under the trees, next to the bar. Rare and wonderful wines, such as Vine Cliff, are sold in the deli, along with ultraluxe rose soaps and other bath products, assorted pastas, pizzas, roasted potatoes, vegetable panini, vegetable lasagna, abundant salads, and an appealing selection of microwavable and take-out goodies. On the terrace under the trees, the tables are cheerfully accented with Italian herbs growing in cachepots. *A fave:* the linguine pomodoro, with fresh tomatoes, spinach-tomato sauce, and a dollop of mascarpone.

In the Kea Lani Hotel, 4100 Wailea Alanui, Wailea. ℂ **808/875-4100.** Reservations recommended. Main courses $13–$20 lunch; $17–$36 dinner; $17–$19 pizzas. AE, DC, DISC, MC, V. Daily lunch (open seasonally) noon–3pm, dinner 5:30–10pm, and bar daily 11am–10pm.

SeaWatch ⭐ ISLAND CUISINE SeaWatch is a good choice from morning to evening, and it's one of the more affordable stops in tony Wailea. You'll dine on the terrace or in a high-ceilinged room, on a menu that carries the tee-off-to-the-19th-hole crowd with ease. From breakfast on, it's a celebration of island bounty: Maui onions on the bagels and lox, kalua pork and Maui onions in the scrambled eggs, crab cake Benedict with roasted pepper hollandaise. Lunchtime sandwiches, pastas, salads, wraps, and soups are moderately priced, and you get 360-degree views to go with them. The cashew chicken wrap with mango chutney is a winner, but if that's too Pan-Asian for you, try the tropical fish quesadilla or the grilled fresh-catch sandwich with Kula lime aioli. Save room for the bananas Foster.

100 Wailea Golf Club Dr., Wailea. ℂ **808/875-8080.** www.seawatchrestaurant.com. Reservations required for dinner. Main courses $4–$12 breakfast; $6.50–$15 lunch; $23–$30 dinner. AE, DC, MC, V. Daily 8am–10pm.

Worth a Splurge
Ferraro's at Seaside ⭐ *Kids* ITALIAN This was a masterstroke for Four Seasons: authentic Italian fare in a casual outdoor tropical setting, with a drop-dead gorgeous view of the ocean and the West Maui Mountains. Ferraro's is not inexpensive, but the food is first-rate, whether you try the oregano-marinated shrimp with avocado or the linguine puttanesca. Mango margaritas, generous salads, such as the Maine lobster with avocado and toasted sourdough, and sandwiches or half-pound burgers cater to the poolside crowd at lunch. But at dinnertime, the choices intensify. The fish selection is noteworthy: pepper-crusted ahi, grilled sea scallops and steamed mussels with saffron risotto cake, and poached snapper with red onion–orange marmalade. It won't be easy to choose.

In the Four Seasons Resort Maui at Wailea, 3900 Wailea Alanui Dr., Wailea. ℂ **808/874-8000.** Reservations recommended. Lunch entrees $15–$22; dinner $25–$46. AE, DC, DISC, MC, V. Daily 11:30am–4pm, 4–6pm (pupu menu), and 6–9pm.

Joe's Bar & Grill ⭐⭐ AMERICAN GRILL The 360-degree view spans the golf course, tennis courts, ocean, and Haleakala—a worthy setting for Beverly Gannon's style of American home cooking with a regional twist. The hearty staples include excellent mashed potatoes, lobster, fresh fish, and filet mignon, but the meatloaf (a whole loaf, like Mom used to make) seems to upstage them all. The Tuscan white-bean soup is superb, and the tenderloin, with roasted portobellos, mashed potatoes with whole garlic, and a Pinot Noir demiglace, is American home cooking at its best. Daily specials could be grilled ahi with white truffle–Yukon mashed potatoes or sautéed mahimahi with shrimp bisque and sautéed spinach. If chocolate cake is on the menu, you should definitely spring for it.

In the Wailea Tennis Club, 131 Wailea Ike Place, Wailea. ℂ **808/875-7767.** Reservations recommended. Main courses $23–$33. AE, DC, DISC, MC, V. Daily 5:30–9:30pm.

Longhi's ⭐⭐ ITALIAN This is a great alternative to the high-priced restaurants in the surrounding resorts. The open-air restaurant, with restaurateur Bob Longhi's trademark black-and-white checkered floor, provides a great way to start the day. Breakfasts here are something you want to wake up to: perfect baguettes, fresh-baked cinnamon rolls (one is enough for two people), and eggs Benedict or Florentine (with hollandaise for those not counting calories). Lunch is either an Italian banquet (ahi torino prawns amaretto and a wide variety of pastas) or fresh salads and sandwiches. Dinner (overlooking the water) is where Longhi shines, with a long list of fresh-made pasta dishes, seafood platters, and beef and chicken dishes (like filet mignon with béarnaise or veal sauté). Leave room for the daily dessert specials. Unlike Longhi's restaurant in Lahaina, this is not a verbal menu recited by your waitperson, but a real menu that you can hold and study as you plan your culinary adventure. If you come on Saturday night, stay for the live music; the place rocks until 1:30am.

The Shops at Wailea, 3750 Wailea Alanui Dr., Wailea. ⓒ **808/891-8883**. www.longhi-maui.com. Reservations recommended for dinner. Main courses $18–$35. AE, DC, MC, V. Mon–Fri 8am–10pm; Sat 7:30am–1:30am; Sun 7:30am–10pm.

Nick's Fishmarket Maui ★★ SEAFOOD   Hawaii's newest Nick's has the perfect balance of visual sizzle and memorable food. A private room with attractive murals seats 50, and the round bar, where you can sit facing the ocean, is highlighted with minimalist dangling amber lights, one of the friendliest touches in Wailea. Stefanotis vines create shade on the terrace, and the sunset views are superb. This is a classic seafood restaurant that sticks to the tried and true (*not* an overwrought menu), but stays fresh with excellent ingredients and a high degree of professionalism in service and preparation. The Greek Maui Wowie salad gets my vote as one of the top salads in Hawaii. The opakapaka has been a Nick's signature for eons, and the fresh salmon, scallops, Hawaiian lobster tails, and chicken, beef, and lamb choices offer ample choices for diners, who find themselves in a fantasy setting on the South Maui shoreline. We love the onion vichyssoise with taro swirl and a hint of *tobiko* (flying-fish roe), and the bow-tied servers bearing almond-scented cold towels.

In the Fairmont Kea Lani Hotel, 4100 Wailea Alanui, Wailea. ⓒ **808/879-7224**. www.tri-star-restaurants.com. Reservations recommended. Main courses $25–$50; prix-fixe dinners $55–market price. AE, DC, DISC, MC, V. Mon–Thurs 5:30–10pm; Fri–Sat 5:30–10:30pm, bar until 11pm.

Spago ★★ HAWAIIAN/CALIFORNIA/PACIFIC REGIONAL   California meets Hawaii in this open air, contemporary-designed eatery featuring fresh, local Hawaii ingredients prepared under the culinary watch of master chef Wolfgang Puck. The room, formerly Seasons Dining Room, has been stunningly transformed into a sleek modern layout using stone and wood in the open-air setting overlooking the Pacific Ocean. The cuisine lives up to Puck's reputation of using traditional Hawaiian dishes with his own brand of cutting-edge innovations. Open for dinner only, the menu features an unbelievable coconut soup with local lobster, keffir, chili and galangal. For entrees, try the whole steamed fish served with chili, ginger, and baby choy sum; the incredible Kona lobster with sweet-and-sour banana curry, coconut rice, and dry-fried green beans; or the grilled *côte de bouef* with braised celery, armagnac, peppercorns, and *pommes aligot*. The wine and beverage list is well thought out and extensive. Save room for dessert (don't pass up the warm guanaja chocolate tart with Tahitian vanilla-bean ice cream). Make reservations as soon as you land on the island, if not before—this place is popular.

Four Seasons Resort Maui, 3900 Wailea Alanui Dr., Wailea. ⓒ **808/879-2999**. www.wolfgangpuck.com. Reservations required. Entrees $27–$48. AE, DC, DISC, MC, V. Daily 5:30–9pm.

UPCOUNTRY MAUI

To locate the restaurants reviewed below, see the "Upcountry Maui" map on p. 371.

HALIIMAILE (ON THE WAY TO UPCOUNTRY MAUI)
Worth a Splurge
Haliimaile General Store ✿ *Kids* AMERICAN   More than a decade later, Bev Gannon, one of the 12 original Hawaii Regional Cuisine chefs, is still going strong at her foodie haven in the pineapple fields. You'll dine at tables set on old wood floors under high ceilings (sound ricochets fiercely here), in a peach-colored room emblazoned with works by local artists. The food, a blend of eclectic American with ethnic touches, puts an innovative spin on Hawaii Regional Cuisine. Even the fresh-catch sandwich on the lunch menu is anything but prosaic. The sashimi Napoleon and the house salad, island greens with mandarin oranges, onions, toasted walnuts, and blue-cheese crumble, are notable items on a menu that bridges Hawaii with Gannon's Texas roots.

Haliimaile Rd., Haliimaile. ✆ 808/572-2666. www.haliimailegeneralstore.com. Reservations recommended for dinner. Lunch $10–$20; dinner $20–$30. AE, DC, DISC, MC, V. Mon–Fri 11am–2:30pm; daily 5:30–9:30pm.

MAKAWAO AND PUKALANI
Casanova Italian Restaurant ✿ ITALIAN   The nexus of upcountry dining and nightlife, Casanova is Makawao's citadel of hip. It's casual, too, with terrific food and music and a tiny veranda with a few stools, always full, in front of a deli at Makawao's busiest intersection. The restaurant contains a stage, dance floor, restaurant, and bar—and food to love and remember. This is pasta heaven; try the spaghetti fradiavolo or the spinach gnocchi in a fresh tomato-Gorgonzola sauce. Other choices include a huge pizza selection, grilled lamb chops in an Italian mushroom marinade, every possible type of pasta, and luscious desserts. Our personal picks on a stellar menu: fresh Kula spinach sautéed with butter, pine nuts, and Parmesan cheese; polenta with radicchio (the mushrooms and cream sauce are fabulous!); and tiramisu, the best on the island.

1188 Makawao Ave., Makawao. ✆ 808/572-0220. Reservations recommended for dinner. Main courses $10–$24; 12-inch pizzas from $10. AE, DC, DISC, MC, V. Mon–Sat 11:30am–2pm and 5:30–9pm; Sun 5:30–9pm; deli Mon–Sat 7:30am–6pm, Sun 8:30am–6pm. Lounge daily 5:30pm–12:30am or 1am; dancing Wed–Sat 9:45pm–1am.

Super-Cheap Eats
'Aha'aina Upcountry Cafe AMERICAN/LOCAL   Pukalani's inexpensive, casual, and very popular cafe features simple, home-cooked comfort food, such as humongous hamburgers, chicken katsu, fresh-fish tacos, sesame-crusted ahi, chicken tortilla soup (with homemade tortillas), home-baked bread, fresh muffins, and local faves, such as saimin, loco moco, and shoyu chicken. If you're up early, breakfast is dreamy, with fluffy pancakes and big egg dishes.

In the Andrade Building, 7 Aewa Place (just off Haleakala Hwy.), Pukalani. ✆ 808/572-2395. Breakfast $5–$10; lunch $6.50–$15. MC, V. Tues–Sat 7am–2pm, Sun 7am–1pm.

KULA (AT THE BASE OF HALEAKALA NATIONAL PARK)
Kula Lodge HAWAII REGIONAL/AMERICAN   Don't let the dinner prices scare you; the Kula Lodge is equally enjoyable, if not more so, at breakfast and lunch, when the prices are lower and the views through the picture windows have an eye-popping intensity. The million-dollar vista spans the flanks of Haleakala, rolling 3,200 feet down to central Maui, the ocean, and the West Maui Mountains. The Kula Lodge has always been known for its breakfasts: fabulous eggs Benedict, including a vegetarian version with Kula onions, shiitake mushrooms, and scallions; legendary banana mac-nut pancakes; and a highly recommended tofu scramble with green onions, Kula vegetables, and garlic chives. If possible, go for sunset cocktails and watch the colors

change into deep end-of-day hues. When darkness descends, a roaring fire and lodge atmosphere add to the coziness of the room. The dinner menu features "small plates" of Thai summer rolls, seared ahi, and other starters. Sesame-seared ono, Cuban-style spicy swordfish with rum-soaked bananas, and miso salmon with wild mushrooms are seafood attractions, but there's also pasta, rack of lamb, filet mignon, and free-range chicken breast.

Haleakala Hwy. (Hwy. 377), Kula. © **808/878-2517.** Reservations recommended for dinner. Main courses $7.50–$16 breakfast; $11–$18 lunch; $14–$28 dinner. AE, DC, DISC, MC, V. Daily 6:30am–9pm.

Super-Cheap Eats

Cafe 808 *Kids* AMERICAN/LOCAL

Despite its out-of-the-way location (or perhaps because of it), Cafe 808 has become the universal favorite among upcountry residents of all ages. The breakfast coffee group, the lunchtime crowd, kids after school, and dinner regulars all know it's the place for tasty home-style cooking with no pretensions: chicken lasagna, smoked-salmon omelet, famous burgers (teriyaki, hamburger, cheeseburger, garden burger, mahimahi, taro), roast pork, smoked turkey, and a huge selection of local-style specials. Regulars rave about the chicken katsu, saimin, and beef stew. The few tables are sprinkled around a room with linoleum-tile floors, hardwood benches, plastic patio chairs, and old-fashioned booths—rough around the edges in a pleasing way.

Lower Kula Rd. (past Holy Ghost Church, across from Morihara Store), Kula. © **808/878-6874.** Burgers from $4; main courses $5.50–$9.95. No credit cards. Daily 6am–8pm.

Grandma's Coffee House COFFEEHOUSE/AMERICAN

Back in 1918, when she was 16 years old, Alfred Franco's grandmother started what is now a five-generation coffee business. Today, this tiny wooden coffeehouse, still fueled by homegrown Haleakala coffee beans, is the quintessential roadside oasis. Grandma's offers espresso, hot and cold coffees, home-baked pastries, inexpensive pasta, sandwiches (including sensational avocado and garden burgers), homemade soups, fresh juices, and local plate-lunch specials that change daily. Rotating specials include Hawaiian beef stew, ginger chicken, saimin, chicken curry, lentil soup, and sandwiches piled high with Kula vegetables. While the coffee is legendary, we think the real story here is the lemon squares and the pumpkin bread.

At the end of Hwy. 37 (about 6 miles before the Tedeschi Vineyards in Ulupalakua), Keokea. © **808/878-2140.** Most items less than $8.95. MC, V. Daily 7am–5pm.

Kula Sandalwoods Restaurant ✿ AMERICAN

Chef Eleanor Loui, a graduate of the Culinary Institute of America, makes hollandaise sauce every morning from fresh upcountry egg yolks, sweet butter, and Myers lemons, which her family grows in the yard above the restaurant. This is Kula cuisine, with produce from the backyard and everything made from scratch: French toast with home-baked Portuguese sweet bread; hotcakes or Belgian waffles with fresh fruit; baguettes; open-faced country omelets; hamburgers drenched in a special cheese sauce made with grated sharp cheddar; and an outstanding veggie burger. The grilled chicken breast sandwich is marvelous, served with soup of the day and Kula mixed greens. Dine in the gazebo or on the terrace, with dazzling views in all directions, including, in the spring, a yard dusted with lavender jacaranda flowers and a hillside ablaze with fields of orange akulikuli blossoms.

15427 Haleakala Hwy. (Hwy. 377), Kula. © **808/878-3523.** Breakfast $6.95–$9.75; lunch $7.25–$13; Sun brunch $6.95–$9.75. MC, V. Mon–Sat 6:30am–2pm; Sun brunch 6:30am–noon.

EAST MAUI: THE ROAD TO HANA
PAIA

Charlie's Restaurant ♠ AMERICAN/MEXICAN   Although Charlie's (named after Charlie P. Woofer, a Great Dane) is open for breakfast, lunch, and dinner, breakfast is really the time to come here. Located in downtown Paia, Charlie's is a cross between a 1960s hippie hangout, a windsurfer power-breakfast spot, and a honkytonk bar (which does get going after dark). Before you head out to Hana, head for Charlie's for a larger-than-life breakfast (eggs, potatoes, toast, and coffee will set you back only $7, and your probably won't be able to eat it all). They have plenty of fancy espresso drinks, but the plain old coffee is excellent. Lunch is burgers, sandwiches, calzones, or pizza. Dinner is grilled fish or steak—hearty, but nothing to write home about. You will see all walks of life here, from visitors on their way to Hana at 7am to buff windsurfers eating mounds of food at noon to Willie Nelson on his way to the bar to play a tune.

142 Hana Hwy., Paia. © **808/579-9453**. Breakfast items around $3.75–$12; lunch items $7.95–$12; dinner main courses $10–$22. AE, DISC, MC, V. Daily 7am–10pm. Food at the bar until 12:30am.

Jacques North Shore ♠♠ *(Value)* SEAFOOD/SUSHI   Of the numerous restaurants which have come and gone over the years at this location, this eclectic, outdoor eatery is my favorite. Jacques is difficult to pin down; some have called it a hipper, cheaper version of the upscale Mama's Fish House. The clientele tend to be trendy, hard-body windsurfers; blonde, tan surfers; and chic North Shore residents. Visitors who wander in generally leave with a smile. The decor is patio dining under a big circus tent. Some might be distracted by the hostess and servers (20-something beauty queens dressed in "barely there" clothes), but the main attraction is the food. Do not miss the North Shore pumpkin fish (fish, bananas, and oranges served with a ginger pumpkin sauce and miso butter), Greek pasta (roasted bell peppers, roasted garlic, and feta cheese over orrechiette pasta), or one of the fabulous vegetarian entrees like the vegetable curry (with tofu, bananas, and oranges). The sushi bar (closed Sun–Mon) whips out a mean spicy ahi roll and a died-and-gone-to-heaven California roll.

120 Hana Hwy., Paia. © **808/579-8844**. Main courses $11–$20. AE, DC, DISC, MC, V. Daily 11:30am–3pm and 5–10pm. Sushi bar Tues–Sat 5:30–10pm.

Milagros Food Company ♠ SOUTHWESTERN/SEAFOOD   Milagros has gained a following with its great home-style cooking, upbeat atmosphere, and highly touted Margaritas. Sit outdoors and watch the parade of Willie Nelson look-alikes ambling by as you tuck into the ahi creation of the evening, a combination of Southwestern and Pacific Rim styles and flavors accompanied by fresh veggies and Kula greens. Blackened ahi taquitos, pepper-crusted ono pasta, blue shrimp tostadas, and sandwiches, salads, and combination plates are some of the offerings here. For breakfast, the Olive Oyl spinach omelet or the huevos rancheros, served with home fries, is recommended. We love Paia's tie-dyes, beads, and hippie flavor, and this is the front-row seat for it all. Watch for happy hour, with its cheap and fabulous Margaritas.

Hana Hwy. and Baldwin Ave., Paia. © **808/579-8755**. Breakfast around $7; lunch $6–$10; dinner $15–$20. AE, MC, V. Daily 8am–10pm.

Moanai Bakery & Cafe ♠♠ LOCAL/EUROPEAN   Moanai gets high marks for its stylish concrete floors, high ceilings, booths and cafe tables, and fabulous food. Don Ritchey, formerly a chef at Haliimaile General Store, has created the perfect Paia eatery, a casual bakery/cafe that highlights his stellar skills. All the bases are covered:

saimin, omelets, wraps, pancakes, and fresh-baked goods in the morning; soups, sandwiches, pasta, and satisfying salads for lunch; and for dinner, varied selections with Asian and European influences and fresh island ingredients. The lemongrass-grilled prawns with green papaya salad are an explosion of flavors and textures, the roasted vegetable Napoleon is gourmet fare, and the Thai red curry with coconut milk, served over vegetables, seafood, or tofu, comes atop jasmine rice with crisp rice noodles and fresh sprouts to cool the fire. Ritchey's Thai-style curries are richly spiced and intense. We also vouch for his special gift with fish: The nori-sesame crusted opakapaka, with wasabi beurre blanc, is cooked, like the curry, to perfection. All this and entertainment 3 nights a week, ranging from jazz to vintage Hawaiian to Latin.

71 Baldwin Ave., Paia. © **808/579-9999.** Reservations recommended for dinner. Breakfast $4.60–$9.95; lunch $5.95–$9.95; dinner main courses $7.95–$24. MC, V. Tues–Sun 8am–9pm and Mon 8am–2:30pm.

Paia Fish Market SEAFOOD   This really is a fish market, with fresh fish to take home and cooked seafood, salads, pastas, fajitas, and quesadillas to take out or enjoy at the few picnic tables inside the restaurant. It's an appealing and budget-friendly selection: Cajun-style fresh catch, fresh-fish specials (usually ahi or salmon), fresh-fish tacos and quesadillas, and seafood and chicken pastas. You can also order hamburgers, cheeseburgers, fish and chips (or shrimp and chips), and wonderful lunch and dinner plates, cheap and tasty. Peppering the walls are photos of the number one sport here, windsurfing.

110 Hana Hwy., Paia. © **808/579-8030.** Lunch and dinner plates $6.95–$20. DISC, MC, V. Daily 11am–9:30pm.

Super-Cheap Eats
Cafe des Amis ★ *Value* CREPES/SALADS   This Paia newcomer quickly became known as the place for healthy and tasty lunches that are kind to the pocketbook. Crepes are the star here, and they are popular: spinach with feta cheese; scallops with garlic and chipotle chile; shrimp curry with coconut milk; and dozens more choices, including breakfast crepes and dessert crepes (banana/chocolate, strawberries and cream, caramelized apples with rum). Equally popular are the salads (niçoise, Greek, and Caesar) and smoothies (peach/banana/raspberry and mango/banana/pineapple). The crepes come with a house salad, and at $6.50 to $8.50, that's a deal.

42 Baldwin Ave., Paia. © **808/579-6323.** Crepes $6.50–$8.50. DISC, MC, V. Mon–Sat 8:30am–8:30pm.

ELSEWHERE ON THE HANA ROAD
Super-Cheap Eats
Nahiku Coffee Shop, Smoked Fish Stand, and Ti Gallery ★ *Finds* SMOKED KABOBS   What a delight to stumble across this trio of comforts on the long drive to Hana! The small coffee shop purveys locally-made baked goods, several flavors of Maui-grown coffee, banana breads made in the neighborhood, organic tropical fruit smoothies, and the Original and Best Coconut Candy made by Hana character Jungle Johnny. Next door, the Ti Gallery sells locally-made Hawaiian arts and crafts, such as pottery and koa-wood vessels. The barbecue smoker, though, is our favorite part of the operation. It puts out superb smoked and grilled fish, fresh and locally caught, sending seductive aromas out into the moist Nahiku air. The teriyaki-based marinade, made by the owner, adds a special touch to the fish (ono, ahi, and marlin). Also a hit are the island-style, two-hand tacos of fish, beef, and chicken, served with about six condiments, including cheese, jalapeños, and salsa. When available, fresh corn on the cob from Kipahulu is served, and grabbed up apace. There are a few roadside picnic

tables, or you can take your lunch on the road for a beachside picnic in Hana. These are not jerkylike smoked meats; the process keeps the kabobs moist while retaining the smoke flavor. The breadfruit—sliced, wrapped in banana leaf, and baked—can be bland and starchy (like a baked potato), but it's a stroke of genius to give visitors a taste of this important Polynesian staple.

Hana Hwy. (past mile marker 28), Nahiku. No phone. Kabobs $3 each. No credit cards. Coffee shop daily 9am–5:30pm; fish stand Sat–Wed 10am–5pm; gallery daily 10am–5pm.

Pauwela Cafe *Finds* INTERNATIONAL   It's easy to get lost while searching out this wonderful cafe, but it's such a find. I never dreamed you could dine so well with such pleasing informality. The tiny cafe with a few tables indoors and out has a strong local following for many reasons. Three local boys purchased this well-loved cafe from the original owners in 2004. Brandon Shim is the chef (formerly with Tommy Bahamas in Wailea) and trained under previous owner Chris Speere at the Maui Community College Culinary Arts School. Chef Brandon certainly has learned well. Nearly everything in this tiny cafe is made from scratch. Breakfasts feature such scrumptious items as *pain perdu* (French bread in orange-vanilla custard for $6), veggie frittata ($6) and Belgian waffles ($5.75). Lunch is a great collection of salads ($5.25–$7.50 range) and sandwiches, where the scene-stealing kalua turkey sandwich consists of moist, smoky, shredded turkey with cheese on home-baked French bread and covered with a green-chili and cilantro sauce. Also available are burgers, (including a taro burger for veggies), chicken quesadillas, and veggie burritos. Dinner entrees include a range of cuisines from chicken quesadilla ($6.75) to veggie lasagna ($8) to Cajun grilled mahi ($9) and taro burger ($6.50). Because this cafe is located in an industrial center of sailboard and surfboard manufacturers, you may find a surf legend dining at the next table. The cafe is a little less than 1½ miles past the Haiku turn-off and a half-mile up on the left.

375 W. Kuiaha Rd. (off Hana Hwy., past Haiku Rd.), Haiku. © **808/575-9242**. Breakfast $4.25–$7; lunch $5.25–$7.50; dinner $6.50–$9. MC, V. Mon–Fri 7am–2:30pm, Tues–Fri 5–8pm and Sun 8am–2pm.

Worth a Splurge

Mama's Fish House ★★ HAWAIIAN   The restaurant's entrance, a cove with windsurfers, tide pools, white sand, and a canoe resting under palm trees, is a South Seas fantasy worthy of Gauguin. The interior features curved lauhala-lined ceilings, walls of split bamboo, lavish arrangements of tropical blooms, and picture windows to let in the view. With servers wearing Polynesian prints and flowers behind their ears, and the sun setting in Kuau Cove, Mama's mood is hard to beat. The fish is fresh (the fishermen are credited by name on the menu!) and prepared Hawaiian style, with tropical fruit or baked in a macadamia-nut and vanilla-bean crust, or in a number of preparations involving ferns, seaweed, Maui onions, and roasted kukui nut. Menu items include mahimahi laulau with luau leaves (taro greens) and Maui onions, baked in ti leaves and served with kalua pig and Hanalei poi—the best. Deep-water ahi could be seared with coconut and lime, while ono "caught by Keith Nakamura along the 40-fathom ledge near Hana" comes in Hana ginger teriyaki with mac nuts and crisp Maui onion. Other special touches include the use of Molokai sweet potato, Hana breadfruit, organic lettuces, Haiku bananas, and fresh coconut, which evoke the mood and tastes of old Hawaii.

799 Poho Place (just off the Hana Hwy.), Kuau. © **808/579-8488**. Reservations recommended for lunch, required for dinner. Main courses $29–$36 lunch, $32–$49 dinner. AE, DC, DISC, MC, V. Opens daily at 11am, last seating at 9pm (light menu 2:30–4:45pm).

HANA

There aren't many choices in Hana.

Hana Ranch Restaurant *Overrated* AMERICAN   Part of the Hotel Hana-Maui operation, the Hana Ranch Restaurant is the informal alternative to the hotel's beleaguered dining room. Dinner choices include New York steak, prawns and pasta, and Pacific Rim options like spicy shrimp wontons or the predictable fresh-fish poke. The warmly received Wednesday Pizza Night and the luncheon buffets are the most affordable prospects: baked mahimahi, pita sandwiches, chicken stir-fry, cheeseburgers, and club and fresh-catch sandwiches. It's not an inspired menu, and the service can be practically nonexistent when the tour buses descend during lunch rush. There are indoor tables as well as two outdoor pavilions that offer distant ocean views. At the adjoining take-out stand, fast-food classics prevail: teriyaki plate lunch, mahimahi sandwich, cheeseburgers, hot dogs, and ice cream.

Hana Hwy., Hana. © 808/248-8255. Reservations required Fri–Sat. Main courses $18–$33. AE, DISC, MC, V. Daily 7–10am and 11am–3pm; Wed and Fri–Sat 6–8:30pm. Take-out counter open Wed and Fri–Sat 6am–4pm, Mon–Tues, Thurs, and Sun 6am–7pm.

5 Beaches

Maui has more than 80 accessible beaches, from black to luxurious golden sands; there's even a rare red-sand beach. All are accessible to the public, as provided by Hawaiian law, and most have facilities. Below we've listed our favorites.

For beach toys and equipment, contact the **Activity Warehouse** (© 800/343-2087; www.travelhawaii.com), which has branches in Lahaina at 578 Front St., near Prison Street (© 808/667-4000), and in Kihei at Azeka Place II, on the mountain side of Kihei Road near Lipoa Street (© 808/875-4000). Beach chairs rent for $2 a day, coolers (with ice) for $2 a day, and a host of toys (Frisbees, volleyballs, and more) for $1 a day.

WEST MAUI
KAANAPALI BEACH ☆

Four-mile-long Kaanapali is one of Maui's best beaches, with grainy gold sand as far as the eye can see. The beach parallels the sea channel through most of its length, and a paved beach walk links hotels and condos, open-air restaurants, and the Whalers Village shopping center. Because Kaanapali is so long and broad, and because most hotels have adjacent swimming pools, the beach is crowded only in pockets—there's plenty of room to find seclusion. Summertime swimming is excellent. The best snorkeling is around Black Rock, in front of the Sheraton, where the water's clear, calm, and populated with clouds of tropical fish.

Facilities include outdoor showers; you can also use the restrooms at the hotel pools. Various beach-activities vendors line up in front of the hotels. Parking is a problem, though. There are two public entrances: At the south end, turn off Honoapiilani Highway into the Kaanapali Resort, and pay for parking here; or continue on Honoapiilani Highway, turn off at the last Kaanapali exit at the stoplight near the Maui Kaanapali Villas, and park next to the beach signs indicating public access.

KAPALUA BEACH ☆☆☆

The beach cove that fronts the Kapalua Bay Hotel and Villas is the stuff of dreams: a golden crescent bordered by two palm-studded points. The sandy bottom slopes gently to deep water at the bay mouth; the water's so clear that you can see where the gold sands turn to green and then deep blue. Protected from strong winds and currents by the lava-rock promontories, Kapalua's calm waters are ideal for snorkelers and swimmers of all ages and abilities, and the bay is big enough to paddle a kayak around in without getting into the more challenging channel that separates Maui from Molokai. Waves come in just right for riding, and fish hang out by the rocks, making it great for snorkeling.

The beach is accessible from the hotel on one end, which provides shaded sun chairs and a beach-activities center for its guests, and a public access way on the other. It isn't so wide that you burn your feet getting in or out of the water, and the inland side is edged by a shady path and cool lawns. Outdoor showers are stationed at both ends. Parking is limited to about 30 spaces in a small lot off Lower Honoapiilani Road, by Napili Kai Beach Club, so arrive early. Next door is a nice, but pricey, oceanfront restaurant, **Kapalua's Bay Club.** Facilities include showers, restrooms, lifeguards, a rental shack, and plenty of shade.

SOUTH MAUI

Wailea's beaches may seem off-limits, hidden from plain view as they are by an intimidating wall of luxury resorts, but they're all open to the public by law. Look for the SHORELINE ACCESS signs along **Wailea Alanui Drive,** the resort's main boulevard.

KAMAOLE III BEACH PARK 🏖

Three beach parks—Kamaole I, II, and III—stand like golden jewels in the front yard of the funky seaside town of Kihei, which, all of a sudden, is sprawling like suburban blight. The beaches are the best thing about Kihei. These three are popular with local residents and visitors alike because they're easily accessible. On weekends, they're jampacked with fishermen, picnickers, swimmers, and snorkelers. The most popular is Kamaole III, or "Kam-3." The biggest of the three beaches, with wide pockets of gold sand, it's the only one with a children's playground and a grassy lawn. Swimming is safe here, but scattered lava rocks are toe-stubbers at the water line, and parents should make sure their kids don't venture too far out, as the bottom slopes off quickly. Both the north and south shores are rocky fingers with a surge big enough to attract fish and snorkelers; the winter waves appeal to bodysurfers. Kam-3 is also a wonderful place to watch the sunset. Facilities include restrooms, showers, picnic tables, barbecue grills, and lifeguards. There's plenty of parking on South Kihei Road across from the Maui Parkshore condos.

WAILEA BEACH 🏖

Wailea is the best golden-sand crescent on Maui's sunbaked southwestern coast. One of five beaches within Wailea Resort, Wailea is big, wide, and protected on both sides by black-lava points. It's the front yard of the Four Seasons Wailea and the Grand Wailea Resort Hotel and Spa, Maui's most elegant and outrageous beach hotels, respectively. From the beach, the view out to sea is magnificent, framed by neighboring Kahoolawe and Lanai and the tiny crescent of Molokini, probably the most popular snorkel spot in these parts. The clear waters tumble to shore in waves just the right size for gentle riding, with or without a board. From shore, you can see Pacific humpback whales in season (Dec–Apr) and unreal sunsets nightly. Facilities include restrooms, outdoor showers, and limited free parking at the blue SHORELINE ACCESS sign, which points toward Wailea Alanui Drive.

Beaches & Outdoor Pursuits on Maui

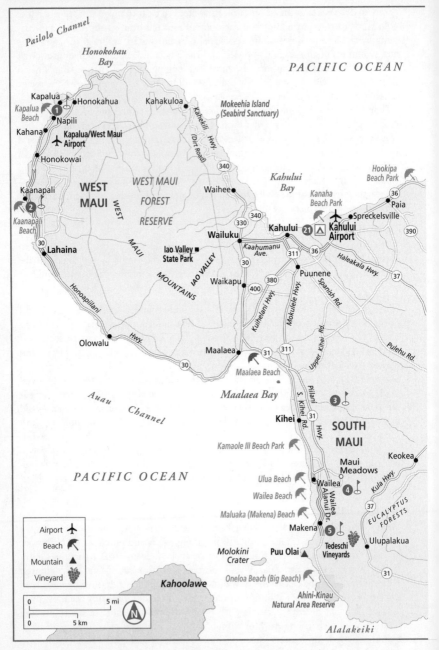

Pailolo Channel

Honokohau Bay

PACIFIC OCEAN

Kapalua
Kapalua Beach ①
Napili
Honokahua
Kahakuloa
Mokeehia Island (Seabird Sanctuary)

Kahana

Kapalua/West Maui Airport

Honokowai

WEST MAUI

WEST MAUI FOREST RESERVE

Kahekili Hwy. (Dirt Road)

340

Waihee

Kahului Bay

Kanaha Beach Park

Hookipa Beach Park

36

Paia

Kaanapali ②
Kaanapali Beach

340

WEST MAUI MOUNTAINS

330

Wailuku

Iao Valley State Park

Kahului

21

Kahului Airport

Spreckelsville

390

30

Lahaina

IAO VALLEY

Kaahumanu Ave.

311

36

Haleakala Hwy.

37

Honoapiilani Hwy.

Waikapu

30

380

400

Puunene

Mokulele Hwy.

Spanish Rd.

Pulehu Rd.

Olowalu

30

Maalaea
31

311

Kulhelani Hwy.

Upper Kihei Rd.

Maalaea Beach

Auau Channel

Maalaea Bay

Kihei

S. Kihei Rd.

Piilani Hwy.

③

SOUTH MAUI

Keokea

Kamaole III Beach Park

Maui Meadows

PACIFIC OCEAN

Ulua Beach
Wailea Beach
Maluaka (Makena) Beach

Wailea

Wailea Alanui Dr.

④

Kula Hwy.

37

EUCALYPTUS FORESTS

Makena ⑤

Tedeschi Vineyards

Ulupalakua

Molokini Crater

Puu Olai ▲

Oneloa Beach (Big Beach)

31

Legend:
Airport ✈
Beach
Mountain ▲
Vineyard 🍇

0 ___ 5 mi
0 ___ 5 km
N

Kahoolawe

Ahini-Kinau Natural Area Reserve

Alalakeiki

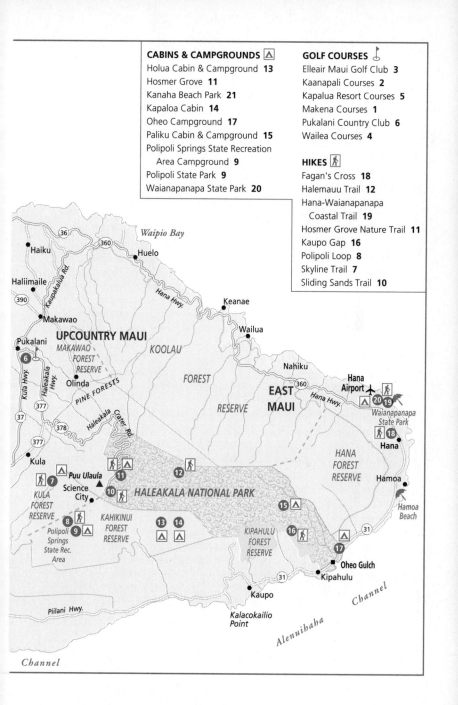

CABINS & CAMPGROUNDS ◮
Holua Cabin & Campground **13**
Hosmer Grove **11**
Kanaha Beach Park **21**
Kapaloa Cabin **14**
Oheo Campground **17**
Paliku Cabin & Campground **15**
Polipoli Springs State Recreation
   Area Campground **9**
Polipoli State Park **9**
Waianapanapa State Park **20**

GOLF COURSES ⛳
Elleair Maui Golf Club **3**
Kaanapali Courses **2**
Kapalua Resort Courses **5**
Makena Courses **1**
Pukalani Country Club **6**
Wailea Courses **4**

HIKES 🚶
Fagan's Cross **18**
Halemauu Trail **12**
Hana-Waianapanapa
   Coastal Trail **19**
Hosmer Grove Nature Trail **11**
Kaupo Gap **16**
Polipoli Loop **8**
Skyline Trail **7**
Sliding Sands Trail **10**

Waipio Bay

(36)
Haiku
(360)
Huelo
Haliimaile
Kaupakalua Rd.
(390)
Makawao
Keanae
Hana Hwy.
Wailua
UPCOUNTRY MAUI
Pukalani
(6)
*MAKAWAO
FOREST
RESERVE*
KOOLAU
Nahiku
Kula Hwy.
Haleakala Hwy.
Olinda
FOREST
Hana
Airport ✈
(360)
Hana Hwy.
◮ 🚶
(20) (19)
PINE FORESTS
(377)
(37)
Haleakala
RESERVE
**EAST
MAUI**
*Waianapanapa
State Park*
🚶 (18)
Hana
(378)
Haleakala
Crater Rd.
(377)
Kula
Puu Ulaula ◮ 🚶 ◮
(7) 🚶 Science (11)
🚶 (12)
*HANA
FOREST
RESERVE*
*KULA
FOREST
RESERVE*
City
(10) 🚶
HALEAKALA NATIONAL PARK
Hamoa
◮ (15)
(8) 🚶
(9) ◮
Polipoli
Springs
State Rec.
Area
*KAHIKINUI
FOREST
RESERVE*
(13) (14)
◮ ◮
(16) 🚶
◮
(17)
*Hamoa
Beach*
*KIPAHULU
FOREST
RESERVE*
(31)
■ Oheo Gulch
Kipahulu
Piilani Hwy.
(31)
Kaupo
*Kalacokailio
Point*
Channel
Alenuihaha
Channel

405

Cheap Thrills: What to See & Do for Free (or Almost) on Maui

- **Greet the Rising Sun from Atop Haleakala.** Get up early, bundle up, fill a thermos full of hot java, and drive up the 37 miles from sea level to 10,000 feet to witness the birth of yet another day. The sky turns from inky black to muted charcoal as a small sliver of orange forms on the horizon. There's something about standing up so high, breathing in the rarefied air, and watching the first rays of light streak across the sky, that makes a Haleakala sunrise a mystical experience of the first magnitude.

- **Browse the Maui Swap Meet.** Every Saturday from 7am to noon, you can browse among the 100-plus booths at the Maui Swap Meet on Puunene Avenue, next to the Kahului Post Office. On hand are plenty of home-baked goods, fragrant cut flowers, some junk, and a few treasures. It's a great way to spend a couple of hours. Admission is just 50¢.

- **Watch for Whales.** No need to shell out megabucks for a whale-watching cruise—you can see these majestic mammals breach and spyhop from shore. One of the best places is McGregor Point, the scenic point at mile marker 9 along Honoapiilani Highway, just outside of Maalaea in South Maui. The humpbacks arrive as early as November, but the majority travel through Maui's waters from mid-December to mid-April, with a few stragglers hanging around until May.

- **Swim with the Fishes.** The calm waters off Kapalua Beach are an ideal place for swimming and snorkeling. The bay is defined by two outstretched arms of black lava at either end that keep the sea calm, and the white-sand, crescent-shaped beach, bordered by graceful palms, is postcard-perfect. Go early in the day for the best water conditions.

- **Take a Dip in the Seven Sacred Pools.** There are actually more than seven of these fern-shrouded waterfall pools, and they're all beautiful. They spill seaward at Oheo Gulch, on the rainy eastern flanks of Haleakala. Some visitors try to swim in the pools that are nearest the sea; if you do, keep an eye on the sky overhead, so a sudden cloudburst doesn't send you cascading out to sea.

- **Venture Back in Time in the Historic Port Town of Lahaina.** In the 1800s, when whaling was at its height, seafarers swarmed into this tiny town and missionaries fought to stem the spread of their evil. It was a wild time, and Lahaina was an exciting place to be. The Lahaina Restoration Society, in the Master's Reading Room on Front and Dickenson streets, will give you a free map that will let you discover those wild whaling days for yourself. A few of the historic sites have an admission fee (the highest is $3), but most are free.

- **Watch Windsurfers Pirouette Over the Waves at Hookipa.** Just off the Hana Highway past Paia is Hookipa Beach, known the world over as a mecca for windsurfers. The great waves and consistent wind draw top windsurfers from around the globe. Watch in awe as these colorful sailboarders ride down the face of waves, then turn into the wind and flip into the air rotating 360 degrees. It's the best free show in town.

ULUA BEACH ★

One of the most popular beaches in Wailea, Ulua is a long, wide, crescent-shaped, gold-sand beach between two rocky points. When the ocean's calm, Ulua offers Wailea's best snorkeling; when it's rough, the waves are excellent for bodysurfers. The ocean bottom is shallow and gently slopes down to deeper waters, making swimming generally safe. The beach is usually occupied by guests of nearby resorts. In high season (Christmas–Mar and June–Aug), it's carpeted with beach towels and packed with sunbathers; like sardines in cocoa butter. Facilities include showers and restrooms. Beach equipment is available for rent at the nearby Wailea Ocean Activity Center. Look for the blue SHORELINE ACCESS sign on South Kihei Road, near Renaissance Wailea Beach Resort; a tiny parking lot is nearby.

MALUAKA BEACH (MAKENA BEACH) ★

On the southern end of Maui's resort coast, development falls off dramatically, leaving a wild, dry countryside of green kiawe trees. The Maui Prince sits in isolated splendor, sharing Makena Resort's 1,800 acres with only a couple of first-rate golf courses and a necklace of perfect beaches. The strand nearest the hotel is Maluaka Beach, often called Makena, notable for its beauty and its views of Molokini Crater, the offshore islet, and Kahoolawe, the so-called "target" island (it was used as a bombing target from 1945 until the early 1990s). This is a short, wide, palm-fringed crescent of golden, grainy sand set between two black-lava points and bounded by big sand dunes topped by a grassy knoll. The swimming in this mostly calm bay is considered the best on Makena Bay, which is bordered on the south by Puu Olai Cinder Cone and historic Keawalai Congregational Church. The waters around Makena Landing, at the north end of the bay, are particularly good for snorkeling. Facilities include restrooms, showers, a landscaped park, on-duty lifeguards, and roadside parking. Along Makena Alanui, look for the SHORELINE ACCESS sign near the hotel, turn right, and head down to the shore.

ONELOA BEACH (BIG BEACH) ★★

Oneloa, meaning "long sand" in Hawaiian, is one of the most popular beaches on Maui. Locals call it "Big Beach"—it's 3,300 feet long and more than 100 feet wide. Mauians come here to swim, fish, sunbathe, surf, and enjoy the view of Kahoolawe and Lanai. Snorkeling is good around the north end, at the foot of Puu Olai, a 360-foot cinder cone. During storms, however, big waves lash the shore, and a strong rip current sweeps the sharp drop-off, posing a danger for inexperienced open-ocean swimmers. There are no facilities except for portable toilets, but there's plenty of parking. To get here, drive past the Maui Prince Hotel to the second dirt road, which leads through a kiawe thicket to the beach.

On the other side of Puu Olai is **Little Beach,** a small pocket beach where assorted nudists work on their all-over tans, to the chagrin of uptight authorities. You can get a nasty sunburn and a lewd-conduct ticket, too.

EAST MAUI
HOOKIPA BEACH PARK ★

On the Hana Highway, 2 miles past Paia , is one of the most famous windsurfing sites in the world. Because of its hard, constant wind and endless waves, Hookipa attracts top windsurfers and wave jumpers from around the globe. Surfers and fishermen also enjoy this small, gold-sand beach at the foot of a grassy cliff, which provides a natural amphitheater for spectators. Except when competitions are being held, weekdays are the best times to watch the daredevils fly over the waves. When waves are flat, snorkelers and divers explore the reef. Facilities include restrooms, showers, pavilions, picnic tables, barbecues, and parking.

WAIANAPANAPA STATE PARK

This beach park is off the Hana Highway, 4 miles before Hana, and takes its name from the legend of the Waianapanapa Cave, where Chief Kaakea, a jealous and cruel man, suspected his wife, Popoalaea, of having an affair. Popoalaea left her husband and hid herself in a chamber of the Waianapanapa Cave. She and her attendant ventured out only at night for food. Nevertheless, a few days later, Kaakea was passing by the area and saw the shadow of the servant. Knowing he had found his wife's hiding place, Kaakea entered the cave and killed her. During certain times of the year, the water in the tide pool turns red, commemorating Popoalaea's death. (Scientists claim, less imaginatively, that the water turns red due to the presence of small red shrimp.)

Waianapanapa State Park's 120 acres contain 12 cabins (p. 379), a caretaker's residence, a beach park, picnic tables, barbecue grills, restrooms, showers, a parking lot, a shoreline hiking trail, and a black-sand beach (the sand is actually small, black pebbles). This is a wonderful area for shoreline hikes (bring insect repellent, as the mosquitoes are plentiful) and picnicking. Swimming is generally unsafe, though, due to strong waves and rip currents. Because Waianapanapa is crowded on weekends with local residents and their families, as well as tourists, weekdays are generally a better bet.

HAMOA BEACH 🏖

This half moon–shaped, gray-sand beach (a mix of coral and lava) in a truly tropical setting is a favorite of sunbathers seeking rest and refuge. The Hotel Hana-Maui maintains the beach and acts as though it's private, which it isn't—so just march down the lava-rock steps and grab a spot on the sand. James Michener called it "a beach so perfectly formed that I wonder at its comparative obscurity." The 100-foot-wide beach is three football fields long and sits below 30-foot black-lava sea cliffs. Surf on this unprotected beach breaks offshore and rolls in, making it a popular surfing and bodysurfing area. Hamoa is often swept by powerful rip currents. The calm left side is best for snorkeling in summer. The hotel has numerous facilities for guests; there's an outdoor shower and restrooms for non-guests. Parking is limited. Look for the Hamoa Beach turnoff from Hana Highway.

6 Watersports

For general advice on the activities listed below, see "The Active Vacation Planner," in chapter 2.

The **Activity Warehouse** (© 800/343-2087; www.travelhawaii.com), which has branches in Lahaina at 578 Front St., near Prison Street (© 808/667-4000), and in Kihei at Azeka Place II, on the mountain side of Kihei Road near Lipoa Street (© 808/875-4000), rents everything from beach chairs and coolers to kayaks, boogie boards, and surfboards.

Snorkel Bob's (www.snorkelbob.com) has snorkel gear, boogie boards, and other ocean toys at four locations: 1217 Front St., Lahaina (© 808/661-4421); Napili Village, 5425-C Lower Honoapiilani Hwy., Napili (© 808/669-9603); in North Kihei at Azeka Place II, 1279 S. Kihei Road #310, S. Kihei Rd. (© 808/875-6188); and in South Kihei/Wailea at the Kamaole Beach Center, 2411 S. Kihei Rd., Kihei (© 808/879-7449). All locations are open daily from 8am to 5pm. If you're island hopping, you can rent from a Snorkel Bob's location on one island and return to a branch on another.

BOATING

Maui is big on snorkel cruises. The crescent-shaped islet called **Molokini** is one of the best snorkel and scuba spots in Hawaii. Trips to the island of **Lanai** (see chapter 8) are also popular for a day of snorkeling. Always remember to bring a towel, swimsuit, sunscreen, and hat on a snorkel cruise; everything else is usually included. If you'd like to go a little deeper than snorkeling allows, consider trying **Snuba.** Most of these snorkel boats offer it for an additional cost; it's usually around $50 for a half-hour or so.

For fishing charters, see "Sportfishing," below.

America II ✪ This U.S. contender in the 1987 America's Cup race is a true racing boat—a 65-foot, 12-meter sailing yacht offering four different 2-hour trips in winter, three in summer: a **morning sail,** an **afternoon sail,** and a **sunset sail,** plus **whale-watching** in winter. These are sailing trips. No snorkeling—just the thrill of racing with the wind. Complimentary bottled water, soda, and chips are available.

Lahaina Harbor, slip 5. ℂ **888/667-2133** or 808/667-2195. www.galaxymall.com/stores/americaii. Trips $33 adults, $17 children 12 and under.

Maui Classic Charters ✪✪ Maui Classic Charters offers morning and afternoon **snorkel-sail cruises to Molokini** on *Four Winds II,* a 55-foot, glass bottom catamaran, for $79 adults ($49 children 3–12 years) for the morning sail and $40 adults ($30 children) in the afternoon. *Four Winds* trips include a continental breakfast; a barbecue lunch; complimentary beer, wine, and soda; complimentary snorkeling gear and instruction; and sportfishing along the way.

Those looking for speed should book a trip on the fast, state-of-the-art catamaran, *Maui Magic.* The company offers a 5-hour snorkel journey to both Molokini and La Perouse for $99 for adults and $79 for children ages 5 to 12, including a continental breakfast; barbecue lunch; beer, wine, and soda; snorkel gear; and instruction. During **whale season** (Dec 22–Apr 22), the Maui Magic Whale Watch, a 1½ hour trip with beverages, is $40 for adults and $30 for children ages 3 to 12 years.

Maalaea Harbor, slip 55 and slip 80. ℂ **800/736-5740** or 808/879-8188. www.mauicharters.com. Prices vary depending on cruise.

Pacific Whale Foundation This not-for-profit foundation supports its whale research by offering **whale-watch cruises** and **snorkel tours,** some to Molokini and Lanai. It operates a 65-foot power catamaran called *Ocean Spirit,* a 50-foot sailing catamaran called *Manute'a,* and a sea kayak. There are 15 daily trips to choose from, offered from December through May, out of both Lahaina and Maalaea harbors.

101 N. Kihei Rd., Kihei. ℂ **800/942-5311** or 808/879-8811. www.pacificwhale.org. Trips from $20 adults, $15 children ages 7–12; 6 years and under free; snorkeling cruises from $30.

Pride of Maui For a high-speed, action-packed snorkel-sail experience, consider the *Pride of Maui.* These 5½-hour **snorkel cruises** take in not only **Molokini,** but also Turtle Bay and Makena for more snorkeling; the cost is $86 for ages 13 and up and $53 for children ages 3 to 12. Continental breakfast, barbecue lunch, gear, and instruction are included. They also have an afternoon Molokini cruise ($35 for ages 13 and up and $27 children ages 3–12, plus an optional lunch for an additional $5), an evening cocktail cruise ($47 for ages 13 and up and $20 for children ages 2–12) and, during whale season, a whale-watching cruise ($26 for ages 13 and up and $17 for children ages 3–12).

Maalaea Harbor. ✆ **877/TO-PRIDE** or 808/875-0955. www.prideofmaui.com. Prices vary; see above.

Scotch Mist Sailing Charters This 50-foot Santa Cruz sailboat offers 2-hour sail/snorkels. Prices include snorkel gear, juice, fresh pineapple spears, Maui chips, beer, wine, and soda.

Lahaina Harbor, slip 2. ✆ **808/661-0386**. www.scotchmistsailingcharters.com. Sail trips $35 adults, $18 children ages 5–12; sunset sail $45.

Trilogy Ocean Sports Lanai *★★★* *Kids* Trilogy offers our favorite **snorkel-sail trips.** Hop aboard its 50-foot catamaran for a 90-mile sail from Lahaina Harbor to **Lanai's Hulopoe Beach,** a terrific marine preserve, for a fun-filled day of sailing, snorkeling, swimming, and **whale-watching** (in season, of course). This is the only cruise that offers a personalized ground tour of the island, and the only one with rights to take you to Hulopoe Beach. The full-day trip costs $179 for adults, half-price for children ages 3 to 12. Ask about overnighters to Lanai.

Trilogy also offers snorkel-sail trips to **Molokini,** one of Hawaii's best snorkel spots. This half-day trip leaves from Maalaea Harbor and costs $101 for adults, half-price for kids ages 3 to 12, including breakfast and a barbecue lunch. There's also a late-morning half-day snorkel/sail off Kaanapali Beach for the same price.

These are the most expensive sail/snorkel cruises on Maui, but they're worth every penny. The crews are fun and knowledgeable, and the boats comfortable and well-equipped. All trips include breakfast (Mom's homemade cinnamon buns) and a very good barbecue lunch (shipboard on the half-day trip, on land on the Lanai trip). Note, however, that you will be required to wear a flotation device no matter how good your swimming skills are. If this bothers you, go with another outfitter.

✆ **888/MAUI-800** or 888/628-4800. www.sailtrilogy.com. Prices and departure points vary with cruise.

DAY CRUISES TO MOLOKAI

You can travel across the seas by ferry from Maui's Lahaina Harbor to Molokai's Kaunakakai Wharf on the ***Molokai Princess*** (✆ **800/275-6969** or 808/667-6165; www.mauiprincess.com). The 100-foot yacht, certified for 149 passengers, is fitted with the latest generation of gyroscopic stabilizers, making the ride smoother. The ferry makes the 90-minute journey from Lahaina to Kaunakakai daily; the cost is $85 adult roundtrip and $43 for children ages 3 to 12 roundtrip. Or, you can choose to tour the island from two different package options: Cruise-Drive, which includes round-trip passage and a rental car for $169 for the driver, $80 per additional adult passenger and $40 for children; or the Alii Tour, which is a guided tour in an air-conditioned van plus lunch for $169 for adults and $109 for children.

They also offer ferry transportation, then a van to the trail head of the switchback trail leading down to the Kalaupapa Peninsula for a hiking-tour of the Kalaupapa Leprosy Settlement for $299 per person, which includes hiking down to the Settlement and then flying out back to Maui; and $249 per person to hike in and hike out. See "The Legacy of Father Damien: Kalaupapa National Historic Park" on p. 483 for more information about the settlement.

DAY CRUISES TO LANAI

In addition to **Trilogy Ocean Sports Lanai** (see above), the following boats specialize in day trips to the island of Lanai.

Expeditions Lahaina/Lanai Passenger Ferry ⚓ *Value*   The cheapest way to Lanai is the ferry, which runs five times a day, 365 days a year. It leaves Lahaina at 6:45am, 9:15am, 12:45pm, 3:15pm, and 5:45pm; the return ferry from Lanai's Manele Bay Harbor leaves at 8am, 10:30am, 2pm, 4:30pm, and 6:45pm. The 9-mile channel crossing takes between 45 minutes and an hour, depending on sea conditions. Reservations are strongly recommended. Baggage is limited to two checked bags and one carry-on. Call **Lanai City Service** (© **800/800-4000** or 808/565-7227) to arrange a car rental or bus ride when you arrive.

Boat: Lahaina Harbor. Office: 658 Front St., Suite 127, Lahaina, HI 96761. © **808/661-3756**. www.go-lanai.com. Round-trip from Maui to Lanai $50 adults, $40 children 2–11 (children under 2 years are free).

BODYBOARDING (BOOGIE BOARDING) & BODYSURFING

In winter, Maui's best bodysurfing spot is **Mokuleia Beach,** known locally as Slaugh-terhouse because of the cattle slaughterhouse that once stood here, not because of the waves—although these waves are for expert bodysurfers only. Take Honoapiilani Highway just past Kapalua Bay Resort; various trails will take you down to the pocket beach.

Good bodyboarding can be found at **Baldwin Beach Park,** just outside Paia. Storms from the south bring fair bodysurfing conditions and great bodyboarding to the leeward side of Maui: **Oneloa Beach** (or Big Beach) in Makena, **Ulua** and **Kamaole III** in Kihei, and **Kapalua** beaches are all good choices.

OCEAN KAYAKING

Gliding silently over the water, propelled by a paddle, seeing Maui from the sea the way the early Hawaiians did—that's what ocean kayaking is all about. One of Maui's best kayak routes is along the **Kihei Coast,** where there's easy access to calm water. Mornings are always best, as the wind comes up around 11am, making seas choppy and paddling difficult.

For the uninitiated, our favorite kayak-tour operator is **Makena Kayak Tours** ⚓ (© **877/879-8426** or 808/879-8426; makenakyak@aol.com). Professional guide Dino Ventura leads a 2½-hour trip from Makena Landing and loves taking first-timers over the secluded coral reefs and into remote coves. His wonderful tour will be a high-light of your vacation. It costs $55, including refreshments and snorkel and kayak equipment.

South Pacific Kayaks, 2439 S. Kihei Rd., Kihei (© **800/776-2326** or 808/875-4848; www.mauikayak.com), is Maui's oldest kayak-tour company. Its expert guides lead ocean-kayak trips that include lessons, a guided tour, and snorkeling. Tours run from 2½ to 5 hours and range in price from $65 to $139. South Pacific also offers kayak rentals starting at $30 a day.

In Hana, **Hana-Maui Sea Sports** (© **808/248-7711;** www.hana-maui-seasports. com) runs 2-hour tours of Hana's coastline on wide, stable "no roll" kayaks, with snor-keling, for $89 per person. They also feature kayak surfing lessons for $89.

OCEAN RAFTING

If you're semiadventurous and looking for a more intimate experience with the sea, try ocean rafting. The inflatable rafts hold 6 to 24 passengers. Tours usually include snor-keling and coastal cruising. One of the best (and most reasonable) outfitters is **Hawai-ian Ocean Raft** (© **888/677-RAFT** or 808/667-2191), which operates out of Lahaina Harbor. The best deal is the 5-hour morning tour for $70 for adults, $50 for children ages 5 to 12; it includes three snorkeling stops and time spent searching for dolphins.

SCUBA DIVING

Everyone dives **Molokini,** a marine-life park and one of Hawaii's top dive spots. This crescent-shaped crater has three tiers of diving: a 35-foot plateau inside the crater basin (used by beginning divers and snorkelers), a wall sloping to 70 feet just beyond the inside plateau, and a sheer wall on the outside and backside of the crater that plunges 350 feet. This underwater park is very popular, thanks to calm, clear, protected waters and an abundance of marine life, from manta rays to clouds of yellow butterfly fish.

Stop by any location of **Maui Dive Shop** ✦ (www.mauidiveshop.com)—Maui's largest diving retailer, with everything from rentals to scuba-diving instruction to dive-boat charters—for a free copy of the 24-page *Maui Dive Guide.* Inside are maps and details of the 20 best shoreline and offshore dives and snorkel sites, each ranked for beginner, intermediate, or advanced snorkelers/divers. Maui Dive Shop has branches in Kihei at Azeka Place II Shopping Center, 1455 S. Kihei Rd. (© **808/879-3388**), and Kamaole Shopping Center (© **808/879-1533**); in Lahaina at Lahaina Cannery Mall (© **808/661-5388**); and in the Honokowai Market Place (© **808/661-6166**). Other locations include Whalers Village, Kaanapali (© **808/661-5117**), and Kahana Gateway, Kahana (© **808/669-3800**).

For personalized diving, **Ed Robinson's Diving Adventures** ✦ (© **800/635-1273** or 808/879-3584; www.mauiscuba.com) is the only Maui company rated one of *Scuba Diver* magazine's top 10 best dive operators for 5 years straight. Ed, a widely published underwater photographer, offers specialized charters for small groups. Two-tank dives are $120 ($135 with equipment); his dive boats depart from Kihei Boat Ramp.

If Ed is booked, call **Severns Diving** ✦ (© **808/879-6596;** www.mikeseverns diving.com) for small (maximum 12 people, divided into 2 groups of 6), personal diving tours on a 38-foot Munson/Hammerhead boat with freshwater shower. Pauline Fiene-Severns is a biologist who makes diving in Hawaii not only fun but also educational (check out her spectacular underwater photography book, *Molokini Island*). In her 25-plus years of operation, the company has been accident-free. Two-tank dives are $110 (with equipment).

SNORKELING

Snorkeling on Maui is easy—there are so many great spots where you can just wade in the water with a face mask and look down to see the tropical fish. Mornings are best, as local winds don't kick in until around noon. Maui's best snorkeling beaches include **Kapalua Beach;** along the Kihei coastline, especially at **Kamaole Beach Park III;** and along the Wailea coastline, particularly at **Ulua Beach.** For an off-the-beaten-track experience, head south to **Makena Beach;** the bay is filled with clouds of tropical fish, and, on weekdays, the waters are virtually empty.

The snorkeling at **Black Rock at Kaanapali** ✦ is worth the inflated rates at the parking lots that buffer this beach. The prominent craggy cliff at the Sheraton Maui Hotel doesn't just end when it plunges into the ocean. Underwater, the sheer wall continues, creating one of the west side's best snorkeling areas: Turtles, rays, and a variety of snappers and goat fish cruise along the sandy bottom. In the crevices, ledges, and holes of the rock wall, you can find eels, shrimp, lobster, and a range of rainbowed tropical fish.

Snorkel Bob's (www.snorkelbob.com) and the **Activity Warehouse** will rent you everything you need; see the introduction to this section for locations. Also see "Scuba Diving," above, for Maui Dive Shop's free booklet on great snorkeling sites.

Two truly terrific snorkel spots are difficult to get to but worth the effort, as they're home to Hawaii's tropical marine life at its best:

MOLOKINI 🐠🐠   This sunken crater sits like a crescent moon fallen from the sky, almost midway between Maui and the uninhabited island of Kahoolawe. Molokini stands like a scoop against the tide and serves, on its concave side, as a natural sanctuary and marine-life preserve for tropical fish. Snorkelers commute daily in a fleet of dive boats. Molokini is accessible only by boat; see "Boating," above, for outfitters that can take you here. Expect crowds in the high season.

AHIHI-KINAU NATURAL PRESERVE 🐠🐠   In Ahihi Bay, you can't miss this 2,000-acre state natural area reserve in the lee of Cape Kinau, on Maui's rugged south coast, where, in 1790, Haleakala spilled red-hot lava that ran to the sea. Fishing is strictly forbidden here, and the fish know it; they're everywhere in this series of rocky coves and black-lava tide pools. To get here, drive south of Makena past Puu Olai to Ahihi Bay, where the road turns to gravel (and sometimes seems like it'll disappear under the waves). At Cape Kinau, three four-wheel-drive trails lead across the lava flow; take the shortest one, nearest La Pérouse Bay. If you have a standard car, drive as far as you can, park, and walk the remainder of the way. Après-snorkel, check out La Pérouse Bay on the south side of Cape Kinau, where the French admiral La Pérouse became the first European to set foot on Maui. A lava-rock pyramid known as Pérouse Monument marks the spot.

When the whales aren't around, **Captain Steve's Rafting Excursions** (📞 808/667-5565; www.captainsteves.com) offers 2-hour whale-watching excursions out of Lahaina Harbor. Take the early-bird trip at 7:30am, and spot some whales for only $35 per person (regular rates are $45 for adults, $35 for children 12 and under).

SPORTFISHING

Marlin, tuna, ono, and mahimahi await the baited hook in Maui's coastal and channel waters. No license is required; just book a sportfishing vessel out of Lahaina or Maalaea harbors. Most charter boats that troll for big game fish carry six passengers max.

The best way to book a sportfishing charter is through the experts; the best booking desk in the state is **Sportfish Hawaii** 🐠 (📞 877/388-1376 or 808/396-2607; www.sportfishhawaii.com), which not only books boats on Maui, but on all islands. These fishing vessels have been inspected and must meet rigorous criteria to guarantee that you will have a great time. Prices range from $850 to $950 for a full-day exclusive charter (you, plus 5 friends, get the entire boat to yourself); it's $599 to $750 for a half-day exclusive.

SUBMARINE DIVES

Plunging 100 feet below the surface of the sea in a state-of-the-art, high-tech submarine is a great way to experience Maui's magnificent underwater world, especially if you're a non-swimmer. **Atlantis Submarines** 🐠, 658 Front St., Lahaina (📞 800/548-6262, 888/REAL-SUB, or 808/667-7816; www.goatlantis.com), offers trips out of Lahaina Harbor every hour, on the hour, from 9am to 2pm; $80 for adults and $40 for children under 12 (children must be at least 3 ft. tall). Allow 2 hours for this underwater adventure. This is not a good choice if you're claustrophobic.

An Expert Shares His Secrets: Maui's Best Dives

Ed Robinson, of Ed Robinson's Diving Adventures (see above), knows what makes a great dive. Here are five of his favorites on Maui:

Hawaiian Reef   This area off the Kihei-Wailea Coast is so named because it hosts a good cross-section of Hawaiian topography and marine life. Diving to depths of 85 feet, you'll see everything from lava formations and coral reef to sand and rubble, plus a diverse range of both shallow and deep-water creatures. It's clear why this area was so popular with ancient Hawaiian fishermen: Large helmet shells, a healthy garden of antler coral heads, and big schools of snapper are common.

Third Tank   Located off Makena Beach at 80 feet, this World War II tank is one of the most picturesque artificial reefs you're likely to see around Maui. It acts like a fish magnet: Because it's the only large, solid object in the area, any fish or invertebrates looking for a safe home come here. Surrounding the tank is a cloak of schooling snapper and goat fish just waiting for a photographer with a wide-angle lens. For its small size, the Third Tank is loaded with more marine life per square inch than any site off Maui.

Molokini Crater   The backside is always done as a live boat-drift dive. The vertical wall plummets from more than 150 feet above sea level to around 250 feet below. Looking down to unseen depths gives you a feeling for the vastness of the open ocean. Pelagic fish and sharks are often sighted, and living coral perches on the wall, which is home to lobsters, crabs, and a number of photogenic black-coral trees at 50 feet.

There are actually two great dive sites around Molokini Crater. Named after common chub or rudderfish, **Enenue Side** gently slopes from the surface to about 60 feet, then drops rapidly to deeper waters. The more shallow

SURFING

Expert surfers visit Maui in winter, when the surf's really up. The best surfing beaches include **Honolua Bay,** north of the Kapalua Resort (the third bay past the Ritz-Carlton Kapalua, off the Honoapiilani Hwy., or Hwy. 30); **Lahaina Harbor** (in summer, there'll be waves just off the channel entrance with a south swell); **Maalaea,** just outside the breakwall of the Maalaea Harbor (a clean, world-class left); and **Hookipa Beach,** where surfers get the waves until noon (after that—in a carefully worked-out compromise to share this prized surf spot—the windsurfers take over).

Always wanted to learn to surf, but didn't know whom to ask? Call the **Nancy Emerson School of Surfing** (© **808/244-SURF** or 808/874-1183; www.surfclinics. com). Nancy has been surfing since 1961, and has even been a stunt performer for various movies, including *Waterworld*. She's pioneered a new instructional technique called "Learn to Surf in One Lesson"—you can, really. It's $75 per person for a 2-hour group lesson; private 2-hour classes are $160.

In Hana, **Hana-Maui Ocean Activities** (© **808/248-7711**) has private lessons taught by a certified ocean lifeguard for $89 for a 2-hour lesson.

area is an easy dive, with lots of tame butterfly fish. It's also the home of Morgan Bentjaw, one of our friendliest moray eels. Enenue Side is often done as a live boat-drift dive to extend the range of the tour. Diving depths vary. Divers usually do a 50-foot dive, but on occasion, advanced divers drop to the 130-foot level to visit the rare boarfish and the shark condos.

Almost every kind of fish found in Hawaii can be seen in the crystalline waters of **Reef's End.** It's an extension of the rim of the crater, which runs for about 200 yards underwater, barely breaking the surface. Reef's End is shallow enough for novice snorkelers and exciting enough for experienced divers. The end and outside of this shoal drop off in dramatic terraces to beyond diving range. In deeper waters, there are shark ledges (at varying depths) and dozens of eels, some of which are tame, including moray, dragon, snowflake, and garden eels. The more shallow inner side is home to Garbanzo, one of the largest and first eels to be tamed. The reef is covered with cauliflower coral; in bright sunlight, it's one of the most dramatic underwater scenes in Hawaii.

La Pérouse Pinnacle   In the middle of scenic La Pérouse Bay, site of Haleakala's most recent lava flow, is a pinnacle rising from the 60-foot bottom to about 10 feet below the surface. Getting to the dive site is half the fun: The scenery above water is as exciting as that below the surface. Underwater, you'll enjoy a much diversified dive. Clouds of damselfish and triggerfish will greet you on the surface. Divers can approach even the timid bird wrasse. There are more porcupine puffers here than anywhere else, as well as schools of goat fish and fields of healthy finger coral. La Pérouse is good for snorkeling and long, shallow second dives.

WHALE-WATCHING
The humpback is the star of the annual whale-watching season, which usually begins in December and can last until May.

WHALE-WATCHING FROM SHORE   The best time to whale-watch is between mid-December and April: Just look out to sea. There's no best time of day, but it seems that when the sea is glassy and there's no wind, the whales appear. Once you see one, keep watching in the same vicinity; they may stay down for 20 minutes. Bring a book. And binoculars, if you can. You can rent binoculars for $2 a day at the **Activity Warehouse** (© **800/343-2087;** www.travelhawaii.com), which has branches in Lahaina at 578 Front St., near Prison Street (© **808/667-4000**), and in Kihei at Azeka Place II, on the mountain side of Kihei Road near Lipoa Street (© **808/875-4000**). Some good whale-watching points on Maui are:

McGregor Point   On the way to Lahaina, there's a scenic lookout at mile marker 9 (just before you get to the Lahaina Tunnel); it's a good viewpoint to scan for whales.

Marriott Wailea Beach Resort   On the Wailea coastal walk, stop at this resort to look for whales through the telescope installed as a public service by the Hawaii Island Humpback Whale National Marine Sanctuary.

Olowalu Reef   Along the straight part of Honoapiilani Highway, between McGregor Point and Olowalu, you'll see whales leap out of the water. Sometimes, their appearance brings traffic to a screeching halt: People abandon their cars and run down to the sea to watch, causing a major traffic jam. If you stop, pull off the road so others may pass.

Puu Olai   It's a tough climb up this coastal landmark near the Maui Prince Hotel, but you're likely to be well rewarded: This is the island's best spot for offshore whale-watching. On the 360-foot cinder cone overlooking Makena Beach, you'll be at the right elevation to see Pacific humpbacks as they dodge Molokini and cruise up Alalakeiki Channel between Maui and Kahoolawe. If you don't see one, you'll at least have a whale of a view.

WHALE-WATCHING CRUISES   For a closer look, take a whale-watching cruise. Just about all of Hawaii's snorkel and dive boats become whale-watching boats in season; some of them even carry professional naturalists on board so you'll know what you're seeing. For the best options, see "Boating," above.

WHALE-WATCHING BY RAFT   Seeing a humpback whale from an ocean kayak or raft is awesome. **Captain Steve's Rafting Excursions** (© **808/667-5565**) offers 2-hour whale-watching excursions out of Lahaina Harbor for $45 for adults, $35 for children ages 12 and under. Take the early-bird trip at 7:30am, and spot some whales for only $35 per person.

WINDSURFING

Maui has Hawaii's best windsurfing beaches. In winter, windsurfers from around the world flock to the town of **Paia** to ride the waves; **Hookipa Beach,** known all over the globe for its brisk winds and excellent waves, is the site of several world-championship contests. **Kanaha,** west of Kahului Airport, also has dependable winds. When the winds turn northerly, **Kihei** is the spot to be; some days, you can spot whales in the distance behind the windsurfers. The northern end of Kihei is best: **Ohukai Park,** the first beach as you enter South Kihei Road from the northern end, not only has good winds, but also parking, a long strip of grass to assemble your gear, and good access to the water. Experienced windsurfers here are found in front of the **Maui Sunset Condo**, 1032 S. Kihei Rd., near Waipuilani Street (a block north of McDonald's), which has great windsurfing conditions but a very shallow reef (not good for beginners).

   Hawaiian Island Surf and Sport, 415 Dairy Rd., Kahului (© **800/231-6958** or 808/871-4981; www.hawaiianisland.com), offers lessons, rentals, and repairs. Other shops that offer rentals and lessons are **Hawaiian Sailboarding Techniques,** 425 Koloa St., Kahului (© **800/968-5423** or 808/871-5423; www.hstwindsurfing.com), with 2½-hour lessons from $79 and equipment rental from $46 a day; and **Maui Windsurf Co.,** 22 Hana Hwy., Kahului (© **800/872-0999** or 808/877-4816; www. maui-windsurf.com), which has complete equipment rental (board, sail, rig harness, and roof rack) from $45 and 1½- or 2½-hour lessons ranging from $75.

   For daily reports on wind and surf conditions, call the **Wind and Surf Report** at © **808/877-3611.**

7 Hiking & Camping

In the past 3 decades, Maui has grown from a rural island to a fast-paced resort destination, but its natural beauty remains largely inviolate; there are still many places that can be explored only on foot. Those interested in seeing the backcountry—complete with virgin waterfalls, remote wilderness trails, and quiet, meditative settings—should head for Haleakala's upcountry or the tropical Hana Coast.

Camping on Maui can be extreme (inside a volcano) or benign (by the sea in Hana). It can be wet, cold, and rainy; or hot, dry, and windy—often, all on the same day. If you're heading for Haleakala, remember that U.S. astronauts trained for the moon inside the volcano; bring survival gear. You'll need your swimsuit and rain gear if you're bound for Waianapanapa. Bring your own gear, as there are no places to rent camping equipment on Maui.

For more information on Maui camping and hiking trails and to obtain free maps, contact **Haleakala National Park,** P.O. Box 369, Makawao, HI 96768 (📞 **808/572-4400;** www.nps.gov/hale), and the **State Division of Forestry and Wildlife,** 54 S. High St., Wailuku, HI 96793 (📞 **808/984-8100;** www.hawaii.gov). For information on trails, hikes, and camping, and permits for state parks, contact the **Hawaii State Department of Land and Natural Resources,** State Parks Division, P.O. Box 621, Honolulu, HI 96809 (📞 **808/587-0300;** www.state.hi.us/dlnr); note that you can get information from the website but cannot obtain permits there. For information on Maui County Parks, contact **Maui County Parks and Recreation,** 1580-C Kaahumanu Ave., Wailuku, HI 96793 (📞 **808/243-7380;** www.mauimapp.com).

GUIDED HIKES   If you'd like a knowledgeable guide to accompany you on a hike, call **Maui Hiking Safaris** 🏃 (📞 **888/445-3963** or 808/573-0168; www.mauihiking safaris.com). Owner Randy Warner takes visitors on half- and full-day hikes into valleys, rainforests, and coastal areas. Randy's been hiking around Maui for more than 15 years and is wise in the ways of Hawaiian history, native flora and fauna, and vulcanology. His rates are $59 to $69 for a half-day and $89 to $109 for a full day, and include day packs, rain parkas, snacks, water, and, on full-day hikes, sandwiches.

Maui's oldest hiking guide company is **Hike Maui** 🏃 (📞 **808/879-5270;** www.hikemaui.com), headed by Ken Schmitt, who pioneered guided hikes on the Valley Isle. Hike Maui offers five different hikes a day, ranging from an easy 1-mile to a 3-hour hike to a waterfall ($65) to a strenuous, full-day hike in Haleakala Crater ($145). All prices include equipment and transportation.

About 1,500 years ago, the verdant Kahakuloa Valley was a thriving Hawaiian village. Today, only a few hundred people live in this secluded hamlet, but old Hawaii still lives on here. Explore the valley with **Ekahi Tours** (📞 **888/292-2422** or 808/877-9775; www.ekahi.com). Your guide, a Kahakuloa resident and a Hawaiiana expert, walks you through a taro farm, explains the mystical legends of the valley, and provides you with a peek into ancient Hawaii. The 7½-hour Kahakuloa Valley Tour is $80 for adults, $60 for children under 12; snacks, beverages, and hotel pickup are included.

For information on hikes given by the **Hawaii Sierra Club** on Maui, call 📞 **808/573-4147;** www.hi.sierraclub.org.

HALEAKALA NATIONAL PARK 🏃🏃🏃

For complete coverage of the national park, see p. 433.

INTO THE WILDERNESS: SLIDING SANDS & HALEMAUU TRAILS

Hiking into Maui's dormant volcano is the best way to see it. The terrain inside the wilderness area of the volcano, which ranges from burnt-red cinder cones to ebony-black lava flows, is simply spectacular. There are some 27 miles of hiking trails, two camping sites, and three cabins.

Entrance to Haleakala National Park is $10 per car. The rangers offer free guided hikes, which are a great way to learn about the unusual flora and geological formations here. Briefing sessions on culture, history, and flora are given daily at 9:30, 10:30, and 11:30am at the Summit Visitors Building, 11 miles up from the Visitor's Information Center. Every Tuesday and Friday at 9am, there's a 2-hour, 2-mile guided cinder desert hike (meet at Sliding Sands Trailhead, next to the summit parking lot). Every Monday and Thursday at 9am, there's a 3-hour, 3-mile guided Waikamoi Cloud Forest hike (meet at Hosmer Grove) to view rare native birds and plants. Wear sturdy shoes and be prepared for wind, rain, and intense sun. Bring water and a hat. Additional options include full-moon hikes and star-program hikes. For details, call the park at ✆ 808/572-4400.

Try to arrange to stay at least 1 night in the park; 2 or 3 nights will allow you more time to explore the fascinating interior of the volcano (see below for details on the cabins and campgrounds in the wilderness area of the valley). If you want to venture out on your own, the best route takes in two trails: into the crater along **Sliding Sands Trail,** which begins on the rim at 9,800 feet and descends into the belly of the beast, to the valley floor at 6,600 feet; and back out along **Halemauu Trail.** Hardy hikers can consider making the 11.3-mile, one-way descent, which takes 9 hours, and the equally-as-long returning ascent, in a day. The rest of us will extend this steep hike to 2 days. The descending and ascending trails aren't loops; the trail heads are miles (and several thousand ft. in elevation) apart, so you'll need to make transportation arrangements in advance. Before you set out, stop at park headquarters to get camping and hiking updates.

The trail head for Sliding Sands is well marked and the trail is easy to follow over lava flows and cinders. As you descend, look around: the view is breathtaking. In the afternoon, waves of clouds flow into the Kaupo and Koolau gaps. Vegetation is spare to nonexistent at the top, but the closer you get to the valley floor, the more vegetation you'll see: bracken ferns, pili grass, shrubs, even flowers. On the floor, the trail travels across rough lava flows, passing by rare silversword plants, volcanic vents, and multicolored cinder cones.

The Halemauu Trail goes over red and black lava and past vegetation, such as evening primrose, as it begins its ascent up the valley wall. Occasionally, riders on horseback use this trail. The proper etiquette is to step aside and stand quietly next to the trail as the horses pass.

Some shorter and easier hiking options include the half-mile walk down the **Hosmer Grove Nature Trail** or the first mile or two down **Sliding Sands Trail,** which gives you a hint of what lies ahead. (Even this short hike is exhausting at the high altitude.) A good day hike is **Halemauu Trail** to Holua Cabin and back, an 8-mile, half-day trip.

STAYING IN THE WILDERNESS AREA   Most people stay at one of two tent campgrounds, unless they get lucky and win the lottery—the lottery, that is, for one of the three wilderness cabins. For more information, contact **Haleakala National Park,** P.O. Box 369, Makawao, HI 96768 (✆ 808/572-4400; www.nps.gov/hale).

Cabins It can get really cold and windy down in the valley (see "A Word of Warning About the Weather"), so try for a cabin. They're warm, protected from the elements, and reasonably priced. Each has 12 padded bunks (but no bedding; bring your own), a table, chairs, cooking utensils, a two-burner propane stove, and a wood-burning stove with firewood (you may also have a few cockroaches). The cabins are spaced so that each one is an easy walk from the other: Holua cabin is on the Halemauu Trail, Kapalaoa cabin on Sliding Sands Trail, and Paliku cabin on the eastern end by the Kaupo Gap. The rates are $40 a night for groups of one to six, $80 a night for groups of 7 to 12.

The cabins are so popular that the National Park Service has a lottery system for reservations. Requests for cabins must be made 3 months in advance (be sure to request alternate dates). You can request all three cabins at once; you're limited to 2 nights in one cabin and 3 nights total in the wilderness each month.

Campgrounds If you don't win the cabin lottery, all is not lost, as there are three tent-camping sites that can accommodate you: two in the wilderness and one just outside at Hosmer Grove. There is no charge for tent camping.

Hosmer Grove, located at 6,800 feet, is a small, open, grassy area surrounded by a forest. Trees protect campers from the winds, but nights still get very cold; sometimes there's ice on the ground up here. This is the best place to spend the night in a tent if you want to see the Haleakala sunrise. Come up the day before, enjoy the park, take a day hike, and then turn in early. The enclosed-glass summit building opens at sunrise for those who come to greet the dawn—a welcome windbreak. Facilities at Hosmer Grove include a covered pavilion with picnic tables and grills, chemical toilets, and drinking water. No permits are needed, and there's no charge—but you can only stay for 3 nights in a 30-day period.

The two tent-camping areas inside the volcano are **Holua,** just off Halemauu at 6,920 feet; and **Paliku,** just before the Kaupo Gap at the eastern end of the valley, at 6,380 feet. Facilities at both campgrounds are limited to pit toilets and non-potable catchment water. Water at Holua is limited, especially in summer. No open fires are allowed inside the volcano, so bring a stove if you plan to cook. Tent camping is restricted to the signed area. No camping is allowed in the horse pasture. The inviting grassy lawn in front of the cabin is off-limits. Camping is free, but limited to 2 consecutive nights, and no more than 3 nights a month inside the volcano. Permits are issued at Park Headquarters, daily from 8am to 3pm, on a first-come, first-served basis on the day you plan to camp. Occupancy is limited to 25 people in each campground.

HIKING & CAMPING AT KIPAHULU (NEAR HANA)

In the East Maui section of Haleakala National Park, you can set up at **Oheo Campground,** a first-come, first-served, drive-in campground with tent sites for 100 near the ocean. It has a few tables, barbecue grills, and chemical toilets. No permit is required, but there's a 3-night limit. No food or drinking water is available, so bring your own. Bring a tent as well—it rains 75 inches a year here. Contact **Kipahulu Ranger Station,** Haleakala National Park, HI 96713 (© **808/248-7375;** www.nps. gov/hale), for information.

HIKING FROM THE SUMMIT If you hike from the crater rim down **Kaupo Gap** to the ocean, more than 20 miles away, you'll pass through several climate zones. On a clear day, you can see every island except Kauai on the trip down.

APPROACHING KIPAHULU FROM HANA   If you drive to Kipahulu, you'll have to approach it from the Hana Highway, as it's not accessible from the summit. From the ranger station, it's a short hike above the famous **Oheo Gulch** (which was misnamed the Seven Sacred Pools in the 1940s) to two spectacular waterfalls. The first, **Makahiku Falls,** is easily reached from the central parking area: The trail head begins near the ranger station. Pipiwai Trail leads you up to the road and beyond for a half-mile to the overlook. If you hike another 1½ miles up the trail across two bridges and through a bamboo forest, you reach **Waimoku Falls.** It's a good uphill hike, but press on to avoid the pool's crowd. In hard rain, streams swell quickly. Always be aware of your surroundings.

GUIDED HIKES   The rangers at Kipahulu conduct a 1-mile hike to the **Bamboo Forest** ✿ at 9am daily; half-mile hikes or orientation talks are given at noon, 1:30, 2:30, and 3:30pm daily; and a 4-mile round-trip hike to **Waimoku Falls** takes place on Saturday at 9:30am. All programs and hikes begin at the ranger station. Again, always call in advance to make sure the hike will take place that day by contacting the **Kipahulu Ranger Station,** Haleakala National Park, HI 96713 (© **808/248-7375;** www.nps.gov/hale).

SKYLINE TRAIL, POLIPOLI SPRINGS STATE RECREATION AREA

This is some hike—strenuous, but worth every step if you like seeing the big picture. It's 8 miles, all downhill, with a dazzling 100-mile view of the islands dotting the blue Pacific, plus the West Maui Mountains, which seem like a separate island.

The trail is just outside Haleakala National Park at Polipoli Springs State Recreation Area; however, you access it by going through the national park to the summit. It starts just beyond the Puu Ulaula summit building on the south side of Science City and follows the southwest rift zone of Haleakala from its lunarlike cinder cones to a cool redwood grove. The trail drops 3,800 feet on a 4-hour hike to the recreation area in the 12,000-acre Kahikinui Forest Reserve. If you'd rather drive, you'll need a four-wheel-drive vehicle.

There's a campground at the recreation area at 6,300 feet. No fee or reservations are required, but your stay must be limited to 5 nights. Tent camping is free, but you'll need a permit. One 10-bunk cabin is available for $45 a night for one to four guests ($5 for each additional guest); it has a cold shower and a gas stove, but no electricity or drinking water (bring your own). To reserve, write the **State Parks Division,** 54 High St., Room 101, Wailuku, HI 96793, or call © **808/984-8109** Monday through Friday between 8am and 4pm.

POLIPOLI STATE PARK ✿

One of the most unusual hiking experiences in the state can be found at Polipoli State Park, part of the 21,000-acre Kula and Kahikinui Forest Reserve on the slope of Haleakala. At Polipoli, it's hard to believe that you're in Hawaii: First of all, it's cold, even in summer, since the elevation is 5,300 to 6,200 feet; second, this former forest of native koa, ohia, and mamane trees, which was overlogged in the 1800s, was reforested in the 1930s with introduced species: pine, Monterey cypress, ash, sugi, red adler, redwood, and several varieties of eucalyptus. The result is a cool area, with muted sunlight filtered by towering trees.

The **Polipoli Loop** is an easy 5-mile hike that takes about 3 hours; dress warmly for it. Take the Haleakala Highway (Hwy. 37) to Keokea and turn right onto Highway 337; after less than a half-mile, turn on Waipoli Road, which climbs swiftly. After

10 miles, Waipoli Road ends at the Polipoli State Park campgrounds. The well-marked trail head is next to the parking lot, near a stand of Monterey cypresses; the tree-lined trail offers the best view of the island.

Polipoli Loop is really a network of three trails: Haleakala Ridge, Plum Trail, and Redwood Trail. After a half-mile of meandering through groves of eucalyptus, black-wood, swamp mahogany, and hybrid cypress, you'll join the Haleakala Ridge Trail, which, about a mile into the trail, joins with the Plum Trail (named for the plums that ripen in June and July). This trail passes through massive redwoods and by an old Conservation Corps bunkhouse and a run-down cabin before joining up with the Redwood Trail, which climbs through Mexican pine, tropical ash, Port Orford cedar, and—of course—redwood.

Camping is allowed with a $5-per-night permit from the **State Parks Division,** 54 S. High St., Room 101, Wailuku, HI 96793 (© **808/984-8109**). There's one cabin, available by reservation.

KANAHA BEACH PARK CAMPING

One of the few Maui County camping facilities on the island is Kanaha Beach Park, located next to the Kahului Airport. The county has two separate areas for camping: seven tent sites on the beach and an additional 10 tent sites inland. This well-used park is a favorite of windsurfers, who take advantage of the strong winds that roar across this end of the island. Facilities include a paved parking lot, portable toilets, outdoor showers, barbecue grills, and picnic tables. Camping is limited to no more than 3 consecutive days; the permit fee is $3 per adult and 50¢ per child, per night, and can be obtained from the **Maui County Parks and Recreation Department,** 1580-C Kaahumanu Ave., Wailuku, HI 96793 (© **808/243-7389;** www.mauimapp. com). The 17 sites book up quickly; reserve your dates far in advance (the county will accept reservations a year in advance).

WAIANAPANAPA STATE PARK ⭑⭑

Tucked in a tropical jungle, on the outskirts of the little coastal town of Hana, is Waianapanapa State Park, a black-sand beach set in an emerald forest.

The **Hana-Waianapanapa Coast Trail** is an easy 6-mile hike that takes you back in time. Allow 4 hours to walk along this relatively flat trail, which parallels the sea, along lava cliffs and a forest of lauhala trees. The best time to take the hike is either in the early morning or late afternoon, when the light on the lava and surf makes for great photos. Midday is the worst time; not only is it hot (lava intensifies the heat), but there's also no shade or potable water available.

There's no formal trail head; join the route at any point along the Waianapanapa Campground and go in either direction. Along the trail, you'll see remains of an ancient *heiau* (temple), stands of lauhala trees, caves, a blowhole, and a remarkable plant, *naupaka,* which flourishes along the beach. Upon close inspection, you'll see that the naupaka have only half blossoms; according to Hawaiian legend, a similar plant living in the mountains has the other half of the blossoms. One ancient expla-nation is that the two plants represent never-to-be-reunited lovers: As the story goes, the couple bickered so much that the gods, fed up with their incessant quarreling, banished one lover to the mountain and the other to the sea.

Waianapanapa has 12 cabins and a tent campground. Go for the cabins (p. 379), as it rains torrentially here, sometimes turning the campground into a mud-wrestling arena. Tent-camping is $5 per night but limited to 5 nights in a 30-day period. Permits are available from the **State Parks Division,** 54 S. High St., Room 101, Wailuku, HI 96793 (© **808/984-8109**). Facilities include restrooms, outdoor showers, drinking water, and picnic tables.

HANA: THE HIKE TO FAGAN'S CROSS

This 3-mile hike to the cross erected in memory of Paul Fagan, the founder of Hana Ranch and Hotel Hana-Maui, offers spectacular views of the Hana Coast, particularly at sunset. The uphill trail starts across Hana Highway from the Hotel Hana-Maui. Enter the pastures at your own risk; they're often occupied by glaring bulls with sharp horns and cows with new calves. Watch your step as you ascend this steep hill on a Jeep trail across open pastures to the cross and the breathtaking view.

8 Golf & Other Affordable Outdoor Activities

GOLF

Maui's world-famous golf courses can be played for less than $100 a round. My advice: Play in the afternoon, when discounted twilight rates are in effect. There's no guarantee you'll get 18 holes in, especially during the winter when it's dark by 6pm, but you'll have an opportunity to experience these challenging courses at half the usual fee. Golfers traveling on a budget should also consider the island's municipal and private courses, some of which are listed below.

For last-minute and discount tee times, call **Stand-by Golf** (© **888/645-BOOK** or 808/874-0600; www.stand-bygolf.com) between 7am and 9pm. Stand-by offers discounted (from 10%–40%), guaranteed tee times for same-day or next-day golfing.

CENTRAL MAUI

Waiehu Municipal Golf Course *Value*   This public, oceanside, par-72 golf course is like playing two different courses: The first 9 holes, built in 1930, are set along the dramatic coastline, while the back 9 holes, added in 1966, head toward the mountains. It's a fun course that probably won't challenge your handicap. The only hazard here is the wind, which can rip off the ocean and play havoc with your ball. The only hole that can raise your blood pressure is the 511-yard, par-5 4th hole, which is very narrow and very long. To par here, you have to hit a long accurate drive, then another long and accurate fairway drive, and finally a perfect pitch over the hazards to the greens (yeah, right).

Facilities include a snack bar, driving range, practice greens, golf-club rental, and clubhouse. Since this is a public course, the greens fees are low—but getting a tee time is tough.

P.O. Box 507, Wailuku, HI 96793. © **808/244-5934.** Greens fees $25 Mon–Fri; $30 Sat–Sun and holidays. From the Kahului Airport, turn right on the Hana Hwy. (Hwy. 36), which becomes Kaahumanu Ave. (Hwy. 32). Turn right at the stoplight at the junction of Waiehu Beach Rd. (Hwy. 340). Go another 1½ miles, and you'll see the entrance on your right.

WEST MAUI

Kaanapali Courses *★*   Both courses at Kaanapali offer a challenge to all golfers, from high handicappers to near-pros. The par-72, 6,305-yard **North Course** is a true Robert Trent Jones, Jr. design: an abundance of wide bunkers; several long, stretched-out tees; and the largest, most contoured greens on Maui. The tricky 18th hole (par 4, 435 yd.) has a water hazard on the approach to the green. The par-72, 6,250-yard **South Course** is an Arthur Jack Snyder design; although shorter than the North

Course, it requires more accuracy on the narrow, hilly fairways. It also has a water hazard on its final hole, so don't tally up your scorecard until the final putt is sunk.

Facilities include a driving range, putting course, and clubhouse with dining. Weekday tee times are best.

Off Hwy. 30, Kaanapali. © **808/661-3691.** www.kaanapali-golf.com. Greens fees $150 (North Course), $142 (South Course); Kaanapali guests pay $130 (North), $117 (South); twilight rates for the South Course are $85 after noon for everyone; after 2pm twilight rates are $77 (North), $74 (South) for everyone. At the 1st stoplight in Kaanapali, turn onto Kaanapali Pkwy.; the 1st building on your right is the clubhouse.

Kapalua Resort Courses ★★★   The views from these three championship courses are worth the greens fees alone. The par-72, 6,761-yard **Bay Course** (© **808/ 669-8820**) was designed by Arnold Palmer and Ed Seay. This course is a bit forgiving, with its wide fairways; the greens, however, are difficult to read. The well-photographed 5th overlooks a small ocean cove; even the pros have trouble with this rocky par-3, 205-yard hole. The par-71, 6,632-yard **Village Course** (© **808/669-8830**), another Palmer/Seay design, is the most scenic of the three courses. The hole with the best vista is the 6th, which overlooks a lake with the ocean in the distance. But don't get distracted by the view—the tee is between two rows of Cook pines. The **Plantation Course** (© **808/669-8877**), site of the Mercedes Championships, is a Ben Crenshaw/Bill Coore design. This 6,547-yard, par-73 course, set on a rolling hillside, is excellent for developing your low shots and precise chipping.

Facilities for all three courses include locker rooms, a driving range, and an excellent restaurant. Weekdays are your best bet for tee times.

Off Hwy. 30, Kapalua. © **877/KAPALUA.** www.kapaluamaui.com. Greens fees: $185 ($130 for hotel guests) at the Village ($85 twilight rate); $200 ($140 for guests) Bay course ($90 twilight rate); $250 ($160 for guests) at the Plantation Course ($100 twilight rate).

SOUTH MAUI

Elleair Maui Golf Club   Sitting in the foothills of Haleakala, just high enough to afford spectacular ocean vistas from every hole, this course (formerly known as the Silversword Golf Club) is for golfers who love the views as much as the fairways and greens. It's very forgiving. *Just one caveat:* Go in the morning. Not only is it cooler, but more important, it's also less windy. In the afternoon, the winds bluster down Haleakala with great gusto. This is a fun course to play, with some challenging holes (the par-5, 2nd hole is a virtual minefield of bunkers, and the par-5, 8th hole shoots over a swale and then uphill).

1345 Piilani Hwy. (near Lipoa St. turnoff), Kihei. © **808/874-0777.** Greens fees: $100; twilight rates (after 1pm) are $80; 9-hole rates are $60.

Makena Courses ★★   Here you'll find 36 holes of "Mr. Hawaii Golf"—Robert Trent Jones, Jr.—at its best. Add to that spectacular views: Molokini islet looms in the background, humpback whales gambol offshore in winter, and the tropical sunsets are spectacular. The par-72, 6,876-yard **South Course** has a couple of holes you'll never forget. The view from the par-4 15th hole, which shoots from an elevated tee 183 yards downhill to the Pacific, is magnificent. The 16th hole has a two-tiered green that's blind from the tee 383 yards away (that is, if you make it past the gully off the fairway). The par-72, 6,823-yard **North Course** is more difficult and more spectacular. The 13th hole, located partway up the mountain, has a view that makes most golfers stop and stare. The next hole is even more memorable: a 200-foot drop between tee and green.

Facilities include a clubhouse, a driving range, two putting greens, a pro shop, lockers, and lessons. Beware of weekend crowds.

On Makena Alanui Dr., just past the Maui Prince Hotel. © 808/879-3344. www.maui.net/~makena/. Greens fees: North Course $170 ($95–$140 for Makena Resort guests), twilight fees (after 2pm) are $95 ($80 for guests); South Course $180 ($105–$150 for resort guests), twilight fees (after 2pm) are $105 ($90 for guests). Guest rates vary seasonally, with higher rates in the winter.

Wailea Courses 🏌️🏌️   There are three courses to choose from at Wailea. The **Blue Course,** a par-72, 6,758-yard course designed by Arthur Jack Snyder and dotted with bunkers and water hazards, is for duffers and pros alike. The wide fairways appeal to beginners, while the undulating terrain makes it a course everyone can enjoy. A little more difficult is the par-72, 7,078-yard championship **Gold Course,** with narrow fairways, several tricky dogleg holes, and the classic Robert Trent Jones, Jr. challenges: natural hazards, like lava-rock walls, and native Hawaiian grasses. The **Emerald Course,** also designed by Robert Trent Jones, Jr., is Wailea's newest, with tropical landscaping and a player-friendly design.

With 54 holes to play, getting a tee time is slightly easier on weekends than at other resorts, but weekdays are best (the Emerald Course is usually the toughest to book). Facilities include two pro shops, restaurants, locker rooms, and a complete golf training facility.

Wailea Alanui Dr. (off Wailea Iki Dr.), Wailea. © 888/328-MAUI or 808/875-7450. www.waileagolf.com. Greens fees: Blue Course $175 ($135 resort guests), twilight $100 ($90 resort guests); Gold Course $185 ($145 resort guests); Emerald Course $185 ($145 resort guests).

UPCOUNTRY MAUI
Pukalani Country Club   This cool, par-72, 6,962-yard course at 1,100 feet offers a break from the resorts' high greens fees, and it's really fun to play. The 3rd hole offers golfers two different options: a tough iron shot from the tee (especially into the wind), across a gully (yuck!) to the green; or a shot down the side of the gully across a second green into sand traps below. (Most people choose to shoot down the side of the gully; it's actually easier than shooting across a ravine.) High handicappers will love this course, and more experienced players can make it more challenging by playing from the back tees. Facilities include club and shoe rentals, practice areas, lockers, a pro shop, and a restaurant.

360 Pukalani St., Pukalani. © 808/572-1314. www.pukalanigolf.com. Greens fees, including cart, are $60 for 18 holes before 11am; $55 11am–2pm; $45 after 2pm; 9-holes is $35. Take the Hana Hwy. (Hwy. 36) to Haleakala Hwy. (Hwy. 37) to the Pukalani exit; turn right onto Pukalani St. and go 2 blocks.

BICYCLING
If you want to venture out on your own, cheap rentals—$10 a day for cruisers and $20 a day for mountain bikes—are available from the **Activity Warehouse** (© 800/343-2087; www.travelhawaii.com), which has branches in Lahaina at 602 Front St., near Prison Street (© 808/667-4000), and in Kihei at Azeka Place II, on the mountain side of Kihei Road near Lipoa Street (© 808/875-4000).

For information on bikeways and maps, check out **www.bikehawaii.com** or get a copy of the *Maui County Bicycle Map,* which has information on road suitability, climate, mileage, elevation changes, bike shops, safety tips, and various bicycling routes. The map is available for $7.50 ($6.25 for the map and $1.25 for postage), bank checks or money orders only, from **Tri Isle R, C, and D Council,** Attn: Bike Map Project, 200 Imi Kala St., Suite 208, Wailuku, HI 96793.

CRUISING HALEAKALA ⭐

It's not even close to dawn, but here you are, rubbing your eyes awake, riding in a van up the long, dark road to the top of Maui's sleeping volcano. It's colder than you ever thought possible for a tropical island. The air is thin. You stomp your chilly feet while you wait, sipping hot coffee. Then comes the sun, exploding over the yawning Haleakala Crater, big enough to swallow Manhattan—a mystic moment you won't soon forget. Now you know why Hawaiians named the crater the House of the Sun. But there's no time to linger: Decked out in your screaming-yellow parka, you mount your mechanical steed and test its most important feature, the brakes—because you're about to coast 37 miles down a 10,000-foot volcano.

Cruising down Haleakala, from the lunarlike landscape at the top past flower farms, pineapple fields, and eucalyptus groves, is quite an experience—and just about any-body can do it. This is a safe, no-strain bicycle trip that requires some stamina in the colder, wetter winter months but is fun for everyone in the warmer months—the key word being *warmer.* In winter and the rainy season, conditions can be harsh, especially on the top, with below-freezing temperatures and 40 mph winds.

(Kids) Especially for Kids

Taking a Submarine Ride (p. 294)   Atlantis Submarines takes you and the kids down into the shallow coastal waters off Lahaina in a real sub, where you'll see plenty of fish (and maybe even a shark!). They'll love it, and you'll stay dry the entire time.

Riding the Sugarcane Train   This ride will appeal to small kids as well as train buffs of all ages. A steam engine pulls open passenger cars of the Lahaina/Kaanapali & Pacific Railroad on a 30-minute, 12-mile round-trip through sugar cane fields between Lahaina and Kaanapali. The conductor sings and calls out the landmarks, and along the way, you can see Molokai, Lanai, and the backside of Kaanapali. Tickets are $16 for adults, $8.75 for kids ages 3 to 12; call (C) **808/661-0089.**

Searching for Stars   After sunset, the stars over Kaanapali shine big and bright, because the tropical sky is almost pollutant-free and no big-city lights interfere with the cosmic view. Amateur astronomers can probe the Milky Way, see the rings of Saturn and Jupiter's moons, and scan the Sea of Tranquility in a 60-minute star search on the world's first recreational, computer-driven telescope. This cosmic adventure takes place nightly at the **Hyatt Regency Maui,** 200 Nohea Kai Dr. ((C) **808/661-1234**), at 8, 9, and 10pm. If you are staying at the hotel, it is $20 for adults and $10 for children under 12; for non-guests it's $25 for adults and $15 for children.

Getting a Dragonfly's View (p. 429)   Kids will think this is too much fun to be educational. Don a face mask and get the dizzying perspective of what a dragonfly sees as it flies over a mountain stream, or watch the tiny oopu fish climb up a stream at the **Hawaii Nature Center** ((C) **808/244-6500**) in beautiful Iao Valley, where you'll find some 30 hands-on, interactive exhibits and displays of Hawaii's natural history.

Maui's oldest downhill company is **Maui Downhill** ℱ (© **800/535-BIKE** or 808/871-2155; www.mauidownhill.com), which offers a sunrise safari bike tour, including continental breakfast and brunch, starting at $150 (book online and save $48). If it's all booked up, try **Maui Mountain Cruisers** (© **800/232-6284** or 808/871-6014; www.mauimountaincruisers.com), which has sunrise trips at $130 (book online and save $35), or **Mountain Riders Bike Tours** (© **800/706-7700** or 808/242-9739; www.mountainriders.com), with sunrise rides for $115 (book online and save $17). All rates include hotel pickup, transport to the top, bicycle, safety equipment, and meals. Wear layers of warm clothing—there may be a 30°F (16°C) change in temperature from the top of the mountain to the ocean.

If you want to avoid the crowd, call **Haleakala Bike Company** (© **888/922-2453;** www.bikemaui.com), which will outfit you with the latest gear and take you up the mountain (sometimes to the top, sometimes not, be sure to ask where you will be dropped off), but, after making sure you are secure on the bike, will let you ride down by yourself at your own pace. Trips range from $65 to $85; they also have bicycle rentals to tour other parts of Maui on your own.

HORSEBACK RIDING

Maui offers spectacular adventure rides through rugged ranchlands, into tropical forests, and to remote swimming holes. One of our favorites is **Piiholo Ranch,** in Makawao (© **866/572-5544** or 808/357-5544; www.piiholo.com). A working cattle ranch, owned by the *kamaaina* (long-time resident) Baldwin family, this is a horseback-riding adventure with a variety of different rides to suit your ability; from the morning picnic ride, a 3½-hour ride on the ranch and a picnic lunch for $160 per person to private rides, including working with the cowboys to round up the cattle, at $190 per person, per hour.

If you're out in Hana, don't pass up the **Maui Stables** ℱℱ, in Kipahulu, a mile past Oheo Gulch (© **808/248-7799;** www.mauistables.com). Not only do they offer two rides daily (9:30am and 1pm) through the mountains above Kipahulu Valley, but you also get a fantastic historical and cultural tour through the unspoiled landscape. It is an experience you will not forget. Both rides are $150. If you enjoy your ride, remember to kiss your horse and tip your guide.

For those horse lovers who are looking for the ultimate encounter, check out Frank Levinson's **Maui Horse Whisperer Experience** (© **808/572-6211;** www.mauihorses.com), which includes a seminar on the language of the horse, $200 for half-day and $300 for full-day workshops. No horse aficionado should pass it up.

Again, if you enjoy your ride, remember to kiss your horse and tip your guide.

HALEAKALA ON HORSEBACK If you'd like to ride down into Haleakala's crater, contact **Pony Express Tours** ℱ (© **808/667-2200** or 808/878-6698; www.ponyexpresstours.com), which offers a variety of rides down to the crater floor and back up, from $155 to $190 per person. Shorter 1- and 2-hour rides are also offered at Haleakala Ranch, located on the beautiful lower slopes of the volcano, for $95 and $115. If you book via the Internet, you get 10% off. Pony Express provides well-trained horses and experienced guides, and accommodates all riding levels. You must be at least 10 years old, weigh no more than 230 pounds, and wear long pants and closed-toe shoes.

WAY OUT WEST ON MAUI: RANCH RIDES We recommend riding with **Mendes Ranch & Trail Rides** ℱ, 3530 Kahekili Hwy., 4 miles past Wailuku

(© **808/244-7320**). The 300-acre Mendes Ranch is a real-life working cowboy ranch complete with rainbows, waterfalls, palm trees, coral-sand beaches, lagoons, tide pools, a rainforest, and its own volcanic peak (more than a mile high). Allan Mendes, a third-generation wrangler, will take you from the edge of the rainforest out to the sea. On the way, you'll cross tree-studded meadows, where Texas longhorns sit in the shade, and pass a dusty corral, where Allan's father, Ernest, a champion roper, may be breaking in a wild horse. Allan keeps close watch, turning often in his saddle to make sure everyone is happy. He points out flora and fauna and fields questions, but generally just lets you soak up Maui's natural splendor in golden silence. The morning ride, which lasts 3 hours and ends with a barbecue back at the corral (the perfect ranch-style lunch after a morning in the saddle), is $130; the 2½-hour afternoon ride costs $85, including snacks.

SPELUNKING

Don't miss the opportunity to see how the Hawaiian Islands were made by exploring a million-year-old underground lava tube/cave. Chuck Thorne, of **Maui Cave Adventures** ★ (© **808/248-7308;** www.mauicave.com), offers several tours of this unique geological feature. After more than 10 years of leading scuba tours through underwater caves around Hawaii, Chuck discovered some caves on land that he wanted to show visitors. When the land surrounding the largest cave on Maui went on the market in 1996, Chuck snapped it up and started his own tour company. The shortest (and cheapest) tour is a self-guided 30- to 45-minute tour for just $12, and kids as young as 6 years old can do it. His 75-minute walking tour ($29; no children under 6) is a fun, safe, and easy stroll through a huge, extinct lava tube with 40-foot ceilings. This is a geology lesson you won't soon forget—Chuck is a longtime student of the science of volcano-speleology and can discuss every little formation in the cave. He supplies all the equipment you'll need: lights, hard hats, gloves, and water bottles. For those looking for a longer experience, his "Wild Adventure Tours" are 2½ hours and cost $79 (no one under 15). Wear long pants and closed shoes, and bring your camera.

TENNIS

Maui has excellent public tennis courts; all are free and available from daylight to sunset (a few are even lit for night play until 10pm). The courts are available on a first-come, first-served basis; when someone's waiting, limit your play to 45 minutes. For a complete list of public courts, call **Maui County Department of Parks and Recreation** (© **808/243-7230**). Most public courts require a wait and are not conveniently located near the major resort areas, so most visitors are likely to play at their own hotels for a fee. The exceptions to that caveat are in Kihei (which has courts in Kalama Park on South Kihei Rd., and in Waipualani Park on West Waipualani Rd., behind the Maui Sunset Condo), in Lahaina (courts are in Malu'uou o lele Park, at Front and Shaw sts.), and Hana (courts are in Hana Park, on the Hana Hwy.).

Private tennis courts are available at most resorts and hotels on the island. The **Kapalua Tennis Garden and Village Tennis Center,** Kapalua Resort (© **808/669-5677;** www.kapaluamaui.com), is home to the Kapalua Open, which features the largest purse in the state, and is played on Labor Day weekend. Court rentals are $10 an hour for resort guests and $12 an hour for non-guests. The staff will match you up with a partner if you need one. In Wailea, try the **Wailea Tennis Club,** 131 Wailea Iki Place (© **808/879-1958**), with 11 Plexipave courts. Court fees are $12 per player.

9 Seeing the Sights

CENTRAL MAUI

Central Maui isn't exactly tourist central; this is where real people live. Most likely, you'll land here and head directly to the beach. However, there are a few sights worth checking out if you feel like a respite from the sun 'n' surf.

KAHULUI

Under the airport flight path, next to Maui's busiest intersection and across from Costco and Kmart in Kahului's new business park, is a most unlikely place: the **Kanaha Wildlife Sanctuary,** Haleakala Highway Extension and Hana Highway (© 808/984-8100). Look for the parking area off Haleakala Highway Extension (behind the mall, across the Hana Hwy. from Cutter Automotive), and you'll find a 50-yard trail that meanders along the shore to a shade shelter and lookout. Look for the sign proclaiming this the permanent home of the endangered black-neck Hawaiian stilt, whose population is now down to about 1,000. Naturalists say this is a good place to see endangered Hawaiian Koloa ducks, stilts, coots, and other migrating shorebirds. For a quieter, more natural-looking wildlife preserve, see the **Kealia Pond National Wildlife Preserve** in Kihei (see below).

WAILUKU & WAIKAPU

Wailuku, the historic gateway to Iao Valley, is worth a visit for a little antiquing and a visit to the **Bailey House Museum** ✶, 2375–A Main St. (© 808/244-3326). Missionary and sugar planter Edward Bailey's 1833 home—an architectural hybrid of stones laid by Hawaiian craftsmen and timbers joined in a display of Yankee ingenuity—is a treasure trove of Hawaiiana. Inside, you'll find an eclectic collection, from precontact artifacts like scary temple images, dogtooth necklaces, and a rare lei, made of tree snail shells, to latter-day relics like Duke Kahanamoku's 1919 redwood surfboard and a koa-wood table given to U.S. President Ulysses S. Grant, who had to refuse it because he couldn't accept gifts from foreign countries. There's also a gallery devoted to a few of Bailey's landscapes, painted from 1866 to 1896, which capture on canvas a Maui we can only imagine today. It's open Monday through Saturday from 10am to 4pm; admission is $5 for adults, $4 for seniors, and $1 for children ages 6 to 12; children under 6 are free.

About 3 miles south of Wailuku lies the tiny, one-street village of Waikapu, which has two attractions that are worth a peek. Relive Maui's past by taking a 40-minute narrated tram ride around fields of pineapple, sugarcane, and papaya trees at **Maui Tropical Plantation,** 1670 Honoapiilani Hwy. (© 800/451-6805 or 808/244-7643; www.mauitropicalplantation.com), a real working plantation open daily from 9am to 5pm. A shop sells fresh and dried fruit, and a restaurant serves lunch. Admission is free; the tram tours, which start at 10am and leave about every 45 minutes, are $9.50 for adults, $3.50 for kids ages 3 to 12.

Marilyn Monroe and Frank Lloyd Wright meet for dinner every night at one of Maui's most unusual buildings, the **Waikapu Golf and Country Club,** 2500 Honoapiilani Hwy. (© 808/244-2011). Neither actually set foot on Maui, but these icons of architecture and glamour share a Hawaiian legacy. Wright designed this place for a Pennsylvania family in 1949, but it was never constructed. In 1957, Marilyn and her husband, Arthur Miller, wanted it built for them in Connecticut, but they separated the following year. When Tokyo billionaire Takeshi Sekiguchi went shopping at

Taliesen West for a signature building to adorn his 18-hole golf course, he found the blueprints and had Marilyn's Wright house cleverly redesigned as a clubhouse. A horizontal in a vertical landscape, it doesn't quite fit the setting, but it's still the best-looking building on Maui today.

IAO VALLEY ☆

A couple of miles north of Wailuku, where the little plantation houses stop and the road climbs ever higher, Maui's true nature begins to reveal itself. The transition from suburban sprawl to raw nature is so abrupt that most people who drive up into the valley don't realize they're suddenly in a rainforest. After the hot tropic sun, the air is moist and cool, and the shade a welcome comfort. This is Iao Valley, a 6.2-acre state park whose great nature, history, and beauty have been enjoyed by millions of people from around the world for more than a century. Iao ("Supreme Light") Valley, 10 miles long and encompassing 4,000 acres, is the eroded volcanic caldera of the West Maui Mountains. The head of the valley is a broad circular amphitheater where four major streams converge into Iao Stream. At the back of the amphitheater is rain-drenched Puu Kukui, the West Maui Mountains' highest point. No other Hawaiian valley lets you go from seacoast to rainforest so easily. This peaceful valley, full of tropical plants, rainbows, waterfalls, swimming holes, and hiking trails, is a place of solitude, reflection, and escape for residents and visitors alike.

To get here from Wailuku, take Main Street to Iao Valley Road to the entrance to the state park.

Two paved walkways loop into the massive green amphitheater, across the bridge of Iao Valley Stream, and along the stream itself. This paved, one-third-mile loop is Maui's easiest hike—you can take your grandmother on this one. The leisurely walk will allow you to enjoy lovely views of the Iao Needle and the lush vegetation. Others often proceed beyond the state park border and take two trails deeper into the valley, but the trails enter private land, and NO TRESPASSING signs are posted.

The feature known as **Iao Needle** is an erosional remnant consisting of basalt dikes. This phallic rock juts an impressive 2,250 feet above sea level. Youngsters play in **Iao Stream,** a peaceful brook that belies its bloody history. In 1790, King Kamehameha the Great and his men engaged in the bloody battle of Iao Valley to gain control of Maui. When the battle ended, so many bodies blocked Iao Stream that the battle site was named Kepaniwai, or "damming of the waters." An architectural heritage park of Hawaiian, Japanese, Chinese, Filipino, and New England–style houses stands in harmony by Iao Stream at **Kepaniwai Heritage Garden.** This is a good picnic spot, with plenty of tables and benches. You can see ferns, banana trees, and other native and exotic plants in the **Iao Valley Botanic Garden** along the stream.

WHEN TO GO   The park is open daily from 7am to 7pm. Go early in the morning or late in the afternoon, when the sun's rays slant into the valley and create a mystical mood. You can bring a picnic and spend the day, but be prepared at any time for a tropical cloudburst, which often soaks the valley and swells both waterfalls and streams.

INFORMATION & VISITOR CENTERS   For information, contact **Iao Valley State Park,** State Parks and Recreation, 54 High St., Room 101, Wailuku, HI 96793 (© **808/984-8100**). The **Hawaii Nature Center,** 875 Iao Valley Rd. (© **808/244-6500;** www.hawaiinaturecenter.org), home to the Iao Valley Nature Center, features hands-on, interactive exhibits and displays relating the story of Hawaiian natural history;

it's an important stop for all who want to explore Iao Valley. Hours are daily from 10am to 4pm; admission is $6 for adults and $4 for children ages 4 to 12.

WEST MAUI
HISTORIC LAHAINA

Back when "there was no God west of the Horn," Lahaina was the capital of Hawaii and the Pacific's wildest port. Today, it's a milder version of its old self—mostly a hustle-bustle of whale art, timeshares, and "Just Got Lei'd" T-shirts. We're not sure the rowdy whalers would be pleased. But if you look hard, you'll still find the historic port town they loved, filled with the kind of history that inspired James Michener to write his best-selling epic novel *Hawaii*.

See the map of Lahaina on p. 356.

Baldwin Home Museum ⭐   The oldest house in Lahaina, this coral-and-rock structure was built in 1834 by Rev. Dwight Baldwin, a doctor with the fourth company of American missionaries to sail 'round the Horn to Hawaii. Like many missionaries, he came to Hawaii to do good—and did very well for himself. After 17 years of service, Baldwin was granted 2,600 acres in Kapalua for farming and grazing. His ranch manager experimented with what Hawaiians called *hala-kahiki,* or pineapple, on a 4-acre plot; the rest is history. The house looks as if Baldwin has just stepped out for a minute to tend a sick neighbor down the street.

Next door is the **Master's Reading Room,** Maui's oldest building. This became visiting sea captains' favorite hangout once the missionaries closed down all of Lahaina's grog shops and banned prostitution. By 1844, once hotels and bars started reopening, it lost its appeal. It's now the headquarters of the **Lahaina Restoration Foundation** (© **808/661-3262**), a plucky band of historians who try to keep this town alive and antique at the same time. Stop in and pick up a self-guided walking-tour map, which will take you to Lahaina's most historic sites.

120 Dickenson St. (at Front St.). © **808/661-3262**. Admission $3 adults, $2 seniors, $5 family. Daily 10am–4:30pm.

Banyan Tree   Of all the banyan trees in Hawaii, this is the greatest of all—so big that you can't get it in your camera's viewfinder. It was only 8 feet tall when it was planted in 1873 by Maui Sheriff William O. Smith to mark the 50th anniversary of Lahaina's first Christian mission. Today, the big old banyan from India is more than 50 feet tall, has 12 major trunks, and shades two-thirds of an acre in Courthouse Square.

At the Courthouse Building, 649 Wharf St.

Maluuluolele Park   At first glance, this Front Street park appears to be only a hot, dry, dusty softball field. But under home plate is an edge of Mokuula, where a royal compound once stood more than 100 years ago, now buried under tons of red dirt and sand. Here, Prince Kauikeaolui, who ascended the throne as King Kamehameha III when he was only 10, lived with the love of his life, his sister, Princess Nahienaena. Missionaries took a dim view of incest, which was acceptable to Hawaiian nobles in order to preserve the royal bloodline. Torn between love for her brother and the new Christian morality, Nahienaena grew despondent and died at the age of 21. King Kamehameha III, who reigned for 29 years—longer than any other Hawaiian monarch—presided over Hawaii as it went from kingdom to constitutional monarchy, and as power over the islands shifted from island nobles to missionaries, merchants, and sugar planters. Kamehameha died in 1854; he was 39. In 1918, his royal compound, containing a mausoleum and artifacts of the kingdom, was demolished and covered with dirt to create a public park. The baseball team from Lahainaluna School, the first American school founded by missionaries west of the Rockies, now plays games on the site of this royal place, still considered sacred to many Hawaiians.

Front and Shaw sts.

A WHALE OF A PLACE IN KAANAPALI

If you haven't seen a real whale yet, go to **Whalers Village,** 2435 Kaanapali Pkwy., an oceanfront shopping center that has adopted the whale as its mascot. You can't miss it: A huge, almost life-size metal sculpture of a mother whale and two nursing whalettes greets you. A few more steps, and you're met by the looming, bleached-white bony skeleton of a 40-foot sperm whale; it's pretty impressive.

On the second floor of the mall is the **Whale Center of the Pacific** (© **808/661-5992**), a museum celebrating the "Golden Era of Whaling" (1825–60). Harpoons and scrimshaw are on display; the museum has even re-created the cramped quarters of a whaler's seagoing vessel. Open during mall hours, daily from 9:30am to 10pm; admission is free.

KAPALUA

For generations, West Maui meant one thing: pineapple. Hawaii's only pineapple cannery today, **Maui Pineapple Co.,** offers tours of its plantation through the Kapalua Resort Activity Center (© **808/669-8088**). Real plantation workers lead the 2½-hour tours. You'll learn about the history of West Maui, facts about growing and harvesting pineapple, and lots of trivia about plantation life; you can even pick and harvest your own pineapple. The tour, which departs from the Kapalua Villas Reception Center, 500 Office Rd., is offered twice daily Monday through Friday. It costs $29; children must be at least 12.

THE SCENIC ROUTE TO WEST MAUI: THE KAHEKILI HIGHWAY

The usual road to West Maui from Wailuku is the Honoapiilani Highway, which takes you across the isthmus to Maalaea and around to Lahaina, Kaapanali, and Kapalua. But those wanting a back-to-nature driving experience should go the other way, along the **Kahekili Highway** (Hwy. 340). (*Highway* is a bit of a euphemism for this paved but somewhat precarious road.)

Drive north from Wailuku to Waiehu and onto this road named for King Kahekili, who built houses out of the skulls of his enemies. The true wild nature of Maui is on full display here. The narrow and winding road weaves for 20 miles along an ancient Hawaiian coastal footpath to Honokohau Bay, at the island's northernmost tip, past blowholes, sea stacks, seabird rookeries, and the imposing 636-foot Kahakaloa headland. On the land side, you'll pass high cliffs, deep valleys dotted with plantation houses, cattle grazing on green plateaus, old wooden churches, taro fields, and houses hung with fishing nets. It's slow going (you can drive only about 10 mph along the road), but it's probably the most beautiful drive in Maui. Your rental-car company might try to deter you, but it's not really a hard drive (don't go if it has been raining), and the views are spectacular.

At Honokohau, pick up Highway 30 and continue on to the West Maui resorts; the first one you'll reach is Kapalua (above).

SOUTH MAUI
MAALAEA
Maui Ocean Center 🎯🎯 *Kids*   This 5-acre facility houses the largest aquarium in Hawaii and features one of Hawaii's largest predators: the tiger shark. Exhibits are geared toward the residents of Hawaii's ocean waters. As you walk past the three dozen or so tanks and countless exhibits, you'll slowly descend from the "beach" to the deepest part of the ocean, without ever getting wet. Start at the surge pool, where you'll see shallow-water marine life like spiny urchins and cauliflower coral, then move on to the reef tanks, turtle pool, "touch" pool (with starfish and urchins), and eagle-ray pool before reaching the star of the show: the 100-foot-long, 600,000-gallon main tank featuring tiger, gray, and white-tip sharks, as well as tuna, surgeonfish, triggerfish, and numerous other tropicals. The most phenomenal thing about this tank is that the walkway goes right through it—so you'll be surrounded on three sides by marine creatures. A very cool place, and well worth the time. Some new additions are a hammerhead exhibit where juvenile scalloped hammerhead sharks are on display and the Shark Dive Maui Program, where certified SCUBA divers plunge into the aquarium with sharks, stingrays and tropical fish (yes, you too can dive with sharks), while friends and family watch safely from the other side of the glass. *Helpful hint:* Buy your tickets online and bypass the long admission lines.

Maalaea Harbor Village, 192 Maalaea Rd. (the triangle between Honoapiilani Hwy. and Maalaea Rd.) 🅒 808/270-7000. www.mauioceancenter.com. Admission $21 adults, $18 seniors, $14 children 3–12. Daily 9am–5pm (until 6pm July–Aug).

KIHEI
Captain George Vancouver "discovered" Kihei in 1778, when it was only a collection of fishermen's grass shacks on the hot, dry, dusty coast (hard to believe, eh?). A **totem pole** stands today where he's believed to have landed, across from Aston Maui Lu Resort, 575 S. Kihei Rd. Vancouver sailed on to "discover" British Columbia, where a great international city and harbor now bear his name.

West of the junction of Piilani Highway (Hwy. 31) and Mokulele Highway (Hwy. 350) is **Kealia Pond National Wildlife Preserve** (🅒 **808/875-1582**), a 700-acre U.S. Fish and Wildlife wetland preserve where endangered Hawaiian stilts, coots, and ducks hang out and splash. These ponds work two ways: as bird preserves and as sedimentation basins that keep the coral reefs from silting from runoff. You can take a self-guided tour along a boardwalk dotted with interpretive signs and shade shelters, through sand dunes, and around ponds to Maalaea Harbor. The boardwalk starts at the outlet of Kealia Pond on the ocean side of North Kihei Road (near mile marker 2 on Piilani Hwy.). Among the Hawaiian waterbirds seen here are the black-crowned high heron, Hawaiian coot, Hawaiian duck, and Hawaiian stilt. There are also shorebirds like sanderlings, Pacific golden plovers, ruddy turnstones, and wandering tattlers. From July to December, the hawksbill turtle comes ashore here to lay her eggs.

WAILEA
The best way to explore this golden resort coast is to rise with the sun and head for Wailea's 1½-mile **coastal nature trail** 🎯, stretching between the Kea Lani Hotel and the kiawe thicket just beyond the Renaissance Wailea. It's a great morning walk, a serpentine path that meanders uphill and down past native plants, old Hawaiian habitats, and a billion dollars' worth of luxury hotels. You can pick up the trail at any of the resorts or from clearly marked SHORELINE ACCESS points along the coast. The best

time to go is when you first wake up; by midmorning, the coastal trail is too often clogged with pushy joggers, and it grows crowded with beachgoers as the day wears on. As the path crosses several bold, black-lava points, it affords new vistas of islands and ocean; benches allow you to pause and contemplate the view across Alalakeiki Channel, which jumps with whales in season. Sunset is another good time to hit the trail.

MAKENA

A few miles south of Wailea, the manicured coast turns to wilderness; now you're in Makena. Once cattle were driven down the slope from upland ranches, lashed to rafts, and sent into the water to swim to boats that waited to take them to market. Now, **Makena Landing** ⚐ is the best place to launch kayaks bound for La Pérouse Bay and Ahihi-Kinau preserve.

From the landing, go south on Makena Road; on the right is **Keawali Congregational Church** (☏ 808/879-5557), built in 1855, with walls 3 feet thick. Surrounded by ti leaves, which, by Hawaiian custom, provide protection, and built of lava rock with coral used as mortar, this church sits on its own cove with a gold-sand beach. It always attracts a Sunday crowd for its 9:30am Hawaiian-language service.

A little farther south on the coast is **La Pérouse Monument,** a pyramid of lava rocks that marks the spot where French explorer Admiral Comte de la Pérouse set foot on Maui in 1786. The first Westerner to "discover" the island, he described the "burning climate" of the leeward coast, observed several fishing villages near Kihei, and sailed on into oblivion, never to be seen again; some believe he may have been eaten by cannibals in what now is Vanuatu. To get here, drive south past Puu Olai to Ahihi Bay, where the road turns to gravel. Go another 2 miles along the coast to La Pérouse Bay; the monument sits amid a clearing in black lava at the end of the dirt road.

HOUSE OF THE SUN: HALEAKALA NATIONAL PARK ★★★

At once forbidding and compelling, Haleakala ("House of the Sun") National Park is Maui's main natural attraction. More than 1.3 million people a year go up the 10,023-foot-high mountain to peer down into the crater of the world's largest dormant volcano. (Haleakala is officially considered active, even though it has not rumbled since 1790.) That hole would hold Manhattan.

But there's more to do here than just stare into a big black hole: Just going up the mountain is an experience. Where else on the planet can you climb from sea level to 10,000 feet in just 37 miles, or a 2-hour drive? The snaky road passes through big, puffy, cumulus clouds to offer magnificent views of the isthmus of Maui, the West Maui Mountains, and the Pacific Ocean.

Many drive up to the summit in predawn darkness to watch the **sun rise over Haleakala** ★★; others coast down the 37-mile road from the summit on a bicycle with special brakes (see "Bicycling," p. 424). Hardy adventurers hike and camp inside the crater's wilderness (see "Hiking & Camping," p. 417). Those bound for the interior should bring their survival gear, for the terrain is raw, rugged, and punishing—not unlike the moon.

JUST THE FACTS

Haleakala National Park extends from the summit of Mount Haleakala down the volcano's southeast flank to Maui's eastern coast, beyond Hana. There are actually two separate and distinct destinations within the park: **Haleakala Summit** and the

Kipahulu coast (see "Tropical Haleakala: Oheo Gulch at Kipahulu," p. 442). The summit gets all the publicity, but Kipahulu draws crowds, too—it's lush, green, and tropical, and home to Oheo Gulch (also known as Seven Sacred Pools). No road links the summit and the coast; you have to approach them separately, and you need at least a day to see each place.

WHEN TO GO   At the 10,023-foot summit, weather changes fast. With wind chill, temperatures can be freezing any time of year. Summer can be dry and warm; winter can be wet, windy, and cold. Before you go, get current weather conditions from the park (© **808/572-4400**) or the **National Weather Service** (© **808/871-5054**).

From sunrise to noon, the light is weak, but the view is usually free of clouds. The best time for photos is in the afternoon, when the sun lights the crater and clouds are few. Go on full-moon nights for spectacular viewing.

But this is Mother Nature, not Disneyland, so there are no guarantees or schedules. Especially in winter, some mornings may be misty or rainy, and sunrise viewing may be obscured. It's the luck of the draw.

ACCESS POINTS   Haleakala Summit is 37 miles, or a 1½- to 2-hour drive, from Kahului. To get here, take Highway 37 to Highway 377 to Highway 378. For details on the drive, see "The Drive to the Summit," below. Pukalani is the last town for water, food, and gas.

The **Kipahulu** section of Haleakala National Park is on Maui's east end near Hana, 60 miles from Kahului on Highway 36 (Hana Hwy.). Due to traffic and rough road conditions, plan on 4 hours for the drive, one-way. For complete information, see "The Road to Hana" (see p. 437) and "Tropical Haleakala: Oheo Gulch at Kipahulu" on p. 442.

At both entrances to the park, the admission fee is $5 per person or $10 per car, good for a week of unlimited entry.

INFORMATION, VISITOR CENTERS & RANGER PROGRAMS   For information before you go, contact **Haleakala National Park,** Box 369, Makawao, HI 96768 (© **808/572-4400;** www.nps.gov/hale).

At 7,000 feet, 1 mile from the park entrance, is **Haleakala National Park Headquarters** (© **808/572-4400**); open daily from 7:30am to 4pm. Stop here to pick up information on park programs and activities, get camping permits, and, occasionally, see a Hawaiian nene bird. Restrooms, a pay phone, and drinking water are available.

The **Haleakala Visitor Center,** open daily from sunrise to 3pm, is near the summit, 11 miles past the park entrance. It offers a panoramic view of the volcanic landscape, with photos identifying the various features, and exhibits that explain the area's history, ecology, geology, and vulcanology. Park staff members are often on hand to answer questions. Restrooms and water are available.

Rangers offer excellent, informative, and free **naturalist talks** at 9:30, 10:30, and 11:30am daily in the summit building. For information on **hiking** and **camping** possibilities, including wilderness cabins and campgrounds, see "Hiking & Camping" on p. 417.

THE DRIVE TO THE SUMMIT

If you look on a Maui map, almost in the middle of the part that resembles a torso, there's a black, wiggly line that looks like this: WWWWWW. That's **Highway 378,** also known as **Haleakala Crater Road**—one of the fastest-ascending roads in the world. This grand corniche has at least 33 switchbacks; passes through numerous climate

Tips   Descending from the Crater

When driving down the Haleakala Crater Road, be sure to put your car in low gear; that way, you won't destroy your brakes by riding them the whole way down.

zones; goes under, in, and out of clouds; takes you past rare silversword plants and endangered Hawaiian geese sailing through the clear, thin air; and offers a view that extends for more than 100 miles.

Going to the summit takes 1½ to 2 hours from Kahului. No matter where you start out, you'll follow Highway 37 (Haleakala Hwy.) to Pukalani, where you'll pick up Highway 377 (aka Haleakala Hwy.), which you'll take to Highway 378. Along the way, expect fog, rain, and wind. You may encounter stray cattle and downhill bicyclists. Fill up your gas tank before you go—the only gas available is 27 miles below the summit at Pukalani. There are no facilities beyond the ranger stations—not even a coffee urn in sight. Bring your own food and water.

Remember, you're entering a high-altitude wilderness area. Some people get dizzy due to the lack of oxygen; you might also suffer lightheadedness, shortness of breath, nausea, or worse: severe headaches, flatulence, and dehydration. People with asthma, pregnant women, heavy smokers, and those with heart conditions should be especially careful in the rarefied air. Bring water and a jacket or a blanket, especially if you go up for sunrise. Or you might want to go up to the summit for sunset, which is also spectacular.

At the **park entrance,** you'll pay an entrance fee of $10 per car (or $2 for a bicycle). About a mile from the entrance is **Park Headquarters,** where an endangered **nene,** or Hawaiian goose, may greet you with its unique call. With its black face, buff cheeks, and partially webbed feet, the gray-brown bird looks like a small Canada goose with zebra stripes; it brays out "nay-nay" (thus its name), doesn't migrate, and prefers lava beds to lakes. More than 25,000 nenes once inhabited Hawaii, but habitat destruction and predators (hunters, pigs, feral cats and dogs, and mongooses) nearly caused their extinction. By 1951, there were only 30 left. Now protected as Hawaii's state bird, the number of wild nene on Haleakala numbers fewer than 250—the species remains endangered.

Beyond headquarters are **two scenic overlooks** on the way to the summit; stop at Leleiwi on the way up and Kalahaku on the way back down, if only to get out, stretch, and get accustomed to the heights. Take a deep breath, look around, and pop your ears. If you feel dizzy or drowsy or get a sudden headache, consider turning around and going back down.

Leleiwi Overlook ✦ is just beyond mile marker 17. From the parking area, a short trail leads you to a panoramic view of the lunarlike crater. When the clouds are low and the sun is in the right place, usually around sunset, you may experience a phenomenon known as the "Specter of the Brocken"—you can see a reflection of your shadow, ringed by a rainbow, in the clouds below. It's an optical illusion caused by a rare combination of sun, shadow, and fog that occurs in only three places on the planet: Haleakala, Scotland, and Germany.

The best place to see a rare **silversword** is 2 miles farther along **Kalahaku Overlook** ✦. You can turn into this overlook only when you are descending from the top. The silversword is the punk of the plant world, its silvery bayonets displaying tiny, purple bouquets—like a spacey artichoke with attitude. This botanical wonder proved irresistible to humans, who gathered them in gunnysacks for Chinese potions, British specimen collections, and just for the sheer thrill of having something so rare. Silverswords grow only in Hawaii, take from 4 to 50 years to bloom, and then, usually between May and October, send up a 1- to 6-foot stalk with a purple bouquet of sunflower-like blooms. They're now very rare, so don't even think about taking one home.

Continue on, and you'll quickly reach **Haleakala Visitor Center,** which offers spectacular views. You'll feel as if you're at the edge of the earth. But don't turn around here; the actual summit's a little farther on, at **Puu Ulaula Overlook** 🐝🐝🐝 (also known as Red Hill), the volcano's highest point, where you'll find a mysterious cluster of buildings officially known as Haleakala Observatories, but unofficially called **Science City.** If you go up for sunrise, the building at Puu Ulaula Overlook, a triangle of glass that serves as a windbreak, is the best viewing spot. After the daily miracle of sunrise—the sun seems to rise out of the vast ocean (hence the name "House of the Sun")—you can see all the way across Alenuihaha Channel to the often snowcapped summit of Mauna Kea on the Big Island.

UPCOUNTRY MAUI

Come upcountry and discover a different side of Maui: On the slopes of Haleakala, cowboys, planters, and other country people make their homes in serene, neighborly communities like **Makawao** and **Kula,** a world away from the bustling beach resorts. Even if you can't spare a day or two in the cool, upcountry air, there are some sights that are worth a look on your way to or from the crater. Shoppers and gallery hoppers might want to spend more time here; see section 10 of this chapter.

See the "Upcountry Maui" map on p. 371.

Kula Botanical Garden 🐝   You can take a self-guided, informative, leisurely stroll through more than 700 native and exotic plants—including three unique collections of orchids, proteas, and bromeliads—at this 5-acre garden. It offers a good overview of Hawaii's exotic flora in one small, cool place.

Hwy. 377, south of Haleakala Crater Rd. (Hwy. 378), ½ miles from Hwy. 37. ℂ **808/878-1715.** Admission $5 adults, $1 children 6–12. Daily 9am–4pm.

Tedeschi Vineyards and Winery 🐝   On the southern shoulder of Haleakala is **Ulupalakua Ranch,** a 20,000-acre spread once owned by legendary sea captain James Makee, celebrated in the Hawaiian song and dance *Hula O Makee.* Wounded in a Honolulu waterfront brawl in 1843, Makee moved to Maui and bought Ulupalakua. He renamed it Rose Ranch, planted sugar as a cash crop, and grew rich. Still in operation, the ranch is now home to Maui's only winery, established in 1974 by Napa vintner Emil Tedeschi, who began growing California and European grapes here and producing serious still and sparkling wines, plus a silly wine made of pineapple juice. The rustic grounds are the perfect place for a picnic. Pack a basket before you go. Settle in under the sprawling camphor tree, pop the cork on a Blanc du Blanc, and toast your good fortune in being here.

Off Hwy. 37 (Kula Hwy.). ℂ **808/878-6058.** www.mauiwine.com. Daily 9am–5pm. Free tastings. Tours 10:30am–1:30pm.

EAST MAUI & HEAVENLY HANA

In and around Hana, you'll find a lush tropical rainforest dotted with cascading waterfalls and sparkling blue pools, skirted by red- and black-sand beaches.

THE ROAD TO HANA ★★★

Top down, sunscreen on, radio tuned to a little Hawaiian music on a Maui morning. It's time to head out to Hana along the Hana Highway (Hwy. 36), a wiggle of a road that runs along Maui's northeastern shore. The drive takes at least 3 hours from Lahaina or Kihei—but take all day. Going to Hana is about the journey, not the destination.

There are wilder roads, steeper roads, and more dangerous roads, but in all of Hawaii, no road is more celebrated than this one. It winds 50 miles past taro patches, magnificent seascapes, waterfall pools, botanical gardens, and verdant rainforests, and ends at one of Hawaii's most beautiful tropical places.

The outside world discovered the little village of Hana in 1926, when the narrow coastal road, carved by pickax-wielding convicts, opened. The mud-and-gravel road, often subject to landslides and washouts, was paved in 1962, when tourist traffic began to increase; it now sees 1,000 cars and dozens of vans a day, according to storekeeper Harry Hasegawa. That translates into half a million people a year, which is way too many. Go at the wrong time, and you'll be stuck in a bumper-to-bumper rental-car parade—peak traffic hours are midmorning and midafternoon year-round, especially on weekends.

In the rush to "do" Hana in a day, most visitors spin around town in 10 minutes and wonder what all the fuss is about. It takes time to take in Hana, play in the waterfalls, sniff the tropical flowers, hike to bamboo forests, and view the spectacular scenery. Stay overnight if you can, and meander back in a day or two. If you really must do the Hana Highway in a day, go just before sunrise and return after sunset.

Tips: Practice aloha. Give way at one-lane bridges, wave at oncoming motorists, let the big guys in 4×4s have the right of way—it's just common sense, brah. If the guy behind you blinks his lights, let him pass. And don't honk your horn—in Hawaii, it's considered rude.

THE JOURNEY BEGINS IN PAIA   Before you even start out, fill up your gas tank. Gas in Paia is mucho expensive, and it's the last place for gas until you get to Hana, some 54 bridges and 600 hairpin turns down the road.

Paia was once a thriving sugar-mill town. The mill is still here, but the population shifted to Kahului in the 1950s when subdivisions opened there, leaving Paia to shrivel up and die. But the town refused to give up, and it has proven its ability to adapt to the times. Now chic eateries and trendy shops stand next door to the old ma-and-pa establishments. Plan to be here early, around 7am, when **Charley's** ★, 142 Hana Hwy. (✆ **808/579-9453**), opens. Enjoy a big, hearty breakfast for a reasonable price.

WINDSURFING MECCA   Just before mile marker 9 is **Hookipa Beach Park** ★, where top-ranked windsurfers come to test themselves against the forces of nature: thunderous surf and forceful wind. On nearly every windy day, after noon (the board surfers have the waves in the morning), you can watch dozens of windsurfers twirling and dancing in the wind like colored butterflies. To watch them, do not stop on the highway, but go past the park and turn left at the entrance on the far side of the beach. You can either park on the high grassy bluff or drive down to the sandy beach and park alongside the pavilion. Facilities include restrooms, a shower, picnic tables, and a barbecue area.

INTO THE COUNTRY   Past Hookipa Beach, the road winds down into **Maliko Gulch** at mile marker 10. At the bottom of the gulch, look for the road on your right,

The Road to Hana

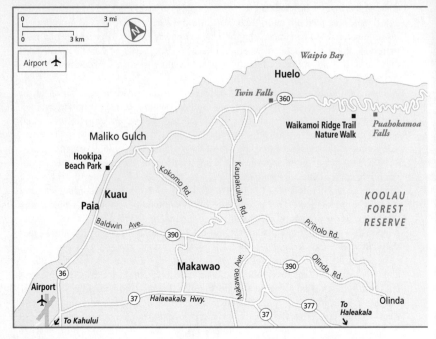

0   3 mi
0   3 km

Airport ✈

Waipio Bay

Huelo

Twin Falls ■ 360

Waikamoi Ridge Trail
Nature Walk ■

Puahokamoa
Falls ■

Maliko Gulch

Hookipa
Beach Park ■

Kokomo Rd.

Kaupakulua Rd.

KOOLAU
FOREST
RESERVE

Kuau

Paia

Baldwin Ave.

390

Pi'iholo Rd.

Makawao

Makawao Ave.

390

Olinda Rd.

36

Airport
✈

37   *Halaeakala Hwy.*

377

To
Haleakala
↓

Olinda

✈ *To Kahului*

37

which will take you out to **Maliko Bay.** Take the first right, which goes under the bridge and past a rodeo arena and on to the rocky beach. There are no facilities here except a boat-launch ramp. In the 1940s, Maliko had a thriving community at the mouth of the bay, but its residents rebuilt farther inland after a strong tidal wave wiped it out.

Back on the Hana Highway, for the next few miles, you'll pass through the rural area of **Haiku:** Banana patches, forests of guavas and palms, avocados, too. Just before mile marker 15 is the **Maui Grown Market and Deli** (© **808/572-1693**), a good stop for drinks or snacks for the ride.

JAWS   If it's winter and the waves are up (like 60 feet or so), here's your chance to watch tow-in surfing off Pauwela Point at an area known as Jaws (yes, like it will chew you up), where expert tow-in surfers battle the mammoth waves. To get there, make a small detour off the Hana Highway by turning left at Hahana Road, between mile marker 13 and 14. When the paved road ends, the dirt road is private property (Maui Land and Pine) and the pineapple fields are there to grow pineapple, not to park cars, so you may have to hike in about a 1½ miles to get close to the ocean. Practice aloha; do not park in the pineapple fields, do not pick or even touch the pineapple (picking would be stealing), and be very careful close to the oceanside cliffs.

At mile marker 16, the curves begin, one right after another. Slow down and enjoy the view of bucolic rolling hills, mango trees, and vibrant ferns. After mile marker 16, the road is still called the Hana Highway, but the number changes from Highway 36 to Highway 360, and the mile markers go back to 0.

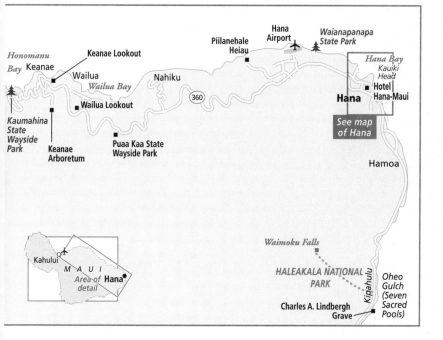

A GREAT PLUNGE ALONG THE WAY   A dip in a waterfall pool is everybody's tropical-island fantasy. The first great place to stop is **Twin Falls** ☂, at mile marker 2. Just before the wide, concrete bridge, pull over on the mountain side and park (but not in front of the sign that says DO NOT BLOCK DRIVEWAY). Although you will see several cars parked in the area and a steady line of people going up to the falls, be aware that this is **private property** and trespassing is illegal in Hawaii. If you decide that you want to "risk-it," from the gate, you can walk 3 to 5 minutes to the waterfall and pool, or continue on another 10 to 15 minutes to the second, larger waterfall and pool (don't go in if it has been raining).

HIDDEN HUELO   Just before mile marker 4, on a blind curve, look for a double row of mailboxes on the left-hand side by the pay phone. Down the road lies a hidden Hawaii of an earlier time, where an indescribable sense of serenity prevails. Hemmed in by Waipo and Hoalua bays is the remote community of **Huelo** ☂. This fertile area once supported a population of 75,000; today, only a few hundred live among the scattered homes here, where a handful of B&Bs cater to a trickle of travelers (see section 3 of this chapter).

The only reason Huelo is even marked is the historic 1853 **Kaulanapueo Church.** Reminiscent of New England architecture, this coral-and-cement church, topped with a plantation-green steeple and a gray tin roof, is still in use, although services are held just once or twice a month. It still has the same austere, stark interior of 1853: straight-backed benches, a no-nonsense platform for the minister, and no distractions on the walls to tempt you from paying attention to the sermon. Next to the church is a small graveyard, a personal history of this village in concrete and stone.

KOOLAU FOREST RESERVE   After Huelo, the vegetation seems lusher, as though Mother Nature had poured Miracle-Gro on everything. This is the edge of the **Koolau Forest Reserve.** *Koolau* means "windward," and this certainly is one of the greatest examples of a lush windward area: The coastline here gets about 60 to 80 inches of rain a year, as well as runoff from the 200 to 300 inches that falls farther up the mountain. Here you'll see trees laden with guavas, as well as mangoes, java plums, and avocados the size of softballs. The spiny, long-leafed plants are hala trees, which the Hawaiians used for weaving baskets, mats, and even canoe sails.

From here on out, there's a waterfall (and one-lane bridge) around nearly every turn in the road, so drive slowly and be prepared to stop and yield to oncoming cars.

DANGEROUS CURVES   About a half-mile after mile marker 6, there's a sharp U-curve in the road, going uphill. The road is practically one-lane here, with a brick wall on one side and virtually no maneuvering room. Sound your horn at the start of the U-curve to let approaching cars know you're coming. Take this curve, as well as the few more coming up in the next several miles, very slowly.

Just before mile marker 7 is a forest of waving **bamboo.** The sight is so spectacular that drivers are often tempted to take their eyes off the road. Be very cautious. Wait until just after mile marker 7, at the **Kaaiea Bridge** and stream below, to pull over and take a closer look at the hand-hewn stone walls. Then turn around to see the vista of bamboo.

A GREAT FAMILY HIKE   At mile marker 9, there's a small state wayside area with restrooms, a pavilion, picnic tables, and a barbecue area. The sign says KOOLAU FOR-EST RESERVE, but the real attraction here is the **Waikamoi Ridge Trail** ⚸, an easy ¾-mile loop. The start of the trail is just behind the QUIET TREES AT WORK sign. The well-marked trail meanders through eucalyptus, ferns, and hala trees.

SAFETY WARNING   I used to recommend another waterfall, **Puohokamoa Falls,** at mile marker 11, but not anymore. Unfortunately what once was a great thing has been overrun by hordes of not-so-polite tourists. You will see cars parking on the already dangerous, barely-two-lane Hana Highway a half a mile before the waterfall. Slow down after the 10 mile marker. As you get close to the 11 mile marker, the road becomes a congested one-lane road due to visitors parking on this narrow highway. Don't add to the congestion by trying to park; there are plenty of other great water-falls, just drive slowly and safely through this area.

CAN'T-MISS PHOTO OPS   Just past mile marker 12 is the **Kaumahina State Wayside Park** ⚸. This is not only a good pit stop (restrooms are available) and a won-derful place for a picnic (with tables and a barbecue area), but also a great vista point. The view of the rugged coastline makes an excellent shot—you can see all the way down to the jutting Keanae Peninsula.

Another mile, and a couple more bends in the road, and you'll enter the Hono-manu Valley, with its beautiful bay. To get to the **Honomanu Bay County Beach Park** ⚸, look for the turnoff on your left, just after mile marker 14, as you begin your ascent up the other side of the valley. The rutted dirt-and-cinder road takes you down to the rocky black-sand beach. There are no facilities here. Because of the strong rip currents offshore, swimming is best in the stream inland from the ocean. You'll con-sider the drive down worthwhile as you stand on the beach, well away from the ocean, and turn to look back on the steep cliffs covered with vegetation.

KEANAE PENINSULA & ARBORETUM   At mile marker 17, the old Hawaiian village of **Keanae** 🐾🐾 stands out against the Pacific like a place time forgot. Here, on an old lava flow graced by an 1860 stone church and swaying palms, is one of the last coastal enclaves of native Hawaiians. They still grow taro in patches and pound it into poi, the staple of the old Hawaiian diet; they still pluck *opihi* (limpet) from tide pools along the jagged coast and cast throw-nets at schools of fish.

At nearby **Keanae Arboretum,** Hawaii's botanical world is divided into three parts: native forest; introduced forest; and traditional Hawaiian plants, food, and medicine. You can swim in the pools of Piinaau Stream, or press on along a mile-long trail into Keanae Valley, where a lovely tropical rainforest waits at the end.

WAIANAPANAPA STATE PARK 🐾🐾   On the outskirts of Hana, shiny black-sand Waianapanapa Beach appears like a vivid dream, with bright-green jungle foliage on three sides and cobalt blue water lapping at its feet. The 120-acre park on an ancient lava flow includes sea cliffs, lava tubes, arches, and that beach—plus a dozen rustic cabins. If you're interested in staying here, see "Accommodations You Can Afford," p. 353. Also see "Beaches," p. 402 and "Hiking & Camping," p. 417.

HANA 🐾🐾🐾

Green, tropical Hana, which some call heavenly, is a destination all its own; a small coastal village in a rainforest inhabited by 2,500 people, many part-Hawaiian. Beautiful Hana enjoys more than 90 inches of rain a year—more than enough to keep the scenery lush. Banyans, bamboo, breadfruit trees—everything seems larger than life, especially the flowers, like wild ginger and plumeria. Several roadside stands offer exotic blooms for $1 a bunch. Just "put money in box." It's the Hana honor system.

The last unspoiled Hawaiian town on Maui is, oddly enough, the home of Maui's first resort, which opened in 1946. Paul Fagan, owner of the San Francisco Seals baseball team, bought an old inn and turned it into the **Hotel Hana-Maui,** which gave Hana its first and, as it turns out, last taste of tourism. Others have tried to open hotels and golf courses and resorts, but Hana, which is interested in remaining Hana, always politely refuses. There are a few B&Bs here, though; see section 3 of this chapter.

A wood-frame 1871 building that served as the old Hana District Police Station now holds the **Hana Museum Cultural Center,** 4974 Uakea Rd. (© 808/248-8622; www.planet-hawaii.com/hana). The center tells the history of the area, with some excellent artifacts, memorabilia, and photographs. Also stop in at **Hasegawa General Store,** a Maui institution.

On the green hills above Hana stands a 30-foot-high white cross made of lava rock. The cross was erected by citizens in memory of Paul Fagan, who helped keep the town alive. The 3-mile hike up to **Fagan's Cross** provides a gorgeous view of the Hana coast, especially at sunset, when Fagan himself liked to climb this hill. See p. 422 for details.

Most day-trippers to Hana miss the most unusual natural attraction of all: **Red Sand Beach** 🐾, officially named Kaihalulu Beach, which means "roaring sea." It's truly a sight to see. The beach is as red as a Ferrari at a five-alarm fire. It's on the ocean side of Kauiki Hill, just south of Hana Bay, in a wild, natural setting in a pocket cove. Kauiki, a 390-foot-high volcanic cinder cone, lost its seaward wall to erosion and spilled red cinders everywhere, creating the red sands. Before you put on your bathing suit, there are three things to know about this beach: You have to trespass to get here (which is against the law), due to recent heavy rains there have been several serious

Hana

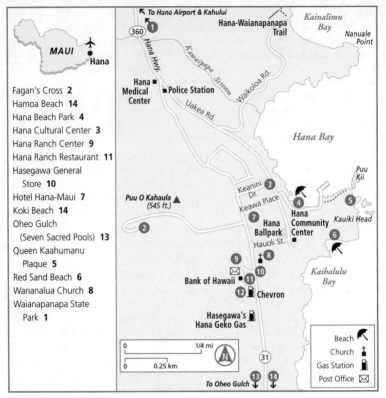

Fagan's Cross **2**
Hamoa Beach **14**
Hana Beach Park **4**
Hana Cultural Center **3**
Hana Ranch Center **9**
Hana Ranch Restaurant **11**
Hasegawa General
 Store **10**
Hotel Hana-Maui **7**
Koki Beach **14**
Oheo Gulch
 (Seven Sacred Pools) **13**
Queen Kaahumanu
 Plaque **5**
Red Sand Beach **6**
Wananalua Church **8**
Waianapanapa State
 Park **1**

injuries on the muddy, slippery train (enter at your own risk, it can be extremely dangerous), and nudity (also illegal in Hawaii—arrests have been made) is common here.

If you are determined to go, ask for permission at the Hotel Hana Maui. And ask about the conditions on the trail (which drops several stories down to the ocean rocks). To reach the beach, put on solid walking shoes (no flip-flops) and walk south on Uakea Road, past the Hotel Hana-Maui to the end of the parking lot for Sea Ranch Cottages. Turn left, cross an open field past an old cemetery, and follow a well-worn path down a narrow cliff trail. In this private, romantic setting, some beachgoers shed their clothes, so try not to be offended.

TROPICAL HALEAKALA: OHEO GULCH AT KIPAHULU

If you're thinking about heading out to the so-called Seven Sacred Pools, out past Hana at the Kipahulu end of Haleakala National Park, let's clear this up right now: There are more than seven pools—about 24, actually—and *all* water in Hawaii is considered sacred. It's all a PR campaign that has spun out of control into contemporary myth. Folks here call it by its rightful name, **Oheo Gulch** ⋒⋒⋒, and visitors sometimes refer to it as Kipahulu, which is actually the name of the area where Oheo Gulch is located. No matter what you call it, it's beautiful. This dazzling series of pools and cataracts is so popular that it now has its own roadside parking lot.

From the ranger station, it's just a short hike above the famous Oheo Gulch to two spectacular **waterfalls.** Check with park rangers before hiking up to or swimming in the pools, and always keep an eye on the water in the streams. The sky can be sunny near the coast, but floodwaters travel 6 miles down from the Kipahulu Valley, and the water level can rise 4 feet in less than 10 minutes. It's not a good idea to swim in the pools in winter.

Makahiku Falls is easily reached from the central parking area; the trail head begins near the ranger station. **Pipiwai Trail** leads up to the road and beyond for a half-mile to the overlook. If you hike another 1½ miles up the trail across two bridges and through a bamboo forest, you reach **Waimoku Falls.** It's a good uphill hike, but press on to avoid the pool's crowd.

ACCESS POINTS   Even though Oheo is part of Haleakala National Park, you cannot drive here from the summit. Oheo is about 30 to 50 minutes beyond Hana town, along Highway 31. The admission fee to enter is $5 per person or $10 per car. The Highway 31 bridge passes over some of the pools near the ocean; the others, plus magnificent 400-foot Waimoku Falls, are uphill, via an often-muddy, but rewarding, hour-long hike (see "Hiking & Camping," above). Expect showers on the Kipahulu coast.

VISITOR CENTER   The **Kipahulu Ranger Station** (© **808/248-7375**) is staffed from 9am to 5pm daily. Restrooms are available, but no drinking water. Here you'll find park-safety information, exhibits, and books. Rangers offer a variety of walks and hikes year-round; check at the station for current activities. Tent camping is permitted in the park; see section 7 of this chapter, "Hiking & Camping," for details.

BEYOND OHEO GULCH

A mile past Oheo Gulch on the ocean side of the road is **Lindbergh's Grave.** First to fly across the Atlantic Ocean, Charles A. Lindbergh (1902–74) found peace in the Pacific; he settled in Hana, where he died of cancer in 1974. The famous aviator is buried under river stones in a seaside graveyard behind the 1857 **Palapala Hoomau Congregational Church.**

Those of you who are continuing on around Maui to the fishing village of **Kaupo** and beyond should be warned that Kaupo Road, or Old Piilani Highway (Hwy. 31), is rough and unpaved, often full of potholes and ruts. There are no goods or services until you reach **Ulupalakua Ranch,** where there's a winery, a general store, and a gas station, which is likely to be closed. Before you attempt this journey, ask around about road conditions, or call the **Maui Public Works Department** (© **808/248-8254**) or the **Police Department** (© **808/248-8311**). This road frequently washes out in the rain. Most rental-car companies forbid you from taking their cars on this road (they don't want to trek all the way out here to get you if your car breaks down), so you'd really be better off retracing your route back through Hana. But, if conditions are good, it can be a pretty drive in the spring (it tends to be dry and boring in summer).

10 Shops & Galleries

The island of Maui is a shopaholic's dream as well as an arts center, with a large number of resident artists who show their works in dozens of galleries and countless gift shops. Maui is also an agricultural cornucopia, producing Kula onions, upcountry protea, Kaanapali coffee, world-renowned potato chips, and many other taste treats that are shipped worldwide.

As with any popular visitor destination, you'll have to wade through bad art and mountains of trinkets, particularly in Lahaina and Kihei, where touristy boutiques line the streets between rare pockets of treasures. If you shop in south or west Maui, expect to pay resort prices, clear down to a bottle of Evian or sunscreen.

And don't ignore Central Maui, home to some first-rate boutiques. Watch Wailuku, which is poised for a resurgence—if not now, then soon. The town has its infusion of creative and cultural energy, and a major promenade/emporium on Main Street is in the works. The Kaahumanu Center, in neighboring Kahului, is becoming more fashionable by the month.

Upcountry, Makawao's boutiques are worth seeking out, despite some attitude and high prices. The charm of shopping on Maui has always rested in the small, independent shops and galleries that crop up in surprising places.

CENTRAL MAUI
KAHULUI

Kahului's best shopping is concentrated in two places. Almost all of the shops listed below are at one of the following centers:

The once rough-around-the-edges **Maui Mall,** 70 E. Kaahumanu Ave. (© **808/ 877-7559**), is the talk of Kahului. Newly renovated, it's now bigger and better, and has retained some of our favorite stores while adding a 12-screen movie megaplex that features current releases as well as art-house films. The mall is still a place of everyday good things, from **Long's Drugs** to **Star Market** to **Tasaka Guri Guri,** the decades-old purveyor of inimitable icy treats, neither ice cream nor shave ice, but something in between.

Queen Kaahumanu Center, 275 Kaahumanu Ave. (© **808/877-3369**), 5 minutes from the Kahului Airport on Highway 32, offers more than 100 shops, restaurants, and theaters. Its second-floor Plantation District offers home furnishings and accessories, and gift and accessories shops. Kaahumanu covers all the bases, from the arts and crafts to a **Foodland Supermarket** and everything in-between: a thriving food court; the island's best beauty supply, **Lisa's Beauty Supply & Salon** (© **808/877-6463**), and its sister store for cosmetics, **Madison Avenue Day Spa and Boutique** (© **808/873-0880**); mall standards like **Sunglass Hut, Radio Shack,** and **Local Motion** (surf and beach wear—including the current fad, women's board shorts, a combination of hot pants and men's surf trunks); and standard department stores like **Macy's** and **Sears** and great specialty shops like **Sharper Image.**

Apricot Rose   The former Caswell-Massey has changed its name but still offers the same selection of products for beauty and home: unique Maui-made soaps and bath products that use tropical fragrances and botanicals. Choose from hundreds of specialty products, from decadent bath salts to Damask rose shampoo and bath gels, eye creams, body lotions, sachets, candles, perfume bottles, potpourris, triple-milled soaps, and more. You can also get handsome, custom-designed baskets at no extra charge. Kaahumanu Center. © 808/877-7761.

Cost Less Imports   Natural fibers are ubiquitous in this newly expanded corner of the Maui Mall, three times larger than before. Household accessories include lauhala, bamboo blinds, grassy floor and window coverings, shoji-style lamps, burlap yardage, baskets, Balinese cushions, Asian imports, and top-of-the-line, made-on-Maui soaps and handicrafts. Japanese folk curtains, called *noreng,* are among the diverse items you'll find here; it's a good source of tropical and Asian home decor. In the Maui Mall. © 808/877-0300.

Lightning Bolt Maui Inc.   Here's an excellent selection of women's board shorts, aloha shirts, swimwear, sandals and shoes, and all necessary accoutrements for fun in the sun. Quality labels such as Patagonia and high-tech, state-of-the-art outdoor gear and moccasins attract adventurers heading for the chilly hinterlands as well as the sun-drenched shores. 55 Kaahumanu Ave. ✆ **808/877-3484.**

Maui County Store   *Attention:* T-shirt collector:—here's your chance to get official Maui County Police and Fire logo T-shirts and other Maui County logo shirts. Plus logo wear from the University of Hawaii and other Made-in-Maui items. This fundraising store (helps the police and fire departments) is staffed by students from Maui Community College learning retail sales. Prices are great, money goes to a good cause, the students get to learn a trade, and you get to take home excellent souvenirs from your Maui vacation. Maui Mall, 70 Kaahumanu Ave., Kahului. ✆ **808/877-6669.** www.maui countystore.com.

Maui Swap Meet   The Maui Swap Meet is a large and popular event. After Thanksgiving and throughout December, the number of booths nearly explodes into the hundreds and the activity reaches fever pitch. The colorful Maui specialties include vegetables from Kula and Keanae, fresh taro, plants, proteas, crafts, household items, homemade ethnic foods, and baked goods, including some fabulous fruit breads. Every Saturday from 7am to noon, vendors spread out their wares in booths and under tarps, in a festival-like atmosphere that is pure Maui with a touch of kitsch. Between the cheap Balinese imports and New Age crystals and incense, you may find some vintage John Kelly prints and 1930s collectibles. Admission is 50¢, and if you go early while the vendors are setting up, no one will turn you away. As we went to press, the Maui Swap Meet owners were in negotiations to stay in their long-time location on Puunene Ave., but they may be forced to move. Please contact them first to make sure they are still there S. Puunene Ave. (next to the Kahului Post Office). ✆ **808/877-3100.**

Summerhouse   Sleek and chic, tiny Summerhouse is big on style: casual and party dresses; separates by Russ Berens, FLAX, Kiko; and Tencel jeans by Signatur—the best. During the holiday season the selection gets dressy and sassy, but it's a fun browse year-round. We adore the hats, accessories, easy-care clothing, and up-to-the-minute evening dresses. The high-quality T-shirts are always a cut above. The casual selection is well suited to the island lifestyle. In the Dairy Center, 395 Dairy Rd. ✆ **808/871-1320.**

WAILUKU

Located at the gateway to Iao Valley, Wailuku is the county seat, the part of Maui where people live and work. Wailuku's attractive vintage architecture, smattering of antiques shops, and mom-and-pop eateries imbue the town with a down-home charm noticeably absent in the resort areas of west, south, and upcountry Maui. The community spirit fuels festivals throughout the year and is slowly attracting new businesses, but Wailuku is still a work in progress. Of course there's junk, but a stroll along Main and Market streets usually turns up a treasure or two. It's a mixed bag, but a treasure hunt, too.

Bailey House Gift Shop   For made-in-Hawaii items, Bailey House is a must-stop. It offers a thoroughly enjoyable browse through authoritative Hawaiiana, in a museum that's one of the finest examples of missionary architecture, dating from 1833. Gracious gardens, rare paintings of early Maui, wonderful programs in Hawaiian arts and culture, and a restored hand-hewn koa canoe await visitors. The shop, a small space of discriminating taste, packs a wallop with its selection of remarkable gift items, from Hawaiian music to exquisite woods, traditional Hawaiian games to pareus and books. Prints by the legendary Hawaii artist Madge Tennent, lauhala hats hanging in midair, hand-sewn pheasant hatbands, jams and jellies, Maui cookbooks, and an occasional Hawaiian quilt are some of the treasures to be found here. Bailey House Museum Shop, 2375–A Main St. © 808/244-3326.

Bird of Paradise Unique Antiques   Owner Joe Myhand loves furniture, old Matson liner menus, blue willow china, kimonos for children, and anything nostalgic that happens to be Hawaiian. The furniture in the strongly Hawaiian collection ranges from 1940s rattan to wicker and old koa—those items tailor-made for informal island living and leisurely moments on the lanai. Myhand also collects bottles and mails his license plates all over the world. The collection ebbs and flows with his finds, keeping buyers waiting in the wings for his Depression glass, California pottery from the 1930s and 1940s, old dinnerware, perfume bottles, vintage aloha shirts, and vintage Hawaiian music on cassettes. 56 N. Market St. © 808/242-7699.

Brown-Kobayashi   Graceful living is the theme here. Prices range from a few dollars to the thousands in this 750-square-foot treasure trove. The owners have added a fabulous selection of antique stone garden pieces that mingle quietly with Asian antiques and old and new French, European, and Hawaiian objects. Although the collection is eclectic, there is a strong cohesive aesthetic that sets Brown-Kobayashi apart from other Maui antiques stores. Japanese kimonos and obis, Bakelite and Peking glass beads, breathtaking Japanese lacquerware, cricket carriers, and cloisonne are among the delights here. Exotic and precious Chinese woods (purple sandalwood and huanghauali) glow discreetly from quiet corners, and an occasional monarchy-style lidded milo bowl comes in and flies out. 160–A N. Market St. © 808/242-0804.

Gottling Ltd.   Karl Gottling's shop specializes in Asian antique furniture, but you can also find smaller carvings, precious stones, jewelry, netsuke, opium weights, and finds in all sizes. One cabinet had 350-year-old doors; a 17th-century Buddha lent an air of serenity next to a 150-year-old Chinese cabinet. Ming dynasty ceramics, carved wooden apples ($15), and a Persian rug ($65,000) give you an idea of the range of possibilities here. 34 N. Market St. © 808/ 244-7779.

Sig Zane Designs Wailuku   Sig Zane is synonymous with the best in aloha wear. As we went to press, Sig announced that he will be moving his Waiiluku store to Kahului, so be sure to check before you head out for this wonderful store, looking for a T-shirt, pareu, duffel bag, aloha shirt, or muumuu, you'll find it at Sig Zane. The staff is helpful and willing to share the background of each design, so you will learn much about the culture, botany, mythology, and beauty of the Islands. 53 Market St. © 808/249-8997.

CENTRAL MAUI EDIBLES

The **Star Market** and **Long's Drugs** in the Maui Mall, **Foodland** in the Kaahumanu Center, and **Safeway** at 170 E. Kamehameha Ave. will satisfy your ordinary grocery needs. On Saturday, you may want to check out the **Maui Swap Meet** (see above).

Down to Earth Natural Foods, 305 Dairy Rd. (© 808/877-2661), has fresh organic produce, a bountiful salad bar, sandwiches and smoothies, vitamins and supplements, fresh-baked goods, chips and snacks, whole grains, and more.

Established in 1941, the **Ooka Super Market,** 1870 Main St., Wailuku (© 808/ 244-3931), Maui's ultimate home-grown supermarket, is a mom-and-pop business that has grown by leaps and bounds but still manages to keep its neighborhood flavor. Ooka sells inexpensive produce (fresh Maui mushrooms for a song), fresh island seafood, and Maui specialties such as manju and mochi. Proteas cut the same day, freesias in season, hydrangeas, fresh leis, torch ginger from Hana, upcountry calla lilies in season, and multicolored anthuriums are offered at what is one of Maui's finest and most affordable retail flower selections. Prepared foods are also a hit: bentos and plate lunches, roast chicken and laulau, and specialties from all the islands. The fish is fresh, and the seaweed, poi, Kula persimmons in fall, fresh Haiku mushrooms, and dried marlin from Kona are among the local delicacies that make Ooka a Maui favorite.

Maui's produce has long been a source of pride for islanders, and **Ohana Farmers Market,** Kahului Shopping Center, next to Ah Fook's Super Market (© **808/878-3189**), is where you'll find a fresh, inexpensive selection of Maui-grown fruit, vegetables, flowers, and plants. Crafts and gourmet foods add to the event, and the large monkeypod trees provide welcome shade.

Located in the northern section of Wailuku, **Takamiya Market,** 359 N. Market St. (© **808/244-3404**), is much loved by local folks and visitors with adventurous palates, who often drive all the way from Kihei to stock up on picnic fare and mouthwatering ethnic foods for sunset gatherings. Unpretentious home-cooked foods from East and West are prepared daily and served on plastic-foam plates. From the chilled-fish counter come fresh sashimi and poke, and in the renowned assortment of prepared foods are mounds of shoyu chicken, tender fried squid, roast pork, kalua pork, laulau, Chinese noodles, fiddlehead ferns, and Western comfort foods, such as corn bread and potato salad.

WEST MAUI
LAHAINA
Lahaina's merchants and art galleries go all out from 7 to 9pm on Fridays, when **Art Night** brings an extra measure of hospitality and community spirit. The Art Night openings are usually marked with live entertainment and refreshments and a livelier-than-usual street scene.

If you're in Lahaina on the second or last Thursday of the month, stroll by the front lawn of the **Baldwin Home,** 120 Dickenson St. (at Front St.), for an opportunity to meet the gregarious senior citizens of Lahaina, who gather from 10am to 4pm to demonstrate lei-making and sell their floral creations.

What was formerly a big, belching pineapple cannery is now a maze of shops and restaurants at the northern end of Lahaina town, known as the **Lahaina Cannery Mall,** 1221 Honoapiilani Hwy. (© **808/661-5304**). Find your way through the T-shirt and sportswear shops to **Lahaina Printsellers,** home of antique originals, prints, paintings, and wonderful 18th- to 20th-century cartography, representing the largest collection of engravings and antique maps in Hawaii. Follow your nose to **Sir Wilfred's Coffee House,** where you can unwind with espresso and croissants, or head for **Compadres Bar & Grill,** where the margaritas flow freely and the Mexican food is tasty (p. 385). **Shoes, Sandals & Slippers by Roland's** may surprise you with its selection of footwear, everything from Cole-Haan sophisticates to inexpensive sandals. At the recently expanded food court, the new **Compadres Taqueria** sells Mexican food to go, while **L & L Drive-Inn** sells plate lunches near Greek, pizza, Vietnamese, and Japanese food booths. There's also a **Long's Drugs** and a **Safeway.**

The **Lahaina Center,** 900 Front St. (© **808/667-9216**), is fairly new and still a work in progress. It's located north of Lahaina's most congested strip, where Front

Street begins. Across the street from the center, the seawall is a much-sought-after front-row seat to the sunset. There's plenty of free validated parking and easy access to more than 30 shops, a salon, restaurants, a nightclub, and a four-plex movie-theater complex. **Ruth's Chris Steak House** has opened its doors in Lahaina Center, and **Maui Brews** serves lunch and dinner and offers live music nightly except weekends. Among the shopping stops: **Banana Republic,** the **Hilo Hattie Fashion Center** (a dizzying emporium of aloha wear), **McInerny** (wonderfully discounted designer clothes), **ABC Discount Store,** and a dozen other recreational, dining, and entertainment options.

The conversion of 10,000 square feet of parking space into the re-creation of a traditional Hawaiian village is a welcome touch of Hawaiiana at Lahaina Center. With the commercialization of modern Lahaina, it's easy to forget that it was once the capital of the Hawaiian kingdom and a significant historic site. The village, called **Hale Kahiko,** features three main *hale,* or houses: a sleeping house; the men's dining house; and the crafts house, where women pounded lauhala for mats and baskets. Construction of the houses consumed 10,000 feet of ohia wood from the island, 20 tons of pili grass, and more than 4 miles of handwoven coconut sennit for the lashings. Artifacts, weapons, a canoe, and indigenous trees are among the authentic touches in this village, which can be toured privately or with a guide.

Lahaina Arts Society Galleries   With its membership of more than 185 Maui artists, the nonprofit Lahaina Arts Society is an excellent community resource. Changing monthly exhibits in the Banyan Tree and Old Jail galleries offer a good look at the island's artistic well: two-dimensional art, fiber art, ceramics, sculpture, prints, jewelry, and more. In the shade of the humongous banyan tree in the square across from Pioneer Inn, "Art in the Park" fairs are offered every second and fourth weekend of the month. 648 Wharf St. ✆ **808/661-3228.**

Lei Spa Maui   It has expanded to include two massage rooms and shower facilities, making it a day spa offering facials and other therapies. It's a good sign that 95% of the beauty and bath products sold are made on Maui, and that includes Hawaiian Botanical Pikake shower gel; kukui and macadamia-nut oils; Hawaiian potpourris; mud masks with Hawaiian seaweed; and a spate of rejuvenating, cleansing potions for hair and skin. Aromatherapy body oils and perfumes are popular, as are the handmade soaps and fragrances of torch ginger, plumeria, coconut, tuberose, and sandalwood. Scented candles in coconut shells, inexpensive and fragrant, make great gifts. 505 Front St. ✆ **808/661-1178.**

Martin Lawrence Galleries   The front is garish, with pop art, kinetic sculptures, and bright, carnivalesque glass objects. Toward the back of the gallery, however, there's a sizable inventory of two-dimensional art and some plausible choices for collectors of Keith Haring, Andy Warhol, and other pop artists. The focus is pop art and national and international artists. In the Lahaina Market Place, 126 Lahainaluna Rd. ✆ **808/661-1788.**

Na Mea Hawaii   The best of Hawaii can be found here, if not in the striking Tutuvi silk-screened dresses and shirts, then in the delicately patterned shawls and scarves of Maile Andrade that depict Hawaiian scenes and traditions on velvet. Arts, crafts, gifts and clothing, all made by Hawaii artists, fill this cozy niche of Lahaina in the historic Baldwin House on Front Street. Whether it's a beautifully made lauhala bag, a colorful muumuu, a Hawaii-themed book, or a pheasant hat lei made by master feather lei makers Mary Lou Kekuewa and Paulette Kahalepuna, Na Mea Hawaii offers Hawaii at its best. 120 Dickensen St. ✆ **808/661-5707.**

The Old Lahaina Book Emporium   What a bookstore! Chockablock with used books in stacks, shelves, counters, and aisles, this bookstore is a browser's dream. More than 25,000 quality used books are lovingly housed in this shop, where owner JoAnn Carroll treats books and customers well. Prices are low, and the selection is diverse. The store is 95% used books and 100% delight. Specialties include Hawaiiana, fiction, mystery, sci-fi, and military history, with substantial selections in cookbooks, children's books, and philosophy/religion. You could pay as little as $2 for a quality read, or a whole lot more for that rare first edition. 505 Front St. ✆ **808/661-1399.**

Totally Hawaiian Gift Gallery   This gallery makes a good browse for its selection of Niihau shell jewelry, excellent Hawaiian CDs, Norfolk pine bowls, and Hawaiian quilt kits. Hawaiian quilt patterns sewn in Asia (at least they're honest about it) are labor-intensive, less expensive, and attractive, although not totally Hawaiian. Hawaiian-quilt-patterned gift wraps and tiles, perfumes and soaps, handcrafted dolls, and koa accessories are of good quality, and the artists, such as Kelly Dunn (Norfolk wood bowls), Jerry Kermode (wood), and Pat Coito (wood) are among the tops in their fields. In the Lahaina Cannery Mall, 1221 Honoapiilani Hwy. ✆ **808/667-2558.**

Village Galleries in Lahaina   The nearly 30-year-old Village Galleries is the oldest continuously running gallery on Maui, and it's esteemed as one of the few galleries with consistently high standards. Art collectors know this as a respectable showcase for regional artists; the selection of mostly original two- and three-dimensional art offers a good look at the quality of work originating on the island. The newer contemporary gallery offers colorful gift items and jewelry. An additional location is in the Ritz-Carlton Kapalua, 1 Ritz-Carlton Dr. (✆ **808/669-1800**). 120 and 180 Dickenson St. ✆ **808/661-4402** and 808/661-5559.

KAANAPALI

On a recent trip we were somewhat disappointed with upscale **Whalers Village,** 2435 Kaanapali Pkwy. (✆ **808/661-4567**). Although it offers everything from whale blubber to Prada and Ferragamo, it is short on local shops, and parking at the nearby lot is expensive. The complex is home to the Whalers Village Museum with its interactive exhibits and 40-foot sperm whale skeleton, but shoppers come for the designer thrills and beachfront dining. You can find most of the items featured in the shops in Lahaina and can avoid the parking hassle and the high prices by skipping this "not-worth-the-time-or-money" shopping center.

Our favorite shoe store, **Sandal Tree,** has its third store in Whalers Village. (You can skip Whaler's Village and shop at the other two stores, on at Hyatt Regency Maui and the other, Grand Wailea Resort in Wailea.)

Ki'i Gallery   Some of the works are large and lavish, such as the Toland Sand prisms for just under $5,000 and the John Stokes handblown glass. Those who love glass in all forms, from handblown vessels to jewelry, will love a browse through Ki'i. We found Pat Kazi's work in porcelain and found objects, such as the mermaid in a teacup, inspired by fairy tales and mythology, both fantastic and compelling. The gallery is devoted to glass and original paintings and drawings; roughly half of the artists are from Hawaii. In the Hyatt Regency Maui, 200 Nohea Kai Dr. ✆ 808/661-4456.

Sandal Tree   It's unusual for a resort shop to draw local customers on a regular basis, but the Sandal Tree attracts a flock of footwear fanatics who come here from throughout the islands for rubber thongs and Top-Siders, sandals and dressy pumps, athletic shoes and hats, designer footwear, and much more. Sandal Tree also carries a generous selection of Mephisto and Arche comfort sandals, Donald Pliner, Anne Klein, Charles Jourdan, and beach wear and casual footwear for all tastes. Accessories range from fashionable knapsacks to avant-garde geometrical handbags—for town and country, day and evening, kids, women, and men. Prices are realistic, too. In Whalers Village, 2435 Kaanapali Pkwy. © 808/667-5330. Also in Grand Wailea Resort, 3850 Wailea Alanui Dr., Wailea; and in the Hyatt Regency Maui, 200 Nohea Kai Dr.

FROM KAANAPALI TO KAPALUA

Those driving north of Kaanapali toward Kapalua will notice the **Honokowai Marketplace** on Lower Honoapiilani Road, only minutes before the Kapalua Airport. There are restaurants and coffee shops, a dry cleaner, the flagship **Star Market, Hula Scoops** for ice cream, a few clothing stores, and the sprawling **Hawaiian Interiorz.**

Nearby **Kahana Gateway** is an unimpressive mall built to serve the condominium community that has sprawled along the coastline between Honokowai and Kapalua. If you need women's swimsuits, however, **Rainbow Beach Swimwear** is a find. It carries a selection of suits for all shapes, at lower-than-resort prices, slashed even further during the frequent sales.

Honolua Store Walk on the old wood floors peppered with holes from golf shoes and find your everyday essentials: bottled water, stationery, mailing tape, jackets, chips, wine, soft drinks, paper products, fresh fruit and produce, and aisles of notions and necessities. With picnic tables on the veranda and a take-out counter offering deli items—more than a dozen types of sandwiches, salads, and budget-friendly breakfasts—there are always long lines of customers. Golfers and surfers love to come here for the morning paper and coffee. 502 Office Rd. (next to the Ritz-Carlton Kapalua). © 808/669-6128.

Kapalua Shops Shops have come and gone in this small, exclusive, and once-chic shopping center, now much quieter than in days past. The closing of elegant Mandalay is a big loss. The **Elizabeth Dole Gallery** has loads of Dale Chihuly studio glass, fabulous and expensive, a dramatic counterpoint to **South Seas Trading Post** and its exotic artifacts such as New Guinea masks, Balinese beads, tribal jewelry, lizard-skin drums, and coconut-shell carvings with mother-of-pearl inlay. Otherwise, it's slim pickings for shoppers in Kapalua. In the Kapalua Bay Hotel and Villas. © 808/669-1029.

Village Galleries Maui's finest exhibit their works here and in the other two Village Galleries in Lahaina. Take heart, art lovers: There's no clichéd marine art here. Translucent, delicately turned bowls of Norfolk pine gleam in the light, and George Allan, Betty Hay Freeland, Fred KenKnight, and Pamela Andelin are included in the pantheon of respected artists represented in the tiny gallery. Watercolors, oils, sculptures, handblown glass, Niihau shell leis, jewelry, and other media are represented. The Ritz-Carlton's monthly Artist-in-Residence program features gallery artists in demonstrations and special hands-on workshops—free, including materials. In the Ritz-Carlton Kapalua, 1 Ritz-Carlton Dr. © 808/669-1800.

SOUTH MAUI
KIHEI

Kihei is one long strip of strip malls. Most of the shopping here is concentrated in the **Azeka Place Shopping Center** on South Kihei Road. Fast foods abound at Azeka, as do tourist-oriented clothing shops like **Crazy Shirts.** Across the street, **Azeka Place II** houses several prominent attractions, including the popular upscale restaurant A Pacific Cafe, **General Nutrition Center,** the **Coffee Store,** and a cluster of specialty shops with everything from children's clothes to shoes, sunglasses, beauty services, and swimwear. Also on South Kihei Road is the **Kukui Mall,** with movie theaters, **Waldenbooks,** and **Whaler's General Store.**

Hawaiian Moons Natural Foods   Hawaiian Moons is an exceptional health-food store, as well as a mini-supermarket with one of the best selections of Maui products on the island. The tortillas are made on Maui (and good!), and much of the produce here, such as organic vine-ripened tomatoes and organic onions, is grown in the fertile upcountry soil of Kula. There's also locally grown organic coffee, gourmet salsas, Maui shiitake mushrooms, organic lemon grass and okra, Maui Crunch bread, free-range Big Island turkeys and chickens (no antibiotics or artificial nasties), and fresh Maui juices. Cosmetics are top-of-the-line: a staggering selection of sunblocks, fragrant floral oils, kukui-nut oil from Waialua on Oahu, and Island Essence made-on-Maui mango-coconut and vanilla-papaya lotions, the ultimate in body pampering. The salad bar is one of the most popular food stops on the coast. 2411 S. Kihei Rd. ℂ 808/875-4356.

Tuna Luna   There are treasures to be found in this small cluster of tables and booths where Maui artists display their work. Ceramics, raku, sculpture, glass, koa-wood books and photo albums, jewelry, soaps, handmade paper, and fiber-art accessories make great gifts to go. Something to watch for: Maui Metal handcrafted journals, aluminum books with designs of hula girls, palms, fish, and sea horses. Tuna Luna also has a new booth in the back pavilion. In Kihei Kalama Village, 1941 S. Kihei Rd. ℂ **808/874-9482.**

WAILEA
CY Maui   Women who like washable, flowing clothing in silks, rayons, and natural fibers will love this shop, formerly the popular Manikin in Kahului. If you don't find what you want on the racks of simple bias-cut designs, you can have it made from the bolts of stupendous fabrics lining the shop. Except for a few hand-painted silks, everything in the shop is washable. In The Shops at Wailea, 3750 Wailea Alanui Dr, A-30. ℂ **808/891-0782.**

Grand Wailea Shops   The sprawling Grand Wailea Resort is known for its long arcade of shops and galleries tailored to hefty pocketbooks. However, gift items in all price ranges can be found at Lahaina Printsellers (for old maps and prints), Dolphin Galleries, H. F. Wichman, Sandal Tree, and Napua Gallery, which houses the private collection of the resort owner. Ki'i Gallery is luminous with studio glass and exquisitely turned woods, and **Sandal Tree** raises the footwear bar. At Grand Wailea Resort, 3850 Wailea Alanui Dr. ℂ 808/875-1234.

The Shops at Wailea   This is the big shopping boost that resort-goers have been awaiting for years. Chains still rule (**The Gap, Louis Vuitton, Banana Republic, Tiffany, Crazy Shirts, Honolua Surf Co.**), but there is still fertile ground for the inveterate shopper in the nearly 60 shops in the complex. **Martin & MacArthur** (furniture and gift gallery) has landed in Wailea as part of a retail mix that is similar to Whalers Village. The high-end resort shops sell expensive souvenirs, gifts, clothing, and accessories for a life of perpetual vacations. 3750 Wailea Alanui. ℂ **808/891-6770.**

UPCOUNTRY MAUI
MAKAWAO
Besides being a shopper's paradise, Makawao is the home of the island's most prominent arts organization, the **Hui No'eau Visual Arts Center,** 2841 Baldwin Ave. (ℂ **808/572-6560;** www.huinoeau.com). Designed in 1917 by C. W. Dickey, one of Hawaii's most prominent architects, the two-story, Mediterranean-style stucco home

that houses the center is located on a sprawling 9-acre estate called Kaluanui. Its tree-lined driveway features two of Maui's largest hybrid Cook and Norfolk Island pines. A legacy of Maui's most prominent *kamaaina* (old-timers), Harry and Ethel Baldwin, the estate became an art center in 1976. Visiting artists offer lectures, classes, and demonstrations, all at reasonable prices, in basketry, jewelry making, ceramics, painting, and other media. Classes on Hawaiian art, culture, and history are also available. Call ahead for schedules and details. The exhibits here are drawn from a wide range of disciplines and multicultural sources, and include both contemporary and traditional art from established and emerging artists. The gift shop, featuring many one-of-a-kind works by local artists and artisans, is worth a stop. Hours are Monday through Saturday from 10am to 4pm.

Collections This long-time Makawao attraction is showing renewed vigor after more than 2 decades on Baldwin Avenue. It's one of our favorite Makawao stops, full of gift items and spirited clothing reflecting the ease and color of island living. Its selection of sportswear, soaps, jewelry, candles, and tasteful, marvelous miscellany reflects good sense and style. Dresses (including up-to-the-moment Citron in cross-cultural and vintage-looking prints), separates, home and bath accessories, sweaters, and a shop full of good things make this a Makawao must. 3677 Baldwin Ave. (✆ **808/572-0781.**

Cuckoo for Coconuts The owner's quirky sense of humor pervades every inch of this tiny shop, barely bigger than a walk-in closet and brimming with vintage collectibles, gag gifts, silly coconuts, 1960s and 1970s aloha wear, tutus, sequined dresses, vintage wedding gowns, and all sorts of oddities. Things we've seen here: an Elvira wig, very convincing; a raffia hat looking suspiciously like a nest, with blue eggs on top; and some vintage aloha shirts that would make a collector drool. 1158 Makawao Ave. (✆ **808/573-6887.**

Gallery Maui Follow the sign down the charming shaded pathway to a cozy gallery of top-notch art and crafts. Most of the works here are by Maui artists, and the quality is outstanding. About 30 artists are represented: Wayne Omura and his Norfolk pine bowls, Pamela Hayes's watercolors, Martha Vockrodt and her wonderful paintings, a stunning Steve Hynson dresser of curly koa and ebony. The two- and three-dimensional original works reflect the high standards of gallery owners Deborah and Robert Zaleski (a painter), who have just added to their roster the talented ceramic artist David Stabley. 3643–A Baldwin Ave. (✆ **808/572-8092.**

Gecko Trading Co. Boutique The selection here is eclectic and always changing: One day it's St. John's Wort body lotion and mesh T-shirts in a dragon motif, the next it's Provence soaps and antique lapis jewelry. You never know what you'll find in this tiny boutique; we've seen everything from handmade crocheted bags from New York to Mexican hammered-tin candle holders. The prices are reasonable, the service is friendly, and it's more homey than glammy. 3621 Baldwin Ave. (✆ **808/572-0249.**

Holiday & Co. Attractive women's clothing in natural fibers hangs from racks, while jewelry to go with it beckons from the counter. Recent finds include elegant fiber evening bags, luxurious bath gels, easygoing dresses and separates, Dansko clogs, shawls, shoes, soaps, aloha shirts, books, picture frames, and jewelry. 3681 Baldwin Ave. (✆ **808/572-1470.**

Hot Island Glassblowing Studio & Gallery You can watch the artist transform molten glass into works of art and utility in this studio in Makawao's Courtyard, where an award-winning family of glassblowers built its own furnaces. It's fascinating to watch the shapes emerge from glass melted at 2,300°F. The colorful works displayed range from small paperweights to large vessels. Four to five artists participate in the demonstrations, which begin when the furnace is heated, about half an hour before the studio opens at 9am. 3620 Baldwin Ave. ℂ 808/572-4527.

Hurricane This boutique carries clothing, gifts, accessories, and books that are two steps ahead of the competition. Tommy Bahama aloha shirts and aloha print dresses; Sigrid Olsen's knitted shells, cardigans, and extraordinary silk tank dresses; hats; art by local artists; a notable selection of fragrances for men and women; and hard-to-find, eccentric books and home accessories are part of the Hurricane appeal. 3639 Baldwin Ave. ℂ 808/572-5076.

Maui Hands Maui hands have made 90% of the items in this shop/gallery. Because it's a consignment shop, you'll find Hawaii-made handicrafts and prices that aren't inflated. The selection includes paintings, prints, jewelry, glass marbles, native-wood bowls, and tchotchkes for every budget. This is an ideal stop for made-on-Maui products and crafts of good quality. The original **Maui Hands** is in Makawao at the Courtyard, 3620 Baldwin Ave. (ℂ 808/572-5194); another Maui Hands can be found in Paia, at 84 Hana Hwy. (ℂ 808/ 579-9245).

The Mercantile The jewelry, home accessories (especially the Tiffany-style glass-and-shell lamps), dinnerware, Italian linens, plantation-style furniture, and clothing here are a salute to the good life. The exquisite bedding, rugs, and furniture include hand-carved armoires, down-filled furniture and slipcovers, and a large selection of Kiehl's products. The clothing—comfortable cottons and upscale European linens— is for men and women, as are the soaps, which include Maui Herbal Soap products and some unusual finds from France. Maui-made jams, honey, soaps and ceramics, and Jurlique organic facial and body products are among the new winners. 3673 Baldwin Ave. ℂ 808/572-1407.

Sherri Reeve Gallery and Gifts If you want to take a little bit of the beauty of Maui home with you, stop by this open aired gallery. Artist Sherri Reeve grew up in Hawaii (the local phone book featured her art on the cover one year) and she has captured the vibrant color and feel of the islands. You can find everything here from inexpensive cards, hand-painted tiles, and T-shirts to original works and limited editions. 3669 Baldwin Ave. ℂ 808/572-8931. www.sreeve.com.

Viewpoints Gallery Maui's only fine-arts cooperative showcases the work of 20 established artists in an airy, attractive gallery located in a restored theater with a courtyard, glassblowing studio, and restaurants. The gallery features two-dimensional art, jewelry, fiber art, stained glass, paper, sculpture, and other media. This is a fine example of what can happen in a collectively supportive artistic environment. 3620 Baldwin Ave. ℂ 808/572-5979.

FRESH FLOWERS IN KULA

Proteas are a Maui trademark and an abundant crop on Haleakala's rich volcanic slopes. They also travel well, dry beautifully, and can be shipped worldwide with ease. Among Maui's most prominent sources is **Sunrise Protea** (ℂ 808/876-0200), in Kula. It offers a walk-through garden and gift shops, friendly service, and a larger-than-usual selection. Freshly cut flowers arrive from the fields on Tuesday and Friday afternoons. You can order individual blooms, baskets, arrangements, or wreaths for shipping all over the world. (Next door, the Sunrise Country Market offers fresh local fruits, snacks, and sandwiches, with picnic tables for lingering.)

Proteas of Hawaii (© **808/878-2533**), another reliable source, offers regular walking tours of the University of Hawaii Extension Service gardens across the street in Kula.

Outside of Kula, **Ooka Super Market** (p. 446) and the Saturday-morning **Maui Swap Meet** (p. 445) are among the best and least expensive places for tropical flowers of every stripe.

UPCOUNTRY EDIBLES

Working folks in Makawao pick up spaghetti and lasagna, sandwiches, salads, and changing specials from the **Rodeo General Store,** 3661 Baldwin Ave. (© **808/572-7841**). At the far end of the store is the oenophile's bonanza, a superior wine selection housed in its own temperature-controlled cave.

Down to Earth Natural Foods, 1169 Makawao Ave. (© **808/572-1488**), always has fresh salads and sandwiches, a full section of organic produce (Kula onions, strawberry papayas, mangos, and lychees in season), bulk grains, beauty aids, herbs, juices, snacks, tofu, seaweed, soy products, and aisles of vegetarian and health foods. Whether it's a smoothie or a salad, Down to Earth has fresh, healthful, vegetarian offerings.

In the more than 6 decades that the **T. Komoda Store and Bakery,** 3674 Baldwin Ave. (© **808/572-7261**), has spent in this spot, untold numbers have creaked over the wooden floors to pick up Komoda's famous cream puffs. Old-timers know to come early, or they'll be sold out. Then the cinnamon rolls, doughnuts, pies, and chocolate cake take over. Pastries are just the beginning; poi, macadamia-nut candies and cookies, and small bunches of local fruit keep the customers coming.

EAST MAUI: ON THE ROAD TO HANA

Biasa Rose Boutique   You'll find unusual gift items and clothing with a tropical flair: capri pants in bark cloth, floating plumeria candles, retro fabrics, dinnerware, handbags and accessories, and stylish vintage-inspired clothes for kids. If the aloha shirts don't get you, the candles and handbags will. You can also custom-order clothing from a selection of washable rayons. 104 Hana Hwy. © **808/579-8602.**

Hemp House   Clothing and accessories made of hemp, a sturdy and sensible fiber, are finally making their way into the mainstream. The Hemp House has as complete a selection as you can expect to see in Hawaii, with "denim" hemp jeans, lightweight linen-like trousers, dresses, shirts, and a full range of sensible, easy-care wear. 16 Baldwin Ave. © **808/579-8880.**

Maui Crafts Guild   The old wooden storefront at the gateway to Paia houses crafts of high quality and in all price ranges, from pit-fired raku to bowls of Norfolk pine and other Maui woods, fashioned by Maui hands. Artist-owned and -operated, the guild claims 25 members who live and work on Maui. Basketry, hand-painted fabrics, jewelry, beadwork, traditional Hawaiian stone work, pressed flowers, fused glass, stained glass, copper sculpture, banana bark paintings, pottery of all styles, and hundreds of items are displayed in the two-story gift gallery. Upstairs, sculptor Arthur Dennis Williams displays his breathtaking work in wood, bronze, and stone. Everything can be shipped. **Aloha Bead Co.** (© **808/579-9709**), in the back of the gallery, is a treasure trove for beadworkers. 43 Hana Hwy. © **808/579-9697.**

Moonbow Tropics   If you're looking for a tasteful aloha shirt, go to Moonbow. The selection consists of a few carefully culled racks of the top labels in aloha wear, in fabrics ranging from the finest silks and linens to Egyptian cotton and spun rayons. Silk pants, silk shorts, vintage print neckwear, and an upgraded women's selection hang on colorful racks. The jewelry pieces, ranging from tanzanite to topaz, rubies to moonstones, are mounted in unique settings made on-site. 36 Baldwin Ave. © 808/579-8592.

HANA

Hana Coast Gallery *(Finds)*   This gallery is an esthetic and cultural experience that informs as it enlightens. Tucked away in the posh hideaway hotel, the gallery is known for its high level of curatorship and commitment to the cultural art of Hawaii. There are no jumping whales or dolphins here—and, except for a section of European and Asian masters (Renoir, Japanese woodblock prints), the 3,000-square-foot gallery is devoted entirely to Hawaii artists. Dozens of well-established local artists display their sculptures, paintings, prints, feather work, stone work, and carvings in displays that are so natural they could well exist in someone's home. Director-curator Patrick Robinson (of impeccable artistic integrity) has expanded the selection of koa wood furniture in response to the ongoing revival of the American Crafts Movement with a Hawaiian/Japanese influence. Stellar artists Tai Lake from the Big Island and Randall Watkins from Maui are among those represented.

Connoisseurs of hand-turned bowls will find the crème de la crème of the genre here: J. Kelly Dunn, Ron Kent, Todd Campbell, Ed Perrira, and Gary Stevens. You won't find a better selection elsewhere under one roof. The award-winning gallery has won accolades from the top travel and arts magazines in the country (*Travel and Leisure, Arts & Antiques* magazine) and has steered clear of trendiness and unfortunate tastes. In the Hotel Hana-Maui. © 808/248-8636.

Hasegawa General Store   Established in 1910, immortalized in song since 1961, burned to the ground in 1990, and back in business in 1991, this legendary store is indefatigable and more colorful than ever in its fourth generation in business. The aisles are choked with merchandise: coffee specially roasted and blended for the store, Ono Farms organic dried fruit, fishing equipment, every tape and CD that mentions Hana, the best books on Hana to be found, T-shirts, beach and garden essentials, baseball caps, film, baby food, napkins, and other necessities for the Hana life. Hana Hwy. © 808/248-8231.

11 Maui After Dark

The island's most prestigious entertainment venue is the $28 million **Maui Arts and Cultural Center,** in Kahului (© 808/242-7469; www.mauiarts.org). Bonnie Raitt has performed here, as have B. B. King, Hiroshima, Pearl Jam, Ziggy Marley, Lou Rawls, the American Indian Dance Theatre, Jonny Lang, and Tony Bennett, not to mention Keali'i Reichel and the finest in local and Hawaii talent. The center is as precious to Maui as the Met is to New York, with a visual-arts gallery, an outdoor amphitheater, offices, rehearsal space, a 300-seat theater for experimental performances, and a 1,200-seat main theater. Whether it's hula, the Iona Pear Dance Company, Willie Nelson, or the Maui Symphony Orchestra, only the best appear here. The center's activities are well publicized locally, so check the *Maui News* or ask your hotel concierge what's going on during your visit.

Except for **Casanova** in Makawao and **Maui Brews** in Lahaina, nightlife options on this island are limited. The major hotels generally have lobby lounges offering Hawaiian music, soft jazz, or hula shows beginning at sunset.

If **Hapa, Willie K.** and **Amy Gilliom,** or the soloist **Keali'i Reichel** are playing anywhere on their native island, don't miss them; they're among the finest Hawaiian musicians around today.

AT THE MOVIES

Movie buffs still rejoice over the infusion of celluloid at the 12-screen movie megaplex at the **Maui Mall,** 70 E. Kaahumanu Ave. (© 808/249-2222), in Kahului, which comes complete with comfortable reclining seats. The megaplex features current releases. The **Maui Film Festival** presents "Academy House" films for the avant-garde, ultra hip movie buff Wednesday nights at the **Maui Art and Cultural Center,** 1 Cameron Way (just off Kahului Beach Rd.), Kahului (© 808/572-3456; www.maui filmfestival.com), usually followed by live music and poetry readings. In the summer, either around Memorial Day weekend or in June, the Maui Film Festival also puts on nights of cinema under the stars in Wailea.

Film buffs can check the local newspapers to see what's playing at the other theaters around the island (or go to www.mauigateway.com/~rw/movie): the **Kaahumanu Theatres,** in the Kaahumanu Center in Kahului (© 808/873-3133); the **Kukui Mall Theatre,** 1819 S. Kihei Rd., in Kihei (© 808/875-4533); the Wallace Theatres in Lahaina at the **Wharf Cinema Center,** 658 Front St. (© 808/249-2222); and the **Front Street Theatres** at the Lahaina Center, 900 Front St.

AT THE THEATER

It's not Broadway, but Maui does have live community theater at the **Iao Theater,** 68 N. Market St., in Wailuku (© 808/244-8680; or © 808/242-6969 for the box office and program information; www.mauionstage.com). Shows range from locally written productions to well-known plays to musicals.

WEST MAUI: LAHAINA

The buzz in Lahaina is **'Ulalena** ☆, Maui Myth and Magic Theatre, 878 Front St. (© 808/661-9913; www.ulalena.com), a riveting evening of entertainment that weaves Hawaiian mythology with drama, dance, and state-of-the-art multimedia capabilities in a brand-new, multimillion-dollar theater. Polynesian dance, original music, acrobatics, and chant, performed by a local and international cast, combine to create an evocative experience that often leaves the audience speechless. It's interactive, with dancers coming down the aisles, drummers and musicians in surprising corners, and mind-boggling stage and lighting effects that draw the audience in. Some special moments: the goddesses dancing on the moon, the white sail of the first Europeans, the wrath of the volcano goddess, Pele, the labors of the field-worker immigrants. The story unfolds seamlessly. At the end, you'll be shocked to realize that not a single word of dialogue was spoken. Performances are Tuesday through Saturday at 6:30pm only. Tickets are $48 to $68 for adults and $28 to $48 for children ages 12 and under.

A very different type of live entertainment is **Warren & Annabelle's,** 900 Front St. (near Ruth Chris' Steakhouse and Hard Rock Cafe), Lahaina (© 808/667-6244; www.hawaiimagic.com), a magic/comedy cocktail show with illusionist Warren Gibson and "Annabelle," a ghost from the 1800s who plays the grand piano (even taking requests from the audience) as Warren dazzles you with his sleight-of-hand magic. Appetizers, desserts and cocktails are available (either as a package or a la carte). Check in is 5pm. Show-only price is $45. You must be 21 years old to attend, although they occasionally have a 4pm family show (minimum age is 6 years) without food or cocktails (generally during major school holidays); call for details.

The **Kaanaplai Beach Hotel** has a wonderful show called **Kupanaha** that is perfect for the entire family. It features the renowned magicians Jody and Kathleen Baran and their entire family, including child prodigy magicians Katrina and Crystal. The dinner show features magic, illusions, and the story of the Hawaii fire goddess, Pele, presented through hula and chant performed by the children of the Kano'eau Dance Academy. The shows are Tuesday through Saturday from 5 to 8pm; tickets are $69 to $79 for adults, $49 for teens, and $29 for children ages 6 to 12 (free for children 5 and under). Included in the ticket price is dinner (entree choices include island fish, roasted stuffed chicken, steak and shrimp, or a vegetarian dish, with keiki menu available). For reservations and tickets, call (📞 **808/661-0011** or www.kbhmaui.com.

Not many visitors get to experience the art of Hawaiian storytelling, but the Ritz-Carlton Kapalua has a weekly series called **The Legends of Kaulula'au,** every Sunday at 4 and 6:30pm, that is not to be missed. In old Hawaii, legends and family history would be passed down from generation to generation orally. "Mo'olelo," or the art of storytelling, would captivate the listeners and the storyteller would receive the same attention a movie star gets today. In the Legends of Kaulula'au, Hawaiian actor Moses Goods puts on this one-man play with agility and a spellbinding performance as he acts all the parts in the legend of Kaulula'au, a mischievous child who was banded to the island of Lanai. Lanai at that time, according to the legend, was inhabited by ghosts. Kaulula'au not only defeats the ghosts but he goes on to become the chief of Lanai and Maui. Tickets for this hour-long performance are $30, available by calling 📞 **888/808-1055.**

Maui Brews (📞 **808/667-7794**) draws the late-night crowd to its corner of the Lahaina Center with swing, salsa, reggae, and jams—omnivorous music, either live or with a DJ every night. The restaurant serves breakfast, lunch, and dinner beginning at 7:30am, and happy hour wails from 3 to 7pm, with $1 drafts and $1 wells. The nightclub opens at 9pm and closes at 2am. For recorded information on entertainment (which changes, so it's a good idea to phone ahead), call 📞 **808/669-2739.**

The **Hard Rock Cafe,** 900 Front St. (📞 **808/667-7400**), occasionally offers live music, so it wouldn't hurt to call them to see if something's up. Usually they feature mainland bands, normally on weekends after 10pm.

At **Longhi's** (📞 **808/667-2288;** www.longhis.com), live music spills out into the streets from 9:30pm on weekends. It's usually salsa or jazz, but call ahead to confirm. Other special gigs can be expected if rock-and-rollers or jazz musicians who are friends of the owner happen to be passing through.

You won't have to ask what's going on at **Cheeseburger in Paradise** (📞 **808/661-4855**), the two-story green-and-white building at the corner of Front and Lahainaluna streets. Just go outside and you'll hear it. Loud, live, and lively, tropical rock blasts into the streets and out to sea nightly from 4:30 to 11pm.

UPCOUNTRY MAUI

Upcountry in Makawao, the party never ends at **Casanova,** 1188 Makawao Ave. (📞 **808/572-0220**), the popular Italian ristorante where the good times roll. The newly renovated bar area has large booths, all the better for socializing around the stage and dance floor. If a big-name mainland band is resting up on Maui following a sold-out concert on Oahu, you may find its members setting up for an impromptu night here. DJs take over on Wednesday (ladies' night) and, on Thursday, Friday, and Saturday, live entertainment draws fun-lovers from even the most remote reaches of the island. Entertainment starts at 9:45pm and continues to 1:30am. Expect good blues, rock 'n' roll, reggae, jazz, Hawaiian, and the top names in local and visiting entertainment. Elvin Bishop, the local duo Hapa, Los Lobos, and many others have filled Casanova's stage. The cover is usually $5. Come Sunday afternoons, 3 to 6pm, for excellent live jazz.

Another place for live music in the Upcountry area is the **Stopwatch Sports Bar,** 1127 Makawao Ave (© **808/572-1380**), which has live music from 9pm on Fridays and Saturdays.

PAIA & CENTRAL MAUI

In the unlikely location of Paia, **Moanai Bakery & Café** (71 Baldwin Ave., © **808/ 579-9999**), not only has some of the best and most innovative cuisine around, but recently it has added live music: vintage Hawaiian from 6:30 to 9pm on Wednesday; smooth jazz and hot blues on from 6:30 to 9pm on Friday; and flamingo guitar and gypsy violin from 6 to 9pm on Sunday. There's no cover; just come and enjoy. Also in Paia, **Charley's Restaurant,** 142 Hana Hwy. (© **808/579-9453**), features an eclectic selection of music from country and western (Willie Nelson has been seen sitting in) to fusion/reggae to rip roaring rock 'n' roll; call for details. Other venues for live music in Paia include **Jacque's,** 120 Hana Hwy. (© **808/579-8844**), and **Sand Bar and Grill,** 89 Hana Hwy. (© **808/579-8742**).

In Central Maui, the **Kahului Ale House,** 355 E. Kamehameha Ave. (© **808/877-9001**), features karaoke on Sunday, Monday, and Wednesday from 10pm to 2am, live music on Thursday and Friday (call for times), and a DJ on Saturday from 10pm.

Other locations for live music include Mañana **Garage,** 33 Lono Ave., in Kahului (© **808/873-0220**) which has live music Wednesday through Saturday nights from 6:30pm on, and **Sushi Go,** in the Queen Kaahumanu Shopping Center, 275 Kaahumanu Ave., in Kahului (© **808/877-8744**), which also features live music on Friday and Saturday nights from 6:30 to 8:30pm.

HANA

Nightlife in Hana is pretty sparce. The only exception is the **Hotel Hana-Maui** (© **808/248-8211**), which features Hawaiian music in the Paniolo Lounge, Thursday through Sunday, 6:30 to 9:30pm, and has a hula show every Thursday and Sunday from 7:30 to 8:15pm in the main dining room.

8

Molokai:
The Most Hawaiian Isle

Born of volcanic eruptions 1½ million years ago, Molokai remains a time capsule on the eve of the 21st century. It has no deluxe resorts, no fancy restaurants, no stoplights or movie theaters, no air-conditioners, and no buildings taller than a coconut tree. Less is definitely more on this languid island—and, fortunately for budget travelers, Molokai has remained one of Hawaii's most affordable vacation destinations.

Molokai lives up to its reputation as the most Hawaiian place chiefly through its lineage; there are more people here of Hawaiian blood than anywhere else. This slipper-shaped island was the cradle of Hawaiian dance (the hula was born here) and the ancient science of aquaculture. An aura of ancient mysticism clings to the land

here, and the old ways still govern life. The residents survive by taking fish from the sea and hunting wild pigs and axis deer on the range. Some folks still catch fish in throw nets and troll the reef for squid. Modern Hawaii's high-rise hotels, shopping centers, and other trappings of tourism haven't been able to gain a foothold here.

The slow-paced, simple life of the people and the absence of contemporary landmarks are what attracts those in search of the "real" Hawaii. But what makes them stand in awe is this little island's diverse natural wonders: Hawaii's highest waterfall and greatest collection of fish ponds; the world's tallest sea cliffs; plus sand dunes, coral reefs, rainforests, hidden coves——and empty, gloriously empty beaches.

EXPLORING THE "MOST HAWAIIAN" ISLE

Only 38 miles from end to end and just 10 miles high, Molokai stands like a big green wedge in the blue Pacific. It has an east side, a west side, a backside, and a topside. Formed by three volcanic eruptions, the long, narrow island is like yin and yang: One side is a flat, austere, arid desert; the other is a lush, green, steepled tropical Eden. But the volcanic gods weren't done with Molokai until a third eruption produced the island's "thumb"—a peninsula jutting out of the steep cliffs of the north shore, like a punctuation mark on the island's geological story.

On the red-dirt southern plain, where most of the island's 6,000 residents live, the rustic village of **Kaunakakai** looks like the set of an old Hollywood Western, with sun-faded clapboard houses and horses tethered in tall grass on the side of the road. At mile marker 0, in the center of town, the island is divided into East and West so dramatically that an arid cactus desert lies on one side, and a lush coco-palm jungle on the other.

Eastbound, along the **coastal highway** named for King Kamehameha V, are Gauguin-like, palm-shaded cottages, set on small coves or near fish ponds; spectacular vistas that take in Maui, Lanai, and Kahoolawe; and a fringing coral reef visible through the crystal-clear waves.

Out on the sun-scorched west end is the island's lone destination resort, **Kaluakoi,** overlooking a gold-sand beach with water usually too rough to swim in. The old hill-top plantation town of **Maunaloa** has been razed and rebuilt as a gentrified planta-tion community, complete with an expensive country lodge with a pricey dining room. Cowboys still ride the range on **Molokai Ranch,** a 53,000-acre spread, while adventure travelers and outdoor-recreation buffs stay at the tentalows on the ranch property and spend their days mountain biking, kayaking, horseback riding, sailing, hiking, snorkeling, and just vegetating on the endless white-sand beaches.

Elsewhere around the island, in hamlets like **Kualapuu,** old farmhouses with pickup trucks in the yards and sleepy dogs under the shade trees stand amid row crops of papaya, coffee, and corn—just like farm towns in Anywhere, USA.

But that's not all there is. The "backside" of Molokai is a rugged wilderness of spec-tacular beauty. On the outskirts of **Kaunakakai,** the land rises gradually from sea-level fish ponds to cool uplands and the Molokai Forest, long ago stripped of sandalwood for the China trade. All that remains is an indentation in the earth that natives shaped like a ship's hull, a crude matrix that gave them a rough idea of when they'd cut enough sandalwood to fill a ship (it's identified on good maps as Luanamokuiliahi, or Sandalwood Boat).

The land inclines sharply to the lofty mountains and the nearly mile-high summit of Mount Kamakou, and then ends abruptly with emerald-green cliffs, which plunge into a lurid aquamarine sea dotted with tiny deserted islets. These breathtaking 3,250-foot **sea cliffs,** the highest in the world, stretch 14 majestic miles along Molokai's north shore, laced by waterfalls and creased by five pristine valleys—Halawa, Papalaua, Wailau, Pelekunu, and Waikolu—once occupied by early Hawaiians who built stone terraces and used waterfalls to irrigate taro patches.

Long after the sea cliffs were formed, a tiny volcano erupted out of the sea at their feet and spread lava into a flat, leaf-like peninsula called **Kalaupapa**—the infamous leper exile where Father Damien de Veuster of Belgium gave his life caring for the afflicted in the 1860s. A few people remain in Molokai's "thumb" by choice, keeping it tidy for the daily company that arrives on mules and small planes.

WHAT A VISIT TO MOLOKAI IS *REALLY* LIKE

There's plenty of aloha on Molokai, but the so-called "friendly island" remains ambivalent about vacationers. One of the least-visited Hawaiian islands, Molokai wel-comes visitors on its own take-it-or-leave-it terms and makes few concessions beyond that of gracious host; it never wants to attract too big of a crowd, anyway. A sign at the airport offers the first clue: SLOW DOWN, YOU ON MOLOKAI NOW—a caveat to heed on this island, where life proceeds at its own pace.

Rugged, red-dirt Molokai isn't for everyone, but anyone who likes to explore remote places and seek their own adventures should love it. The best of the island can only be seen on foot, mule, or horse, or via kayak or sailboat. The sea cliffs are only accessible by sea in the summer, when the Pacific is calm, or via a 10-mile trek through the Wailau Valley—an adventure only a handful of hardy hikers attempt each year. The great Kamakou Preserve is open just once a month, by special arrange-ment with the Nature Conservancy. Even Moomomi, which holds bony relics of pre-historic flightless birds and other *Lost World* creatures, needs a guide to divulge the secrets of the dunes.

Molokai

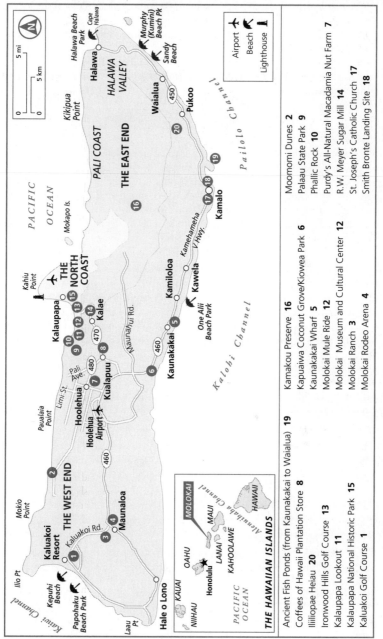

Airport ✈
Beach ☀
Lighthouse 🗼

Moomomi Dunes **2**
Palaau State Park **9**
Phallic Rock **10**
Purdy's All-Natural Macadamia Nut Farm **7**
R.W. Meyer Sugar Mill **14**
St. Joseph's Catholic Church **17**
Smith Bronte Landing Site **18**

Kamakou Preserve **16**
Kapuaiwa Coconut Grove/Kiowea Park **6**
Kaunakakai Wharf **5**
Molokai Mule Ride **12**
Molokai Museum and Cultural Center **12**
Molokai Ranch **3**
Molokai Rodeo Arena **4**

THE HAWAIIAN ISLANDS

Ancient Fish Ponds (from Kaunakakai to Waialua) **19**
Coffees of Hawaii Plantation Store **8**
Iliiliopae Heiau **20**
Ironwood Hills Golf Course **13**
Kalaupapa Lookout **11**
Kalaupapa National Historic Park **15**
Kaluakoi Golf Course **1**

Those in search of nightlife have come to the wrong place; Molokai shuts down after sunset. The only public diversions are softball games under the lights of Mitchell Pauole Field, movies at Maunaloa, and the few restaurants that stay open after dark, serving everything from local brew to pizza.

The "friendly" island may captivate you—on the other hand, you may leave with your head shaking, never to return. It all depends on how you approach Molokai. Either way, take it slow.

1 Orientation

ARRIVING

BY PLANE Molokai has two airports, but you'll most likely fly into **Hoolehua Airport,** which everyone calls "the Molokai Airport." It's on a dusty plain about 6 miles from Kaunakakai town. Twin-engine planes offer daily service, **Island Air** (© **800/ 323-3345** from the mainland, or 800/652-6541 inter-island; www.islandair.com), with seven direct flights a day from Honolulu and two direct flights from Maui. **Molokai Air Shuttle** (© **808/545-4988**) has four to five flights a day from Honolulu in small planes. **Pacific Wings** (© **888/575-4546** from the mainland, or 808/873-0877 from Maui; www.pacificwings.com), with one daily flight from Honolulu to the Kalaupapa Peninsula (see p. 484 for tours of Kalaupapa).

BY BOAT You can travel across the seas by ferry from Maui's Lahaina Harbor to Molokai's Kaunakakai Wharf on the ***Molokai Princess*** (© **800/275-6969** or 808/ 667-6165; www.mauiprincess.com). The 100-foot yacht, certified for 149 passengers, is fitted with the latest generation of gyroscopic stabilizers, making the ride smoother. The ferry makes the 90-minute journey from Lahaina to Kaunakakai daily; the cost is $85 adult round-trip and $43 children ages 3 to 12 round-trip. Or you can choose to tour the island from two different package options: Cruise/Drive, which includes round-trip passage and a rental car for $169 for the driver, $80 per additional adult passenger and $40 for children; or the Alii Tour, which is a guided tour in an air-conditioned van plus lunch for $169 for adults and $109 for children.

VISITOR INFORMATION

The **Molokai Visitors Association,** P.O. Box 960, Kaunakakai, HI 96748 (© **800/ 800-6367** from the U.S. mainland and Canada, 800/553-0404 inter-island, or 808/ 553-3876; www.molokai-hawaii.com) can give you all the information you need on what to see and do while you're on Molokai. If you want to drop by and see them when you are on the island, they are located in the Moore Cemter, 2 Kamoi Ave., Suite 200, in beautiful downtown Kaunakakai.

THE ISLAND IN BRIEF

KAUNAKAKAI Dusty vehicles—mostly pickup trucks—are parked diagonally along Ala Malama Street. It could be any small town, except it's Kaunakakai, the closest thing Molokai has to a business district. Friendly Isle Realty and Friendly Isle Travel offer islanders dream homes and vacations; Rabang's Filipino Food posts bad checks in the window; antlered deer-head trophies guard the grocery aisles at Misaki's Market; and Kanemitsu's, the town's legendary bakery, churns out fresh loaves of onion-cheese bread daily.

Once an ancient canoe landing, Kaunakakai was the royal summer residence of King Kamehameha V. The port town bustled when pineapple and sugar were king, but those days, too, are gone. With its Old West–style storefronts laid out in a 3-block grid on a flat, dusty plain, Kaunakakai is a town from the past. At the end of Wharf Road is Molokai Wharf, a picturesque place to fish, photograph, and just hang out.

Kaunakakai is the dividing point between the lush, green East End and the dry, arid West End. On the west side of town stands a cactus, and on the east side of town there's thick, green vegetation.

THE NORTH COAST   Upland from Kaunakakai, the land tilts skyward and turns green, with scented plumeria in yards and glossy coffee trees all in a row, until it blooms into a true forest—and then abruptly ends at a great precipice, falling 3,250 feet to the sea. The green sea cliffs are creased with five V-shaped crevices so deep that light is seldom seen (to paraphrase a Hawaii poet). The north coast is a remote, forbidding place, with a solitary peninsula—**Kalaupapa**—once the home for exiled lepers (it's now a national historical park). This region is easy on the eyes, difficult to visit. It lies at a cool elevation, and frequent rain squalls blow in from the ocean. In summer, the ocean is calm, providing great opportunities for kayaking, fishing, and swimming, but during the rest of the year, giant waves come rolling onto the shores.

THE WEST END   This end of the island, home to **Molokai Ranch,** is miles of stark desert terrain, bordered by the most beautiful white-sand beaches in Hawaii. The rugged rolling land slopes down to Molokai's only destination resort, **Kaluakoi,** a cul-de-sac of condos clustered around a 30-year-old seafront hotel (temporarily closed when we went to press) near 3-mile-long Papohaku, the island's biggest beach. On the way to Kaluakoi, you'll find **Maunaloa,** a 1920s-era pineapple-plantation town that's in the midst of being transformed into a master-planned community, Maunaloa Village, with an upscale lodge, triplex theater, restaurants, and shops. The West End is dry, dry, dry. It hardly ever rains, but when it does (usually in the winter), expect a downpour and lots of red mud.

THE EAST END   The area east of Kaunakakai becomes lush, green, and tropical, with golden pocket beaches and a handful of cottages and condos that are popular with thrifty travelers. With this voluptuous landscape comes rain. However, most storms are brief (15-min.) affairs that blow in, dry up, and disappear. Winter is Hawaii's rainy season, so expect more rain during January to March, but even then, the storms usually are brief and the sun comes back out.

Beyond Kaunakakai, the two-lane road curves along the coast past piggeries, palm groves, and a 20-mile string of fish ponds as well as an ancient *heiau,* Damien-built churches, and a few contemporary condos by the sea. The road ends in the glorious **Halawa Valley,** one of Hawaii's most beautiful valleys.

FAST FACTS

Molokai and Lanai are both part of Maui County. For **local emergencies,** call ⓒ 911. For non-emergencies, call the **police** at ⓒ 808/553-5355, the **fire department** at ⓒ 808/553-5601, or **Molokai General Hospital,** in Kaunakakai, at ⓒ 808/553-5331.

Downtown Kaunakakai has a **post office** (ⓒ **808/553-5845**) and several banks, including the **Bank of Hawaii** (ⓒ **808/553-3273**), which has a 24-hour ATM.

2 Getting Around

Getting around Molokai isn't easy if you don't have a rental car, and rental cars are often hard to find on Molokai. On holiday weekends—and remember, Hawaii celebrates different holidays than the rest of the United States (see "Holidays," on p. 31)—car-rental agencies simply run out of cars. Book before you go. There's no municipal transit or shuttle service, but a 24-hour taxi service is available.

CAR-RENTAL AGENCIES Rental cars are available from **Budget** (© **808/567-6877**) and **Dollar** (© **808/567-6156**); both agencies are located at the Molokai Airport. Nonchain operators include: **Molokai Outdoors** (© **877/553-4477** or 808/553-4477; www.molokai-outdoors.com); prices range from $25 a day for a compact to $65 a day for a 4×4 Jeep. We also recommend **Island Kine** (© **808/553-5242;** www.molokai-car-rental.com)—not only are the cars cheaper, but Barbara Shonely and her son, Steve, also give personalized service. They'll meet you at the Molokai Airport, take you to their office in Kaunakakai, and recommend specific outfitters for your activities. The used cars are in excellent condition (to quote Barbara: "I would drive every one of them with my grandkids") and are air-conditioned. Vans and pickup trucks are also available. You won't need a four-wheel-drive vehicle unless you're planning some specialized hiking, but, if that's the case, Island Kine has what you're looking for.

TAXI & TOUR SERVICES Molokai Off-Road Tours & Taxi (© **808/553-3369;** www.molokai.com/offroad) offers regular taxi service, an airport shuttle ($8 per person one-way to Molokai Ranch Lodge; and $8.50 per person one-way to Kaunakakai), and island tours (the Molokai highlights tour is $49 per person).

3 Accommodations You Can Afford

Molokai is Hawaii's most affordable island; in fact, hotel prices here are lower than those on any other island. Plus, because there are so few restaurants, most hotel rooms and condos come with kitchens, which can save you a bundle on dining costs.

The options on Molokai are mostly B&Bs, condos, a few quaint oceanfront vacation rentals, an aging resort, and a very expensive lodge. For camping on Molokai, you have two options: the upscale tentalows offered by Molokai Ranch, or, for hardy souls, camping with your own tent at the beach or in the cool upland forest (see "Hiking & Camping," p. 478). We've listed our top picks below; you may want to contact **Molokai Visitors Association** (see section 1 of this chapter) for additional options.

Note: Taxes of 11.42% will be added to your hotel bill. Parking is free.

KAUNAKAKAI

A'ahi Place *Value* Just outside of the main town of Kaunakakai and up a small hill lies this dream vacation cottage, complete with a wicker-filled sitting area, a kitchen, and two full-size beds in the bedroom. Two lanais make great places to just sit and enjoy the stars at night. The entire property is surrounded by tropical plants, flowers, and fruit trees. You also get a great continental breakfast (home-grown Molokai coffee, fresh-baked goods, fruit from the property) in the kitchen, so you can enjoy it at your leisure. For those who seek a quiet place (no phone or TV to distract you), this is the place. And for those who wish to explore Molokai, the central location is perfect.

P.O. Box 2006, Kaunakakai, HI 96748. © 808/553-8033. www.molokai.com/aahi. 1 unit. $75 double. Continental breakfast $10 extra. Extra person $20. 3-night minimum. No credit cards. *In room:* Kitchen, fridge, coffeemaker, no phone.

Hotel Molokai ⚶ This nostalgic Hawaiian motel complex is composed of a series of modified A-frame units, nestled under coco palms along a gray-sand beach with a great view of Lanai. The Travel Advantage Network purchased this property a couple of years ago, and immediately spent $270,000 upgrading the rooms with new phones, televisions, decorations, and roof coverings. The rooms are basic (be sure to ask for one with a ceiling fan), and each has a lanai. The mattresses are on the soft side, the sheets thin, and the bath towels rough, but you're on Molokai—and this is the only hotel in Kaunakakai. The kitchenettes, with coffeemaker, toaster, pots, and two-burner stove, can save you money on eating out.

Kamehameha V Hwy. (P.O. Box 1020), Kaunakakai, HI 96748. © 800/367-5004 on the mainland, 800/272-5275 in Hawaii, or 808/553-5347. Fax 800/477-2329. www.hotelmolokai.com. 45 units. $90–$175 double. Extra bed/crib $17. AE, DC, DISC, MC, V. **Amenities:** Fairly good and reasonably priced restaurant with bar; outdoor pool; watersports equipment/rentals; bike rentals; activities desk; babysitting; coin-op washer/dryers. *In room:* A/C, TV, dataport, kitchenette (in some rooms), fridge, coffeemaker, hair dryer, iron, safe.

Ka Hale Mala Bed-and-Breakfast *Value*   In a subdivision just outside town (off Kamehameha V Highway, before mile marker 5) is this large four-room unit, with a private entrance through the garden and a Jacuzzi just outside. Inside, you'll find white rattan furnishings, room enough to sleep four, and a full kitchen. The helpful owners, Jack and Cheryl, meet all guests at the airport like long-lost relatives. They'll happily share their homegrown, organic produce; we recommend paying the extra $5 for the breakfast here. The owners can also supply a couple of bikes and snorkel and picnic gear.

7 Kamakana Place (P.O. Box 1582), Kaunakakai, HI 96748. © and fax 808/553-9009. www.molokai-bnb.com. 1 unit. $70 double without breakfast; $80 double with breakfast. Extra person $10. No credit cards. **Amenities:** Jacuzzi. *In room:* TV, kitchen, fridge, coffeemaker.

GREAT DEALS FOR FAMILIES
Molokai Shores Suites *Kids*   Basic units with kitchens and large lanais face a small gold-sand beach in this quiet complex of three-story Polynesian-style buildings, less than a mile from Kaunakakai. Alas, the beach is mostly for show (offshore, it's shallow mud flats underfoot), fishing, or launching kayaks, but the swimming pool and barbecue area come with an ocean view, and the spacious units make this a good choice for families. Well-tended gardens, spreading lawns, and palms frame a restful view of fish ponds, offshore reefs, and neighbor islands. The central location can be a plus, minimizing driving time from the airport or town, and it's convenient to the mule ride, as well as the lush East End countryside. There's no daily maid service. Check the website for Internet-only discounts. We have gotten some letters complaining about the lack of maintenance and cleanliness; the management swears that they are taking steps to correct these deficiencies.

Kamehameha V Hwy. (P.O. Box 1037), Kaunakakai, HI 96748. © 800/535-0085 or 808/553-5954. Fax 808/553-5954. www.marcresorts.com. 102 units. $169 1-bedroom apt (sleeps up to 4); $250 2-bedroom apt (up to 6). Discounted rates for weekly and extended stays, plus corporate, military, and senior discounts. AE, DC, MC, V. **Amenities:** Putting green; salon; coin-op washer/dryers. *In room:* TV, kitchen, fridge, coffeemaker, iron.

THE WEST END

Paniolo Hale ★ *Finds*   Tucked into a verdant garden on the dry west end, this condo complex has the advantage of being next door to a while-sand beach and a golf course. The two-story, old-Hawaii ranch-house design is airy and homey, with oak floors and walls of folding-glass doors that open to huge screened verandas, doubling your living space. The one- and two-bedroom units come with two bathrooms and accommodate three or four easily. Some units have hot tubs on the lanai. All are spacious, comfortably furnished, and well equipped, with full kitchens and washer/dryers.

Believe It or Not: High-Priced Camping

This was a great idea: a unique eco-adventure that combines camping and outdoor activities with the amenities of a resort. The **Beach Village at Molokai Ranch** (© **888/627-8082** or 808/660-2824; fax 808/552-2773; www.molokai ranch.com) features camping on an exclusive private beach, with very upscale "camping" accommodations. The Beach Village offers "tentalows" (safari-type tents mounted on wooden platforms). This is yuppie camping—with queen or twin beds, ceiling fans, solar-powered lights, private bathrooms with composting toilets, and solar hot-water showers, plus big decks with lounge chairs, personal hammocks for two, and picnic tables. There's even daily maid service! A big pavilion down at the beach has all-you-can-eat buffet meals three times a day, plus nightly entertainment under the stars.

When the ranch first opened these camps in 1997, the price included airport pickup, meals, and a large menu of outdoor activities (horseback riding, mountain biking, hiking, sailing, snorkeling, kayaking, and other adventures). It was all-inclusive and quite a deal at $185 per person.

Today the prices have risen to an astounding $268 for garden tentalows, $308 (near the beach) to $358 (directly on the beach) double or single occupancy (plus the ubiquitous "resort fee" of $15 a day), and meals and activities are no longer included. Children 17 and under do stay free (with an adult), and children 12 and under also eat free, when accompanied by an adult. Meal prices are $15 for breakfast, $15 for lunch, and $31 for dinner. It starts to add up: Two adults staying in the least expensive room will spend $315 a day—including tax and $15 daily resort fee—just on the room! With meals, and tax (before any tipping), add another $127 a day; it comes out to $442 a day for two—and that's not including any activities you may want to do. That's pretty expensive "camping."

Now that the ranch has taken over the reins again, the new management promises many changes (including money-saving package deals). We hope they return to the all-inclusive policy, priced closer to camping than to luxury accommodations.

The whole place overlooks the Kaluakoi Golf Course (recently reopened), a green barrier that separates these condos from the rest of Kaluakoi Resort. Out front, Kepuhi Beach is a scenic place for walkers and beachcombers, but the seas are too hazardous for most swimmers. A pool, paddle tennis, and barbecue facilities are on the property, which adjoins open grassland countryside.

As with most condominiums in a rental pool, the quality and upkeep of the individually-owned units can vary widely. When booking, spend some time talking with the friendly people at Molokai Vacation Rentals so that you can get a top-quality condo that has been renovated recently.

Lio Place (next door to Kaluakoi Resort), Kaluakoi, HI 96770. Reservations: c/o Molokai Vacation Rentals, P.O. Box 1979, Kaunakakai, 96748. © **800/367-2984** or 808/553-8334. Fax 808/553-3783. www.molokai-vacation-rental. com. 77 units. $105–$145 double studio; $130–$195 1-bedroom apt (sleeps up to 4); $225 2-bedroom apt (up to 6).

3-night minimum; 1-week minimum Dec 20–Jan 5. AE, MC, V. **Amenities:** Outdoor pool; nearby golf course. *In room:* TV, kitchen, fridge, coffeemaker, washer/dryers.

GREAT DEALS FOR FAMILIES

Families should also consider our favorite place to stay on Molokai, **Paniolo Hale** (see above), which has one- and two-bedroom apartments that can sleep up to six.

Ke Nani Kai Resort ★ *Kids*   This place is great for families, who will appreciate the space. The large apartments are set up for full-time living with real kitchens, washer/dryers, VCRs, attractive furnishings, and breezy lanais. There's a huge pool, a volleyball court, tennis courts, and golf on the neighboring Kaluakoi course. These condos are farther from the sea than other local accommodations, but still just a brief walk from the beach. The two-story buildings are surrounded by parking and garden areas. The only downside: Maid service is only every third day.

In the Kaluakoi Resort development, Kaluakoi Rd., off Hwy. 460 (P.O. Box 289), Maunaloa, HI 96770. Reservations: c/o Molokai Vacation Rentals, P.O. Box 1979, Kaunakakai, 96748. ☎ 800/367-2984 or 808/553-8334. Fax 808/553-3783. www.molokai-vacation-rental.com. 100 units. $95–$105 1-bedroom apt (sleeps up to 4); $120–$135 2-bedroom apt (up to 6). AE, DC, DISC, MC, V. **Amenities:** Outdoor pool; golf course; 2 tennis courts; Jacuzzi. *In room:* TV, kitchen, fridge, coffeemaker, washer/dryers.

THE EAST END

Aloha Beach House ★★ *Finds*   This is the place to stay on Molokai. Nestled on the lush East End of Molokai lies this Hawaiian-style beach house sitting right on the white-sand beach of Waialua. Perfect for families, this impeccably decorated two-bedroom, 1,600-square-foot beach house has a huge open living/dining/kitchen area that opens out to an old-fashioned porch for meals or just sitting in the comfy chairs and watching the clouds roll by. It's fully equipped, from the complete kitchen (including a dishwasher), to a VCR (plus a library of videos), to all the beach toys you can think of. It's located close to The Neighborhood Store in case you need to pick up something or don't feel like cooking and want to eat out.

Located just after mile marker 19. Reservations: c/o The Rietows, P.O. Box 79, Kilauea, Hi 96754. ☎ 888/828-1008 or 808/828-1100. Fax 808/828-2199. www.molokaivacation.com. 1 2-bedroom house (sleeps up to 5). $220 (for up to 5) plus $95 cleaning fee. 3-night minimum. No credit cards. *In room:* TV, kitchen, fridge, coffeemaker, washer/dryer.

Country Cottage at Puu O Hoku Ranch ★ *Kids*   Escape to a working cattle ranch! *Puu o Hoku* ("Star Hill") Ranch, which spreads across 14,000 acres of pasture and forests, is the last place to stay before Halawa Valley—it's at least an hour's drive from Kaunakakai along the shoreline. Two acres of tropically landscaped property circle the ranch's rustic cottage, which boasts breathtaking views of rolling hills and the Pacific Ocean. The wooden cottage features comfortable country furniture, a full kitchen, two bedrooms (one with a double bed, one with two twins), two bathrooms, and a separate dining room on the enclosed lanai. TVs and VCRs are available on request. We recommend stargazing at night, watching the sunrise in the morning, and hiking, swimming, or a game of croquet in the afternoon. For larger parties, there's a four-bedroom, three-bathroom (sleeps up to eight) unit on the property. Horseback riding is available at the ranch.

Kamehameha V Hwy., at mile marker 25. Reservations: P.O. Box 1889, Kaunakakai, HI 96748. ☎ 808/558-8109. Fax 808/558-8100. www.puuohoku.com. 1 unit. $140 double for two-bedroom cottage. Extra person $20. 2-night minimum. No credit cards. **Amenities:** Swimming pool. *In room:* TV/VCR available on request, kitchen, fridge, coffeemaker.

Dunbar Beachfront Cottages ★★ *Kids*   This is one of the most peaceful, comfortable, and elegant properties on Molokai's East End, and the setting is simply stunning. Each of these two green-and-white plantation-style cottages sits on its own secluded beach—you'll feel like you're on your own private island. The Puunana Cottage has a king bed and two twins, while the Pauwalu has a queen and two twins. Each has a full kitchen, VCR, ceiling fans, comfortable tropical furniture, large furnished deck (perfect for whale-watching in winter), and views of Maui, Lanai, and Kahoolawe across the channel.

Kamehameha V Hwy., past mile marker 18. Reservations: c/o Kip and Leslie Dunbar, HC01 Box 901, Kaunakakai, HI 96748. (℃ **800/673-0520** or 808/558-8153. Fax 808/558-8153. www.molokai-beachfront-cottages.com. 2 2-bedroom cottages (each sleeps up to 4). $170 cottage ($75 cleaning fee). 3-night minimum. No credit cards. *In room:* TV, kitchen, fridge, coffeemaker, washer/dryer.

Kamalo Plantation Bed-and-Breakfast 🌾 *(Value* Glenn and Akiko Foster's (no relation to the author) 5-acre spread includes an ancient *heiau* ruin in the front yard, plus leafy tropical gardens and a working fruit orchard. Their Eden-like property is easy to find: It's right across the East End road from Father Damien's historic St. Joseph church. The plantation-style cottage is tucked under flowering trees and surrounded by swaying palms and tropical foliage. It has its own lanai, a big living room with a queen sofa bed, and a separate bedroom with a king bed, so it can sleep four comfortably. The kitchen is fully equipped (it even has spices), and there's a barbecue outside. A breakfast of fruit and freshly baked bread is served every morning. There's no TV reception, but the cottage does have a VCR, radio, and CD and cassette player.

Kamehameha V Hwy., just past mile marker 10 (HC01, Box 300), Kaunakakai, HI 96748. (℃ and fax **808/558-8236**. www.molokai.com/kamalo. 1 cottage. $85 cottage. Rate includes continental breakfast. Extra person $10. 2-night minimum. No credit cards. *In room:* Kitchen, fridge, coffeemaker, hair dryer.

Moanui Beach House 🌾 *(Kids* If you're looking for a quiet, remote beach house, this is it. The genial Fosters, who have lived in the islands for many years, run the popular Kamalo Plantation Bed-and-Breakfast (see above). They recently purchased and renovated this two-bedroom beach house, right across the street from a secluded white-sand cove beach. The A-frame has a shaded lanai facing the ocean, a screened-in lanai on the side of the house, a full kitchen, and an ocean view that's worth the price alone. The Fosters leave a "starter supply" of breakfast foods for guests (fruit basket, home-baked bread, tropical fruit juices, tea, and coffee).

Kamehameha V Hwy., at mile marker 20. Reservations: c/o Glenn and Akiko Foster, HC01, Box 300, Kaunakakai, HI 96748. (℃ and fax **808/558-8236**. www.molokai.com/kamalo. 1 2-bedroom unit. $140 double. Extra person $20. 3-night minimum. No credit cards. *In room:* TV, kitchen, fridge, coffeemaker, hair dryer, iron.

GREAT DEALS FOR FAMILIES

Families might also want to consider **Dunbar Cottages** (see above), two wonderful two-bedroom cottages by the sea.

Wavecrest Resort *(Kids* These condos—some of them newly remodeled, some in need of remodeling—are in three-story tropical structures surrounded by lawns, palms, mountainous inland slopes, and the solitude of the island's lush East End. The units, individually decorated by the owners, come with full kitchens, large lanais, and either garden or ocean views. If the complex is full, it can be noisy. Wavecrest is more remote than Molokai Shores—it's about 12 miles of leisurely driving to Kaunakakai (translation: 30-plus minutes), 7 more to the airport, and a substantial drive to West End activities—but more appropriately tropical than West End properties. Fortunately, there's a small store on the property for snacks or drinks and video rentals, as well as two lighted tennis courts and a swimming pool. The haunting views of the three neighboring islands really provide a unique sense of place, but the shoreline here isn't Molokai's best for swimming.

Kamehameha V Hwy. Reservations: c/o Molokai Resorts, P.O. Box 893, Kaunakakai HI 96748. ℭ **800/600-4158** or 808/553-3666. Fax 808/553-3867. www.wavecresthawaii.com. 126 units. $75 1-bedroom apt (up to 4; $40 cleaning fee). MC, V. **Amenities:** Outdoor swimming pool; tennis courts; small general store; coin-op laundry. *In room:* TV, kitchen, fridge, coffeemaker.

4 Great Deals on Dining

Molokai is strong on adventure, the outdoors, and the get-away-from-it-all feeling. No traffic lights and honking horns here, nor long lines at overbooked, self-important restaurants. But when it comes to dining, Molokai is not nirvana. Even with the first upscale hotel and dining room open in Maunaloa, Molokai's culinary offerings are spare.

A lot of people like it that way and acknowledge that the island's character is unchangeably rugged and natural. But a few years ago, when the renovated Hotel Molokai unveiled a tropical fantasy of an oceanfront dining room, the islanders thought this was the height of culinary pleasure. And it quickly became the island's busiest restaurant.

In 1999, when the Molokai Ranch opened the Lodge, it introduced the concept of Molokai having its own gourmet culinary cuisine, using local ingredients in not only traditional Molokai preparations but also in other ethnic styles of cooking.

Even with these new developments, Molokai has retained its glacial pace of change. The culinary offerings of the island are dominated by mom-and-pop eateries, nothing fancy, most of them fast-food or takeout places, and many of them with a home-cooked touch. Lovers of the fast lane might consider this aspect of the island's personality a con rather than a pro, but they wouldn't choose to come here, anyway. Molokai is for those who want to get away from it all, who consider the lack of high-rises and traffic lights a welcome change from the urban chaos that keeps nibbling at the edges of the more popular and populated islands. Sybarites, foodies, and pampered oenophiles had best lower their expectations upon arrival, or turn around and leave the island's natural beauty to nature lovers.

Personally, I like the unpretentiousness of the island; it's an oasis in a state where plastic aloha abounds. Most Molokai residents fish, collect seaweed, grow potatoes and tomatoes, and prepare for backyard luaus. Unlike Lanai (see chapter 9), which is small and rural but offers sophisticated dining in the two classy hotels, Molokai provides no such mix of innocence and erudition. Molokai doesn't pretend to be anything more than a combination of old ways and an informal lifestyle that's closer to the land than to a chef's toque.

You'll even find a certain defiant stance against the trappings of modernity. Although some of the best produce in Hawaii is grown on this island, you're not likely to find much of it served in its restaurants, other than in the takeout items at Outpost Natural Foods, at the Molokai Pizza Cafe (one of the most pleasing eateries on the island), or the Hotel Molokai. The rest of the time, content yourself with ethnic or diner fare—or by cooking for yourself. The many visitors who stay in condos find that it doesn't take long to sniff out the best sources of produce, groceries, and fresh fish to fire up at home when the island's other dining options are exhausted. The "Edibles" sections in "Shopping" (later in this chapter) will point you to the places where you can pick up foodstuffs for your own island-style feast.

Molokai's restaurants are inexpensive or moderately priced, and several of them do not accept credit cards. Regardless of where you eat, you certainly won't have to dress up. In most cases, I've listed just the town rather than the street address because, as you'll see, street addresses are as meaningless on this island as fancy cars and sequins. Reservations are not accepted unless otherwise noted.

KAUNAKAKAI

Hotel Molokai ⭐ AMERICAN/ISLAND   On the ocean, with a view of Lanai, torches flickering under palm trees, and tiny fairy lights lining the room and the neighboring pool area, the Hotel Molokai's dining room evokes the romance of a South Seas fantasy. It's a casual room, providing the only nightlife in Kaunakakai (p. 491) and the most pleasing ambience on the island. Lunch choices stick to the basics; most promising are salads (Big Island organic greens) and sandwiches, from roast beef to grilled mahimahi. As the sun sets and the torches are lit for dinner, the menu turns to heavier meats, ribs, fish, and pasta. Try the fresh catch, Korean kalbi ribs, barbecued pork ribs, New York steak, coconut shrimp, or garlic chicken. Temper your expectations of culinary excellence, and you're sure to enjoy a pleasing, but not perfect, dinner in an atmosphere that's unequaled on the island.

On Kamehameha V Hwy. ② 808/553-5347. Reservations recommended for dinner. Main courses $7–$8 lunch, $12–$19 dinner. AE, DC, MC, V. Daily 7–10am, 11am–2pm, and 6–9pm; bar until 10:30pm.

Molokai Pizza Cafe ⭐ *Kids* PIZZA   It's still the gathering place, with excellent pizzas and sandwiches that have made it a Kaunakakai staple as well as one of our favorite eateries on the island. The best-selling pies are the Molokai (pepperoni and cheese), the Big Island (pepperoni, ham, mushroom, Italian sausage, bacon, and vegetables), and the Molokini (plain cheese slices). Pasta, sandwiches, and specials round out the menu. Our personal fave is the vegetarian Maui pizza, but others tout the fresh-baked submarine and pocket sandwiches and the gyro pocket with spinach pie. Sunday is prime-rib day, Wednesday is Mexican, and Hawaiian plates are sold on Thursdays. Coin-operated cars and a toy airplane follow the children's theme, but adults should feel equally at home with the very popular barbecued baby back rib plate and the fresh-fish dinners. Children's art and letters in the tiled dining room add an entertaining and charming touch. Free delivery to the Hotel Molokai is a welcome development.

In Kahua Center, on the old Wharf Rd. ② 808/553-3288. Large pizzas $13–$23. No credit cards. Sun 11am–10pm; Mon–Thurs 10am–10pm; Fri–Sat 10am–11pm.

SUPER-CHEAP EATS

Kamoi Snack-N-Go *Kids* ICE CREAM/SNACKS   The Kamoi specialty: sweets and icy treats. Ice cream made by Dave's on Oahu comes in flavors such as green tea, lychee sherbet, *ube* (a brilliant purple color, made from Okinawan sweet potato), haupia, mango, and many other tropical—and traditional—flavors. Schoolchildren, and their parents, line up for the cones, shakes, floats, sundaes, and popular Icee floats served at this tiny snack shop. No tables, but there are aisles of candies.

In Kamoi Professional Center. ② 808/553-3742. Ice cream $1.65–$3.40. MC, V. Mon–Sat 9am–9pm; Sun noon–9pm.

Kanemitsu's Bakery & Restaurant ⭐ BAKERY/DELI   Morning, noon, and night, this local legend fills the Kaunakakai air with the sweet smells of baking. Taro lavosh is the hot seller, joining Molokai bread—developed in 1935 in a cast-iron, kiawe-fired oven—as a Kanemitsu signature. Flavors range from apricot-pineapple to mango (in season), but the classics remain the regular white, wheat, cheese, sweet, and onion-cheese breads. For those who like their bread warm, the bread mixes offer a way to take Molokai home. In the adjoining coffee shop/deli, all sandwiches come on their own freshly baked buns and breads. The hamburgers, egg-salad sandwiches, mahi burgers, and honey-dipped fried chicken are popular and cheap.

Kanemitsu's has a life after dark, too. Whenever anyone on Molokai mentions "hot bread," he's talking about the hot-bread run at Kanemitsu's, the surreal late-night ritual for die-hard bread lovers. Those in the know line up at the bakery's back door beginning at 10:30pm, when the bread is whisked hot out of the oven and into waiting hands. You can order your fresh bread with butter, jelly, cinnamon, or cream cheese, and the bakers will cut the hot loaves down the middle and slather on the works so it melts in the bread. *Hint:* The cream cheese and jelly bread makes a fine substitute for dessert.

79 Ala Malama St. ⓒ **808/553-5855.** Most items less than $5.50. No credit cards. Restaurant Wed–Sun 5:30–11:30am; bakery Wed–Mon 5:30am–6:30pm.

Molokai Drive-Inn AMERICAN/TAKEOUT   It is a greasy spoon, but it's one of the rare drive-up places with fresh *akule* (mackerel) and ahi (when available), plus fried saimin at budget-friendly prices. The honey-dipped fried chicken is a favorite among residents, who also come here for the floats, shakes, and other artery-clogging choices. But don't expect much in terms of ambience: This is a fast-food takeout counter with the smells of frying in the surrounding air—and it doesn't pretend to be otherwise.

Kaunakakai. ⓒ **808/553-5655.** Most items less than $7.75. No credit cards. Mon–Thurs 5:30am–10pm; Fri–Sun 6am–10:30pm.

Outpost Natural Foods ⭐ VEGETARIAN   The healthiest and freshest food on the island is served at the lunch counter of this health-food store, around the corner from the main drag on the ocean side of Kaunakakai town. The tiny store abounds in Molokai papayas, bananas, herbs, potatoes, watermelon, and other local produce, complementing its selection of vitamins, cosmetics, and health aids, as well as bulk and shelf items. But the real star is the closet-size lunch counter. The salads, burritos, tempeh sandwiches, vegetarian potpie, tofu-spinach lasagna, and mock chicken, turkey, and meatloaf (made from oats, sprouts, seeds, and seasonings) are testament to the fact that vegetarian food need not be boring. A must for health-conscious diners and shoppers.

70 Makaena Place. ⓒ **808/553-3377.** Most items less than $5. AE, DISC, MC, V. Sun–Fri 10am–3pm.

Sundown Deli DELI   From "gourmet saimin" to spinach pie, Sundown's offerings are home-cooked and healthful, with daily specials that include vegetarian quiche, spanakopita, vegetarian lasagna, and club sandwiches. The sandwiches (like smoked turkey and chicken salad) and several salads (Caesar, Oriental, stuffed tomato) are served daily, with a soup that changes by the day (clam chowder, Portuguese bean, cream of broccoli). Vitamins, T-shirts, and snacks are sold in this tiny cafe, but most of the business is takeout.

145 Puali St. (across the street from Veteran's Memorial Park). ⓒ **808/553-3713.** Sandwiches, soups, and salads $3.95–$7.50. AE, MC, V. Mon–Fri 10:30am–4pm; Sat 10:30am–2pm.

THE WEST END
WORTH A SPLURGE

Maunaloa Room 🌴 MOLOKAI REGIONAL   Molokai has never had anything resembling fine dining, but this restaurant changes the picture. It's in the island's first upscale hotel, the Lodge at Molokai Ranch, a 22-room lodge fashioned after a ranch owner's private home in the cool hills of Maunaloa, where you can see Oahu past the rolling ranchlands and the ocean. Fresh Molokai ingredients come in cross-cultural preparations. Breakfast features banana-stuffed Molokai sweetbread, French toast, or eggs with taro hash. The dinner menu includes entrees like fresh fish prepared with ling hing mui chutney; Hawaiian snapper with tropical fruit salsa and ginger lime butter; grilled Korean kal bi ribs with kim chee; New York steak with garlic butter; even vegetarian dishes like fried tofu in peanut oil with sweet chili sauce. Sunday night is Wok's Cooking, with an all-you-can-eat buffet featuring a wok station with stir-fried vegetables, chicken, shrimp and beef. The room's rustic, lodgelike ambience fits the paniolo (cowboy/Western) surroundings, and Hawaiian proverbs stenciled on the walls are a nice cultural touch.

The Lodge at Molokai Ranch, Maunaloa. ✆ **888/627-8082** or 808/660-2824. Reservations recommended for dinner. Main course $7.50–$16 breakfast; $10 lunch sandwiches (served in bar); $19–$29 dinner; $20 Sun buffet ($10 for children under 12). AE, DC, DISC, MC, V. Mon–Sat. 7–10am and 6–9pm; Sun 7–10 am, 5–9pm buffet; bar lunch service 10am–4pm.

EN ROUTE TO THE NORTH COAST

Kualapuu Cook House 🌴 AMERICAN   An old wagon in front of a former plantation house marks this down-home eatery, now takeout only. Local residents flock here for the oversized servings. Breakfasts feature giant omelets, homemade corned beef hash and, for those who dare, The Works—buttermilk pancakes, eggs, and home fries (you'll either be fueled for the day, or ready to take a nap). Lunch can be either a burger or sandwich or one of their humongous plate lunches of pork katsu or chicken, served up with rice, of course.

Farrington Hwy., 1 block west of Hwy. 470, Kalapuu. ✆ **808/567-9655.** Most items under $15. No credit cards. Mon 7am-2pm, Tues–Sat 7am–8pm.

THE EAST END
SUPER-CHEAP EATS

Neighborhood Store 'N Counter 🌴 *Kids* AMERICAN   The Neighborhood Store is nothing fancy, and that's what we love about it. This store/lunch counter appears like a mirage near mile marker 16 in the Pukoo area en route to the East End. Picnic tables under a royal poinciana tree are a wonderful sight, and the food does not disappoint. The place serves omelets, Portuguese sausage, and other breakfast specials (brunch is very popular), then segues into sandwiches, salads, mahimahi plates, and varied over-the-counter lunch offerings. Favorites include the mahimahi plate lunch, the chicken katsu, and the Mexican plate, each one with a tried-and-true home-cooked flavor. There are daily specials, ethnic dishes, and some vegetarian options, as well as burgers (including a killer veggie burger), saimin, and legendary desserts. Made-on-Maui Roselani ice cream is a featured attraction, and we hear raves over the Portuguese doughnut dessert, a deep-fried doughnut filled with ice cream. A Molokai treasure, The Neighborhood Store is also the only grocery store on the East End (see "Shopping," p. 488).

Pukoo. ✆ **808/558-8498.** Most items less than $6.95; bento $7.30. No credit cards. Daily 8am–6pm.

5 Beaches

With imposing sea cliffs on one side and lazy fish ponds on the other, Molokai has little room for beaches along its 106-mile coast. Still, a big gold-sand beach flourishes on the West End, and you'll find tiny pocket beaches on the East End. The emptiness of Molokai's beaches is both a blessing and a curse: The seclusion means no lifeguards.

KAUNAKAKAI
ONE ALII BEACH PARK

This thin strip of sand, once reserved for the *alii* (chiefs), is the oldest public beach park on Molokai. You'll find One Alii Beach Park (*One* is pronounced *o-nay,* not *won*) by a coconut grove on the outskirts of Kaunakakai. Safe for swimmers of all ages and abilities, it's often crowded with families on weekends, but it can be all yours on weekdays. Facilities include outdoor showers, restrooms, and free parking.

THE WEST END
PAPOHAKU BEACH 🏝🏝

Nearly 3 miles long and 100 yards wide, gold-sand Papohaku Beach is one of the biggest in Hawaii (17-mile-long Polihale Beach on Kauai is the biggest). It's great for walking, beachcombing, picnics, and sunset watching year-round. The big surf and rip tides make swimming risky, except in summer, when the waters are calmer. Go early in the day when the tropic sun is less fierce and the winds calm. The beach is so big that you may never see another soul except at sunset, when a few people gather on the shore in hopes of spotting the elusive green flash, a natural wonder that takes place when the horizon is cloud free. Facilities include outdoor showers, restrooms, picnic grounds, and free parking.

KEPUHI BEACH

Golfers see this picturesque golden strand in front of the Kaluakoi Resort and Golf Course as just another sand trap, but sunbathers like the semiprivate grassy dunes; they're seldom, if ever, crowded. Beachcombers often find what they're looking for here, but swimmers have to dodge lava rocks and risk rip tides. Oh, yes—look out for errant golf balls. There are no facilities or lifeguards, but cold drinks and restrooms are handy at the resort.

THE EAST END
SANDY BEACH 🏝

Molokai's most popular swimming beach—ideal for families with small kids—is a roadside pocket of gold sand protected by a reef, with a great view of Maui and Lanai. You'll find it off the King Kamehameha V Highway (Hwy. 450) at mile marker 20. There are no facilities—just you, the sun, the sand, and the surf.

MURPHY BEACH PARK (KUMIMI BEACH PARK)

In 1970, the Molokai Jaycees wanted to create a sandy beach park with a good swimming area for the children of the East End. They chose a section known as Kumimi Beach, which was owned by the Puu o Hoku Ranch. The beach was a dump, literally. The ranch owner, George Murphy, immediately gave his permission to use the site as a park; the Jaycees cleaned it up and built three small pavilions, plus picnic tables and barbecue grills. Officially, the park is called the George Murphy Beach Park (shortened to Murphy Beach Park over the years), but some old-timers still call it Kumimi Beach, and, just to make things real confusing, some people call it Jaycees Park.

Cheap Thrills: What to See & Do for Free (or Almost) on Molokai

- **Travel Back in Time on the Pepeopae Trail.** This awesome hike takes you through the Molokai Forest Reserve and back a few million years to a time before any human or creature set foot on the island. Along the misty trail (actually a boardwalk across the bog), expect close encounters of the wildlife kind: mosses, sedges, violets, lichens, and knee-high ancient ohias.
- **Soak in the Warm Waters off Sandy Beach.** On Molokai's East End, about 20 miles outside of Kaunakakai—just before the road starts to climb to Halawa Valley—lies a small pocket of white sand known as Sandy Beach. Submerging yourself in the warm, calm waters (an outer reef protects the cove) is a sensual experience par excellence—and it's absolutely free.
- **Stroll the Sands at Papohaku.** Go early, when the tropical sun isn't so fierce, and stroll this 3-mile stretch of unspoiled golden sand on Molokai's West End. It's one of the longest beaches in Hawaii. The big surf and rip currents make swimming somewhat risky, but Papohaku is perfect for walking, beachcombing, and sunset watching.
- **Snorkel among Clouds of Butterfly Fish.** You don't have to pay for a boat ride or an expensive guide to explore the calm waters at Kumimi Beach on the East End. Just don a snorkel, mask, and fins and head to the reef, where you'll find lots of exotic tropical fish, including long-nosed butterfly fish (*lau wiliwili nukunuku oioi*), saddle wrasses (*hinalea lau wili*), and convict tang (*manini*).
- **Venture into the Garden of Eden.** Drive the 30 miles of road along Molokai's East End. Take your time. Stop to smell the flowers and pick guavas by the side of the road. Pull over for a swim. Wave at every car you pass and every person you see. At the end of the road, stand on the beach at Halawa Valley and see Hawaii as it must've looked around A.D. 650, when the first people arrived in the islands.
- **Celebrate the Ancient Hula.** Molokai is the birthplace of the hula, the heartbeat of Hawaiian culture. While most visitors to Hawaii never get to see the real thing, it's possible to see it here—once a year, on the third Saturday in May, when Molokai celebrates the birth of the hula at its Ka Hula Pikoi Festival. The day-long festival at Papohaku Beach Park includes dance, music, food, and crafts.
- **Kayak along the North Shore.** This is the Hawaii of your dreams: waterfalls thundering down sheer cliffs, remote sand beaches, miles of tropical

No matter what you call it, this small park is shaded by ironwood trees that line a white-sand beach. It's generally a very safe swimming area. On calm days, snorkeling and diving are great outside the reef. Fishermen are also frequently spotted here looking for papio and other island fish.

vegetation, and the sounds of the sea splashing on your kayak and the wind whispering in your ear. The best times to go are late March and early April, or in summer, especially August to September, when the normally galloping ocean lies down flat.

- **Hike into Kalaupapa.** Even if you can't afford to ride a mule or to fly into Kalaupapa, don't pass up the opportunity to see this hauntingly beautiful peninsula. It takes nothing more than a pair of hiking boots, a permit (available at the trail head), and some grit. Hike down the 2½-mile trail (with 26 switchbacks, it can be a bit tricky) to Molokai's famous leper colony. The views are breathtaking: You'll see the world's highest sea cliffs and waterfalls plunging thousands of feet into the ocean. If you're afraid of heights, catch the views from the Kalaupapa Lookout.

- **Sample the Local Brew.** Saunter up to the Espresso Bar at the Coffees of Hawaii Plantation Store in Kualapuu for a fresh cup of java made from beans that were grown, processed, and packed on this 450-acre plantation. While you sip, survey the vast collection of native crafts.

- **Taste Aloha at a Macadamia Nut Farm.** It could be the owner, Tuddie Purdy, and his friendly disposition, that make the macadamia nuts here taste so good. Or it could be his years of practice in growing, harvesting, and shelling them on his 1½-acre farm. Either way, Purdy produces a perfect crop. You can see how he does it on a short, free tour of Purdy's All Natural Macadamia Nut Farm in Hoolehua, just a nut's throw from the airport.

- **Talk Story with the Locals.** The number-one favorite pastime of most islanders is "talking story," or exchanging experiences and knowledge. It's an old Hawaiian custom that brings people, and generations, closer together. You can probably find residents more than willing to share their wisdom with you while fishing from the wharf at Kaunakakai, hanging out at Molokai Fish & Dive, or having coffee at any of the island's restaurants.

- **Post a Nut.** Why send a picturesque postcard to your friends and family back home when you can send a fresh coconut? The Hoolehua Post Office will supply the free coconuts, if you'll supply the $3.95 postage fee.

- **Watch the Sunset from a Coconut Grove.** Kapuaiwa Coconut Beach Park, off Maunaloa Highway (Hwy. 460), is a perfect place to watch the sunset. The sky behind the coconut trees fills with a kaleidoscope of colors as the sun sinks into the Pacific. Be careful where you sit, though: Falling coconuts could have you seeing stars well before dusk.

HALAWA BEACH PARK ✿

At the foot of scenic Halawa Valley is this beautiful black-sand beach with a palm-fringed lagoon, a wave-lashed island offshore, and a distant view of the West Maui Mountains across the Pailolo Channel. The swimming is safe in the shallows close to shore, but, where the waterfall stream meets the sea, the ocean is often murky and unnerving. A winter swell creases the mouth of Halawa Valley on the north side of the bay and attracts a crowd of local surfers. Facilities are minimal; bring your own water. To get here, take King Kamehameha V Highway (Hwy. 450) east to the end.

6 Watersports

The best place to rent beach toys (snorkels, boogie boards, beach chairs, fishing poles, and more) is **Molokai Outdoors Activities,** in the lobby of Hotel Molokai, just outside Kaunakakai (© 877/553-4477 or 808/553-4477; www.molokai-outdoors.com). They have everything you'll need for a day at the beach and can also give you advice on where to find a great swimming beach or where the waves are breaking. Another good place to check out is **Molokai Fish & Dive,** Kaunakakai (© 808/553-5926; www.molokaifishanddive.com), a mind-boggling store filled with outdoor gear. You can rent snorkels, fishing gear, and even ice chests here. This is also a hot spot for fishing news and tips on what's running where.

For general advice on the activities listed below, see "The Active Vacation Planner," in chapter 2.

BODYBOARDING (BOOGIE BOARDING) & BODYSURFING
Molokai has only three beaches that offer ridable waves for body boarding and bodysurfing: Papohaku, Kepuhi, and Halawa. Even these beaches are only for experienced bodysurfers, due to the strength of the rip currents and undertows. You can rent boogie boards with fins for just $5 a day, or $19 a week, at **Molokai Outdoors Activities,** in the lobby of Hotel Molokai, just outside Kaunakakai (© 877/553-4477 or 808/553-4477; www.molokai-outdoors.com).

OCEAN KAYAKING
During the summer months, when the waters on the north shore are calm, Molokai offers some of the most spectacular kayaking in Hawaii. You can paddle from remote valley to remote valley, spending a week or more exploring the exotic terrain. However, most of Molokai is for the experienced kayaker only. You must be adept in paddling through open ocean swells and rough waves.

Molokai Outdoors Activities, in the lobby of Hotel Molokai, just outside Kaunakakai (© 877/553-4477 or 808/553-4477; www.molokai-outdoors.com), has sunset tours ($47 per person) of the ancient Hawaii fish ponds and a coastline tour ($61 per person). They also rent kayaks; rates start at $12 an hour and $26 a day.

On the West End, the **Lodge at Molokai Ranch** (© 888/627-8082 or 808/660-2824; www.molokairanch.com) offers a range of ocean-kayaking trips with snorkeling from $75 to $85.

SAILING
Molokai Charters (© 808/553-5852) offers a variety of sailing trips on *Satan's Doll,* a 42-foot sloop: 2-hour sunset sails for $40 per person, half a day of sailing and whale-watching for $50 (mid-Dec to mid-Mar), and a full-day sail to Lanai with swimming and snorkeling for $90 (which includes lunch, cold drinks, snacks, and all equipment). Owners Richard and Doris Reed have been sailing visitors around Molokai's waters since 1975.

SCUBA DIVING
Want to see turtles or manta rays up close? How about sharks? Molokai resident Bill Kapuni has been diving the waters around the island his entire life; he'll be happy to

show you whatever you're brave enough to encounter. **Bill Kapuni's Snorkel and Dive,** Kaunakakai (✆ **808/553-9867**), can provide gear, a boat, and even instruction. Two-tank dives in his 22-foot Boston whaler cost $125 and include Bill's voluminous knowledge of the legends and lore of Hawaii. You can also just rent tanks for $11 a day.

On the West End, **The Lodge at Molokai Ranch** (✆ **888/627-8082** or 808/660-2824; www.molokairanch.com) offers scuba-diving trips from $125 to $275.

SNORKELING

When the waters are calm, Molokai offers excellent snorkeling; you'll see a wide range of butterfly fish, tangs, and angelfish. Good snorkeling can be found—when conditions are right—at many of Molokai's beaches (see the box titled "Molokai's Best Snorkel Spots," below). **Molokai Outdoors Activities** (✆ **877/553-4477** or 808/553-4477; www.molokai-outdoors.com) offer the least-expensive snorkel gear for rent ($9 a day for fins, mask and snorkel, or $37 a week). Molokai Outdoors also offers snorkel/kayak tours for $130 per person.

For snorkeling tours on a boat, contact **Bill Kapuni's Snorkel & Dive,** Kaunakakai (✆ **808/553-9867**), which charges $65 for a 2½-hour trip. Walter Naki of **Molokai Action Adventures** (✆ **808/558-8184**) offers leisurely snorkeling, diving,

Molokai's Best Snorkel Spots

Most Molokai beaches are too dangerous for snorkeling in winter, when big waves and strong currents are generated by storms that sweep down from Alaska. From mid-September to April, stick to Murphy Beach Park (also known as Kumimi Beach Park) on the East End. In summer, roughly May to mid-September, when the Pacific Ocean takes a holiday and turns into a flat lake, the whole west coast of Molokai opens up for snorkeling. Mike Holmes, of Molokai Ranch & Fun Hogs Hawaii, says the best spots are as follows:

Kawaikiunui, Ilio Point, and **Pohaku Moiliili** (West End)   These are all special places seldom seen by even those who live on Molokai. You can reach Kawaikiunui and Pohaku Moiliili on foot after a long, hot, dusty ride in a four-wheel-drive vehicle, but it's much easier and quicker to go by sea. See above for places to rent a kayak and get advice. It's about 2 miles as the crow flies from Pohaku Moiliili to Ilio Point.

Kapukahehu (Dixie Maru) Beach (West End)   This gold-sand family beach is well protected, and the reef is close and shallow. The name Dixie Maru comes from a 1920s Japanese fishing boat stranded off the rocky shore. One of the Molokai Ranch cowboys hung the wrecked boat's nameplate on a gate by Kapukahehu Beach, and the name Dixie Maru stuck. To get here, take Kaluakoi Road to the end of the pavement, and then take the footpath 100 yards to the beach.

Murphy (Kumimi) Beach Park ✿ (East End)   This beach is located between mile markers 20 and 21, off Kamehameha V Highway (Hwy. 450). The reef here is easily reachable, and the waters are calm year-round.

and swimming trips in his 21-foot Boston whaler for $100 per person for a 4- to 6-hour custom tour.

SPORTFISHING

Molokai's waters can provide prime sporting opportunities, whether you're looking for big-game sportfishing or bottom fishing. When customers are scarce, Captain Joe Reich, who has been fishing the waters around Molokai for decades, goes commercial fishing, so he always knows where the fish are biting. He runs **Alyce C Sportfishing** out of Kaunakakai Harbor (© **808/558-8377**; www.alycecsportfishing.com). A full day of fishing, for up to six people, is $400, a three quarters-day is $350, and a half-day is $300. You can usually persuade him to do a whale-watching cruise during the winter months.

For fly-fishing or light-tackle reef-fish trolling, contact Walter Naki at **Molokai Action Adventures** (© **808/558-8184**). Walter's been fishing his entire life and loves to share his secret spots with visiting fishermen—he knows *the* place for bonefishing on the flats. A full-day trip in his 21-foot Boston whaler, for up to four people, is $300.

For deep-sea fishing, contact **Fun Hogs Hawaii** (© **808/567-6789**). Fun Hogs has fishing excursions on a 27-foot, fully equipped sportfishing vessel. Prices are $365 for six passengers for 4 hours, $417 for 6 hours, and $550 for 8 hours.

If you just want to try your luck casting along the shoreline, **Molokai Outdoors Activities,** in the lobby of Hotel Molokai, just outside Kaunakakai (© **877/553-4477** or 808/553-4477; www.molokai-outdoors.com), offers the least expensive rent for fishing poles ($5 a day, or $24 for the week), and can tell you where they're biting.

SURFING

Depending on the time of year and the wave conditions, Molokai can offer some great surfing for the beginner, as well as the expert. **Molokai Outdoors Activities,** in the lobby of Hotel Molokai, just outside Kaunakakai (© **877/553-4477** or 808/553-4477; www.molokai-outdoors.com), not only will know where the waves are, but they also rent gear: soft surfboards ($13 a day), short surfboards ($20 a day), and long boards ($24 a day). Good surfing spots include Kaunakakai Wharf in town, Hale O Lono Beach and Papohaku Beach on the West End, and Halawa Beach on the East End.

7 Hiking & Camping

HIKING MOLOKAI'S PEPEOPAE TRAIL

Molokai's most awesome hike is the **Pepeopae Trail** 👫👫, which takes you back a few million years. On the cloud-draped trail (actually a boardwalk across the bog), you'll see mosses, sedges, native violets, knee-high ancient ohias, and lichens that evolved in total isolation over eons. Eerie intermittent mists blowing in and out will give you an idea of this island at its creation.

The narrow boardwalk, built by volunteers, protects the bog and keeps you out of the primal ooze. Don't venture off it; you could damage this fragile environment or get lost. The 3-mile round-trip takes about 90 minutes to hike—but first you have to drive about 20 miles from Kaunakakai, deep into the Molokai Forest Preserve, on a four-wheel-drive road. *Don't try this with a regular rental car.* Plan a full day for this outing. Better yet, go on a guided nature hike with the **Nature Conservancy of**

Tips   A Tip for the Adventurous

If it's action you crave, call **Molokai Action Adventures** (© **808/558-8184**). Island guide Walter Naki will take you skin diving, reef trolling, kayaking, hunting, or hiking into Molokai's remote hidden valleys. Hiking tours are $50 per person for 4 hours; the number of participants is limited to no more than four. Not only does Walter know Molokai like the back of his hand, but he also loves being outdoors and talking story with visitors; he'll tell you about the island, the people, the politics, the myths, and anything else you want to know.

Hawaii, which guards this unusual ecosystem. For information, write to the Nature Conservancy at 1116 Smith St., Suite 201, Honolulu, HI 96817. No permit is required for this easy hike. Call ahead (© **808/537-4508** or 808/553-5236) to check on the condition of the ungraded four-wheel-drive, red-dirt road that leads to the trail head and to let people know that you'll be up there.

To get here, take Highway 460 west from Kaunakakai for 3½ miles and turn right before the Maunawainui Bridge onto the unmarked Molokai Forest Reserve Road (sorry, there aren't any road signs). The pavement ends at the cemetery; continue on the dirt road. After about 2 to 2½ miles, you'll see a sign telling you that you are now in the Molokai Forest Reserve. At the Waikolu Lookout and picnic area, which is just over 9 miles on the Molokai Forest Reserve Road, sign in at the box near the entrance. Continue on the road for another 5 miles to a fork in the road with the sign PUU KOLEKOLE pointing to the right side of the fork. Do not turn right; instead, continue straight at the fork, which will lead to the clearly marked trail head. The drive will take about 45 minutes.

HIKING TO KALAUPAPA

This hike to the site of Molokai's famous leper colony is like going down a switchback staircase with what seems like a million steps. You don't always see the breathtaking view because you're too busy watching your step. It's easier going down (surprise!)—in about an hour, you'll go 2½ miles, from 2,000 feet to sea level. The trip up sometimes takes twice as long. The trail head starts on the *mauka* (inland) side of Highway 470, just past the Mule Barn (you can't miss it). Check in here at 7:30am, get a permit, and go before the mule train departs. You must be 16 or older (it's an old state law that kept kids out of the leper colony) and should be in good shape. Wear good hiking boots or sneakers; you won't make it past the first turn in sandals.

HIKING THE WEST END

Molokai's entire West End, some 53,000 acres, is opening to hike tours through **The Lodge at Molokai Ranch** (© **888/627-8082** or 808/660-2824; www.molokairanch. com), which offers a range of hikes to fit different abilities. Prices range from $45 for an easy 2- to 3-hour hike to $85 for advanced hikes along the sea-cliff coast.

Molokai Outdoors Activities, in the lobby of Hotel Molokai, just outside Kaunakakai (© **877/553-4477** or 808/553-4477; www.molokai-outdoors.com) has a range of hikes from the Halawa Cultural hike at $75 to an East End Cultural tour and waterfall hike for $180.

CAMPING

Bring your own camping equipment, as none is available for rent on the island.

AT THE BEACH

One of the best year-round places to camp on Molokai is **Papohaku Beach Park** ✿, on the island's West End. This drive-up seaside site makes a great getaway. Facilities include restrooms, drinking water, outdoor showers, barbecue grills, and picnic tables. Groceries and gas are available in Maunaloa, 6 miles away. Kaluakoi Resort is a mile away. Get camping permits by contacting **Maui County Parks Department,** P.O. Box 526, Kaunakakai, HI 96748 (© **808/553-3204**). Camping is limited to 3 days, but if nobody else has applied, the time limit is waived. The cost is $3 a person per night.

IN AN IRONWOOD FOREST

At the end of Highway 470 is the 234-acre piney woods known as **Palaau State Park** ✿✿, home to the Kalaupapa Lookout (the best vantage point for seeing the historic leper colony if you're not hiking or riding a mule in). It's airy and cool in the park's ironwood forest, where many love to camp at the designated state campground. Camping is free, but you'll need a permit from the **State Division of Parks** (© **808/ 567-6618**). For more on the park, see p. 483.

GOLF

If you didn't bring your clubs, you can rent them from $6 a day ($24 for the week) from **Molokai Rentals and Tours,** Kaunakakai (© **808/553-5663;** www.molokai-rentals.com).

Golf is one of Molokai's best-kept secrets; it's challenging and fun, tee times are open, and the rates are lower than your score will be. After being closed for a number of years, the **Kaluakoi Golf Course** (© **808/552-0255**) is open again. After extensive renovation (repairs to irrigation, newly planted grass, redesigned bunkers, and narrower fairways), all 18-hole are again in play. Most of the work was cosmetic, and the Ted Robinson–designed course is still as challenging as ever. Using the natural terrain and narrow fairways, there are some tough bunkers and water hazards to maneuver around. The first 9 holes are at sea level, with panoramic views over the isolated 3-mile, white-sand Papohaku Beach, with the island of Oahu in the distance. A stiff wind is often present as this course provides a scenic and challenging experience. The back 9 holes play up along lush green hillsides, over a tropical gulch, and back down to the shore. Kaluakoi offers driving range, practice area, and three sets of tees making this course playable for all levels of golfers. Greens fees are $70 with cart.

The real find in golf courses is the **Ironwood Hills Golf Course,** off Kalae Highway (© **808/567-6000**). It's located just before the Molokai Mule Ride Mule Barn, on the road to the Lookout. One of the oldest courses in the state, Ironwood Hills (named after the two predominant features of the course, ironwood trees and hills) was built in 1929 by Del Monte Plantation for its executives. This unusual course, which sits in the cool air at 1,200 feet, delights with its rich foliage, open fairways, and spectacular views of the rest of the island. If you play here, use a trick developed by the local residents: After teeing off on the 6th hole, just take whatever clubs you need to finish playing the hole and a driver for the 7th hole, and park your bag under a tree. The climb to the 7th hole is steep—you'll be glad that you're only carrying a few clubs. Greens fees are $15 for 9 holes, $20 for 18 holes. Cart fees are $7 for 9 holes, $14 for 18. You can also rent a hand cart for just $2.50. Club rentals are $7 for 9 holes and $12 for 18.

BICYCLING

Molokai is a great place to see by bicycle. The roads are not very busy and there are great places to pull off the road and take a quick dip. **Molokai Outdoors Activities,** in the lobby of Hotel Molokai, just outside Kaunakakai (© **877/553-4477** or 808/553-4477; www.molokai-outdoors.com), offers a bike/kayak tour of the East End of Molokai, with snorkeling. All gear, lunch, guide, and transportation are $140. Bike rentals are $13 an hour, $26 a day, or $113 a week, and include a complimentary bicycle rack for your rental.

The best mountain biking in the state is on the trails of **The Lodge at Molokai Ranch** (© **888/627-8082** or 808/660-2824; www.molokairanch.com). Imagine 53,000 acres with inter-crossing trails that weave up and down the West End to the beach—simply spectacular. Guided tours range from $45 for 2 to 3 hours and bike rentals are $35 a day.

HORSEBACK RIDING

One of the most scenic places to go riding on Molokai is **Pu'u O Hoku Ranch** (© **808/558-8109;** www.puuohoku.com), about 25 miles outside Kaunakakai on the East End. Guided trail rides pass through green pasture on one of the largest working ranches on Molokai, then head up into the high mountain forest. Don't forget your camera: There are plenty of scenic views of waterfalls, the Pacific Ocean, and the islands of Maui and Lanai in the distance. Rates are $55 for an hour-long ride, $75 for a 2-hour ride, and $120 for a beach adventure.

For those looking for a little more than just a horseback ride, **The Lodge at Molokai Ranch** (© **888/627-8082** or 808/660-2824; www.molokairanch.com) offers a "Paniolo Roundup." You can learn horsemanship from the ranch's working cowboys and compete in traditional rodeo games; the half-day adventure is $85. Two-hour trail rides also are $85.

TENNIS

The only two tennis courts on Molokai are located at the **Mitchell Pauole Center,** in Kaunakakai (© **808/553-5141**). Both are lit for night play and are available free on a first-come, first-served basis, with a 45-minute time limit if someone is waiting. You can rent a racket for just $4 a day ($16 a week) from **Molokai Rentals and Tours,** HC01 Box 28, Kaunakakai (© **808/553-5663;** www.molokai-rentals.com). You can also rent tennis rackets and balls from **Molokai Outdoors Activities,** in the lobby of Hotel Molokai, just outside Kaunakakai (© **877/553-4477** or 808/553-4477; www.molokai-outdoors.com).

8 Seeing the Sights

IN & AROUND KAUNAKAKAI

Kapuaiwa Coconut Grove/Kiowea Park ★ *Kids* This royal grove—a thousand coconut trees on 10 acres planted in 1863 by the island's high chief Kapua'iwa (later, King Kamehameha V)—is a major roadside attraction. The shoreline park is a favorite subject of sunset photographers and visitors who delight in a hand-lettered sign that warns: DANGER: FALLING COCONUTS. In its backyard, across the highway, stands Church Row: seven churches, each a different denomination, clear evidence of the missionary impact on Hawaii.

Along Maunaloa Hwy. (Hwy. 460), 2 miles west of Kaunakakai.

Post-A-Nut 🎈 Postmaster Margaret Keahi-Leary will help you say "Aloha" with a dried Molokai coconut. Just write a message on the coconut with a felt-tip pen, and she'll send it via U.S. mail over the sea. Coconuts are free, but postage is $3.95 for a mainland-bound 2-pound coconut.

Hoolehua Post Office, Puu Peelua Ave. (Hwy. 480), near Maunaloa Hwy. (Hwy. 460). © **808/567-6144.** Mon–Fri 7:30–11:30am and 12:30–4:30pm.

Purdy's All-Natural Macadamia Nut Farm (Na Hua O'Ka Aina) 🎈 *Finds* The Purdys have made macadamia-nut buying an entertainment event, offering tours of the 1½-acre homestead and giving lively demonstrations of nutshell-cracking in the shade of their towering trees. The tour of the 70-year-old nut farm explains the growth, bearing, harvesting, and shelling processes, so that by the time you bite into the luxurious macadamia nut, you'll have more than a passing knowledge of its entire life cycle.

Lihipali Ave. (behind Molokai High School), Hoolehua. © **808/567-6601.** www.visitmolokai.com. Free admission. Mon–Fri 9:30am–3:30pm; Sat 10am–2pm; closed on holidays.

THE NORTH COAST

Even if you don't get a chance to see Hawaii's most dramatic coast in its entirety—not many people do—you shouldn't miss the opportunity to glimpse it from the **Kalaupapa Lookout** at Palauu State Park. On the way, there are a few diversions (arranged here in geographical order).

EN ROUTE TO THE NORTH COAST

Coffees of Hawaii Plantation Store The defunct Del Monte pineapple town of Kualapuu is rising again—only this time, coffee is the catch, not pineapple. Located in the cool foothills, Coffees of Hawaii has planted coffee beans on 600 acres of former pineapple land. The plantation is irrigating the plants with a high-tech, continuous water and fertilizer drip system. You can see it all on the walking tour; call 24 hours in advance to set up. The Plantation Store sells arts and crafts from Molokai. Stop by the Espresso Bar for a Mocha Mama (Molokai coffee, ice, chocolate ice cream, chocolate syrup, whipped cream, and chocolate shavings on top). It'll keep you going all day—maybe even all night.

Hwy. 480 (near the junction of Hwy. 470). © **800/709-BEAN** or 808/567-9241. www.molokaicoffee.com. Walking tour $7 adults, $3.50 children 5–12. Tours Mon–Sat 9:30am and 11:30am; Sun 11:30am only. Store open Mon–Fri 7am–4pm; Sat 8am–4pm; Sun 10am–4pm.

Molokai Museum and Cultural Center En route to the California Gold Rush in 1849, Rudolph W. Meyer, a German professor, came to Molokai, married the high chieftess Kalama, and began to operate a small sugar plantation near his home. Now on the National Register of Historic Places, this restored 1878 sugar mill, with its century-old steam engine, mule-driven cane crusher, copper clarifiers, and redwood evaporating pan (all in working order), is the last of its kind in Hawaii. The mill also houses a museum that traces the history of sugar growing on Molokai and features special events, such as wine tastings every 2 months, taro festivals, an annual music festival, and occasional classes in ukulele making, loom weaving, and sewing. Call for a schedule.

Meyer Sugar Mill, Hwy. 470 (just after the turnoff for the Ironwood Hills Golf Course, and 2 miles below Kalaupapa Overlook), Kalae. © **808/567-6436.** Admission $2.50 adults, $1 students. Mon–Sat 10am–2pm.

Palaau State Park ⚐   This 234-acre piney-woods park, 8 miles out of Kaunakakai, doesn't look like much until you get out of the car and take a hike, which really puts you between a rock and a hard place. Go right, and you end up on the edge of Molokai's magnificent sea cliffs, with its panoramic view of the well-known Kalaupapa leper colony; go left, and you come face to face with a stone phallus.

If you have no plans to scale the cliffs by mule or on foot (see "Hiking & Camping," p. 478), the **Kalaupapa Lookout** ⚐⚐⚐ is the only place from which to see the former place of exile. The trail is marked, and historic photos and interpretive signs will explain what you're seeing.

It's airy and cool in the ironwood forest, where camping is free at the designated state campground. You'll need a permit from the **State Division of Parks** (© **808/567-6618**). Not many people seem to camp here, probably because of the legend associated with the **Phallic Rock** ⚐. At 6feet high and pointed at an angle that means business, Molokai's famous Phallic Rock is a legendary fertility tool that appears to be working today. According to Hawaiian legend, a woman who wishes to become pregnant need only spend the night near the rock and . . . voilà! It's probably just a coincidence, of course, but Molokai does have a growing number of young, pregnant women.

Phallic Rock is at the end of a well-worn uphill path that passes an ironwood grove and several other rocks that vaguely resemble sexual body parts. No mistaking the big guy, though. Supposedly, it belonged to Nanahoa, a demigod who quarreled with his wife, Kawahuna, over a pretty girl. In the tussle, Kawahuna was thrown over the cliff, and both husband and wife were turned to stone. Of all the phallic rocks in Hawaii and the Pacific, this is the one to see. It's featured on a postcard with a tiny, awe-struck Japanese woman standing next to it.

At the end of Hwy. 470.

THE LEGACY OF FATHER DAMIEN: KALAUPAPA NATIONAL HISTORIC PARK ⚐⚐⚐

An old tongue of lava that sticks out to form a peninsula, Kalaupapa became infamous because of man's inhumanity to victims of a formerly incurable contagious disease.

King Kamehameha V sent the first lepers—nine men and three women—into exile on this lonely shore, at the base of ramparts that rise like temples against the Pacific, on January 6, 1866. More than 11,000 lepers arrived between 1865 and 1874, dispatched to disfigure and die in one of the world's most beautiful—and lonely—places. They called Kalaupapa "The Place of the Living Dead."

Leprosy is actually one of the world's least contagious diseases, transmitted only by direct, repetitive contact over a long period of time. It's caused by a germ, *Mycobacterium leprae,* which attacks the nerves, skin, and eyes, and is found mainly, but not exclusively, in tropical regions. American scientists found a cure for the disease in the 1940s.

Before science intervened, there was Father Damien. Born to wealth in Belgium, Joseph de Veuster traded a life of excess for exile among lepers; he devoted himself to caring for the afflicted at Kalaupapa. Father Damien, as he became known, volunteered to go out to the Pacific in place of his ailing brother. Horrified by the conditions in the leper colony, Father Damien worked at Kalaupapa for 11 years, building houses, schools, and churches, and giving hope to his patients. He died on April 15, 1889, in Kalaupapa, of leprosy. He was 49.

A hero nominated for Catholic sainthood, Father Damien is buried not in his tomb next to Molokai's St. Philomena Church, but in his native Belgium. Well, most of him anyway. His hand was recently returned to Molokai, however, and was reinterred at Kalaupapa as a relic of his martyrdom.

This small peninsula is probably the final resting place of more than 11,000 souls. The sand dunes are littered with grave markers, sorted by the religious affiliation— Catholic, Protestant, Lutheran, Buddhist—of those who died here. But so many are buried in unmarked graves that no accurate census of the dead exists.

Kalaupapa is now a National Historic Park (© 808/567-6802; www.nps.gov/kala) and one of Hawaii's richest archaeological preserves, with sites that date to A.D. 1000. About 60 former patients chose to remain in the tidy village of whitewashed houses with statues of angels in their yards. The original name for their former affliction, leprosy, was officially banned in Hawaii by the State Legislature in 1981. The name used now is "Hansen's disease," for Dr. Gerhard Hansen of Norway, who discovered the germ in 1873. The few remaining residents of Kalaupapa still call the disease leprosy, although none are too keen on being called lepers.

Kalaupapa welcomes visitors who arrive on foot, by mule, or by small plane. Father Damien's St. Philomena church, built in 1872, is open to visitors, who can see it from a yellow school bus driven by resident tour guide Richard Marks, an ex-seaman and sheriff who survived the disease. You won't be able to roam freely, and you'll be allowed to enter only the museum, the craft shop, and the church.

MULE RIDES TO KALAUPAPA   The first turn's a gasp, and it's all downhill from there. You can close your eyes and hold on for dear life, or slip the reins over the pommel and sit back, letting the mule do the walking down the precipitous path to Kalaupapa National Historic Park.

Even if you have only one day to spend on Molokai, spend it on a mule. This is an expensive outing, but it's a once-in-a-lifetime ride. The cliffs are taller than a 300-story skyscraper, but Buzzy Sproat's mules go safely up and down the narrow 3-mile trail daily, rain or shine. Starting at the top of the nearly perpendicular ridge (1,600 ft. high), the sure-footed mules step down the muddy trail, pausing often on the 26 switchbacks to calculate their next move—and always, it seems to us, veering a little too close to the edge. Each switchback is numbered; by the time you get to number four, you'll catch your breath, put the mule on cruise control, and begin to enjoy Hawaii's most awesome trail ride.

The mule tours are offered once daily starting at 8am, and they last until about 3:30pm. It costs $165 per person for the all-day adventure, which includes the round-trip mule ride, a guided tour of the settlement, a visit to Father Damien's church and grave, lunch at Kalawao, and souvenirs. To go, you must be at least 16 years old and physically fit. Contact **Molokai Mule Ride** ☆☆☆, 100 Kalae Hwy., Suite 104, on Hwy. 470, 5 miles north of Hwy. 460 (© **800/567-7550,** or 808/567-6088 from 8–10pm; www.muleride.com). Advance reservations (at least 2 weeks ahead) are required.

SEEING KALAUPAPA BY PLANE   The fastest and easiest way to get to Kalaupapa is by hopping on a plane and zipping to Kalaupapa airport. From here, you can pick up the same Kalaupapa tour that the mule riders and hikers take. **Molokai Mule Ride** ☆☆☆, 100 Kalae Hwy., Suite 104, on Highway 470, 5 miles north of Highway 460 (© **800/ 567-7550,** or 808/567-6088 from 8–10pm; www.muleride.com) will pick you up at the

Kalaupapa airport and take you to some of the area's most scenic spots, including Kalawao, where Father Damien's church still stands, and the town of Kalaupapa. Packages include a round-trip flight to Kalaupapa, entry permits, historical park tour with Damien Tours, and a light picnic lunch, and cost $299 from Honolulu. All visitors must be at least 16 years old.

SEEING KALAUPAPA BY FERRY/HIKING   From Maui take the *Molokai Princess* Ferry to Molokai (© **800/275-6969** or 808/667-6165; www.mauiprincess. com), where you are met and transported by van to the top of the 1700-foot sea cliffs. Here, you hike down the 3-mile trail to the Kalaupapa National Historic Park; at the park you are met by Damien Tours and given a van tour of the peninsula, during which you'll visit Father Damien's St. Philomena Church, see his early gravesite, and hear the stories of struggle and courage of the residents of Kalaupapa. The only catch is you have to hike back up the 1,700-foot cliffs, where you are picked up by the van and returned to the ferry dock for the trip back to Maui. This fabulous experience really should be undertaken only by the physically fit (it will take about an hour hiking down and another 1½ hours to hike back up). Cost for ferry, transportation, tour, and lunch is $249 (participants must be 16 years or older). If you would like to hike in, tour, then fly back to Maui, the fee is $299.

THE WEST END
MAUNALOA
In the first and only urban renewal on Molokai, the 1920s-era pineapple-plantation town of Maunaloa is being reinvented. Streets are getting widened and paved, and curbs and sidewalks are being added to serve a new tract of houses. Historic Maunaloa is becoming Maunaloa Village—there's already a town center with a park, a restaurant, a triplex movie theater, a gas station, a KFC, and an upscale lodge.

This master-planned village will also have a museum and artisans' studios—uptown stuff for Molokai. Jonathan Socher's **Big Wind Kite Factory** (p. 491) is keeping his kites and books wrapped in cellophane against constant clouds of red dust raised by construction crews.

ON THE NORTHWEST SHORE: MOOMOMI DUNES
Undisturbed for centuries, the Moomomi Dunes, on Molokai's northwest shore, are a unique treasure chest of great scientific value. The area may look like just a pile of sand as you fly over on the final approach to Hoolehua Airport, but Moomomi Dunes is much more than that. Archaeologists have found adz quarries, ancient Hawaiian burial sites, and shelter caves; botanists have identified five endangered plant species; and marine biologists are finding evidence that endangered green sea turtles are coming out from the waters once again to lay eggs here. The greatest discovery, however, belongs to Smithsonian Institute ornithologists, who have found bones of prehistoric birds—some of them flightless—that existed nowhere else on earth.

Accessible by Jeep trails that thread downhill to the shore, this wild coast is buffeted by strong afternoon breezes. It's hot, dry, and windy, so take water, sunscreen, and a windbreaker.

At Kawaaloa Bay, a 20-minute walk to the west, there's a broad, golden beach that you can have all to yourself. *But, due to the rough seas, stay out of the water.* The 920-acre preserve is accessible via monthly guided nature tours led by the **Nature Conservancy of Hawaii;** call © **808/553-5236** or 808/524-0779 for an exact schedule and details.

To get here, take Highway 460 (Maunaloa Hwy.) from Kaunakakai; turn right onto Highway 470, and follow it to Kualapuu. At Kualapuu, turn left on Highway 480 and go through Hoolehua Village; it's 3 miles to the bay.

THE EAST END

The East End is a cool and inviting green place that's worth a drive to the end of King Kamehameha V Highway (Hwy. 450). Unfortunately, the trail that leads into the area's greatest natural attraction, Halawa Valley, is now off-limits.

A HORSEBACK RIDE TO ILIILIOPAE HEIAU

On horseback (where the elevated view is magnificent), you bump along a dirt trail through an incredible mango grove, bound for an ancient temple of human sacrifice. This temple of doom—right out of *Indiana Jones*—is Iliiliopae, a huge rectangle of stone made of 90 million rocks, overlooking the once-important village of Mapulehu and four ancient fish ponds. The wagon glides under the perfumed mangoes, then heads uphill through a kiawe forest filled with Java plums to the *heiau* (temple), which stands across a dry stream bed under cloud-spiked Kaunolu, the 4,970-foot island summit.

Hawaii's most powerful *heiau* attracted *kahunas* (priests) from all over the islands. They came to learn the rules of human sacrifice at this university of sacred rites. Contrary to Hollywood's version, historians say that the victims here were always men, not young virgins, and that they were strangled, not thrown into a volcano, while priests sat on lauhala mats watching silently. Spooky, eh?

This is the biggest, oldest, and most famous *heiau* on Molokai. The massive 22-foot-high stone altar is dedicated to Lono, the Hawaiian god of fertility. The *heiau* resonates with *mana* (power) strong enough to lean on. Legend says Iliiliopae was built in a single night by a thousand men who passed rocks hand over hand through the Wailau Valley from the other side of the island; each received a shrimp (*'opae*) in exchange for the rock (*ili'ili*). Others say it was built by Menehunes, mythic elves who accomplished Herculean feats.

After the visit to the temple, your own horse takes you back to the mango grove. Contact **Molokai Wagon Rides,** King Kamehameha V Highway (Hwy. 450), at mile marker 15, Kaunakakai, HI 96748 (© **808/558-8380**). The tour is $40 per person via wagon (minimum 10 people) or $50 per person on horseback. The hour-long ride goes up to the *heiau*, then beyond it to the top of the mountain for those breathtaking views, and finally back down to the beach.

KAMAKOU PRESERVE

It's hard to believe, but close to the nearly mile-high summit here, it rains more than 80 inches a year—enough to qualify as a rainforest. The Molokai Forest, as it was historically known, is the source of 60% of Molokai's water. Nearly 3,000 acres from the summit to the lowland forests of eucalyptus and pine are now held by the Nature Conservancy, which has identified 219 Hawaiian plants that grow here exclusively. The preserve is also the last stand of the endangered Molokai thrush (*olomao*) and Molokai creeper (*kawawahie*).

To get to the preserve, take the Forest Reserve road from Kaunakakai. It's a 45-minute, four-wheel-drive trip on a dirt trail to Waikolu Lookout Campground; from here, you can venture into the wilderness preserve on foot across a boardwalk on a 1½-hour hike (see "Hiking Molokai's Pepeopae Trail," earlier in this chapter). For more information, contact the **Nature Conservancy** (© **808/553-5236**).

EN ROUTE TO HALAWA VALLEY

No visit to Molokai is complete without at least a passing glance at the island's **ancient fish ponds,** a singular achievement in Pacific aquaculture. With their hunger for fresh fish and lack of ice or refrigeration, Hawaiians perfected aquaculture in 1400, before Christopher Columbus "discovered" America. They built gated, U-shaped stone and coral walls on the shore to catch fish on the incoming tide; they would then raise them in captivity. The result: A constant, ready supply of fresh fish.

The ponds, which stretch for 20 miles along Molokai's south shore and are visible from Kamehameha V Highway (Hwy. 450), offer insight into the island's ancient population. It took something like a thousand people to tend a single fish pond, and more than 60 ponds once existed on this coast. All the fish ponds are named; a few are privately owned. Some are silted in by red-dirt runoff from south coast gulches; others have been revived by folks who raise fish and seaweed.

The largest, 54-acre **Keawa Nui Pond,** is surrounded by a 3-foot-high, 2,000-foot-long stone wall. **Alii Fish Pond,** reserved for kings, is visible through the coconut groves at One Alii Beach Park (p. 473). From the road, you can see **Kalokoeli Pond,** 6 miles east of Kaunakakai on the highway.

Moments **Halawa Valley: A Hike Back in History**

"There are things on Molokai, sacred things, that you may not be able to see or may not hear, but they are there," said Pilipo Solotario, who was born and raised in Halawa Valley, and survived the 1946 tsunami that barreled into the ancient valley. "As Hawaiians, we respect these things."

If people are going to "like Molokai," Solotario feels it is important that they learn about the history and culture; that is part of the secret of appreciating the island.

"I see my role, and I'm 67 years old, as educating people, outsiders on our culture, our history," he said at the beginning of his cultural hike into his family property in Halawa Valley. "To really appreciate Molokai you need to understand and know things so that you are *pono;* you are right with the land and don't disrespect the culture. Then, then you see the real Molokai."

Solotario and his family, who own the land in the valley, are the only people allowed to hike into Halawa. They lead daily tours, which begin at the County Park pavilion, with a history of the valley, a discussion of the Hawaiian culture, and a display of the fruits, trees, and other flora you will be seeing in the valley. As you hike through the valley, Solotario stops to point out historical and cultural aspects, including chanting in Hawaiian before entering a sacred heiau. At the falls, after another brief chant, visitors can swim in the brisk waters of the waterfall. Cost for the 4-hour tour is $75. Contact **The Lodge at Molokai Ranch** (⟲ **888/627-8082** or 808/660-2824; www.molokai ranch.com). Bring insect repellant, water, a snack, and a swimsuit. Don't forget your camera.

Note that if you venture away from the County Park into the valley on your own, you are trespassing and can be prosecuted.

Our Lady of Sorrows Catholic Church, one of five built by Father Damien on Molokai and the first outside Kalaupapa, sits across the highway from a fish pond. For a closer look, park in the church lot (except on Sundays).

St. Joseph's Catholic Church   The afternoon sun strikes St. Joseph's Church with such a bold ray of light that it looks as if God is about to perform a miracle. This little 1876 wood-frame church is one of four Father Damien built "topside" on Molokai. Restored in 1971, the church stands beside a seaside cemetery, where feral cats play under the gaze of a Damien statue amid gravestones decorated with flower leis.

King Kamehameha V Hwy. (Hwy. 450), just after mile marker 10.

Smith Bronte Landing Site   In 1927, Charles Lindbergh soloed the Atlantic Ocean in a plane called *The Spirit of St. Louis* and became an American hero. That same year, Ernie Smith and Emory B. Bronte took off from Oakland, California, on July 14 in a single-engine Travelair aircraft named *The City of Oakland,* headed across the Pacific Ocean for Honolulu, 2,397 miles away. The next day, after running out of fuel, they crash-landed upside-down in a kiawe thicket on Molokai, but emerged unhurt to become the first civilians to fly to Hawaii from the U.S. mainland. The 25-hour, 2-minute flight landed Smith and Bronte a place in aviation history—and on a roadside marker on Molokai.

King Kamehameha V Hwy. (Hwy. 450), at mile marker 11, on the *makai* (ocean) side.

HALAWA VALLEY 🥾

Of the five great valleys of Molokai, only Halawa, with its two waterfalls, golden beach, sleepy lagoon, great surf, and offshore island, is easily accessible. Unfortunately, the trail through fertile Halawa Valley, which was inhabited for centuries, and on to the 250-foot Moaula Falls has been closed for some time. There is one operator who conducts very expensive tours, but we have received so many letters of complaint (and have been personally stood up by him after a confirmed reservation) that we no longer recommend you use him.

You can spend a day at the county beach park, but do not venture into the valley on your own. In a kind of 21st-century *kapu,* the private landowners in the valley, worried about slip-and-fall lawsuits, have posted NO TRESPASSING signs on their property.

To get to Halawa Valley, drive north from Kaunakakai on Highway 450 for 30 miles along the coast to the end of the road, which descends into the valley past Jersalema Hou Church. If you'd just like a glimpse of the valley on your way to the beach, there's a scenic overlook along the road: After Puuo Hoku Ranch, at mile marker 25, the narrow, two-lane road widens at a hairpin curve, and you'll find the overlook on your right; it's 2 miles more to the valley floor.

9 Shopping

KAUNAKAKAI

Molokai Surf, Molokai Island Creations, Molokai Imports (which has great, inexpensive lauhala bags and local lemons), and **Lourdes** are clothing and gift shops in close proximity to one another in downtown Kaunakakai, where most of the retail shops sell T-shirts, muumuus, surf wear, and informal apparel. For food shopping, there are several good options. Since many visitors stay in condos, knowing the grocery stores is especially important. Other than that, serious shoppers will be disappointed, unless they love kites or native-wood vessels. The following are Kaunakakai's notable stores.

Imamura Store   Wilfred Imamura, whose mother founded this store, recalls the old railroad track that stretched from the pier to a spot across the street. "We brought our household things from the pier on a hand-pumped vehicle," he recalls. His store, appropriately, is a leap into the past, a marvelous amalgam of precious old-fashioned things. Rubber boots, Hawaiian-print tablecloths, Japanese tea plates, ukulele cases, plastic slippers, and even coconut bikini tops line the shelves. But it's not all nostalgia: The Molokai T-shirts, jeans, and palaka shorts are of good quality and inexpensive, and the pareu fabrics are a find. In Kaunakakai. ℭ 808/553-5615.

Molokai Drugs   David Mikami, whose father-in-law founded the pharmacy in 1935, has made this more than a drugstore. It's a gleaming, friendly stop full of life's basic necessities, with generous amenities such as a phone and a restroom for passersby (!). Here you'll find the best selection of guidebooks, books about Molokai, and maps, as well as greeting cards, paperbacks, cassette players, flip-flops, and every imaginable essential. The Mikamis are a household name on the island, not only because of their pharmacy, but also because the family has shown exceptional kindness to the often economically-strapped Molokaians. In Kamoi Professional Center. ℭ 808/553-5790.

Molokai Fish & Dive   Here you'll find the island's largest selection of T-shirts and souvenirs, crammed in among fishing, snorkeling, and outdoor gear that you can rent or buy. Find your way among the fishnets, boogie boards, diving equipment, bamboo rakes, beach towels, postcards, juices and soft drinks, disposable cameras, and staggering miscellany of this chockablock store. One entire wall is lined with T-shirts, and the selection of Molokai books and souvenirs is extensive. The staff is happy to point out the best snorkeling spots of the day. In Kaunakakai. ℭ 808/553-5926.

Molokai Surf   This brand-new, wooden building now houses Molokai Surf and its selection of skateboards, surf shorts, sweatshirts, sunglasses, T-shirts, footwear, boogie boards, backpacks, and a broad range of clothing and accessories for life in the surf and sun. In Kaunakakai. 130 Kamehameha V Hwy. ℭ 808/553-5093.

Take's Variety Store   If you need luggage tags, buzz saws, toys, candy, cloth dolls, canned goods, canteens, camping equipment, hardware, batteries, candles, pipe fittings, fishing supplies—whew!—and other products for work and play, this 52-year-old variety store is the answer. You may suffer from claustrophobia in the crowded, dusty aisles, but Take's carries everything. In Kaunakakai. ℭ 808/553-5442.

EDIBLES

Friendly Market Center   You can't miss this salmon-colored wooden storefront on the main drag of "downtown" Kaunakakai, where people of all generations can be found just talking story in the Molokai way. Friendly's has an especially good selection of produce and healthy foods—from local poi to Glenlivet. Blue-corn tortilla chips, soy milk, organic brown rice, a good selection of pasta sauces, and Kumu Farms macadamia-nut pesto, the island's stellar gourmet food, are among the items that surpass standard grocery-store fare. In Kaunakakai. ℭ 808/553-5595.

Misaki's Grocery and Dry Goods   Established in 1922, this third-generation local legend is one of Kaunakakai's two grocery stores. Some of its notable items: chopped garlic from Gilroy, California, fresh luau leaves (taro greens), fresh okra, Boca burgers, large Korean chestnuts in season, gorgeous bananas, and an ATM. The fish section includes akule and ahi, fresh and dried, but the stock consists mostly of meats, produce, baking products, and a humongous array of soft drinks.

Moments **The Hot Bread Run**

For years, local residents have lined up waiting for Molokai Bread to be taken from the oven. Molokai's well-known and well-loved export, Molokai Bread—developed in 1935 in a cast-iron, kiawe-fired oven—is the signature product of **Kanemitsu Bakery** (© **808/553-5855;** 79 Ala Malama St.). Flavors range from apricot-pineapple to mango (in season), but the classics remain the regular white, wheat, cheese, sweet, and onion-cheese breads. Kanemitsu's is part of Molokai's night life, too. Whenever anyone on Molokai mentions "hot bread," he's talking about the hot-bread run at Kanemitsu's, the late-night ritual for die-hard bread lovers. Those in the know line up at the bakery's back door beginning at 10:30pm, when the bread is whisked hot out of the oven and into waiting hands. You can order your fresh bread with butter, jelly, cinnamon, or cream cheese, and the bakers will cut the hot loaves down the middle and slather on the works so it melts in the bread. The cream cheese and jelly bread makes a fine substitute for dessert.

Liquor, stationery, candies, and paper products round out the selection of this full-service grocery. In Kaunakakai. © **808/553-5505.**

Molokai Wines & Spirits   This is your best bet on the island for a decent bottle of wine. The shop offers 200 labels, including Caymus, Silver Oak, Joseph Phelps, Heitz, Bonny Doon, and a carefully-culled European selection. *Wine Spectator* reviews are tacked to some of the selections, which always helps, and the snack options include imported gourmet cheeses, salami, and Carr's biscuits. In Kaunakakai. © **808/553-5009.**

EN ROUTE TO THE NORTH COAST

Coffees of Hawaii Plantation Store and Espresso Bar   This is a fairly slick—for Molokai—combination coffee bar, store, and gallery for more than 30 artists and craftspeople from Molokai, Maui, and the Big Island. Sold here are the Malulani Estate and Muleskinner coffees that are grown, processed, and packed on the 500-acre plantation surrounding the shop, as well as Hawaii-grown flavored coffees. (See p. 431 for details on plantation tours.) You may find better prices on coffee at other retail outlets, but the gift items are worth a look: pikake and plumeria soaps from Kauai, perfumes and pure beeswax candles from Maui, koa bookmarks and hair sticks, and pottery, woods, and baskets. Hwy. 480 (near the junction of Hwy. 470), Kualapuu. © **800/709-BEAN** or 808/567-9023.

Molokai Museum Gift Shop   The restored 1878 sugar mill sits 1,500 feet above the town of Kualapuu. It's a considerable drive from town, but a good cause for those who'd like to support the museum and the handful of local artisans who sell their crafts, fabrics, cookbooks, quilt sets, and other gift items in the tiny shop. There's also a modest selection of cards, T-shirts, coloring books, and, at Christmas, handmade ornaments made of lauhala and koa. Meyer Sugar Mill, Hwy. 470 (just after the turnoff for the Ironwood Hills Golf Course, and 2 miles below Kalaupapa Overlook), Kalae. © **808/567-6436.**

EDIBLES

Kualapuu Market   This market, in its third generation, is a stone's throw from the Coffees of Hawaii store. It's a scaled-down, one-stop shop with wine, food, and necessities—and a surprisingly presentable, albeit small, assortment of produce, from Molokai sweet potatoes to Ka'u navel oranges in season. The shelves are filled with canned goods, propane, rope, hoses, paper products, and baking goods, reflecting the uncomplicated, rural lifestyle of the area. In Kualapuu. (C) 808/567-6243.

THE WEST END

A Touch of Molokai   We were pleasantly surprised by the selection of gift items in this hotel shop. The surf shorts and aloha shirts are better than the norm, with attractive, up-to-date choices by Jams, Quiksilver, and other name brands. Tencel dresses, South Pacific shell necklaces (up to $400), and a magnificent, hand-turned milo bowl also caught our attention. Most impressive are the wiliwili, kamani, and soap-berry leis and a handsome array of lauhala bags, all made on Molokai. At Kaluakoi Hotel & Golf Club. (C) 808/552-0133.

Big Wind Kite Factory & the Plantation Gallery   Jonathan and Daphne Socher, kite designers and inveterate Bali-philes, have combined their interests in a kite factory/import shop that dominates the commercial landscape of Maunaloa, the reconstituted plantation town. Maunaloa's naturally windy conditions make it ideal for kite-flying classes, which are offered free when conditions are right. The adjoining Plantation Gallery features local handicrafts, such as milo-wood bowls, locally made T-shirts, Hawaii-themed sandblasted glassware, baskets of lauhala and other fibers, and Hawaiian-music CDs. There are also many Balinese handicrafts, from jewelry to clothing and fabrics. In Maunaloa. (C) 808/552-2634.

Maunaloa General Store   Maunaloa's only general store sells everything from paper products to batteries, dairy products, frozen and fresh meats, wine, canned goods, and a cross section of necessities. In Maunaloa. (C) 808/552-2346.

Molokai Ranch Logo Shop   Located next to the ranch's bike rentals in a recently renovated wooden building, this shop can outfit you for life's great adventures. North Face parkas, Bullfrog sunscreens, saddle blankets, Teva sandals, bicycle helmets, swimwear, T-shirts, kites, walking sticks, and camping gear for all kinds of conditions line the shelves. The food items and souvenirs are equally diverse: mugs, magnets, CDs and cassettes, Buckeye corn bread, pasta, Molokai Ranch toffees, mobiles, toys, plastic buckets, lidded koa boxes, Dr. Bronner's soaps, Muleskinner coffees, coconut-shell soap dishes, picture frames, and other attractive gifts to go. In Maunaloa. (C) 808/552-2791.

THE EAST END

The Neighborhood Store 'N Counter   The Neighborhood Store, the only grocery on the East End, sells batteries, film, aspirin, cookies, beer, Molokai produce, candies, paper products, and other sundries. There's good food pouring out of the kitchen for the breakfast and lunch counter, too. See p. 472 for a restaurant review. In Pukoo. (C) 808/558-8498.

10 Molokai After Dark

Hotel Molokai, in Kaunakakai ((C) 808/553-5347), offers live entertainment, from local musicians, poolside and in the dining room on Friday from 4pm to 11pm. With its South Seas ambience and poolside setting, it's become the island's premier venue for local and visiting entertainers.

Molokai musicians to watch for include **Pound for Pound,** a powerful group of artists, each over 250 pounds. The members are lead vocalist Jack Stone, Shane

Dudoit, Danny Reyes, John Pele, and Alika Lani. As popular off-island as on, they perform Hawaiian, reggae, country, and contemporary Hawaiian numbers, many of them originals. Their CD, *100% Molokai,* has become a local legend.

Darryl Labrado is a teen phenomenon and the island's rising star; he sings and plays the ukulele to a huge local following. And **Pa'a Pono,** with its contemporary Hawaiian and reggae sounds, is a familiar name on the local nightlife circuit. *Molokai Now,* a CD anthology of original music from Molokai, is a terrific memento for those who love the island and its music.

Movie buffs, too, finally have a place to call their own on Molokai. **Maunaloa Cinemas** (© **808/552-2707**) is a triplex theater that shows first-run movies in the middle of Maunaloa town—four screenings a day at each of the three theaters. Also in Maunaloa, the lounge at **The Lodge at Molokai Ranch** (© **888/627-8082** or 808/660-2824) offers live music Friday and Saturday, from 7 to 9pm, ranging from Hawaiian songs to keiki hula.

9

Lanai: A Different Kind of Paradise

Lanai is not an easy place to reach. There are no direct flights from the mainland. It's almost as if this quiet, gentle oasis—known, paradoxically, for both its small-town feel and its celebrity appeal—demands that its visitors go to great lengths to get here in order to ensure that they will appreciate it.

Lanai (pronounced lah-*nigh*-ee), the nation's biggest defunct pineapple patch, now claims to be one of the world's top tropical destinations. It's a bold claim, since so little is here. Don't expect a lot of dining or accommodations choices (Lanai has even fewer than Molokai). There are no stoplights here and barely 30 miles of paved road. This almost virgin island is unspoiled by what passes for progress, except for a tiny 1920s-era plantation village—and, of course, the village's fancy new arrivals: two first-class luxury hotels where room rates hover around $400 a night.

As soon as you arrive on Lanai, you'll feel the small-town coziness. People wave to every car; residents stop to "talk story" with their friends; fishing and working in the garden are considered priorities in life; and leaving the keys in the car's ignition is standard practice.

For generations, Lanai was little more than a small village, owned and operated by the pineapple company, surrounded by acres of pineapple fields. The few visitors to the island were either relatives of the mainly Filipino residents or occasional weekend hunters. Life in the 1960s was pretty much the same as in the 1930s. But all that changed in 1990, when the Lodge at Koele, a 102-room hotel resembling an opulent English Tudor mansion, opened its doors, followed a year later by the 250-room Manele Bay Hotel, a Mediterranean-style luxury resort overlooking Hulopoe Bay. Overnight, the isolated island was transformed: Corporate jets streamed into the tiny Lanai Airport, former plantation workers were retrained in the art of serving gourmet meals, and the population of 2,500 swelled with transient visitors and outsiders coming to work in the island's new hospitality industry. Microsoft billionaire Bill Gates chose the island for his lavish wedding—and sleepy Lanai went on the map as a vacation spot for the rich and powerful.

But don't be put off by the publicity: Lanai isn't just about top-dollar resorts and fancy meals. A handful of B&Bs and local cafes in the time-mellowed plantation town called Lanai City have opened their doors to travelers seeking simpler pleasures. And the island is overflowing with extraordinary natural beauty. It's so much more than just a luxury beach resort. And it's the traveler who comes to discover the island's natural wonders, local lifestyle, and other inherent joys who's bound to have the most genuine island experience.

1 Orientation

ARRIVING

BY PLANE   No matter where you're coming from, you'll have to make a connection in Honolulu or Kahului (on Maui), where you can easily catch a small plane for the 25-minute flight to Lanai's airport. Twin-engine planes are the only air service to Lanai. **Island Air** (© **800/652-6541** or 808/565-6744; www.islandair.com) offers seven flights a day from Honolulu. For more details on these airlines—including details on how to get the cheapest fares—see "Getting There & Getting Around" and "Money-Saving Package Deals," in chapter 2.

You'll touch down in Puuwai Basin, once the world's largest pineapple plantation; it's about 10 minutes by car to Lanai City and 25 minutes to Manele Bay.

BY BOAT   A round-trip on **Expeditions Lahaina/Lanai Passenger Ferry** (© **808/ 661-3756**) takes you between Maui and Lanai for $50. The ferry service runs five times a day, 365 days a year, between Lahaina and Lanai's Manele Bay harbor. The ferry leaves Lahaina at 6:45, 9:15am, 12:45, 3:15, and 5:45pm; the return ferry from Lanai's Manele Bay Harbor leaves at 8, 10:30am, 2, 4:30, and 6:45pm. The 9-mile channel crossing takes 45 minutes to an hour, depending on sea conditions. Reservations are strongly recommended. Baggage is limited to two checked bags and one carry-on.

VISITOR INFORMATION

Lanai Visitors Bureau, P.O. Box 631436, Lanai City, HI 96763, or 431 7th St., Suite A, Lanai City (© **800/947-4774** or 808/565-7600; fax 808/565-9316; www.visit lanai.net) and the **Hawaii Visitors and Convention Bureau** (© **800/GO-HAWAII** or 808/923-1811; www.gohawaii.com) will both provide brochures, maps, and island guides. For a free *Road and Site Map* of hikes, archaeological sites, and other sights, contact the **Castle and Cooke Resorts,** P.O. Box 310, Lanai City, HI 96763 (© **808/ 565-3000;** www.lanai-resorts.com).

THE ISLAND IN BRIEF

Inhabited Lanai is divided into three parts—Lanai City, Koele, and Manele—and two distinct climate zones: hot and dry, and cool and misty.

Lanai City (pop. 2,800) sits at the heart of the island at 1,645 feet above sea level. It's the only place on the island where you'll find services. Built in 1924, this plantation village is a tidy grid of quaint tin-roofed cottages in bright pastels, with roosters penned in tropical gardens of banana, lilikoi, and papaya. Many of the residents are Filipino immigrants who worked the pineapple fields and imported the art, culture, language, food, and lifestyle of the Philippines. Their clapboard homes are excellent examples of historic preservation; the whole town looks like it's been kept under a bell jar.

Around Dole Park Square, a charming village square lined with towering Norfolk and Cook Island pines, plantation buildings house general stores with basic necessities as well as two banks, and a police station with a jail that consists of three blue-and-white wooden outhouse-sized cells with padlocks.

In the nearby cool upland district of **Koele** is the Lodge at Koele, standing alone on a knoll overlooking pastures and the sea at the edge of a pine forest, like a grand European manor. The other bastion of indulgence, the Manele Bay Hotel, is on the sunny southwestern tip of the island at **Manele.** You'll get more of what you expect from Hawaii here—beaches, swaying palms, mai tais, and the like.

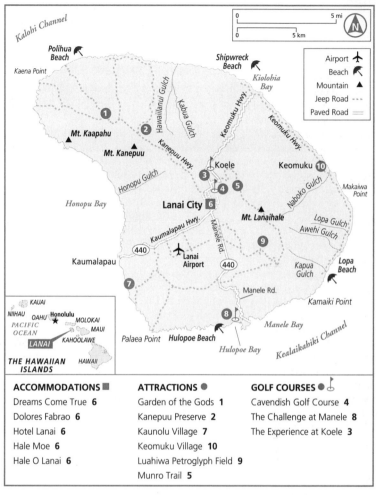

ACCOMMODATIONS ▪

Dreams Come True **6**

Dolores Fabrao **6**

Hotel Lanai **6**

Hale Moe **6**

Hale O Lanai **6**

ATTRACTIONS ●

Garden of the Gods **1**

Kanepuu Preserve **2**

Kaunolu Village **7**

Keomuku Village **10**

Luahiwa Petroglyph Field **9**

Munro Trail **5**

GOLF COURSES ● ⛳

Cavendish Golf Course **4**

The Challenge at Manele **8**

The Experience at Koele **3**

FAST FACTS: Lanai

American Express There's no local office on the island.

Dentists Emergency dental care is available from **Dr. James Sagawa** (☎ **808/565-6418**).

Doctors If you need a doctor, contact the **Lanai Family Health Center** (☎ **808/565-6423**).

Emergencies Dial ☎ **911** for police, fire, and ambulance service. The **Poison Control Center** can be reached at ☎ **800/362-3585**.

Hospitals The **Lanai Community Hospital** (© **808/565-6411**) has emergency services available around the clock.

Police For non-emergencies, call © **808/565-6428.**

Weather For current weather conditions, call © **808/565-6033.**

See "Fast Facts: The Hawaiian Islands" in chapter 2 for more information.

2 Getting Around

With so few paved roads here, you'll need a four-wheel-drive vehicle if you plan on exploring the island's remote shores, its interior, or the summit of Mount Lanaihale. Even if you only have 1 day on Lanai, rent one and see the island.

Both cars and four-wheel-drive vehicles are available at the **Dollar Rent-A-Car** desk at **Lanai City Service,** 1036 Lanai Ave. (© **800/588-7808** for Dollar reservations, or 808/565-7227 for Lanai City Service). Expect to pay about $60 a day for the least-expensive car available, a Nissan Sentra, and $129 to $145 a day for a four-wheel-drive Jeep or SUV (both these rates drop 10% if you rent for a week or more). *Be warned:* Gas is expensive on Lanai and those four-wheel-drive vehicles get terrible mileage. Since everything in Lanai City is within walking distance, it makes sense to rent a Jeep only for the days you want to explore the island.

Though it's fun to rent a car and explore the island, it's possible to stay here and get to the beach without one. The two big resort hotels run shuttle vans around the island, but only for their guests. If you are staying at The Lodge at Koele or Hotel Lanai, the free shuttles to Manele Bay Hotel run every hour. From the Manele Bay Hotel, you walk over to Hulopoe Beach. When you want to return, you just catch the hourly shuttle (it may run on the half-hour from Manele Bay Hotel) back to Lanai City.

If you're staying elsewhere, you can walk to everything in Lanai City and take a taxi to the beach. **Lanai City Service** (© **808/565-7227**) will provide transportation from Lanai City to Hulopoe Beach for $10 per person one-way (you can arrange with them when you want to be picked up, or walk over to the Manele Bay Hotel and phone them to come get you—or you can most likely get a ride back up to Lanai City with a local). Whether or not you rent a car, sooner or later you'll find yourself at Lanai City Service. This all-in-one grocery store, gas station, rental-car agency, and souvenir shop serves as the island's Grand Central Station. Here you can pick up information, directions, maps, and all the local gossip.

3 Accommodations You Can Afford

There aren't a whole lot of options on Lanai. As we mentioned earlier, the island is dominated by two big, fabulous, ultra-luxurious resorts—the **Lodge at Koele** (© **800/321-4666** or 808/565-7300; www.islandoflanai.com) and the **Manele Bay Hotel** (© **800/321-4666** or 808/565-7700; www.islandoflanai.com), both of which cater to the celebrity set and carry pretty hefty rack rates. But don't lose hope just yet. There are a handful of affordable choices in town: the small but charming Hotel Lanai and some affordable B&Bs, all of which are discussed below.

A free guest shuttle links the island's three hotels (the two mega-resorts and the Hotel Lanai), the beach park, the village, the golf courses, and the airport; however, you can only use it if you're staying at one of the fancy resorts or the Hotel Lanai. If you're staying at a B&B and don't plan on renting a car for your entire stay, you might ask your hosts if they'll pick you up from the airport; several will be happy to comply. Once you're in Lanai City, everything is within walking distance.

Don't forget to add 11.42% in taxes to all accommodation bills.

Dreams Come True ★ *Finds*   This quaint plantation house is tucked away among papaya, banana, lemon, and avocado trees in the heart of Lanai City, at 1,620 feet. Hosts Susan and Michael Hunter have filled their house with Southeast Asian antiques collected on their travels. Both are jewelers, and they operate a working studio on the premises. Two of the three bedrooms feature a four-poster canopied bed, with an additional single bed (perfect for a small family), while the third has just one queen bed. The common area looks out on the garden and is equipped with both TV and VCR. Breakfast usually consists of freshly-baked bread with homemade jellies and jams, tropical fruit, juice, and coffee.

547 12th St. (P.O. Box 525), Lanai City, HI 96763. © **800/566-6961** or 808/565-6961. Fax 808/565-7056. www.dreams cometruelanai.com. 4 units. $99 double; $380 entire house. Rates include full breakfast. Extra person $25.. AE, DISC, MC, V. *In room:* No phone.

Hotel Lanai ★ *Kids*   This hotel lacks the facilities of Lanai's two upscale resorts, but it's perfect for families and other vacationers who can't afford to spend $400 to $500 a night. Just a few years ago, the Hotel Lanai, on a rise overlooking Lanai City, was the only place to stay and eat unless you knew someone who lived on the island. Built in the 1920s for VIP plantation guests, this clapboard, plantation-era relic has retained its quaint character and lives on as a country inn. A well-known chef from Maui, Henry Clay Richardson, is the inn's owner and the dining room's executive chef (see review on p. 498).

The guest rooms are extremely small, but clean and newly decorated, with Hawaiian quilts, wood furniture, and ceiling fans. The most popular are the lanai units, which feature a shared lanai with the room next door. All rooms have ceiling fans and private, shower-only bathrooms. The small, one-bedroom cottage, with a TV and bathtub, is perfect for a small family.

The hotel serves as a down-home crossroads where total strangers meet local folks on the lanai to drink beer and talk story, or play the ukulele and sing into the dark, tropic night. Often, a curious visitor in search of an authentic experience will join the party and discover Lanai's very Hawaiian heart. Guests have the use of the complimentary shuttle to the Lodge at Koele, the Manele Bay Hotel, the golf courses (at which they get the same low rates given to guests at the two resorts), and the beach.

828 Lanai Ave. (P.O. Box 630520), Lanai City, HI 96763. © **800/795-7211** or 808/565-7211. Fax 808/565-6450. www. hotellanai.com. 11 units. $105–$135 double; $175 cottage double. Rates include continental breakfast. Extra person $10. AE, MC, V. Airport shuttle $25 round-trip. **Amenities:** Excellent restaurant; intimate bar; access to 2 resort golf courses on the island and the 9-hole golf course in town; nearby tennis courts; complimentary snorkeling equipment.

OTHER BED-AND-BREAKFAST OPTIONS

Delores Fabrao *Finds*   Delores offers two rooms: a downstairs family room with a double bed, two twin beds, and two couches with private bathroom that sleeps six; and an upstairs room with a double bed and a shared bathroom. No breakfast is provided, but you have the run of the house, including the kitchen, where you're welcome to cook meals for yourself.

538 Akahi St. (P.O. Box 398), Lanai City, HI 96763. © **808/565-6134.** 2 units (1 with shared bathroom). $50 single; $55 double; $100 for 4. No credit cards.

Hale Moe *(Finds)*   Momi Suzuki has made two bedrooms in her Lanai City home available to guests. One room has a queen bed, and the other has two twins; both have private bathrooms. If Momi isn't working, she happily picks up her guests from the airport and lets them use her two bicycles to roam around Lanai.

502 Akolu Place (P.O. Box 196), Lanai City, HI 96763. ℂ 808/565-9520. 2 units. $80–$90 double. Rates include continental breakfast. No credit cards.

Hale O Lanai *(Value)*   This relatively new two-bedroom, two-bathroom house, which can sleep up to six, can be all yours. It comes equipped with a complete kitchen (including dishwasher and microwave oven) and washer/dryer. This is really a vacation rental, so no breakfast is provided. Rates depend on the number of guests and the length of your stay.

405 Lanai Ave., Lanai City. Reservations: c/o Hawaii Beachfront Vacation Homes, 46–535 Haiku Plantations Place, Kaneohe, HI 96744. ℂ 808/247-3637. Fax 808/235-2644. www.hibeach.com. 1 house. $115–$135. No credit cards. *In room:* Kitchen, fridge, coffeemaker, washer/dryer.

4 Great Deals on Dining

Lanai offers some of the best dining in Hawaii, and most of it, of course, is pricey. The gap between upscale-luxe and down-home diner is vast. But Lanai is a curious mix of innocence and sophistication, with strong cross-cultural elements that liven up its culinary offerings. On this island of three hotels, a handful of stores, and fewer than 3,000 residents, you can go from a greasy-spoon breakfast to a five-star dinner in less than a mile and a few hundred feet in altitude. Since this is a budget guide, and since this is the smallest island you can visit, you'll notice that the dining options will be noticeably slim. Because there are so few restaurants on this island, they're simply listed alphabetically.

Henry Clay's Rotisserie *(★★)* COUNTRY CUISINE   Henry Clay Richardson, a New Orleans native, has made some welcome changes to Lanai's dining landscape with his rustic inn in the middle of Lanai City. It's very popular and always full. Maybe that's because it's the only option on Lanai that occupies the vast gap between deli/diner and upscale-luxe.

The menu focuses on American country fare: fresh meats, seafood, and local produce in assertive preparations. Appetizers and entrees reflect Cajun, regional, and international influences, particularly the Rajun Cajun Clay's shrimp, a fiery concoction of hefty shrimp in a spiced tomato broth. The meats, which could be rabbit, quail, venison, osso buco, beef, or chicken, are spit-roasted on the rotisserie. Gourmet pizzas and salads occupy the lighter end of the spectrum. Diners rave about the fresh catch in lemon butter caper sauce; we loved the eggplant Creole, presented with perfect sugar snap peas on a bed of herbed angel-hair pasta.

In the Hotel Lanai. 828 Lanai Ave., Lanai City. ℂ 808/565-7211. www.hotellanai.com. Main courses $19–$33. MC, V. Daily 5:30–9pm.

Manele Bay Clubhouse *(★)* PACIFIC RIM   The view from the alfresco tables here may be the best on the island, encompassing Kahoolawe, Haleakala, on Maui, and, on an especially clear day, the peaks of Mauna Kea and Mauna Loa on the Big Island. Dinner may be prohibitively expensive on your budget. But lunch is a good alternative. Lighter fare prevails: salads and sandwiches, burgers, Caesar with chicken, herbed chicken sandwich on sourdough, fish and chips, excellent shrimp spring rolls, and fresh catch of the day on sourdough bread. The clubhouse is casual, the view of the ocean is awe inspiring, and it's a great gathering place to talk about your day on the course.

In the Challenge at Manele Clubhouse. (☎ **808/565-2230**. Reservations recommended. Lunch entrees $10–$22; dinner entrees $25–$38. AE, DC, MC, V. Lunch daily 10:30am–3:30pm; pupu appetizer menu daily 3:30–5:30pm; dinner Thurs–Mon 5:30–9pm.

Pele's Other Garden ✶✶ (*Value*) DELI/BISTRO   This popular Lanai City eatery has added a patio with umbrella tables outside and expanded the kitchen in the back, so there's a lot more seating than there used to be—and a fuller menu to match. Owners Mark and Barbara have turned Pele's Other Garden from a small sandwich shop to a full-scale deli and bistro. Daily soup and menu specials, excellent pizza, fresh organic produce, fresh juices, and special items such as top-quality black-bean burritos, roasted red peppers, and stuffed grape leaves are some of the features that make Pele's Other Garden a Lanai City must. At lunch, the pizzas and sandwiches are still top-drawer and popular. Sandwiches are made with wraps or whole-wheat, rye, sourdough, or French bread, all baked on the island and delivered fresh daily; the turkey is free-range. In the evening, you dine on china at cloth-covered tables, and the menu expands to include pastas (bow-tie pasta with butterflied garlic shrimp, fettuccine with smoked salmon), pizza, and salads. The fire truck-yellow building is easy to spot along tree-shaded Dole Park.

Dole Park, 811 Houston St., Lanai City. (☎ **808/565-9628**. Most lunch items less than $7, dinner items $17–$20. AE, DISC, MC, V. Mon–Fri 10am–2:30pm and 5–8pm; Sat dinner only 5–8pm.

SUPER-CHEAP EATS

Blue Ginger Cafe COFFEE SHOP   Famous for its mahimahi sandwiches and inexpensive omelets, Blue Ginger is a very local, very casual, and moderately-priced alternative to Lanai's fancy hotel restaurants. The four tables on the front porch face the cool Norfolk pines of Dole Park and are always filled with locals who talk story from morning to night. The tiny cafe is often jammed from 6 to 7am with construction workers on their way to work. The offerings are solid, no-nonsense, everyday fare: fried saimin (no MSG, a plus), very popular hamburgers on homemade buns, and mahimahi with capers in a white-wine sauce. Blue Ginger also serves a tasty French toast of homemade bread, vegetable lumpia (the Filipino version of a spring roll), and Mexican specials. The stir-fried vegetables—a heaping platter of fresh, perfectly cooked veggies, including summer squash and fresh mushrooms—are a hit.

409 Seventh St. (at Lilima St) Lanai City. (☎ **808/565-6363**. Breakfast items under $7.50; lunch under $10; and dinner less than $15. No credit cards. Daily 6am–8pm.

Café 565 PIZZA/SUB SANDWICHES   This colorful pizzeria, with hot and cold sub sandwiches, spills out of the old house and into the umbrella tables in the front yard. Named after Lanai's phone prefix, 565, the pizzas here are the real thing, baked in pizza ovens, and the sub sandwich rolls are baked fresh every day. Daily plate-lunch specials and great salads complete the menu. In the works were plans to add a children's menu, calzones, thick-crust pizza, and sushi.

408 Eighth St. (at Ilima St.), Lanai City. (☎ **808/565-6622**. Sub sandwiches $5–$10; pizza $13–$20. No credit cards. Mon–Fri 10am–3pm and 5–8pm.

Canoes Lanai LOCAL   Formerly Tanigawa's, this ma-and-pa eatery may have changed its name, but it still remains the landmark that it's been since the 1920s. In those days, the tiny storefront sold canned goods and cigarettes; the 10 tables, hamburgers, and Filipino food came later. This hole-in-the-wall is a local institution, with a reputation for serving local-style breakfasts. The fare—fried rice, omelets, short stack, and simple ham and eggs—is more greasy spoon than gourmet, but it's friendly to the pocketbook.

419 Seventh St., Lanai City. ⓒ 808/565-6537. Breakfast less than $8.50; lunch sandwiches $2.50–$8.50; burgers $2–$5. No credit cards. Thurs–Tues 6:30am–1pm.

Coffee Works ⭐ COFFEE HOUSE   Oahu's popular Ward Warehouse coffeehouse has opened a new branch in Lanai City with a menu of espresso coffees and drinks, ice cream (from gelatos to local brands, like Cascade Ice Cream, made in Honolulu), and a small selection of pastries. It's Lanai City's new gathering place, a tiny cafe with tables and benches on a pleasing wooden deck surrounded by tall pines and a stone's throw from Dole Park. Formerly a plantation house, the structure fits in with the surrounding plantation homes in the heart of Lanai City. There are some nice gift items available, including T-shirts, tea infusers, Chai, teapots, cookies, and gourmet coffees.

604 Ilima (across from Post Office), Lanai City. ⓒ **808/565-6962**. Most items under $5. AE, DC, DISC, MC, V. Mon–Sat 6am–4pm.

WORTH A SPLURGE

Ihilani ⭐⭐ MEDITERRANEAN   A number of top Hawaii chefs (such as Phillippe Padovani and Edwin Goto) have each added their style of melding Mediterranean with Island cuisine during their tenure here. The result is Lanai's top gourmet restaurant in a formal atmosphere (resort wear recommended) with inspiring food at eye-popping prices. Standouts include appetizers like homemade goat cheese and spinach ravioli with roasted eggplant and asparagus salad in a sun-dried tomato cilantro sauce ($13), or terrine of foie gras with pear d'anjou, Madeira wine gelee, and warm toasted black truffle brioche ($23). My favorite entree is the baked onaga and citrus in a sea-salt crust ($38), they also have a mouth watering Lanai venison foursome: chop, loin, saddle, and stew ($41). The prix-fixe menu is very complete and comes with selected wines.

In the Manele Bay Hotel. ⓒ **808/565-2296**. Reservations strongly recommended. Resort attire recommended. Main courses $23–$40; prix-fixe menu $85 without wine, $135 with wine. AE, DC, MC, V. Tues–Sat 6–9:30pm.

5 Beaches

If you like big, wide, empty, gold-sand beaches and crystal-clear, cobalt-blue water full of bright tropical fish—and who doesn't?—go to Lanai. With 18 miles of sandy shoreline, Lanai has some of Hawaii's least crowded and most interesting beaches.

HULOPOE BEACH ⭐⭐⭐

In 1997, Stephen Leatherman of the University of Maryland ranked Hulopoe the best beach in the United States. It's easy to see why. This palm-fringed, gold-sand beach is bordered by black-lava fingers, protecting swimmers from the serious ocean currents that sweep around Lanai. In summer, Hulopoe is perfect for swimming, snorkeling, or just lolling about; the water temperature is usually in the mid-70s. Swimming is usually safe, except when swells kick up in winter. The bay at the foot of the Manele Bay Hotel is a protected marine preserve, and the schools of colorful fish know it. So do the spinner dolphins that come here to play, as well as the humpback whales that

Cheap Thrills: What to See & Do for Free (or Almost) on Lanai

- **Snorkel Hulopoe Beach.** Crystal-clear water teems with brilliant tropical fish off a postcard-perfect beach. There are tide pools to explore, waves to play in, and other surprises—like a pod of spinner dolphins that often makes a splashy entrance.

- **Explore the Garden of the Gods.** Eroded by wind, rain, and time, this geologic badlands is worth visiting at sunrise or sunset, when the low light plays tricks on the land—and your mind.

- **Hike the Munro Trail.** The 11-mile Munro Trail is a lofty, rigorous hike along the rim of an old volcano, across a razorback ridge through a cloud forest, which offers big views of the nearby islands. Some hike the ridge to see the rainforest, others take a four-wheel-drive to spend more time on top of the island to, maybe, catch a rare five-island view.

- **Camp under the Stars.** The campsites at Hulopoe Beach Park are about as close to the heavens as you can get. The sound of the crashing surf will lull you to sleep at night, while the sound of chirping birds will wake you in the morning. If you're into roughing it, this is the most affordable way to experience Lanai.

- **Watch the Whales at Polihua Beach.** Located on the northern coast, this beach—which gets its name from the turtles that nest here—is a great place to spend the day scanning the ocean for whales during the winter months.

- **Play a Quick 9.** At the quirky Cavendish Golf Course, just walk up to the first tee, leave a donation ($5–$10) in the wooden box, and hit away. For 9 rugged holes, it's not such a bad deal—especially when you consider the $200 greens fees you'll have to cough up at the other two island courses.

cruise by in winter. Hulopoe is also Lanai's premier beach park, with a grassy lawn, picnic tables, barbecue grills, restrooms, showers, and ample parking. You can camp here, too.

HULOPOE'S TIDE POOLS Some of the best lava-rock tide pools in Hawaii are found along the south shore of Hulopoe Bay. These miniature Sea Worlds are full of strange creatures: asteroids (sea stars) and holothurians (sea cucumbers), not to mention spaghetti worms, Barber Pole shrimp, and Hawaii's favorite local delicacy, the opihi, a tasty morsel also known as the limpet. Youngsters enjoy swimming in the enlarged tide pool at the eastern edge of the bay. When you explore tide pools, do so at low tide. Never turn your back on the waves. Wear tennis shoes or reef walkers, as wet rocks are slippery. Collecting specimens in this marine preserve is forbidden, so don't take any souvenirs home.

SHIPWRECK BEACH ✷

This 8-mile-long windswept strand on Lanai's northeastern shore—named for the rusty ship, *Liberty*, stuck on the coral reef—is a sailor's nightmare and a beachcomber's dream. The strong currents yield all sorts of flotsam, from Japanese handblown-glass fish floats and rare pelagic paper nautilus shells to lots of junk. This is also a great place to spot whales from December to April, when the Pacific humpbacks cruise in from Alaska to winter in the calm offshore waters. The road to the beach is paved most of the way, but you really need a four-wheel-drive to get down here.

POLIHUA BEACH ✸

So many sea turtles once hauled themselves out of the water to lay their eggs in the sun-baked sand on Lanai's northwestern shore that Hawaiians named the beach here *Polihua*, or "egg nest." Although the endangered green sea turtles are making a comeback, they're seldom seen here now. You're more likely to spot an offshore whale (in season) or the perennial litter that washes up onto this deserted beach at the end of Polihua Road, a 4-mile Jeep trail. There are no facilities except fishermen's huts and driftwood shelters. Bring water and sunscreen. Beware the strong currents, which make the water unsafe for swimming. This strand is ideal for beachcombing (those little green-glass Japanese fishing-net floats often show up here), fishing, or just being alone.

6 Watersports

Lanai has Hawaii's best water clarity because it lacks major development and has low rainfall and runoff, and because its coast is washed clean daily by the sea current known as "The Way to Tahiti." But the strong sea currents pose a threat to swimmers, and there are few good surf breaks. Most of the aquatic adventures—swimming, snorkeling, scuba diving—are centered on the somewhat protected south shore, around Hulopoe Bay.

The only outfitter for watersports is **Trilogy Lanai Ocean Sports** ✸ (© 888/ **MAUI-800** or 808/565-9303; www.visitlanai.com).

OCEAN KAYAKING

Discover the thrill of kayaking with **Trilogy's** guided trips into Lanai's complex eco-systems and unique flora and fauna (see contact information above). You'll either paddle along Lanai's magnificent south shore to explore the water and sea caves at Kahekili Ho'e, where 1,000-foot sea cliffs still hide the bones of ancient Hawaiians; or you'll travel along the north shore at Shipwreck Beach, one of the longest barrier reefs in Hawaii, where you can explore the shipwreck and paddle your kayak amongst the numerous turtles who frequent the reef. Both trips offer lunch, sodas and snacks, single and double kayaks, and snorkeling gear. Cost is $125 (half-price for children 3–15), $75 for non-paddlers who join the tour and enjoy a guided hike along the coast.

SAILING/SNORKELING

Trilogy Lanai Ocean Sports ✸ (see contact information above), which has built a well-deserved reputation as the leader in sailing/snorkeling cruises in Hawaii, has a morning **snorkel sailing trip** on Monday, Wednesday, and Friday from 8:45am to 1pm and on Saturday from 10am to 2:30pm on board their luxury custom sailing catamarans. The trips along Lanai's protected coastline include sailing past hundreds of spinner dolphins and into some of the best snorkeling sites in the world. The $110 price (half-price for children 3–15) includes breakfast, lunch, sodas, snacks, snorkel gear and instruction. In the evening, Trilogy offers a **sunset sail** for $59 per person (children ages 3–5 half price).

SCUBA DIVING

Two of Hawaii's best-known dive spots are found in Lanai's clear waters, just off the south shore: **Cathedrals I** and **II,** so named because the sun lights up an underwater grotto like a magnificent church. **Trilogy Lanai Ocean Sports** ✈ (see above for contact information) offers several different kinds of sailing, diving, and snorkeling trips on catamarans and from their new 32-foot, high-tech, jet-drive ocean raft. At the crack of dawn (6:30am–8am) on Tuesday, Thursday and Saturday, Trilogy has its own version of "sunrise services" at the Cathedrals. Not only is this the best time of day to dive this incredible area, but there are virtually no other dive boats in the water at this time. Cost is $95.

For those wanting to sleep in, **Trilogy** offers an afternoon dive (3–6pm) on Monday, Wednesday, and Friday for the serious diver looking for a two-tank dive in the areas that have made Lanai famous. Cost is $130 and includes sodas, snacks, scuba gear and a dive master. Non-certified divers can check out Trilogy's Discover Scuba (Mon–Fri, 10am) for $169; certified divers can join in for $159 from the boat; and $95 for non-certified and $85 for certified divers from the beach.

SNORKELING

Hulopoe is Lanai's best snorkeling spot. Fish are abundant in the marine-life conservation area. Try the lava-rock points at either end of the beach and around the lava pools. Newcomers can get lessons from **Triology's Beach Snorkeling Class** (Mon–Fri, 10am); after the lessons, there's a 30-minute guided reef tour. The cost is $30 ($15 for children under 15), including all equipment.

SPORTFISHING

Jeff Menze will take you out on the 28-foot Omega boat *Spinning Dolphin* (© 808/ 565-6613). His fishing charters cost $400 for six people for 4 hours, or $600 for six people for 8 hours.

WHALE-WATCHING

Year-round, **Trilogy** offers 1½-hour adventures on a 32-foot, 26-passenger, rigid-hulled inflatable boat. From late December through April, they are on the lookout for whales. But, the remainder of the year, schools of spinner dolphins are featured on this Blue Water Marine Mammal Watch. The cost is $75 (half-price for children 3–15).

7 Hiking & Camping

HIKING
A LEISURELY MORNING HIKE

The 3-hour **Koele Nature Hike** starts by the reflecting pool in the backyard of the Lodge at Koele and takes you on a 5-mile loop through a cathedral of Norfolk Island pines, into Hulopoe Valley, past wild ginger, and up to Koloiki Ridge, with its panoramic view of Maunalei Valley and Molokai and Maui in the distance. You're welcome to take the hike even if you're not a guest at the Lodge. Neither is the trail head obvious—just keep going *mauka* (inland) toward the trees—nor the path clearly marked, but the concierge will give you a free map. We suggest doing this hike in the morning, before the clouds usually roll in, marring visibility at the top and increasing your chance of being caught in a downpour.

THE CHALLENGING MUNRO TRAIL

This tough, 11-mile (round-trip) uphill climb through the groves of Norfolk pines is a lung-buster, but if you reach the top, you'll be rewarded with a breathtaking view of Molokai, Maui, Kahoolawe, the peaks of the Big Island, and—on a really clear day—Oahu in the distance. Figure on 7 hours. The trail begins at Lanai Cemetery along Keomoku Road (Hwy. 44) and follows Lanai's ancient caldera rim, ending up at the island's highest point, Lanaihale. Go in the morning for the best visibility. After 4 miles, you'll get a view of Lanai City. The weary retrace their steps from here, while the more determined go the last 1⅓ miles to the top. Diehards head down Lanai's steep south-crater rim to join the highway to Manele Bay. For more details on the Munro Trail—including information on four-wheel-driving it to the top—see p. 506.

AN EASY SELF-GUIDED NATURE TRAIL

This self-guided nature trail in the Kanepuu Preserve is about a 10- to 15-minute walk through eight stations, with interpretive signs explaining the natural or cultural significance of what you're seeing. The trail head is clearly marked on the Polihua Road on the way to the Garden of the Gods. Kanepuu is one of the last remaining examples of the type of forest that once covered the dry lowlands throughout the state. There are some 49 plant species here that are found only in Hawaii. The **Nature Conservancy** (© 808/565-7430) conducts guided hikes every month; call for details.

GUIDED HIKES

The **Lodge at Koele** (© 808/5657300; www.lanai-resorts.com) has a 2½-hour Koloiki Ridge Nature hike through 5 miles of the upland forests of Koele at 11am daily. Fee is $15.

The **Manele Bay Hotel** (© 808/565-7700; www.lanai-resorts.com) has a 1½-hour fitness hike along an old fisherman's trail at 9am Tuesday and Friday, led by Joe West, wildlife and outdoor photographer extraordinaire. Bring your camera and ask Joe for photographing tips. The fee is $15.

CAMPING AT HULOPOE BEACH PARK

There is only one legal place to camp on Lanai: Hulopoe Beach Park, which is owned by Castle and Cooke Resorts. To camp in this exquisite beach park, with its crescent-shaped, white-sand beach bordered by kiawe trees, contact **Wendell Sarme–Park Manager,** Castle and Cooke Resorts, P.O. Box 630310, Lanai City, HI 96763 (© 808/565-2970; www.lanai-resorts.com). There's a $5 registration fee, plus a charge of $5 per person, per night. Hulopoe has six campsites; each can accommodate up to six people. Facilities include restrooms, running water, showers, barbecue areas, and picnic tables.

8 Golf & Other Affordable Outdoor Pursuits

GOLF

Lanai has two challenging championship courses, the **Experience at Koele** (© 808/565-4653) and the **Challenge at Manele** (© 808/565-2222). Both are well respected in the golfing world; however, non-guest greens fees at both courses are $200 for 18 holes. For most visitors, this is not exactly affordable golf.

If you're looking for a quick, inexpensive fix, you can tee it up at **Cavendish Golf Course** (no phone), located next to the Lodge at Koele in Lanai City. It's a quirky par-36, 9-hole public course with not only no clubhouse or club pros, but also no tee times, score cards, or club rentals. To play, just show up, put a donation ($5–$10 would be nice) into the little wooden box next to the first tee, and hit away. The 3,071-yard course was designed by E. B. Cavendish and built by the Dole plantation, in 1947, for its employees. The greens are a bit bumpy—nothing will roll straight here—but the views of Lanai are great, and the temperatures are usually quite mild.

BICYCLING

Road-bike treks are available through the **Lodge at Koele** (© 808/565-7300), which also has mountain bikes to rent for $8 an hour, $35 for 4 hours (includes backpack and lunch), and $40 to $55 for 8 hours.

For general information about bike trails, check out **www.bikehawaii.com**.

HORSEBACK RIDING

Horses can take you to many places in Lanai's unique landscape that are otherwise unreachable, even in a four-wheel-drive vehicle. The **Stables at Koele** (© 808/565-4424) offers various rides, including group rides that are a slow, gentle walk, starting at $65 for a 1½-hour trip. We recommend the 2-hour **Paniolo Trail Ride,** which takes you into the hills surrounding Koele. You'll meander through guava groves and patches of ironwood trees; catch glimpses of axis deer, quail, wild turkeys, and Santa Getrudis cattle; and end with panoramic views of Maui and Lanai. The cost is $75. Private rides (where you can canter, gallop, and trot) are $90 per person for 1 hour and $150 per person for 2 hours. Long pants and shoes are required; safety helmets are provided. Bring a jacket, as the weather is chilly and rain is frequent. Children must be at least 9 years old and 4 feet tall. The maximum weight limit is 250 pounds.

TENNIS

Public courts, lit for night play, are available in Lanai City at no charge; call © 808/565-6979 for reservations. Guests staying at the Lodge at Koele or the Manele Bay Hotel have complimentary tennis privileges at either the Tennis Center at Manele, with its six Plexipaved courts, a fully equipped pro shop, and tournament facilities; or at the courts at Koele. Instruction is available for $25 for a clinic, $65 for a private 1-hour lesson. Courts are complimentary for hotel guests. For information, call © 808/565-2072.

9 Seeing the Sights

You'll need a four-wheel-drive vehicle to reach all the sights listed below. Renting a Jeep is an expensive proposition on Lanai—from $129 to $145 a day—so we suggest that you rent one just for the day (or days) you plan on sightseeing; otherwise, it's easy enough to get to the beach and around Lanai City without your own wheels. For details on vehicle rentals, see "Getting Around," p. 496.

GARDEN OF THE GODS ⭐

A dirt four-wheel-drive road leads out of Lanai City, through the now uncultivated pineapple fields, past the Kanepuu Preserve (a dry-land forest preserve teeming with rare plant and animal life) to the so-called Garden of the Gods, out on Lanai's north shore. This place has little to do with gods, Hawaiian or otherwise. It is, however, the ultimate rock garden: a rugged, barren, beautiful place full of rocks strewn by volcanic forces and shaped by the elements into a variety of shapes and colors—brilliant reds, oranges, ochres, and yellows.

Ancient Hawaiians considered this desolate, windswept place an entirely supernatural phenomenon. Scientists, however, have other, less-colorful explanations. Some call the area an "ongoing post-erosional event;" others say it's just "plain and simple badlands." Take a four-wheel-drive ride out here and decide for yourself.

Go early in the morning or just before sunset, when the light casts eerie shadows on the mysterious lava formations. Drive west from the Lodge on Polihua Road; in about 2 miles, you'll see a hand-painted sign that'll point you in the right direction, left down a one-lane, red-dirt road through a kiawe forest and past sisal and scrub to the site.

FIVE ISLANDS AT A SINGLE GLANCE: THE MUNRO TRAIL ⍟

In the first golden rays of dawn, hop into a 4×4 and head out on the two-lane black-top toward Mount Lanaihale, the 3,370-foot summit of Lanai. Your destination is the Munro Trail, the narrow, winding ridge trail that runs across Lanai's razorback spine to the summit. From here, hopefully, you'll get a rare treat: On a clear day, you can see all of the main islands in the Hawaiian chain except Kauai.

When it rains, the Munro Trail becomes slick and boggy, with major washouts. Rainy-day excursions often end with a rental Jeep on the hook of the island's lone tow truck—and a $250 tow charge. You could even slide off into a major gulch and never be found, so don't try it. But in late August and September, when trade winds stop and the air over the islands stalls in what's called a *kona* condition, Mount Lanaihale's suddenly visible peak becomes an irresistible attraction.

When you're on Lanai, look to the summit. If it's clear in the morning, get a four-wheel-drive vehicle and take the Munro Trail to the top. Look for a red-dirt road off Manele Road (Hwy. 440), about 5 miles south of Lanai City; turn left and head up the ridge line. No sign marks the peak, so you'll have to keep an eye out. Look for a wide spot in the road and a clearing that falls sharply to the sea.

The islands stand in order on the flat blue sea: Kahoolawe, Maui, the Big Island of Hawaii, and Molokini's tiny crescent. Even the summits show. You can also see the silver domes of Space City on Haleakala in Maui; Puu Moaulanui, the tongue-twisting summit of Kahoolawe; and, looming above the clouds, Mauna Kea on the Big Island. At another clearing farther along the thickly forested ridge, all of Molokai, including the 4,961-foot summit of Kamakou, and the faint outline of Oahu (more than 30 miles across the sea) are visible. You actually can't see all five in a single glance anymore, as a thriving pine forest blocks the view. For details on hiking the trail, see p. 504.

LUAHIWA PETROGLYPH FIELD

Lanai is second only to the Big Island in its wealth of prehistoric rock art, but you'll have to search a little to find it. Some of the best examples are on the outskirts of Lanai City, on a hillside site known as Luahiwa Petroglyph Field. The characters you'll see incised on 13 boulders in this grassy 3-acre knoll include a running man, a deer, a turtle, a bird, a goat, and even a rare, curly-tailed Polynesian dog (a latter-day wag has put a leash on him—some joke).

To get here, take the road to Hulopoe Beach. About 2 miles out of Lanai City, look to the left, up on the slopes of the crater, for a cluster of reddish-tan boulders (believed to form a rain *heiau*, or shrine, where people called up the gods Ku and Hina to nourish their crops). A cluster of spiky century plants marks the spot. Look for the Norfolk pines on the left side of the highway, turn left on the dirt road that veers across the abandoned pineapple fields, and after about 1 mile, take a sharp left by the water tanks. Drive for another half-mile, and then veer to the right at the V in the road. Stay on this upper road for about a third of a mile; you'll come to a large cluster of boulders on the right side. It's just a short walk up the cliffs (wear walking or hiking shoes) to the petroglyphs. Exit the same way you came. Go between 3pm and sunset for ideal viewing and photo ops.

KAUNOLU VILLAGE

Out on Lanai's nearly vertical, Gibraltar-like sea cliffs is an old royal compound and fishing village. Now a national historic landmark and one of Hawaii's most treasured ruins, it's believed to have been inhabited by King Kamehameha the Great and hundreds of his closest followers about 200 years ago. It's a hot, dry, dusty, slow-going, 3-mile, 4×4 drive from Lanai City to Kaunolu, but the miniexpedition is worth it. Take plenty of water, don a hat for protection against the sun, and wear sturdy shoes.

Ruins of 86 house platforms and 35 stone shelters have been identified on both sides of Kaunolu Gulch. The residential complex also includes the Halulu Heiau temple, named after a mythical man-eating bird. His Majesty's royal retreat is thought to have stood on the eastern edge of Kaunolu Gulch, overlooking the rocky shore facing Kahekili's Leap, a 62-foot-high bluff named for the mighty Maui chief who leaped off cliffs as a show of bravado. Nearby are burial caves, a fishing shrine, a lookout tower, and many warrior-like stick figures carved on boulders. Just offshore stands the telltale fin of little Shark Island, a popular dive spot that teems with bright tropical fish and, frequently, sharks.

Excavations are underway to discover more about how ancient Hawaiians lived, worked, and worshipped on Lanai's leeward coast. Who knows? The royal fishing village may yet yield the bones of King Kamehameha. His burial site, according to legend, is known only to the moon and the stars.

KANEPUU PRESERVE

This ancient forest on the island's western plateau is so fragile, you can only visit once a month, and, even then, only on a guided hike. Kanepuu, which has 48 species of plants unique to Hawaii, survives under the Nature Conservancy's protective wing. Botanists say the 590-acre forest is the last dry lowland forest in Hawaii; the others have all vanished, trashed by axis deer, agriculture, or "progress." Among the botanical marvels of this dry forest are the remains of *olopua* (native olive), *lama* (native ebony), *mau hau hele* (a native hibiscus), and the rare *'aiea* trees, which were used for canoe parts.

Due to the forest's fragile nature, guided hikes are led only 12 times a year, on a monthly, reservations-only basis. Contact the **Nature Conservancy Oahu Land Preserve** manager at 1116 Smith St., Suite 201, Honolulu, HI 96817 (© **808/537-4508**), to reserve.

OFF THE TOURIST TRAIL: KEOMOKU VILLAGE

If you're sunburnt lobster red, have read all the books you packed, and are starting to get island fever, take a little drive to Keomoku Village, on Lanai's east coast. You'll really be off the tourist trail. All that's in Keomoku, a ghost town since the mid-1950s, is a 1903 clapboard church in disrepair, an overgrown graveyard, an excellent view across the 9-mile Auau Channel to Maui's crowded Kaanapali Beach, and some very empty beaches that are perfect for a picnic or a snorkel. This former ranching and fishing village of 2,000 was the first non-Hawaiian settlement on Lanai, but it dried up after droughts killed off the Maunalei Sugar Company. The village, such as it is, is a great little escape. Follow Keomoku Road for 8 miles to the coast, turn right on the sandy road, and keep going for 5⅔ miles.

10 Shopping

Central Bakery ⭐ *(Finds)*   This is the mother lode of the island's baked delights, the bakery that is, well, central to Lanai's dining pleasure. If you've noshed on the fantastic sandwiches at Lodge at Koele's Terrace or any of the stellar desserts at its formal dining room or at Manele Bay Hotel, you've enjoyed goodies from Central Bakery. The bakery supplies all breads, all breakfast pastries, specialty ice creams and sorbets, all banquet desserts, and restaurant desserts on the island. Although it's not your standard retail outlet, you can call in advance, place your order, and pick it up. They prefer as much notice as possible (preferably 48 hours), but in a pinch will take a 24-hour order. Breads range from walnut onion ($4.50) to roasted potato bacon ($4.50) to olive onion ($4.50). They also have cookies (chocolate chip, oatmeal, coconut, all for 50¢), brownies (50¢), muffins, croissants (including chocolate croissants), Danish, and scones, plus an assortment of breakfast pastries (pineapple turnover, hazelnut roll, mascarpone apricot Danish, pistachio chocolate roll and others). 1311 Fraser Ave., Lanai City. ⓒ **808/565-3920.**

Dis 'N Dat ⭐⭐ *(Finds)*   Dis (Barry) and Dat (Susie) visited Lanai from Florida to look at buying a retirement home. They found their home and moved to Lanai to retire. That did not last. A few years later, outgoing Barry and his wife started searching for unusual, finely crafted teak and exotic wood sculptures and carvings. Along the way, they took a shine to mobiles and wind chimes, the more outrageous, the better. Then they started collecting handmade jewelry, stained glass, and unique garden ornaments and home decor. All this lead to this eclectic store, which you have to see to believe. Meeting Barry is worth the trip alone. This also is the biggest collection of Hawaii slipper necklaces, earrings, anklets, and bracelets. You'll also find T-shirts, pottery, ceramics, batik scarves, hula lamps and whimsical dragonfly lamps, woven baskets, and even waterfalls. You can't miss this vivid green shop with hanging chimes and mobiles leading the way to the front door. 418 Eighth Ave (at Kilele St.), Lanai City. ⓒ **866-DISNDAT** or 808/565-9170.

Gifts with Aloha   Phoenix and Kimberly Dupree's store of treasures offers fabulously stylish hats and hatbands, T-shirts, swimwear, quilts, Jams World dresses, children's books and toys, Hawaii-themed books, pareus, candles, aloha shirts, picture frames, handbags, ceramics, dolls, and art by local artists. The sumptuous white-lehua honey from the Big Island is available here, as are jams and jellies by Lanai's Fabrao House. The made-on-Maui soaps and bath products—in gardenia, pikake, and plumeria fragrances—make great gifts to go. Dole Park, 363 Seventh St. ⓒ **808/565-6589.**

Heart of Lanai Gallery   Denise Hennig, the resident artist at Hotel Lanai, displays her own photographs and watercolors of landscapes, people, and the lifestyle of Lanai's plantation past, as well as the work of other local Lanai artists, at her afternoon teas, Tuesday through Saturday from 2:30 to 4:30pm. You can drop by and enjoy a cup of tea with her as she shows you the art she is displaying that week. Her home/gallery is located behind the hospital in a bright yellow house. 758 Queens St., Lanai City. ⓒ **808/565-7815.** www.lanaionline.com/Merchants/heart_of_lanai.htm.

High Lights   Located one block off Seventh Street, across the street from Coffee Works is this island-style beauty salon and supply store. Owner Katharina Oriol has been working in beauty salons since 1975 and offers a full service salon with hair cuts, styling, highlighting, manicures, pedicures, waxing, and so on, Plus, she carries a wide selection of beauty products for hair and skin, and cosmetics. She welcomes walk-ins. 617 Ilima Ave., Lanai City. © 808/565-7207.

International Food & Clothing   Come here for the basics: groceries, housewares, T-shirts, hunting and fishing supplies, over-the-counter drugs, wine and liquor, paper goods, and hardware. We were pleasantly surprised by the extraordinary candy and bubble-gum section, the beautiful local bananas in the small produce section, the surprisingly extensive selection of yuppie soft drinks (Sobe, Snapple, and others), and the best knife-sharpener we've seen—handy for the Lanai lifestyle. 833 Ilima Ave. © 808/ 565-6433.

Lanai Art Center ★ *Finds*   This wonderful center was organized in 1989 to provide a place where both residents and visitors can come to create art. The center offers classes and studio time in ceramics, painting and drawing, calligraphy, woodworking, photography, silk and textile painting, watercolor, and glass. Plus, the center has an impressive schedule of visiting instructors from writers to folk artists (quilting, lei-making, and instrument-making) to oil painters. Check out their reasonably-priced classes (generally in the $25 range) or browse in the gallery for excellent deals on works by Lanai residents. 333 Seventh St., Lanai City. © 808/565-7503.

Lanai Marketplace   Everyone on Lanai, it seems, is a backyard farmer. From 7 to 11am or noon on Saturday, they all head to this shady square to sell their dewy-fresh produce, home-baked breads, plate lunches, and handicrafts. This is Lanai's version of the green market: petite in scale, but charming, and growing.

Dolores Fabrao's jams and jellies, under the **Fabrao House** label (© **808/565-6134** for special orders), are a big seller at the market and at the resort gift shops where they're sold. The exotic flavors include pineapple-coconut, pineapple-mango, papaya, guaivi (strawberry guava), poha (gooseberry) in season, passion fruit, Surinam cherry, and the very tart karamay jelly. All fruits are grown on the island. Dole Square.

The Local Gentry   Open since December 1999, Jenna Gentry's wonderful boutique is the first of its kind on the island, featuring clothing and accessories that are not the standard resort-shop fare. You'll find fabulous silk aloha shirts by Iolani; mahogany wood lamps; mermaids and hula girls; Putumayo separates (perfect for Hawaii) in easy-care fabrics; a fabulous line of silk aloha shirts by Tiki; top-quality hemp-linen camp shirts; inexpensive sarongs; and the Tommy Bahama line for men and women. There are also great T-shirts, swimwear, jewelry, bath products, picture frames, jeans, chic sunglasses, and offbeat sandals. 363 Seventh St. © 808/565-9130.

Mike Carroll Gallery   If he is on the island, you will find Mike Carroll at work on his original oil paintings, which generally depict Lanai's landscape. After a successful 22-year career as a professional artist in Chicago, Carroll moved to Lanai and has been painting the beauty and the lifestyle of the island ever since. You'll find an extensive selection of his original work, some limited editions, prints and notecards, plus a dozen or so of Maui and Lanai's top artists and even some locally-made, one-of-a-kind jewelry. 443 Seventh St., Lanai City. © 808/565-7122. www.mikecarrollgallery.com.

Pine Isle Market   A local landmark for two generations, Pine Isle specializes in locally-caught fresh fish, but you can also find fresh herbs and spices, canned goods, electronic games, ice cream, toys, zoris, diapers, paint, cigars, and other basic essentials of work and play. The fishing section is outstanding, with every lure imaginable. 356 Eighth St. © **808/565-6488.**

11 Lanai After Dark

The only regular nightlife venues are the Lanai Playhouse, at the corner of Seventh and Lanai avenues in Lanai City, and the two resorts, the Lodge at Koele and Manele Bay Hotel.

The **Lanai Playhouse** (© **808/565-7500**) is a historic 1920s building that has won awards for its renovations. When it opened in 1993, the 150-seat venue stunned residents by offering first-run movies with Dolby sound—quite contemporary for anachronistic Lanai. Lanai Playhouse usually, but not always, shows two movies each evening from Friday to Tuesday (to Wed in summer), at 6:30 and 8:30pm, with occasional Sunday and Monday matinees; if a 3-hour movie is on, it's shown at 7:30pm. Tickets are $7 for adults and $4.50 for kids and seniors. The playhouse is also the venue for occasional special events.

The **Lodge at Koele** has stepped up its live entertainment. In the lodge's **Great Hall,** in front of its manorial fireplaces, local artists bring contemporary Hawaiian, classical, and other genres to listeners who sip port and fine liqueurs while sinking into plush chairs. The special programs are on weekends, but throughout the week, some form of nightly entertainment takes place from 7 to 10pm.

Occasionally special events will bring in a few more nightlife options. During the annual **Pineapple Festival,** generally the first weekend in July, some of Hawaii's best musicians arrive to show their support for Lanai (see "Hawaii Calendar of Events," in chapter 2). Other special events include the **Aloha Festival** (www.alohafestivals.com), which takes place either the end of September or the first week in October, and the **Christmas Festival,** the first Saturday in December (contact **Lanai Visitors Bureau,** P.O. Box 631436, Lanai City, HI 96763, or 431 Seventh St., Suite A, Lanai City © **800/947-4774** or 808/565-7600; fax 808/565-9316; www.visitlanai.net for more information).

10

Kauai: The Garden Isle

On any list of the world's most spectacular islands, Kauai ranks right up there with Bora Bora, Huahine, and Rarotonga. It's full of paradoxes and contradictions. It's a small island, but to adequately see it, you have to take to the air and view it from a helicopter. It gets more than its fair share of tropical downpours, but that just means it's lush and green—and that there's a profusion of rainbows. Kauai feels remote, but it's just a 30-minute plane ride from the urban bustle of Honolulu.

All the tropical elements are here: moody rainforests, majestic cliffs, jagged peaks, emerald valleys, palm trees swaying in the breeze, daily rainbows, and spectacular golden beaches. Sunrise birdsong, essence of ginger and plumeria, Technicolor sunsets, sparkling waterfalls—you don't just go to Kauai, you absorb it with every sense.

Kauai's great natural beauty derives from its inevitable decline and erosion. Ten million years of wind and rain and epic hurricanes have carved the landscape, shaping now-dormant volcanoes into jagged peaks and reducing giant boulders into miles of soft, white-sand beaches. On September 11, 1992, Hurricane Iniki eroded the island by a century in a single day. Kauai's fabled Na Pali Coast is said to be the fastest-eroding land on earth. Born at the beginning of the archipelago, Kauai is enjoying its last days in the sun—"days" that will last at least a million years or more. Still, the very best time to enjoy Kauai is right now—and nearly a million people do each year.

Essentially a single large shield volcano that rises 3 miles above the sea floor, Kauai lies 90 miles across open ocean from Oahu, but it seems at least a half-century removed in time. The oldest and most remote of the main islands, it's often called "the separate kingdom," because it stood alone and resisted King Kamehameha's efforts to unite Hawaii. It took a royal kidnapping to take the Garden Isle. After King Kamehameha the Great died, his son, Liholiho, ascended the throne. He gained control of Kauai by luring Kauai's king, Kaumualii, aboard the royal yacht and sailing to Oahu; once there, Kaumualii was forced to marry Kaahumanu, Kamehameha's widow, thereby uniting the islands.

Today, the independent spirit lives on in Kauai, which refuses to surrender its soul to overdevelopment, preferring instead to take care of residents first and visitors second, which it does very well. A Kauai rule of thumb holds that no building may exceed the height of a coconut tree, between three and four stories. That restriction keeps Kauai from becoming another Miami or Waikiki. As a result, the island's natural beauty, not its palatial beach hotels, is still the attention-grabber. Its laid-back lifestyle hasn't been altered. There's no real nightlife, no opulent shopping malls. But there's the verdant jungle, the endless succession of gorgeous beaches, the grandeur of Waimea Canyon, and the drama of the magnificent Na Pali

Coast. Even at Princeville, an opulent marble-and-glass luxury hotel does little more than frame the natural glory of Hanalei's spectacular 4,000-foot-high Namolokama mountain range.

Kauai's beauty has won a supporting role in more than 50 Hollywood films, from *South Pacific* and *Blue Hawaii* to *Jurassic Park*. But it's not just another pretty face: The island's raw wilderness is daunting, its seas challenging, its canyons forbidding; two-thirds of this island is impenetrable. This is the island for active visitors, with watersports galore; miles of trails for hikers, bicyclists, and horseback riders, winding through rainforests, along ocean cliffs, and across remote beaches;

and a range of golf courses, from championship links to funky local courses where chickens roam the greens and balls wind up embedded in coconut trees.

This great green place remains a sanctuary for native birds and plants, fish, and, in a larger sense, even humans. This is the destination for those who need a place to relax and heal jangled nerves. There are miles and miles of sandy beaches, perfect for just sitting and meditating while the waves roll onto the shore. There are quiet spots in the forest to listen to the rain dance on the leaves, and there are laid-back, lazy days that end with the sun sinking into the Pacific amid a blaze of glorious tropical color.

1 Orientation

The final approach to Lihue Airport is dramatic; try to sit on the left side of the aircraft, where passengers are treated to an excellent view of the Haupu Ridge, Nawiliwili Bay, and Kilohana Crater. **United Airlines** (© **800/225-5825;** www.ual.com) offers direct service to Kauai, with daily flights from Los Angeles. **American Airlines** (© **800/433-7300;** www.aa.com) has direct flights from Los Angeles and San Francisco. **Pleasant Holidays** (© **800/742-9244;** www.pleasantholidays.com), one of Hawaii's largest travel companies offering low-cost airfare and package deals, has two weekly nonstop flights from Los Angeles and San Francisco using American Trans Air. All other airlines land in Honolulu, where you'll have to connect to a 30-minute inter-island flight to Kauai's Lihue Airport. Between the two inter-island jet carriers, **Aloha Airlines** (© **800/367-5250,** 808/245-3691, or 808/484-1111; www.alohaair.com) and **Hawaiian Airlines** (© **800/367-5320,** 808/245-1813, or 808/838-1555; www.hawaiianair.com), there is a flight at least every hour to Lihue. The third alternative is **Island Air** (© **800/323-3345** or 808/484-2222; www.islandair.com), with a fleet of 37-seat de Havilland DASH-8 propeller aircraft flying one direct flight a day from Honolulu to Lihue, three direct flights from Kahului, Maui and indirect flights from both Kona and Hilo on the Big Island.

All of the major car-rental companies have branches at Lihue Airport; see section 2 of this chapter, "Getting Around," and "Getting There & Getting Around" in chapter 2 for details on renting in Hawaii. If you're not renting a car (although you should be), call the **Kauai Taxi Company** (© **808/246-9554**) for airport pickup.

VISITOR INFORMATION

The **Kauai Visitors Bureau** is located on the first floor of the Watumull Plaza, 4334 Rice St., Suite 101, Lihue, HI 96766 (© **808/245-3971;** fax 808/246-9235; www.kauai visitorsbureau.org). For a free official *Kauai Vacation Planner* or recorded information, call © **800/262-1400.** The **Poipu Beach Resort Association,** P.O. Box 730, Koloa, HI 96756 (© **888/744-0888** or 808/742-7444; http://poipu-beach.org), will also send you a free guide to accommodations, activities, shopping, and dining in the Poipu Beach area.

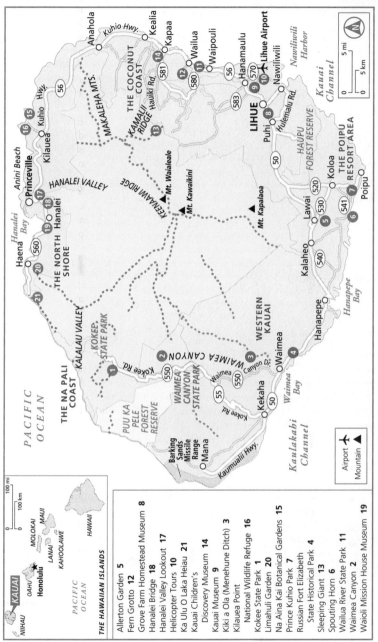

If you'd like to learn more about Kauai before you go, contact the **Kauai Historical Society,** 4396 Rice St., Lihue, HI 96766 (© **808/245-3373**). The group maintains a video-lending library that includes material on a range of topics, including Hawaiian legends, ghost stories, archaeology, and travelogues on individual areas around Kauai. Mainland residents can borrow tapes for up to 3 weeks. Rates are $1 for society members, $2.50 for nonmembers; shipping and handling costs $5.

THE ISLAND IN BRIEF

Kauai's main resort areas are all quite different in climate, price, and accommodations, but it's a wide, wonderful range. On the south shore, dry and sunny **Poipu** is anchored by perfect beaches. This is the place to stay if you like the ocean, watersports, and plenty of sunshine. The **Coconut Coast,** on the east coast of Kauai, has the most condos, shops, and traffic—it's where all the action is. Hanalei, up on the **North Shore,** is rainy, lush, and quiet, with spectacular beaches and deep wilderness. Because of its remote location, the North Shore is a great place to get away from it all—but unless you like spending a lot of your vacation time in the car, it's not a great place from which to explore the rest of the island.

LIHUE & ENVIRONS

Lihue is where most visitors first set foot on the island. This red-dirt farm town, the county seat, was founded by sugar planters and populated by descendants of Filipino and Japanese cane cutters. It's a plain and simple place, with used-car lots and mom-and-pop shops. It's also the source of bargains: inexpensive lodging, great deals on dining, and some terrific shopping buys. One of the island's most beautiful beaches, **Kalapaki Beach,** is just next door at **Nawiliwili,** by the island's main harbor.

THE POIPU RESORT AREA

POIPU BEACH   On Kauai's sunny South Shore, this is a pleasant if sleepy resort destination of low-rise hotels set on gold-sand pocket beaches. Well-done, master-planned Poipu is Kauai's most popular resort, with the widest variety of accommodations, from luxury hotels to B&Bs and condos. It offers 36 holes of golf, 38 tennis courts, and two outstanding restaurants. This is a great place for watersports, and a good base from which to tour the rest of Kauai. The only drawback is that the North Shore is about 1 to 1½ hours away.

KOLOA   This tiny old town of gaily painted sugar shacks, just inland from Poipu Beach, is where the Hawaiian sugar industry was born more than a century-and-a-half ago. The mill is closed, but this showcase plantation town lives on as a tourist attraction, with delightful shops, an old general store, and a vintage Texaco gas station with a 1930s Model A truck in place, just like in the good old days.

KAHALEO/LAWAI   Just a short 10- to 15-minute drive inland from the beach at Poipu lie the more residential communities of Lawai and Kalaheo. Quiet subdivisions line the streets, restaurants catering to locals dot the area, and life revolves around family and work. Good bargains on B&Bs and a handful of reasonably-priced restaurants can be found here.

WESTERN KAUAI

This region, west of Poipu, is more remote than its eastern neighbor and lacks its terrific beaches. But it's home to one of Hawaii's most spectacular natural wonders, **Waimea Canyon** (the "Grand Canyon of the Pacific"), and, farther upland and inland, one of its best parks, **Kokee State Park.**

HANAPEPE   For a quick trip back in time, turn off Highway 50 at Hanapepe, once one of Kauai's biggest towns. Founded by Chinese rice farmers, it's so picturesque that it was used as a backdrop for the miniseries *The Thornbirds*. Hanapepe makes a good rest stop on the way to or from Waimea Canyon. It has galleries selling antiques as well as local art and crafts, including Georgio's surfboard art and coconut-grams. Nearby, at **Salt Pond Beach Park,** Hawaiians since the 17th century have dried a red-dish sea salt in shallow, red-clay pans. This is a great place to swim, snorkel, and—maybe—observe an ancient industry still in practice.

WAIMEA   This little coastal town, the original capital of Kauai, seems to have quit the march of time. Dogs sleep in the street while old pickups rust in front yards. The ambience is definitely laid-back. A stay in Waimea is peaceful and quiet (especially at the Waimea Plantation Cottages on the beach), but the remote location means this isn't the best base if you want to explore the other regions of Kauai, such as the North Shore, without a lot of driving.

On his search for the Northwest Passage in 1778, British explorer Captain James Cook dropped anchor at Waimea and discovered a sleepy village of grass shacks. In 1815, the Russians arrived and built a fort here (now a national historic landmark), but they didn't last long: A scoundrel named George Anton Scheffer tried to claim Kauai for Russia, but he was exposed as an impostor and expelled by King Kamehameha I.

Today, even Waimea's historic relics are spare and simple: a statue of Cook along-side a bas-relief of his ships, the rubble foundation of the Russian fort, and the remains of an ancient aqueduct unlike any other in the Pacific. Except for an overabundance of churches for a town this size, there's no sign that Waimea was selected as the first landing site of missionaries in 1820.

THE COCONUT COAST

The eastern shore of Kauai, north of Lihue, is a jumble of commerce and condos strung along the coast road named for Prince Kuhio, with several small beaches beyond. Almost anything you need, and a lot of stuff you can live without, can be found along this coast, which is known for its hundreds of coconut trees waving in the breeze. It's popular with budget travelers, with myriad B&Bs and affordable hotels and condos to choose from, and it offers great restaurants and the island's major shopping areas.

KAPAA   The center of commerce on the east coast and the capital of the Coconut Coast condo-and-hotel district, this restored plantation town looks just like an antique. False-front wooden stores line both sides of the highway; it looks as though they've been here forever—until you notice the fresh paint and new roofs and realize that everything has been rebuilt since Hurricane Iniki smacked the town flat in 1992. Kapaa has made an amazing comeback without losing its funky charm.

THE NORTH SHORE

Kauai's North Shore may be the most beautiful place in Hawaii. Exotic seabirds, a half-moon bay, jagged peaks soaring into the clouds, and a mighty wilderness lie around the bend from the Coconut Coast, just beyond a series of one-lane bridges traversing the tail ends of waterfalls. There's only one road in and out, and only two towns, Hanalei and Kilauea—the former by the sea, the latter on a lighthouse cliff that's home to a bird preserve. Sun seekers may fret about all the rainy days, but Princeville Resort offers elegant shelter and two golf courses where you can play through rainbows.

KILAUEA   This village is home to an antique lighthouse, tropical-fruit stands, little stone houses, and Kilauea Point National Wildlife Refuge, a wonderful seabird preserve. The rolling hills and sea cliffs are hideaways for the rich and famous, including Bette Midler and Sylvester Stallone. The village itself has its charms: The 1892 Kong Lung Company, Kauai's oldest general store, sells antiques, art, and crafts; and you can order a jazzy Billie Holiday Pizza to go at Kilauea Bakery and Pau Hana Pizza.

ANINI BEACH   This little-known residential district on a 2-mile reef (the biggest on Kauai) offers the safest swimming and snorkeling on the island. A great beach park is open to campers and day-trippers, and there's a boat ramp where locals launch sampans to fish for tuna. On Sundays, there's polo in the park and the sizzle of barbecue on the green. Several residents host guests in nearby B&Bs.

PRINCEVILLE   A little overwhelming for Kauai's wild North Shore, Princeville Resort is Kauai's biggest project, an 11,000-acre development set on a high plain overlooking Hanalei Bay. This resort community includes a luxury Sheraton hotel, 10 condo complexes, new timeshare units around two championship golf courses, cliffside access to pocket beaches, and one B&B right on the golf course.

HANALEI   Picture-postcard Hanalei is the laid-back center of North Shore life and an escapist's dream; it's also the gateway to the wild Na Pali Coast. Hanalei is the last great place on Kauai yet to face the developer's blade of progress. At **Hanalei Bay,** sloops anchor and surfers play year-round. The 2-mile-long crescent beach, the biggest indentation on Kauai's coast, is ideal for kids in summer, when the wild winter surf turns placid. Hanalei still retains the essence of its original sleepy, end-of-the-road charm. On either side of two-lane Kuhio Highway, you'll find just enough shops and restaurants to sustain you for a week's visit—unless you're a hiker, surfer, or sailor, or have some other preoccupation that just might keep you here the rest of your life.

HAENA   Emerald-green Haena isn't a town or a beach but an ancient Hawaiian district, a place of exceptional natural beauty and the gateway to the Na Pali Coast. It's the perfect tropical escape, and everybody knows it: Old house foundations and temples, now covered by jungle, lie in the shadow of new million-dollar homes of movie stars and musicians like Jeff Bridges and Graham Nash. This idyllic, 4-mile coast has lagoons, bays, great beaches, spectacular snorkeling, a botanical garden, and the only North Shore resort that's right on the sand, the Hanalei Colony Resort.

THE NA PALI COAST

The road comes to an end, and now it begins. Kauai's **Na Pali Coast** (*na pali* means "the cliffs") is a place of extreme beauty and Hawaii's last true wilderness. Its majestic splendor will forever remain unspoiled because no road will ever traverse it. You can enter this state park only on foot or by sea. Serious hikers—and we mean *very* serious—tackle the ancient 11-mile-long trail down the forbidding coast to Kalalau Valley. The lone, thin trail that creases these cliffs isn't for the faint of heart or anyone afraid of heights. Those of us who aren't up to it can explore the wild coast in an inflatable rubber Zodiac, a billowing sailboat, a high-powered catamaran, or a hovering helicopter, which takes you for the ride of your life.

2 Getting Around

You need a car to see and do everything on Kauai. Luckily, driving here is easy. There are only two major highways, each beginning in Lihue. From Lihue Airport, turn right, and you'll be on Kapule Highway (Hwy. 51), which eventually merges into Kuhio Highway (Hwy. 56) a mile down. This road will take you to the Coconut Coast and through the North Shore, before dead-ending at Kee Beach, where the Na Pali Coast begins.

If you turn left from Lihue Airport and follow Kapule Highway (Hwy. 51), you'll pass through Lihue and Nawiliwili. Turning on Nawiliwili Road (Hwy. 58) will bring you to the intersection of Kaumualii Highway (Hwy. 50), which will take you to the south and southwest sections of the island. This road doesn't follow the coast, however, so if you're heading to Poipu (and most people are), take Maluhia Road (Hwy. 520) south.

Kaumualii Highway (Hwy. 50) continues all the way to Waimea, where it then dwindles to a secondary road before dead-ending at the other end of the Na Pali Coast.

To get to Waimea Canyon, take either Waimea Canyon Road (Hwy. 550), which follows the western rim of the canyon and affords spectacular views, or Kokee Road (Hwy. 55) up through Waimea Canyon and to Kokee State Park, at more than 4,000 feet; the roads join about halfway.

CAR RENTALS   All of the major car-rental agencies are represented on Kauai. See section 1, "55 Money-Saving Tips" in chapter 2; tips 14 through 20 will help you get the best deal on a car rental. Also see "Car Rentals" under section 12, "Getting There & Getting Around," in chapter 2; it has a list of agencies, plus details on insurance and driving rules. The rental desks are just across the street from Lihue Airport, but you must go by van to collect your car. For deep discounts on weekly car-rental rates, call **Hookipa Haven Vacation Services** (© **800/398-6284;** www.hookipa.com). Rates in low season (Jan, Apr 16–June, and Aug 21–Dec 18) are $148 a week; they jump up to $160 in high season.

MOTORCYCLE RENTALS   The best place to find a customized, cherried-out Harley is **Activity Warehouse,** which has three locations: Kapaa, Princeville and Lihue (© **808/822-4000;** www.travelhawaii.com) and rents Harleys from $65 for 3 hours to $179 for 24 hours. They also have mopeds ($20 for 2 hours, $50 for 24 hours), mountain bikes (from $10 a day), Jeeps ($39 for 4 hours and $69 for 24 hours), even a Ferrari ($275 for 6 hours and $425 for 24 hours).

OTHER TRANSPORTATION OPTIONS   Kauai Taxi Company (© 808/246-9554) offers taxi, limousine, and airport-shuttle service. **Kauai Bus** (© 808/241-6410;** www.kauai.hawaii.gov) operates a fleet of 15 buses that serve the entire island. Taking the bus may be practical for day trips, if you know your way around the island, but you can't take anything larger than a shopping bag aboard, and the buses don't stop at any of the resort areas—but they do serve more than a dozen coastal towns between Kekaha, on the southwest shore, all the way to Hanalei. Buses run, more or less, hourly from 5:30am to 6pm. The fare is $1.50 for adults or 75¢ for seniors, students, and passengers with disabilities.

FAST FACTS: Kauai

American Express There's no local office on the island.

Dentists Emergency dental care is available from **Dr. Mark A. Baird,** 4–9768 Kuhio Hwy., Kapaa (℡ **808/822-9393**), and **Dr. Michael Furgeson,** 4347 Rice St., Lihue (℡ **808/246-6960**).

Doctors Walk-ins are accepted at **Kauai Medical Clinic,** 3–3420 Kuhio Hwy., Suite B, Lihue (℡ **808/245-1500,** or 808/245-1831 after hours). You can also try the **North Shore Clinic,** Kilauea and Oka roads, Kilauea (℡ **808/828-1418**); **Koloa Clinic,** 5371 Koloa Rd. (℡ **808/742-1621**); **Eleele Clinic,** 3292 Waialo Rd. (℡ **808/335-0499**); or **Kapaa Clinic,** 3–1105 Kuhio Hwy. (℡ **808/822-3431**).

Emergencies Dial ℡ **911** for police, fire, and ambulance service. The **Poison Control Center** can be reached at ℡ **800/362-3585.**

Hospitals **Wilcox Health System,** 3420 Kuhio Hwy., Lihue (℡ **808/245-1100**), has emergency services available around the clock.

Police For non-emergencies, call ℡ **808/245-9711.**

Post Office The main post office is at 4441 Rice St., Lihue. To find the branch office nearest you, call ℡ **800/ASK-USPS.**

Weather For current weather conditions, call ℡ **808/245-6001.** For marine conditions, call ℡ **808/245-3564.**

See "Fast Facts: The Hawaiian Islands" in chapter 2 for more information.

3 Accommodations You Can Afford

Deals abound on Kauai. A family of four can share a luxury one-bedroom apartment on the beach at Hanalei for less than $53 each per night (at the Hanalei Colony Resort), and a couple can have a quaint cottage in a quiet residential area of Kapaa, on the Coconut Coast, for as little as $50 for two (at the Hibiscus Hollow). Some visitors may spend $339 or more for a room facing the scenic Kalapaki Beach—but you can have one just across the street from this picture-perfect beach for $85 double (at the Garden Island Inn).

Numerous bed-and-breakfasts have sprung up on Kauai, offering great accommodations at budget prices. Staying in a B&B is not only a good way to meet other visitors to the islands, but a great way to get to know the interesting characters who own and run the B&Bs themselves; they include farmers, artists, psychotherapists, acupuncturists, and numerous doctors.

Before you book, be sure to read "The Island in Brief," beginning on p. 514 of this chapter; it'll help you settle on a location. Also check out chapter 2, section 1, "55 Money-Saving Tips"; tips 21 to 39 have valuable advice on booking your accommodations. Also in chapter 2, section 14, "Tips on Accommodations" (starting on p. 62) defines the various types of options and points you to the state's best booking agencies.

When planning your vacation on Kauai, don't forget to add the 11.42% tax to all accommodation rates. Don't worry about parking; on Kauai it's generally free and usually no problem, unless noted otherwise.

LIHUE & ENVIRONS

Garden Island Inn ★ *Finds*   This bargain-hunter's delight is located 2 miles from the airport, 1 mile from Lihue, and within walking distance of shops and restaurants. The spacious rooms are decorated with island-style furniture, bright prints, and fresh tropical flowers (grown right on the grounds). Each unit contains a fridge, microwave, wet bar, TV, coffeemaker, and ocean view; some have private lanais, and the suites have sitting areas. The grounds are filled with flowers and banana and papaya trees (and you're welcome to take from the pile of fruit at the front desk). Owner Steve Layne offers friendly service, lots of advice on activities (the entire staff happily uses their connections to get you discounts), and even complimentary use of beach gear, golf clubs (a course is nearby, as are tennis courts), and coolers. If they are booked, ask about their two-bedroom condo nearby for $135 to $155 per night.

3445 Wilcox Rd. (across the street from Kalapaki Beach, near Nawiliwili Harbor), Lihue, HI 96766. ℂ **800/648-0154** or 808/245-7227. Fax 808/245-7603. www.gardenislandinn.com. 21 units (private bathrooms have shower only). $85–$135 double. Extra person $5. AE, DISC MC, V. **Amenities:** Complimentary watersports equipment; activities desk. *In room:* A/C, TV, fridge, coffeemaker, hair dryer, iron.

SUPER-CHEAP SLEEPS

Motel Lani *Value*   For a no-frills bed and shower, this place will do the job. You won't find a little basket of toiletries in the bathroom or a mint on your pillow, but you will get a clean, basic room (no TV) for as little as $34. This small, concrete-block motel mainly serves inter-island travelers and a few visitors on a budget. The location, on a busy street right in the heart of Lihue, isn't bad—the airport is just a 5-minute drive away, making this a good rest stop if you have an early-morning flight—but the beach is a significant schlep away. For $50, you can get a room with a kitchenette.

4240 Rice St. (P.O. Box 1836), Lihue, HI 96766. ℂ **808/245-2965.** 9 units (with shower only). $34–$52 double. No credit cards. *In room:* A/C, fridge, kitchenette (some rooms).

Tip Top Motel *Value*   The Tip Top is an institution on Kauai. Their motto, "Over 75 years of service on the island of Kauai," lets you know they've been around a while. The two-story, concrete-tile building, with a cafe on the first floor, provides very basic accommodations: twin beds (with solid, hard mattresses), shower, A/C in the window, and a dresser. Don't look for expensive carpeting here—just institutional linoleum tile. But for $45, you're still getting your money's worth. Guests are usually inter-island business travelers who like the convenience of the central Lihue location, just 5 minutes from the airport.

3173 Akahi St., Lihue, HI 96766. ℂ **808/245-2333.** Fax 808/246-8988. 30 units (with shower only). $45 double. MC, V. From the airport, follow Ahukini Rd.; turn left on Akahi St. **Amenities:** Coffee shop. *In room:* A/C, TV, no phone.

THE POIPU RESORT AREA

Kauai Cove ★ *Value*   These immaculate cottages, located just 300 feet from the Koloa Landing, next to the Waikomo Stream, are the perfect private getaway. Each studio has a full kitchen, private lanai (with barbecue grill), and big bamboo four-poster bed. The cozy rooms feature beautiful hardwood floors, tropical decor, and cathedral ceilings. It's close enough that you can walk to sandy beaches, great restaurants, and shopping, yet far enough off the beaten path that privacy and quiet are assured.

2672 Puuholo Rd., Poipu, HI 96756. ℂ and fax **800/624-9945** or 808/742-2562. www.kauaicove.com. 3 units. $95–$125 double. 3-night minimum. DISC, MC, V. **Amenities:** Use of pool, tennis courts and hot tub nearby. *In room:* A/C, TV, dataport, kitchen, fridge, coffeemaker, CD player.

Lihue

Koloa Landing Cottages (Kids)   Most return guests at Koloa Landing Cottages have become close friends with former-hosts Hans and Sylvia Zeevat, who started this vacation cottage rental business in 1978. Ellie and Bret Knopf took over the property in 2001 and have brought the five cottages, nestled in the tropical landscaping, back to their original glory. Located across the street from a beach that offers great snorkeling and diving, the cottages range from a studio to a 1,100-square-foot, two-bedroom/two-bathroom home that can sleep up to six. All units have full kitchens. Larger units also have private decks. The units exude comfort; they're outfitted with the practical furniture of tropical beach houses—great for flopping down with a good book. Since the Knopfs have four kids of their own, they welcome families.

2704–B Hoonani Rd. (near the Hoonani Rd. Bridge), Koloa, HI 96756. © **800/779-8773** or 808/742-1470. www. koloa-landing.com. 1 studio, 3 cottages, 1 house. $105–$185. 4-night minimum. No credit cards. **Amenities:** Washer/dryer facilities. *In room:* TV, kitchen, fridge, coffeemaker.

Marjorie's Kauai Inn (★) (Finds)   This quiet property, perched on the side of a hill, is just 10 minutes from Poipu Beach and 5 minutes from Old Koloa Town. From its large lanai, it offers stunning views over the rolling pastures and the Lawai Valley. Every unit has a kitchenette, dining table, ceiling fan, and lanai. The new Sunset View unit has a separate sitting area and a futon sofa for extra guests. On the hillside is a

Poipu Resort Area Accommodations

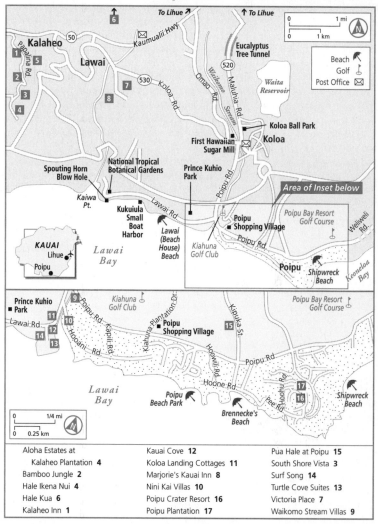

Aloha Estates at Kalaheo Plantation **4**	Kauai Cove **12**	Pua Hale at Poipu **15**
Bamboo Jungle **2**	Koloa Landing Cottages **11**	South Shore Vista **3**
Hale Ikena Nui **4**	Marjorie's Kauai Inn **8**	Surf Song **14**
Hale Kua **6**	Nini Kai Villas **10**	Turtle Cove Suites **13**
Kalaheo Inn **1**	Poipu Crater Resort **16**	Victoria Place **7**
	Poipu Plantation **17**	Waikomo Stream Villas **9**

huge, 50-foot swimming pool, perfect for lap swimming. But the best reason to stay here is Marjorie Ketcher herself. "Do more than one fun thing a day!" is Marjorie's motto, and she makes sure that her guests are out diving, snorkeling, sightseeing, hiking, dining, dancing, or enjoying one of the hundreds of other things she can recommend. This establishment is not suitable for children. In 2005, Marjorie sold this great B&B, but she is staying on to manage it through most of 2006.

P.O. Box 866 (off Hailima Rd., adjacent to the National Tropical Botanical Garden), Lawai, HI 96765. ☎ 800/717-8838 or 808/332-8838. www.marjorieskauaiinn.com. 3 units. $100–$130 double. Rates include continental breakfast on 1st day. Extra person $20. 2-night minimum. No credit cards. **Amenities:** Pool Jacuzzi,. *In room:* TV, kitchenette, fridge, coffeemaker, hair dryer.

Poipu Plantation *(Value)*   This tropical property has three bed-and-breakfast rooms in the main house and separate apartment vacation rentals on the same property. The large rooms in the house are reminiscent of the old plantation days, with shining wooden floors, huge bathrooms, and lots of privacy. Breakfast is served in the dining room; you're also welcome to take yours out on the lanai. The impeccably decorated one- and two-bedroom apartments are huge and come with big lanais, big living rooms, big separate bedrooms (with shoji doors), full kitchens, and big bathrooms; gleaming hardwood floors, air-conditioning, and ocean views add to the value. Located in the heart of Poipu, within walking distance of beaches and water activities, golf, tennis, shops, and restaurants, Poipu Plantation is an excellent choice for budget vacationers.

1792 Pee Rd., Koloa, HI 96756. ℰ **800/634-0263** or 808/742-6757. Fax 808/742-8681. www.poipubeach.com. 3 units, 9 apts. $95 double; $120–$145 1-bedroom; $175–$190 2-bedroom for 4. Rates include continental breakfast. Extra person $20. 3-night minimum. MC, V. From Poipu Rd., turn toward the ocean onto Pee Rd. **Amenities:** Hot tub. *In room:* A/C, TV/VCR, kitchen, fridge, coffeemaker.

Pua Hale at Poipu *(Finds)*   Created by an artist and designed by an engineer, Pua Hale is a large (850 sq. ft.) cottage on a quiet, dead-end street, just 2 blocks from Poipu Beach. Artist/photographer Carol Ann Davis and her husband, engineer Walter Briant, took an empty space in their yard and created an open, airy cottage with an Asian-influenced interior. The cottage is surrounded by a high fence to ensure privacy; entrance is through a rustic wooden gate draped with colorful bougainvillea. The large main room has a complete kitchen at one end, and living and dining areas (with a queen sofa-bed) at the other. The bathroom has a wonderful tiled Japanese furo (sunken tub) for soaking, as well as a shower. A real bonus is the intimate, curved lanai overlooking Japanese gardens blooming with ginger, heliconia, and plumeria. Other pluses include a barbecue, stereo, and laundry facilities. Poipu beaches, shopping, and restaurants are just a walk away.

2381 Kipuka St., Koloa, HI 96756. ℰ **800/745-7414** or 808/742-1700. Fax 808/742-7392. www.kauai-puahale.com. 1 cottage. $125 double ($60 cleaning fee). Extra person $10. 4-night minimum. DISC, MC, V. From Poipu Rd., turn left on Kipuka St. (just past shopping center). No children under 8. **Amenities:** Washer/dryer. *In room:* A/C, TV/VCR, kitchen, fridge, coffeemaker, iron.

Surf Song *(Value)*   Located in a quiet residential neighborhood amongst million-dollar oceanfront homes, these three studios and one apartment unit offer excellent value for your vacation dollar. Each unit has a private lanai, queen bed, and a sleeper sofa (some even have ocean views). The studios have kitchenettes with microwave, coffeemaker, small refrigerator, and other appliances; the apartment has a full kitchen. The units all face a courtyard, landscaped with tropical flowers, with a picnic table and barbecue. It's walking distance to the beach, and a 2-minute drive to restaurants and shops in Poipu Resort Area.

5135 Ho'ona Rd., Poipu Beach, HI 96756. ℰ **877/373-2331** or 808/742-2331. Fax 808/826-6033. www.surf song.com. 4 units. $70–$130 double. No credit cards. 3-night minimum. **Amenities:** Washer and dryer. *In room:* TV, kitchenette or kitchen, fridge, coffeemaker.

Victoria Place *(Finds)*   The reason to stay here? Two words: Edee Seymour. It's easy to see why she won the Kauai Chamber of Commerce's Aloha Spirit Award. She lavishes her guests with attention and aloha. Her spacious, skylit, U-shaped house wraps around the swimming pool and garden. Three bedrooms, located in one wing of the home, open onto the pool area, which is surrounded by flowering walls of

---

Value The Queen of Condos

One of the easiest ways to find lodging in the Poipu Beach area is to contact **Grantham Resorts**, 3176 Poipu Rd., Koloa, HI 96756 (© **800/325-5701** or 808/742-2000; fax 808/742-9093; www.grantham-resorts.com), which handles more than 100 "hand-picked" rental units for 12 different condo developments, plus dozens of vacation homes, ranging from quaint cottages to elite resort homes. Owner Nancy Grantham has high standards for her rental units and offers extremely fair prices. If the properties are not maintained to her standards, Nancy has no problem taking the units (and, in one case, an entire condominium project) out of her selected rentals. The condos start at $89 for a basic two-bedroom, garden-view unit in low season, and vacation homes start at $185 and go up to $1,140 for exquisite multi-million dollar ocean homes. There's a 5-night minimum for condos and a 7-night minimum for homes.

If you're staying on Kauai for 5 days, ask Grantham Resorts about the "Frommer's Silver Rate," large one- and two-bedroom condos, well-equipped (full kitchen, washer/dryer, wet bar, TV, phone, most with Hospitality High-Speed Internet Service and DVDs), starting as low as $99 a night for one-bedroom and $129 for two-bedroom garden-view condos, or $135 a night for one-bedroom or two-bedroom ocean-view condos. (see "Nihi Kai Villas" and "Waikomo Stream Villas" below). There's not a better deal on Kauai. Kudos to Nancy for these fabulous vacation bargains.

---

bougainvillea, hibiscus, gardenia, and ginger. So why is the price is so low? Guests share the TV, the phone, and a refrigerator in the common area. Edee also rents a secluded studio apartment (dubbed "Victoria's Other Secret") down a private path; it contains a king bed, shower-only bathroom, kitchen, and TV. Edee's breakfasts are truly a big deal: at least five different tropical fruits, followed by something from the oven, such as homemade bread, scones, or muffins. Most of her guests are returnees. As a couple from Germany told us, "Once you stay with Edee, every place else is cold and indifferent."

3459 Lawai Loa Lane (off Koloa Rd./Hwy. 530), Koloa. Reservations: c/o P.O. Box 930, Lawai, HI 96765. © **808/332-9300**. Fax 808/332-9465. www.hshawaii.com/kvp/victoria. 4 units. $90 double; $125 studio apt. Rates include yummy full breakfast. Extra person $15. No credit cards. No children under 15. **Amenities:** Outdoor pool; beach toys. *In room:* No phone.

AMAZING DEALS ON WEEK-LONG STAYS

Nihi Kai Villas 🏄 *Value* *Kids*   Nancy Grantham, owner of Grantham Resorts, is a marketing genius. She's offering the deal of the decade on these large, two-bedroom units just 200 yards from the beach. If you stay 7 nights, the rate for these big, well-equipped two-bedroom apartments is an unbelievable $115 a night. You may not be getting new carpet, new furniture, new drapes, or a prime beachfront location, but you *are* getting a clean, well-cared-for unit with a full kitchen, washer/dryer, and TV/VCR, all at an unbeatable price. The sofa bed in the living room allows you to comfortably sleep six. The property is a 2-minute walk from Brennecke's Beach (great for bodysurfing) and a block from Poipu Beach Park. On-site amenities include an oceanfront swimming pool, tennis and paddle courts, and a barbecue and picnic area. Within a 5-minute drive are two great golf courses, several restaurants, and loads of shopping.

1870 Hoone Rd. Reservations: c/o Grantham Resorts, 3176 Poipu Rd., Suite 1, Koloa, HI 96756. © **800/325-5701** or 808/742-2000. Fax 808/742-9093. www.grantham-resorts.com. 70 units. $135–$199 1-bedroom double; $135–$259 2-bedroom for 4. 5-night minimum. Ask about Frommer's "Silver Rate" (5-night minimum). DC, DISC, MC, V. From Poipu Rd., turn toward the ocean on Hoowili Rd., then left on Hoone Rd.; Nihi Kai Villas is just past Nalo Rd. on Hoone Rd. **Amenities:** Outdoor pool; nearby golf course; tennis courts; Jacuzzi; activities desk, concierge. *In room:* TV/VCR, dataport, kitchen, coffeemaker, iron, washer/dryer.

Poipu Crater Resort *(Value)*   Attention travelers on a budget: two-bedroom garden-view units for just $89 a night in low season (okay, $99 midseason and a still unbe-lievable $109 in high season) is a deal you can't pass up. This resort consists of 15 duplexes in a tropical garden setting. Each unit is about 1,500 square feet with living area, kitchen, large lanai, bathroom and guest bedroom downstairs, and master bed-room and bathroom upstairs. Each has a full kitchen (with microwave), as well as a washer/dryer and VCR. The complex has a swimming pool, tennis and paddle ball courts, sauna, table-tennis tables, and barbecues. Poipu Beach is a bout a 10-minute walk away, and the entire Poipu Beach Resort area (offering everything from restau-rants to golf courses) is within a 5-minue drive. The only caveats are no maid service and no air conditioning. Pick up the phone right now and reserve a unit before the rest of the world beats you to it.

2330 Hoohu Rd., Poipu. Reservations: c/o Grantham Resorts, 3176 Poipu Rd., Suite 1, Koloa, HI 96756. © **800/ 325-5701** or 808/742-2000. Fax 808/742-9093. www.grantham-resorts.com. 30 units. $89–$99 1-bedroom garden view. 5-night minimum. Ask about Frommer's "Silver Rate" (5-night minimum). DC, DISC, MC, V. From Poipu Rd., turn toward the ocean on Hoowili Rd., then left on Hoone Rd.; continue on Hoone Rd., past the bends, where the road is now called Pee Rd; turn left off Pee Rd. onto Hoohu Rd. **Amenities:** Outdoor pool; nearby golf course; tennis courts; sauna; barbecue area. *In room:* TV/VCR, kitchen, coffeemaker, iron, washer/dryer, CD player.

Waikomo Stream Villas ★ *(Kids)* *(Value)*   Nancy Grantham has one more fabulous trick up her sleeve: these 800- to 900-square-foot one-bedroom apartments, which comfortably sleep four, and larger two-bedroom units, which sleep six. Tucked into a lush tropical garden setting, these spacious, well-decorated units have everything you could possibly need on your vacation: full kitchen, VCR, washer/dryer, and private lanai. The complex—which has both adults' and children's pools, tennis courts, and a barbecue area—is adjacent to the Kiahuna Golf Club and just a 5-minute walk from restaurants, shopping, and Poipu's beaches and golf courses.

2721 Poipu Rd. (just after entry to Poipu, on ocean side of Poipu Rd.), Poipu. Reservations: c/o Grantham Resorts, 3176 Poipu Rd., Suite 1, Koloa, HI 96756. © **800/325-5701** or 808/742-2000. Fax 808/742-9093. www.grantham-resorts. com. 60 units. $99–$145 1-bedroom for 4; $129–$175 2-bedroom for 6. 5-night minimum. Ask about Frommer's "Sil-ver Rates." DC, DISC, MC, V. **Amenities:** 2 outdoor pools (1 for children, 1 for adults); tennis courts; Jacuzzi; activities desk, concierge. *In room:* TV/VCR, dataport, kitchen, fridge, coffeemaker, washer/dryer.

WORTH A SPLURGE
Turtle Cove Suites *(Value)* ★★What makes this property so incredible is not only the fabulous location (overlooking the stream and ocean) but also the great eye of the interior designer. It also helps that owner Joe Sylvester and his wife own a furniture and fine-arts store to choose the "perfect" items for their four units. Our favorite of the units, located on a quiet street, away from the crowds, is the 1,100-square-foot oceanfront suite with a full kitchen and private Jacuzzi, original art on the walls, and

a zillion little touches that make this place seem more like a home than a vacation rental. All the units (even the $100 one) have lanais, use of the swimming pool and Jacuzzi, and feature top-of-the-line material like slate from India, four poster beds, and marble bathrooms. At these prices, these units are a deal. Book in advance.

P.O. Box 1899, Poipu Beach, 96756. ℂ **866/294-2733.** www.kauaibeachrentals.com. 4 units. $135–$240. 4-night minimum. AE, DC, DISC, MC, V. **Amenities:** Pool, Jacuzzi, coin-operated washer/dryer. *In room:* TV/VCR, kitchens (in some), kitchenettes (in some), fridge, coffeemaker, microwave.

ELSEWHERE ON THE SOUTH COAST

Aloha Estates at Kalaheo Plantation *Value*   This is a love story. Part one: A Japanese visitor, LeeAnn, meets stained-glass artist James Hargraves while on vacation on Oahu. They fall in love and marry. Part two: While visiting Kauai, they discover a 1924 plantation house and fall in love with it. They lovingly restore the old house and convert it into a bed-and-breakfast filled with 1920s and 1930s furniture and fabrics, and James's stained-glass work. There's a room to fit everyone's needs and budget, from a small $45 room with king bed, kitchenette, private entrance, stereo, VCR, and lanai, to a $75 room with full kitchen, private entrance, hot tub, VCR, stereo, and private lanai overlooking the koi pond. Part 3: Guests arrive, and fall in love with this grand old house themselves . . . and everyone lives happily ever after (at least while they're on Kauai!).

4579 Puuwai Rd. (P.O. Box 872), Kalaheo, HI 96741. ℂ and fax **808/332-7812.** www.kalaheo-plantation.com. 6 units. $45–$75 double. Extra person $10. 2-night minimum. No credit cards. Turn off Hwy. 50 toward the mountain onto Puuwai Rd. at Steve's Mini-Mart, then turn right immediately again to stay on Puuwai Rd. *In room:* TV, kitchenette, fridge, coffeemaker, iron (on request).

Bamboo Jungle *Finds*   New owners Lucy and Carrie Ryan recently took over this property, a jungle of verdant plants, a quaint gazebo, a 82-foot lap pool, and an impeccably-decorated old plantation-era house. They are making the much-needed repairs and renovations to the rooms, where each one has a private entrance and French doors opening onto a private lanai with an ocean view. The netting over the beds creates a romantic mood and serves a functional purpose (it keeps Hawaii's insects on their side of the sleeping quarters). Accommodations range from a single room with deck to a studio with minikitchen. There are no phones in the units, but you can use the house phone. Breakfast is served in the "great room" inside the house. The next renovation will be to the gardens and yard. Golf and tennis courts are nearby. Note that there is no air-conditioning, which 350 days of the year is fine, but on the days the trade winds stop blowing, it's not so great.

3829 Waha Rd. Reservations: P.O. Box 737, Kalaheo, HI 96741. ℂ **888/332-5115** or 808/332-5515. www.kauai-bedandbreakfast.com. 3 units. $110–$150 double. 3-night minimum (in rooms), 5-night minimum (in suite). MC, V. From Hwy. 50, turn left at the traffic light onto Papalina Rd., then right on Waha Rd. **Amenities:** Outdoor pool; Jacuzzi. *In room:* TV, kitchenette (in 1 room), coffeemaker, no phone.

Hale Ikena Nui *Value*   Patti Pantone opened this 1,000-square-foot, self-contained guest suite on the first floor of their home in 1995 and had instant success. It has a private entrance, a full-size kitchen (with dishwasher), and large dining room and living room areas. With a queen bed and a queen-size sofa-bed, the unit easily sleeps four. Outside, on the private lanai, are a gas barbecue and all the beach and picnic equipment you could possibly need. Throw in a full-size washer/dryer, and you can see why this place is so popular. In 1996, she also opened a room upstairs in their house for people looking for less space and a smaller bite out of their budget. The

room has a huge walk-in closet, plus gives you run of the house, including the gourmet kitchen.

3957 Ulualii St. (P.O. Box 171), Kalaheo, HI 96741. ℂ **800/550-0778** or 808/332-9005. Fax 808/332-0911. www.kauai vacationhome.com. 1 unit, 1 apt (with shower only). $75 double (includes continental breakfast); $95 double apt (includes continental breakfast on 1st day). Extra person $15. 3-night minimum for apt only. MC, V. At the 11-mile marker on Hwy. 50, turn down Papalina Rd. toward the ocean; continue for 1⅕ miles; turn right on Waha Rd., then left on Ulualii St. **Amenities:** Washer/dryer. *In room (apartment only):* TV, kitchen, fridge, coffeemaker, iron.

Hale Kua ⭐ (*Value*) This is for people who love the beach—at a distance—and want to sleep in the quiet and cool climate of the hills of Lawai Valley, away from the maddening crowds. If you want to stay in a forest, wake up to the sound of the birds singing, and see incredible sunsets each night, one of the five units in three different houses may be for you. Hale Kua features a two-story house with a complete three-bedroom home with big kitchen, wraparound eating bar, walk-in closets, washer/dryer, and a view of the bucolic rolling hills; downstairs are two separate one-bedroom units with full kitchens, wraparound lanai, washer/dryer, with the sound of birds serenading you all day long. Next door, hosts Bill and Cathy Cowern own an 8-acre tree farm, where there is a one-bedroom separate cottage and a studio apartment in their large home. The beach is just a 10-minute drive down the hill. If you are looking for privacy and all the comforts to nestle into a honeymoon or family accommodation, you won't find anything better at this price.

4896-E Kua Rd., Lawai, HI 96765. ℂ **800/440-4353** or 808/332-8570. www.halekua.com. 5 units. $105 1-bedroom apt for 2; $115 1-bedroom cottage for 2; $125 3-bedroom unit for 2 ($5 extra per person). 5-night minimum in cottage Dec 15–Jan 15. No credit cards. **Amenities:** Barbecue areas. *In-room:* TV/VCR/DVD, kitchen, fridge, microwave, coffeemaker, washer/dryer.

Kalaheo Inn ⭐ (*Kids*) (*Value*) What a deal! Located in the town of Kalaheo, a 12-minute drive from world-famous Poipu Beach, a 5-minute drive from the Kukuiolono Golf Course, and within walking distance of shops and restaurants, the inn is a comfortable 1940s motel that was totally remodeled in 1999 and converted into apartment units with kitchenettes. In 2005, they replaced the beds with Simmons "heavenly" mattresses and put hair dryers in the bathrooms, new refrigerators in all the rooms, and gave the place a polishing. Owners Chet and Tish Hunt couldn't be friendlier, handing out complimentary beach towels, beach toys, and even golf clubs to guests (links are nearby). They love families and have a storeroom full of games to keep the kids entertained. This is a must-stay for vacationers on a budget.

4444 Papalina Rd. (just behind the Kalaheo Steakhouse), Koloa, HI 96756. ℂ **888/332-6023** or 808/332-6023. Fax 808/742-6432. www.kalaheoinn.com. 15 units. $65 double studio with kitchenette; $75–$85 1-bedroom with kitchenette; $105 2-bedroom; $145 3-bedroom with full kitchen. AE, MC, V. **Amenities:** Complimentary watersports equipment; children's games; coin-op washer/dryers. *In room:* TV, kitchen or kitchenette, fridge, coffeemaker, hair dryer, iron, no phone.

South Shore Vista ⭐ (*Kids*) Host Margy Parker has been the executive director of the Poipu Beach Resort Association since 1982, and she knows what guests need to be happy and comfortable on vacation. The one-bedroom apartment, with ocean and mountain views, is in Margy's home. The list of pluses for this place includes a separate bedroom with a queen bed and full bathroom, private entry, big lanai with ocean view, living area with fold-out couch (the unit can sleep up to four), VCR, and fully-equipped kitchenette. Margy stocks breakfast provisions such as coffee, tea, cereal, and fresh papayas and limes from her garden. Located on a quiet residential street, South Shore Vista is 2 blocks from the Kukuiolono Park and Golf Course (with jogging and walking paths through Hawaiian and Japanese gardens and 9 holes of golf for an unbelievable $9), 10 minutes from Poipu beaches, 40 minutes from Waimea Canyon, and 25 minutes from the airport. Margy is a walking encyclopedia of knowledge on island activities, including new activities and undiscovered adventures. You can't go wrong staying here.

4400 Kai Ikena Dr., Kalaheo, HI 96741. ✆ **808/332-9339.** Fax 808/332-7771. www.southshorevista.com. 1 apt. $84 double. Rate includes continental breakfast. Extra person $10 (children $5). 3-night minimum. No credit cards. After the 11-mile marker on Hwy. 50, turn toward the ocean on Papalina Rd.; continue for nearly a mile to Kai Ikena Dr. *In room:* TV/VCR, kitchen, fridge, coffeemaker, hair dryer, iron.

SUPER CHEAP SLEEPS

Seaview Suite *Value*   If you are on a really tight budget, you can still stay in the popular south shore area. Located in a private home, in a residential area about a 10-minute drive from the beach, is this budget place with two small, but affordable, rooms. The Seaview Suite, a large studio with separate bedroom area divided by sliding shoji doors, contains a full kitchen, big bathroom, walk-in closet, and a private lanai with barbecue. Downstairs, owner Monica has added a tiny "ti suite" for those on a very strict budget. The small one-room unit has a tiny kitchenette (microwave and full-size refrigerator), a queen bed, and just enough room for a single bed and TV. Great for the frugal crowd that plans to come home only to sleep. Monica will do one complimentary load of laundry per week for her guests, and she has lots of beach paraphernalia she's happy to loan out.

3913 Ulualii St., Kalaheo, 96741. ✆ and fax **808/332-9744.** www.vrbo.com/53989. 2 units. $65 for small studio; $75 for larger studio. 3 night minimum. No credit cards. **Amenities:** Complimentary watersports equipment. *In room:* TV/VCR, full kitchen in one unit/kitchenette in other, fridge, coffeemaker, phone.

GREAT DEALS FOR FAMILIES

Waimea Plantation Cottages ✿ *Kids*   This beachfront vacation retreat is like no other in the islands: Among groves of towering coco palms sit clusters of restored sugar-plantation cottages, dating from the 1880s to the 1930s and bearing the names of their original plantation-worker dwellers. The lovely cottages have been transformed into cozy, comfortable guest units with period rattan and wicker furniture and fabrics from the 1930s, sugar's heyday on Kauai. Each has a furnished lanai and a fully-equipped modern kitchen and bathroom; some units are oceanfront. Facilities include an oceanfront pool, tennis courts, and laundry room. The only downsides: the black-sand beach, which is lovely, but not conducive to swimming (the water is often murky at the Waimea River mouth), and the location, at the foot of Waimea Canyon Drive—its remoteness can be very appealing, but the North Shore is 1½ hours away. Golf courses and tennis courts, however, are much closer.

9400 Kaumualii Hwy. (P.O. Box 367), Waimea, HI 96796. ✆ **800/9-WAIMEA** or 808/338-1625. Fax 808/338-2338. www.waimea-plantation.com. 48 units. $140–$160 hotel room double; $140 studios with kitchenette double; $195–$310 1-bedroom double; $240–$370 2-bedroom (sleeps up to 4); $280–$415 3-bedroom (up to 5); $405–$465 4-bedroom (up to 8); $620–$730 5-bedroom (up to 9). Extra person $20. Children under 18 stay free. AE, DC, DISC, MC, V. **Amenities:** Restaurant; bar; large outdoor pool; activities desk; coin-op washer/dryers; dry cleaning. *In room:* TV, dataport, kitchen, fridge, coffeemaker, iron, safe.

SUPER-CHEAP SLEEPS

Kokee Lodge *Value*   This is an excellent choice, especially if you want to do some hiking in Waimea Canyon and Kokee State Park. There are two types of cabins here: The older ones have dormitory-style sleeping arrangements (and resemble a youth hostel), while the new ones have two separate bedrooms each. Both styles sleep six and come with cooking utensils, bedding, and linens. We recommend the newer units, which have wood floors, cedar walls, and more modern kitchen facilities (some are wheelchair-accessible as well). There are no phones or TVs in the units, but there is a pay phone at the general store. You can purchase firewood for the cabin stove at Kokee Lodge, where there's a restaurant that's open for continental breakfast and lunch every day. There's also a cocktail lounge, a general store, and a gift shop. Light sleepers, you've been warned—this area is home to lots of roosters, which crow at dawn's first light.

P.O. Box 819, Waimea, HI 96796. ℂ 808/335-6061. 12 cabins. $35–$45 double. Cleaning fee of $15. Extra person $5. 5-night maximum. AE, DC, DISC, MC, V. *In room:* Kitchen, fridge, coffeemaker, no phone.

THE COCONUT COAST

Alohilani Bed-and-Breakfast ★ *Finds* Owner Sharon Mitchell has furnished her B&B, which sits amid 6 peaceful acres at the very end of a country road, with antiques and other beautiful pieces. Her separate cottage is a large room decorated in country charm with a full kitchen, sleeper sofa, and adorable antique bed with its own teddy bear. Our favorite suite is the open, airy Sunshine Atrium, with its floor-to-ceiling windows and arched French glass doors opening onto a lanai that overlooks the entire valley. The white-tiled room has a queen bed, a sleeper sofa, a small fridge, and a microwave.

1470 Wanaao Rd., Kapaa, HI 96746. ℂ 800/533-9316 or 808/823-0128. Fax 808/823-0128. www.hawaiian. net/~alohila. 3 units. $99–$109 double suite; $109 double cottage. Rates include continental breakfast. Extra person $10. 3-night minimum. MC, V. From Kuhio Hwy. (Hwy. 56), turn left onto Kawaihau Rd.; go about 4 miles, then turn left again on Wanaao Rd. **Amenities:** Jacuzzi. *In room:* TV, kitchenette, fridge, coffeemaker, hair dryer, no phone.

Hotel Coral Reef *Value* Here's a budget choice right on the beach. This small, unpretentious hotel faces a grassy lawn, coconut trees, and a white-sand beach. It offers economical rooms and friendly service in an ideal location, within walking distance of shops, restaurants, golf, and tennis, and just 50 yards away from good swimming and snorkeling. There's even an 8-mile bike path that starts right on the grounds. Of the two wings in the hotel, we prefer the oceanfront one, which has big rooms that overlook the beach through sliding-glass lanai doors. The two-room units have a separate bedroom and a living room with a sofa bed—perfect for families. Linda Warriner, owner and gracious hostess of this quaint hotel, is always happy to give you pointers on how to stretch your budget and still have a good time on Kauai.

1516 Kuhio Hwy. (at the northern end of Kapaa, between mile markers 8 and 9), Kapaa, HI 96746. ℂ 800/843-4659 or 808/822-4481. Fax 808/822-7705. www.hotelcoralreef.com. 21 units. $99–$149 double; from $159 suite. Extra person $25. Children 12 and under stay free in parents' room. Room/car packages available. AE, DC, MC, V. **Amenities:** Activities desk; coin-op washer/dryers. *In room:* A/C, TV, fridge, coffeemakers, safes (in oceanfront rooms).

Inn Paradise *Finds* Out in the country, about a 10- to 15-minute drive from the beach, Inn Paradise is a plantation-style building with a wraparound lanai that houses three guest units on 3½ landscaped acres. The units range from the one-room "Prince," with a tiny kitchenette tucked away in a closet, to the large, two-bedroom "King," which has a full kitchen. Carefully decorated rooms with sparkling tile floors and a quiet, relaxing ambience come together to make this property a good budget choice. The large deck overlooks the flower-filled grounds and a valley dotted with fruit trees beyond. An added bonus: A hot tub for soaking after a long day of sightseeing.

Coconut Coast Accommodations

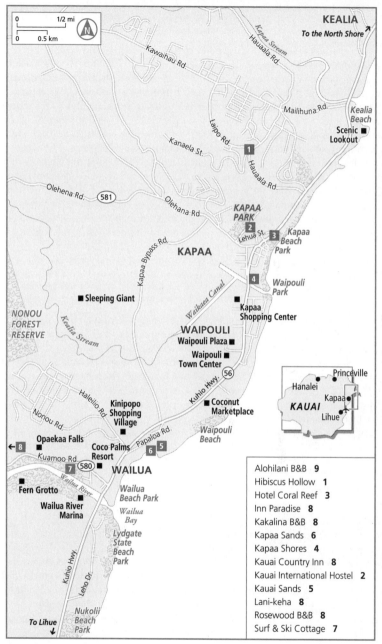

0   1/2 mi
0   0.5 km

KEALIA
To the North Shore

Kapaa Stream
Hauaala Rd.
Kawaihau Rd.

Mailihuna Rd.
Kealia Beach
Scenic Lookout

Laipo Rd.
Kanaela St.
Hauaala Rd.

1

Olehena Rd. (581)
Olehana Rd.

KAPAA PARK
2
Lehua St.
3 Kapaa Beach Park

KAPAA

Kapaa Bypass Rd.

■ Sleeping Giant

4 Waipouli Park

Waikaea Canal
Kapaa Shopping Center

NONOU FOREST RESERVE

Kealia Stream

WAIPOULI
Waipouli Plaza ■
Waipouli Town Center ■

Kuhio Hwy. (56)

Haleilio Rd.
Nonou Rd.
Kinipopo Shopping Village ■

■ Coconut Marketplace

Waipouli Beach

Opaekaa Falls ■
←**8** ■
Kuamoo Rd.
Coco Palms Resort ■
Papaloa Rd.
6 **5**

7 (580)   WAILUA

Wailua River

■ Fern Grotto
Wailua River Marina ■

Wailua Beach Park

Wailua Bay

Lydgate State Beach Park

Kuhio Hwy.
Leho Dr.

To Lihue ↓
Nukolii Beach Park

Princeville
Hanalei
Kapaa
KAUAI
Lihue

Alohilani B&B   **9**
Hibiscus Hollow   **1**
Hotel Coral Reef   **3**
Inn Paradise   **8**
Kakalina B&B   **8**
Kapaa Sands   **6**
Kapaa Shores   **4**
Kauai Country Inn   **8**
Kauai International Hostel   **2**
Kauai Sands   **5**
Lani-keha   **8**
Rosewood B&B   **8**
Surf & Ski Cottage   **7**

Makana Rd., Kapaa. Reservations: c/o Hawaii's Best Bed-and-Breakfasts, P.O. Box 563, Kamuela, HI 96743. © 800/ 262-9912 or 808/885-4550. Fax 808/885-9912. www.bestbnb.com. 3 units. $70–$95 double. Rates include welcome basket with fruit, juice, cereal, bread or muffins. Extra person $10. 2-night minimum. No credit cards. **Amenities:** Hot tub; washer/dryer. *In room:* TV, kitchen, fridge, coffeemaker.

Kakalina's Bed and Breakfast *(Finds* Nestled in the foothills of Mount Waialeale, about a 10-minute drive from the beach, is this 3-acre flower farm and bed-and-breakfast. You can just imagine the view: flowers, flowers, and more flowers. The most popular unit is Hale Akahi, a two-room unit located under Kathy and Bob Offley's round home, on the ground floor. You enter through an enclosed wooden porch, which has a spectacular view of the verdant valley; the apartment is decorated in white wicker furniture with brilliant tropical flowers splashing color throughout. The views are breathtaking, and the king bed is comfortable, but the draw here is the bathroom: A huge, blue-tile tub, big enough to soak in, and surrounded by green plants, makes this unit one of a kind. Also on the property, in a separate cottage, is Hale Elua, a studio with a queen bed, a full kitchen, and a breakfast nook with a view of the flower gardens, a mountain lake, and the ocean in the distance; a queen-size futon can accommodate extra guests. A third unit with separate bedroom has a full kitchen, so breakfast is not included.

6781 Kawaihau Rd., Kapaa, HI 96746. © 800/662-4330 or 808/822-2328. Fax 808/823-6833. www.kakalina.com. 3 units. $90–$155 double. Rates include continental breakfast in 2 units. Extra person $15. 2-night minimum. MC, V (with 5% processing fee). Turn left off Kuhio Hwy. (Hwy. 56) onto Kawaihau Rd. and go 4½ miles. **Amenities:** Activity desk; car-rental desk; laundry service. *In room:* TV/VCR, kitchen, fridge, coffeemaker, hair dryer, iron, no phone.

Kapaa Sands ☆ *(Finds* This boutique (just 24 units) offers condo units right on the ocean with all the comforts of home at bargain prices. Each unit is decorated by their owners, but they are all comfortable (some studio units have pull-down beds to take advantage of the living space) and have everything you need for a vacation. The bathrooms tend to be tiny, but the kitchens are roomy enough. Ask for a unit on the ocean; they cost a bit more, but are worth the few extra dollars. On-site amenities include a fresh water swimming pool, laundry facilities, maid service, and a very friendly staff, happy to point out where to eat and things to do.

380 Papaloa Rd., Kapaa, HI 96746. © 800/222-4901 or 808/822-4901. Fax 808/822-1556. www.kapaasands.com. 24 units. $110–$128 studio double; $147–$168 2-bedroom units for 4. Extra person $10. 3-night minimum Dec 15–Mar 15. MC, V. **Amenities:** Swimming pool; barbecue area; laundry facilities. *In-room:* TV, kitchen, fridge, microwave, coffeemaker, dishwasher.

Kauai Country Inn ☆☆ *(Finds* Run to the phone right now and book this place! Hard to believe that, nestled in the rolling hills behind Kapaa, this old-fashioned country inn exists. Not only does it exist, but hosts Mike and Martina Hough, refugees from the fast life of running an international advertising agency in Los Angeles, have taken their considerable creative talents and produced a slice of paradise on 2 acres. Each of the four suites is uniquely decorated in Hawaiian art deco with a touch of humor, complete with hardwood floors, private bathrooms, kitchen or kitchenette, your own computer with high-speed Internet connection, and lots of little amenities that will make you break out into laughter at the Hough's sense of humor. Everything is top drawer from the furniture to the Sub-Zero refrigerator. They recently added a two-bedroom, country cottage for families with young children. The grounds are immaculate, and you can pick as much organic fruit as you want from the abundance of mango, guava, lilikoi, starfruit, oranges, and lemons. *Beatle fans take note:* Mike has been collecting memorabilia for decades and has the only private Beatle Museum in the state (including a Mini Cooper S car owned by Brian Epstein, the Beatles manager, original paintings by John Lennon, and a host of books, records, movies, tapes, T-shirts, and other interesting and unusual rare items). And for those missing the family pooch, Annie, the staff golden retriever, personally greets each guest like her long lost friend.

6440 Olohena Rd., Kapaa, HI 96746. (✆) **808/821-0207.** www.kauaicountryinn.com. 4 units and 1 2-bedroom cottage. $95–$145 1- and 2-bedroom suites double; $245 2-bedroom cottage for 6. $15 extra person in suites. 3-night minimum suites; 5-night minimum cottage. Discount car rentals available. AE, MC, V. *In room:* TV/VCR/DVD, computer with high-speed connection, kitchen or kitchenette, fridge, coffeemaker, hair dryer, iron.

Kauai Sands   These modest, motel-style accommodations will do just fine for budget travelers who want a basic, clean room with a central location. Right on the ocean, next door to the Coconut Marketplace, the Kauai Sands is located near tennis courts and a golf course. The small rooms have simple furniture (two doubles or twin beds), ceiling fans, and small refrigerators; most have tiny lanais. Do *not* pay rack rates; for the best deal here, go on the Internet and get a room and car package starting from $99.

420 Papaloa Rd., Kapaa, HI 96746. (✆) **800/560-5553** or 808/822-4951. Fax 808/882-0978. www.sand-seaside.com. 200 units. $125–$160 double. Room/car packages available from $99. MC, V. **Amenities:** Restaurant; bar; 2 small outdoor pools; exercise room; coin-op washer/dryers. *In room:* A/C, TV, kitchenette (some units), fridge.

Lani-keha ⭐ *Finds*   Step back in time to the 1940s, when old Hawaiian families lived in open, airy, rambling homes on large plots of land lush with fruit trees and sweet-smelling flowers. This gracious age is still alive and well in Lani-keha, a *kamaaina* (old-timer) home with an open living/game/writing/dining room, with oversized picture windows to take in the views, and bedrooms with private bathrooms. The house is elegant yet casual, with old-style rattan furniture—practicality and comfort outweigh design aesthetics. The large communal kitchen has everything a cook could want, even a dishwasher. All the guests share the TV/VCR and single phone in the living area.

848 Kamalu Rd. (Hwy. 581), Kapaa, HI 96746. (✆) **800/821-4898** or 808/822-1605. Fax 808/822-2429. www.lanikeha.com. 3 units. $65 double. Rates include continental breakfast. Extra person $15. 3-night minimum. No credit cards. From Kuhio Hwy. (Hwy. 56), turn left at the stoplight at Coco Palms onto Hwy. 580 (Kuamoo Rd.); go 3 miles; turn right at Hwy. 581 (Kamalu Rd.) and go 1 mile. **Amenities:** Washer/dryer. *In room:* No phone.

Rosewood Bed-and-Breakfast ⭐ *Finds*   This lovingly restored, century-old plantation home, set on an acre of tropical flowers, lily ponds, and waterfalls, has accommodations to suit everyone. There's a Laura Ashley–style room in the main house along with two private cottages: one a miniature of the main house, with oak floors and the same Laura Ashley decor; the other is a little grass shack set in a tropical garden, with an authentic thatched roof and an outside shower. There's also a bunkhouse with three separate small rooms with a shared shower and toilet. Hostess Rosemary Smith also has a list of other properties she manages. *Note:* Smoking is not permitted on the property.

872 Kamalu Rd., Kapaa, HI 96746. (✆) **808/822-5216.** Fax 808/822-5478. www.rosewoodkauai.com. 7 units (3 with shared bathroom). $85 double in main house (includes continental breakfast); $45–$55 double in bunkhouse; $115–$150 cottage double (sleeps up to 4); $135 2-bedroom cottage (sleeps 4); $200 3-bedroom home (sleeps 6) Extra person $15. 3-night minimum. No credit cards. From Kuhio Hwy. (Hwy. 56), turn left at the stoplight at Coco Palms onto Hwy. 580 (Kuamoo Rd.); go 3 miles; at junction of Hwy. 581 (Kamalu Rd.), turn right; go 1 mile and look for the yellow house on the right with the long picket fence in front. *In room:* TV (in cottage), kitchen (in cottage), kitchenette (in bunkhouse), fridge, coffeemaker, hair dryer (in cottage), iron (in cottage), no phone.

Royal Garden Cottages *(Finds)*   Down a quiet private road in beautiful Wailua (just minutes from the beaches and the Wailua River) lies a little bit of paradise: three cozy, comfortable houses surrounded by lush gardens and flowering fruit trees. The two cottages have twin beds that can be combined into one king, a well-equipped kitchenette, ceiling fans, and garden views. One cabin has a TV and phone; the other is for those looking to get away from the distractions of the outside world. There's also a unit in the main house with two bedrooms and two bathrooms. Guests are encouraged to pick all the bananas, avocados, breadfruit, pomelo, and lemons they can eat.

147 Royal Dr. (off Hwy. 580), Kapaa, HI 96746. (✆) **808/245-5758.** Fax 303/444-5931. www.royaldrive.com. 3 units (2 with shower only). $85 double cottage; $110 2-bedroom house for 2, $125 for 4, $140 for 6. Additional cleaning fee: $50 cottage, $75 house. Children 15 and younger stay free. 3-night minimum (cottage), 4-night minimum (house). No credit cards. From Kuhio Hwy. (Hwy. 56), turn left at the stoplight at Coco Palms on to Hwy. 580 (Kuamoo Rd.); go 2⅖ miles and turn left on Royal Drive. **Amenities:** Complimentary use of laundry facilities. *In room:* TV/VCR, kitchen, fridge, coffeemaker, iron.

Surf & Ski Cottage *(★) (Value)*   Even if you aren't a kayaking/water-skiing/watersports enthusiast, this is still a fantastic place to stay. Right on the Wailua River, surrounded by fruit trees and tropical plants, Surf & Ski Cottage is an adorable 22×22-foot, self-contained guesthouse. Essentially one large room (with separate bathroom), the open, airy, high-ceilinged cottage has a complete kitchen, a TV, and a queen bed. Located close to the old Coco Palms Resort, the cottage is within walking distance of Kapaa's shops, restaurants, and beaches. Kenny and Kathy Terheggen, the owners of Kauai Water Ski & Surf Co. (who also live on the property), are a wealth of information on nearly everything to do on Kauai. If you plan to play in the water, this is the place to stay—cottage guests get a 20% discount on all outdoor equipment and activities at Kauai Water Ski & Surf Co. (including water-skiing, kayaking, and surf lessons, plus bodyboard and snorkel rentals, and much more), which could really save you a lot of dough.

Ohana St. (in Wailua River Lots), off Hwy. 580 (Kuamoo Rd.), Kapaa. Reservations: c/o Kauai Water Ski & Surf Co., 4–356 Kuhio Hwy., Kapaa, HI 96746. (✆) **800/344-7915** or 808/822-3574. Fax 808/822-3574. surfski@aloha.net. 1 cottage (with shower only). $65 double. 4-night minimum. AE, DC, DISC, MC, V. *In room:* TV, kitchenette, fridge, coffeemaker, hair dryer, iron.

SUPER-CHEAP SLEEPS

Hibiscus Hollow *(★) (Value)*   Yes, Virginia, the price is $50. And no—there's nothing wrong with this place. It's the best budget buy, not just in Kauai, but in the entire state of Hawaii. Book this place.

A studio with one-bedroom is attached to the main house in a residential area. Hibiscus Hollow has a living room (with queen-size sleeper couch); a separate bedroom; a kitchenette with refrigerator, coffeemaker, microwave, and everything you need to make and serve a meal; and a large lanai with picnic table and chairs, barbecue, and chaise lounges. The only drawback that we could find was the street noise—but at $50 a day, you'll be able to afford earplugs.

So what's the deal? Greg and Sue Liddle are nice people who think $50 is a fair price (and hundreds of happy guests agree with them). They moved to Kauai in 1990 and wanted a place where their customers could stay (they're in the surfboard and dog-grooming businesses). One thing led to another, and now they offer their cute cottage as a vacation rental. The Kapaa location is perfect: close to beaches, restaurants, trails, and shopping. If you stay for a week, the price drops—believe it or not—to $44 a night!

4906 Laipo Rd., Kapaa, HI 96746. (C) **808/823-0925.** www.a1vacations.com/hibiscushollow/1. 1 unit (with shower only). $50 double. Extra person $10. 3-night minimum. No credit cards. From Kuhio Hwy. (Hwy. 56), take the first left after Kapaa Fish and Chowder House (Hauaala St.), then go left again on Laipo Rd. *In room:* TV/VCR, kitchen, fridge, coffeemaker.

Kauai International Hostel *Value*   Located in the heart of Kapaa, a block from the beach, this hostel provides clean rooms in a friendly atmosphere. Guests are generally European backpackers. This low-rise building has a very clean kitchen and laundry facilities, a TV, a pool table, and a barbecue area; just 1 block from the highway, it's within walking distance of shops and restaurants. In addition to the bunk-bed dorm rooms, there are private rooms for two (with shared bathrooms). Airport pick-up is available ($10 for 2, $15 for 3), and long-term (a week or more) rates make this bargain hostel even more affordable.

4532 Lehua St. (off Kuhio Hwy.), Kapaa, HI 96746. (C) **808/823-6142.** www.hostels.com/kauaihostel. 30 bunk beds, 5 private rooms (shared bathrooms with showers only). $20 dorm single; $50 private double. MC, V. **Amenities:** Coin-op laundry facilities; community kitchen with fridge and coffeemaker; community TV. *In-room:* No phone.

GREAT DEALS FOR FAMILIES

Kapaa Shores ★ *Kids*   These apartments are located right on the beach in the heart of Kapaa. Even the budget units have a partial view of the ocean, but oceanfront units are available for a bit more money. The one-bedrooms can comfortably sleep four, while the two-bedrooms can sleep as many as six (the sofa in each unit pulls out into a queen-size bed). All units are in excellent shape and come with fully equipped modern kitchens and large lanais, where you can enjoy a sunrise breakfast or sunset cocktails. On-site amenities include a large pool, a tennis court, a family-size hot tub, a shuffleboard court, laundry facilities, and barbecues. Golf courses, restaurants, and bars are nearby.

900 Kuhio Hwy. (between mile markers 7 and 8). Reservations: c/o Garden Island Properties, 4–928 Kuhio Hwy., Kapaa, HI 96746. (C) **800/801-0378** or 808/822-4871. Fax 808/822-7984. www.kauaiproperties.com. 84 units. $115–$125 1-bedroom; $140–$163 2-bedroom. 5-night minimum. MC, V. **Amenities:** Outdoor pool; tennis courts; Jacuzzi; salon; coin-op washer/dryers. *In room:* TV/VCR or TV/DVD, dataport (some rooms), kitchen, fridge, coffeemaker, iron.

THE NORTH SHORE

Bed, Breakfast & Beach at Hanalei Bay *Finds*   On a quiet street in a residential area, just 150 yards from Hanalei Bay, lies one of the best deals on the North Shore. The three guest rooms in Carolyn Barnes's three-story house range from a 700-square-foot suite with a 360-degree view to a miniapartment on the ground floor with a kitchenette and an outdoor shower. The location couldn't be better (some guests don't even bother to rent a car). It's a 4-minute walk to Hanalei Bay's 2-mile-long beach and a 10-minute walk to the shops and restaurants of Hanalei. For families, Carolyn also has a cozy two-bedroom, one-bathroom house a couple of blocks away.

P.O. Box 748, Hanalei, HI 96714. (C) 808/826-6111. www.bestofhawaii.com/hanalei. 4 units. $85–$135 double room (includes continental breakfast); extra person $15. $1,000 a week for cottage (for 2); extra person $100 a week. 2- to 3-night minimum for rooms, 7-night minimum in cottage. No credit cards. *In room:* TV, no phone.

Hale Ho'o Maha *Finds*   Kirby Guyer and her husband, Toby, have a spacious four-bedroom, three-bathroom home on 5 acres. It's filled with Hawaiian and South Pacific artifacts and features a fireplace, a library, and a 150-gallon saltwater aquarium (it's more entertaining than TV). The rooms are uniquely decorated and priced with budget travelers in mind. We recommend the Pineapple Room, with its 7-foot round bed (with custom-quilted pineapple spread and matching handmade area rug) and an ocean view from the large picture window. The landscaped grounds feature a stream and a pond, and there's a waterfall across the street. Kirby has everything you need, from beach chairs to surfboards; you'll also have access to a complete kitchen. Within spitting distance are two remarkable white-sand beaches; also close by are golf courses, riding stables, restaurants, and markets. *Warning:* The property is next to the main highway; light sleepers may be bothered by traffic noise.

P.O. Box 422 (on Kalihiwai Rd., off Kuhio Hwy. at mile marker 24), Kilauea, HI 96754. © **800/851-0291** or 808/828-1341. Fax 808/828-2046. www.aloha.net/~hoomaha. 4 units (2 with shared bathroom). $75–$95 double. Rates include continental breakfast. Extra person $15. AE, DC, MC, V. **Amenities:** Laundry facilities. *In room:* TV, hair dryer.

Hanalei Inn   Despite its very romantic sounding name, the Hanalei Inn is an attempt at frugal accommodations in this very "high end" neighborhood. Located on the sometimes noisy main highway, the "inn" is a series of old, very basic rooms. The majority of rooms are small studios with bed, small kitchenette, tiny bathroom, and TV—period. The rooms are clean, but unless you have run totally out of money, this would not be our first choice of accommodations. For those on a shoestring budget and looking for hostel-type accommodations, they have a few rooms that offer "bed and bathroom" only (no cooking facilities), which are even tinier than the already small units.

5-5468 Kuhio Hwy., Hanalei, HI 96714. © **808/826-9333.** www.hanaleiinn.com. 4 units. $99 studio with kitchenettes, $89 bed and bathroom only. MC, V. **Amenities:** Barbecue; pavilion; hammocks; coin-op laundry facilities. *In room:* TV, kitchenette, fridge, no phones.

North Country Farms 🍴 (Kids)   In the rolling green hills outside of Kilauea, on a 4-acre organic vegetable, fruit, and flower farm, Lee Roversi and her family have a private, handcrafted, redwood cottage for rent. This restful spot is an excellent choice, both in terms of comfort and value, especially for a family. The cottage has hardwood floors, a large lanai with garden views, a compact kitchenette for cooking (Lee stocks fruit, juice, muffins, croissants, fresh eggs, coffee, and tea for breakfast), and a separate bedroom with a beautiful Hawaiian quilt on the queen bed. The couch in the living room turns into two separate beds, so the cottage can easily sleep four (children are welcome). Outside is another shower for washing off the sand from the beach. The only thing the cottage lacks is a TV, but since it's so close to beaches, hiking, shopping, and restaurants, you're likely to find yourself too tired at the end of the day to watch the tube anyway.

Kahlili Makai St. (P.O. Box 723, off Kuhio Hwy. at mile marker 22), Kilauea, HI 96754. © **808/828-1513.** Fax 808/828-0805. 1 cottage. $120 double. Rate includes fixings for breakfast, plus fruits and veggies from organic farm. Extra person $5. Children under 16 stay free in parents' room. No credit cards. *In room:* Kitchen, fridge, coffeemaker, hair dryer, iron.

GREAT DEALS FOR FAMILIES
Hanalei Colony Resort 🍴 (Kids)   Picture this: A perfect white-sand beach is just steps from your door, and lush tropical gardens, jagged mountain peaks, and fertile jungle serve as your backdrop. Welcome to Haena, Kauai's northernmost town and gateway to the famous Na Pali Coast, with miles of hiking trails, fabulous sunset views, and great beaches. This 5-acre resort is the place to stay if you're looking to experience the magic of the enchanting North Shore. The units are unbelievably spacious—six people could sleep comfortably. Each has a private lanai (the less-expensive

budget units face the garden), a full kitchen, a dining area, a living room, and ceiling fans (the area is blessed with cooling trade winds, so air-conditioning isn't necessary). The atmosphere is quiet and relaxing: no TVs, stereos, or phones. The property has a barbecue and picnic area. Guests have access to complimentary beach mats and towels, a lending library, and children's toys, puzzles, and games (plus badminton and croquet for the entire family). A restaurant and deli are next door. The entire property is undergoing a massive renovation and, when it is completed, the rates for this ocean-front property will probably increase; so book it while it is still affordable.

5–7130 Kuhio Hwy. Reservations: c/o P.O. Box 206, Hanalei, HI 96714. ⓒ **800/628-3004** or 808/826-6235. Fax 808/826-9893. www.hcr.com. 48 units. $210–$375 2-bedroom apt for 4. Rate includes continental breakfast once a week. 7th night free. Extra person $15. 5-night minimum June 1–Sept 8 and Dec 20–Jan 4. AE, MC, V. **Amenities:** Good-size outdoor pool; Jacuzzi; coin-op washer/dryers. *In room:* Kitchen, fridge, coffeemaker, no phone.

SUPER-CHEAP SLEEPS

YMCA of Kauai–Camp Naue ★ *Value*   Attention, campers, hikers, and backpackers: This is the ideal spot to stay before or after conquering the Na Pali Trail, or if you just want to spend a few days lounging on fabulous Haena Beach. This Y camp site sits right on the ocean, on 4 grassy acres ringed with ironwood and kumani trees and bordered by a sandy beach that offers excellent swimming and snorkeling in the summer (the ocean here turns really rough in the winter). Camp Naue has two bunkhouses overlooking the beach; each has four rooms with 10 to 12 beds. The facilities are co-ed, with separate bathrooms for men and women. There's no bedding here, so bring your sleeping bag and towels. Large groups frequently book the camp, but if there's room, the Y will squeeze you into the bunkhouse or offer tent space. Also on the grounds is a beachfront pavilion and a campfire area with picnic tables. You can pick up basic supplies in Haena, but it's best to stock up on groceries and other necessities in Lihue or Hanalei. Remember, this is the Y, not the Ritz; they only have one employee who handles all the bookings plus everything else related to the Y activities. The best way to find out if they have space available is to call (DO NOT e-mail, DO NOT send a letter). The Y simply is not set up to answer mail. Instead, a few months before your trip, call and they will let you know if space in the campsite or the bunkhouse will be available.

On Kuhio Hwy., 4 miles west of Hanalei and 2 miles from the end of the road, Haena. YMCA, P.O. Box 1786, Lihue, HI 96766. ⓒ **808/246-9090.** 50 bunk beds (with shared bathroom), 1 cabin, tent camping. $12 per bunk; $12 tent camping. No credit cards.

WORTH A SPLURGE

Aloha Sunrise Inn/Aloha Sunset Inn ★★ *Finds*   Hidden on the North Shore are these two unique cottages nestled on a quiet 7-acre farm with horses, fruit trees, flowers, and organic vegetables. We highly recommend both of these darling bungalows. Each is fully furnished with hardwood floors, top-of-the-line bedding, tropical island–style decor, a complete kitchen, washer/dryer, and everything you can think of to make your stay heavenly (from all the great videos you've been meaning to watch to an excellent CD library). Close enough to activities, restaurants, and shopping, yet far enough away to feel the peace and quiet of a Hawaii of yesteryears. Hosts Allan and Catherine Rietow, who have lived their entire lives in the islands, can help you plan your stay, give you money-saving tips, and even hand out complimentary masks, snorkels, boogie boards and other beach toys and point you to their favorite beaches. Note that these cottages are not appropriate for children.

P.O. Box 79, Kilauea, HI 96754. © **888/828-1008** or 808/828-1100. Fax 808/828-2199. www.kauaisunrise.com. 2 1-bedroom cottages. $145–$170 double ($60 cleaning fee). 3-night minimum. No credit cards. **Amenities:** Washer/dryer. *In room:* TV/VCR in one cottage, cable TV in other cottage, kitchen, fridge, coffeemaker, hair dryer, iron.

Hanalei Surf Board House ★★ *Finds*   Book now; this place is so fabulous that it will go fast! Just a block from the beach, these two incredibly-decorated studio units are a steal at $150. Host Simon Potts is a former record company executive from England, who thinks he has retired to Hawaii. He's the hardest working retired guy we have ever met. First thing he did was ask the kids he coaches in soccer if they had any old surfboards; he even offered a few bucks. Potts got enough surfboards to line them all standing up next to each other to create the most unusual fenced-in yard in Hawaii. Next, Potts turned to decorating—one studio is filled with whimsical "cowgirl" decor and the other in pure Elvis Presley memorabilia. Both units have kitchenettes, 300-channel televisions, free high-speed Internet access, DVDs, barbecues, and backyard lanais. But the best reason to stay here (besides the 2-minute walk to either the beach or downtown Hanalei) is Simon himself; his stories about the record industry will keep you howling with laughter for hours.

5459 Weke Rd., Hanalei. © **808/826-9825**. simon.potts@verison.net. 2 units. $150 double. 2-night minimum. No credit cards. *In room:* TV, DVD, kitchenette, fridge, coffeemaker, free high-speed Internet connection.

4 Great Deals on Dining

Except for Lihue, the plate-lunch center of the island, dining on Kauai is centered on the island's shores: Poipu on the south, Kapaa on the east, and Hanalei on the north. And that's a good thing, because on Kauai, street names seem irrelevant and locations are determined by trees, erstwhile mom-and-pop stores, and other landmarks of rural life. Follow the winding (and often traffic-choked) road and you'll find the tried-and-true temples of Hawaii Regional Cuisine amid plate-lunch palaces and a new, post-hippie breed of affordable, top-quality eateries that cook healthy, fresh, and tasty.

While Roy's and Casa Blanca, both in Poipu, Beach House in neighboring Lawai, Hanapepe Café in Hanapepe, and Café Coco in Wailua remain Kauai's foodie stalwarts, there are some excellent choices at all levels of the food chain. Most of the island's newcomers are moderately priced and have cropped up along the island's one main road.

On your jaunt across the island, you'll find affordable choices in every town, from hamburger joints to *saimin* (noodles in broth topped with scrambled eggs, onions, and sometimes pork) stands to busy neighborhood diners. As long as you don't expect filet mignon on a fish-and-chips budget, it shouldn't be difficult to please both your palate and your pocketbook.

For condo dwellers who are preparing their own meals, we've featured a variety of markets and shops around Kauai—including some wonderful greenmarkets and fruit stands—where you can pick up the island's best foodstuffs. These are listed in section 10 of this chapter, "Shops & Galleries," on p. 586.

In the listings below, reservations are not required unless noted otherwise.

LIHUE & ENVIRONS
For a map of Lihue, see p. 520.

Barbecue Inn ★ AMERICAN/JAPANESE/PACIFIC RIM   Watch for the specials at this more than 60-year-old family restaurant, where everything from soup to dessert is made in the Sasakis' kitchen. You can still get an inexpensive hamburger for lunch, but there are also fancier specials on the wide-ranging menu, including complete dinners for $8 to $24 and entrees such as grilled fresh ahi or ono and macadamia-nut chicken. The familiar favorites remain as well (oxtail soup, Japanese-style dinners, chow mein, roast turkey). Locally grown organic greens are a big hit, and specialty salads are a welcome addition. Several-course dinner combinations of Japanese and American favorites draw long lines.

2982 Kress St. (off Rice St.), Lihue. © 808/245-2921. Main courses $7–$13 lunch, $8–$24 dinner. MC, V. Mon–Thurs 7:30am–1:30pm and 5–8:30pm; Fri–Sat 7:30am–1:30pm and 4:30–8:45pm.

Duke's Canoe Club ⭐ STEAK/SEAFOOD   It's hard to go wrong at Duke's. Part of a highly successful restaurant chain (including Duke's Canoe Club in Waikiki, and three similar restaurants on Maui), this oceanfront oasis is the hippest spot in town, with a winning combination of great view, affordable menu, attractive salad bar, popular music, and very happy happy hour. The noontime bestseller is stir-fried cashew chicken, but the fresh mahi burger and the grilled chicken quesadilla are front-runners, too. The inexpensive fish tacos are a major attraction, and the five or six varieties of fresh catch a night are a highlight, served in several different preparations—a great value. Hawaiian musicians serenade diners nightly, while downstairs in the Barefoot Bar, traditional and contemporary Hawaiian music adds to the cheerful atmosphere. On Tropical Fridays, tropical drinks go for $3.50 from 4 to 6pm, when live music stirs up the joint.

In the Kauai Marriott Resort & Beach Club, 3610 Rice St., Nawiliwili. © 808/246-9599. Reservations recommended for dinner. Lunch $4–$11; dinner $8–$28. Taco Tuesdays 4–6pm, with $2.50 fish tacos and $2.50 draft beer. AE, DISC, MC, V. Barefoot Bar daily 11am–11pm; main dining room daily 5–10pm.

Hanamaulu Restaurant CHINESE/JAPANESE/SUSHI   When passing this restaurant, you'd never know that serene Japanese gardens with stone pathways and tatami-floored teahouses are hidden within. You can dine at the sushi bar, American style, or in the teahouses for lunch or dinner, but you must call ahead for teahouse dining. At lunch, enter a world of chop suey, wontons, teriyaki chicken, and sukiyaki (less verve than value), along with many other choices in budget-friendly Japanese and Chinese plate lunches. Special Japanese and Chinese menus can be planned ahead for groups of up to 60 people, who can dine at low tables on tatami floors in a Japanese-garden setting. Old-timers love this place, and those who came here in diapers are now stopping in for after-golf pupu and beer.

3–4291 Kuhio Hwy., Hanamaulu. © 808/245-2511. Reservations recommended. Main courses $6–$15. MC, V. Tues–Fri 10am–1pm; daily 4:30–8:30pm.

Kauai Chop Suey CANTONESE   This long time Kauai favorite recently closed, then reopened under new management. The huge menu has something for everyone: chow mein, Cantonese shrimp, roast duck, lemon chicken, and hundreds of choices of Cantonese noodles, soups, sweet-and-sours, foo-yongs, and stir-fries.

In the Harbor Mall, 3501 Rice St., Nawiliwili. © 808/245-8790. Most dishes $6–$9. No credit cards. Tues–Sat 11am–2pm and 4:30–9pm; Sun 4:30–9pm.

Restaurant Kiibo JAPANESE   Neither a sleek sushi bar nor a plate-lunch canteen, Kiibo is a neighborhood staple with inexpensive, unpretentious, tasty, home-style Japanese food served in a pleasant room accented with Japanese folk art. You can dine on sushi, ramen, sukiyaki, tempura, teriyaki, or the steamed egg-rice-vegetable marvel called *oyako donburi.* There are satisfying, affordable lunch specials and teishoku specials of mackerel, salmon, soup, dessert, and other condiments.

299 Umi St., Lihue. © **808/245-2650.** Main courses $5–$19. MC, V. Mon–Fri 11am–1:30pm; Mon–Sat 5:30–9pm.

SUPER-CHEAP EATS

Dani's Restaurant AMERICAN/HAWAIIAN Formica all the way, and always packed for breakfast, Dani's is the pancake palace of Lihue: banana, pineapple, papaya, and buttermilk, plus sweet-bread French toast and kalua-pig omelets. Regulars know that fried rice is offered on Thursday only, and that the papaya hotcakes are always a deal. At lunch, Hawaiian specials—laulau, kalua pig, lomi salmon, and beef stew, in various combinations—dominate the otherwise standard American menu of fried foods and sandwiches.

4201 Rice St., Lihue. © **808/245-4991.** Main courses $3.30–$8.50. MC, V. Mon–Fri 5am–1:30pm; Sat 5am–1pm.

Hamura's Saimin Stand ✺ SAIMIN If there were a saimin hall of fame, Hamura's would be it. It's a cultural experience, a renowned saimin stand where fans line up to take their place over steaming bowls of this island specialty at a few U-shaped counters that haven't changed in decades. The saimin and teriyaki barbecue sticks attract an all-day, late-night, pre- and postmovie crowd. The noodles come heaped with vegetables, wontons, hard-boiled eggs, sweetened pork, vegetables, and several condiment combinations. We love the casualness of Hamura's and the simple pleasures it consistently delivers.

2956 Kress St., Lihue. © **808/245-3271.** Most items less than $5. No credit cards. Mon–Thurs 10am–11pm; Fri–Sat 10am–midnight; Sun 10am–9pm.

Kako's ✺ SAIMIN Wonderful home-cooked broth and noodles are the Kako's signature. Saimin aficionados are ecstatic that this former Hanapepe fixture has reopened, this time in Lihue. After a long absence, the new installation—just as tiny and just as good as the original—is cause for applause. Owner Dorothea Hayashi uses a secret recipe to make her broth from scratch, and the noodles, also house-made and fresh, are the perfect accompaniment. When teamed with her teriyaki chicken sticks, the saimin and wonton min are pure heaven for noodle lovers. Kako's Saimin was a west-side phenom for years until Hurricane Iniki turned out the lights. The saimin comes with a choice of toppings, such as barbecued chicken, cabbage, sliced eggs, and green onions. Old-fashioned, home-style hamburgers like Mom used to make, flavored with onions mixed into the patties, are flying out the door for just over a couple of bucks.

2980 Ewalu St., Lihue. © **808/246-0404.** Saimin $3–$5.50. No credit cards or checks. Mon–Sat 10:30am–2pm.

Kalapaki Beach Hut *(Kids* AMERICAN This place is tricky to find (look for the anchor chain out in front of the blue building), but the money you'll save makes it worth the hunt. Started in 1990, by Steve and Sharon Gerald, as Kalapaki Beach Burgers, the tiny eatery started adding more items and then evolved into serving breakfast. This "hut" has window service and a few tables downstairs and more upstairs (with an ocean view out the screen windows). It's basic fare, served on paper plates with plastic cutlery at cheap, cheap prices. Breakfasts are hearty omelets, pancakes, and numerous egg dishes. Lunches are heavy on the hamburgers (prepared 10 different ways), lots of sandwiches, a few healthy salads, and fish and chips. The kids get their own menu. This casual restaurant welcomes people in their bathing suits and flip-flops.

3474 Rice St., Nawiliwili. © **808/246-6330.** Breakfast $3.95–$6.95; lunch $3.50–$7.50. AE, DISC, MC, V. Tues–Sun 7am–8pm; Mon 7am–9pm.

Ma's Family *(Finds* LOCAL/HAWAIIAN   This is a family affair, not only for the clients, but also for Ma (aka Akiyo Honjo), who works alongside her kids and grandkids in this tiny, off-the-beaten-track restaurant. The place is packed with local residents, lining up for Ma's filling breakfast at super-cheap prices; coffee is free (something you don't see anymore in Hawaii). Ma's lunches included everything from hamburgers to local favorites (teriyaki beef, loco moco, and noodle dishes) to Hawaiian dishes like kalua pork and lomi salmon.

4277 Haleani St., Lihue. ✆ **808/245-3142.** Most dishes under $6. No credit cards. Mon–Fri 5am–1:30pm, Sat–Sun 5–11:30am.

Tip Top Café/Bakery *(Kids* LOCAL   This small cafe/bakery (also the lobby for the Tip Top Motel) has been serving local customers since 1916. The best deal is their breakfasts: Most items are $5 or under, and their macadamia pancakes are known throughout Kauai. Lunch ranges from pork chops to teriyaki chicken, but their specialty is oxtail soup. For a real treat, stop by the bakery (where you pay your bill) and take something home. (We recommend the freshly baked *malasadas*.)

3173 Akahi St., Lihue. ✆ **808/245-2333.** Breakfast items under $5; lunch entrees under $6. MC, V. Tues–Sun 6:30am–2pm.

WORTH A SPLURGE

Aroma ★★ *(Kids* ECLECTIC/PACIFIC RIM   Chef/owner Robert Moler spent a lot of time cooking for the inter-island cruise ship in Hawaii and picked up a variety of cooking styles that he displays in his second-floor restaurant, across the street from the ocean, in the Harbor Mall. Open for mouthwatering breakfast (try the cherry hill French toast, stuffed with dried cherries and cream cheese), hearty lunches, and dinner, Aroma's has something for everyone on the menu, from pork osso buco to a vegetarian seared tofu tower to fresh island fish in a coconut mint and orange beurre blanc sauce. Plus the open-aired restaurant has a kids menu (hamburger, hot dogs, grilled barbecue chicken, and grilled cheese sandwiches). Be sure to make reservations, even if you're just coming for lunch.

Harbor Mall, 3501 Rice St. (across from the entrance to the Kauai Marriott), 2nd floor, Nawiliwili. ✆ **808/245-9192.** Reservations recommended for lunch and dinner. Main courses $3.75–$9.75 breakfast, $5.95–$12 lunch, $16–$27 dinner. AE, DC, DISC, MC, V. Thurs–Sun 8am–11am; Tues–Sun 11:30am–3pm; daily 5–9pm.

Gaylord's ★ CONTINENTAL/PACIFIC RIM   It's expensive, so go here for lunch. One of Kauai's most splendid examples of *kamaaina* (old-time) architecture, Gaylord's is the anchor of a 1930s plantation manager's estate on a 1,700-acre sugar plantation. You'll enter a complex of shops, galleries, and a living room of Hawaiian artifacts and period furniture. The private dining room has a lavish table, always elegantly set, as if Queen Liliuokalani were expected at any minute; another room accommodates private parties. The main dining room, which winds around a flagstone courtyard overlooking rolling lawns and purple mountains, serves American classics (New York steak, rack of lamb, prime rib) along with pasta, fresh seafood, and lavish desserts. The ambience, historic surroundings, and soothing views from the terrace make Gaylord's a special spot for lunch, when salads, soups, fresh fish, Oliver Shagnasty's signature baby back ribs, burgers, sandwiches, and lighter fare predominate. Daily specials include international dishes, such as kalua pork and Mexican fajitas, and fresh island fish in various cross-cultural preparations.

At Kilohana, 3–2087 Kaumualii Hwy., Lihue. ✆ **808/245-9593.** Reservations recommended. Main courses $6.95–$12 lunch; $17–$30 dinner. AE, DC, DISC, MC, V. Mon–Sat 11am–3pm and 5–9pm; Sun 9:30am–3pm (brunch) and 5–9pm.

Plate Lunch Palaces

If you haven't yet come face to face with the local phenomenon called *plate lunch,* Kauai is a good place to start. Like saimin, the plate lunch is more than a gastronomic experience—it's a part of the local culture. Lihue is peppered with affordable plate-lunch counters that serve this basic dish: two scoops of rice, potato or macaroni salad, and a beef, chicken, fish, or pork entree—all on a single plate. Although heavy gravies are usually *de rigueur,* some of the less traditional purveyors have streamlined their offerings to include healthier touches, such as lean, grilled fresh fish. Pork cutlets and chicken, or beef soaked in teriyaki sauce, however, remain staples, as does the breaded and crisply fried method called *katsu,* as in chicken katsu. Most of the time, *fried* is the operative word; that's why it's best to be ravenously hungry when you approach a plate lunch, or it can overpower you. At its best, a plate lunch can be a marvel of flavors, a saving grace after a long hike; at its worst, it's a plate-size grease bomb.

The following are the best plate-lunch counters on Kauai. How fortunate that each is in a different part of the island!

The **Koloa Fish Market,** 5482 Koloa Rd. (© **808/742-6199**), is in southern Kauai, on Koloa's main street. A tiny corner stand with plate lunches, prepared foods, and two stools on a closet-size veranda, it sells excellent fresh fish poke, Hawaiian-food specials, and seared ahi to go. It's gourmet fare masquerading as takeout. Daily specials may include sautéed ahi or fresh opakapaka with capers, and regular treats include crisp-on-the-outside, chewy-on-the-inside poi dumplings (when poi is available), one of life's consummate pleasures. For a picnic or outing on the south shore, this is a good place to start.

On the Hanamaulu side of Lihue, across the street from Wal-Mart, look for the prim, gray building that reads **Fish Express,** 3343 Kuhio Hwy. (© **808/ 245-9918**). It's astonishing what you'll find here for the price of a movie: Cajun-style grilled ahi with guava basil, fresh fish grilled in a passion-orange-tarragon sauce, fresh fish tacos in garlic and herbs, and many other delectables, all served with rice, salad, and vegetables. The Hawaiian plate lunch (laulau or kalua pork, lomi salmon, ahi poke, rice or poi) is a top seller, as are the several varieties of smoked fish, everything from ahi to swordfish. The owners marinate the fish in soy sauce, sugar, ginger, and garlic (no preservatives), and smoke it with kiawe wood. The fresh fish specials, at $6.95, come in six preparations and are done and flavored to perfection. At the chilled counter you can choose freshly sliced sashimi and many styles of poke, from scallop, ahi, and octopus to exotic marinated crab. This is a potluck bonanza that engages even newcomers, who point and order while regulars pick up sweeping assortments of seafood appetizers on large platters. They're all fresh and at good prices, especially for Friday-afternoon *pau hana* (after-work) parties.

In east Kauai's Kapaa town, the indispensable **Pono Market,** 4–1300 Kuhio Hwy. (© **808/822-4581**), has similarly enticing counters of sashimi, poke, Hawaiian food, sushi, and a diverse assortment of take-out fare. It's known for its flaky *manju* (sweet potato and other fillings in baked crust), apple turnovers, sandwiches, excellent boiled peanuts, pork and chicken laulau, and plate lunches—shoyu chicken, sweet-and-sour spareribs, pineapple-glazed chicken, teriyaki fish, and so on. The potato-macaroni salad (regulars buy it by the pound for barbecues and potlucks) and roast pork are top sellers. Pono Market is as good as they come. If they're available, pick up Taro Ko taro chips: made in Hanapepe, hard to find, and worth hand-carrying home.

At **Mark's Place,** 1610 Haleukana St. in Puhi Industrial Park (© **808/245-2722**), just southwest of Lihue, island standards (Korean-style chicken, teriyaki beef, beef stew, chicken katsu) come with brown rice (or white) and salad for $5 or $5.50. The selection, which changes daily, always includes two salad and three entree choices as well as hot sandwiches (chicken, beef, and hamburgers) and the ever-popular bentos. Mark's is a take-out and catering operation, so don't expect table seating.

Lihue, the island's county and business seat, is full of ethnic eateries serving inexpensive plate lunches, everything from *bento* (rice with beef, chicken, or fish, arranged in a lidded box) to Hawaiian, Korean, and Chinese food. **Local Boy's Restaurant & Deli,** 3204 Kuhio Hwy (© **808/246-8898**), is a budget bonanza and a popular stop for jumbo-size appetites. They offer generous servings of noodles (ramen, several types of chow mein, vegetarian fried noodles); barbecued chicken, beef, and spare ribs by the pound; sandwiches; mini- and regular- (big) sized plate lunches, and local favorites such as chili and beef stew. The Korean plate is very popular, a heroic serving of short ribs, chicken, and teriyaki beef, and kim chee for a mere $6.75. The $4 miniplate of teriyaki chicken is very large, for a mini, and, although not boneless and skinless, tasty. **Po's Kitchen,** 4100 Rice St. (© **808/246-8617**), offers Japanese specials: cone sushi, chicken katsu, teriyaki beef plates, and bentos. One block away, **Garden Island BBQ,** 4252–A Rice St. (© **808/245-8868**), is the place for Chinese plate lunches and local staples, such as barbecued or lemon chicken and teriyaki steak, as well as soups and tofu dishes.

In the Kukui Grove Center, at Kaumualii Highway (Hwy. 50) and Old Nawiliwili Road, **Joni-Hana** (© **808/245-5213**) is famous for its specials—nearly 20 a day! The tiny counter serves fried noodles, lemon-shoyu *ono* (wahoo), teriyaki everything, and many other local dishes. It's arguably the busiest place on the mall.

THE POIPU RESORT AREA

Brennecke's Beach Broiler ⭐ AMERICAN/SEAFOOD   Cheerful petunias in window boxes and second-floor views of Poipu Beach are pleasing touches at this seafood-burger house, a longtime favorite (for more than 15 years). Of course, it helps that the best hamburgers on the south shore are served here, as well as excellent vegetarian selections. Quality is consistent in the kiawe-broiled steak, fresh fish, and vegetarian gourmet burger. It's so casual that you can drop in before or after the beach and dine on nachos and peppers, fresh-fish sandwiches, kiawe-broiled fish and kebabs, prime rib, pasta, build-your-own gourmet burgers, and the salad bar. Look for the early dinner (4–6pm) and happy-hour specials daily, and the Alaskan king crab and prime rib theme nights.

2100 Hoone Rd. (across from Poipu Beach Park). ℂ **808/742-7588.** www.brenneckes.com. Main courses $9–$30. AE, DC, DISC, MC, V. Daily 11am–10pm (street-side deli takeout daily 8am–9pm).

Brick Oven Pizza PIZZA   A Kalaheo fixture for nearly 25 years, Brick Oven is the quintessential mom-and-pop business, serving pizza cooked directly on the brick hearth, brushed with garlic butter and topped with real cheeses and long-simmering sauces. This is the real thing! You have a choice of whole-wheat or white crust, plus many toppings: house-made Italian sausage, Portuguese sausage, bay shrimp, anchovies, smoked ham, vegetarian options, and more. The result: very popular pizza, particularly when topped with fresh garlic and served with Gordon Biersch beer. The seafood-style pizza-bread sandwiches are big at lunch, and the "Super Pizza" with everything on it—that's *amore.*

2–2555 Kaumualii Hwy. (Hwy. 50), Kalaheo (inland from Poipu). ℂ **808/332-8561.** Sandwiches less than $7.40; pizzas $10–$31. MC, V. Tues–Sun 11am–10pm.

Joe's on the Green ⭐ *Finds* AMERICAN   Psst! We'll let you in on a secret. This "hidden" eatery is mainly known to local residents, who flock here for breakfast or for lunch after a round of golf. They don't want the secret to get out because then their local hangout will be flooded with tourists. Breakfasts are a bargain, especially if you go before 9am and get the early bird special for $4.99. This is the place to go for breakfast; not only do you have a great setting—outdoors overlooking the golf course—but the menu has everything you could possibly want, from fluffy pancakes (banana-macadamia nut are the best) to biscuits-'n'-gravy to healthy tofu scramble. (The coffee keeps coming, so your cup is never empty.) Lunch is popular because of a range of sandwiches (from fresh fish to Joe's Mama Burger to "a dog named Joe," which is a quarter-pounder with sauerkraut and Cleveland stadium mustard), salads (build your own), and desserts. (Do not pass up the large, warm chocolate chip cookie.) Joe recently added dinner on Wednesday and Thursday nights with live Hawaiian music.

2545 Kiahuna Plantation Dr., at the Kiahuna Golf Club Clubhouse, Poipu. ℂ **808/742-9696.** Breakfast $4.95–$9.50, lunch $5.50–$9.50, dinner $6.95–$18. MC, V. Daily, breakfast 7–11:30am, lunch 11:30am–2:30pm, and happy hour 3–5:30pm; Wed–Thurs, dinner 5:30–8:30pm.

Keoki's Paradise STEAK/SEAFOOD   It's sprawling and lively and has improved with the years, with lunch favorites that include a fresh ahi sandwich, fresh-fish tacos, Thai shrimp sticks, and chicken Caesar salad—all good and affordable. In the evenings, regulars tout the fresh fish crusted in lemongrass, basil, and bread crumbs. When it's time for dessert, the original Hula pie, from Kimo's in Lahaina, is an ever-sinful presence. The cafe in the bar area serves lighter fare and features live Hawaiian music on Thursday and Friday nights and Sunday afternoon.

In Poipu Shopping Village, 2360 Kiahuna Plantation Dr., Poipu. © 808/742-7534. Reservations recommended. Main courses $6–$12 lunch, $16–$27 dinner. AE, DC, DISC, MC, V. Daily 5–10pm in the main dining room and cafe menu daily 11am–11pm.

Pomodoro ☆ ITALIAN   Pomodoro is the Italian magnet of the west side; a small, casual, and intimate second-floor dining room with a bar, potted plants, soft lighting, and pleasing Italian music. It's a warm, welcoming place where Hawaiian hospitality meets European flavors: homemade garlic focaccia, homemade mozzarella, chicken saltimbocca, and homemade pastas (cannelloni, manicotti, and excellent lasagna, the house specialty). Whether you order the veal, chicken, scampi, calamari, or very fresh, organic green salads, you'll appreciate the wonderful home-style flavor and the polite, efficient servers.

In Rainbow Plaza, Kaumualii Hwy. (Hwy. 50), Kalaheo (inland from Poipu). © 808/332-5945. Reservations recommended. Main courses $12–$22. MC, V. Daily 5:30–10pm.

Tomkats Grille AMERICAN/GRILL   Fried appetizers, inexpensive New York steak, rotisserie chicken, seafood salad with fresh catch, and sandwiches and burgers are among the offerings at the Grille, in a serene garden setting in Old Koloa Town. Old-fashioned brews are big here—everything from Watney's to Samuel Adams to Guinness Stout plus two dozen others; all the better to wash down the spicy jalapeños stuffed with cream cheese. For the reckless: the Cats' Combo, a basket of jumbo onion rings, mozzarella sticks, zucchini, and mushrooms, all dangerously fried. Recently they have added breakfast.

5404 Koloa Rd., Old Koloa Town. © 808/742-8887. Main courses $11–$37. MC, V. Daily 7am–10pm. Happy hour daily 3–6pm; bar daily until midnight.

SUPER-CHEAP EATS
Kalaheo Coffee Co. & Cafe COFFEEHOUSE/CAFE   John Ferguson has long been one of our favorite Kauai chefs, and his cafe is a coffee lover's fantasy: Kauai Estate Peaberry, Kona dark roast, Maui's Kaanapali Estate, Molokai Estate, Guatemalan French roast, Colombian, Costa Rican, Sumatran, and African coffees—you can visit the world on a coffee bean! The coffeehouse also serves masterful breakfasts: Bonzo Breakfast Burritos (sautéed ham, peppers, mushrooms, onions, and olives scrambled with cheese and served with salsa and sour cream), veggie omelets with sundried tomatoes and mushrooms, Belgian waffles, and bagels. At lunch, the fabulous grilled-turkey burgers (heaped with grilled onions and mushrooms on a sourdough bun) are the headliner on a list of winners. Fresh-from-the-garden salads brighten up the day. The tasty, inexpensive soup changes daily. The cinnamon "knuckles" (baked fresh daily), lilikoi cheesecake, and fresh apple pie and carrot cake are more reasons to stop by.

2–2436 Kaumualii Hwy. (Hwy. 50), Kalaheo (inland from Poipu). © 808/332-5858. Most items less than $8. DISC, MC, V. Mon–Fri 6am–2:30pm; Sat–Sun 6:30am–2pm.

WORTH A SPLURGE
The Beach House ☆☆☆ HAWAII REGIONAL   The Beach House remains the south shore's premier spot for sunset drinks, appetizers, and dinner—a treat for all the senses. The oceanfront room is large, accented with oversize sliding-glass doors, with old Hawaii Regional favorites on the menu. Come for cocktails or early dinner, when you can still see the sunset and perhaps a turtle or two bobbing in the waves. Menus change daily and include Kauai asparagus salad, seared crusted macadamia-nut

mahimahi with miso sauce, sea scallops with lemongrass and kaffir lime, and the Beach House crab cake with mint sambal butter sauce and grilled tomato compote. "Local boy paella" features fresh seafood with home-style fried rice and seafood saffron broth. Desserts shine too, so be warned: The molten chocolate desire is a hot chocolate tart that comes warm and wonderful, and the Kalúha taro cheesecake is tangy with lilikoi crème fraîche.

5022 Lawai Rd., Poipu. ✆ 808/742-1424. Reservations recommended. Main courses $19–$32. AE, DC, MC, V. Daily 5:30–9pm.

Roy's Poipu Bar & Grill ★★ EURO-ASIAN   This is a loud, lively room with ceiling fans, marble tables, works by local artists, and a menu tailor-made for foodies. The signature touches of Roy Yamaguchi (of Roy's restaurants in Oahu, Big Island, Maui, Tokyo, New York, and Guam) are abundantly present: an excellent, progressive, and affordable wine selection; fresh local ingredients prepared with a nod to Europe, Asia, and the Pacific; and service so efficient it can be overbearing. Because appetizers (such as nori-seared ahi with black-bean sauce, spinach-shiitake ravioli, and crisp shrimp cakes with butter sauce) are a major part of the menu, you can sample Roy's legendary fare without breaking the bank. The three dozen nightly specials invariably include eight fresh-fish dishes a night, prepared at least five or six different ways.

In Poipu Shopping Village, 2360 Kiahuna Plantation Dr. ✆ 808/742-5000. www.roysrestaurant.com. Reservations recommended. Main courses $19–$29. AE, DC, DISC, MC, V. Daily 5:30–9:30pm.

WEST & SOUTHWEST KAUAI

Green Garden AMERICAN/ISLAND   This Hanapepe landmark continues a decades-old tradition of offering local fare amid layers of foliage inside and out. A riot of fishing balls suspended in nets, plants everywhere, and a labyrinthine dining room make for a unique environment. The Green Garden is known for its inexpensive fresh-fish sandwiches and lilikoi-cream pies and, at dinner, the kiawe-grilled fresh-fish specials (onaga, opakapaka, and ehu) that come with soup and salad.

Hwy. 50, Hanapepe. ✆ 808/335-5422. Reservations recommended for 4 or more. Entrees $15–$30. AE, MC, V. Wed–Mon 5–9pm.

Hanapepe Cafe & Espresso Bar ★★ GOURMET VEGETARIAN/ITALIAN   The couple who ran this delectable, wholesome vegetarian in a casual, winning ambience wanted to sell this icon and move back to the mainland. They used the same good sense in selecting a buyer as they did in creating their menu. They passed this one-of-a-kind restaurant to Andrea Pisciotta, a former waitress in the restaurant who loved the place and wanted to continue the tradition. The first thing Pisciotta did was upgrade the facilities, repainted the walls, put in new artwork, introduced fish on the menu, and added dinners on Friday nights with live entertainment. It's packed at lunchtime, when people come for the several varieties of garden burger. They have elevated this modest staple to gourmet status: You can top yours with sautéed mushrooms, grilled onions, pesto, fresh-grated Parmesan, and other choices. Other lunch notables: fresh rosemary home fries, a heroic grilled vegetable sandwich, and whole roasted garlic heads. On the Friday night dinner menu, the Italian specialties shine: Southwestern-style lasagna (with green chilies, polenta, and sun-dried tomatoes); lasagna quattro formaggio with spinach, mushrooms, and four cheeses; crepes; and the nightly special with the cafe's famous marinara sauce—terrific choices all. There's no liquor license, so if you want wine, bring your own.

3830 Hanapepe Rd., Hanapepe. ℂ 808/335-5011. Reservations recommended for dinner. Lunch main courses $6.50–$10; dinner main courses $16–$24. MC, V. Mon–Thurs 11am–3pm; Fri 11am–2pm and 6–9pm.

Toi's Thai Kitchen THAI/AMERICAN   A west Kauai staple, Toi's has gained a following for its affordable, authentic Thai food and a casual atmosphere. Tucked into a corner of a small shopping complex, Toi's serves savory dishes utilizing fresh herbs and local ingredients, many of them from the owner's garden. Popular items include the house specialty, Toi's Temptation (home-grown herbs, coconut milk, lemongrass, and your choice of seafood, meat, or tofu), the vegetable curries, shrimp satay, and ginger-sauce nua: your choice of seafood, meat, or tofu in a fresh ginger stir-fry. Most of the rice, noodle, soup, curry, and main-course selections allow you to choose from among pork, chicken, seafood, beef, or vegetarian options. All dishes come with green-papaya salad, dessert, and a choice of jasmine, sticky, or brown rice.

In the Eleele Shopping Center, Eleele. ℂ 808/335-3111. Main courses $10–$17. DC, MC, V. Mon–Sat 10:30am–2pm and 5:30–9:30pm.

Waimea Brewing Company ECLECTIC   The popular brewery in the Waimea Plantation Cottages is a welcome addition to the dry west side, serving pub fare with a multiethnic twist: "small plates" for grazing, composed of smoked-chicken quesadillas, fried calamari, gado-gado skewers, and a goat-cheese dip with taro leaves; and "big plates" of roasted chicken, steak, short ribs, and kalua pork. In between are soups, noodles, salads, and sandwiches, including fresh catch. The beer is brewed on the premises. It's a pleasant stop, one of the top two places in Waimea for dinner.

In Waimea Plantation Cottages, 9400 Kaumualii Hwy., Waimea. ℂ 808/338-9733. Main courses $10–$30. AE, DC, DISC, MC, V. Daily 11am–9pm.

Wrangler's Steakhouse (Kids STEAKHOUSE   Good service and pleasant veranda seating are among the pluses of this family-run operation. Western touches abound: a wagon in the loft, log-framed booths with gas lanterns, and lauhala *paniolo* hats in the made-in-Hawaii gift shop. A combination of cowboy, plantation, and island traditions, Wrangler's serves steak—lots of it, big, and hand-selected cuts—and adds some island touches, from shrimp tempura to beef teriyaki, imu-style roast pork with cabbage, and grilled mahimahi sandwiches, smoky and tender. Families like Wrangler's for its multicourse dinners that won't break the bank.

9852 Kaumualii Hwy., Waimea. ℂ 808/338-1218. Lunch $8–$12; dinner main courses $17–$30. AE, DISC, MC, V. Mon–Thurs 11am–8:30pm; Fri 11am–9pm; Sat 5–9pm.

SUPER CHEAP EATS

Wong's Restaurant CHINESE/JAPANESE/DELI/BAKERY   "Eat at Wong's, you can't go Wrong" proclaims the menu to this long-time island institution. Wong's has all the bases covered for the breakfast, lunch, and dinner they serve: They feature both Japanese and Chinese dishes and have one of the best deli's and bakery (Omoide's Deli and Bakery) on the property (great for picking up picnic fixings and sandwiches for the beach); the bakery has one of the world's best homemade *lilikoi* (passion fruit) chiffon pies (worth the drive alone to sample this piece of heaven). Wong's is not known for its ambience; in fact, it looks like a typical Chinese restaurant, one big giant cafeteria-size room. If you go at the wrong time, you'll find the tour buses love this place and it can be crowded. But the portions are huge, the prices right, and the service smiling. They have take-out available.

1–3543 Kaumualii Hwy., Hanapepe. ℂ 808/335-5066. Main courses under $8. Tues–Sun 6am–9pm.

THE COCONUT COAST

Caffè Coco 🐸 GOURMET BISTRO   This gets our vote for the most charming ambience on Kauai, with gourmet fare cooked to order, and at cafe prices. Food gets a lot of individual attention here. Caffè Coco appears just off the main road at the edge of a cane field in Wailua, its backyard shaded by pomelo, avocado, mango, tangerine, lychee, and banana trees, with a view of the Sleeping Giant Mountain. The trees provide many of the ingredients for the muffins, chutneys, salsas, and fresh-squeezed juices that Ginger Carlson whips up in her kitchen. Seats are indoors (beyond the black-light art gallery!) or on the gravel-floored back courtyard, where tiki torches flicker at night. From interior design to cooking, this is clearly a showcase for Carlson's creativity. The food is excellent, with vegetarian and other healthful delights such as spanakopita, Greek salad and fish wraps, macadamia nut–black sesame ahi with wasabi cream, and an excellent tofu-and-roast-veggie wrap. Although the regular menu is limited, there are many impressive specials. Service can be, to say the least, laid-back. Next door, Carlson's sister runs **Bambulei,** a vintage shop of treasures (see "Shops & Galleries," p. 586).

4–369 Kuhio Hwy., Wailua. ✆ 808/822-7990. Reservations recommended for 4 or more. Main courses $7–$21; specials usually less than $20. MC, V. Tues–Fri 11am–9pm; Sat–Sun 5–9pm.

Coconuts Island Style Grill 🐸 AMERICAN/ECLECTIC   Kauai's newest sensation is right on the highway, next to Taco Bell, where fans line up for the happy-hour pupu and affordable, tasty fare. Coconuts is upbeat and busy, with a cheerfully tropical dining room of bamboo ceilings and coconut everything: bar floor, fixtures, furniture, and lights. There are lots of wines by the glass, good beers on tap, and a wide-ranging menu, including the best-selling teriyaki-dipped fresh salmon, a fresh catch for only $19 (oven-roasted, with kaffir lime broth and wasabi mashed potatoes), and an excellent seafood chowder. Grilled polenta with herb pesto and braised spinach, the burger with house-made potato chips, and shrimp cakes are also popular. The appetizer menu—nine items, from baby back ribs to lobster ravioli—is a hit from the time the doors open at 4pm.

4–919 Kuhio Hwy., Wailua. ✆ 808/823-8777. Reservations accepted only for 6 or more. Main courses $11–$27. AE, DC, MC, V. Daily 4–10pm.

Kapaa Fish & Chowder House AMERICAN   The passion-fruit Margaritas (pioneered and perfected here), the garden setting, and the coconut shrimp served with mango-chutney sauce make this a pleasant stop at the north end of Kapaa town. Families love to gather in the outdoor garden patio for celebratory send-offs and reunions, but it's also ideal for a spontaneous stop for appetizers and a cold beer or Margarita. The choices: steamer clams, mounds of iced shrimp, fresh catch with exotic salsas, and spicy New York pepper steak—surf-and-turf all the way.

4–1639 Kuhio Hwy., Kapaa. ✆ 808/822-7488. Reservations recommended. Main courses $13–$29. AE, DISC, MC, V. Daily 11:30am–9pm.

The King and I THAI   This medium-size restaurant, in a small and nondescript roadside complex, serves reasonably priced specials and vegetarian selections, including spring rolls, salads, curries, and stir-fries. The owners grow their own herbs for the savory curries and seasonings on the menu. At dinner, the pad Thai noodles with shrimp have a special touch and are a popular counterpoint to the red, green, and yellow curries. The vegetarian menu is generous—everything from noodles to spring rolls to curries and eggplant/tofu—but most diners come back for the Evil Jungle Prince, in its sauce of coconut milk, spices, and kaffir-lime leaves.

In Waipouli Plaza, 4–901 Kuhio Hwy. ✆ 808/822-1642. Reservations recommended. Main courses $6–$13. AE, DC, DISC, MC, V. Daily 4:30–9:30pm.

Mema THAI/CHINESE   For those looking for a casual dining experience with something exotic but priced reasonably, this is your place. This family-run restaurant is decorated with a profusion of plants and flowers and wait-servers dressed in traditional Thai costumes. The large menu offers some 50 different appetizers, a range of curries (we recommend the house curry, a Siam-style panans curry with lime leaves, lemongrass, and coconut milk), and a host of traditional Thai and Chinese specialties. Most of the dishes can be ordered mild, medium, or spicy with either vegetables, tofu, chicken, pork, beef, shrimp, or seafood.

4-369 Kuhio Hwy., Kapaa. ✆ 808/823-0899. Main courses $8.95–$18. Mon–Fri 11am–2pm. Daily 5–9pm.

Norberto's El Cafe (Value MEXICAN   The lard-free, home-style Mexican fare here includes top-notch chiles rellenos with homemade everything, vegetarian selections by request, and, if you're lucky, fresh-fish enchiladas. All of the sauces are made from scratch, and the salsa comes red-hot with homegrown chile peppers fresh from the chef's garden. Norberto's signature is the spinachy Hawaiian taro-leaf enchiladas, a Mexican version of laulau, served with cheese and taro or with chicken.

4–1373 Kuhio Hwy., Kapaa. ✆ 808/822-3362. Reservations recommended for parties of 6 or more. Main courses $4.75–$9.45; complete dinners $14–$18. AE, DISC, MC, V. Mon–Sat 5–9pm.

Sukhothai Restaurant THAI/VIETNAMESE/CHINESE   Curries, saimin, Chinese soups, satays, Vietnamese *pho,* and a substantial vegetarian menu are a few of the features of this unobtrusive—but extremely popular—Thai restaurant. Menu items appeal to many tastes and include 85 Vietnamese, Chinese, and Thai choices, along with much-loved curries and the best-selling pad Thai noodles. The coconut/lemongrass/kaffir lime soups (eight choices) are the Sukhothai highlights, along with the red and green curries.

In the Kapaa Shopping Center (next to Kapaa's Big Save Market), 4–1105 Kuhio Hwy., Kapaa. ✆ 808/821-1224. Main courses $8–$17. AE, DC, DISC, MC, V. Daily 10:30am–3pm and 5–9pm.

Wailua Marina Restaurant AMERICAN   This is a strange but lovable place, anti-nouvelle to the end. We recommend the open-air seating along the Wailua River, where you can watch the riverboats heading for the Fern Grotto over sandwiches (mahimahi is a favorite) and salads. The interior is cavernous, with a high ceiling and stuffed fish adorning the upper walls—bordering on weird, but we love it anyway. The salad bar makes the place friendlier to dieters and vegetarians; otherwise, you'll find the Alaskan king crab legs with filet mignon (or filet paired with lobster tail), stuffed prawns, famous hot lobster salad, steamed mullet, teriyaki spareribs, and some 40 other down-home items heavy in the sauces and gravies. Although the open salad bar is a meal in itself, the more reckless can try the mayo-laden minilobster salad appetizer, the crab-stuffed mushrooms, or the baked stuffed island chicken. ***Bargain-hunters tip:*** The early bird specials (5–6pm) start at $9 for spaghetti dinner and go up to $11 for a mixed plate of shrimp tempura, chicken yakitori, and teriyaki top sirloin.

5971 Kuhio Hwy., Wailua. ✆ 808/822-4311. Reservations recommended. Lunch $7–$10; dinner main courses $9–$29. AE, MC, V. Tues–Sun 10:30am–2pm and 5–8:30pm.

SUPER-CHEAP EATS

Aloha Diner HAWAIIAN   It's funky and quirky and claims legions of fans for its authentic Hawaiian plates. Lunch and dinner specials offer samplings of kalua pig, laulau, lomi salmon, fried whole *akule* (big-eyed scad, hooked not netted), and other Hawaiian dishes. Saimin and wonton min are the other favorites at this tiny diner, where steaming dishes and perspiring faces are cooled by electric fans whirring over Formica tables. Although the Aloha Diner may intimidate the uninitiated, it's pure comfort for lovers of Hawaiian food.

971–F Kuhio Hwy., Waipouli. © 808/822-3851. Most items less than $7.50. No credit cards. Mon–Sat 10:30am–2:30pm; Tues–Sat 5:30–9pm.

Bubba Burgers *Kids* AMERICAN   Here at the house of Bubba they dish out humor, great T-shirts, and burgers nonpareil, along with tempeh burgers for vegetarians. Grilled fresh-fish sandwiches cater to the sensible, fish-and-chips to the carefree, and fish burgers to the undecided. But old-fashioned hamburgers are still the main attraction. You can order the Slopper (open-faced with chili), the half-pound Big Bubba (three patties), the Hubba Bubba (with rice, hot dog, and chili—a Bubba's plate lunch), and others. Chicken burgers, Bubba's famous Budweiser chili, and other American standards are also served up here, where the burger is king, attitude reigns, and lettuce and tomato cost extra. And for a burger joint, it's big on fish, too, with a daily trio of fresh-fish specials, fish burgers, and fish-and-chips.

4–1421 Kuhio Hwy., Kapaa. © 808/823-0069. All items less than $7. MC, V. Daily 10:30am–8pm.

Blossoming Lotus VEGETARIAN   In the tranquil atmosphere of wooden floors, muted music, and lots of inspiring quotes framed on the walls is this organic gourmet vegan and "live food" cuisine restaurant. Even if you are not a born-again vegetarian, you'll like this place of interesting cuisine. Appetizers include spring rolls filled with fresh garden veggies with a Thai dipping sauce and a cosmic corn bread packed with cilantro and chiles. Entrees range from a coconut curry to daily pizza. Lots of salads and wraps/sandwiches and sinful-looking (but healthy) desserts round out the always changing menu. Or as one of the many framed quotes on the wall puts it: "Nothing will benefit human health and increase the chances for survival of life on Earth as much as the evolution to a vegetarian diet," according to Albert Einstein.

1384 Kuhio Hwy., Kapaa. © 808/822-7678. Entrees $5–$12. MC, V. Wed–Mon 11am–10pm.

Kountry Kitchen AMERICAN   Forget counting calories when you sit down to the brawny omelets here. You can choose your own fillings from several possibilities, among them a kimchi omelet with cream cheese and several vegetable, meat, and cheese combinations. Sandwiches and American dinners (steak, fish, and chicken) are standard coffeehouse fare, but there are sometimes fresh-fish specials that stand out. *Caveat:* Sit as far away from the grill as possible; the smell of grease travels—and clings to your clothes.

1485 Kuhio Hwy., Kapaa. © 808/822-3511. Main courses $6–$9. MC, V. Daily 6am–1:30pm.

Mermaids Cafe ★ *Value* HEALTHFUL/ISLAND STYLE. Don't you love places that use fresh local ingredients, make everything to order, and barely charge anything for all that trouble? A tiny sidewalk cafe with brisk takeout and a handful of tables on Kapaa's main drag, Mermaids takes kaffir lime, lemongrass, local lemons (Meyers when available), and organic herbs, when possible, to make the sauces and beverages to go with its toothsome dishes. Sauces are lively and healthful, such as the peanutty satay made with lemon juice instead of fish sauce and served in the tofu or chicken satay, chicken coconut curry plate, and chicken satay wrap. The seared ahi wrap is made with the chef's special blend of garlic, jalapeño, lemongrass, kaffir lime, basil, and cilantro, then wrapped in a spinach tortilla—fabulous. The fresh-squeezed lemonade is made fresh daily, and you can choose white or organic brown rice. These special touches elevate the simple classics to dreamy taste sensations; if you don't believe me, try the coconut custard French toast, made with Hawaiian guava-taro bread and served with fresh local fruit, custardy and divine.

1384 Kuhio Hwy, Kapaa. ✆ **808/821-2026**. Main courses $7.95–$9.95. DC, MC, V. Daily 11am–9pm.

Olympic Café AMERICAN   Impossible to imagine anyone walking away from this casual eatery hungry. Serving huge breakfasts and filling lunches, the Olympic is known for big portions and small prices. Breakfast features a range of espresso drinks, pancakes, omelettes, and egg dishes. Lunch includes sandwiches, burgers, salads, and a range of wraps. Stop by for a drink; they have smoothies, juice, Italian sodas, specialty teas, and a menu of specialty coffee drinks. Recently they moved upstairs and are now on the second floor overlooking Kapaa.

1387 Kuhio Hwy., Kapaa. ✆ **808/822-2825**. Breakfast under $8; lunch $6–$11. Daily 6am–3pm.

Ono Family Restaurant (Kids AMERICAN   Breakfast is a big deal here, with eggs Florentine (two poached eggs, blanched spinach, hollandaise sauce) leading the pack, and eggs Canterbury (much like eggs Benedict, but with more ingredients) following close behind. The Garden Patch, a dollop of fried rice topped with fresh steamed vegetables, scrambled eggs, and hollandaise sauce, is a real conscience-buster. Steak and eggs; banana, coconut, and macadamia-nut pancakes; and dozens of omelet choices also attract throngs of loyalists.

Lunch is no slouch either, with scads of fish, veggie, steak, tuna, and turkey sandwiches to choose from, and Ono beef or buffalo burgers with various toppings highlighting the menu. The gourmet hamburger with fries and soup demands an after-lunch siesta.

4–1292 Kuhio Hwy., Kapaa. ✆ **808/822-1710**. Most items less than $9. AE, DC, DISC, MC, V. Daily 7am–1:30pm.

Waipouli Deli & Restaurant (Value AMERICAN/JAPANESE   Modest home-style cooking at low, low prices attracts throngs of local folks who love the saimin, pancakes, and $3 "rice bowls" with chili, teriyaki beef, chicken katsu, or "anything," says the owner. The saimin is great here, especially the miso saimin special (but hold the Spam, please!), a hefty bowl of steaming noodles with tofu, vegetables, and a boiled egg. There are always inexpensive dinner specials, ranging from sukiyaki to roast chicken. This place is crowded from breakfast to closing.

In Waipouli Town Center, Waipouli. ✆ **808/822-9311**. Most lunch items less than $7; dinner less than $10. No credit cards. Daily 7am–2pm; Tues–Sat 5–8:30pm.

WORTH A SPLURGE

Hukilau Lanai STEAK/SEAFOOD   The owners of Gaylord's in Kilohana have opened this restaurant in the Kauai Coast Resort and feature local products and produce of Kauai, promising that the dishes "are made from scratch in our kitchen." The menu features a wide selection of appetizers from spinach and lauau leaf dip (a creamy cheese dip with luau leaf, spinach, and tomato relish served in a homemade bread bowl) to prosciutto, basil, and prawns (jumbo shrimp wrapped with thinly sliced Italian ham and fresh basil). Entrees feature a range of fresh fish, beef, chicken, and pork dishes. Save room for dessert, especially the goat cheese tart.

Kauai Coast Resort, Kapaa. (© **808/822-0600.** Main course $14–$23. MC, V. Tues–Sun 5–9pm. Live music Wed and Fri 6:30–9:30pm. Comedy show Thurs 7pm.

EN ROUTE TO THE NORTH SHORE

Duane's Ono-Char Burger *(Kids) (Value)* HAMBURGER STAND   We can't imagine Anahola without this roadside burger stand; it's been serving up hefty, all-beef burgers for generations. (And now there are Boca burgers, too.) The teriyaki sauce and blue cheese are only part of the secret of Duane's beefy, smoky and legendary ono charburgers, which come in several styles: teriyaki, mushroom, cheddar, barbecue, and the Special, with grilled onions, sprouts, and two cheeses. The broiled fish sandwich (another marvel of the seasoned old grill) and the marionberry ice-cream shake, a three-berry combo, are popular lighter fare.

On Kuhio Hwy., Anahola. (© **808/822-9181.** Hamburgers $4.15–$6.45. MC, V. Mon–Sat 10am–6pm; Sun 11am–6pm.

THE NORTH SHORE

Hanalei Dolphin Restaurant & Fish Market *⚓* SEAFOOD   Hidden behind a gallery called Ola's are this fish market and adjoining steak-and-seafood restaurant, on the banks of the Hanalei River. Particularly inviting are the fresh-fish sandwiches, served under umbrellas at river's edge. Most appealing (besides the river view) are the appetizers: artichokes steamed or stuffed with garlic, butter, and cheese; buttery stuffed mushrooms; and ceviche fresh from the fish market, with a jaunty dash of green olives. From fresh catch to baked shrimp to Alaskan king crab and chicken marinated in soy sauce, the Dolphin has stayed with the tried and true.

5144 Kuhio Hwy., Hanalei. (© **808/826-6113.** Main courses $16–$36. MC, V. Daily 11am–10pm. Fish market daily 11am–7pm.

Hanalei Gourmet AMERICAN   The wood floors, wooden benches, and blackboards of the old Hanalei School, built in 1926, are a haven for today's Hanalei hipsters noshing on the Tu Tu Tuna (far-from-prosaic tuna salad with green beans, potatoes, niçoise olives, and hard-boiled eggs); fresh grilled ahi sandwiches; roasted eggplant sandwiches; chicken-salad boats (in papaya or avocado, with macadamia nuts and sans mayonnaise); and other selections. This is an informal cross-cultural tasting, from stir-fried veggies over udon to Oriental ahi-pasta salad to artichoke hearts fried in beer batter. Big Tim's burger is big, and the sandwich selection, on fresh-baked bread, hits the timeless deli faves, from roast beef and pastrami to smoked turkey and chicken salad. The TV over the bar competes with the breathtaking view of the Hanalei Mountains and waterfalls, and the wooden floors keep the noise level high (the music on the sound system can be almost deafening). Nightly live music adds to the fun.

In the Old Hanalei Schoolhouse, 5–5161 Kuhio Hwy., Hanalei. (© **808/826-2524.** Main courses $7–$23. DC, DISC, MC, V. Sun–Thurs 8am–10:30pm; Fri–Sat 8am–11:30pm.

Kilauea Bakery & Pau Hana Pizza *⚓* PIZZA/BAKERY   When owner, baker, and avid diver Tom Pickett spears an ono and smokes it himself, his catch appears on the Billie Holiday pizza, guaranteed to obliterate the blues with its brilliant notes of Swiss chard, roasted onions, Gorgonzola-rosemary sauce, and mozzarella. And the much-loved bakery continues to put out guava sourdough, Hanalei poi sourdough, fresh chive–goat-cheese–sun-dried-tomato bread, blackberry–white chocolate scones, and other fine baked goods. The breads go well with the soups and hot lunch specials, and the pastries with the new full-service espresso bar, which serves not only the best of the bean, but also blended frozen drinks and such up-to-the-minute voguish things as iced chai and Mexican chocolate smoothies (with cinnamon). We also love the fresh vegetables in olive oil and herbs, baked in a baguette; the olive tapenade; and the classic scampi pizza with tiger prawns, roasted garlic, capers, and cheeses. The Picketts have added a small dining room, and the few outdoor picnic tables under umbrellas are as inviting as ever. The macadamia nut butter cookies and lilikoi fruit danishes are sublime.

In Kong Lung Center, Kilauea Rd. (off Hwy. 56 on the way to the Kilauea Lighthouse), Kilauea. ℂ **808/828-2020.** Pizzas $11–$30. MC, V. Daily 6:30am–9pm.

Neide's Salsa and Samba BRAZILIAN/MEXICAN   Tucked away in the very back of the Hanalei Center is a "hot" eatery dishing up Brazilian cuisine like *muqueca* (fresh fish with coconut sauce), *ensopado* (baked chicken and vegetables), or *bife acebolado* (beef steak with onions), plus the usual popular Mexican dishes like enchiladas and burritos. Big portions, friendly service, and reasonable prices make this a good bet.

Hanalei Center, Hanalei. ℂ **808/826-1851.** Entrees $9–$15. MC, V. Daily noon–2:30pm and 5–9:30pm.

Sushi & Blues ⭐ SUSHI/PACIFIC RIM   This second-floor oasis has copper tables and a copper-topped bar, large picture windows for gazing at the Hanalei waterfalls, and, most important, chefs who know their sushi. Traditional sushi, fusion sushi, and hot Pacific Rim dishes for those who aren't sushi lovers please diners of every stripe. Big hits: the temaki hand rolls; the Las Vegas roll, a heroic composition of ahi, hamachi, and avocado, dipped in tempura batter and quickly fried, hot on the outside and chilled on the inside; the Rainbow Roll, a super-duper California roll with eight different types of fish; and fresh fish prepared several ways, in fusion flavorings involving mango, garlic, sake, sesame, coconut, passion fruit, and other Pacific Rim preparations. The action fires up Wednesday, Thursday, Saturday, and Sunday from 8:30pm on, with live music, from Hawaiian to blues, jazz to rock 'n' roll.

In Ching Young Village, Hanalei. ℂ **808/826-9701.** www.sushiandblues.com. Reservations recommended for parties of 6 or more. Main courses $18–$23; sushi rolls $4 and up. MC, V. Daily 6–10pm. Live music from 8:30pm on.

Zelo's Beach House ⭐ STEAK/SEAFOOD   Good food, concrete floors, window tables with flower boxes, seating on the deck with mountain views: what's not to like? Along with Sushi & Blues, Zelo's is the hippest, most popular spot in Hanalei, a "beach house" spiced up with South Pacific kitsch, a wide variety of coffee drinks, excellent mai tais, and sliding doors all around. The congenial bar area has a tin roof and ironwood poles, and a one-person canoe hangs overhead. Gourmet burgers, pastas, steaks, 50 different microbrews and 30 tropical drinks, a wonderful salad in a large clam-shaped bowl, warm bread, seafood chimichangas, and a good seafood chowder are some of the attractions. Zelo's is always packed, and when happy hour rolls around (3:30–5:30pm), the inexpensive tap beers and tacos start flowing. A children's menu, appetizers and entrees in all price ranges, and the new Martini Madness menu make Zelo's a Hanalei must, especially if you can snag a table on the deck.

Kuhio Hwy. and Aku Rd., Hanalei. ℂ **808/826-9700.** Reservations recommended for parties of 6 or more. Main courses $8–$12 lunch, $9–$25 dinner. MC, V. Winter daily 11am–9:30pm; summer daily 11am–10pm.

SUPER-CHEAP EATS

Bubba Burgers *Value Kids* AMERICAN   Green picnic tables and umbrellas thatched with coconut leaves stand out against the yellow walls of Bubba's, the burger joint with attitude. The burgers are as flamboyant as the exterior. This North Shore version of the Kapaa fixture (see p. 548) has the same menu, same ownership, and same high-quality, all-beef, burgers that have made the original such a smashing success.

In Hanalei Center (on the town's main road), Hanalei. ℂ 808/826-7839. All items less than $7. MC, V. Daily 10:30am–6pm.

Hanalei Mixed Plate AMERICAN   The popular take-out stand in the heart of Hanalei is known for its Caesar salad, kalua pork and cabbage, and shoyu ginger chicken—hearty flavors in plate-lunch style, inexpensive and tasty. The flame-broiled burgers, beef hot dogs, and German bratwurst are known throughout Hanalei, where surfers and expats line up throughout the day.

5-5190 Kuhio Hwy. (next to Ching Young Village), Hanalei. ℂ 808/826-7888. Plate lunch $5.95–$7.95; sandwiches $6.95–$11. No credit cards. Daily 10:30am–9pm.

Hanalei Wake-Up Cafe AMERICAN   It's a surfer's pre-cowabunga breakfast call. Dawn patrol begins with pancakes, omelets, quesadillas, killer fresh-fruit smoothies, the Hang Ten Special (eggs and toast with bacon or Portuguese sausage), macadamia nut cinnamon rolls, and a legendary French toast, all custard and topped with exotic fruit. It's cheap and easy, with the popular papaya bowl—papaya, yogurt, and granola—one of the simple hits. The informal cafe is lined with historic photos of the town from the 1900s, and the crowd is decidedly laid-back and briny.

5144 Kuhio Hwy. (at Aku Rd.), Hanalei. ℂ 808/826-5551. Most items less than $8. No credit cards. Daily 6am–11:30am.

WORTH A SPLURGE

La Cascata AMERICAN MEDITERRANEAN/SOUTHERN ITALIAN   The North Shore's special-occasion restaurant is sumptuous—a Sicilian spree in Eden. Try to get here before dark, so you can enjoy the views of Bali Hai, the persimmon-colored sunset, and the waterfalls of Waialeale, all an integral part of the feast. Click your heels on the terra-cotta floors, take in the trompe l'oeil vines, train your eyes through the concertina windows, and pretend you're being served on a terrazzo in Sicily. The menu dazzles quietly with its Mediterranean-inspired offerings and fresh local ingredients. Polenta, charred peppers, Kauai asparagus, organic Kauai vegetables, risottos, ragouts, grilled fresh fish, and vegetable Napoleons are colorful and tasty, and beautifully presented.

In the Princeville Resort, 5520 Ka Haku Rd., Princeville. ℂ 808/826-9644. Reservations recommended for dinner. Main courses $24–$38; 3-course prix-fixe dinner $56. AE, DC, DISC, MC, V. Daily 6–9:30pm.

5 Beaches

Ancient Kauai is what geologists call "post-erosional"—which means eons of wind and rain have created a geological masterpiece with some fabulous beaches, like Hanalei, Kee, and Kalapaki. All are accessible to the public, as provided by Hawaii law, and many have facilities.

For beach toys and equipment, head to **Activity Warehouse,** 788 Kuhio Hwy. (across from McDonald's), Kapaa (ℂ **800/688-0580** or 808/822-4000; www.travelhawaii.com), with branches in Princeville and Lihue.

LIHUE'S BEST BEACH
KALAPAKI BEACH 🏖

Any town would pay a fortune to have a beach like Kalapaki, one of Kauai's best, in its backyard. But little Lihue turns its back on Kalapaki; there's not even a sign pointing the way through the trafficky labyrinth to this graceful half moon of golden sand at the foot of the Marriott Resort & Beach Club. A quarter-mile long and 50 yards wide, Kalapaki is protected by a jetty and patrolled by lifeguards, making it very safe for swimmers. The waves are good for surfing when there's a winter swell, and the view from the sand—of the steepled, 2,200-foot peaks of the majestic Haupu Ridge that shield Nawiliwili Bay—is awesome. Kalapaki is the best beach not only in Lihue, but also on the whole east coast. From Lihue Airport, turn left onto Kapule Highway (Hwy. 51) to Rice Street, turn left, and go to the entrance of the Marriott; pass the hotel's porte cochere and turn right at the SHORELINE ACCESS sign. Facilities include lifeguards, free parking, restrooms, and showers; food and drink are available nearby at **JJ's Broiler.**

THE POIPU RESORT AREA
MAHAULEPU BEACH 🏖🏖🏖

Mahaulepu is the best-looking unspoiled beach on Kauai, and possibly in the whole state. Its 2 miles of reddish-gold, grainy sand line the southeastern shore at the foot of 1,500-foot-high Haupu Ridge, just beyond the Hyatt Regency Poipu and McBryde sugarcane fields, which end in sand dunes and a forest of casuarina trees. Almost untouched by modern life, Mahaulepu is a great escape from the real world. It's ideal for beachcombing and shell hunting, but swimming can be risky, except in the reef-sheltered shallows 200 yards west of the sandy parking lot. There's no lifeguard, no facilities—just great natural beauty everywhere you look. (This beach is where George C. Scott portrayed Ernest Hemingway in the movie *Islands in the Stream.*) While you're here, see if you can find the Hawaiian petroglyph of a voyaging canoe carved in the beach rock.

To get here, drive past the Hyatt Regency Poipu, 3 miles east on a red-dirt road, past the golf course and stables. Turn right at the T intersection; go 1 mile to the big sand dune, turn left, and drive a half-mile to a small lot under the trees.

POIPU BEACH PARK 🏖🏖

Big, wide Poipu is actually two beaches in one; it's divided by a sandbar, called a *tombolo.* On the left, a lava-rock jetty protects a sandy-bottom pool that's perfect for children; on the right, the open bay attracts swimmers, snorkelers, and surfers. And everyone likes to picnic on the grassy lawn graced by coconut trees. You'll find excellent swimming, small tide pools for exploring, great reefs for snorkeling and diving, good fishing, nice waves for surfers, and a steady wind for windsurfers. Poipu attracts a daily crowd, but the density seldom approaches Waikiki levels, except on holidays. Facilities include restrooms, showers, picnic areas, **Brennecke's Beach Broiler** nearby (p. 542), and free parking in the red-dirt lot. To get here, turn on Poipu Beach Road, then turn right at Hoowili Road.

WESTERN KAUAI
SALT POND BEACH PARK

Hawaii's only salt ponds still in production are at Salt Pond Beach, just outside Hanapepe. Generations of locals have come here to swim, fish, and collect salt crystals that are dried in sunbeds. The tangy salt is used for health purposes and to cure fish and season food. The curved reddish-gold beach lies between two rocky points and features a protected reef, tide pools, and gentle waves. Swimming here is excellent, even for children; this beach is also good for diving, windsurfing, and fishing. Amenities include a lifeguard, showers, restrooms, camping area, picnic area, pavilion, and parking lot. To get here, take Highway 50 past Hanapepe and turn on Lokokai Road.

POLIHALE STATE PARK ↟

This mini-Sahara on the western end of the island is Hawaii's biggest beach: 17 miles long and as wide as three football fields. This is a wonderful place to get away from it all, but don't forget your flip-flops—the midday sand is hotter than a lava flow. The golden sands wrap around Kauai's northwestern shore from Kekaha plantation town, just beyond Waimea, to where the ridgebacks of the Na Pali Coast begin. The state park includes ancient Hawaiian *heiau* (temple) and burial sites, a view of the "forbidden" island of Niihau, and the famed **Barking Sands Beach,** where footfalls sound like a barking dog. (Scientists say that the grains of sand are perforated with tiny echo chambers, which emit a "barking" sound when they rub together.) Polihale also takes in the Pacific Missile Range Facility, a U.S. surveillance center that snooped on Russian subs during the Cold War, and Nohili Dune, which is nearly 3 miles long and 100 feet high in some places.

Be careful in winter, when high surf and rip currents make swimming dangerous. The safest place to swim is **Queen's Pond,** a small, shallow, sandy-bottom inlet protected from waves and shore currents. There are facilities for camping, as well as restrooms, showers, picnic tables, and pavilions. To get here, take Highway 50 past Barking Sands Missile Range and follow the signs through the sugarcane fields to Polihale. Local kids like to burgle rental cars out here, so don't leave tempting valuables in your car.

THE COCONUT COAST

LYDGATE STATE PARK ↟

This seacoast park has a rock-wall fish pond that blunts the open ocean waves and provides the only safe swimming and the best snorkeling on the eastern shore. The 1-acre beach park, near the mouth of the Wailua River, is named for the Rev. J. M. Lydgate (1854–1922), founder and first pastor of Lihue English Union Church, who likely would be shocked at the public display of flesh here. This popular park is a great place for a picnic or for kite flying on the green. It's 5 miles north of Lihue on Kuhio Highway (Hwy. 56); look for the turnoff just before the Kauai Resort Hotel. Facilities include a pavilion, restrooms, outdoor showers, picnic tables, barbecue grills, lifeguards, and parking.

THE NORTH SHORE

ANINI BEACH COUNTY PARK ↟↟

Anini is Kauai's safest beach for swimming and windsurfing. It's also one of the island's most beautiful: It sits on a blue lagoon at the foot of emerald cliffs, looking more like Tahiti than almost any other strand in the islands. This 3-mile-long, gold-sand beach is shielded from the open ocean by the longest, widest fringing reef in Hawaii. With shallow water, 4 to 5 feet deep, it's also the very best snorkel spot on Kauai, even for beginners; on the northwest side, a channel in the reef runs out to the deep blue water with a 60-foot drop that attracts divers. Beachcombers love it, too: Seashells, cowries, and sometimes even rare Niihau shells can be found here. Anini has a park, a campground, picnic and barbecue facilities, and a boat-launch ramp; several B&Bs and vacation rentals are nearby. Follow Kuhio Highway (Hwy. 56) to Kilauea; take the second exit, called Kalihiwai Road (the first dead-ends at Kalihiwai Beach), and drive a half-mile toward the sea; turn left on Anini Beach Road.

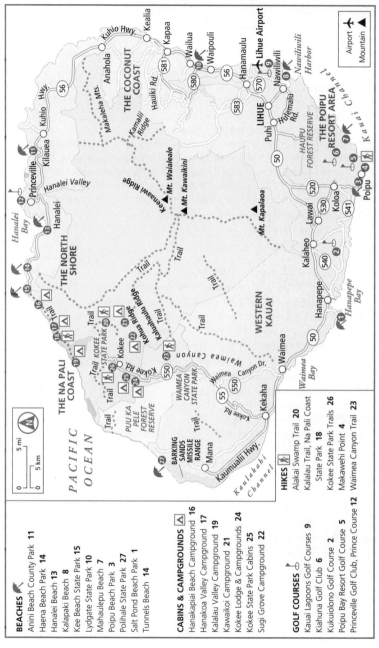

BEACHES

Anini Beach County Park **11**
Haena Beach Park **14**
Hanalei Beach **13**
Kalapaki Beach **8**
Kee Beach State Park **15**
Lydgate State Park **10**
Mahaulepu Beach **7**
Poipu Beach Park **3**
Polihale State Park **27**
Salt Pond Beach Park **1**
Tunnels Beach **14**

CABINS & CAMPGROUNDS

Hanakapiai Beach Campground **16**
Hanakoa Valley Campground **17**
Kalalau Valley Campground **19**
Kawaikoi Campground **21**
Kokee Lodge & Campgrounds **24**
Kokee State Park Cabins **25**
Sugi Grove Campground **22**

GOLF COURSES

Kauai Lagoons Golf Courses **9**
Kiahuna Golf Club **6**
Kukuiolono Golf Course **2**
Poipu Bay Resort Golf Course **5**
Princeville Golf Club, Prince Course **12**

HIKES

Alakai Swamp Trail **20**
Kalalau Trail, Na Pali Coast State Park **18**
Kokee State Park Trails **26**
Makawehi Point **4**
Waimea Canyon Trail **23**

555

Cheap Thrills: What to See & Do for Free (or Almost) on Kauai

- **Snorkel Kee Beach.** For a few dollars a day, you can rent a mask, fin, and snorkel and enter a magical underwater world, where brilliant fish dart here and there across coral in water clear as day. A slow-moving turtle may even stop by to check you out.

- **Walk on a Sleeping Giant.** According to ancient Hawaiian legend, a huge giant named Puni laid down for a quick nap near the Wailua River. The villagers tried to wake him by throwing rocks at him; unfortunately, the rocks landed in Puni's mouth and choked him to death—so the giant lies for eternity by the river. You can take an easy family hike up this fabled mountain (which really does look like a giant in repose) to a fabulous view.

- **Catch a Glimpse of Hawaii's Bird Life.** The best places for bird-watching are Kokee State Park, where, if you're lucky, you can spot the apapane, iwi, amakihi, anianiau, and elepaio, as well as the very popular moa (or Kauai chicken); and Kilauea Point National Wildlife Refuge, a great place to spot red-footed boobies, wedge-tailed shearwaters, frigate birds, laysan albatross, and the white-tailed tropic bird.

- **Hike Waimea Canyon, the Grand Canyon of the Pacific.** Ansel Adams would have loved this ageless desert canyon, carved by an ancient river. Sunlight plays against its rustic red cliffs, burnt-orange pinnacles, and blue-green valleys. There's nothing else like it in the islands.

- **Wander Around a High Mountain Forest.** Kokee State Park, through Waimea Canyon at the end of Highway 550, is a combination rainforest and bog up around 4,000 feet. The park's 45 miles of trails offer everything from casual nature strolls to hardy camping and hiking adventures among the redwoods.

- **Stroll Through Hawaiian History.** Old Waimea town is where Captain James Cook "discovered" the Hawaiian islands, where Russians once built a fortress, and where New England missionaries arrived in 1820 to save the heathens. A self-guided hour-long walking tour of historic Waimea is available at Waimea Public Library, Kaumaualii Highway (© 808/338-6848).

- **Watch for Whales from Land.** There's no need to spend big bucks to go out in a boat to spot these mighty mammals. Mahaulepu Beach, in the Poipu area, offers excellent viewing conditions to spot whales, who cruise by from December through April.

HANALEI BEACH 🏖🏖

Gentle waves roll across the face of half-moon Hanalei Bay, running up to the wide, golden sand; sheer volcanic ridges laced by waterfalls rise to 4,000 feet on the other side, 3 miles inland. Is there any beach with a better location? Celebrated in song and hula and featured on travel posters, this beach owes its natural beauty to its age—it's an ancient sunken valley with post-erosional cliffs. Hanalei Bay indents the coast a full

- **Take a Long Walk on a Short (but Historic) Pier.** Hanalei's 1910 pier was once a major shipping port for local farmers. Today, the rebuilt pier makes a great platform for swimming, fishing, and diving. The pier is at the Black Pot Beach end of Hanalei, where in olden days, local families would camp on the beach all summer and always have something cooking in a "black pot" on the shore.
- **Journey into Eden.** For a glimpse of the spectacularly remote Na Pali Coast, you need only hike the first 2 miles along the Kalalau Trail into the first tropical valley, Hanakapiai. Hardier hikers may want to venture another 2 miles to the Hanakapiai Waterfalls and pools. *Beware:* The Na Pali's natural beauty is so enticing that you may want to keep going—but the trail is *extremely* difficult after Hanakapiai.
- **Catch a Poipu Wave.** Vividly turquoise, curling and totally tubular, big enough to hang ten yet small enough to bodysurf, the waves at Poipu are endless in their attraction. Grab a Boogie Board—rentable for just dollars a day—or simply jump in and go with the flow.
- **Go Spelunking where Evil Spirits Once Roamed.** Across from Haena State Park is the Maniniholo Dry Cave, which extends several hundred yards into the vertical cliff. The cave is composed of a main cavern, which allows you to stand up when you first enter and then gets smaller and smaller as you move further into the cave. The legend behind the cave is that a spirit had stolen fish left by Menehune fishermen for a village; to capture the evil spirit, the Menehune started digging from the top of the cliff as well as from the bottom, hoping to trap him in the middle. The result? The dry cave. Some legends say that the Menehune captured the evil spirit; others say it still roams the cave.
- **Watch the Hula.** The Coconut Market Place, on Kuhio Highway (Hwy. 56) between mile markers 6 and 7, hosts free hula shows everyday at 5pm. Get there early to get a good seat for the hour-long performances of both *kahiko* (ancient) and *auwana* (modern) hula. The real show-stoppers are the *keiki* (children) who perform. Don't forget your camera!
- **Bid the Sun Aloha.** Polihale State Park hugs Kauai's western shore for some 17 miles. It's a great place to bring a picnic dinner, stretch out on the sand, and toast the sun as it sinks into the Pacific, illuminating the island of Niihau in the distance.

1 mile inland and runs 2 miles point to point, with coral reefs on either side and a patch of coral in the middle—plus a sunken ship that belonged to a king, so divers love it. Swimming is excellent year-round, especially in summer, when Hanalei Bay becomes a big, placid lake. The aquamarine water's also great for bodyboarding, surfing, fishing, windsurfing, canoe paddling, kayaking, and boating (a boat ramp is on the west bank of the Hanalei River). The area known as Black Pot, near the pier, is

particularly good for swimming, snorkeling, and surfing. Facilities include a pavilion, restrooms, picnic tables, and parking. This beach is always packed with both locals and visitors, but you can usually find your own place in the sun by strolling down the shore; the bay is big enough for everyone.

To get here, take Kuhio Highway (Hwy. 56), which becomes Highway 560 after Princeville. In Hanalei town, make a right on Aku Road just after Tahiti Nui, then turn right again on Weke Road, which dead-ends at the parking lot for the Black Pot section of the beach; the easiest beach access is on your left.

TUNNELS BEACH & HAENA BEACH PARK ★★

Postcard-perfect, gold-sand Tunnels Beach is one of Hawaii's most beautiful. When the sun sinks into the Pacific along the fabled peaks of Bali Ha'i, there's no better-looking beach in the islands: You're bathed in golden rays that butter-up the blue sky, bounce off the steepled ridges, and tint the pale clouds hot pink. Catch the sunset from the pebbly sand beach or while swimming in the emerald-green waters, but do catch it. Tunnels is excellent for swimming nearly year-round and is safe for snorkeling, since it's protected by a fringing coral reef (the waters can get rough in winter, though). The long, curvy beach is sheltered by a forest of ironwoods that provide welcome shade from the tropic heat.

Around the corner is grainy-gold-sand Haena Beach Park, which offers excellent swimming in summer and great snorkeling amid clouds of tropical fish. But stay out of the water in winter, when the big waves are dangerous. Haena also has a grassy park for camping, making it especially popular for camping. Noise-phobes will prefer Tunnels.

Take Kuhio Highway (Hwy. 56), which becomes Highway 560 after Princeville. Tunnels is about 6 miles past Hanalei town, after mile marker 8 on the highway (look for the alley with the big wood gate at the end), and Haena is just down the road. Tunnels has no facilities, but Haena has restrooms, outdoor showers, barbecue grills, picnic tables, and free parking (no lifeguard, though).

KEE BEACH STATE PARK ★★

Where the road ends on the North Shore, you'll find a dandy little reddish-gold beach almost too beautiful to be real. Don't be surprised if it looks familiar; it was featured in *The Thornbirds*. Kee (*kay*-ay) is on a reef-protected cove at the foot of fluted volcanic cliffs. Swimming and snorkeling are safe inside the reef, but dangerous outside; those North Shore waves and currents can be killers. This park has restrooms, showers, and parking, but no lifeguard. To get here, take Kuhio Highway (Hwy. 56), which becomes Highway 560 after Princeville; Kee is about 7½ miles past Hanalei.

6 Watersports

Several outfitters on Kauai not only offer equipment rentals and tours but also give out expert information on weather forecasts, sea and trail conditions, and other important matters for hikers, kayakers, sailors, and other backcountry adventurers. For watersports questions and equipment rental, contact **Kayak Kauai Outbound,** 1 mile past Hanalei Bridge on Highway 560, in Hanalei (© **800/437-3507** or 808/826-9844; www.kayakkauai.com), the outfitters' center in Hanalei. They also have their own private dock (the only one on Kauai) for launching kayaks and canoes. In Kapaa contact **Kauai Water Ski & Surf Co.,** Kinipopo Shopping Village, 4–356 Kuhio Hwy. (on the ocean side of the highway), Kapaa (© **808/822-3574;** www.kauaiwaterskisurfandkayak.com). In the Lihue and Poipu areas, go with **Snorkel**

Bob's Kauai at 4–734 Kuhio Hwy. (just north of Coconut Plantation Marketplace), Kapaa (© **800/262-7725** or 808/823-9433; www.snorkelbob.com), and in Koloa at 3236 Poipu Rd. (just south of Poipu Shopping Village), near Poipu Beach (© **808/ 742-2206**).

For general advice on the activities listed below, see "The Active Vacation Planner," in chapter 2.

BODYBOARDING (BOOGIE BOARDING) & BODYSURFING

The best places for bodysurfing and boogie boarding are **Kalapaki Beach** (near Lihue) and **Poipu Beach.** In addition to the rental shops listed above, one of the most inexpensive places to rent boogie boards is the **Activity Warehouse,** 788 Kuhio Hwy. (across from McDonald's), Kapaa (© **800/343-2087** or 808/822-4000; www.travel hawaii.com), and branches in Princeville and Lihue, where they go for $2 to $6 a day or **Snorkel Bob's** (see above) for just $15 a week.

BOATING

One of Hawaii's most spectacular natural attractions is Kauai's **Na Pali Coast.** Unless you're willing to make an arduous 22-mile hike (see p. 569), there are only two ways to see it: by helicopter (see "A Bird's-Eye View of Waimea Canyon & the Na Pali Coast" on p. 575 for details on this splurge) or by boat. Picture yourself cruising the rugged Na Pali coastline in a 42-foot ketch-rigged yacht under full sail, watching the sunset as you enjoy a tropical cocktail, or speeding through the aquamarine water in a 40-foot trimaran as porpoises play off the bow. Or, even more exciting: cruising just above the water in a fast, low-slung rubber Zodiac, just like Jacques Cousteau.

When the Pacific humpback whales make their annual visit to Hawaii from December to March, they swim right by Kauai. In season, most boats on Kauai—including sailboats and Zodiacs—combine **whale-watching** with their regular adventures.

Kauai has many freshwater areas that are accessible only by boat, including the Fern Grotto, Wailua State Park, Huleia and Hanalei national wildlife refuges, Menehune Fish Pond, and numerous waterfalls. If you want to strike out on your own, **Paradise Outdoor Adventures,** 4–1596 Kuhio Hwy., Kapaa (© **800/66-BOATS** or 808/822-0016; www.kayakers.com), has 40 different rental boats to choose from, like the popular Boston whaler (six-person capacity) for $295 a day, plus kayaks and sea cycles. Included are all the amenities, such as safety equipment, coolers, dry bags (for cameras, wallets, towels), and a comprehensive orientation on where to go. The staff will even deliver the boat to the Wailua River at no extra charge.

For sportfishing charters, see "Fishing," below. For tours of the Fern Grotto, see p. 580.

Captain Andy's Sailing Adventures ★   Captain Andy operates a 55-foot, 49-passenger catamaran out of two locations on the south shore. The **snorkel/picnic cruise,** a 5½-hour cruise to the **Na Pali Coast,** from May to October, costs $129 for adults and $89 for children 2 to 12, and includes a deli-style lunch, snorkeling, and drinks. There's also a 4-hour Na Pali Coast **dinner sunset cruise** that sets sail for $95 for adults and $70 for children, and a 2-hour pupu cocktail sunset sail with drinks and pupu for $59 adults and $40 children. They also offer 6-hour Na Pali Zodiac cruise on inflatable boats for $129 to $159 adults and $89 to $106 children 5 to 12 years old.

Kukuiula Small Boat Harbor, Poipu; and Port Allen, Eleele. © **800/535-0830** or 808/335-6833. www.capt-andys.com. Prices vary depending on trip.

Holoholo Charters This outfitter has taken over several boats and features both swimming/snorkeling sailing charters as well as powerboat charters to the Na Pali Coast. The 5½-hour sailing trips take place on a 48-foot catamaran called *Leila,* and are offered both in the morning (with a continental breakfast and lunch) and afternoon (big buffet lunch) for $119 adults and $85 children. The 7-hour power-boat trip is on the 61-foot vessel *Holoholo,* and not only cruises the Na Pali Coast but then crosses the channel to the forbidden island of Niihau, where they stop to snorkel. A continental breakfast, buffet lunch, and snorkel equipment is included in the price: $169 adults, $119 children. They've recently added at 42-foot sailboat that does a 5 1/2 hour cruise of the Na Pali Coast with snorkeling for $99 adults and $69 kids ages 2-12. They also provide complimentary shuttle service to and from your hotel.

Port Allen, Eleele. ℂ 800/848-6130 or 808/335-0815. www.holoholocharters.com. Prices and departure points vary depending on trip.

Liko Kauai Cruises ★ *Kids* Liko offers more than just a typical whale-watching cruise; this is a 4-hour combination **Na Pali Coast tour**–deep-sea fishing–historical lecture–whale-watching extravaganza with lunch. It all happens on a 49-foot power catamaran (with only 24 passengers). In addition to viewing the whales, you'll glimpse sea caves, waterfalls, lush valleys, and miles of white-sand beaches; you'll also make stops along the way for snorkeling.

Kekaha Small Boat Harbor, Waimea. ℂ 888/SEA-LIKO or 808/338-0333. Fax 808/338-1327. www.liko-kauai.com. Na Pali Trips $110 adults, $75 children 4–12 (lunch included).

FISHING

DEEP-SEA FISHING Kauai's fishing fleet is smaller and less well recognized than others in the islands, but the fish are still out there. All you need to bring is your lunch and your luck. The best way to book a sportfishing charter is through the experts; the best booking desk in the state is **Sportfish Hawaii** ★ (ℂ 877/388-1376 or 808/396-2607; www.sportfishhawaii.com), which books boats not only on Kauai, but on all islands. These fishing vessels have been inspected and must meet rigorous criteria to guarantee that you will have a great time. Prices range from $1050 for a full-day exclusive charter (you and five of your closest friends get the entire boat to yourselves), $850 for a three-quarter day or $650 for a half-day exclusive. Frankly, the fishing is better off the Kona coast and the prices are more reasonable too.

FRESHWATER FISHING Freshwater fishing is big on Kauai, thanks to its dozens of "lakes," which are really man-made reservoirs. Regardless, they're full of large-mouth, small-mouth, and peacock bass (also known as *tucunare*). The **Puu Lua Reservoir,** in Kokee State Park, also has rainbow trout and is stocked by the state every year. Fishing for rainbow trout in the reservoir has a limited season: It begins on the first Saturday in August and lasts for 16 days, after which you can only fish on weekends and holidays through the last Sunday in September.

Before you rush out and get a fishing pole, you have to have a **Hawaii Freshwater Fishing License,** available through the **State Department of Land and Natural Resources,** Division of Aquatic Resources, P.O. Box 1671, Lihue, HI 96766 (ℂ 808/241-3400) or online at www.hawaii.gov/dlnr/dar/licenses.htm, or through any fishing-supply store like **Lihue Fishing Supply,** 2985 Kalena St., Lihue (ℂ 808/245-4930); **Waipouli Variety,** 4–901 1-A Kuhio Hwy., Kapaa (ℂ 808/822-1014); or **Westside Sporting Goods,** 9681 Kaumualii Hwy., Waimea (ℂ 808/338-1411). A 7-day tourist license costs $10 for adults and $4 for kids ages 9 to 15. When you get your license, pick up a copy of the booklet *State of Hawaii Freshwater Fishing Regulations*. Another great little book to get is *The Kauai Guide to Freshwater Sport Fishing*, by Glenn Ikemoto, available for $2.50 plus postage from **Magic Fishes Press,** P.O. Box 3243, Lihue, HI 96766. If you would like a guide, **Sportfish Hawaii** (✆ 877/ 388-1376 or 808/396-2607; www.sportfishhawaii.com), has guided bass-fishing trips starting at $265 per person for a half-day and $375 for a full day.

KAYAKING

Kauai is made for kayaking. You can take the Huleia River into **Huleia National Wildlife Refuge** (located along the eastern portion of the Huleia Stream where it flows into Nawiliwili Bay). It's the last stand for Kauai's endangered birds, and kayak is the only way to see it. The adventurous can head to the Na Pali Coast, featuring majestic cliffs, empty beaches, open-ocean conditions, and monster waves. Or you can just go out and paddle around Hanalei Bay.

Kayak Kauai Outbound ⚓, a mile past Hanalei Bridge on Highway 560, in Hanalei (✆ 800/437-3507 or 808/826-9844; www.kayakkauai.com), has a range of tours for independent souls. The shop's experts will be happy to take you on a guided kayaking trip or to tell you where to go on your own. Equipment rental starts at $28 for a one-person kayak and $52 for a two-person ocean kayak per day. Kayak lessons are $50 per person per hour. Tours (some including snacks) start at $115 per person and include transportation and lunch for the all-day excursion. Kayak Kauai also has its own private dock (the only one on Kauai) for launching kayaks and canoes.

Rick Haviland, who gained fame after he was mentioned in Paul Theroux's book *The Happy Isles of Oceania,* is the owner of **Outfitters Kauai** ⚓, 2827A Poipu Rd. (Poipu Plaza, a small five-shop mall before the road forks to Poipu/Spouting Horn), Poipu (✆ 888/742-9887 or 808/742-9667; www.outfitterskauai.com), which has a bunch of different kayaking tours. A full-day trip along the entire Na Pali Coast (summer only) costs $185 per person and includes a guide, lunch, drinks, and equipment. Another kayak tour takes you up a jungle stream and involves a short hike to waterfalls and a swimming hole; it's $94 (children, ages 5–14, $72) including lunch, snacks, and drinks. Outfitters Kauai also rents river kayaks by the day ($40).

The cheapest place to rent kayaks is the **Activity Warehouse,** 788 Kuhio Hwy. (across from McDonald's), Kapaa (✆ 808/822-4000; www.travelhawaii.com), where a one-person kayak goes for $10 a day and a two-person kayak is $15. **Kauai Water Ski & Surf Co.,** Kinipopo Shopping Village, 4–356 Kuhio Hwy. (on the ocean side), Kapaa (✆ 808/ 822-3574; www.kauaiwaterskisurfandkayak.com); or **Pedal 'n Paddle,** Ching Young Village Shopping Center, Hanalei (✆ 808/826-9069; http://pedalnpaddle.com).

PADDLING INTO HULEIA NATIONAL WILDLIFE REFUGE   Ride the Huleia River through Kauai's 240-acre Huleia National Wildlife Refuge, the last stand of Kauai's endangered birds, with **True Blue,** Nawiliwili Harbor (✆ 888/245-1707 or 808/245-9662; www.kauaifun.com). You paddle up the picturesque Huleia (which appeared in *Raiders of the Lost Ark* and the remake of *King Kong*) under sheer pinnacles that open into valleys full of lush tropical plants, bright flowers, and hanging vines. Look for great blue herons and Hawaiian gallinules taking wing. The 4½-hour voyage, which starts at Nawiliwili Harbor, is a great trip for all—but especially for movie buffs, birders, and great adventurers under 12. It's even safe for nonswimmers. Wear a swimsuit, T-shirt, and boat shoes. The cost is $89 for adults, $36 for children 8 to 12. The prices include a picnic snack, juice, kayak, life vest, and guide services

SCUBA DIVING

Diving on Kauai is dictated by the weather. In winter, when heavy swells and high winds hit the island, it's generally limited to the more protected south shore. Probably the best-known site along the south shore is **Caverns,** located off the Poipu Beach resort area. This site consists of a series of lava tubes interconnected by a chain of archways. A constant parade of fish streams by (even shy lionfish are spotted lurking in crevices), brightly hued Hawaiian lobsters hide in the lava's tiny holes, and turtles swim past.

In summer, when the north Pacific storms subside, the magnificent North Shore opens up, and you can take a boat dive locally known as the **Oceanarium,** northwest of Hanalei Bay, where you'll find a kaleidoscopic marine world in a horseshoe-shaped cove. From the rare (long-handed spiny lobsters) to the more common (taape, conger eels, and nudibranches), the resident population is one of the more diverse on the island. The topography, which features pinnacles, ridges, and archways, is covered with cup corals, black-coral trees, and nooks and crannies enough for a dozen dives.

Because the best dives on Kauai are offshore, we recommend booking a two-tank dive off a dive boat. **Bubbles Below Scuba Charters,** 6251 Hauaala Rd., Kapaa (© 808/ 822-3483; www.bubblesbelowkauai.com), specializes in highly personalized, small-group dives, with an emphasis on marine biology. The 35-foot boat *Kaimanu* is a custom-built Radon dive boat that comes complete with a hot shower. Two-tank boat dives cost $110 ($25 more if you need gear); nondivers can come along for the ride for $50. In summer (May–Sept) Bubbles Below offers a three-tank trip for experienced divers–only to the "forbidden" island of Niihau, 90 minutes by boat from Kauai. You should be comfortable with vertical drop-offs, huge underwater caverns, possibly choppy surface conditions, and significant currents. You should also be willing to share water space with the resident sharks. The all-day, three-tank trip costs $260, including tanks, weights, dive computer, lunch, drinks, and marine guide (if you need gear, it's $25 more). On the south side, call **Fathom Five Adventures,** 3450 Poipu Rd. (next to the Chevron), Koloa (© 808/742-6991; www.fathomfive.com).

GREAT SHORE DIVES FROM KAUAI If you want to rent your own equipment for shore dives, it will probably cost around $25 to $40 a day. Try **Dive Kauai,** 4–976 Kuhio Hwy., Kapaa (© 808/822-0452); or **Fathom Five Adventures,** 3450 Poipu Rd. (next to the Chevron), Koloa (© 808/742-6991).

Spectacular shoreline dive sites on the North Shore include **Kee Beach/Haena Beach Park** (where the road ends), one of the most picturesque beaches on the island. On a calm summer day, the drop-off near the reef begs for underwater exploration. Another good bet is **Tunnels Beach,** also known as Makua Beach. It's off Highway 560, just past mile marker 8; look for the short dirt road (less than a half-mile) to the beach. The wide reef here makes for some fabulous snorkeling and diving, but again, only during the calm summer months. **Cannons Beach,** east of Haena Beach Park (use the parking for Haena, located across the street from the Dry Cave near mile marker 9 on Hwy. 560), has lots of vibrant marine life in its sloping offshore reef.

On the south shore, head to **Tortugas** (located directly in front of Poipu Beach Park) if you want to catch a glimpse of sea turtles. **Koloa Landing** has a horseshoe-shaped reef that's teeming with tropical fish. **Sheraton Caverns** (located off the Sheraton Kauai) is also popular, due to its three large underwater lava tubes, which are usually filled with marine life.

SNORKELING

See the intro to this section for locations of **Snorkel Bob's.**

For great shoreline snorkeling, try the reef off **Kee Beach/Haena Beach Park,** located at the end of Highway 560. **Tunnels Beach,** about a mile before the end of Highway 560 in Haena, has a wide reef that's great for poking around in search of tropical fish. Be sure to check ocean conditions—don't go if the surf is up or if there's a strong current. **Anini Beach,** located off the northern Kalihiwai Road (between mile markers 25 and 26 on Kuhio Hwy., or Hwy. 56), just before the Princeville Airport, has a safe, shallow area with excellent snorkeling. **Poipu Beach Park** has some good snorkeling to the right side of Nukumoi Point—the tombolo area, where the narrow strip of sand divides the ocean, is best. If this spot is too crowded, wander down the beach in front of the old Waiohai resort; if there are no waves, this place is also hopping with marine life. **Salt Pond Beach Park,** off Highway 50 near Hanapepe, has good snorkeling around the two rocky points, home to hundreds of tropical fish.

SURFING

Hanalei Bay's winter surf is the most popular on the island, but it's for experts only. **Poipu Beach** is an excellent spot to learn to surf; the waves are small and—best of all—nobody laughs when you wipe out. Check with the local surf shops or call the **Weather Service** (© 808/245-3564) to find out where surf's up.

Surf lessons are available for $60 for a 1½-hour session, including all-day use of equipment (board, wet-suit top, and carrying rack for your car), from **Windsurf Kauai,** in Hanalei (© 808/828-6838). Poipu is also the site of numerous surfing schools; the oldest and best is **Margo Oberg's School of Surfing,** at the Nukumoi Surf Shop, across from Brennecke's Beach (© 808/742-8019; www.surfonkauai.com). Margo charges $50 for 2 hours of group instruction, including surfboard and leash; she guarantees that by the end of the lesson, you'll be standing and catching a wave.

Equipment is available for rent (ranging from $5 an hour or $20 a day for "soft" beginner boards to $7.50 an hour or $30 a day for hard boards for experienced surfers) from **Nukumoi Surf Shop,** across from Brennecke's Beach, Poipu Beach Park (© 888/384-8810 or 808/742-8019; www.brenneckes.com/nukumoi.html); **Hanalei Surf Co.,** 5–5161 Kuhio Hwy. (across from Zelo's Beach House Restaurant in Hanalei Center), Hanalei (© 808/826-9000); and **Pedal 'n Paddle,** Ching Young Village Shopping Center, Hanalei (© 808/826-9069). The cheapest place to rent a board is the **Activity Warehouse,** 788 Kuhio Hwy. (across from McDonald's), Kapaa (© 808/822-4000; www.travelhawaii.com), where they start at $5 a day.

TUBING

Back in the days of the sugar plantations, on really hot days, if no one was looking, local kids would grab inner tubes and jump in the irrigation ditches crisscrossing the cane fields and get an exciting ride. Today you can enjoy this (formerly illegal) activity by "tubing" the flumes and ditches of the old Lihue Plantation through **Kauai Backcountry Adventures** (© 888/270-0555 or 808/245-2506; www.kauaibackcountry.com). Passengers are taken in four-wheel-drive vehicles high into the mountains above Lihue and look at vistas generally off-limits to the public. At the flumes you will be outfitted with a giant tube, gloves, and headlamp (for the long passageways through the tunnels). All you do is jump in the water and the gentle gravity-feed flow will carry you through forests, into tunnels, and finally to a mountain swimming hole, where a picnic lunch is served. The 3-hour tours are $92 and appropriate for anyone ages 5 to 95. Swimming is not necessary, as all you do is relax and drift downstream.

WATER-SKIING

Hawaii's only freshwater water-skiing is on the Wailua River. Ski boats launch from the boat ramp in Wailua River State Park, directly across from the marina. **Kauai Water Ski & Surf Co.,** Kinipopo Shopping Village, 4–356 Kuhio Hwy., Kapaa (© **800/ 344-7915** or 808/822-3574; www.kauaiwaterskisurfandkayak.com), rents equipment and offers lessons and guided tours; it's $55 for a half-hour trip and $100 for an hour.

WINDSURFING

Anini Beach is one of the safest beaches for beginners to learn windsurfing. Lessons and equipment rental are available at **Anini Beach Windsurfing and Kitesurfing** (© **808/826-WIND** or 808/8269463). Owner Foster Ducker has been teaching windsurfing for nearly a decade, he has special equipment to help beginners learn the sport. A 1-hour lesson is $50 and includes equipment and instruction. If you fall in love with the sport and want to keep going, he'll rent the equipment for $25 an hour or $50 for the rest of the day. For those experienced windsurfers, who don't want to cart their equipment half way around the globe, he will rent windsurfing equipment for $25 an hour or $75 a day. Serious windsurfers should head to **Hanalei Bay** or **Tunnels Beach** on the North Shore.

For the real adventurous, Ducker also is a certified instructor in kitesurfing; he claims he can get people up and on the water in just one lesson. His introduction to kitesurfing is 5 hours long and costs $400 for one person and $600 for two.

7 Hiking & Camping

Kauai is an adventurer's delight. The island's greatest tropical beauty isn't easily reachable; you've got to head out on foot and find it. For more information on Kauai's hiking trails, contact the **State Division of Parks,** P.O. Box 1671, Lihue, HI 96766 (© **808/274-3446;** www.hawaii.gov/dlnr/dsp/kauai.html); the **State Division of Forestry and Wildlife,** P.O. Box 1671, Lihue, HI 96766 (© **808/274-3077;** www. dofaw.net/); **Kauai County Parks and Recreation,** 4193 Hardy St., Lihue, HI 96766 (© **808/241-6670;** www.k12.hi.us/~pworks/parksandrec/); or the **Kokee Lodge Manager,** P.O. Box 819, Waimea, HI 96796 (© **808/335-6061**).

Kayak Kauai Outbound ⚓, a mile past Hanalei Bridge on Highway 560 in Hanalei (© **800/437-3507** or 808/826-9844; fax 808/822-0577; www.kayakkauai.com), is the premier all-around outfitter on the island. It's staffed by local experts who keep track of weather forecasts and sea and trail conditions; they have a lot more pertinent information that hikers, campers, and other backcountry adventurers need to know. Plus they have guided hiking tours starting at $81 per person. If you don't plan to bring your own gear, you can rent it here or at **Pedal 'n Paddle,** in Hanalei (© **808/826-9069;** www.pedalnpaddle.com). If you want to buy camping equipment, head for **Ace Island Hardware,** at Princeville Shopping Center (© **808/826-6980**).

GUIDED HIKES   You can join a guided hike with the Kauai chapter of the **Sierra Club,** P.O. Box 3412, Lihue, HI 96766 (© **808/246-8748;** www.hi.sierraclub.org), which offers two to three different hikes every month, varying from an easy family moonlit beach hike to a moderate 4-mile trip up some 1,100 feet to 8-mile-plus treks for serious hikers only. The club also does guided hikes of Kokee State Park (see

> **Tips A Warning About Flash Floods**
>
> When it rains on Kauai, the waterfalls rage and rivers and streams overflow, caus-
> ing flash floods on roads and trails. If you're hiking, avoid dry streambeds, which
> flood quickly and wash out to sea. Before going hiking, camping, or sailing, espe-
> cially in the rainy season (Nov–Mar), check the weather forecast by calling
> © 808/245-6001.

below), usually on weekends. As there's no staffed office, the best way to contact the
chapter is to check the website; outings are usually listed 3 to 6 months in advance,
with complete descriptions of the hike, the hike leader's phone number, and what to
wear and bring. You can also check the daily newspaper, the *Garden Island,* for a list
of hikes in the Community Calendar section. Generally, the club asks for a donation
of $3 per person per hike for nonmembers, $1 for members. It also does service work
(clearing trails, picking up trash) on the hikes, so you may spend an hour doing service work, then 2 to 3 hours hiking. Last year, the club took three service-work trips
along the Na Pali Coast trail to help maintain it.

Hawaiian Wildlife Tours 🕊 (© **808/639-2968;** cberg@pixi.com) is environmental education in action. Biologist Dr. Carl Berg will take you out into the woods and
down to the shoreline to see Kauai's native and vanishing species, from forest birds and
flora to hoary bats, monk seals, and green sea turtles. His personalized tours last from
2 hours to a week and are tailored around the season and weather, your physical abilities, and what you want to see. He leads tours to Hanalei taro fields to see wetland
birds, to Crater Hill to see nene geese, to Mahaulepu to see wildflowers in the sand
dunes, to Kilauea Lighthouse to see oceanic birds, and much more. Rates are $45 per
couple, per hour.

Other options for guided hikes include **Princeville Ranch Hiking Adventures**
(© **808/826-7669;** www.kauai-hiking.com), which offers various hikes on 2,000
acres of private property, such as a 3-hour hike to a waterfall (plus another hour swimming) for $79; and **Kauai Nature Adventures** (© **888/233-8365** or 808/742-8305;
www.kauainaturetours.com), which leads a geological-history excursion, a tour of
Kauai's environments from the mountain to the ocean, and a Mahaulepu coast hike,
all lead by scientists, costing $87 for adults and $54 for children 12 and under, plus a
host of other tours ranging in price up to $97 for adults and $64 for children.

THE POIPU RESORT AREA
MAKAWEHI POINT 🕊

Like a ship's prow, Makawehi Point juts out to sea on the east side of Keoneloa Beach
(known locally as Shipwreck Beach), which lies in front of the Hyatt Regency Poipu.
This 50-foot-high sand-dune bluff attracts a variety of people: pole fishers, whale-
watchers, those who just like the panoramic views of the Pacific, and daredevils who
test their courage by leaping off the cliff into the waves (don't try it).

The trail head begins on the east end of Shipwreck Beach, past the Hyatt. It's an
easy 10-minute walk up to Makawehi Point; after you take in the big picture, keep
going uphill along the ridge of the sand dunes (said to contain ancient Hawaiian burial sites), past the coves frequented by green sea turtles and endangered Hawaiian
monk seals, through the coastal pine forest, and past World War II bunkers to the very

top. Now you can see Hauupu Ridge and its 2,297-foot peak, the famously craggy ridgeline that eerily resembles Queen Victoria's profile, and, in the distance, Mahaulepu Beach, one of the best looking in Hawaii. Inland, three red craters dimple the green fields; the one in the middle, the biggest, Pu'u Huni Huni, is said to have been the last volcano to erupt on Kauai—but it was so long ago that nobody here can remember when.

WESTERN KAUAI
WAIMEA CANYON TRAILS
On a wet island like Kauai, a dry hike is hard to find. But in the desert-dry gulch of Waimea Canyon, known as the Grand Canyon of the Pacific (once you get here, you'll see why—it's pretty spectacular), you're not likely to slip and slide in the muck as you go.

CANYON TRAIL   You want to hike Hawaii's Grand Canyon, but you only have so much time. Well, then, take the Canyon Trail to the east rim for a breathtaking view into the 3,000-foot-deep canyon. Park your car at the top of Halemanu Valley Road (located between mile markers 14 and 15 on Waimea Canyon Road, about a mile down from the museum). Walk down the not very clearly marked trail on the 3⅔-mile round-trip, which takes 2 to 3 hours and leads to Waipoo Falls (as does the hike below) and back. We suggest going in the afternoon, when the light is best.

HIKE TO WAIPOO FALLS ⚐   The 3-hour round-trip family hike to Waipoo Falls is one of Kauai's best hikes. The two-tiered, 800-foot waterfall that splashes into a natural pool is worth every step it takes to get here. To find the trail, drive up Kokee Road (Hwy. 550) to the Puu Hina Hina Outlook; a quarter mile past the lookout, near a NASA satellite tracking station on the right, a two-lane dirt road leads to the Waipoo Falls trail head. From here, the trail winds gently through a jungle dotted with wild yellow orchids and flame-red torch ginger before it leads you out on a descending ridgeback that juts deep into the canyon. At the end of the promontory, take a left and push on through the jungle to the falls; at the end, reward yourself with a refreshing splash in the pool.

KOKEE STATE PARK
At the end of Highway 550, which leads through Waimea Canyon to its summit, lies a 4,640-acre state park of high-mountain forest wilderness (3,600 ft.–4,000 ft. above sea level). The rainforest, bogs, and breathtaking views of the Na Pali coastline and Waimea Canyon are the draw at Kokee. This is the place for hiking—among the 45 miles of maintained trails are some of the best hikes in Hawaii. Official trail maps of all the park's trails are for sale for 50¢ at the **Kokee Natural History Museum** (© **808/335-9975**).

   A few words of advice: Always check current trail conditions; up-to-date trail information is available on a bulletin board at the Kokee Natural History Museum. Stay on established trails; it's easy to get lost here. Get off the trail well before dark. Carry water and rain gear—even if it's perfectly sunny when you set out—and wear sunscreen.

AWAAWAPUHI TRAIL   This 3¼-mile hike (6½ miles round-trip) takes about 3 hours each way and is considered strenuous by most, but offers a million-dollar view. Look for the trail head at the left of the parking lot, at mile marker 17 between the museum and Kalalau Lookout. The well-marked and -maintained trail now sports quarter-mile markers, and you can pick up a free plant guide for the trail at the museum. The trail drops about 1,600 feet through native forests to a thin precipice right at the very edge of the Na Pali cliffs for a dramatic and dizzying view of the tropical valleys and blue Pacific 2,500 feet below. It's not recommended for anyone with vertigo (although a railing will keep you from a major slip and fall). Go early, before clouds obscure the view, or late in the day; the chiaroscuro sunsets are something to behold.

The Awaawapuhi can be a straight-out-and-back trail or a loop that connects with the **Nualolo Trail** (3¾ miles), which provides awesome views and leads back to the main road between the ranger's house and the Kokee cabins, which is about a mile and a half from where you started. So you can hike the remaining 1½ miles along the road or hitch a ride if you decide to do the entire loop but can't make it all the way.

HALEMANU-KOKEE TRAIL   This trail takes you on a pleasant, easy-to-moderate 2⅖-mile round-trip walk through a native koa and ohia forest inhabited by native birds. The trail head is near mile marker 15; pick up the Faye Trail, which leads to this one. The Halemanu-Kokee links Kokee Valley to Halemanu Valley (hence the name); along the way, you'll see a plum orchard, valleys, and ridges.

PIHEA TRAIL   This is the park's flattest trail, but it's still a pretty strenuous 7⅖-mile round-trip. A new boardwalk on a third of the trail makes it easier, especially when it's wet. The trail begins at the end of Highway 550 at Puu o Kila Lookout, which overlooks Kalalau Valley; it goes down at first, and then flattens out as it traces the back ridge of the valley. Once it enters the rainforest, you'll see native plants and trees. It intersects with the Alakai Swamp Trail (below). If you combine both trails, figure on about 4 hours in and out.

ALAKAI SWAMP TRAIL 🛈   If you want to see the "real" Hawaii, this is it—a big swamp that's home to rare birds and plants. The trail allows a rare glimpse into a wet, cloud-covered wilderness preserve where rainfall of 460 inches a year is common. This 7-mile hike used to take 5 hours of sloshing through the bog, with mud up to your knees. Now a boardwalk protects you from the shoe-grabbing mud. Come prepared for rain. (The only silver lining is that there are no mosquitoes above 3,000 ft.)

The trail head is off Mohihi (Camp 10) Road, just beyond the Forest Reserve entrance sign and the Alakai Shelter picnic area. From the parking lot, the trail follows an old World War II four-wheel-drive road. Stick to the boardwalk, as this is a fragile eco-area (not to mention the mud). At the end of the 3½-mile slog, if you're lucky and the clouds part, you'll have a lovely view of Wainiha Valley and Hanalei from Kilohana Lookout.

Campgrounds & Wilderness Cabins in Kokee

CABINS & TENT CAMPGROUNDS   Camping facilities include state campgrounds (one next to Kokee Lodge, and four more primitive backcountry sites), one private tent area, and the **Kokee Lodge,** which has 12 cabins for rent at very reasonable rates. At 4,000 feet, the nights are cold, particularly in winter; because no open fires are permitted at Kokee, the best deal is the cabins (see "Accommodations You Can Afford," p. 518, for details). The **Kokee Lodge Restaurant** is open daily from 9am to 3:30pm for continental breakfast and lunch. Groceries and gas aren't available in Kokee, so stock up in advance, or you'll have to make the long trip down the mountain.

The **state campground** at Kokee allows tent camping only. Permits can be obtained from a state parks office on any island; on Kauai, it's at 3060 Eiwa St., Room 306, Lihue, HI 96766 (© **808/274-3444;** www.hawaii.gov/dlnr/dsp/fees.html). The permits are $5 per night; the time limit is 5 nights in a single 30-day period. Facilities include showers, drinking water, picnic tables, a pavilion with tables, restrooms, barbecues, sinks for dishwashing, and electric lights.

Tent camping at **Camp Sloggett,** owned by the Kauai YWCA, 3094 Elua St., Lihue, HI 96766 (© **808/335-6060;** fax 808/245-5961; http://campingkauai.com), is available for $10 per person per night (children under 5 stay free). The sites are on 1½ acres of open field, with a covered pit for fires and a barbecue area, plus volleyball and badminton nets. There's also a hostel-style accommodation at the **Weinburg Bunkhouse,** with bunk beds, separate toilets, showers, and kitchenettes ($20 per person). To get here, continue on the highway past park headquarters and take the first right after the Kokee Lodge. Follow the dirt road and look for the wooden CAMP SLOGGETT sign; turn right and follow the bumpy road past the state cabins into a large clearing.

BACKCOUNTRY CAMPING   The more primitive backcountry campgrounds include **Sugi Grove** and **Kawaikoi,** located about 4 miles from park headquarters on the Camp 10 Road, an often muddy and steep four-wheel-drive road. Sugi Grove is located across the Kawaikoi Stream from the Kawaikoi campsite. The area is named for the sugi pines, which were planted in 1937 by the Civilian Conservation Corps. This is a shady campsite with a single picnic shelter, a pit toilet, a stream, and space for several tents. The Kawaikoi site is a 3-acre open grass field, surrounded by Kokee plum trees and forests of koa and ohia. Facilities include two picnic shelters, a composting toilet, and a stream that flows next to the camping area. There is no potable water—bring in your own, or treat the stream water.

Permits, which are $5 per night, are available through the **State Parks Office,** 3060 Eiwa St., Lihue, HI 96766 (© **808/241-3444;** www.hawaii.gov/dlnr/dsp/fees.html). You're limited to 5 nights in any 30-day period.

BEACH CAMPING AT POLIHALE STATE PARK

Polihale holds the distinction of being the westernmost beach in the United States. The beach is spectacular—some 300 feet wide in summer, with rolling sand dunes (some as high as 100 ft.), and the islands of Niihau and Lehua just offshore. Bordered by a curtain of Na Pali Coast cliffs on the north, razor-sharp ridges and steep valleys to the east, and the blue Pacific on the south and west, this is one of the most dramatic camping areas in the state.

The campgrounds for tent camping are located at the south end of the beach, affording privacy from the daytime beach activities. There's great swimming in summer (even then, be on the lookout for waves and rip currents, as there are no lifeguards), some surfing (the rides are usually short), and fishing. The camping is on sand, although there are some kiawe trees for shade. (*Warning:* Kiawe trees drop long thorns, so make sure you have protective footwear.) Facilities include restrooms, showers, picnic tables, barbecues, and a spigot for drinking water. You can purchase supplies about 15 miles away in Waimea.

Permits, which are $5 per night, are available through the **State Parks Office,** 3060 Eiwa St., Lihue, HI 96766 (© **808/241-3444;** www.hawaii.gov/dlnr/dsp/fees.html). You're limited to 5 nights in any 30-day period. To reach the park from Lihue, take Highway 50 west to Barking Sands Pacific Missile Range. Bear right onto the paved road, which heads toward the mountains. There will be small signs directing you to Polihale; the second sign will point to a left turn onto a dirt road. Follow this for about 5 miles; at the fork in the road, the campgrounds are to the left and the beach park is to the right.

THE COCONUT COAST
THE SLEEPING GIANT TRAIL

This hardy hike takes you up the fabled mountain known as Sleeping Giant (which really does look like a giant resting on his back) to a fabulous view. The trail will gain 1,000 feet in altitude on a clearly marked trail (be sure to stay on the trail). The climb is steep and steadily uphill (remember you are climbing up a mountain), but the view at the top is well worth the constant incline. To get to the trail head, turn mauka (toward the mountain) off Kuhio Highway (Hwy. 56) onto Haleilio Road (between Wailua and Kapaa, just past mile marker 6); follow Haleilio Road for 1¼ miles to the parking area, at telephone pole number 38. From here, signs posted by the State of Hawaii Division of Forestry and Wildlife lead you over the 1¾-mile trail, which ends at a picnic table and shelter. The panoramic view is breathtaking. Be sure to bring water—and a picnic, if you like.

THE NORTH SHORE
NA PALI COAST STATE PARK

Simply put, the Na Pali Coast is the most beautiful part of the Hawaiian Islands. Hanging valleys open like green-velvet accordions, and waterfalls tumble to the sea from the 4,120-foot-high cliffs; the experience is both exhilarating and humbling. Whether you hike in, fly over, or take a boat cruise past, be sure to see this park.

Established in 1984, Na Pali Coast State Park takes in a 22-mile stretch of fluted cliffs that wrap around the northwest shore of Kauai between Kee Beach and Polihale State Park. Volcanic in origin, carved by wind and sea, "the cliffs" (*na pali* in Hawaiian), which heaved out of the ocean floor 200 million years ago, stand as constant reminders of majesty and endurance. Four major valleys—Kalalau, Honopu, Awaawapuhi, and Nualolo—crease the cliffs.

Unless you boat or fly in (see "Boating" on p. 559, or "A Bird's-Eye View of Waimea Canyon & the Na Pali Coast" on p. 575), the park is accessible only on foot—and it's not easy. An ancient footpath, the **Kalalau Trail,** winds through this remote, spectacular 6,500-acre park, ultimately leading to Kalalau Valley. Of all the green valleys in Hawaii, and there are many, only Kalalau is a true wilderness, probably the last wild valley in the islands. No road goes here, and none ever will. The remote valley is home to long-plumed tropic birds, golden monarch butterflies, and many of Kauai's 120 rare and endangered species of plants. The hike into the Kalalau Valley is grueling and takes most people 6 to 8 hours one-way.

Despite its inaccessibility, this journey into Hawaii's wilderness has become increasingly popular since the 1970s. Overrun with hikers, helicopters, and boaters, the Kalalau Valley was in grave danger of being loved to death. Strict rules about access have been adopted. The park is open to hikers and campers only on a limited basis, and you must have a permit (though you can hike the first 2 miles, to Hanakapiai Beach, without a permit). Permits are $10 per night and are issued in person at the **Kauai State Parks Office,** 3060 Eiwa St., Room 306, Lihue, HI 96766 (✆ **808/274-3444;** www.hawaii.gov/dlnr/dsp/fees.html). You can also request one by writing **Kauai Division of State Parks** at the address listed above. For more information, contact **Hawaii State Department of Land and Natural Resources,** 1151 Punchbowl St., Room 130, Honolulu, HI 96813 (✆ **808/587-0320**).

HIKING THE KALALAU TRAIL ★★

The trail head is at Kee Beach, at the end of Highway 560. Even if you only go as far as Hanakapiai, bring water.

THE FIRST 2 MILES: TO HANAKAPIAI BEACH   Do not attempt this hike unless you have adequate footwear (closed-toe shoes at least; hiking shoes are best), water, a sun visor, insect repellent, and adequate hiking clothes (shorts and T-shirt are fine, your bikini is not). It's only 2 miles to Hanakapiai Beach, but the first mile's all uphill. This tough trail takes about 2 hours one-way and dissuades many, but everyone should attempt at least the first half-mile, which gives a good hint of the startling beauty that lies ahead. Day hikers love this initial stretch, so it's usually crowded. The island of Niihau and Lehua Rock are often visible on the horizon. At mile marker 1, you'll have climbed from sea level to 400 feet; now it's all downhill to Hanakapiai Beach. Sandy in summer, the beach becomes bouldery when winter waves scour the coast. There are strong currents and no lifeguards, so swim at your own risk. You can also hike another 2 miles inland from the beach to **Hanakapiai Falls,** a 120-foot cascade. Allow 3 hours for that stretch.

THE REST OF THE WAY   Hiking the Kalalau is the most difficult and challenging hike in Hawaii, and one you'll never forget. Even the Sierra Club rates the 22-mile round-trip into Kalalau Valley and back as "strenuous"—this is serious backpacking. Follow the footsteps of ancient Hawaiians along a cliff-side path that's a mere 10 inches wide in some places, with sheer 1,000-foot drops to the sea. One misstep, and it's *limu* ("seaweed") time. Even the hardy and fit should allow at least 2 days to hike in and out (see below for camping information). Although the trail is usually in good shape, go in summer when it's dry; parts of it vanish in winter. When it rains, the trail becomes super slippery, and flash floods can sweep you away.

A park ranger is now on-site full time at Kalalau Beach to greet visitors, provide information, oversee campsites, and keep trails and campgrounds in order.

CAMPING IN KALALAU VALLEY & ALONG THE NA PALI COAST

You must obtain a camping permit, $5 per night, available through the **State Parks Office,** 3060 Eiwa St., Lihue, HI 96766 (© 808/241-3444). You're limited to 5 nights in any 30-day period. The camping season runs roughly from May or June to September (depending on the site). All campsites are booked almost a year in advance, so call or write well ahead of time. Stays are limited to 5 nights. Camping areas along the Kalalau Trail include **Hanakapiai Beach** (facilities are pit toilets, and water is from the stream; use iodine tablets to treat it), **Hanakoa Valley** (no facilities, water from the stream), **Milolii** (no facilities, water from the stream), and **Kalalau Valley** (composting toilets, several pit toilets, and water from the stream). Keep your camping permit with you at all times.

8 Great Golf & Other Affordable Outdoor Activities

GOLF

Kauai is a golfer's paradise; Robert Trent Jones, Jr. called it "the best island for golf there is." To get the most out of your travel dollar, book an afternoon tee-time at reduced or twilight rates (you can save up to 50% off).

For last-minute and discount tee times, call **Stand-by Golf** (© 888/645-BOOK; www.stand-bygolf.com) between 7am and 9pm. Stand-by offers discounted (up to 50% off greens fees), guaranteed tee times for same-day or next-day golfing.

In the listings below, the cart fee is included in the greens fee unless otherwise noted.

LIHUE & ENVIRONS

Kauai Lagoons Golf Courses   Choose between two excellent Jack Nicklaus–designed courses: the **Mokihana Course** (formerly known as the Lagoons Course), for the recreational golfer, or the **Kauai Kiele Championship Course** 🏌, for the low handicapper. The 6,942-yard, par-72 Mokihana is a links-style course with a bunker that's a little less severe than Kiele; emphasis is on the short game. The Kiele is a mixture of tournament-quality challenge and high-traffic playability; it winds up with one of Hawaii's most difficult holes, a 431-yard, par-4 played straightaway to an island green.

Facilities include a driving range, lockers, showers, a restaurant, a snack bar, a pro shop, practice greens, a clubhouse, and club and shoe rental; transportation from the airport is provided.

Kalapaki Beach, Lihue (less than a mile from Lihue Airport). ⓒ **800/634-6400** or 808/241-5061. www.kauai lagoonsgolf.com. Greens fees at Mokihana Course: $120 ($75 for guests of the Kauai Marriott; $85 for guests of other hotels and condos on Kauai) and $75 twilight; for the Kiele Course: $170 ($130 for Marriott guests; $145 for guests of other hotels and condos on Kauai) and $110–$115 twilight. From the airport, make a left on Kapule Hwy. (Hwy. 51) and look for the sign on your left.

THE POIPU RESORT AREA

Kiahuna Golf Club   This par-70, 6,353-yard Robert Trent Jones, Jr.–designed course plays around four large archaeological sites, ranging from an ancient Hawaiian temple to the remains of a Portuguese home and crypt built in the early 1800s. This Scottish-style course has rolling terrain, undulating greens, 70 sand bunkers, and near-constant winds. The 3rd hole, a par-3, 185-yarder, goes over Waikomo Stream. At any given time, just about half the players on the course are Kauai residents, the other half visitors. Facilities include a driving range, practice greens, and a snack bar.

2545 Kiahuna Plantation Dr. (adjacent to Poipu Resort area), Koloa. ⓒ **808/742-9595.** www.kiahunagolf.com. Greens fees: $90, twilight rates $50 (times for twilight rates may vary throughout the year). Take Hwy. 50 to Hwy. 520, bear left into Poipu at the fork in the road, and turn left onto Kiahuna Plantation Dr.

Kukuiolono Golf Course *(Finds)*   This is a fun 9-hole course in a spectacular location with scenic views of the entire south coast. You can't beat the price—$7 for the day, whether you play 9 holes or 90. The course is in Kukuiolono Park, a beautiful wooded area donated by the family of Walter McBryde. In fact, you'll see McBryde's grave on the course, along with some other oddities, like wild chickens, ancient Hawaiian rock structures, and Japanese gardens. Of course, there are plenty of trees to keep you on your game. When you get to the second tee box, check out the coconut tree dotted with yellow, pink, orange, and white golf balls that have been driven into the bark. Don't laugh—your next shot might add to the decor! This course shouldn't give you many problems—it's excellently maintained and relatively straightforward, with few fairway hazards. Facilities include a driving range, practice greens, club rental, a snack bar, and a clubhouse.

Kukuiolono Park, Kalaheo. ⓒ **808/332-9151.** Greens fees: $8 for the day; optional cart rental is $7 for 9 holes. Take Hwy. 50 into the town of Kalaheo; turn left on Papalina Rd., drive up the hill for nearly a mile, and watch for the sign on your right; the entrance has huge iron gates and stone pillars—you can't miss it.

Poipu Bay Resort Golf Course 🏌🏌   This 6,959-yard, par-72 course with a links-style layout is the home of the PGA Grand Slam of Golf. Designed by Robert Trent Jones, Jr., this challenging course features undulating greens and water hazards on eight of the holes. The par-4 16th hole has the coastline weaving along the entire left side. You can take the safe route to the right and maybe make par (but more likely bogey), or you can try to take it tight against the ocean and possibly make it in two. The most striking (and the most disrespectful) hole is the 201-yard, par-3 on the 17th, which has a tee built on an ancient Hawaiian stone formation. Facilities include a restaurant, a locker room, a pro shop, a driving range, and putting greens.

2250 Ainako St. (across from the Hyatt Regency Kauai), Koloa. ℂ 808/742-8711. www.kauai-hyatt.com. Greens fees: $185 ($125 Hyatt Regency guest); $120 afternoon play noon–3pm ($110 Hyatt Regency guest); $65 twilight rate after 3pm. Take Hwy. 50 to Hwy. 520; bear left into Poipu at the fork in the road; turn right on Ainako St.

THE NORTH SHORE
Princeville Golf Club, Prince Course ★★
Here's your chance to play one of the best golf courses in Hawaii. This Robert Trent Jones, Jr.–designed devil of a course sits on 390 acres molded to create ocean views from every hole. Some holes have a waterfall backdrop to the greens, others shoot into the hillside, and the famous par-4 12th has a long tee shot off a cliff to a narrow, jungle-lined fairway 100 feet below. This is the most challenging course on Kauai; accuracy is key here. Most of the time, if you miss the fairway, your ball's in the drink. "The average vacation golfer may find the Prince Course intimidating, but they don't mind, because it's so beautiful," Jones says. Facilities include a restaurant, a health club and spa, lockers, a clubhouse, a golf shop, and a driving range.

Princeville. ℂ 800/826-1105 or 808/826-5070. www.princeville.com/play/prince_desc.html. Greens fees: $175 ($150 for Princeville resort guests and $130 for Princeville Hotel guests) for the Prince Course; $125 ($110 for Princeville resort guests and $105 for Princeville Hotel guests) for the Makai Course. Take Hwy. 56 to mile marker 27; the course is on your right.

BIKING
There are a couple of great places on Kauai for two-wheeling: the **Poipu area,** which has wide, flat roads and several dirt-cane roads (especially around Mahaulepu); and the cane road between **Kealia Beach** and **Anahola,** north of Kapaa. For information on bikeways and maps, contact Ann Leighton, chair of the **Garden Island Resource, Conservation and Development Infrastructure Committee** (ℂ 808/639-3249).

The following places rent mountain bikes, from a low of $10 a day for cruisers to $15 to $20 a day for mountain bikes (with big discounts for multiple-day rentals): **Outfitters Kauai,** 2827A Poipu Rd. (look for the small five-shop mall before the road forks to Poipu/Spouting Horn), Poipu (ℂ 808/742-9667; www.outfitterskauai.com); and **Kauai Cycle and Tour,** 1379 Kuhio Hwy., Kapaa (ℂ 808/821-2115; www.bike hawaii.com/kauaicycle). For a great selection of high-quality mountain bikes at reasonable prices, it's worth the drive to **Pedal 'n Paddle,** in Hanalei (ℂ 808/826-9069; www.pedalnpaddle.com), which has not only high-grade Kona mountain bikes with Shimano components but also bikes with front-end suspension systems. Rentals start at $10 a day or $30 a week and include helmet, bike lock, and car rack. The shop even has kids' 20-inch BMX bikes. The knowledgeable folks here are more than happy to provide you with free maps and tell you about the best biking spots on the island.

GUIDED BIKE TOURS **Outfitters Kauai** ★ (ℂ 808/742-9667; www.outfitters kauai.com) offers a fabulous downhill bike ride from Waimea Canyon to the ocean. The 12-mile trip (mostly coasting) begins at 6am, when the van leaves the shop in Poipu and heads up to the canyon. By the time you've scarfed down the fresh-baked muffins and coffee, you're at the top of the canyon, just as the sun is rising over the rim—it's a remarkable moment. The tour makes a couple of stops on the way down for short, scenic nature hikes. You'll be back at the shop around 10am. The sunset trip follows the same route. Both tours cost $90 per adult; $70 children 12 to 14.

BIRDING

Kauai provides some of Hawaii's last sanctuaries for endangered native birds and oceanic birds, such as the albatross. If you didn't bring your binoculars, you can rent some at **Activity Warehouse,** 788 Kuhio Hwy. (across from McDonald's), Kapaa (© **800/343-2087** or 808/822-4000; www.travelhawaii.com), where rentals start at 99¢ a day.

At **Kokee State Park,** a 4,345-acre wilderness forest at the end of Highway 550 in southwest Kauai, you have an excellent chance of seeing some of Hawaii's endangered native birds. You might spot the apapane, a red bird with black wings and a curved black bill; or the iwi, a red bird with black wings, orange legs, and a salmon-colored bill. Other frequently seen native birds are the honeycreeper, which sings like a canary; the amakihi, a plain, olive-green bird with a long, straight bill; and the anianiau, a tiny yellow bird with a thin, slightly curved bill. The most common native bird at Kokee is the moa, or red jungle fowl, brought as domestic stock by ancient Polynesians. Ordinarily shy, they're quite tame in this environment. David Kuhn leads custom hikes, pointing out Hawaii's rarest birds on his **Terran Tours** (© **808/335-3313;** dkuhn99@hotmail.com), which range from a half-day to 3 days and feature endemic and endangered species.

Kilauea Point National Wildlife Refuge ⚑, a mile north of Kilauea on the North Shore (© **808/828-1413;** http://pacificislands.fws.gov/wnwr/kkilaueanwr.html), is a 200-acre headland habitat that juts above the surf and includes cliffs, two rocky wave-lashed bays, and a tiny islet that serves as a jumping-off spot for seabirds. You can easily spot red-footed boobies, which nest in trees, and wedge-tailed shearwaters, which burrow in nests along the cliffs. You may also see the great frigate bird, the Laysan albatross, the red-tailed tropic bird, and the endangered nene. Native plants and the Kilauea Point Lighthouse are highlights as well. The refuge is open from 10am to 4pm daily (closed on Thanksgiving, Christmas, and New Year's Day); admission is $3. Recently, the refuge temporarily suspended their popular 1-hour **guided hikes** up to the 568-foot summit of Crater Hill, which affords spectacular views. Call to see if they have resumed their hikes, which had taken place Monday through Thursday at 10am (the only fee is the $3 admission to the refuge), but you must make a reservation (© **808/828-0168**). To get here, turn right off Kuhio Highway (Hwy. 56) at Kilauea, just after mile marker 23; follow Kilauea Road to the refuge entrance.

Peaceful Hanalei Valley is home to Hawaii's endangered Koloa duck, gallinule, coot, and stilt. The **Hanalei National Wildlife Refuge** (© **808/828-1413;** http://pacificislands.fws.gov/wnwr/khanaleinwr.html) also provides a safe habitat for migratory shorebirds and waterfowl. It's not open to the public, but an interpretive overlook along the highway serves as an impressive vantage point. Along Ohiki Road, which begins at the west end of the Hanalei River Bridge, you'll often see white cattle egrets hunting crayfish in streams.

HORSEBACK RIDING

Only on Kauai can you ride a horse across the wide-open pastures of a working ranch under volcanic peaks and rein up near a waterfall pool. No wonder Kauai's *paniolo* (cowboys) smile and sing so much. Near the Poipu area, **CJM Country Stables,** 1731

Kelaukia St. (1⅗ miles beyond the Hyatt Regency Kauai), Koloa (© **808/742-6096;** www.cjmstables.com), offers both 2- and 3-hour escorted Hidden Valley beach rides. You'll trot over Hidden Valley ranch land, past secluded beaches and bays, along the Hauupu Ridge, across sugarcane fields, and to Mahaulepu Beach; it's worth your time and money just to get out to this seldom seen part of Kauai. The Secret Beach and Breakfast Ride costs $105 and includes breakfast. The 2-hour Hidden Beach Ride is $90. There's also a 3½-hour swim/beach/picnic ride for $115.

Princeville Ranch Stables, Highway 56 (just after the Princeville Airport), Hanalei (© **808/826-6777;** www.princevilleranch.com), has a variety of outings. The 1½-hour country ride takes in views of the Hanalei mountains and the vista of Anini Beach ($65), while the 3-hour adventure meanders along the bluffs of the North Shore to Anini Beach, where you tie off your horse and take a short stroll to the beach ($110). The 4-hour Waterfall Picnic Ride crosses ranch land, takes you on a short (but steep) hike to swimming pools at the base of waterfalls, and then feeds you a picnic lunch for $120. Riders must be in good physical shape, and don't forget to put your swimsuit on under your jeans. The Princeville Ranch Stables also offers other adventures, ranging from the less strenuous wagon rides to a cattle-drive ride.

TENNIS

The **Kauai County Parks and Recreation Department,** 4444 Rice St., Suite 150, Lihue (© **808/241-6670**), has a list of the nine county tennis courts around the island, all of which are free and open to the public. Private courts that are open to the public include the **Princeville Tennis Club,** Princeville Hotel (© **808/826-3620;** www.princeville.com), which has six courts available for $15 per person ($12 for guests) for 90 minutes. On the south side, try **Hyatt Regency Kauai Resort and Spa,** Poipu Resort (© **808/742-1234;** www.kauai-hyatt.com), which has four courts, available for $30 an hour; and **Kiahuna Swim and Tennis Club,** Poipu Road (just past the Poipu Shopping Village on the left), Poipu Resort (© **808/742-9533**), which has 10 courts renting for $10 per person per hour.

9 Seeing the Sights

No matter how much time you have on Kauai, make it a priority to see the North Shore. No doubt about it—this is Hawaii at its best. **Hanalei and the North Shore beaches** *❀❀❀* are, hands-down, Kauai's top attraction (see "Paradise Found: The North Shore," beginning on p. 582). The frequent rains are responsible for some of the most stunning scenery in the world. Even if you're staying in Southwest Kauai, be sure to spend at least a day driving the road to Hanalei; you'll want to leave time for at least a half dozen North Shore stops along the way.

ISLAND TOURS

Four-Wheel-Drive Backroad Adventure *❀*　If you want to get off the beaten path and see the "hidden" Kauai, this 4-hour tour follows a figure-eight path around Kauai, from Kilohana Crater to the Mahaulepu coastline. The tour, done in a four-wheel-drive van, not only stops at Kauai's well-known scenic spots, but also travels on sugarcane roads (on private property), taking you to places most people who live on Kauai have never seen. The guides are well versed in everything from native plants to Hawaiian history. Bring plenty of film.

Aloha Kauai Tours, 1702 Haleukana St., Lihue, HI 96766. ☎ **800/452-1113** or 808/245-8809. www.alohakauai
tours.com. Tours $65 adults, $50 children under 13. 11 and under; lunch is included.

A BIRD'S-EYE VIEW OF WAIMEA CANYON &
THE NA PALI COAST

If you can possibly afford the splurge, don't leave Kauai without seeing it from a helicopter. It's expensive, but worth it. It's also one of the only ways to glimpse Kauai's
fabled Na Pali coast, now that the number of boat trips has been curtailed. You can
take home memories of the thrilling ride up and over the Kalalau Valley on Kauai's
wild North Shore, and into the 5,200-foot vertical temple of Mount Waialeale, the
most sacred place on the island and the wettest spot on earth (and in some cases, you
can even take a video of your ride home). All flights leave from Lihue Airport.

Blue Hawaiian ★★★   Blue Hawaiian has been the Cadillac of helicopter tour companies on Maui and the Big Island for more than a decade, and recently they have
expanded their operations to Kauai. I strongly recommend that you try to book with
them first. Their operation is first-class, and the equipment is state-of-the-art in Hawaii:
American Eurocopter ECO-Star, which reduces noise in the helicopter by 50% and
allows 23% more interior room. Plus the craft has individual Business Class style seats,
two-way communication with the pilot, and expansive glass for incredible views. The
50-minute flights first journeys to Hanapepe Valley, then continues on to Mana Waia-
puna, commonly referred to as "Jurassic Park Falls." Next it's up the Olokele Canyon,
then on to the Waimea Canyon, the famed "Grand Canyon of the Pacific." Most of the
flight then will be along the Na Pali Coast, before heading out to the Bali Hai Cliffs, and
the pristine blue waters of Hanalei Bay and the Princeville Resort area. If the weather
gods are on your side, you've got to see the highest point on Kauai: Mt Waialeale, the
wettest spot on earth, with an average rainfall of 450 to 500 inches annually. Your flight
will take you right into the center of the crater with its 5,000-foot walls towering above
and its 3,000-foot waterfalls surrounding you, something you will remember forever.

Harbor Mall staging area, 3501 Rice St., Lihue (take off from the Lihue Airport). ☎ **800/745-2583** or 808/245-5800.
www.bluehawaiian.com. 50-min. tour $210 ($179 if you book online).

Air Kauai Helicopters ★   Since 1988, Chuck DiPiazza has been flying visitors over
Kauai without an incident. He flies custom-designed A-STAR helicopters with high-
back leather seats and huge windows (37% larger than most helicopters). The pilot sits
on the left side of the helicopter (instead of the usual position on the right), which not
only allows a better view but also more leg room. Another plus: All his helicopters
have BOSE Acoustic Noise Canceling Stereo Headsets. Ask for Captain Chuck; his
commentaries are informative and down to earth, he welcomes questions, and he loves
to show off his multi-CD disk player, combining the "right" music to the tour.

3651 Ahukini Rd., Lihue. ☎ **800/972-4666** or 808/246-4666. www.airkauai.com. The 60-min. tour is $253, but men-
tion Frommer's and they will discount it to $190.

Island Helicopters ★   Curt Lofstedt has been flying helicopter tours of Kauai for
nearly 3 decades. He personally selects and trains professional pilots with an eye not
only to their flying skills but also to their ability to share the magic of Kauai. All flights
are in either the four-passenger Bell Jet Ranger III or the six-passenger Aerospatiale
ASTAR, with extra-large windows and stereo headsets to hear the pilot's personal narration. You'll be able to relive your memories of the Na Pali Coast and Nualolo Aina
(the Valley of the Lost Tribes) with a complimentary video of your trip.

Lihue Airport, Lihue. (℄ **800/829-5999** or 808/245-8588. www.islandhelicopters.com. 55-min. island tour $250. Mention Frommer's and receive 37% off.

Jack Harter ☝   The pioneer of helicopter flights on Kauai, Jack was the guy who started the sightseeing-via-helicopter trend. On the 60-minute tour, he flies a four-passenger Bell Jet Ranger Model 204 (with just installed "scenic view" windows), a six-seater A-star, or a Eurocopter AS350BA A-star. The 90-minute tour (in the Bell Jet Ranger only) hovers over the sights a bit longer than the 60-minute flight, so you can get a good look, but we found the shorter tour pretty sufficient.

4231 Ahukini Rd., Lihue. (℄ **888/245-2001** or 808/245-3774. www.helicopters-kauai.com. 60- to 65-min. tour $199; 90- to 95-min. tour $269 (book on the Internet and save up to 15%).

Ohana Helicopter Tours   Hawaiian-born pilot Bogart Kealoha delights in showing his island his way—aboard one of his four-passenger Bell Jet Rangers or his six-passenger Aerospatiale A-Star helicopter. You're linked to a customized audio entertainment system through individual headsets with narration as you swoop over and through 12-mile-long Waimea Canyon on a memorable sightseeing flight that also includes the valleys and waterfalls of the Na Pali Coast.

Anchor Cove Shopping Center, 3416 Rice St., Lihue. (℄ **800/222-6989** or 808/245-3996. www.ohana-helicopters. com. 50-min. tour $185; 65-min tour $240.

Will Squyres Helicopter Tours   The 60-minute flight starts in Lihue and takes you through Waimea Canyon, along the Na Pali Coast, and over Waialeale Crater and the two sets of waterfalls that appeared in *Fantasy Island*. Will's A-star six-passenger copter has side-by-side seats (nobody sits backward and everybody gets a window seat) and enlarged windows. A veteran pilot, Will has flown several thousand hours over Kauai since 1984 and knows the island, its ever-changing weather conditions, and his copters.

3222 Kuhio Hwy., Lihue. (℄ **888/245-4354** or 808/245-8881. www.helicopters-hawaii.com. 60-min. Grand Tour of Kauai $208.

LIHUE & ENVIRONS

Grove Farm Homestead Museum   You can experience a day in the life of an 1860s sugar planter on a visit to Grove Farm Homestead, which shows how good life was (for some, anyway) when sugar was king. This is Hawaii's best remaining example of a sugar-plantation homestead. Founded in 1864 by George N. Wilcox, a Hanalei missionary's son, Grove Farm was one of the earliest of Hawaii's 86 sugar plantations. A self-made millionaire, Wilcox died a bachelor in 1933, at age 94. His estate looks much like it did when he lived here, complete with period furniture, plantation artifacts, and Hawaiiana.

4050 Nawiliwili Rd. (Hwy. 58) at Pikaka St. (2 miles from Waapa Rd.), Lihue. (℄ **808/245-3202.** Requested donation $5 adults, $2 children under 12. Tours offered Mon and Wed–Thurs at 10am and 1pm; reservations required.

Kauai Museum ☝ *Kids*   The history of Kauai is kept safe in an imposing Greco-Roman building that once served as the town library. This great little museum is worth a stop before you set out to explore the island. It contains a wealth of historical artifacts and information tracing the island's history from the beginning of time through Contact (when Captain James Cook "discovered" Kauai in 1778), the monarchy period, the plantation era, and the present. You'll hear tales of the Menehune (the mythical elflike people who were said to build massive stoneworks in a single night) and see old poi pounders and idols, relics of sugar planters and *paniolos*, a nice seashell collection, old

Hawaiian quilts, feather leis, a replica of a plantation worker's home, and much more—even a model of Cook's ship, the HMS *Resolution,* riding anchor in Waimea Bay. Vintage photographs by W. J. Senda, a Japanese immigrant, show old Kauai, while a contemporary video, shot from a helicopter, captures the island's natural beauty.

4428 Rice St., Lihue. © 808/245-6931. www.kauaimuseum.org. Admission $5 adults, $4 seniors, $3 students 13–17, $1 children 6–12. Mon–Fri 9am–4pm; Sat 10am–4pm. Admission is free on "Family Day," the 1st Sat of every month.

THE POIPU RESORT AREA

No Hawaii resort has a better entrance: On Maluhia Road, eucalyptus trees planted in 1911 as a wind break for sugarcane fields now form a monumental **tree tunnel.** The leafy green, cool tunnel starts at Kaumualii Highway; you'll emerge at the golden-red beach.

Prince Kuhio Park   This small roadside park is the birthplace of Prince Jonah Kuhio Kalanianaole, the "People's Prince," whose March 26 birthday is a holiday in Hawaii. He opened the beaches of Waikiki to the public in 1918 and served as Hawaii's second territorial delegate to the U.S. Congress. What remains here are the foundations of the family home, a royal fish pond, and a shrine where tributes are still paid in flowers.

Lawai Rd., Koloa. Just after mile marker 4 on Poipu Rd., veer to the right of the fork in the road; the park is on the right side.

Spouting Horn ★ *Kids*   This natural phenomenon is second only to Yellowstone's Old Faithful. It's quite a sight—big waves hit Kauai's south shore with enough force to send a spout of funneled saltwater 10 feet or more up in the air; in winter, the water can get as high as six stories.

Spouting Horn is different from other blowholes in Hawaii, in that it has an additional hole that blows air that sounds like a loud moaning. According to Hawaiian legend, this coastline was once guarded by a giant female lizard (*Mo'o*); she would gobble up any intruders. One day, along came Liko, who wanted to fish in this area. Mo'o rushed out to eat Liko. Quickly, Liko threw a spear right into the giant lizard's mouth. Mo'o then chased Liko into a lava tube. Liko escaped, but legend says Mo'o is still in the tube, and the moaning sound at Spouting Horn is her cry for help.

At Kukuiula Bay, beyond Prince Kuhio Park (see above).

Discover the Legendary Little People

According to ancient Hawaiian legend, among Kauai's earliest settlers were the Menehune, a race of small people who worked at night to accomplish magnificent feats. Above Nawiliwili Harbor, the **Menehune Fish Pond**—which, at one time, extended 25 miles—is said to have been built in just 1 night, with two rows of thousands of Menehune passing stones hand to hand. The Menehune were promised that no one would watch them work, but one person did; when they discovered the spy, they stopped working immediately, leaving two gaps in the wall. From Nawiliwili Harbor, take Hulemalu Road above Huleia Stream; look for the HAWAII CONVENTION AND VISITORS BUREAU marker at a turnoff in the road, which leads to the legendary fish pond. Kayakers can paddle up Huleia Stream to see it up close.

Allerton Garden of the National Tropical Botanical Garden ☆ Discover an extraordinary collection of tropical fruit and spice trees, rare Hawaiian plants, and hundreds of varieties of flowers at the 186-acre preserve known as **Lawai Gardens,** said to be the largest collection of rare and endangered plants in the world. Adjacent, **McBryde Garden,** a royal home site of Queen Emma in the 1860s, is known for its formal gardens, a delicious kind of colonial decadence. It's set amid fountains, streams, waterfalls, and European statuary. Endangered green sea turtles can be seen here (their home in the sea was wiped out years ago by Hurricane Iniki). The tours are fascinating for green thumbs and novices alike.

Visitor Center, Lawai Rd. (across the street from Spouting Horn), Poipu. ℂ 808/742-2623. www.ntbg.org. Guided 2½-hr. tours by reservation only, Mon–Sat at 9am, 10am, 1pm, and 2pm. Self-guided tours of McBryde Garden Mon–Sat 9am–4pm, $15 (trams into the valley leave once an hour on the half-hour, last tram 2:30pm); guided tour Mon 9:30am, $30. Reserve a week in advance in peak months of July–Sept.

WESTERN KAUAI
WAIMEA TOWN

If you'd like to take a self-guided tour of this historic town, stop at the **Waimea Library,** at mile marker 23 on Highway 50, to pick up a map and guide to the sites.

Kiki a Ola (Menehune Ditch) Hawaiians were expert rock builders, able to construct elaborate edifices without using mortar. They formed long lines and passed stones hand over hand, and lifted rocks weighing tons with ropes made from native plants. Their feats gave rise to fantastic tales of Menehune; elflike people hired by Hawaiian kings to create massive stoneworks in a single night—reputedly for the payment of a single shrimp (see "Discover the Legendary Little People," above). An excellent example of ancient Hawaiian construction is Kiki a Ola, the so-called Menehune Ditch, with cut and dressed stones that form an ancient aqueduct that still directs water to irrigate taro ponds. Historians credit the work to ancient Hawaiian engineers who applied their knowledge of hydraulics to accomplish flood control and irrigation. Only a 2-foot-high portion of the wall can be seen today; the rest of the marvelous stonework is buried under the roadbed.

From Hwy. 50, go inland on Menehune Rd.; a plaque marks the spot about 1½ miles up.

Russian Fort Elizabeth State Historical Park To the list of all who tried to conquer Hawaii, add the Russians. In 1815, a German doctor tried to claim Kauai for Russia. He even supervised the construction of a fort in Waimea, but he and his handful of Russian companions were expelled by Kamehameha I a couple of years later. Now a state historic landmark, the Russian Fort Elizabeth (named for the wife of Russia's Czar Alexander I) is on the eastern headlands overlooking the harbor, across from Lucy Kapahu Aukai Wright Beach Park. The fort, built Hawaiian style with stacked lava rocks in the shape of a star, once bristled with cannons; it's now mostly in ruins. You can take a free, self-guided tour of the site, which affords a keen view of the west bank of the Waimea River, where Captain Cook landed, and of the island of Niihau across the channel.

Hwy. 50 (on the ocean side, just after mile marker 22), east of Waimea.

THE GRAND CANYON OF THE PACIFIC: WAIMEA CANYON ★★★

The great gaping gulch known as Waimea Canyon is quite a sight. This valley, known for its reddish lava beds, reminds everyone who sees it of the Grand Canyon. Kauai's version is bursting with ever-changing color, just like its namesake, but it's smaller—only a mile wide, 3,567 feet deep, and 12 miles long. A massive earthquake sent all the streams flowing into a single river that ultimately carved this picturesque canyon. Today, the Waimea River—a silver thread of water in the gorge, sometimes a trickle, often a torrent, but always there—keeps cutting the canyon deeper and wider, and nobody can say what the result will be 100 million years from now.

You can stop by the road and look at the canyon, hike down into it, or swoop through it in a helicopter. For more information, see "Hiking & Camping" (p. 564), "Horseback Riding" (p. 573), and "A Bird's-Eye View of Waimea Canyon & the Na Pali Coast" (p. 575).

THE DRIVE THROUGH WAIMEA CANYON & UP TO KOKEE

By car, there are two ways to visit Waimea Canyon and reach Kokee State Park, 20 miles up from Waimea. From the coastal road (Hwy. 50), you can turn up Waimea Canyon Drive (Hwy. 550) at Waimea town, or you can pass through Waimea and turn up Kokee Road (Hwy. 55) at Kekaha. The climb is very steep from Kekaha, but Waimea Canyon Drive, the rim road, is narrower and rougher. A few miles up, the two merge into Kokee Road.

The first good vantage point is **Waimea Canyon Lookout,** located between mile markers 10 and 11 on Waimea Canyon Road. From here, it's another 6 miles to Kokee. There are a few more lookout points along the way that also offer spectacular views, such as **Puu Hina Hina Lookout,** between mile markers 13 and 14, at 3,336 feet; be sure to pull over and spend a few minutes pondering this natural wonder. (The giant white object that looks like a golf ball and defaces the natural landscape is a radar station left over from the Cold War.)

KOKEE STATE PARK

It's only 16 miles from Waimea to Kokee, but it's a whole different world because the park is 4,345 acres of rainforest. You'll enter a new climate zone, where the breeze has a bite and trees look quite continental. You're in a cloud forest on the edge of the Alakai Swamp, the largest swamp in Hawaii, on the summit plateau of Kauai. Days are cool and wet, with intermittent bright sunshine, not unlike Seattle on a good day. Bring your sweater, and, if you're staying over, be sure you know how to light a fire (overnight lows dip into the 40s).

The forest is full of native plants, such as mokihana berry, ohia lehua tree, iliau (similar to Maui's silversword), and imports like Australia's eucalyptus and California's redwood. Pigs, goats, and black-tailed deer thrive in the forest, but the moa, or Polynesian jungle fowl, is the cock of the walk.

Right next to Kokee Lodge (which lies on the only road through the park, about a mile before it ends) is the **Kokee Natural History Museum** (© **808/335-9975;** www.kokee.org), open daily from 10am to 4pm (free admission). This is the best place to learn about the forest and Alakai Swamp before you set off hiking in the wild. The museum shop has great trail information and local books and maps, including the official park trail map. We recommend getting the *Pocket Guide on Native Plants on the Nature Trail for Kokee State Park* and the *Road Guide to Kokee and Waimea Canyon State Park.*

A **nature walk** is the best intro to this rainforest; it starts behind the museum at the rare Hawaiian koa tree. This easy, self-guided walk of about one-tenth of a mile takes about 20 minutes if you stop and look at all the plants, identified along the way.

Two miles above Kokee Lodge is **Kalalau Lookout** ✯, the spectacular climax of your drive through Waimea Canyon and Kokee. When you stand at the lookout, below you is a work in progress that began at least five million years ago. It's hard to stop looking; the view is breathtaking, especially when light and cloud shadows play across the red-and-orange cliffs.

There's lots more to see and do up here: Anglers fly-fish for rainbow trout, and hikers tackle the 45 trails that lace the Alakai Swamp (see "Watersports" on p. 558 or "Hiking & Camping" on p. 564). That's a lot of ground to cover, so you might want to plan on staying over. If pitching a tent is too rustic for you, the wonderful **cabins** set in a grove of redwoods are one of the best lodging bargains in the islands (see "Accommodations You Can Afford," p. 518). The restaurant at **Kokee Lodge** is open for continental breakfast and lunch, daily from 9am to 3:30pm.

For advance information, contact the **State Division of Parks,** P.O. Box 1671, Lihue, HI 96766 (✆ **808/335-5871**); and the **Kokee Lodge Manager,** P.O. Box 819, Waimea, HI 96796 (✆ **808/335-6061**). The park is open daily year-round. The best time to go is early in the morning, to see the panoramic view of Kalalau Valley from the lookout at 4,000 feet, before clouds obscure the valley and peaks.

THE COCONUT COAST

Fern Grotto   This is one of Kauai's oldest (since 1946) and most popular tourist attractions. Several times daily a 157-passenger motorized barge takes people up and down the river on a 90-minute, 2½-mile, river trip to a natural amphitheater filled with ferns. A steady flow of water from a plantation created reservoir above the cavern keeps them happy and growing. The drought of the past few years, coupled with the closing of the plantation, and thus cutting off the supply of water, made the place dry up. But the Hawaii Tourism Authority and Kauai County are spending $440,000 to refurbish the Fern Grotto. The grotto is the source of many Hawaiian legends and a popular site for weddings. The Smith family now has a monopoly on the tours, as a circuit court judge evicted the Waialeale Boat Tours from the river in August 2004 because the company had not paid rent for use of the state-owned marina and Fern Grotto State Park for more than 4 years (and owed more than $100,000).

Smith's Motor Boats (✆ 808/821-6892; www.smithskauai.com) Wailua Marina. Daily 9am–3:30pm. Admission $16 adults, $8 children 2–12; reservations recommended. At the mouth of the Wailua River; turn off Kuhio Hwy. (Hwy. 56) into Wailua Marine State Park.

WAILUA RIVER STATE PARK

Ancients called the Wailua River "the river of the great sacred spirit." Seven temples once stood along this 20-mile river, which is fed by 5,148-foot Mount Waialeale, the wettest spot on earth. You can go up Hawaii's biggest navigable river by boat or kayak (see "Boating" on p. 559 and "Kayaking" on p. 561), or drive Kuamoo Road (Hwy. 580; sometimes called the King's Highway), which goes inland along the north side of the river from Kuhio Highway (Hwy. 56)—from the northbound lane, turn left at the stoplight just before the ruins of Coco Palms Resort. Kuamoo Road goes past the *heiau* (temple) and historical sites to Opaekaa Falls and Keahua Arboretum, a State Division of Forestry attempt to reforest the watershed with native plants.

The entire district from the river mouth to the summit of Waialeale was once royal land. This sacred, historical site was believed to be founded by Puna, a Tahitian priest who, according to legend, arrived in one of the first double-hulled voyaging canoes to come to Hawaii, established a beachhead, and declared Kauai his kingdom. All of

Moments Pilgrimage to a Hindu Temple

Believe it or not, a sacred Hindu temple is being carved out of rocks from India and constructed on the banks of the Wailua River. The **San Marga Iraivan Temple** is being built to last "a thousand years or more" on the 458-acre site of the Saiva Siddhanta Church monastery. Not expected to be completed until 2010, the Chola-style temple is the result of a vision by the late Satguru Sivaya Subramuniyaswami, known to his followers as Gurudeva, the founder of the church and its monastery. He specifically selected this site in 1970, recognizing that the Hawaiians also felt the spiritual power of this place, which the Hawaiians call *pihanakalani* (where heaven touches the earth).

The concrete foundation is 68 feet by 168 feet and 3 feet thick, designed not to crack under the weight of the 3.2 million-pound temple, dedicated to the Hindu god Shiva. The public is welcome to the monastery temple, open daily from 9am to noon. There also is a weekly guided tour of the grounds that includes the San Marga Iraivan Temple. The weekly tours vary depending on the retreat schedule at the monastery. For information, call ⓒ **808/822-3012**, ext. 198, or visit www.saivasiddhanta.com/hawaii.

A few suggestions if you plan to visit: carry an umbrella (it's very rainy here), wear what the Hindus call "modest clothing" (certainly no shorts, short dresses, T-shirts, or tank tops); Hindu dress is ideal. Also, there are lots of people around, so don't leave valuables in your car.

How to get there: Turn mauka (left, inland) off Kuhio Highway (Hwy. 56) at the lights, just after crossing over the bridge, onto Kuamoo Road (between Coco Palms Hotel and the Wailua River). Continue up the hill for just over 4 miles. One-quarter mile past the 4-mile marker, turn left on Kaholalele Road and go 1 block to the end of the road. The Information Center is at 107 Kaholalele Rd. Park on Temple Lane; enter the open pavilion. A guide will be there to escort you through the monastery. You can also visit the Sacred Rudraksha Forest at 7345 Kuamo'o Rd. for meditation (open 6am–6pm) or the Nepalese Ganesha Shrine and Bangalore Gallery, which are located at 107 Kaholalele Rd.

Kauai's *alii* (royalty) are believed to be descended from Puna. Here, in this royal settlement, are remains of the seven temples, including a sacrificial *heiau,* a planetarium (a simple array of rocks in a celestial pattern), the royal birthing stones, and a stone bell to announce a royal birth. (You can still ring the bell—many people have—but you should be prepared to make an announcement when it stops ringing.)

There's a nice overlook view of 40-foot **Opaekaa Falls** ★★ 1½ miles up Highway 580. This is probably the best-looking drive-up waterfall on Kauai. With the scenic peaks of Makaleha mountains in the background and a restored Hawaiian village on the river banks, these falls are what the tourist-bureau folks call an "eye-popping" photo op.

Near Opaekaa Falls overlook is **Poliahu Heiau,** the large lava-rock temple of Kauai's last king, Kaumualii, who died on Oahu in 1824 after being abducted by King Kamehameha II. If you stop here, you'll notice two signs. The first, an official 1928

Kids Kauai Children's Discovery Museum

This is every parent's dream: an enthralling, hands-on learning adventure to take kids on rainy days (hey, it's so much fun, the kids will be begging to come back even on sunny days). The **Kauai Children's Discovery Museum,** located under the Whale Tower, in the Kauai Village Shopping Center, in Kapaa (© 808/823-8222; ww.kcdm.org), arose out of a grass roots community effort to have a fun place where kids could learn about science, culture, arts, technology and nature. Not only are the hands-on, interactive exhibits thrilling to kids, but it's a great place for your kids to interact and meet children from Kauai. The 7,000-square-foot play-center is open Tuesday through Saturday, 9am to 5pm, and during school breaks they also are open on Monday, 7am to 5pm. In addition to the exhibits, which range from playing with Hawaiian musical instruments to participating in virtual reality television to hiding out in a "magic tree house" and reading a book (there's even a baby area for kids four and under), there also are *Keiki* Camps (Children Camps), where you can leave the kids all day and they will take them out to various outings to the beach and to points of interest. Admission is $3.50 for kids and $4.50 for adults, with family memberships available.

bronze territorial plaque, says that the royal *heiau* was built by Menehunes, which it explains parenthetically as "Hawaiian dwarves or brownies." A more recent, hand-painted sign warns visitors not to climb on the rocks, which are sacred to the Hawaiian people.

SLEEPING GIANT

If you squint your eyes just so as you pass the 1,241-foot-high Nounou Ridge, which forms a dramatic backdrop to the coastal villages of Wailua and Waipouli, you can see the fabled Sleeping Giant. On Kuhio Highway, just after mile marker 7, around the mini-mall complex Waipouli Town Center, look *mauka* (inland) and you may see what appears to be the legendary giant named Puni, who, as the story goes, fell asleep after a great feast. If you don't see it at first, visualize it this way: His head is Wailua and his feet are Kapaa. For details on an easy hike, suitable for the entire family, to the top of the Sleeping Giant, see "Hiking & Camping," p. 564.

PARADISE FOUND: THE NORTH SHORE ★★★
ON THE ROAD TO HANALEI

The first place everyone should go on Kauai is Hanalei. The drive along **Kuhio Highway** (Hwy. 56, which becomes Hwy. 560 after Princeville to the end of the road), displays Kauai's grandeur at its absolute best. Just before Kilauea, the air and the sea change, the light falls in a different way, and the last signs of development are behind you. Now there are roadside fruit stands, a little stone church in Kilauea, two roadside waterfalls, and a long, stiltlike bridge over the Kalihiwai Stream and its green river valley.

If you don't know a guava from a mango, stop in Kilauea at the cool, shady **Guava Kai Plantation,** at the end of Kuawa Road (© **808/828-6121**), for a refreshing, free treat. After you take a walk through the orchards and see what a guava looks like on the tree, you can sample the juice of this exotic pink tropical fruit (which also makes a great jam or jelly—sold here, too). The plantation is open daily from 9am to 5pm.

Birders might want to stop off at **Kilauea Point National Wildlife Refuge,** a mile north of Kilauea, and the **Hanalei National Wildlife Refuge,** along Ohiki Road, at the west end of the Hanalei River Bridge. (For details, see "Birding," on p. 573.) In the Hanalei Refuge, along a dirt road on a levee, you can see the **Hariguchi Rice Mill,** now a historic treasure.

Now the coastal highway heads due west and the showy ridgelines of Mount Nama-hana create a grand amphitheater. The two-lane coastal highway rolls over pastures of grazing cattle, past a tiny airport and the luxurious Princeville Hotel.

Five miles past Kilauea, just past the Princeville Shopping Center, is **Hanalei Valley Lookout** ✰. Big enough for a dozen cars, this lookout attracts crowds of people who peer over the edge into the 917-acre Hanalei River Valley. So many shades of green: rice green, taro green, and green streams lace a patchwork of green ponds that back up to green-velvet Bali Ha'i cliffs. Pause to catch the first sight of taro growing in irrigated ponds; maybe you'll see an endangered Hawaiian black-necked stilt. Don't be put off by the crowds; this is definitely worth a look.

Farther along, a hairpin turn offers another scenic look at Hanalei town; then you cross the **Hanalei Bridge.** The Pratt truss steel bridge, pre-fabbed in New York City, was erected in 1912; it's now on the National Registry of Historic Landmarks. If it ever goes out, the nature of Hanalei will change forever; currently, this rusty, one-lane bridge (which must violate all kinds of Department of Transportation safety regula-tions) isn't big enough for a tour bus to cross. Good bridge etiquette calls for you to stop before crossing the bridge to make sure no cars are coming. If cars in front of you are crossing the bridge, the rule of thumb is that three to five cars go at one time, and then traffic should stop and give the cars on the other side of the bridge an opportu-nity to cross. You're on vacation, so what's your hurry?

You'll drive slowly past the **Hanalei River banks** and Bill Mowry's **Hanalei Buf-falo Ranch,** where 200 American bison roam in the tropic sun; you may even see buf-falo grazing in the pastures on your right. The herd is often thinned to make buffalo patties. (You wondered why there was a Buffalo Burger on the Ono Family Restaurant menu, didn't you?)

Just past Tahiti Nui, turn right on Aku Road before Ching Young Village, then take a right on Weke Road; **Hanalei Beach Park** ✰, one of Hawaii's most gorgeous, is a half block ahead on your left. Swimming is excellent here year-round, especially in summer, when Hanalei Bay becomes a big, placid lake; for details, see "Beaches," p. 552.

If this exquisite 2-mile-long beach doesn't meet your expectations, head down the highway, where the next 7 miles of coast yield some of Kauai's other spectacular beaches, including **Lumahai Beach** ✰, of *South Pacific* movie fame; **Tunnels Beach** ✰, where the 1960s puka-shell necklace craze began; and **Haena Beach Park** ✰, a fabulous place

---

Impressions

Puff, the magic dragon lived by the sea, and frolicked in the autumn mist in a land called Hanalei . . .

—Peter, Paul, and Mary, "Puff, the Magic Dragon"

Kauai's North Shore: Princeville & Hanalei

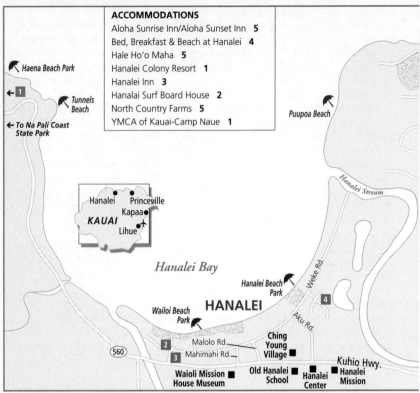

ACCOMMODATIONS
Aloha Sunrise Inn/Aloha Sunset Inn **5**
Bed, Breakfast & Beach at Hanalei **4**
Hale Ho'o Maha **5**
Hanalei Colony Resort **1**
Hanalei Inn **3**
Hanalai Surf Board House **2**
North Country Farms **5**
YMCA of Kauai-Camp Naue **1**

Haena Beach Park

Tunnels Beach

To Na Pali Coast State Park

Puupoa Beach

Hanalei Stream

Hanalei Princeville
Kapaa
KAUAI
Lihue

Hanalei Bay

Hanalei Beach Park

HANALEI

Wailoi Beach Park

Weke Rd.

Aku Rd.

560

Malolo Rd.
Mahimahi Rd.

Ching Young Village ■

Kuhio Hwy.

Waioli Mission House Museum ■

Old Hanalei School ■

Hanalei Center ■

Hanalei Mission ■

to kick back and enjoy the waves, particularly in summer (see "Beaches," p. 552). Once you've found your beach, stick around until sundown, and then head back to one of the North Shore's restaurants for a mai tai and a fresh seafood dinner. Another day in paradise.

ATTRACTIONS ALONG THE WAY

Ka Ulu O Laka Heiau   On a knoll above the boulders of Kee Beach stands a sacred altar of rocks, often draped with flower leis and ti-leaf offerings, dedicated to Laka, the goddess of hula. Dancers (men and women) of Hawaii's hula *halau* (schools) climb the cliff, bearing small gifts of flowers. In Hawaiian myths, Lohiau, a handsome chief, danced here before the fire goddess Pele; their passion became *Haena,* which means "the heat." The site is filled with what Hawaiians call *mana,* or power.

From the west side of Kee Beach, take the footpath across the big rocks almost to the point; then climb the steep grassy hill.

Limahuli Garden of the National Tropical Botanical Garden   Out on Kauai's far North Shore, beyond Hanalei and the last wooden bridge, there's a mighty cleft in the coastal range where ancestral Hawaiians lived in what can only be called paradise. Carved by a waterfall stream known as Limahuli, the lush valley sits at the foot of steepled cliffs that Hollywood portrayed as Bali Hai in the film classic *South Pacific.* This small, almost secret garden is ecotourism at its best. It appeals not just to

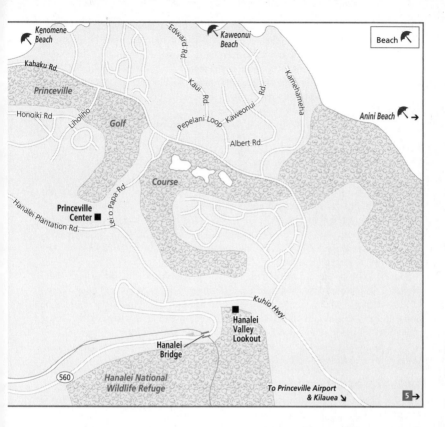

green thumbs but to all who love Hawaii's great outdoors. Here botanists hope to save Kauai's endangered native plants. You can take the self-tour to view the plants, which are identified in Hawaiian and English. From taro to sugarcane, the mostly Polynesian imports tell the story of the people who cultivated the plants for food, medicine, clothing, shelter, and decoration. In addition, Limahuli's stream is sanctuary to the last five species of Hawaiian freshwater fish.

Visitor Center, ½ mile past mile marker 9 on Kuhio Hwy. (Hwy. 560), Haena. © **808/826-1053.** Fax 808/826-1394. www.ntbg.org. Admission $10 self-guided, $15 guided; free for children 12 and under. Open Tues–Fri and Sun 10am–4pm. Advance reservations required for 2½-hr. guided tours. During peak seasons of July–Sept, book at least a week ahead.

Na Aina Kai Botanical Gardens ★★★ *Finds*   Do not miss this incredible, magical garden on some 240 acres, sprinkled with some 70 life-size (some larger than life-size) whimsical bronze statues, hidden off the beaten path of the North Shore. This is the place for both avid gardeners as well as people who think they don't like botanical gardens. They have everything: waterfalls, pools, arbors, topiaries, colonnades, gazebos, a maze you will never forget, a lagoon with spouting fountains, a Japanese teahouse, and an enchanting path along a bubbling stream to the ocean. The imaginary, fairy-tale creativity that has gone into these grounds will be one of your fondest memories of Kauai. A host of different tours is available, from 1½ hours ($25) to 5 hours ($70) long, ranging from casual, guided strolls to riding in the covered CarTram to treks from one end of the gardens to the ocean. Currently the tours are open to adults and children 13 years and older. For younger kids there is a magical tropical children's garden with a gecko hedge maze, a tropical jungle gym, a treehouse in a rubber tree, and a 16-foot tall Jack-and-the-Beanstalk Giant with a 33-foot wading pool below. It's only open 3 days a week; book a tour before you leave for Hawaii so you won't be disappointed.

4101 Wailapa Rd. (write: P.O. Box 1134), Kilauea, HI 96754. 📞 808/828-0525. Fax 808/828-0815. www. naainakai.com. Open Tues–Thurs 8am–5pm. Tours vary. Advance reservations strongly recommended. To get there from Lihue, drive north past mile marker 21 and turn right on Wailapa Rd. At road's end drive through the iron gates. From Princeville, drive south 6½ miles and take the 2nd left past mile marker 22 on Wailapa Rd. At road's end drive through the iron gates.

Waioli Mission House Museum   If you're lucky and time your visit just right, you can visit this 150-year-old mission house, which serves today as a living museum. It's a real treasure. Others in Honolulu are easier to see, but the Waioli Mission House retains its sense of place and most of its furnishings, so you can really get a clear picture of what life was like for the New England missionaries who came to Kauai to convert the heathens to Christianity.

Most mission houses are small, dark Boston cottages that violate the tropical sense of place. This two-story wood-frame house, built in 1836 by Abner and Lucy Wilcox of New Bedford, Massachusetts, is an excellent example of hybrid architecture. The house features a lanai on both stories, with a cookhouse in a separate building. It has a lava-rock chimney, ohia-wood floors, and Hawaiian koa furniture.

Kuhio Hwy. (Hwy. 560), just behind the green Waioli Huia Church, Hanalei. 📞 808/245-3202. Free admission (donations gratefully accepted). Tours: Mon, Wed, and Thurs, 10am and 1pm. Reservations required.

THE END OF THE ROAD

The real Hawaii begins where the road stops. This is especially true on Kauai—for at the end of Highway 56, the spectacular **Na Pali Coast** begins. To explore it, you have to set out on foot, by boat, or by helicopter. For details on experiencing this region, see "Hiking & Camping" (p. 564), "Boating" (p. 559), and "A Bird's-Eye View of Waimea Canyon & the Na Pali Coast" (p. 575).

10 Shops & Galleries

Shopping is a pleasure on this island. Where else can you browse vintage Hawaiiana practically in a cane field, buy exquisite home accessories in an old stone building built in 1942, and get a virtual agricultural tour of the island through city-sponsored green markets that move from town to town throughout the week, like a movable feast? At Kauai's small, tasteful boutiques, you can satisfy your shopping ya-yas in concentrated spurts around the island. This is a bonanza for the boutique shopper, the one who appreciates the thrill of the hunt.

"Downtown" Kapaa continues to flourish, and Hanalei, touristy as it is, is still a shopping destination. (Ola's and Yellowfish make up for the hurricane of trinkets and trash in Hanalei.) Kilauea, with Kong Lung Store and the fabulous new Lotus Gallery, is the style center of the island. The Kaua'i Heritage Center of Hawaiian Culture & the Arts makes it possible for visitors to escape the usual imitations, tourist traps, and clichés in favor of authentic encounters with the real thing: Hawaiian arts, Hawaiian cultural practices, and Hawaiian elders and artists.

GREEN MARKETS & FRUIT STANDS   The county of Kauai sponsors regular weekly **Sunshine Markets** (© **808/241-6390;** www.kauai.hawaii.gov) throughout the island, featuring fresh Kauai **Sunrise papayas** (sweeter, juicier, and redder than most), herbs and vegetables used in ethnic cuisines, exotic fruit such as rambutan and atemoya, and the most exciting development in pineapple agriculture, the low-acid white pineapple called **Sugarloaf,** rarer these days but still spottily available. These markets, which sell the full range of fresh local produce and flowers at rock-bottom prices, present the perfect opportunity to see what's best and what's in season. Farmers sell their bounty from the backs of trucks or at tables set up under tarps.

The biggest market is at **Kapaa New Town Park,** in the middle of Kapaa town, on Wednesday at 3pm. The Sunshine Market in **Lihue,** held on Friday at 3pm at the Vidhina Stadium Parking Lot, is close in size and extremely popular. The schedule for the other markets: **Koloa Ball Park,** Monday at noon; **Kalaheo Neighborhood Center,** Papalina Road off Kaumualii, Tuesday at 3pm; **Hanapepe Park,** Thursday at 3pm; **Kilauea Neighborhood Center,** Keneke off Lighthouse Road, Thursday at 4:30pm; and **Kekaha Neighborhood Center,** Elepaio Road, Saturday at 9am. Whenever possible, go early and shop briskly, especially at the Koloa Market, which draws hundreds of shoppers.

On the North Shore, Kilauea is the agricultural heart of the island, with two weekly green markets: the county-sponsored **Sunshine Market,** Thursday at 4:30pm at the Kilauea Neighborhood Center; and the private Kilauea Quality Farmers Association (mostly organic growers) **Farmers' Market,** Saturday from 11:30am to 1:30pm behind the Kilauea Post Office. Everything in the wide-ranging selection is grown or made on Kauai, from rambutan and long beans to sweet potatoes, corn, lettuce, and salsas and chutneys.

Also on the North Shore, about ¼ mile past Hanalei in an area called Waipa, the **Hawaiian Farmers of Hanalei**—anywhere from a dozen to 25 farmers—gather along the main road with their budget-friendly, just-picked produce. This market is held every Tuesday at 2pm. You'll find unbelievably priced papayas (in some seasons, several for a dollar, ready to eat), organic vegetables, inexpensive tropical flowers, avocados and mangoes in season, and, when possible, fresh seafood. The best of the best, in season, are rose apples, mountain apples, and the orange-colored papaya lilikoi.

On the south shore, we're hearing great things about the two adorable fruit stands in Lawai, where you can find inexpensive bananas (sometimes $1.25 a hand!), papayas, and avocados along an old country road. The fruit is cheerfully displayed, and sometimes it's sold on the honor system—leave the money if no one is there. This is country style nonpareil. (From Kaumualii Hwy., turn at the corner where Mustard's Last Stand is—Lauoho Rd.—then take the first right.) In Kauai jargon, directions would be: "Go to that old road where the old post office was, near Matsuura Store, the old manju place. . . ."

Closer to the resorts, in Poipu, with a view across asparagus fields and the chiseled ridges of Haupu Mountain, the **Poipu Southshore Market** sells produce, some of it by Haupu Growers, daily from 10am to 6pm on Koloa Bypass Road. Haupu Growers is the major supplier of Kauai asparagus, and this is where you'll find it. Asparagus season begins in October.

LIHUE & ENVIRONS

DOWNTOWN LIHUE   The gift shop of the **Kauai Museum,** 4428 Rice St. (© **808/245-6931**), is your best bet for made-on-Kauai arts and crafts, from Niihau-shell leis to woodwork, lauhala and coconut products, and more. The master of lauhala weaving, Esther Makuaole, weaves regularly in the gallery on Monday and Wednesday from 9am to 1:30pm.

About a mile north of the Lihue Airport, on Highway 56 (Kuhio Hwy.), **Kauai Fruit & Flower** is a great stop for flowers, including the rare Kauai maile in season, coconut drums the owner makes himself, Hawaiian gourds *(ipu)*, cut flowers for shipping, and Kauai fruit, such as papayas and pineapples. Other products include lauhala gift items, teas, Kauai honey, Kauai salad dressings, jams and jellies, and custom-made gift baskets.

The **Kukui Grove Center,** at Kaumualii Highway (Hwy. 50) and Old Nawiliwili Road, was once the commercial center of the island, but it's been staggering under the weight of change. It may be in for some good juju now that Steve Case (of AOL Time Warner) has bought landowner Grove Farm. Until they make some changes, however, there remain many empty spaces. **Long's Drugs** provides for basic needs, and the **Kauai Products Store** (© 808/246-6753) is a fount of local handicrafts (about 60% Kauai artists) and a respectable showcase for made-on-the-island products, such as soaps, paintings, clothing, coffee, Kukui guava jams, fabrics, and Niihau-shell leis. The Hawaiian quilts are made in the Philippines but designed by Kauai families. You'll find everything from a $1,200 teak table to bamboo chairs and koa ukulele by Raymond Rapozo in Kealia, who does stunning work. Beware the macadamia-nut fudge, found only at Kauai Products Store: It's rich, sweet, and irresistible. Across the mall is the **Deli and Bread Connection** (© 808/245-7715), which sells soups, sandwiches, and deli items as well as pots, china, and hundreds of kitchen gadgets.

KILOHANA PLANTATION Kilohana, the 35-acre Tudor-style estate that sprawls across the landscape in Puhi, on Highway 50 between Lihue and Poipu, is an architectural marvel that houses a sprinkling of galleries and shops. At the **Country Store,** on the ground level, you'll find island and American crafts of decent quality, koa accessories, pottery, and Hawaii-themed gift items. On the other side of Gaylord's, the **Kilohana and Kahn galleries** offer a mix of crafts and two-dimensional art, from originals to affordable prints, at all levels of taste.

THE POIPU RESORT AREA

Expect mostly touristy shops in Poipu, the island's resort mecca; here you'll find T-shirts, souvenirs, black pearls, jewelry, and the usual quota of tired marine art and trite hand-painted silks.

Exceptions: The formerly characterless **Poipu Shopping Village,** at 2360 Kiahuna Plantation Dr., is shaping up to be a serious shopping stop. **Hale Mana** is a glorious collection of hard-to-find gift items of excellent taste: fabulous incense sticks from Provence (lavender, amber, vanilla), antique picture frames, lacquer boxes, beaded bags, unique candles, sterling-silver chopsticks, sake sets, pillows, masks, Hawaiian handmade paper, and jewelry by Kauai artist Adove. The staggering selection also includes dramatic acrylic jewelry that looks like elk horn, one-of-a-kind jewelry and purses by Maya, gemlike sake cups, cotton yukata, silk kimono, snuff bottles, and diaphanous silk dresses that you won't find elsewhere in Hawaii. Also in Poipu Shopping Village, the tiny **Bamboo Lace** boutique lures the fashionistas; its resort wear and accessories can segue from Hawaii to the south of France in one easy heartbeat. Across the courtyard, **Sand People** is great for understated resort wear (such as Tencel jeans) and Indonesian coconut picture frames, while the newly renovated **Overboard** rides the wave of popularity in aloha wear and surf stuff.

The shopping is surprisingly good at the **Hyatt Regency Kauai,** with the footwear mecca **Sandal Tree, Water Wear Hawaii** for swim stuff, **Reyn's** for top-drawer aloha shirts, **Kauai Kids** for the children, and **McInery,** an institution in Hawaii for aloha wear.

Across the street from Poipu Beach, on Hoone Road, **Nukumoi Surf Shop** is a pleasant surprise: an excellent selection of sunglasses, swimwear, surf equipment, and watersports regalia, and not just for the under-20 crowd.

In neighboring **Old Koloa Town,** you'll find everything from **Lappert's Ice Cream** and **Island Soap and Candle Works** (where you can watch them make soap and candles) to **Crazy Shirts** and **Sueoka Store** on Koloa's main drag, Koloa Road. Just walk the long block for gifts, souvenirs, sun wear, groceries, soaps and bath products, and everyday necessities, but don't expect dazzling temptations.

On Poipu Road between Koloa and Poipu, in the tiny Poipu Plaza mini-mall, nestled next to **Sea Sport Divers** and **Outfitters Kauai,** the **Kukuiula Store** is a stop for everything from produce and sushi to paper products, sunscreen, beverages, and groceries. Occasionally, when the fishermen drop by, the store offers fresh sliced sashimi and poke, quite delicious and popular for sunset picnickers and nearby condo residents.

In Kalaheo, condo dwellers and locals are flocking to the nondescript, single building, **Medeiros Farms,** 4365 Papalina Rd. (✆ **808/332-8211**), for everything they raise and make: chicken, range-fed beef, eggs, Italian pork, and Portuguese sausages. The meats are hailed across the island and the prices are good. Medeiros Farms chicken is so good it's mentioned on some of the chichi menus on the island. Just up the street is **The Bread Box,** 4447 Papalina Rd. (✆ **808/332-9000**), for just-baked breads (a deal at $3.25), gooey mac-nut rolls ($1.50), a huge variety of muffins (poppyseed, blueberry, honey oat, etc.) and wonderfully light and flaky croissants (only $1).

WESTERN KAUAI

HANAPEPE   This West Kauai hamlet is becoming a haven for artists, but finding them requires some vigilance. The center of town is off Highway 50; turn right on Hanapepe Road just after Eleele if you're driving from Lihue. First, you'll smell the sumptuous lavender **Taro Ko Chips Factory** ✿, located in an old green plantation house, 3940 Hanapape Rd. Cooking in a tiny, modest kitchen at the east end of town, these famous taro chips are handmade by the farmers who grow the taro in a nearby valley. Despite their breakable nature, these chips make great gifts to go. To really impress them back home, get the lihi mung–flavored chips.

Farther on, Hanapepe Road is lined with gift shops and galleries, including **Koa Wood Gallery** and its koa furniture, koa photo albums, and Norfolk pine bowls; and the corny but cherubic **Aloha Angels,** where everything is angel-themed or angel-related. The **Kauai Village Gallery** offers abstract and surreal paintings by Kauai artist Lew Shortridge, while nearby **Kauai Fine Arts** offers an odd mix that works: antique maps and prints of Hawaii, authentic Polynesian tapa, rare wiliwili-seed leis, old Matson liner menus, and a few pieces of contemporary island art. Down the street, the **Kim Starr Gallery,** showing only Kim Starr's oil paintings, pastels, drawings, and limited-edition graphics, is a strong positive note in Hanapepe's art community. Taking a cue from Maui's Lahaina, where every Friday night is Art Night, Hanapepe's gallery owners and artists recently instituted the **Friday Night Art Walk** every Friday from 6 to 9pm. Gallery owners take turns hosting this informal event along Hanapepe Road.

WAIMEA   Neighboring Waimea is filled more with edibles than art, with Kauai's favorite native supermarket, **Big Save,** serving as the one-stop shop for area residents and passersby heading for the uplands of Kokee State Park, some 4,000 feet above this sea-level village. A cheerful distraction for lovers of Hawaiian collectibles is **Collectibles and Fine Junque,** on Highway 50, next to the fire station on the way to Waimea Canyon. This is where you'll discover what it's like to be the proverbial bull in a china shop (even a knapsack makes it hard to get through the aisles). Heaps of vintage linens, choice aloha shirts and muumuus, rare glassware (and junque, too), books, ceramics, authentic 1950s cotton chenille bedspreads, and a back room full of bargain-priced secondhand goodies always capture our attention. You never know what you'll find in this tiny corner of Waimea.

Up in Kokee State Park, the gift shop of the **Kokee Natural History Museum** (© 808/335-9975) is *the* stop for botanical, geographical, historical, and nature-related books and gifts, not only on Kauai, but on all the islands. Audubon bird books, hiking maps, and practically every book on Kauai ever written line the shelves.

THE COCONUT COAST

As you make your way from Lihue to the North Shore, you'll pass **Bambulei** (© 808/823-8641), bordering the canefield in Wailua next to Caffè Coco. Watch for the sign just past the Wailua intersection, across from Kintaro's Restaurant. Bambulei houses a charming collection of 1930s and 1940s treasures—everything from Peking lacquerware to exquisite vintage aloha shirts to lamps, quilts, jewelry, parrot figurines, and zany salt and pepper shakers. If it's not vintage, it will look vintage, and it's bound to be fabulous. Vintage muumuus are often in perfect condition, and dresses go for $20 to $2,000.

Wood turner **Robert Hamada** (© 808/822-3229) works in his studio at the foot of the Sleeping Giant, quietly producing museum-quality works with unique textures and grains. His skill, his lathe, and more than 60 years of experience bring luminous life to the kou, milo, kauila, camphor, mango, and native woods he logs himself. Hamada was honored by the Kauai Museum in May 2001, when his private collection of woods was displayed in the main lobby in honor of his 80th birthday.

KAPAA   Moving toward Kapaa on Highway 56 (Kuhio Hwy.), don't get your shopping hopes up; until you hit Kapaa town, quality goods are slim in this neck of the woods. The **Coconut Marketplace** features the ubiquitous Elephant Walk gift shop, Gifts of Kauai, and various other underwhelming souvenir and clothing shops sprinkled among the sunglass huts. Our favorite shop here is the unassuming **Overboard,** a small but tasteful boutique with great aloha shirts by Kahala, Tommy Bahama, Duke Kahanamoku, and other top labels for men and women.

Nearby, set back from the main road across from Foodland supermarket, **Marta's Boat** is one of the island's more appealing boutiques for children and women. The shop is a tangle of accessories, toys, chic clothing, and unusual gift items.

In the green-and-white wooden storefronts of nearby **Kauai Village,** you'll find everything from **Wyland Galleries'** trite marine art to yin chiao Chinese cold pills and organic produce at **Papayas Natural Foods.** Although its prepared foods are way overpriced, Papayas carries the full range of health-food products and is your only choice in the area for vitamins, prepared health foods to go, health-conscious cosmetics, and bulk food items. **ABC, Long's Drugs,** and **Safeway** are the familiar anchors for groceries and staples.

A stone's throw from that is the **Waipouli Variety Store,** Kapaa's version of Maui's fabled Hasegawa General Store—a tangle of fishing supplies, T-shirts and thongs, beach towels, and souvenirs. Fishermen love this store as much as cookie lovers swear by nearby **Popo's Cookies,** the best store-bought cookies on the island. Popo's chocolate-chip, macadamia-nut, chocolate–macadamia nut, chocolate-coconut, almond, peanut butter, and other varieties of butter-rich cookies are among the most sought-after food items to leave the island.

And Kapaa town is full of surprises. On the main strip, across from Sunnyside Market, you'll find the recently expanded **Kela's Glass Gallery** (© 808/822-4527), the island's showiest showplace for handmade glass in all sizes, shapes, and prices, with the most impressive selection in Hawaii. Go nuts over the vases and studio glass pieces, functional and nonfunctional, and then stroll along this strip of storefronts to **Kebanu Gallery** (© 808/823-6820), **Hula Girl** (© 808/822-1950), and **South China Sea Trading Company** (© 808/823-8655), and see if you can resist their wares. While Kebanu's pottery, fountains, candleholders, jewelry, wood works, and glass works are attractive gifts to go, South China's Asian accents make you want to move in for good. Here's the South China seascape: everything from mosquito netting to carved doors, inexpensive bead necklaces to a coconut inlaid armoire for $2,500. We love the fragrance of rush and reed; the amber tones of Indonesian, Vietnamese and Filipino crafts; the coconut rice paddles and kitchen accessories; and the sumptuous Indonesian silk sarongs, of high quality and reasonable prices. Meanwhile, at Hula Girl, a wonderful whimsy prevails: aloha shirts (very pricey, however), vintage-looking luggage covered with decals of old Hawaii, Patrice Pendarvis prints, zoris, sunglasses, and shells.

Down the street, **Earth Beads,** on the main drag (Hwy. 56), sells beads, jewelry, gemstones, and crafts materials, along with a small selection of gifts and accessories. Across the street is the town's favorite fashion stop, **Island Hemp & Cotton,** where Hawaii's most stylish selection of this miracle fabric is sold: gorgeous silk-hemp dresses, linen-hemp sportswear, hemp aloha shirts, Tencel clothing, T-shirts, and wide-ranging, attractive, and comfortable clothing and accessories that have shed the hippie image. It's also a great store for gift items, from Balinese leather goods to handmade paper, jewelry, luxury soaps, and natural-fiber clothing for men and women. A few doors to the north, **Orchid Alley** gets our vote for most adorable nursery on the island. A narrow alcove opens into a greenhouse of phalaenopsis, oncidiums, dendrobiums, and dozens of brilliant orchid varieties for shipping or hand-carrying.

THE NORTH SHORE

Kauai's North Shore is the premier shopping destination on the island. Stylish, sophisticated galleries and shops, such as **Kong Lung,** in a 1942 Kilauea stone building (the last to be built on the Kilauea Plantation) off Highway 56 on Kilauea Road (© 808/828-1822), have launched these former hippie villages as top-drawer shopping spots. Save your time, energy, and, most of all, discretionary funds for this end of the island. Kong Lung, through all its changes, including pricier merchandise in every category, remains a showcase of design, style, and quality, from top-of-the-line dinnerware and bath products to aloha shirts, jewelry, ceramics, women's wear, stationery, and personal and home accessories. The book selection is fabulous, and the home accessories—sake sets, tea sets, lacquer bowls, handblown glass, and pottery—are unequaled in Hawaii. It's expensive, but browsing here is a joy.

Directly behind Kong Lung is newcomer **Lotus Gallery** (© 808/828-9898), a showstopper for lovers of antiques and designer jewelry. The serenity and beauty will envelop you from the moment you remove your shoes to step in the door and onto the bamboo floor. There are gems, crystals, Tibetan art, antiques and sari clothing from India, 12th-century Indian bronzes, temple bells, Oriental rugs, pearl bracelets—items from $30 to

$50,000. Owners Kamalia (jewelry designer) and Tsajon Von Lixfeld (gemologist) have a staggering sense of design and discovery.

In Hanalei, at **Ola's,** by the Hanalei River on the Kuhio Highway (Hwy. 560) after the bridge, before the main part of Hanalei town (© **808/826-6937**), Sharon and Doug Britt, an award-winning artist, have amassed a head-turning assortment of American and island crafts, including Doug's paintings and the one-of-a-kind furniture that he makes out of found objects, driftwood, and used materials. Britt's works—armoires, tables, lamps, bookshelves—often serve as the display surfaces for others' work, so look carefully. Lundberg Studio handblown glass, exquisite jewelry, intricately wrought pewter switch plates, sensational handblown goblets, and many other fine works fill this tasteful, seductive shop. Be on the lookout for the wonderful koa jewel boxes by local woodworker Tony Lydgate.

From health foods to groceries to Bakelite jewelry, the **Ching Young Village Shopping Center,** in the heart of Hanalei, covers a lot of bases. It's more funky than fashionable, but Hanalei, until recently, has never been about fashion. People take their time here, and there are always clusters of folks lingering at the few tables outdoors, where tables of Kauai papayas beckon from the entrance of **Hanalei Health and Natural Foods.** Next door, **Hot Rocket** is ablaze with aloha shirts, T-shirts, Reyn Spooner and Jams sportswear, flamingo china, backpacks and pareus, swimwear, and, for collectors, one of the finest collections of Bakelite accessories you're likely to see in the islands.

Next door to Ching Young Village is **On the Road to Hanalei** (© **808/826-7360**), worth your time to wander around and check out the unusual T-shirts (great gifts to take home because they don't take up much suitcase space), scarves, jewelry, and other unique gifts.

Across the street in the **Hanalei Center,** the standout boutique is the **Yellowfish Trading Company** (© **808/826-1227**), where owner Gritt Benton's impeccable eye and zeal for collecting are reflected in the 1920s to 1940s collectibles: menus, hula-girl nodders, hula lamps, rattan and koa furniture, vases, bark-cloth fabric, retro pottery and lamp bases, must-have vintage textiles, and wonderful finds in books and aloha shirts.

11 Kauai After Dark

Suffice it to say that you don't come to Kauai to trip the light fantastic. This is the island for winding down—from New York, Houston, or even the hiking trails of Kokee or the Na Pali Coast. But there are a few nightlife options.

As the former plantation community, and now county seat, Lihue is a place where local residents live and work. For action after sunset, music, dancing, and bars, the hotels and resorts are the primary players. There are a few local places, but generally all is quiet in Lihue after dark.

The **Coconut MarketPlace,** 4–484 Kuhio Hwy., Kapaa (© **808/822-3641**), has a free hula show every day at 5pm.

The **Kauai Marriott Resort & Beach Club,** 3610 Rice St., Nawiliwili (© **808/245-5050**), has a host of nightlife activities, including a torch–lighting ceremony and sunset hula show on the beach every Monday and Thursday. **Duke's Canoe Club's Barefoot Bar** (© **808/246-9599**) has traditional and contemporary Hawaiian music nightly. On Tropical Fridays, tropical drinks go for $4 from 4 to 6pm, when live music stirs up the joint.

The south shore, with the sunset view and miles of white sand beaches, is a great place for nightlife. At the far end of Poipu, the **Stevenson's Library** at the **Hyatt Regency Kauai Resort and Spa,** 1571 Poipu Rd., Koloa (© **808/742-1234;** www.kauai-hyatt.com), is the place for an elegant after-dinner drink with live jazz nightly from 8 to 11pm.

Also in Poipu, **Keoki's Paradise,** in the Poipu Shopping Village, 2360 Kiahuna Plantation Dr. (© **808/742-7534**), offers live music Thursday and Friday evenings from 8:30 to 10pm, with the cafe menu available from 11am to 11:30pm. Hawaiian, reggae, and contemporary music draw the 21-and-over dancing crowd.

The **Poipu Shopping Village** also offers free hula performances every Tuesday and Thursday at 5pm in the outdoor courtyard.

Down the street at **Sheraton Kauai Resort,** 2440 Hoonani Rd. (© **808/742-1661**), **The Point,** on the water, is the Poipu hotspot. Live music Wednesday through Saturday with dancing to a range of different artists from contemporary Hawaiian to good ole rock 'n' roll.

Beyond Poipu, in the old plantation community of Hanapepe, every Friday is **Hanapepe Art Night** from 5 to 9pm. Each one is unique. Participating galleries take turns being the weekly "host gallery," offering original performances or demonstrations, which become the theme for that art night. All the galleries are lit up and decked out, giving the town a special atmosphere. Enjoy a stroll down the streets of quaint, historic Hanapepe Town and meet the local artists. Also in Hanapepe on Friday nights, the **Hanapepe Cafe & Espresso Bar,** 3830 Hanapepe Rd. (© **808/ 335-5011**), is open for dinner from 6 to 9pm and has live music.

Up on the North Shore, Hanalei has some action, primarily at **Sushi & Blues,** in Ching Young Village (© **808/826-4105**). Reggae, rhythm and blues, rock, and good music by local groups draw dancers and revelers Wednesday, Thursday, and Sunday from 8:30pm on. The format changes often here, so call ahead to see who's playing.

Across the street, the **Hanalei Gourmet,** in the Old Hanalei Schoolhouse, 5–5161 Kuhio Hwy. (© **808/826-2524**), has live music every night. Down the road, **Tahiti Nui** (© **808/826-6277**), is a great place to "experience" old Hawaii. Stop by for an exotic drink, and "talk story" with the owner, Louise Marston, who actually is from Tahiti.

Just down the road, Princeville has several nightlife spots. **Hanalei Bay Resort,** 5380 Honoiki St. (© **808/826-6522;** www.hanaleibayresort.com), is a music lover's gem, with a Sunday Jazz Jam in its **Happy Talk Lounge** from 3 to 7pm and again on Saturday from 6:30 to 9:30pm.

Over at the **Princeville Resort Kauai,** 5520 Kahaku Rd. (© **808/826-9644;** www.princeville.com), in the main lobby, the **Living Room** (filled with comfy, overstuffed furniture), has a range of nightlife activities, like a Hawaiian ceremony of chanting, dancing, and an entertaining talk on Hawaiian culture, from 6:30pm on Tuesday, Thursday, and Sunday, and other island-related entertainment from 7 to 11pm the rest of the week.

Appendix:
Hawaii in Depth

Today, other tropical islands are closing in on the 50th state's position as the world's premier beach destination. But Hawaii isn't just another pretty place in the sun. There's an undeniable quality ingrained in the local culture and lifestyle—the quick smiles to strangers, the feeling of family, the automatic extension of courtesy and tolerance. It's the aloha spirit.

1 History 101

Paddling outrigger canoes, the first ancestors of today's Hawaiians followed the stars and birds across a trackless sea to Hawaii, which they called "the land of raging fire." Those first settlers were part of the great Polynesian migration that settled the vast triangle of islands stretching from New Zealand in the southwest to Easter Island in the east to Hawaii in the north. No one is sure exactly when they came to Hawaii from Tahiti and the Marquesas Islands, some 2,500 miles to the south, but a dog-bone fish hook found at the southernmost tip of the Big Island has been carbon-dated to A.D. 700.

An entire Hawaiian culture arose from these settlers. Each island became a separate kingdom. The inhabitants built temples, fish ponds, and aqueducts to irrigate taro plantations. Sailors became farmers and fishermen. The *alii* (high-ranking chiefs) created a caste system and established taboos. Ritual human sacrifices were common.

THE "FATAL CATASTROPHE" No ancient Hawaiian ever imagined a *haole* (a white person; literally, one with "no breath") would ever appear on one of these "floating islands." But then one day, in 1779, just such a person sailed into Waimea Bay on Kauai, where he was welcomed as the god Lono.

The man was 50-year-old Captain James Cook, already famous in Britain for "discovering" much of the South Pacific. Now on his third great voyage of exploration, Cook had set sail from Tahiti northward across uncharted waters to find the mythical Northwest Passage that was said to link the Pacific and Atlantic oceans. On his way, Cook stumbled upon the Hawaiian Islands quite by chance. He named them the Sandwich Islands, for the Earl of Sandwich, first lord of the admiralty, who had bankrolled the expedition.

Overnight, Stone-Age Hawaii entered the age of iron. Gifts were presented and objects traded: nails for fresh water, pigs, and the affections of Hawaiian women. The sailors brought syphilis, measles, and other diseases to which the Hawaiians had no natural immunity, thereby unwittingly wreaking havoc on the native population.

After his unsuccessful attempt to find the Northwest Passage, Cook returned to Kealakekua Bay on the Big Island, where a fight broke out over an alleged theft, and the great navigator was killed by a blow to the head. After this "fatal catastrophe," the British survivors sailed home. But Hawaii was now on the sea charts. French, Russian, American, and other traders on the fur route between Canada's Hudson Bay Company and China anchored in Hawaii to get fresh water. More trade—and more disastrous liaisons—ensued.

Two more sea captains left indelible marks on the islands: The first was American John Kendrick, who, in 1791, stripped Hawaii of its sandalwood and sailed to China. The second captain was Englishman George Vancouver, who, in 1793, left cows and sheep, which spread out to the high-tide lines. King Kamehameha I sent to Mexico and Spain for cowboys to round up the wild livestock, thus beginning the islands' *paniolo* (Hawaiian cowboy) tradition.

The tightly woven Hawaiian society, enforced by royalty and religious edicts, began to unravel after the death in 1819 of King Kamehameha I, who had used guns seized from a British ship to unite the islands under his rule. One of his successors, Queen Kaahumanu, abolished the old taboos, thus opening the door for religion of another form.

STAYING TO DO WELL   In April 1820, God-fearing missionaries arrived from New England, bent on converting the pagans. Intent on instilling their brand of rock-ribbed Christianity on the islands, the missionaries clothed the natives, banned them from dancing the hula, and nearly dismantled their ancient culture. They tried to keep the whalers and sailors out of the bawdy houses, where a flood of whiskey quenched fleet-sized thirsts, and the virtue of native women was never safe. They taught reading and writing, created the 12-letter Hawaiian alphabet, started a printing press, and began recording the islands' history, until then only an oral account in remembered chants.

Children of the missionaries became the islands' business leaders and politicians. They married Hawaiians and stayed on in the islands, causing one wag to remark that the missionaries "came to do good and stayed to do well." In 1848, King Kamehameha III proclaimed the Great Mahele (division), which enabled commoners and, eventually, foreigners to own crown land. In two generations, more than 80% of all private land was in *haole* hands. Sugar planters imported waves of immigrants to work the fields as contract laborers. The first Chinese came in 1852, followed by Japanese in 1885, and Portuguese in 1878.

King David Kalakaua was elected to the throne in 1874. This popular "Merrie Monarch" built Iolani Palace in 1882, threw extravagant parties, and lifted the prohibitions on the hula and other native arts. For this, he was much loved. He also gave Pearl Harbor to the United States; it became the westernmost bastion of the U.S. Navy. In 1891, King Kalakaua visited chilly San Francisco, caught a cold, and died in the royal suite of the Sheraton Palace. His sister, Queen Liliuokalani, assumed the throne.

A SAD FAREWELL   On January 17, 1893, a group of American sugar planters and missionary descendants, with the support of gun-toting U.S. Marines, imprisoned Queen Liliuokalani in her own palace, where she penned the sorrowful lyric "Aloha Oe," Hawaii's song of farewell. The monarchy was dead.

A new republic was established, controlled by Sanford Dole, a powerful sugarcane planter. In 1898, through annexation, Hawaii became an American territory ruled by Dole. His fellow sugarcane planters, known as the Big Five, controlled banking, shipping, hardware, and every other facet of economic life on the islands.

Oahu's central Ewa Plain soon filled with row crops. The Dole family planted pineapple on its vast acreage. Planters imported more contract laborers from Puerto Rico (1900), Korea (1903), and the Philippines (1907–31). Most of the new immigrants stayed on to establish families and become a part of the islands. Meanwhile, the native Hawaiians became a landless minority.

For nearly a century on Hawaii, sugar was king, generously subsidized by the U.S. government. The sugar planters dominated the territory's economy, shaped its social fabric, and kept the islands in a colonial-plantation era with bosses and field hands. But the workers eventually struck for higher wages and improved working conditions, and the planters found themselves unable to compete with cheap third-world labor costs.

THE TOURISTS ARRIVE Tourism proper began in the 1860s. Kilauea volcano was one of the world's prime attractions for adventure travelers, who rode on horseback 29 miles from Hilo to peer into the boiling hellfire. In 1865, a grass version of Volcano House was built on the Halemaumau Crater rim to shelter visitors; it was Hawaii's first tourist hotel. But tourism really got off the ground with the demise of the plantation era.

In 1901, W. C. Peacock built the elegant beaux-arts Moana Hotel on Waikiki Beach, and W. C. Weedon convinced Honolulu businessmen to bankroll his plan to advertise Hawaii in San Francisco. Armed with a stereopticon and tinted photos of Waikiki, Weedon sailed off in 1902, for 6 months of lecture tours to introduce "those remarkable people and the beautiful lands of Hawaii." He drew packed houses. A tourism-promotion bureau was formed, in 1903, and about 2,000 visitors came to Hawaii that year.

Steamships were Hawaii's tourism lifeline. It took 4½ days to sail from San Francisco to Honolulu. Streamers, leis, and pomp welcomed each Matson liner at downtown's Aloha Tower. Well-heeled visitors brought trunks, servants, even their Rolls-Royces, and stayed for months. Hawaii amused the idle rich with personal tours, floral parades, and shows spotlighting that naughty dance, the hula.

Beginning in 1935 and running for the next 40 years, Webley Edwards' weekly live radio show, "Hawaii Calls," planted the sounds of Waikiki—surf, sliding steel guitar, sweet Hawaiian harmonies, drumbeats—in the hearts of millions of listeners in the United States, Australia, and Canada.

By 1936, visitors could fly to Honolulu from San Francisco on the *Hawaii Clipper,* a seven-passenger Pan American Martin M-130 flying boat, for $360 one-way. The flight took 21 hours, 33 minutes. Modern tourism was born, with five flying boats providing daily service. The 1941 visitor count was a brisk 31,846 through December 6.

WORLD WAR II & ITS AFTERMATH On December 7, 1941, Japanese Zeros came out of the rising sun to bomb American warships based at Pearl Harbor. This was the "day of infamy" that plunged the United States into World War II.

The aftermath of the attack brought immediate changes to the islands. Martial law was declared, stripping the Big Five cartel of its absolute power in a single day. Feared to be spies, Japanese Americans and German Americans were interned in Hawaii as well as in California. Hawaii was "blacked out" at night, Waikiki Beach was strung with barbed wire, and Aloha Tower was painted in camouflage. Only young men bound for the Pacific came to Hawaii during the war years. Many came back to graves in a cemetery called Punchbowl.

The postwar years saw the beginnings of Hawaii's faux culture. Harry Yee invented the Blue Hawaii cocktail and dropped in a tiny Japanese parasol. Vic Bergeron created the mai tai, a rum and fresh-lime-juice drink, and opened Trader Vic's, America's first theme restaurant that featured the art, decor, and food of Polynesia. Arthur Godfrey picked up a ukulele and began singing *hapa-haole* tunes on early TV shows. Burt Lancaster and Deborah Kerr made love in the surf at Hanauma Bay in 1954's *From Here to Eternity.* In 1955, Henry J. Kaiser built the Hilton Hawaiian Village, and the 11-story high-rise Princess Kaiulani Hotel opened on a site where the real princess once played. Hawaii greeted 109,000 visitors that year.

STATEHOOD In 1959, Hawaii became the 50th of the United States. That year also saw the arrival of the first jet airliners, which brought 250,000 tourists to the fledgling state. The personal touch that had defined aloha gave way to the sheer force of numbers. Waikiki's room count virtually doubled in 2 years, from 16,000, in 1969, to 31,000 units, in 1971; more followed before city fathers finally clamped a growth lid on the world's most famous resort. By 1980, annual arrivals had reached four million.

In the early 1980s, the Japanese began traveling overseas in record numbers, and they brought lots of yen to spend. Their effect on sales in Hawaii was phenomenal: European boutiques opened branches in Honolulu, and duty-free shopping became the main supporter of Honolulu International Airport. Japanese investors competed for the chance to own or build part of Hawaii. Hotels sold so fast and at such unbelievable prices that heads began to spin with dollar signs.

In 1986, Hawaii's visitor count passed five million. Just 2 years later, it went over six million. Expensive fantasy megaresorts bloomed on the neighbor islands like giant artificial flowers, swelling the luxury market with ever-swankier accommodations.

The highest visitor count ever recorded was 6.9 million in 1990, but the bubble burst, in early 1991, with the Gulf War and worldwide recessions. In 1992, Hurricane Iniki devastated Kauai, which is only now staggering back to its feet. Airfare wars sent Americans to Mexico and the Caribbean. Overbuilt with luxury hotels, Hawaii slashed its room rates, giving middle-class consumers access to high-end digs at affordable prices—a trend that continues as Hawaii struggles to stay atop the tourism heap.

2 Hawaii Today

A CULTURAL RENAISSANCE A conch shell sounds, a young man in a bright feather cape chants, torch lights flicker at sunset on Waikiki Beach, and hula dancers begin telling their graceful centuries-old stories. It's a cultural scene out of the past come to life once again—for Hawaii is enjoying a renaissance of hula, chant, and other aspects of its ancient culture.

The biggest, longest, and most elaborate celebrations of Hawaiian culture are the Aloha Festivals, which encompass more than 500 cultural events from August through October. "Our goal is to teach and share our culture," says Gloriann Akau, who manages the Big Island's Aloha Festivals. "In 1946, after the war, Hawaiians needed an identity. We were lost and needed to regroup. When we started to celebrate our culture, we began to feel proud. We have a wonderful culture that had been buried for a number of years. This brought it out again. Self-esteem is more important than making a lot of money."

In 1985, native Hawaiian educator, author, and *kupuna* George Kanahele started integrating Hawaiian values into hotels like the Big Island's Mauna Lani and Maui's Kaanapali Beach Hotel. (A *kupuna* is a respected elder with leadership qualities.) "You have the responsibility to preserve and enhance the Hawaiian culture, not because it's going to make money for you, but because it's the right thing to do," Kanahele said. "Ultimately, the only thing unique about Hawaii is its Hawaiianess. Hawaiianess is our competitive edge."

From general managers to maids, resort employees went through hours of Hawaiian cultural training. They held focus groups to discuss the meaning of *aloha*—the Hawaiian concept of unconditional love—and applied it to their work and their lives. Now many hotels have joined the movement and instituted Hawaiian programs. No longer content with teaching hula as a joke, resorts now employ a real *kumu hula* (hula teacher) to instruct visitors and have a *kupuna* take guests on treks to visit *heiau* (temples) and ancient petroglyph sites.

3 Life & Language

Plantations brought so many different people to Hawaii that the state is now a rainbow of ethnic groups. Living here are Caucasians, African Americans, American Indians, Eskimos, Japanese, Chinese, Filipinos, Koreans, Tahitians, Vietnamese, Hawaiians, Samoans, Tongans, and other Asian and Pacific islanders. Add a few Canadians, Dutch, English, French, Germans, Irish, Italians, Portuguese, Scottish, Puerto Ricans, and Spaniards. Everyone's a minority here.

THE HAWAIIAN LANGUAGE

Almost everyone here speaks English, so except for pronouncing the names of places, you should have no trouble communicating in Hawaii.

But many folks in Hawaii now speak Hawaiian as well, for the ancient language is making a comeback. All visitors will hear the words *aloha* and *mahalo* (thank you). If you've just arrived, you're a *malihini*. Someone who's been here a long time is a *kamaaina*. When you finish a job or your meal, you are *pau* (over). On Friday, it's *pau hana*, work over. You put *pupu* (Hawaii's version of hors d'oeuvres) in your mouth when you go *pau hana*.

The Hawaiian alphabet, created by the New England missionaries, has only 12 letters: the five regular vowels (a, e, i, o, and u) and seven consonants (h, k, l, m, n, p, and w). The vowels are pronounced in the Roman fashion, that is, *ah, ay, ee,* oh, and *oo* (as in "too")—not *ay, ee, eye, oh,* and *you,* as in English. For example, *huhu* is pronounced *who-who.* Most vowels are sounded separately, though some are pronounced together, as in Kalakaua: *Kah-lah-cow-ah.*

WHAT *HAOLE* MEANS When Hawaiians first saw Western visitors, they called the pale-skinned, frail men *haole,* because they looked so out of breath. In Hawaiian, *ha* means *breath,* and *ole* means an absence of what precedes it. In other words, a lifeless-looking person. Today, the term *haole* is generally a synonym for Caucasian or foreigner and is used casually without any intended disrespect. However, if uttered by an angry stranger who adds certain adjectives (like "stupid"), the term can be construed as a mild racial slur.

SOME HAWAIIAN WORDS Here are some basic Hawaiian words that you'll often hear in Hawaii and see throughout this book. For a more complete list of Hawaiian words, point your Web browser to **www.geocities.com/~olelo/hltable ofcontents.html** or **www.hisurf.com/ hawaiian/dictionary.html.**

PIDGIN: 'EH FO'REAL, BRAH

If you venture beyond the tourist areas, you might hear another local tongue: pidgin English. A conglomeration of slang and words from the Hawaiian language, pidgin developed as a method sugar

Basic Glossary

akamai   smart
alii   Hawaiian royalty
aloha   greeting or farewell
halau   school
hale   house or building
heiau   Hawaiian temple or place of worship
hui   club, assembly
kahuna   priest or expert
kamaaina   old-timer
kapa   tapa, bark cloth
kapu   taboo, forbidden
keiki   child
lanai   porch or veranda
lomilomi   massage

mahalo   thank you
makai   a direction, toward the sea
malihini   stranger, newcomer
mana   spirit power
mauka   a direction, toward the mountains
muumuu   loose-fitting gown or dress
nene   official state bird, a goose
ono   delicious
pali   cliff
paniolo   Hawaiian cowboy(s)
wiki   quick

planters used to communicate with their Chinese laborers in the 1800s.

"Broke da mouth" (tastes really good) is the favorite pidgin phrase and one you might hear; "'Eh fo'real, brah" means "It's true, brother." You could be invited to hear an elder "talk story" (relating myths and memories) or to enjoy local treats like "shave ice" (a tropical snow cone) and "crack seed" (highly seasoned preserved fruit). But since pidgin is really the province of the locals, your visit to Hawaii is likely to pass without your hearing much pidgin at all.

4 A Taste of Hawaii

TRIED & TRUE: HAWAII REGIONAL CUISINE

Hawaii's tried-and-true baseline remains Hawaii Regional Cuisine (HRC), established in the mid-1980s in a culinary revolution that catapulted Hawaii into the global epicurean arena. The international training, creative vigor, fresh ingredients, and cross-cultural menus of the 12 original HRC chefs have made the islands a dining destination applauded and emulated nationwide. (In a tip of the toque to island tradition, *ahi*—a word ubiquitous in Hawaii—has replaced *tuna* on many chic New York menus.) And other options have proliferated at all levels of the local dining spectrum: Waves of new Asian residents have transplanted the traditions of their homelands to the fertile soil of Hawaii, resulting in unforgettable taste treats true to their Thai, Vietnamese, Japanese, Chinese, and Indo-Pacific roots. When combined with the bountiful, fresh harvests from sea and land for which Hawaii is known, these ethnic and culinary traditions take on renewed vigor and a cross-cultural, uniquely Hawaiian quality.

Hawaii Regional Cuisine has evolved as Hawaii's singular cooking style, what some say is this country's current gastronomic, as well as geographic, frontier. It highlights the fresh seafood and produce of Hawaii's rich waters and volcanic soil, the cultural traditions of Hawaii's ethnic groups, and the skills of well-trained chefs who broke ranks with their European predecessors to forge new ground in the 50th state.

Fresh ingredients are foremost here. Farmers and fishermen work together to provide steady supplies of just-harvested seafood, seaweed, fern shoots, vine-ripened tomatoes, goat cheese, lamb, herbs, taro, gourmet lettuces, and countless harvests from land and sea. These ingredients wind up in myriad forms on ever-changing menus, prepared in Asian and Western culinary styles. Exotic fruits introduced by recent Southeast Asian emigrants—such as sapodilla, soursop, and rambutan—are beginning to appear regularly in Chinatown markets. Aquacultural seafood, from seaweed to salmon to lobster, is a staple on many menus. Additionally, fresh-fruit sauces (mango, lychee, papaya, pineapple, guava), ginger-sesame-wasabi flavorings, corn cakes with sake sauces, tamarind and fish sauces, coconut-chile accents, tropical-fruit vinaigrettes, and other local and newly arrived seasonings from Southeast Asia and the Pacific impart unique qualities to the preparations.

Here's a sampling of what you can expect to find on a Hawaii Regional menu: seared Hawaiian fish with lilikoi shrimp butter; taro-crab cakes; Pahoa corn cakes; Molokai sweet-potato or breadfruit vichyssoise; Ka'u orange sauce and Kahua Ranch lamb; fern shoots from Waipio Valley; Maui onion soup and Hawaiian bouillabaisse, with fresh snapper, Kona crab, and fresh aquacultural shrimp; blackened ahi summer rolls; herb-crusted onaga; and gourmet Waimanalo greens, picked that day. You may also encounter locally made cheeses, squash and taro risottos, Polynesian imu-baked foods, and guava-smoked meats. If there's pasta or risotto or rack of lamb on the menu, it could be *nori* (red algae) linguine with *opihi* (limpet) sauce, or risotto with local seafood served in taro cups, or rack of lamb in cabernet and *hoisin* sauce (fermented soybean, garlic, and spices). Watch for ponzu sauce, too; it's lemony and zesty, a welcome new staple on local menus.

PLATE LUNCHES & MORE: LOCAL FOOD

At the other end of the spectrum is the vast and endearing world of "local food." By that, we mean plate lunches and poke, shave ice and saimin, bento lunches and manapua—cultural hybrids all.

Reflecting a polyglot population of many styles and ethnicities, Hawaii's idiosyncratic dining scene is eminently inclusive. Consider Surfer Chic: Barefoot in the sand, in a swimsuit, you chow down on a **plate lunch** ordered from a lunch wagon, consisting of fried mahimahi, "two scoops rice," macaroni salad, and a few leaves of green, typically julienned cabbage. (Generally, teriyaki beef and shoyu chicken are options.) Heavy gravy is often the condiment of choice, accompanied by a soft drink in a paper cup. Like **saimin**—the local version of noodles in broth topped with scrambled eggs, green onions, and, sometimes, pork—the plate lunch is Hawaii's version of high camp.

Because this is Hawaii, at least a few licks of *poi*—cooked, pounded taro (the traditional Hawaiian staple crop)—and the other examples of indigenous cuisine are a must. Other **native foods** include those from before and after Western contact, such as *laulau* (pork, chicken, or fish steamed in ti leaves), *kalua* pork (pork cooked in a Polynesian underground oven known here as an *imu*), *lomi* salmon (salted salmon with tomatoes and green onions), squid *luau* (cooked in coconut milk and taro tops), *poke* (cubed raw fish seasoned with onions and seaweed and the occasional sprinkling of roasted *kukui* nuts), *haupia* (creamy coconut pudding), and *kulolo* (steamed pudding of coconut, brown sugar, and taro).

Bento, another popular quick meal available throughout Hawaii, is a compact, boxed assortment of picnic fare usually consisting of neatly arranged sections of rice, pickled vegetables, and fried chicken, beef, or pork. Increasingly, however, the bento is becoming more health-conscious, as in macrobiotic bento lunches or vegetarian brown-rice bentos. A derivative of the modest lunch box for Japanese immigrants who once labored in the sugar and pineapple fields, bentos are dispensed everywhere, from department stores to corner delis and supermarkets.

Also from the plantations come **manapua,** a bready, doughy sphere filled with tasty fillings of sweetened pork or sweet beans. In the old days, the Chinese "manapua man" would make his rounds with bamboo containers balanced on a rod over his shoulders. Today, you'll find white or whole-wheat manapua containing chicken, vegetables, curry, and other savory fillings.

The daintier Chinese delicacy **dim sum** is made of translucent wrappers filled with fresh seafood, pork hash, and vegetables, served for breakfast and lunch in Chinatown restaurants. The Hong Kong–style dumplings are ordered fresh and hot from bamboo steamers from invariably brusque servers who move their carts from table to table. Much like hailing a taxi in Manhattan, you have to be quick and loud for dim sum.

For dessert or a snack, particularly on Oahu's north shore, the prevailing choice is **shave ice,** the island version of a snow cone. Particularly on hot, humid days, long lines of shave-ice lovers gather for the rainbow-colored cones heaped with finely shaved ice and topped with sweet tropical syrups. (The sweet-sour *li hing mui* flavor is a current rage.) The fast-melting mounds, which require prompt, efficient consumption, are quite the local summer ritual for sweet tooths.

AHI, ONO & OPAKAPAKA: A HAWAIIAN SEAFOOD PRIMER

The seafood in Hawaii has been described as the best in the world. In Janice Wald Henderson's pivotal book *The New Cuisine of Hawaii,* acclaimed chef Nobuyuki Matsuhisa (chef/owner of Matsuhisa in Beverly Hills and Nobu in Manhattan and London) writes, "As a chef who specializes in fresh seafood, I am in awe of the quality of Hawaii's fish; it is unparalleled anywhere else in the world." And why not? Without a doubt, the islands' surrounding waters, including the waters of the remote northwestern Hawaiian Islands, and a growing aquaculture industry contribute to the high quality of the seafood here.

The reputable restaurants in Hawaii buy fresh fish daily at predawn auctions or from local fishermen. Some chefs even catch their ingredients themselves. "Still wiggling" or "just off the hook" are the ultimate terms for freshness in Hawaii. The fish can then be grilled over *kiawe* (mesquite) or prepared in innumerable other ways.

Although most menus include the Western description for the fresh fish used, most often the local nomenclature is listed, turning dinner for the uninitiated into a confusing, quasi-foreign experience. To help familiarize you with the menu language of Hawaii, a basic glossary of island fish is below.

5 The Natural World: An Environmental Guide to the Islands

The first Hawaiian Islands were born of violent volcanic eruptions that took place deep beneath the ocean's surface, about 70 million years ago—more than 200 million years after the major continental land masses had been formed. As soon as the islands emerged, Mother Nature's fury began to carve beauty from

Fish Glossary

ahi   yellowfin or bigeye tuna, important for its use in sashimi and poke at sushi bars and in Hawaii Regional Cuisine

aku   skipjack tuna, heavily used by local families in home cooking and poke

ehu   red snapper, delicate and sumptuous, yet lesser known than opakapaka

hapuupuu   grouper, a sea bass whose use is expanding from ethnic to nonethnic restaurants

hebi   spearfish, mildly flavored, and frequently featured as the "catch of the day" in upscale restaurants

kajiki   Pacific blue marlin, also called *au,* with a firm flesh and high fat content that make it a plausible substitute for tuna in some raw fish dishes and as a grilled item on menus

kumu   goatfish, a luxury item on Chinese and upscale menus, served *en papillote* or steamed whole, Oriental style, with sesame oil, scallions, ginger, and garlic

mahimahi   dolphin fish (the game fish, not the mammal) or dorado, a classic sweet, white-fleshed fish requiring vigilance among purists, because it's often disguised as fresh when it's actually "fresh-frozen"—a big difference

monchong   bigscale or sickle pomfret, an exotic, tasty fish, scarce but gaining a higher profile on Hawaiian Island menus

nairagi   striped marlin, also called *au;* good as sashimi and in poke, and often substituted for ahi in raw-fish products

onaga   ruby snapper, a luxury fish, versatile, moist, and flaky

ono   wahoo, firmer and drier than the snappers, often served grilled and in sandwiches

opah   moonfish, rich and fatty, and versatile—cooked, raw, smoked, and broiled

opakapaka   pink snapper, light, flaky, and luxurious, suited for sashimi, poaching, sautéing, and baking; the best-known upscale fish

papio   jack trevally, light, firm, and flavorful and favored in island cookery

shutome   broadbill swordfish, of beeflike texture and rich flavor

tombo   albacore tuna, with a high fat content, suitable for grilling and sautéing

uhu   parrot fish, most often encountered steamed, Chinese style

uku   gray snapper of clear, pale-pink flesh, delicately flavored and moist

ulua   large jack trevally, firm-fleshed and versatile

barren rock. Untiring volcanoes spewed forth rivers of fire that cooled into stone. Severe tropical storms, some with hurricane-force winds, battered and blasted the cooling lava rock into a series of shapes. Ferocious earthquakes flattened, shattered, and reshaped the islands into precipitous valleys, jagged cliffs, and recumbent flatlands. Monstrous surf and gigantic tidal waves rearranged and polished the lands above and below the reaches of the tide.

It took millions of years for nature to shape the familiar form of Diamond Head on Oahu, Maui's majestic peak of Haleakala, the waterfalls of Molokai's northern side, the reefs of Hulopoe Bay on Lanai, and the lush rainforests of the Big Island. The result is an island chain like no other—a tropical landscape rich in unique flora and fauna, surrounded by a vibrant underwater world.

THE ISLAND LANDSCAPES

OAHU   Oahu is the third-largest island in Hawaii (behind the Big Island and Maui). As the home of Honolulu, it's also the most urban island, with a population of nearly 900,000. Oahu is defined by two mountain ranges: the Waianae Ridge in the west, and the jagged Koolaus in the east, which form a backdrop for Honolulu. These ranges divide the island into three different environments. The windward (eastern) side is lush with greenery, ferns, tropical plants, and waterfalls. On the leeward (western) side, the area between the Waianae Range and the ocean is drier, with sparse vegetation, little rainfall, and an arid landscape. Between the two mountain ranges lies the central Ewa Valley; it's moderate in temperature and vibrant with tropical plants, agricultural fields, and trees.

HAWAII, THE BIG ISLAND   By far the largest island at some 4,034 square miles (and still growing), the Big Island is twice the size of all the other islands combined. Here you'll find every type of climate zone existing in Hawaii. It's not uncommon for there to be 12 feet of snow on the two largest mountain peaks, 13,796-foot Mauna Kea and 13,680-foot Mauna Loa. These mountains are the tallest in the state; what's more, when measured from their true base on the ocean floor, they reach 32,000 feet, making them the tallest mountains in the

world. The 4,077-foot Kilauea volcano has been continuously erupting since January 3, 1983, and has added more than 600 acres of new land to the Big Island since then. Just a few miles from the barely cooled barren lava lies a pristine rainforest. On the southern end of the island is an arid desert. The rest of the island contains tropical terrain; white-, black-, and even green-sand beaches; windswept grasslands; and productive farming and ranching areas growing tropical fruits, macadamia nuts, coffee, and ornamental flowers.

MAUI   When two volcanoes—Mauna Kahalawai, a 5,277-foot ancient volcano in the West Maui Mountains, and 10,000-foot Haleakala—flowed together a million or so years ago, the event created a "Valley Isle" with a range of climates from arid desert to tropical rainforest. This 728-square-mile island is the only place in the world where you can drive from sea level to 10,000 feet in just 38 miles, passing from tropical beaches through sugar and pineapple plantations and rolling grassy hills up past the timber line to the lunarlike surface of the top of Haleakala. In addition to 33 miles of public beaches on the south and west shores, Maui is home to the arid lands of Kihei, the swampy bogs of the West Maui Mountains, the rainforest of Hana, and the desert of Kaupo.

MOLOKAI   Roughly the shape and size of Manhattan, Molokai is 37 miles long and 10 miles wide, with a "thumb" protruding out of the North Shore. The North Shore begins on the west, with miles of white-sand beaches that fringe a desertlike landscape. The thumb—the Kalaupapa Peninsula—is cut off by a fence of cliffs, some 2,000 feet tall, that line the remainder of the north side. Molokai can be divided into two areas: the dry west end; and the rainy, tropical east and north ends. Its highest point is Mount Kamakou, at 4,970 feet.

LANAI This small, kidney bean–shaped island—only 13 miles wide by 17 miles long—rises sharply out of the ocean, with cliffs on the west side that rise to a high point of 3,370 feet. Lanai slopes down to sea level on the east and south sides. The only town, Lanai City, sits in the clouds at 1,600 feet. The island's peak is covered with Norfolk pines and is usually shrouded in clouds, while the arid beaches survive on minimal rainfall. One area in particular stands out: the Garden of the Gods, just 7 miles from Lanai City, where oddly strewn boulders lie in the amber- and ocher-colored dirt and bizarre stone formations dot the landscape. The ancient Hawaiians formed romantic legends explaining this enigma, but modern-day scientists still debate its origins.

KAUAI This compact island, 25 miles long by 33 miles wide, has Mount Waialeale, the island's highest point at nearly 5,000 feet and the earth's wettest spot, with more than 400 inches of rain annually. Just west of Mount Waialeale is the barren landscape of Waimea Canyon, dubbed "the Grand Canyon of the Pacific"—the result of the once 10,000-foot-tall Olokele shield volcano, which collapsed and formed a *caldera* (crater) some 3,600 feet deep and 14 miles across. Peaks and craters aren't Kauai's only distinctive landscape features, though: Miles of white-sand beaches rim most of the island, with majestic 2,700-foot cliffs—the spectacular Na Pali Coast—completing the circle. Lush tropical jungle inhabits the north side of the island, while balmy, palm tree–lined beaches are located in the south.

THE FLORA OF THE ISLANDS

Hawaii is filled with sweet-smelling flowers, lush vegetation, and exotic plant life.

AFRICAN TULIP TREES Even from afar, you can see the flaming red flowers on these large trees, which can grow to be more than 50 feet tall. Children in Hawaii love them because the buds hold water—they use the flowers as water pistols.

ANGEL'S TRUMPETS These small trees can grow up to 20 feet tall, with an abundance of large (up to 10 in. in diameter) pendants—white or pink flowers that resemble, well, trumpets. The Hawaiians call them *nana-honua,* which means "earth gazing." The flowers, which bloom continually from early spring to late fall, have a musky scent. *Beware:* All parts of the plant are poisonous and contain a strong narcotic.

ANTHURIUMS One of Hawaii's most popular cut flowers, anthuriums originally came from the tropical Americas and the Caribbean islands. There are more than 550 species, but the most popular are the heart-shaped red, orange, pink, white, and even purple flowers with tail-like spathes. Look for the heart-shaped green leaves in shaded areas. These exotic plants have no scent but will last several weeks as cut flowers. Anthuriums are particularly prevalent on the Big Island.

BANYAN TREES Among the world's largest trees, banyans have branches that grow out and away from the trunk, forming descending roots that grow down to the ground to feed and form additional trunks, making the tree very stable during tropical storms. The banyan in the courtyard next to the old Court House in Lahaina, Maui, is an excellent example of a spreading banyan—it covers two-thirds of an acre.

BIRDS OF PARADISE These natives of Africa have become something of a trademark of Hawaii. They're easily recognizable by the orange and blue flowers nestled in gray-green bracts, looking somewhat like birds in flight.

BOUGAINVILLEA Originally from Brazil, these vines feature colorful, tissue-thin bracts, ranging in color from majestic purple to fiery orange, that hide tiny white flowers. A good place to spot them is on the Big Island, along the Queen Kaahumanu Highway stretching from Kona Airport to Kailua-Kona.

BREADFRUIT TREES A large tree—more than 60 feet tall—with broad, sculpted, dark-green leaves, the famous breadfruit produces a round, head-size green fruit that's a staple in the diets of all Polynesians. When roasted or baked, the whitish-yellow meat tastes somewhat like a sweet potato.

BROMELIADS There are more than 1,400 species of bromeliads, of which the pineapple plant is the best known. "Bromes," as they're affectionately called, are generally spiky plants ranging in size from a few inches to several feet in diameter. They're popular not only for their unusual foliage but also for their strange and wonderful flowers. Used widely in landscaping and interior decoration, especially in resort areas, bromeliads are found on every island.

COFFEE Hawaii is the only state that produces coffee commercially. Coffee is an evergreen shrub with shiny, waxy, dark-green, pointed leaves. The flower is a small, fragrant white blossom that develops into half-inch berries that turn bright red when ripe. Look for coffee at elevations above 1,500 feet on the Kona side of the Big Island and on large coffee plantations on Kauai, Molokai, Oahu, and Maui.

GINGER White and yellow ginger flowers are perhaps the most fragrant in Hawaii. Usually found in clumps growing 4 to 7 feet tall in areas blessed by rain, these sweet-smelling, 3-inch-wide flowers are composed of three dainty petal-like stamens and three long, thin petals. Ginger is so prevalent that many people assume it is native to Hawaii; actually, it was introduced in the 19th century from the Indonesia-Malaysia area. Look for white and yellow ginger from late spring to fall. If you see ginger on the side of the road, stop and pick a few blossoms—your car will be filled with a divine fragrance the rest of the day.

HELICONIA Some 80 species of the colorful heliconia family came to Hawaii from the Caribbean and Central and South America. The bright yellow, red, green, and orange bracts overlap and appear to unfold like origami birds. The most obvious heliconia to spot is the lobster claw, which resembles a string of boiled crustacean pincers. Another prolific heliconia is the parrot's beak; growing to about hip height, it's composed of bright-orange flower bracts with black tips. Look for parrot's beaks in spring and summer.

HIBISCUS The 4- to 6-inch hibiscus flowers bloom year-round and come in a range of colors, from lily white to lipstick red. The flowers resemble crepe paper, with stamens and pistils protruding spire-like from the center. Hibiscus hedges can grow up to 15 feet tall. The yellow hibiscus is Hawaii's official state flower.

JACARANDA Beginning around March and sometimes lasting until early May, these huge, lacy-leaved trees metamorphose into large clusters of spectacular lavender-blue sprays. The bell-shaped flowers drop quickly, leaving a majestic purple carpet beneath the tree.

MACADAMIA A transplant from Australia, macadamia nuts have become a commercial crop in recent decades in Hawaii, especially on the Big Island and Maui. The large trees—up to 60 feet tall—bear a hard-shelled nut encased in a leathery husk, which splits open and dries when ripe.

MONKEYPOD TREES The monkeypod is one of Hawaii's most majestic trees; it grows more than 80 feet tall and 100 feet across. Seen near older homes and in parks, the leaves of the monkeypod drop in February and March. Its wood is a favorite of woodworking artisans.

NIGHT-BLOOMING CEREUS   Look along rock walls for this spectacular night-blooming flower. Originally from Central America, this vinelike member of the cactus family has green scalloped edges and produces foot-long white flowers that open as darkness falls and withers as the sun rises. The plant also bears an edible red fruit.

ORCHIDS   To many minds, nothing says Hawaii more than orchids. The orchid family is the largest in the entire plant kingdom. The most widely grown variety—and the major source of flowers for leis and garnishes for tropical libations—is the vanda orchid. The vandas used in Hawaii's commercial flower industry are generally lavender or white, but they grow in a rainbow of colors, shapes, and sizes. The orchids used for corsages are the large, delicate cattleya; the ones used in floral arrangements—you'll probably see them in your hotel lobby—are usually dendrobiums. On the Big Island, don't pass up a chance to wander through the numerous orchid farms around Hilo.

PANDANUS (HALA)   Called *hala* by Hawaiians, pandanus is native to Polynesia. Thanks to its thick trunk, stiltlike supporting roots, and crown of long, swordlike leaves, the hala tree is easy to recognize. In what is quickly becoming a dying art, Hawaiians weave the *lau* (leaves) of the hala into hats, baskets, mats, bags, and the like.

PLUMERIA   Also known as frangipani, this sweet-smelling, five-petal flower, found in clusters on trees, is the most popular choice of lei makers. The Singapore plumeria has five creamy-white petals, with a touch of yellow in the center. Another popular variety, ruba—with flowers from soft pink to flaming red—is also used in leis. When picking plumeria,

be careful of the sap from the flower, as it's poisonous and can stain clothes.

PROTEA   Originally from South Africa, this unusual oversized shrub comes in more than 40 different varieties. The flowers of one species resemble pincushions; those of another look like a bouquet of feathers. Once dried, proteas will last for years.

SILVERSWORD   This very uncommon and unusual plant is seen only on the Big Island and in the Haleakala Crater on Maui. This rare relative of the sunflower family blooms between July and September. The silversword in bloom is a fountain of red-petaled, daisylike flowers that turn silver soon after blooming.

TARO   Around pools, near streams, and in neatly planted fields, you'll see these green heart-shaped leaves, whose dense roots are a Polynesian staple. The ancient Hawaiians pounded the roots into *poi*. Originally from Sri Lanka, taro is not only a food crop, but is also grown for ornamental reasons.

THE FAUNA OF THE ISLANDS

When the first Polynesians arrived in Hawaii between A.D. 500 and 800, scientists say they found some 67 varieties of endemic Hawaiian birds, a third of which are now believed to be extinct. What's even more astonishing is what they didn't find—there were no reptiles, amphibians, mosquitoes, lice, fleas, or even a cockroach.

There were only two endemic mammals: the hoary bat and the monk seal. The **hoary bat** must have accidentally blown to Hawaii at some point, from either North or South America. It can still be seen during its early evening forays, especially around the Kilauea Crater on the Big Island.

The **Hawaiian monk seal,** a relative of warm-water seals found in the Caribbean and the Mediterranean, was nearly slaughtered into extinction for its skin and oil during the 19th century. These seals have recently experienced a minor population explosion; sometimes they even turn up at various beaches throughout the state. They're protected under federal law by the Marine Mammals Protection Act. If you're fortunate enough to see a monk seal, just look; don't disturb one of Hawaii's living treasures.

The first Polynesians brought a few animals from home: dogs, pigs, and chickens (all were for eating), as well as rats (stowaways). All four species are still found in the Hawaiian wild today.

BIRDS

More species of native birds have become extinct in Hawaii in the last 200 years than anywhere else on the planet. Of 67 native species, 23 are extinct and 30 are endangered. Even the Hawaiian crow, the **alala,** is threatened.

The **aeo,** or Hawaiian stilt—a 16-inch-long bird with a black head, black coat, white underside, and long pink legs—can be found in protected wetlands like the Kanaha Wild Life Sanctuary on Maui (where it shares its natural habitat with the Hawaiian coot), the Kealia Pond on Maui, and the Hanalei National Wildlife Refuge on Kauai, which is also home to the Hawaiian duck. Other areas in which you can see protected birds are the Kipuku Puaulu (Bird Park) and the Olaa Rain Forest, both in Hawaii Volcanoes National Park on the Big Island, and at Goat Island bird refuge off Oahu, where you can see wedge-tailed shearwaters nesting.

Another great birding venue is Kokee State Park on Kauai. Various native birds that have been spotted include some of the 22 species of the native honey creepers, whose songs fill the forest. Frequently seen are the **apapane** (a red bird with black wings and a curved black bill), **iiwi** (another red bird with black wings but with orange legs and a salmon-colored bill), **amakihi** (a plain olive-green bird with a long, straight bill), and **anianiau** (a tiny yellow bird with a thin, curved bill). Also in the forest is the **elepaio,** a small, gray flycatcher with an orange breast and an erect tail. A curious fellow, the elepaio comes out to investigate any unusual whistles. The most common native bird at Kokee—and the most easily seen—is the **moa,** or red jungle fowl, a chicken brought to Hawaii by the Polynesians.

To get a good glimpse of the seabirds that frequent Hawaii, drive to Kilauea Point on Kauai's North Shore. Here, you can easily spot **red-** and **white-footed boobies, wedge-tailed shearwaters, frigate birds, red-tailed tropic birds,** and the **Laysan albatross.**

The **nene** is Hawaii's state bird. It's being brought back from the brink of extinction through strenuous protection laws and captive breeding. A relative of the Canada goose, the nene stands about 2 feet high and has a black head and yellow cheek, a buff neck with deep furrows, a grayish-brown body, and clawed feet. It gets its name from its nasal, two-syllable call, "nay-nay." The approximately 500 nenes in existence can be seen in only three places: at Haleakala National Park on Maui, at Mauna Kea State Park bird sanctuary, and on the slopes of Mauna Kea on the Big Island.

The Hawaiian short-eared owl, the **pueo,** which grows to between 12 and 17 inches, can be seen at dawn and dusk on Kauai, Maui, and the Big Island, when the black-billed, brown-and-white bird goes hunting for rodents. Pueos are highly regarded by Hawaiians; according to legend, spotting a pueo is a good omen.

SEA LIFE

Approximately 680 species of fish are known to inhabit the waters around the Hawaiian Islands. Of those, approximately 450 species stay close to the reef and inshore areas.

CORAL The reefs surrounding Hawaii are made up of various coral and algae.

The living coral grows through sunlight that feeds a specialized alga, which in turn allows the development of the coral's calcareous skeleton. The reef, which takes thousands of years to develop, attracts and supports fish and crustaceans, which use it for food and habitat. Mother Nature can batter the reef with a strong storm or large waves, but humans—through seemingly innocuous acts such as touching the coral—have proven far more destructive.

The corals most frequently seen in Hawaii are hard, rocklike formations named for their familiar shapes: antler, cauliflower, finger, plate, and razor coral. Wire coral looks like a randomly bent wire growing straight out of the reef. Some coral appears soft, such as tube coral; it can be found in the ceilings of caves. Black coral, which resembles winter-bare trees or shrubs, is found at depths of more than 100 feet.

REEF FISH   Of the approximately 450 types of reef fish here, about 27% are native to Hawaii and are found nowhere else in the world. During the millions of years it took for the islands to sprout up from the sea, ocean currents—mainly from Southeast Asia—carried thousands of marine animals and plants to Hawaii's reef; of those, approximately 100 species not only adapted, but also thrived.

Some species are much bigger and more plentiful than their Pacific cousins, and many developed unique characteristics. Some, like the lemon or milletseed butterfly fish, developed specialized schooling and feeding behaviors. Hawaii's native fish are often surprisingly common: You can see the saddleback wrasse, for example, on virtually any snorkeling excursion or dive in Hawaiian waters. You're likely to spot one or more of the following fish while underwater:

Angel fish, often mistaken for butterfly fish, can be distinguished by the spine, located low on the gill plate. These fish are very shy; several species live in colonies close to coral for protection.

Blennies are small, elongated fish, ranging from 2 to 10 inches long, with the majority in the 3- to 4-inch range. Blennies are so small that they can live in tide pools; you might have a hard time spotting one.

Butterfly fish, among the most colorful of the reef fish, are usually seen in pairs (scientists believe they mate for life) and appear to spend most of their day feeding. There are 22 species of butterfly fish, of which three (bluestripe, lemon or milletseed, and multiband or pebbled butterfly fish) are endemic. Most butterfly fish have a dark band through the eye and a spot near the tail resembling an eye, meant to confuse their predators (moray eels love to lunch on them).

Moray and **conger eels** are the most common eels seen in Hawaii. Morays are usually docile except when provoked or when there's food or an injured fish around. Unfortunately, some morays have been fed by divers and—being intelligent creatures—associate divers with food; thus, they can become aggressive. But most morays like to keep to themselves, hidden in their hole or crevice. While morays may look menacing, conger eels look downright happy, with big lips and pectoral fins (situated so that they look like big ears) that give them the appearance of a perpetually smiling face. Conger eels have crushing teeth so they can feed on crustaceans; since they're sloppy eaters, they usually live with shrimp and crabs that feed off the crumbs they leave.

Parrot fish, one of the largest and most colorful of the reef fish, can grow up to 40 inches long. They're easy to spot—their front teeth are fused together, protruding like buck teeth and resembling a parrot's beak. These unique teeth allow them to feed by scraping algae from rocks and coral. The rocks and coral pass through the parrot fish's system, resulting in fine sand. In fact, most of the white sand found in Hawaii is parrot-fish waste; one large parrot fish can produce a ton of sand a year. Native parrot-fish species include yellowbar, regal, and spectacled.

Scorpion fish are what scientists call "ambush predators": They hide under camouflaged exteriors and ambush their prey. Several kinds sport a venomous dorsal spine. These fish don't have a gas bladder, so when they stop swimming, they sink—that's why you usually find them "resting" on ledges and on the ocean bottom. Although they're not aggressive, an inattentive snorkeler or diver could feel the effects of those venomous spines—so be very careful where you put your hands and feet in the water.

Surgeonfish, sometimes called *tang,* get their name from the scalpel-like spines located on each side of the body near the base of the tail. Some surgeonfish have a rigid spine, while others have the ability to fold the spines against the body until they're needed for defense purposes. Several surgeonfish, such as the brightly colored yellow tang, are boldly colored; others are adorned in more conservative shades of gray, brown, or black. The only endemic surgeonfish—and the most abundant in Hawaiian waters—is the convict tang, a pale white fish with vertical black stripes (like a convict's uniform).

Wrasses are a very diverse family of fish, ranging in length from 2 to 15 inches. Wrasses can change gender from female (when young) to male. Some have brilliant coloration that changes as they age. Several types of wrasse are endemic to Hawaii: Hawaiian cleaner, shortnose, belted, and gray (or old woman).

GAME FISH Hawaii is known around the globe as *the* place for big-game fish—marlin, swordfish, and tuna—but its waters are also great for catching other offshore fish like mahimahi, rainbow runner, and wahoo;

coastal fish like barracuda and scad; bottom fish like snappers, sea bass, and amberjack; and inshore fish like trevally and bonefish.

Six kinds of **billfish** are found in the offshore waters around the islands: Pacific blue marlin, black marlin, sailfish, broadbill swordfish, striped marlin, and shortbill spearfish. Hawaii billfish range in size from the 20-pound shortbill spearfish and striped marlin to the 1,805-pound Pacific blue marlin, the largest marlin ever caught with rod and reel in the world.

Tuna ranges in size from small (a pound or less) mackerel tuna used as bait (Hawaiians call them *oioi*) to 250-pound yellowfin ahi tuna. Other local species of tuna are bigeye, albacore, kawakawa, and skipjack.

Other types of fish, also excellent for eating, include **mahimahi** (also known as dolphin fish or dorado), in the 20- to 70-pound range; **rainbow runner,** from 15 to 30 pounds; and **wahoo** (*ono*), from 15 to 80 pounds. Shoreline fishermen are always on the lookout for **trevally** (the state record for a giant trevally is 191 lb.), **bonefish, ladyfish, threadfin, leatherfish,** and **goatfish.** Bottom fishermen pursue a range of **snapper**—red, pink, gray, and others—as well as **sea bass** (the state record is a whopping 563 lb.) and **amberjack** (which weigh up to 100 lb.).

WHALES Humpback whales are the popular visitors who come to Hawaii to mate and calve every year, beginning in November and staying until spring (Apr or so), when they return to their summer home in Alaska. On every island, you can take winter whale-watching cruises that will let you observe these magnificent leviathans close up. You can also spot their signature spouts from shore as they expel water in the distance. Humpbacks grow to up to 45 feet long, so when they breach (propel their entire body out of the water) or even wave a fluke, you can see it for miles.

Humpbacks are among the biggest whales found in Hawaiian waters, but other whales—such as pilot, sperm, false killer, melon-headed, pygmy killer, and beaked—can be seen year-round, especially in the calm waters off the Big Island's Kona Coast. These whales usually travel in pods of 20 to 40 animals and are very social, interacting with one another on the surface.

SHARKS   Yes, there *are* sharks in Hawaii, but you more than likely won't see one unless you're specifically looking. About 40 different species of sharks inhabit the waters surrounding Hawaii, ranging from the totally harmless whale shark (at 60 ft., the world's largest fish), which has no teeth and is so docile that it frequently lets divers ride on its back, to the not-so-docile, infamous, and extremely uncommon great white shark. The most common sharks seen in Hawaii are white-tip reef sharks, gray reef sharks (about 5 ft. long), and black-tip reef sharks (about 6 ft. long).

HAWAII'S ECOSYSTEM PROBLEMS

Officials at Hawaii Volcanoes National Park on the Big Island saw a potential problem a few decades ago with people taking a few rocks home with them as "souvenirs." To prevent this problem from escalating, the park rangers created a legend that the fiery volcano goddess, Pele, did not like people taking anything (rocks, chunks of lava) from her home, and bad luck would befall anyone disobeying her wishes. There used to be a display case in the park's visitor center filled with letters from people who had taken rocks from the volcano, relating stories of all the bad luck that followed. Most of the letters begged Pele's forgiveness and instructed the rangers to please return the rock to the exact location that was its original home.

Unfortunately, Hawaii's other ecosystem problems can't be handled as easily.

MARINE LIFE   Hawaii's beautiful and abundant marine life has attracted so many visitors that they threaten to overwhelm it. A great example of this overenthusiasm is Oahu's beautiful **Hanauma Bay.** Crowds flock to this marine preserve, which features calm, protected swimming and snorkeling areas loaded with tropical reef fish. Its popularity forced government officials to limit admissions and charge an entrance fee. Commercial tour operators have also been restricted in an effort to balance the people-to-fish ratio.

Another marine-life conservation area that suffers from overuse is **Molokini,** a small crater off the coast of Maui. In the 1970s, residents made the area a conservation district in order to protect the unique aquarium-like atmosphere of the waters inside the arms of the crater. Unfortunately, once it was protected, everyone wanted to come here just to see what was worth special protection. Twenty-five years ago, one or two small six-passenger boats made the trip once a day to Molokini; today, it's not uncommon to sight 20 or more boats, each carrying 20 to 49 passengers, moored inside the tiny crater. One tour operator has claimed that, on some days, it's so crowded that you can actually see a slick of suntan oil floating on the surface of the water.

Hawaii's **reefs** have faced increasing impact over the years as well. Runoff of soil and chemicals from construction, agriculture, erosion, and even heavy storms can blanket and choke a reef, which needs sunlight to survive. In addition, the intrusion of foreign elements—caused by such things as breaks in sewage lines—can cause problems; human contact with the reef can also upset the ecosystem. Coral, the basis of the reef system, is very fragile; snorkelers and divers grabbing onto it can break off pieces that took decades to form. Feeding the fish can also upset the balance of the ecosystem (not to mention upsetting the digestive systems of the fish). In areas where they're fed, the normally shy reef fish become more aggressive, surrounding divers and demanding food.

FLORA   The rainforests are among Hawaii's most fragile environments. Any intrusion—from hikers carrying seeds on their shoes to the rooting of wild boars—can upset the delicate balance of these complete ecosystems. In recent years, development has moved closer and closer to the rainforests. On the Big Island, people have protested the invasion of bulldozers and the drilling of geothermal wells in the Wao Kele O Puna rainforest for years, claiming that the damage done is irreparable.

FAUNA   The biggest impact on the fauna in Hawaii is the decimation of native birds by feral animals, which have destroyed the birds' habitats, and by mongooses, which have eaten the birds' eggs and young. Government officials are vigilant about snakes because of the potential damage they can do to the remaining bird life.

Index

THE NEW TRAVELOCITY GUARANTEE

EVERYTHING YOU BOOK WILL BE RIGHT, OR WE'LL WORK WITH OUR TRAVEL PARTNERS TO MAKE IT RIGHT, RIGHT AWAY.

*To drive home the point,
we're going to use the word "right" in every single sentence.*

Let's get right to it. Right to the meat! Only Travelocity guarantees everything about your booking will be right, or we'll work with our travel partners to make it right, right away. Right on!

Here's a picture taken smack dab right in the middle of Antigua, where the guarantee also covers you.

The guarantee covers all but one of the items pictured to the right.

For example, what if the ocean view you booked actually looks out at a downright ugly parking lot? You'd be right to call – we're there for you. And no one in their right mind would be pleased to learn the rental car place has closed and left them stranded. Call Travelocity and we'll help get you back on the right track.

Now, you may be thinking, "Yeah, right, I'm so sure." That's OK; you have the right to remain skeptical. That is until we mention help is always right around the corner. Call us right off the bat, knowing that our customer service reps are there for you 24/7. Righting wrongs. Left and right.

Now if you're guessing there are some things we can't control, like the weather, well you're right. But we can help you with most things – to get all the details in righting,* visit **travelocity.com/guarantee**.

*Sorry, spelling things right is one of the few things not covered under the guarantee.

I'd give my right arm for a guarantee like this, although I'm glad I don't have to.

travelocity
You'll never roam alone.

IF YOU BOOK IT, IT SHOULD BE THERE.

Only Travelocity guarantees it will be, or we'll work
with our travel partners to make it right, right away.
So if you're missing a balcony or anything else you
booked, just call us 24/7. **1-888-TRAVELOCITY.**

travelocity
You'll never roam alone.